Admiralty Record®

Volume 6

PUBLISHED ADMIRALTY OPINIONS OF
THE SUPREME COURT OF THE UNITED STATES AND
THE UNITED STATES COURTS OF APPEALS ISSUED DURING
THE CALENDAR YEAR

2018

Cite as: 6 Adm. R. _____

REPORTED BY KIRK N. AURANDT, ESQ.
MEMBER OF THE BAR IN LOUISIANA AND PENNSYLVANIA

ADMIRALTY RECORD PUBLISHING COMPANY, L.L.C.
MANDEVILLE, LOUISIANA, U.S.A.

ISSN 2334-5411
ISBN 978-1-7337790-0-5

Admiralty record: published admiralty opinions of the Supreme Court of the United States and the United States Courts of Appeals issued during the calendar year ... Mandeville, Louisiana, U.S.A.: Admiralty Record Publishing Company, LLC, 2014-

KF1104 .A75
ISSN: 2334-5411

https://lccn.loc.gov/2014200303

Preface

Volume 6—the sixth annual edition of the Admiralty Record®—reports the published admiralty opinions of the United States Courts of Appeals that were issued during the calendar year 2018. There were no admiralty opinions from the Supreme Court of the United States in 2018. The opinions reported are the original majority, concurring, and dissenting opinions of the Court, with only minor changes in formatting to better suit a dual-column presentation. The pagination found in the Court's original opinion is indicated by the number contained inside of black brackets, *see, e.g.*, **[—15—]**. The pagination found in the official Reporter is indicated by the number contained inside of black braces, *see, e.g.*, **{–15–}**. Also, where applicable, I have added parallel citations to opinions reported in this Volume and in prior Volumes of the Admiralty Record®.

The decision to select an opinion to appear in Volume 6 of the Admiralty Record® was made solely by me following an examination of those opinions that each of the above-named courts designated for publication in 2018. Every effort has been made to ensure inclusion of all 2018 federal appellate court admiralty opinions that were designated for publication; however, to the extent that a relevant admiralty opinion has been inadvertently overlooked or otherwise mistakenly omitted, the error is regretted and is solely my own. A few opinions from appeals in civil cases that technically may not have fallen under a federal district court's admiralty or maritime jurisdiction have been reported if they touched upon admiralty matters, or were otherwise deemed to be of potential interest to the admiralty practitioner. Additionally, several opinions from criminal cases involving maritime crimes and civil cases arising under the Federal Employers' Liability Act have been included.

To assist the reader in locating those opinions from 2018 involving subject matters of interest, I have prepared an Index to the opinions. I have also prepared Tables of Authority, which supply page references to the cases, statutes, and rules cited in each opinion. Prior to relying upon any of the opinions reported herein, the reader is reminded to verify the current status of any particular case as valid precedent by checking the case with a reliable citator.

Additional copies of Volume 1 (covering 2013), Volume 2 (covering 2014), Volume 3 (covering 2015), Volume 4 (covering 2016), Volume 5 (covering 2017), Volume 6 (covering 2018), and succeeding-year Volumes may be ordered at www.admiraltyrecord.com. I hope that the Admiralty Record® will continue to be a valuable and ready reference source for not only the admiralty practitioner, but for anyone who is interested in reading the published admiralty opinions of the federal appellate courts.

Kirk N. Aurandt, Esq.

This page intentionally left blank

TABLE OF CONTENTS[1]

(CASES ARRANGED CHRONOLOGICALLY BY COURT)

PAGE

[1] In 2018, there were no published admiralty opinions from the Supreme Court of the United States and the United States Courts of Appeals for the Eighth and Federal Circuits.

This page intentionally left blank

United States Court of Appeals for the First Circuit

United States Court of Appeals
for the First Circuit

No. 16-2350

UNITED STATES
vs.
DE LA CRUZ-GUTIÉRREZ

Appeal from the United States District Court for the District of Puerto Rico

Decided: January 31, 2018

Citation: 881 F.3d 221, 6 Adm. R. 2 (1st Cir. 2018).

Before HOWARD, Chief Judge, TORRUELLA, and KAYATTA, Circuit Judges.

[—2—] **{-222-}** TORRUELLA, Circuit Judge: **{-223-}**

Defendant-appellant Adolfo De la Cruz-Gutiérrez ("De la Cruz") pled guilty to possession with intent to distribute five kilograms or more of cocaine, in violation of 21 U.S.C. §§ 841(a)(1) and (b)(1)(A); and importation of five kilograms or more of cocaine into the United States, in violation of 21 U.S.C. §§ 952(a), 960(a)(1) and (b)(1)(B). The district court sentenced him to a 120-month term of imprisonment, in the middle of his United States Sentencing Guidelines ("U.S.S.G." or "Guidelines") imprisonment range. De la Cruz now appeals, challenging the district court's denial of a mitigating role adjustment under U.S.S.G. § 3B1.2, and the substantive reasonableness of his sentence. After careful consideration, we affirm.

I. Factual Background

Because De la Cruz pled guilty, our discussion of the relevant facts draws from the change-of-plea colloquy, the unchallenged portions of the Presentence Investigation Report ("PSR"), and the transcript of the sentencing hearing. *See United States v. Fernández-Santos*, 856 F.3d 10, 14 n.1 (1st Cir. 2017).

On January 7, 2016, Border Patrol agents responded to information they had received regarding drug-smuggling activity at a beach in Isabela, Puerto Rico. There, the agents discovered an abandoned twenty-two-foot fiberglass vessel with a single sixty **[—3—]** horsepower outboard motor. In close proximity to the vessel, the agents observed De la Cruz, a Venezuelan national and resident of the Dominican Republic, who had worked for several years as a fisherman, attempting to flee the scene. The agents detained De la Cruz and searched the backpack he was carrying, which revealed two cell phones, a global positioning system ("GPS"), and cocaine. Agents from several law enforcement agencies searched the beach and found five bales of cocaine hidden in the nearby brush, weighing 153.78 kilograms in total. Its estimated value was $10,848,859.74. During a post-arrest interview, De la Cruz admitted that he traveled from the Dominican Republic to Puerto Rico to smuggle the cocaine. According to De la Cruz, he traveled with two other individuals (one of them known as "Tin"),[1] all three individuals took turns navigating the vessel,[2] and he was offered $20,000 for his role in the trip. **[—4—]**

De la Cruz was indicted on January 13, 2016, for possession with intent to distribute five kilograms or more of cocaine, in violation of 21 U.S.C. §§ 841(a)(1) and **{-224-}** (b)(1)(A); and importation of five kilograms or more of cocaine into the United States, in violation of 21 U.S.C. §§ 952(a), 960(a)(1) and (b)(1)(B). De la Cruz pled guilty to both counts of the indictment. After a series of procedural events—including the issuance of a PSR, De la Cruz's objections to some aspects of the PSR, the issuance of an amended PSR and an addendum to the PSR, as well as De la Cruz's

[1] The two individuals allegedly traveling with De la Cruz were not apprehended. De la Cruz told law enforcement that both of them drowned during the trip from the Dominican Republic to Puerto Rico. The record is devoid of any evidence corroborating De la Cruz's statement.

[2] In this interview, De la Cruz stated that he had been hired as a captain. When faced with the possibility of receiving a two-level sentencing enhancement for his role as a captain under U.S.S.G. § 2D1.1(b)(3)(C), De la Cruz recanted his prior statement and, instead, claimed that Tin was the captain, and that he had recruited De la Cruz "to engage in any task required of him."

filing a sentencing memorandum[3]—De la Cruz filed a motion requesting that the district court grant him a three-level reduction for his role in the offense.[4] In his motion, De la Cruz alleged that he was entitled to a three-level reduction under U.S.S.G. § 3B1.2—as opposed to the two-level reduction the probation officer had proposed in the amended PSR—because his participation in the criminal activity was less than that of a minor participant (although not minimal). The government responded that it would defer to the court's discretion because, "based on the totality of the evidence collected at the scene and **[—5—]** the post arrest statements of [De la Cruz, it did] not have enough information to determine if [De la Cruz] was a minor participant in the smuggling venture." On October 6, 2016, the district court denied De la Cruz's motion as to the mitigating role adjustment. The court determined that De la Cruz was not even eligible for the two-level minor role reduction that the probation officer had recommended. In essence, the district court concluded that the record before it contained "no factual basis to justify classifying [De la Cruz] as a minor participant versus the participation of the other two persons who he claims accompanied him in the smuggling venture." To the contrary, according to the court, the record reflected that all three participants, including De la Cruz, were no "ordinary mules but, rather, persons of trust within the organization."

The sentencing hearing took place on October 13, 2016. There, De la Cruz renewed his request for a mitigating role adjustment. After the district court stated that it would not award the adjustment, De la Cruz argued for a downwardly variant sentence "to what would have been [his] sentence had the Court granted the role adjustment." The district court then calculated De la Cruz's Guidelines sentencing range ("GSR"). It determined that De la Cruz's base offense level was thirty-six under U.S.S.G. § 2D1.1(c)(2) because the offense involved "the possession and **[—6—]** importation of at least 150 kilograms but less than 450 kilograms of cocaine." The court granted a two-level reduction because De la Cruz complied with the provisions in 18 U.S.C. §§ 3553(f)(1)-(5) and U.S.S.G. §§ 5C1.2(a)(1)-(5) (the safety valve). Finally, it granted a three-level reduction pursuant to U.S.S.G. §§ 3E1.1(a) and (b) due to De la Cruz's acceptance of responsibility, resulting in a total offense level of thirty-one. This, in conjunction with De la Cruz's criminal history category of I, yielded a GSR of 108 to 135 months of imprisonment.

The court then addressed De la Cruz's request for a variant sentence. In so doing, it considered the 18 U.S.C. § 3553(a) sentencing factors, emphasizing De la Cruz's personal history and characteristics, including his status as a first offender, and the nature of the offense. Ultimately, the court denied De la Cruz's request for a downwardly variant sentence and sentenced De la Cruz to 120 months of imprisonment, **{-225-}** in the middle of the GSR. This timely appeal followed.

II. Discussion

A. Procedural Reasonableness of De la Cruz's Sentence

We review preserved challenges to the reasonableness of a sentence "under a deferential abuse-of-discretion standard." *United States v. Battle*, 637 F.3d 44, 50 (1st Cir. 2011) (quoting *Gall v. United States*, 552 U.S. 38, 41 (2007)). Under this **[—7—]** deferential standard, "we first determine whether the sentence imposed is procedurally reasonable and then determine whether it is substantively reasonable." *United States v. Coleman*, 854 F.3d 81, 84 (1st Cir. 2017) (quoting *United States v. Clogston*, 662 F.3d 588, 590 (1st Cir. 2011)). Procedural errors include: "failing to calculate (or improperly calculating) the Guidelines range, treating the Guidelines as mandatory, failing to consider the § 3553(a) factors, selecting a sentence based on clearly erroneous facts, or failing to adequately explain the chosen sentence—including an explanation for any deviation from the Guidelines range." *United States v.*

[3] Because, in general, these issues are not relevant to the present appeal, we do not delve into them.

[4] De la Cruz's motion included another issue not relevant to this appeal.

Reyes-Rivera, 812 F.3d 79, 86 (1st Cir. 2016) (quoting *United States v. Martin*, 520 F.3d 87, 92 (1st Cir. 2008)). In the course of determining whether the district court committed procedural error, "we afford de novo review to the sentencing court's interpretation and application of the sentencing guidelines, assay the court's factfinding for clear error, and evaluate its judgment calls for abuse of discretion." *United States v. González-Rodríguez*, 859 F.3d 134, 137 (1st Cir. 2017) (quoting *United States v. Ruiz-Huertas*, 792 F.3d 223, 226 (1st Cir. 2015)).

De la Cruz argues that, by failing to grant him a minor role reduction, the district court improperly calculated his GSR and, thus, his sentence is procedurally unreasonable. De la Cruz **[—8—]** now presses for a two-level minor role reduction, instead of the three-level reduction he requested below.

The Guidelines allow a court to award a two-level reduction to a defendant who was a minor participant in the criminal activity in question.[5] U.S.S.G. § 3B1.2. In the past, we have required a defendant seeking a minor role reduction to prove by a preponderance of the evidence that he was "both less culpable than his cohorts in the particular criminal endeavor and less culpable than the majority of those within the universe of persons participating in similar crimes." *United States v. Trinidad-Acosta*, 773 F.3d 298, 315-16 (1st Cir. 2014) (quoting *United States v. Santos*, 357 F.3d 136, 142 (1st Cir. 2004)). Effective November 1, 2015, Amendment 794 to the Guidelines adopted a more lenient approach, then-followed by the Seventh and Ninth Circuits. Per that amendment, "when determining mitigating role, the defendant is to be compared with other participants 'in the criminal activity'" and not with the typical offender. U.S.S.G. App. C Supp., Amend. 794 (effective Nov. 1, 2015). Although De **[—9—]** la Cruz embraced the two-part test in his opening brief, his challenge fails even under Amendment 794's more lenient standard.

Because determining one's role in an offense is a fact-specific inquiry, "we rarely reverse a district court's decision regarding whether to apply a minor role **{–226–}** adjustment." *United States v. Bravo*, 489 F.3d 1, 11 (1st Cir. 2007) (citing *United States v. Tom*, 330 F.3d 83, 95 (1st Cir. 2003)); *see also United States v. Pérez*, 819 F.3d 541, 546, 4 Adm. R. 20, 21 (1st Cir. 2016) ("[B]attles over a defendant's status . . . will almost always be won or lost in the district court." (second alteration in original) (quoting *United States v. Graciani*, 61 F.3d 70, 75 (1st Cir. 1995))). A defendant will "only prevail on appeal by demonstrating that the district court's determination as to his role in the offense was clearly erroneous." *United States v. González-Soberal*, 109 F.3d 64, 74 (1st Cir. 1997) (quoting *United States v. López-Gil*, 965 F.2d 1124, 1131 (1st Cir. 1992)). De la Cruz cannot meet that burden.

De la Cruz alleges that the district court's denial of a mitigating role adjustment was clearly erroneous because, although "[h]e played a role," it was "not one that made him any more valuable or essential—or culpable—than any other crewmember." De la Cruz further argues that the district court's decision not to impose a sentencing enhancement for "captain" under **[—10—]** U.S.S.G. § 2D1.1(b)(3)(C) "was an acknowledgement that even if [he] operated the boat[,] he was clearly not in charge." Because he was not in charge, his argument goes, someone else (he claims it was Tin) was more culpable than him and thus it was clearly erroneous for the district court to deny him a mitigating role adjustment.

De la Cruz's argument fails for several reasons. First, De la Cruz seems to believe that he is entitled to a minor role reduction as long as he was not a more culpable participant. Yet, this is simply not the standard. To be entitled to the role reduction, De la Cruz had to prove that he was *less* culpable than his cohorts. Merely not being more culpable than his cohorts falls short of meeting the standard. *See Bravo*, 489 F.3d at

[5] The Guidelines also provide for a four-level reduction to a defendant whose participation in the criminal activity was minimal, and a three-level reduction if the defendant's participation was between minor and minimal. *See* U.S.S.G. § 3B1.2.

11 (affirming denial of role reduction where, despite being crewmembers and not the captain, defendants failed to demonstrate that any of them were less culpable than the other crewmembers). De la Cruz's concession before the district court that "[a] third individual also performed a role substantially similar to [De la Cruz]" makes evident that he did not meet his burden and thus defeats his claim. Second, assuming as true that someone else, and not De la Cruz, was the captain of the vessel, it does not necessarily follow that De la Cruz and the captain were not "equal partners in the criminal activity." *See Pérez*, 819 F.3d at 545-46, 4 Adm. R. at 21 **[—11—]** (holding that the fact that Pérez's co-defendant "was deemed the 'captain' of the craft does not undermine the sentencing court's finding that they were equal partners in the criminal activity" (citing *Bravo*, 489 F.3d at 11)). Third, the fact that someone else might have been more culpable than De la Cruz does not necessarily mean that De la Cruz's participation was minor. *See United States v. García-Ortiz*, 657 F.3d 25, 29-30 (1st Cir. 2011) ("The fact that some other accomplice may be more culpable than the defendant does not necessarily mean that the defendant's role in the offense is minor."); *see also United States v. Meléndez-Rivera*, 782 F.3d 26, 29 (1st Cir. 2015) (noting that "a defendant need not be the key figure in a conspiracy in order to be denied [a role reduction]").

Likewise, De la Cruz's comparison of his role in the criminal activity to that of a "'mule'—who does little more than knowingly transport drugs during one leg of the trip," leads him nowhere. The district court expressly rejected this characterization as an ordinary mule and De la Cruz has failed to show that this determination was clearly erroneous. Based on the record before it—including De la Cruz's participation in a multimillion dollar smuggling **{–227–}** venture involving bringing more than $10,000,000-worth of cocaine aboard a small vessel with a single outboard motor for a hazardous voyage at sea—the district court **[—12—]** reasonably inferred that De la Cruz was no "Johnny-come-late[ly]" or an ordinary mule, but rather that he, as well as his cohorts, were "persons of trust within the organization." Although De la Cruz does not agree with the inferences the district court drew, and provides alternate explanations, where, as here, the record supports at least two permissible inferences, "the sentencing court's choice among supportable alternatives cannot be clearly erroneous." *Pérez*, 819 F.3d at 546, 4 Adm. R. at 21 (finding no clear error in the district court's denial of a mitigating role adjustment where the district court "mentioned the large quantity of drugs, the trust that the drug owners obviously placed in the appellant, and the appellant's expertise in 'how to handle the boat'"); *United States v. Vargas*, 560 F.3d 45, 51 (1st Cir. 2009) (noting that the "large quantity of drugs hauled by the appellant . . . was a relevant datum in assessing [the defendant's] role in the conspiracy"). Furthermore, De la Cruz's attempt to minimize his role is undermined by his concession that "[a]ll three participants took turns 'navigating'" the vessel, that they all "look[ed] at the GPS" and partook in steering the vessel, and "that one or both of the other participants took a turn steering" the vessel when De la Cruz became tired.

In any event, even if De la Cruz had been an ordinary mule, our precedent is clear that merely being a courier does not **[—13—]** automatically entitle a defendant to a mitigating role adjustment. *See Vargas*, 560 F.3d at 51 (noting that couriers are not automatically entitled to mitigating role adjustments, that "[s]ome couriers are more central to the plot than others," and that "[a] defendant who participates in only one phase of a conspiracy may nonetheless be found to play a non-minor role"); *United States v. De La Cruz*, 249 F. App'x 833, 835 (1st Cir. 2007) (upholding denial of minor role reduction where defendant's role "was limited 'to aid[ing] in the transportation of drugs from one point to the other'" (alteration in original)); *González-Soberal*, 109 F.3d at 73 (noting that couriers are not automatically entitled to a reduction).

In light of the above, we conclude that the district court's denial of a mitigating role adjustment was not clearly erroneous.

B. Substantive Reasonableness of De la Cruz's Sentence

In his other claim of error, De la Cruz challenges the substantive reasonableness of his sentence. Although De la Cruz did not preserve this claim below, because the standard of review for unpreserved challenges to the substantive reasonableness of a sentence is murky, we assume—favorably to him—that our review is for abuse of discretion. *See Ruiz-Huertas*, 792 F.3d at 228. **[—14—]**

A sentence is substantively reasonable if it rests on "a plausible sentencing rationale and a defensible result." *Martin*, 520 F.3d at 96. Successfully challenging the substantive reasonableness of a sentence is a heavy burden that "grows even heavier where, as here, the sentence falls within a properly calculated GSR." *United States v. Cortés-Medina*, 819 F.3d 566, 572 (1st Cir. 2016) (citing *Clogston*, 662 F.3d at 592-93); *see also United States v. Llanos-Falero*, 847 F.3d 29, 36 (1st Cir. 2017) (noting that within-the-Guidelines sentences "deserve[] 'a presumption of reasonableness'" (quoting *Cortés-Medina*, 819 F.3d at 572)). De la Cruz has failed to carry his heavy burden. **{–228–}**

De la Cruz concedes that he was awarded safety valve relief under 18 U.S.C. § 3553(f) and U.S.S.G. § 5C1.2, and that the district court appropriately considered this when calculating his GSR, resulting in a lower applicable GSR. He claims, however, that by sentencing him to 120 months of imprisonment, which would have been his statutory minimum term had he not qualified for safety valve relief, the district court "arbitrarily nullified" the "benefit" of the safety valve and imposed a substantively unreasonable sentence.

The safety valve provision of 18 U.S.C. § 3553(f) requires a court to disregard an applicable mandatory sentence if the court finds at sentencing that the defendant meets the five **[—15—]** specified criteria, none of which are at issue here. *See* 18 U.S.C. §§ 3553(f)(1)-(5). Its purpose is to "'mitigate the harsh effect of mandatory minimum sentences' on first-time, low-level offenders in drug trafficking schemes." *United States v. Padilla-Colón*, 578 F.3d 23, 30 (1st Cir. 2009) (quoting *United States v. Ortiz-Santiago*, 211 F.3d 146, 150 (1st Cir. 2000)). In addition, the Guidelines provide for a two-level reduction in the offense level of a defendant that qualifies for safety valve relief. *See* U.S.S.G. §§ 2D1.1 and 5C1.2.

De la Cruz's contention that the district court disregarded the safety valve relief and imposed the statutory minimum sentence is belied by the record. Here, the district court explicitly found at sentencing that De la Cruz qualified for safety valve relief under 18 U.S.C. § 3553(f), and applied a two-level reduction to the GSR calculation, which lowered De la Cruz's GSR to 108 to 135 months of imprisonment.[6] The record reflects that the district court did not consider itself constrained by the statutory minimum of 120 months of imprisonment. On the contrary, it was aware that it could impose a guideline or variant sentence. In fact, the district court considered De la Cruz's request for a variant sentence, but ultimately denied it. **[—16—]** The record clearly shows that, in determining De la Cruz's sentence, the district court considered all the § 3553(a) sentencing factors and concluded, based on these factors, that a mid-range sentence was warranted. That the mid-range sentence turned out to coincide with what would have been the minimum sentence had the safety-valve relief not applied is inconsequential in light of the entire record, which lacks a single reference (explicit or implicit) indicating that the district court considered itself bound by, or that it relied on, a mandatory minimum sentence.

De la Cruz does not dispute that, in determining his sentence, the district court considered all the factors listed in 18 U.S.C. § 3553(a). *See Clogston*, 662 F.3d at 592 (noting that where, as here, the district court states that it has considered all of the § 3553(a) factors, "[s]uch a statement 'is entitled to some weight'" (quoting *United*

[6] Had the safety valve relief not applied, De la Cruz's GSR would have been 135 to 168 months of imprisonment.

States v. Dávila-González, 595 F.3d 42, 49 (1st Cir. 2010))). He argues, however, that even though the district court emphasized some of the sentencing factors—such as the nature and characteristics of the offense and his personal history and characteristics—it "had no intention of allowing" De la Cruz's personal characteristics to "impact the sentence" and, instead, focused primarily on the nature of the offense (including the amount of drugs involved, worth over **[—17—]** $10,000,000). De la Cruz's argument thus goes to how the district court weighed the sentencing factors. And we have repeatedly **{–229–}** held that "[a] criminal defendant is entitled to a weighing of the section 3553(a) factors that are relevant to his case, not to a particular result." *Dávila-González*, 595 F.3d at 49 (alteration omitted) (quoting *United States v. Carrasco-De-Jesús*, 589 F.3d 22, 29 (1st Cir. 2009)). Nor is the sentence unreasonable because the district court elaborated upon some factors more than others, especially where, as here, it imposed a within-the-range sentence. *See United States v. Murphy-Cordero*, 715 F.3d 398, 402 (1st Cir. 2013) ("[A] within-the-range sentence typically requires a less elaborate explanation than a variant sentence.").

Lastly, De la Cruz compares his case to *United States v. Torres-Rivera*, 661 F. App'x 727 (1st Cir. 2016), in what seems to be an attempt to argue sentencing disparity. In *Torres-Rivera*, the defendant was also convicted of a drug offense and qualified for safety-valve relief. *Id.* at 728-29. De la Cruz notes that Torres-Rivera was also sentenced to 120 months of imprisonment, and appears to argue that receiving the same sentence as Torres-Rivera was unreasonable because, unlike Torres-Rivera, he "had no managerial duties," he "was involved in one incident only," and he "had no duties regarding the money [that others] . . . expected to glean from selling the cocaine." But De la Cruz's argument is **[—18—]** inapposite. De la Cruz is not similarly situated to Torres-Rivera, whose GSR was 87 to 108 months of imprisonment, *id.* at 729, lower than De la Cruz's. By sentencing Torres-Rivera to 120 months, *id.*, the district court upwardly departed from the Guidelines and thus treated Torres-Rivera more harshly in relation to his GSR than De la Cruz, who received a mid-range sentence. *See United States v. Bedini*, 861 F.3d 10, 21 (1st Cir. 2017) (noting that "'[a] well-founded claim of disparity' must compare 'apples . . . to apples'" (alterations in original) (quoting *United States v. Mateo-Espejo*, 426 F.3d 508, 514 (1st Cir. 2005))).

Because we find that Appellant's mid-range sentence was within the universe of reasonable and defensible sentences, *United States v. Torres-Landrúa*, 783 F.3d 58, 69 (1st Cir. 2015), we reject De la Cruz's substantive reasonableness challenge.

III. Conclusion

In sum, the district court did not clearly err in denying De la Cruz a minor role adjustment, and his sentence was substantively reasonable. We thus affirm his sentence.

Affirmed.

United States Court of Appeals
for the First Circuit

No. 15-2025

UNITED STATES
vs.
SARMIENTO-PALACIOS

Appeal from the United States District Court for the District of Puerto Rico

Decided: March 16, 2018

Citation: 885 F.3d 1, 6 Adm. R. 8 (1st Cir. 2018).

Before **HOWARD**, Chief Judge, **TORRUELLA**, and **BARRON**, Circuit Judges.

[—2—] {–2–} HOWARD, Chief Judge: **{–3–}**

Johnny Sarmiento-Palacios pleaded guilty to two cocaine-related charges under the Maritime Drug Law Enforcement Act ("MDLEA"). On appeal, Sarmiento claims that (1) Congress exceeded its constitutional authority in promulgating the MDLEA; (2) Amendment 794 to the U.S. Sentencing Commission Guidelines ("the Guidelines") is retroactive, so he should be re-sentenced under the Sentencing Commission's amended guidance; or, in the alternative, (3) section 3B1.2 of the Sentencing Guidelines is void for vagueness. Although we find Sarmiento's constitutional challenges to MDLEA and section 3B1.2 meritless, because we agree that Amendment 794 is retroactive, we vacate his sentence and remand for re-sentencing.

I. Background

A. Facts and Procedural History

In August 2013, United States Coast Guard personnel stationed aboard a Dutch warship encountered a "go-fast" vessel[1] dead in the Caribbean Sea's international waters. Because the vessel bore no indicia of nationality, the Coast Guard conducted a right-of-visit[2] approach. The Coast Guard found Sarmiento and **[—3—]** two codefendants—as well as over 600 kilograms of cocaine in plain view—on the vessel. The Coast Guard arrested the three men and seized the contraband.

In March 2015, Sarmiento entered a straight plea of guilty (that is, without a plea agreement) for (1) conspiracy to possess cocaine with the intent to distribute; and (2) aiding and abetting the same, all on a vessel subject to United States jurisdiction. *See* 46 U.S.C. §§ 70501 *et seq.*; 18 U.S.C. § 2. At his sentencing hearing in August 2015, Sarmiento argued for a two-level reduction because he was a "minor participant" in the offense and was "substantially less culpable than the average participant." *See* U.S.S.G. § 3B1.2(b) & cmt. n.3(A) (2014). Sarmiento emphasized that he had no criminal record prior to his arrest and that he was almost entirely blind. As such, he argued that he was both too inexperienced and too ill-suited to play more than a minor role in the charged crimes.

The district court rejected this argument, citing the "substantial amount of drugs" at issue. It sentenced Sarmiento to 135 months' imprisonment on each count—at the bottom of the guidelines sentencing range—to run concurrently. This timely appeal followed. **[—4—]**

II. Analysis

A. Sarmiento's MDLEA Challenge

Sarmiento briefly suggests that because Congress exceeded its constitutional **{–4–}** authority under Article I when it promulgated the MDLEA, the United States lacked jurisdiction to prosecute him. *See United States v. Cardales-Luna*, 632 F.3d 731, 739-51 (1st Cir. 2011) (Torruella, J., dissenting). But even if this skeletal challenge has been

[1] "This is a small boat, customized with additional engines and fuel tanks for added speed and range. Experience tells us that such boats play a large role in the drug trade." *United States v. González*, 311 F.3d 440, 444 n.3 (1st Cir. 2002).

[2] This "doctrine of international maritime common law . . . bestows a nation's warship with the authority to hail and board an unidentified vessel to ascertain its nationality." *United States* **[—3—]** *v. Matos-Luchi*, 627 F.3d 1, 21 (1st Cir. 2010) (Lipez, J., dissenting) (citation omitted).

properly presented to us, *see United States v. Zannino*, 895 F.2d 1, 17, it is unavailing.

At his change of plea hearing, Sarmiento admitted that he was apprehended on "a vessel without nationality," and he makes no effort to contest that admission on appeal. Further, Sarmiento concedes that the MDLEA is a valid exercise of Congress's Article I powers, at least in cases of "piracy, slave trading, and stateless vessels." *See United States v. Matos-Luchi*, 627 F.3d 1, 6 (1st Cir. 2010) ("[A] refusal to claim nationality renders [an] unflagged vessel stateless and so within federal jurisdiction."); *see also Cardales-Luna*, 632 F.3d at 751 (Torruella, J., dissenting). Because Sarmiento's "valid guilty plea relinquishes any claim that would contradict the 'admissions necessarily made upon entry of a voluntary plea of guilty,'" *Class v. United States*, No. 16-424, slip op. at 8 (U.S. Feb. 21, 2018) (quoting *United States v. Broce*, 488 U.S. 563, 573-74 (1989)), his challenge to the MDLEA must fail. **[—5—]**

B. Guidelines Amendment 794

"Normally, the sentencing judge is to apply the guidelines version in effect at the time of sentencing." *United States v. Crudup*, 375 F.3d 5, 8 (1st Cir. 2004). The district court did just that when rejecting Sarmiento's argument for a reduction under U.S.S.G. § 3B1.2(b) (2014). But "a reviewing court may give effect to post-sentencing guideline amendments that clarify, without purporting substantive change, the pertinent guideline provision." *Crudup*, 375 F.3d at 8.

Here, about three months after Sarmiento's sentencing, the Sentencing Commission enacted Amendment 794, which altered section 3B1.2's commentary. *See* U.S.S.G. supp. to App. C, amend. 794, at 116-18 (2015) [hereinafter Amendment 794]. The amendment added language to the commentary notes that, among other things, explained that the mitigating-role reduction should apply to defendants who are "substantially less culpable than the average participant *in the criminal activity*" and listed five "non-exhaustive . . . factors" that courts "should consider" when determining whether a defendant qualifies for the reduction. *Id.* at 116 (emphasis added). Sarmiento argues that, under this new guidance, he would have received the two-level reduction that the sentencing court denied.

Amendment 794 must be "clarifying" in order to apply retroactively to Sarmiento—that is, it must "change[] nothing **[—6—]** concerning the legal effect of the guidelines, but merely clarif[y] what the Commission deems the guidelines to have already meant." *Crudup*, 375 F.3d at 8 (quoting *United States v. Smaw*, 22 F.3d 330, 333 (D.C. Cir. 1994)). All of the other circuits that have considered this question have determined that Amendment 794 is clarifying, and therefore retroactive.[3] We agree.

An amendment's retroactivity is a "case-specific inquiry" because "a clear-cut demarcation rarely can be drawn between an amendment which is a mere clarification and one which effects a substantive **{–5–}** change. . . . [O]ften we must weigh various factors and any conflicting indicia of the Commission's intent." *Id.* at 9. Our caselaw suggests four such factors: (1) whether the amendment is listed in U.S.S.G § 1B1.10; (2) the Commission's characterization of the amendment; (3) whether the amendment conflicts with our circuit precedent; and (4) whether the Commission takes sides in a circuit split—and if so, how. *Crudup*, 375 F.3d at 9-10 (citing cases). We next examine these factors, keeping in mind that a "guideline amendment is either substantive or it is not," and that we are ultimately seeking the "significance of the amendment as a whole." *United States v. Cabrera-Polo*, 376 F.3d 29, 32 (1st Cir. 2004) (citation omitted). **[—7—]**

1. Section 1B1.10(d)

Section 1B1.10(d) lists amendments that the Commission designates as retroactive. *See Crudup*, 375 F.3d at 9. The Commission did not include Amendment 794 in section

[3] *See United States v. Quintero-Leyva*, 823 F.3d 519, 523 (9th Cir. 2016); *United States v. Carter*, 662 F. App'x 342, 349 (6th Cir. 2016); *United States v. Casas*, 632 F. App'x 1003, 1005 (11th Cir. 2015) (per curiam).

1B1.10(d)'s 2015 version (the first published after Amendment 794), which is "some evidence" that the Commission considered the amendment to be substantive, not clarifying. *Id.* But whether an amendment is listed in section 1B1.10(d) is not dispositive, as "courts may ascribe retroactive effect to an amendment not listed . . . if other evidence independently suggests that the Commission intended it as a clarification." *Id.* Such evidence exists here.

2. The Commission's characterization

Amendment 794 does not contain the words "clarify" or "clarification," and the government suggests that the Commission's failure to use these words shows that the Commission intended the amendment to be substantive. But our caselaw is not this formalistic. Rather than requiring the Commission to use any specific language when drafting guidelines amendments, the inquiry is more holistic: we care about whether the Commission "expressed [or] implied that [the amendment] is a clarification." *Crudup*, 375 F.3d at 9. Indeed, even if the Commission expressly designated Amendment 794 as either "clarifying" or "substantive" (which it did not), we would consider that label worthy of "considerable weight" but "not controlling." *Id.* **[—8—]**

We agree with the Ninth, Sixth, and Eleventh Circuits that Amendment 794's language "indicates that the Commission intended it to be a clarifying amendment." *Quintero-Leyva*, 823 F.3d at 523. The amendment's stated purpose is to "provide[] additional guidance to sentencing courts in determining whether a mitigating role adjustment applies" because the Commission determined that sentencing courts were applying section 3B1.2 "more sparingly than the Commission intended." Amendment 794 at 117. Besides providing a "non-exhaustive list of factors" for courts to consider when applying the mitigating-role reduction, *id.*, the amendment eliminated prior commentary language that "may have had the unintended effect of discouraging courts from applying" the adjustment when appropriate. *Id.* at 118. By using this language, the Commission implied that Amendment 794 was a clarification of section 3B1.2, and the fact that the Commission never expressly used the word "clarify" does not change the amendment's overall intent.

3. Conflict with our circuit precedent

We have considered an amendment's conflict with our circuit precedent as a "factor . . . [that] would weigh in favor of characterizing [the amendment] as substantive." *Crudup*, 375 F.3d at 10. Amendment 794 clearly conflicts with our precedent. *See* Amendment 794 at 117 (discussing **{-6-}** *United States v. Santos*, 357 F.3d 136, 142 (1st Cir. 2004)). But in *Crudup*, we recognized that **[—9—]** this interpretive principle was idiosyncratic to our circuit and applied it in a situation where "there [was] no other evidence that the Commission intended [for the amendment] to be a clarification." 375 F.3d at 10 n.3. Here, on the other hand, the evidence indicates the amendment's clarifying purpose, so we give this factor less weight.

4. Taking sides in a circuit split

When, as here, the Commission weighs in on a circuit split by "intimat[ing] that [some] circuits correctly apprehended the Commission's original intent underlying the pre-amendment guideline" and that circuits on the other side of the split "had misinterpreted that original intent," the amendment's likely purpose is clarification, not substantive change. *Id.* at 10.

Amendment 794 addressed a circuit split over section 3B1.2's pre-amendment guideline commentary, which allowed a sentencing court to apply the mitigating-role reduction when the defendant was "substantially less culpable than the average participant." U.S.S.G. § 3B1.2, cmt. n.3(A) (2014). Some circuits evaluated the "average participant" by looking only at the other participants in the defendant's actual activity; other circuits, including ours, looked also to the "universe of persons participating in similar crimes" to define the average participant. Amendment 794 at 117 (describing the circuit split and citing cases). The amendment "generally adopt[ed]" the former [—10—] approach by revising the application note to read: "substantially less culpable than the average participant *in the criminal activity.*" *Id.* (emphasis added).

This factor weighs in Sarmiento's favor because the Commission did not merely "assert[] that it follow[ed]" the winning circuits' holdings. *Crudup*, 375 F.3d at 10 (second alteration in original) (internal quotation marks omitted). Rather, the Commission determined that the "mitigating role [was] applied inconsistently and more sparingly *than the Commission intended*," so it promulgated the amendment to "promote consistency" in section 3B1.2's application. Amendment 794 at 117-18 (emphasis added). In other words, the Commission did not resolve the circuit split by creating "a new blanket rule . . . going beyond any circuit's reading of the previous rule," but instead issued a "clarification in favor of one view or the other." *United States v. Godin*, 522 F.3d 133, 135 (1st Cir. 2008) (describing such a resolution of a circuit split as clarifying).

Having considered these factors, and looking at the "significance of the amendment as a whole," *Cabrera-Polo*, 376 F.3d at 32 (quotation omitted), we agree with Sarmiento that Amendment 794 clarifies the Commission's original intent regarding section 3B1.2 and therefore applies retroactively.

The government argues in the alternative that Sarmiento would have been denied the minor-role reduction even in light of [—11—] Amendment 794, but we think it prudent to leave that determination in the hands of the able district court judge. Accordingly, a remand is justified to allow the sentencing court the opportunity to consider the "Commission's current policy position[,] . . . [which] may have some influence on the judge's ultimate discretionary choice of sentence." *United States v. Ahrendt*, 560 F.3d 69, 79 (1st Cir. 2009) (quoting *Godin*, 522 F.3d at 136).[4] {–7–}

III. Conclusion

Although Sarmiento's MDLEA contention is unavailing, we agree that because Amendment 794 is clarifying, not substantive, it is retroactively applicable. We therefore ***vacate*** the district court's sentence and ***remand*** for resentencing under the Commission's clarified guidance, as reflected in Amendment 794.

(Reporter's Note: Concurring Opinion follows on p. 12).

[4] Because we remand on the basis of Sarmiento's argument about the retroactivity of Amendment 794, we need not address his argument in the alternative that section 3B1.2 is void for vagueness. *See United States v. Vidal-Reyes*, 562 F.3d 43, 48 (1st Cir. 2009).

[—12—] {-7-} **TORRUELLA**, Circuit Judge, concurring:

I write separately to highlight that I join the majority opinion's holding that the United States had jurisdiction to prosecute Sarmiento *solely because* Sarmiento has conceded that he was aboard "a vessel without nationality" when the Coast Guard apprehended him. As I have previously explained, Congress exceeded its authority under Article I of the Constitution in attempting to extend criminal jurisdiction via the MDLEA to conduct outside of the United States lacking any nexus to the United States and over which the United States does not enjoy universal jurisdiction. *See United States v. Cardales-Luna*, 632 F.3d 731, 739-42 (Torruella, J., dissenting) (1st Cir. 2011). And while the United States (like all nations) does have universal jurisdiction over stateless vessels, I also reiterate that "the MDLEA's definition of 'statelessness' goes far beyond what is recognized by international customs or convention." *Id.* at 747 (citing Eugene Kontorovich, *Beyond the Article I Horizon: Congress's Enumerated Powers and Universal Jurisdiction over Drug Crimes*, 93 Minn. L. Rev. 1191, 1228 (2009)).

Thus, it is only by virtue of Sarmiento's concession that he was aboard a stateless vessel that I am able to join the panel in concluding that the United States has jurisdiction over crimes taking place aboard a vessel crewed by Dominican and Venezuelan nationals that was stopped by a Dutch warship in international waters in the middle of the Caribbean Sea.

United States Court of Appeals
for the First Circuit

No. 16-2470

SAWYER BROS., INC.
vs.
ISLAND TRANSPORTER, LLC

Appeal from the United States District Court for the District of Maine

Decided: April 3, 2018

Citation: 887 F.3d 23, 6 Adm. R. 13 (1st Cir. 2018).

Before **BARRON**, **SELYA**, and **LIPEZ**, Circuit Judges.

[—2—] {-26-} LIPEZ, Circuit Judge: **{-27-}**

Sawyer Brothers, Inc. hired Island Transporter, LLC to ferry three construction vehicles and their drivers from Rockland, Maine to North Haven, Maine. The M/V ISLAND TRANSPORTER encountered rough seas while traversing Penobscot Bay, and two of the vehicles tipped over onto the vessel's port bulwark. Sawyer Brothers, Inc., and its owners Ryan and Ross Sawyer (collectively, "Sawyer Brothers"), subsequently filed this maritime action, claiming that the ship captain was negligent and seeking damages for property loss and emotional distress.

Following a bench trial, the district court found in favor of Sawyer Brothers and awarded $257,154.03 in damages, including $100,000 for the Sawyers' emotional distress. On appeal, Island Transporter, LLC and M/V ISLAND TRANSPORTER (collectively, "Island Transporter") challenge both the district court's negligence finding and its damages award.

With the exception of one minor damages issue, we agree with the district court's well-reasoned decision, including its determination on an issue of first impression in our circuit—that a plaintiff within the zone of danger can recover for negligent infliction of emotional distress in maritime cases. We therefore affirm its judgment in substantial part, vacating only one element of the damages award. **[—3—]**

I.

In December 2014, Sawyer Brothers was hired to construct a foundation in North Haven, an island in Penobscot Bay.[1] It engaged Island Transporter to ferry a cement truck, a Mack truck, and a pickup truck, along with the Sawyers themselves and the cement truck's driver, from Rockland Harbor to North Haven Harbor. The M/V ISLAND TRANSPORTER began its run to North Haven on the morning of December 11, 2014, with Richard Morse as its captain and James McIntyre as its mate.

The National Oceanic and Atmospheric Administration ("NOAA") provides mariners with weather information by making periodic forecasts and publishing data from weather buoys. For forecasting purposes, NOAA divides the ocean into forecast areas, two of which are relevant to this case. The route taken by the M/V ISLAND TRANSPORTER that morning fell within the southern portion of the Penobscot Bay area. The Coastal Waters area from Stonington to Port Clyde ("Coastal Waters") borders the Penobscot Bay area to the south.

At the time the vessel departed—approximately 8:30 a.m.—the most recent forecast from NOAA predicted southerly **[—4—]** winds of 10-20 knots with waves of 2-4 feet for the Penobscot Bay area. For the Coastal Waters area, NOAA predicted significantly higher waves of 8-11 feet, with wind gusts up to 30 knots. These predicted wave heights represent the average of the highest one third of all waves—a measurement known as "significant wave height." Thus, when a forecast predicts waves of 2-4 feet, it is reasonable to expect some waves to be higher than 4 feet.

NOAA also publishes data from weather buoys maintained by the North Eastern Regional Association of Coastal Ocean

[1] We summarize the background facts of this case only to the extent necessary to contextualize our analysis. For a more detailed recitation, *see Sawyer Brothers, Inc. v. M/V Island Transporter*, No. 15-cv-00338-NT, 2016 WL 6537575 (D. Me. Nov. 3, 2016).

Observing Systems. One such buoy, known as the F01 buoy, is proximate to the route taken by the M/V ISLAND TRANSPORTER. Data from the buoy is published **{-28-}** hourly online and on the radio. At 7:30 a.m. on December 11, 2014, the buoy recorded a significant wave height of 6.3 feet, with 10.7 seconds between waves, and wind speeds of 18.7 knots. At 8:30 a.m., the significant wave height was 6.7 feet, with 5.3 seconds between waves. By 9:30 a.m., the significant wave height had increased to 7.1 feet, with 5.3 seconds between waves.

Captain Morse relied on the forecast for the Penobscot Bay area the morning of December 11, but disregarded the Coastal Waters forecast because his route did not cross into that area. It was part of Captain Morse's normal routine to check the F01 buoy's data, though he has no specific recollection of checking the buoy's data on that particular morning. In any event, Captain **[—5—]** Morse determined that the forecast allowed for safe passage to North Haven, and he arrived at Rockland Harbor to load the vehicles and passengers.

Once aboard, Ryan Sawyer sat in Sawyer Brothers' 1987 Mack truck, which was situated at the vessel's bow, with the truck's cabin facing forward. The truck was mounted with a 1992 Copma knuckleboom crane, capable of extending 68 feet and lifting 2,400 pounds. Ross Sawyer sat in Sawyer Brothers' pick-up truck, which was located in the middle of the vessel, facing the stern. Dana Martin, who is not a party to this suit, sat in his loaded cement truck, which was situated at the vessel's stern, with the truck's cabin facing forward toward the bow. Mate McIntyre placed chocks at all three vehicles' wheels to help stabilize them for the trip. He did not take the additional precaution of chaining the vehicles to the "D rings" located on the vessel's deck.

Conditions were mild as the vessel left the dock. Once the ship cleared the protected waters of Rockland Harbor and entered the stretch of open water between the mainland and North Haven, calm seas gave way to a far more tumultuous environment. Video captured on Ryan Sawyer's cellphone shows the vessel's bow dipping up and down, as sizeable waves crash aboard, peppering the Mack truck's windshield with sheets of ocean water. As Ryan Sawyer continued to film, a sequence of waves hit the starboard side of the ship and caused the truck to tip toward the vessel's port side **[—6—]** until the vehicle struck the port bulwark. The truck rested diagonally against the bulwark, with the driver-side door angled downward and the passenger-side door angled upward. Ryan Sawyer feared that he would be trapped in the truck's cabin as it went overboard, or as the ship capsized. After a minute or two, he was able to escape the cabin by standing on the side of the driver's seat, pushing open the passenger-side door, lifting himself out of the cabin, and jumping down to the deck.

At the other end of the vessel, Dana Martin was sitting inside the cement truck as it also tipped over, striking the portside bulwark, and resting against it diagonally.[2] Martin honked the truck's horn to alert everyone to the situation, and then managed to exit the truck's cabin through its driver-side door. Ross Sawyer watched the scene unfold and feared that the cement truck and the Mack truck would tip overboard with Martin and his brother trapped inside. He also feared that the ship would capsize, and he would drown.

Although the weight of the vehicles against the portside bulwark caused the M/V ISLAND TRANSPORTER to develop **{-29-}** a significant list of 37 degrees, Captain Morse navigated the ferry to North Haven harbor without further incident. The Sawyers **[—7—]** managed to walk away physically uninjured, but their Mack truck sustained enough damage that their insurer would later deem it a total loss.

Sawyer Brothers filed suit against Island Transporter in August 2015, alleging negligence and seeking damages for its Mack truck, lost profits, damaged construction

[2] This case does not involve damages for the cement truck. Though the record does not disclose whether the cement truck was owned by Dana Martin or his employer, neither is a party in the case.

supplies, and emotional distress. Following a three-day bench trial, the district court found that Captain Morse was negligent in failing to lash down the Mack truck and the cement truck. It awarded Sawyer Brothers $126,859.03 for replacing the Mack truck, $5,025 for damaged plywood panels that the Mack truck was carrying, $25,270 for lost profits, and $100,000 for emotional distress. Island Transporter now appeals the district court's finding of negligence and each damages award.

II.

A. Standard of Review

Island Transporter challenges the subsidiary factual findings upon which the district court based its negligence determination. Where a district court conducts a bench trial and serves as the factfinder, we review its factual findings for clear error. *See N. Ins. Co. of N.Y. v. Point Judith Marina, LLC*, 579 F.3d 61, 67 (1st Cir. 2009); *Sierra Fria Corp. v. Donald J. Evans, P.C.*, 127 F.3d 175, 181 (1st Cir. 1997). Accordingly, we will set aside a trial court's factual findings only if "after careful **[—8—]** evaluation of the evidence, we are left with an abiding conviction that those determinations and findings are simply wrong." *N. Ins. Co. of N.Y.*, 579 F.3d at 67 (quoting *Jackson v. United States*, 156 F.3d 230, 232-33 (1st Cir. 1998)).

Island Transporter's challenge to the district court's damages award rests on both factual and legal grounds. We review the district court's factual determinations in fixing damages for clear error. *See La Esperanza de P.R., Inc. v. Perez y Cia. de P.R., Inc.*, 124 F.3d 10, 21 (1st Cir. 1997); *Reilly v. United States*, 863 F.2d 149, 166 (1st Cir. 1988). We review its legal conclusions de novo. *See Lawton v. Nyman*, 327 F.3d 30, 42 (1st Cir. 2003) ("The district court's method of calculating damages in this case is essentially a conclusion of law, to which we give full review.").

B. Negligence

While the familiar elements of negligence—duty, breach, causation, and damages—apply in maritime cases, we look to "the principles of maritime negligence" to provide substance to each element. *La Esperanza de P.R., Inc.*, 124 F.3d at 17; *see also Canal Barge Co. v. Torco Oil Co.*, 220 F.3d 370, 376 (5th Cir. 2000) (reciting the elements of negligence in a maritime case). Thus, under maritime negligence law, "a shipowner owes the duty of exercising reasonable care towards those lawfully aboard the vessel who are not members of the crew." *Kermarec v. Compagnie* **[—9—]** *Generale Transatlantique*, 358 U.S. 625, 630 (1959). A private carrier, such as Island Transporter, also assumes a duty "to exercise due care in the protection of the goods committed to [its] care." *Commercial Molasses Corp. v. N.Y. Tank Barge Corp.*, 314 U.S. 104, 110 (1941). "Under this standard, the degree of care required must be in proportion to the apparent risk." *Muratore v. M/S Scotia Prince*, 845 F.2d 347, 353 (1st Cir. 1988). A captain breaches his duty of reasonable care "if he 'makes a decision which nautical experience and good seamanship would condemn as inexpedient and unjustifiable at the time and under the circumstances.'" **{-30-}** *DiMillo v. Sheepscot Pilots, Inc.*, 870 F.2d 746, 748 (1st Cir. 1989) (alteration omitted) (quoting *The Lizzie D. Shaw*, 47 F.2d 820, 822 (3d Cir. 1931)). We have long recognized that, for a captain, the duty of reasonable care clearly includes a "duty to monitor and take into account weather conditions." *Id.*

The district court found that Captain Morse breached his duty of care by failing to utilize the M/V ISLAND TRANSPORTER'S D-rings to lash down the construction vehicles. This negligence determination was based in part upon the district court's subsidiary finding that the weather conditions that caused the incident were foreseeable. More specifically, the court determined that the weather information available to Captain Morse would have apprised him of a likelihood of rough seas. The **[—10—]** district court also found that the incident was not caused by two unforeseeable rogue waves.

Island Transporter challenges both of these subsidiary factual findings. It asserts that the weather information available to Captain Morse would not have apprised him of rough seas along his route, and maintains that the incident was caused by two unpredictable rogue waves. Under its view of the facts, Island Transporter argues that Captain Morse did not breach his duty of care because the incident was unforeseeable.

1. Available Weather Information

The district court determined that Captain Morse could have reasonably anticipated 5-7.5 foot seas on the voyage. It reached this conclusion by averaging the 2-4 foot seas forecasted for the Penobscot Bay area and the 8-11 foot seas forecasted for the Coastal Waters area. Island Transporter believes this calculation was clearly erroneous because the M/V ISLAND TRANSPORTER'S route remained entirely within the Penobscot Bay area. Thus, according to Island Transporter, only that area's forecast was relevant to Captain Morse. Given the much calmer 2-4 foot predicted seas, he could not have reasonably foreseen the conditions the M/V ISLAND TRANSPORTER would encounter.

Island Transporter's position overlooks an abundance of testimony suggesting that the Coastal Waters forecast was relevant to assessing the sea conditions along the vessel's route. Though **[—11—]** the route fell entirely within Penobscot Bay, it came close to the northern border of the Coastal Waters area. The wind on the morning of December 11 was blowing from a southerly direction; that is, from the open seas of the Coastal Waters area toward the Penobscot Bay area. Maine State Ferry Captain Almer Dinsmore testified that, given the direction of the wind and the route's proximity to the Coastal Waters area, the Coastal Waters forecast was highly relevant to assessing the predicted weather conditions along the route. He opined that it would have been unreasonable in those circumstances for a ship captain to rely solely on the Penobscot Bay forecast.

Other witnesses echoed this sentiment. Both Mate McIntyre and Maine State Ferry Service Port Captain Daniel McNichol represented that they rely on both areas' forecasts when they sail comparable routes. Island Transporter's own weather expert testified that it would be unreasonable to think there would be an abrupt transition—from 2-4 foot seas in Penobscot Bay to 8-11 foot seas in the Coastal Waters area—right at the boundary of the two zones.[3] Island Transporter's nautical expert similarly testified on cross examination **{-31-}** that it would be a mistake to rely solely on the Penobscot Bay forecast. Even Captain Morse conceded **[—12—]** that it is generally prudent to rely on more than one piece of weather information in making navigational decisions, and that the Coastal Waters forecast is in some circumstances relevant to the Rockland-to-North Haven route.

Given this testimony, the district court's finding that the information available to Captain Morse would have apprised him of a likelihood of rough conditions did not rest on a clearly erroneous view of the facts. To the contrary, the record contains ample testimony to support the court's conclusion that the Coastal Waters area forecast was relevant to predicting the weather conditions along the M/V ISLAND TRANSPORTER'S route.

2. The Rogue Wave Theory

Island Transporter challenges the district court's finding that the incident was not caused by two "rogue waves." A rogue wave is classified as such if it is more than twice the significant wave height. Although the record does not reveal precisely how often rogue waves occur, expert testimony established that so-called "extreme waves"—those reaching about double the significant wave height—occur once every thousand waves. Rogue waves are not only larger, but also rarer than extreme waves.

The only evidence at trial supporting Island Transporter's rogue wave theory was Captain Morse's testimony. He testified that two rogue waves hit the vessel in quick

[3] Sawyer Brothers elicited this testimony after it called Island Transporter's weather expert, Ken McKinley, as a witness in its case-in-chief.

succession, **[—13—]** causing the cement truck and the Mack truck to tip against the port bulwark. According to Captain Morse, these waves were 12-15 feet high, and anomalous compared to the other waves the vessel had encountered.

The district court found Captain Morse's testimony to be not credible for a number of reasons. It noted that Captain Morse was the only witness who testified to having seen the rogue waves. The court also stated that the Coast Guard incident report filed by Island Transporter identified the offending waves as being 10-12 feet, not 12-15 feet. Such waves were foreseeable—not rogue—considering the predicted wave heights for the Penobscot Bay and Coastal Waters areas, as well as the F01 buoy data. Perhaps most damaging to Captain Morse's testimony is the video recorded by Ryan Sawyer from the Mack truck's cabin. The district court observed that the video depicted a series of similarly sized waves, not two anomalous swells.

We have repeatedly said that "in a bench trial, credibility calls are for the trier." *Carr v. PMS Fishing Corp.*, 191 F.3d 1, 7 (1st Cir. 1999). We see no basis here for deviating from that principle. Indeed, the district court aptly supported its credibility assessment by finding that Ryan Sawyer's video, the weather data, the Coast Guard report, and the lack of corroborating testimony contradicted Captain Morse's position. **[—14—]** Our review of that evidence confirms that the court's decision to reject the rogue wave theory was not clearly erroneous.

C. Damages for the Mack Truck

The district court awarded Sawyer Brothers $126,859.03 for the loss of its Mack truck, after finding that the truck's fair market value could not be established, and using as the relevant measure of damages Sawyer Brothers' replacement cost. The court assessed that cost as $206,859.03. It then deducted $80,000 to account for Sawyer Brothers' insurance recovery, resulting in the $126,859.03 award. **{-32-}**

Island Transporter challenges this award on three grounds. First, it assails the district court's finding that the truck's fair market value could not be reasonably established. Second, it argues that the court committed legal error by failing to deduct the Mack truck's salvage value from Sawyer Brothers' damages. Third, it challenges the court's decision to treat Sawyer Brothers as the real party in interest for its Mack truck, asserting instead that the company's insurer was the real party in interest.

1. Fair Market Value vs. Replacement Cost

The parties agree that the ordinary measure of damages under maritime law for property deemed a total loss is the property's fair market value, less its salvage value. *See Dimillo*, 870 F.2d at 752 ("[W]here a vessel is adjudged a complete loss, **[—15—]** the damages will be derived by calculating the vessel's value and deducting therefrom the salvage proceeds, if any there be."); *Texas Co. v. R. O'Brien & Co.*, 242 F.2d 526, 527 (1st Cir. 1957) (stating that "the normal measure of damages is the vessel's fair market value").[4] Courts determine fair market value based on the price paid for comparable property on the open market. *See Standard Oil Co. of N.J. v. S. Pac. Co.*, 268 U.S. 146, 155 (1925); *Moench v. Marquette Transp. Co. Gulf-Inland*, 838 F.3d 586, 592, 4 Adm. R. 281, 283 (5th Cir. 2016). If fair market value cannot be determined, courts may resort to alternative measures of damages. *See, e.g., Standard Oil*, 268 U.S. at 155 ("Where there is no market

[4] In addressing the damages analysis for the Mack truck, both the parties and the district court relied primarily on case law dealing with damaged vessels. *See, e.g., Standard Oil Co. of N.J. v. S. Pac. Co.*, 268 U.S. 146 (1925); *Dimillo*, 870 F.2d at 746; *Greer v. United States*, 505 F.2d 90 (5th Cir. 1974). Although the Mack truck is not a vessel, the rule for measuring damages to cargo is materially similar to the rule for measuring damages to vessels. *See Columbia Brick Works, Inc. v. Royal Ins. Co. of Am.*, 768 F.2d 1066, 1068–69 (9th Cir. 1985) (explaining that the proper measure of damages for cargo is based on market value, but that courts may use other indicators of value when market price proves inaccurate).

value, . . . other evidence is resorted to."); *Moench*, 838 F.3d at 592, 4 Adm. R. at 283.[5]

Island Transporter argues that the evidence at trial allowed the district court to establish the Mack truck's fair market value, making the court's decision to resort to replacement **[—16—]** cost erroneous. Specifically, Island Transporter contends that the court should have relied on its valuation expert's estimate of the truck's fair market value, or on Ryan Sawyer's lay testimony regarding fair market value.

Island Transporter's expert assessed the Mack truck's fair market value at $38,000. He reached this figure by employing a peculiar methodology. Sawyer Brothers had filed an insurance claim following the incident, and its insurer took possession of the Mack truck as part of the claim's settlement. A third party then listed the truck for sale for $39,500. The valuation expert used this listing as the benchmark to estimate the Mack truck's fair market value. However, the expert testified that when he made this estimate, he did not realize that the Mack truck had been listed for sale in its damaged condition.

The district court rejected the expert's valuation, finding that his methodology **{-33-}** was "seriously discredit[ing]." We agree. The expert erroneously assessed the value of the undamaged Mack truck based on its listing price in its damaged condition. Given his flawed methodology, the district court was not obligated to rely on the expert's conclusion in awarding damages for the Mack truck.

Ryan Sawyer also offered an opinion as to the Mack truck's value. Disputing the valuation expert's $38,000 estimate, Ryan opined that the truck was worth $80,000 to $90,000. He then **[—17—]** testified at length about his attempts to find a replacement truck, explaining that—to suit Sawyer Brothers' needs—the company required a truck with a minimum 68-foot crane, a flatbed to hold equipment, four outriggers, and certain other features. The truck would also have to be capable of passing Department of Transportation and Occupational Safety and Health Administration safety inspections. Despite reviewing truck listings for months, Ryan stated that he could not find a replacement that met these specifications. Eventually, he located a 2006 Sterling crane truck in Wisconsin. Sawyer Brothers purchased and then modified the truck to suit its needs, at a total cost of $206,859.03, according to the district court. Ryan testified that this was the least expensive truck he could locate.

In finding that the Mack truck's fair market value could not be reasonably established, the district court did not mention Ryan Sawyer's testimony that the truck was worth $80,000 to $90,000. This omission does not undermine the court's finding. As an initial matter, the phrase "fair market value" is a term of art under maritime law. It refers to a specific measure of valuation, based on the price of "contemporaneous sales of like property . . . bought and sold in the market." *Standard Oil*, 268 U.S. at 155. Ryan, a lay witness, was not provided with this definition when he testified, and offered no indication that the basis for his valuation was sales of "like property." *Id.* Indeed, **[—18—]** when asked by Sawyer Brothers' attorney to provide a basis for his estimate, Ryan appeared not to understand the line of questioning.

Apparently realizing that Ryan would not be able to articulate a basis for his valuation, Sawyer Brothers' attorney began asking him about the unique features of the Mack truck, and his prolonged search for replacing it. As noted above, Ryan responded to this line of questioning by explaining that he was unable to find any comparable trucks on the market after months of searching. In other words, Ryan testified, at considerable length, that the market lacked any sales of "like property" that could be used to establish the Mack truck's fair market value. *Id.* This fact is precisely what justified the district court's decision to resort to an alternative measure of damages. The balance of Ryan's testimony thus under-

[5] *See also Ill. Cent. R.R. v. Crail*, 281 U.S. 57, 64–65 (1930) ("The test of market value is at best but a convenient means of getting at the loss suffered. It may be discarded and other more accurate means resorted to, if, for special reasons, it is not exact or otherwise not applicable.").

mined his lay assessment of the truck's fair market value and supported the court's finding that the fair market value could not be established. For these reasons, the district court was not obligated to rely on his estimate of the truck's value.[6]

2. The Salvage Value Deduction

As noted, the district court determined that Sawyer Brothers' replacement cost was $206,859.03. It then reduced that **[—19—]** amount by $80,000 to account for the company's insurance recovery, and awarded Sawyer Brothers $126,859.03 for the Mack truck. Island Transporter argues that the district court should have also reduced the **{-34-}** award by the Mack truck's salvage value, which it asserts was $39,500. *See Dimillo*, 870 F.2d at 752. We do not agree.

A careful review of the record shows that Sawyer Brothers forfeited the Mack truck's salvage value to its insurer following the incident. Ryan Sawyer testified that Sawyer Brothers filed a claim with its insurance company, and the insurer deemed the Mack truck a total loss. Sawyer Brothers then settled its insurance claim for $80,000, and—importantly—the insurer took possession of the damaged Mack truck as a condition of the payment. The salvage value thus became the insurer's property, and the district court correctly abstained from further reducing the damages award.

3. Real Party in Interest

Pursuant to Federal Rule of Civil Procedure 17(a), all civil actions must be "prosecuted in the name of the real party in interest." When an insurer has paid the entire loss suffered by its insured, the insurer becomes the real party in interest. *See United States v. Aetna Cas. & Sur. Co.*, 338 U.S. 366, 380–81 (1949); *State Farm Mut. Liab. Ins. Co. v. United States*, 172 F.2d 737, 739 (1st Cir. 1949). However, when an insurer pays only part of the loss suffered by its insured, the insured remains a real **[—20—]** party in interest together with the insurer. *See Aetna Cas. & Sur. Co.*, 338 U.S. at 381; *State Farm Mut. Liab. Ins. Co.*, 172 F.2d at 739.

Island Transporter argues that Sawyer Brothers is not a real party in interest because Sawyer Brothers' insurer paid its entire loss. However, the district court properly found that Sawyer Brothers' loss exceeded its gross insurance recovery by $126,859.03. Sawyer Brothers was thus a real party in interest because its insurer paid only part of its loss.

D. Damaged Panels

The district court awarded Sawyer Brothers $5,025 for plywood panels that it found were damaged in the incident. The only evidence offered by Sawyer Brothers pertaining to the damaged plywood panels was the testimony of Ryan Sawyer. He testified that the Mack truck was carrying 63 eight-foot plywood panels, which cost an average of $120.50 each.[7] Ryan estimated that approximately 80% of the panels were damaged on the voyage, but declared that Sawyer Brothers continued to use the panels in their damaged condition. This was so, he explained, even though the use of damaged panels generally results in a reduced quality of work. **[—21—]**

Based on this testimony, the district court found that the incident caused damage to approximately 50 eight-foot panels. It multiplied this quantity by a $120.50 per-panel cost to reach a total of $6,025. The court then reduced this amount by $1,000 to account for its finding that Sawyer Brothers continued to use "some" of the damaged panels. That is to say, the district court did not award damages for panels that it found Sawyer Brothers continued to use on construction projects.

---

[6] Island Transporter does not challenge the district court's choice of replacement cost as the alternative measure of damages, so we do not reach that issue.

[7] More precisely, Ryan testified that the truck was carrying 126 four-foot panels, and that the four-foot panels were made by cutting eight-foot panels in half. He estimated that the eight-foot panels cost between $118 and $123 each.

The district court's findings regarding the cost of the panels and the number of panels damaged are consistent with Ryan Sawyer's testimony, but its finding regarding Sawyer Brothers' continued use of the panels is not. It mistakenly concluded that Sawyer Brothers only continued to use *some* of the damaged panels, when Ryan testified that the company continued **{-35-}** to use *all* of the damaged panels. Moreover, Ryan Sawyer did not indicate that the diminished quality of work caused by using damaged panels resulted in any injury to Sawyer Brothers—for example, in the form of increased labor costs or decreased revenue. For these reasons, the district court's $5,025 award for damaged panels rests on a clearly erroneous view of the facts.

E. Lost Profits

The district court awarded Sawyer Brothers $25,270 in damages for the cost of additional labor, and for certain jobs it declined, because it could not use its Mack truck. In challenging **[—22—]** this award, Island Transporter alludes to the maritime-law maxim that when a vessel is a total loss, the owner cannot recover lost-profit damages. *See The Umbria*, 166 U.S. 404, 421-22 (1897). It argues that the rule applies to the lost profits caused by the damage to Sawyer Brothers' Mack truck. We disagree.

In *The Umbria*, the Supreme Court declined to award damages for the "probable profits" of a charter agreement entered into shortly before a collision rendered the Iberia vessel a total loss. *Id.* at 421. Lost profits, the Court explained, "may be considered in cases of delay occasioned by a partial loss, where the question is as to the value of the use of the vessel pending her repairs." *Id.* But, where a vessel is a total loss,

> the recovery of such profits is limited to the voyage which the vessel is then performing; since, if the owner were entitled to recover the profits of a future voyage or charter, there would seem to be no limit to such right so far as respects the time of its continuance; and, if the vessel were under a charter which had months or years to run, the allowance of the probable profits of such charter might work a great practical injustice to the owner of the vessel causing the injury.

Id. at 422.

This old rule of maritime law survives to the present day. *See, e.g., A & S Transp. Co. v. Tug Fajardo*, 688 F.2d 1, 2 (1st Cir. 1982); *Matter of P & E Boat Rentals, Inc.*, 872 F.2d 642, 648 (5th Cir. 1989). Its purpose, as stated in *The Umbria*, is to protect tortfeasors from incurring overly speculative or excessive **[—23—]** liability, particularly when they damage vessels that have months, or years, of work under agreement. 166 U.S. at 422. The owner of such a vessel is instead expected to promptly acquire a replacement to fulfill its chartered obligations. *See Barger v. Hanson*, 426 F.2d 640, 642 (9th Cir. 1970) ("[The law] considers that ships are commodities bought and sold in the market, and that one may be purchased to take the place of one lost . . . ." (quoting *The Hamilton*, 95 F. 844, 845 (E.D.N.Y. 1899))).

The rule of *The Umbria* does not apply in this case for an obvious reason. Sawyer Brothers' Mack truck was not a vessel. It was cargo aboard a vessel.[8] Island Transporter cites no case that applies *The Umbria's* rule to cargo, and we see no basis for extending the rule to such cases.

Moreover, even in the context of vessels, we have recognized that "arguments may be made, pro and con, for [the rule's] soundness as an original proposition." **{-36-}** *A & S Transp. Co.*, 688 F.2d at 3. For example, ordinary principles of mitigation would seem to resolve the problems involving excessive or speculative damages identified by the Court.

[8] As we observed, *supra* note 4, this distinction was not significant in valuing the Mack truck because the well-established rules for valuing cargo and vessels are materially similar. In contrast, Island Transporter now seeks to extend to cargo cases a principle of damages that has traditionally applied only to vessels. Its position thus places the distinction between vessels and cargo at the forefront.

Indeed, in *Barger*, **[—24—]** the Ninth Circuit declined to apply the rule of *The Umbria* in a vessel case in part because the plaintiff had mitigated his damages "as quickly as possible." 426 F.2d at 642. Though we have since declined to follow *Barger's* decision to depart from the "well-established" rule in vessel cases, the Ninth Circuit's reasoning and our prior reference to the rule's questionable soundness counsel against extending it to new ground. *A & S Transp. Co.*, 688 F.2d at 3 (noting that the rule is "too well-established to be altered now, at least at our level").

We thus uphold the district court's award of lost profit damages.[9]

F. Emotional Distress

The district court awarded the Sawyers each $50,000 in damages for their emotional distress. Island Transporter challenges this award, raising several issues related to the standard of liability for negligent infliction of emotional distress ("NIED") claims under the general maritime law in the **[—25—]** First Circuit. We uphold the award. In doing so, we conclude that maritime plaintiffs within the "zone of danger" can recover for NIED in the First Circuit.

1. The NIED Cause of Action

As a threshold matter, the district court assumed that a claim for NIED is cognizable under the general maritime law in the First Circuit. It was correct to do so. We recognized a plaintiff's right to recover for NIED under the general maritime law in *Petition of the U.S. (Petition)*, 418 F.2d 264, 269 (1st Cir. 1969). The plaintiff in *Petition* was a crewman who nearly died in the cold seas after his vessel capsized. *Id.* at 267. Following the incident, the plaintiff became "very depressed and emotionally upset," and was diagnosed with "severe neurosis of an anxiety reaction type with depressive features." *Id.* The district court awarded the plaintiff damages due to his emotional distress and accompanying physical symptoms, and the defendant appealed. *Id.* at 267-68.

Surveying the common-law treatment of NIED claims, we observed that it was "almost uniformly recognized that recovery may be had for the physical consequences of mental disturbance, at least where there is some contemporaneous physical impact also resulting from [a] defendant's negligence." *Id.* at 268. In other words, we described the general state of the law as imposing two limitations on a plaintiff's ability to recover for NIED. First, **[—26—]** the plaintiff had to experience a physical impact from the defendant's negligence during the incident in question. Second, the plaintiff's emotional distress had to have a "physical consequence" that is "susceptible of objective determination." *Id.* at 269.

We determined that the *Petition* plaintiff's "substantial jolt," and the impact from being "thrown into the water as the boat capsized," were both "sufficient to **{-37-}** satisfy the test applied by jurisdictions following the impact rule." *Id.* at 268. Since the plaintiff satisfied the physical impact test, we found it "unnecessary to decide whether a contemporaneous physical impact" was "required as a prerequisite to recovery" for NIED in the First Circuit. *Id.* at 269. We then proceeded to the physical consequence issue and concluded that the plaintiff's "definite nervous disorder" was a sufficiently "physical" injury to permit recovery. *Id.*

By affirming the district court's damages award, our decision in *Petition* recognized a cause of action for NIED under the general maritime law. However, *Petition* left the contours of the cause of action unresolved. It expressly declined to decide whether a

[9] We also reject Island Transporter's contention that Sawyer Brothers failed to mitigate its damages. The district court rebuffed this argument after finding that Sawyer Brothers' cost to rent a suitable replacement truck would have been $3,800 per month, plus a $10,000 delivery fee. The court concluded that these costs made renting a replacement truck to perform Sawyer Brothers' lost work unreasonable. We find no error in this conclusion. In addition, we note that the district court carefully circumscribed Sawyer Brothers' damages award to the approximately six-week period following the incident, declining to include lost profits that it considered speculative or too attenuated.

contemporaneous physical impact was a prerequisite to recovery. And, because the *Petition* plaintiff suffered physical consequences from his emotional distress, we had no occasion to determine whether a plaintiff can recover for NIED without showing **[—27—]** physical consequences within the meaning of *Petition*. This was the state of our maritime NIED jurisprudence at the time this case was tried. We recognized the cause of action, but had yet to define its boundaries.[10]

2. The Zone of Danger Test

This case compels us to confront the first issue left open by *Petition*: whether a plaintiff can recover for NIED under the general maritime law without sustaining a contemporaneous physical impact. The district court awarded the Sawyers emotional distress damages based on their presence within the "zone of danger," not based upon any physical impact. Island Transporter asks us to adopt the physical impact test, and to accordingly vacate the district court's damages award.

The "zone of danger" test applied by the district court limits recovery for emotional injury to those "who are placed in immediate risk of physical harm by that conduct." *Consol. Rail Corp. v. Gottshall*, 512 U.S. 532, 548 (1994). In *Gottshall*, the Supreme Court held that the zone of danger test applies to NIED claims brought under the Federal Employers' Liability Act **[—28—]** ("FELA"), 45 U.S.C. §§ 51-60. *Id.* at 554. Section 1 of the FELA provides railroad employees with a cause of action when they are injured or killed as a result of their employers' negligence. 45 U.S.C. § 51. The Jones Act provides a parallel cause of action for seamen, 46 U.S.C. § 30104, and incorporates by reference the standard of liability under the FELA. *Id.* ("Laws of the United States regulating recovery for personal injury to, or death of, a railway employee apply to an action under this section."). Thus, we have declared that "[c]aselaw developed under both statutes guides subsequent interpretation of either of them." *Ellenwood*, 984 F.2d at 1281 n.15 (citing *Mitchell v. Trawler Racer, Inc.*, 362 U.S. 539, 547 (1960)); *see also Butynski v. Springfield Terminal Ry. Co.*, 592 F.3d 272, 277 n.2 (1st Cir. 2010) ("[P]recedent under the Jones Act is deemed instructive in FELA cases, and vice versa.").

The zone of danger test, as articulated in *Gottshall*, therefore applies to seamen alleging NIED under the Jones Act. Given its application to seamen, we see no principled **{-38-}** basis for imposing the more restrictive physical impact test upon passengers alleging NIED under the general maritime law. *See Miles v. Apex Marine Corp.*, 498 U.S. 19, 24 (1990) ("[L]egislation has always served as an important source of . . . admiralty principles."); *Chan v. Soc'y Expeditions, Inc.*, 39 F.3d 1398, 1407–08 (9th Cir. 1994) ("[W]e look to . . . maritime statutes for guidance in **[—29—]** determining what remedies should be available in an admiralty case . . . that falls outside the ambit of statutory maritime law.").

In so concluding, we join two circuits and a number of district courts in recognizing that, post-*Gottshall*, a plaintiff within the zone of danger may recover for NIED under the general maritime law. *See Chaparro v. Carnival Corp.*, 693 F.3d 1333, 1338 (11th Cir. 2012) (per curiam); *Stacy v. Rederiet Otto Danielsen, A.S.*, 609 F.3d 1033, 1035 (9th Cir. 2010); *Blair v. NCL (Bahamas) Ltd.*, 212 F. Supp. 3d 1264, 1271 (S.D. Fla. 2016); *Nieto-Vincenty v. Valledor*, 22 F. Supp. 3d 153, 160 (D.P.R. 2014); *Smith v. Carnival Corp.*, 584 F. Supp. 2d 1343, 1355 (S.D. Fla. 2008); *Douville v. Casco Bay Island Transit*, 1998 A.M.C. 2775, 2781 (D.N.H. 1998); *Williams v. Carnival Cruise Lines, Inc.*, 907 F. Supp. 403, 406 (S.D. Fla. 1995).[11] **[—30—]**

---

[10] Our more recent pronouncements on the maritime NIED cause of action are consistent with *Petition*. *See Ellenwood v. Exxon Shipping Co.*, 984 F.2d 1270, 1282 (1st Cir. 1993) (declining to decide whether "a seaman may recover emotional distress damages *without showing a physical injury*" (emphasis added)); *Fairest-Knight v. Marine World Distribs., Inc.*, 652 F.3d 94, 102 n.7 (1st Cir. 2011) (refusing to decide whether plaintiffs had made out a cognizable cause of action for NIED).

[11] This case does not require us to determine whether *Gottshall* counsels against applying the more permissive "relative bystander" test to general maritime cases. *Gottshall*, 512 U.S. at 548. That test allows plaintiffs to recover "for emotional

3. The Scope of the Zone of Danger

Island Transporter next contends that the district court clearly erred[12] in finding that the Sawyers were within the zone of danger when the construction vehicles tipped and the M/V ISLAND TRANSPORTER took on a 37-degree list in tumultuous seas. A plaintiff is within the zone of danger if he sustains a physical impact, or is "placed in immediate risk of physical harm" by a defendant's negligent conduct. *Gottshall*, 512 U.S. at 548. Plaintiffs facing immediate physical peril or the reasonable apprehension thereof are within the zone of danger. *See Metro-North Commuter R.R. Co. v. Buckley*, 521 U.S. 424, 430 (1997) (noting that the zone of danger cases cited by *Gottshall* all involved "a threatened physical contact that caused, or might have caused, immediate traumatic harm"); *Gottshall*, 512 U.S. at 555 ("The zone of danger test also is consistent with FELA's central focus on physical perils."). Indeed, it is oft repeated that "a near miss may be as frightening as a direct hit." *Gottshall*, 512 U.S. at 547 (quoting **{-39-}** Richard N. Pearson, *Liability to Bystanders for Negligently Inflicted Emotional Harm—A Comment on the Nature of Arbitrary Rules*, 34 U. Fla. L. Rev. 477, 488 (1982)). **[—31—]**

Courts applying the test in maritime cases have consistently found that plaintiffs on board vessels that experience near misses are within the zone of danger. In *Stacy*, for example, the Ninth Circuit held that a fisherman sufficiently alleged he was in the zone of danger when a ship narrowly avoided hitting his fishing boat, only to collide with a nearby vessel. 609 F.3d at 1034-37. Similarly, the plaintiff in *In re Clearsky Shipping Corp.* was aboard a docked casino boat as a vessel collided with a nearby wharf. No. Civ. 96-4099, 2002 WL 31496659, *1 (E.D. La. Nov. 7, 2002). The plaintiff was "obviously in the 'zone of danger'" as she attempted to exit the casino boat and witnessed the other vessel coming directly toward her. *Id.* at *3.

In another near-miss case, a class of passengers sued a cruise line after they experienced a severe storm on their voyage. *Williams*, 907 F. Supp. at 404. The court found that the passengers "[met] the first part of the zone of danger test in that they were placed in immediate risk of physical impact by [the cruise line's] conduct." *Id.* at 407. Finally, the case of *Hutton v. Norwegian Cruise Line Ltd.* goes beyond a near miss and involves an actual collision. 144 F. Supp. 2d 1325 (S.D. Fla. 2001). There, a proposed class of passengers sued when their cruise ship collided with another vessel. *Id.* at 1326. The lead plaintiffs were sleeping in their cabin at the time of the collision, and then went to their muster (emergency) station, where they saw the other **[—32—]** vessel in flames. *Id.* The court found that when the ships collided the lead plaintiffs "were certainly within the zone of danger," as they "were frightened and were placed in immediate risk of physical harm by the Defendant's negligent conduct." *Id.* at 1328.

It is fair to characterize the Sawyers' experience on board the M/V ISLAND TRANSPORTER as involving more immediate peril than any of the cases summarized above. They were aboard a relatively small ferry as it attempted to traverse a sea roiled by large waves. Ryan Sawyer was in the cabin of his Mack truck as its passenger-side wheels lifted off the ground, causing the vehicle to tip against the vessel's bulwark. Ross Sawyer

---

distress brought on by witnessing the injury or death of a third party (who typically must be a close relative of the bystander) that is caused by the defendant's negligence." *Id.* at 549. *Gottshall* rejected the relative bystander test in the context of the FELA, in large part because "it would be a rare occurrence for a [railroad] worker to witness during the course of his employment the injury or death of a close family member." *Id.* at 556. This reasoning does not necessarily translate to general maritime law, where "it is not at all 'unlikely' that a person involved in a maritime accident—as opposed to a railroad worker covered by FELA—would have occasion to witness the death or serious injury of a close family member." *Stacy*, 609 F.3d at 1040 n.1 (Hall, J., dissenting). For this reason, there *may* be a "principled basis" for not extending **[—30—]** *Gottshall* to general maritime relative bystander cases, though we do not decide that issue here.

[12] Whether a plaintiff was within the zone of danger presents a fact-dominated mixed question of law and fact, resulting in clear error review. *See Sierra Fria Corp.*, 127 F.3d at 181 (explaining that fact-dominated mixed questions are reviewed for clear error).

watched as the Mack truck and cement truck tipped with his brother and co-worker inside their respective cabins. Both Sawyers reasonably feared that the vehicles would go overboard, or that the vessel—listing significantly to its port—would capsize. Given this series of events, the district court did not clearly err by determining that the Sawyers were within the zone of danger.

4. The Physical Consequences Requirement

The second issue left open by *Petition* was whether a plaintiff can recover for NIED under the general maritime law without showing physical consequences of his emotional distress. The district court assumed that this requirement applied to the Sawyers' NIED claims, concluded that the brothers satisfied the requirement, and awarded each of them $50,000. Island Transporter **[—33—]** contends that the district court clearly erred by finding that the Sawyers showed physical consequences of their emotional distress, and argues that the brothers cannot recover damages for NIED absent such a showing.

Whether the physical consequences requirement applies to NIED claims under the general maritime law is a matter of some disagreement among the federal courts. *See, e.g.*, **{-40-}** *Tassinari v. Key W. Water Tours, L.C.*, 480 F. Supp. 2d 1318, 1321-22 (S.D. Fla. 2007) (collecting cases). As in *Petition*, this case does not require us to resolve that issue in the First Circuit. For reasons that we will explain, it was not clearly erroneous for the district court to conclude that the Sawyers satisfied the physical consequences requirement. Given that their NIED claims succeed regardless of whether the requirement applies, we, like the district court, assume, without deciding, that the requirement applies in this case.

The term "physical" in the physical consequences requirement "is not used in its ordinary sense." *Id.* at 269. Its meaning includes both consequences of emotional distress that are traditionally "physical"—e.g., heart attacks or ulcers—and other conditions that are "susceptible of objective determination." *Id.* For example, emotional distress may "physically" manifest as a psychological condition—i.e., a nervous disorder or a stress disorder—so long as the condition **[—34—]** is capable of objective determination. *See id.* (categorizing psychoneurosis as a "physical" condition); *Haught v. Maceluch*, 681 F.2d 291, 299 n.9 (5th Cir. 1982) (noting that "physical injury" extends to nervous disorders, and deciding that "depression, nervousness, weight gain, and nightmares" were "sufficient to constitute physical injury" under Texas law).[13] Whether a particular condition falls within the NIED definition of a "physical" consequence presents a fact-intensive question, requiring case-by-case assessment. *Cf. Atchison, Topeka & Santa Fe Ry. Co. v. Buell*, 480 U.S. 557, 570 (1987) (opining that "broad pronouncements" in the area of emotional distress claims "may have to bow to the precise application of developing legal principles to the particular facts at hand").

Here, we need not probe the physical consequences requirement's outer boundaries. The district court found that the Sawyers experienced several symptoms properly classified as "physical." It found that Ross Sawyer experienced ongoing gastrointestinal distress, pain in his limbs, and pain in his chest. As to Ryan Sawyer, the district court concluded that he had a bout of stress-induced shingles accompanied by a high fever and pain that felt like a heart attack. Several courts have found **[—35—]** that plaintiffs with comparable or lesser symptomology satisfied the physical consequences requirement. *See, e.g.*, *Whalley v. Sakura*, 804 F.2d 580, 587 (10th Cir. 1986) (finding requirement satisfied where plaintiff had loss of energy, fatigue, decreased mobility, sleep disturbance, and significant depression); *Doe v. Trs. of the Univ. of Pa.*, 270 F. Supp. 3d 799, 828 (E.D. Pa. 2017) (allowing claim to survive dismissal where plaintiff's alleged physical consequences consisted of "depression, extreme anxiety, loss of the ability to concentrate, intense feelings of hopelessness

---

[13] *See also Sullivan v. Bos. Gas Co.*, 605 N.E.2d 805, 808-11 (Mass. 1993); *Vance v. Vance*, 408 A.2d 728, 733-34 (Md. 1979); *Corso v. Merrill*, 406 A.2d 300, 307 (N.H. 1979); Restatement (Second) of Torts § 436A cmt. c (1965).

and sadness, and the inability to sleep through the night"); *Terry v. Carnival Corp.*, 3 F. Supp. 3d 1363, 1370 (S.D. Fla. 2014) (allowing emotional distress claim to survive summary judgment where plaintiffs alleged physical consequences in the form of continuous sleep deprivation and nightmares); *Sullivan*, 605 N.E.2d at 806, 810 (Mass. 1993) (finding that symptoms such as sleeplessness, gastrointestinal distress, and nightmares allowed a plaintiff to survive summary judgment). These cases are consistent with the Restatement (Second) of Torts' position that "long continued nausea or headaches may amount to physical **{-41-}** illness, which is bodily harm; and even long continued mental disturbance, as for example in the case of repeated hysterical attacks, or mental aberration, may be classified by the courts as illness, notwithstanding their mental character." Restatement (Second) of Torts § 436A cmt. c (1965). **[—36—]**

Furthermore, the district court noted that experts for both parties opined that Ross Sawyer could be diagnosed with Post-Traumatic Stress Disorder ("PTSD") as a result of the incident. One of the experts also testified that Ryan Sawyer could be diagnosed with PTSD. A PTSD diagnosis with accompanying symptoms has been found sufficient to satisfy the physical consequences requirement. *See Walters v. Mintec/Int'l*, 758 F.2d 73, 78 (3d Cir. 1985) (affirming emotional distress award in product liability case based on PTSD diagnosis, headaches, insomnia, and nightmares); *Sullivan*, 605 N.E.2d at 806-07, 810 (finding that plaintiff with PTSD and related symptoms could proceed to trial on NIED claim).

Given the substantial body of law approving of comparable symptomologies, it was not clearly erroneous for the district court to conclude that both brothers satisfied the physical consequences requirement.[14] **[—37—]**

5. Summary

In sum, we hold that plaintiffs within the zone of danger may recover for NIED under the general maritime law. We also uphold the district court's findings that the Sawyers were within the zone of danger, and that they experienced physical consequences of emotional distress. Island Transporter does not challenge the amount of the district court's award. Accordingly, we affirm the district court's judgment awarding $50,000 to Ryan Sawyer and $50,000 to Ross Sawyer for their emotional distress.

III. Conclusion

For the reasons discussed above, we affirm the district court's finding of negligence, and its award of damages for the Mack truck, lost profits, and emotional distress. We vacate the district court's damages award for the plywood panels, and remand with instructions to enter judgment consistent with this opinion. The parties shall bear their own costs on appeal.

So ordered.

---

[14] In reaching this conclusion, we reject Island Transporter's contention that the district court clearly erred by determining that the Sawyers' symptoms were caused by the incident, rather than other work-related stresses, or their investment years earlier in a Ponzi scheme. We also reject Island Transporter's assertion that the district court errantly relied on Maine law. Although the court stated that Maine law does not impose the physical consequences requirement, it did not ultimately follow that precedent.

This page intentionally left blank

United States Court of Appeals for the Second Circuit

United States Court of Appeals
for the Second Circuit

No. 15-3777

DS-RENDITE
vs.
ESSAR CAPITAL AMERICAS INC.

Appeal from the United States District Court for the Southern District of New York

Decided: February 6, 2018

Citation: 882 F.3d 44, 6 Adm. R. 28 (2d Cir. 2018).

Before **KATZMANN**, Chief Judge, **WINTER**, and **RAGGI**, Circuit Judges.[1]

[—2—] {–46–} WINTER, Circuit Judge:

DS-Rendite Fonds Nr. 108 VLCC Ashna GmbH & Co Tankschiff KG ("DS-Rendite") appeals from Judge Daniels's denial of its motion for an attachment and garnishment **{–47–}** order under Rule B of the Supplemental Rules for Admiralty or Maritime Claims and Asset Forfeiture Actions. We affirm.

BACKGROUND

We assume that the facts alleged in the underlying complaint are true. *Ashcroft v. Iqbal*, 556 U.S. 662, 679 (2009); *Transfield ER Cape Ltd. v. Indus. Carriers, Inc.*, 571 F.3d 221, 222 (2d Cir. 2009) (recognizing "[b]ecause maritime attachments are granted on the pleadings, we assume all allegations in the complaint to be true" (internal quotation marks omitted)). On or about November 2, 2009, DS-Rendite chartered the M/T Ashna to Energy Transportation International Limited ("ETIL") pursuant to a Time Charter ("Charter"). That same day, Essar Shipping Limited ("ESL") entered into a **[—3—]** novation agreement assuming the obligations of ETIL in the event ETIL defaulted on the Charter. Approximately five years later, Essar Shipping and Logistics Limited ("ESLL")[2] guaranteed the obligations of ETIL and ESL arising under the Charter. ESLL also agreed to guarantee subsequent settlement agreements between DS-Rendite, ETIL, and ESL resulting from ETIL and ESL's alleged failure to pay the charter-hire costs due under the Charter. DS-Rendite then made "repeated demand[s]" for payment. App'x at 12.

Appellant's complaint asserted a claim for breach of a maritime contract against appellees ETIL, ESL, and ESLL and simultaneously sought a maritime attachment and garnishment order against Essar Capital Americas Inc., Essar Capital LLC, Essar Group LLC, Essar Minerals, Inc., Essar Steel Algoma Inc., and Essar Trading Inc. (collectively "Garnishees") in the amount of $10,586,346.63. On September 8, 2015, the district court denied the motion for attachment. After the district court's denial of a motion for reconsideration, this appeal followed.

DISCUSSION

This is a classic *quasi in rem* proceeding. The plaintiff is seeking to assert a claim against a defendant, over whom the court does not (otherwise) have **[—4—]** personal jurisdiction, by seizing property of the defendant (alleged here to be in the hands of a third party). Although Rule B states that it applies to "an *in personam* action," Fed. R. Civ. P. Supp. R. B(1), a maritime *in personam* claim is more appropriately styled a *quasi in rem* action. "[T]he nature of the jurisdiction the court acquires by a Rule B attachment is properly denominated '*quasi in rem*' because any judgment rendered is limited to the value of the attached property." *Teyseer Cement Co. v. Halla Mar. Corp.*, 794 F.2d 472, 477 (9th Cir. 1986); *see Maryland Tuna Corp. v. MS Benares*, 429 F.2d 307, 311 (2d Cir. 1970) (action brought under Rule B is *quasi in rem*); *Eng'g Equip. Co. v. S.S. Selene*, 446 F. Supp. 706, 709 n.9 (S.D.N.Y. 1978) (same). In fact, Rule E, which governs *quasi in rem* actions, "applies to actions *in personam* with process of maritime attachment and garnishment." Fed. R. Civ. P. Supp. R. E(1); see Peter Friedenberg, *The Use of Maritime Attachment as a Jurisdictional Device*, 12 Cornell Int'l L.J.

[1] Appellees have not entered an appearance in this case.

[2] Appellant's complaint refers to "ESSL" as guaranteeing ETIL and ESL's obligations, App'x at 12, but we assume that it means "ESLL."

329, 332 (1979) ("It should be emphasized that, despite the language in Rule B limiting its scope to claims brought *in personam*, the Rule is in fact a classic example of *quasi in rem* jurisdiction." (internal quotation marks omitted)). **[—5—] {-48-}**

The concept of *quasi in rem* jurisdiction evolved in the Lord Mayor's Court in London and "served the useful purpose of mitigating the rigors of securing personal jurisdiction" over elusive defendants. Paul D. Carrington, *The Modern Utility of Quasi in Rem Jurisdiction*, 76 Harv. L. Rev. 303, 304-05 (1962). In a *quasi in rem* proceeding, "a thing owned by a specified person is seized as a basis for exercising jurisdiction to decide a claim against the owner." Restatement (Second) of Judgments § 6 cmt. a (1982).

The *quasi in rem* device has proved particularly useful in admiralty, where defendants are so often transitory that the "process of foreign attachment is known of old in admiralty." *Swift & Co. Packers v. Compania Colombiana Del Caribe, S.A.*, 339 U.S. 684, 693 (1950). Without the use of maritime attachment to provide jurisdiction over defendants' properties, many plaintiffs would not be compensated for meritorious claims, *see id.* (citing *Manro v. Almeida*, 23 U.S. 473, 489 (1825)), and international commerce would be diminished. The *quasi in rem* device, in modern form, is now provided by Rule B.

In a Rule B proceeding, "the *res* is the only means by which a court can obtain jurisdiction over the defendant." *Shipping Corp. of India v. Jaldhi Overseas Pte Ltd.*, 585 F.3d 58, 69 (2d Cir. 2009). So, "[o]nce that property or its **[—6—]** substitute security is released, the court has no jurisdiction over the defendant." *Teyseer*, 794 F.2d at 477; *cf. The Rock Island Bridge*, 73 U.S. 213, 215 (1867) ("The lien and the proceeding *in rem* are, therefore, correlative—where one exists, the other can be taken, and not otherwise."); *see generally* Gilmore & Black, *The Law of Admiralty* 622 (2d ed. 1975). If a plaintiff is not able to successfully attach the defendant's property under Rule B, the district court lacks jurisdiction over the defendant. Indeed, if the defendant is subject to typical *in personam* jurisdiction, Rule B cannot be used. *STX Panocean (UK) Co. v. Glory Wealth Shipping Pte Ltd.*, 560 F.3d 127, 130-31 (2d Cir. 2009). At stake in this appeal, therefore, is not only the availability of property to satisfy any judgment that might be entered but also jurisdiction over a defendant to adjudicate a judgment.

With regard to the standard of review, existing case law in this circuit relates only to removal of Rule B attachments. *See India S.S. Co. v. Kobil Petroleum Ltd.*, 663 F.3d 118, 121 (2d Cir. 2011); *Jaldhi*, 585 F.3d at 66. That established standard is that removal is reviewed under an abuse of discretion standard. We see no reason why this standard should not apply to the grant or denial of Rule B attachments as well. Of course, findings of adjudicative facts found in a Rule E hearing are reviewed for clear error, while conclusions of law **[—7—]** are reviewed *de novo*. *Allied. Mar., Inc. v. Descatrade SA*, 620 F.3d 70, 74 (2d Cir. 2010); *see Man Ferrostaal, Inc. v. M/V Akili*, 704 F.3d 77, 82 (2d Cir. 2012). However, where the ultimate judgment involves the weighing and balancing of several factual and legal issues—for example, the issuance of preliminary injunctive relief—the standard of review is abuse of discretion. *See SG Cowen Sec. Corp. v. Messih*, 224 F.3d 79, 81 (2d Cir. 2000). Granting of a Rule B attachment, as discussed *infra*, whether on the pleadings or after a Rule E hearing requires such weighing and balancing.

To secure an *ex parte* order of attachment under Rule B, a plaintiff "bears the burden of establishing a right to attachment." *Jensen v. Rollinger*, No. 13 Civ. 1095 (DAE), 2014 WL 4539660, at *2 (W.D. Tex. Sept. 11, 2014). The Rule requires **{-49-}** the following showing. First, a plaintiff must file a "verified complaint praying for attachment" and "an affidavit stating that, to the affiant's knowledge, or on information and belief, the defendant cannot be found within the district." Fed. R. Civ. P. Supp. R. B(1)(a) and (b). Second, the complaint "may contain a prayer for process to attach the defendant's tangible or intangible personal property—up to the amount sued for—in the hands of garnishees named in the process." *Id.* at Supp. R. B(1)(a). Finally, the district court must then "review the complaint **[—8—]** and affidavit and, if the conditions of . . . Rule B appear to exist, enter an order so stating and authorizing process of attachment and garnishment." *Id.* at Supp. R. B(1)(b). If an attachment is ordered, "any person claiming an interest in [the attached property] shall be entitled to a prompt hearing at which the plaintiff shall be required to show why the arrest or attachment should not be vacated or other relief granted." *Id.* at Supp. R. E(4)(f) ("Rule E hearing").

The issue in the present matter is whether appellant's complaint and affidavit make legally sufficient allegations that identifiable property of the defendants, tangible or intangible, is "in the hands of garnishees." *Id.* at Supp. R. B(1)(a). We conclude that the allegations are not sufficient.

As a general matter, the pleading requirements under Rule B are said to be easily met. *See Aqua Stoli Shipping Ltd. v. Gardner Smith Pty Ltd.*, 460 F.3d 434, 443 (2d Cir. 2006), *overruled on other grounds by Shipping Corp. Of India Ltd. v. Jaldhi Overseas Pte Ltd.*, 585 F.3d 58 (2d Cir. 2009) ("Maritime parties are peripatetic, and their assets are often transitory . . . [resulting in] a relatively broad maritime attachment rule, under which the attachment is quite easily obtained."); *ContiChem LPG v. Parsons Shipping Co.*, 229 F.3d 426, 433–34 (2d Cir. 2000) (finding that to meet the Rule B requirements "little else [other than the **[—9—]** affidavit and complaint] is required and there need only be a hearing after the attachment is served").

However, there are limits to the ease of attachment under Rule B. An existing attachment order is not valid where the attachment and garnishment is "served before the garnishee comes into possession of the property," *Reibor Int'l Ltd. v. Cargo Carriers (KACZ-CO.) Ltd.*, 759 F.2d 262, 263 (2d Cir. 1985) (affirming the vacatur of an attachment order), or where the garnishees do not "owe[] a debt to the defendant at the time the order is served." *ContiChem*, 229 F.3d at 434 (citing *Reibor*, 759 F.2d at 266) (same).

Courts have also recognized the need for limits to prevent abuse. *See Maersk, Inc. v. Neewra, Inc.*, 443 F. Supp. 2d 519, 527 (S.D.N.Y. 2006)("The ease with which a prima facie case for attachment can be made . . . creates a real risk of abusive use of the maritime remedy.") (citation, alteration, and internal quotations omitted). As a result, district courts have often initially granted attachment and then used Rule E hearings to determine whether the requirements of Rule B were in fact met. *See, e.g., Transportes Navieros y Terrestres S.A. de C.V. v. Fairmount Heavy Transp., N.V.*, 572 F.3d 96, 100-03 (2d **[—10—]** Cir. 2009); *Aqua Stoli*, 460 F.3d at 438; *Tide Line, Inc. v. Eastrade Commodities, Inc.*, 2007 A.M.C. 252, 260-61 (S.D.N.Y. 2006).

In recent years, moreover, perhaps in response to motions for broad attachments based entirely on conclusory allegations as to the property to be attached, district courts have required a minimal specificity of factual allegations identifying the defendant's property to be attached before issuing Rule B attachments and holding Rule E hearings. *See* **{-50-}** *Marco Polo Shipping Co. Pte. v. Supakit Prod. Co.*, 2009 A.M.C. 639, 641 (S.D.N.Y. 2009); *see also Optimum Shipping & Trading S.A. v. Prestige Marine Servs. PTE. Ltd.*, No. 08 Civ. 9533 (JSR), 2010 WL 3469542, at *1 (S.D.N.Y. Aug. 24, 2010); *DBCN v. Enersur S.A.*, No. 09 Civ. 8359 (RJS), 2009 WL 3254447, at *2–3 (S.D.N.Y. Oct. 9, 2009); *Deval Denizcilik Ve Ticaret A.S. v. Sensy Freeight SRL*, No. 09 Civ. 7314 (LAK), 2009 WL 2633661, at *2–3 (S.D.N.Y. Aug. 26, 2009); *Arctic Ocean Int'l, Ltd. v. High Seas Shipping Ltd.*, 622 F. Supp. 2d 46, 52 (S.D.N.Y. Mar. 30, 2009); *Peninsula Petroleum Ltd. v. New Econ Line PTE Ltd.*, No. 09 Civ. 1375 (PGG), 2009 WL 702840, at *3 (S.D.N.Y. Mar. 17, 2009) (adopting the "reasoning and holding of *Marco Polo*"). **[—11—]**

Marco Polo held that a plaintiff seeking to maintain an existing Rule B attachment "must at least set forth enough facts to render it plausible that the defendant's funds [are] present in the district." *Marco Polo*, 2009 A.M.C. at 641. In applying this standard, courts have held that "[m]ore is required to demonstrate a 'plausible' entitlement to a maritime attachment than . . . conclusory allegations." *Peninsula Petroleum*, 2009 WL 702840, at *2 (quoting *Bell Atlantic Corp. v. Twombly*, 550 U.S. 544, 570 (2007)). Specifically, a plaintiff must allege facts showing "that it is plausible to believe that Defendant's property will be 'in the hands of' garnishees in the Southern District of New York at the time the requested writ of attachment is served or during the time that service is effected." *Id.* To meet that standard some identification of the "property" is needed.

Neither Rule B nor Rule E provide pleading standards regarding the identification of the property to be attached and garnished. Each rule seems to assume that at least the nature of the property is known. We agree with the application of *Twombly* standards to the identification of the property to be attached under Rule B. *See Twombly*, 550 U.S. at 570 (requiring plaintiffs to plead "enough facts to state a claim to relief that is plausible on its face"). In **[—12—]** order to render the garnishee's possession of identifiable property of the defendant plausible, the facts alleged must provide sufficient specificity either as to the nature of the business relationship between the garnishee(s) and the defendant and/or the nature of the defendant's property subject to the attachment.

The present complaint fails to meet that standard. It alleges only in entirely conclusory fashion that the alleged garnishees do business with the defendants. The complaint alleges that "[e]ach of the Garnishees, on information and belief, holds property of Essar," namely "funds held by . . . Garnishee[s] which are due and owing to Defendants." App'x at 11, 13. The district court denied the motion for attachment, finding that these entirely conclusory allegations "d[id] not provide a sufficient basis to conclude that there are attachable assets in this District." *Id.* at 22.

When DS-Rendite moved for reconsideration, its brief in support of the motion contained new factual allegations.[3] The brief stated that "Essar Group," an entity nowhere mentioned in the complaint, "is an indisputably large **[—13—]** multinational corporation with thousands of affiliates and subsidies." *Id.* at 28. "Furthermore," appellant **{-51-}** contended, "given that Defendants are subsidiaries or affiliates of Essar Group, and the Garnishees are also subsidiaries or affiliates of Essar Group, it is highly likely that the Garnishees owe money to Defendants, and thus have attachable assets within this District." *Id.*[4] The district court found that these assertions also failed to "sufficiently allege[] that Defendants are entitled to a debt owed by the Garnishees." *Id.* at 35.

We agree. The complaint's caption lists six companies as garnishees but nowhere alleges facts about the commercial ventures of the garnishees or their business relationships, much less transactions with the three companies named as defendants. *Id.* at 10. Instead, the complaint states only in conclusory terms that "[e]ach of the Garnishees, on information and belief, holds property of Essar," but does not allege facts explaining why any one of those six companies would hold property of "Essar," which is actually three separate companies. *Id.* at 11. **[—14—]**

Even assuming *arguendo* that, as a general matter, the defendants and garnishees are somehow "affiliates or subsidiaries" of the same "group"—an allegation, as noted *supra*, absent from appellant's complaint—it does not

[3] For the sake of efficiency, we assume the allegations contained only in appellant's briefs and not in their complaint are properly before us. They are not. *See Puglisi v. United States*, 586 F.3d 209, 217-18 (2d Cir. 2009); *Pani v. Empire Blue Cross Blue Shield*, 152 F.3d 67, 71 (2d Cir. 1998).

[4] In a footnote, DS-Rendite revealed the paucity of its allegations by stating: "For instance, Garnishee Essar Steel Algoma, Inc. actively engages in business transactions with Essar Group affiliate, Essar Steel Minnesota LLC," another company nowhere mentioned in the complaint, and "[t]hus, it is more than likely that the similar Essar Group affiliates interact similarly in transacting business with other Essar Group affiliates." App'x at 28 n.2.

follow that there is a specific entitlement of one of the defendants to a debt owed by a garnishee, *see Alaska Reefer Mgmt. LLC v. Network Shipping Ltd.*, 68 F. Supp. 3d 383, 387 (S.D.N.Y. 2014), much less a debt that would be in the possession of the garnishee "at the time the order is served," *ContiChem*, 229 F.3d at 434. As the district courts found in *DBCN* and *Deval Denizcilik*, entitlement to an attachment must be based on more than "a conclusory allegation that, on the basis of general industry practices, it is anticipated and expected that Defendants will have property in this District [in the possession] of . . . garnishees during the pendency of the requested order." *DBCN*, 2009 WL 3254447, at *2 (quotation marks omitted); *see Deval Denizcilik*, 2009 WL 2633661, at *2.

In *Marco Polo*, the Southern District likewise rejected the contention that "any likelihood short of impossibility that the defendant's funds could be restrained in the future is sufficient to meet the requirement that the defendant's property be found within the district." 2009 A.M.C. at 641. In that regard, we note that DS-Rendite fails to allege facts that defendants have *ever* transferred **[—15—]** funds through New York—from garnishees or otherwise. *See Peninsula Petroleum*, 2009 WL 702840, at *2 (citing cases in this circuit in which plaintiff's allegations met the plausibility standard).

While the availability of a swift Rule E hearing may, in a district court's discretion, allow room for a relaxed pleading standard with regard to an attachment, the pleading must provide targeted guidance as to the property that is the subject of the hearing. As appellant's district court brief in support of the motion for reconsideration made clear by presenting new factual allegations not pleaded in the complaint, *see* Note 4, *supra*, a Rule E hearing in this matter would have no focus and be little more than a prolonged fishing expedition.

CONCLUSION

For the reasons stated above, it was within the district court's discretion to **{–52–}** deny appellant's motion for an order of maritime attachment and garnishment. Should appellant wish to renew its application, appellant may file a complaint and motion according to the standards set forth in this opinion. We affirm.

United States Court of Appeals
for the Second Circuit

No. 16-3125

D'AMICO DRY LTD.
VS.
PRIMERA MAR. (HELLAS) LTD.

Appeal from the United States District Court for the Southern District of New York

Decided: March 29, 2018

Citation: 886 F.3d 216, 6 Adm. R. 33 (2d Cir. 2018).

Before **KATZMANN**, Chief Judge, **JACOBS**, and **LIVINGSTON**, Circuit Judges.

[—3—] {-217-} **LIVINGSTON**, Circuit Judge:

Plaintiff-Appellant d'Amico Dry Limited ("d'Amico") is a shipping company and Defendant-Appellee Primera Maritime (Hellas) Limited ("Primera") is a ship management company. In 2008, d'Amico sold a derivative financial instrument known as a forward freight agreement ("FFA") to Primera. Under the FFA, d'Amico was obligated to pay Primera if the mean market rates for shipping on certain types of vessels on certain routes during certain months exceeded an agreed-upon rate. In turn, Primera was obligated to pay d'Amico if the market rate was less than the agreed-upon rate. When Primera failed to pay d'Amico as required under the agreement, d'Amico terminated the FFA and **{-218-}** obtained a judgment against Primera in an English court. Then, seeking to enforce the judgment, d'Amico sued Primera and its alleged alter egos and successors-in-interest in the United States District Court for the Southern District of New York. D'Amico asserted subject matter jurisdiction under 28 U.S.C. § 1333(1), which empowers federal district courts to hear admiralty cases. The **[—4—]** district court dismissed the case for lack of subject matter jurisdiction because the judgment was rendered by a commercial (not admiralty) court and the underlying claim was nonmaritime under English law. On appeal, this Court vacated the dismissal and remanded for the district court to determine in the first instance whether the underlying claim was maritime under U.S. law.

After a four-day bench trial, the district court again dismissed the case for lack of subject matter jurisdiction. The district court concluded that the agreement between d'Amico and Primera was not a maritime contract falling within § 1333(1)'s jurisdictional grant because d'Amico had not proven it made the agreement to protect against the risk that specific vessels in d'Amico's fleet would be underemployed during the period of the FFA.

On appeal, d'Amico argues that the FFA was a maritime contract because, on the facts found by the district court at trial, the agreement with Primera was a hedge against another risk: d'Amico's exposure to shifts in the market price for shipping on certain routes. We agree: the combination of d'Amico's identity as a market participant with the substance of the agreement establishes that the FFA was part of d'Amico's shipping business. Because the FFA's principal objective was maritime commerce, it is a maritime contract and claims arising from it fall **[—5—]** within our admiralty jurisdiction. *See Norfolk S. Ry. Co. v. Kirby*, 543 U.S. 14, 23–24 (2004). We therefore VACATE the judgment of the district court and REMAND for proceedings consistent with this opinion.

BACKGROUND

I. Factual Background[1]

D'Amico, incorporated in Ireland, owns and operates dry bulk shipping vessels. In 2008 and 2009, when the events underlying this lawsuit occurred, d'Amico's fleet included approximately thirty vessels—including ten to twelve "Panamax" vessels. Panamax vessels have the maximum dimensions that can traverse the Panama Canal. They transport commodities such as coal, minerals, and grains to destinations all over the globe. D'Amico owned about half of its fleet, and

[1] Unless otherwise noted, the factual background presented here is derived from the stipulated facts and uncontroverted evidence presented at trial.

chartered the rest of its vessels long term. D'Amico employed the vessels it controlled in various ways—in part through long-term time charters, but also on the spot market through single-trip-voyage or short-duration charters.

As a shipping company, d'Amico is exposed to the ebbs and flows of shipping prices, including the risk that the market rate for shipping on a route its **[—6—]** vessels ply will sink significantly. According to d'Amico's 2008 Directors' Report, the company used FFAs "to mitigate movements in the 'physical market'" that could harm its business. Joint App'x 739; *see also id.* at 751 (noting that d'Amico "uses derivative financial instruments to partially hedge its exposure to . . . market risks"). An FFA is a contract for the difference between a contract rate and a settlement rate. The contract rate is a rate agreed upon by the parties. The settlement rate is the market **{-219-}** rate for freight carried by a certain type of vessel, traveling a certain route (or group of routes), during a certain time period in the future. Because FFAs are not commitments to perform shipping services, any individual or entity (including one with no other tether to maritime commerce) can trade in FFAs. FFAs are traded over the counter rather than on regulated exchanges. In 2008, when the FFA at issue here was made, most FFAs were concluded bilaterally rather than through a clearinghouse, so each party bore the risk that its counterpart would fail to meet its obligations under the contract. There was no general requirement that these transactions be secured, although a prospective trader could request assurances from a potential counterparty.[2] **[—7—]**

In September 2008, d'Amico sold an FFA to Primera, a ship management company incorporated in Liberia and operating in Greece ("the d'Amico-Primera FFA"). The d'Amico-Primera FFA covered forty-five days in the first quarter of 2009. The contract rate was $55,750 per day. The FFA was to be settled monthly; the settlement rate was the mean of the daily published Baltic Panamax Index ("BPI") for all days of the pertinent month. The BPI is one of several indices published daily by the Baltic Exchange, a London-based organization that provides maritime market information. The BPI, which is based on reports from independent freight brokers about the freight market's performance, incorporates rates for shipping on standard routes travelled by Panamax carriers. For each month that the settlement rate exceeded the contract rate, d'Amico, as seller, was obligated to pay Primera, as buyer, the difference between the two rates. If instead the contract rate exceeded the settlement rate, Primera would have to pay the difference to d'Amico.

For the first month of the FFA, January 2009, the latter came to pass as the late-2008 financial crisis had sunk freight rates from historic crests in the mid-2000s. When Primera breached by failing to pay the amount due for January 2009, d'Amico terminated the contract and sued Primera in the English High Court **[—8—]** of Justice, as provided for in the contract. On June 19, 2009, the English court issued a judgment in favor of d'Amico for $ 1,766,278.54 plus costs.

II. Procedural History

In September 2009, d'Amico filed this lawsuit against Primera in the United States District Court for the Southern District of New York, seeking enforcement of the English judgment. The following December, d'Amico filed an amended complaint adding several individual and entity defendants, which d'Amico sought to hold liable for the English judgment as Primera's alleged alter egos and successors-in-interest.

In 2011, the defendants moved to dismiss the case for lack of subject matter jurisdiction. The district court granted the motion, holding that it lacked jurisdiction under the principle recognized in *Penhallow v. Doane's Adm'rs*, 3 U.S. (3 Dall.) 54, 97 (1795), which permits admiralty courts to enforce judgments issued by their foreign counterparts. *D'Amico Dry Ltd. v. Primera Mar. (Hellas) Ltd.*, No. 09-cv-7840-JGK, 2011 WL 1239861, at *2–3 (S.D.N.Y. Mar. 28, 2011). According to the district court, *Penhallow* did not apply

[2] By contrast, today nearly all FFA trades are made through clearinghouses, under circumstances which dramatically reduce counterparty risk.

because the English judgment was neither rendered by an admiralty court nor based on a claim deemed maritime by English law. *Id.* at *3–4. After judgment, **{-220-}** d'Amico moved for reconsideration, **[—9—]** arguing the district court had jurisdiction under 28 U.S.C. § 1333 because the d'Amico-Primera FFA was a maritime contract under U.S. law. *D'Amico Dry Ltd. v. Primera Mar. (Hellas) Ltd.*, No. 09-cv-7840-JGK, 2011 WL 3273208, at *4 (S.D.N.Y. Aug. 1, 2011). The district court denied this motion, holding that a judgment enforcement action is separate from the underlying substantive action, and that "a suit to enforce a judgment rendered on a maritime claim is not itself maritime in nature." *Id.*

On appeal, this Court vacated the district court's judgment dismissing the case, holding that "under § 1333, United States courts have jurisdiction to enforce a judgment of a foreign non-admiralty court if the claim underlying that judgment would be deemed maritime under the standards of U.S. law." *D'Amico Dry Ltd. v. Primera Mar. (Hellas) Ltd.*, 756 F.3d 151, 153, 2 Adm. R. 69, 69 (2d Cir. 2014). In the absence of binding precedent on the question, we identified "strong theoretical and practical reasons for assessing the maritime nature of the claim under U.S. admiralty standards." *Id.* at 160, 2 Adm. R. at 75. On the theoretical side, we emphasized the constitutional (and statutory) policy of allowing U.S. federal courts to hear claims deemed maritime by U.S. law, as well as traditional choice-of-law and international-comity principles. *Id.* at 160–61, 2 Adm. R. at 75–76. On the practical side, we **[—10—]** expressed concern about the costly litigation that would result if subject matter jurisdiction turned on the characterization of the claim under foreign law and we emphasized the special need for certainty in light of § 1333's exclusive jurisdictional grant. *Id.* at 161–62, 2 Adm. R. at 76–77. We therefore remanded the case for the district court to determine in the first instance whether "the underlying claim on the FFA is deemed maritime under the standards of U.S. law." *Id.* at 162, 2 Adm. R. at 77.

In May 2016, the district court held a four-day bench trial during which it received evidence on the remaining issues in this case, including whether the d'Amico-Primera FFA is a maritime contract under U.S. law.[3] On this point, the district court considered both documentary evidence and testimony from the principals of d'Amico and Primera and an expert witness about d'Amico's purpose for entering the agreement.

D'Amico's witness on this issue was Luciano Bonaso ("Bonaso"), d'Amico's general manager when the d'Amico-Primera FFA was made. In that role, he supervised the arrangement of employment for vessels as well as their **[—11—]** management and purchase. He maintained spreadsheets to keep track of both the fleet's physical commitments and d'Amico's FFA trades. Bonaso testified that to his best recollection, d'Amico's "intention" for entering the d'Amico-Primera FFA was "to hedge" its physical position "against certain days" in the opening months of 2009. Joint App'x 71. He explained that d'Amico sold an FFA that was to be settled each month against that month's mean BPI because the FFA was made to hedge against risk d'Amico faced in the Panamax segment of its business, on "routes that contribute to the index for the settlement," which "was consistent with the employment for [d'Amico's] spot vessels . . . at the time." *Id.* at 70. Bonaso also testified that in 2008, d'Amico derived approximately "[t]wo to three percent" of its revenue from FFAs, *id.* at 69, and d'Amico **{-221-}** was not "speculating in FFAs" although a separate entity, d'Amico Finance, was doing so, *id.* at 75.[4] **[—12—]**

---

[3] The other issues at trial were whether the district court should recognize the English judgment and order interest in accord with English law; if so, whether the non-Primera defendants were liable for the English judgment as alter egos or successors-in-interest of Primera; and whether the district court should enter default judgments against non-appearing defendants alleged to be alter egos or successors-in-interest of Primera.

[4] As discussed *infra*, the district court refused to credit portions of Bonaso's testimony—including, particularly, those concerning d'Amico's purpose for selling the d'Amico-Primera FFA—because there were inconsistencies among Bonaso's testimony and his earlier statements, and because the

Primera offered expert testimony from Karina Albers ("Albers"), a consultant in the maritime-freight field as evidence that the d'Amico-Primera FFA was nonmaritime. Albers testified that, based on her experience with the FFA market, d'Amico's FFA trading behavior in 2008 and 2009 did not support the conclusion that it used FFAs to hedge its shipping business.

According to Albers, a vessel owner's FFA qualifies as a hedge only if the owner uses the FFA to protect against the underemployment of specific vessels at specific times. Although she claimed that the specific vessels to be protected by an FFA need not be recorded at the time of the trade for the trade to be a hedge, she admitted that "for . . . an expert to testify" at a later date that the owner was using a specific FFA as a hedge in this particular way, the specific vessels would need to be documented somewhere. Joint App'x 323.

Albers testified that in addition to hedging specific assets, FFAs can be used as a tool for "redistributing market risk" in general. *Id.* at 320. But she also claimed that if a vessel owner sold FFAs because of concern about the risk of a declining market, but "d[id]n't have [a] specific vessel in mind and . . . d[id]n't connect the FFA with [a] specific vessel," then the owner was "speculating,"—not hedging. *Id.* at 323. Albers further acknowledged that "an owner [could] go **[—13—]** into an FFA as a hedge and then change his mind," but asserted that when the owner "changes his mind and . . . closes it out, it's not a hedge any longer." *Id.* at 326.

In its post-trial order, the district court acknowledged that the proper inquiry was "whether the 'principal objective' of the contract is the furtherance of maritime commerce." *D'Amico*, 201 F. Supp. 3d at 408 (quoting *Kirby*, 543 U.S. at 25). The district court nonetheless adopted the view that an FFA was a maritime contract only if the FFA was made to hedge against "market risks relating to the employment" of specific vessels. *Id.* at 411. Rejecting Bonaso's testimony about d'Amico's reason for entering the agreement, *id.* at 405–06, and accepting Albers's characterization of d'Amico's trading behavior as speculating rather than hedging, the district court concluded that there was "no credible evidence that" the d'Amico-Primera FFA's "principal objective . . . was to further maritime commerce," *id.* at 412.

The district court rejected as "not credible" Bonaso's testimony about d'Amico's reasons for entering the FFA because, in its view, Bonaso's trial testimony was both "inconsistent" with his previous statements and "belied by the actual facts" of d'Amico's trading behavior. *Id.* at 405. Bonaso's testimony **[—14—]** was "inconsistent," in the district court's view, because he had made conflicting statements in his pretrial depositions and declarations. *Id.* at 405–06. For example, Bonaso had incorrectly stated the number of days the d'Amico-Primera FFA concerned. *Id.* at 406. The district court deemed this error "significant" because it undermined Bonaso's claim that "he carefully **{-222-}** calculated the number of days that he wanted to cover with an FFA to protect against the underuse of his fleet." *Id.* In a deposition, Bonaso had also underreported the number of FFAs d'Amico had entered into for the first quarter of 2009. *Id.* at 406, 412. According to the court, Bonaso's testimony was "belied by the actual facts" of d'Amico's FFA trading behavior, *id.* at 405, in two ways. First, despite Bonaso's earlier statement in a deposition that d'Amico only sold FFAs, the evidence revealed that d'Amico bought them as well. *Id.* at 412. Second, Bonaso's claim that he intended the d'Amico-Primera FFA to protect against the risk of underemployed vessels was not credible because d'Amico closed its position two days later, securing its earnings at that time and leaving "no financial protection for unemployed or 'underemployed' vessels or any vessels at all in the first quarter of 2009." *Id.* at 407; *see also id.* at 411. Disregarding Bonaso's claims about the purpose behind the d'Amico-Primera FFA, the district court

statements were, in the district court's view, inconsistent with d'Amico's trading behavior. *D'Amico Dry Ltd. v. Primera Mar. (Hellas) Ltd.*, 201 F. Supp. 3d 399, 405–07 (S.D.N.Y. 2016). On appeal, d'Amico does not challenge the district court's credibility findings (or, for that matter, any of the district court's factual findings).

instead credited Albers's testimony **[—15—]** that d'Amico's "trading pattern was typical of a derivatives trader" rather than a shipowner "hedging a physical position in the freight market." *Id.* at 412.

Concluding d'Amico had failed to prove the d'Amico-Primera FFA was a maritime contract, the district court held that it lacked federal maritime jurisdiction to enforce the English judgment. *Id.* at 412. Without reaching the remaining issues, the district court dismissed the case. *Id.* D'Amico appealed.

During the pendency of the appeal, on September 14, 2016, Primera sent a letter to d'Amico explaining that Primera believed this appeal to be frivolous, and expressing its intent to move for sanctions if d'Amico failed to withdraw the appeal. D'Amico held fast, and in February 2017 Primera moved for sanctions against d'Amico for purportedly filing a frivolous appeal based on false testimony and distortion of the relevant decisions.[5] D'Amico opposed the request for sanctions. The motion was referred to our panel.

DISCUSSION

The district court acknowledged that, under *Kirby*, the appropriate inquiry is whether the principal objective of the agreement is maritime commerce. **[—16—]** *D'Amico*, 201 F. Supp. 3d at 408 (citing *Kirby*, 543 U.S. at 25). But the court held that, to establish the "principal objective" of the d'Amico-Primera FFA, d'Amico had to prove that its subjective purpose for entering the agreement was to hedge against the underemployment of specific vessels in its fleet. *Id.* at 411.

We review *de novo* "[w]hether a suit falls within federal subject matter jurisdiction," *D'Amico*, 756 F.3d at 155 n.2, 2 Adm. R. at 71 n.2, and we conclude that the district court conceived of its maritime contract jurisdiction too narrowly. Despite the extensive evidence presented at trial, the essential facts in this case are few: First, d'Amico, a shipping company, sold a freight-derivative valued by reference to freight rates. And, second, the fluctuation of those rates was a risk inherent in d'Amico's shipping operations. Given the alignment between d'Amico's identity and the substance of the agreement, the d'Amico-Primera FFA was plainly made as part of d'Amico's shipping business, and its principal objective is promoting maritime commerce. Because the d'Amico-Primera FFA was a maritime contract, the district court erred by dismissing **{-223-}** this case for lack of subject matter jurisdiction. **[—17—]**

I

The U.S. Constitution extends the federal judicial power to "all Cases of admiralty and maritime jurisdiction." Art. III, § 2, cl. 1. By statute, Congress has empowered federal district courts to hear "[a]ny civil case of admiralty or maritime jurisdiction." 28 U.S.C. § 1333(1). This grant provides for jurisdiction over claims arising from maritime contracts. *See Fireman's Fund Ins. Co. v. Great Am. Ins. Co. of N.Y.*, 822 F.3d 620, 632, 4 Adm. R. 70, 76 (2d Cir. 2016). The resolution of this appeal turns, therefore, on a deceptively simple question: is the d'Amico-Primera FFA a maritime contract?

The question is clear, but the law is murky. There is no "clean line[]" of demarcation "between maritime and nonmaritime contracts." *Kirby*, 543 U.S. at 23. Instead, general principles steer our "case-by-case approach" for determining whether an agreement is a maritime contract. *Folksamerica Reins. Co. v. Clean Water of N.Y., Inc.*, 413 F.3d 307, 311 (2d Cir. 2005). We consult "precedent and usage [for] help[] insofar as they exclude or include certain common types of contract." *Id.* (brackets omitted) (quoting *Kossick v. United Fruit Co.*, 365 U.S. 731, 735 (1961)). But when our quest to categorize an agreement draws us into uncharted waters, ultimately "the answer 'depends upon the nature and character **[—18—]** of the contract,' and the true

[5] Primera moved for sanctions pursuant to Federal Rule of Appellate Procedure 38; 28 U.S.C. § 1927; and this Court's inherent power to issue sanctions, *see Chambers v. NASCO, Inc.*, 501 U.S. 32, 44 (1991).

criterion is whether it has 'reference to maritime service or maritime transactions.'" *Kirby*, 543 U.S. at 24 (ellipsis omitted) (quoting *N. Pac. S.S. Co. v. Hall Bros. Marine Ry. & Shipbldg. Co.*, 249 U.S. 119, 125 (1919)). In other words, we ask whether the "principal objective" of the agreement is "maritime commerce." *Id.* at 25; *see id.* at 23–24. The Supreme Court has cautioned that this inquiry is "conceptual" and not constrained by the location of contract performance or a vessel's involvement in the dispute. *Id.* at 24. Our beacon is "the purpose of the jurisdictional grant—to protect maritime commerce." *Folksamerica*, 413 F.3d at 311 (citing *Exxon Corp. v. Cent. Gulf Lines, Inc.*, 500 U.S. 603, 608 (1991); *Sisson v. Ruby*, 497 U.S. 358, 367 (1990)).

We discern enough maritime flavor in the d'Amico-Primera FFA to conclude that there is federal subject matter jurisdiction over this case. Where the identity of at least one party (here, d'Amico's identity as a shipping business) aligns with the substance of the agreement (here, the parties' respective estimations of the market rate for freight on vessels and certain routes integral to at least one party's business), the resulting agreement is distinctly briny. Thus, when a party that is exposed to fluctuating shipping prices in its operations enters **[—19—]** into an FFA to be settled against a future value of the market to which it is exposed, the FFA is part of that party's shipping business and a maritime contract.

Here, undisputedly, at least one of the contracting parties is primarily engaged in the shipping business. Indeed, both fit this description: Primera is a ship management company; d'Amico owns and operates vessels that ship commodities worldwide. Bonaso, d'Amico's general manager, testified that trading FFAs generated just two or three percent of d'Amico's revenue in 2008. D'Amico's primary business is shipping. Because of its participation in the shipping industry, d'Amico is exposed to shifts in shipping prices.

The parties' identities as shipping outfits provide further context for the agreement. In particular, the collateral for the d'Amico-Primera **{-224-}** FFA was likely vessels. As was ordinary at the time, no security was required for the agreement. Each party bore the risk that its counterparty would default. But because the parties to the contract owned vessels, the counterpart party could pursue the shirker's vessels for satisfaction of the debt—as apparently happened here. *See D'Amico*, 201 F. Supp. 3d at 407 ("Since 2009, vessels connected to the defendants in this case were attached in the Central District of California, the Eastern and Southern Districts of Texas, and the Eastern District of Louisiana."). **[—20—]**

As to the substance of the agreement, the d'Amico-Primera FFA not only refers to maritime transactions generally, but also reflects the specific contours of d'Amico's shipping business. As already explained, the agreement concerns the market price for shipping goods on certain types of vessels along certain routes during certain months. The very vessels and routes referred to in the agreement reflect a segment of d'Amico's physical shipping business: the settlement rate is the mean price for shipping via a type of vessel employed (Panamax vessels) and a group of routes plied (the standard routes traveled by Panamax vessels) by d'Amico at the time of the contract. Bonaso testified that he sold an FFA to be measured against the BPI—as opposed to another of the several indices published by the Baltic Exchange—because of this congruity. His explanation is consistent with Albers's testimony that a vessel owner shielding itself from price risk would sell an FFA settled against the rate for shipping on routes travelled by its vessels.[6]

---

[6] The district court found that Bonaso's testimony supporting d'Amico's claim that it used the d'Amico-Primera FFA "not for simple financial speculations but rather as a means to hedge against the possible underuse of its fleet and, thereby, to promote maritime commerce" was "not credible." *D'Amico*, 201 F. Supp. 3d at 405. We do not read the district court's decision as finding all aspects of Bonaso's testimony not credible. Indeed, the district court relied on Bonaso's testimony for some of its findings of fact. *See, e.g., id.* at 402–03. Considering the record, we see no reason to conclude that the district court rejected Bonaso's

[—21—] These design choices support d'Amico's claim that—as stated in d'Amico's 2008 Director's Report—d'Amico used FFAs like this one to temper its "expos[ure] to movements in market prices arising from its operations." Joint App'x 739.

Regardless of the district court's conclusion that d'Amico did not use this (or any) FFA to hedge risk in the manner endorsed by Albers, we are of the view that d'Amico's sale of an FFA valued against market shipping rates to which it was exposed in its operations was directed toward managing risks inherent in its shipping business. Said differently, as a component of d'Amico's shipping business, the FFA's principal objective was facilitating maritime commerce. In these circumstances, we have no doubt that the d'Amico-Primera FFA was "'entered into in connection with [a] maritime commercial venture and [is] therefore maritime in nature,'" *Williamson v. Recovery Ltd. P'ship*, 542 F.3d 43, 49 (2d Cir. 2008) (quoting *Williamson v. Recovery Ltd. P'ship*, No. 06-cv-5724(LTS)(FM), 2007 WL 102089, at *2 (S.D.N.Y. Jan. 16, 2007)). Federal subject matter jurisdiction therefore exists here.[7] [—22—] {-225-}

This conclusion is consistent with our reasoning in the maritime insurance context. On facts like those here, an FFA bears some resemblance to a maritime insurance policy. Specifically, FFAs shield "against the vagaries of future maritime price fluctuations," *Flame S.A. v. Freight Bulk Pte. Ltd.*, 762 F.3d 352, 354, 2 Adm. R. 117, 117 (4th Cir. 2014), just as maritime insurance policies protect against losses like shipwreck or liability for discharging pollutants into the sea. We routinely conclude that insurance policies covering marine risks fall within our maritime jurisdiction. *See, e.g., Fireman's Fund Ins.*, 822 F.3d at 634, 4 Adm. R. at 78 (stating that insurance "for pollution coverage for a [floating dry-dock, a] structure used in vessel repair and maintenance . . . directly implicate[d] the business of maritime commerce"); *Folksamerica*, 413 F.3d at 310, 323 (holding that an insurance policy covering a ship tank cleaning company was a maritime contract). We see no compelling reason to treat a contract designed to ameliorate the risks posed by a fluctuating market differently from one drafted to protect against financial devastation from the realization of physical risks. [—23—]

The only other circuit to resolve the question of whether an FFA may qualify as a maritime contract reached a similar conclusion. *See Flame S.A.*, 762 F.3d at 363, 2 Adm. R. at 125. In *Flame S.A.*, the plaintiff entered four FFAs, the counterparty breached, and the plaintiff obtained a judgment against the counterparty from an English court. *Flame S.A. v. Indus. Carriers, Inc.*, No. 2:13-cv-658, 2014 WL 108897, at *1 (E.D. Va. Jan. 10, 2014). Then, the plaintiff sued in U.S. federal court and obtained an attachment of a vessel belonging to the counterparty's alleged alter ego. *Id.* A motion to vacate the attachment order on the ground that the district court lacked subject matter jurisdiction was denied; the district court observed that the FFAs were "singularly concerned with shipping routes," and that the plaintiff had apparently used them "primarily for hedging the risks inherent in [its] shipping business." *Id.* at *3. Therefore, the dispute implicated the court's admiralty jurisdiction. *Id.* On interlocutory appeal, the Fourth Circuit affirmed. *Flame S.A.*, 762 F.3d at 363, 2 Adm. R. at 125. The affirmance rested on two characteristics of the FFAs in that case: First, both parties to the agreements were shipping businesses. *See id.* at 362 & n.9, 2 Adm. R. at 124–25 & n.9. Second, it followed from the parties' identities as shipping businesses and the contents of the agreements that the parties "did not create the FFAs as mere financial speculators, but as a component of their shipping [—24—] businesses." *Id.* at 362, 2 Adm. R. at 124. In

---

testimony about why this FFA was to be settled against the BPI.

[7] As should be clear from the foregoing analysis, even if d'Amico's counterparty were not in the shipping business, the instrument would remain designed to function as a hedge against risks inherent in maritime commerce under our holding. This accords with the roughly analogous maritime insurance context (discussed herein), where the [—22—] inquiry is not whether the issuer writes only maritime policies, but instead what coverage the policy provides. *See, e.g., Folksamerica*, 413 F.3d at 314–15.

other words, the purpose of the FFAs was essentially inferable from the identities of the parties and the substance of their agreements. *See id.*, 2 Adm. R. at 124. The court of appeals, therefore, easily affirmed the district court's conclusion that the purpose of the agreements was to hedge against the risks of the shipping business. *See id.*, 2 Adm. R. at 124.

Here, the crux of the district court's holding was that the d'Amico-Primera FFA did not satisfy the "principal objective" test because d'Amico failed to establish that—subjectively—it made the agreement to protect against the underemployment of specific vessels. *See D'Amico*, 201 F. Supp. 3d at 407, 412. The district court cast its holding in broad terms about the absence of evidence that d'Amico used FFAs to hedge risk at all. *Id.* at 411. But a closer examination reveals that the district court based its holding primarily on its determination that d'Amico's "trading pattern" resembled the behavior of "a derivatives trader" rather than of "a shipowner who was hedging a physical position in the freight market." *Id.* at 412.

There are two key flaws in this analysis. First, as already explained, the risks that a shipping company faces in the conduct of **{-226-}** its business are not limited to the risk that any particular vessel will remain docked. Shipping companies **[—25—]** like d'Amico are exposed to, among other things, broader shifts in shipping prices. We see no reason to distinguish among instruments designed to mitigate these related risks. Second, the north star for maritime contract jurisdiction is an agreement's relationship with maritime commerce, not its tie to any particular vessel (or seaman, or shipment). Requiring a connection with a specific vessel is in tension with *Kirby*'s express instruction that the existence of maritime contract jurisdiction cannot be resolved by resort to questions like whether a vessel was involved in the dispute or where the contract was made or meant to be performed. 543 U.S. at 23–24; *see also Folksamerica*, 413 F.3d at 323–24 (holding that an insurance policy is a maritime contract even when it does not cover an identified vessel or shipment).

Our approach also avoids the serious practical consequences of anchoring subject matter jurisdiction to a party's intent in making an FFA. The nature of a party's principal business and the substance of a contract can likely be ascertained from relatively uncomplicated documentary evidence. Resting the question of maritime contract jurisdiction on a party's subjective intent in making an agreement, however, invites a far more complex evidentiary showing. A district court might be forced to hold a hearing (or receive evidence during trial) in nearly **[—26—]** every case before determining its jurisdiction. The record below illustrates this problem perfectly: the district court heard extensive testimony from the respective principals of d'Amico and Primera on their respective reasons for making the agreement, as well as expert testimony interpreting d'Amico's trading behavior. The necessity for such a showing is not limited to this case because, as the district court acknowledged, whether a party used an FFA to manage risk or to speculate (or for any other purpose) is not apparent from the face of the agreement. *See D'Amico*, 201 F. Supp. 3d at 404–05. Even where the record of a party's trading behavior initially appears to reflect what might be labeled speculative or risk-hedging behavior, the parties would likely seek to contradict that impression with additional evidence, including live testimony. For example, a trade made with the purpose of hedging in the manner required by the district court—that is, held open for enough time to ensure vessel employment—would not necessarily resemble such a hedge if, for example, the trader soon after changed his mind about the tenor of the market. We are disinclined to promote expensive litigation to resolve the threshold question of jurisdiction. *See D'Amico*, 756 F.3d at 161, 2 Adm. R. at 76 ("[Q]uestions of subject matter jurisdiction should be amenable to quick and relatively certain resolution."). **[—27—]**

Allowing subjective purpose to govern also risks rendering jurisdiction unpredictable. Because the best evidence of a contracting party's intent might be testimony, the existence of jurisdiction could turn primarily on the credibility of a witness (or witnesses)—

as it did here. That credibility could be easily undermined on cross-examination, especially when witnesses are asked to explain their motivations for decisions made years before.[8] **{-227-}**

Another troubling implication of the district court's position is that the purpose behind a contract—and with it, the existence of federal jurisdiction—may shift over the lifetime of the agreement. After all, Albers testified that an owner selling an FFA "can go into a hedge, but when he changes his mind and if he closes it out, it's not a hedge any longer." Joint App'x 326. Similarly, because a party **[—28—]** may close its position by making a new contract with a third party, the district court's position would allow a contract to be divested of its maritime character—and federal courts divested of their jurisdiction over a claim arising from that contract—by a separate, later-in-time agreement. Uncertainty is a particularly acute concern in this context because "§ 1333 vests admiralty jurisdiction *exclusively* in the federal courts," which means "parties concerned about uncertain federal jurisdiction cannot, as is generally the case, avoid the problem by bringing suit in a state court of concurrent (and unquestionable) jurisdiction." *D'Amico*, 756 F.3d at 162, 2 Adm. R. at 77. Moreover, a rule rendering jurisdiction readily manipulated or ephemeral destabilizes contract enforcement, undermining the very purpose of § 1333's jurisdictional grant, "'the protection of maritime commerce,'" *Exxon Corp.*, 500 U.S. at 608 (quoting *Sisson*, 497 U.S. at 367).

Finally, Primera argues that "it is significant that other [non-U.S.] jurisdictions have uniformly held that FFAs are not maritime contracts." Appellee's Br. at 20. The last time this case was before us, we considered the "general proposition" that there exists "widespread agreement throughout the world" about which matters are maritime and concluded that it was not controlling. *D'Amico*, 756 F.3d at 160, 2 Adm. R. at 75–76. Our analysis bears repeating here: **[—29—]**

> [T]here is no assurance that some other nation might not define its own maritime jurisdiction more broadly, or more narrowly, than we do. It seems reasonable to assume that the Framers of the Constitution and Congress wanted to ensure that matters deemed maritime *under our laws* have access to our federal courts. There is no reason to suppose that the Founders or Congress would have wished to exclude from the admiralty jurisdiction matters that U.S. law deems maritime, merely because another nation does not consider them maritime.

Id., 2 Adm. R. at 75–76. In addition, it seems reasonable that our admiralty jurisdiction might sweep more broadly than that of foreign jurisdictions in light of our federal system. Our "touchstone" for the interpretation of maritime contracts "is a concern for the uniform meaning of maritime contracts" throughout the United States. *Kirby*, 543 U.S. at 28. For this reason, a maritime contract is governed by federal substantive law unless the dispute is "inherently local." *Id.* at 27. Excluding FFAs from our admiralty jurisdiction would require parties seeking to enforce them in the United States to litigate in state courts, subject to varying state laws. Primera's position completely ignores the burden that litigating in the **{-228-}** shadow

[8] The timing of testimony is a key distinction between this context and another—diversity of citizenship—in which jurisdiction turns in part on a party's intent and, potentially, credibility. Specifically, in the diversity jurisdiction context, "[a]n individual's citizenship . . . is determined by his domicile" which is "'the place where a person has his true fixed home and principal establishment, and to which, whenever he is absent, he has the *intention* of returning.'" *Palazzo ex rel. Delmage v. Corio*, 232 F.3d 38, 42 (2d Cir. 2000) (emphasis added) (quoting *Linardos v. Fortuna,* 157 F.3d 945, 948 (2d Cir. 1998)). But the intent-to-remain inquiry is likely less susceptible to manipulation because a party's citizenship is analyzed at the time the suit is filed, *Grupo Dataflux v. Atlas Glob. Grp., L.P.*, 541 U.S. 567, 570 (2004), not at the time of a contract underlying the suit. Because the latter is in the more distant past, the memories of those with knowledge relevant to the jurisdictional inquiry may be less crisp and the truth harder to discern.

of such variation could impose on FFA investors involved in the shipping business.

In sum, we are persuaded that the d'Amico-Primera FFA is a maritime contract. One of the many threats to d'Amico's shipping business was the risk **[—30—]** that shipping rates would decline. Through the agreement, d'Amico expressed its view that the market rate for shipping in one of its business segments would not exceed a certain rate. The agreement ensured that if market conditions meant d'Amico chartered some of its vessels for less during the relevant period, it would recover the difference between its prediction and the actual state of the market. The absence of evidence that d'Amico used the FFA to hedge against the underuse of specific vessels is irrelevant. D'Amico's risks as a shipping business are more generalized than the risk that a particular vessel is under-employed. In any event, there is no requirement that a maritime contract concern a particular vessel, seaman, or shipment. *See, e.g.*, *Flame S.A.*, 762 F.3d at 362, 2 Adm. R. at 124 (citing *Kirby*, 543 U.S. at 23). Finally, the practical consequences of permitting a party's subjective intent to determine the maritime nature of a contract tug firmly against applying such a rule. We therefore conclude that the d'Amico-Primera FFA is a maritime contract, over which the district court had admiralty jurisdiction pursuant to § 1333.[9] **[—31—]**

II

One final matter remains: Primera seeks sanctions against d'Amico, arguing that this appeal is frivolous because it is based on Bonaso's discredited testimony and lacks any basis in law. Primera asks this Court to sanction d'Amico pursuant to Federal Rule of Appellate Procedure 38; 28 U.S.C. § 1927; and our inherent authority to manage the litigation before us, *see Chambers v. NASCO, Inc.*, 501 U.S. 32, 44 (1991). We have ordered sanctions not only where an appeal is "'patently frivolous'" but also where "the conduct of the sanctioned litigant or attorney evinces bad faith or an egregious disrespect for the Court or judicial process." *Ransmeier v. Mariani*, 718 F.3d 64, 68 (2d Cir. 2013) (quoting *Gallop v. Cheney*, 642 F.3d 364, 370 (2d Cir. 2011)).

There is no basis for sanctioning d'Amico here. Primera's first contention—that d'Amico improperly relies upon Bonaso's discredited testimony about d'Amico's purpose for entering the FFA—is incorrect. As already explained, d'Amico's argument (indeed, our holding) is that evidence about the subjective purpose for entering into an FFA is irrelevant to the question of admiralty jurisdiction. We disagree, moreover, with Primera's claim that the assertion for which d'Amico cited a snippet of Bonaso's trial testimony—that **[—32—]** d'Amico "used the FFA in dispute as a component of its shipping business" and used FFAs in its "shipping business . . . to manage . . . freight rate fluctuations," Appellant's Br. at 33 (citing Joint App'x 68–69)—is inconsistent with the district court's conclusion that there was no credible evidence that d'Amico used the d'Amico-Primera FFA "to hedge its shipping business or to protect its physical shipping positions," *D'Amico*, 201 F. Supp. 3d at 411. As stated above, the district court concluded merely that there was no evidence that d'Amico "hedged" in the specific way described by **{-229-}** Albers, a determination that is not relevant to our conclusion.

In addition, we reject Primera's claim that this appeal was frivolous. In the first place, we found d'Amico's claim to be meritorious. But even if we had affirmed the district court's decision, sanctions are inappropriate in an appeal—such as this one—that presents a substantial question of first impression in this Court. *See Clarendon Nat'l Ins. Co. v. Kings Reins. Co., Ltd.*, 241 F.3d 131, 135 (2d Cir. 2001); *Upton v. IRS*, 104 F.3d 543, 547 (2d Cir. 1997) (per curiam).

[9] Because we conclude that, even assuming the district court's factual findings were correct, its legal conclusion was erroneous, we have no occasion to consider d'Amico's further contention that Albers's testimony did not satisfy the requirements of Federal Rule of Evidence 702.

CONCLUSION

For the foregoing reasons, we VACATE the district court's judgment and REMAND for further proceedings consistent with this opinion.

United States Court of Appeals
for the Second Circuit

No. 16-3923

ING BANK N.V.
vs.
M/V TEMARA[1]

Appeal from the United States District Court for the Southern District of New York

Decided: June 13, 2018

Citation: 892 F.3d 511, 6 Adm. R. 44 (2d Cir. 2018).

Before **PARKER, WESLEY,** and **LIVINGSTON,** Circuit Judges.

[—3—] {-514-} PARKER, Circuit Judge:

This appeal requires us to decide which parties are entitled to a maritime lien under the Commercial Instruments and Maritime Liens Act ("CIMLA"), 46 U.S.C. § 31301 *et seq.*

In 2014, the charterer of a vessel contracted with a supplier to buy bunkers (marine fuel). To fulfill its obligation, the contract supplier subcontracted with an intermediary, who, in turn, subcontracted with another entity, the physical supplier, who then delivered the bunkers. After the bunkers were delivered, but before anyone was paid, the contract supplier and the intermediary entered bankruptcy. In order to get paid, the assignee of the contract supplier and the physical supplier asserted competing maritime liens against the vessel. We must decide which party was entitled to do so.

The assignee of the contract supplier and the physical supplier cross-moved for summary judgment. The United States District Court for the Southern District of New York (Katherine B. Forrest, *Judge*) concluded that neither the contract supplier (and, thus, its assignee) nor the physical supplier were entitled under CIMLA to maritime liens and denied their motions for summary **[—4—]** judgment. Without providing notice to the parties, the District Court then *sua sponte* entered summary judgment in favor of the vessel. **{-515-}**

We affirm in part, vacate in part, and remand for further proceedings. We agree with the District Court that the subcontractor physical supplier was not entitled to a maritime lien because it did not provide the bunkers on the order of an entity specified in CIMLA. However, we disagree with the District Court that the bunker contract supplier—and, thus, its assignee—was not entitled to seek a maritime lien. A contractor is entitled to assert a maritime lien under CIMLA when it contracts with an entity specified in the statute for the delivery of necessaries and those necessaries are delivered pursuant to that arrangement, even if by a subcontractor. We also conclude that the District Court's *sua sponte* entry of summary judgment was error.

BACKGROUND[2]

This appeal flows from the collapse of O.W. Bunker and Trading A/S ("O.W. Denmark") and its international subsidiaries (collectively with its international subsidiaries, the "O.W. Bunker Group"), a world-wide operation which was in the business of supplying bunkers to ships operating in **[—5—]** international commerce. Following the collapse of the O.W. Bunker Group, many of its customers were unsure where to direct payment and, because they faced competing claims from various unpaid parties, those customers were concerned that their vessels would be subject to arrest while the payment issues were sorted out.

CIMLA provides to a specific class of creditors a special type of statutory lien—a maritime lien—as security for a discrete category of debts. Under CIMLA, a party who provides necessaries (such as bunkers) to a vessel is entitled to assert a maritime lien. 46 U.S.C. § 31342. A maritime lien grants a provider of necessaries a suite of powerful rights: the right to arrest the vessel, to have it

[1] The Clerk of Court is respectfully directed to amend the caption as above.

[2] "JA" refers to the parties' joint appendix. "SA" refers to ING's supplemental appendix.

sold, and to be paid from the proceeds. Maritime liens promote maritime commerce by providing additional recourse—beyond *in personam* claims against counterparties—by enabling the assertion of a lien directly against the vessel, thereby encouraging the prompt payment of debts and the existence of a reliable market for the servicing and supplying of vessels, which are obviously essential to maritime commerce. Unpaid entities who have supplied necessaries but who do not qualify for maritime liens may have *in personam* claims. However, due to **[—6—]** the complexities of international maritime commerce, collection on these claims can be considerably more problematic than is the case with maritime liens.

The relevant chain of events began in October 2014 when Copenship Bulkers A/S ("Copenship"), the time-charterer of the M/V TEMARA (the "TEMARA," or the "Vessel"), contracted with a contract supplier, O.W. Denmark, for the delivery of 400 metric tons of bunkers to the Vessel in Balboa, Panama. After receiving the order, O.W. Denmark issued a sales order to Copenship confirming the details of the sale. The confirmation lists O.W. Denmark as the "seller," Copenship as the "buyer," and CEPSA International B.V. ("CEPSA")[3] as the "supplier." The confirmation provided that "acceptance of the marine bunkers by the vessel . . . shall be deemed to constitute acceptance of the said general terms[.]" The confirmation reflected the agreed-upon price for the fuel—$536.00 per metric ton—and specified that payment would be due 30 days after delivery. **{-516-}** The sales agreement between O.W. Denmark and the charterer was governed by the "OW Bunker Group Terms and Conditions of sale **[—7—]** [sic] for Marine Bunkers Edition 2013" (the "O.W. Terms"). JA at 103–14. Clause L.4(a) of the O.W. Terms ("Clause L.4(a)") made them fluid by providing that:

> These Terms and Conditions are subject to variation in circumstances where the physical supply of the Bunkers is being undertaken by a third party which insists that the Buyer is also bound by its own terms and conditions. In such circumstances, these Terms and Conditions shall be varied accordingly, and the Buyer shall be deemed to have read and accepted the terms and conditions imposed by the said third party.

Id. at 111.

In the next step of the transaction, O.W. Denmark subcontracted with its subsidiary, O.W. USA, for the purchase of the bunkers. O.W. USA issued a sales order confirmation to O.W. Denmark, listing O.W. Denmark as the "buyer" and O.W. USA as the "seller." The confirmation reflected a price of $529.00 per metric ton and called for payment within 30 days of delivery.[4] **[—8—]**

In the third and final stage of the transaction, O.W. USA subcontracted with the physical supplier, CEPSA, for the actual delivery of the bunkers. CEPSA issued a confirmation to O.W. USA listing CEPSA as the "seller," O.W. USA as the "buyer," and reflecting a price of $526.00 per metric ton. O.W. USA then memorialized the transaction in its own confirmation. Neither confirmation referenced O.W. Denmark or the charterer of the Vessel, but both referenced the Vessel. CEPSA physically supplied the bunkers to the Vessel and CEPSA provided a bunker receipt that the Vessel's chief engineer signed and stamped with the names of the Vessel and its owner.

Following delivery of the bunkers, each party in the contractual chain invoiced its respective counterparty, at different prices, reflecting a markup at each stage of the transaction: O.W. Denmark invoiced the

[3] CEPSA Panama, S.A. originally filed the intervenor complaint, but the District Court determined that the real party-in-interest was CEPSA International B.V.

[4] Notably, ING failed to present the actual contract constituting this link in the contractual chain to the District Court on its motion for summary judgment; it only presented the actual contract as part of its motion for reconsideration, which the District Court declined to consider when it denied the motion. *See* Order, *ING Bank N.V. v. M/V TEMARA*, No. 16-cv-95 (S.D.N.Y. Nov. 28, 2016), ECF Dkt. 181.

charterer, Copenship, JA at 115 ($536 per metric ton); O.W. USA invoiced O.W. Denmark, JA at 130 ($529 per metric ton); and CEPSA invoiced O.W. USA, JA at 90 ($526 per metric ton). As the invoices came due, O.W. Denmark entered insolvency proceedings in Denmark, the O.W. Bunker Group collapsed, and the various O.W. Bunker Group entities then entered insolvency proceedings around the world. **[—9—]**

In December 2013, almost a year before the O.W. Bunker Group's collapse, ING Bank N.V. ("ING") and O.W. Denmark entered into a $700 million revolving credit agreement, funded by a syndicate of lenders, which provided working capital for the O.W. Bunker Group. ING contends that the credit agreement was secured by, among other things, an assignment of O.W. Bunker Group receivables from the bunker transactions it had conducted—including the right to payment for the bunkers delivered to the Vessel. No one has received payment for those bunkers.

In May 2015, ING, as assignee of O.W. Denmark, filed a complaint *in rem* against the Vessel in the United States District Court for the District of Maryland, asserting a maritime lien against the Vessel for the bunkers delivered by CEPSA. ING **{-517-}** moved for a warrant of arrest, and the Vessel was then arrested in Baltimore, Maryland. A few days later, CEPSA, intervened to assert a competing maritime lien claim and an *in personam* breach of contract claim against ING. To secure the release of the Vessel pending the adjudication of the competing claims, its owner posted security, and the vessel was released. **[—10—]**

In September 2015, ING moved for partial summary judgment on its lien claim and on CEPSA's claims and CEPSA cross-moved for summary judgment. In January 2016, as these motions were still pending, the case was transferred to the Southern District of New York. By June 2016, several other actions arising out of the collapse of the O.W. Bunker Group involving similar claims were pending before the District Court. The District Court entered an order coordinating them, and among other things, directed ING to move for partial summary judgment to test the validity of its maritime lien.

Initially, the District Court considered CEPSA's entitlement to a maritime lien. The District Court granted ING's motion for summary judgment, dismissed CEPSA's maritime lien claim and denied its cross-motion for summary judgment. *See ING Bank N.V. v. M/V TEMARA*, 203 F. Supp. 3d 355 (S.D.N.Y 2016) (the "August 2016 Order").[5] Noting that CIMLA requires that a party asserting a maritime lien must have provided the necessaries upon the order of owner of the vessel or a person authorized by the owner, the District Court **[—11—]** determined that CEPSA was not entitled to a maritime lien because it provided the bunkers on the order of O.W. USA, an intermediary who was neither an owner nor the authorized agent of the owner. *See id.* at 365. The District Court also dismissed CEPSA's alternative claim that it was entitled to recover on a theory of unjust enrichment and on equitable principles, reasoning that because maritime liens are creations of CIMLA whose terms are strictly construed, generalized equitable concerns do not trump the express provisions of the statute.

Turning to ING's (as assignee of O.W. Denmark) assertion of a maritime lien, the District Court concluded that O.W. Denmark had not "provided" necessaries to the Vessel within the meaning of CIMLA and thus could not assert a maritime lien. The District Court found that there was a lack of evidence with respect to O.W. Denmark's "arrangements down the chain" and that O.W. Denmark could not, without proof of a fully intact contractual chain, be deemed to have provided necessaries as required by CIMLA. *See ING Bank, N.V. v. M/V TEMARA*, No. 16-cv-95,

[5] At the same time, the District Court issued opinions in other O.W. Bunker Group related matters, dismissing the physical suppliers' claims in those actions. *See Aegean Bunkering (USA) LLC v. M/T AMAZON*, No. 14-cv-9447, 2016 WL 4471895 (S.D.N.Y. Aug. 24, 2016); Order, *O'Rourke Marine Servs. L.P., LLP v. M/V COSCO HAIFA*, No. 15-cv-2992 (S.D.N.Y. Aug. 24, 2016), ECF Dkt. 103.

2016 WL 6156320, at *8 (S.D.N.Y. Oct. 21, 2016) (the "October 2016 Order"). In other words, the District Court concluded that the **[—12—]** record was uncertain as to how financial obligations and terms and conditions moved down the chain from O.W. Denmark, the contract supplier, to CEPSA, the physical supplier (through the intermediary, O.W. USA). Based on this view of the record, the District Court reasoned that O.W. Denmark did not take on any risk—financially or in terms of necessaries provided—in connection with the provision of bunkers to the Vessel since "it never assumed title or possession of the bunkers, it never obligated itself to pay the actual physical supplier, and it never supplied the bunkers." **{-518-}** *See id.* at *3. Concluding that a provider of necessaries must have taken on some risk in the transaction, the District Court denied O.W. Denmark's claim for a maritime lien because it was "steps removed from the physical provision of bunkers and never . . . had a tangible financial risk with regard to them[.]" *See id.* at *6; *id.* at *7 ("The case law does not support awarding a maritime lien in a non-risk—and therefore non-protective—circumstance.").

After denying ING's motion for partial summary judgment, the District Court *sua sponte*—and without giving ING notice or an opportunity to respond—entered summary judgment against ING and in favor of the Vessel, **[—13—]** even though the Vessel had not moved for summary judgment. Subsequently, ING moved for reconsideration and sought to supplement that factual record with additional information in order to complete the contractual links missing from its original motion. The District Court denied the motion without entertaining further submissions or briefing. Order, *ING Bank N.V. v. M/V TEMARA*, No. 16-cv-95 (S.D.N.Y. Nov. 28, 2016), ECF Dkt. 181. This appeal followed.

STANDARD OF REVIEW

We review a district court's grant of summary judgment *de novo*. *Process Am., Inc. v. Cynergy Holdings, LLC*, 839 F.3d 125, 133 (2d Cir. 2016). "Summary judgment is proper 'if the movant shows that there is no genuine dispute as to any material fact and the movant is entitled to judgment as a matter of law.'" *Id.* (quoting Fed. R. Civ. P. 56(a)). We construe the evidence in the light most favorable to the non-moving party and draw all reasonable inferences in its favor. *June v. Town of Westfield*, 370 F.3d 255, 257 (2d Cir. 2004). **[—14—]**

DISCUSSION

A maritime lien is a "special property right in the vessel, arising in favor of the creditor by operation of law as security for a debt or claim," which "arises when the debt arises[.]" *Itel Containers Int'l Corp. v. Atlanttrafik Express Serv. Ltd.*, 982 F.2d 765, 766 (2d Cir. 1992) (quoting *Equilease Corp. v. M/V SAMPSON*, 793 F.2d 598, 602 (5th Cir. 1986) (en banc)). Unlike other security arrangements, a maritime lien tends to benefit both the ship and its creditors. "On the one hand, it enables ships to obtain repairs and supplies on its own account that might not otherwise be available." *Id.* at 768 (citing *Piedmont & Georges' Creek Coal Co. v. Seaboard Fisheries Co.*, 254 U.S. 1, 9 (1920)). On the other hand, it endows the creditor with a "special property" in the ship that comes into existence when the debt arises and gives the creditor the right to have the ship sold so that the creditor's debt may be paid out of the proceeds of the sale. *Id.* (quoting *The Poznan*, 9 F.2d 838, 842 (2d Cir. 1925), *rev'd on other grounds sub nom., New York Dock Co. v. Steamship Poznan*, 274 U.S. 117 (1927)); *see also* Schoenbaum, Thomas, J., *Admiralty and Maritime Law* § 9-1, at 684 (5th ed. 2011); 2-II Benedict on Admiralty § 22 (2017). **[—15—]**

CIMLA is the statutory basis for maritime liens. CIMLA provides that "a person providing necessaries to a vessel on the **{-519-}** order of the owner or a person authorized by the owner . . . has a maritime lien on the vessel [and] may bring a civil action in rem to enforce the lien . . . ." 46 U.S.C. § 31342(a). Specifically, CIMLA requires three elements for a maritime lien: (1) that the goods or services at issue were "necessaries," (2) that the entity "provid[ed]" the necessaries to a vessel; and (3) that the entity provided the necessaries "on the order of the owner or a person authorized by the owner." *Id.; see Barcliff LLC v. M/V DEEP BLUE*, 876 F.3d 1063, 1068, 5 Adm. R. 518, 521 (11th Cir. 2017). CIMLA defines "persons . . . presumed to have authority to procure necessaries for a vessel" as "(1) the owner; (2) the master; (3) a person entrusted with the management of the vessel at the port of supply; or (4) an officer or agent appointed by—(A) the owner; (B) a charterer; (C) an owner pro hac vice; or (D) an agreed buyer in possession of the vessel." 46 U.S.C. § 31341(a). "Necessaries" include, among other things, bunkers. *See Hapag-Lloyd Aktiengesellschaft v. U.S. Oil Trading LLC*, 814 F.3d 146, 151 n.13, 4 Adm. R. 62, 65 n.13 (2d Cir. 2016); *see also* 46 U.S.C. § 31301(4). **[—16—]**

Maritime liens arise only by operation of law and not by contract. *Bominflot, Inc. v. The M/V HENRICH S*, 465 F.3d 144, 146 (4th Cir. 2006) ("[M]aritime liens are *stricti juris* and cannot be created by agreement between the parties; instead, they arise by operation of law[.]"); *accord Newell v. Norton*, 70 U.S. 257, 262 (1865) ("Maritime liens are not established by the agreement of the parties. . . . They are consequences attached by law to certain contracts, and are independent of any agreement between the parties that such liens shall exist."). Maritime liens are disfavored by the law, and are thus construed under the doctrine of *stricti juris*, meaning that the statutory requirements are construed strictly and may not be expanded by "construction, analogy or inference." *Itel Containers*, 982 F.2d at 768 (quoting *Piedmont*, 254 U.S. at 12). The primary purpose of maritime liens is to facilitate maritime commerce by reducing the counterparty risk associated with supplying a vessel that may not return to the same port again. Strict construction of CIMLA, among other things, is intended to prevent a proliferation of liens, something that might otherwise be a significant hindrance to maritime commerce. *See id.* **[—17—]**

A. Contract Supplier's Claims (O.W. Denmark)

Whether ING, as O.W. Denmark's purported assignee, is entitled to assert a maritime lien against the Vessel depends on whether O.W. Denmark is entitled to assert such a lien. The key to this inquiry is whether an entity such as O.W. Denmark which agreed to supply necessaries and then contracts with one or more intermediaries to supply them can itself be deemed to have "provided" necessaries under CIMLA. We conclude that the answer, guided by straightforward principles of contract law, is yes. A maritime lien may be asserted by an entity when that entity contracts with a vessel's owner, charterer, or other statutorily-authorized person for the provision of necessaries and the necessaries are supplied pursuant to that agreement even if by another party.

The Restatement (Second) of Contracts offers the following apt illustration: "A contracts to deliver to B coal of a specified kind and quality. A delegates the performance of this duty to C, who tenders to B coal of specified kind and quality. The tender has the effect of a tender by A." Restatement (Second) of Contracts § 318 cmt. a., illus. 2 (Am. Law Inst. 1981). In other words, a supplier may provide necessaries to a vessel indirectly through a subcontractor because **[—18—]** when a subcontractor does so pursuant to its contract with a contractor, the subcontractor's performance is attributable to the contractor. *See Galehead, Inc. v. M/V ANGLIA*, 183 F.3d 1242, 1245 (11th Cir. 1999) (observing that a contract supplier "'provided' necessaries to the vessel under the contract irrespective of how, or by whom, the delivery was carried out"); *see also* **{–520–}** *Clearlake Shipping PTE Ltd. v. O.W. Bunker (Switzerland) SA*, 239 F. Supp. 3d 674, 691 (S.D.N.Y. 2017) (concluding that a contractor need not have supplied fuel to have a lien, so long as it, "through a chain of separate, but clearly documented transactions, caused its subcontractors to deliver the necessaries to the vessels"); *Exxon Corp. v. Cent. Gulf Lines, Inc.*, 780 F. Supp. 191, 194 (S.D.N.Y. 1991).

That is what occurred here. O.W. Denmark agreed to supply bunkers to the Vessel on the order of Copenship, the charterer. O.W. Denmark then subcontracted its obligations to O.W. USA, which, in turn, subcontracted with CEPSA for the actual delivery of the bunkers and who in fact delivered the bunkers. Accordingly, we hold that O.W. Denmark was a provider of necessaries under CIMLA and may assert a maritime lien against the Vessel. *See also Barcliff*, 876 F.3d at 1074, 5 Adm. R. at 526 (holding that an O.W. Bunker Group entity acting as a contract **[—19—]** supplier could assert a maritime lien against a vessel because it "provided the bunkers to the vessel within the meaning of § 31341(a)").

The District Court reached a different result. It concluded that O.W. Denmark, in subcontracting for the provision of the bunkers to the Vessel, did not "provide" the bunkers to the Vessel since it did not incur any financial risk down the contractual chain. *See* October 2016 Order, 2016 WL 6156320, at *7 (observing that "if Party A subcontracts to Party B for bunkers for a vessel, and B subcontracts to C . . . in order for Party A to have a maritime lien . . . the contractual chain between A and C (or D) must be traceable and intact, ultimately placing A at financial risk for the bunkers provided" (alteration in original)). We disagree with this application of CIMLA. To assert a maritime lien, all a bunker contractor must establish is that it contracted with a statutorily-authorized person for the delivery of bunkers and that the bunkers were delivered pursuant to that contractual arrangement. Here, there is no question that the Vessel's charterer and O.W. Denmark entered into a contract to deliver bunkers to the Vessel. And, there is no question that those bunkers were **[—20—]** delivered pursuant to that arrangement. Thus, O.W. Denmark is entitled to assert a maritime lien under CIMLA.

The District Court's risk analysis was beside the point. In any event, the contractual chain in the record reflects routine commercial risk. Had O.W. USA (through CEPSA) failed to deliver, O.W. Denmark would have been liable to Copenship for the breach. O.W. Denmark bore the risk of O.W. USA's nonperformance (and, also, CEPSA's) and would have had to find an alternate bunker supplier if they failed to deliver. Moreover, O.W. Denmark would have had to pay O.W. USA even in the event that Copenship failed to pay it (and bankruptcy had not intervened). Insofar as the District Court determined that some additional proof of financial risk (over and above the contract itself) on the part of the bunker contractor was required, we conclude that such proof is not required by CIMLA.

Accordingly, we conclude that the District Court erred in denying ING's motion for partial summary judgment on its entitlement to a maritime lien. **[—21—]**

B. Physical Supplier's Claims (CEPSA)

CEPSA claimed that it is entitled to a maritime lien for the bunkers it supplied, or, in the alternative, that it is entitled to recovery based upon equitable principles, such as unjust enrichment. We do not agree. Because there is no dispute that CEPSA physically provided bunkers to the Vessel, "CEPSA's entitlement to a maritime lien turns on whether it furnished **{-521-}** those bunkers 'on the order of the owner or a person authorized by the owner'" August 2016 Order, 203 F. Supp. 3d at 364 (quoting 46 U.S.C. § 31342(a)). We agree with the District Court that CEPSA, as a subcontractor, is not entitled to a maritime lien because it provided the bunkers at the direction of O.W. USA rather than at the direction of the owner or the charterer of the Vessel, or any other statutorily-authorized person. It is a "long-recognized rule that the services of an independent subcontractor [generally] do not give rise to a maritime line." 1 Admiralty & Mar. Law § 9-3 (5th ed.) Every circuit to have considered the issue agrees. *See Barcliff*, 876 F.3d at 1071, 5 Adm. R. at 523 ("Where the owner directs a general contractor to provide necessaries to its vessel, a subcontractor retained by the general contractor to . . . provide the supplies is generally not entitled to a **[—22—]** maritime line."); *Cianbro Corp. v. George H. Dean, Inc.*, 596 F.3d 10, 17 (1st Cir. 2010); *Lake Charles Stevedores, Inc. v. PROFESSOR VLADIMIR POPOV MV*, 199

F.3d 220, 229 (5th Cir. 1999); *S.C. State Port Auth. v. M/V TYSON LYKES*, 67 F.3d 59, 61 (4th Cir. 1995); *Port of Portland v. M/V PARALLA*, 892 F.2d 825, 828 (9th Cir. 1989).

Despite the weight of authority to the contrary, CEPSA claims nevertheless that it is entitled to a maritime lien for the bunkers it supplied. Alternatively, CEPSA claims that it is entitled to recovery based upon equitable principles, such as unjust enrichment. We reject both of these arguments.

The District Court correctly concluded that there is no genuine dispute of material fact as to whether CEPSA provided the bunkers at the direction of O.W. USA. The record contained the sales order confirmation that CEPSA issued to O.W. USA and the purchase order confirmation that O.W. USA issued to CEPSA. On CEPSA's sales order confirmation, O.W. USA is listed as the "buyer" and CEPSA is listed as the "supplier." *See* JA at 65 (CEPSA sales order confirmation). O.W. USA's confirmation to CEPSA is to the same effect. *See id.* at 66 (O.W. USA purchase order confirmation). These documents indicate that CEPSA entered **[—23—]** into a bilateral transaction with O.W. USA and none of them indicate that O.W. USA was the owner of the Vessel or an agent of the owner or any other statutorily-authorized person. The nomination, confirmations of purchase and sale, and invoice all denominate O.W. USA as the "buyer" and CEPSA as the "seller." None of the pertinent documents refer to O.W. Denmark or the charterer. In other words, CEPSA points us to no credible evidence that the charterer of the Vessel agreed to be bound by O.W. USA's purchase of the bunkers.[6] *See Lake Charles Stevedores*, 199 F.3d at 229 (subcontracting suppliers "hired by those general contractors are generally not entitled to assert a lien on their own behalf, unless it can be shown that an entity authorized to bind the ship controlled the selection of the subcontractor and/or its performance"). For these reasons, we agree with the District Court's conclusion that CEPSA was acting as a subcontractor of O.W. USA (which itself was a subcontractor of O.W. **[—24—]** Denmark) when it delivered **{–522–}** the bunkers to the Vessel and is, therefore, not entitled to a maritime lien.[7]

Nor can CEPSA show that it was acting on the order of O.W. USA, as agent of the vessel owner. *See id.* at 229; *Marine Fuel Supply & Towing, Inc. v. M/V KEN LUCKY*, 869 F.2d 473, 477–78 (9th Cir. 1988). To resist this conclusion, CEPSA argues that the terms and conditions in its (bilateral) agreement with O.W. USA bind not just O.W. USA, but also the Vessel, the charterer, and O.W. Denmark (and ING, as O.W. Denmark's assignee). Specifically, CEPSA contends that the terms of the contract between CEPSA and O.W. USA apply to the Vessel through Clause L.4(a) of the O.W. Terms. In essence, CEPSA argues that, assuming those terms pass through to and apply to the Vessel, then the Vessel had knowledge of those terms and approved and accepted them, making any O.W. Bunker Group entity an agent of the Vessel such that CEPSA, in contracting with O.W. USA, provided the bunkers on the order of a statutorily-authorized person. This chain of contract argument fails because, as we have seen, maritime liens are solely **[—25—]** creatures of statute. If a party does not comply with the express provisions of CIMLA, it is not entitled to a maritime lien. Generalized principles of contract law can not be used to work around those provisions. *See Itel Containers*, 982 F.2d at 768 (a maritime lien

---

[6] CEPSA's argument that the Vessel's chief engineer's signature or CEPSA's delivery receipt evidences a directive from the Vessel (or an authorized agent of the owner) fails to raise a genuine issue of material fact. Acknowledgment of delivery merely shows that the bunkers reached the ship and is merely evidence of "acceptance of performance under a pre-existing contract." *Clearlake*, 239 F. Supp. 3d at 689. A signature on a delivery receipt alone is not enough to show that the parties intended to alter in any way the established contractual chain well-documented by order confirmations and invoices.

[7] We also note, as the District Court cogently observed, that if we were to allow a subcontractor—without any indication that a statutorily-authorized entity provided direction—to assert a maritime lien, we would be subjecting vessels to arrest on the basis of disputes between contractors and their subcontractors, or in this case, a dispute between a subcontractor and a sub-subcontractor. *See* August 2016 Order, 203 F. Supp. 3d at 367.

"aris[es] by operation of law . . . [and] is therefore *stricti juris*").

CEPSA's related agency argument fails as well. CEPSA contends that its terms and conditions pass up the contractual chain, and thus the O.W. Bunker Group entities (O.W. Denmark and O.W. USA) became its agents for the supply of the bunkers directly to the Vessel. In other words, the charterer (or the Vessel) ordered the bunkers directly from CEPSA through O.W. Denmark and O.W. USA. We are not persuaded. We see no support in the record for the proposition that either or both of O.W. Denmark and O.W. USA were acting as CEPSA's agent when (i) O.W. Denmark took the initial order for bunkers from the charterer of the Vessel, (ii) O.W. Denmark subcontracted with O.W. USA for delivery, and (iii) O.W. USA then sub-subcontracted with CEPSA. All we see is a series of counterparty transactions. **[—26—]**

CEPSA also argues that since it supplied the bunkers, it is entitled to recovery from the Vessel on a theory of unjust enrichment. The District Court properly determined that CEPSA could not prevail on this theory. The District Court determined, and CEPSA confirms on appeal, that the only relief sought is a maritime lien against the Vessel *in rem*. But, as the District Court correctly determined, an unjust enrichment claim must be asserted *in personam*. Although unjust enrichment claims are available under maritime law as *in personam* claims, *Gulf Oil Trading Co. v. Creole Supply*, 596 F.2d 515, 519 (2d Cir. 1979), *in rem* maritime liens "cannot be conferred on the theory of unjust enrichment or subrogation." 2-II Benedict on Admiralty § 24 (2017); *see also Mullane v. Chambers*, 438 F.3d 132, 136 n.5 (1st Cir. 2006) (observing that the plaintiffs "mistakenly thought that their maritime lien theories could create equitable liens"); *The Eurana*, 1 F.2d 684, 686 (3d Cir. 1924) ("Maritime liens . . . cannot **{-523-}** be conferred on the theory of unjust enrichment or subrogation.").

Finally, CEPSA's other equitable arguments also fail. Observing that equitable principles are "central" to admiralty law, CEPSA contends that it would be a "manifest injustice" to allow ING to recover the funds that are owed **[—27—]** CEPSA, the entity that provided the bunkers, in circumstances where ING delivered nothing and supposedly incurred no commercial risk or obligation. CEPSA Opening Br. at 24. While maritime law is indeed grounded in equity, we disagree that equitable principles mean that CEPSA is entitled to a *de facto* maritime lien under CIMLA when the statue unambiguously provides otherwise. As the District Court correctly observed, courts have consistently rejected the concept of an equitable maritime lien. *C.f. The Bird of Paradise*, 72 U.S. 545, 555 (1866); *O'Rourke Marine Servs. L.P., LLP v. M/V COSCO HAIFA*, 179 F. Supp. 3d 333, 336–37 (S.D.N.Y. 2016). We do as well because maritime liens are strictly creatures of statute and "cannot be extended argumentatively, or by analogy or inference." *Osaka Shosen Kaisha v. Pac. Exp. Lumber Co.*, 260 U.S. 490, 500 (1923).

We are not unsympathetic to CEPSA's position. After all, it supplied the bunkers and our conclusion means it gets no lien and very likely could find itself at the end of the day with an uncollectible receivable. But this result is a frequent one in insolvencies: an unsecured entity such as CEPSA, who took an unsecured credit risk, stands in line behind secured lenders. **[—28—]**

C. *Sua Sponte* Grant of Summary Judgment to Vessel

Finally, we conclude that the District Court erred when it, *sua sponte*, granted summary judgment in favor of the Vessel. *See* October 2016 Order, 2016 WL 6156320, at *9 (citing *Bridgeway Corp. v. Citibank*, 201 F.3d 134, 140 (2d Cir. 2000)). Federal Rules of Civil Procedure 56(a) and 56(b)-(e) set out the procedures that apply when a party moves for summary judgment and when a district court decides a such a motion. But when a party does not move for summary judgment, Rule 56(f) controls and "provide[s] express procedures governing the grant of summary judgment independent of a motion." *Swatch Grp. Mgmt. Servs. Ltd. v. Bloomberg L.P.*, 756

F.3d 73, 80 n.2 (2d Cir. 2014). Rule 56(f) provides:

> **Judgment Independent of the Motion.** After giving notice and a reasonable time to respond, the court may:
>
> (1) grant summary judgment for a nonmovant;
> (2) grant the motion on grounds not raised by a party; or
> (3) consider summary judgment on its own after identifying for the parties material facts that may not be genuinely in dispute.

Fed. R. Civ. P. 56(f). **[—29—]**

As we recently stated, this Rule requires "that a court may grant summary judgment *sua sponte* only '[a]fter giving notice and a reasonable time to respond' and 'after identifying for the parties material facts that may not be genuinely in dispute.'" *In re 650 Fifth Ave. and Related Props.*, 830 F.3d 66, 96 (2d Cir. 2016) (quoting Fed. R. Civ. P. 56(f) (alteration in original)). The Supreme Court has emphasized that prior notice is a prerequisite to a *sua sponte* grant of summary judgment. *See Celotex Corp. v. Catrett*, 477 U.S. 317, 326 (1986) ("[D]istrict courts are widely acknowledged to possess the power to enter summary judgments *sua sponte*, so long as the losing party was on notice that [it] had to **{-524-}** come forward with all of [its] evidence."). In addition to providing notice, a district court is also required to "identify[] for the parties material facts that may not be genuinely in dispute" before entering summary judgment *sua sponte*. Fed. R. Civ. P. 56(f)(3).[8]

A district court's failure to provide adequate notice is almost always reversible error, as it is here. A notice-free, *sua sponte* entry of summary judgment is "firmly discouraged" and is limited only to situations when there is no indication that the party against whom summary judgment would be entered **[—30—]** could present evidence that would affect the summary judgment determination. *Bridgeway Corp.*, 201 F.3d at 139; *see also Coach Leatherware Co. v. AnnTaylor, Inc.*, 933 F.2d 162, 167–68 (2d Cir. 1991); *Schwan-Stabilo Cosmetics GmbH v. Pacificlink Int'l Corp.*, 401 F.3d 28, 33 (2d Cir. 2005); *In re 650 Fifth Ave.*, 830 F.3d at 96–97.[9]

The District Court's notice-free *sua sponte* grant of summary judgment in this case was ill-advised. It concluded that the record before it did not contain documentation regarding the arrangement between O.W. Denmark and the other entities down the contractual chain to CEPSA. It then concluded that this lack of documentation was fatal to ING's assertion of a maritime lien by failing to establish a "traceable and intact" contractual chain that would ultimately place O.W. Denmark, ING's assignor, at financial risk for the bunkers. *See* October 2016 Order, 2016 WL 6156320, at *6.

ING put forth evidence that tended to establish its relationships down the contractual chain. ING submitted, as an exhibit to its S.D.N.Y. Local Civil Rule 56.1 statement in support of its motion for summary judgment, a declaration of **[—31—]** Claus Erik Mortensen, in which he attested that contractual relationships existed between the contract supplier (O.W. Denmark), the subcontractor (O.W. USA), and the physical supplier of the bunkers to the Vessel (CEPSA). *See* SA at 40–41, ¶¶ 16–18. Although specifics were not provided, he attested that O.W. USA was a "subcontractor" of O.W. Denmark and that CEPSA was a "sub-subcontractor of [O.W. Denmark] for the delivery of bunkers to [the Vessel]." *Id.* at 41, ¶ 18. These facts were incorporated into ING's Rule 56.1 statement, and the Vessel did not

[8] The advisory committee notes to Rule 56(f) provide that "[i]n many cases it may prove useful first to invite a motion; the invited motion will automatically trigger the regular procedure of [Rule 56(c)]." Fed. R. Civ. P. 56, Advisory Committee Notes (2010 Amendments).

[9] *In re 650 Fifth Ave.*, 830 F.3d at 96–97 ("We have emphasized that 'care should be taken by the district court to determine that the party against whom summary judgment is rendered has had a full and fair opportunity to meet the proposition that there is no genuine issue of material fact to be tried.'" (quoting *Schwan-Stabilo Cosmetics GmbH*, 401 F.3d at 33)).

dispute them in its Rule 56.1 counter statement. Further, in its motion for reconsideration, ING submitted an additional declaration and offered documentation regarding the details of the contractual arrangements O.W. Denmark had with its subcontractors.

Thus, when the District Court granted summary judgment, it knew from the Mortensen declaration that some evidence existed concerning the contractual arrangements between O.W. Denmark and the entities down the chain. Insofar as the District Court concluded it required additional documentation on this point, the information ING presented at a minimum should have alerted the District Court **{–525–}** that, given notice and an opportunity to do so, ING could have **[—32—]** provided additional information on an issue the District Court considered dispositive. The availability of this information was confirmed when ING provided it on its motion for reconsideration. To be sure, district courts are ordinarily not required to accept evidence on motions to reconsider that could have been adduced earlier. But here the District Court's failure to follow Rule 56(f) was not a technical lapse. By *sua sponte* entering summary judgment without affording ING the opportunity to present its relevant evidence, the District Court denied ING the procedures to which it was entitled under Rule 56.

CONCLUSION

For the foregoing reasons, we **AFFIRM IN PART**, **VACATE IN PART**, and **REMAND** to the District Court for further proceedings consistent with this opinion.

United States Court of Appeals
for the Second Circuit

No. 16-3944

ING BANK N.V.
vs.
M/V MARITIME KING

Appeal from the United States District Court for the Southern District of New York

Decided: July 9, 2018

Citation: 894 F.3d 506, 6 Adm. R. 54 (2d Cir. 2018).

Before **PARKER, WESLEY,** and **LIVINGSTON,** Circuit Judges.

[—2—] {-507-} PER CURIAM:

BACKGROUND

ING Bank, N.V. ("ING") and Chemoil Adani Pvt. Ltd. ("Chemoil") appeal from a judgment of the United States District Court for the Southern District of New York (Katherine B. Forrest, *J.*). The District Court granted summary judgment to defendant *in rem* M/V MARITIME KING (the "Vessel") on a competing maritime lien claim brought against it by ING and Chemoil under the Commercial Instruments and Maritime Liens Act ("CIMLA"), 46 U.S.C. § 31301 *et seq.*, arising from the provision of bunkers (marine **[—3—]** fuel) to the Vessel. *See ING Bank, N.V. v. M/V TEMARA*, No. 16-cv-95, 2016 WL 6156320 (S.D.N.Y. Oct. 21, 2016).[1] The District Court also reduced the principal amount and interest rate posted by CldN Cobelfret S.A. ("Cobelfret"), the charterer of the Vessel, to secure the Vessel's release from arrest. *See ING Bank N.V. v. M/V VOGE FIESTA*, No. 16-cv-2051, 2016 WL 8136300 (S.D.N.Y. Oct. 20, 2016).

In October 2014, Cobelfret contracted with O.W. Bunker (Switzerland) S.A. ("O.W. Switzerland") to supply bunkers to the Vessel. To do so, O.W. Switzerland utilized the services of an intermediary, O.W. Middle East DMCC, which, in turn, selected a local supplier, Chemoil, to physically supply the bunkers. Chemoil supplied the bunkers to the Vessel in November 2014.

Cobelfret did not pay for the bunkers and ING, as the purported assignee of O.W. Switzerland,[2] filed a complaint *in rem* **[—4—]** against the Vessel in the United States District Court for the District of Maryland, seeking a maritime lien for the amounts owed. Chemoil intervened in that **{-508-}** proceeding and asserted a competing maritime lien for the same bunkers and the Vessel was arrested. To secure the release of the Vessel, Cobelfret agreed to post security. The court fixed the security at $235,804.29, the full amount requested by ING, and in addition required Cobelfret to post 6% per annum as interest in accordance with Federal Rules of Civil Procedure Supplemental Rules for Admiralty and Maritime Claims ("Fed. R. Civ. P. Admiralty Supp."), Rule E(5).

The case was eventually transferred to the Southern District of New York, where ING moved for summary judgment on its maritime lien claim. The District Court denied ING's motion and instead *sua sponte* granted summary judgment to the Vessel. The District Court also entered an order reducing the security to $147,202.47 and reducing the interest rate from 6% to 3.5% per annum. ING argues on this appeal that the District Court erred in reducing the security. We disagree. **[—5—]**

DISCUSSION

"We review *de novo* the constructions of the statutes and rules and the conclusions of law

[1] The issues raised on appeal in response to the order denying ING's maritime lien claim and granting summary judgment, *sua sponte*, to the Vessel are addressed in a companion summary order.

[2] In December 2013, eleven months before O.W. Bunker & Trading A/S ("O.W. Bunker Group") declared bankruptcy, ING and O.W. Bunker Group entered into a $700 million revolving credit agreement, funded by a syndicate of lenders, which provided working capital for O.W. Bunker Group. ING contends that the Credit Agreement was secured by, among other things, an assignment of O.W. Bunker Group's receivables from the bunker transactions it had conducted—including the right to payment for the bunkers delivered to the Vessel.

upon which the district court based its decision." *Transportes Navieros y Terrestres S.A. de C.V. v. Fairmont Heavy Transp., N.V.*, 572 F.3d 96, 100 (2d Cir. 2009). "Where the district court has made no error of law, we review its decision to reduce a maritime attachment for abuse of discretion." *Id.*

The purposes of a maritime attachment are twofold: "first, to gain jurisdiction over an absent defendant, and second, to assure satisfaction of a judgment." *Aqua Stoli Shipping Ltd. v. Gardner Smirth Pty Ltd.*, 460 F.3d 434, 437 (2d Cir. 2006) (overruled on other grounds in *Shipping Corp. of India v. Jaldhi Overseas Pte. Ltd.*, 585 F.3d 58 (2d Cir. 2009)). When a vessel is restrained pursuant to an order of a maritime attachment, "any person claiming an interest in it shall be entitled to a prompt hearing at which the plaintiff shall be required to show why the arrest or attachment should not be vacated or other relief granted consistent with these rules." Fed. R. Civ. P. Admiralty Supp. R. E(4)(f). Under Rule E(5), the vessel may be released on the giving of security. When the parties cannot agree to the amount of **[—6—]** security, a court "shall fix the principal sum of the bond or stipulation at an amount sufficient to cover the amount of the plaintiff's claim fairly stated with accrued interest and costs." Fed. R. Civ. P. Admiralty Supp R. E(5)(a). This Rule goes on to provide that:

> [T]he principal sum shall in no event exceed (i) twice the amount of the plaintiff's claim or (ii) the value of the property on due appraisement, whichever is smaller. The bond or stipulation shall be conditioned for the payment of the principal sum and interest thereon at 6 per cent per annum.

Id. Where, as here, security is posted and a vessel is released, Rule E(6) empowers the court to reduce security. Rule E(6) provides that the court "may, on motion and hearing, for good cause shown, reduce the amount of security given."

After security is set, the circumstances or the conditions that initially supported security at a particular level can change. Rule E(6) is intended to accommodate such changes. On one hand, the amount set by a court typically places a cap on a plaintiff's recovery. On the other hand, a court must be mindful that excessive security is inherently unfair and restrains funds that a vessel's owner is entitled to use for other purposes. *See Transportes*, 572 F.3d at 108-09 ("Absent district court discretion to . . . reduce the security based on a **[—7—]** weighing of the equities . . . it would work inestimable hardship on the defendant **{-509-}** if a plaintiff could obtain an attachment for any amount it claimed in damages."). Rule E(6) is intended to afford courts the flexibility to balance these competing interests. As the District Court noted, "[i]n exercising discretion to reduce security under Rule E(6), courts strive to strike this balance carefully and equitably." *M/V VOGE FIESTA*, 2016 WL 8136300, at *2.

Given these considerations, we have broadly instructed that when a court is requested to reduce security under Rule E(6), it should assess the reasonableness of plaintiff's damages claim and "weigh other equitable considerations." *Transportes*, 572 F.3d at 111. The reason for this flexibility is that "limiting a district court's discretion to set or reduce a security in the same way that we have limited its discretion under Rule E(4)(f) creates a substantial and unnecessary risk that plaintiffs will abuse the maritime attachment power." *Id.* at 108.

Here, the District Court found that Cobelfret had shown "good cause" for reducing security. The District Court assessed the reasonableness of ING's damages claim and noted that "rather than reduce security by a proxy or rule of thumb, the Court shall require **[—8—]** an accounting of the statutorily permitted components of security to ensure that ING may recover its due under a favorable judgment (if any), while also preventing inequitable over-securitization." *M/V VOGE FIESTA*, 2016 WL 8136300, at *2. The District Court also explained its choice of assigning 3.5% (the prime rate at the time that it issued its opinion on October 20, 2016, taking into account recent inflation rates) as opposed to the 6% rate mentioned in Rule

E(5). *See id.*, at *1 n.1 ("Accrued interest is intended to ensure fair compensation, not windfall profit.").

The District Court did not violate either Rule E(5) or E(6) when it lowered the interest rate. As mentioned, Rule E(5)(a) requires that the "bond or stipulation" be conditioned upon the payment of the principal sum, plus "interest thereon at 6 per cent per annum." ING argues that the 6% interest rate required by E(5)(a) cannot be changed pursuant to Rule E(6). We do not agree. Rule E(5) governs the initial setting of security. Rule E(6), on the other hand, broadly accommodates changed circumstances by affording district courts the discretion to lower or raise security for "good cause shown." We see no reason to constrict this latitude by rewriting Rule **[—9—]** E(6) to exempt the appropriate interest rate from the "good cause" calculus. We therefore conclude that the District Court committed no legal error in imposing an interest rate other than the 6% rate mentioned in Rule E(5). Nor did the District Court abuse its discretion in determining that there was "good cause shown" for reducing the interest rate to 3.5%.

CONCLUSION

For these reasons, we AFFIRM the District Court's judgment reducing security.

United States Court of Appeals
for the Second Circuit

No. 16-1356

LEOPARD MARINE & TRADING, LTD.
vs.
EASY ST. LTD.

Appeal from the United States District Court for the Southern District of New York

Decided: July 13, 2018

Citation: 896 F.3d 174, 6 Adm. R. 57 (2d Cir. 2018).

Before **POOLER, PARKER,** and **LIVINGSTON,** Circuit Judges.

[—3—] {-178-} POOLER, Circuit Judge:

We decide here whether Easy Street Ltd., a Cypriot fuel supply company, has a valid maritime lien against a vessel, the M/V Densa Leopard (the "Vessel"). A maritime lien is "[a] lien on a vessel," given for one of several purposes, including "to secure the claim of a creditor who provided maritime services to the vessel." Black's Law Dictionary 1065 (10th ed. 2014). In this case, the Vessel's owner, Leopard Marine & Trading, Ltd., a Maltese company, sued for a declaratory judgment that Easy **{-179-}** Street may not exercise the maritime lien because of laches. The United States District Court for the Southern District of New York (Rakoff, *J.*), sitting in admiralty, declined to abstain on grounds of international comity in deference to an ongoing suit in Panama in which Easy Street has attempted to exercise the lien. The district court then issued a declaration that laches has extinguished the lien. **[—4—]**

We determine that the federal courts have jurisdiction to declare a maritime lien unenforceable; that abstention on the basis of international comity is not required in this case; and that the district court did not abuse its discretion in ruling that laches extinguished the lien. We thus AFFIRM the district court's judgment.

BACKGROUND

I. Factual Background

This case arises from an ocean vessel's unpaid fuel bill. In 2011, the Vessel's owner, Leopard Marine, chartered[1] the Vessel to Allied Maritime, Inc., thus allowing Allied to operate the Vessel for a period of time. As part of the chartering agreement, Allied gave Leopard Marine a cargo lien worth the amount owed for using the Vessel.

On August 23, 2011, Allied bought fuel for the Vessel from Easy Street in Mejillones, Chile, at a price of $848,847.60. Allied agreed to pay Easy Street for the fuel by September 26, 2011. By purchasing the fuel, a maritime lien arose on the Vessel in Easy Street's favor, which would allow Easy Street to seize the **[—5—]** Vessel pursuant to the lien if the fuel bill went unpaid. *See Itel Containers Int'l Corp. v. Atlanttrafik Exp. Serv. Ltd.*, 982 F.2d 765, 766 (2d Cir. 1992) ("A maritime lien is[] a special property right in the vessel, arising in favor of the creditor by operation of law as security for a debt or claim. The lien arises when the debt arises, and grants the creditor the right to appropriate the vessel, have it sold, and be repaid the debt from the proceeds."). Under American law, Allied, as the charterer of the Vessel, could give third parties such liens even without the Vessel's owner's consent. *See* 46 U.S.C.A. §§ 31341, 31342.

Allied returned the Vessel to Leopard Marine on November 4, 2011, with significant fuel left in it. On December 2, 2011, Leopard Marine provided Allied a payment credit of $409,853.10 for the fuel's value, and Allied made the final payment for use of the Vessel, which was set off in part by the fuel credit.

Allied did not pay Easy Street—the fuel provider—when the fuel invoice was due, and Easy Street undertook efforts to recover the amount owed under the invoice. Demitrios Chasampalis, the only full-time employee of Easy Street in 2011, stated that he sent

[1] To "charter," in this context, refers to "[t]he leasing or hiring of . . . [a] ship[] or other vessel." Black's Law Dictionary 284 (10th ed. 2014).

electronic notices and attended "about 100 meetings," "in person . . . [i]n Allied offices," between when the invoice was issued in 2011 **[—6—]** and sometime in 2012. App'x at 240, 246-47. During the meetings, which occurred "almost every two [or] three days," he "demanded payment of the invoice," among other outstanding issues between the two companies. App'x at 249-50. He testified that he did not seek "a settlement" of the money that was owed, but instead demanded payment of the invoice in full. App'x at 249-50. On March 16, 2012 and April 20, 2012, evidently after scores of in-person meetings had already been held, Allied sent two written notices to Easy Street, each promising to pay within a month. App'x at 321-24. But Allied did not honor either of the **{-180-}** notices, and ultimately never paid the fuel bill.

On April 15, 2012, Allied entered into involuntary bankruptcy proceedings following a motion by third-party creditors. On November 6, 2012, a Greek court declared Allied bankrupt, and ruled that Allied was "considered (retrospectively) to have stopped payments to its creditors since [January 1, 2012]." App'x at 325. The parties agree that seeking recovery from the bankruptcy estate would be futile.

Easy Street never considered suing Allied before its bankruptcy, at least in part because of the companies' strong ties to each other. Chasampalis stated that **[—7—]** the relationship between Allied and Easy Street was "such that they had me like their son," and that he "believed in them." App'x at 254.

It was also not until at least September of 2012, after Allied entered into involuntary bankruptcy proceedings, that Easy Street considered pursuing remedies against Leopard Marine, and began tracking the Vessel for arrest. Although there is some dispute as to when Easy Street first informed Leopard Marine that Allied's bill was unpaid, the earliest Easy Street claims to have done so was in October of 2013. In any event, Easy Street sent Leopard Marine an email on March 30, 2015, demanding payment of $1,394,807.76—the amount of the unpaid fuel bill plus interest and legal fees.

During 2011 and 2012, the Vessel passed through a number of ports where Easy Street could have arrested it and exercised the maritime lien. Easy Street conceded in the district court that the Vessel was in the Port of Vancouver, Canada, from March 17, 2012 until March 22, 2012, in Panama from April 4, 2012 to April 5, 2012, and in Brazil from June 5, 2012 to June 12, 2012. The district court noted, and Easy Street does not dispute, that exercise of its maritime lien **[—8—]** would have been legally possible—even if costly and protracted—in each of those ports.

On April 19, 2015, Easy Street arrested the Vessel in Panama, exercising its maritime lien for the unpaid fuel in an in rem action there.[2] The next day, Leopard Marine commenced this action, seeking a declaratory judgment that Easy Street's lien is barred by laches, and also seeking attorneys' fees and costs.

II. Proceedings Below

This appeal reviews two orders entered by the district court. The first denied Easy Street's motion to dismiss, brought under two theories: international comity and lack of personal jurisdiction. *Leopard Marine & Trading, Ltd. v. Easy St., Ltd.*, No. 15-cv-3064, 2015 WL 4940109 (S.D.N.Y. Aug. 6, 2015) (hereinafter "Motion to Dismiss Order"). Easy Street first argued that the Panamanian courts had already exercised jurisdiction over part of the proceedings, and so the district court should abstain from considering the case, either through dismissal or stay. The district court concluded that this case did not raise the "exceptional circumstances" necessary for abstention. The court also determined that it had **[—9—]** personal jurisdiction because of a United States forum selection clause in the fuel supply contract between Easy Street and Allied, even though Leopard Marine was not a party to that contract. The court reasoned that, because American law allows a party chartering a vessel to bind the vessel's owner to contracts, Easy Street should have foreseen that Leopard Marine, the Vessel's owner, might

[2] Leopard Marine was required to post a bond worth more than two million dollars in Panama to serve as security for the release of the Vessel.

later seek to enforce any favorable provision—including a choice-of-law provision—in a contract between Easy Street and Allied. **{-181-}**

The second order considered whether, on the basis of laches, Easy Street should be foreclosed from enforcing its maritime lien against the Vessel. *Leopard Marine & Trading, Ltd. v. Easy St. Ltd.*, No. 15-cv-3064, 2016 WL 3144058 (S.D.N.Y. Apr. 8, 2016) ("Summary Judgment Order"). The court concluded that laches barred the exercise of the lien, as Easy Street had delayed exercising the lien and the delay prejudiced Leopard Marine. The court focused, in particular, on the fact that Easy Street waited until after Allied had gone bankrupt to exercise the lien, which eliminated a number of otherwise reasonable means of repayment. Had Leopard Marine known that Easy Street intended to enforce the lien on the Vessel to be repaid for the fuel, Leopard Marine could have exercised its own **[—10—]** lien against Allied's cargo pursuant to the chartering agreement, or pursued an arbitration against Allied in London. But after Allied entered bankruptcy, these were no longer realistic possibilities.

Easy Street appealed the district court's decisions not to abstain on grounds of international comity, and to bar exercise of the lien on grounds of laches.

DISCUSSION

I. Federal Jurisdiction

While the parties did not raise any jurisdictional challenges in the district court, "[w]e have an independent obligation to consider the presence or absence of subject matter jurisdiction *sua sponte*." *In re Quigley Co., Inc.*, 676 F.3d 45, 50 (2d Cir. 2012). To do so, we consider whether there is jurisdiction in admiralty over a suit brought under the Declaratory Judgment Act, 28 U.S.C. § 2201, to adjudicate maritime lien rights within an in personam action.[3] **[—11—]**

The Declaratory Judgment Act provides that "[i]n a case of actual controversy within its jurisdiction . . . any court of the United States . . . may declare the rights and other legal relations of any interested party seeking such declaration." 28 U.S.C. § 2201(a). In enacting the Declaratory Judgment Act, "Congress enlarged the range of remedies available in the federal courts but did not extend their jurisdiction." *Skelly Oil Co. v. Phillips Petroleum Co.*, 339 U.S. 667, 671 (1950). Thus, "the requirements of jurisdiction—the limited subject matters which alone Congress had authorized the District Courts to adjudicate—were not impliedly repealed or modified." *Id.* at 672. Therefore, "if, but for the availability of the declaratory judgment procedure," there would be no jurisdiction over the issues involved in the suit, then "jurisdiction is lacking." **[—12—] {-182-}** *Franchise Tax Bd. of State of Cal. v. Constr. Laborers Vacation Tr. for S. Cal.*, 463 U.S. 1, 16 (1983) (quotation marks omitted).

To decide whether federal jurisdiction exists to entertain a claim for declaratory relief, courts follow *Skelly Oil*'s approach to "conceptually realign the declaratory judgment parties and claims and analyze them as they would appear in a coercive suit." *Garanti Finansal Kiralama A.S. v. Aqua Marine & Trading Inc.*, 697 F.3d 59, 67 (2d Cir. 2012); *see also Skelly Oil*, 339 U.S. at 672

[3] We note that Congress provided, in the provisions pertaining to maritime liens within the Commercial Instruments and Maritime Liens Act ("CIMLA"), *see* 46 U.S.C. § 31341 et seq., statutory bases for the origination, enforcement, and discharge of maritime liens, certain of which will be discussed in due course. Some courts have treated these provisions as conferring federal question **[—11—]** jurisdiction—in addition to admiralty jurisdiction—where a declaration is sought under CIMLA's provisions as to the invalidity of a lien. *See Cianbro Corp. v. George H. Dean, Inc.*, 596 F.3d 10, 11 (1st Cir. 2010) (noting, in a case requesting declaratory judgment regarding maritime lien, that "[b]ecause . . . we are required to interpret the Maritime Lien Act to resolve the issues presented, this controversy is deemed properly before us."). Here, however, Leopard Marine does not claim that it has satisfied the requirements for a declaratory judgment pursuant to 46 U.S.C. § 31343(c), and the parties have not otherwise suggested that we have federal question jurisdiction based on CIMLA. Thus, we address only the question of whether we have admiralty jurisdiction over this dispute.

("If Phillips sought damages from petitioners or specific performance of their contracts, it could not bring suit in a United States District Court on the theory that it was asserting a federal right. . . . [S]uch a suit would 'arise' under the State law governing the contracts."). Thus, if the defendant in a declaratory suit could have sued in federal court, seeking non-declaratory relief on the same claims pressed in the declaratory suit, then federal courts have jurisdiction over the declaratory action. *See Garanti Finansal*, 697 F.3d at 68 ("[W]e have summarized the law as follows: a complaint seeking a declaratory judgment is to be tested, for purposes of the well-pleaded complaint rule, as if the party whose adverse action the declaratory **[—13—]** judgment plaintiff apprehends had initiated a lawsuit against the declaratory judgment plaintiff." (internal quotation marks omitted)).

Although the *Skelly Oil* "conceptual realign[ment]" heuristic originated in federal question jurisdiction, this Court recently applied it in assessing admiralty suits. *Id.* at 68-71. While noting that it is not perfectly tailored to the admiralty context, *id.*, we explained that if "*Skelly Oil*'s simple and effective analysis applied only to federal-question jurisdiction, many admiralty litigants (and judges hearing admiralty cases) would miss out on the salutary effects of the [Declaratory Judgment Act]." *Id.* at 70.

In the present case, Leopard Marine, owner of the Vessel, sues seeking a declaration that Easy Street may not enforce its maritime lien. The precedents of *Skelly Oil* and *Garanti Finansal* teach that we must ask, to assure ourselves of jurisdiction, whether Easy Street could have brought a coercive suit in federal court to enforce its lien, i.e., to become owner of the vessel.[4] **[—14—]**

Authorities concur that a maritime lien may be enforced only through an action in rem—that is, by proceeding against the vessel itself. *See, e.g.*, 8-VII Joshua S. Force & Steven F. Friedell, Benedict on Admiralty § 7.01 (2017) ("Maritime liens do not exist apart from their ability to be enforced *in rem* in admiralty."); *The Rock Island Bridge*, 73 U.S. 213, 215 (1867) ("The lien and the proceeding *in rem* are, therefore, correlative—where one exists, the other may be taken, and not otherwise."). Generally speaking, "[a]n action in rem . . . [t]o enforce [a] maritime lien" requires court officials to "arrest . . . the vessel or other property that is the subject of the action." Fed. R. Civ. P. Supp. Adm. R. C (1)(a), (3)(a)(i). Here, the question is whether the Vessel's absence from the district would have precluded a suit by Easy Street to exercise its lien, and, if so, whether we lack jurisdiction to consider the "realigned" suit brought by Leopard Marine seeking that the lien be declared unenforceable.[5] **[—15—]** **{-183-}**

The Supreme Court has referred to in rem jurisdiction as a device of legal fiction intended to promote access to courts. "The fictions of *in rem* forfeiture were developed primarily to expand the reach of the courts and to furnish remedies for aggrieved parties . . . ." *Republic Nat'l Bank of Miami v. United States*, 506 U.S. 80, 87 (1992) (citations

[4] In this context, the "exercise" or "enforcement" of a maritime lien refers to a lienholder's action to become the owner of the vessel. It does not refer, for example, to a declaration of rights in a lien, such as that sought in the present case.

[5] In applying the *Skelly Oil* test, courts typically ask whether an action could lie if brought by the defendant in the declaratory action against the plaintiff in the declaratory action. *Garanti Finansal*, 697 F.3d at 68. Here, we encounter an unusual situation: since maritime liens may be exercised only in rem, the realigned non-declaratory suit would not involve Leopard Marine as a party, but would instead involve the Vessel. But, for purposes of declaratory judgment actions regarding maritime liens, courts permit the vessels' owners to serve as **[—15—]** plaintiffs in place of the vessels themselves. *See Cianbro*, 596 F.3d at 11 (permitting the vessels' owners to serve as plaintiffs-intervenors in an appeal in a declaratory action adjudicating rights in a maritime lien). Although *Cianbro* arose under the declaratory procedure permitted for liens by 46 U.S.C. § 31343, which we discuss more fully below, that statute does not prescribe that owners be permitted to serve as plaintiffs in declaratory actions. We think the conclusion that the vessel's owner may serve as plaintiff in a declaratory action applies just as well to declaratory actions such as this one that are not brought under Section 31343.

omitted). One "purpose[] of the fiction, among others, has been to allow actions against ships where a person owning the ship could not be reached." *Continental Grain Co. v. The FBL-585*, 364 U.S. 19, 23 (1960). As such, "a fiction born to provide convenient forums should not be transferred into a weapon to defeat that very purpose." *Id.* As discussed below, we conclude that our jurisdictional analysis squarely aligns with these principles.

Courts often speak as though physical presence of the res within the territorial jurisdiction of the district court, along with the attachment of the res, is **[—16—]** a hard-and-fast jurisdictional prerequisite for an action in rem, particularly in admiralty. *See, e.g., In re Millenium Seacarriers, Inc.*, 419 F.3d 83, 94 (2d Cir. 2005) ("[S]ubject matter jurisdiction lies in the district court where the vessel or other *res* is located, but that jurisdiction does not attach until the vessel is arrested within the jurisdiction."); *Dow Chem. Co. v. Barge UM-23B*, 424 F.2d 307, 311 (5th Cir. 1970) ("Attachment subjecting the res to the jurisdiction of the court is a prerequisite to a finding of in rem liability."); *The Resolute*, 168 U.S. 437, 439 (1897) ("Jurisdiction . . . . [a]s applied to a suit in rem for the breach of a maritime contract . . . presupposes—First, that the contract sued upon is a maritime contract; and, second, that the property proceeded against is within the lawful custody of the court."). But significant authority clarifies an exception: that, "[i]f the *res* is absent from the district, this . . . jurisdictional defect can be waived if the owner of the *res* voluntarily appears" and "waive[s]" the "presence requirement." 29-704 Moore's Federal Practice - Civil § 704.02 (2017); *Hapag-Lloyd Aktiengesellschaft v. U.S. Oil Trading LLC*, 814 F.3d 146, 153–54, 4 Adm. R. 62, 67 (2d Cir. 2016) ("To obtain jurisdiction . . . a court must either seize the *res* or obtain the consent of the owner or other person asserting a right of possession."). **[—17—]**

In *Hapag-Lloyd*, this court considered a complex interpleader suit, part of which resolved the validity of a number of maritime liens. 814 F.3d at 149, 4 Adm. R. at 66–67. We held that the consent of a vessel's owner to the adjudication of rights in a maritime lien was sufficient for the court to exercise in rem jurisdiction, regardless of whether the vessel itself was present:

> [The] argument—that *both* parties' consent is necessary in cases where the party initiating suit is the owner of the **{-184-}** *res* that the lienholder seeks to arrest—relies on cases holding that where a lienholder brings a claim, both parties' consent is "sufficient" for a court to exercise *in rem* jurisdiction without seizure of the *res.* That is not inconsistent, however, with other cases indicating that only the owner's consent is necessary. *In rem* jurisdiction is "a customary elliptical way of referring to jurisdiction over the interests of persons in a thing." *Shaffer v. Heitner*, 433 U.S. 186, 207 (1977). To obtain jurisdiction over that interest, a court must either seize the *res* or obtain the consent of the owner or other person asserting a right of possession. This principle is demonstrated by the many cases in which *in rem* jurisdiction has been held waived without seizure when the owner appears without contesting jurisdiction. *See, e.g., United States v. Republic Marine, Inc.*, 829 F.2d 1399, 1402 (7th Cir. 1987); *Cactus Pipe & Supply Co. v. M/V Montmartre*, 756 F.2d 1103, 1107–08 (5th Cir. 1985); *cf. Continental Grain Co. v. The FBL-585*, 364 U.S. 19, 22–27 (1960). By initiating an interpleader concerning certain *in rem* claims and posting adequate security for those claims, [the plaintiff] consented to the District Court's jurisdiction over its interests, which is sufficient to confer jurisdiction.

Id., 4 Adm. R. at 66–67 (internal quotation marks and citations omitted; other citations abridged). **[—18—]**

There is admittedly some question as to whether the rule of *Hapag-Lloyd* applies here. That opinion largely discussed the interpleader statute—which created some of the controversy over jurisdiction in rem[6]—and the present case is unrelated to the interpleader mechanism. We nonetheless conclude that *Hapag-Lloyd*'s rule applies in the present case for a number of reasons. **[—19—]**

To begin, although *Hapag-Lloyd* dealt heavily with interpleader issues, it stated specifically that it considered, for reasons other than just the interpleader requirements, whether in rem jurisdiction existed:

> [The appellee] argues that [the appellant] conflates subject matter and *in rem* jurisdiction, which are distinct. While it is true that some elements of the arguments overlap, [the appellant] makes two arguments: first, the amount of the bond is insufficient under § 1335[, **{–185–}** the interpleader statute,] to confer subject matter jurisdiction . . . and second, even if it is sufficient under § 1335, it is insufficient to constitute a substitute *res* for the vessels themselves . . . .

814 F.3d at 153 n.20, 4 Adm. R. at 66 n.20 (internal citations omitted). The Court also otherwise separated its resolution of the appellant's argument as to "the sufficiency of the District Court's *in rem* jurisdiction," *id.* at 153, 4 Adm. R. at 66, from the resolution of the "principal argument" related to interpleader, *see id.* at 151, 4 Adm. R. at 64–65. The Court's discussion of the in rem question thus resolved the argument, as the district court framed it, "that the Court could not adjudicate the *in rem* claims against the Vessels . . . because . . . the Vessels were never arrested or present in this jurisdiction and the [opposing parties] did not consent to substitute the amounts on deposit for the [vessels] that are the subjects of their maritime liens." *UPT Pool Ltd. v. Dynamic Oil Trading (Singapore) PTE. Ltd.*, No. 14-CV-9262, 2015 WL **[—20—]** 4005527, at *5 (S.D.N.Y. July 1, 2015), *aff'd sub nom. Hapag-Lloyd Aktiengesellschaft v. U.S. Oil Trading LLC*, 814 F.3d 146, 4 Adm. R. 62 (2d Cir. 2016). That issue is nearly identical to the one in this case regarding whether the vessel's presence may be waived if in rem jurisdiction is to be exercised. *Hapag-Lloyd*'s holding thus applies here.

The reasoning of *Hapag-Lloyd* also demonstrates why its rule should apply in this suit. The rule in *Hapag-Lloyd* draws on two lines of doctrine. The first acknowledges that an action in rem, while ostensibly a suit against property itself, is in reality a convenient means of targeting the owner's interest in the property. *See Continental Grain*, 364 U.S. at 26 (noting that an action in rem against a barge is "an alternative way of bringing the owner into court"); *Shaffer*, 433 U.S. at 207 (noting that "the phrase, 'judicial jurisdiction over a thing', is a customary elliptical way of referring to jurisdiction over the interests of persons in a thing" (brackets omitted)). A corollary is that a main purpose

[6] The district court's opinion noted that the parties raised two separate arguments based on in rem jurisdiction. The first argument related to whether "the Court could . . . adjudicate the *in rem* claims against the Vessels . . . because, in many cases, the Vessels were never arrested or present in this jurisdiction and the Objecting Claimants did not consent to substitute the amounts on deposit for the *res* that are the subjects of their maritime liens." *UPT Pool Ltd. v. Dynamic Oil Trading (Singapore) PTE. Ltd.*, No. 14-CV-9262, 2015 WL 4005527, at *5 (S.D.N.Y. July 1, 2015), *aff'd sub nom. Hapag-Lloyd Aktiengesellschaft v. U.S. Oil Trading LLC*, 814 F.3d 146, 4 Adm. R. 62 (2d Cir. 2016). The second argument, which raised an in rem argument related to the interpleader statute, was that "the Court lacks subject matter jurisdiction to adjudicate . . . statutory *in rem* claims against the Vessels under 28 U.S.C. § 1335" because "*in rem* claims against the Vessels are 'separate and distinct' from any *in personam* claims against the Vessel Interests and therefore are not amenable to resolution as part of an interpleader, which requires adverse claims arising out of a single obligation." *Id.* We also mentioned the presence of both of these arguments, albeit in a summary fashion. *Hapag-Lloyd*, 814 F.3d at 151, 4 Adm. R. at 64–65 ("[Appellant's] principal argument is that, because [some] claims to payment arise from statutory *in rem* liens . . . [and others] arise from the supply contracts (and thus are correctly characterized . . . as being *in personam* in nature), its codefendants are not claiming entitlement to *the same* money, property, or benefit of the instrument or obligation."); 153, 4 Adm. R. at 66 ("[Appellant] also challenges the sufficiency of the District Court's *in rem* jurisdiction.").

of personifying vessels in admiralty—a practice that might otherwise be derided as "irrational" and "atavistic"—is "to allow actions against ships where a person owning the **[—21—]** ship could not be reached."[7] *Continental Grain*, 364 U.S. at 23. Accordingly, the Supreme Court does not strictly apply the requirement that the vessel remain present in the district, if its absence would not threaten the owner's participation in the suit.

In *Continental Grain*, the Court permitted transfer of an in rem action from one district to another under 28 U.S.C. 1404(a), which states that "a district court may transfer any civil action to any other district . . . where it might have been brought." *Id.* at 20-21, 26-27. This was true even though the in rem action could not "have been brought" initially in the transferee district, as the vessel was not located there when the plaintiff filed suit. *Id.* at 22. The Court emphasized that its decision to ignore the vessel's physical location served practical and salutary purposes; a contrary ruling demanding physical presence of the res as an absolute jurisdictional requirement would merely have "provide[d] a shelter for in rem admiralty proceedings in **{-186-}** costly and inconvenient forums." *Id.* at 27. The **[—22—]** *Continental Grain* Court noted that "the fiction appears to have no relevance whatever in a District Court's determination of where a case can most conveniently be tried. A fiction born to provide convenient forums should not be transferred into a weapon to defeat that very purpose." *Id.* at 23 (also observing that "[t]he concept of the ship as a distinct juridical entity" is no more than "a convenient conceptual tool."). *Continental Grain*—ignored by the dissent—supports our conclusion that a vessel owner's agreement to have its rights in property adjudicated in the forum is sufficient to confer in rem jurisdiction.

The second line of precedent undergirding *Hapag-Lloyd* is one that explains vessel attachment rules governing in rem actions as rules for service of process rather than independent jurisdictional requirements. *See, e.g., The St. Lawrence*, 66 U.S. 522, 529 (1861) (noting that in a prior decision, *The General Smith*, 17 U.S. 438 (1819), it was understood that "the right to proceed against the property [was] regarded as a mere question of process and not of jurisdiction"). In *United States v. Republic Marine, Inc.*, the Seventh Circuit held that, even where "jurisdiction [is] never gained over [a vessel] by the supplemental admiralty rules of attachment," that "alone . . . is not enough to prove lack of jurisdiction over the **[—23—]** vessel." 829 F.2d 1399, 1402 (7th Cir. 1987). The court went on to explain that "a vessel may waive jurisdiction *in rem* by appearing in the action and failing to raise the defense of lack of jurisdiction over the party in a timely fashion."[8] *Id.* Voluminous authority supports this proposition in the admiralty context. *See Porsche Cars N. Am. Inc. v. Porsche.net*, 302 F.3d 248, 256 (4th Cir. 2002) ("[I]n admiralty and civil forfeiture cases, for years courts have held that objections to in rem jurisdiction may be waived."); *Cactus Pipe and Supply Co. v. M/V Montmartre*, 756 F.2d 1103, 1107-11 (5th Cir. 1985) ("A claimant . . . can waive the necessity of in rem seizure and consent to jurisdiction so far as its interest in the vessel is concerned."); *Reed v. Steamship Yaka*, 307 F.2d 203, 204 (3d Cir. 1962), *rev'd on other grounds*, 373 U.S. 410 (1963) ("While the power of an

[7] This is to say nothing of the origin of the personification of vessels. Evidently, this legal fiction was an application of more widespread rules assigning responsibility to inanimate objects for their own harmful acts. *See* Oliver Wendell Holmes, Jr., The Common Law 24-30 (Dover ed. 1991) (1881). But it is of course not unusual that the later understanding and employment of a rule differs significantly from the rule's initial purpose. *Id.* at 5.

[8] Although the Seventh Circuit spoke in *Republic Marine* of the vessel's "appearance," we do not take this statement as referring to an actual, physical appearance, but instead as the common legal term of art that refers to participation in the litigation of an action whether or not one is physically present. *See Republic Marine*, 829 F.2d at 1402 ("Of course, the general rule in civil actions is now (and has been for some time) that any appearance in an action is a general appearance, and although the special appearance has not been abolished with respect to admiralty and maritime claims, its preservation requires explicit affirmative acts restricting its appearance." (internal citations omitted)).

admiralty court to exercise authority over a ship normally depends upon the arrest of the **[—24—]** ship within the court's territorial jurisdiction, a claimant can waive this requirement and consent to jurisdiction so far as its interest in the vessel is concerned."); *The Willamette*, 70 F. 874, 878 (9th Cir. 1895), *decree modified,* 72 F. 79 (9th Cir. 1895); *see also Farwest Steel Corp. v. Barge Sea Span 241*, 769 F.2d 620, 622 (9th Cir. 1985) (noting rule that courts have exercised in rem jurisdiction over vessels where "the *res,* while beyond the court's territorial jurisdiction, was owned by a party actually before the court, over whom the court already held *in personam* jurisdiction"); *Farwest Steel Corp. v. Barge Sea-Span 241*, 828 F.2d 522, 524 (9th Cir. 1987) (noting that an "exception" to the requirements of territorial presence and attachment of the res in order for a court to **{-187-}** possess in rem jurisdiction "is established by the consent of the vessel's owner to in rem jurisdiction.").[9] **[—25—]**

We are cognizant of the unusual position that actions in rem occupy within admiralty jurisdiction. Pursuant to the Judiciary Act of 1789, the federal courts have exclusive jurisdiction over in rem actions within admiralty jurisdiction. *See* Charles J. Black, Jr., Admiralty Jurisdiction: Critique and Suggestions, 50 Colum. L. Rev. 259, 263, 265-66 (1950); *Knapp, Stout & Co. v. McCaffrey*, 177 U.S. 638, 642–43 (1900); *Am. Dredging Co. v. Miller*, 510 U.S. 443, 446–47 (1994) ("An *in rem* suit against a vessel is . . . distinctively an admiralty proceeding, and is hence within the exclusive province of the federal courts."); *see also* 28 U.S.C. § 1333.[10] On the other hand, state courts share with the federal courts jurisdiction over most actions in personam. *See* 1 Thomas J. Schoenbaum, Admiralty & Mar. Law § 3-2 (5th ed. 2016); *Am. Dredging Co.*, 510 U.S. at 447 ("In exercising *in personam* jurisdiction . . . a state court may adopt such remedies, and **[—26—]** attach to them such incidents, as it sees fit so long as it does not attempt to make changes in the substantive maritime law." (internal quotation marks and ellipsis omitted)). Additionally, in rem jurisdiction is sometimes necessary to establish subject matter jurisdiction in admiralty. That situation arises when a suit's only basis of admiralty jurisdiction is enforcement of a maritime lien, since maritime liens can only be enforced through proceedings in rem. *See, e.g.*, 8-VII Benedict on Admiralty § 7.01 (2017). This differs from most other settings, where in rem jurisdiction emphatically "deal[s] with personal and not subject matter jurisdiction." *Falise v. Am. Tobacco Co.*, 241 B.R. 48, 62 (E.D.N.Y. 1999) (citing *Cargill, Inc. v. Sabine Trading & Shipping Co., Inc.*, 756 F.2d 224, 228–29 (2d Cir. 1985)).

Since in rem jurisdiction is necessary, in this case, for subject matter jurisdiction in admiralty, our dissenting colleague argues that our ruling impermissibly gives parties permission to waive challenges to subject matter jurisdiction. That is not so. We reiterate the reasoning above. If the requirement that a vessel be arrested is a mere matter of service of process, and a practical means of getting at the owner's property, then there is no reason that it could

[9] In *Ventura Packers, Inc. v. F/V Jeanine Kathleen*, 424 F.3d 852, 860-61 (9thCir. 2005), the Ninth Circuit, following *Republic National Bank of Miami,* held that the conditions for in rem jurisdiction—territorial presence and attachment—need only be present at the commencement of a lawsuit, and that if res departs the district and evades the clutches of the court, or if the court releases the res or the substitute res, then the court still retains jurisdiction over the case. That the res's owner can consent to the exercise of jurisdiction despite the absence of the res is reinforced by this principle, under which a court's control over the res is not required during the duration of a lawsuit and possible appeal.

[10] The provenance of this rule is the "saving to suitors" clause of the Judiciary Act of 1789, which, much like its modern successor in 28 U.S.C. § 1333, gave the district courts "exclusive original cognizance of all civil causes of admiralty and maritime jurisdiction . . . saving to suitors, in all cases, the right of a common law remedy, where the common law is competent to give it." 1 Stat. 76 (1789). The "saving to suitors" clause was interpreted to allow state courts to adjudicate admiralty cases other than "an admiralty proceeding *in rem*" because such a proceeding "is in no sense a common-law remedy." *The Hine*, 71 U.S. 555, 571 (1866); *see also* 1 Thomas J. Schoenbaum, Admiralty & Mar. Law § 3-2 (5th ed. 2016).

not **[—27—]** be waived under appropriate circumstances. That is not the same as allowing the parties **{–188–}** to waive the requirement of in rem jurisdiction itself where, as here, it is necessary for subject matter jurisdiction. The dissent's major error is to conflate these two wildly different requirements—arrest and in rem jurisdiction. In many other areas of the law, in rem jurisdiction cannot require an arrest or seizure since the property is intangible. *Cf. Hanson v. Denckla*, 357 U.S. 235, 247 (1958) (noting, in discussion of in rem jurisdiction, that "[i]n considering restrictions on the power to tax, this Court has concluded that 'jurisdiction' over intangible property is not limited to a single State"). Despite the dissent's suggestion to the contrary, there is no fundamental rule that actual seizure or possession of an object is always required for in rem jurisdiction over it. *See Mullane v. Cent. Hanover Bank & Tr. Co.*, 339 U.S. 306, 312 (1950) ("Distinctions between actions in rem and those in personam are ancient and originally expressed in procedural terms what seems really to have been a distinction in the substantive law of property under a system quite unlike our own. . . . American courts have sometimes classed certain actions as in rem because personal service of process was not required, and at other times have held personal service of process not **[—28—]** required because the action was in rem."). In short, the vessel's arrest is simply not a matter of jurisdiction itself. It therefore can be waived, even though the requirement of subject matter jurisdiction obviously cannot be waived.

Other, less direct, considerations support our conclusion that jurisdiction exists over this case. One is a realization that, absent a rule permitting the vessel's owner to waive its arrest to confer jurisdiction in declaratory judgment actions, the Declaratory Judgment Act would seem not to apply to most maritime lien disputes. The Federal Rules of Civil Procedure permit seizure of a vessel for actions in rem. *See* Fed. R. Civ. P. Supp. Adm. R. C(3)(a)(i) ("If the conditions for an in rem action appear to exist, the court must issue an order directing the clerk to issue a warrant for the arrest of the vessel or other property that is the subject of the action."). But they apparently lack a procedure for the situation here: an in personam action where the court's jurisdiction is *not* in rem, but *derivative* of theoretically-possible jurisdiction in rem. If any substitute exists, it would be some lesser requirement—perhaps that a vessel appear in the district, or that the owner produce property of equivalent value—but without court process ensuring the vessel's continued presence. But if so, then the vessel, **[—29—]** and the court's jurisdiction, would remain only at the owner's pleasure. One can imagine the impracticality of requiring a federal judge to scan the harbor for the physical basis of the court's jurisdiction before issuing any order. And, of course, upon the whiff of an impending adverse judgment, both the vessel and the court's jurisdiction would likely set sail. *Cf. Lozman v. City of Riviera Beach, Fla.*, 133 S. Ct. 735, 744, 1 Adm. R. 2, 6 (2013) ("Admiralty law . . . provides special attachment procedures lest a vessel avoid liability by sailing away."). Under this rule, declaratory suits regarding maritime liens would be unworkable as a practical matter. We think such a result "would . . . contravene the well settled rule that the Declaratory Judgment Act should be liberally construed to accomplish its purpose of providing a speedy and inexpensive method of adjudicating legal disputes without invoking coercive remedies and that it is not to be interpreted in any narrow or technical sense." *Garanti Finansal*, 697 F.3d at 70. **{–189–}**

We observe, also, that the Congress has passed a statute permitting declaratory judgment actions in admiralty for the adjudication of rights in maritime liens recorded with the Secretary of the Department of Homeland Security. 46 U.S.C. § 31343(c)(2) ("The district courts of the United States shall **[—30—]** have jurisdiction over a civil action in Admiralty to declare that a vessel is not subject to a lien claimed under subsection (b) of this section, or that the vessel is not subject to the notice of claim of lien, or both, regardless of the amount in controversy or the citizenship of the parties."). The existence and application of this statute demonstrates that the availability of declaratory actions to adjudicate claims in liens is neither legally dubious nor likely to be disruptive to maritime commerce. *See, e.g., Cianbro Corp. v. George H. Dean, Inc.*, 596 F.3d 10, 11 (1st Cir. 2010) (considering, under Section 31343(c)(2), an appeal of a district court's order that "issued a declaratory judgment to the effect that [two] Vessels were not subject to a maritime lien"). We do not take the existence of Section 31343 to limit the possibility that declaratory actions will be available for liens *not* recorded with the Secretary, as the statute contains a savings clause stating that it "does not alter in any respect the law pertaining to the establishment of a maritime lien, the remedy provided by such a lien, or the defenses thereto." 46 U.S.C. § 31343(f). And "[t]he purpose of a savings clause is . . . to nix an inference that the statute in which it appears is intended to be the exclusive remedy for harms caused by the **[—31—]** violation of the statute." *PMC, Inc. v. Sherwin-Williams Co.*, 151 F.3d 610, 618 (7th Cir. 1998).

Finally, we note that the rule we today endorse has been applied by our district courts in declaratory actions in past years. *See Kristensons-Petroleum, Inc. v. Sealock Tanker Co., Ltd.*, 304 F. Supp. 2d 584, 590 (S.D.N.Y. 2004). And the remedy we are describing—in personam adjudication of rights in a maritime lien—is available through the interpleader statute under *Hapag-Lloyd*. 814 F.3d 146, 4 Adm. R. 62.

The dispute considered here is one seeking a declaration that a maritime lien is not enforceable. We have no occasion to discuss what, if any, authority the Declaratory Judgment Act provides courts to issue other declarations regarding maritime liens. But we are satisfied that the federal courts possess jurisdiction to adjudicate the dispute before us.

II. Abstention Pursuant to International Comity

Easy Street contends that the district court erred in denying its motion to dismiss or stay the case in deference to the Panamanian proceedings on grounds of international comity. "We review a district court's decision to extend or deny **[—32—]** comity to a foreign proceeding for abuse of discretion." *Finanz AG Zurich v. Banco Economico S.A.*, 192 F.3d 240, 246 (2d Cir. 1999).

"International comity has been described by the Supreme Court as 'the recognition which one nation allows within its territory to the legislative, executive or judicial acts of another nation, having due regard both to international duty and convenience, and to the rights of its own citizens or of other persons who are under the protection of its laws.'" *JP Morgan Chase Bank v. Altos Hornos de Mex., S.A. de C.V.*, 412 F.3d 418, 423 (2d Cir. 2005) (quoting *Hilton v. Guyot*, 159 U.S. 113, 164 (1895)). "[I]nternational comity is clearly concerned with maintaining amicable working relationships between nations, a shorthand for good neighbourliness, common courtesy and mutual respect between those who **{-190-}** labour in adjoining judicial vineyards." *Id.* (internal quotation marks omitted). "We have stated that the doctrine is not an imperative obligation of courts but rather is a discretionary rule of practice, convenience, and expediency." *Id.* (internal quotation marks omitted).

"While the doctrine can be stated clearly in the abstract, in practice we have described its boundaries as 'amorphous' and 'fuzzy.'" *Royal & Sun All. Ins.* **[—33—]** *Co. of Can. v. Century Int'l Arms, Inc.*, 466 F.3d 88, 92 (2d Cir. 2006) (citation omitted). "Generally, concurrent jurisdiction in United States courts and the courts of a foreign sovereign does not result in conflict" requiring dismissal or stay of a case for comity concerns. *Id.* "The mere existence of parallel foreign proceedings does not negate the district courts' 'virtually unflagging obligation . . . to exercise the jurisdiction given them.'" *Id.* (quoting *Colo. River Water Conservation Dist. v. United States*, 424 U.S. 800, 817 (1976)). In particular, "parallel proceedings in the same in personam claim should ordinarily be allowed to proceed simultaneously, at least until a judgment is reached in one which can be pled as res judicata in the other." *Id.* (brackets omitted).

In order for a court to decline jurisdiction on grounds of international comity, it must find "exceptional circumstances exist that justify the surrender of that jurisdiction." *Id.* at 93. "The exceptional circumstances that would support such a surrender must, of course, raise considerations which are not generally present as a result of parallel litigation, otherwise the routine would be considered exceptional, and a district court's unflagging obligation to exercise its jurisdiction would become merely a polite request." *Id.* "We have recognized one **[—34—]** discrete category of foreign litigation that generally requires the dismissal of parallel district court actions—foreign bankruptcy proceedings"—because "[a] foreign nation's interest in the equitable and orderly distribution of a debtor's property is an interest deserving of particular respect and deference." *Id.* at 93-94 (internal quotation marks omitted).

Easy Street makes two arguments as to why the district court should have relinquished jurisdiction in favor of either dismissal or a stay of the case while the Panamanian in rem proceeding was ongoing. First, Easy Street claims that this case satisfies a list of factors articulated in *Royal & Sun,* factors that guide the analysis of whether international comity militates against exercising jurisdiction. The *Royal & Sun* opinion articulated those factors as follows:

> In the context of parallel proceedings in a foreign court, a district court should be guided by the principles upon which international comity is based: the proper respect for litigation in and the courts of a sovereign nation, fairness to litigants, and judicial efficiency. Proper consideration of these principles will no doubt require an evaluation of various factors, such as [1] the similarity of the parties, [2] the similarity of the issues, [3] the order in which the actions were filed, [4] the adequacy of the alternate forum, [5] the potential prejudice to either party, [6] the convenience of the parties, [7] the connection between the litigation and the United States, and [8] the connection between the litigation and the foreign jurisdiction. This list is not exhaustive, and a district court should examine the **[—35—]** "totality of the circumstances" to determine whether the specific facts before it are sufficiently exceptional to justify abstention.

Royal & Sun, 466 F.3d at 94 (internal citations omitted). Easy Street contends that each factor in this list weighs in favor **{-191-}** of dismissal or stay of the American action in favor of the Panamanian suit. In particular, Easy Street argues that: (1) the parties and (2) the issues are identical in the actions; (3) the Panamanian suit was filed first, and the laches issue had already been briefed in Panama when the motion to dismiss was filed in the United States; (4) the district court expressly stated that Panamanian courts could ably handle the dispute; (5) Easy Street suffered prejudice, as Leopard Marine filed a suit in the United States to cause Easy Street significant expense in litigating duplicative suits in multiple locations and languages; (6) neither party has a connection to the United States, and both are inconvenienced by litigating here; (7) the court should not determine that the United States has a strong connection to the case simply because American law will govern it; and (8) Panama has greater connection to the case, particularly because of its exclusive jurisdiction over any in rem action resolving ownership of the Vessel. **[—36—]**

Easy Street argues that, in addition to satisfying the above-enumerated factors, this case presents "exceptional circumstances" favoring abstention, as required by *Royal & Sun,* because the Panamanian courts have exercised in rem jurisdiction over the Vessel. In support of the proposition that a foreign court's exercise of in rem jurisdiction is an "exceptional circumstance," Easy Street cites a number of cases suggesting that, in at least some circumstances, exercise of in rem jurisdiction "disables other courts of coordinate jurisdiction from exercising a like power." *Farmers' Loan & Tr. Co. v. Lake St. Elevated R.R. Co.,* 177 U.S. 51, 61 (1900); *Moses H. Cone Mem'l Hosp. v. Mercury Constr. Corp.,* 460 U.S. 1, 15 (1983); *Woodford v. Cmty. Action Agency of Greene Cty., Inc.,* 239 F.3d 517, 522 (2d Cir. 2001) (noting that, in an abstention analysis, the court should consider "whether the controversy involves a res over which one of the courts has assumed jurisdiction") (citing *Colo. River Water Conservation Dist. v. United States*, 424 U.S. 800, 818 (1976)). Easy Street contends that the district court has essentially displaced the Panamanian courts' power to exercise jurisdiction over the res in this case, which it claims is inconsistent with the doctrine of international comity. **[—37—]**

We have some doubt as to whether all eight factors from *Royal & Sun* unproblematically weigh in favor of deferring to the Panamanian proceedings. In particular, the district court concluded—and Easy Street does not dispute—that American law governs the case, which creates some connection between the United States and this suit. We have noted that "public interest" weighs in favor of having "a case heard in a forum at home with the law that must govern the case." *Blanco v. Banco Indus. de Venez., S.A.*, 997 F.2d 974, 983 (2d Cir. 1993) (internal quotation marks and ellipsis omitted).

We have even greater doubt that the fact of a foreign proceeding in rem is, without more, enough of an "exceptional circumstance" to merit abstention in an American in personam action on grounds of international comity.

The general rule is that "concurrent proceedings" regarding the same question are "tolerat[ed]." *China Trade & Dev. Corp. v. M.V. Choong Yong*, 837 F.2d 33, 36 (2d Cir. 1987). It is true that this rule admits of "[a] long-standing exception," *id.*, that "if the two suits are in rem, or quasi in rem . . . the jurisdiction of the one court must yield to that of the [first to consider the action]," *Princess Lida of Thurn & Taxis v. Thompson*, 305 U.S. 456, 466 (1939). The **[—38—]** **{-192-}** exception, which some have called the "prior exclusive jurisdiction" doctrine, *Chapman v. Deutsche Bank Nat. Tr. Co.*, 651 F.3d 1039, 1043 (9th Cir. 2011), emerged "because of the threat a second action poses to the first court's basis for jurisdiction." *China Trade*, 837 F.2d at 36 (citing *Donovan v. City of Dallas*, 377 U.S. 408 (1964), and *Princess Lida*, 305 U.S. 456). The "threat" emerges because "if the two suits are in rem, or quasi in rem . . . the court, or its officer, has possession or must have control of the property which is the subject of the litigation in order to proceed with the cause and grant the relief sought," which means that both courts cannot claim jurisdiction of the same property, and so "the jurisdiction of the one court must yield to that of the other." *Princess Lida*, 305 U.S. at 466; *see also Carvel v. Thomas & Agnes Carvel Found.*, 188 F.3d 83, 85-86 (2d Cir. 1999) (discussing *Princess Lida*'s rule and describing it as "a prudential doctrine of abstention"). "The logical and practical difficulty of two courts simultaneously vying for possession or control of the same property is the key" to the conflict. *United States v. $79,123.49 in U.S. Cash & Currency*, 830 F.2d 94, 97 (7th Cir. 1987); *see also Hagan v. Lucas*, 35 U.S. 400, 403 (1836) ("A most injurious conflict of jurisdiction would be likely, often, to arise between the federal and the state **[—39—]** courts; if the final process of the one could be levied on property which had been taken by the process of the other.").

But the prior exclusive jurisdiction doctrine does not generally apply to situations where one action is in rem and the other in personam. The adjudication of rights in personam simply does not impede the possession or control of the property required for maintenance of an in rem action. The Supreme Court explained as much in a conflict between state and federal courts in *United States v. Klein*, 303 U.S. 276 (1938). In *Klein*, a state court in Pennsylvania exercised jurisdiction to declare the escheat of funds, even though the funds had been deposited into the registry of a federal court to satisfy a judgment in a federal suit. *Id.* at 277. The United States appeared in the state case, and moved to dismiss "on the ground that the state court was without jurisdiction to escheat moneys in the custody of the United States or of its courts." *Id.* at 279. The Supreme Court of Pennsylvania held that the state court could exercise jurisdiction to declare escheat of the funds, because "exercise of that jurisdiction involved no interference with the federal court and no attempted control over **[—40—]** funds in its custody." *Id.* The United

States Supreme Court agreed, explaining as follows:

> While a federal court which has taken possession of property in the exercise of the judicial power conferred upon it by the Constitution and laws of the United States is said to acquire exclusive jurisdiction, the jurisdiction is exclusive only in so far as restriction of the power of other courts is necessary for the federal court's appropriate control and disposition of the property. Other courts having jurisdiction to adjudicate rights in the property do not, because the property is possessed by a federal court, lose power to render any judgment not in conflict with that court's authority to decide questions within its jurisdiction and to make effective such decisions by its control of the property. Similarly a federal court may make a like adjudication with respect to property in the possession of a state court.

Id. at 281 (internal citations omitted). In short, even when property is **{-193-}** within the "possession" and "exclusive jurisdiction" of one court, a second court does not "lose power to render any judgment not in conflict with [the first] court's authority to decide questions within its jurisdiction and to make effective such decisions by its control of the property." *Id.* In *Klein*, declaration of rights in the funds did not impede another court's possession and control of the funds themselves. **[—41—]**

Courts of appeals invariably reach the same conclusion, stating more broadly the principle that one court's exercise of jurisdiction in rem does not prevent other courts from declaring rights in the res within an in personam action. The First Circuit, although recognizing that "a court cannot exercise jurisdiction over a *res* that is already subject to the *in rem* jurisdiction of another court," has stated that "if only one of the actions is *in rem*, and the other is *in personam*, the cases may proceed simultaneously." *United States v. One 1986 Chevrolet Van*, 927 F.2d 39, 44 (1st Cir. 1991). Similarly, the Seventh Circuit understands *Klein* and other precedent to mean that "if only one of the actions is *in rem* or *quasi in rem*, both cases may proceed side by side." *$79,123.49 in U.S. Cash*, 830 F.2d at 97 (citing *Klein*, 303 U.S. 276).

The same principle governs this case. The Panamanian proceeding is one in rem, but the present case, an action in personam, merely adjudicates *rights* in the res. Our declaration of rights in the res does not impair the Panamanian court's possession of the res or its authority over it. The prior exclusive jurisdiction doctrine does not apply, and thus does not create an exceptional circumstance that would permit abstention. **[—42—]**

This case is admittedly unusual. Plaintiff comes to court seeking a declaration in personam. But the suit, if filed as a non-declaratory action by defendant, would likely be brought in rem, and, had it been brought in rem, the prior exclusive jurisdiction doctrine might well counsel in favor of abstention. We have, moreover, not required an absolute jurisdictional bar for a case's circumstances to be sufficiently "exceptional" that they merit abstention. One could thus argue that the close kinship of this case to a proceeding in rem gives reason enough for us to abstain as though it *were* a second proceeding adjudicating the same res. But the doctrine of prior exclusive jurisdiction—and the exceptional circumstances it might present justifying abstention—derive from the practicalities of in rem proceedings, not from the character of rights those proceedings adjudicate. Despite its similarity to an in rem proceeding, this case does not require us to keep custody over any property, either in actuality or constructively. We thus pose no challenge to the foreign court's possession of the res. For comity purposes, this suit is no different from an ordinary proceeding in personam running parallel to an in rem adjudication. And that situation, without more, is not "exceptional." **[—43—]**

Accordingly, the district court did not abuse its discretion in declining to abstain in deference to the Panamanian proceedings.

III. Laches

Easy Street next contends that the district court incorrectly determined that laches barred execution of its maritime lien. "Laches . . . . is an equitable defense that bars a plaintiff's equitable claim where he is guilty of unreasonable and inexcusable delay that has resulted in prejudice to the defendant." *Ikelionwu v. United States*, 150 F.3d 233, 237 (2d Cir. 1998) (internal quotation marks omitted).

A. Standard of Review

"The existence of laches is a factual question that requires the court to **{-194-}** weigh the equities of each case." 8-VII Benedict on Admiralty § 7.01 (7th ed. 2017). Because of the case-specific nature of the doctrine, we review for abuse of discretion a district court's rulings regarding laches. *DeSilvio v. Prudential Lines, Inc.*, 701 F.2d 13, 15 (2d Cir. 1983) ("[The district court] granted summary judgment in appellee's favor, finding DeSilvio had been guilty of laches. . . . Determinations relating to a claim of laches ordinarily are left to the discretion of the trial court. These rulings may not be overturned unless the trial court has **[—44—]** abused its discretion." (internal citations omitted)); *see also Czaplicki v. The Hoegh Silvercloud*, 351 U.S. 525, 534 (1956) ("[T]he existence of laches is a question primarily addressed to the discretion of the trial court."). Abuse of discretion is a high standard and is met only when the district court "based its ruling on an erroneous view of the law or on a clearly erroneous assessment of the evidence, or rendered a decision that cannot be located within the range of permissible decisions." *In re Sims*, 534 F.3d 117, 132 (2d Cir. 2008) (quotations omitted).

Easy Street notes that our opinion in *Ivani Contracting Corp. v. City of N.Y.* appeared to say that summary judgment granted based on laches should be reviewed de novo. 103 F.3d 257, 259 (2d Cir. 1997) ("We review the district court's grant of summary judgment *de novo*. . . . Ivani argues that the district court erred in holding that laches could bar its claims. We agree."). But in *Ivani Contracting Corp.*, we held that "laches is not available to bar . . . claims for damages under [42 U.S.C.] § 1983," *id.* at 262, and thus decided the legal permissibility of applying laches to a class of legal claims rather than the appropriateness of a laches ruling on the facts of a particular case. Consequently, *Ivani Contracting Corp.* does not detract from the statement of law in *DeSilvio*. We **[—45—]** review laches rulings dependent on the facts and equities of a given case for abuse of discretion.[11]

B. Laches Defense to Easy Street's Lien

We next consider whether the district court correctly held that laches extinguished Easy Street's maritime lien.

"There is no fixed period of time that must elapse for a suit to be barred by the doctrine of laches." 8-VII Benedict on Admiralty § 7.01 (7th ed. 2017). The ultimate test for laches is whether there has been (1) inexcusable delay in exercising a lien and (2) prejudice to the party against whom the lien would be enforced. *Czaplicki*, 351 U.S. at 533 ("Where there has been no inexcusable delay in seeking a remedy and where no prejudice to the defendant has ensued from **[—46—]** the mere passage of time, there should be no bar to relief."); *DeSilvio*, 701 F.2d at 15. "[T]hese two factors are not to be viewed independently." *Larios v. Victory Carriers, Inc.*, 316 F.2d 63, 67 (2d Cir. 1963). Even where there has **{-195-}** been delay, "[a] weak

---

[11] Easy Street also relies on *Hermes Int'l v. Lederer de Paris Fifth Ave., Inc.*, where we stated that a de novo standard of review applied to summary judgment based on laches. 219 F.3d 104, 107 (2d Cir. 2000). But there, too, we held that a laches argument foundered at "a dispositive, threshold inquiry" of whether the party seeking application of laches "[came] into equity . . . with clean hands." *Id.* We explained that the "clean hands" question was one that "bars further consideration of the laches defense" rather than serving as "a mere factor to be weighed in balancing the equities." *Id.* Thus, much like in *Ivani Contracting*, de novo review was appropriate because our ruling did not concern the district court's analysis of the equities in the case, but instead made a ruling on the basis of a dispositive legal question at the threshold.

excuse may suffice if there has been no prejudice; an exceedingly good one might still do even when there has been some." *Id.* As the Fifth Circuit observed in *Point Landing, Inc. v. Alabama Dry Dock & Shipbuilding Co.*, "[l]aches is much more than time. It is time plus prejudicial harm, and the harm is not merely that one loses what he otherwise would have kept, but that delay has subjected him to a disadvantage in asserting and establishing his claimed right or defense." 261 F.2d 861, 865 (5th Cir. 1958).

"[I]n deciding whether maritime claims are barred by laches, courts of admiralty will use local limitation statutes as a rule-of-thumb." *Larios*, 316 F.2d at 66 (quoting *Oroz v. Am. President Lines, Ltd.*, 259 F.2d 636, 639 (2d Cir. 1958)). "When the suit has been brought after the expiration of the state limitation period, a court applying maritime law asks why the case *should* be allowed to proceed; when the suit, although perhaps long delayed, has nevertheless been brought within the state limitation period, the court asks why it *should not* be." *Id.* **[—47—]** (emphasis added); *see also Federal Treasury Enterprise Sojuzplodoimport v. Spirits Int'l B.V.*, 809 F.3d 737, 745-46 ("If the most closely analogous state statute of limitations has not run, the presumption of laches does not attach and the defendant bears the burden of proving the defense.").

The district court held—and the parties do not dispute—that the relevant local statute of limitations is Section 83 of the New York Lien Law. That statute states as follows:

> Every lien for a debt shall cease if the vessel navigates the western or northwestern lakes, or either of them, or the Saint Lawrence river, at the expiration of six months after the first of January next succeeding the time when the debt was contracted, and *in case of any other vessel, at the expiration of twelve months after the debt was contracted*. If, upon the expiration of the time herein limited in either of such cases, such vessel shall be absent from the port at which the debt was contracted, the lien shall continue until the expiration of *thirty days after the return of such vessel to such port*. If proceedings are instituted for the enforcement of the lien within the time herein limited, such lien shall continue until the termination of such proceedings.

N.Y. Lien Law § 83 (emphasis added).

The district court noted that Allied purchased fuel from Easy Street in Mejillones, Chile and never returned there. Under the New York statute, when the "vessel [is] absent from the port at which the debt was contracted" one year **[—48—]** after the debt was contracted, "the lien shall continue until the expiration of thirty days after the return of such vessel to such port." N.Y. Lien Law § 83. Because the Vessel never returned to Mejillones, it was absent from that port one year after the debt was contracted. Consequently, the court treated the statute of limitations as never having expired. Easy Street agreed with this conclusion.[12] The district **{-196-}** court nonetheless concluded that the delay and prejudice to Leopard Marine in the enforcement of the lien were so great that laches should be applied. Easy Street protests that decision.

Laches decisions are largely limited to the facts of each case. But a few principles emerge from past decisions. A key consideration in deciding whether delay is excusable is whether the lienor failed to "exercise[]

[12] Leopard Marine suggests that the New York statute should be understood as providing a limitations period of twelve months, and a *tolling* period that extends until thirty days after the vessel returns to the port where the transaction occurred. Leopard Marine then suggests that we should not apply state-law tolling rules, but should instead look to tolling rules from federal maritime statutes to supplement state statutes of limitations.

Although this Court has suggested that both the 12-month period and the additional period (that operates until the vessel returns to port) are considered part of the New York limitations period in laches decisions based on Section 83 of the New York lien law, *see The Owyhee*, 66 F.2d 399, 400 (2d Cir. 1933), we need not address the point: Leopard Marine prevails even on Easy Street's more generous view of the New York limitations period.

reasonable diligence **[—49—]** in arresting" the vessel. *Barwil ASCA v. M/V SAVA*, 44 F. Supp. 2d 484, 488 (E.D.N.Y. 1999). At a minimum, that generally requires that a lienor had an opportunity to enforce the lien. *See The Everosa*, 93 F.2d 732, 735 (1st Cir. 1937) (noting that a significant factor in deciding whether laches bars exercise of a lien against a vessel's bona fide purchaser is whether the lienor had "a reasonable opportunity to enforce" the lien) (quoting *Magee v. The Lyndhurst*, 48 F. 839, 840 (S.D.N.Y. 1892)).[13] For example, in *The Gertrude*, the Fifth Circuit denied a laches defense where the owner hid a boat "for the purpose of preventing its seizure in libel proceedings." 38 F.2d 946, 947 (5th Cir. 1930). Although some courts have said, as an extension of this principle, that "lienors are not required to attempt to enforce their liens in foreign waters," *Bermuda Exp., N.V. v. M/V Litsa (Ex. Laurie U)*, 872 F.2d 554, 559 (3d Cir. 1989), we have not said so as a strict matter, and have never said as much in contemporary times. *But see The Slingsby*, 120 F. 748, **[—50—]** 753 (2d Cir. 1903) (finding laches inapplicable because the vessel spent little time "within the jurisdiction . . . between the injury and the libel").

A laches defense may be justifiable where delay diminishes a party's ability to absorb a loss. *See* Uisdean R. Vass & Xia Chen, *The Admiralty Doctrine of Laches*, 53 La. L. Rev. 495, 518 (1992) (noting that, among "[t]he most typical cases of prejudice are where the defendant has . . . lost the right to contribution or indemnity [or] lost the right to pass on costs to its customers"). This may happen, for example, because lawsuits against third parties no longer lie. *See Murphy v. Int'l Freighting Corp.*, 182 F. Supp. 636, 640 (D. Mass. 1960) (noting that "plaintiff's delay in bringing his action has seriously prejudiced defendant," in part because "[d]efendant has been unable to determine with certainty the stevedore who loaded the vessel at its previous port of call, who might be liable to defendant"), *aff'd sub nom. Murphy v. A/S Sobral*, 283 F.2d 392 (1st Cir. 1960); *United Fruit Co. v. The M. D. Whiteman*, 125 F. Supp. 898, 900 (E.D. La. 1954) (noting that delay was prejudicial because, by the time the claim was pressed, insurance coverage was time-barred). Reflecting that principle, this court has said that "a person asserting a maritime lien on a chartered vessel is obliged to move promptly, so that the **[—51—]** owner may effectively pursue his rights of indemnification against the charterer." **{-197-}** *United States v. S.S. Lucie Schulte*, 343 F.2d 897, 901 n.3 (2d Cir. 1965).

The district court considered also the principle that if a lienholder, "instead of proceeding with reasonable diligence to arrest the vessel, preferred to collect in personam, such delay, occasioned by such choice, cannot be overlooked if . . . libelant now seeks to proceed in rem." *The Mendotta II*, 13 F. Supp. 1019, 1020 (E.D.N.Y. 1935); *see also The Owyhee*, 66 F.2d 399, 401 (2d Cir. 1933) (ruling that the creditor's "attempt to collect" from the vessel's owner "was obviously an alternative and was independent of [the lienholder's] rights as a lienor," and thus was "no justification for the delay" in exercising the lien). We think that principle is sound in many cases, though it must be applied carefully. The choice of whether to pursue a remedy in rem, or instead to proceed informally or by in personam legal action against the debtor, typically lies in the lienholder's hands. It is thus inequitable for others to bear the costs of that choice. On the other hand, in many cases, pursuit of a remedy in rem is far more costly than pursuit of monetary payment, and also far more disruptive to commerce. *See The Clinton*, 160 F. 421, 422 (5th Cir. 1908) ("A maritime lien is a powerful instrument. It **[—52—]** enables a creditor . . . to attach and seize a vessel, even though . . . she is loaded with freight and filled with passengers and about to proceed upon a

---

[13] We note that, "where the lien is to be enforced to the detriment of a [bona fide] purchaser for value, without notice of the lien, the defence [of laches] will be held valid under shorter time, and a more rigid scrutiny of the circumstances of the delay, than when the claimant is the owner at the time the lien accrued." *The Key City*, 81 U.S. 653, 660 (1871). Nevertheless, cases setting out the rules that apply when the vessel's owner is a bona fide purchaser, *see The Everosa*, 93 F.2d at 735, are still instructive for cases such as the one at present, where the owner has remained the same from the time the lien arose.

voyage. It gives him power to inflict almost irreparable injury upon the debtor . . . ."). A rule requiring lienholders to pursue in rem remedies whenever possible would likely cause great waste. For that reason, we have said that "[w]here an *owner* and a lienholder have come to an . . . arrangement for payment of an undisputed lien claim . . . failure to litigate the lien should be excused so long as the arrangement is being carried out," and that "[t]o hold the opposite would be an unwise policy, injurious alike to vessel owner and lienholder." *In re Marine Transit Corp.*, 94 F.2d 7, 10 (2d Cir. 1938) (emphasis added). We certainly decline to adopt any rule that requires the lienor to bear the costs of *any* failure to pursue a remedy in rem, even where such pursuit would have been unreasonable.

Applying those principles to the facts of this case, we determine that the district court did not abuse its discretion. Allied's fuel bill was initially due September 26, 2011, a bit more than one month after the fuel was contracted for. Easy Street does not dispute the district court's determination that Easy Street failed to inform Leopard Marine until at least the latter half of 2013 that Allied **[—53—]** had never paid the bill. Consequently, when Allied delivered the Vessel to Leopard Marine in November of 2011, Leopard Marine was unaware of Allied's failure to pay its outstanding fuel bill. Thus, Leopard Marine credited Allied with $409,853.10 for the value of fuel on board the Vessel.

Easy Street's failure even to inform Leopard Marine of Allied's non-payment of the fuel bill within the first few months prejudiced Leopard Marine, as reflected in several of the laches principles articulated above. First, had Leopard Marine known in late 2011 that Allied had failed to pay Easy Street, Leopard Marine could have declined to give Allied a credit for the value of the fuel left in the Vessel when it returned. Second, Leopard Marine also could have exercised its lien over Allied's cargo, pursuant to the chartering agreement, at the time of the Vessel's redelivery. In other words, Easy Street's lack of notice eliminated two of Leopard Marine's possible remedies against Allied, and thus diminished Leopard Marine's ability to absorb any loss. Although Easy Street's failure to inform Leopard Marine of the nonpayment does not relate strictly to delay in **{-198-}** exercising the lien, it weighs heavily on the equities of the case. **[—54—]**

After that point, Easy Street's conduct with respect to Allied bespoke an odd mixture of extreme alarm and lack of pursuit of any meaningful remedy. As noted above, Demitrios Chasampalis, Easy Street's only full-time employee in 2011, went to roughly one hundred in-person meetings at Allied's offices, beginning around the invoice's issuance in 2011 and ending sometime in 2012. He demanded full payment of the invoice instead of any settlement of the debt, but never received any payment at all. Easy Street also received two written assurances of payment, neither of which was honored. Yet Easy Street did not think to sue Allied, instead trusting the close relationship between the companies and, evidently, between the persons running them. Only after Allied entered involuntary bankruptcy proceedings did Easy Street begin tracking the Vessel, and it was not until long after Allied's bankruptcy that Easy Street requested payment from Leopard Marine. Moreover, as the district court noted, and as Easy Street does not successfully dispute, there were several opportunities before Allied's bankruptcy to seize the Vessel in a port that would have honored the lien. **[—55—]**

The facts of this case implicate the principle the district court applied: where a lienor chooses to take time to proceed in personam or informally, trusting that the indebted party—here, the charterer—is good for its commitments, the vessel's owner should not bear the costs of that choice. *See The Mendotta II*, 13 F. Supp. at 1020. In this case, the lienor gave a close, long-term business partner more trust and leeway than circumstances merited. If the lien were now to be exercised, that trust and leeway—and the delay they occasioned—would prejudice Leopard Marine.

Moreover, Easy Street failed to respect our guidance in *S.S. Lucie Schulte*, that "a person asserting a maritime lien on a chartered vessel is obliged to move promptly, so that the owner may effectively pursue his rights of indemnification against the charterer." 343 F.2d at 901 n.3. Had Easy Street instead exercised the lien before Allied's bankruptcy in November 2012, Leopard Marine would have had some chance to recover from Allied through an arbitration, or exercise of the cargo liens, before Allied's bankruptcy. That is no longer a possibility. Easy Street's actions are even more striking because of its failure to notify Leopard Marine of Allied's debt in any way until at least October 2013. By that time— **[—56—]** more than a year after Easy Street began tracking the Vessel—any possible recovery against Allied was long gone. Had Easy Street merely notified Leopard Marine of the debt when it began tracking the Vessel, Leopard Marine may have had a greater chance of recovery from Allied.

Easy Street emphasizes that the Greek court administering Allied's bankruptcy proceedings stated that "all payments to any creditors of Allied . . . ceased retrospectively as of January 1, 2012," Appellant's Br. at 7, and suggests that, because of this "retrospective" ruling, Leopard Marine could not have recovered anything from Allied after that date, Appellant's Br. at 37. But Easy Street provides no explanation of what a "retrospective" stoppage of payments means, or how it affected the likelihood of recovery. Although Easy Street cites a legal opinion from a Greek lawyer, the opinion simply restates what Easy Street's brief claims: that the bankruptcy court "considered [Allied] (retrospectively) to have stopped payments to its creditors since [January 1, 2012]." App'x at 325. The legal opinion then concludes only that, "[a]ssuming that Leopard Marine . . . was not made aware of East Street['s] . . . **{-199-}** outstanding claim against Allied for the [fuel] Easy Street supplied . . . until *March 30, 2015* . . . any attempt by Leopard to **[—57—]** make a claim in the Allied bankruptcy proceeding [after *that* time] would have been futile." App'x at 326 (emphasis added). The document contains no statements regarding whether Leopard Marine could have pressed claims against Allied before November of 2012, and, if so, what the value of those claims might have been.

Leopard Marine responds to Easy Street's argument with expert testimony that, before the November 6, 2012 bankruptcy order issued, there was no prohibition on suit against Allied, at least in certain forums, and that Leopard Marine might also have exercised liens against Allied's cargo during the period. App'x at 557-558. Easy Street does not dispute these assertions in any direct way. In the district court, Easy Street agreed that Leopard Marine could have brought claims against Allied at any time before November 6, 2012, but did so "subject to the reservation that Allied['s] . . . bankruptcy declaration was deemed retroactive to January 1, 2012." *See* App'x at 569 ¶ 38; App'x at 351 ¶ 38. The record establishes that Easy Street's delay deprived Leopard Marine of remedies it could have availed itself of, including causes of action against Allied in certain forums and the right to exercise liens on Allied's cargo, until the Greek **[—58—]** bankruptcy court issued its order on November 6, 2012, which purportedly extinguished, nunc pro tunc, the payments Allied still needed to make to its creditors from January 1, 2012. Easy Street has not called into question the viability or value of these causes of action. The elimination of viable causes of action that would permit a party to absorb a loss weighs heavily in determining that prejudice exists. *See S.S. Lucie Shulte*, 343 F.2d at 901 n.3. It was thus not an abuse of discretion for the district court to conclude that Easy Street's failure to take any action with respect to Leopard Marine during this period prejudiced Leopard Marine by depriving it of these remedies.

We do not think the district court committed clear error in discerning that Leopard Marine suffered additional prejudice because it lost the opportunity to assert causes of action against Allied. The record clearly demonstrates that Easy Street's delay deprived Leopard Marine of causes of action that it otherwise could have used until November of 2012. Easy Street has not included any factual material raising a genuine question as to the viability or value of those causes of action. And, as noted earlier, foreclosure of causes of action that would permit a party to absorb a loss has widely been weighed in determining whether **[—59—]** prejudice exists. *See S. S. Lucie Schulte,* 343 F.2d at 901 n.3. We do not depart from that sensible principle here.

Because of the significant prejudice caused by Easy Street's delay in exercising the lien, the district court did not abuse its discretion in ruling that laches extinguished the lien.

CONCLUSION

We have reviewed Easy Street's other arguments and have determined that they are meritless. The district court's judgment is AFFIRMED.

(Reporter's Note: Dissenting Opinion follows on p. 76).

[—1—] {-199-} LIVINGSTON, Circuit Judge, dissenting:

"[P]arties may not confer subject matter jurisdiction on [an Article III] court by consent." *Cable Television Ass'n of N.Y., Inc. v. Finneran*, 954 F.2d 91, 94 (2d Cir. 1992); *accord Steel Co. v. Citizens for a Better Env't*, 523 U.S. 83, 95 (1998); {-200-} *Ins. Corp. of Ireland v. Compagnie des Bauxites de Guinee*, 456 U.S. 694, 702 (1982) ("[N]o action of the parties can confer subject-matter jurisdiction upon a federal court. Thus, the consent of the parties is irrelevant . . . ."); *Doe v. United States*, 833 F.3d 192, 196 (2d Cir. 2016); *New York v. Shinnecock Indian Nation*, 686 F.3d 133, 138 (2d Cir. 2012); *Bay Shore Union Free Sch. Dist. v. Kain*, 485 F.3d 730, 733 (2d Cir. 2007). By holding that the Maltese owner of a vessel arrested in Panama can satisfy a United States maritime court's *in rem* subject matter jurisdiction requirement simply by consenting to adjudication, the majority departs from this fundamental and "well established" rule. *See Woods v. Rondout Valley Cent. Sch. Dist. Bd. of Educ.*, 466 F.3d 232, 238 (2d Cir. 2006).

In so doing, the majority forgets that we are "courts of limited jurisdiction whose power is limited strictly," especially in the maritime context. *See Garanti Finansal Kiralama A.S. v. Aqua Marine & Trading Inc.*, 697 F.3d 59, 64–65 (2d Cir. 2012) (quoting *Ahmed v. Holder*, 624 F.3d 150, 154 (2d Cir. 2010)). Unlike in other [—2—] settings, where *in rem* jurisdiction typically is a matter of personal, and not subject matter jurisdiction, in this appeal, our subject matter jurisdiction depends on our jurisdiction over the *res* (*i.e.*, the Densa Leopard ship). Because we lack jurisdiction over the *res*, and thus are without subject matter jurisdiction, I respectfully dissent.

A

I agree with the majority's declaratory judgment analysis, *see* Maj. Op. at 10–14, and so do not belabor this point. Briefly, "the Declaratory Judgment Act does not by itself confer subject matter jurisdiction on the federal courts." *Correspondent Servs. Corp. v. First Equities Corp.*, 442 F.3d 767, 769 (2d Cir. 2006) (per curiam). Instead, a declaratory judgment action is available only in cases where there is an independent jurisdictional basis over the underlying dispute. *See Skelly Oil Co. v. Phillips Petroleum Co.*, 339 U.S. 667, 671 (1950) (explaining that the Declaratory Judgment Act "enlarged the range of remedies available in the federal courts but did not extend their jurisdiction"). "[A] complaint seeking a declaratory judgment is to be tested . . . as if the party whose adverse action the declaratory judgment plaintiff apprehends had initiated a lawsuit against the declaratory judgment plaintiff." *Fleet Bank v. Burke*, 160 F.3d 883, 886 (2d Cir. 1998). In other words, we must "examine the structure of the suit that would ultimately take place if it were [—3—] not forestalled by the declaratory judgment action"; "[i]f that suit could not be brought in federal court, we do not have jurisdiction in the analogous declaratory judgment action[,] [but] [i]f the suit could be brought in federal court, we [do] have jurisdiction . . . ." *Garanti*, 697 F.3d at 70 (internal citations omitted). The dispositive question, then, is whether the declaratory judgment defendant, here Easy Street Ltd. ("Easy Street"), a Cypriot bunker supply company, could have brought a coercive suit to enforce its maritime lien under the district court's admiralty jurisdiction, *see* Maj. Op. at 13–14. It could not.

B

A maritime lien is a "lien on a vessel, given to secure the claim of a creditor who provided maritime services to the vessel or who suffered an injury from the vessel's use." *Maritime Lien, Black's Law Dictionary* 1065 (10th ed. 2014). Unlike a standard lien, which is a device to secure a creditor's interests against a debtor, the distinct legal fiction created by the maritime lien is that the vessel itself is the obligor. *See* {-201-} *Piedmont & George's Creek Coal Co. v. Seaboard Fisheries Co.*, 254 U.S. 1, 10 (1920) ("A vessel may be made liable in rem for supplies, although the owner can be made liable therefor in personam, since the dealer may rely upon the credit [—4—] of both."); *see also id.* at 8–9 (discussing the historical development of the maritime lien).

As a result, as the majority acknowledges, *see* Maj. Op. at 13, the maritime lien itself (as distinct from any related contractual obligation) may be enforced only in a federal *in rem* proceeding against the vessel. *See, e.g., Am. Dredging Co. v. Miller*, 510 U.S. 443, 446–47 (1994) ("An *in rem* suit against a vessel is, we have said, distinctively an admiralty proceeding, and is hence within the exclusive province of the federal courts." (citing *The Moses Taylor*, 71 U.S. 411, 431 (1866))); *Madruga v. Super. Ct.*, 346 U.S. 556, 560 (1954) ("Admiralty's jurisdiction is exclusive . . . as to those maritime causes of action begun and carried on as proceedings in rem, that is, where a vessel or thing is itself treated as the offender and made the defendant by name or description in order to enforce a lien." (citations and internal quotation marks omitted)); *Norton v. Switzer*, 93 U.S. 355, 356 (1876) ("[T]he jurisdiction of the admiralty courts to enforce a maritime lien is exclusive, and cannot be exercised in any other mode than by a proceeding *in rem*."); *In re Millenium Seacarriers, Inc.*, 419 F.3d 83, 93 (2d Cir. 2005) (Sotomayor, *J.*) ("Traditional admiralty principles suggest that only a federal admiralty court acting *in rem* has the jurisdiction to quiet title to a vessel conclusively by **[—5—]** extinguishing its maritime liens.").[1] As the Supreme Court has elsewhere expressed it, "[t]he lien and the proceeding in rem are . . . correlative—where one exists, the other may be taken, and not otherwise." *The Rock Island Bridge*, 73 U.S. 213, 215 (1867); *accord DS-Rendite Fonds Nr. 108 VLCC Ashna GMBH & Co Tankschiff KG v. Essar Capital Americas Inc.*, 882 F.3d 44, 48, 6 Adm. R. 28, 29 (2d Cir. 2018). This view is reinforced by the text of the statute that would underlie Easy Street's hypothetical suit, which, by its terms, permits only *in rem* enforcement of a maritime lien for necessaries. 46 U.S.C. § 31342(a)(2); *see also Piedmont,* 254 U.S. at 12 ("The maritime lien is . . . . stricti juris and will not be extended by construction, analogy or inference.").

Here, we have admiralty jurisdiction to hear Leopard Marine's declaratory judgment action only if Easy Street could have brought an affirmative suit in the district court to enforce its maritime lien. The inquiry is straightforward: because **[—6—]** a maritime lien is enforced *in rem*, absent federal court jurisdiction over the *res*, Easy Street could not have proceeded against the Densa Leopard *in rem*. *See, e.g.,* **{-202-}** *United States v. One Assortment of 89 Firearms*, 465 U.S. 354, 363 (1984) (noting that *in rem* jurisdiction traditionally has been "dependent upon seizure of a physical object"). In other words, in this admiralty appeal, where our jurisdiction stems from 28 U.S.C. § 1333, our subject matter jurisdiction depends on our jurisdiction over the Densa Leopard (which was arrested in Panama and is not here). And because we lack jurisdiction over the Densa Leopard, we lack jurisdiction to adjudicate the parallel declaratory judgment action. *See Medtronic, Inc. v. Mirowski Family Ventures, LLC*, 134 S. Ct. 843, 848 (2014) ("The relevant question [in examining jurisdiction underlying declaratory judgment actions] concerns the nature of the threatened action in the absence of the declaratory judgment suit.").

The majority seeks to avoid this simple conclusion by reconceptualizing admiralty *in rem* jurisdiction as "a mere matter of service of process, and a practical means of getting at the owner's property." Maj. Op. at 26. But that view conflates the *in rem* jurisdiction that is necessary here for *subject matter* jurisdiction with the *in rem* jurisdiction that is often necessary for *personal* jurisdiction. Admittedly, the distinction between these two concepts can be thin—as evidenced by the

---

[1] Numerous well-established authorities confirm this rule. *See, e.g.*, 8-VII Joshua S. Force & Steven F. Friedell, *Benedict on Admiralty* § 7.01[A] (2017) ("Maritime liens do not exist apart from their ability to be enforced *in rem* in admiralty."); 1 Thomas J. Schoenbaum, *Admiralty & Maritime Law* § 9-1 (5th ed. 2011 & Supp. 2017) (noting that a maritime lien "adheres to the maritime property even through changes of ownership until it is either executed through the *in rem* legal process available in admiralty or is somehow extinguished by operation of law"); *see also* Griffith Price, *The Law of Maritime Liens* 1 (1940) (noting that a maritime lien is "enforced by means of an action in rem"); Grant Gilmore & Charles L. Black, Jr., *The Law of Admiralty* § 9–2 at 588 (2d ed. 1975) (explaining that maritime liens "can be 'executed' (which is the admiralty terminology for 'foreclosed') only by an admiralty court acting *in rem*[]"); *id.* at 622.

cases [—7—] cited by the majority that discuss *in rem* jurisdiction solely in the context of *personal* jurisdiction. *See, e.g.*, *Shaffer v. Heitner*, 433 U.S. 186, 207 (1977) (addressing the due process constraints on *personal* jurisdiction rather than the distinct issue of subject matter jurisdiction in admiralty); *United States v. Republic Marine, Inc.*, 829 F.2d 1399, 1402 (7th Cir. 1987) ("*[A]s with other forms of jurisdiction over the party*, a vessel may waive jurisdiction in rem by appearing in the action and failing to raise the defense of lack of jurisdiction over the party in a timely fashion." (emphasis added) (internal citation omitted)). But the distinction is a critical one. After all, a party can satisfy a federal court's personal jurisdiction requirement by consent; it cannot, however, satisfy a federal court's subject matter jurisdiction requirement by doing the same. *See, e.g.*, *Ins. Corp. of Ireland*, 456 U.S. at 702–03.

Our case law makes clear that in an *in rem* admiralty action where our jurisdiction comes from 28 U.S.C. § 1333, jurisdiction over the *res* is fundamental to our *subject matter* jurisdiction. As then-Judge Sotomayor explained, "[l]ienors seeking to bring an admiralty action *in rem* face stringent access requirements before securing the aid of the federal court to enforce their liens." *Millennium Seacarriers*, 419 F.3d at 94. Specifically, she emphasized, "subject matter jurisdiction lies in the district court *where the vessel or other* res *is located*[.]" *Id.* [—8—] (emphasis added); *see also Mackensworth v. S.S. Am. Merch.*, 28 F.3d 246, 252 (2d Cir. 1994) ("Subject matter jurisdiction in an *in rem* action in admiralty lies in the district court where the vessel or other res is located."). And, on top of the stringent subject matter jurisdictional requirement that the *res* must be located in the district, then-Judge Sotomayor added, "jurisdiction does not attach until the vessel is arrested within the jurisdiction." *Millennium Seacarriers*, 419 F.3d at 94; *see also Burns Bros. v. Long Island R. Co.*, 176 F.2d 950 (2d Cir. 1949) (per curiam) (holding, under the predecessor to the current admiralty rules, that because "there has been no arrest of the vessel . . ., jurisdiction to enter a decree in rem is lacking"). Thus, much as a declaratory judgment action turning on federal question jurisdiction is limited by the jurisdictional prerequisites of the well-pleaded complaint rule, *see Skelly Oil*, 339 U.S. at 671–72, the availability of a declaratory judgment action turning on admiralty jurisdiction is bound by the constraints **{–203–}** on our jurisdiction under 28 U.S.C. § 1333, including the requirement that a plaintiff proceed on a maritime lien *in rem*. And even when both parties in a suit "are satisfied to present their dispute[] to [a] federal court[], the parties cannot confer subject matter jurisdiction where the Constitution and Congress [—9—] have not." *Doe*, 833 F.3d at 196 (quoting *Wynn v. AC Rochester*, 273 F.3d 153, 157 (2d Cir. 2001)).

By holding to the contrary, the majority broadly expands our admiralty jurisdiction. According to the majority, there is no requirement for a ship ever to have been remotely near the United States before it can be subject to a federal court's *in rem* subject matter jurisdiction. As a result, whenever a foreign owner of a foreign ship in a foreign country believes that a maritime lien proceeding brought by a foreign party in a foreign court is going poorly, the shipowner can simply come to our shores and acquire a declaratory judgment. *Cf.* Richard H. Fallon, Jr. et al., *Hart and Wechsler's The Federal Courts and the Federal System* 872–73 (7th ed. 2015) (noting that the purpose of federal admiralty jurisdiction is to *further* international cooperation). Similarly, given federal courts' general obligation to hear cases within their jurisdiction, when two foreign parties locked in a dispute over a maritime lien asserted against a foreign ship agree that it should be heard in New York—regardless of the ship's location—a federal court here now must presumably arbitrate that dispute and expend judicial resources to do so. *See, e.g.*, *Susan B. Anthony List v. Driehaus*, 134 S. Ct. 2334, 2347 (2014) ("'[A] federal court's obligation to hear and decide' cases within its jurisdiction 'is virtually [—10—] unflagging.'" (quoting *Lexmark Int'l, Inc. v. Static Control Components, Inc.*, 134 S.Ct. 1377, 1386 (2014))). The holding here thus comes very close to transforming our Circuit into an

"International Court of Maritime Liens" with universal jurisdiction. Needless to say, absent further guidance from Congress, we should hesitate before reading our grant of subject matter jurisdiction so broadly. *See Garanti*, 697 F.3d at 64–65 (noting that "[t]here is always a 'presumption against jurisdiction,'" and that our "venerable case law" consequently strictly limits our maritime jurisdiction (quoting *Miller v. United States*, 78 U.S. 268, 299 (1870))).[2] The Supreme Court has cautioned against reading jurisdictional statutes in a way that would cause us to become "the *custos morum* of the whole world." **{-204-}** *Kiobel v. Royal* **[—11—]** *Dutch Petroleum Co.*, 569 U.S. 108, 123 (2013) (quoting *United States v. The La Jeune Eugenie*, 26 F. Cas. 832, 847 (No. 15,551) (C.C. Mass. 1822) (Story, *J.*)). The majority, however, would have us become something quite similar: a "*custos navium*."

[2] The majority cites 46 U.S.C. § 31343(c)(2) in an attempt to show that it would be "neither legally dubious nor likely to be disruptive to maritime commerce" to allow Leopard Marine to seek a declaratory judgment in this case. Maj. Op. at 29. But § 31343(c)(2) is of no help to the majority. As an initial matter, that statute only provides jurisdiction to adjudicate lien claims on vessels that, unlike the Densa Leopard, are owned by *American* entities. *See* 46 U.S.C. §§ 12103, 31343(a), 31343(b), 31343(c)(2). But even more importantly, § 31343(c)(2) merely grants federal courts jurisdiction to hear *in personam* suits to *extinguish* alleged maritime liens, while we have subject matter jurisdiction in this declaratory judgment action only if Easy Street could have brought an *in rem* suit to *enforce* its alleged maritime lien. *See, e.g.*, *Millenium Seacarriers*, 419 F.3d at 102 (recognizing that "proceedings other than *in rem* admiralty actions [can] extinguish[] individual lienors' rights to their maritime liens"); *Rainbow Line, Inc. v. M/V Tequila*, 480 F.2d 1024, 1028 (2d Cir. 1973) ("*[I]n rem* jurisdiction in the admiralty exists only to *enforce* a maritime lien . . . ." (emphasis added)). That § 31343 "does not alter in any respect the law pertaining to the *establishment* of a maritime lien," 46 U.S.C. § 31343(f) (emphasis added), reveals that the statute is of no moment to the instant dispute—that is, whether Easy Street could have brought such an *in rem* action.

C

The closest jurisdictional argument—and the crux of the majority's analysis—turns on our decision in *Hapag-Lloyd Aktiengesellschaft v. U.S. Oil Trading LLC*, 814 F.3d 146, 4 Adm. R. 62 (2d Cir. 2016). I agree with the majority's candid observation that "[t]here is admittedly some question as to whether the rule of *Hapag-Lloyd* applies here." Maj. Op. at 17. There, a shipowner, Hapag-Lloyd, had entered into bunker supply contracts with O.W. Bunker & Trading A/S ("O.W. Denmark"). *Hapag-Lloyd*, 814 F.3d at 148, 4 Adm. R. at 62. When O.W. Denmark went bankrupt, U.S. Oil Trading LLC ("USOT"), the O.W. Denmark subcontractor who had actually provided the bunkers to the Hapag-Lloyd ships, instituted *in rem* proceedings around the country seeking to enforce its maritime liens against Hapag-Lloyd's vessels. *Id.* at 148–49, 4 Adm. R. at 62–63. In response, Hapag-Lloyd filed an interpleader action in district court, posted bond for the amount claimed, and moved for an anti-suit injunction against the various *in rem* actions. *Id.* at 149–50, 4 Adm. R. at 63. USOT appealed, arguing that, absent jurisdiction over the *res*, there was no basis for the district court to exercise jurisdiction over its *in* **[—12—]** *rem* claims, and that an anti-suit injunction stemming from the interpleader action was inappropriate.

In resolving the matter, we first recognized that only minimal diversity of the parties is necessary to an interpleader action, 28 U.S.C. § 1335(a)(1), and that, given the parties' respective domiciles, we clearly had *in personam* jurisdiction to adjudicate the merits of the contract claims running between O.W. Denmark and Hapag-Lloyd—contract claims that O.W. Denmark was pressing in connection with the bunkers provided by USOT. *Id.* at 150–51, 4 Adm. R. at 63–65. We explained further that since any *in rem* claim to collect on USOT's maritime liens was "inextricably interrelated" to any merits determination on O.W. Denmark's contract claims, jurisdiction under the interpleader action was appropriate even if the resolution of these contract claims would not necessarily (absent the interpleader action) have extinguished USOT's maritime liens. *Id.* at 152, 4 Adm. R. at 65. Finally, we rejected USOT's argument that, because the district court did not have *in rem* jurisdiction, it could not rule on the validity of USOT's maritime liens. *Id.* at 153, 4 Adm. R. at 66. Although we identified the general rule reflected in *Millennium Seacarriers* that "subject matter jurisdiction lies in the district court where the vessel or other *res* is located, [and] that jurisdiction does not attach until the vessel is arrested within the jurisdiction," **[—13—]** we held this rule inapplicable to a case, like Hapag-Lloyd's, in which the party instituting the action had (1) initiated a jurisdictionally appropriate interpleader; (2) posted adequate security for those claims; and (3) consented to the court's jurisdiction over its interests in the *res*. *See id.* at 153–54, 4 Adm. R. at 66–67.

Although we upheld jurisdiction in *Hapag-Lloyd*, that case did not modify our admiralty jurisdiction precedents, and instead depended on the flexibility of the interpleader mechanism. Critically, unlike here, in *Hapag-Lloyd* we *did* have *in personam* jurisdiction to review the merits of O.W. Denmark's contract claims against Hapag-Lloyd.[3] Since the basic predicate **{-205-}** for the interpleader action—minimal diversity of the parties—was already present, the panel in *Hapag-Lloyd* considered only whether the interpleader mechanism permitted the district court to exert jurisdiction over USOT's linked and "inextricably interrelated," *id.* at 152, 4 Adm. R. at 65 (internal quotation marks omitted), and "inextricably intertwined," *id.* at 153, 4 Adm. R. at 66, *in rem* claims.

Furthermore, the factors which were present in *Hapag-Lloyd* and supported our jurisdiction over the *res* there despite the general rule demanding *in rem* **[—14—]** jurisdiction are not present in this appeal. In particular, Leopard Marine does not appear to have (1) submitted to the jurisdiction of the federal courts other than for purposes of determining the viability of Easy Street's claims against the *Densa Leopard* (as Leopard Marine does not suggest that an action could be maintained against *it* as party to the original bunker fuel supply contract); or (2) posted bond to serve as a substitute *res* in place of the Densa Leopard.[4] *See id.* at 153–54 & n.20, 4 Adm. R. at 66 & n.20. Without such grounds for jurisdiction, and in light of "the long standing principle that the Declaratory Judgment Act . . . does not expand the jurisdiction of the federal courts," I would conclude that Leopard Marine cannot bring a viable declaratory judgment action. *Albradco, Inc. v. Bevona*, 982 F.2d 82, 85 (2d Cir. 1992) (citations and internal quotation marks omitted).

To be sure, the majority seizes on certain language in *Hapag-Lloyd* to support its different view. Relying in part on *Hapag-Lloyd*'s language that "[*i*]*n rem* jurisdiction is a customary elliptical way of referring to jurisdiction over the interests of persons in a thing," Maj. Op. at 17 (citation and internal quotation **[—15—]** marks omitted), the majority surmises that Leopard Marine can manufacture admiralty jurisdiction simply by consenting to a judicial determination as to whether Easy Street's efforts to attach Leopard Marine's interest in the Densa Leopard are barred by laches.

However, the cases cited in *Hapag-Lloyd* and by the majority are largely beside the point in assessing our subject matter jurisdiction and leave me unpersuaded. For instance, as noted above, *Shaffer* involved due process constraints on *personal* jurisdiction and not the issue here: subject matter jurisdiction in admiralty. 433 U.S. 186. And,

[3] Leopard Marine does not (and could not) argue that the bunker fuel supply contract (to which it was not a party) permits *in personam* jurisdiction over it in this case, nor does it ask for a judicial declaration of what Easy Street's *contractual* rights—as distinct from its *maritime lien*—might be.

[4] The absence of these two factors here easily distinguishes *Continental Grain Co. v. The FBL-585*, 364 U.S. 19 (1960), an inapposite venue case resorted to by the majority. Unlike here, where there is no possible *in personam* claim, in *Continental Grain* an *in rem* claim merely was joined with an already pending, jurisdictionally appropriate *in personam* claim against a barge owner. And, again unlike here, in *Continental Grain* there was a substitute *res*.

to take other examples, in both *Republic Marine, Inc.*, 829 F.2d 1399, and *Cactus Pipe & Supply Co. v. M/V Montmartre*, 756 F.2d 1103 (5th Cir. 1985), out-of-circuit cases relied on in *Hapag-Lloyd* (and by the majority), the vessel was present in the relevant district (unlike the Densa Leopard) and thus—wholly apart from and unrelated to the subject matter jurisdiction inquiry—the "*vessel* [could] waive jurisdiction *in rem* by appearing in the action and failing to raise the defense of lack of jurisdiction *over the party* in a timely fashion," *Republic Marine*, 829 F.2d at 1402 (emphases added).

Nothing in the supposedly "[v]oluminous authority" cited by the majority (none of **{-206-}** which comes from the Supreme Court or our Circuit), Maj. Op. at 22–23, **[—16—]** purports to supplant the bedrock and binding tenet that—even though consent can confer *personal* jurisdiction—consent cannot create *subject matter* jurisdiction. *See, e.g., Ins. Corp. of Ireland*, 456 U.S. at 702; *Shinnecock Indian Nation*, 686 F.3d at 138. Indeed, all of the circuits pointed to by the majority—the Third, Fourth, Fifth, Seventh, and Ninth—have unsurprisingly affirmed that, unlike in the personal jurisdiction context, the parties' consent *cannot* establish subject matter jurisdiction. *See, e.g., Coffin v. Malvern Fed. Sav. Bank*, 90 F.3d 851, 854 (3d Cir. 1996) ("[J]urisdiction cannot be conferred by consent."); *Brickwood Contractors, Inc. v. Datanet Eng'g, Inc.*, 369 F.3d 385, 390 (4th Cir. 2004) (en banc) ("Subject-matter jurisdiction cannot be conferred by the parties, nor can a defect in subject-matter jurisdiction be waived by the parties."); *Elam v. Kansas City S. Ry. Co.*, 635 F.3d 796, 802 (5th Cir. 2011) ("Litigants cannot bestow subject matter jurisdiction on federal courts by waiver or consent."); *DeBartolo v. Healthsouth Corp.*, 569 F.3d 736, 740 (7th Cir. 2009) (noting that "[s]ubject-matter jurisdiction is not an issue that can be brushed aside or satisfied by agreement between the litigants"); *City of Colton v. Am. Promotional Events, Inc.-W.*, 614 F.3d 998, 1006 n.6 (9th Cir. 2010) ("It is well established that subject matter jurisdiction cannot be expanded or contracted by prior action or consent of the parties." (citation and internal quotation marks **[—17—]** omitted)). The cases on which the majority relies are thus correctly read to involve personal jurisdiction rather than dramatically to expand our subject matter jurisdiction in admiralty.

In sum, *Hapag-Lloyd* provides no authority for the step the majority takes today. Here we ask if we would have admiralty jurisdiction under 28 U.S.C. § 1333 over Easy Street's affirmative suit to enforce its maritime lien, whereas in *Hapag-Lloyd*, we asked how far federal court jurisdiction extends under the interpleader statute, "which is remedial and to be liberally construed." *State Farm Fire & Cas. Co. v. Tashire*, 386 U.S. 523, 533 (1967). I am mindful that a smattering of language in the older case law provides some consolation to the majority, such as a statement from Chief Justice Taney that "the right to proceed against the property [is] regarded as a mere question of process and not of jurisdiction." *The St. Lawrence*, 66 U.S. 522, 529 (1861) (cited in the Maj. Op. at 21–22). But because, as described above, the weight of our case law militates in the other direction, I remain convinced that *Hapag-Lloyd* was decided in the specific (and liberal) procedural context of interpleader actions and instead would conclude that nothing in *Hapag-Lloyd*, or elsewhere, confers jurisdiction in this appeal.

* * * **[—18—]**

The majority concedes that: (1) "subject matter jurisdiction obviously cannot be waived," Maj. Op. at 27; (2) "in rem jurisdiction is necessary, in this case, for [our] subject matter jurisdiction in admiralty," *id.* at 25; and (3) the *res* (the ship) was arrested in Panama and is not here, nor is there a substitute *res* in its place. In nonetheless holding that we have *in rem* jurisdiction over a *res* (a foreign ship in a foreign country owned by a foreign party) that is not here, the majority gives short shrift to our precedent's explicit teaching that, for lienors bringing an admiralty action *in rem*, "subject matter jurisdiction lies in the district court where the vessel or other *res* is located," *Millennium Seacarriers*, 419 F.3d at 94 (Sotomayor, *J.*); *see also Mackensworth*, 28 F.3d at 252 ("Subject matter jurisdiction in an *in rem* action **{-207-}** in admiralty lies in the district court where the vessel or other res is located."). And in dispensing with any semblance of a requirement that our *in rem* jurisdiction demands a *res* within this country (much less our Circuit), the majority has propagated an astonishing jurisdictional theory: any owner of any ship subject to a maritime lien proceeding anywhere in the world can now—without limitation **[—19—]** and without any connection to the United States—seek a declaratory judgment in the Second Circuit. Because this cannot be right, I respectfully dissent.[5]

---

[5] Having determined that we lack jurisdiction, I proceed no further and express no view on the majority's discussion of international comity abstention and laches, *see* Maj. Op. at 30–57.

United States Court of Appeals
for the Second Circuit

No. 17-0922

U.S. OIL TRADING LLC
vs.
M/V VIENNA EXPRESS

Appeal from the United States District Court for the Southern District of New York

Decided: December 19, 2018

Citation: 911 F.3d 652, 6 Adm. R. 83 (2d Cir. 2018).

Before **KEARSE, CABRANES,** and **LOHIER,** Circuit Judges.

[—6—] {-654-} KEARSE, Circuit Judge: **{-655-}**

In these appeals, U.S. Oil Trading LLC ("USOT" or "U.S. Oil")—the plaintiff in No. 17-0922, and an interpleader defendant in No. 17-0931—challenges (a) orders entered in the United States District Court for the Southern District of New York, Valerie E. Caproni, *Judge*, denying USOT's motions for summary judgment on its claims of entitlement to maritime liens for physically supplying marine fuel ("bunkers") to certain vessels owned or chartered by interpleader plaintiff Hapag-Lloyd Aktiengesellschaft ("Hapag"), and (b) partial final judgments entered on May 2, 2017, dismissing USOT's maritime-lien claims. Pursuant to the Commercial Instruments **{-656-}** and Maritime Liens Act ("CIMLA"), 46 U.S.C. § 31301 *et seq.*, which permits a maritime lien to be asserted by "a person providing necessaries to a vessel on the order of the owner or a person authorized by the owner," *id.* § 31342(a)—*see also Hapag-Lloyd Aktiengesellschaft v. U.S. Oil Trading LLC*, 814 F.3d 146, 151 n.13, 4 Adm. R. 62, 65 n.13 (2d Cir. 2016) ("[f]or the purposes of § 31342, bunkers are 'necessaries'")—the district court denied USOT's motions for summary judgment and entered the partial judgments dismissing USOT's claims for liens, ruling that USOT had not provided the fuel to the vessels on the order of the owner or a person authorized by the owner to place such an order. On appeal, USOT contends that the district court erred in finding it was not **[—7—]** entitled to maritime liens in the absence of a direct contractual or agency relationship with the vessels or with an authorized entity specified in CIMLA, arguing principally that it was entitled to the liens because Hapag's purchase orders specified that the physical supplier of the fuel was to be USOT. For the reasons that follow, we conclude that purchase orders and admissions by Hapag in these actions permit a finding that Hapag directed that USOT be the subcontractor to supply the fuel, thereby bringing USOT within an established exception that allows maritime liens to be asserted by subcontractors whose selection was controlled or directed by the vessel's owner/charterer or authorized agent. We therefore vacate the judgment and remand for trial on the issue of whether Hapag directed that USOT be the physical supplier.

I. BACKGROUND

The present cases are among many that have their origin in the financial collapse of O.W. Bunker & Trading A/S ("O.W. Denmark") and its subsidiaries and affiliates (collectively the "O.W. Bunker Group"), a global network of traders and suppliers of bunkers. *See generally ING Bank N.V. v. M/V TEMARA*, 892 F.3d 511, 515, 6 Adm. R. 44, 44 **[—8—]** (2d Cir. 2018) ("*Temara*"); *see also Chemoil Adani Pvt. Ltd. v. M/V MARITIME KING*, No. 16-3944, 2018 WL 3359609 (2d Cir. July 10, 2018) ("*Chemoil*"); *Aegean Bunkering (USA) LLC v. M/T AMAZON*, 730 F. App'x 87 (2d Cir. 2018) ("*Aegean*"); *O'Rourke Marine Services L.P. v. M/V COSCO HAIFA*, 730 F. App'x 89 (2d Cir. 2018) ("*O'Rourke*"). Except as indicated below, the following facts, drawn from statements submitted by various parties pursuant to Rule 56.1 of the Local Rules for the Southern District of New York ("Rule 56.1 Statements"), are not in dispute.

A. *USOT's Delivery of Bunkers to Hapag Vessels*

In the fall of 2014, Hapag was the owner and operator of the M/V VIENNA EXPRESS and the M/V SOFIA EXPRESS, and was the time charterer of the M/V SEASPAN HAMBURG and the M/V SANTA ROBERTA (collectively the "Subject Vessels" or "Vessels"). The O.W. Bunker Group, an international operation that both supplied bunkers to ships and arranged the supply of bunkers by others, included O.W. Denmark, O.W. Bunker Germany GmbH ("O.W. Germany" or "OWG"), and O.W. Bunker USA Inc. ("O.W. USA"). USOT was in the business of physically supplying bunkers to oceangoing vessels. **[—9—]**

In September–October 2014, Hapag, upon receiving fuel replenishment requests from the masters of the respective Vessels, solicited fuel supply bids from a number of potential counterparties. In response, O.W. Germany and several others submitted bids. O.W. Germany, to do so, had requested quotes from its affiliate O.W. USA, which was in charge of the O.W. Bunker **{-657-}** Group's bunker procurement in the Americas. O.W. USA, to obtain the necessary information, had contacted physical suppliers, including USOT. For two of the Hapag Vessels, O.W. Germany submitted several bids, each bid describing fuel to be provided by a different physical supplier; for each of the four Vessels, O.W. Germany submitted one bid that listed USOT as the physical supplier. Hapag analyzed the submitted responses in internal spreadsheets that set out for each bid the bidder, the price, details as to fuel quality, and the identity of the physical supplier.

For each of the Subject Vessels, Hapag accepted the O.W. Germany bid that identified the physical supplier as USOT. For each contract, Hapag sent O.W. Germany a purchase order that stated that the supplier would be USOT. (*See* Hapag's Interpleader Complaint ¶ 20, Exhibit 2 ("SUPPLIER: US OIL"); *id.* ¶ 23, Exhibit 3 (same); *id.* ¶ 26, Exhibit 4 ("SUPPLIER: US Oil"); *id.* ¶ 30, Exhibit 5 (same).) After receiving the purchase orders, O.W. Germany sent Hapag sales order **[—10—]** confirmations that listed the buyer as Hapag, the seller as O.W. Germany, and the supplier as USOT. (*See* Hapag's Response to USOT's 56.1 Statement ¶¶ 42–43, 74–75, 105–06, 136–37.)

In order to fulfill its contracts with Hapag for the supply of bunkers to the Vessels, O.W. Germany then subcontracted to purchase the bunkers from O.W. USA. (*See* OWG's Rule 56.1 Statement and USOT's Response ¶¶ 36, 72, 103, 133; *see, e.g., id.* ¶ 39 (as to the SEASPAN HAMBURG, "on October 10, 2014, after entering into a contract with Hapag, . . . OW Germany advised . . . OW USA that OW Germany had sold to Hapag at a price of $534 per metric ton, and requested that OW USA purchase the bunker stem offered by USOT")).

With respect to these fuel orders for the four Subject Vessels, USOT delivered the ordered bunkers in October 2014. USOT, on the premise that it had made the sales to O.W. Denmark, sent invoices to O.W. Denmark (O.W. Germany contends instead that USOT sold to O.W. USA); O.W. USA sent invoices to O.W. Germany; O.W. Germany sent invoices to Hapag. On November 7, 2014, O.W. Denmark entered bankruptcy; bankruptcy filings by other members of the O.W. Bunker Group followed. On November 6, Hapag had paid O.W. Germany for the bunkers delivered to the SANTA ROBERTA; O.W. Germany received no **[—11—]** payments with respect to the other three Vessels. USOT has received no payments for the bunkers it supplied to any of the four Vessels.

B. *The District Court's Dismissal of USOT's Lien Claims*

Following the collapse of the O.W. Bunker Group, Hapag, faced with the prospect of competing *in rem* claims by USOT and by O.W. Germany or its lender-assignee, commenced its present interpleader action against USOT, O.W. Germany, O.W. Denmark, and others. Hapag provided security for the amounts due for the bunkers delivered to the Subject Vessels, in the form of a bond with respect to three of the Vessels and a letter of undertaking with respect to the fourth. Hapag requested a determination by the court as to which of the claimants was entitled to recover against the posted security, and a declaratory judgment that Hapag and the Vessels are discharged from all liability with respect to the supply of the bunkers. The court ordered that the interpleader funds would serve as a substitute *res*. *See Clearlake Shipping PTE Ltd. v. O.W. Bunker (Switzer-*

land) SA, 239 F.Supp.3d 674, 678 n.3 (S.D.N.Y. 2017) ("*Clearlake*"). **{-658-}**

USOT commenced its present action *in rem* in the United States District Court for the Western District of Washington against the VIENNA EXPRESS and the **[—12—]** SOFIA EXPRESS and commenced a similar *in rem* action in the Central District of California against the SEASPAN HAMBURG and the SANTA ROBERTA, seeking to assert maritime liens for the amounts due on the bunkers USOT had delivered to the Vessels. The action filed in Washington was transferred to the Southern District of New York (or "Southern District"); the other action is being held in abeyance in light of the numerous suits pending before several judges in the Southern District, *see generally Clearlake*, 239 F.Supp.3d at 678 ("24 interpleader cases [involving O.W. Bunker Group] . . . were pending before [Judge Caproni] as of June 30, 2015").

Following consolidated discovery proceedings, the parties, at the request of the court, identified test cases for the efficient decision of significant legal issues with respect to the *in rem* claims. *See generally id.* at 678–79. To the extent pertinent to these appeals, USOT's present *in rem* action and Hapag's interpleader action were among those so identified; motions for summary judgment were filed by USOT and O.W. Germany, with each interested party (including Hapag) filing Rule 56.1 Statements as to allegations they disputed and facts they contended were undisputed.

O.W. Germany, opposing USOT's lien claims, contended that USOT could not meet the CIMLA lien prerequisite that USOT show that it provided the bunkers to the Vessels "on the order of" an owner or a person authorized by the **[—13—]** owner to order them, 46 U.S.C. § 31342(a). O.W. Germany asserted—and USOT agreed, to an extent—that USOT had no contract with Hapag or anyone authorized to act as Hapag's agent in the ordering of bunkers. USOT conceded that it did not enter into a contract with Hapag for the bunker sales at issue here (*see, e.g.*, USOT's Rule 56.1 Statement and Hapag's Response ¶ 7), and that Hapag placed these fuel orders with O.W. Germany and did not contract with O.W. USA, or O.W. Denmark, or USOT (*see* USOT's Response to OWG's 56.1 Statement ¶¶ 26, 69, 100, 130).

However, in response to O.W. Germany's Rule 56.1 Statement asserting that USOT had no "account or direct business relationship with Hapag in October 2014," USOT stated:

> Admits that USOT did not have an account with Hapag, but denies that USOT did not have a direct business relationship with Hapag in October 2014. The undisputed record shows that Hapag, as the Vessels' owner or charterer, analyzed and compared the price and quality of the bunkers offered by USOT with the price and quality offered by other suppliers, and then ***selected USOT to deliver the bunkers to Hapag's Vessels***. . . . Hapag specifically named USOT as the supplier of the bunkers on its . . . purchase orders, which Hapag prepared well ***before*** each delivery.

(USOT's Response to OWG's Rule 56.1 Statement ¶ 14 (emphases in original).) USOT also noted that "[t]he sales order confirmations prepared by O.W. Germany and sent **[—14—]** to Hapag" for each delivery specified that the physical supplier would be "USOT." (*Id.*) For the same reasons, USOT also disputed O.W. Germany's assertion that "Hapag did not instruct OW Germany . . . to use USOT . . . for the supply of bunker fuel to [the relevant] vessels . . . and did not control the selection of a physical supplier," reiterating, *inter alia*, that Hapag in its purchase orders, and O.W. Germany in its sales confirmations, had specifically named USOT as the physical supplier for the bunkers ordered. **{-659-}** (USOT's Response to OWG's Rule 56.1 Statement ¶ 19.)

In addition, while USOT admitted that "Hapag never advised USOT" that O.W. Germany or O.W. USA would be acting as Hapag's agents for the bunker purchases (OWG's Rule 56.1 Statement and USOT's Response ¶ 31), USOT denied O.W. Germany's assertion that "Hapag never authorized or appointed OW Germany or OW USA as agents to order bunker fuel on Hapag's behalf" (USOT's Response to OWG's Rule 56.1 Statement ¶ 30). USOT stated that "[t]he undisputed record shows that O.W. Germany and O.W. USA were cloaked with at least implied authority while procuring the subject bunkers for Hapag's account." (USOT's Response to OWG's Rule 56.1 Statement ¶ 30 (citing evidence of discussions between USOT and O.W. USA).) USOT also argued that other entities with which it had contact—including Hapag's port coordinator Norton Lilly International, Inc. ("Norton Lilly"), which **[—15—]** forwarded the Hapag bunker orders in emails to USOT, and the Vessels' masters or chief engineers who gave USOT receipts upon delivery of the bunkers—possessed at least implied or apparent authority to bind the Vessels with respect to orders of bunkers.

USOT argued further that as it had physically supplied the fuel, the price of which was in the range of approximately $1.3–$1.5 million for each Vessel—and that as O.W. Germany was merely a middleman that could earn only a small fraction of the value of the fuel—USOT, rather than O.W. Germany, was entitled to the maritime liens as a matter of equity.

In its opinion in *Clearlake*, to the extent pertinent to these two appeals, the district court denied USOT's motions for summary judgment, rejecting its claims for maritime liens because USOT did not provide the bunkers "on the order" of the Vessels or their agents. 239 F.Supp.3d at 684–90 (internal quotation marks omitted). The court stated that maritime liens arise exclusively under CIMLA, that such liens are construed narrowly under the doctrine of *stricti juris*, and that CIMLA "typically require[s]" a finding of "a direct contractual or agency nexus between the supplier and the vessel or its agents." *Id.* at 684. It determined that, because USOT acted as a subcontractor, it "lack[ed] a direct connection to the [Vessels]." *Id.* at 685. **[—16—]**

The court—referring to O.W. Denmark and its international subsidiaries collectively as "O.W.," and collectively to the vessels, their owners, or authorized agents as the "Vessel Interests"—noted that USOT contended that it in fact had "a direct relationship . . . to the Vessel Interests":

> Because USOT was identified as O.W.'s supplier in internal analyses prepared by Hapag[] personnel, USOT contends that it, rather than O.W., was nominated as the supplier. . . . USOT [was also] identified as the supplier in the order confirmations exchanged by O.W. and the Vessel Interests.

Id. at 686. The court found this contention unpersuasive:

> Direct contacts between . . . Physical Suppliers and agents of the vessel can be relevant if they demonstrate a direct contractual or agency relationship. For example, *when a vessel requires a contractor to use a specific subcontractor there may be a basis to argue that the contractor engaged the subcontractor with actual authority from the vessel*, creating a direct link between the vessel and the subcontractor. *See Port of Portland*[*v. M/V PARALLA*], 892 F.2d [825,] 828 [(9th Cir. 1989)] ("[*A*]*n owner can still become responsible for the services of a subcontractor, if the owner has ordered the general contractor to retain that subcontractor*." (citing **{-660-}** *The Juniata*, 277 F. 438, 440 (D. Md. 1922))). But evidence that the supplier was known to the vessel and coordinated with the vessel to satisfy its obligations to a third party does not establish a legally significant relationship between the vessel and subcontractors. *See Integral Control Sys.*[*v. Consolidated Edison Co.*], 990 F.Supp [295,] 299-300 [(S.D.N.Y. 1998)] (subcontractor's selection must be "ordered" by the vessel (quoting Port of Portland, 892 F.2d at 828)) . . . . **[—17—]**

Clearlake, 239 F.Supp.3d at 686–87 (footnote omitted) (emphases ours). The court concluded that

> [*a*]*t best* (from [USOT's] perspective), the summary judgment record shows that the Vessel Interests viewed . . . USOT as [an] *acceptable* supplier[]. *There is no evidence that the Vessel Interests required O.W. to use [USOT] to satisfy its obligations* or that [USOT was] directly engaged by agents of the Vessel Interests. *To the contrary, the evidence on this point is that the Vessel Interests were indifferent to the identity of the supplier*[]. The representatives of each of the Vessel Interests *testified that the physical supplier was O.W.'s choice. . . .* [W]hen O.W. provided bids to Hapag[], it included multiple different suppliers, depending on the port of call. For example, in Los Angeles, O.W. used O.W. itself, and in Oakland it used P66. . . . *The uncontradicted testimony from the Vessel Interests is that they saw the choice of physical supplier as essentially O.W.'s to make.* . . . In short, *the inclusion of [USOT] on the confirmations provided by O.W. and the Vessel Interests does not amount to a "selection" by the Vessel Interests of . . . USOT.*

Id. at 688 (emphases ours). The court added that

> [t]he evidence that the Vessel Interests were *aware* of [USOT's] identit[y] and *tacitly* "selected" [it] is potentially a question of fact, particularly as to Hapag[], which included USOT in internal analyses of competing bids. If a question of fact exists on this point, however, it is not material. There is no dispute that the Vessel Interests did not contract with [USOT], and [*USOT does*] *not argue that the contracts required O.W. to use* [*USOT*] *as supplier*[].

Id. at 688 n.11 (emphases added). **[—18—]**

The district court also rejected contentions by USOT that it was entitled to rely on theories of apparent or implied authority or on principles of equity. *See id.* at 686 n.10, 688–89, 692–94. The court concluded:

> In sum, while the Court sympathizes with [USOT], which apparently believed that [it] held maritime liens and may be financially harmed by this Court's holding that [it does] not, the contractual relationships between the parties in this case are clear, and those relationships must be respected. [USOT] delivered the bunkers to the [V]essels at the direction of O.W. [USOT did not enter] into a contract with the Vessel Interests or their agents, and *the undisputed evidence is that the Vessel Interests did not require O.W. to use [USOT]*. These back-to-back contracts were intended, in part, to avoid multilateral obligations that could embroil the [V]essels in litigation between suppliers. It is unfortunate that it may be that [USOT] . . . will suffer from O.W.'s bankruptcy . . . . Ultimately, however, that is not a reason for the Court to depart from the Second Circuit's strict approach to maritime liens.

Id. at 689–90 (emphasis added).

Effectively granting summary judgment against USOT on its maritime-lien claims, the court entered a partial final judgment **{-661-}** in both the *in rem* action brought by USOT and the interpleader action brought by Hapag, ruling "that USOT does not possess maritime liens pursuant to [CIMLA] against the vessels M/V SANTA ROBERTA, M/V VIENNA EXPRESS, M/V SEASPAN HAMBURG, or the M/V SOFIA **[—19—]** EXPRESS," and "dismissing [USOT's] maritime lien claims." Partial Final Judgment, May 2, 2017, at 2.

II. DISCUSSION

On appeal, USOT contends principally (1) that the district court erred in concluding that USOT did not show that it had a sufficient contractual nexus with the Vessels' owner/charterer or agents to entitle it to assert maritime liens under the "plain" language of CIMLA (USOT briefs on appeal in No. 17-0922, at 21, and No. 17-0931, at 25); (2) that the court overlooked parts of the record in determining whether USOT was a subcontractor that was entitled to a maritime lien; and (3) that the court should have concluded that USOT is entitled to assert the requested maritime liens as a matter of equity.

Reviewing the district court's summary dismissal of USOT's maritime-lien claims *de novo*, construing the record in the light most favorable to USOT as the party against which summary judgment was entered, and drawing all reasonable inferences in its favor, *see, e.g.*, *Temara*, 892 F.3d at 518, 6 Adm. R. at 47; *June v. Town of Westfield*, 370 **[—20—]** F.3d 255, 257 (2d Cir. 2004), we reject USOT's first and third arguments, which are largely foreclosed by our recent decision in *Temara*; but we find merit in the second.

A. *CIMLA, Contracts, and Equitable Principles*

As discussed in *Temara*, "[a] maritime lien is a special property right in [a] vessel, arising in favor of the creditor by operation of law as security for a debt or claim, which arises when the debt arises," 892 F.3d at 518, 6 Adm. R. at 47 (internal quotation marks omitted). The primary function of such liens "is to facilitate maritime commerce by reducing the . . . risk associated with supplying a vessel that may not return to the same port again." *Id.* at 519, 6 Adm. R. at 48. "Maritime liens arise only by operation of law and not by contract," and are "construed under the doctrine of *stricti juris*, meaning that the statutory require-ments are construed strictly and may not be expanded by construction, analogy[,] or inference." *Id.*, 6 Adm. R. at 48 (internal quotation marks omitted).

CIMLA provides, *inter alia*, that "a person providing necessaries to a vessel on the order of the owner or a person authorized by the owner . . . has a maritime lien on the vessel [and] may bring a civil action in rem to enforce the lien." 46 U.S.C. § 31342(a). It provides, to the extent at issue here, that the following are "persons [who] are presumed to have authority to procure necessaries for a vessel": **[—21—]**

(1) the owner;

(2) the master;

(3) a person entrusted with the management of the vessel at the port of supply; or

(4) an officer or agent appointed by—

(A) the owner; [or]

(B) a charterer . . . .

Id. § 31341(a). There being no question that fuel bunkers are necessaries, and no question in these cases that the bunkers were provided to the Subject Vessels by USOT, the only question under the language of CIMLA was whether USOT did so "on the order of" Hapag or a person authorized by Hapag. **{–662–}**

We conclude, substantially for the reasons stated by the district court in *Clearlake*, which parallel those leading our Court to answer such a question in the negative in *Temara*, that the district court correctly ruled that USOT did not adduce evidence that it was ordered to provide the bunkers by Hapag or by an agent authorized by Hapag to order bunkers. As described in Part I.B. above, there is no dispute that, for the Subject Vessels, Hapag ordered the bunkers from O.W. Germany; that O.W. Germany ordered the bunkers from O.W. USA; that O.W. USA ordered the **[—22—]** bunkers from USOT; and that USOT had no contract with Hapag or with O.W. Germany. Although USOT argues that it complied with a chain of contracts for orders that originated with the Vessels' owner or charterer, we agree with the district court that in each of the contracts requiring USOT to deliver the bunkers, USOT's counterparty was neither Hapag nor O.W. Germany. USOT in fact acted upon orders placed by an intermediary between itself and O.W. Germany, and the intermediary was not authorized by the Vessels' owner or charterer to order bunkers for the Vessels.

We also reject, substantially for the reasons stated by the district court, *see Clearlake*, 239 F.Supp.3d at 689, USOT's argument that either communications from Hapag's port agent Norton Lilly in arranging for delivery, or receipts issued by a Vessel's master or chief engineer acknowledging USOT's bunker deliveries, constituted evidence that USOT provided the bunkers on the order of an agent of the Vessels. *See generally Temara*, 892 F.3d at 521 n.6, 6 Adm. R. at 50 n.6. Coordinating delivery and acknowledging receipt do not indicate that the persons so coordinating and/or acknowledging had placed the bunker orders or been authorized by the owner to do so. **[—23—]**

Finally, the district court properly rejected USOT's additional arguments for entitlement to maritime liens purely as a matter of equity. As we stated in *Temara*, such liens cannot properly be conferred on the basis of equitable principles such as unjust enrichment. *See id.* at 522–23, 6 Adm. R. at 51; *id.* at 523, 6 Adm. R. at 51 (rejecting "the concept of an equitable maritime lien").

B. *The Subcontractor Rule and Its Exception*

In rejecting USOT's claims for maritime liens, the district court noted that "[s]ubcontractors who deal with a contractor or a middle-man lack a direct connection to the vessel," and that "there is a considerable body of law . . . that a subcontractor cannot assert a maritime lien." *Clearlake*, 239 F.Supp.3d at 685 (internal quotation marks omitted) (citing, *inter alia*, *Lake Charles Stevedores, Inc. v. PROFESSOR VLADIMIR POPOV MV*, 199 F.3d 220, 229–30 (5th Cir. 1999) ("*Lake Charles*"), *cert. denied*, 529 U.S. 1130 (2000); and 2 *Benedict on Admiralty* § 40 (7th ed. 1997)). The district court applied this general rule, stating that

> [w]hile a subcontractor may "provide" necessaries to the vessel, its counterparty is the contractor, not any of the parties authorized by Section 31341(a) to encumber the vessel. *See Lake Charles*, 199 F.3d at 230 (explaining that the "nature of the relationship **[—24—]** between each pair of entities" determines whether a party provides necessaries "on the order" of the vessel).

Clearlake, 239 F.Supp.3d at 685 (footnote omitted).

1. *The Exception to the General Rule*

There is, however, an exception to the general rule: "The sole exception to the rule against the subcontractor lien will **{-663-}** occur where the subcontractor has been engaged by a general contractor in circumstances *where the general contractor was acting as an agent at the direction of the owner to engage specific subcontractors*," *Farwest Steel Corp. v. Barge Sea-Span 241*, 828 F.2d 522, 526 (9th Cir. 1987) ("*Farwest*") (emphasis added), *cert. denied*, 485 U.S. 1034 (1988), *i.e.*, where "an entity authorized to bind the ship *controlled the selection* of the subcontractor and/or its performance," *Lake Charles*, 199 F.3d at 229 (emphasis added). *See, e.g.*, *Port of Portland v. M/V PARALLA*, 892 F.2d 825, 828 (9th Cir. 1989) ("*Port of Portland*") (the subcontractor may be entitled to a lien "if the owner has ordered the general contractor to retain that subcontractor"). Thus, under this "minimal exception," *Cianbro Corp. v. George H. Dean, Inc.*, 596 F.3d 10, 17 (1st Cir. 2010) ("*Cianbro*"), a subcontractor is not entitled to assert a maritime lien "unless it can be shown that an entity authorized to bind the ship controlled the selection of the subcontractor and/or its performance," *id.* (internal quotation marks **[—25—]** omitted); *Valero Marketing & Supply Co. v. M/V ALMI SUN*, 893 F.3d 290, 293, 6 Adm. R. 205, 206 (5th Cir. 2018) ("*Valero*") (internal quotation marks omitted). The "exception to th[e] general rule . . . applies when the vessel owner directs the general contractor to use a particular subcontractor." *Bunker Holdings Ltd. v. Yang Ming Liberia Corp.*, 906 F.3d 843, 846, 6 Adm. R. 386, 387 (9th Cir. 2018) ("*Yang Ming*").

The subcontractor exception does not apply where there is no significant evidence "that the owner intended that [the physical supplier] be engaged as a subcontractor," *Farwest*, 828 F.2d at 526. The owner/charterer's mere awareness of a particular subcontractor does not show that the vessel controlled or directed the subcontractor's selection or intended to do so. *See*, *e.g.*, *Valero*, 893 F.3d at 295, 6 Adm. R. at 208; *Cianbro*, 596 F.3d at 17–18. Mere knowledge that a particular subcontractor will be used "has never been held to be sufficient to establish a lien." *Port of Portland*, 892 F.2d at 828 (citing *Farwest*, 828 F.2d at 526).

In *Temara*, citing, *inter alia*, *Lake Charles*, 199 F.3d at 229; *Cianbro*, 596 F.3d at 17; and *Port of Portland*, 892 F.2d at 828, we stated the "long-recognized rule that the services of an independent subcontractor *generally* do not give rise to a maritime li[en]" and noted the exception for a subcontractor who "can . . . show[] that an entity authorized to bind the ship controlled the selection of the subcontractor and/or its **[—26—]** performance," 892 F.3d at 521, 6 Adm. R. at 49, 50 (internal quotation marks and brackets omitted) (emphasis ours); *see also id.* at 522 n.7, 6 Adm. R. at 50 n.7 (no subcontractor maritime lien "without any indication that a statutorily-authorized entity provided direction"). We referred to the subcontractor exception again several times in other recent decisions in the O.W. Bunker Group related appeals, while noting that the evidence in their respective records was insufficient to trigger the exception. *See, e.g., O'Rourke*, 730 F. App'x at 91 ("O'Rourke did not supply the bunkers upon the order of a statutorily authorized person, thus failing to meet CIMLA's third requirement for a maritime lien. . . . *Nor did it adduce evidence that a statutorily authorized person controlled the selection* of O'Rourke as the physical supplier." (emphasis added)); *Aegean*, 730 F. App'x at 89 ("Nor did [Aegean] adduce evidence that a statutorily authorized person *controlled the selection* of Aegean as the physical supplier." (emphasis added)); *Chemoil*, 2018 WL 3359609, at *2 ("*no*[] . . . *evidence* that a statutorily authorized person *controlled the selection* of Chemoil as the physical supplier" (emphases added)). **{-664-}**

As is evident from the above statements of the requirements for application of the subcontractor exception, the exception is rooted in the same concerns that are reflected in the elements set out in CIMLA: For the exception to apply so as to afford the subcontractor a lien on the vessel, there must have been (a) **[—27—]** an order or direction (b) by the owner/charterer of the vessel or its authorized agent, that the particular subcontractor be used. "[T]he mere fact that an entity [who is given that order or direction] is a general contractor will not preclude it from being an agent under proper circumstances." *Port of Portland*, 892 F.2d at 828. "In th[e] scenario" in which "the vessel owner directs the general contractor to use a particular subcontractor," "the general contractor essentially acts as the owner's agent and thus exercises authority to bind the vessel." *Yang Ming*, 906 F.3d at 846, 6 Adm. R. at 387. As to the provision of necessaries, proper application of the subcontractor exception is thus within the scope of CIMLA.

2. *The Record in the Present Cases Involving USOT*

The district court in the present cases adverted to the subcontractor exception, *see Clearlake*, 239 F.Supp.3d at 687 ("[a]n owner can still become responsible for the services of a subcontractor, if the owner has ordered the general contractor to retain that subcontractor" (quoting *Port of Portland*, 892 F.2d at 828)), but concluded that the exception was not applicable. We note that in *Clearlake*, the district court was addressing four test cases and dealing with maritime-lien claims asserted by two physical suppliers—USOT in the cases that are the subject of the present appeals, and NuStar Energy Services, Inc. ("NuStar") in the other two cases—and in some critical **[—28—]** instances the court made findings collectively with respect to "the Vessel Interests" and "the Physical Suppliers," 239 F.Supp.3d at 688–90, without distinguishing among the various owner/charterers or between USOT and NuStar. We consider here only the record that was created in the USOT cases.

Insofar as concerns USOT, the court viewed the record as showing

- that USOT "d[id] not argue that the [Hapag] contracts required O.W. to use [USOT] as supplier[]," *id.* at 688 n.11;

- that there was "no evidence that the Vessel Interests required O.W. to use [USOT] to satisfy its obligations," *id.* at 688;

- that, although "aware of [USOT's] identit[y]," Hapag only "*tacitly* 'selected' [USOT]," *id.* at 688 n.11 (emphasis added);

- that "the *undisputed* evidence" was "that the Vessel Interests did not require O.W. to use [USOT]," *id.* at 690 (emphasis added);

- that there was "uncontradicted" evidence that Hapag viewed "the choice of physical supplier as essentially O.W.'s to make," *id.* at 688;

- that Hapag "w[as] indifferent to the identity of the supplier[]," *id.*;

- that "[*a*]*t best*," Hapag "viewed . . . USOT as "acceptable," *id.* (emphasis added); and

- that "the inclusion of [USOT] on the confirmations provided by . . . [Hapag] d[id] not amount to a 'selection' by the Vessel Interests of . . . USOT," *id.* **[—29—]**

Although in the two companion appeals being decided today we agree that the district court correctly viewed the records in the NuStar cases as not warranting application of the subcontractor exception, *see Clearlake Shipping PTE Ltd. v. NuStar Energy Services, Inc.*, No. 17-1458, 6 Adm. R. 93 (2d Cir. Dec. 19, 2018), and *Nippon Kaisha Line Ltd. v.* **{-665-}** *NuStar Energy Services, Inc.*, No. 17-1378 (2d Cir. Dec. 19, 2018), we do not share the above view of the record in the instant cases involving USOT.

First, USOT did argue that the Hapag purchase orders to O.W. Germany required O.W. Germany to use USOT as the physical supplier. USOT directly "[*d*]*enie*[*d*]" O.W. Germany's assertion that "*Hapag did not instruct OW Germany . . . to use USOT . . .* for the supply of bunker fuel to [the relevant] vessels . . . and did not control the selection of a physical supplier." (USOT's Response to OWG's Rule 56.1 Statement ¶ 19 (emphases added).) USOT added—to this response as well as others—that the

> undisputed record shows that *Hapag, as the Vessels' owner or charterer*, analyzed and compared the price and quality of the bunkers offered by USOT with the price and quality offered by other suppliers, and then ***selected USOT to deliver the bunkers to Hapag's Vessels***. . . . Hapag specifically named USOT as the supplier of the bunkers on its . . . purchase orders, which Hapag prepared well ***before*** each delivery. **[—30—]**

(USOT's Response to OWG's Rule 56.1 Statement ¶ 19 (first emphasis added; second and third emphases in original); *id.* ¶¶ 14, 20; USOT's Response to Hapag's Rule 56.1 Counter-Statement ¶¶ 186, 191, 193, 197, 198, 200, 204, 211, 212, 214, 231, 232.)

Second, viewing the record in the light most favorable to USOT as the party against which summary judgment was granted, we cannot agree that it shows as a matter of law that when Hapag decided to award the bunkers contracts to O.W. Germany, Hapag was "indifferent" to who would be the physical supplier and merely "tacitly" accepted USOT as a name of which it was merely "aware" because it had been introduced by O.W. Germany in the initial bidding. The notion that Hapag did not care who supplied the fuel—although cultivated in the deposition testimony of Hapag's fuel purchasing director Norbert Kock who stated that it was "not [Hapag's] business" to "care about what happened downstream of O.W. Germany in terms of dealing with subcontractors, physical suppliers" (Deposition of Norbert Kock at 138)—is belied by, *inter alia*, Kock's sworn declarations, twice pointing out the importance of fuel quality to a ship's performance (*see* Declaration of Norbert Kock dated June 15, 2016, ¶ 13; Declaration of Norbert Kock dated July 27, 2015, ¶ 5).

Third, the record contradicts the views that Hapag's selection of USOT as physical supplier was only "tacit[]," that there was "no evidence" of Hapag's **[—31—]** directing O.W. Germany to use USOT as the physical supplier, and that there was "undisputed" evidence that Hapag did not so direct. To begin with, as shown in Part I.A. above quoting exhibits to Hapag's Interpleader Complaint, each of the Hapag purchase orders themselves expressly listed USOT—and only USOT—as the "SUPPLIER." In addition, O.W. Germany, in its responding sales confirmations likewise listed USOT and only USOT as the physical supplier. While the sales confirmations standing alone would not suffice to permit a conclusion that the selection of USOT had been ordered or directed by Hapag, they provide support for a conclusion that the language in Hapag's purchase orders, listing USOT and only USOT, evinced an instruction.

Finally, USOT in its Rule 56.1 Statement asserted that Hapag, in issuing purchase orders that listed USOT and only USOT as the supplier for the four Vessels, "expressly confirm[ed]" that USOT was to be the physical supplier. Hapag disputed the characterization, stating that it "denies **{–666–}** its purchase order 'confirms' that USOT will act as the 'supplier'"; however, in each response, Hapag also said "Hapag admits that its purchase order lists the identity of USOT as the physical supplier." (Hapag's Response to USOT's Rule 56.1 Statement ¶ 38 (re SANTA ROBERTA), ¶ 71 (re VIENNA EXPRESS), ¶ 102 (re SEASPAN HAMBURG), ¶ 133 (re SOFIA EXPRESS)). **[—32—]** Without more, Hapag's listing of USOT in the purchase orders could perhaps have been viewed as merely suggestive. But in each of those same Rule 56.1 responses as to the meaning of its purchase orders, Hapag went on to state that

> O.W. Germany was *permitted* . . . to find a substitute fuel of similar specifications and price ***if*** USOT was unable to act as the physical supplier.

(Emphases added.) The plain syntactical implication of this statement by Hapag is that unless USOT was unable to perform, O.W. Germany's use of a physical supplier other than USOT was not permitted.

We see nothing in the record to compel the conclusion that Hapag did not control the selection of the physical supplier; and Hapag's own admissions may permit a conclusion that it instructed O.W. Germany to use USOT as the physical supplier unless USOT could not perform.

CONCLUSION

We have considered all of the parties' arguments on these appeals and, except to the extent indicated above, have found them to be without merit. For the reasons stated, we affirm the district court judgment insofar as it concluded that **[—33—]** USOT did not adduce evidence that it was ordered to provide the bunkers by Hapag or by an agent authorized by Hapag to order bunkers. We further affirm the district court's conclusion that maritime liens cannot properly be conferred on the basis of equitable principles such as unjust enrichment. We vacate and remand the district court judgment on the issue of whether Hapag directed that USOT be the physical supplier pursuant to the exception to the subcontractor rule.

United States Court of Appeals
for the Second Circuit

No. 17-1458

CLEARLAKE SHIPPING PTE LTD.
VS.
NUSTAR ENERGY SERVS., INC.

Appeal from the United States District Court for the Southern District of New York

Decided: December 19, 2018

Citation: 911 F.3d 646, 6 Adm. R. 93 (2d Cir. 2018).

Before **KEARSE, CABRANES,** and **LOHIER,** Circuit Judges.

[—4—] {-648-} KEARSE, Circuit Judge:

Interpleader defendant NuStar Energy Services, Inc. ("NuStar"), a physical supplier of marine fuel ("bunkers") to two vessels time-chartered by interpleader plaintiff Clearlake Shipping PTE Ltd. ("Clearlake"), appeals from orders and an April 18, 2017 partial final judgment of the United States District Court for the Southern District of New York, Valerie E. Caproni, *Judge*, denying NuStar's motion for summary judgment and dismissing its claims to maritime liens against the vessels. The district court ruled that, under the Commercial Instruments and Maritime Liens **[—5—]** Act ("CIMLA"), 46 U.S.C. § 31301 *et seq.*, NuStar was not entitled to maritime liens because it provided the fuel "on the order of" an entity other than "the owner or a person authorized by the owner" of the vessels, *id.* § 31342(a). *See Clearlake Shipping PTE Ltd. v. O.W. Bunker (Switzerland) SA*, 239 F.Supp.3d 674 (S.D.N.Y. 2017) ("*Clearlake*"). On appeal, NuStar contends principally that it was entitled to the claimed liens in light of CIMLA's plain text and purpose and as a matter of equity, regardless of NuStar's lack of contractual privity with the vessels' owner or charterer or their agent. We see no error in the district court's interpretation of CIMLA or its ruling that maritime liens may not properly be granted based on principles of equity. And given that—unlike the physical supplier in two companion appeals, U.S. Oil Trading LLC v. M/V VIENNA EXPRESS, No. 17-0922, and Hapag-Lloyd Aktiengesellschaft v. U.S. Oil Trading LLC, No. 17-0931, which are also decided today *sub nom. U.S. Oil Trading LLC v. M/V VIENNA EXPRESS*, --- F.3d --- , 6 Adm. R. 83 (2d Cir. 2018) ("*USOT*")—NuStar has not pointed to evidence that the owner or charterer or their agent directed that NuStar be the physical supplier for the vessels in question, we affirm, as NuStar's claims are not meaningfully distinguishable from those rejected in *ING Bank N.V. v. M/V TEMARA*, 892 F.3d 511, 6 Adm. R. 44 (2d Cir. 2018) ("*Temara*"). **[—6—]**

I. BACKGROUND

This case is one of the many resulting from the financial collapse of O.W. Bunker & Trading A/S ("O.W. Denmark") and its subsidiaries and affiliates (collectively the "O.W. Bunker Group"), an international operation that both supplied bunkers to ships and arranged the supply of bunkers by others. *See generally Temara*, 892 F.3d at 515, 6 Adm. R. at 44. In the wake of bankruptcy filings by O.W. Bunker Group members, interpleader actions were initiated by numerous **{-649-}** owners or charterers of vessels, including the present action by Clearlake, seeking judicial resolution of the competing claims to payment asserted by physical suppliers and by O.W. Bunker Group members that had engaged the physical suppliers. *See, e.g., Clearlake*, 239 F.Supp.3d at 678 ("24 interpleader cases [involving O.W. Bunker Group] . . . were pending before [Judge Caproni] as of June 30, 2015"). In the present case, the following facts, drawn from statements submitted by various parties pursuant to Rule 56.1 of the Local Rules for the Southern District of New York ("Rule 56.1 Statements"), are not in dispute.

In October 2014, Clearlake, charterer of the M/V HELLAS GLORY and the M/V VENUS GLORY (collectively the "Vessels"), acting through its agent AS Tarcona ("Tarcona"), placed orders for fuel bunkers for the Vessels with O.W. Bunker **[—7—]** (Switzerland) SA ("O.W. Switzerland"). O.W. Switzerland, in turn, issued purchase orders to its affiliate O.W. Bunker USA, Inc. ("O.W. USA"). O.W. USA then issued purchase orders to NuStar.

Local agents for the Vessels coordinated the deliveries by NuStar. In late October, NuStar delivered the ordered bunkers to the Vessels.

NuStar did not directly contract with Clearlake or with O.W. Switzerland. In early November 2014, NuStar invoiced O.W. USA for the bunkers; O.W. USA invoiced O.W. Switzerland; O.W. Switzerland invoiced Clearlake. On November 7, O.W. Denmark filed for bankruptcy; bankruptcy filings by other members of the O.W. Bunker Group followed. Neither NuStar nor any O.W. Bunker Group entity has been paid for NuStar's bunker deliveries to Clearlake's Vessels.

Clearlake brought the present interpleader action against NuStar, O.W. Switzerland, O.W. USA, and others. In the district court, this case and three others—one other involving NuStar and two involving U.S. Oil Trading LLC ("USOT")—were selected to serve as test cases for the efficient resolution of the various *in rem* claims. Following coordinated discovery, and summary judgment motions by NuStar, USOT, and O.W. Bunker entities that had dealt with the vessels' owners or charterers, the district court addressed these four cases in its opinion in *Clearlake*. **[—8—]**

The court stated that maritime liens arise exclusively under CIMLA, that such liens are construed narrowly under the doctrine of *stricti juris*, and that CIMLA "typically require[s]" a finding of "a direct contractual or agency nexus between the supplier and the vessel or its agents." *Clearlake*, 239 F.Supp.3d at 684. The court determined that NuStar had performed as a subcontractor that "lack[ed] a direct connection to the [Vessels]," noting the general rule that a subcontractor cannot assert a maritime lien. *Id.* at 685.

Adverting to an exception to that general rule, the court noted that "'[a]n owner can still become responsible for the services of a subcontractor, if the owner has ordered the general contractor to retain that subcontractor,'" *id.* at 687 (quoting *Port of Portland v. M/V PARALLA*, 892 F.2d 825, 828 (9th Cir. 1989) (*"Port of Portland"*)). However, insofar as is pertinent to the present appeal, the court stated that the record showed at best that Clearlake was merely "aware" that NuStar had been named by O.W. Switzerland as the physical supplier and that Clearlake accepted NuStar only "tacitly." *Clearlake*, 239 F.Supp.3d at 688 n.11. Seeing no evidence in the record that Clearlake had required O.W. Switzerland to use NuStar as the physical supplier, the court concluded that the subcontractor exception was not applicable to NuStar. **[—9—]**

Accordingly, the district court denied NuStar's motion for summary judgment **{-650-}** and effectively granted summary judgment against NuStar on its maritime-lien claims against Clearlake, entering a partial final judgment dismissing those claims.

II. DISCUSSION

On appeal, NuStar contends principally that it was entitled to maritime liens against the Clearlake Vessels in light of CIMLA's plain text and purpose and as a matter of equity, regardless of a lack of contractual privity between NuStar and Clearlake or its agent. We reject these contentions substantially for the reasons stated by the district court in *Clearlake*.

We see no error in the district court's interpretation of CIMLA or its ruling that maritime liens may not properly be granted based on principles of equity. NuStar's contentions as to the proper interpretation of CIMLA are foreclosed by our recent decision in *Temara*, which involved events not substantially dissimilar to those here. *See generally* 892 F.3d at 519, 6 Adm. R. at 48 (CIMLA's "statutory requirements are construed strictly and may not be expanded by construction, analogy[,] or inference" (internal **[—10—]** quotation marks omitted)); *id.* at 522-23, 6 Adm. R. at 51 (rejecting the concept of entitlement to maritime lien through application of principles of equity).

Nor do we see any error in the district court's conclusion that the exception to the general rule against a subcontractor's entitlement to a maritime lien did not apply to NuStar. As discussed in *USOT*,

> a subcontractor is not entitled to assert a maritime lien "*unless* it can be shown that *an entity authorized to bind the ship controlled the selection of the subcontractor and/or its performance*."

--- F.3d at xxx, 6 Adm. R. at 89 (quoting *Cianbro Corp. v. George H. Dean, Inc.*, 596 F.3d 10, 17 (1st Cir. 2010) ("*Cianbro*"), and *Valero Marketing & Supply Co. v. M/V ALMI SUN*, 893 F.3d 290, 293, 6 Adm. R. 205, 206 (5th Cir. 2018) ("*Valero*") (emphases ours)).

> "The sole exception to the rule against the subcontractor lien will occur where the subcontractor has been engaged by a general contractor in circumstances *where the general contractor was acting as an agent at the direction of the owner to engage specific subcontractors*" . . . .

USOT, --- F.3d at xxx, 6 Adm. R. at 89 (quoting *Farwest Steel Corp. v. Barge Sea-Span 241*, 828 F.2d 522, 526 (9th Cir. 1987) ("*Farwest*") (emphasis in *USOT*), *cert. denied*, 485 U.S. 1034 (1988)). The exception is applicable "if the owner has ordered the general contractor to retain that subcontractor." *Port of Portland*, 892 F.2d at 828; *see, e.g., Bunker Holdings Ltd. v. Yang Ming Liberia Corp.*, 906 F.3d 843, 846, 6 Adm. R. 386, 387 (9th Cir. 2018) (the "exception to th[e] **[—11—]** general rule . . . applies when the vessel owner directs the general contractor to use a particular subcontractor").

As indicated in *Temara* and our other recent decisions in appeals involving fuel suppliers and O.W. Bunker Group entities, a subcontractor is not allowed to assert a maritime lien "without any indication that *a statutorily-authorized entity provided direction*" that that subcontractor be used. *Temara*, 892 F.3d at 522 n.7, 6 Adm. R. at 50 n.7 (emphasis added); *see, e.g., O'Rourke Marine Services L.P. v. M/V COSCO HAIFA*, 730 F. App'x 89, 91 (2d Cir. 2018) (affirming denial of maritime-lien claim by a physical supplier that did not "adduce evidence that *a statutorily authorized person controlled* [*its*] *selection . . . as the physical supplier*" (emphases added)); *Aegean Bunkering (USA) LLC v. M/T AMAZON*, 730 F. App'x 87, 89 (2d Cir. 2018) (same); *Chemoil Adani Pvt. Ltd. v. M/V MARITIME KING*, No. 16-3944, 2018 WL 3359609, at *2 (2d Cir. July 10, 2018) (same where there was "*no*[] . . . **{–651–}** *evidence that a statutorily authorized person controlled the selection* of Chemoil *as the physical supplier*" (emphases added)).

Thus, the subcontractor exception does not apply where there is no significant evidence "that the owner intended that [the physical supplier] be engaged as a subcontractor." *Farwest*, 828 F.2d at 526. Mere awareness by the vessel's owner, charterer, or authorized agent that a particular physical supplier would be used is not **[—12—]** sufficient to permit a conclusion that they had such intent or that they controlled or directed the subcontractor's selection. *See, e.g., Valero*, 893 F.3d at 295, 6 Adm. R. at 208; *Cianbro*, 596 F.3d at 17–18; *Port of Portland*, 892 F.2d at 828 (mere knowledge that a particular subcontractor will be used "has never been held to be sufficient to establish a lien").

Insofar as NuStar was concerned, the district court correctly applied these principles in *Clearlake* to conclude that NuStar did not fall within the subcontractor exception. The court viewed the record as showing

- that NuStar "*d*[*id*] *not argue* that the [Clearlake/Tarcona] contracts *required* O.W. to use [NuStar] as supplier[]," 239 F.Supp.3d at 688 n.11 (emphases added);

- that there was "*no evidence* that [Clearlake or Tarcona] *required* O.W. to use [NuStar] to satisfy its obligations," *id.* at 688 (emphases added);

- that, although "aware of [NuStar's] identit[y]," Clearlake/Tarcona only "tacitly 'selected' [NuStar]," *id.* at 688 n.11; and

- that "the undisputed evidence" was "that [Clearlake/Tarcona] did not require O.W. to use [NuStar]," *id.* at 690.

We see no error in these findings. Although we reach a different conclusion on the subcontractor-exception issue today in the appeals brought by USOT, we do so based on differences between the records in the NuStar and USOT cases. **[—13—]**

In the USOT cases, Hapag-Lloyd Aktiengesellschaft ("Hapag"), the owner or charterer of the USOT-supplied vessels, issued to O.W. Bunker Germany GmbH ("O.W. Germany") purchase orders that named USOT as the physical supplier. *See USOT*, --- F.3d at xxx, 6 Adm. R. at 84. And in response to USOT's motion for summary judgment relying on the purchase orders, Hapag described these orders as meaning that O.W. Germany was "permitted" to use some other supplier "***if*** USOT was unable to act as the physical supplier," *id.* at xxx, 6 Adm. R. at 92 (internal quotation marks omitted) (emphasis in *USOT*).

We see no similar evidence or admission by Clearlake in the present case. Whereas the record in the USOT cases contained copies of the purchase orders issued by the owner/charterer Hapag, *see, e.g., Clearlake*, 239 F.Supp.3d at 682 ("The agreements between Hapag[] and O.W. Germany identify O.W. Germany as the seller, Hapag[] as buyer, and USOT as supplier."), NuStar here has pointed not to purchase orders issued by Clearlake or Tarcona but rather to the sales order confirmations issued by O.W. Switzerland. The district court stated that "[t]he Clearlake-O.W. Switzerland transactions are memorialized in . . . sales order confirmations," and it cited only to O.W. Switzerland documents. *Id.* at 680. Thus, we are aware of no evidence to suggest, much less confirm, that Clearlake or Tarcona **[—14—]** identified NuStar as the physical supplier in any purchase order. Nor has NuStar pointed to any other evidence in the record to support a conclusion that Clearlake or Tarcona directed O.W. Switzerland to use NuStar as the physical supplier.

The closest that NuStar came to claiming that Tarcona directed the use of NuStar was asserting (a) that, several days in **{-652-}** advance of delivery to the Clearlake Vessels, "Tarcona *knew* . . . that NuStar was the designated physical supplier of the bunkers it had ordered" (*see* NuStar Rule 56.1 Statement ¶¶ 11, 12 (emphasis added)), and (b) that Tarcona "*accepted* NuStar as the physical supplier of the bunkers it had ordered" (*id.* ¶ 13 (emphasis added)). As discussed above, however, evidence merely of such awareness and acceptance is insufficient to show that the vessel owner/charterer or its agent controlled the selection of the physical supplier or that they ordered or directed that NuStar be used.

CONCLUSION

We have considered all of NuStar's arguments on this appeal and have found them to be without merit. The partial final judgment is affirmed.

United States Court of Appeals for the Third Circuit

United States Court of Appeals
for the Third Circuit

No. 16-3470

IN RE FRESCATI SHIPPING CO., LTD.

Appeal from the United States District Court for the Eastern District of Pennsylvania

Decided: March 29, 2018

Citation: 886 F.3d 291, 6 Adm. R. 98 (3d Cir. 2018).

Before **SMITH**, Chief Judge, **HARDIMAN**, Circuit Judge, and **BRANN**, District Judge.*

* The Honorable Matthew W. Brann, United States District Judge for the Middle District of Pennsylvania, sitting by designation.

[—5—] **{-294-}** **SMITH**, Chief Judge: **{-295-}**

Table of Contents

[—6—]

I. Introduction

After a 1,900-mile journey from Venezuela to Paulsboro, New Jersey, the M/T *Athos I*, a single-hulled oil tanker, had come within 900 feet of its intended berth when it struck an abandoned anchor on the bottom of the Delaware River. The anchor pierced the *Athos I*'s hull, causing approximately 264,000 gallons of crude oil to spill into the river.

The cost of cleaning up the spill was $143 million. We are presented with the question of how to apportion responsibility for that cost between three parties. The first party comprises not only the shipowner, Frescati Shipping Company, Ltd., but also the ship's manager, Tsakos Shipping & Trading, S.A. (collectively, "Frescati"). Frescati, through an intermediary, contracted to deliver crude oil to the second party, which is made up of several affiliated companies—CITGO Asphalt Refining Company, CITGO Petroleum Corporation, and CITGO East Coast Oil Corporation (collectively, "CARCO"). The oil shipment was to be delivered to CARCO at its marine terminal in Paulsboro. After the oil spill, Frescati paid for the cleanup effort, and was eventually reimbursed $88 million by the third party to this litigation, the United States, pursuant to the Oil Pollution Act (OPA) of 1990, 33 U.S.C. § 2701 *et seq.* Frescati and the United States now seek to recover their cleanup costs from CARCO. **[—7—]**

II. Background

a. Facts[1]

The M/T *Athos I* was a single-hulled tanker ship, measuring approximately 748 feet long and 105 feet wide.[2] As owner of the ship, Frescati chartered it to an intermediary which assigned it to a tanker pool. **{-296-}** CARCO sub-chartered the *Athos I* from the tanker pool to deliver a shipment of crude oil from Puerto Miranda, Venezuela, to CARCO's berth in Paulsboro, New Jersey. CARCO was the shipping customer as well as the wharfinger who operated the berth.

The *Athos I*, carrying CARCO's shipment, left Venezuela in mid-November 2004 under the command of the ship's master, Captain Iosif Markoutsis. CARCO had **[—8—]** in-

[1] The facts are undisputed unless otherwise noted.

[2] Single-hulled tanker ships drew the attention of regulators and the public in the wake of the 1989 *Exxon Valdez* oil spill off the Alaskan coast; the *Exxon Valdez*, like the *Athos I*, was a single-hulled tanker. Single-hulled ships were initially subjected to extra regulation, *see, e.g.*, 33 C.F.R. § 157.455, but have since been phased out of operation in the United States in favor of double-hulled ships. *See* 46 U.S.C. § 3703a.

structed the *Athos I* to load to a draft[3] of 37 feet or less in Venezuela, and provided a warranty that the ship would be able to safely reach the berth in Paulsboro as long as it arrived with a draft of 37 feet or less. When the *Athos I* left Venezuela, it had a draft of 36′ 6″. Over the course of the *Athos I*'s journey, the ship burned fuel and the crew consumed fresh water. As the ship grew lighter, it rode higher on the water. By the time it reached the entrance to the Delaware Bay, the *Athos I* was drawing 36′ 4″. Because the fuel and fresh water were consumed from tanks located in the stern, or rear, of the ship, the *Athos I* was no longer sailing at an even keel; it was "trimmed by the bow," meaning that the bow, or front of the ship, was deeper in the water than the ship's stern. To return the ship to an even keel, the *Athos I* took on approximately 510 metric tons of ballast to tanks in the rear of the ship. Although the parties dispute how much the *Athos I* was drawing as it approached CARCO's berth, the District Court found that the added ballast brought the ship's draft to 36′ 7″.

The *Athos I* reached the entrance to the Delaware Bay without incident on November 26th. All vessels **[—9—]** traveling north from the Delaware Bay to the Delaware River are required to use a Delaware River Pilot to navigate the waters. At the appropriate time, a local river pilot, Captain Howard Teal, Jr. boarded the ship and guided it up the Delaware River until it reached a section of the river near CARCO's berth. At that point, a local docking pilot, Captain Joseph Bethel, replaced Captain Teal and began to navigate the ship to its berth at Paulsboro. Captains Teal and Bethel both engaged Captain Markoutsis in conversations about the *Athos I*, its passage from the Delaware Bay to the Paulsboro berth, water depth, underkeel clearance, and other local conditions. The substance and sufficiency of those conversations are disputed by the parties.

CARCO's berth is on the New Jersey side of the Delaware River, directly across from Philadelphia International Airport. To reach the berth from the main river channel, ships must pass through an anchorage immediately adjacent to the berth. The anchorage, known as Federal Anchorage Number 9 or the Mantua Creek Anchorage, is a federally-designated section of the river in which ships may anchor; it is periodically surveyed for depth and dredged by the Army Corps of Engineers, as Corps resources allow. No government agency is responsible for preemptively searching for unknown obstructions to navigation in the anchorage, although the Coast Guard, the National Oceanic and Atmospheric **[—10—]** Administration (NOAA), and the Corps of Engineers work together to remove or mark obstructions when they are discovered. Anyone who wishes to search for obstructions in the anchorage may do so, but anyone wishing to dredge in the anchorage requires a permit from the Corps of Engineers. **{–297–}**

It was in this anchorage on November 26, 2004, at 9:02 p.m., that the allision occurred.[4] The *Athos I* was only 900 feet—not much more than the ship's length—from CARCO's berth. The ship was "just about dead in the water" as Captain Bethel slowly positioned it to dock. Suddenly, the ship began to list and oil appeared in the river. At the time of the allision, the ship was in the middle of a 180° rotation, guided by tugboats, and moving astern and to port (backwards and to the ship's left). The path taken by the *Athos I* through the anchorage passed, at its shallowest point, over a 38-foot shoal. Most of the anchorage was deeper, and the depth of the river at the site of the allision was at least 41.65 feet at the time.

Captain Bethel immediately called the Coast Guard to alert them to the spill, while Captain Markoutsis rushed to the engine room and transferred oil from the breached **[—11—]** cargo tank into another tank. The crew of the *Athos I* was eventually able to stop

---

[3] A ship's draft is the measurement from the water line to the bottom of the ship's hull, known as the keel. As a ship loads cargo, it becomes heavier and sits lower in the water. Its draft thereby increases.

[4] An allision is "[t]he contact of a vessel with a stationary object such as an anchored vessel or a pier." *Allision*, BLACK'S LAW DICTIONARY (10th ed. 2014).

the leak, but not before 264,321 gallons of crude oil had spilled into the Delaware River.

The cleanup effort began almost immediately. Although it was ultimately successful, it took months to complete and the efforts of thousands of workers at a cost of $143 million. The cause of the allision was not discovered until more than a month later, when an abandoned anchor was discovered on the riverbed. The search for the obstruction that caused the allision proved difficult. An experienced sonar operator using side-scan sonar conducted the first search shortly after the allision, but did not recognize the anchor.[5] A second search by the **[—12—]** same operator, conducted several weeks later, eventually discovered the anchor with the use of side-scan sonar in combination with divers and magnetometers. The anchor weighed approximately nine tons and was 6′ 8″ long, 7′ 3″ wide, and 4′ 6″ high. It has since been removed from the river.

The parties dispute the positioning of the anchor at the time of the allision. An anchor like the one that punctured the *Athos I* has two stable positions. It can sit at rest in the "flukes-up" or "flukes-down" position. A flukes-up anchor stands almost upright on its crown, with the flukes pointed upward at a 65° angle, while a flukes-down anchor has essentially tipped over, with both the crown and flukes of the anchor lying horizontally on the riverbed. In the flukes-up position, the anchor sticks up approximately seven feet above the riverbed, but in the flukes-down position, it rises only about 3′ 5″ above the riverbed. The District Court found that the anchor was flukes-up at the time of the allision, but CARCO asserts that the anchor was flukes-down, pointing to side-scan sonar data gathered as part of a geophysical study of the Delaware River that showed the anchor was flukes-down in 2001, three years before the allision.[6] The anchor was **[—13—]** **{-298-}** also flukes-down when it was discovered after the allision. Between 2001 and the allision in 2004, 241 vessels went to CARCO's Paulsboro berth, and many others have anchored in the anchorage over the years. The District Court theorized that one of those anchored ships could have dragged its own anchor chain along the riverbed, catching on the abandoned anchor and shifting its position. The court ultimately concluded that although the actual cause of the anchor's movement would never be known, at some point between the geophysical study in 2001 and the allision in 2004, the anchor shifted from flukes-down to flukes-up. A flukes-down anchor would not have allided with the *Athos I* if the *Athos I*'s draft was less than 37 feet; a flukes-up anchor would have.

Now, more than thirteen years after the allision, the *Athos I* has been scrapped, the anchor removed from the river, and the oil spill cleaned up. What remains is this case for apportionment of cleanup costs.

b. Procedural History

This case, like the *Athos I*, has been on a long journey. Over the past thirteen years, the matter has been to trial before two different judges and heard on appeal **[—14—]** before two separate panels of this Court. We briefly summarize that history.

Litigation began shortly after the allision in January, 2005, when Frescati filed a "Petition for Exoneration from or Limitation of Liability." CARCO and others filed claims for damages associated with the spill. Frescati

[5] Side-scan sonar is used to locate objects on the sea floor and works like a camera, but using sound instead of light to form an image. Single-beam sonar, by contrast, uses sound to measure the depth along a single line traced by a sounding mechanism known as a towpath. If an obstruction is not located along the towpath, it would not be detected, and even if the towpath crossed an obstruction, the data would simply show a depth change rather than the obstruction itself. Before the allision, CARCO used single-beam sonar to survey its berthing area and a small portion of the anchorage. The government typically used single-beam sonar when it surveyed the anchorage for depth and dredging purposes.

[6] The anchor was identified in the geophysical study data only after the allision occurred. The parties agree that in 2001, the anchor was flukes-down, and that no one was **[—13—]** aware of the anchor's existence before the allision—except, perhaps, the still-unidentified owner who abandoned it.

then filed a counterclaim against CARCO for its damages. The United States eventually reimbursed Frescati for some of its cleanup expenses pursuant to the OPA, and filed suit against CARCO as a partial subrogee to some of Frescati's claims. The claims of Frescati and the United States against CARCO were consolidated with CARCO's counterclaims and defenses, forming the litigation as it exists today.

The case was first tried in a forty-one-day bench trial before the Honorable John P. Fullam. Judge Fullam found that CARCO was not liable for the casualty in contract, tort, or otherwise; Frescati and the United States appealed. On appeal, we affirmed in part, vacated in part, and remanded the case because the District Court had failed to make appropriate findings of fact and conclusions of law as required by Fed. R. Civ. P. 52(a)(1). *In re Frescati*, 718 F.3d 184, 189, 196–97, 1 Adm. R. 80, 80–81, 86–87 (3d Cir. 2013).

We determined, among other things, that Frescati was a third-party beneficiary of CARCO's safe berth warranty, and that the allision occurred in the approach to **[—15—]** CARCO's terminal, meaning that CARCO had an unspecified duty of care to Frescati in tort. We remanded for the District Court to determine whether Frescati met the conditions for the safe berth warranty to apply. We also asked the District Court, if necessary, to determine the appropriate duty of care CARCO owed Frescati and whether CARCO breached that duty. 718 F.3d at 214–15, 1 Adm. R. at 102–03.

Judge Fullam retired before the case was remanded. Upon its return to the District Court, the case was assigned to the Honorable Joel H. Slomsky as a successor judge pursuant to Fed. R. Civ. P. 63. Under the terms of that rule, Judge Slomsky certified his familiarity with the record and recalled more than twenty witnesses over the course of a thirty-one-day proceeding. **{-299-}**

The District Court held that CARCO was liable to Frescati, and the United States as Frescati's subrogee, for breach of contract. CARCO's contract included a provision known as a safe berth warranty, which, for purposes of this appeal, warrantied that CARCO's berth would be safe for the *Athos I* as long as the ship had a draft of 37 feet or less and Frescati did not cause the allision through bad navigation or negligent seamanship. The District Court concluded that CARCO breached the warranty because the *Athos I* had a draft of 36′ 7″ at the time of the allision, exercised good navigation and seamanship, and yet still hit an anchor within the geographic area covered by the warranty. On appeal, **[—16—]** CARCO argues that the *Athos I* had a draft much deeper than the warrantied depth of 37 feet, and that Frescati demonstrated negligent seamanship by violating several federal maritime regulations relating to underkeel clearance and safe navigation.

The District Court also found CARCO liable in tort to Frescati,[7] concluding that CARCO had a duty, as operator of the berth, to search for obstructions in the approach to its berth. Specifically, the District Court concluded that CARCO had a duty to use side-scan sonar to search for unknown obstructions to navigation in the approach to its berth, and to remove any such obstructions or warn invited ships—like the *Athos I*—of their presence. Because CARCO had not taken any action to search for obstructions, the District Court held CARCO liable in tort—for the same amount for which it was liable in contract. The District Court's contract and tort holdings independently support the judgment for Frescati.

CARCO, in a motion for partial summary judgment before the District Court, asked that its liability, like Frescati's, be limited under the OPA. Because CARCO did not raise the defense until after the first trial and **[—17—]** appeal, almost a decade into this litigation, the District Court held that the defense was waived, and in the alternative, that it failed on the merits.

The District Court did, however, partially credit CARCO's equitable recoupment defense

[7] The United States is not a party to the tort claim, pursuant to a partial settlement agreement it reached with CARCO in 2009.

against the United States. CARCO argued that the conduct of three federal agencies—the Coast Guard, NOAA, and the Army Corps of Engineers—misled CARCO into believing that the United States was maintaining the anchorage free of obstructions. In addition, CARCO argued that equity requires the United States to bear the cost of the cleanup rather than CARCO. The District Court ultimately reduced the United States' recovery against CARCO by 50%, rather than acceding to CARCO's request to eliminate its liability entirely.

Finally, the District Court held that Frescati was entitled to prejudgment interest at the federal postjudgment rate rather than the higher U.S. prime rate requested by Frescati.

The District Court ultimately awarded Frescati $55,497,375.95[8] on the claims of **{-300-}** breach of contract and **[—18—]** negligence, plus prejudgment interest of $16,010,773.75, for a total judgment of $71,508,149.70. The United States, after the court's 50% reduction, was awarded $43,994,578.66 on its subrogated breach of contract claim, with prejudgment interest of $4,620,159.98, for a total judgment of $48,614,738.64.

All three parties now appeal. We will affirm the District Court's judgment in favor of Frescati on the breach of contract claim and the prejudgment interest award, as well as the District Court's denial of CARCO's motion for partial summary judgment on its limitation of liability defense. We will vacate the District Court's judgment in favor of Frescati on the negligence claim. We will affirm in part the District Court's judgment in favor of the United States with respect to CARCO's liability on the subrogated breach of contract claim, but because **[—19—]** CARCO's equitable recoupment defense fails, we will reverse and remand for further proceedings to recalculate damages and prejudgment interest.

III. Jurisdiction and Standard of Review

The District Court had admiralty jurisdiction pursuant to 28 U.S.C. § 1333(1). We have jurisdiction over this appeal under 28 U.S.C. § 1291.

"On appeal from a bench trial, we review a district court's findings of facts for clear error and exercise plenary review over conclusions of law." *Norfolk S. Ry. Co. v. Pittsburgh & W. Va. R.R.*, 870 F.3d 244, 253 (3d Cir. 2017). "A finding of fact is clearly erroneous when it is completely devoid of minimum evidentiary support displaying some hue of credibility or bears no rational relationship to the supportive evidentiary data." *VICI Racing, LLC v. T-Mobile USA, Inc.*, 763 F.3d 273, 283 (3d Cir. 2014); *In re Frescati*, 718 F.3d at 196, 1 Adm. R. at 86.

IV. The Safe Berth Warranty

CARCO promised that the *Athos I* would be directed to a location "she may safely get (always afloat)," a promise known as a safe port or safe berth warranty. JA at 1211. Such a promise provides, among other things, "protection against damages to a ship incurred in an unsafe port to which the warranty applies." *In re Frescati*, 718 F.3d at 197, 1 Adm. R. at 87. **[—20—]**

> A port is deemed safe where the particular chartered vessel can proceed to it, use it, and depart from it without, in the absence of abnormal weather or other occurrences, being exposed to dangers which cannot be avoided by good navigation and seamanship.

[8] Frescati's liability under the OPA for the cost of cleaning up the spill was limited to approximately $45 million. The United States reimbursed it for the remaining $88 million of its qualifying cleanup expenses. In addition to the $45 **[—18—]** million in OPA damages, Frescati also incurred roughly $10 million in damages that fell outside the scope of the OPA's liability cap—third-party claims; cleanup expenses for recreational boats; the cost of removing the anchor and the pump casing from the riverbed; a settlement with a nearby nuclear power plant that had to shut down; unrepaired hull damage to the *Athos I*, and other miscellaneous expenses. Frescati's contract recovery of $55 million was based on both its OPA and non-OPA damages.

> Whether a port is safe refers to the particular ship at issue, and goes beyond the immediate area of the port itself to the adjacent areas the vessel must traverse to either enter or leave. In other words, a port is unsafe—and in violation of the safe berth warranty—where the named ship cannot reach it without harm (absent abnormal conditions or those not avoidable by adequate navigation and seamanship).

Id. at 200, 1 Adm. R. at 89–90 (quotations and citations omitted). "[T]he safe berth warranty is an express assurance made without regard to the amount of diligence taken by the charterer." *Id.* at 203, 1 Adm. R. at 92. For our purposes, a safe berth warranty promises that a ship with a draft less than the warrantied depth is covered by the warranty in the absence of bad navigation or negligent seamanship.

Our prior opinion called for the District Court to resolve three issues on remand: the draft limit beyond which the safe berth **{-301-}** warranty would not apply; the actual draft of the *Athos I* at the time of the allision; and whether **[—21—]** the warranty was negated by bad navigation or negligent seamanship. *Id.* at 204–05, 204 n.20, 1 Adm. R. at 93–94, 93 n.20.

As an initial matter, the District Court found that the safe berth warranty applied to ships drawing less than 37 feet, a finding neither party challenges on appeal. The remaining issues, then, are whether the *Athos I* had a draft of less than 37 feet, and if it did, whether bad navigation or negligent seamanship by Frescati negated the warranty.

a. The Draft of the *Athos I*

The District Court found that the *Athos I* had a draft of 36′ 7″ at the time of the allision. The court based this finding on the undisputed draft of the *Athos I* at the time of its departure from Puerto Miranda—36′ 6″—as well as expert testimony regarding the condition of the ship and its estimated draft at Paulsboro.[9] **[—22—]**

CARCO challenges the District Court's determination of the *Athos I*'s draft, arguing that the District Court improperly based its finding on a speculative assumption about the orientation of the abandoned anchor. Specifically, CARCO disputes the District Court's finding that the anchor shifted from a flukes-down position to a flukes-up position sometime between 2001 and the allision in 2004, a shift that caused the anchor to intrude within the 37-foot safe depth promised by CARCO. CARCO argues that the District Court failed to make a finding as to the precise mechanism by which the anchor shifted from flukes-down to flukes-up. The anchor's orientation matters; if the accident occurred while the anchor was flukes-down, the *Athos I* necessarily would have had a draft that exceeded the scope of CARCO's warranty.[10] **[—23—]**

Broadly speaking, the District Court made three findings of fact related to the anchor's orientation. First, the court and parties agree that, three years before the allision, the anchor was in the flukes-down position.[11] Second, the District Court found that at some

[9] Frescati's expert, Anthony Bowman, developed the Seamaster software program, which allows him to enter the measurements of a ship—including the weight, dimensions, and strength of all its constituent parts, such as the hull, cargo, and supplies—and calculate, among other things, a ship's draft. Having considered the ship's records, information about the ballast tanks, and his own software, Bowman testified that at the time of the allision, **[—22—]** the Athos I had a draft of 36′ 7″. The District Court credited his testimony.

[10] The District Court made undisputed findings of fact as to the height of the anchor in a flukes-down position (41 inches or 3.42 feet) and the depth of the river at the time and location of the allision (41.65 feet). Assuming for the moment that the anchor was flukes-down, as CARCO argues, the allision would not have occurred unless the *Athos I* had a draft of at least 38.23 feet, or just under **[—23—]** 38′ 3″, significantly in excess of the warrantied draft of 37 feet.

[11] Experts for both sides were able to identify the flukes-down anchor in a sonar scan performed in 2001 as part of an independent geophysical study.

point before the allision, the anchor shifted into the flukes-up position. Finally, after the allision, the anchor was eventually discovered back in the flukes-down position—perhaps unsurprising, given the force of its encounter with the *Athos I*.

CARCO attacks the second finding, arguing that there was insufficient evidence in the record to support the District Court's suggestion that a "sweeping anchor chain" could have caught the anchor and shifted it into the flukes-up position.[12] **[—24—] {-302-}**

We find CARCO's arguments unconvincing, primarily because the "sweeping anchor chain" theory, however plausible or implausible, is not necessary to sustain the District Court's finding. Let us imagine a piece of furniture (a sofa, perhaps, or an armchair) that has fallen off the back of a pickup truck onto a roadway. One driver reports seeing the furniture in the right lane. A while later, a second driver hits the furniture. The second driver asserts that the furniture was in the left lane when he struck it, and provides evidence to that effect. A highway patrolman **[—25—]** shows up later and finds the furniture once again in the right lane. A court may find, without committing error, that the furniture was in the right lane and moved to the left without making a specific finding as to the precise method by which the furniture moved from one lane to the other. Perhaps another driver hit it; perhaps a pedestrian tried to move it out of the road but did not finish the job. When credible evidence shows that the second driver was driving in the left lane, a finding to that effect does not become error because the furniture was in the right lane when the first driver passed, or changed position after—or because of—the encounter with the second driver.

Here, the record contains sufficient evidence to support the finding that the anchor was, in fact, flukes-up at the time of the allision. How exactly the anchor changed position does not impact our sufficiency determination. As an initial matter, the movement of the *Athos I* at the time of the allision and the damage to its hull are sufficient to show that the anchor was flukes-up. And substantial evidence unrelated to the anchor showed that the *Athos I* was drawing 36′ 7″ at the time of the allision—a draft at which the allision would not have occurred had the anchor been flukes-down. That is enough to support the District Court's finding that the anchor moved from flukes-down to flukes-up.

The movement of the ship and damage to its hull shows that the anchor must have been flukes-up. The **[—26—]** District Court found that the *Athos I* was moving astern and to port at the time of the allision, a finding CARCO does not challenge. Based on that movement, the scoring left by the anchor on the hull, the size and shape of the two holes the anchor created, and the damage to the anchor itself also supported the District Court's finding that the anchor must have been flukes-up at the time of the allision. CARCO's own expert witness, on cross-examination, testified that if the *Athos I* were moving astern and to port, the damage to the *Athos I*'s hull would necessarily require a flukes-up anchor.[13] JA at 1021–22. **{-303-}**

[12] Ships at anchor move with the tide, back and forth as the tide comes in and goes out. The anchor chain drags or "sweeps" across the riverbed as the ship floats, potentially shifting the position of objects on the riverbed, and leaving scour marks on the riverbed. Anchor chains also move **[—24—]** along the river bottom when the anchor is pulled back onto the ship. CARCO, for its part, characterizes the idea that an anchor chain might have moved the abandoned anchor as "fantastical," "inexplicabl[e]," an "astonishing assertion," "facially implausible," "pure and wild speculation," "pure speculation," "conjecture," "speculative and unsupported," and, once again, "implausible." CARCO Opening Br. 4, 53–55; CARCO Reply Br. 32. The District Court pointed out that scour marks were found on the river bottom near the site of the allision, but ultimately decided only that the anchor was in the flukes-up position at the time of the allision. JA at 78 ("Although the actual cause of the anchor's movement to a 'flukes-up' position will never be known, the Court finds that at some point after December 2001, this movement occurred and the anchor was positioned in a 'flukes-up' orientation when it allided with the Athos I.").

[13] CARCO's theory at trial, abandoned on appeal, was that the ship was *not* moving astern and to port.

Nor did the District Court base its finding of a 36′ 7″ draft on the flukes-up anchor alone. While CARCO argues that the anchor was flukes-down, and that therefore the *Athos I* must have had a deep draft, the reverse is also true. If the *Athos I* had a draft of 36′ 7″, then the anchor must have been flukes-up. The District Court credited expert testimony that the ship had a 36′ 7″ draft. The ballast tanks contained no extra liquid that would have affected the ship's draft, a finding that CARCO does not challenge on appeal. The ship left Puerto Miranda with a draft of 36′ 6″. Visual observation of the ship by experts and crewmembers immediately after the allision suggested the *Athos I* had a 36′ 7″ draft before the allision. And, on **[—27—]** appeal, CARCO fails to offer any suggestion as to how the draft might have increased by more than a foot without the crew's knowledge or any evidence that the ballast tanks were faulty.[14]

We conclude there was no clear error in the District Court's determination that the *Athos I* had a draft of 36′ 7″ at the time of the allision. The ship was, therefore, within the scope of CARCO's safe berth warranty.

b. Frescati's Seamanship

A safe berth warranty applies only in the absence of bad navigation or negligent seamanship. CARCO argues on appeal that Frescati violated several maritime regulations related to the operation of single-hulled tankers, and that those regulatory violations serve as sufficient proof of negligent seamanship. The District Court concluded that Frescati did not violate any relevant regulations, and enforced the safe berth warranty. We **[—28—]** agree with the District Court that Frescati did not violate any relevant regulations.

On appeal, CARCO argues specifically that Frescati violated two federal regulations: 33 C.F.R. § 157.455 and 33 C.F.R. § 164.11. Section 157.455 applied to certain single-hulled tankers during the period they were being phased out of operation, while § 164.11 applies to certain ships above 1,600 gross tons. 33 C.F.R. §§ 157.400, 164.01. Both sections applied to the *Athos I* at the time of the allision.

Section 157.455 requires the owner or operator of a single-hulled tanker to provide certain written guidance to the ship's master for purposes of estimating the tanker's underkeel clearance.[15] **{-304-}** 33 C.F.R.

[14] The *Athos I* passed safely over a 38-foot shoal less than fifteen minutes before the allision. JA at 203. It seems that if the *Athos I* had a draft deep enough to hit the flukes-down anchor (a minimum of 38.23 feet, *see* supra note 10), it would have encountered the 38-foot shoal before it ever encountered the anchor. A flukes-down anchor would have been deeper than the 38-foot shoal even at the anchor's shallowest point. JA at 77, 78, 85.

[15] 33 C.F.R. § 157.455(a)–(b) reads:

(a) The owner or operator of a tankship, that is not fitted with a double bottom that covers the entire cargo tank length, shall provide the tankship master with written under-keel clearance guidance that includes—
   (1) Factors to consider when calculating the ship's deepest navigational draft; **[—29—]**
   (2) Factors to consider when calculating the anticipated controlling depth;
   (3) Consideration of weather or environmental conditions; and
   (4) Conditions which mandate when the tankship owner or operator shall be contacted prior to port entry or getting underway; if no such conditions exist, the guidance must contain a statement to that effect.

(b) Prior to entering the port or place of destination and prior to getting underway, the master of a tankship that is not fitted with the double bottom that covers the entire cargo tank length shall plan the ship's passage using guidance issued under paragraph (a) of this section and estimate the anticipated under-keel clearance. The tankship master and the pilot shall discuss the ship's planned transit including the anticipated under-keel clearance. An entry must be made in the tankship's official log or in other **[—30—]** onboard documentation reflec-

§ 157.455(a). It also **[—29—]** **[—30—]** requires the master to use that guidance to plan the ship's passage, estimate the underkeel clearance, consult with the relevant pilots who will guide the ship to its berth, and make a log entry reflecting discussion of the ship's underkeel clearance with the pilot. 33 C.F.R. § 157.455(b). Section 164.11 mandates that the master ensure the pilot is informed of certain information, including the ship's draft and tidal conditions.[16] 33 C.F.R. § 164.11. **[—31—]**

CARCO argues that Frescati was responsible for three specific violations, each of which allegedly caused the allision. First, CARCO claims that Frescati failed to adequately plan the ship's passage. Second, CARCO claims that Frescati failed to estimate the *Athos I*'s underkeel clearance. Finally, CARCO claims that Frescati failed to ensure that an adequate master-pilot exchange occurred, and made no log entry that would reflect such an exchange.

With respect to planning the passage, CARCO argues that 33 C.F.R. § 157.455 requires a written voyage plan. Frescati allegedly violated that requirement by failing to finalize an official voyage plan document using the Tsakos Voyage Plan form contained in the Tsakos Vessel Operation Procedures Manual. *See* JA at 1178–85.

The text of § 157.455 undermines CARCO's argument. The regulation does not itself require a *written* voyage plan. Paragraph (a) of the regulation requires that Frescati create "written under-keel clearance guidance," which must contain "factors to consider" when evaluating **[—32—]** draft, water depth, and weather conditions. Paragraph (b) requires that the master plan the ship's passage using those "factors to consider" in the guidance required by paragraph (a). Nowhere does this regulation require that the master's passage plan be in writing; the only reference to a writing in paragraph (b) comes in the requirement that some official log of the master-pilot conference be recorded. CARCO conflates the passage plan requirement of paragraph (b)—to consider certain relevant factors when planning—with the "Voyage Plan" form contained in Frescati's Vessel Operation Procedures Manual. *See* JA at 1180. The Voyage Plan form focuses on plotting the course of the vessel from berth to berth; paragraphs (a) and (b) of the regulation, on the other hand, serve to create a reference list for the ship's master of relevant factors to consider when estimating underkeel clearance.

Frescati satisfied the requirements of paragraph (a) by providing written underkeel clearance guidance in Section 3.4[17] of its Vessel Operation Procedures Manual. **{-305-}** JA at 1191. The Manual appropriately lists factors to consider, including "sea state and swell," "tidal **[—33—]** conditions," and "the effect of squat,"[18] and suggests to the master

---

> ting discussion of the ship's anticipated passage.

33 C.F.R. § 157.455(a)–(b).

[16] 33 C.F.R. § 164.11 reads:

> The owner, master, or person in charge of each vessel underway shall ensure that:
>
> . . . .
>
> (k) If a pilot other than a member of the vessel's crew is employed, the pilot is informed of the draft, maneuvering characteristics, and peculiarities of the vessel and of any abnormal circumstances on the vessel that may affect its safe navigation. **[—31—]**
>
> . . .
>
> (n) Tidal state for the area to be transited is known by the person directing movement of the vessel . . . .

33 C.F.R. § 164.11.

[17] The Vessel Operation Procedures Manual appears to contain a typographical error listing the appropriate section as 2.4 rather than 3.4, as it appears in the Table of Contents. *See* JA at 1189, 1191.

[18] "Squat is a hydrodynamic phenomenon, which occurs when a ship is moving through the waters. As a ship moves forward, it displaces a volume of water. The displaced water rushes under the keel of the ship and creates a low pressure area causing the ship to sink down toward the riverbed. The faster a ship is moving, the more the ship will sink down towards the riverbed. This process

that 10% or 5% underkeel clearance margins would typically be appropriate. *Id.*

Furthermore, Frescati satisfied the planning requirement of paragraph (b) because the *Athos I*'s master, Captain Markoutsis, considered factors like the sea state, tidal condition, and the effect of squat. Even though CARCO provided a safe berth warranty for a draft up to 37 feet, Captain Markoutsis loaded the ship to only 36′ 6″ because he was "afraid" of a 37-foot draft, and eventually entered the Delaware River with a draft of 36′ 7″. *In re Frescati,* 718 F.3d at 204, 1 Adm. R. at 93. The charts in the *Athos I* were marked with the 38-foot controlling draft in the anchorage. JA at 992. Captain Teal, the river pilot, testified that he and Captain Markoutsis discussed the draft, wind, visibility, and tides. We agree with the District Court that Frescati fully complied with the planning requirement of **[—34—]** § 157.455(b)—that is, to use the factors listed in the Vessel Operating Procedures Manual when planning the passage.

CARCO's second argument is that Frescati violated § 157.455(b) because Captain Markoutsis failed to estimate the *Athos I*'s underkeel clearance. The District Court did not err in finding that Captain Markoutsis had estimated underkeel clearance. Captain Markoutsis discussed the draft, tidal conditions, and anticipated underkeel clearance with Captain Teal. JA at 801–802. They estimated that the ship would have at least 1.5 meters' clearance—nearly five feet. *Id.* Captains Bethel and Markoutsis also discussed the draft and believed they would have sufficient clearance. JA at 833, 837. CARCO highlights that there is no evidence of *written* underkeel clearance estimates, but § 157.455 does not require written estimates.

Finally, CARCO argues that the master-pilot exchange required by § 157.455 and § 164.11 was inadequate. In general, master-pilot exchanges are intended to allow the master to share the navigational characteristics of his ship with the pilot who will be guiding it, and for the pilot to share local conditions such as weather, depth, and the tide with the master. Section 157.455(b) requires that "[t]he tankship master and the pilot shall discuss the ship's planned transit including the anticipated under-keel clearance. An entry must be made **[—35—]** in the tankship's official log or in other onboard documentation reflecting discussion of the ship's anticipated passage." 33 C.F.R. § 157.455(b). Section 164.11 requires that the master ensure that

> [i]f a pilot other than a member of the vessel's crew is employed, the pilot is informed of the draft, maneuvering characteristics, and peculiarities of the vessel and of any abnormal circumstances on the vessel that may affect its safe navigation. . . . [and that the] [t]idal state for the area to be transited is known by the person directing movement of the vessel.

33 C.F.R. § 164.11(k), (n).

Captain Markoutsis was responsible for discussing the draft, underkeel clearance, maneuvering characteristics, and tidal **{-306-}** state with the two pilots who guided the *Athos I.* The testimony shows that Captain Markoutsis did so, discussing all the relevant information with both pilots, and that he recorded the conversation on the signed Pilot Card, which served as sufficient documentation of the master-pilot conference. The District Court additionally credited Frescati's expert witness, Captain Betz, who observed both Captain Teal and Captain Bethel testify. Captain Betz opined that the **[—36—]** master-pilot exchanges were adequate and customary in all respects.

Frescati operated the *Athos I* with neither bad navigation nor negligent seamanship. Nevertheless, the allision occurred. The District Court did not err in concluding that the allision resulted from a breach of CARCO's safe berth warranty.

causes a ship to be closer to the riverbed by increasing a vessel's draft." JA at 70 (citations omitted).

V. Wharfinger Negligence

CARCO wore two hats in its dealings with Frescati, as a shipping customer and as a wharfinger. These dual roles exposed CARCO to liability under two independent legal theories. CARCO's first role, as a shipping customer that contracted with Frescati for delivery of a shipment of crude oil, resulted in CARCO's liability under the contractual safe berth warranty, discussed above. The second, as the wharfinger for the Paulsboro berth that was the *Athos I*'s intended destination, resulted in the District Court's finding of negligence and CARCO's corresponding liability in tort.

Both theories of liability independently support the District Court's judgment against CARCO. As a result, our decision to affirm the judgment based on CARCO's contractual liability means that we are not required to delve into the District Court's tort analysis. However, having reviewed that analysis, we harbor serious doubts **[—37—]** about the appropriateness of the court's proposed duty of care. For that reason, we are compelled to make clear that we will affirm the District Court's judgment based solely on CARCO's breach of contract.

A wharfinger's duty is more limited than that of a shipping customer who has provided a safe berth warranty. As we previously wrote:

> In the tort context, . . . a wharfinger is not a guarantor of a visiting ship's safety, but is bound to use reasonable diligence in ascertaining whether the berths themselves and the approaches to them are in an ordinary condition of safety for vessels coming to and lying at the wharf. This is not an unconstrained mandate to ensure safe surroundings or warn of hazards merely in the vicinity. Instead, a visiting ship may only expect that the owner of a wharf has afforded it a safe approach. In being invited to dock at a particular port, a vessel should be able to enter, use and exit a wharfinger's dock facilities without being exposed to dangers that cannot be avoided by reasonably prudent navigation and seamanship.

In re Frescati, 718 F.3d at 207, 1 Adm. R. at 96 (quotations and citations omitted). In short, and as a general matter, a wharfinger's **[—38—]** duty is to use reasonable diligence to ascertain whether the approach to its berth is safe for an invited vessel.[19]

We remanded for the District Court to determine in the first instance what reasonable diligence required of CARCO under the circumstances of this case, and whether CARCO breached that standard. **{-307-}** *Id.*, 1 Adm. R. at 99. On remand, the District Court concluded that

> a reasonably prudent terminal operator should periodically scan the approach to its dock for hazards to navigation as long as ships are being invited there. In this case, the standard would require that side-scan sonar be used to search the approach for obstructions that are potential hazards to navigation. If an obstruction is located, a terminal operator is then required to remove it, and if the terminal operator cannot remove it, notice of the hazard must be given to **[—39—]** incoming ships by marking it as a hazard and/or warning ships of its presence.

JA at 132. Because CARCO did nothing to look for obstructions, the District Court held that it had breached its duty.

The District Court chose its standard by determining what the "demands of reasonableness and prudence" required. JA at 129. Citing Judge Learned Hand's famous formula from *United States v. Carroll Towing*, 159 F.2d 169 (2d Cir. 1947), the court concluded that the precaution of a preemptive side-scan sonar search would be less

[19] We previously determined that the allision occurred in the approach to CARCO's berth—the geographic area within which a wharfinger's duty exists—and as a result, CARCO had a duty to use reasonable diligence to provide the *Athos I* with a safe approach. *In re Frescati*, 718 F.3d at 211, 1 Adm. R. at 99.

burdensome than the probability of an allision multiplied by the serious harm caused by a spill of toxic substances like crude oil.

We have doubts about the District Court's balancing of the cost of preventative measures on one hand and the cost of potential accidents on the other. The court found that a general scan of the approach to CARCO's berth and the berth itself would have cost between $7,500 and $11,000, and would have prevented the allision. Yet in this very case, the targeted scan of the area where the allision occurred, conducted only eight days after the allision, did not identify the anchor. The first set of 93 side-scan sonar passes conducted by Frescati's expert, John Fish—at a cost of $38,577—identified a pump casing on the river bottom. The anchor, however, went **[—40—]** unrecognized.[20] We do not share the District Court's confidence that a general $11,000 scan of the approach and berth would have "recognized" the anchor with sufficient clarity to prevent the allision, given that a targeted $38,000 scan for obstructions failed to do so.

Beyond the questionable utility of side-scan sonar as applied to this case, we doubt whether imposing a specific duty to require side-scan sonar would be useful for wharfingers in the ordinary course of their business. Single-hulled vessels like the *Athos I* present unique risks, and have been treated with special care by regulators. *See, e.g.*, 33 C.F.R. § 157.455. Today, as a result of those unique risks, such vessels are no longer permitted to operate in the waters of the United States. *See* 46 U.S.C. § 3703a (banning single-hulled oil tankers in the waters of the United States after January 1, 2015). Furthermore, side-scan sonar is not the only method available to detect and recognize obstructions, as the District Court pointed out.[21] Even if we were to accept the court's balancing of **[—41—]** cost, risk, and the magnitude of the potential harm, the high standard set forth in **{-308-}** this case—involving a risky single-hulled vessel—would not necessarily apply to future cases, which will necessarily involve only double-hulled vessels.[22]

We are not unsympathetic to the position in which we placed the District Court by asking it to specify the duty of care at play in this case. The District Court has conscientiously complied. And we stand by our previous holding that CARCO had some duty to use reasonable diligence to provide the *Athos I* with a safe approach to its **[—42—]** berth—a duty it may or may not have breached. *In re Frescati*, 718 F.3d at 211, 1 Adm. R. at 99. Nevertheless, given CARCO's independent liability in contract and our decision to affirm on that basis, we will once again decline to outline precisely what CARCO's duty of reasonable diligence entailed.

VI. Subrogation and Equitable Recoupment

This litigation does not implicate the interests of only Frescati and CARCO. The United States reimbursed Frescati for $88 million in cleanup expenses above the liability limit established by the OPA. Consequently, the United States became subrogated to

---

[20] Fish testified that the side-scan sonar equipment "detected" the anchor, but neither he nor anyone else "recognized" it until after the second set of scans were taken. JA at 927.

[21] The court determined that CARCO should have used side-scan sonar to search for obstructions, but seemed willing to accept that other methods of searching for **[—41—]** obstructions might accomplish the same purpose. It noted that "side-scan sonar . . . is not the only method available in the industry to search for hazardous debris. . . . Since the standard of care involves factual issues, the methods may vary when the conditions in the approach to each terminal are examined." JA at 132 n.109.

[22] Indeed, five years after the *Athos I* allision, the Norwegian tanker *SKS Satilla*, carrying nearly 42 million gallons of crude oil, allided with a sunken oil rig in the Gulf of Mexico, sustaining "substantial damage to the port side of her hull." Findings of Fact and Conclusions of Law, *In re Ensco Offshore Co.*, No. 4:09-CV-2838, ECF No. 185 at 3, ¶¶ 6–7 (S.D. Tex. Sept. 30, 2014). But "[b]ecause the SATILLA [was] a double hulled vessel[,] . . . there was no discharge of crude oil." *Id.* at 3, ¶ 9.

Frescati's claims, and joined the fray by filing suit against CARCO in 2008.[23] **[—43—]**

Frescati initially paid for the oil spill cleanup costs as a "responsible party" under the OPA. *See* 33 U.S.C. § 2702(a). The OPA allows a responsible party like Frescati to limit its liability to a specified sum; any cleanup costs above that amount are reimbursed out of the Oil Spill Liability Trust Fund.[24] *See* 33 U.S.C. § 2704. Under this **[—44—]** scheme, Frescati's liability for the cost of the oil spill cleanup was limited to approximately **{-309-}** $45 million. The Trust Fund reimbursed Frescati for its remaining cleanup costs, which totaled approximately $88 million. The United States then became statutorily "subrogated to all rights, claims, and causes of action that the claimant [Frescati] has under any other law." 33 U.S.C. § 2715(a). The United States pursued these claims against CARCO as a "person who is liable, pursuant to any law, to the compensated claimant [Frescati] or to the Fund, for the cost or damages for which the compensation was paid." 33 U.S.C. § 2715(c).

Pursuant to the partial settlement agreement, the United States limited itself to the same contractual claims Frescati asserted. Because CARCO was liable to Frescati in contract, it was also liable to the United States for the amount the Trust Fund had reimbursed Frescati: nearly $88 million. But CARCO asserted a defense against the United States it did not assert against Frescati—equitable **[—45—]** recoupment—and in response, the District Court reduced the United States' judgment by 50%. Both CARCO and the United States appealed. CARCO argues that the District Court erred by not eliminating the United States' recovery, while the United States argues that the District Court should have left the contract judgment untouched and denied CARCO any equitable remedy. We conclude that the District Court erred by reducing the United States' judgment by 50%. The United States is entitled to a full recovery.

a. Subrogation and Subrogee-Specific Defenses

As an initial matter, we note that the dispute between CARCO and the United States presents an unusual question about the nature of subrogation. Subrogation itself is not unusual; in general terms, it "simply means substitution of one person for another; that is, one person is allowed to stand in the shoes of another and assert that person's rights against a third party." *US Airways v. McCutchen*, 569 U.S. 88, 97 n.5 (2013). Most often, it arises in the insurance context as a

---

[23] The United States and CARCO reached a partial settlement agreement before the first trial. Both the United States and CARCO agreed to forgo any negligence claims they might have had against one another. The parties agreed that the United States would pursue only its contract claim against CARCO. As a result, the United States' judgment against CARCO was based solely on CARCO's contractual liability under the safe berth warranty. CARCO, for its part, reserved in the settlement agreement

> each and every substantive and procedural right available to a defendant . . . including **[—43—]** but not limited to the right to raise affirmative defenses under any theory or doctrine of law or equity, the right to assert setoff or recoupment and the right to assert compulsory or non-compulsory counterclaims other than a Claim for Contribution or Indemnity . . . .

JA at 391.

[24] The Oil Spill Liability Trust Fund, administered by the Coast Guard, serves much like insurance for the oil transportation industry. Companies that import oil into the United States pay a per-barrel fee into the Trust Fund. When a tanker vessel spills oil, the OPA assigns liability for the cleanup to a "responsible party"—typically the owner of the vessel from which the oil spilled. The responsible party is liable for all cleanup costs associated with the spill. If the costs exceed a liability cap established by the OPA, the Trust Fund reimburses the responsible party for all expenses above the statutory cap. Liability under the OPA does not preclude a responsible party from **[—44—]** bringing any claims it has against a third party under any other law. The United States, to the extent the Trust Fund has reimbursed the responsible party's costs, steps into the shoes of the responsible party as subrogee and may pursue claims against a third party as if it were the responsible party. Any recovery won by the United States is returned to the Trust Fund to cover future oil spill reimbursements.

procedural mechanism to allow an insurer (the subrogee) to step into the shoes of its insured (the subrogor) after it has compensated the insured for harm caused by a third party. The subrogee, having stepped into the shoes of the subrogor, is entitled to assert all of the subrogor's rights and claims against the responsible third party. Likewise, **[—46—]** the third party—now defending an action brought by the subrogee—is entitled to assert every defense it otherwise could have raised against the subrogor. In that vein, the third party's liability to a subrogee cannot be greater than it would have been to the subrogor. Restatement (Third) of Restitution & Unjust Enrichment § 24.

All that is unexceptional. The unusual question presented here is whether a third party may assert a defense against a subrogee that it could *not* assert against the subrogor. As we discussed above, CARCO is liable to Frescati, the subrogor, in contract. Consequently, CARCO is liable to the United States, the subrogee, under that very same contract. But CARCO wishes to assert a defense against the United States—namely, that equitable recoupment requires the United States to bear the loss rather than CARCO because of the allegedly misleading conduct of three federal agencies—that it could not assert against Frescati.

The United States makes a related argument. Its position is that the equitable recoupment defense, predicated as it is on the conduct of federal agencies rather than the contractual relationship between Frescati and the United States, violates the **{-310-}** statutory subrogation provision of the OPA. Specifically, the United States argues that it is entitled to "all [of Frescati's] rights, claims, and causes of action" under the OPA. 33 U.S.C. § 2715(a). Frescati's contractual right is not limited by CARCO's claims **[—47—]** against the Coast Guard, NOAA, and the Army Corps of Engineers; the United States asserting Frescati's contractual right should also not be so limited, and to do otherwise would infringe on the United States' statutory entitlement. When Frescati has the right to a full recovery under its contract, the argument goes, so does the United States.

We agree. CARCO may only assert defenses against the United States' subrogated claims which it could have asserted against Frescati—including any equitable recoupment defense it could have asserted against Frescati. In its capacity as a subrogee, the United States should be subject to the same treatment as Frescati. Just as the United States, as subrogee, may only assert Frescati's claims, CARCO, as defendant, is not entitled to extra defenses because the United States asserts Frescati's claims rather than Frescati itself. Of course, no party is exempt from the Federal Rules of Civil Procedure. The United States is subject to the ordinary procedural rules governing counterclaims and third-party complaints, and the OPA does not bar CARCO from asserting whatever claims it has against the United States using those recognized procedural mechanisms where appropriate.[25] **[—48—]**

In this case, the only claim asserted by the United States is Frescati's contract claim. *In re Frescati*, 718 F.3d at 189, 1 Adm. R. at 80; JA at 390. It follows that CARCO's equitable recoupment defense must be directed toward the United States' contract claim. *See* 718 F.3d at 214, 1 Adm. R. at 102 (declining to preclude CARCO from raising "equitable defense[s] to the Government's subrogation claims"). If CARCO had other cognizable claims against the three federal agencies involved in regulating the Delaware River and the anchorage, sounding in tort or otherwise, it was free to assert them in a third-party

[25] This issue is complicated by the fact that the specific defense asserted by CARCO, equitable recoupment, is sometimes pleaded as a defense, and sometimes as a **[—48—]** counterclaim. We do not mean to imply that CARCO should have pleaded equitable recoupment as a counterclaim rather than a defense. However it is pleaded, "recoupment is in the nature of a defense arising out of some feature of the transaction upon which the plaintiff's action is grounded," and here, the plaintiff's action is grounded in Frescati's contractual right. *Bull v. United States*, 295 U.S. 247, 262 (1935). To the extent CARCO had cognizable claims against the Coast Guard, NOAA, and the Army Corps of Engineers, it should have asserted those claims directly, rather than as a defense to Frescati's now-subrogated contract claim.

complaint or counterclaim, just as the United States was free to pursue other claims against CARCO.[26] In that light, we proceed to analyze CARCO's **[—49—]** equitable recoupment **{-311-}** defense as it applies to the United States' contractual rights.

b. Equitable Recoupment

Equitable recoupment is a "principle that diminishes a party's right to recover a debt to the extent that the party holds money or property of the debtor to which the party has no right."[27] *In re Frescati*, 718 F.3d at **[—50—]** 214 n.35, 1 Adm. R. at 102 n.35. For an equitable recoupment defense to succeed, the defendant must possess a claim against the plaintiff arising from the same transaction or occurrence as the plaintiff's suit, seeking relief of the same kind as that sought by the plaintiff, in an amount no greater than that **[—51—]** sought by the plaintiff. *See Livera v. First Nat'l State Bank of New Jersey*, 879 F.2d 1186, 1195 (3d Cir. 1989).

CARCO's equitable recoupment defense faces at least two serious obstacles. As an initial matter, the United States questions whether CARCO possesses a "claim" against it, rather than a generalized request for the court to balance the equities. Second, the United States questions whether CARCO seeks relief of the same kind as the United States. On both points, CARCO fails to meet its burden.

CARCO's claim, such as it is, appears to be that the equities favor CARCO, and require the United States to bear the cost of the spill. CARCO argues that the United States, through the Coast Guard, NOAA, and the Army Corps of Engineers, had responsibility for maintaining the anchorage where the allision occurred free of obstructions. In the alternative, if the agencies were not responsible to preemptively search for obstructions, CARCO argues they should have more explicitly made clear that they were not conducting such searches. CARCO asserts that it reasonably believed, based on the agencies' conduct, that the agencies were maintaining the anchorage free of obstructions. Additionally, CARCO argues that equity **[—52—]** requires the Oil Spill Liability Trust Fund to bear the cost of the cleanup rather than CARCO.[28] **[—53—]** **{-312-}**

---

[26] CARCO was also free to waive its claims against the United States, and vice versa. Indeed, both CARCO and **[—49—]** the United States waived certain rights in the 2009 partial settlement agreement, including CARCO's waivers of the rights to bring a "Claim for Contribution or Indemnity . . . whether based on principles of common law, contract, quasi-contract or tort," and "demand that the court reduce or offset the damages awarded to the United States . . . based on evidence that the negligence or fault of the United States in failing to detect, mark and/or remove underwater obstructions to navigation . . . caused or contributed to the ATHOS I Incident." JA at 389. At an earlier stage in the litigation, the United States argued that CARCO's equitable recoupment defense amounted to a violation of the settlement agreement. The United States eventually waived that argument by failing to raise it at the first trial, and so we need not consider it today. *In re Frescati*, 718 F.3d at 214, 1 Adm. R. at 102.

[27] A classic example of recoupment is a situation in which the statute of limitations is different for two related claims **[—50—]** arising out of the same transaction—when, for example, the statute of limitations period during which the United States may file a claim against a taxpayer for underpayment of the income tax is longer than the period during which a taxpayer may file a claim for a refund of overpayment of the estate tax. The taxpayer (in this case, the estate of a decedent) pays the estate tax and final year's income tax. Sometime later, after the statute of limitations has run on the estate tax overpayment but not the income tax underpayment, the government claims the taxpayer owes additional income tax for the taxpayer's final year. Due to the increased income tax liability for the year, the taxpayer now owes less in estate tax—but the statute of limitations has already run, and the taxpayer cannot amend the estate tax return. In an action brought by the government to recover the extra income tax owed, the taxpayer may assert an equitable recoupment defense for the amount of the overpayment of the estate tax, even though the statute of limitations has run and the taxpayer would not otherwise have been able to recover the overpayment. *See generally Bull v. United States*, 295 U.S. 247 (1935).

[28] Though it is not necessary to our holding, we note that these equities do not appear to favor CARCO. As to agency regulation and maintenance of the anchorage where the allision occurred, the District Court held that the agencies did not have a

Equitable recoupment requires more than just a request to balance the equities. CARCO points out that although equitable recoupment most often arises in the context of offsetting monetary claims, as in tax or bankruptcy cases, it is not necessarily limited to those situations. *See, e.g., Oneida Indian Nation of New York v.* **[—54—]** *New York*, 194 F. Supp. 2d 104, 136–37 (N.D.N.Y. 2002) (allowing an equitable recoupment defense in the context of offsetting requests for declaratory judgments in a land rights case). But CARCO still must assert some cognizable claim, rather than simply a request for the Court to reduce the United States' damages in the interest of equity. Here, CARCO has failed to do so.

Neither does CARCO seek the same kind of relief as the United States. The United States seeks contractual relief, to which it is entitled by operation of statute. *See* 33 U.S.C. § 2715. CARCO, by contrast, seeks equitable relief, or (on another reading) essentially tort-based relief grounded in misrepresentation by the agencies. The mismatched relief sought by CARCO and the United States does not support CARCO's equitable recoupment defense.

The requirement that a defendant seek the same kind of relief as has been sought in the plaintiff's claim is a fundamental requisite for recoupment. The defense is not intended to be a catch-all to allow any claims otherwise barred by time, settlement, or statute to be heard as equity seems to require. Equitable recoupment is intended to allow only truly similar claims arising from the same transaction to offset one another in the interest of equity between the parties. As noted, equitable recoupment is well-suited for disputes in which two claims arise out of the same taxable event or the same contractual obligation, **[—55—]** as often seen in tax or bankruptcy cases. When, as here, the plaintiff seeks relief on a contract, the defendant may not resort to equitable recoupment as a means to assert a non-contractual claim, whether sounding in an equitable-balancing analysis, in tort, or otherwise.

CARCO has failed to meet its burden of establishing an equitable recoupment defense. It is liable to the United States in full. **{-313-}**

VII. Limitation of Liability under the Oil Pollution Act

CARCO argues that a provision of the OPA, 33 U.S.C. § 2702(d)(2)(B), limits its liability in this case to the same extent to which Frescati's liability was limited—approximately $45 million. Because CARCO did not raise this defense with the requisite

---

duty to maintain the anchorage free of obstructions. The United States does not preemptively search for obstructions in the anchorage, it is not responsible for doing so, and it did not tell CARCO that it would do so. To the extent CARCO believed otherwise, CARCO simply misunderstood the regulatory structure and the responsibilities (and indeed, the capabilities) of the agencies.

Additionally, to the extent—if at all—that the Coast Guard, NOAA, and the Army Corps of Engineers were responsible for the *Athos I* oil spill, reducing the recovery of the United States in this case would not be equitable. Beyond our concerns relating to subrogation (equity would certainly not favor reducing Frescati's recovery under these circumstances), such a decision would impose liability on the Oil Spill Liability Trust Fund, not the responsible agencies. Any recovery based on the United States' subrogated claim flows back to the Trust Fund, out of which the United States originally reimbursed Frescati. 26 U.S.C. § 9509(b)(3). The Trust Fund is not intended (or **[—53—]** allowed by statute) to be used as a slush fund to cover the liabilities of federal agencies. *See* 33 U.S.C. § 2712 ("Uses of the Fund").

As a final point, the purpose of the Trust Fund is not to absorb the cost of cleaning up oil spills; indeed, almost the opposite is true. The OPA creates a strict liability regime for responsible parties, while capping that liability at a set amount. But the Trust Fund was not designed to bear those costs indefinitely; the subrogation provision of 33 U.S.C. § 2715 allows the United States, on behalf of the Trust Fund, to pursue any claim a responsible party could have brought against a third party under any law, in order to recover the money paid out by the Trust Fund and preserve the Trust Fund's ability to respond quickly to spills in the future. The OPA is intended to quickly compensate victims of spills, minimize environmental damage, and internalize the costs of oil spills within the oil industry. The subrogation provision serves those purposes by letting cleanup costs fall upon the liable party, rather than with the Trust Fund.

clarity until nearly ten years after this litigation began, the District Court concluded that CARCO waived it. We agree that the defense was waived.

A District Court's holding that an affirmative defense has been waived is reviewed for abuse of discretion. *Cetel v. Kirwan Financial Group, Inc.*, 460 F.3d 494, 506 (3d Cir. 2006). Waiver is appropriate if the party raising the defense did not do so at a "pragmatically sufficient time" and if the opposing party would be prejudiced if the defense were allowed. *Charpentier v. Godsil*, 937 F.2d 859, 864 (3d Cir. 1991). **[—56—]**

Whether CARCO raised its defense at a pragmatically sufficient time requires us to determine *when* CARCO first raised the § 2702(d)(2)(B) defense. CARCO argues that it first raised the limitation defense in its 2005 answer to Frescati's Amended Counterclaim by referring to the OPA. The District Court concluded that CARCO's answer contained nothing that would have put Frescati or the United States on notice that CARCO planned to rely on a limitation of liability defense. In general, "[a]n affirmative defense . . . 'need not be articulated with any rigorous degree of specificity, and is sufficiently raised for purposes of [Fed. R. Civ. P. 8] by its bare assertion.' " *Moody v. Atl. City Bd. of Educ.*, 870 F.3d 206, 218 (3d Cir. 2017) (quoting *Zotos v. Lindbergh Sch. Dist.*, 121 F.3d 356, 361 (8th Cir. 1997)). Nevertheless, the party asserting the defense must actually do so, and in a way that gives fair notice of that defense.

CARCO relies on the averment listed as its "Seventh Separate Defense," which reads simply: "The claims and causes of action set forth in the plaintiffs' Amended Counterclaim are barred in whole or in part by the provisions of the Oil Pollution Act of 1990, 33 U.S.C. § 2701, et seq." JA at 355. Noticeably absent from this general averment is any specific citation to the limitation of liability defense or even a description of the nature of the defense. This is significant, because the OPA includes a number of potential affirmative defenses. *See, e.g.*, 33 **[—57—]** U.S.C. § 2702(b) (limiting scope of damages for which the OPA imposes liability); § 2702(c) (excluding certain oil spills from OPA liability); § 2702(d)(1)(A) (shifting liability under the OPA to a solely responsible third party); § 2702(d)(2) (limiting the liability of certain parties under the OPA); § 2703 ("Defenses to liability"). CARCO's general reference to the entirety of the OPA did not provide adequate information from which Frescati could determine that CARCO was seeking to limit its liability under § 2702(d)(2)(B). Nor did CARCO develop this defense at any point before the first trial. For that reason, CARCO's unspecified reference to the OPA did not provide the requisite fair notice to Frescati.

Furthermore, Frescati would be prejudiced if the defense were allowed. As the District Court found, if CARCO had asserted its defense in a timely fashion, fifteen days of depositions and trial testimony from seven witnesses could have been avoided, along with the OPA damages phase of the first trial.[29] **[—58—] {-314-}**

CARCO did not clearly assert the limitation defense until nearly a decade after this action commenced, and over a year after the first trial and appeal had concluded. The District Court appropriately concluded that CARCO had not raised the defense at a pragmatically sufficient time, and that Frescati would be prejudiced if the defense were allowed. The District Court did not abuse its discretion in finding the defense waived.[30]

---

[29] Allowing CARCO to assert the defense after failing to raise it at a practicable time wastes the District Court's resources as well.

> Affirmative defenses must be raised as early as practicable, not only to avoid prejudice, but also to promote judicial economy. If a **[—58—]** party has a successful affirmative defense, raising that defense as early as possible, and permitting a court to rule on it, may terminate the proceedings at that point without wasting precious legal and judicial resources.

Robinson v. Johnson, 313 F.3d 128, 137 (3d Cir. 2002).

[30] It is worth noting that the United States similarly waived a defense by its failure to raise an

VIII. Prejudgment Interest Rate

The District Court awarded Frescati prejudgment interest of just over $16 million. Frescati, in its cross-appeal from the District Court's judgment, argues that the District Court erred by using the federal postjudgment **[—59—]** interest rate set by 28 U.S.C. § 1961(a) to determine the amount of the prejudgment interest award. Specifically, Frescati argues that the District Court improperly believed itself bound to use the federal postjudgment rate rather than the higher U.S. prime rate because Frescati did not present evidence of its borrowing costs.

An award of prejudgment interest is reviewed for abuse of discretion. *Ambromovage v. United Mine Workers of Am.*, 726 F.2d 972, 981–82 (3d Cir. 1984); *see also Sun Ship, Inc. v. Matson Nav. Co.*, 785 F.2d 59, 63 (3d Cir. 1986). When selecting an interest rate, the District Court must keep in mind that the rate and corresponding award "must be compensatory rather than punitive." *Del. River & Bay Auth. v. Kopacz*, 584 F.3d 622, 634 (3d Cir. 2009).

Here, the District Court awarded Frescati prejudgment interest at the one-year Treasury rate—the same rate used as the federal postjudgment interest rate. *See* 28 U.S.C. § 1961(a). Importantly, the District Court found that the postjudgment rate would "fairly and adequately compensate Frescati for its losses." JA at 183.

Frescati argues that, in the absence of evidence of borrowing costs, we should require the use of the U.S. prime rate. We grant that, had the District Court chosen to use the prime rate, it would not have abused its discretion even without extensive proof of borrowing costs. *Taxman* **[—60—]** *v. Bd. of Educ.*, 91 F.3d 1547, 1566 (3d Cir. 1996) (en banc). Indeed, the prime rate is commonly used to approximate the cost the defendant would have paid to borrow in the market, and at least one court appears to require it. *See, e.g.*, *Gorenstein Enters., Inc. v. Quality Care-USA, Inc.*, 874 F.2d 431 (7th Cir. 1989) (requiring use of the prime rate in certain circumstances); *see also Forman v. Korean Air Lines Co.*, 84 F.3d 446, 450–51 (D.C. Cir. 1996) ("[T]he prime rate is not merely *as* appropriate as the Treasury Bill rate, but *more* appropriate . . . ."). In this Circuit, however, a district court is not constrained to the use of only the prime rate: "[i]n exercising [its] discretion, . . . the court may be guided by the rate set out in **{–315–}** 28 U.S.C. § 1961." *Sun Ship*, 785 F.2d at 63; *Taxman*, 91 F.3d at 1566 ("[A] court 'may' use the post-judgment standards of 28 U.S.C. § 1961(a) [to calculate prejudgment interest, though] it is not compelled to do so.").[31]

The District Court determined that the federal postjudgment rate "fairly and adequately compensate[s] **[—61—]** Frescati for its losses." JA at 183. Under our Court's precedent, the District Court acted within its discretion.

IX. Conclusion

The District Court's order dated August 17, 2016 will be affirmed in part, vacated in part, and reversed in part. The District Court's judgment in favor of Frescati on the breach of contract claim and the prejudgment interest award will be affirmed. The District Court's judgment in favor of Frescati on the negligence claim will be vacated. The District Court's judgment in favor of the United States will be affirmed in part with respect to CARCO's liability on the subrogated breach of contract claim, but the judgment will be reversed and remanded for further proceedings in light of our equitable recoupment ruling for the purpose of recalculating damages and prejudgment interest. The District Court's order dated April 9, 2015, denying CARCO's motion for

argument in the first trial. We previously held that the United States waived its right to object to CARCO's equitable recoupment defense on the basis that it violated the terms of the partial settlement agreement. *In re Frescati*, 718 F.3d at 214, 1 Adm. R. at 102.

[31] Nor was it an abuse of discretion for the District Court to adopt a variable interest rate. Interest accumulated for more than a decade, and during that time prevailing interest rates changed substantially.

partial summary judgment on its limitation of liability defense, will be affirmed.

United States Court of Appeals
for the Third Circuit

No. 16-4195

LIBERTY WOODS INT'L, INC.
vs.
MOTOR VESSEL OCEAN QUARTZ

Appeal from the United States District Court for the District of New Jersey

Decided: May 4, 2018

Citation: 889 F.3d 127, 6 Adm. R. 117 (3d Cir. 2018).

Before **MCKEE, AMBRO,** and **ROTH,** Circuit Judges.

[—2—] {-127-} **ROTH,** Chief Judge: **{-128-}**

Liberty Woods International (LWI) brought suit for cargo damage sustained during a trip to Camden, New Jersey, on the Ocean Quartz (Vessel). Liability for the damage is governed by the carrier's bill of lading, which contains a forum selection clause requiring suit to be brought in South Korea. LWI instead sought to bring an *in rem* suit against the Vessel in the District of New Jersey, arguing that the foreign forum selection clause violates the Carriage of Goods by Sea Act (COGSA) because South Korea does not allow *in rem* **[—3—]** suits. The District Court dismissed the case, and for the following reasons, we will affirm.

I.

LWI purchased plywood veneer sheets, which it shipped to Camden, New Jersey, on the Vessel. Dalia Ship Holding owns the Vessel; however, in a chain of chartering, Dalia bareboat chartered[1] the Vessel to Star Bulk, which in turn time chartered it to Daiichi, which in turn time chartered it to SK Shipping. SK Shipping issued a bill of lading which specified that "[a]ny claim, dispute, suit or action concerning goods carried under this Bill of Lading, whether based upon breach of contract, tort, or otherwise shall be brought before the Seoul District Court in Korea." Both parties agree that LWI's cargo is covered by this bill of lading.

In February 2013, the Vessel arrived in Camden, and LWI discovered that its cargo was damaged. Believing the damage was caused by improper stowage, LWI threatened to arrest the Vessel. In lieu of an arrest, the Japan Ship Owners' Mutual Protection & Indemnity Association (JSO) issued to LWI and its insurers a letter of undertaking (LOU) on behalf of the Vessel, which could be used to satisfy any judgment against the Vessel *in rem* up to and including $2.75 million.

On December 23, 2015, LWI filed suit in the District of New Jersey against the Vessel *in rem* and Dalia *in personam*. Dalia answered on behalf of the *in rem* defendant. **[—4—]** LWI later learned that it could not recover *in personam* against Dalia because of the bareboat charter. While LWI could have filed an *in personam* suit against S.K. Shipping in South Korea, it chose not to. At argument, counsel admitted that this was a strategic move on its part, because LWI felt that its suit would not be successful in South Korea.

The Vessel moved to dismiss the New Jersey suit based on the forum selection clause in the bill of lading. LWI argued that enforcing the forum selection clause would violate section 3(8) of COGSA. In relevant part, this section states:

> Any clause, covenant, or agreement in a contract of carriage relieving the carrier *or the ship* from liability for loss or damage to or in connection with the goods, arising from negligence, fault, or failure in the duties and obligations provided in this section, or lessening such liability otherwise than as provided in this Act, shall be null and void and of no effect. A benefit of insurance in favor of the carrier, or similar clause, shall be **{-129-}** deemed to be a clause relieving the carrier from liability.[2]

[1] Bareboat chartering transfers complete control and operation of the vessel from the owner to the bareboat charterer without imposing liability for the acts of the charterer.

[2] Note to 46 U.S.C. § 30701, Title I, Section 8 (emphasis added).

LWI argued that this provision invalidates the foreign forum selection clause because South Korea does not recognize *in rem* suits. On November 9, 2016, the District Court granted the motion to dismiss under Rule 12(b)(3). LWI appealed. **[—5—]**

II.[3]

A.

In granting the motion to dismiss, the District Court erred in interpreting COGSA by confusing it with the Harter Act, a precursor to COGSA. COGSA was modeled after the Brussels Convention for the Unification of Certain Rules Relating to Bills of Lading (Hague Rules).[4] In 2006, COGSA was relocated from 46 U.S.C. §§ 1300 *et seq.*, to a note after 46 U.S.C. § 30701.[5] During this same period, the Harter Act was also moved from 46 U.S.C. §§ 190-196 to 46 U.S.C. §§ 30701-30707. As a result, COGSA was amended, not merely relocated. The relocated Harter Act provisions were the "amended" COGSA provisions. Upon analyzing 46 U.S.C. §§ 30704 and 30705, the District Court held that Congress modified COGSA's language so that it no longer **[—6—]** prohibited limiting a ship's liability.[6] That, however, was a misinterpretation of COGSA.

B.

Nevertheless, we will affirm the judgment because the foreign forum selection clause here does not violate COGSA.

While foreign forum selection clauses were originally disfavored under COGSA, the Supreme Court later adopted a policy that better reflected the need to respect the competence of foreign forums to resolve disputes. In the seminal case of *Indussa Corp. v. S.S. Ranborg*, the Second Circuit held a foreign forum selection clause to be invalid because it "put[] 'a high hurdle' in the way of enforcing liability, and thus [was] an effective means for carriers to secure settlements lower than if cargo [owners] could sue in a convenient forum."[7] After *Indussa*, courts of appeal uniformly adopted this reasoning to invalidate foreign forum selection clauses[8] until the Supreme Court overruled *Indussa* in *Vimar Seguros y Reaseguros, S.A. v. M/V Sky Reefer*. **[—7—]**

Sky Reefer held that a foreign arbitration **{-130-}**[9] clause would not lessen carrier liability in violation of COGSA solely because litigating abroad would be more costly.[10] While acknowledging that a choice of forum and choice of law clause would be invalid as against public policy if they operated as a "prospective waiver of a party's right to pursue statutory remedies,"[11] the Court noted that "the historical judicial resistance to foreign forum selection clauses has little place in an era when . . . businesses . . . now operate in world markets."[12] Moreover, the Court stated that it would be "out of keeping with the objects of the [Hague Rules] for the courts of this country to interpret COGSA to

---

[3] The District Court exercised jurisdiction under 28 U.S.C. §§ 1332(a)(2) and1333(1), and we have jurisdiction under 28 U.S.C. § 1291. We exercise plenary review over the District Court's construction of COGSA, *see e.g., United States v. Cooper*, 396 F.3d 308, 310 (3d Cir. 2005) (citation omitted), and review the District Court's decision to dismiss a complaint on the basis of forum non conveniens for abuse of discretion, *Windt v. Qwest Comms Int'l, Inc.*, 529 F.3d 183, 189 (3d Cir. 2008) ("This Court reviews a district court's dismissal of a complaint on *forum non conveniens* grounds for abuse of discretion." (citations omitted)).

[4] *Vimar Seguros y Reaseguros, S.A. v. M/V Sky Reefer*, 515 U.S. 528, 536 (1995).

[5] 200 A.L.R. Fed. 249 (2005) (noting the original locations for COGSA and the Harter Act).

[6] App. 14 ("Therefore, it is evident from the plain language of COGSA that 'the carrier' may not limit its liability through provisions inserted into a bill of lading. 46 U.S.C.A. §§ 30704, 30705. Congress did not make the same requirement of 'the ship.'").

[7] 377 F.2d 200, 203 (2d Cir. 1967) (internal citation omitted).

[8] *Sky Reefer*, 515 U.S. at 533 (collecting cases).

[9] While *Sky Reefer* involved a foreign arbitration clause, the Supreme Court noted that "foreign arbitration clauses are but a subset of foreign forum selection clauses in general[.]" *Id.* at 534 (citation omitted).

[10] *Id.*

[11] *Id.* at 540 (internal quotation marks and citation omitted).

[12] *Id.* at 537-38 (first omission in original) (internal quotation marks and citation omitted).

disparage the authority or competence of international forums for dispute resolution."[13] Accordingly, the Court held that while COGSA prohibited lessening the "liability for loss or damage . . . arising from negligence, fault, or failure in the duties and obligations provided in this section,"[14] COGSA did not address the "means and costs of enforcing that liability."[15] "The relevant question . . . is whether the substantive law to **[—8—]** be applied will reduce the carrier's obligations to the cargo owner below what COGSA guarantees."[16]

LWI argues, however, that the forum selection clause here violates COGSA because *in rem* suits are themselves a substantive right guaranteed by the statute. In the alternative, LWI seems to argue that mandating a South Korean forum will effectively limit the Vessel's liability. We consider each argument in turn.

1.

LWI claims that COGSA designates *in rem* suits as substantive rights, which are violated by the instant forum selection clause. We disagree. As LWI concedes, when the plain language of a statute is clear, the text should govern.[17] An examination of the plain language of section 3(8) shows that the clause clearly protects both carrier and ship liability; any clause completely eliminating or lessening ship liability runs afoul of COGSA.[18] This does not mean, however, that section 3(8) guarantees the right to an *in rem* suit. Rather, COGSA protects ship *liability*, not any particular vehicle for imposing it. The text does not mention *in rem* suits, nor require any specific remedy for enforcing ship liability. Indeed, such an interpretation would run counter to *Sky Reefer*'s holding that COGSA does not protect procedural **[—9—]** means for enforcing liability. Insofar as prohibiting *in rem* suits makes enforcing ship liability more costly or less convenient, *Sky Reefer* explicitly held that liability is not improperly lessened by procedural **{-131-}** costs.[19]

While LWI acknowledges that section 3(8) protects against lessening of ship liability, it cites this language as establishing a substantive right to *in rem* suits without adequately explaining this analytic leap. LWI argues in its brief that *in rem* suits are well established and important features of maritime law in the United States. It maintains that nothing in section 3 excludes *in rem* rights or limits *in rem* rights against the ship to a procedural device for the enforcement of an *in personam* defendant's liability. This argument turns the necessary discussion on its head; arguing that absence of express limitations grants a substantive right, especially in light of *Sky Reefer*'s limitations, is woefully inadequate.

In addition to the textual reasons for concluding that COGSA does not grant the substantive right to *in rem* suits, there are strong policy considerations that caution against such an interpretation. Requiring *in rem* suits would essentially invalidate numerous foreign forum selection clauses, as many countries do not acknowledge *in rem* suits.[20] **[—10—]** Indeed, the United States is one of the few countries that do recognize *in rem* suits. Imposing this idiosyncratic procedural requirement on other countries would be needlessly parochial. For these reasons, we conclude that COGSA section

[13] *Id.* at 537.

[14] *Id.* at 534 (omission in original).

[15] *Id.*

[16] *Id.* at 539 (citation omitted).

[17] *Cooper*, 396 F.3d at 310 (citation omitted).

[18] Note to 46 U.S.C. § 30701, Title I, Section 3(8) (prohibiting "[a]ny clause, covenant, or agreement in a contract of carriage relieving the carrier or the ship from liability[.]").

[19] *Sky Reefer*, 515 U.S. at 534 (noting the difference "between applicable liability principles and the forum in which they are to be vindicated").

[20] *See, e.g., Thyssenkrupp Materials NA, Inc. v. M/V KACEY*, 236 F. Supp. 3d 835, 840 (S.D.N.Y. 2017) (acknowledging that Greek law does not recognize *in rem* actions); *Uniwire Trading LLC v. M/V Wladyslaw Orkan*, 622 F. Supp. 2d 15, **[—10—]** 21 (S.D.N.Y. 2008) (acknowledging that Polish law does not recognize *in rem* suits); *Matter of Topgallant Lines, Inc.*, 154 B.R. 368, 380 (S.D. Ga. 1993), *aff'd sub nom. McAllister Towing v. Ambassador*, 20 F.3d 1175 (11th Cir. 1994) (acknowledging that German law does not recognize *in rem* suits).

3(8)'s substantive protections[21] encompass ship liability, not *in rem* suits specifically as the instrument to seek that recovery.[22] **[—11—]**

2.

LWI argues that even if *in rem* suits are not a substantive right, the forum selection clause here *effectively* relieves or lessens ship liability by not recognizing *in rem* actions, in violation of COGSA. Once again, we disagree.

While *in rem* suits might appear to be an obvious way to impose ship liability, courts have recognized other avenues for imposing liability in situations where *in rem* suits are prohibited. Courts have recognized plaintiffs' ability to obtain LOUs in lieu of bringing an *in rem* suit when they are precluded from doing so by arbitration clauses, which functionally prohibit **{-132-}** *in rem* suits.[23] For example, in *Thyssen Inc. v. Calypso Shipping Corporation, S.A.*, the Second Circuit held that an arbitration clause did not violate COGSA because the plaintiff accepted an LOU as full security of its claims and could have recovered against the ship pursuant to the LOU. The Second Circuit reasoned that "[a] letter of undertaking replaces the vessel as the *res* and moots the question of the need for separate *in rem* claim."[24] This Circuit similarly held that "[g]enerally, once a[n] LOU is issued, the letter becomes a complete substitute for the *res* and the maritime lien transfers from the vessel to the LOU."[25] **[—12—]**

As the Vessel argues, LWI could have obtained an LOU that would provide security for an *in personam* suit in South Korea. Moreover, the Vessel produced an unchallenged affidavit by Korean lawyer Byung-Suk Chung, claiming that South Korean law allows a party to "obtain[] security from vessel interests by arresting a vessel or attaching other assets in a foreign jurisdiction . . . to act as security for an *in personam* judgment to be obtained in the Seoul District Court."[26] Because LWI would then be able to collect from the Vessel using the LOU, the forum selection clause would not lessen or relieve the ship's liability in violation of COGSA.

In response, LWI raises a narrow argument: LWI concedes that obtaining an LOU is an accepted practice that is functionally equivalent to arresting a ship in an *in rem* suit.[27] Further, LWI does not argue that the forum selection clause prevented LWI from arresting the Vessel and obtaining a bond or an LOU. Instead, LWI argues that the forum selection clause eliminated ship liability *in this case*, because LWI received an LOU that secured only an *in rem* judgment

---

[21] For this reason, and because LWI has not argued that any other statute creates a substantive right to *in rem* suits, we reject LWI's argument that the forum selection clause functions as a prospective waiver of a statutory remedy, as prohibited by *Sky Reefer*.

[22] We join the Ninth Circuit in so holding. The Ninth Circuit upheld a forum selection clause specifying that Korean law would govern in *Fireman's Fund Insurance Co. v. M.V. DSR Atlantic*, holding that an *in rem* proceeding was merely a "means . . . of enforcing [COGSA] liability." 131 F.3d 1336, 1339-40 (9th Cir. 1997), *as amended* (Mar. 10, 1998) (internal quotation marks and citation omitted) (omission in original). The Ninth Circuit found no COGSA violation because the vessel presented uncontroverted evidence that Korean law was at least as favorable to the plaintiff as COGSA. *Id.* at 1340. The Ninth Circuit summarily confirmed this holding in *Kukje Hwajae Ins. Co., Ltd. v. M/V/ Hyundai Liberty*, 408 F.3d 1250, 1255 (9th Cir. 2005).

[23] *Petroleos Mexicanos Refinacion v. M/T KING A*, 554 F.3d 99, 108 (3d Cir. 2009) ("An *in rem* action is cognizable only in federal court; therefore the vessel could not have been a party to the *in personam* arbitration." (citing *Madruga v. Superior Court*, 346 U.S. 556, 560 (1954))).

[24] *Thyssen, Inc. v. Calypso Shipping Corp., S.A.*, 310 F.3d 102, 107 (2d Cir. 2002) (citations omitted).

[25] *Petroleos*, 554 F.3d at 104 (citations omitted).

[26] App. 119.

[27] LWI's counsel admitted that the LOU is limited to the amount "you could get if you actually arrested the vessel. So what you get in a letter of undertaking is exactly the same thing that you get when you arrest the vessel . . .." Audio Recording of Oral Arguments held July 11, 2017 at 5:50-6:15, http://www.ca3.uscourts.gov/oral-argument-recordings. Additionally, the Federal Rules of Civil Procedure Supplemental Rules allow for a similar procedure.

against the Vessel. LWI does not allege that it could not have obtained an LOU unencumbered by this restriction. Indeed, **[—13—]** LWI's inability to recover seems to be a consequence of its own deliberate inaction: First, it refused to file an *in personam* suit against S.K. Shipping in South Korea. Second, it did not obtain an LOU that would be applicable to an *in personam* suit. LWI's own willful limitation of alternatives, not the forum selection clause, has eliminated its ability to recover. For this reason, we hold that the forum selection clause did not effectively lessen or eliminate the Vessel's liability and that it is valid under COGSA.

Because LWI has not raised any other arguments as to how the District Court abused its discretion in enforcing the forum selection clause, we will affirm the District Court's dismissal of the suit.

IV.

In this case, we are asked to support an interpretation of COGSA that would invalidate **{-133-}** a host of foreign forum selection clauses for the sake of a procedural device available in few countries besides the United States. Where parties have contracted to bring suit abroad, the U.S. must be cognizant of its status as a member of a global community and respect the competence of other jurisdictions to adjudicate claims. In light of this and in light of the fact that the forum selection clause did not lessen or eliminate ship liability for cargo damage, we decline to impose LWI's restrictive interpretation of COGSA. COGSA does not invalidate the forum selection clause simply because the selected jurisdiction does not acknowledge *in rem* suits. For this reason, we will affirm the District Court's order, dismissing the action.

(Reporter's Note: Concurring Opinion follows on p. 122).

[—1—] {-133-} **AMBRO,** Circuit Judge, concurring:

For a maritime creditor an action *in rem* is a procedure for obtaining pre-judgment security and post-judgment enforcement. In the global shipping business the debtor's ship is typically the main asset on which a judgment-creditor can rely to collect from a defendant located perhaps on the other side of the world. A court can easier locate, bring within its jurisdiction, and arrest the ship than a defendant's other foreign assets.

It is no surprise then that maritime law supplies *in rem* liability against a ship, that is, permits an action naming the ship as though it were the defendant. As is relevant here, in the United States a ship can be liable *in rem* for cargo damage, the idea being that the ship impliedly ratified the shipping contract when the carrier loaded the cargo onboard. *See Man Ferrostaal, Inc. v. M/V Akili*, 704 F.3d 77, 83 (2d Cir. 2012); *see also Pioneer Import Corp. v. Lafcomo*, 49 F.Supp. 559, 561–62 (S.D.N.Y. 1943), *aff'd*, 138 F.2d 907 (2d Cir. 1943) ("A lien against the ship arises for damage to cargo caused by improper storage.").

The Carriage of Goods by Sea Act, or COGSA, assumes the availability of an action against the ship. Indeed, § 3 of COGSA is titled, "Responsibilities and Liabilities of Carrier *and Ship*." (emphasis added). And under § 3(8), the parties to a contract for shipping goods by sea cannot agree to lessen or relieve the liability of the "carrier or the ship." However, an action *in rem* is only one way to impose liability on a ship. Although South Korean law does not allow *in rem* suits, Liberty Woods International concedes that equivalent security for *in personam* suits is available. As it chose not to pursue this avenue for relief, I agree with my colleagues that any lessening of the ship's liability is the fault of Liberty Woods, not the selection of a foreign forum.

If, however, a forum-selection clause were to operate such that a shipper could never enforce the selected forum's judgment against the value of the ship that carried the shipper's damaged goods, the clause would be unenforceable per COGSA § 3(8). *See Vimar Seguros y Reaseguros, S.A. v. M/V Sky Reefer*, 515 U.S. 528, 540 (1995) ("[W]ere we persuaded that the choice-of-forum and choice-of-law clauses operated in tandem as a prospective waiver of a party's right [—2—] to pursue statutory remedies, we would have little hesitation in condemning the agreement as against public policy." (internal quotations and ellipsis omitted)). My concern is that, in another case, the common shipping industry practice of chartering and sub-chartering a ship risks placing it and its owner beyond the reach of the designated forum's *in personam* jurisdiction. Here, because sub-charterer SK Shipping Co. Ltd. operated the Ocean Quartz, the parties agree that its owner, Dalia Ship Holding S.A., bears no liability {-134-} for damage to Liberty Woods' cargo. This naturally leads to a question: if Dalia Ship Holding bears no liability, how could Liberty Woods attach Dalia Ship's property—that is, the Ocean Quartz—to enforce a judgment against someone else (*i.e.*, SK Shipping)?

As noted, the parties do not contest that Liberty Woods could have enforced a judgment obtained in South Korea against the Ocean Quartz's value. So there is no reason to question that proposition here. But I am not convinced it will hold in every case. It is easy to imagine a shipowner contending that a personal judgment against a sub-charterer several steps removed should not be enforceable against the owner's vessel. The use of so-called "bareboat" or "demise" charter agreements, in which a shipowner surrenders control of the vessel to the charterer (and ultimately any sub-charterer down the line) and disclaims carrier liability, heightens the concern. An owner can credibly "seek to use the bareboat charter as a shield against *in personam* liability." *Backhus v. Transit Cas. Co.*, 532 So. 2d 447, 449 (La. Ct. App. 1988), *aff'd*, 549 So. 2d 283 (La. 1989). If the sub-charterer has few assets or becomes insolvent, the shipper might be left high and dry without compensation for damage to its cargo.

A suit *in rem* provides a means of cutting through a web of sub-charter agreements to impose liability on the ship directly and vindicate § 3(8)'s command (and thereby protect shippers in the face of judgment-proof sub-charterers). Other jurisdictions may provide other procedural vehicles to deliver these protections (as apparently South Korea does). In my view, COGSA requires that a shipper have some means to assess liability for damaged goods against the value of the ship. Because Liberty Woods has not explained why it would be impossible to vindicate its rights in the designated forum, I agree with my colleagues that we must affirm the dismissal of its *in rem* action.

This page intentionally left blank

United States Court of Appeals for the Fourth Circuit

United States Court of Appeals
for the Fourth Circuit

No. 16-1773

MOODY
vs.
HUNTINGTON INGALLS INC.

On Petition for Review of an Order of the Benefits Review Board

Decided: January 3, 2018

Citation: 879 F.3d 96, 6 Adm. R. 126 (4th Cir. 2018).

Before **GREGORY,** Chief Judge, **NIEMEYER,** and **AGEE,** Circuit Judges.

[—2—] {-97-} **GREGORY,** Chief Judge:

Russell L. Moody, a shipyard employee, suffered a workplace injury but did not undergo surgery until after he retired. He sought disability benefits for the two-month, post-surgery period during which he was not medically cleared for work. The Department of Labor's Benefits Review Board denied his disability claim under the Longshore and Harbor Workers' Compensation Act (the "LHWCA" or "Act"). 33 U.S.C. §§ 901, 902(10), 908. The sole question on appeal is whether voluntary retirement before the onset of a workplace injury's debilitating effects precludes the existence of a "disability." 33 U.S.C. § 902(10). We hold that it does not and reverse and remand.

I.

A.

Appellant Russell Moody began working for Appellee Huntington Ingalls Inc. ("Huntington") in 1966, when he was only 20 years old. He continued to work for Huntington for 45 years, as a rigger, a welder, and a truck driver. In June 2011, Huntington assigned Moody to a new shift. On Aug. 1, 2011, unhappy with the shift, Moody gave his requisite 90-day notice of retirement, effective Oct. 31, 2011.

During that 90 day-window, on Sep. 19, 2011, Moody injured his right shoulder in the shipyard. While using the steering wheel of his truck to pull himself into the driver's seat, Moody tore his rotator cuff along with other parts of his shoulder. Even though the injury required surgery, Moody continued to work as a driver and received his normal wages. On Oct. 31, he retired from the shipyard as planned. **[—3—]**

On Dec. 13, 2011, Moody underwent shoulder surgery. According to his physician, Moody needed to remain "out of work" until Feb. 16, 2012 to recover from surgery. J.A. 154, 171–72. Moody could then work with certain limitations from Feb. 17 to Mar. 28 and with no restrictions thereafter. Since his retirement from the shipyard, Moody has not worked or pursued any job opportunities.

Huntington paid for the costs of surgery but refused to pay Moody temporary total disability benefits for the post-operation recovery period from Dec. 13 to Feb. 16. Huntington does not dispute that the injury was otherwise a compensable, workplace injury under the LHWCA that would have entitled Moody to disability benefits had he undergone surgery prior to retirement. *See* 33 U.S.C. § 903.

B.

Moody brought his claim for temporary total disability benefits before an administrative law judge ("ALJ") in the Department of Labor. 33 U.S.C. § 919(d) (providing for ALJs). To demonstrate a **{-98-}** compensable "disability" under the LHWCA, Moody must show that he suffered an "incapacity because of injury to earn . . . wages." 33 U.S.C. § 902(10).

The ALJ ruled in Moody's favor and awarded temporary benefits. He concluded that Moody was totally incapacitated during the recovery period and that his workplace injury caused the incapacity. He also noted that Moody performed his duties in good faith even while injured and that, had Moody undergone surgery immediately, Huntington would have had to pay disability benefits in addition to the wages of a replacement driver. Although the ALJ found that Moody voluntarily retired for reasons unrelated to his injury, **[—4—]** he ultimately concluded that retirement is irrelevant to the definition of "disability" under the LHWCA.

However, the Board, on appeal, disagreed and concluded that Moody was not entitled to any disability benefits because he voluntarily retired before the onset of his workplace injury's debilitating effects. The Board reasoned that voluntary retirement results in a total loss of ability to earn wages, such that no injury could cause any further loss of economic capacity. This appeal followed.[1]

II.

We have jurisdiction to review direct appeals from the Benefits Review Board under 33 U.S.C. § 921(c). The factual findings of the ALJ are reviewed for substantial evidence. *See v. Washington Metro. Area Transit Auth.*, 36 F.3d 375, 380 (4th Cir. 1994). "Review of legal questions is de novo, and no deference is due to the Board's legal conclusions." *Newport News Shipbuilding & Dry Dock Co. v. Riley*, 262 F.3d 227, 231 (4th Cir. 2001). Because the ALJ's factual findings are not disputed and are supported by substantial **[—5—]** evidence, we proceed directly to the BRB's legal conclusion that voluntary retirement made Moody ineligible for disability benefits.

A.

For matters of statutory interpretation, we first "look to the statutory text, and absent a different definition, we interpret statutory terms 'in accordance with their ordinary meaning.'" *PETA v. United States Dep't of Agric.*, 861 F.3d 502, 509 (4th Cir. 2017) (quoting *Sebelius v. Cloer*, 569 U.S. 369, 376 (2013)). Under the LHWCA, "'[d]isability' means incapacity because of injury to earn the wages which the employee was receiving at the time of injury in the same or any other employment." 33 U.S.C. § 902(10). Nothing in the statute expressly addresses retirement or its timing: the only reference to time requires the assessment of earning capacity at the time of injury, not the time of retirement. *Id.* Instead, the Board and Huntington would insert a new requirement into the statute by misconstruing the plain meaning of "incapacity" and the real-world significance of retirement. **{-99-}**

The ordinary meaning of "incapacity" precludes the Board's and Huntington's interpretation that an employee's retirement necessarily makes him incapable of earning any wages. 33 U.S.C. § 902(10). "Incapacity," as used today and circa 1927 when the LHWCA was passed, has meant "inability," "incompetence," and "incapability." Oxford English Dictionary (1933). There is no dispute that, apart from the two-month recovery period, Moody had the ability, competence, and capability of being a truck driver and earning wages on the days before and after his retirement. Retirement, quite simply, is not **[—6—]** inherently debilitating. By focusing on the voluntary nature of Moody's retirement, both the Board and Huntington Ingalls confuse being *unwilling* with being *unable*.

Huntington and the Board also erroneously equate loss of earning capacity with loss of actual earnings. Moody's injury did not cause him to lose any income during his recuperation, but it did deprive him of the ability to work. In asking the Court to interpret incapacity as actual wage loss, Huntington cites cases that characterize "disability" as an "economic harm." *E.g., Metro. Stevedore Co. v. Rambo*, 521 U.S. 121, 126 (1997); *Norfolk Shipbuilding & Drydock Corp. v. Hord*, 193 F.3d 797, 799–802 (4th Cir. 1999). However, Huntington omits that those cases specifically define "economic harm" as lost capacity to earn wages, not actual economic loss. *See Rambo*, 521 U.S. at 126

[1] Following oral argument in this case, Huntington Ingalls opted to pay Moody the benefits for the two-month recovery period and moved to dismiss the case as moot. Moody opposed the motion. We deny that motion and proceed with the merits because Huntington Ingalls has not shown that the challenged conduct is not likely to recur, particularly given the BRB's several decisions erroneously interpreting "disability" under the LHWCA. *See Friends of the Earth, Inc. v. Laidlaw Envtl. Servs. (TOC), Inc.*, 528 U.S. 167, 190 (2000); *see, e.g., Christie v. Georgia-Pacific Co.*, BRB No. 16-0321, 2017 WL 2572359, at *2 (Mar. 7, 2017); *Eason v. Huntington Ingalls Inc.*, BRB No. 16-0082, 2016 WL 8315589, at *3 (Sept. 20, 2016).

("The Act speaks of this economic harm as 'disability,' defined as the 'incapacity because of injury to earn [] wages.'"); *Hord*, 193 F.3d at 800 ("The Act provides compensation not for the injury itself, but for the economic harm suffered as a result of the decreased ability to earn wages."). In any event, our interpretation of the LHWCA does not deprive "disability" of its economic character. Rather than compensating Moody for a torn rotator cuff, the LHWCA mandates compensation for the lost earning capacity—an economic injury—that he suffers as a result of the torn rotator cuff.

As the Supreme Court has held, "[c]apacity, and thus disability, is not necessarily reflected in actual wages earned after injury, and when it is not, the factfinder under the Act must make a determination of disability that is reasonable and in the interest of justice, and one that takes account of the disability's future effects." *Rambo*, 521 U.S. at 127–28. The *Rambo* Court held that an employee may still be eligible to receive disability benefits **[—7—]** under the LHWCA even if his post-injury wages are higher than his pre-injury wages, upon a determination that the employee's earning capacity is likely to fall below pre-injury levels in the future. *Id.* at 128. Similarly, in this case, actual wage loss does not fully capture the loss of capacity caused by Moody's shoulder injury. The ALJ here followed *Rambo*'s instruction in deciding that the interests of justice and public policy weigh in favor of granting benefits. *See* J.A. 59–60. To decide otherwise would not only deprive Moody of his rightful benefits but would also confer a windfall on Huntington: it is undisputed that Moody would have received disability benefits had he undergone surgery immediately, rather than discharging his duties in good faith, and Huntington would have had to pay for another driver. *Id.*

The fact that Moody did not actually work or seek job opportunities after retirement does not change the analysis. That fact goes to actual economic loss but not incapacity. Because the LHWCA compensates workers for their inability to earn wages due to injury, workers are entitled to disability benefits when an injury is sufficient to preclude the possibility of working. Here, Moody could have changed **{–100–}** his mind and chosen to work even after retiring, perhaps in a job that offered better hours. *See Rambo*, 521 U.S. at 132 (holding that LHWCA contains "mandate to account for the future effects of disability" when fashioning disability awards). His shoulder injury and the resulting surgery took that choice away from him for at least two months. The law compensates that deprivation of economic choice when it is caused by workplace injury.

In sum, voluntary retirement is not a form of total incapacity. As the Board has determined in the past, retirement status, standing alone, is irrelevant to earning capacity **[—8—]** and the determination of "disability" under 33 U.S.C. § 902(10). *See Raymond Harmon v. Sea-Land Service Inc.*, 31 BRBS 45 (May 14, 1997) ("The sole relevant inquiry in this case with regard to claimant's burden of proof on disability is whether claimant's work injury precludes his return to his usual work."); *Robert Carrion v. SSA Marine Terminals, LLC.*, BRB No. 12-0601, 2013 WL 3479992, at *4 (June 25, 2013) ("The only relevant inquiry . . . is whether claimant's work injury precludes his return to his usual work.").

B.

Huntington also argues that the original purpose of the LHWCA was to compensate workers for actual wage loss. It theorizes that the LHWCA was modeled after the New York Workers' Compensation Act ("the NYWCA") and that the NYWCA only compensated actual wage loss. While the LHWCA adopted many provisions from the NYWCA, the legislative history cited by Huntington also shows that there were points of departure. H.R. Rep. No. 69-1190 at 2–3 (1926). Instead, the purpose of the LHWCA was not to emulate the NYWCA *per se* but to enact a "humanitarian legislation" that afforded workers with "protection" that was "almost universally recognized as necessary in the interest of social justice between employer and employee." *Id.* at 3.

Indeed, the Supreme Court has recognized that "the LHWCA represents a compromise between the competing interests of disabled laborers and their employers." *Potomac Elec. Power Co. v. Dir., Office of Workers' Comp. Programs*, 449 U.S. 268, 281–82 (1980). Under this compromise, employees give up the possibility of greater damages in tort litigation "in return for the certainty of compensation payments." *Id.* at 281–82, n. 24 (quoting 1 M. Norris, The Law of Maritime Personal Injuries § 55, at 102 (3d ed. 1975)); **[—9—]** *see* 33 U.S.C. § 905 (making recovery under the LHWCA the exclusive remedy for covered employees). We give effect to that compromise by applying the plain text of the statute and by adopting the interpretation that affords greater certainty of coverage if the text is ambiguous. *See Sidwell v. Express Container Servs., Inc.*, 71 F.3d 1134, 1140 (4th Cir. 1995) (recognizing that interpretation under the LHWCA should "achieve the 'broad' remedial purposes for which the legislation was enacted") (quoting *P. C. Pfeiffer Co. v. Ford*, 444 U.S. 69, 74, 78 (1979)). Here, we give effect to the plain text of the LHWCA and conclude that earning capacity is distinct from actual wages.

In sum, Huntington has not shown, and the Court has not found, any evidence that the LHWCA modeled its definition of "disability" after the NYWCA's. The legislative history surrounding the LHWCA does not suggest a conclusion contrary to the clear definition of "disability" and the plain meaning of "incapacity" under 33 U.S.C. § 902(10). **{–101–}**

III.

Because we hold that the Benefits Review Board misinterpreted 33 U.S.C. § 902(10), we reverse and remand for further proceedings as may be appropriate.

REVERSED AND REMANDED

United States Court of Appeals
for the Fourth Circuit

No. 17-1075

HICKERSON
VS.
YAMAHA MOTOR CORP., U.S.A.

Appeal from the United States District Court for the District of South Carolina at Anderson

Decided: February 20, 2018

Citation: 882 F.3d 476, 6 Adm. R. 130 (4th Cir. 2018).

Before **MOTZ, AGEE,** and **FLOYD,** Circuit Judges.

[—2—] {-478-} AGEE, Circuit Judge:

Deborah Meek Hickerson sustained serious internal injuries in a personal watercraft ("PWC") accident and filed a complaint in the District of South Carolina against the manufacturers of the PWC, Yamaha Motor Corporation, U.S.A. and Yamaha Motor Co., Ltd. (collectively "Yamaha"). In her complaint, Hickerson alleged product liability claims under South Carolina law for design and warning defects. The district court excluded Hickerson's proffered expert testimony and entered summary judgment in favor of Yamaha on all claims. Hickerson then filed a motion to reconsider under Federal Rule of Civil Procedure 59(e), which the district court also denied. On appeal, Hickerson contends the district court erred in requiring expert testimony on her claims and in failing to conduct an appropriate *Daubert* analysis before excluding her expert's testimony. *See Daubert v. Merrell Dow Pharm., Inc.*, 509 U.S. 579 (1993). For the reasons below, we affirm the judgment of the district court.

I.

A.

This appeal follows a motion for summary judgment. Accordingly, we view the facts in the light most favorable to Hickerson, the nonmoving party below. *See Anderson v. Liberty Lobby, Inc.*, 477 U.S. 242, 248 (1986).

The PWC at issue, a 2011 Yamaha VXS WaveRunner, has on-craft warnings, which are repeated in the operator's manual, that advise riders to wear protective clothing **[—3—]** to avoid internal injuries. The following warning (reproduced below) appears on the PWC's front glove box:

> WEAR PROTECTIVE CLOTHING. Severe internal injuries can occur if water is forced into body cavities as a result of falling into water or being near jet thrust nozzle. Normal swimwear does not adequately protect against forceful water entry into rectum or vagina. All riders must wear a wet suit bottom or clothing that provides equivalent protection (See Owner's Manual).

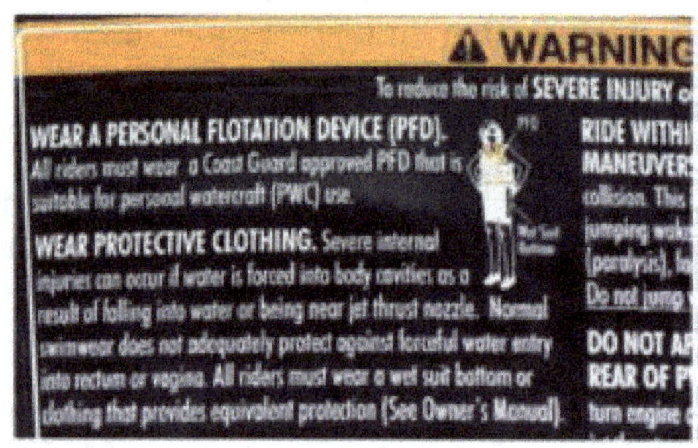

J.A. 716. The PWC's rear boarding platform also bears a warning label (reproduced below) stating that "[s]evere internal injuries can occur" and passengers must "[w]ear a wetsuit bottom or clothing that provides equivalent protection."

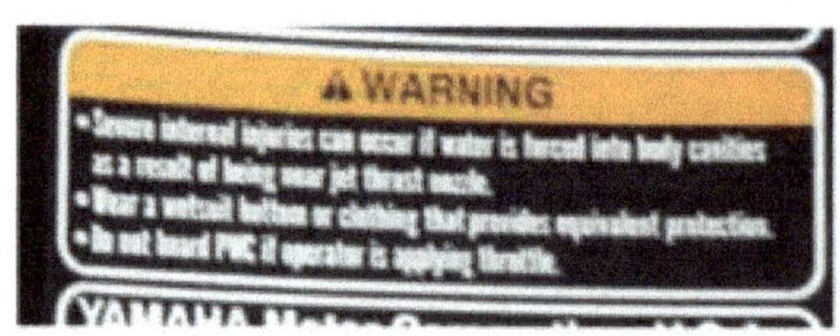

[—4—] J.A. 716. **{-479-}**

The PWC and accompanying owner's manual also contained warnings that only three people may ride the craft at a time, the operator should be at least sixteen years old, and a person should not ride after consuming alcohol.

In 2012, Hickerson was a passenger riding the PWC on Lake Hartwell, South Carolina. She fell off the back of the PWC into the jet thrust behind it and suffered injuries to her rectum, perineum, vagina, anus, and colon ("orifice injuries"). She underwent eight weeks of medical procedures and recovery.

When she was injured, Hickerson was wearing a bikini and no wetsuit. It is undisputed that she was the fourth passenger on the PWC, a ten-year-old was driving, and Hickerson had consumed alcohol prior to riding. Hickerson admitted that she did not read any on-craft or manual warnings before riding the PWC.

B.

Hickerson, a South Carolina resident, filed her complaint in federal court based on diversity of citizenship with Yamaha. *See* 28 U.S.C. § 1332. In her complaint, Hickerson pleaded state law claims of strict liability, negligence, and breach of warranties based on the PWC's allegedly inadequate warnings and defective design.

During discovery, Hickerson proffered the expert testimony of Dr. Anand Kasbekar, a mechanical engineer familiar with PWCs who has been retained as an expert in dozens of various product liability cases. Dr. Kasbekar represented that he intended to give several opinions: that the PWC's warnings were inadequate, that a set of alternative warnings was better, and that design alterations like a contoured seat and hand straps **[—5—]** would have made the PWC safer. The district court found Dr. Kasbekar qualified to testify as an expert on PWC warnings and design based on his relevant experience in engineering, forensic analysis, and warnings testimony.

However, in response to a motion in limine by Yamaha, the district court excluded Dr. Kasbekar's proffered opinion for a set of alternative warnings as unreliable under *Daubert. Hickerson v. Yamaha Motor Corp., U.S.A.*, No. 8:13-cv-02311-JMC, 2016 WL 4123865 (D.S.C. July 29, 2016). The district court explained that because Dr. Kasbekar's proposals were neither tested nor based on "specific relevant research or studies," they bore no indicia of reliability. *Id.* at *5; *see Daubert,* 509 U.S. at 597. In its written opinion on the motion in limine excluding the alternative warning opinion, the district court mentioned Dr. Kasbekar's separate inadequate warning opinion. However, the court did not expressly exclude the inadequate warning opinion.

Later, in awarding summary judgment to Yamaha, the district court revisited the issue of whether Dr. Kasbekar's proposed inadequate warning opinion was admissible. *Hickerson v. Yamaha Motor Corp., U.S.A.*, No. 8:13-cv-02311-JMC, 2016 WL 4367141 (D.S.C. Aug. 16, 2016). The court noted that Hickerson's claim of a warning inadequacy "implicate[s] the study of human factors and other industry standards . . . generally beyond the common knowledge of a jury." *Id.* at *3. Thus, the district court expected expert testimony to support any claim of inadequate warnings. But Dr. Kasbekar's inadequate warning opinion was not supported by studies, research, or other scientific basis of verification necessary to establish reliability for *Daubert* purposes. Indeed, because "[t]he primary evidence [Hickerson] presented . . . to support her inadequate **[—6—]** warnings claims was, in fact, in the form of expert testimony from Dr. Anand Kasbekar" and the proposed warning system opinion was excluded **{–480–}** as unreliable, the district court was "hard-pressed to discern a 'genuine dispute as to any material fact'" on Hickerson's warnings claims. *Id.* at *3–4. The district court then excluded the proffered inadequate warning opinion and awarded summary judgment to Yamaha on all the warnings claims.

On the defective design claim, the court held that South Carolina continues to follow Comment j to § 402A of the Restatement (Second) of Torts, which, in the district court's view, allows adequate product warnings to "cure" alleged design defects. The court next observed that because Hickerson had not produced admissible evidence that the PWC's warnings were inadequate, "the product's warnings [were] adequate as a matter of law." *Id.* at *6. Consequently, under Comment j, the adequate warnings cured any alleged design defects so that the PWC could not be deemed defectively designed. Because strict liability, negligence, and breach of warranties claims require "proof of a defective condition," the court granted judgment as a matter of law on all of Hickerson's claims. *Id.*

Hickerson filed a motion to reconsider under Rule 59(e), claiming the district court's rulings were clearly erroneous because Hickerson had provided sufficient evidence to withstand summary judgment and a product with adequate warnings can still be unreasonably dangerous under South Carolina law. *See Hickerson v. Yamaha Motor Corp., U.S.A.*, No. 8:13-cv-02311-JMC, 2016 WL 7324684 (D.S.C. Dec. 16, 2016). The district court rejected Hickerson's argument that Dr. Kasbekar's inadequate warning opinion could rest on his own "specialized skill, training, and experiences" without any **[—7—]** relevant scientific support. *Id.* at *7. It also rejected Hickerson's "mere disagreement with the court's interpretation of South Carolina law" on the application of Comment j. *Id.* at *12. Having reviewed its rulings, the district court denied the motion.

Hickerson timely appealed, and we have jurisdiction pursuant to 28 U.S.C. § 1291. Federal courts sitting in diversity apply the substantive state law that would apply had the plaintiff filed the case in state court. *Stonehocker v. Gen. Motors Corp.*, 587 F.2d 151, 154 (4th Cir. 1978). The Parties agree that South Carolina products liability law applies to the issues in this case.

II.

On appeal, Hickerson challenges the district court's exclusion of Dr. Kasbekar's opinions, its grant of summary judgment, and its denial of her motion for reconsideration.

We review the exclusion of expert testimony for abuse of discretion. *See Gen. Elec. Co. v. Joiner*, 522 U.S. 136, 143 (1997). Trial judges serve a "gatekeeping" function and have "considerable leeway" in excluding evidence. *Kumho Tire Co. v. Carmichael*, 526 U.S. 137, 152 (1999). Expert testimony must be "based on sufficient facts or data," and the expert must arrive at his opinions by properly applying "reliable principles and methods" to the facts. *See* Fed. R. Evid. 702.

Because Hickerson appeals the district court's exclusion of Dr. Kasbekar's testimony as unreliable, we consider the following *Daubert* factors pertaining to the reliability of evidence:

> (1) whether a theory or technique can be or has been tested; (2) whether it **[—8—]** has been subjected to peer review and publication; (3) whether a technique has a high known or potential rate of error and whether there are standards controlling **{–481–}** its operation; and (4) whether the theory or technique enjoys general acceptance within a relevant scientific community.

Cooper v. Smith & Nephew, Inc., 259 F.3d 194, 199 (4th Cir. 2001) (citing *Daubert*, 509 U.S. at 592–94). The Rule 702 inquiry is "a flexible one," and the *Daubert* factors are "helpful, not definitive." *Kumho*, 526 U.S. at 150–51; *see Daubert*, 509 U.S. at 493. When applying these standards, courts "should be conscious of two guiding, and sometimes competing, principles[:] Rule 702 was intended to liberalize the introduction of relevant expert evidence [and] expert witnesses have the potential to be both powerful and quite misleading." *Westberry v. Gislaved Gummi AB*, 178 F.3d 257, 261 (4th Cir. 1999).

We review the district court's entry of summary judgment de novo. *Higgins v. E.I. DuPont de Nemours & Co.*, 863 F.2d 1162, 1167 (4th Cir. 1988). Summary judgment is appropriate when no genuine issues of material fact exist and the moving party is entitled to judgment as a matter of law. Fed. R. Civ. P. 56(a). We review the denial of a motion to reconsider for abuse of discretion. *Ingle ex rel. Estate of Ingle v. Yelton*, 439 F.3d 191, 197 (4th Cir. 2006).

III.

We turn first to Hickerson's warnings claims for which she sought to introduce expert opinion testimony as to the inadequacy of the PWC's existing warnings and that alternative warnings should have been used. Hickerson offered Dr. Kasbekar as her **[—9—]** expert, and he proffered to opine that the existing warnings were inadequate in location, content, and form. These deficiencies, according to Dr. Kasbekar, inhibited passengers' ability to see the warnings and appreciate the danger of riding a PWC without a wetsuit. He also intended to offer a proposed set of alternative PWC warnings that he claimed would have better informed passengers of the PWC's danger. The district court excluded the alternative warning opinion as unreliable and later similarly excluded his inadequate warning opinion, which was "ostensibly . . . ground[ed]" on the alternative warning opinion. 2016 WL 4367141, at *3.

A.

Hickerson contends the district court abused its discretion by failing to conduct a proper *Daubert* analysis before excluding Dr. Kasbekar's inadequate warning opinion. She argues the court mistakenly held that the proposed inadequate warning opinion was based only on the excluded alternative warning opinion when, in fact, Dr. Kasbekar had formulated his inadequate warning opinion by drawing on his experience, training, testing, and knowledge of PWC industry standards. Yamaha responds that the district court appropriately excluded the inadequate warning opinion because it was unsupported with any scientific indicia of reliability. To that point, Yamaha noted that Dr. Kasbekar's claim for the inadequacy of the glove box and rear craft warnings hinged chiefly on their location; however, his only support for that proposition was his already excluded alternative warning opinion. The district court did not abuse its discretion when it excluded Dr. Kasbekar's inadequate warning opinion. **[—10—]**

Dr. Kasbekar had concluded in his expert report that the existing warnings on the PWC were inadequate because passengers could more easily see a warning located directly on the seat instead of warnings appearing on the glove box and at the rear of the craft. He also concluded that the warnings were "congested" and confused important information that passengers should read before riding the PWC. J.A. **{-482-}** 161. Yet, aside from his alternative warning opinion—the exclusion of which Hickerson does not challenge on appeal—Dr. Kasbekar supported his inadequate warning opinion with no research, data, or scientific theories. The district court observed,

> outside of the warnings expert testimony, there is little to no evidence in the record on which this court can rely to conclude that there is a genuine factual dispute as to whether the product was 'unreasonably dangerous' based on Defendants' failure to provide an adequate warning concerning the product's use.

2016 WL 4367141, at *4. Dr. Kasbekar had not tested his inadequate warning opinion and admitted he provided no research to support the notion that passengers read a seat warning more often than glove box or rear craft warnings, especially if "read means . . . read and comprehend it." J.A. 163–64. Even his opinion that the wetsuit depicted in the on-craft warnings should be black rather than white was based solely on his personal recollection that he had never seen a white wet suit. He could not reliably opine that the PWC warnings with white wetsuit images are inadequate because he failed to provide relevant testing or research and his alternative warning opinion featuring a black wetsuit—which could support the inadequacy of the existing warnings—had been excluded. Dr. Kasbekar's own testimony established that his opinions lacked the markers **[—11—]** of reliability Rule 702 and *Daubert* require to prevent an expert from misleading a jury with unproven conjecture.

Furthermore, the district court concluded Hickerson presented "little to no evidence beyond Dr. Kasbekar's excluded testimony" to support her claim that the PWC's warnings were defective. 2016 WL 7324684, at *4. She was unable to refute Yamaha's evidence that the Boating Safety Advisory Council and

Coast Guard had approved the PWC's warnings and uniform labels. As illustrated above, the warnings on the PWC plainly warn of the danger of the orifice injuries Hickerson sustained. The district court noted that, in the absence of any evidence to the contrary, "it would be difficult . . . to accept that a jury could find that the warnings' direct and specific verbiage and its multiple locations on both the front and rear parts of the PWC rendered them inadequate." 2016 WL 4367141, at *4. The district court properly concluded that the PWC's warnings were adequate as a matter of law.

B.

Hickerson also contends the district court erred in requiring expert testimony at all to support her warnings claims. Because South Carolina only requires expert testimony when issues are beyond a jury's general knowledge and most jurors will have had exposure to various warnings, Hickerson posits the jury here did not need expert testimony to determine whether the PWC's warnings were adequate. Yamaha responds that the district court did not err because the issue of the adequacy of the warnings could only be submitted to the jury once admissible evidence had been presented that they were inadequate. **[—12—]**

While the district court noted expert testimony was "in this particular case . . . important" and was "perhaps the most appropriate form of evidence to support" the inadequacy of the PWC's warnings, the district court did not end its analysis there. 2016 WL 7324684, at *9. After it excluded Dr. Kasbekar's proffered opinions as unreliable, the court also looked for other warnings evidence in the record but was "hard-pressed to discern a genuine factual dispute on the issue precisely because [his] **{-483-}** opinion testimony was the primary evidence Plaintiff presented on the issue and because there is little to no evidence in the record on the issue beyond his testimony." *Id.* (internal citations omitted). The district court did not exclude Hickerson's warnings claims merely because they lacked expert testimony; rather, it required her to support those claims with *any* admissible evidence. In this regard, Hickerson simply failed.

C.

Hickerson relied to her detriment on Dr. Kasbekar's expert testimony as the exclusive support for her warnings claims. Because "the question of the adequacy of the warning" does not reach the jury unless "evidence has been presented that the warning was inadequate," and Hickerson failed to present such evidence, her warnings claims could not withstand summary judgment. *Allen v. Long Mfg. NC, Inc.*, 505 S.E.2d 354, 357 (S.C. Ct. App. 1998). The district court did not err in awarding summary judgment to Yamaha on the defective warnings claims. **[—13—]**

IV.

We turn next to Hickerson's defective design claims. The Parties' core disagreement concerns whether claims of defective design are defeated when product warnings are deemed legally adequate, as occurred in this case. Our judicial function in a diversity case such as this is cabined by a bedrock principle of federalism: "In adjudicating non-federal questions, a federal court must apply the law of the state." *United States v. Little*, 52 F.3d 495, 498 (4th Cir. 1995). Thus, we will apply South Carolina law to resolve this inquiry.

South Carolina's Defective Products Act ("the Act") imposes strict liability on manufacturers of defectively designed products. S.C. Code § 15-73-10, *et seq.* This Act codified § 402A of the Restatement (Second) of Torts, whose comments the South Carolina General Assembly also adopted as the expression of its legislative intent for the Act. S.C. Code § 15-73-30 ("Comments to § 402A of the Restatement of Torts, Second, are incorporated herein by reference thereto as the legislative intent of this chapter."); *Aldana v. RJ Reynolds Tobacco Co.*, No. 2:06-3366-CWH, 2008 WL 1883404, at *1 (D.S.C. Apr. 25, 2008). The disputed provision, Comment j to § 402A, states in pertinent part: "Where warning is given, the seller may reasonably assume that it will be read and heeded; and a product bearing such a warning, which is safe for use if it is followed, is not in defective condition, nor is it unreasonably dangerous." Restatement (Second) of Torts § 402A cmt. j (Am. Law Inst. 1965).

Advancing a number of policy arguments, Hickerson contends Comment j allows her to bring defective design claims even if her defective warnings claims fail. **[—14—]** Specifically, she argues that design claims are independent of any warning claim. As a consequence, Hickerson represents that allowing good warnings to trump bad design would "subordinat[e] design safety to warnings." Appellant's Br. 14. Her counsel also speculates that William Prosser, the drafter of the Restatement (Second) of Torts, simply erred in drafting Comment j and did not intend for it to say what it says. In response, Yamaha notes that Comment j's plain text, and the South Carolina court decisions applying it, allow a product manufacturer to rely on a legally adequate warning to avoid liability for an alleged defective design.

Hickerson calls Comment j "ambiguous" in passing but offers no textual support for her position. Appellant's Br. 6. Even a cursory examination of Comment j refutes her label. On its face, Comment j provides **{–484–}** that an adequate *warning* makes a product "safe for use if [the warning] is followed." § 402A cmt. j. A product seller who puts such a *warning* on his product is entitled to "reasonably assume that [the warning] will be read and heeded." *Id.* The *warning* also makes the product "not in defective condition, nor . . . unreasonably dangerous." *Id.* The application of Comment j to design defect claims thus relies entirely upon the adequacy of a product warning.

Consistent with Comment j's text, the South Carolina Court of Appeals has repeatedly applied its plain language to confirm that an adequate warning operates to "cure" a product's alleged design defects. *E.g., Curcio v. Caterpillar, Inc.*, 543 S.E.2d 264, 269 (S.C. Ct. App. 2001) ("[A] product is not unreasonably dangerous if accompanied by adequate warnings that, if followed, make the product safe for use."), *rev'd on other grounds*, 585 S.E.2d 272 (S.C. 2003); *Allen*, 505 S.E.2d at 359 (stating a **[—15—]** manufacturer need not "refine a product which is made safe for use by an adequate warning so that the product does not need a warning to be safe"); *Anderson v. Green Bull, Inc.*, 471 S.E.2d 708, 710 (S.C. Ct. App. 1996) ("A product bearing a warning that the product is safe for use if the user follows the warning is neither defective nor unreasonably dangerous; therefore, the seller is not liable for any injuries caused by the use of the product if the user ignores the warning."); *Claytor v. Gen. Motors Corp.*, 286 S.E.2d 129, 132 (S.C. Ct. App. 1982) ("If [inherently dangerous products] are properly prepared, manufactured, packaged and accompanied with adequate warnings and instructions, they cannot be said to be defective.").

This Court has likewise understood Comment j to shield a manufacturer from liability for product defects if the product contains an adequate warning. *See Phelan v. Synthes (U.S.A.),* 35 F. App'x 102, 109–10 (4th Cir. 2002) (per curiam) (citing *Allen* and *Anderson* for the principle that a product with an adequate warning is not defective or unreasonably dangerous). The South Carolina district courts have ruled similarly. *Priester v. Futuramic Tool & Eng'g Co.*, No. 2:14-cv-01108-DCN, 2017 WL 1135134, at *6 (D.S.C. Mar. 27, 2017); *Alford v. Lowe's Home Ctrs., Inc.*, No. 8:13-1787-BHH, 2014 WL 5305825, at *2 (D.S.C. Oct. 15, 2014) (recognizing the principle as articulated in *Anderson* and *Claytor*); *Aldana*, 2008 WL 1883404, at *1 (rejecting the plaintiff's theory "that an adequate warning does not preclude liability for a defective design claim"). *But see Marshall v. Lowe's Home Ctrs., LLC*, No. 4:14-cv-04585-RBH, 2016 WL 4208090, at *20 & n.29 (D.S.C. Aug. 10, 2016) ("Comment j and the South Carolina cases **[—16—]** interpreting it simply recognize an adequate warning *may* preclude liability for a defective design claim.").

Although the Supreme Court of South Carolina has not applied Comment j to the precise issue before us, the South Carolina Court of Appeals has consistently applied

Comment j in similar South Carolina products liability cases. When the highest court of a state has not indicated how it would decide an issue, we follow the law of intermediate state courts, like the South Carolina Court of Appeals, absent "persuasive data" that the highest court would rule differently. *Little*, 52 F.3d at 498.

Under South Carolina law, a product manufacturer is entitled to assume that its warnings will be read and heeded. § 402A cmt. j. Hickerson admitted she did not read the PWC's warnings, and even if she had, she produced no admissible evidence that they were legally inadequate. *See Allen*, 505 S.E.2d at 357 (allowing issue of **{-485-}** warning adequacy to go to the jury only if accompanied by admissible evidence of inadequacy). Thus, the PWC's warnings were adequate as a matter of law. Consequently, even if we assume, without deciding, that the PWC was defectively designed, Comment j allows Yamaha to avoid liability for any design defects because the PWC's warnings were legally adequate such that, "if [they were] followed, [the PWC was] not in defective condition, nor [was] it unreasonably dangerous" when Hickerson was injured. *See* § 402A cmt. j.

Nevertheless, Hickerson urges us to rewrite the text of Comment j despite its lack of facial ambiguity. She would have us ignore the uniform decisions of the South Carolina Court of Appeals based on her counsel's academic theories and policy **[—17—]** arguments. She has presented no "persuasive data" that the Supreme Court of South Carolina would apply Comment j differently, yet she essentially asks us to do what that court has not done—overrule the South Carolina Court of Appeals on a question of South Carolina law. This we cannot do. Federal courts "should not create or expand [a] [s]tate's public policy." *St. Paul Fire & Marine Ins. Co. v. Jacobson*, 48 F.3d 778, 783 (4th Cir. 1995). Comment j means what it says and functions to cure the PWC's alleged design defects. Accordingly, the district court did not err in granting summary judgment on Hickerson's design defect claims.[1]

V.

Hickerson based her claims of strict liability, negligence, and breach of warranties on theories of warning and design defects. Because the record is devoid of admissible evidence on either theory of defect, the district court properly entered summary judgment for Yamaha on all claims, and its judgment is

AFFIRMED.

---

[1] Though the district court's ruling on Yamaha's motion in limine underpinned the court's summary judgment ruling, Hickerson does not appeal the disposition of the motion in limine. And because the district court correctly disposed of the motion for summary judgment, it similarly did not abuse its discretion in denying Hickerson's motion for reconsideration.

United States Court of Appeals
for the Fourth Circuit

No. 17-4061

UNITED STATES
vs.
OCEANIC ILLSABE LTD.

Appeal from the United States District Court for the Eastern District of North Carolina at Wilmington

Decided: May 7, 2018

Citation: 889 F.3d 178, 6 Adm. R. 137 (4th Cir. 2018).

Before **TRAXLER, KING,** and **HARRIS,** Circuit Judges.

[—3—] {-181-} KING, Circuit Judge: **{-182-}**

In 2016, Oceanic Illsabe Limited ("Oceanic") and Oceanfleet Shipping Limited ("Oceanfleet") (together, the "Appellants")— two closely related corporate entities headquartered in Greece—were each convicted of nine criminal offenses by a jury in eastern North Carolina. Those crimes were directly committed by the supervisory personnel in the Engine Department of the M/V OCEAN HOPE (the "Ocean Hope," or the "Vessel")—an oceangoing cargo ship owned and operated by the Appellants. The offenses of conviction arose from and are related to illegal discharges of large quantities of oily pollutants from the Vessel into the ocean. Oceanic and Oceanfleet maintain on appeal that the prosecution failed to sufficiently prove that they are criminally responsible for the offenses lodged against them. The Appellants also contend that the district court erred in imposing fines and other penalties at sentencing. As explained below, we affirm the convictions and sentences.

I.

A.

We begin with a brief review of some pertinent legal and factual background for this prosecution. The United States is a signatory to the 1973 International Convention for the Prevention of Pollution from Ships, as amended in 1978 ("MARPOL"). MARPOL's primary purpose is to eliminate pollution of the oceans by discharges of oily wastes. To that end, MARPOL—an abbreviation for "marine pollution"—requires its **[—4—]** member states to punish under domestic law any violations of MARPOL that occur on oceangoing ships, and to provide for penalties that will discourage additional violations.

In compliance with MARPOL, our Congress enacted in 1980 the Act to Prevent Pollution from Ships ("APPS"). APPS provides that foreign ships in the navigable waters of the United States are subject to the discharge requirements of federal law pertaining to oily pollutants. *See* 33 U.S.C. § 1902(a)(2).[1] With respect to discharges of such pollutants that occur outside our navigable waters, the Coast Guard can assert jurisdiction when a foreign ship fails to make complete and accurate entries in the ship's Oil Record Book. *Id.* § 1908(a).[2]

MARPOL and federal law both require all oceangoing ships exceeding 400 gross tons to maintain an Oil Record Book. *See* 33 C.F.R. § 151.25(a). The Oil Record Book must be fully updated any time a ship's crewmembers engage in certain "machinery space operations," including the disposal of oily pollutants and wastes. *Id.* § 151.25(d).[3]

[1] For convenience, we refer to the oily waste products of oceangoing ships, such as bilge water and sludge, as "oily wastes," "oily mixtures," "oily pollutants," or simply as "pollutants."

[2] Section 1908(a) of Title 33 of the United States Code provides that "a person who knowingly violates [APPS], or the regulations issued thereunder commits a . . . felony."

[3] Pursuant to Section 151.25(h) of Title 33 of the Code of Federal Regulations, "[e]ach operation [mandated in section 151.25(d)] shall be fully recorded without delay in the Oil Record Book so that all the entries in the book appropriate to that operation are completed." Section 151.25(d) provides that

> [e]ntries shall be made in the Oil Record Book on each occasion, on a tank to tank basis if appropriate, whenever any of the following machinery space

(Continued) **[—5—]**

[—5—] Because oceangoing ships {-183-} generate large quantities of oily pollutants and wastes, their Oil Record Books are required to be updated "without delay." *Id.* § 151.25(h).

The applicable regulations prescribe how to properly dispose of specific waste products, including bilge water and sludge. *See* 33 C.F.R. § 151.10(a). Bilge water is created when water accumulates at the bottom of a ship and combines with oily mixtures that have leaked and dripped from the engine fuel systems. *Id.* § 151.05. Bilge water must be collected and stored in tanks onboard the ship and then processed through two pollution control devices, the Oil Water Separator (the "Separator") and the Oil Content Monitor (the "Content Monitor"). *Id.* § 151.10(a)(5)-(6). If, after passing through the Separator, the Content Monitor measures only negligible quantities of oil, bilge water can be legally discharged into the ocean. *Id.* Sludge—that is, the oil residue left over after bilge water has been processed through the Separator—must either be incinerated onboard the vessel or offloaded in port to a licensed hauler and disposal facility. *See* MARPOL, Annex VI, Reg. 16.1. The foregoing disposal activities must always be assiduously recorded in the ship's Oil Record Book. [—6—]

B.

On April 14, 2016, the grand jury in the Eastern District of North Carolina returned the operative nine-count indictment in this case and charged Oceanic, Oceanfleet, and two of the Ocean Hope's supervisory personnel (the "Indictment"). The indicted supervisory personnel were Chief Engineer Rustico Ignacio and Second Engineer Cassius Samson of the Engine Department. The charges against the defendants included conspiracy to commit offenses against the United States, failure to fully and accurately maintain (and aiding and abetting the failure to fully and accurately maintain) the Ocean Hope's Oil Record Book, a charge of obstruction of justice by falsification of (and aiding and abetting the falsification of) the Oil Record Book, making false statements to Coast Guard investigators, a second obstruction of justice charge for making false statements to Coast Guard investigators, and four charges of witness tampering. Samson was subjected to eight charges—all the counts alleged except Count Six—while Chief Ignacio was subjected to five charges—Counts One, Two, Three, Six and Nine. More specifically, the nine offenses alleged in the Indictment were as follows:

- Count One—Conspiracy to violate APPS and obstruct justice, in violation of 18 U.S.C. § 371;
- Count Two—Violating APPS by failing to fully and accurately maintain—and by aiding and abetting the failure to fully and accurately maintain—the Oil Record Book, in violation of 33 U.S.C. § 1908(a), 18 U.S.C. § 2, and 33 C.F.R. § 151.25 (the "Failure to Maintain charge");[4] [—7—] {-184-}

operations take place on any ship to which this section applies - (1) Ballasting or cleaning of fuel oil tanks; (2) Discharge of ballast containing an oily mixture or cleaning water from fuel oil tanks; (3) Disposal of oil residue; (4) Discharge overboard or disposal otherwise of bilge water that has accumulated in machinery spaces; (5) Bunkering of fuel or bulk lubricating oil; and (6) Any failure, and the reasons for, of the oil filtering equipment.

See 33 C.F.R. § 151.25(d).

[4] Section 2 of Title 18, commonly referred to as the aiding and abetting statute, is actually titled "Principals," and provides that

(Continued) [—7—]

(a) Whoever commits an offense against the United States or aids, abets, counsels, commands, induces or procures its commission, is punishable as a principal.

(b) Whoever willfully causes an act to be done which if directly performed by him or another would be an offense against the United States, is punishable as a principal.

- Count Three—Obstructing justice by falsification of—and by aiding and abetting the falsification of—the Ocean Hope's Oil Record Book, in violation of 18 U.S.C. §§ 1519 and 2 (the "Obstruction by Falsification charge");[5]

- Count Four—False statements to Coast Guard investigators, in violation of 18 U.S.C. § 1001(a)(2);

- Count Five—Obstructing justice by making false statements to Coast Guard investigators, in violation of 18 U.S.C. § 1505; and

- Counts Six through Nine—Four offenses of witness tampering, in violation of 18 U.S.C. § 1512(b)(3).

Oceanic and Oceanfleet were charged in each of the nine counts with being vicariously liable for the illegal activities of Chief Engineer Ignacio and Second Engineer Samson, who were acting within the scope of their agency and employment. At the conclusion of the pretrial proceedings, the four defendants—Oceanic, Oceanfleet, Chief Ignacio, and Samson—were jointly tried before a jury in Wilmington. **[—8—]**

C.

The trial lasted several days and concluded on September 1, 2016. The jury heard approximately twenty witnesses and was presented with numerous exhibits and records.[6] The witnesses confirmed that, sometime in April 2015, the Ocean Hope embarked on a voyage from Bangladesh in southern Asia to Wilmington in eastern North Carolina. During that trip, the Engine Department's subordinate crewmembers—at the direction of Chief Engineer Ignacio and Second Engineer Samson—ignored the waste disposal procedures required by MARPOL and APPS and illegally discharged large quantities of oily pollutants into the ocean. Several crewmembers confirmed that, after the Vessel's arrival in Wilmington, they were instructed by Chief Ignacio and Samson to make false statements to the Coast Guard investigators about the illegal discharges. The Oil Record Book of the Ocean Hope was not accurately maintained and was systematically falsified. The trial evidence proving those unlawful activities is summarized below.

1.

The jury learned that the Ocean Hope was owned by Oceanic, a Liberian corporation with its principal place of business in Greece. In October 2009, Oceanic contracted with its parent entity, Oceanfleet—a Marshall Islands corporation headquartered in Greece—to provide commercial ship management services to the Ocean Hope. Oceanic and Oceanfleet retained a staffing agency in the Philippines to **[—9—]** provide seafarers (i.e., employees) to operate and maintain the Ocean Hope. Several of those employees were the subordinate crewmembers in the Vessel's Engine Department, and worked under the supervision of Chief Engineer Ignacio and Second Engineer Samson.

The Engine Department was staffed by eight crewmembers. The crewmembers generally wore uniforms with the name "Oceanfleet" affixed thereon. The prosecution emphasized that the Department's crewmembers confirmed to the jury that **{-185-}** they were employed by either Oceanic or Oceanfleet, or by both Appellants. For example, Second Engineer Samson confirmed that his salary came from both Oceanic and Oceanfleet. Samson said that the name "Oceanic Illsabe" was written on his employment contract, and that Oceanfleet operated the Ocean Hope for the duration of his employment. The subordinate crewmembers understood that they were employed by Oceanfleet.

[5] When we refer herein to falsification of the Oil Record Book—as alleged for example in Count Three of the Indictment—such references include knowing concealment, covering up, making false entries, and omissions of required entries in the Oil Record Book.

[6] The facts recited herein are derived from the trial record and are presented in the light most favorable to the government, as the prevailing party. *See United States v. Singh*, 518 F.3d 236, 241 n.2 (4th Cir. 2008).

All of the Engine Department crewmembers were required to comply with the Oceanfleet Safety Management System Manual (the "Oceanfleet Manual"), which had the name "Oceanfleet" emblazoned on nearly every page. The Oceanfleet Manual explained the chain of command on the Ocean Hope and emphasized that "orders are given and expected to be obeyed down the chain of command without hesitation or question." *See* G.A. 344.[7] At the apex of the Department's hierarchy was Chief **[—10—]** Engineer Ignacio, followed by Second Engineer Samson. Chief Ignacio and Samson were responsible for managing the day-to-day operations of the Department. Further down the chain were third engineer Menente, fourth engineer Sarduma, two "oilers" named Villar and Villegas, a "fitter" named Belleza, and a "wiper" named Reyes.

In his supervisory capacity, Chief Engineer Ignacio was responsible for ensuring the Engine Department's compliance with all required safety and pollution control procedures. Pursuant to the Oceanfleet Manual, Chief Ignacio was also responsible for tracking the generation, transfer, and disposal of all oily pollutants produced onboard the Ocean Hope. Chief Ignacio was specifically required by the Oceanfleet Manual to fully and accurately record the completion of those tasks in the Vessel's Oil Record Book.[8]

2.

Evidence of the Ocean Hope's organizational structure provided the foundation for the government's theory of the vicarious criminal liability of the Appellants. The prosecution proved that the supervisory personnel in the Ocean Hope's Engine **[—11—]** Department—that is, Chief Engineer Ignacio and Second Engineer Samson—oversaw and regularly directed illegal discharges of bilge water and sludge into the ocean. The prosecution also proved that Chief Ignacio and Samson committed the offense alleged in the Failure to Maintain charge by contravening the provisions of § 1908(a) of Title 33 and § 2 of Title 18, by aiding and abetting the failure to fully and accurately maintain the Ocean Hope's Oil Record Book. Similarly, the evidence proved that Chief Ignacio and Samson committed the Obstruction by Falsification charge, in violation **{–186–}** of §§ 1519 and 2 of Title 18.[9] In addition, Chief Ignacio and Samson had corruptly persuaded their subordinate crewmembers in the Engine Department to make false statements to the Coast Guard investigators in Wilmington. Those false statements were made on behalf of the Appellants in a corrupt endeavor to conceal the pollution offenses that had occurred on the Ocean Hope.

---

[7] Three separate appendixes have been filed in these appeals and are referred to herein. Our references to the "J.A. __" refer to the contents of the Joint Appendix. Our citations to the "G.A. __" refer to the contents of the Government's Supplemental Appendix, which was filed by the prosecutors. Finally, our references to the "S.A. __"

(Continued) **[—10—]**

refer to the contents of the Sealed Appendix, which contains the presentence reports (the "PSRs") for Oceanic and Oceanfleet which are sealed.

[8] Pursuant to MARPOL and APPS, maintenance of the Oil Record Book must be assigned to "[t]he master or other person having charge of [the] ship." *See* 33 C.F.R. § 151.25(j). Although the master of the ship (or other person in charge of the ship) is the person directly responsible for proper maintenance of the Oil Record Book, the Oceanfleet Manual purported to assign that duty to the Chief Engineer of the Ocean Hope, that is, Chief Engineer Ignacio. Notwithstanding the provisions of the Oceanfleet Manual, the Appellants had no authority to override the applicable legal principles or reassign to the Chief Engineer any responsibilities placed on the ship's master under federal law.

[9] The obstruction of justice offense alleged in the Obstruction by Falsification charge is defined in § 1519 of Title 18, and provides, in pertinent part, that

> [w]hoever knowingly alters, destroys, . . . conceals, covers up, falsifies, or makes a false entry in any record . . . with the intent to impede, obstruct, or influence the investigation . . . within the jurisdiction of any . . . agency of the United States . . . shall be [punished as provided by law].

a.

The evidence proved that illegal discharges of bilge water and sludge consistently occurred during the Vessel's trip to Wilmington. For example, Second Engineer Samson, with Chief Engineer Ignacio's approval, directed oiler Villegas to pump unprocessed bilge water directly into the ocean two to three times each week, using the Ocean Hope's **[—12—]** general service pump.[10] When third engineer Menente questioned Samson about why they had not been using the Separator, Samson replied that they only used the Separator in Port when surveyors came aboard to inspect the viability of the Vessel's waste disposal equipment.[11] As Menente explained, if the Separator "wasn't used"—that is, if it was clean—there would not be "any problems with the survey" in Port. *See* G.A. 85.[12]

The evidence also proved that Chief Engineer Ignacio and Second Engineer Samson directed their underlings in the Engine Department to improperly and illegally dispose of sludge. The prosecution emphasized a specific illegal discharge of sludge—corroborated with pictures, but never recorded in the Oil Record Book—that occurred on or about June 14, 2015. On that occasion, oiler Villar informed Samson that the **[—13—]** sludge level in one of the sludge storage tanks was high. In response, Samson directed Villar and wiper Reyes to connect a "magic pipe"—that is, a surreptitious bypass hose—between the Ocean Hope's sludge pump and an illegal onboard discharge valve on the storage tank. After Villar and Reyes connected the magic pipe, Samson ordered them to run the sludge pump. When the Department's **{-187-}** crewmembers ran the sludge pump, suction from the magic pipe drew sludge from the storage tank's illegal discharge valve and channeled it directly into the ocean. On that occasion, Villar and Reyes, acting at the direction of Samson, polluted the ocean with approximately ten cubic meters (2640 gallons) of sludge.

Third engineer Menente corroborated the illegal dumping of sludge from the Ocean Hope on June 14. When Menente began his shift in the Engine Room just before midnight that evening, he—along with oiler Villegas—saw the magic pipe connected to the illegal discharge valve on the sludge tank. Menente—who was immediately suspicious—captured pictures and videos of the magic pipe and its surreptitious valve connection. Sometime later, Menente saw the magic pipe in the trash after it had been disconnected from the illegal valve on the sludge tank. At that time, Menente had Villegas record a video of Menente removing part of the magic pipe from the trash for use as evidence. Menente sent those pictures and videos to his wife, and they were placed in evidence by the prosecutors. A day or two after the illegal June 14 sludge disposal from the Ocean Hope, Second Engineer Samson directed Reyes to destroy the incriminating evidence by throwing the magic pipe overboard. Reyes complied with Samson's order and pitched the magic pipe into the sea. **[—14—]**

---

[10] Of note, during the leg of the Vessel's voyage from Korea to Panama, only one of the two bilge water storage tanks onboard the Vessel was available for bilge water storage. The second bilge water storage tank then contained diesel fuel because, while refueling in Korea, more diesel fuel was received onboard than could be stored in the designated diesel fuel tank. As a result, the extra diesel fuel was placed in the second bilge water storage tank, limiting the Ocean Hope's available storage space for bilge water. The storage tank limitations, coupled with the Vessel's inability to properly use the Separator, enhanced the need for the Engine Department supervisors to direct the dumping of excess oily pollutants into the ocean.

[11] Pursuant to MARPOL, surveyors are obliged to "ensure that the structure, equipment, systems, fittings, arrangements and material fully comply with the applicable requirements." *See* MARPOL, Annex I, Reg. 6.1.1. If a ship is unfit to go to sea, the surveyor must take corrective action.

[12] When the Ocean Hope arrived in Wilmington in July 2015, the Oil Record Book accurately reflected that the Separator had not been used since the Vessel visited China four months earlier in February 2015. Because an updated copy of the Oil Record Book was delivered to Oceanfleet headquarters on a weekly basis, Oceanfleet was aware that the Separator was not being used on the Ocean Hope.

b.

The evidence also proved that Chief Engineer Ignacio and Second Engineer Samson had conspired to falsify and fail to accurately maintain the Ocean Hope's Oil Record Book. By way of example, oiler Villar was responsible for measuring the bilge water and sludge levels in the Vessel's seven storage tanks, a process known as "sounding the tanks." Each time Villar did so, he was required to prepare a record of the measurements called a "sounding slip." Samson routinely directed Villar to falsely reduce the measurements recorded on the sounding slips. Chief Ignacio, meanwhile, would reduce those measurements even further when he recorded them in the Oil Record Book.

The prosecution also proved that Chief Engineer Ignacio and Second Engineer Samson failed to make required entries in the Ocean Hope's Oil Record Book. For example, the Oil Record Book did not reflect that Second Engineer Samson had frequently directed the subordinate crewmembers to discharge unprocessed bilge water and sludge directly into the ocean, including the unlawful discharge of sludge on June 14, 2015.[13] Similarly, although entries were required to be made in the Oil Record Book **[—15—]** when diesel fuel was pumped into the bilge water storage tank, those incidents were never recorded.[14]

The applicable regulations also require oceangoing ships to record any "failure, and the reasons for, of the oil filtering equipment" in the Oil Record Book. *See* 33 C.F.R. § 151.25(d)(6). The government proved that, on about July 2, 2015, before reaching Panama, Chief Engineer Ignacio and the Vessel's Master, a man named **{-188-}** Tabacaru, alerted Oceanfleet headquarters that the Separator was not functioning properly. That alert was never recorded in the Oil Record Book.

D.

1.

The prosecution also proved that Chief Engineer Ignacio and Second Engineer Samson sought to conceal their illicit activities from the Coast Guard both before and after the Ocean Hope's arrival in Wilmington on July 15, 2015. In the course of the voyage from Panama to Wilmington, the Engine Department's subordinate crewmembers were gathered together on the Ocean Hope and instructed on how to avoid problems during the expected Port State Control Examination by the Coast Guard (the "Port Examination"). Oceanfleet assisted in this endeavor by providing a checklist for the crewmembers to use in their preparations for the Port Examination in Wilmington. The **[—16—]** Oceanfleet checklist specified several tasks to be addressed prior to entering Port. Those included: (1) ensuring that the engine room was clean and free from oil traces; (2) repairing oil leakages "permanently (if possible)"; (3) ensuring that the Oil Record Book was in order; and (4) removing oily plastic pipes. *See* G.A. 358-63. An Oceanfleet official also provided Chief Engineer Ignacio with an example of an entry for the Oil Record Book that should pass the expected Coast Guard inspection. Chief Ignacio was advised to "enter . . . on a weekly basis" in the Oil Record Book that the Separator was "tested and found satisfactory." *See* G.A. 351. Such weekly entries, of course, would be fictitious.

While the Ocean Hope was in Port in Panama, two senior Oceanfleet officials, a "Superintendent" named Prouzos and a "Port Captain" named Trousas, came aboard and travelled on the final leg to Wilmington. During their time onboard, they directed the Engine Department's subordinate crew-members to perform certain tasks in

13 The fact that Chief Engineer Ignacio and Second Engineer Samson knowingly made false entries in—and failed to make required entries in—the Ocean Hope's Oil Record Book, and that they aided and abetted such falsifications and omissions, provided strong evidentiary support for the charges alleged in Counts Two and Three.

14 The fact that Chief Engineer Ignacio and Second Engineer Samson aided and abetted each other and the Vessel's Master in failing to fully and accurately maintain the Oil Record Book provided strong evidentiary support for the Failure to Maintain charge alleged in Count Two.

preparation for the Port Examination—such as painting and cleaning the engine room. Of note, those officials never sought to verify whether the Engine Department had complied with MARPOL and APPS and the proper oil pollution disposal procedures during the Vessel's trip from Bangladesh.

2.

Two Coast Guard investigators—a Lieutenant named March and a Chief Warrant Officer named Libbert—testified extensively about the Port Examination and about interviewing the Engine Department crewmembers. In early July 2015, before the Ocean Hope arrived in Wilmington, the Coast Guard had been tipped off about illegal **[—17—]** discharges of oily pollutants—particularly sludge—from the Vessel in mid-June during its trip from Bangladesh. The informant was the spouse of third engineer Menente. Menente had forwarded his wife the photographs and videos he made of the magic pipe being used as a bypass hose on the Ocean Hope to illegally dump sludge overboard.

Immediately after initiating its Port Examination on July 15, the Coast Guard discovered that some of the Ocean Hope's firehoses were defective. Warrant Officer Libbert explained that third engineer Menente soon approached him and arranged to meet privately with the investigators. Menente then fully cooperated with the Coast Guard investigators, providing them with the pictures and videos he had taken of the magic pipe, plus the piece of the magic pipe that he had removed. Menente showed the Coast Guard investigators where and how the magic pipe had been used to dump sludge into the ocean from **{-189-}** the Ocean Hope. After interviewing Menente, the Coast Guard investigators sounded the holding tanks and discovered that one of the bilge water tanks actually contained diesel fuel. As Lieutenant March confirmed, Menente's interview and that discovery prompted an expansion of the Port Examination into a criminal investigation.

E.

1.

The Coast Guard's criminal investigation included interviews of the Engine Department's crewmembers. Before the Coast Guard investigators could fully interview oiler Villegas, however, Chief Engineer Ignacio directed Villegas to lie to the **[—18—]** investigators and deny any knowledge of illegal pollution discharges from the Vessel.[15] Second Engineer Samson then approached Villegas, as well as fourth engineer Sarduma, and directed each of them to give false statements to the Coast Guard investigators. Villegas and Sarduma were each ordered by Samson to lie to the investigators about the use of the Separator onboard the Vessel.[16] Chief Ignacio and Samson also spoke with oiler Villar and wiper Reyes and directed both of them to deny any knowledge of unlawful sludge discharges from the Ocean Hope.[17] As a result of those corrupt efforts, each of the subordinate crewmembers in the Engine Department—except for third engineer Menente—initially lied to the Coast Guard investigators. The subordinate crewmembers who initially made false statements, however, later recanted and testified truthfully before the jury. At trial, they admitted participating in illegal pollution discharges from the Ocean Hope and confirmed that they had been ordered by their superiors to lie to the Coast Guard investigators. **[—19—]**

---

[15] The fact that oiler Villegas was directed by Chief Engineer Ignacio to make false statements to the Coast Guard investigators at Wilmington provided evidentiary support for the witness tampering offense alleged in Count Six.

[16] The fact that oiler Villegas and fourth engineer Sarduma were directed by Second Engineer Samson to make false statements to the Coast Guard investigators at Wilmington provided evidentiary support for the witness tampering offenses alleged in Counts Seven and Eight.

[17] The fact that oiler Villar and wiper Reyes were directed by Chief Engineer Ignacio and Second Engineer Samson to lie to the Coast Guard investigators at Wilmington provided evidentiary support for the witness tampering offense alleged in Count Nine.

Second Engineer Samson, on the other hand, lied extensively to Lieutenant March during his interview about the illegal pollution activities onboard the Ocean Hope. For example, Samson told Lieutenant March that he did not know why there was oil residue in the overboard discharge equipment on the Vessel. Samson also falsely advised the Coast Guard investigators that the Ocean Hope's Separator had never been bypassed.[18] At trial, Samson testified falsely in each of those respects. Samson also denied connecting the magic pipe to the sludge tank and told the jury that he was unaware of any sludge being dumped directly overboard from the Ocean Hope. Samson denied ordering any Engine Department crewmembers to pump unprocessed bilge water into the ocean, and he maintained that he had not ordered anyone to lie to the Coast Guard investigators. **{-190-}** Regarding the sounding slips, Samson falsely asserted that the sounding slips went directly to Ignacio, and maintained that he (Samson) never saw them.

2.

Put succinctly, the Coast Guard confirmed that the Oil Record Book contained a plethora of inaccurate and false information, and the investigation revealed that a vast amount of inculpatory information had not been properly recorded therein. The jury heard, for example, that—according to the Oil Record Book—the Ocean Hope had not offloaded sludge since September of 2014, about seven months before the Vessel's **[—20—]** departure from Bangladesh. The Oil Record Book also reflected the daily use of the Ocean Hope's incinerator to burn sludge. The jury was advised that frequent or daily use of a ship's incinerator, however, was "not a common thing to see," and the frequent use revealed by the Oil Record Book "struck [the Coast Guard investigator] as extremely odd." *See* G.A. 250. The Coast Guard's investigation also confirmed that the insulation on the incinerator was cracked and defective, and that such a defect would prevent sludge from burning properly.

The evidence proved that Chief Engineer Ignacio had destroyed most of the sounding slips delivered to him by oiler Villar. Indeed, Chief Ignacio was able to provide the Coast Guard with only four sounding slips during the investigation in Wilmington. Furthermore, those sounding slips failed to match any entries in the Oil Record Book. For example, the amount of sludge in the sludge tank on July 13, 2015, was falsely recorded in the Oil Record Book as 4.9 cubic meters. The sounding slip for that date provided to Chief Ignacio by oiler Villar, however, revealed that the sludge tank then contained more than 7.0 cubic meters of sludge.

The Coast Guard's investigation also revealed that the sludge pump was illegally equipped with an extra flange.[19] A flange is normally used to connect a pipe to equipment or other pipes, and is usually welded to its location. Superintendent Prouzos **[—21—]** approached Lieutenant March in Wilmington and asked to see the piping diagram of where the illegal extra flange on the sludge pump of the Ocean Hope had been discovered. The extra flange was the one that had been connected to the magic pipe during the illegal discharge of sludge from the Ocean Hope on June 14, 2015. The extra flange, however, was not shown on the Vessel's piping diagrams. And its absence rendered those diagrams false, in violation of the federal regulations. The prosecution emphasized that, under the evidence, Oceanic and Oceanfleet had owned and operated the Vessel for several years with the illegal third flange affixed to the sludge pump. During that period, no steps had been

[18] Second Engineer Samson's series of false statements to the Coast Guard investigators at Wilmington provided evidentiary support for the false statements offense alleged in Count Four, as well as strong support for the obstruction of justice offense alleged in Count Five.

[19] Second Engineer Samson misled the Coast Guard investigators when he falsely advised Lieutenant March that he did not know about the extra flange on the Ocean Hope's sludge pump. That fact provided further evidentiary support for the false statements offense alleged in Count Four, as well as the obstruction of justice offense alleged in Count Five.

taken by the Appellants to rectify that problem.[20] **{-191-}**

F.

1.

Oceanic and Oceanfleet argued at trial that they were not vicariously criminally liable for any of the problems revealed by the Coast Guard's investigation. The Appellants asserted that they had been wrongly prosecuted for misconduct that was confined to the Engine Department crewmembers and unknown to Oceanic and Oceanfleet. More specifically, the Appellants denied all responsibility and blamed Chief Engineer Ignacio and Second Engineer Samson for the charges in the Indictment. **[—22—]**

Oceanic and Oceanfleet called four trial witnesses, unsuccessfully seeking to convince the jury that the misconduct of Chief Engineer Ignacio, Second Engineer Samson, and the Engine Department's subordinate crewmembers had been concealed from them. The Appellants fruitlessly argued that none of the crewmembers had alerted them to any misconduct onboard the Vessel, and they maintained that they were not legally bound by any criminal activities of their Engine Department supervisors or subordinate crewmembers. Oceanic and Oceanfleet also asked the district court to rule, as a matter of law, that the sole employer of the crewmembers was Oceanic. That request was denied.

In support of their joint defense, Oceanic and Oceanfleet introduced the MARPOL certificates of Chief Engineer Ignacio and Second Engineer Samson, as well as other Engine Department crewmembers, apparently seeking to show that the Appellants had hired qualified employees that could reasonably be relied upon. One witness asserted that the "company's policy was for zero pollution from the vessel." *See* J.A. 307. The Appellants also sought to show that some of the subordinate crewmembers in the Engine Department had improper motives. For example, third engineer Menente's wife was allegedly seeking a visa into this country when she provided the Coast Guard with evidence of the Ocean Hope's illegal pollution of the ocean.

2.

During the trial proceedings, Oceanic and Oceanfleet made a series of motions—pursuant to Rule 29 of the Rules of Criminal Procedure—for judgments of acquittal. In support thereof, the Appellants argued that they could not be vicariously liable for the **[—23—]** criminal conduct of any of the Engine Department crewmembers.[21] Each of those motions was denied. After the evidence was presented, the parties rested and the lawyers argued their competing positions to the jury.

In its instructions, the district court explained that it was the jury's duty "to decide whether the government has proved beyond a reasonable doubt the specific facts necessary to find each of the defendants guilty of the crimes charged." *See* J.A. 353. With reference to Oceanic and Oceanfleet, the jury was instructed on the vicarious liability issues that arise in these appeals. The jury was advised that,

> [i]n addition to the required elements of each offense, in order for you to find either [Oceanic or Oceanfleet] guilty of any of these charges, the government

[20] After being informed by the Coast Guard of the oil pollution activities and Oil Record Book falsifications onboard the Ocean Hope revealed by the Port Examination in Wilmington, Oceanfleet's Prouzos and Trousas promptly left for Europe. Before leaving, however, Prouzos blamed the criminal revelations made to him by the Coast Guard on those "F-ing Filipinos." *See* G.A. 254. Neither Prouzos nor Trousas had any further involvement in the Port Examination.

[21] With respect to the Failure to Maintain charge in Count Two, Oceanic and Oceanfleet supported their Rule 29 motions in their appellate submissions by asserting that Master Tabacaru of the Ocean Hope was the "only person . . . with the legal obligation to maintain the Oil Record Book." *See* Br. of Appellants 38. They argued that, because the proof of that charge was that Chief Engineer Ignacio and Second Engineer Samson were the real culprits and neither served as the Vessel's Master, Count Two had not been proven.

{-192-} must prove each of the following three elements:

> One, that the offense charged was committed by an agent or employee of [Oceanic or Oceanfleet];
>
> Second, in committing the offense, the agent or employee intended, at least in part, to benefit [Oceanic or Oceanfleet];
>
> And third, the agent or employee acted within his or their authority.

See J.A. 362.[22] **[—24—]**

In connection with that instruction, the district court explained to the jury that "an agent or employee of a corporation may act for his own benefit while also acting for the benefit of an organization." *See* J.A. 363. It also instructed that "[a]n act is within the authority of an agent or employee if it concerns a matter the organization generally entrusted to that agent or employee. The organization need not have actually authorized or directed the particular act." *Id.* The jury was instructed that, even if an act was illegal or "contrary to [Oceanic and/or Oceanfleet's] instructions" or "against . . . general policies," that fact would not absolve the Appellants of criminal responsibility. *Id.* The jury was advised that it could "consider . . . how carefully [Oceanic and/or Oceanfleet] tried to enforce [the policies and instructions it had in place]" in assessing whether employees or agents of Oceanic or Oceanfleet had acted with the intent to benefit the Appellants or only to benefit themselves. *Id.*

In instructing the jury on the Failure to Maintain charge in Count Two, the district court explained that, "the government does not contend that the defendants physically committed the acts charged," but "instead . . . contends that the defendants willfully caused another person, specifically the master, or captain . . . to physically commit the crime in violation of" the aiding and abetting statute. *See* J.A. 373-74. The court then proceeded to quote the provisions of § 2(b) of Title 18 to the jury. *Id.* at 373. In instructing the jury on Count Three, the court reiterated that it had "already explained the aiding and abetting statute," but then quoted "the other part of aiding and abetting" by reading the language of § 2(a) of Title 18. *Id.* at 377. Although the Appellants **[—25—]** unsuccessfully objected to certain aspects of the jury instructions, they have not pursued any of those issues on appeal.

On September 1, 2016, after completing its deliberations, the jury returned guilty verdicts on each of the nine charged offenses. Those verdicts, as relevant here, included the nine convictions of Oceanic and Oceanfleet.

G.

1.

Prior to the sentencing proceedings, separate PSRs were prepared for Oceanic and Oceanfleet. Because of the sentencing issues being pursued in these appeals, the PSRs must be reviewed in some detail.

According to the PSRs, neither Oceanic nor Oceanfleet had an effective program to prevent or detect violations, and neither of them had self-reported the violations or cooperated with the investigation. For both Oceanic and Oceanfleet, the PSRs applied Sentencing Guidelines § 3D1.2(c), which explains the concept of grouping as to closely related offenses of conviction. The offenses of conviction of the Appellants were grouped into "Count Group 1: Obstruction of Justice and Aiding and {-193-} Abetting" for Guidelines calculation purposes. *See* S.A. 16, 40. Importantly, the PSRs explained that obstruction of justice is not listed in Guidelines § 8C2.1—the permissible fine guideline—as an offense category concerning the imposition of criminal fines against corporations. *Id.* Thus, the permissible fines against Oceanic and Oceanfleet were determined by applying Guidelines § 8C2.10. That Guideline provides that, for any

---

[22] According to the government, the jury instructions were primarily drawn from our decision in *United States v. Singh*, 518 F.3d 236 (4th Cir. 2008).

conviction not covered under Guidelines § 8C2.1, the sentencing court will determine the **[—26—]** appropriate fine by applying the provisions of 18 U.S.C. §§ 3553 and 3572. *Id.* According to the PSRs, the statutory maximum fine against Oceanic and Oceanfleet on each of their convictions was $500,000. *Id.* at 17, 41.

The PSRs then assessed self-reported, unaudited financial information that was submitted by Oceanic and Oceanfleet. The PSRs concluded that Oceanic was "profitable until the instant offense," and that Oceanfleet was profitable until 2014. *See* S.A. 15, 39. The PSRs also revealed that Oceanic and Oceanfleet—in the context of these proceedings—had posted a surety bond of $500,000 for the Ocean Hope. *Id.* Under its provisions, that bond could be applied towards fines imposed as punishment. Oceanic's PSR concluded that it was "capable of paying a significant fine in installments if the corporate defendant is placed on probation." *Id.* at 24. Similarly, Oceanfleet's PSR found that it was "capable of paying a fine in installments." *Id.* at 40.

The information provided to the sentencing court by the United States Attorney in his sentencing memorandum convincingly revealed that Oceanic was a shell entity created by Oceanfleet to serve as the registered owner of the Ocean Hope. For example, a maritime credit reporting agency characterized Oceanic as being "understood to form part of the wider group of Oceanfleet," *see* G.A. 374, and "controlled by the same principals," *id.* at 376. The PSRs also revealed a significant overlap in the management personnel of Oceanic and Oceanfleet. Of importance, Oceanic's PSR said that "Oceanic appear[ed] to be a special-purpose corporate entity that is, for all relevant purposes, under the management and control of Oceanfleet." *See* S.A. 4. Although Oceanic and **[—27—]** Oceanfleet objected to certain aspects of their PSRs, they did not object to how the PSRs handled the grouping of offenses issue.

2.

The sentencing court adopted the PSRs and, on January 11, 2017, conducted the sentencing proceedings at issue here. Oceanic was ordered to pay $675,000 in fines, plus $225,000 in restitution to the Gray's Reef National Marine Sanctuary Foundation. Oceanfleet's fines and restitution were significantly greater than those assessed against Oceanic. Oceanfleet was thus ordered to pay $1,350,000 in fines, plus $450,000 in restitution to the same foundation. Oceanic and Oceanfleet were each sentenced to probationary terms of five years, but probation could be terminated after one year if certain conditions were satisfied. As a special condition of probation, Oceanic and Oceanfleet ships were barred from ports in the United States until the financial aspects of their sentences were satisfied. This special condition extended to "all vessels managed by [Oceanic or Oceanfleet] and/or any successor, assignee, subcontractor, acquirer, affiliate or other entity related to either defendant by reason of shared or common ownership, management or control." *See* J.A. 529, 535.

Oceanic and Oceanfleet have timely appealed the criminal judgments entered **{-194-}** against them.[23] We possess jurisdiction pursuant to 28 U.S.C. § 1291. **[—28—]**

II.

A.

In these appeals, Oceanic and Oceanfleet each present a single challenge to their convictions. That is, they maintain that the evidence was insufficient to prove corporate criminal liability. More specifically, they argue that the jury was not entitled to find beyond a reasonable doubt—with respect to any of the offenses in the Indictment—that any Ocean Hope crewmember was acting pursuant to corporate authority or with an intent to benefit Oceanic or Oceanfleet. The Appellants also assert that the sentencing

[23] The Ocean Hope supervisors who were convicted—Chief Engineer Ignacio and Second Engineer Samson—did not appeal their convictions or sentences.

court erred in four respects in imposing penalties. They contend that the court erred: (1) in grouping the various offenses; (2) by failing to consider Oceanic and Oceanfleet's independent financial conditions and separate abilities to pay the fines imposed; (3) by imposing erroneously disparate fines on Oceanfleet compared to fines on similarly situated defendants; and (4) by imposing a special condition of probation that improperly impacted related third parties.

B.

In reviewing the sufficiency of evidence in a criminal prosecution, we look for a clear prosecutorial failure. *See United States v. Jones*, 735 F.2d 785, 791 (4th Cir. 1984). Indeed, reversal of a conviction on grounds of insufficient evidence should be confined to cases where the prosecution's failure is clear. *Id.* We are obliged to sustain a guilty verdict "if there is substantial evidence, taking the view most favorable to the Government, to support it." *See United States v. Bolden*, 325 F.3d 471, 485 (4th Cir. 2003). In making an evidence sufficiency analysis, we ask only "whether there is **[—29—]** evidence that a reasonable finder of fact could accept as adequate and sufficient to support a conclusion of a defendant's guilt beyond a reasonable doubt." *See United States v. Foster*, 507 F.3d 233, 245 (4th Cir. 2007). Our precedent is that an appellant faces "a heavy burden" in challenging evidence sufficiency. *Id.*

In assessing a challenge to a sentencing court's application of the Sentencing Guidelines, we review the court's factual findings for clear error and its legal conclusions de novo. *See United States v. Allen*, 446 F.3d 522, 527 (4th Cir. 2006). We assess for abuse of discretion the reasonableness of fines imposed on a defendant. *See United States v. Walker*, 83 F.3d 94, 95 (4th Cir. 1996). If an appellant has failed to properly object and preserve an issue in the district court, we review the appellate contention for plain error only. *See United States v. Martinez*, 277 F.3d 517, 524 (4th Cir. 2002); *see also* Fed. R. Crim. P. 52(b). And we review special conditions of probation for abuse of discretion. *See United States v. Dotson*, 324 F.3d 256, 259 (4th Cir. 2003).

III.

A.

We begin our analysis by examining the contention that there is insufficient evidentiary support for the convictions of Oceanic and Oceanfleet. The Appellants each argue that the trial evidence was insufficient to prove their vicarious liability for the criminal activities of Chief Engineer Ignacio and Second Engineer Samson. In assessing the **{-195-}** liability of a corporate defendant, we adhere to the principles explained, inter alia, in *United States v. Singh*, 518 F.3d 236 (4th Cir. 2008) and *United States v. Automated Med.* **[—30—]** *Labs., Inc.*, 770 F.2d 399 (4th Cir. 1985). Consistent therewith, we are obliged to apply the legal proposition that "a corporation is liable for the criminal acts of its employees and agents done within the scope of their employment with the intent to benefit the corporation." *See Singh*, 518 F.3d at 249 (internal quotation marks omitted). Corporate liability can also arise "if the employee or agent has acted for his own benefit as well as that of his employer." *Id.* at 250.

1.

We first assess whether the prosecution presented sufficient evidence to prove that Chief Engineer Ignacio and Second Engineer Samson were agents or employees of Oceanfleet and Oceanic. The Appellants argue that Chief Ignacio and Samson were employed by Oceanic only, and that they were not agents or employees of Oceanfleet for purposes of vicarious liability. The evidence, however, when viewed in the proper light, proved that both Oceanic and Oceanfleet were their employers.

By way of example, the Oceanfleet Manual provided that Oceanfleet was "entitled to use or appoint [to the Ocean Hope] any agents or sub-contractors as it shall deem fit." *See* J.A. 406. Samson confirmed that his paychecks came from both Oceanic and Oceanfleet, and that "Oceanic Illsabe" was written on his employment contract. Samson explained that, while working aboard the Ocean Hope, he understood that Oceanfleet was the operator of the Vessel. The crewmembers understood that they were employed by Oceanfleet. Samson—as well as third engineer Menente and fitter Belleza—confirmed that the uniforms worn by crewmembers of the Ocean Hope bore the name Oceanfleet. Of great importance, the Oceanfleet Manual was provided to the Ocean Hope **[—31—]** crewmembers by Oceanfleet itself. And the Oil Record Book updates were provided to Oceanfleet officials on a weekly basis. Put succinctly, the evidence was more than sufficient to prove that the Engine Department crewmembers were employed by both Oceanic and Oceanfleet.

2.

a.

Next, we must assess whether Chief Engineer Ignacio and Second Engineer Samson were acting within the scope of their employment when they committed the various criminal offenses charged in the Indictment. We have broadly defined the term "scope of employment" for purposes of vicarious criminal liability, and the term includes, for example, "acts on the corporation's behalf in performance of the agent's general line of work." *See Automated Med. Labs., Inc.*, 770 F.2d at 407. We therefore need to decide whether the jury heard sufficient evidence to reasonably find that the actions of Chief Ignacio and Samson fell within their "general line of work" aboard the Ocean Hope.

It was Chief Engineer Ignacio's responsibility, as required by the Oceanfleet Manual, to implement and ensure compliance by all Engine Department crewmembers with the relevant safety and pollution prevention procedures. Pursuant to the Oceanfleet Manual, Chief Ignacio was personally in charge of maintaining a complete and accurate Oil Record Book on the Ocean Hope. Similarly, Second Engineer Samson acknowledged that he was obligated—on behalf of Oceanic and Oceanfleet—to supervise and carry out his duties pursuant to the Oceanfleet Manual. And Samson **{-196-}** had to ensure that the **[—32—]** Department's subordinate crewmembers complied with all applicable environmental policies.

The evidence proved that the Ocean Hope's Oil Record Book contained false and inaccurate entries, and that it was not accurately maintained. The evidence also proved that the Engine Department's subordinate crewmembers had been trained that "orders are given and expected to be obeyed down the chain of command without hesitation or question," as required by the Oceanfleet Manual. *See* G.A. 344. As a result, the subordinate crewmembers acted within the scope of their employment in complying with the directives of Chief Ignacio and Samson.

b.

Oceanic and Oceanfleet nonetheless contend on appeal that the activities of Chief Engineer Ignacio and Second Engineer Samson exceeded the scope of their duties, in that the Engine Department crewmembers had acted illegally and contrary to company policies. The Appellants also argue that they are not vicariously liable because the Department's crewmembers did not report any illegal conduct to responsible corporate officials at Oceanic or Oceanfleet. Those contentions are meritless.

The fact that the actions of the Engine Department crewmembers were illegal or contrary to corporate policy does not absolve either Oceanic or Oceanfleet of criminal responsibility. *See Automated Med. Labs.*, 770 F.2d at 407 (explaining that, although an agent acting within the scope of his employment acted unlawfully "and contrary to corporate policy," that fact did not "absolve [the company] of legal responsibility for [the agent's] acts"). In a somewhat analogous situation, the Second Circuit recognized that **[—33—]** "crew members acted within their authority to maintain the engine room, discharge waste, and record relevant information when they used [a] 'magic [pipe].'"

See United States v. Ionia Mgmt., 555 F.3d 303, 309 (2nd Cir. 2009).

Consistent with the district court's instructions, the jury weighed the purported corporate policies of Oceanic and Oceanfleet. And the jury was entitled to find—on the evidence—that none of those policies absolved the Appellants of criminal liability. Put simply, Chief Engineer Ignacio and Second Engineer Samson consistently ordered the subordinate crewmembers to violate MARPOL, APPS, various federal criminal statutes, and the applicable regulations.[24]

The evidence was that Oceanfleet received and reviewed the Ocean Hope's Oil Record Book on a weekly basis, and that the Appellants made recommendations to the Engine Department crewmembers on how to satisfy the Coast Guard's inspection. From those weekly updates of the Oil Record Book, Oceanfleet was on notice of multiple oddities. For example, Oceanfleet was aware that the Separator had broken on about July 2, 2015, and thus knew that the Separator's malfunction on that occasion was not properly recorded in the Oil Record Book. Oceanfleet also knew that the Oil Record Book falsely reflected that the Ocean Hope had not offloaded sludge since September 2014. And Oceanfleet knew that the incinerator was being used on a daily basis. The **[—34—]** Appellants, however, never inquired about any of these suspicious events. In the circumstances, the jury was entitled to infer the worst as to **{-197-}** Oceanic and Oceanfleet. That view, in favor of the prosecution, was that the Appellants were well aware of the systematic criminal misconduct of their supervisors concerning the Oil Record Book.

Oceanic and Oceanfleet also contend on appeal that Chief Engineer Ignacio and Second Engineer Samson consistently acted only to benefit themselves and not to benefit either Oceanic or Oceanfleet. We have never required the prosecution to prove, however, that a corporate defendant, "presumably as represented by its upper level officers and managers, had an intent separate from that of its lower level employees." *See United States v. Basic Constr. Co.*, 711 F.2d 570, 573 (4th Cir. 1983). As long as the corporate agent intends, at least in part, to benefit his employer, the corporate entity can be criminally liable, even if the agent is also acting for his own benefit. *See Singh*, 518 F.3d at 249 ("The appropriate scope of employment of such an employee or agent has been defined to include all those acts falling within the employee's or agent's general line of work, when they are motivated—at least in part—by an intent to benefit the corporate employer." (internal quotation marks omitted)). Importantly, the trial court's careful instructions to the jury were entirely consistent with that established legal principle.

In assessing the evidence for sufficiency, "[w]e review both direct and circumstantial evidence, and accord the government all reasonable inferences from the facts shown to those sought to be established." *See United States v. Cone*, 714 F.3d 197, 212 (4th Cir. 2013). The trial evidence was more than sufficient for the jury to infer that the intended beneficiaries of the illegal conduct on the Ocean Hope were Oceanic and **[—35—]** Oceanfleet. By way of example, the jury knew of the Appellants' profound concern with avoiding the detainment of the Ocean Hope in Wilmington because of the Coast Guard investigation. To avoid that problem, Oceanfleet provided the Engine Department's crewmembers with a checklist to complete before arriving in Wilmington. It also provided Chief Engineer Ignacio with sample Oil Record Book entries, which were themselves false and fraudulent.

Oceanfleet had a Port Captain and a Superintendent board the Ocean Hope in Panama to oversee the Vessel's preparations for the Coast Guard in Wilmington. Second Engineer Samson advised the Engine

[24] The jury also heard from three Engine Department subordinate crewmembers who were fearful of reporting illegal misconduct on the Vessel. For example, fourth engineer Sarduma and oiler Villegas both told the jury that they were afraid to report the illegal activities they saw occurring onboard the Ocean Hope. *See* G.A. 173a, 178, 196.

Department's subordinate crewmembers not to use the Separator unless it was for survey, in order to keep the Separator clean for the Port Examination. And Samson advised the subordinate crewmembers not to tell the Coast Guard investigators about illegal discharges of sludge. In those circumstances, the jury was entitled to find that Chief Engineer Ignacio and Samson intended to prevent the Coast Guard from finding any deficiencies onboard the Ocean Hope which might cause the Vessel to be detained or delayed in Wilmington.

In sum, voluminous false entries were made in the Ocean Hope's Oil Record Book. And the Oil Record Book was not maintained accurately and completely. Instructions from Chief Engineer Ignacio and Second Engineer Samson to the subordinate crewmembers were that they had to lie to the Coast Guard investigators. Additional false statements were made by Samson that constituted incriminating efforts—attributable to the Appellants—to assist the Vessel in passing the Port Examination. *See Automated Med. Labs.*, 770 F.2d at 407 (concluding that an agent was acting in part **[—36—]** to benefit his employer when the employer's "well-being" rested on "its lack of difficulties with the FDA"). Even if Chief Ignacio and Samson had personal motives to obstruct the Coast Guard investigation **{–198–}** (and none were offered or shown)—or if they intended to otherwise conceal their unlawful acts from the Coast Guard investigators—we nevertheless view the evidence in the light most favorable to the prosecution. Viewed in that light, Chief Ignacio and Samson were motivated to benefit Oceanic and Oceanfleet. *See Singh*, 518 F.3d at 249.

c.

In challenging their convictions on the Failure to Maintain charge in Count Two, Oceanic and Oceanfleet pursued a refined contention that they were entitled to judgments of acquittal because Master Tabacaru was the "only person with the legal obligation to maintain the Oil Record Book."[25] To support that proposition, they primarily rely on the Fifth Circuit's decision in *United States v. Fafalios*, which recognized that "[c]hief engineers on foreign-flagged vessels cannot . . . be prosecuted simply for having failed to maintain an oil record book once a ship enters U.S. waters, since 33 C.F.R. § 151.25 assigns that duty explicitly and exclusively to the 'master or other person having charge of the ship.'" *See* 817 F.3d 155, 162, 4 Adm. R. 204, 208 (5th Cir. 2016). Oceanic and Oceanfleet also maintain that, on the evidence presented, Master Tabacaru was not shown to have "knowingly fail[ed] to maintain" the Oil Record Book, nor to have permitted the **[—37—]** supervising crewmembers to falsify any entries made—or omitted to be made—in the Oil Record Book. *See* Br. of Appellants 38. Oceanic and Oceanfleet therefore contend that they cannot be held vicariously liable on the Failure to Maintain charge.

This refined theory of criminal liability must also fail, in that Oceanic and Oceanfleet were proven vicariously liable for the criminal acts of Chief Engineer Ignacio and Second Engineer Samson in aiding and abetting the failure of Master Tabacaru to maintain an accurate Oil Record Book. Indeed, Oceanic and Oceanfleet admit in their appellate submissions that "[t]here is no dispute" that Chief Ignacio and Samson "were permissibly prosecuted and convicted under the aiding and abetting theory of liability for causing the Master to fail to maintain an accurate" Oil Record Book. *See* Br. of Appellants 39. The explicit provisions of § 2(a) of Title 18 further undermine the Appellants' refined contention on Count Two. Since the time that statutory provision was amended in 1951, any distinction between an aider and abettor of an offense, on the one hand, and a principal offender, on the other, has been abolished. *See Standefer v. United States*, 447 U.S. 10, 18 n.11 (1980). That is, "[w]hoever . . . aids [or] abets" the commission of an offense against

[25] As we see it, Oceanic and Oceanfleet properly preserved their refined Count Two contention at trial, arguing to the court that they could not "aid and abet" themselves. *See* J.A. 280-81.

the United States "is punishable as a principal." *See* 18 U.S.C. § 2(a).

As the Fifth Circuit emphasized in its *Fafalios* decision, the crewmembers of a ship, other than the master thereof, "may be prosecuted for aiding and abetting the failure to maintain an accurate" Oil Record Book. *See* 817 F.3d at 162, 4 Adm. R. at 208. And we have already recognized that the criminal actions of Chief Engineer Ignacio and Second Engineer Samson fell within the scope of their duties on the Ocean Hope, and that they intended **[—38—]** for those actions to benefit Oceanic and Oceanfleet. As we have heretofore explained, "[a] person aids and abets a crime when . . . he intends to facilitate the offense's commission." *See* **{-199-}** *BMG Rights Mgmt. (US) LLC v. Cox Communs., Inc.*, 881 F.3d 293, 309 (4th Cir. 2018) (internal quotation marks omitted). Viewed in the proper light, Chief Ignacio and Samson aided and abetted Master Tabacaru's failure to maintain an accurate Oil Record Book. This refined contention of error as to Count Two is therefore also rejected.

d.

Consistent with the foregoing, Oceanic and Oceanfleet are unable to successfully challenge the sufficiency of the trial evidence. The district court thus did not err in denying the various motions for judgments of acquittal, and the guilty verdicts returned by the jury are amply supported by the evidence.

B.

Next, we turn to Oceanic and Oceanfleet's contentions regarding the sentences imposed by the district court.[26] The Appellants claim that the court erred in four respects: **[—39—]**

- by failing to properly group Counts Two and Three as well as Counts Six through Nine (the "grouping contention");
- by failing to consider Oceanic and Oceanfleet's independent financial conditions and separate abilities to pay the fines imposed (the "excessive fine contention");
- by imposing erroneously disparate fines on Oceanfleet compared to fines on similarly situated defendants (the "disparate fine contention");[27] and
- by imposing, as a special condition of probation, a five-year ban from ports in the United States of ships of the Appellants and related third parties (the "probation condition contention").

We will address the sentencing contentions in turn.

1.

In their grouping contention, the Appellants maintain that the sentencing court failed to properly "group" the offenses of conviction. The relevant Guideline provision—USSG § 3D1.2—provides that "counts involving substantially the same harm shall be grouped together in a single Group." Counts are deemed to allege substantially the same harm when, inter alia, "one of the counts embodies conduct that is treated as a specific offense characteristic in, or other adjustment to, the guideline applicable to another of the counts." *See* USSG § 3D1.2(c). Oceanic and Oceanfleet contend that Counts Two and Three and Counts Six through Nine alleged substantially the same criminal conduct, and thus should have been grouped together for sentencing purposes. **[—40—]** Had the court done so, according to Oceanic and Oceanfleet,

[26] When we refer herein to the "sentences" imposed on Oceanic and Oceanfleet, we mean the fines, restitution awards, periods of probation, and conditions of probation. Furthermore, the sentencing court and the parties have variously referred to the fines and restitution awards as fines, financial penalties, special assessments, and community service payments. Because the distinctions between fines and restitution awards do not alter or impact the resolution of these appeals, we sometimes collectively refer to them as "fines" or "financial penalties."

[27] As indicated below, the disparate fine contention is being pursued by Oceanfleet only. Oceanic does not pursue such a contention.

their permissible fines would have been substantially reduced.

Importantly, Oceanic and Oceanfleet did not present the grouping contention to the sentencing court, either by challenging the PSRs or by objecting in the sentencing proceedings. When a defendant **{-200-}** has not properly preserved a sentencing error and failed to provide the lower court with an opportunity to correct the alleged error, we can review the appellate contention for plain error only. *See United States v. Boykin*, 669 F.3d 467, 470 (4th Cir. 2012). In conducting plain error review, we assess: (1) whether there is an error; (2) whether the error is clear or obvious; and (3) whether the error affected the appellant's substantial rights. *See United States v. Olano*, 507 U.S. 725, 734 (1993). To satisfy the third requirement of the plain error test, the appellant must show that the error actually "affected the outcome of the district court proceedings." *Id.* Even when all three of these requirements are satisfied, "we have discretion whether to recognize the error, and should not do so unless the error 'seriously affects the fairness, integrity or public reputation of judicial proceedings.'" *See United States v. Hargrove*, 625 F.3d 170, 184 (4th Cir. 2010) (quoting *Olano*, 507 U.S. at 736).

Put simply, we discern no error in the sentencing court's handling of the grouping question in this case. And Oceanic and Oceanfleet failed—in their appellate submissions—to grapple with the fact that their PSRs actually grouped their offenses of conviction into a single group: "Count Group 1: Obstruction of Justice and Aiding and Abetting." *See* S.A. 16, 40. The Guideline applicable to an obstruction of justice offense directs the court to "determine an appropriate fine by applying the provisions of 18 **[—41—]** U.S.C. §§ 3553 and 3572." *See* USSG § 8C2.10; *see also* USSG § 2J1.2(a); USSG § 8C2.1. Neither § 3553 nor § 3572, however, requires a court to group the offenses of conviction prior to imposing a fine. Rather, those statutes direct the court to consider certain sentencing factors and impose a sentence "sufficient, but not greater than necessary" to serve the ends of justice. *See* 18 U.S.C. § 3553; *see also* 18 U.S.C. § 3572. The record confirms that the court considered those factors, and it then imposed financial penalties—totalling $900,000 for Oceanic and $1,800,000 for Oceanfleet—that were substantially less than the statutory maximum of $4,500,000. *See* 18 U.S.C. § 3571(c)(3) (establishing maximum fine of $500,000 for each felony offense of conviction).[28]

Assuming that the sentencing court erred in grouping Oceanic and Oceanfleet's offenses of conviction, the grouping contention fails to satisfy the requirements of plain error review. *See United States v. Seignious*, 757 F.3d 155, 166 (4th Cir. 2014) (assuming error in context of plain error review and "jumping straight" to second and third prongs of analysis). Put succinctly, the grouping contention is by no means plainly erroneous. A "plain" error is said to be an error so "clear or obvious" that it jumps off the page. *See Puckett v. United States*, 556 U.S. 129, 135 (2009). The Appellants, however, do not even argue on appeal that the court committed an obvious error. Indeed, they have **[—42—]** failed to argue that the grouping contention satisfies any of the requirements of plain error review. In these circumstances, the grouping contention must be rejected.

2.

In their excessive fine contention, Oceanic and Oceanfleet maintain that the sentencing court erred by failing to properly **{-201-}** consider the sentencing factors identified in 18 U.S.C. §§ 3553(a) and 3572. The Appellants objected to their fines at sentencing—after the fines had been imposed—on the ground that neither Oceanic nor Oceanfleet had the financial wherewithal to pay them.[29] The

[28] Section 3571(c)(3) of Title 18 provides for a statutory maximum fine of $500,000 on a corporate defendant convicted of a felony. Oceanic and Oceanfleet were each convicted of nine felonies, resulting in a statutory maximum aggregate fine of $4,500,000 for each of them.

[29] When asked by the district court if there were any objections to the sentence being imposed on Oceanic, its counsel replied "Yes sir. The fine that has been imposed is an improper fine because it is a fine which can never be paid based on the

Appellants thus preserved their excessive fine contention for these appeals, and we assess that contention for abuse of discretion. *See United States v. Walker*, 83 F.3d 94, 95 (4th Cir. 1996).

Pursuant to the PSRs, the criminal conduct of Oceanic and Oceanfleet falls within Sentencing Guidelines § 8C2.10. *See* S.A. 16, 40. That Guideline provision directs a sentencing court to determine appropriate fines for a corporate entity by looking to 18 U.S.C. §§ 3553 and 3572. Section 3553(a) provides that "[t]he court shall impose a sentence sufficient, but not greater than necessary" to reflect the severity of the offense, to provide just punishment for the offense, to deter future criminal conduct, and to protect **[—43—]** the public from future crimes by the defendant. *See* 18 U.S.C. § 3553(a)(2). In pursuing that end, the court should consider several factors, including:

- the nature and circumstances of the offense and the history and characteristics of the defendant;
- the need for the sentence imposed;
- the pertinent policy statements;
- the need to avoid unwarranted sentence disparities among defendants with similar records; and
- the need to provide restitution.

See 18 U.S.C. § 3553(a)(1)-(7). Section 3572 of Title 18, entitled "Imposition of a sentence of fine and related matters," directs a court to consider other factors that are similar to those enumerated in Section 3553.[30]

At the oral argument of these appeals, Oceanic and Oceanfleet maintained that the sentencing court failed to analyze any of the § 3572 factors. That contention—even if valid—would not warrant relief on the excessive fine contention. As we have recognized, specific findings as to each factor in § 3572(a) are unnecessary, and a court "may satisfy [the requirements of § 3572(a)] if it adopts a defendant's presentence investigation report . . . that contains adequate factual findings to allow effective appellate review of the fine or restitution." *See United States v. Castner*, 50 F.3d 1267, **[—44—]** 1277 (4th Cir. 1995). As with the § 3553(a) factors, we need "not vacate [a] sentence simply because the [sentencing] court did not spell out what the context of its explanation made patently obvious." *See United States v. Montes-Pineda*, 445 F.3d 376, 381 (4th Cir. 2006) (internal citations omitted). Put simply, a court "need not robotically tick through § 3553(a)'s every subsection." *Id.* at 380 (internal quotation marks omitted). **{-202-}**

After carefully considering the arguments of the prosecution and the defense, the sentencing court "[found] the basis for the findings contained in the presentence report [to be] credible and reliable, and therefore, adopt[ed] those findings." *See* J.A. 517; 520. And the PSRs contained adequate findings for appellate review, in that they specifically described Oceanic and Oceanfleet's abilities to pay. *See* S.A. 14-15; 38-39. Indeed, neither Oceanic nor Oceanfleet argues that the court misapprehended their abilities to pay the financial penalties imposed.

The financial information with respect to Oceanic and Oceanfleet that is reflected in the PSRs was self-reported and unaudited. Oceanic's PSR indicates that Oceanic sold the Ocean Hope—its only asset—in 2016, a year after the events giving rise to this prosecution. Oceanic reported a profit of nearly $5,000,000 in 2015, indicating that the Ocean Hope was profitable around the time the illegal pollution conduct occurred. Oceanfleet's PSR reflected

company's financial situation." *See* J.A. 523. The lawyer, who represented the Appellants jointly, raised the same objection to the fines imposed on Oceanfleet. *Id.* The court overruled both objections.

[30] For example, § 3572 of Title 18 directs a sentencing court to consider the income, earning capacity, and financial resources of the defendant; the burden that a fine will impose on the defendant; whether restitution is being ordered; the size of the organization; and any measures taken by the organization to prevent a recurrence of offenses.

that it had "10.8 vessels under management and [was] generating significant revenue." *See* S.A. 37. Therefore, Oceanfleet's PSR explained that "based on the continued receipt of revenues," Oceanfleet had the ability to pay a fine "if allowed to do so in installments." *Id.* at 40. The PSRs did not recommend any specific fines for either Oceanic or Oceanfleet. Nonetheless, even if a corporate **[—45—]** defendant has a negative net monthly cash flow at sentencing, that fact "does not necessarily indicate an inability to pay, particularly when their PSRs reflect past success in business and above average earning capacities." *See Castner*, 50 F.3d at 1278.

When calculating the Appellants' aggregate financial penalties—$1,800,000 for Oceanfleet and $900,000 for Oceanic—the sentencing court accepted and understood the factual findings in the PSRs and explained that the court had "considered the statutory issues as well as the factors provided in [§ 3553(a)]." *See* J.A. 517. The court carefully considered the pertinent public interests of "punishment, deterrence and recidivism," which mirror the factors in § 3553(a) that call for providing just punishment and deterrence. *Id.* at 515. The court also weighed the findings of the PSRs which reflect past business success by both Oceanic and Oceanfleet, and confirmed their abilities to pay fines in installments.

The sentencing court also considered the inculpatory findings of the PSRs that explained that "neither company acknowledged the discharges occurred or provided information from their internal investigations to the Coast Guard." *See* S.A. 11, 33. Addressing the illegal extra flange found on the sludge pump, the PSRs revealed that neither Oceanic nor Oceanfleet "took any steps to rectify the piping or . . . ensure that [the Ocean Hope] did not have [an] illegal connection." *Id.* at 7, 31-32. In these circumstances, we perceive no abuse of discretion by the court in the amounts of the financial penalties that were imposed. The excessive fine contention is therefore rejected.

3. **[—46—]**

The disparate fine contention is pursued by Oceanfleet only, and it has two subparts. Both aspects of the disparate fine contention are predicated on the sentencing court's alleged contravention of Section 3553(a)(6) of Title 18. Section 3553(a)(6) requires a sentencing court to consider "the need to avoid unwarranted sentence disparities among defendants with similar records who have been found guilty of similar conduct." *See* 18 U.S.C. § 3553(a)(6). In the first part of its disparate fine contention, Oceanfleet argues that the court erred by imposing a greater fine on Oceanfleet than on Oceanic, in that the Appellants were convicted of the same **{–203–}** offenses. In the second part of that contention, Oceanfleet argues that the court erred by imposing a greater financial penalty on Oceanfleet than was imposed on a corporate defendant convicted of pollution offenses several years ago in the Eastern District of Virginia. *See United States v. Diana Shipping Servs., S.A.*, 985 F. Supp. 2d 719 (E.D. Va. 2013). Because Oceanfleet did not pursue these arguments in the lower court, we review them for plain error only. *See Boykin*, 669 F.3d at 470.

Put simply, the foregoing contentions are nearly spurious. First, assuming the sentencing court plainly erred in imposing a greater financial penalty on Oceanfleet—the parent entity—than it imposed on Oceanic, Oceanfleet has not shown how that error could have affected its substantial rights. *See Seignious*, 757 F.3d at 166. In *Seignious*, we concluded that a criminal defendant's substantial rights were not affected where the defendant could not show that the "amount of restitution the district ordered [the defendant] to pay . . . would have been any different" but for the alleged error. *Id.* Similarly, Oceanfleet cannot show that the court would have imposed a lesser financial **[—47—]** penalty on Oceanfleet had it timely presented its disparity issue to the lower court. Indeed, that court might have agreed with Oceanfleet's disparate fine contention and increased Oceanic's financial penalties to equal those of Oceanfleet. In these circumstances, therefore, we are unable to rule that Oceanfleet's substantial rights were affected. This aspect of the disparate fine contention thus fails under the third prong of plain error review. *See Olano*, 507 U.S. at 732.

The sentencing court also did not err—plainly or otherwise—by imposing a greater fine on Oceanfleet than the court imposed on the defendant in the *Diana Shipping* case. The *Diana* defendant—a ship operator—was convicted of eleven offenses arising from its failure to properly record the disposal of bilge water in its Oil Record Book. *See* 985 F. Supp. 2d at 722. According to Oceanfleet, the *Diana* court imposed an aggregate fine of $1,100,000 on those convictions—approximately $700,000 less than Oceanfleet's aggregate financial penalty. *See* Br. of Appellants 48-49. Oceanfleet requests that we vacate its financial penalty in light of that disparity. We are satisfied to reject that request for at least two reasons.

First, although Oceanfleet and the *Diana* defendant were convicted of similar offenses, the defendant in *Diana* was not shown as similarly situated to Oceanfleet. For example, the *Diana* court credited the defendant for accepting responsibility for the actions of its employees and moving swiftly to implement procedures to preempt additional violations of federal law. *See* Sentencing Tr. at 43, *Diana Shipping Servs., S.A.*, No. 2:13-cr-40 (E.D. Va. Dec. 18, 2013), ECF No. 151. Oceanfleet, by contrast, maintained its innocence throughout the sentencing proceedings, and has never **[—48—]** acknowledged that its environmental safety training and compliance procedures are inadequate to prevent reoccurrences of the criminal conduct that occurred on the Ocean Hope. *See* S.A. 35; *see also* S.A. 38 (specifying in Oceanfleet's PSR that "it does not appear that the corporate defendant had an effective program to prevent or detect violations.").

Second, we are aware of no precedent that requires district courts in separate districts to impose nearly identical fines on corporate defendants convicted of similar criminal offenses. The sentencing court in this case was directed to impose fines on Oceanfleet by applying the sentencing factors set forth in 18 U.S.C. §§ 3553 and 3572. And Section 3572(a)(6) required the **{-204-}** sentencing court to take into account Oceanfleet's "income, earning capacity, and financial resources" in imposing financial penalties. The individualized nature of those factors will necessarily result in different penalties being imposed on different defendants. Indeed, discrepancies in income and earning capacity in all likelihood contributed to the distinctions between the penalties imposed on Oceanfleet—the parent entity of at least ten subsidiary-like entities—and the *Diana* defendant, which was a subsidiary of a large publicly traded company. *See* Def. Sentencing Mem. at 11, *Diana Shipping Servs., S.A.*, No. 2:13-cr-40 (E.D. Va. Nov. 29, 2013), ECF No. 134. In these circumstances, the sentencing court did not err in imposing a greater financial penalty on Oceanfleet than the Virginia federal court apparently imposed on the *Diana* defendant.

4. **[—49—]**

Finally, in their probation condition contention, Oceanic and Oceanfleet argue that it was improper for the sentencing court to impose a ban on ships managed by Oceanfleet and Oceanic from all ports in the United States, for a maximum period of five years, or until they paid their financial penalties. Although we would normally review such an issue for abuse of discretion, the Appellants did not object to the special condition of probation when it was imposed. *See United States v. Dotson*, 324 F.3d 256, 259 (4th Cir. 2003). Therefore, we assess the probation condition contention for plain error only. *See Olano*, 507 U.S. 725, 734.

The Appellants argue that the five-year ban (contingent upon failure to pay financial penalties)—which extended to "all vessels managed by [Oceanic or Oceanfleet] and/or any . . . entity related to either defendant by reason of shared or common ownership, management or control"—improperly punished innocent third parties for the criminal actions of the Appellants. *See* J.A. 529, 535. A sentencing court is, in its discretion, entitled to impose such special conditions so long as they "are reasonably related to the factors set forth in section 3553(a)(1) and (a)(2)." *See* 18 U.S.C. § 3563(b)(22).

As the government emphasizes, the sentencing court's special condition of probation—that extended to any "entity related to either defendant by reason of shared or common ownership, management or control"—was reasonably related to the sentencing factors listed in 18 U.S.C. § 3553(a). *See* J.A. 529, 535. In particular, the special condition was directly tied to the need to "afford adequate deterrence to criminal conduct," "protect the public from further crimes of the defendant," and "provide **[—50—]** restitution to . . . victims." *See* 18 U.S.C. § 3553(a)(2)(B)-(C), (7). The PSRs revealed that it is a common practice for international shippers, such as Oceanfleet, to operate through special-purpose subsidiary entities like Oceanic. Indeed, the PSRs reflect that Oceanfleet manages and controls at least ten other ships in this manner. It was therefore reasonable for the court to conclude that, if its special condition of probation did not extend to other special-purpose entities managed by Oceanfleet, those entities would continue to operate freely in the ports of the United States. The special condition of probation was thus entirely reasonable and its imposition was not an abuse of the court's discretion. Because no error was committed, there can be no plain error. The probation condition contention is therefore also rejected.

IV.

Pursuant to the foregoing, we reject Oceanic and Oceanfleet's various contentions of error regarding their convictions and sentences. We are therefore satisfied **{–205–}** to affirm the criminal judgments that are challenged in these appeals.

AFFIRMED

This page intentionally left blank

United States Court of Appeals for the Fifth Circuit

United States Court of Appeals
for the Fifth Circuit

No. 16-30217

IN RE LARRY DOIRON, INC.

Appeal from the United States District Court for the Western District of Louisiana

Decided: January 8, 2018
Revised: January 11, 2018

Citation: 879 F.3d 568, 6 Adm. R. 160 (5th Cir. 2018) (en banc).

Before **STEWART**, Chief Judge, and **JOLLY***, **DAVIS****, **JONES**, **SMITH**, **DENNIS**, **CLEMENT**, **PRADO**, **OWEN**, **ELROD**, **SOUTHWICK**, **HAYNES**, **GRAVES**, **HIGGINSON** and **COSTA**, Circuit Judges.***

* Judge Jolly, now a Senior Judge of this court, participated in the consideration of this en banc case.
** Judge Davis, now a Senior Judge of this court, is participating as a member of the original panel.
*** Judges Willett and Ho were not on the court when this case was heard en banc.

[—2—] {–569–} DAVIS, Circuit Judge:

We took this case en banc to consider modifying the criteria set forth in *Davis & Sons, Inc. v. Gulf Oil Corp.* for determining whether a contract for performance of specialty services to facilitate the drilling or production of oil or gas on navigable waters is maritime.[1] After briefing and argument, the Court has decided to adopt a simpler, more straightforward test consistent with the Supreme Court's decision in *Norfolk Southern Railway Co. v. Kirby* for making this determination.[2]

I. BACKGROUND

On October 12, 2005, Apache Corporation ("Apache") entered into a blanket master services contract ("MSC") with Specialty Rental Tools & Supply, L.L.P. ("STS"). The MSC included an indemnity provision running in favor of Apache and **{–570–}** its contractors.[3] In early 2011, Apache issued an oral work order directing STS to perform "flow-back" services on a gas well in navigable waters in Louisiana in order to remove obstructions hampering the well's flow. A stationary production platform provided the only access to the gas well. The work order did not require a vessel, and neither Apache nor STS anticipated that a vessel would be necessary to perform the job. **[—3—]**

On February 24, 2011, STS dispatched a two-man crew to perform the work required by the work order. After an unsuccessful day of work, the STS crew determined that some heavy equipment was needed to complete the job and that a crane would be required to lift the equipment into place. Because the production platform was too small to accommodate a crane, the crew suggested to Apache that it engage a barge equipped with a crane to lift the equipment. Apache agreed and contracted with Plaintiff Larry Doiron, Inc. ("LDI"), to provide a crane barge.

The next day, the LDI crew proceeded to the job site on the crane barge POGO and unloaded the equipment requested by the STS crew. After being unsuccessful, however, the STS crew discovered that it needed yet a different piece of equipment, so, with the aid of the crane, both crews began removing the heavy equipment previously unloaded. During this process, the LDI crane operator struck and injured one of the STS crewmembers, Peter Savoie, with the equipment.

Anticipating a claim from Mr. Savoie, LDI filed a limitation of liability proceeding as owner of the crane barge POGO. Savoie filed a claim in the limitation proceeding. LDI, as Apache's contractor, then filed a third-party complaint against STS, seeking indemnity under the terms of the MSC.

LDI filed a motion for summary judgment seeking a declaration that it was entitled to indemnity from STS under the MSC. STS filed a cross-motion for summary judgment seeking a determination that it owed no indemnity. The narrow issue presented was whether the

[1] *See* 919 F.2d 313 (5th Cir. 1990).
[2] *See* 543 U.S. 14 (2004).
[3] A more exhaustive factual background can be found in the panel opinion. *See In re Larry Doiron, Inc.*, 869 F.3d 338, 340–41, 5 Adm. R. 206, 206–07 (5th Cir. 2017).

MSC was a maritime contract. If so, general maritime law permitted enforcement of the indemnity provision. If not, Louisiana law controlled, and the Louisiana Oilfield Indemnity Act ("LOIA") precluded indemnity.[4] The district court concluded that maritime **[—4—]** law applied and awarded LDI indemnity from STS. Our panel affirmed that judgment on appeal. A majority of the active judges then voted to take the case en banc.

II. DISCUSSION

A. Standard of Review

We review de novo a district court's grant of summary judgment.[5] Summary judgment is proper "if the movant shows that there is no genuine dispute as to any material fact and the movant is entitled to judgment as a matter of law."[6] A genuine dispute exists if a reasonable jury could find in favor of the nonmoving party.[7] All facts and evidence are viewed in **{-571-}** the light most favorable to the nonmovant.[8] We turn first to the existing law on maritime contracts in this circuit.

B. Current Law

The issue in this case is whether the Court should apply maritime law or Louisiana law to determine the validity of the indemnity provisions in the MSC. If Louisiana law applies, the indemnity agreement is void as against public policy.[9] If, on the other hand, the contract is maritime and state law does not apply, then the indemnity obligation is enforceable.[10] **[—5—]**

Our cases in this area have long been confusing and difficult to apply. In *Thurmond v. Delta Well Surveyors*, Judge Garwood stated in his concurring opinion that he was "generally in agreement with Judge Wisdom's persuasive opinion, but . . . troubled by the tension, or perhaps outright inconsistency, between many of our opinions in this area."[11] He elaborated that:

> [I]t seems to me that it may be desirable to consider this issue en banc, in order that we may take a more consistent approach to the question of whether and in what circumstances activities in connection with mineral development in state territorial waters are maritime (or perhaps "maritime and local[.]")][12]

Since 1990, we have followed the multi-factor test set forth in *Davis & Sons, Inc. v. Gulf Oil Corp.* ("*Davis & Sons*") to determine whether a contract is a maritime contract.[13] Judge Rubin, in attempting to summarize and make sense of our case law, set forth numerous guiding principles:

> If . . . the contract consists of two parts, a blanket contract followed by later work orders, the two must be interpreted together in evaluating whether maritime or land law is applicable to the interpretation and enforceability of the contract's provisions. The blanket contract is not of itself complete and calls for no specific work. The actual contract between the parties therefore consists of the blanket agreement as modified by the later work order.[14]

---

4 *See* LA. REV. STAT. § 9:2780(A).

5 *James v. State Farm Mut. Auto. Ins. Co.*, 743 F.3d 65, 68 (5th Cir. 2014).

6 FED. R. CIV. P. 56(a).

7 *Anderson v. Liberty Lobby, Inc.*, 477 U.S. 242, 248 (1986).

8 *James*, 743 F.3d at 68.

9 *See* LA. REV. STAT. § 9:2780(A).

10 *See Hoda v. Rowan Cos.*, 419 F.3d 379, 380 (5th Cir. 2005).

LDI also argues that the choice-of-law clause in the MSC, which specifies general maritime law as the applicable law under which to construe the contract, should be enforced even if the contract is nonmaritime in nature. Our case law makes clear that, if the contract is nonmaritime, Louisiana law will govern its construction even in the face of a choice-of-law clause. This is so because enforcement of the choice-of-law clause would violate Louisiana's public policy and directly contravene LOIA. *See Verdine v. Ensco Offshore Co.*, 255 F.3d 246, 254 (5th Cir. 2001).

11 836 F.2d 952, 957 (5th Cir. 1988) (Garwood, J., concurring).

12 *See id.* (quoting *Kossick v. United Fruit Co.*, 365 U.S. 731, 738 (1961)).

13 919 F.2d at 316.

14 *Id.* at 315.

He stated further:

> A contract may either contain both maritime and non-maritime obligations . . . . If separable maritime obligations are imposed . . . , these are maritime obligations that can be separately enforced in admiralty without prejudice to the rest, hence subject to maritime law.[15]
>
> Whether the blanket agreement and work orders, read together, do or do not **{–572–}** constitute a maritime contract depends, as does the **[—6—]** characterization of any other contract, on the nature and character of the contract, rather than on its place of execution or performance. A contract relating to a ship in its use as such, or to commerce or navigation on navigable waters, or to transportation by sea or to maritime employment is subject to maritime law. What constitutes maritime character is not determinable by rubric. The Supreme Court has resorted to the observation that a contract is maritime if it has a genuinely salty flavor.[16]

He concluded his synopsis by distilling these principles into the six-factor test at issue in this appeal:

> Determination of the nature of a contract depends in part on historical treatment in the jurisprudence and in part on a fact-specific inquiry. We consider six factors in characterizing the contract: 1) what does the specific work order in effect at the time of injury provide? 2) what work did the crew assigned under the work order actually do? 3) was the crew assigned to work aboard a vessel in navigable waters? 4) to what extent did the work being done relate to the mission of that vessel? 5) what was the principal work of the injured worker? and 6) what work was the injured worker actually doing at the time of injury?[17]

A number of judges on this Court have since criticized this approach as confusing, particularly the six-factor, fact-intensive test.[18] In *Hoda v. Rowan Cos.*, Judge Jones began the opinion by stating that:

> This appeal requires us to sort once more through the authorities distinguishing maritime and non-maritime contracts in the offshore exploration and production industry. As is typical, the final result turns on a minute parsing of the facts. Whether this is the soundest jurisprudential approach may be doubted, inasmuch as it creates uncertainty, spawns litigation, and hinders the rational calculation of costs and risks by companies **[—7—]** participating in this industry. Nevertheless, we are bound by the approach this court has followed for more than two decades.[19]

Professor David W. Robertson has also pointed out some of the difficulties with the *Davis & Sons* test:

> The six factors are too pointillistic: they have led Fifth Circuit panels down such odd lines of thought as "whether drilling mud services are more akin to wireline work [which has sometimes been viewed as quintessentially nonmaritime] or to casing services."[20]

---

15 *Id.* at 315–16 (internal quotation marks, brackets, and citations omitted).

16 *Id.* at 316 (internal quotation marks and citations omitted).

17 *Id.*

18 *See, e.g., Hodgen v. Forest Oil Corp.*, 87 F.3d 1512, 1523 n.8 (5th Cir. 1996), (collecting cases expressing frustration with the inconsistent analysis of maritime contracts), *overruled on other grounds by Grand Isle Shipyard, Inc. v. Seacor Marine, LLC,* 589 F.3d 778, 788 (5th Cir. 2009) (en banc); *Hoda*, 419 F.3d at 380.

19 419 F.3d at 380.

20 David W. Robertson, *The Outer Continental Shelf Lands Act's Provisions on Jurisdiction, Remedies, and Choice of Law: Correcting the Fifth Circuit's Mistakes,* 38 J. MAR. L. & COM. 487, 545 (2007). For a more detailed criticism of the *Davis & Sons* test, see id. at 540–45.

For a variety of reasons, most of the prongs of the *Davis & Sons* test are unnecessary and unduly complicate the determination of whether a contract is maritime. Judge Southwick's complex factual explication of the prongs in the panel opinion—which we consider below—demonstrates **{-573-}** this point.[21]

The first *Davis & Sons'* prong asks: What does the contract provide?[22] This is clearly an appropriate consideration in any contract case: the language of the contract. In this case, the contract consists of both the blanket MSC and the oral work order, which must be read together.[23]

The second prong asks: What did the crew actually do?[24] Analyzing this prong required the panel to parse the precise facts related to the services **[—8—]** performed under the contract and determine whether those services were inherently maritime. Because none of our previous case law had considered the flow-back services at issue here and whether they were inherently maritime, the panel attempted to analogize flow-back services to other services considered in previous opinions.[25] This required the panel to give a detailed description of both this case and the analogous cases, comparing flow-back services to casing, wireline, and welding services.[26] In doing so, the panel added to the many pages dedicated to similar painstaking analyses in the Federal Reporter.[27] The fact is, none of these services are inherently maritime. As discussed below, the focus should be on whether the contract calls for substantial work to be performed from a vessel.

The third and fourth *Davis & Sons* prongs ask: Was the crew assigned to a vessel in navigable waters, and to what extent was the crew's work related to the mission of the vessel?[28] These facts would be relevant if we were required to decide whether the crew members were seamen but not relevant to whether the employer of the crewmembers entered into a maritime contract. The fifth prong asks: What was the principal work of the injured worker?[29] **[—9—]** Again, this is not relevant to whether the injured worker's *employer* entered into a maritime contract.

The sixth prong asks: What was the injured worker doing when injured?[30] The facts surrounding the accident are relevant to whether the worker was injured in a maritime tort, but they are immaterial in **{-574-}** determining whether the worker's employer entered into a maritime contract.

In our panel opinion, after exhaustively analyzing the facts of this case in light of the six-prong test, we limited our holding to the facts of this case and determined that the contract was maritime primarily because a

---

[21] *See generally In re Doiron*, 869 F.3d., 5 Adm. R. 206.

[22] *Davis & Sons*, 919 F.2d at 316.

[23] STS argues that the following provision in the MSC contemplates the use of a vessel: "IF CONTRACTOR [STS] *USES* ANY VESSELS IN CONNECTION WITH ITS WORK FOR COMPANY OR COMPANY GROUP," additional vessel-related insurance is required. (emphasis added).

This insurance provision on its face has no application because STS did not provide or use a vessel—the vessel and crew were provided by LDI. This provision requiring vessel-related insurance applied to contractors such as LDI.

[24] *Davis & Sons*, 919 F.2d at 316.

[25] *See In re Doiron*, 869 F.3d at 343, 5 Adm. R. at 208–09.

[26] *See id.* at 344–46, 5 Adm. R. at 209–11.

[27] *Compare Thurmond*, 836 F.2d at 956 (finding wireline services nonmaritime in nature); *Domingue v. Ocean Drilling & Expl. Co.*, 923 F.2d 393, 398 (5th Cir. 1991) (same), *with Corbitt v. Diamond M. Drilling Co.*, 654 F.2d 329, 332 (5th Cir. Unit A Aug. 1981) (finding casing services to be maritime in nature), *and Campbell v. Sonat Offshore Drilling, Inc.*, 979 F.2d 1115, 1124–25 (5th Cir. 1992) (same); *see also* Kenneth G. Engerrand, *Primer of Remedies on the Outer Continental Shelf*, 4 LOY. MAR. L.J. 19, 61–63 (2005) (noting that historically, some service contracts are considered maritime in nature, including drilling and workover, casing, catering, repair, and well-site supervision, while other services contracts are traditionally nonmaritime in nature, including wireline work, testing and completion operations).

[28] *Davis & Sons*, 919 F.2d at 316.

[29] *See id.*

[30] *Id.*

vessel was essential to the completion of the job.[31]

C. *Kirby*

Fortunately, the Supreme Court's opinion in *Norfolk Southern Railway Co. v. Kirby* lights a path to a simpler, more straightforward method for determining whether a contract is maritime and avoids most of the unnecessary analysis required by *Davis & Sons*.[32] In *Kirby*, the Supreme Court considered a claim for money damages for cargo damaged in a train wreck.[33] Under two coextensive bills of lading, the goods were transported from Australia to Huntsville, Alabama: first by ship from Australia to Savannah, Georgia, and then by rail to Huntsville, Alabama.[34] The question was whether the suit to recover for cargo damaged on the land leg of the trip fell within the Court's admiralty jurisdiction.[35] The Court answered this in the affirmative because both bills of lading were maritime contracts.[36] This was **[—10—]** so, the Court reasoned, because the "primary objective" of these bills was "to accomplish the transportation of goods by sea from Australia to the eastern coast of the United States."[37]

In considering whether the bills of lading were maritime contracts, the Court broadly defined what characterized a contract as maritime. The Court observed that:

> [W]e cannot look to whether a ship or other vessel was involved in the dispute, as we would in a putative maritime tort case. . . . Nor can we simply look to the place of the contract's formation or performance. Instead, the answer "depends upon . . . the nature and character of the contract," and the true criterion is whether it has "reference to maritime service or maritime transactions."[38]

The Court also emphasized that "the fundamental interest giving rise to maritime jurisdiction is the protection of maritime commerce."[39] "The conceptual approach," the Court explained, "vindicates that interest by focusing our inquiry on whether the principal objective of a contract is maritime commerce."[40] The *Kirby* opinion clarified that we should use contract rather than tort principles in determining whether a contract being sued upon is maritime.[41] **[—11—]** **{-575-}**

The Court in *Kirby* rejected the mixed-contract theory applied in some circuits and which was one of the underpinnings of the *Davis & Sons* panel's rationale in formulating its six-prong test. *Davis & Sons* explained that:

> A contract may either contain both maritime and non-maritime obligations or, as in the Gulf-Davis blanket agreement, contemplate future detailed contracts having different characteristics. If separable maritime obligations are imposed by the supplementary contracts, or work orders, these are "maritime obligations [that] can be separately enforced [in admiralty] without prejudice to the rest," hence subject to maritime law.[42]

---

[31] *In re Doiron*, 869 F.3d at 345–47, 5 Adm. R. at 210–12.

[32] *See* 543 U.S. at 22–27.

[33] *See id.* at 18.

[34] *See id.* at 18–21.

[35] *See id.* at 22–24.

[36] *See id.* at 24.

[37] *Id.*

[38] *Id.* (second alteration in original) (quoting *N. Pac. S.S. Co. v. Hall Bros. Marine Ry. & Shipbuilding Co.*, 249 U.S. 119, 125 (1919)); *see also Exxon Corp. v. Cent. Gulf Lines, Inc.*, 500 U.S. 603, 611 (1991) ("[T]he trend in modern admiralty case law . . . is to focus the jurisdictional inquiry upon whether the nature of the transaction was maritime.").

[39] *Kirby*, 543 U.S. at 25 (emphasis removed) (internal quotation marks and citations omitted).

[40] *Id.*

[41] *Id.* at 24. The Court explained that "[g]eography . . . is useful in a conceptual inquiry only in a limited sense: If a bill's *sea* components are insubstantial, then the bill is not a maritime contract." *Id.* at 27.

[42] *See Davis & Sons*, 919 F.2d at 315–16 (footnote omitted).

The *Kirby* court, after disapproving mixed-contract decisions from the Second, Fifth, and Federal Circuit Courts of Appeal,[43] added the following:

> Furthermore, to the extent that these lower court decisions fashion a rule for identifying maritime contracts that depends solely on geography, they are inconsistent with the conceptual approach our precedent requires. Conceptually, so long as a bill of lading requires *substantial* carriage of goods by sea, its purpose is to effectuate maritime commerce—and thus it is a maritime contract. Its character as a maritime contract is not defeated simply because it also provides for some land carriage.[44]

Our cases have long held that the drilling and production of oil and gas on navigable waters from a vessel is commercial maritime activity. For example, in *Theriot v. Bay Drilling Corp.*, we considered a contract for supplying a submersible drilling barge and concluded that the contract was clearly maritime, noting that "[o]il and gas drilling on navigable waters aboard a vessel is recognized to be maritime commerce."[45] We recently affirmed this understanding of commercial maritime activity in *In re Deepwater Horizon*, **[—12—]** where we concluded that maritime law applied in reference to the oil spill that "occurred while the vessel[, Deepwater Horizon,] was engaged in the maritime activity of conducting offshore drilling operations."[46]

III. CONCLUSION

Based on the principles laid out in *Kirby*, we adopt the following two-pronged **{-576-}** test to determine whether a contract in this context is maritime: First, is the contract one to provide services to facilitate the drilling or production of oil and gas on navigable waters? The answer to this inquiry will avoid the unnecessary question from *Davis & Sons* as to whether the particular service is inherently maritime. Second, if the answer to the above question is "yes," does the contract provide or do the parties expect that a vessel will play a substantial role in the completion of the contract?[47] If so, the contract is **[—13—]**

---

[43] *See, e.g.*, *Kuehne & Nagel (AG & Co.) v. Geosource, Inc.*, 874 F.2d 283, 290 (5th Cir. 1989).

[44] *Kirby*, 543 U.S. at 27 (emphasis added) (internal citation omitted).

[45] 783 F.2d 527, 538–39 (5th Cir. 1986).

[46] 745 F.3d 157, 166, 2 Adm. R. 171, 175 (5th Cir. 2014); *see also Boudreaux v. Am. Workover, Inc.*, 664 F.2d 463, 466 (5th Cir. Unit A Dec. 1981) (noting that vessel-related oil and gas drilling and production "is a major industry with peculiar maritime-related problems," and, further, that because it is "an industry that provides approximately 40,000 jobs, and untold millions of dollars in revenues and that takes place primarily upon the navigable waters of the United States," it "bears 'a significant relationship to . . . commerce on navigable waters'") (alteration in original) (footnote and internal citation omitted); *Pippen v. Shell Oil Co.*, 661 F.2d 378, 384 (5th Cir. Unit A Nov. 1981) ("[O]ffshore drilling the discovery, recovery, and sale of oil and natural gas from the sea bottom is maritime commerce . . . ."); *Corbitt*, 654 F.2d at 332 (finding that a contract requiring the furnishing of a casing crew to a submersible drilling barge was a maritime contract); *Transcon. Gas Pipe Line Corp. v. Mobile Drilling Barge*, 424 F.2d 684, 688–91 (5th Cir. 1970) (finding that a drilling and re-work contract requiring the operation and "survey" of a submersible drilling barge was maritime in nature).

[47] When work is performed in part on a vessel and in part on a platform or on land, we should consider not only time spent on the vessel but also the relative importance and value of the vessel-based work to completing the contract. In *Chandris, Inc. v. Latsis*, in formulating the test for whether a worker's connection to a vessel was substantial enough to qualify him as a seaman under the Jones Act, 46 U.S.C. § 30104, the Supreme Court noted:

> [S]ubstantiality in this context is determined by reference to the period covered by the Jones Act plaintiff's maritime employment, rather than by some absolute measure. Generally, the Fifth Circuit seems to have identified an appropriate rule of thumb for the ordinary case: A worker who spends less than about 30 percent of his time in the service of a vessel in navigation should not qualify as a seaman under the Jones Act. This figure of course serves as **[—13—]** no more than a guideline established by years of experience, and departure from it will certainly be justified in appropriate cases.

maritime in nature.[48] We find strong support in *Kirby* for this test, particularly in the following sentence: "Conceptually, so long as a bill of lading requires substantial carriage of goods by sea, its purpose is to effectuate maritime commerce—and thus it is a maritime contract."[49] Also, in *Kirby*, the parties obviously expected a vessel to play a major role in transporting the cargo from Australia to Alabama.[50]

This test places the focus on the contract and the expectations of the parties. This is the proper approach in a contract case and assists the parties in evaluating their risks, particularly their liability under indemnification clauses in the contract.[51] This test also removes from the {-577-} calculus those prongs of the *Davis & Sons* test that are irrelevant, such as whether the service work [—14—] itself is inherently maritime and whether the injury occurred following a maritime tort. Courts need not determine whether this service work has a more or less salty flavor than other service work when neither type is inherently salty.

This does not mean, however, that some of the *Davis & Sons* factors are never relevant. The scope of the contract may be unclear; the extent to which the parties expect vessels to be involved in the work may also be unclear. In resolving these issues, courts may permit the parties to produce evidence of the work actually performed and the extent of vessel involvement in the job. It is also conceivable, for example, that the seamen status of a crew—which is implicated in two of the *Davis & Sons* factors—could be relevant to whether the vessel involvement was a substantial part of the overall contract. If the contract provided only for work to be done by permanent crewmembers aboard a vessel, the substantial vessel involvement issue would ordinarily be answered. If part of the contract work involves work by crewmembers aboard a vessel and part does not, the work by seamen aboard a vessel would be part of the factual mix that the district court could consider in resolving whether the overall contract involved substantial involvement of a vessel.[52]

Applying this new test to this case, the oral work order called for STS to perform downhole work on a gas well that had access only from a platform. After the STS crew began work down hole, the crew encountered an unex-

---

515 U.S. 347, 371 (1995). The district courts may develop a similar rule of thumb in evaluating substantiality in this context. However, we leave this for further development below. The calculus would not include transportation to and from the job site.

[48] *See* Robertson, *supra* note 20, at 547–48.

[49] *See Kirby*, 543 U.S. at 27. Six other circuits have applied *Kirby* to determine whether a contract is a maritime one in various circumstances; though none of those decisions addressed a factual situation similar to that in this case, the approaches in those decision are not inconsistent with this test. *See Fireman's Fund Ins. Co. v. Great Am. Ins. Co.*, 822 F.3d 620, 631–36, 4 Adm. R. 70, 75–80 (2d Cir. 2016) (analyzing whether an insurance contract was maritime); *N.H. Ins. Co. v. Home Sav. & Loan Co.*, 581 F.3d 420, 424–27 (6th Cir. 2009) (same); *Sentry Select Ins. Co. v. Royal Ins. Co.*, 481 F.3d 1208, 1218–20 (9th Cir. 2007) (same); *Flame S.A. v. Freight Bulk Pte. Ltd.*, 762 F.3d 352, 361–63, 2 Adm. R. 117, 123–25 (4th Cir. 2014) (analyzing whether forward freight agreements were maritime contracts); *Odyssey Marine Expl., Inc. v. Unidentified Shipwrecked Vessel*, 636 F.3d 1338, 1340–41 (11th Cir. 2011) (analyzing whether a contract to conduct research pertaining to a shipwrecked vessel was maritime); *Puerto Rico Ports Auth. v. Umpierre-Solares*, 456 F.3d 220, 224–26 (1st Cir. 2006) (analyzing whether a contract to remove a sunken ship from navigable waters was maritime); *see also* ROBERT FORCE & MARTIN J. NORRIS, THE LAW OF MARITIME PERSONAL INJURIES § 1:22 (5th ed. 2017) (discussing *Kirby*'s approach to analyzing maritime contracts).

[50] *See Kirby*, 543 U.S. at 19.

[51] We applied a similar analysis in *Grand Isle Shipyard, Inc. v. Seacor Marine, LLC*, where we held that the focus of the contract, rather than the situs of the injury, was the relevant consideration for the purposes of evaluating the applicability of an indemnity agreement. *See* 589 F.3d at 786–89; *see also* FORCE & NORRIS, *supra* note 49, § 13:9 (discussing cases applying the rule emanating from *Grand Isle Shipyard*).

[52] We deal today only with determining the maritime or nonmaritime nature of contracts involving the exploration, drilling, and production of oil and gas. If an activity in a non-oil and gas sector involves maritime commerce and work from a vessel, we would expect that this test would be helpful in determining whether a contract is maritime.

pected problem that required a vessel and a crane to lift equipment needed to resolve this problem. The use of the vessel to lift the equipment was an insubstantial part of the job and not work the parties expected to be performed. Therefore, **[—15—]** the contract is nonmaritime and controlled by Louisiana law. The LOIA bars indemnity. Accordingly, we reverse the summary judgment in favor of LDI and grant summary judgment in favor of STS, render judgment in favor of STS, and dismiss LDI's third-party complaint against STS.

REVERSED AND RENDERED.

United States Court of Appeals
for the Fifth Circuit

No. 17-30523

MORGAN
VS.
HUNTINGTON INGALLS, INC.

Appeal from the United States District Court for the Middle District of Louisiana

Decided: January 11, 2018

Citation: 879 F.3d 602, 6 Adm. R. 168 (5th Cir. 2018).

Before **SMITH**, **PRADO**, and **HIGGINSON**, Circuit Judges.

[—1—] {-604-} **SMITH**, Circuit Judge:

Defendants Huntington Ingalls, Incorporated ("Huntington Ingalls"), J. Melton Garrett, Albert Bossier, Lamorak Insurance Company, and Murphy Oil USA, Incorporated ("Murphy Oil"), appeal an order of remand in which the district court found removal untimely under 28 U.S.C. § 1446(b)(3). **[—2—]** Defendants contend that removal was timely instituted within thirty days of receipt of a deposition transcript indicating the case might be removable under 28 U.S.C. § 1442(a)(1). Plaintiff Curtis Morgan challenges Murphy Oil's standing to appeal. Because the removal clock began on receipt of the deposition transcript, we vacate the order and remand to the district court for consideration of whether Huntington Ingalls meets the substantive requirements for federal officer jurisdiction. We dismiss Murphy Oil's appeal for want of standing. **{-605-}**

I.

Morgan, a "sheet metal tacker" for Avondale Shipyards[1] in 1966, alleges that his employment exposed him to asbestos and resulted in his contracting asbestos-related mesothelioma among other health problems. On February 23, 2017, Morgan sued seventy-eight defendants, including Huntington Ingalls, former alleged executive officers and insurers of Avondale Shipyards,[2] and Murphy Oil in state court under theories of negligence and strict liability. His pleading did not identify any vessels on which he worked.

Morgan was deposed during eight days from March 9 to April 13, 2017. Avondale specifically questioned him on two days (March 10 and 20). Morgan stated that he worked at Avondale's main yard and on one vessel, a Lykes vessel. He did not remember working on any other vessel. On March 20, Avondale's lawyer questioned Morgan about working on the *USS Huntsville*,[3] but **[—3—]** Morgan could not remember the ship. Avondale showed Morgan medical records indicating he had allegedly worked and been injured on the *USS Huntsville* during his employment. Morgan reiterated that he could not remember the ship. "But if the records indicate that [he] had those injuries aboard the HUNTSVILLE, [he] would agree that [he] worked on the HUNTSVILLE[.]"

On March 28, 2017, Avondale received a link to the deposition transcript. It removed the case on April 27, 2017, which was 30 days after receipt of the transcript but 38 days after the relevant testimony. The basis for the removal was the federal officer removal statute, 28 U.S.C. § 1442, which allows removal of state cases commenced against

> [t]he United States or any agency thereof or any officer . . . of the United States or of any agency thereof, in an official or individual capacity, for or relating to any act under color of such

[1] Avondale's formal identity is Huntington Ingalls Incorporated—formally known as Northrup Grumman Shipbuilding Inc., Northrup Grumman Ship Systems, Inc., Avondale Industries, Inc., Avondale Shipyards, Inc., and Avondale Marine Ways, Inc.

[2] Consistent with the briefs, we hereinafter refer to these parties and Avondale Shipyards collectively as "Avondale."

[3] The *USS Huntsville* was converted in the mid-1960s to support NASA's Apollo manned missions to the moon. The Navy hired Ling-Temco-Vaught Inc. for the "design, preparation of working plans and other data, modification, renovation, and repair" of the **[—3—]** ship. Avondale was in turn hired as a subcontractor for the "design, ... modification, renovation, and repair ..., outfitting and delivery of" the ship.

office or on account of any right, title or authority claimed under any Act of Congress for the apprehension or punishment of criminals or the collection of the revenue.

§ 1442(a)(1).

Morgan contested removal as untimely under § 1446(b)(3) and claimed that the court "lack[ed] federal subject matter jurisdiction under [the federal officer removal statute]." The district court agreed removal was untimely. It determined that section 1446's removal clock began running on the date of the relevant oral testimony. Because removal was untimely, the court remanded and did "not decide whether the[ ] substantive requirements of § 1442 ha[d] been met."

Avondale and Murphy Oil appeal. Morgan moved to dismiss Murphy Oil's appeal, contending that it lacks standing to appeal. We expedited the **[—4—]** appeal because of Morgan's ill health, but he died September 14, 2017. **{-606-}**

II.

It makes little practical difference whether Murphy Oil has standing to appeal. Avondale's standing to appeal is not questioned, so we will still reach the issue of whether the deposition testimony or transcript starts the removal clock. If the case is removable by Avondale, the entire case will be deemed removable, such that Morgan's claims against all other defendants, including Murphy Oil, will be heard in federal court as well.[4]

But, "Article III standing implicates the federal judiciary's power to adjudicate disputes [so] it can be neither waived nor assumed." *Rohm & Hass Texas, Inc. v. Ortiz Bros. Insulation, Inc.*, 32 F.3d 205, 207 (5th Cir. 1994) (footnote omitted). "Merely because a party appears in the district court proceedings does not mean that the party automatically has standing to appeal the judgment rendered by that court."[5] A defendant must meet both constitutional and prudential standing requirements.[6]

"[T]he irreducible constitutional minimum of standing contains three elements[:]" (1) "[T]he plaintiff must have suffered an 'injury in fact'—an invasion of a legally protected interest which is (a) concrete and particularized and **[—5—]** (b) 'actual or imminent, not "conjectural" or "hypothetical"'"; (2) "there must be a causal connection between the injury and the conduct complained of"; and (3) "it must be 'likely,' . . . that the injury will be 'redressed by a favorable decision.'" *Lujan v. Defs. of Wildlife*, 504 U.S. 555, 560–61 (1992) (citations omitted). Murphy Oil has the burden to establish standing. *In re Deepwater Horizon*, 857 F.3d 246, 253, 5 Adm. R. 246, 249 (5th Cir. 2017).

Murphy Oil points to no sufficient "injury in fact." The primary injury it alleges is "a procedural right to remove cases within thirty days of receipt of a deposition transcript." Because it "has, in fact, litigated [this] issue . . . in other personal injury litigation" and "consistently faces situations where a case is potentially removable upon close review of the deposition transcript," Murphy Oil believes that "[t]he district court's ruling . . . impinges on Murphy's procedural removal rights." That is a speculative grievance well short of a concrete injury. *See Defs. of Wildlife*, 504 U.S.

[4] *See Savoie v. Huntington Ingalls, Inc.*, 817 F.3d 457, 463, 4 Adm. R. 225, 228 (5th Cir. 2016) ("[R]emoval of the entire case is appropriate so long as a single claim satisfies the federal officer removal statute.") (citing 14C WRIGHT & MILLER, FED. PRAC. & PROC. Juris. § 3726 (4th ed.) ("Section 1442(a)(1) authorizes removal of the entire case even if only one of the controversies it raises involves a federal officer or agency.")).

[5] *Rohm & Hass*, 32 F.3d at 208. ("[A] party generally may not appeal a district court's order to champion the rights of another, and even '[a]n indirect financial stake in another party's claims is insufficient to create standing on appeal.'") (quoting *Morrison-Knudsen Co. v. CHG Int'l, Inc.*, 811 F.2d 1209, 1214 (9th Cir. 1987)) (alterations in original).

[6] *Bennett v. Spear*, 520 U.S. 154, 162 (1997) ("The question of standing 'involves both constitutional limitations on federal-court jurisdiction and prudential limitations on its exercise.'") (quoting *Warth v. Seldin*, 422 U.S. 490, 498 (1975)).

at 560. The hypothetical potential to confront this issue in future possible litigation with different plaintiffs is too conjectural to constitute an injury in fact.[7]

Further, Murphy Oil "cannot satisfy the demands of Article III by alleging a **{-607-}** bare procedural violation." *Spokeo Inc. v. Robins*, 136 S. Ct. 1540, 1550 (2016). It must also show "some concrete interest that is affected by the deprivation." *Summers v. Earth Island Inst.*, 555 U.S. 488, 496 (2009); *accord Spokeo*, 136 S. Ct. at 1549. Murphy Oil asserts that it "maintains an interest in a federal forum for this and other, future removable litigation," such that "the District Court's remand has now deprived Murphy of its preferred forum." But, Murphy Oil itself has no right to be in federal court in the first place. Only Avondale, its co-defendant, can invoke the federal officer removal statute. Had **[—6—]** Avondale not chosen to remove, Murphy Oil could not have asserted federal officer jurisdiction on Avondale's behalf. Congress granted the right to remove under § 1442 to only certain classes of defendants, none of which includes Murphy Oil.[8] A generalized desire to litigate in federal court, without holding a corresponding right to be in federal court in the first place, is insufficient to satisfy the injury-in-fact prong of Article III. Murphy Oil experienced no concrete and particularized injury sufficient to satisfy the injury-in-fact prong of Article III, so its appeal is dismissed for lack of jurisdiction.

III.

A.

A remand order "is not reviewable on appeal or otherwise, except that an order remanding a case to the State court from which it was removed pursuant to *section 1442* or 1443 of this title shall be reviewable by appeal or otherwise." 28 U.S.C. § 1447(d) (emphasis added). Avondale removed under § 1442(a)(1), so we have appellate jurisdiction.[9]

We review a remand order de novo. *Preston v. Tenet Healthsystem Mem'l Med. Ctr., Inc.*, 485 F.3d 793, 796 (5th Cir. 2007). In cases involving § 1442, the remand order is reviewed "without a thumb on the remand side of the scale."[10] **[—7—]**

Section 1446(b)(1) permits removal "30 days after the receipt by the defendant, through service or otherwise, of a copy of the initial pleading setting forth the claim for relief." "[I]f the case stated by the initial pleading is not removable," a defendant can also remove "within 30 days after receipt . . . of a copy of an amended pleading, motion, order or other paper from which it may first be ascertained that the case is one which is or has become removable." § 1446(b)(3). Avondale removed under the latter provision, claiming that the transcript of Morgan's deposition is "other paper" from which it was able to ascertain that the case was removable under the federal officer statute.

B.

Though this court has not yet confronted the precise question whether oral testimony at a deposition is "other paper" within the meaning of § 1446(b)(3), we have **{-608-}** held that "a transcript of the deposition testimony is 'other paper.'" *S.W.S. Erectors, Inc. v. Infax, Inc.*, 72 F.3d 489, 494 (5th Cir. 1996). Thus, in this case, we review only whether oral

---

[7] *See Rohm & Hass*, 32 F.3d at 211 (finding "greater potential liability should [defendant] ever file for bankruptcy" too "attenuated" to satisfy Article III).

[8] *See* 28 U.S.C. § 1442(a) ("A civil action or criminal prosecution that is commenced in a State court and that is against or directed to any of the following *may be removed by them* . . . .") (emphasis added).

[9] *See Decatur Hosp. Auth. v. Aetna Health Inc.*, 854 F.3d 292, 295–96 (5th Cir. 2017) (noting that although "we ordinarily lack jurisdiction to review a remand order based on [ ] a defect [in removal procedure] . . . the fact that [defendant] relied upon the federal officer removal statute in its notice of removal permits appellate review.").

[10] *Decatur*, 854 F.3d at 295 (quoting *Savoie*, 817 F.3d at 462, 4 Adm. R. at 227); *see also Durham v. Lock-heed Martin Corp.*, 445 F.3d 1247, 1253 (9th Cir. 2006) ("[W]here the timeliness of a federal officer's removal is at issue, we extend section 1442's liberal interpretation to section 1446.").

deposition testimony can constitute other paper, and if so, whether the testimony or the transcript started the removal clock in this instance.[11]

C.

The plain meaning of, purpose of, and policy considerations behind § 1446(b) all support the conclusion that oral testimony at a deposition does not constitute "other paper." "[I]n any case requiring statutory construction, **[—8—]** the High Court has instructed us to adhere to the plain language of the law . . . ."[12] Though "removal statutes are to be construed strictly against removal and for remand[,] [t]his canon does not trump a plain language reading of the statute's terms."[13]

> Except as provided in subsection (c), if the case stated by the initial pleading is not removable, a notice of removal may be filed within 30 days after *receipt* by the defendant, through service or otherwise, of a *copy* of an amended pleading, motion, order or *other paper* from which it may first be *ascertained* that the case is one which is or has become removable.

§ 1446(b)(3) (emphasis added).[14]

"[P]aper" is defined as "[a] written or printed document or instrument." BLACK'S LAW DICTIONARY 1266 (4th ed. 1951).[15] "[R]eceipt" is defined as the "[a]ct of receiving; also, the fact of receiving or being received; that which is received." *Id.* at 1433.[16] "Copy" is defined as "[t]he transcript or double of an original writing." *Id.* at 405. "'Ascertain' means 'to make certain, exact, or precise' or 'to find out or learn with certainty.'"[17] Thus, "ascertain" requires "a **[—9—]** greater level of certainty or that the facts supporting removability be stated unequivocally." *Id.* "[T]he information supporting removal in a copy of an **{-609-}** amended pleading, motion, order or other paper" under § 1446(b)(3)[18] "must be 'unequivocally clear and certain' to start the time limit running." *Id.*

The plain meaning of each of these words suggests that the information giving notice of removal must be contained in a writing. The defendant must actually "receive" a "copy" of the pertinent information. To say that a defendant receives a copy of the information upon oral testimony defies logic. The definition of "paper" contemplates a written "document" or

---

[11] Morgan cites our unpublished decision in *Ameen v. Merck & Co.*, 226 F. App'x 363 (5th Cir. 2007), for support that oral testimony can be "other paper." There, we cited *S.W.S. Erectors*, for the proposition that a deposition was an "other paper." We found "removal [ ] timely, as Appellees removed within 30 days of becoming aware that the case might be removable." *Id.* at 368. That case does not necessarily suggest that the removal clock was triggered by the testimony, but only that removal was timely. To the extent *Ameen* can be read to suggest that oral testimony triggers the removal clock, it is a nonbinding opinion and a misreading of *S.W.S. Erectors*.

[12] *Chapman v. Powermatic, Inc.*, 969 F.2d 160, 164 (5th Cir. 1992) (alteration in original) (quoting *FDIC v. Meyerland Co.* (*In re Meyerland Co.*), 960 F.2d 512, 516 (5th Cir. 1992) (en banc)) (looking to the plain language of § 1446(b)).

[13] *Bosky v. Kroger Tex., LP*, 288 F.3d 208, 211 (5th Cir. 2002) (footnotes omitted) (internal quotation marks omitted) (looking to the plain language of § 1446(b)).

[14] Section 1446 was updated in December 2011 when Congress enacted the Federal Courts Jurisdiction and Venue Clarification Act. Pub. L. No. 112-63, 125 Stat. 758 (2011). There were, however, no substantive changes to the relevant portion of § 1446, only structural changes. H.R. Rep. No. 112-10, at 14 (2011) ("New paragraph 1446(b)(3) is essentially the same as the text of the second paragraph of current subsection 1446(b), except that the 1-year limit on removal in diversity cases is made part of a new subsection ....").

[15] The relevant statutory language was first put into effect in 1949. The 1951 edition of BLACK'S LAW DICTIONARY is the edition closest to the original statutory enactment.

[16] "Receive" is similarly defined as "[t]o take into possession and control; accept custody of." BLACK'S LAW DICTIONARY 1433 (4th ed. 1951).

[17] *Bosky*, 288 F.3d at 211 (quoting WEBSTER'S NINTH NEW COLLEGIATE DICTIONARY 107 (1990)).

[18] At the time of *Bosky*, § 1444(b) did not have subsections but was instead long paragraphs. The 2011 amendment divided § 1444(b) into subsections but did not make a substantive change.

"instrument."[19] The definition of "copy" specifically states that the "double" must be in "writing." Oral testimony is not a written document or instrument. Further, as *Bosky* explains, "ascertain" requires a high level of certainty. Although it is possible that an oral deposition can provide such certainty, transcripts are often the key that a court must use to evaluate disputes over whether the testimony forms the basis for removal.

Moreover, under the *ejusdem generis* canon of statutory construction, "other papers" should be read similarly to "amended pleading, motion, order."[20] All three of those items are generally reduced to a writing—though not always.[21] All, however, are modified by "a copy of," which emphasizes the **[—10—]** written nature of these three documents.[22]

We comply with the plain language "unless 'literal application of a statute will produce a result demonstrably at odds with the intentions of its drafters.'"[23] The removal statute generally favors "reduc[ing] removals."[24] But, "the purpose of the removal statute" is also "to encourage prompt resort to federal court when a defendant first learns" of the facts supporting **{-610-}** removability. *Addo v. Globe Life & Acc. Ins. Co.*, 230 F.3d 759, 762 (5th Cir. 2000). "[D]efendant[s] will be less likely to act on more equivocal information provided in an 'amended pleading, motion, order or other paper' because such a 'protective' removal is no longer necessary to avoid the risk of losing [their] right to removal by the lapse of time." *Bosky*, 288 F.3d at 212. The two competing goals of the removal statute are both to encourage prompt, proper removals and to prevent hasty, improper removals.

It "promotes [both the purpose of § 1446 and] judicial economy" to "reduce 'protective' removals by defendants" and "discourage removals before **[—11—]** their factual basis can be proven by a preponderance of the evidence through a simple and short statement." *Id.* at 211. Here, if we were to require removal on the day of the oral deposition, defendants are likely to remove immediately upon any whiff that removal is proper and before having the chance to review the record and confirm that they in fact can remove.[25] Thus, it promotes the purpose of

---

[19] An instrument is "[a] written document; a formal or legal document in writing, such as a contract, deed, will, bond or lease.... A document or writing which gives formal expression to a legal act or agreement for the purpose of creating, securing, modifying, or terminating a right." BLACK'S LAW DICTIONARY 941 (4th ed. 1951).

[20] *See Chapman*, 969 F.2d at 164 ("[T]he recitation . . . of the words 'amended pleading, motion, order,' before the words 'or other paper[]' [ ] clearly refer[s] to actions normally and logically occurring after the filing of the initial pleading.").

[21] A pleading is a "formal written statement[] of accusation or defense presented by **[—10—]** the parties alternately in an action at law." BLACK'S LAW DICTIONARY 1311 (4th ed. 1951). A motion is "[p]rimarily an application for a rule or order made viva voce to a court or judge, but the term is generally employed with reference to all such applications, whether written or oral." *Id.* at 1164. An order is "[a] mandate, precept; a command or direction authoritatively given; a rule or regulation. . . . Every direction of a court or judge made or entered in writing, and not included in a judgment." *Id.* at 1247.

[22] *Accord Jernigan v. Ashland Oil Inc.*, 989 F.2d 812, 815 (5th Cir. 1993) (explaining that under § 1446(b) "[t]he thirty days is measured from receipt of whatever *writing* . . . constitutes first notice."). *See also* 14C WRIGHT & MILLER, FED. PRAC. & PROC. Juris. § 3731 (4th ed.) ("Although the requisite notice of removability may be communicated to defendants in either a formal or an informal manner, the communication should be in writing."); Adam C. Clanton, *Uncertainty in Federal Removal Procedure: The Riddle of the "Other Paper,"* 71 DEF. COUNS. J. 388, 398 (2004) (explaining that the "plain meaning" of "other paper" cannot include an "oral deposition [as it] is neither written, nor is it printed").

[23] *Chapman*, 969 F.2d at 164 (quoting *Meyerland*, 960 F.2d at 516).

[24] *Bosky*, 288 F.3d at 211–12 (explaining that "removal statutes are to be construed strictly against removal and for remand") (quoting *Eastus v. Blue Bell Creameries, L.P.*, 97 F.3d 100, 106 (5th Cir. 1996)).

[25] Additionally, at the time of its enactment, various "methods of oral notification," such as "[d]epositions, telephone conversations and other oral testimony existed in the litigation process." Clanton, *supra* note 22, at 399. "Congress was quite capable of recognizing the possible disconnect between deposition testimony and deposition transcripts and the effects it would have on

the statute to begin the removal clock on receipt of the transcript.

There are several policy considerations advanced by the parties and the district court. Though all have merit, the considerations favoring the transcript approach are more persuasive. Morgan and the district court primarily rely on the concern expressed in *Huffman v. Saul Holdings Limited Partnership*, 194 F.3d 1072, 1078 (10th Cir. 1999), that "the date of receipt of a transcript may also be subject to manipulation," given that "the applicable rule of civil procedure does not provide a deadline for obtaining a transcript of a deposition, *see* FED. R. CIV. P. 30(b)(2), (f)(2)."[26] Thus, theoretically defendants **[—12—]** could delay ordering the transcripts and thus buy extra time. Based on that policy concern, the Tenth Circuit held that "the **{-611-}** removal period commences with the giving of the testimony."[27]

But, Avondale contends that depositions often last months.[28] Requiring counsel to file on the date of the oral testimony may involve filing before a deposition is complete and all the relevant information is obtained. The length and complexity of a deposition may

---

removal procedure when it . . . include[d] 'other paper.'" *Id.*

[26] The district court and Morgan also reference three cases in the Third, Sixth, and Ninth Circuit as supporting the position that the removal clock begins on the date of the deposition. None of those circuits, however, actually addressed the issue of deposition testimony versus transcript. These cases are better characterized as standing for the general idea that a deposition can constitute an "other paper" than for actually deciding whether the defendant must remove within thirty days of the testimony or the transcript. *See Papp v. Fore-Kast Sales Co.*, 842 F.3d 805, 816 n.10 (3d Cir. 2016) (noting that the plaintiff "concede[d] that answers to deposition questions 'can constitute "other paper" for purposes of triggering the time for removal.'"); *Peters v. Lincoln Elec. Co.*, 285 F.3d 456, 465–66 (6th Cir. 2002) (citing *S.W.S. Erectors* for the proposition that "a plaintiff's responses to deposition questioning may constitute an 'other paper'"); *Carvalho v. Equifax Info. Serv., LLC*, 629 F.3d 876, 886–87 (9th Cir. 2010) ("[A] plaintiff's response to deposition questions can constitute 'other paper'.").

Moreover, these decisions are distinguishable. They involved removals within thirty days of the deposition. *See Papp*, 842 F.3d at 816 n.10 ("As a result, the relevant date for determining the timeliness of Boeing's motion to remove was the September 5, 2013 **[—12—]** deposition of Mary Papp, and Boeing's October 4, 2013 filing was therefore timely."); *Peters*, 285 F.3d at 466 ("Plaintiff does not dispute that Defendant Lincoln filed its Notice of Removal of this case within 30 days of the date of his deposition."); *Carvalho*, 629 F.3d at 887 ("[T]he notice of removal was filed within thirty days of Carvalho's deposition testimony.").

Curiously, the opinions of the district court *a quo* and the Sixth Circuit in *Peters* rest in part on a misquoting of our opinion in *Addo*. Specifically, the district court and the Sixth Circuit represent that the following appears in *Addo*:

> Holding that a plaintiff's deposition testimony may be an "other paper" under § 1446(b) is consistent with the purpose of the removal statute to encourage prompt resort to federal court when a defendant first learns that the plaintiff is alleging a federal claim.

Peters, 285 F.3d at 466. But *Addo* says nothing about "deposition testimony." Instead, the issue was whether a post-complaint demand letter could constitute "other paper" under the removal statute. *See Addo*, 230 F.3d at 761–62. *Addo* actually says, "Holding that a *post-complaint letter, which is not plainly a sham*, may be 'other paper' under § 1446(b) is consistent with the purpose of the removal statute . . . ." *Id.* at 762 (emphasis added) (footnote omitted). *Addo* thus does not answer the question presented.

Morgan separately cites *Atwell v. Boston Sci. Corp.*, 740 F.3d 1160 (8th Cir. 2013). There, the Eighth Circuit quickly held that "oral statements, made at a court hearing and *later transcribed*, like deposition testimony, satisfy § 1446(b)(3)'s 'other paper' requirement." *Id.* at 1162 (emphasis added). It noted, "The thirty-day time limit begins running when a plaintiff 'explicitly discloses' she is seeking a remedy that affords a basis for federal jurisdiction." *Id.* That opinion provides no reasoning, so to the extent it can be read as disagreeing with our approach, it is unpersuasive.

[27] *Huffman*, 194 F.3d at 1078. "[T]he notice of removal was untimely if [the] deposition testimony provided sufficient notice that the amount in controversy exceeded the jurisdictional minimum." *Id.* at 1079.

[28] For instance, in the instant case the pertinent deposition was taken over a period of eight days during a one-month period.

thereby compel defendants to file more protective removals. **[—13—]**

Additionally, a removing defendant bears the burden of pointing to the evidence demonstrating that removal is proper.[29] Where a removal is based on a statement made during the deposition, the transcript will often be used to evidence the alleged statement. Thus, it is counterintuitive to start the clock before obtaining the very evidence the defendant will rely on to support removal. Even under the Tenth Circuit's "notice" standard, it is likely that a district court will need to sift through the deposition to determine whether the answer was "clear and unequivocal" enough to trigger the thirty days.[30] The main way to sift through the deposition will of course be to look at the transcript. In fact, that is exactly what Morgan does in his brief to show that "Avondale was well aware of the implication of [Morgan's] testimony with respect to its planned removal." Morgan devotes nearly two pages to combing the transcript.

Our past cases concerning "other paper" suggest that these latter concerns carry more weight. In *S.W.S. Erectors,* 72 F.3d at 491, along with the deposition issue, we **{-612-}** also addressed whether an affidavit created by the defendant's counsel alleging removable facts "learned during a telephone conversation with [plaintiff's] attorney" was an "other paper" starting the removal clock. We rejected that contention, as "the defendant's subjective knowledge **[—14—]** cannot convert a case into a removable action." *Id.* at 494.[31] Thus, to remove, a defendant needs more than his own averment in a removal petition that a favorable answer was provided during a deposition.[32]

Moreover, *Bosky*, 288 F.3d at 211, counsels against a rule that would increase "protective" removals.[33] Though it is true that the Federal Rules do not set a deadline for obtaining a transcript, that one negative policy implication is not enough to outweigh our precedent, the plain meaning of § 1446(b)(3), and the contrary policy considerations.[34] "In short, a bright-line rule should create a fairer environment for plaintiffs and defendants."[35]

We adopt a bright-line rule today: Section 1446(b)(3)'s removal clock begins ticking upon receipt of the deposition transcript. Avondale thus timely removed within thirty days of receiving the deposition transcript.

IV.

Morgan alternatively requests that we affirm the remand based on Avondale's failure to meet the substantive requirements of federal officer removal. **[—15—]** "It is the general rule, of course, that a federal

---

[29] *See Bosky*, 288 F.3d at 211 ("It should also discourage removals before their factual basis can be proven by a preponderance of the evidence through a simple and short statement of the facts."); § 1446(a) ("[D]efendants desiring to remove . . . shall file . . . a short and plain statement of the grounds for removal ....").

[30] *See Bosky,* 288 F.3d at 211 ("[T]he information supporting removal in a copy of an amended pleading, motion, order or other paper must be 'unequivocally clear and certain' to start the time limit running."); *see also Cole ex rel. Ellis v. Knowledge Learning Corp.*, 416 F. App'x 437, 440 (5th Cir. 2011) (explaining that "[a] discovery response may constitute an 'other paper'" where such response is "'unequivocally clear and certain,' so that defendant may ascertain the action's removability").

[31] *See also Chapman*, 969 F.2d at 163 (noting, in the context of § 1446(b)(1), that "[w]e adopt this rule because we conclude that it promotes certainty and judicial efficiency by not requiring courts to inquire into what a particular defendant may or may not subjectively know").

[32] *See Addo*, 230 F.3d at 762 (noting "our rule that 'other paper' must result from the voluntary act of a plaintiff which gives the defendant notice of the changed circumstances which now support federal jurisdiction.").

[33] *See also Chapman*, 969 F.2d at 163 (adopting a rule for § 1446(b)(1) removal because a contrary rule would "encourage defendants to remove prematurely cases . . . to be sure that they do not accidentally waive their right to have the case tried in a federal court.").

[34] Additionally, § 1446(c)(1) places a one-year deadline on removal for diversity cases, which should help curtail some potential manipulation.

[35] *Bosky,* 288 F.3d at 211 ("[A] clearer threshold promotes judicial economy."); *see also Chapman,* 969 F.2d at 163 ("We believe the better policy is to . . . adopt[ ] a bright line rule . . . .").

appellate court does not consider an issue not passed upon below.'"[36] Because Morgan's death eliminates any need for an expedited appeal, there is "no reason to alter the normal course" of remanding this issue to the district court.[37]

Accordingly, the order of remand to state court is VACATED, and this matter is REMANDED to the district court for further proceedings as needed. We place no limitation on the matters that the district court may address, as needed, on remand.

---

[36] *Humphries v. Elliott Co.*, 760 F.3d 414, 418 (5th Cir. 2014) (quoting *Singleton v. Wulff*, 428 U.S. 106, 120 (1976)). *Accord Savoie*, 817 F.3d at 466, 4 Adm. R. at 230 ("As the district court never had the opportunity to consider whether these defenses are colorable, we will remand to allow it to do so in the first instance.").

[37] *Humphries*, 760 F.3d at 418 (refusing to determine whether federal officer jurisdiction was proper in the context of an expedited appeal).

United States Court of Appeals
for the Fifth Circuit

No. 17-30167

CLAIMANT ID 100187856
vs.
BP EXPLORATION & PROD., INC.

Appeal from the United States District Court for the Eastern District of Louisiana

Decided: January 29, 2018

Citation: --- F.3d ---, 6 Adm. R. 176 (5th Cir. 2018).

Before **STEWART**, Chief Judge, and **JOLLY** and **OWEN**, Circuit Judges.

[—1—] {——} **STEWART**, Chief Judge:

This appeal arises from the class-action settlement program established for civil claims resulting from the Deepwater Horizon Incident ("Spill"). After being denied on every level of review within the Court Supervised Settlement Program ("CSSP"), Plaintiff-Appellant, JAD Contractors, LLC ("JAD"), sought discretionary review from the district court. The district court denied discretionary review. For the reasons that follow, we AFFIRM. **[—2—]**

I. BACKGROUND

The Claims Process

After the Spill, BP and a class of individuals reached a final E&P Settlement Agreement ("Agreement") in May 2012 for those individuals and entities who experienced economic and property damages as a result of the Spill. The Agreement provides for claim resolution using various procedures, depending upon the type of claim and proximity to the Spill. To receive compensation, claimants must submit a claim to the CSSP and show that they are members of the class as defined by the Agreement.

Submitting a claim requires providing verified forms and documentation proof such as tax returns and profit/loss statements. An existing business seeking compensation completes a Business Economic Loss ("BEL") form. Once the documents are submitted the program accountants examine the provided documents to calculate the award amount. The award amount represents the difference between the business's actual profit during the compensable period and the profit it would have expected during that period had the Spill not occurred.

After the CSSP makes a determination about a particular claim's eligibility, either the claimant or BP may avail themselves of a multi-tiered internal review. After multiple levels of review, an appeal panel hears the claims de novo and issues "final" decisions. The district court retains the power of discretionary review, and if the decision is appealed, the court treats the panel's decision like a magistrate judge's report and recommendation. **[—3—]**

The Class

The Agreement provides: "If a person or entity is included . . . in Section 1.2, and their claims meet the descriptions of the Damage Categories in Section 1.3, that entity is a member of the [Class]."[1] Section 1.2 defines the class as:

> All Entities doing business or operating in the Gulf Coast Areas . . . that: are service businesses . . . who performed their full-time services while physically present in the Gulf Coast Areas . . . at any time from April 20, 2010 to April 16, 2012 . . . .

Section 1.3 explains "[e]ntities who meet the geographical descriptions of . . . 1.2 above are included in the Economic Class only if [they experience a l]oss of income, earnings or profits . . . as a result of the **DEEPWATER HORIZON INCIDENT** . . . ."

Exhibit 4A establishes what documents a BEL class member must provide to be eligible for compensation. Exhibit 4B identifies class

[1] JAD claimed to be an existing business, not a start-up or a business that failed as a result of the Spill. As such, this opinion only addresses the provisions and claims pertaining to similarly situated businesses.

members who do not have to show *any* additional evidence of causation and specifies how other class members meet their causation requirements. These are the only causation requirements as we established in *Hutto v. BP Expl. & Prod.*, 753 F.3d 509, 2 Adm. R. 217 (5th Cir. 2014). Exhibit 4C provides program accountants with the framework for compensation.[2] Class members are only entitled to compensation for loss that occurred between May and December 2010. Even still, their compensation is calculated by subtracting actual earnings from the earnings they would have expected had the Spill not occurred. If a class member has no documentary **[—4—]** support of their expected earnings, program accountants cannot calculate compensation.

The Claimant

On June 10, 2013, JAD, a construction company in operation since 2004, timely submitted a BEL claim to the CSSP for damages it incurred in Gulf Coast Economic Zone C. On June 10, 2015, the CSSP sent an incompleteness notice, asking JAD to supplement the information in JAD's profit/loss statements. The same request was sent again on July 21, 2015.[3] On April 04, 2016, a Program Accountant again asked JAD to supplement the documents and explain the absence of revenue between January 2010 and April 2011. On April 12, 2016, another incompleteness notice was sent, to which JAD responded, on April 14, stating it was still in operation and actively seeking work. On May 9, 2016, the CSSP denied JAD's claim because they were "unable to determine causation and/or calculate a compensation amount under the BEL frameworks because [JAD was] not doing business or operating in the Gulf Coast Areas . . . at the time of the Oil Spill, April 20, 2010."

JAD requested re-review. In its decision the administrator reiterated the previous reasoning and further explained that JAD was inactive "from January 2010 through April 2011 because it reported no revenues or variable operating expenses." It additionally reasoned that JAD, in its tax reconciliation, stated it did not have revenue or expenses in 2010. Thus, JAD had "not provided documents indicating that the business was operating at the time of the Oil Spill."

JAD requested reconsideration. This time an administrator denied JAD's reconsideration, stating: **[—5—]**

> The specific requirements for eligibility as a member of the Settlement Class, as laid out in Section 1.2 and Section 1.3 of the Settlement Agreement, have not been satisfied as the claimant has still not provided specific documentation indicating it was doing business or operating in the Gulf Coast areas . . . at the time of the Oil Spill, April 20, 2010.

This was the first time class eligibility was cited as a reason for the denial.

JAD appealed to the appeal panel. Reviewing de novo, the panel affirmed the CSSP's original denial and did not mention class eligibility. The panel instead held that the documents JAD presented were "simply insufficient evidence to support the conclusion that JAD was actively seeking jobs and incurring expenses between January 2010 and April 2011." JAD then sought discretionary review from the district court, which summarily denied the claim. JAD timely appealed.

---

[2] Particularly, Exhibit 4C explains:

> The compensation framework for business claimants compares the *actual profit* of a business during a defined post-spill period in 2010 to the profit that the claimant might have *expected* to earn in the comparable post-spill period of 2010. . . . Compensation Period is selected by the Claimant to include three or more consecutive months *between May and December 2010*.

[3] It is not clear from the record whether this second request was prompted because JAD again submitted insufficient documents or no additional documents at all.

II. DISCUSSION

A. Standard of Review

We review the district court's decision not to exercise discretionary review for abuse of discretion. *See Steering Comm. v. BP Expl. & Prod.*, 785 F.3d 1003, 1011, 3 Adm. R. 325, 329 (5th Cir. 2015). However, when the district court is presented with a purely legal question of contract interpretation, the standard of review is effectively de novo. *See id.*, 3 Adm. R. at 329 (quoting *United States v. Delgado-Nuñez*, 295 F.3d 494, 496 (5th Cir. 2002) ("[A]buse of discretion review of purely legal questions . . . is effectively de novo because a district court by definition abuses its discretion when it makes an error of law."). Yet still, review is not mandatory, *Lake Eugenie Land Dev., Inc. v. BP Expl. & Prod.*, 785 F.3d 986, 999, 3 Adm. R. 341, 350 (5th Cir. 2015), and we may affirm on any ground supported by the record. *Moncrief Oil Int'l Inc. v. OAO Gazprom*, 481 F.3d 309, 311 (5th Cir. 2007).

B. Applicable Law

The district court abuses its discretion in denying review of an appeal if the panel substantially misapplies or misconstrues the Agreement. *See Claimant* **[—6—]** *ID 100212278 v. BP Expl. & Prod., Inc.*, 848 F.3d 407, 410, 5 Adm. R. 202, 203 (5th Cir. 2017). Even if the panel's decision does not constitute a misapplication, if (1) the issue is regularly before the panel; (2) panels have rendered different decisions on the issue; and (3) the issue's resolution will significantly impact the Agreement's administration, the district court may abuse its discretion in declining review. *See id.*

C. Analysis

1. Dormancy & Award Calculation

When parties enter into a settlement agreement, the terms of that agreement govern disputes arising from the agreement's implementation. *See Lake Eugenie*, 785 F.3d at 994, 3 Adm. R. at 345. According to the present Agreement, a claimant's class membership does not guarantee it will receive an award. Once a claimant clears the hurdle of class eligibility, it faces additional obstacles. The Agreement sets compensation calculations and requires the class member to provide certain documents that render program accountants able to calculate an award amount using the agreed upon equation. Upon receipt, the accountants then use those documents to determine the profit the company made in the years before the Spill, review the entity's actual profit during the specified months, and then calculate the award amount, subtracting actual profits from expected profit. Using this calculation, claimants can be class members because they meet the class definition and still receive no compensation because they were inactive during the entire agreed upon compensable period.

Although the period that defines the class ranges from April 20, 2010 to April 16, 2012, the parties agreed that the compensable period is May 2010 through December 2010 for BEL class members. Accordingly, regardless of whether the panel found that JAD's inactivity from April 2010 through April 2011 made it ineligible for the class, program accountants could not have **[—7—]** calculated an amount to award JAD because JAD was inactive during the entire compensable period.

JAD submitted its claim on June 10, 2013. The CSSP asked JAD to supplement the documents multiple times and gave JAD ample opportunity to prove that it was active during the compensable period. The CSSP eventually denied JAD's claim because it was "unable to determine causation and/or calculate a compensation amount under the BEL frameworks because [JAD was] not doing business or operating in the Gulf Coast Areas . . . at the time of the Oil Spill, April 20, 2010." The administrator who conducted re-review found the same. Then the reconsideration administrator, for the first time, found that JAD had not satisfied the requirements for class eligibility. The panel, after receiving even more documents and reviewing the record de novo, did not address class eligibility and found instead that JAD presented insufficient evidence to support the company's assertion that it actively sought work during the compensable period.[4]

This decision was correct. Although JAD sufficiently alleged that it was a business entity located in the Gulf Area between April 2010 and April 2012, it did not provide the CSSP with adequate documentation to calculate profits JAD expected to generate between May and December 2010, as the Agreement required. Program accountants asked JAD to provide documentation showing activity or explaining its inactivity four times between January 2009 and April 2011. When it finally responded, JAD simply stated that it was actively working. At the final level of appeal, it provided additional documents in support of that assertion: insurance documents, a payment request, and invoices for office supplies. These documents were inadequate. The insurance **[—8—]** documents represented a premium refund for insurance predating 2010 and illuminated that JAD was also uninsured from April 2010 through December 2010. JAD had one policy from April 2009 through April 2010, and it renewed in December 2010 through December 2011. So although JAD presented the documents to invoke the inference that it had to be in business since it was insured, the documents did the opposite, showing JAD was not insured during the entire compensable period. The payment request was for work completed before April 2010, and the invoices were dated April 2011, after the compensation period. All of these documents further supported that JAD was inactive during the compensation period, and they did not provide the program accountants with the ability to calculate the profits JAD expected May through December 2010.

Panels consistently deny claims where the entity shows no revenue or expenses for that period and also presents no documentation evidencing an ardent attempt to find work. In 37 APD 2017-370 (Mar. 23, 2017), the panel upheld a commercial real estate lessor's claim denial because the property went without a tenant, no revenue, and minimum expenses. When asked to provide documentation to assist the program accountant in calculating an award amount, the claimant presented insufficient evidence that it was actively seeking a tenant during the compensable period. The panel decided similarly in 23 APD 2015-186 (Nov. 20, 2016), when it upheld the denial of a window cleaning business's claim where the business was inactive during the entire compensable period.

Furthermore, panels consistently reverse denials when BEL claimants demonstrate they actively sought work. Although the commercial real estate lessor in 25 APD 2016-128 (Feb. 24, 2016) had no revenue or expenses from February 2010 through April 2011, the panel reversed the denial because the owner showed that it was actively seeking business during the compensable **[—9—]** period. The same was done in multiple other claims. *See* 26 APD 2016-279 (Apr. 4, 2016) (reversed denial because inactivity from January 2009 through August 2010 did not preclude entity from class membership, it only negatively affected the award amount); 39 APD 2017-742 (2017) (reversed denial of real estate agent's claim even though it had no revenue and expenses for a period of time because it showed that the nature of its work was sporadic). JAD made no attempt to provide similar support, and the documents it offered further supported the panel's decision. Class members who do not provide any documentation explaining their inactivity during the compensable period are consistently denied. Therefore, the panel did not misapply the Agreement in denying JAD's claim, and the district court did not abuse its discretion.

2. Class Membership

Foregoing argument that the CSSP misapplied the Agreement by holding that it was unable to calculate an award, JAD instead offered the same argument as BP. Both BP and JAD aver that the panel found that JAD was not entitled to compensation because it experienced a period of inactivity

[4] JAD argued that the panel required it to be in business on the day of the Spill, April 20, 2010. This is not supported by the record. The panel, in accord with the Agreement, asked JAD to show it was in business May through December 2010.

and, thus, was not a class member. JAD argues that this was an errant decision. BP argues that this was the right one. The panel found that JAD was not entitled to compensation as a result of its inactivity; however, the panel's "why" surrounded the compensation calculation, not class membership.

As previously contested by BP, traceability is again challenged here. *See Hutto*, 753 F.3d at 512–13, 2 Adm. R. at 218. In order for an individual to have standing to bring a case, there must be, *inter alia*, a causal connection between a plaintiff's injury and a defendant's conduct. *See id.* at 513, 2 Adm. R. at 218. In *Hutto*, we held that in class action claims, individuals who meet the class definition maintain traceability and are class members. *Id.* at 512–13, 2 Adm. R. at 218 (citing *Lujan v. Defenders of Wildlife*, 504 U.S. 555, 561 (1992)). The class action claimants simply have to allege causation to **[—10—]** satisfy Article III traceability. *See id.*, 2 Adm. R. at 218 ("Allegations of causation are sufficient to satisfy Article III in a class action complaint and in class action definition.").

The panel did not misapply or misconstrue the Agreement in determining JAD's class status. Contrary to the parties' beliefs,[5] the panel did not conclude that JAD was ineligible for the class. A claimant seeking class membership must only allege that the defendant caused its injury. *Id.* at 513, 2 Adm. R. at 218. The parties agreed that a class member is one who meets the requirements of section 1 of the Agreement. Section 1.2 of the Agreement's plain language says any entity operating in the Gulf area *at any time* from April 20, 2010 through April 16, 2012 is a class member[6] if they experience a loss defined in section 1.3. Section 1.3 of the Agreement further defines class members as those individuals or entities defined in section 1.2 who experienced a loss as a result of the spill.[7]

As established in *Hutto*, claimants simply have to *allege* that they are members of the class. *Id.* at 512–13, 2 Adm. R. at 218. Here, that allegation is made in the parties' agreed-upon claimant form, which requires claimants to certify they meet the class definition under penalty of perjury. JAD completed and signed the forms and thus sufficiently alleged that it was a class member.

The parties' misunderstanding is not without merit. Instead of conducting the analysis piece-by-piece and determining class membership separately from award calculation, the administrator simply gives the reasoning as to why a **[—11—]** claimant would not receive an award. The initial review administrator, the re-review administrator, and the final review panel did not reason that JAD's lack of activity precluded it from the class.[8] Instead the panel stated it could not

[5] JAD makes an argument similar to the one previously made by BP: the class administrator was supposed to use Exhibit 4B to find a causal nexus and approve its claim. This argument fails. We have already held Exhibit 4B causation requirements do not affect class membership. *Hutto*, 753 F.3d at 513, 2 Adm. R. at 218. ("Exhibit 4B . . . [is an] evidentiary framework[] that [has] no effect on the claimants' allegations or on the class definition."). Neither do Exhibit 4C requirements.

[6] JAD easily clears the Section 1.2 hurdle. Although there was some time of inactivity, the parties concede that JAD was operating a business by April 2011 and continues to operate. Thus, JAD operated in the Gulf area between April 20, 2010 and April 16, 2012.

[7] JAD also alleged economic loss, during that time and as a result of the Spill, meeting the Section 1.3 requirements. Therefore, JAD is a class member as defined by the Agreement.

[8] The administrator who conducted the reconsideration did find that JAD was not a member of the class because of the period of inactivity. However, it does not necessarily follow that the panel affirmed for these reasons. The panel conducts a de novo review and makes its own determination. In its decision, the panel did not repeat the language the reconsideration administrator used. It did not mention class eligibility or causation. If the panel followed the reasoning of the reconsideration administrator, this was likely error and a misinterpretation of the Agreement that should have been reviewed by the district court. That methodology goes directly against precedent set by this Court and heightens Article III standing requirements. *See Hutto*, 753 F.3d at 512, 2 Adm. R. at 217. However, this is

calculate an award because of the lack of activity during the compensable period.

Despite BP's familiar argument,[9] JAD's alleged temporary dormancy does not affect its class status. Beyond the established rule that we must "assume arguendo the elements of [each claimant's] legal claim," *Cole v. Gen. Motors Corp.*, 484 F.3d 717, 723 (5th Cir. 2007), the required claim form that a claimant must complete and submit is signed under the penalty of perjury, further establishing that allegations are sufficient. Furthermore, this argument ignores precedent and attempts to set a higher burden for class action claimants in blatant disregard of that same precedent. *Hutto*, 753 F.3d at 512–13, 2 Adm. R. at 217–18.

Accepting JAD's class membership but otherwise denying the claim is in line with other panel decisions. In fact, the panel has explicitly stated that dormancy has no effect on class membership. In 26 APD 2016-279 (Apr. 4, **[—12—]** 2016), the panel reversed an administrator's decision to deny the claim of a commercial real estate lessor, who generated no revenues or expenses from January 2009 through August 2010. The initial reviewer determined that this time of inactivity made the business ineligible for class membership. The panel directly addressed this error saying:

> The fact that the property was not leased from January 2009 through August 2010 is of no real importance as to whether the Claimant is a member of the class. It most certainly is. The issue which appears to stump the Vendor Accountants was the amount of the award.

26 APD 2016-279. Thus, the CSSP has already found that dormancy does not affect class status but only the calculation of the award.

Because JAD's allegations of class membership are sufficient, JAD is a class member. Despite the period of inactivity, the parties concede that JAD provided documentation demonstrating it was operating by April 2011 and continues to operate. So JAD meets section 1.2 requirements. JAD also alleged economic loss as a result of the Spill, meeting the Section 1.3 requirements. Therefore, the CSSP likely did not misapply or misconstrue the agreement because it did not decide that JAD's inactivity precluded it from the class. It instead found that JAD was a class member, who did not provide sufficient documentation for the Program Accountant to calculate an award.[10]

III. CONCLUSION

The district court's judgment is AFFIRMED.

(Reporter's Note: The U.S. Fifth Circuit designated this opinion as a published opinion; however, the opinion does not appear in the official reporter).

likely not the methodology the CSSP undertook because again, only one of the four review panels said that JAD was ineligible to be a part of the class because of its dormancy.

[9] In 2014 BP attempted to argue that if the panel did not ensure that a claim contained a direct causal nexus, its constitutional and contractual rights would be violated. *Hutto*, 753 F.3d at 512–13, 2 Adm. R. at 217–18. Now it argues that here the panel conducted this causal calculation that this court held was inaccurate and ruled in its favor as a result. We again disagree. If the panel acted as BP avers, it committed substantial error reviewable by the district court.

[10] Although there was likely no misapplication of the Agreement, this is likely a question of law that can potentially substantially impact Agreement administration if the CSSP precludes dormant individuals from the class, instead of considering them class members presenting noncompensable claims.

United States Court of Appeals
for the Fifth Circuit

No. 17-20093

SANGHA
VS.
NAVIG8 SHIPMANAGEMENT PRIVATE LTD.

Appeal from the United States District Court for the Southern District of Texas

Decided: February 5, 2018

Citation: 882 F.3d 96, 6 Adm. R. 182 (5th Cir. 2018).

Before **STEWART**, Chief Judge, and **JOLLY** and **OWEN**, Circuit Judges.

[—1—] {-98-} STEWART, Chief Judge:

Plaintiff-Appellant Captain Manjit Sangha ("Cpt. Sangha") challenges both the district court's grant of Defendant-Appellee Navig8 Ship Management Private Limited's ("Navig8") motion to dismiss for lack of personal jurisdiction and for *forum non conveniens*, and the denial of his motion to remand. We conclude that the district court did not err in dismissing Cpt. Sangha's claims and therefore AFFIRM.

I. BACKGROUND

Beginning in June 2009, Cpt. Sangha worked as a mooring master for Navig8 aboard the M/V Miss Claudia ("Miss Claudia") in the Gulf of Mexico. In October 2015, while Cpt. Sangha was working as the master in command of **[—2—]** the Miss Claudia, his vessel collided with another ship, causing damage to both vessels. After this **{-99-}** accident, Navig8 declined to renew Cpt. Sangha's employment contract. He subsequently obtained new employment as a mooring master under a contract with Marine Consulting, LLC ("Marine Consulting").

Several months later, Navig8 learned that Cpt. Sangha, who was then serving on board the M/V Songa Pearl ("Songa Pearl") in his employment with Marine Consulting, would soon be maneuvering in the Gulf of Mexico in a ship-to-ship transfer of bunker fuel alongside the Miss Claudia, his former vessel. That same day, Manish Gupta ("Gupta"), Navig8's Safety Manager, sent an email to Cpt. Sangha's supervisor, Captain Johannes Schild ("Schild"), informing him that Navig8 would prefer not to have Cpt. Sangha in charge of the maneuver with the Miss Claudia because "[t]he collision incident [was] still under legal/insurance proceedings." After additional correspondence in which another Navig8 representative, Prashant Mirchandani ("Mirchandani"), explained that Navig8 only wished to use a different mooring master in all maneuvers involving the Miss Claudia, Cpt. Sangha alleges that Marine Consulting terminated his contract and removed him from the Songa Pearl in the Port of Houston.

Cpt. Sangha filed a petition for damages against Navig8 in the 129th District Court in Harris County, Texas, alleging various tort claims, including tortious interference with his contract as a mooring master with Marine Consulting.[1] Navig8 removed the case from Texas state court to federal district court under 28 U.S.C. § 1441(a), arguing that Cpt. Sangha pleaded a claim **[—3—]** within the original admiralty or maritime jurisdiction of the federal courts under 28 U.S.C. § 1333. Cpt. Sangha sought to remand the case to state court on grounds that the saving-to-suitors clause of the admiralty jurisdiction statute prohibited removal of the case. Navig8 opposed the motion to remand, arguing that Cpt. Sangha's lawsuit, an admiralty action, fell clearly within the province of the removal statute as amended in 2011 and, consequently, Navig8 had a right to remove Cpt. Sangha's claims to federal court. Navig8 thereafter filed a motion to dismiss under, *inter alia*, Federal Rule of Civil Procedure 12(b)(2), arguing (1) that Cpt. Sangha failed to provide details supporting a showing of personal jurisdiction over Navig8, and (2) that the doctrine of *forum non conveniens* warranted dismissal. After limited discovery, the district court dismissed Cpt. Sangha's

[1] Cpt. Sangha also brought claims alleging defamation, tortious interference with his "current and prospective relations and economic advantage" in the maritime industry, intentional infliction of emotional distress, and intentional fraudulent misrepresentation, allegedly resulting in Cpt. Sangha's loss of employment and other damages.

claims, holding that the court lacked personal jurisdiction over Navig8 and, alternatively, that Cpt. Sangha's claims should be dismissed under the doctrine of *forum non conveniens*. This appeal followed.

II. DISCUSSION

A. Subject-Matter Jurisdiction and Order of Determination

On appeal, Cpt. Sangha primarily contends that the district court abused its discretion by foregoing the challenge to subject-matter jurisdiction presented in his motion to remand in favor of the questions of personal jurisdiction and *forum non conveniens* raised in Navig8's motion to dismiss. We disagree.

A district court's decision to address non-merits matters before establishing its own subject-matter jurisdiction is reviewed for abuse of discretion. **{-100-}** *Ruhrgas AG v. Marathon Oil Co.*, 526 U.S. 574, 588 (1999). Although district courts generally determine their own subject-matter jurisdiction before proceeding to a determination on the merits, such a strict sequencing of consideration is not required before a court orders dismissal on non-merits grounds. *Id.* at 584. To that end, the Supreme Court has **[—4—]** consistently held that "there is no mandatory 'sequencing of jurisdictional issues.'" *Sinochem Int'l Co. v. Malay. Int'l Shipping*, 549 U.S. 422, 431 (2007) (quoting *Ruhrgas*, 526 U.S. at 584). Indeed, a federal court has considerable leeway "to choose among threshold grounds for denying audience to a case on the merits." *Id.* (quoting *Ruhrgas*, 526 U.S. at 585). The Supreme Court has expressly approved of addressing personal jurisdiction before subject-matter jurisdiction, *see Ruhrgas*, 526 U.S. at 584–85, and of addressing *forum non conveniens* before other jurisdictional issues, *see Sinochem*, 549 U.S. at 429.

However, neither *Ruhrgas* nor *Sinochem* change the general expectation that federal courts address subject-matter jurisdiction at the outset in the "mine run of cases" and reach other issues first only where the jurisdictional issue is "difficult to determine" and the other grounds are relatively "less burdensome." *Sinochem*, 549 U.S. at 436; *accord Ruhrgas*, 526 U.S. at 587–88 (stating that "expedition and sensitivity to state courts' coequal stature should impel the federal court to dispose of [the issue of subject-matter jurisdiction] first"). That is, although federal courts normally must resolve questions of subject-matter jurisdiction before reaching other threshold issues, this rule is subject to the qualification that courts facing multiple grounds for dismissal should consider "the complexity of subject-matter jurisdiction issues raised by the case, as well as concerns of federalism, and of judicial economy and restraint in determining whether to dismiss claims due to a lack of personal jurisdiction before considering challenges to its subject-matter jurisdiction." *Alpine View Co. Ltd. v. Atlas Copco AB*, 205 F.3d 208, 213 (5th Cir. 2000).

We hold that the district court acted within its discretion in deciding the issues of personal jurisdiction and *forum non conveniens* before that of subject-matter jurisdiction. The district court did not state that Cpt. Sangha's motion to remand presented particularly thorny questions. However, despite Cpt. Sangha's claims to the contrary, the question of subject-matter jurisdiction **[—5—]** presented in this case—whether the saving-to-suitors clause of the federal maritime statute prohibits removal of general maritime claims absent an independent basis for federal jurisdiction in light of Congress's December 2011 amendment to the federal removal statute—is not clear. The vast majority of district courts considering this question have maintained that such lawsuits are not removable. *See Langlois v. Kirby Inland Marine, LP*, 139 F. Supp. 3d 804, 809–10 (M.D. La. 2015) (collecting cases). However, because there is no binding precedent from this circuit, *see Riverside Constr. Co., Inc. v. Entergy Miss., Inc.*, 626 F. App'x 443, 447 (5th Cir. 2015) (noting that "[t]he Fifth Circuit has not yet spoken directly on this issue"), there remains a consequential number of district courts that have held to the contrary. *See, e.g., Ryan v. Hercules Offshore, Inc.*, 945 F. Supp. 2d 772 (S.D. Tex. 2013); *see also Langlois*, 139 F. Supp. 3d at 809 (collecting cases). This disagreement, lopsided as it might be, highlights the conceptual difficulty of and uncertainty surrounding the issue. Accordingly, **{–101–}** we hold that the district court did not abuse its discretion in resolving the issue of personal jurisdiction before establishing whether subject-matter jurisdiction existed.

B. Personal Jurisdiction

This court reviews de novo a district court's determination that it lacks personal jurisdiction. *Pervasive Software, Inc. v Lexware GmbH & Co. KG*, 688 F.3d 214, 219 (5th Cir. 2012) (citing *Stripling v. Jordan Prod. Co.*, 234 F.3d 863, 869 (5th Cir. 2000)).

A non-resident defendant may move to dismiss for lack of personal jurisdiction. If, as here, the court rules on personal jurisdiction without conducting an evidentiary hearing, the plaintiff bears the burden of establishing only a *prima facie* case of personal jurisdiction. *Quick Techs., Inc. v. Sage Grp. PLC*, 313 F.3d 338, 343 (5th Cir. 2002). "The district court is not obligated to consult only the assertions in the plaintiff's complaint in **[—6—]** determining whether a *prima facie* case for jurisdiction has been made. Rather, the district court may consider the contents of the record at the time of the motion . . . ." *Paz v. Brush Engineered Materials, Inc.*, 445 F.3d 809, 812 (5th Cir. 2006) (quoting *Quick Techs., Inc.*, 313 F.3d at 343). "Although jurisdictional allegations must be accepted as true, such acceptance does not automatically mean that a *prima facie* case for [personal] jurisdiction has been presented." *Id.*

There is personal jurisdiction if the state's long-arm statute extends to the defendant and exercise of such jurisdiction is consistent with due process. *Johnston v. Multidata Sys. Int'l Corp.*, 523 F.3d 602, 609 (5th Cir. 2008). "Because the Texas long-arm statute extends to the limits of federal due process, the two-step inquiry collapses into one federal due process analysis." *Id.* Due process requires that the defendant have "minimum contacts" with the forum state (*i.e.*, that the defendant has purposely availed himself of the privilege of conducting activities within the forum state) and that exercising jurisdiction is consistent with "traditional notions of fair play and substantial justice." *Id.* (quoting *Wilson v. Belin*, 20 F.3d 644, 647 (5th Cir. 1994)).

"Minimum contacts" can give rise to either specific jurisdiction or general jurisdiction. *Lewis v. Fresne*, 252 F.3d 352, 358 (5th Cir. 2001). Specific jurisdiction may exist "over a nonresident defendant whose contacts with the forum state are singular or sporadic only *if* the cause of action asserted arises out of or is related to those contacts." *Int'l Energy Ventures Mgmt., L.L.C. v. United Energy Grp., Ltd.*, 818 F.3d 193, 212 (5th Cir. 2016) (citing *McFadin v. Gerber*, 587 F.3d 753, 759 (5th Cir. 2009)). In other words, such jurisdiction exists "when a nonresident defendant has purposefully directed its activities at the forum state and the litigation results from alleged injuries that arise out of or relate to those activities." *Walk Haydel & Assocs., Inc. v. Coastal Power Prod. Co.*, 517 F.3d 235, 243 (5th Cir. 2008) (internal quotation marks omitted). **[—7—]** "[S]pecific jurisdiction is confined to adjudication of issues deriving from, or connected with, the very controversy that establishes jurisdiction." *Goodyear Dunlop Tires Operations, S.A. v. Brown*, 564 U.S. 915, 919 (2011) (quotations omitted).

"A court may assert general jurisdiction over [non-resident defendants] to hear any and all claims against them when their affiliations with the State are so 'continuous and systematic' as to render them essentially at home in the forum State." *Id.* Establishing general jurisdiction is "difficult" and requires "extensive **{–102–}** contacts between a defendant and a forum." *Johnston*, 523 F.3d at 609. "Even repeated contacts with forum residents by a foreign defendant may not constitute the requisite substantial, continuous and systematic contacts required . . . . [V]ague and overgeneralized assertions that give no indication as to the extent, duration, or frequency of contacts are insufficient to support general jurisdiction." *Id.* at 609–10 (quoting *Revell v. Lidov*, 317 F.3d 467, 471 (5th Cir. 2002).

Once a plaintiff establishes minimum contacts between the defendant and the forum state, the burden of proof shifts to the defendant to show that the assertion of jurisdiction is unfair and unreasonable. *Wien Air Alaska, Inc. v. Brandt*, 195 F.3d 208, 215 (5th Cir. 1999). The defendant must make a "compelling case." *Burger King Corp. v. Rudzewicz*, 471 U.S. 462, 477 (1985). In determining whether the exercise of jurisdiction is fair and reasonable, the court must balance: (1) the burden on the nonresident defendant of having to defend itself in the forum, (2) the interests of the forum state in the case, (3) the plaintiff's interest in obtaining convenient and effective relief, (4) the interstate judicial system's interest in the most efficient resolution of controversies, and (5) the shared interests of the states in furthering fundamental social policies. *Id.*; *see also Asahi Metal Indus. Co., Ltd. v. Superior Court of Cal.*, 480 U.S. 102, 115 (1987). **[—8—]**

We hold that Cpt. Sangha did not make a *prima facie* showing of personal jurisdiction. More pointedly, after considering Cpt. Sangha's petition and the record evidence, it is clear that Navig8 is not subject to general jurisdiction in Texas. It is undisputed that Navig8 is not incorporated in Texas, has a foreign principal place of business, has no officers or shareholders in Texas, does not pay taxes in Texas, and does not have an agent for service of process in Texas. To dispute Navig8's jurisdictional defense, Cpt. Sangha submitted an affidavit testifying that he was aware that Navig8 "conducted business routinely out of the Port of Houston" and that Navig8 "does substantial business from and in the Port of Houston in bunkering fuel from the Port of Houston and other ports on Texas to offshore Texas." Cpt. Sangha argues that these statements are not controverted and are therefore sufficient to establish a *prima facie* case of general jurisdiction. Even assuming the veracity of the jurisdictional allegations contained in Cpt. Sangha's petition and affidavit, he has not demonstrated that Navig8's contacts with the state of Texas are "continuous and systematic" enough to support general jurisdiction. *Goodyear*, 564 U.S. at 919. Cpt. Sangha's allegations that Navig8 "conducted business routinely" and does "substantial business" in Texas, without more, merely amount to "vague and overgeneralized assertions" of contacts "that give no indication as to the extent, duration or frequency" of Navig8's contacts. *See Johnston*, 523 F.3d at 609; *see also Panda Brandywine Corp. v. Potomac Elec. Power Co.*, 253 F.3d 865, 869 (5th Cir. 2001) (emphasizing that conclusory allegations of contacts with a forum, even if uncontroverted, cannot establish general jurisdiction). Coupling Cpt. Sangha's insufficient allegations with the difficulty of making a *prima facie* showing of general jurisdiction, we hold that Cpt. Sangha has failed to adequately show that Navig8 should be subject to general jurisdiction in Texas. **[—9—]**

Nor does Cpt. Sangha allege sufficient contacts to show Navig8 is subject to specific jurisdiction in Texas. Cpt. Sangha avers that the intentional torts urged by him "stem from communications from Navig8 **{-103-}** about Captain Sangha, directed toward the State of Texas because Captain Sangha was working under his contract with his employer at the Port of Houston at the time of the tortious conduct," and that "[t]he effect of Navig8's intentional torts were felt in Houston, Texas." Specific jurisdiction "focuses on the relationship among the defendant, the forum, and the litigation." *Monkton Ins. Servs. v. Ritter*, 768 F.3d 429, 432–33 (5th Cir. 2014). This court has previously explained that a defendant does not have minimum contacts with a state when it does not have a physical presence in the state, it did not conduct business in the state, and the contract underlying the business transaction was not signed in the state and did not call for performance in the state. *Id.* at 272. Neither can the plaintiff's *own contacts* with the forum be used to demonstrate contacts by the defendant. *See Walden v. Fiore*, 134 S. Ct. 1115, 1122 (2014) ("We have consistently rejected attempts to satisfy the defendant-focused 'minimum contacts' inquiry by demonstrating contacts between the plaintiff (or third parties) and the forum State.") (citing *Helicopteros Nacionales de Colombia, S.A. v. Hall*, 466 U.S. 408, 417 (1984)).

The contacts Cpt. Sangha identifies to support specific jurisdiction—email communications from two Navig8 representatives located outside the country to Cpt. Sangha's then-supervisor in Alabama, an employment contract between Cpt. Sangha and Marine Consultants allegedly confected in Houston,[2] that the email communications were targeted at a contract formed in Texas, **[—10—]** and that the emails concerned work that was to be performed in Texas—are legally insufficient to support a finding of specific jurisdiction. Navig8's contacts with the state have to be purposeful "and not merely fortuitous," *Walden*, 134 S. Ct. at 1123 (noting that "[d]ue process requires that a defendant be haled into court in a forum State based on his own affiliation with the State, not based on the 'random, fortuitous, or attenuated' contacts he makes by interacting with persons affiliated with the State") (quoting *Burger King*, 471 U.S. at 475). Even though Navig8's email communications happened to affect Cpt. Sangha while he was at the Port of Houston, this single effect is not enough to confer specific jurisdiction over Navig8.

Relatedly, Cpt. Sangha's reliance on the "effects" test of *Calder v. Jones*, 465 U.S. 783 (1984), is unavailing. Cpt. Sangha argues that "[t]his case tracks the *Calder* analysis because committed [sic] an act expressly aimed at work that Capt. Sangha was performing in and from Texas ports, including the Port of Houston, and the harm, including termination[,] was felt in Houston, where Capt. Sangha was picked up after termination." The Supreme Court recently clarified the form that forum contacts must take in intentional tort cases for the effects to be applicable, reiterating that mere injury to a forum resident is not a sufficient connection to the forum. *Walden*, 134 S. Ct. at 1125. "Regardless of where a plaintiff lives or works, an injury is jurisdictionally relevant only insofar as it shows that the defendant has formed a contact with the forum State." *Id.* The proper question is not whether Cpt. Sangha experienced an injury or effect in a particular location, but **{–104–}** whether Navig8's conduct connects it to the forum in a meaningful way. Cpt. Sangha's presence in the Gulf of Mexico/Port of Houston is largely a consequence of *his* relationship with the forum, and not of any actions Navig8 took to establish **[—11—]** contacts with the forum.[3] Accordingly, Cpt. Sangha has failed to establish a *prima facie* case of personal jurisdiction.

Because we affirm on personal jurisdiction grounds, we need not address the district court's *forum non conveniens* analysis.

III. CONCLUSION

For the foregoing reasons, we AFFIRM the district court's judgment dismissing Cpt. Sangha's claims.

---

[2] Record evidence demonstrates that the contract was not confected in Houston. Schild, Cpt. Sangha's supervisor, sent the contract in an email from Alabama. The executed contract indicates the parties signed the agreement in Boca Raton, Florida, Cpt. Sangha's residence. The contract does not specifically provide that Cpt. Sangha's work would be confined to the Gulf of Mexico, nor does it specifically refer to the Port of Houston.

[3] The record indicates that Navig8 was likely aware that the ship-to-ship transfer between its vessel and the Songa Pearl would take place in the Gulf of Mexico right outside of Houston. Map coordinates included in email correspondence between Navig8 representatives and Schild indicate that the cargo transfer would happen on April 9, 2016 "near position: 29 degrees 04.0'N, 094 degrees 41.0'W". The plotting of those coordinates shows that the maneuver Navig8 employees were attempting to remove Cpt. Sangha from would occur just southeast of Houston in the Gulf of Mexico. Even considering this, however, the allegation that the "effects" of Navig8's emails were felt in Houston are nothing more than fortuitous. *See Walden*, 134 S. Ct. at 1125.

United States Court of Appeals for the Fifth Circuit

No. 17-30424

CONTINENTAL INS. CO.
VS.
L&L MARINE TRANSP., INC.

Appeal from the United States District Court for the Eastern District of Louisiana

Decided: February 15, 2018

Citation: 882 F.3d 566, 6 Adm. R. 187 (5th Cir. 2018).

Before **REAVLEY**, **SMITH**, and **OWEN**, Circuit Judges.

[—1—] {-568-} **SMITH**, Circuit Judge:

Three tugs were towing a barge, with one designated as the "lead" tug **[—2—]** and the other two as "assisting" tugs. One of the assisting tugs allided with a bridge fender system and sank. An insurance policy on the lead tug covers damage only to its "tow." Accordingly, we decide the meaning of "tow" for purposes of that insurance contract and whether the assisting tug was the "tow" of the lead tug. The district court held that the assisting tug was the "tow" because of a tort principle known as the "dominant mind" doctrine. We reverse and render.

I.

Three tugs—the M/V MISS DOROTHY, the M/V ANGELA RAE, and the M/V FREEDOM—were traversing the Mississippi River with a barge, FSB 101. The MISS DOROTHY allided with a portion of a bridge fender system and sank, resulting in a total loss. Accordingly, its insurers, Continental Insurance Company ("Continental"), filed a complaint against the ANGELA RAE's owners, L&L Marine Transportation, Incorporated ("L&L"). According to Continental's complaint,

> At the time of the allision, the M/V MISS DOROTHY was assisting the M/V ANGELA RAE, and the M/V FREEDOM, with the towage of FSB 101 . . . . Both the M/V ANGELA RAE and M/V FREEDOM were positioned behind FSB 101, pushing it down the river, and the M/V MISS DOROTHY was positioned at the head of FSB 101.

Most importantly to the present dispute, Continental alleged that "[t]he M/V ANGELA RAE was the lead tug and was responsible for coordination of the tow." Continental further averred that the ANGELA RAE was negligent in several ways, including "failure to keep a proper look out; failure to properly navigate around the Sunshine Bridge fender system; [and] failure to chart and plan a proper and safe route."

Both Atlantic Specialty Insurance Company ("Atlantic Specialty") and P & I Underwriters ("P & I") insured the ANGELA RAE. This is a dispute **[—3—]** between them regarding whose policy covers the incident.[1] Atlantic Specialty is the Hull & Machinery insurer, while P & I provides Protection and Indemnity Insurance. Following the above complaint, Atlantic Specialty denied that its policy covered any liability for the MISS DOROTHY's allision and sinking. Accordingly, P & I filed a complaint against Atlantic Specialty, claiming that the Atlantic Specialty policy did so cover. P & I's coverage complaint was initially consolidated with Continental's tort suit against L&L, then severed by joint motion.

The parties cross-moved for summary judgment, each alleging that the other's policy covered any liability for the loss of the MISS DOROTHY. As relevant here, **{-569-}** Atlantic Specialty's policy insures the ANGELA RAE as follows:

> [I]f the Vessel hereby insured shall come into collision with any other vessel, craft, or structure, floating or otherwise (including her tow); or shall strand her tow or shall cause her tow to come into

[1] As an initial matter, P & I moved for partial summary judgment, insisting that Atlantic Specialty had a duty to defend the insured, L&L. The district court denied that motion in part, reasoning that the Atlantic Specialty Hull & Machinery policy was not a defense policy and created no duty to defend. P & I does not raise that issue on appeal.

> collision with any other vessel, craft, or structure, floating or otherwise, or shall cause any other loss or damage to her tow or to the freight thereof or to the property on board, and the Assured, or the Surety, in consequence of the insured Vessel being at fault, shall become liable to pay and shall pay by way of damages to any other person or persons any sum or sums we, the Underwriters, will pay.

Essentially, the Atlantic Specialty policy covers the following situations: (1) the ANGELA RAE collides with something else, (2) the ANGELA RAE strands her tow, (3) the ANGELA RAE causes her tow to come into collision with anything else, or (4) the ANGELA RAE causes any damage to her tow or to her tow's freight. As Atlantic Specialty maintains, none of those situations occurred. The ANGELA RAE never collided with anything, nor was her tow stranded, subject to collision, or damaged in any way. **[—4—]**

Conversely, P & I's policy is much broader, indemnifying L&L for "[l]iability for loss of or damage to any other vessel or craft, or to property on such other vessel or craft . . . provided such liability does not arise by reason of a contract made by the assured." Yet P & I is suing because *its* policy covers only situations that Atlantic Specialty's does *not*: "Nonwithstanding anything to the contrary contained in this policy, no liability attaches to the Assurer [f]or any loss, damage, or expense which would be payable under the terms of the {Response} form of policy on hull and machinery." It is undisputed that, if Atlantic Specialty's policy does not cover this incident, then P & I's does.

Accordingly, P & I contends that the loss of the MISS DOROTHY falls within the third situation covered by Atlantic Specialty's policy, *i.e.* that the ANGELA RAE caused her "tow" to come into collision with the fender system. P & I reasons that the MISS DOROTHY was the "tow" of the ANGELA RAE—despite being itself a tugboat—because the ANGELA RAE was allegedly the *lead* tug. The district court agreed with P & I and granted it summary judgment. Atlantic Specialty appeals.

II.

As a preliminary matter, the parties dispute whether the so-called "Eight Corners" rule governs this case. Under it, courts "assess whether there is a duty to defend by applying the allegations of the compliant to the underlying policy without resort to extrinsic evidence." *Martco Ltd. P'ship v. Wellons, Inc.*, 588 F.3d 864, 872 (5th Cir. 2009). Put another way, the court determines whether an insurance policy covers an incident by looking to the allegations in the underlying suit's complaint. *See id.* P & I has consistently maintained, before the district court and on appeal, that the rule applies.

For the first time on appeal—and only in its reply brief—Atlantic Specialty disputes the application of the rule. Accordingly, the district court **[—5—]** stated, "The parties do not dispute [that] the allegations in the complaint control which policy is liable for defense costs and coverage." Thus, Atlantic Specialty has waived any quarrel over the applicability of the Eight Corners rule and the controlling nature of **{–570–}** Continental's complaint.[2] Accordingly, we assume the facts in Continental's complaint—the ANGELA RAE was the lead tug; the MISS DOROTHY was assisting the ANGELA RAE with the towage of FSB 101; and the ANGELA RAE

[2] *See Stewart Glass & Mirror, Inc. v. U.S. Auto Glass Disc. Ctrs., Inc.*, 200 F.3d 307, 316–17 (5th Cir. 2000) ("It is a bedrock principle of appellate review that claims raised for the first time on appeal will not be considered."). Even looking past waiver, it is not clear why this disagreement makes an ounce of difference here. The relevant facts are that the ANGELA RAE and the MISS DOROTHY were chartered to tow the barge FSB 101 while the ANGELA RAE was the lead tug. Nowhere does Atlantic Specialty dispute that the ANGELA RAE was the lead tug; all that it contests is the legal import of that fact. According to the district court and P & I, the assisting tugs are the "tow" of the lead tug; conversely, Atlantic Specialty maintains that the assisting tugs are still tugs, not tows. Thus, whether the Eight Corners analysis appertains is irrelevant—we need only ask how to read the word "tow" in Atlantic Specialty's policy.

negligently caused the MISS DOROTHY's allision.

III.

With these facts assumed, we turn to the central issue: Was the MISS DOROTHY the "tow" of the ANGELA RAE for purposes of Atlantic Specialty's policy? Both sides agree that Louisiana law controls.[3] Under Louisiana law, the interpretation of insurance policies is governed by general rules of contract interpretation. *Cadwallader v. Allstate Ins. Co.*, 848 So. 2d 577, 580 (La. 2003). Accordingly, courts "should seek to determine the parties' common intent, as reflected by the words in the policy." *Gabarick v. Laurin Maritime (Am.), Inc.*, 650 F.3d 545, 553 (5th Cir. 2011) (internal quotations omitted). "The words of a contract must be given their generally prevailing meaning" or their technical **[—6—]** meaning "when the contract involves a technical matter."[4] If the words of the contract "are unambiguous and the parties' intent is clear, the insurance contract will be enforced as written."[5]

A.

Because we look for the "plain, ordinary and generally prevailing meaning" or "technical meaning" of the word "tow," we begin with the dictionary. *See Cadwallader*, 848 So. 2d at 580–81. Dictionary definitions almost uniformly point toward the following definition of "tow": a vessel that is being provided extra motive power from another vessel by being pushed or pulled. For example, Black's Law Dictionary defines "towage" as "[t]he act or service of towing ships . . . by means of a small vessel called a *tug*."[6] That indicates that the "tug" is actively "towing" or exerting some force on the "tow." Supporting this, Merriam-Webster defines the verb "tow" as "to draw or pull along behind" or "to move in tow."[7] The Oxford English Dictionary agrees, defining the verb "tow" as **{-571-}** "[t]o draw by force; to pull, drag."[8] Furthermore, Oxford defines the noun "tow" as "[t]he action of towing or fact of being towed" or as "[a] vessel taken in tow; also, string of boats, barges, etc. being towed. Hence also, a string of barges that is pushed rather than pulled."[9] **[—7—]**

Caselaw and treatises support those definitions. The Supreme Court explained tows and towage in *Stevens v. The White City*, 285 U.S. 195, 200 (1932):

> The supplying of power by a vessel, usually one propelled by steam, to tow or draw another is towage. Many vessels, such as barges and canal boats, have no power of their own and are built with a view to receiving their propelling force from other sources. And vessels having motive power often employ auxiliary power to assist them in moving about harbors and docks.[10]

[3] *See Richard v. Dolphin Drilling Ltd.*, 832 F.3d 246, 248, 4 Adm. R. 267, 267 (5th Cir. 2016); *Cal-Dive Int'l, Inc. v. Seabright Ins. Co.*, 627 F.3d 110, 113 (5th Cir. 2010) ("The interpretation of a marine policy of insurance is governed by relevant state law.").

[4] LA. CIV. CODE ANN. art. 2047; *see also Naquin v. Elevating Boats, L.L.C.*, 817 F.3d 235, 238, 4 Adm. R. 221, 222 (5th Cir. 2016); *Cadwallader*, 848 So. 2d at 580.

[5] *Naquin*, 817 F.3d at 238–39, 4 Adm. R. at 222 (quoting *Doerr v. Mobil Oil Corp.*, 774 So. 2d 119, 124 (La. 2000)); *see also* LA. CIV. CODE ANN. art. 2046.

[6] *Towage*, BLACK'S LAW DICTIONARY 1719 (10th ed. 2014).

[7] *Tow*, MERRIAM-WEBSTER (Online ed.), https://www.merriam-webster.com/dictionary/tow.

[8] *Tow*, OXFORD ENGLISH DICTIONARY (Online ed.), http://www.oed.com/view/Entry/203995?rskey=nHWNmf&result=7#eid.

[9] *Tow*, OXFORD ENGLISH DICTIONARY (Online ed.), http://www.oed.com/view/Entry/203993?rskey=nHWNmf&result=5&isAdvanced=false#eid. This dictionary also includes a possibility that "[a] vessel that tows; a tug" is also a defined as a "tow." We discount this because it plainly cannot be the meaning of "tow" in the **[—7—]** contract—any other tug would then be a "tow," including the ANGELA RAE. Even P & I does not read the Atlantic Specialty policy so broadly. And no other dictionary, case, or treaties defines "tow" in a similar way, indicating that this was not what the parties intended.

[10] Similarly, in *Sacramento Navigation Co. v. Salz*, 273 U.S. 326, 328 (1927), the Court defined "[t]owage service" as "the employment of one vessel to expedite the voyage of another."

Fifth Circuit precedent accords with this notion. In *Mississippi Valley Barge Line Co. v. Indian Towing Co.*, 232 F.2d 750, 753 n.5 (5th Cir. 1956), the court noted that "[towage] is the employment of one vessel to expedite the voyage of another." Finally, at least one treatise defines "[t]owage" as "a service rendered by one vessel to aid the propulsion or to expedite the movement of another vessel. The vessel that supplies the power . . . is typically called a *tug*." THOMAS J. SCHOENBAUM, ADMIRALTY AND MARITIME LAW § 12-1 (West 5th ed. 2017) ("SCHOENBAUM").

Therefore, dictionaries, cases, and treatises all point to a common understanding of "tow": some ship or boat that is being provided extra motive power from another ship or boat by being pushed or pulled.[11] As P & I rightly contends, the tow may have its own power—such as cruise ships or tankers being **[—8—]** towed into a harbor—but the ship being towed is designated as the "tow" precisely because it receives auxiliary motive power from the tug or towing vessel.

Under this plain-meaning approach, it is evident that the MISS DOROTHY was *not* the "tow" of the ANGELA RAE. Nowhere **{-572-}** is there indication that the ANGELA RAE was providing the MISS DOROTHY with any motive power or was pushing or pulling her in any way.[12] Rather, Continental's claim is that the ANGELA RAE was the *lead* tug—and that since the MISS DOROTHY was an *assisting* tug, also pulling the barge FSB 101, the ANGELA RAE was responsible for the safe navigation of the MISS DOROTHY. But under those facts, there is no reason to characterize the MISS DOROTHY as the "tow" of the ANGELA RAE.

B.

In the face of this plain meaning uniformly articulated by dictionaries, treatises, and cases alike, P & I urges that we define "tow" as a vessel for whose safe navigation another vessel has responsibility. That is, P & I insists that we apply a maritime tort law concept—the "dominant mind" doctrine—to define "tow" in this insurance contract. We decline that invitation.

In any given flotilla, tugs generally have the following duties to their **[—9—]** tows: reasonable navigation, providing a proper towing apparatus, having a qualified master and crew, following proper towing procedures, etc. SCHOENBAUM § 12-3. In turn, a tow has duties such as providing a seaworthy vessel, being properly manned, and following the instructions of the tug. *Id.* § 12-5.

The dominant mind doctrine usually kicks in where a flotilla—*i.e.* the tugs and tows as unit—causes damage to some third party.[13]

[11] As P & I reads these dictionaries, cases, and treatises, the common thread is that "towage is one vessel with some responsibility for the steering or navigation of another vessel or object." But none of these dictionaries or cases defines "towage" in relation to the responsibilities of a vessel—a concept that P & I inserts without support. Instead, the plain definition of "tow" requires that it be provided some motive power. P & I's reading is without merit.

Furthermore, P & I asserts that its definition of "tow" is the only one that is clean and **[—8—]** easily applied. Yet there is no reason to think that the plain meaning of "tow," articulated above, is not also clean and easily applied. It will likely be plain in almost every case whether one ship is providing another auxiliary momentum. To the contrary, as explained below, it is P & I's definition of "tow" that will likely lead to confusion—there may be instances in which the vessel being towed has responsibility for the navigation of the tug.

[12] P & I claims that the MISS DOROTHY "alleges the MISS DOROTHY, though it had motive power, in effect used the ANGELA RAE as 'auxiliary power to assist [it] in moving about.'" That quotation comes, however, from *Stevens*, 285 U.S. at 200—not from Continental's complaint. We find no indication in the record that the MISS DOROTHY used the ANGELA RAE for extra motive power. Rather, Continental's complaint cuts the other direction. As Continental alleges, the MISS DOROTHY was "traversing the Mississippi River with barge FSB 101 . . . in tow." Thus, Continental's complaint squares with the notion that all three tugs were jointly pulling the barge. And other than this singular allegation by P & I, the parties seem to agree that these are the facts upon which we should decide this case.

[13] *See* SCHOENBAUM § 12-6; *Melbourne Bros. Constr. Co. v. Gnots-Reserve*, 461 So. 2d 1145, 1148

Typically courts hold only the tug liable, given that it is usually in control of the operation, having the duty of reasonable navigation. *Id.* § 12-6. Furthermore, the doctrine can absolve helper tugs of liability "if they are merely following instructions of the tug in charge." *Id.* Yet this is merely a rebuttable presumption—the tow or helper tug may be liable if negligent,[14] or the tow itself may be the dominant mind.[15] Finally, the dominant **{-573-}** mind doctrine can sometimes be used where a tow itself is damaged—in such situations, a tug that was the dominant mind may have had the duty of safely navigating the tow and may be liable.[16] **[—10—]**

According to the district court and P & I, a tug that is the dominant mind of a flotilla, with the accompanying responsibilities, necessarily must view the rest of the flotilla as its "tow." Because Continental avers that the ANGELA RAE was the lead tug and responsible for the navigation of the flotilla, P & I infers that the MISS DOROTHY was the "tow" of the ANGELA RAE. As P & I reasons, the ANGELA RAE owed the same duty of safe navigation to the MISS DOROTHY as it did to the barge, FSB 101—thus, they are both the "tow" of the ANGELA RAE.

We disagree. First, there is little reason to think that these tort duties should govern the meaning of "tow" in Atlantic Specialty's policy. Tort duties are precisely that: responsibilities that the parties owe to each other. But there is no reason to think that these duties then *define* the meaning of "tow." At least in other contexts, there is good reason to think that using tort duties to define contractual terms would be wholly inappropriate.[17]

Of course, some terms of insurance contracts might turn on tort law concepts. If an insurance contract exempts employees who "assault" other employees, then the tort law concept of "assault" is probably at play. Or a contract that indemnifies a party only for acts that they "proximately cause" would likely import that tort concept. But such terms usually derive their primary meaning from the relevant tort principles. Conversely, "tow" has a plain and unambiguous meaning outside tort law or the dominant mind doctrine, as **[—11—]** evidenced by the above-discussed cases, dictionaries, and treatises. Therefore, there is little reason to think that the meaning of "tow" in an insurance contract

---

(La. Ct. App. 5th Cir. 1984); *Dep't of Highways v. S. Shipbuilding Corp.*, 217 So. 2d 497, 500–02 (La. Ct. App. 1st Cir. 1969).

[14] SCHOENBAUM § 12-6; *see also Chitty v. M/V Valley Voyager*, 408 F.2d 1354, 1356–58 (5th Cir. 1969) (finding that a refueling tug, which effectively became the "tow" of the lead tug because it docked with the barge and mostly shut down its engines, was negligent by failing to warn the lead tug of excessive speed); *Commercial Union Ins. Co. v. M/V Bill Andrews*, 624 F.2d 643, 646–48 (similarly finding that a tug was mostly liable for the sinking of a refueling tug that was effectively a tow but that the refueling tug was also somewhat liable); *S. Shipbuilding*, 217 So. 2d at 502 ("[T]he helper tug is not liable for damages proximately caused by the faulty navigation of the superior or dominant vessel unless the helper is guilty of independent fault which contributes to the casualty.").

[15] *See, e.g., Plains Pipeline, L.P. v. Great Lakes Dredge & Dock Co.*, 54 F. Supp. 3d 586, 589–91 (E.D. La. 2014) ("The tow in this instance acted as the 'dominant mind, instructing the tug captains on the location to bring the dredge as well as how the dredge would be anchored.'"). Furthermore, at least in admiralty cases, both tugs can be jointly at fault if neither "surrendered command to the other." *Cenac Towing Co. v. Keystone Shipping Co.*, 404 F.2d 698, 701–02 (5th Cir. 1968).

[16] *See, e.g., Commercial Union*, 624 F.2d at 647 (finding that a tug had duties to a refueling tug that "became an appendage" of the lead tug); *Chitty*, 408 F.2d at 1356–57 (noting the district court's finding that the lead tug was negligent for failing to negotiate a river **[—10—]** bend safely and thus was liable to a refueling tug that effectively became the tow).

[17] For example, take a parent who has a $100,000 life insurance policy with his "children" as the beneficiaries. Assume that the parent is acting as a chaperone for a field trip when he is killed and that the relevant state law of *in loco parentis* imposes the same duty of care on field-trip chaperones that any parent has over a child. Surely the insurance policy does not then distribute the $100,000 equally to all of the children to whom the parent owed that duty. The term "children" in the life insurance policy, everyone would know, would not turn on the tort duty of *in loco parentis*.

should be derived from tort law as opposed to its ordinary definition.[18]

Our conclusion is buttressed by the confusion we encounter when trying to determine how to use tort duties to define "tow." As discussed above, tugs have several duties to their tows, only one of which is the duty of safe navigation. *See* SCHOENBAUM § 12-3. P & I gives no reason to think that the word "tow" should be defined by that duty of safe navigation instead of, for example, the duty to provide a proper towing apparatus. *Cf. id.* Indeed, the duty to provide a proper towing apparatus seems more specific to tows and tugs. And presumably, a lead tug would not have that duty to an assisting tug. **{–574–}**

Furthermore, as mentioned above, the dominant mind doctrine is only a presumption. *See id.* § 12-6. It can be flipped; the tow can become the dominant mind. *See, e.g., Plains Pipeline*, 54 F. Supp. 3d at 591; *cf.* SCHOENBAUM § 12-6. In such cases, it would be absurd to say that the tug is the "tow" of the tow. The word "tow," then, could not be defined by the dominant mind doctrine in every case. And if the word "tow" does not always follow the duties attached to the dominant mind, it is not clear why "tow" should ever be so defined.

There is another reason why using the dominant mind doctrine to define "tow" is strange: The doctrine does not impute the lead tug with *sole* responsibility for the safe navigation of the flotilla. *See* SCHOENBAUM § 12-6. As our caselaw make clear, even tugs that effectively become tows by relying on the lead tug's propulsion still have duties to inform the lead tug of any excessive speed, to use their rudders to avoid catastrophe, and to move to more secure **[—12—]** positions if necessary.[19] Accordingly, both tugs have duties regarding the safe navigation of the flotilla.

The concept of "dominant mind" just helps courts allocate the fault of the tugs, ensure that the lead tug has a duty of safe navigation, and determine who was more negligent. Therefore, because liabilities flowing from the dominant mind doctrine are really a matter of degree rather than kind, it seems odd to use the doctrine as an ontological on/off switch when defining "tow." That is especially true insofar as the assisting tug could possibly be more negligent in those duties regarding safe navigation.

IV.

In sum, "tow" as used in Atlantic Specialty's policy is defined by its plain, ordinary meaning: a vessel that is provided auxiliary motive power by being pushed or pulled. A tug remains a tug when it is tugging (*i.e.*, pushing or pulling), and a tow is a tow only when it is being towed (*i.e.* being pushed or pulled). And because the MISS DOROTHY was not provided any extra motive power, it was not a tow. Atlantic Specialty's policy does not apply.

The summary judgment is REVERSED, and judgment is RENDERED for Atlantic Specialty.

---

[18] Notably, P & I points to no case in which the dominant mind doctrine is used to define "tow" for an insurance contract.

[19] *Commercial Union*, 624 F.2d at 646–48; *Chitty*, 408 F.2d at 1356–58; *S. Shipbuilding*, 217 So. 2d at 502.

United States Court of Appeals for the Fifth Circuit

No. 17-30371

LEGENDRE
vs.
HUNTINGTON INGALLS, INC.

Appeal from the United States District Court for the Eastern District of Louisiana

Decided: March 16, 2018

Citation: 885 F.3d 398, 6 Adm. R. 193 (5th Cir. 2018).

Before **HIGGINBOTHAM, PRADO,** and **HIGGINSON,** Circuit Judges.

[—1—] {-399-} **HIGGINSON,** Circuit Judge:

The Legendre brothers, Stephen, Paul, Ragus, and Percy, Jr., sued appellant Huntington Ingalls, Inc. (Avondale)[1] and other defendants in Louisiana state court. In their complaint, the Legendres alleged that the defendants exposed their sister, Mary Jane Wilde, to asbestos and caused her **[—2—]** to die of mesothelioma. Avondale invoked the federal officer removal statute, 28 U.S.C. § 1442, and removed to the Eastern District of Louisiana. The district court remanded, holding that Avondale failed to show the required "causal nexus" to support federal jurisdiction. We affirm.[2]

I.

In 2016, Mary Jane Wilde died of complications related to mesothelioma. Wilde's father, Percy Legendre, worked at Avondale's shipyard in the 1940s. His responsibilities included working with asbestos insulation in the engine rooms of tugs built for the United States government. The Legendre brothers allege that asbestos fibers clung to their father's clothing and body when he returned home from work each day, and that Wilde was exposed to these fibers at home, causing her disease and eventual death.

In their complaint, the Legendres allege that Avondale failed to warn its employees of the risks of asbestos exposure and failed to implement proper safety procedures for handling asbestos. The district court held, and Avondale does not dispute, that the Legendres' claims sound in negligence, not strict liability.

Avondale removed to the Eastern District of Louisiana, asserting federal jurisdiction **{-400-}** under 28 U.S.C. § 1442, the federal officer removal statute. The Legendre brothers moved to remand. The district court granted the motion, and Avondale now appeals.

II.

"[F]ederal officer removal under 28 U.S.C. § 1442 is unlike other removal doctrines: it is not narrow or limited." *State v. Kleinert*, 855 F.3d 305, 311 (5th Cir. 2017) (quotation marks omitted). We review the district court's remand **[—3—]** order de novo, "without a thumb on the remand side of the scale." *Savoie v. Huntington Ingalls, Inc.*, 817 F.3d 457, 462, 4 Adm. R. 225, 227 (5th Cir. 2016); *see also* 28 U.S.C. § 1447(d) ("[A]n order remanding a case to the State court from which it was removed pursuant to section 1442 . . . of this title shall be reviewable by appeal or otherwise."). Nonetheless, it remains "the defendant's burden to establish the existence of federal jurisdiction over the controversy." *Winters v. Diamond Shamrock Chem. Co.*, 149 F.3d 387, 397 (5th Cir. 1998).

Under § 1442, an action "against or directed to . . . any officer (or any person acting under that officer) of the United States or of any agency thereof, in an official or individual capacity, for or relating to any act under color of such office" may be removed to federal court. 28 U.S.C. § 1442(a)(1). To remove, a defendant must show: "(1) that it is a person within the meaning of the statute, (2) that it has 'a colorable federal defense,' (3) that it 'acted pursuant to a federal officer's directions,' and (4) 'that a causal nexus exists between [its] actions under color of federal

[1] Appellant Huntington Ingalls was formerly known as Avondale. The parties refer to Huntington Ingalls as Avondale, and we follow their lead.

[2] Avondale recently moved to stay the district court's remand order. That motion is denied.

office and the plaintiff's claims.'" *Zeringue v. Crane Co.*, 846 F.3d 785, 789, 5 Adm. R. 193, 194 (5th Cir. 2017) (alteration in original) (quoting *Bartel v. Alcoa S.S. Co.*, 805 F.3d 169, 172, 3 Adm. R. 422, 422 (5th Cir. 2015)). The district court determined that Avondale could not meet the "causal nexus" prong, and therefore did not reach the rest of the test.[3]

In the past, § 1442 permitted removal "only when the state suit was 'for any act under color of such office.'" *Id.* at 793, 5 Adm. R. at 197 (quoting Act of June 25, 1948, ch. 646, 62 Stat. 938 (codified at 28 U.S.C. § 1442)). But Congress amended the **[—4—]** statute in 2011 "to allow the removal of a state suit 'for *or relating to* any act under color of such office.'" *Id.*, 5 Adm. R. at 197 (quoting Removal Clarification Act of 2011, Pub. L. No. 112–51, § 2(b)(2), 125 Stat. 545 (codified at 28 U.S.C. § 1442)). As recognized by the district court, we have interpreted the causal nexus requirement under the modern statute three times.

First was *Bartel v. Alcoa Steamship Co., Inc.*, 805 F.3d 169, 3 Adm. R. 422 (5th Cir. 2015). In that case, merchant mariners sued their former employers in state court. *Id.* at 171, 3 Adm. R. at 422. The mariners alleged that they had been injured by asbestos exposure on vessels owned by the United States Navy, but operated by the civilian employers. *Id.* at 171-72, 3 Adm. R. at 422. The mariners attributed their injuries "to the employers' failure to warn of the dangers of asbestos, to train their crews in using asbestos-containing products, and to adopt procedures for the safe installation and removal of asbestos." **{-401-}** *Id.* at 171, 3 Adm. R. at 422. We found no nexus between these negligence claims and the defendants' actions under color of federal office because the evidence suggested that the government did not issue any "orders relating to safety procedures or asbestos" and that defendants were therefore "free to adopt the safety measures the plaintiffs now allege would have prevented their injuries." *Id.* at 174, 3 Adm. R. at 424.

We revisited the causal nexus requirement in *Savoie v. Huntington Ingalls, Inc.*, 817 F.3d 457, 4 Adm. R. 225 (5th Cir. 2016). That case, like this one, involved alleged asbestos exposure during construction of federal vessels at Avondale's shipyard. *Id.* at 459, 4 Adm. R. at 225. The Savoies brought both negligence and strict liability claims in state court, and Avondale removed citing federal officer jurisdiction. *Id.* at 460, 4 Adm. R. at 225. The district court remanded, finding causal nexus lacking. *Id.* at 460, 462, 4 Adm. R. at 225, 227.

The allegations of federal control in *Savoie* mirror those in this case, and the parties cited much of the same evidence. As to the plaintiffs' negligence claims, this court in *Savoie* "agree[d] with the district court that the federal **[—5—]** government's mandate of asbestos insulation did not cause the shipyard to engage in the challenged conduct." *Id.* at 462, 4 Adm. R. at 227. We described the *Savoie* plaintiffs' negligence allegations as "nearly identical" and "essentially the same as the ones made in *Bartel*[.]" *Id.* at 462-63, 4 Adm. R. at 227–28. We explained that "the Navy neither imposed any special safety requirements on the shipyard nor prevented the shipyard from imposing its own safety procedures." *Id.* at 463, 4 Adm. R. at 228. Accordingly, the Savoies' negligence claims "challenge[d] discretionary acts of the shipyard free of federal interference," and "the government's directions to the shipyard via the contract specifications did not cause the alleged negligence[.]" *Id.*, 4 Adm. R. at 228. These claims therefore could not support removal. *Id.*, 4 Adm. R. at 228. The Savoies' strict liability claims, by contrast, "rest[ed] on the mere use of asbestos." *Id.* at 465, 4 Adm.

[3] The district court did address the "colorable federal defense" prong in a later order denying Avondale's motion to stay the remand order. *Legendre v. Huntington Ingalls Inc.*, 17-2162, 2017 WL 2881324, at *3-5 (E.D. La. July 6, 2017). The court concluded that Avondale could not meet this prong because it failed to allege that the government exercised discretion over any warnings or safety programs at Avondale's shipyard. *Id.* In the same order, the court declined Avondale's renewed invitation to disregard our causal nexus decisions. *See id.* at *2 n.5 (citing J.R.R. Tolkien, *The Fellowship of the Ring* bk. 1, ch. 3 (1954) ("Do not meddle in the affairs of Wizards, for they are subtle and quick to anger.")).

R. at 229. These claims were causally linked to the Navy's requirement that its ships contain asbestos, and therefore supported removal. *Id.* at 465-66, 4 Adm. R. at 230.[4]

Zeringue v. Crane Co., 846 F.3d 785, 5 Adm. R. 193 (5th Cir. 2017), is the final installment in our post-2011 federal officer trilogy. Zeringue sued in state court, asserting that he had been exposed to asbestos while deployed with the U.S. Navy. *Id.* at 788, 5 Adm. R. at 193. Among several other defendants, Zeringue sued Crane, which manufactured valves packed in asbestos for the Navy. *Id.* at 788, 791, 5 Adm. R. at 193, 195. Zeringue asserted strict liability, negligence, and failure to warn claims. *Id.* at 788, 5 Adm. R. at 193. Crane removed under § 1442, asserting that both the valve's design and **[—6—]** the decision to warn lay within the discretion of Crane's federal superior. *Id.*, 5 Adm. R. at 193. The district court remanded, and we reversed. *Id.* at 788-89, 795, 5 Adm. R. at 193, 198.

In *Zeringue*, we recognized that the 2011 amendment shifted the causal nexus calculus: "The plain meaning of the added language broadens the scope of the statute as 'the ordinary meaning of [relating to] is a broad one—"to stand in some relation; to have bearing or concern; to pertain; refer; to bring into association with or connection with."'" *Id.* at 793, 5 Adm. R. at 197 (alteration in original) **{-402-}** (quoting *Morales v. Trans World Airlines, Inc.*, 504 U.S. 374, 383 (1992)); *see also id.*, 5 Adm. R. at 197 ("The 2011 amendment expanded the breadth of acts sufficient to establish a causal nexus even further."). But this broadening, we held, did not eliminate the requirement that the removing party "establish 'a nexus, a "causal connection" between the charged conduct and asserted official authority.'" *Id.*, 5 Adm. R. at 197 (quoting *Jefferson Cty. v. Acker*, 527 U.S. 423, 431 (1999)). Crane met this requirement—at least as to the claims based on mere use of asbestos[5]—because its "relationship with Zeringue derive[d] solely from its official authority to provide parts to the Navy, and that official authority relate[d] to Crane's allegedly improper actions, namely its use of asbestos in those parts." *Id.* at 793-94, 5 Adm. R. at 197–98 (emphasis omitted). Importantly, in *Zeringue* we explicitly reaffirmed *Bartel*. *Id.* at 794, 5 Adm. R. at 198. We described the "charged conduct" in *Bartel* as failing to warn, train, and adopt safety procedures regarding asbestos. *Id.*, 5 Adm. R. at 198. These actions, we explained, were "private conduct that implicated no federal interest" and therefore "an extension of § 1442 to allow [the *Bartel*] defendants to remove would have stretched the causal nexus requirement to the point of irrelevance." *Id.*, 5 Adm. R. at 198. **[—7—]**

III.

The district court correctly held that this sequence of our precedent requires remand of the Legendres' claims. As noted, *Bartel* instructs that § 1442 does *not* support removal where defendant government contractors "were free to adopt the safety measures the plaintiffs now allege would have prevented their injuries." 805 F.3d at 174, 3 Adm. R. at 424. The Legendres provide unrebutted evidence that although the government required Avondale to use asbestos in the construction of the tugs, the government did nothing to restrict Avondale's safety practices. In *Bartel*, the government required the defendants to use ships containing asbestos,

[4] The *Savoie* defendants did not argue that the 2011 amendment to § 1442 altered our pre-existing causal nexus test. *See Savoie v. Huntington Ingalls, Inc.*, 824 F.3d 468, 469 (5th Cir. 2016). In a petition for rehearing, however, the defendants made "a colorable argument that, in regard to the negligence claims, [the] action [wa]s removable because of the 2011 statutory amendment." *Id.* In our order denying rehearing, we clarified that defendants had forfeited this argument, but cautioned that "[n]othing in our opinion should be read as an exposition of the effect of the 2011 amendment on the viability of *Winters* or on the scope of the post-amendment decision in *Bartel* . . . ." *Id.* at 469-70.

[5] "Because 'removal of the entire case is appropriate so long as a single claim satisfies the federal officer removal statute,' we do not determine whether Crane independently established the right to remove Zeringue's failure to warn claim." *Zeringue*, 846 F.3d at 794, 5 Adm. R. at 198 (quoting *Savoie*, 817 F.3d at 463, 4 Adm. R. at 228).

but did nothing to restrict the defendants' safety measures. Between the two, the causal nexus analysis is, as highlighted by us in *Savoie*, "nearly identical." 817 F.3d at 462, 4 Adm. R. at 227.

The Legendres point to unchallenged evidence that Avondale was free to adopt the safety measures the Legendres allege would have prevented their sister's death. The Legendres' expert, a former Navy ship inspector at Avondale, states that "government inspectors neither monitored nor enforced safety regulations" at Avondale. Rather, "[o]n the job safety during the construction of vessels for the United States government was the responsibility of Avondale Shipyards' safety department." Another Navy inspector states in deposition that the Navy was a customer "[j]ust like anybody else" and the purpose of Navy inspections was to ensure that a particular job "was completed and Avondale had done all the work." Avondale does not attempt to rebut this evidence, or to show that the government did in fact limit Avondale's authority to implement safety measures.

Avondale's attempt to distinguish *Bartel* on its facts is unpersuasive. It stresses that the government specifically required Avondale to use asbestos insulation and oversaw construction to ensure that Avondale built the tugs to the government's specifications. But nothing about this arrangement suggests **[—8—]** that Avondale was not **{-403-}** "free to adopt the safety measures the plaintiffs now allege would have prevented their injuries." *Bartel*, 805 F.3d at 174, 3 Adm. R. at 424. Absent such a conflict between federal direction and the Legendres' state-law claims, *Bartel* requires remand.

Perhaps recognizing this factual similarity, Avondale directs most of its energy towards arguing that that *Bartel* is inapposite because it applied pre-2011 precedent and thereby failed to give effect to Congress' new language. This significant argument, presented to us instead of our full court, however, is precluded by our rule of orderliness. "This Court adheres to a 'rule of orderliness,' under which a panel may not overturn a controlling precedent 'absent an intervening change in law, such as by a statutory amendment, or the Supreme Court, or our en banc court.'" *Vaughan v. Anderson Reg'l Med. Ctr.*, 849 F.3d 588, 591 (5th Cir. 2017) (quoting *Sprong v. Fidelity Nat'l Prop. & Cas. Ins. Co.*, 787 F.3d 296, 305 (5th Cir. 2015)). The 2011 amendment was, of course, not "intervening"; *Bartel* was decided after the change and quoted the new "relating to" language. *Bartel*'s articulation of the causal nexus standard, and its requirement that the claimed negligence conflict with a federal directive, was integral to the result. We are therefore bound by the *Bartel* standard. *Cf. E.E.O.C. v. LHC Grp., Inc.*, 773 F.3d 688, 695 (5th Cir. 2014) (rule of orderliness required court to apply earliest Fifth Circuit articulation of "causal nexus" element necessary to establish a prima facie case of discriminatory termination under the ADA).[6]

As the district court responsibly observed, and as we too are bound, because *Bartel* is a published decision of this court, and there has been no **[—9—]** intervening change in law, its causal nexus test controls. Avondale makes no showing that it was not "free to adopt the safety measures the plaintiffs now allege would have prevented their injuries." *Bartel*, 805 F.3d at 174, 3 Adm. R. at 424. Accordingly, Avondale cannot meet the causal nexus prong of the federal officer removal standard and remand was proper.

This conclusion is consistent with both *Savoie* and *Zeringue*. In *Savoie* we relied on *Bartel* to hold that negligence claims nearly identical to those at issue here could not support removal. 817 F.3d at 463, 4 Adm. R. at 228. In *Zeringue* we found federal jurisdiction where plaintiffs asserted liability based on the presence of asbestos in parts the Navy "directed" Crane to provide, while at the

---

[6] As in *Savoie*, the *Bartel* panel worked without the benefit of argument on the effect of the 2011 amendment. But that does not reduce the opinion's binding effect. *See Sykes v. Tex. Air Corp.*, 834 F.2d 488, 492 (5th Cir. 1987) ("The fact that in [a prior decision] no litigant made and no judge considered the fancy argument advanced in this case does not authorize us to disregard our Court's strong rule that we cannot overrule the prior decision.").

same time we explicitly reaffirmed *Bartel.* 846 F.3d at 794, 5 Adm. R. at 198. These cases therefore do not support federal jurisdiction over this case.

IV.

Although we are bound by our precedents, we note that other circuits have read the 2011 amendments to eliminate the old "causal nexus" requirement. The Third Circuit has explained that before 2011, proponents of jurisdiction were required to "show a nexus, a causal connection." *In re Commonwealth's Mot. to Appoint Counsel Against or Directed to Def. Ass'n of Phila.*, 790 F.3d 457, 470 (3d Cir. 2015) (internal quotations omitted). The court contrasted this old, causal requirement with the new statutory language, which—the Third Circuit **{–404–}** held—requires only "a 'connection' or 'association' between the act in question and the federal office." *Id.* at 471; *accord Sawyer v. Foster Wheeler LLC*, 860 F.3d 249, 258, 5 Adm. R. 167, 172–73 (4th Cir. 2017) (applying "connection or association" test). *But see Caver v. Cent. Ala. Elec. Coop.*, 845 F.3d 1135, 1144-45 (11th Cir. 2017) (citing the Third Circuit's "connection or association" language, but applying a "causal connection" test).

A revised approach may have merit. The causal nexus requirement we have continued to apply derives from the pre-2011 "for any act under color of **[—10—]** such office" language. *See Willingham v. Morgan*,395 U.S. 402, 409 (1969)("Past cases have interpreted the 'color of office' test to require a showing of a 'causal connection' between the charged conduct and asserted official authority."); *Acker*, 527 U.S. at 431 ("To qualify for removal, an officer of the federal courts must . . . establish that the suit is *for* an act under color of office. To satisfy [this] requirement, the officer must show a nexus, a causal connection between the charged conduct and asserted official authority." (internal citations, quotation marks, and alterations omitted)). By adding "relating to," Congress preserved a *nexus* requirement, but it is unclear the relationship must be *causal*. Rather, as we have recognized, "relating to" has a broad meaning—"to stand in some relation; to have bearing or concern; to pertain; refer; to bring into association with or connection with." *Zeringue*, 846F.3d at 793, 5 Adm. R. at 197 (internal quotation marks omitted). Nonetheless, under our law as presently controlling on us, Avondale must show a causal connection between the federal officer's direction and the conduct challenged by the Legendres. We affirm as correct the district court's conclusion that Avondale has not made this showing.

V.

The order of the district court is AFFIRMED.

(Reporter's Note: Concurring Opinion follows on p. 198).

[—11—] {-404-} **HIGGINBOTHAM,** Circuit Judge, concurring:

I concur fully with the majority opinion but write to suggest a source of the tension among our opinions; that is, our lack of focus on the colorable federal defense element, the predicate for removal under 28 U.S.C. § 1442. Here, that defense is the federal contractor defense articulated in *Boyle v. United Technologies Corp.*[1] I suggest that case contains all the necessary inquiries.

With these asbestos cases, we encounter three sets of jurisprudence. The first concerns the state-law claim for injuries suffered by exposure to asbestos. The second involves the federal contractor defense asserted by the government's contractor. The third entails the defendant's exercise of its forum choice through removal to {-405-} federal court. Rather than plodding through these areas, district courts, in deciding a motion to remand, are often drawn by the parties into issues concerning the sufficiency of a plaintiff's state-law claim.

To these eyes, the better approach is to begin with the jurisdictional issue; that is, we, in resolving a motion to remand, should first ask if the defendant offers a colorable federal defense, as not doing so tends to invite a [—12—] premature merits determination.[2] For an asbestos case like the one presently before us, resolution is found by close application of the principles set forth in *Boyle*. There, the Court indicated that the overarching inquiry is whether the claimed injury results from a discretionary decision of the government—i.e., whether Lieutenant Boyle's death resulted from the government's decision that led to the defectively designed escape hatch.[3]

Drifting from this inquiry leads to the misapplication of the causal nexus requirement. It is telling that other circuits have read the 2011 amendment to eliminate causal nexus, accenting the point that the causal nexus analysis begins to take the same shape as the colorable federal defense inquiry. It is not so much that we need to abandon causal nexus; rather, the relevant point is that causal nexus has little work to do once a court sequences its analysis to determine the availability of a colorable federal defense—here, the federal contractor defense—at the outset.

It bears emphasis that while the metrics for removal have softened, there has been no retreat from the sharp demands of *Boyle*. The suggested sequencing with firm application of *Boyle* ought to bring much clarity to cases that appear sound in outcome but less than clear in rationale.

---

[1] 487 U.S. 500, 512 (1988) ("Liability . . . cannot be imposed, pursuant to state law, when (1) the United States approved reasonably precise specifications; (2) the equipment conformed to those specifications; and (3) the supplier warned the United States about the dangers in use of the equipment that were known to the supplier but not to the United States."); *see also Jowers v. Lincoln Elec. Co.*, 617 F.3d 346, 352 (5th Cir. 2010) ("The government contractor defense preempts state law and provides a total bar to liability in a failure-to-warn case if a defendant establishes three elements: (1) the federal government exercised discretion and approved warnings for the product; (2) the warnings the defendant provided about the product conformed to the federal government specification; and (3) the defendant warned the federal government about dangers known to the defendant but not the government.") (citing *Boyle*, 487 U.S. at 512)

[2] *See, e.g., Zeringue v. Crane Co.*, 846 F.3d 785, 790, 5 Adm. R. 193, 195 (5th Cir. 2017) (resolving federal colorable defense before answering the causal nexus requirement).

[3] *Boyle*, 487 U.S. at 511.

United States Court of Appeals for the Fifth Circuit

No. 17-40577

UNITED STATES vs. RUIZ-HERNANDEZ

Appeal from the United States District Court for the Southern District of Texas

Decided: May 10, 2018

Citation: 890 F.3d 202, 6 Adm. R. 199 (5th Cir. 2018).

Before **DAVIS, JONES,** and **HIGGINSON,** Circuit Judges.

[—1—] {–206–} HIGGINSON, Circuit Judge:

Galdino Jose Ruiz-Hernandez helped Patricia Cervantes, a Mexican citizen, enter the United States by first taking a boat across the Rio Grande River and then swimming across a ship channel in Brownsville, Texas. While crossing the ship channel, Cervantes was struck by a passing Coast Guard vessel and killed.

Ruiz-Hernandez was indicted for one count of conspiracy to bring in, transport, and harbor an alien resulting in death and one count of transporting an alien within the United States for private financial gain and resulting in death. He went to trial and was found guilty of both counts. He now appeals, challenging his convictions and the application of two sentencing **[—2—]** enhancements under the United States Sentencing Guidelines. Ruiz-Hernandez makes essentially four arguments on appeal: that he did not act in furtherance of Cervantes's unlawful presence in the country; that he did not act for the purpose of financial gain; that Cervantes's death was not reasonably foreseeable; and that his conduct was not the but-for cause of her death. We find those arguments unavailing and affirm.

I.

A.

The Brownsville Ship Channel lies just north of the Rio Grande River and connects the Port of Brownsville with the Gulf of Mexico. It is approximately 40 feet deep and 500 feet wide. The channel is a high-traffic waterway, travelled day and night by various vessels from small fishing boats to large tankers. There are no lights along the channel, making it very dark at night, and there is no posted speed limit. The nearby Brownsville Shrimp Basin, however, a shrimp-boat docking area located on the north side of the ship channel, is designated as a "no-wake zone," meaning that vessels must travel slowly to avoid creating a wake that could damage the banks of the basin or cause the small shrimp boats to come untied.

B.

At 6:15 a.m. on April 24, 2015, Galdino Ruiz-Hernandez approached a security guard in the shrimp basin, telling the guard that someone else had told him that a person had been hit by a boat and needed **{–207–}** help. The guard looked for the injured person, but, because it was still dark at the time, was unsuccessful. About an hour later, Police Officer Rolando Doria received a call from a person who (according to the transcript of Doria's testimony) identified himself as "Galdino Jose Luis Hernandez," stating that a woman had been injured by a vessel in the Brownsville Ship Channel. Doria went to the ship channel, where he was flagged down by Ruiz-Hernandez. Ruiz-Hernandez **[—3—]** directed Doria to the woman's body, which was floating in the channel. Her body had multiple lacerations and her right foot was severed. She had on her person a Mexican voter-identification card identifying her as Patricia Guadalupe Garcia Cervantes.

Later that same morning, Sergeant Jesus Rosas, an investigator with the Cameron County Sheriff's Office, was dispatched to the scene. Ruiz-Hernandez agreed to provide a voluntary statement, and was taken to the sheriff's office. At the time, he was treated as a witness only and not a suspect. He explained to Sergeant Rosas that, at approximately 3:00 a.m. that morning, he and his "distant cousin Pati [Cervantes]" swam across the ship channel wearing inner tubes. Cervantes had told Ruiz-Hernandez that she could not swim very well, but she was about eight feet ahead of Ruiz-Hernandez when a large ship—later identified as a Coast Guard vessel—approached them "travelling very fast and without any light." The ship squarely struck Cervantes. Ruiz-Hernandez found her two minutes later, floating upside down and unresponsive. He tried, unsuccessfully, to resuscitate her, then went to get help.[1]

After reviewing Ruiz-Hernandez's statement, Sergeant Rosas realized that criminal activity could be involved. Rosas read Ruiz-Hernandez his rights, and Ruiz-Hernandez expanded upon his statement. He explained that he "was only doing a favor [for his] cousin Pati [Cervantes]," who wanted to get away from her abusive husband in Mexico. He said that his other cousin, his co-defendant Gabriel Sanchez, had insisted that he help Cervantes. On April 23, 2015, Sanchez picked Ruiz-Hernandez up from work and drove him to Sanchez's mother-in-law's house in Mexico where Cervantes was staying. **[—4—]** They stopped along the way to purchase two inner tubes. A ranchero arrived at the house a little while later, who informed Ruiz-Hernandez that he would charge 6,000 pesos to take Ruiz-Hernandez and Cervantes across the Rio Grande. The ranchero then took Ruiz-Hernandez and Cervantes to a ranch near the river, where they waited until approximately 9:30 p.m. before crossing by boat. When they left the boat, Ruiz-Hernandez and Cervantes walked through brush for four or five hours to get to the ship channel. They inflated their inner tubes and began to swim across. Ruiz-Hernandez insisted that he "just wanted to help [his] cousin cross[] the river and that no one offered to pay [him] any money in return."

On April 28, 2015, the Coast Guard contacted Homeland Security Investigations ("HSI") to assist in investigating Cervantes's death. HSI agent Luz Gonzalez then interviewed Ruiz-Hernandez, who provided a similar account to the one he had provided to Sergeant Rosas. Gonzalez also ran a database query for money-service businesses and discovered that there had been a $650 wire transfer from Eleazar Leon Fernandez in New York to Gabriel Sanchez at a Western Union wire-transfer **{-208-}** outlet in Brownsville on April 22, 2015. Fernandez explained to Gonzalez that he had paid Sanchez a $650 smuggling fee to bring Cervantes—who was his wife's relative—into the country because she was being abused by her husband. Of that $650, $300 was converted into pesos and given to Ruiz-Hernandez, who then gave it to the ranchero who brought Ruiz-Hernandez and Cervantes across the Rio Grande.

In the course of his investigation, Gonzalez obtained a pink inner tube that had been recovered by the Coast Guard near where Cervantes's body was found. At trial, he testified that the inner tube was not big enough to fit around an adult's waist, and that it appeared to be a floatation device intended for children to use in a swimming pool. He also testified that, during his investigation, he learned that Ruiz-Hernandez was not related to Cervantes. **[—5—]** Ruiz-Hernandez was not related to Sanchez either, though they knew each other because they worked together at the nearby Port of Brownsville.

C.

Ruiz-Hernandez was indicted on one count of conspiracy to bring in, transport, and harbor an alien resulting in death and one count of transporting an alien within the United States for private financial gain and resulting in death. He went to trial and, after two days of evidence, was found guilty of both counts. The jury answered three special interrogatories, indicating that they found beyond a reasonable doubt that: (1) the conspiracy count (Count 1) resulted in the death of a person; (2) the substantive count (Count 2) resulted in the death of a person,

[1] At trial, a forensic pathologist testified that Cervantes's death was caused by boat-propeller trauma and drowning. She further testified that Cervantes's injuries were consistent with being struck by the propellers of the Coast Guard vessel.

and (3) the substantive count (Count 2) was committed for private financial gain.

In calculating Ruiz-Hernandez's Guidelines sentencing range, the pre-sentence report ("PSR") added six points to his base offense level pursuant to § 2L1.1(b)(6) of the Sentencing Guidelines for creating a substantial risk of death or serious bodily harm and another 10 points pursuant to § 2L1.1(b)(7) for a resulting death.[2] Ruiz-Hernandez objected to the enhancements, but the district court overruled his objections. The district court did, however, grant Ruiz-Hernandez's motion for a downward departure based on § 5K2.16 for voluntary disclosure of the offense prior to its discovery. Ruiz-Hernandez was sentenced to 80 months, 17 months below the low end of the applicable Guidelines range. **[—6—]**

II.

A.

Ruiz-Hernandez first argues that the evidence was legally insufficient to support his convictions for conspiracy to transport an alien resulting in death (Count One) and transporting an alien for private financial gain and resulting in death (Count Two). Because he did not move at trial for a judgment of acquittal, we review only for whether the convictions constitute a "manifest miscarriage of justice." *United States v. Avants*, 367 F.3d 433, 449 (5th Cir. 2004). "Such a miscarriage 'exist[s] only if the record is "devoid of evidence pointing to guilt," or . . . "because the evidence on a key element of the offense [i]s so tenuous that a conviction would be shocking."'" *United States v. McDowell*, 498 F.3d 308, 312 (alterations in original) (quoting **{-209-}** *United States v. Knezek*, 964 F.2d 394, 400 n.14 (5th Cir. 1992)). And as always when we review the sufficiency of the evidence, our review is deferential to the verdict, viewing all evidence "in the light most favorable to the government, giving the government the benefit of all reasonable inferences and credibility choices." *Id.* (quoting *Knezek*, 964 F.2d at 400 n.14). Applying these standards, we conclude that there was no miscarriage here.

1.

Ruiz-Hernandez first argues that the evidence is insufficient to support his conviction for the conspiracy charge. To obtain a conviction for conspiracy to transport an alien under 8 U.S.C. § 1324(a)(1)(A), "the government must establish that the defendant[] 'agreed with one or more persons to transport or move illegal aliens within the United States in furtherance of their unlawful presence . . . knowingly or in reckless disregard of the fact that such aliens had come to, entered, or remained in the United States in violation of law." *United* **[—7—]** *States v. Chon*, 713 F.3d 812, 818 (5th Cir. 2013) (alteration omitted) (quoting *United States v. Ahmed Khan*, 258 F. App'x 714, 717 (5th Cir. 2007)).

Ruiz-Hernandez argues that the evidence is insufficient to support his conviction because it fails to establish either that he knew that Cervantes's presence in the country was unlawful or that he agreed to act in furtherance of her unlawful presence. However, there was ample evidence from which a rational jury could infer that Ruiz-Hernandez either knew or acted in reckless disregard of the fact that Cervantes's presence was unlawful. They entered the country by crossing the Rio Grande, walking for hours across brush, and swimming across a busy ship channel, all in the middle of the night. A rational jury could conclude that "if [Cervantes] were entitled to enter the United States legally, [s]he would not have utilized this dangerous method of entry." *United States v. Cardenas-Meneses*, 532 F. App'x 505, 512 (5th Cir. 2013).

Furthermore, while Ruiz-Hernandez argues that he acted for the purpose of helping her escape her abusive husband rather than furthering her unlawful presence, § 1324(a)(1)(A) is concerned only with *intent*, not *motive*. "While motive is the inducement to do some act, intent is the mental resolution or determination to do it. When the intent to

[2] The PSR also added an additional two points under § 3C1.1 for obstruction of justice, which is not at issue in this appeal.

do an act that violates the law exists, motive becomes immaterial." *Intent*, Black's Law Dictionary (10th ed. 2014). Here, there was evidence from which a rational jury could infer that Ruiz-Hernandez agreed to transport Cervantes in furtherance of her unlawful presence. For example, there is evidence that he knew or should have known that she was not lawfully entitled to enter the country and that he paid a smuggler to bring himself and Cervantes across the Rio Grande and into the country. Accordingly, we affirm Ruiz-Hernandez's conspiracy conviction.

2.

Ruiz-Hernandez also argues that the evidence is insufficient to support his conviction for the substantive transportation charge. He simply repeats **[—8—]** his argument that the evidence was insufficient to establish that he knew or recklessly disregarded the fact that Cervantes's presence in the United States was unlawful. For the reasons stated above, this argument fails.

3.

Next, Ruiz-Hernandez contends that the evidence is insufficient to support the statutory financial-purpose enhancement **{-210-}** because there was no evidence that he actually received any of the money transferred to Sanchez. Section 1324(a)(1)(B)(i) of Title 8 increases the maximum penalty for transportation of an alien from 5 years to 10 if "the offense was done for the purpose of commercial advantage or private financial gain." 8 U.S.C. § 1324(a)(1)(B)(i). Because § 1324(a)(1)(B)(i) increases the applicable statutory maximum sentence, it must be found by a jury beyond a reasonable doubt, *see United States v. McMillon*, 657 F. App'x 326, 338 (5th Cir. 2016) (citing *Apprendi v. New Jersey*, 530 U.S. 466, 476 (2000)), and we review the enhancement along with the underlying conviction itself for sufficiency of the evidence, *see United States v. Williams*, 449 F.3d 635, 646 (5th Cir. 2006) ("The 'financial gain' fact is an 'element' of a separate, greater offense."); *see also United States v. Allende-Garcia*, 407 F. App'x 829, 834–35 (5th Cir. 2011) (reviewing proof of financial-purpose element for sufficiency of the evidence).

The financial-purpose element requires the government to prove that the defendant sought "to profit or otherwise secure some economic benefit from [the] smuggling endeavor." *United States v. Garcia*, 883 F.3d 570, 574 (5th Cir. 2018) (construing identical language in 8 U.S.C. § 1324(a)(2)(B)(ii)). It does not require proof of *actual* payment, only evidence that the smuggling activity was undertaken for the *purpose* of financial gain. *See id.* at 575; *United States v. Kim*, 435 F.3d 182, 185 (2d Cir. 2006). Furthermore, a jury is free to infer such a purpose from circumstantial evidence, including evidence that the defendant did not previously know the individuals being smuggled, *see Garcia*, **[—9—]** 883 F.3d at 576, and evidence that others in the same smuggling operation had received or would receive money, *see Allende-Garcia*, 407 F. App'x at 833–35. Here, there was such evidence. Ruiz-Hernandez had no prior relationship with Cervantes, and there is evidence that his co-conspirator, Sanchez, received money in exchange for bringing Cervantes into the country. In light of that evidence, there was no miscarriage of justice and we affirm.

4.

In Ruiz-Hernandez's final challenge to his convictions, he argues that the evidence was insufficient to support the statutory enhancement for transportation resulting in death. As with the financial-purpose element, the resulting-in-death element, 8 U.S.C. § 1324(a)(1)(B)(iv), increases the applicable statutory maximum sentence and thus must be submitted to the jury and found beyond a reasonable doubt. *See Williams*, 449 F.3d at 645. As an "'element' of a greater aggravated offense," *id.*, we review the resulting-in-death element for sufficiency of the evidence, *see Cardenas-Meneses*, 532 F. App'x at 509–10; *United States v. De Jesus-Ojeda*, 515 F.3d 434, 444–45 (5th Cir. 2008).

Section 1324(a)(1)(B)(iv) increases the applicable statutory maximum sentence to death or life imprisonment in the case of a violation "resulting in the death of any person." 8 U.S.C. § 1324(a)(1)(B)(iv). Ruiz-Hernandez argues that, in order for that enhancement to apply, the government was required to prove that the resulting death was reasonably foreseeable and that the government failed to do so. We have previously declined to decide whether § 1324(a)(1)(B)(iv) requires foreseeability. *See De Jesus-Ojeda*, 515 F.3d at 444–45. Finding here that Cervantes's death was reasonably foreseeable, we again decline to decide whether the government was required to so prove. **{–211–}**

Ruiz-Hernandez argues that it was not reasonably foreseeable that a Coast Guard vessel—which he contends was operating in violation of speed **[—10—]** limitations, wake restrictions, and lighting requirements[3]—would strike a person swimming across the ship channel. The thrust of his argument is that it is unforeseeable that a government vessel, the presence of which is intended to enforce the law and to protect and assist persons present in the channel, would operate in violation of the law and, in so doing, cause harm. We recognize the tragic irony of the circumstances of Cervantes's death, but, as a legal matter, Ruiz-Hernandez confuses the foreseeability of *harm* with the foreseeability of the *manner* in which harm ultimately occurs. The foreseeability inquiry turns on whether "harm of a general sort to persons of a general class might have been anticipated by a reasonably thoughtful person." *In re Signal Int'l, LLC*, 579 F.3d 478, 492 (5th Cir. 2009). "The precise nature of the [resulting] injury and the manner of its infliction is immaterial . . . , so long as the injury is of a type that, in the circumstances, might reasonably have been expected to occur." *Hall v. Atchison, Topeka & Santa Fe Ry. Co.*, 504 F.2d 380, 385 (5th Cir. 1974). Here, it was reasonably foreseeable that a person swimming across a high-traffic ship channel in the dark of night would be struck by a passing ship.

That the ship's lights were, we assume, not on at the time of the accident does not change our conclusion. The negligent acts of others are foreseeable and thus do not break foreseeability. *See Allied Chem. Corp. v. Hess Tankship Co. of Del.*, 661 F.2d 1044, 1060 (5th Cir. Unit A 1981) ("A subsequent negligent act does not excuse prior negligence except in most unusual circumstances."). A ship travelling at night without lights is not so "extraordinary" that a **[—11—]** reasonable person would not foresee it, *see Becker v. Tidewater, Inc.*, 586 F.3d 358, 372 (5th Cir. 2009) (explaining that only "highly extraordinary" actions will constitute a superseding cause of harm), and does not render Ruiz-Hernandez's conviction a manifest miscarriage of justice. Accordingly, we affirm Ruiz-Hernandez's conviction under § 1324(a)(1)(B)(iv).

B.

Ruiz-Hernandez next challenges the district court's application of two sentencing enhancements under the Sentencing Guidelines. The district court increased his base offense level pursuant to § 2L1.1(b)(6) of the Guidelines for creating a substantial risk of death or serious bodily injury and pursuant to § 2L1.1(b)(7)(D) for conduct resulting in death. Because Ruiz-Hernandez objected to the application of these enhancements below, we review "the district court's interpretation and application of the Sentencing Guidelines *de novo*" and its "findings of fact and its application of the Sentencing Guidelines to those findings of fact . . . for clear error." *United States v. Cedillo-Narvaez*, 761 F.3d 397, 401 (5th Cir. 2014). "Sentencing enhancements must be proven 'by a preponderance of the evidence.'" *United States v. Muniz*, 803 F.3d 709, 712 (5th Cir. 2015) (quoting *United States v. Juarez*, 626 F.3d 246, 251 (5th Cir. 2010)). **{–212–}** "A factual finding is 'not clearly erroneous as long as it is

[3] As summarized above, the evidence at trial showed that there was no speed limit posted in the ship channel and that it, unlike the nearby shrimp basin, is not designated as a no-wake zone. As to lighting, the evidence presented at trial, derived from Ruiz-Hernandez's statement to Sergeant Rosas, was that the ship was travelling "without any light." That was later disputed in the PSR. For purposes of reviewing the sufficiency of the evidence, however, we assume that the ship's lights were not on.

plausible in light of the record read as a whole.'" *Cedillo-Narvaez*, 761 F.3d at 401 (quoting *United States v. McMillan*, 600 F.3d 434, 457–58 (5th Cir. 2010)).

1.

Section 2L1.1(b)(6) provides for an increased base offense level for a defendant convicted of smuggling, transporting, or harboring an alien "if the offense involved intentionally or recklessly creating a substantial risk of death **[—12—]** or serious bodily injury to another person." U.S.S.G. § 2L1.1(b)(6).[4] Ruiz- Hernandez again argues that Cervantes's death must have been reasonably foreseeable in order for § 2L1.1(b)(6) to apply.

Ruiz-Hernandez is correct as a general matter that § 2L1.1(b)(6) requires that a risk of harm be foreseeable. *See De Jesus-Ojeda*, 515 F.3d at 442–43. However, it requires only that *some* risk of death or serious bodily injury be foreseeable, not the specific harm that actually occurred. After all, the enhancement applies for creating a *risk* of harm; no harm at all need actually occur to warrant its application. *See, e.g., United States v. Maldonado-Ochoa*, 844 F.3d 534, 537 (5th Cir. 2016) (affirming application of § 2L1.1(b)(6) where the defendant "started to drive with unrestrained persons lying in the bed of his truck," even though he was pulled over as soon as his vehicle began to move and no one was injured). Accordingly, the relevant inquiry focuses on whether the defendant's conduct "pose[d] inherently dangerous risks to the aliens being transported." *United States v. Solis-Garcia*, 420 F.3d 511, 516 (5th Cir. 2005) (quoting *United States v. Garcia-Guerrero*, 313 F.3d 892, 896 (5th Cir. 2002)). The actual results of the defendant's conduct are irrelevant. *See United States v. Munoz-Tello*, 531 F.3d 1174, 1185 (10th Cir. 2008) ("In assessing whether the enhancement was appropriate, we must focus exclusively on the defendant's *conduct*, ignoring the *results* of that conduct."). As discussed above, it was reasonably foreseeable that a person swimming across a busy ship channel in the dark of night would be struck by a passing ship. Accordingly, we affirm the district court's application of the sentencing enhancement under § 2L1.1(b)(6). **[—13—]**

2.

Section 2L1.1(b)(7) provides for a ten-point increase in the base offense level "[i]f any person died" in the course of the smuggling or transportation offense. U.S.S.G. § 2L1.1(b)(7). Ruiz-Hernandez acknowledges that § 2L1.1(b)(7) requires only that a defendant's conduct be the but-for, not proximate, cause of the resulting death. *See United States v. Ramos-Delgado*, 763 F.3d 398, 401–02 (5th Cir. 2014). However, he contends the evidence shows that the Coast Guard vessel, and not his conduct, was the but-for cause of Cervantes's death. We disagree.

But-for causation exists if the result would not have occurred without the conduct at issue. *See Burrage v. United States*, 134 S. Ct. 881, 888 (2014). A particular result can be caused by multiple necessary factors—multiple but-for causes—yet one of those single factors will still be considered a but-for cause so long as the result would **{–213–}** not have occurred in its absence. *Id.* Here, while the Coast Guard ship was *a* but-for cause of Cervantes's death, she would not have been in its path but for Ruiz-Hernandez's conduct in smuggling her across the ship channel. Accordingly, his conduct was also a but-for cause of her death, and the district court did not err in applying the enhancement under § 2L1.1(b)(7).

III.

For the foregoing reasons, we AFFIRM Ruiz-Hernandez's convictions and his sentence.

[4] Section 2L1.1(b)(6) instructs courts to increase a base offense level "by 2 levels, but if the resulting offense level is less than level 18, increase to level 18." U.S.S.G. § 2L1.1(b)(6). Here, because Ruiz-Hernandez's base offense level before application of this enhancement was 12, its application resulted in a six point increase to level 18.

United States Court of Appeals
for the Fifth Circuit

No. 16-30194

**VALERO MKTG. & SUPPLY CO.
vs.
M/V ALMI SUN**

Appeal from the United States District Court for the Eastern District of Louisiana

Decided: June 19, 2018

Citation: 893 F.3d 290, 6 Adm. R. 205 (5th Cir. 2018).

Before **HIGGINBOTHAM, JONES,** and **HAYNES,** Circuit Judges.

[—1—] {–291–} HIGGINBOTHAM, Circuit Judge:

This case asks whether a bunker supplier, having entered into a contract with a bunker trader that later went bankrupt, is entitled to assert a maritime lien against the vessel that physically received its fuel. Because that supplier cannot show that it provided necessaries "on the order of the owner or a person authorized by the owner," we affirm the district court's denial of a maritime lien. **[—2—]**

I.

While in Corpus Christi, Texas, the Almi Sun (the "Vessel") needed refueling. Almi Tankers S.A., an agent for the Vessel's owner Verna Marine Co. Ltd., contracted with O.W. Bunker Malta, Ltd., a fuel trader, to procure bunkers. During negotiations, Almi Tankers requested the name of the physical supplier, and O.W. Malta named Valero Marketing & Supply Company. O.W. Malta issued a final sales order confirming Valero as the supplier and listing itself as the seller. Another O.W. Bunker entity, O.W. Bunker USA, Inc., then contracted with Valero to purchase the fuel. O.W.'s involvement ended there. Valero coordinated delivery directly with the Vessel, and Vessel agents tested and **{–292–}** verified the bunkers' quality. After delivery was completed, an authorized officer of the Vessel signed the bunkering certificate, and Valero submitted an invoice to O.W. USA.

In early November 2014, Almi Tankers learned that the O.W. Bunker group of companies faced significant financial problems and might be unable to pay Valero. Almi Tankers requested "written confirmation and evidence of payment," and "reserve[d] the right to make remittance directly to the physical supplier and . . . hold any balance due . . . for payment." O.W. Bunker and other related entities filed for bankruptcy shortly thereafter.

Valero then brought this *in rem* action seeking a maritime lien for the amount owed for the bunkering plus interest and fees. Verna appears as the *in rem* claimant of the Vessel defending the action on the Vessel's behalf. Both Valero and Verna moved for summary judgment, and the district court granted summary judgment in favor of Verna. Valero timely appeals. **[—3—]**

II.

We review the "'district court's grant of summary judgment de novo, applying the same standards as the district court.'"[1] Summary judgment is appropriate where "there is no genuine dispute as to any material fact and the movant is entitled to judgment as a matter of law."[2] On summary judgment, we view the evidence in the light most favorable to the nonmovant, and draw all reasonable inferences in the nonmovant's favor.[3]

III.

The Commercial Instruments and Maritime Liens Act ("CIMLA") governs the circumstances under which a party is entitled to a maritime lien. In relevant part, CIMLA states that a person providing necessaries to a vessel "on the order of the owner or a person authorized by the owner" is entitled to a

---

[1] *Green v. Life Ins. Co. of N. Am.*, 754 F.3d 324, 329, 2 Adm. R. 245, 247 (5th Cir. 2014) (quoting *Cooper v. Hewlett-Packard Co.*, 592 F.3d 645, 651 (5th Cir. 2009)).

[2] FED. R. CIV. P. 56(a).

[3] *Cox v. Wal-Mart Stores East, L.P.*, 755 F.3d 231, 233 (5th Cir. 2014).

maritime lien on the vessel.[4] Section 31341(a) lists "persons . . . presumed to have authority to procure necessaries for a vessel:"

> (1) the owner; (2) the master; (3) a person entrusted with the management of the vessel at the port of supply; or (4) an officer or agent appointed by—(a) the owner; (b) a charterer; (c) an owner pro hac vice; or (d) an agreed buyer in possession of the vessel.[5]

We apply the provisions of CIMLA *stricti juris* to ensure that maritime liens are not "lightly extended by construction, analogy, or inference."[6] **{-293-}**

It is not unusual for an entity supplying necessaries to a vessel to lack privity of contract with the owner of that vessel, and to instead contract with **[—4—]** an intermediary. In *Lake Charles*, we recognized two lines of cases that deal with such circumstances: the general/subcontractor line of cases and the principal/agent, or "middle-man," line of cases.[7] To determine which line of cases applies, *Lake Charles* instructs that "it is not whether an intermediary can be expected to supply the necessaries itself that distinguishes instances in which the actual suppliers have liens, but it is rather the nature of the relationship between each pair of entities that are involved in the transaction at issue."[8]

As it happened in *Lake Charles*, ED&F Man Sugar, Inc. entered into an agreement to purchase rice from Broussard Rice Mill, Inc. In that agreement, the parties assigned the responsibility of providing stevedoring services to Broussard. Broussard, working through an agent, awarded Lake Charles Stevedores ("LCS") the bid to load the rice onto the vessel. LCS loaded the rice, and the vessel's agents signed activity sheets and receipts. When Broussard failed to pay, LCS asserted a maritime lien for its services.[9] **[—5—]**

We found those facts to be "more akin to those in which general contractors have been engaged to supply a service and have called upon other firms to assist them in meeting their contractual obligations."[10] Typically, "the general contractor supplying necessaries on the order of an entity with authority to bind the vessel has a maritime lien"; however, "subcontractors hired by those general contractors are generally not entitled to assert a lien on their own behalf, unless it can be shown that an entity authorized to bind the ship controlled the selection of the subcontractor and/or its performance."[11] Because Man Sugar "retained no control over the selection of a stevedoring concern, and Broussard accepted all the risk associated,"

---

4 46 U.S.C. § 31342(a).

5 46 U.S.C. § 31341(a).

6 *Atlantic & Gulf Stevedores, Inc. v. M/V GRAND LOYALTY*, 608 F.2d 197, 200–01 (5th Cir. 1979). In *Atlantic & Gulf Stevedores*, we ruled that a vessel's chief officer is a "person to whom management of the vessel at the port of supply is intrusted" for purposes of section 972 of the Federal Maritime Lien Act—the predecessor to CIMLA. *Id.* at 200–03. In so **[—4—]** holding, we acknowledged the doctrine of *stricti juris* but opined that the Federal Maritime Lien Act "is not to be viewed through the constricting glass of [s]tricti juris" as its "legislative history" required "a more liberal application than that which existed prior to the 1971 amendments to the Maritime Lien Act." *Id.* at 201. We further explained that Congress intended to "make it easier and more certain for stevedores and others to protect their interests by making maritime liens available where traditional services are routinely rendered." *Id.*

In subsequent decisions, however, we have clarified our "respect for the principle of *stricti juris*," counseling against application of the sweeping language set forth in *Atlantic & Gulf Stevedores* to the present case. *See Lake Charles Stevedores, Inc. v. PROFESSOR VLADIMIR POPOV MV*, 199 F.3d 220, 231 (5th Cir. 1999). As we discuss *infra*, *Lake Charles* stands for the rule in our circuit that a subcontractor is generally not entitled to assert a maritime lien "unless it can be shown that an entity authorized to bind the ship controlled the selection of the subcontractor and/or its performance." *Id.* at 229. Because *Lake Charles* is on point, we are guided by its application of *stricti juris* here.

7 *Id.* at 228–29.

8 *Id.* at 230.

9 *Id.* at 222–23.

10 *Id.* at 230.

11 *Id.* at 229.

we held that LCS was not entitled to a maritime lien.[12]

Ken Lucky typifies the middle-man line of cases.[13] In that case, the following sequence of events occurred: Bulkferts, Inc., the vessel's subcharterer, placed an order for fuel with its managing agent, Eurostem Maritime Limited; Eurostem contacted Brook Oil Ltd., a fuel trader; Brook Oil then instructed Gray Bunkering Services to place an order for fuel with Marine Fuel, the physical supplier; Marine Fuel, in turn, asked Gray for assurances about payment before delivery of the bunkers; Gray notified Marine Fuel that it had been "nominated by the owner" of the vessel to supply the fuel; Marine Fuel delivered the **{-294-}** fuel; and the vessel's chief engineer accepted the fuel with the approval of the vessel's master.[14] After having unsuccessfully sought payment, Marine Fuel asserted a maritime lien on the vessel.[15] **[—6—]**

The Ninth Circuit found that Marine Fuel was entitled to a lien because the parties agreed that the order originated from Bulkferts, the subcharterer, an entity with authority to bind the ship.[16] Due to that concession, the Ninth Circuit did not "reach . . . the district court's conclusion that Brook was *not* Bulkfert's agent," concluding that Marine Fuel did not need to "establish agency between Brook and Bulkferts to fall within the scope of one entitled to a maritime lien under [CIMLA]."[17]

IV.

In this case, there is no dispute that bunkers qualify as necessaries and that Valero provided those necessaries to the Vessel. The sole inquiry before us is whether Valero furnished the necessaries to the Vessel "on the order of the owner or a person authorized by the owner." We conclude that it did not.

The record shows that Verna, through its agent Almi Tankers, contacted OW Malta because it was a "reputable bunker trader[]"; that during negotiations, Almi Tankers asked who would be the bunker fuel supplier, and it did not object to Valero's selection; that the sales order confirmation listed Valero as the supplier; that Valero provided the entire bunkering service that Almi Tankers contracted for, with no assistance from O.W. or its affiliates; that the Vessel's agents monitored and tested Valero's performance; and that Almi Tankers expressed concern about O.W.'s ability to pay Valero.

These facts do not demonstrate that Valero provided the bunkers to the Vessel "on the order of the owner or a person authorized by the owner." Valero provided the bunkers at O.W.'s request, and O.W. is not a "person [] presumed **[—7—]** to have authority to procure necessaries[.]"[18] These facts are "more akin to those in which general contractors have been engaged to supply a service and have called upon other firms to assist them in meeting

---

[12] *Id.* at 230.

[13] *Marine Fuel Supply & Towing, Inc. v. M/V KEN LUCKY*, 869 F.2d 473 (9th Cir. 1988).

[14] *Id.* at 475.

[15] *Id.*

[16] *Id.* at 477.

[17] *Id.* The Ninth Circuit separately examined the master's implied authority to incur a lien against the vessel upon accepting the supplies that Marine Fuel delivered, and determined that the master had such authority because a ship's master has *presumed* authority to incur a lien under CIMLA. *Id.* at 477–78.

[18] 46 U.S.C. § 31341(a); *see also ING Bank N.V. v. M/V TEMARA*, No. 16-4019, 2018 WL 2944306, -- F.3d -- , at *6, 6 Adm. R. 44, 49 (2d Cir. June 13, 2018) (finding that physical supplier was not entitled to a maritime lien when it provided necessaries at the direction of an O.W. Bunker entity acting as an intermediary "rather than at the direction of the owner or the charterer of the Vessel, or any other statutorily-authorized person"); *Barcliff, LLC v. M/V DEEP BLUE*, 876 F.3d 1063, 1071, 5 Adm. R. 518, 523 (11th Cir. 2017) (same); *Galehead, Inc. v. M/V ANGLIA*, 183 F.3d 1242, 1245 (11th Cir. 1999) (finding that supplier provided the bunkers at the trader's request, and that the trader is not a "person [] . . . presumed to have authority to procure necessaries"); *Port of Portland v. M/V PARALLA*, 892 F.2d 825, 828 (9th Cir. 1989) (denying maritime lien when supplier dealt with general contractor, not vessel owner or vessel owner's agent).

their contractual obligations."[19] Thus, Valero must show that an entity authorized to bind the ship "controlled [its] selection . . . and/or its performance."[20] The record, **{-295-}** however, proves no more than the Vessel's awareness of Valero, not that the Vessel "controlled" the selection or performance of Valero. Mere awareness does not constitute authorization under CIMLA.[21]

Despite Valero's urging, we decline to apply *Ken Lucky*. As mentioned *supra*, the Ninth Circuit's holding—that the physical supplier could assert a lien—turns on the parties' concession that the physical supplier sold the bunkers to an entity with authority to bind the vessel.[22] Here, Valero dealt with O.W., not with Verna or Almi Tankers, and the record does not establish that O.W. served as Verna's or Almi Tankers' agent.[23] Thus, *Ken Lucky* is inapplicable. **[—8—]**

V.

The dissent says that we fail to follow *Lake Charles* because in that case, "we made clear that the 'subcontractor' line of cases is itself divided into two lines of cases: (1) cases requiring 'an entity with authority to bind the vessel' to *'direct* that the general contractor hire a particular subcontractor in order for that subcontractor to be entitled to a lien'; and (2) cases requiring the subcontractor to be 'identified and accepted by the vessel's owner or charterer prior to performance.'" The dissent's view likely emerges from the following passage in *Lake Charles*:

> In keeping with the notion that subcontractors may acquire liens where the vessel's owners retain control over their selection and/or performance, the Ninth and Second Circuits require that an entity with authority to bind the vessel direct that the general contractor hire a particular subcontractor in order for that subcontractor to be entitled to a lien. *See Port of Portland,* 892 F.2d at 828; *Farwest*, 828 F.2d at 526; *Integral Control Sys.*, 990 F. Supp. at 301. In other cases in which subcontractors have been found to be entitled to a lien, those subcontractors were identified and accepted by the vessel's owner or charterer prior to performance. *See Stevens,* 913 F.2d at 1525, 1534; *Turecamo of Savannah, Inc. v. United States,* 824 F. Supp. 1069, 1072 (S.D. Ga. 1993). Owner involvement in directing, testing, and/or inspecting subcontractor performance has also been cited in support of finding a lien in favor of a subcontractor. *See Stevens*, 913 F.2d at 1535; *cf. Marine Coatings*, 932 F.2d at 1375 n.9 (listing operator's inspecting subcontractor work and giving provisional and final acceptance to work performed by the subcontractor among evidence that supported court's conclusion that a genuine issue of fact existed regarding general contractor's authority to bind the vessel). Based on these cases, we agree with the district court that LCS has not shown it was entitled to a lien under the circumstances presented here.[24]

We do not read *Lake Charles* as the dissent does. To these eyes, the above specifies three factual scenarios that color the general proposition that a **[—9—]** subcontractor is not entitled to a lien, "unless it can be shown that an entity authorized to bind **{-296-}** the ship controlled the selection of the subcontractor and/or its performance."[25] We see no adoption, let alone a clear one, of "two lines of cases" branching from the subcontractor line of cases.

Even assuming that *Lake Charles* divided the subcontractor line of cases into "two lines of cases" *sub silentio,* Valero cannot establish that it falls in either one. Verna, through Almi

---

19 *Lake Charles*, 199 F.3d at 230.

20 *Id.* at 229.

21 *Id.* at 232 (explaining that CIMLA's authority requirement would be rendered meaningless if "awareness that necessaries are being supplied was sufficient, even though those necessaries were procured by an entity without authority to bind the vessel").

22 *Ken Lucky*, 869 F.2d at 477.

23 *Id.*

24 *Lake Charles*, 199 F.3d at 231 (footnote omitted).

25 *Id.* at 229.

Tankers, neither "direct[ed] that the general contractor hire a particular subcontractor" nor "identified and accepted" Valero "prior to performance." The record merely shows that Verna, through Almi Tankers, was aware that Valero would physically supply the bunkers.

The dissent also says that the majority opinion "creates an unnecessary circuit split with the Eleventh Circuit," citing *Galehead* and likening this case to *Marine Coatings* and *Stevens*.[26] Specifically, the dissent states that *Marine Coatings* and *Stevens* reflect the Eleventh Circuit's embrace of the "second line of cases" of the subcontractor line of cases—*i.e.*, cases requiring the subcontractor to be identified and accepted by the vessel's owner or charterer prior to performance. The dissent, however, overlooks *Barcliff*, in which the Eleventh Circuit held that a subcontractor in the same contractual scenario as here was not entitled to a maritime lien.[27] In so holding, the Eleventh Circuit reviewed *Galehead*, *Marine Coatings*, and *Stevens*.[28] In determining the law of the Eleventh Circuit, we prefer its own statement of its law.

To begin, a review of the facts and holding in *Barcliff* dispel any notion that we create a circuit split.[29] Technip UK Limited, the vessel owner, sent a **[—10—]** request to O.W. Bunkers (UK) Limited and two other suppliers seeking bunker fuel. Technip awarded the contract to O.W. UK. Thereafter, O.W. UK entered into a contract with O.W. Bunker USA, Inc., who then contracted with Radcliff, the physical supplier of the bunkers. Like the present case, Radcliff coordinated delivery with the vessel, and upon delivery, the vessel's chief engineer signed a delivery certificate. After O.W. filed for bankruptcy, Radcliff, having gone unpaid and thus finding itself in the same situation as Valero, asserted a maritime lien against the vessel. The Eleventh Circuit ruled that Radcliff was not entitled to a lien because "Radcliff acted on the order of O.W. USA, not Technip."[30]

To reach that holding, the *Barcliff* court reviewed its jurisprudence on maritime liens. It began with the circuit's general rule, as set forth in *Galehead*, which provides: "Where the owner directs a general contractor to provide necessaries to its vessel, a subcontractor retained by the general contractor to perform the work or provide the supplies is generally not entitled to a maritime lien."[31] The *Barcliff* court then noted that *Galehead* recognizes an exception to the general rule. That is, **{–297–}** "where the general contractor is not an agent of the owner, and the owner does not initially order the subcontractor to perform the work, it might still be said that the owner 'somehow authorized' **[—11—]** the work if it 'was sufficiently aware of, and involved in, [the] work that it might be said that [the subcontractor] was working for [the owner].'"[32]

This "significant-and-ongoing-involvement exception" emerged from *Marine Coatings* and *Stevens*. The *Barcliff* court proceeded to review these cases, explaining that *Marine Coatings* "involved extensive maintenance, such as painting, coating, and cleaning" and that *Stevens* involved "repair work."[33] In addition, those cases, the *Barcliff* court

[26] *See Marine Coatings of Ala., Inc. v. United States*, 932 F.2d 1370 (11th Cir. 1991); *Stevens Tech. Servs., Inc. v. United States*, 913 F.2d 1521 (11th Cir. 1990).

[27] *Barcliff*, 876 F.3d at 1071–73, 5 Adm. R. at 523–25.

[28] *Id.*, 5 Adm. R. at 523–25.

[29] *Id.* at 1065–67; 1071–73, 5 Adm. R. at 518–20; 523–25.

[30] *Id.* at 1071, 5 Adm. R. at 523.

[31] *Id.*, 5 Adm. R. at 523. In *Galehead*, Genesis Container Line, a charterer, contacted Polygon Energy Services, Inc. to obtain fuel bunkers for its vessel, and Polygon contacted Establissment Asamar, Ltd. to supply the fuel. Asamar then engaged the physical supplier. This arrangement occurred twice, and Genesis failed to pay Asamar both times. Asamar thereafter assigned its rights to a collection agency, Galehead, who brought suit. 183 F.3d at 1244. The Eleventh Circuit ruled that Galehead was not entitled to a lien, reasoning that "Asamar did not provide the bunkers on order of the owner or an authorized agent." *Id.* at 1245. Rather, the Eleventh Circuit determined that "Asamar provided the bunkers at Polygon's request, and Polygon is not a '"person [] . . . presumed to have authority to procure necessaries[.]"' *Id.* (quoting 46 U.S.C. § 31341(a)).

[32] 876 F.3d at 1071, 5 Adm. R. at 524 (quoting *Galehead*, 183 F.3d at 1245).

[33] *Id.* at 1072, 5 Adm. R. at 524.

observed, involved an owner and a subcontractor that "developed a relationship over an extended period of time as the work progressed."[34] The *Barcliff* court then turned specifically to *Stevens*, noting that "the owner was in contact almost exclusively with the subcontractor because the general contractor did not have the capability to perform the work," and "the owner dealt directly with the subcontractor and its employees directed, inspected, tested, and approved the subcontractor's work on a continuing basis."[35] In short, "the owner's participation with the subcontractor was so substantial that it could not seriously be argued the work was not done on the owner's orders."[36] The *Barcliff* court concluded by acknowledging that "[t]he *Galehead* panel juxtaposed *Marine Coatings* and *Stevens* with cases involving a one-off transaction, 'where the degree of involvement with the owner is minimal or non-existent;'"[37] and that "[o]ne of those cases involved fuel provision."[38]

Against this background, *Marine Coatings* and *Stevens* are inapplicable in light of *Barcliff* and *Galehead*. Though *Barcliff* determined that the physical supplier had waived its argument concerning the *Galehead* exception, no **[—12—]** circuit split results by following the holding in *Barcliff*. We are unaware of a case in the Eleventh Circuit, and the dissent proffers none, that applies *Marine Coatings* and *Stevens* to find that a subcontractor may acquire a lien for a one-off transaction in which the vessel owner was merely aware of the subcontractor's identity.[39] The circuits to have addressed the sequence of contracts before us agree that such physical suppliers are not entitled to a maritime lien.[40]

VI.

We affirm the district court's grant of summary judgment for Verna.

(Reporter's Note: Dissenting Opinion follows on p. 211).

[34] *Id.*, 5 Adm. R. at 524.

[35] *Id.*, 5 Adm. R. at 524 (citing *Stevens*, 913 F.2d at 1525–26, 1535).

[36] *Id.*, 5 Adm. R. at 524 (citing *Stevens*, 913 F.2d at 1525–26, 1535).

[37] *Id.*, 5 Adm. R. at 524 (quoting *Galehead*, 183 F.3d at 1246).

[38] *Id.*, 5 Adm. R. at 524.

[39] *See Galehead*, 183 F.3d at 1246 ("That a charterer of a vessel becomes aware that some work performed was by a party somewhere down the chain of contracting and re-contracting does not give rise to a maritime lien.").

[40] *See ING Bank*, 2018 WL 2944306, at *6–8, 6 Adm. R. at 49–51; *Barcliff*, 876 F.3d at 1071–73, 5 Adm. R. at 523–25.

[—13—] {-298-} HAYNES, Circuit Judge, dissenting:

The majority opinion fails to follow our prior precedent in *Lake Charles Stevedores, Inc. v. Professor Vladimir Popov MV*, 199 F.3d 220, 231 (5th Cir. 1999) and creates an unnecessary circuit split with the Eleventh Circuit. *See Galehead, Inc. v. M/V Anglia*, 183 F.3d 1242, 1245–46 (11th Cir. 1999) (per curiam); *see also Noramco Shipping Corp. v. Bunkers Int'l Corp.*, No. 6:02CV515-ORL-22DAB, 2003 WL 22594419, at *7 (M.D. Fla. Apr. 30, 2003) ("Under Eleventh Circuit jurisprudence, the right of a subcontractor to assert a maritime lien against a vessel for necessaries is not restricted by a rigid rule but instead depends on the degree of involvement between the owner and the subcontractor."). Accordingly, I respectfully dissent.

I agree that Valero is a subcontractor under the "general contractor/subcontractor" line of cases. *Lake Charles* explains the general proposition that "subcontractors hired by those general contractors are generally not entitled to assert a lien on their own behalf, unless it can be shown that an entity authorized to bind the ship controlled the selection of the subcontractor and/or its performance." 199 F.3d at 229. However, this exception is not as narrow as the majority opinion makes it seem. Unmentioned by the majority opinion, in *Lake Charles* we made clear that the "subcontractor" line of cases is itself divided into two lines of cases: (1) cases requiring "an entity with authority to bind the vessel" to "*direct* that the general contractor hire a particular subcontractor in order for that subcontractor to be entitled to a lien"; and (2) cases requiring the subcontractor to be "identified and accepted by the vessel's owner or charterer prior to performance." *Id.* at 231. In the second line of cases, "[o]wner involvement in directing, testing, and/or inspecting subcontractor performance has also been [—14—] cited in support of finding a lien in favor of a subcontractor."[1] *Id.* We clearly adopted both lines of cases but found that the subcontractor in *Lake* Charles did not meet either one. *See id.*

The Eleventh Circuit has embraced the second line of cases. In *Marine Coatings of Alabama v. United States*, the Eleventh Circuit addressed the question of the availability of a subcontractor lien in a repair services contract. 932 F.2d 1370, 1375–76 (11th Cir. 1991). There, the United States Navy entered into Master Ship Repair Contracts with Braswell Shipyards, Inc., that permitted Braswell to hire subcontractors, although "the contracts did not purport to make Braswell an agent of the government." *Id.* at 1732. Braswell subcontracted with Marine Coatings of Alabama, Inc. ("MCI"), for the painting, cleaning, and coating of three vessels, and the United States inspected and approved MCI's work. *Id.* at 1373. The United States paid Braswell, but Braswell filed for Chapter 11 {-299-} without paying MCI. *Id.* Despite being a subcontractor, MCI asserted a maritime lien against the three vessels, and the Eleventh Circuit found "a genuine issue as to whether the government procured MCI's work, authorized the work, or ratified the procurement of MCI's work. Alternatively, there is a genuine issue as to whether Braswell was authorized by the government to procure MCI's work." *Id.* at 1376.

Likewise, in *Stevens Technical Services., Inc. v. United States*, the Sealift Antarctic needed a "major overhaul." 913 F.2d 1521, 1525 (11th Cir. 1990). [—15—] Marine Transport Lines, Inc. ("MTL"), on behalf of the United States government, solicited bids, and

[1] *Compare Galehead*, 183 F.3d at 1245 ("Where the level of involvement between the owner and the third-party provider was significant and ongoing during the pertinent transaction, the courts have found a triable issue of fact about whether the third-party deserved a lien."), *with Cianbro Corp. v. George H. Dean, Inc.*, 596 F.3d 10, 17–18 (1st Cir. 2010) (holding that subcontractor was not entitled to a lien where "the record establishes that [the vessel's owners] did not have any participation in the subcontracting of this work or control over its performance"), *and Bonanni Ship Supply, Inc. v. United States*, 959 F.2d 1558, 1565 (11th Cir. 1992) ("[T]he mere fact of acceptance and full compensation to the prime contractor, absent any allegation that the [vessel's owner] had any knowledge of *performance by the subcontractor plaintiff*, is insufficient to create a genuine issue of material fact regarding whether the plaintiff was a maritime lienor under the MCILA.").

Atlantic submitted a bid that identified Stevens as a subcontractor. *Id.* Atlantic then entered into a memorandum of understanding with Stevens, dividing the work between the two of them. *Id.* Subsequently, Atlantic's bid was accepted and MTL awarded it the contract. *Id.* During the course of the work, government representatives inspected, tested, and approved the work performed by both Atlantic and Stevens. *Id.* at 1525–26. Once work was completed, MTL paid Atlantic, but Atlantic failed to pay Stevens. *Id.* at 1526. Stevens subsequently filed actions against Atlantic *in personam* and against the Sealift Antarctic *in rem*. *Id.* In vacating and remanding for further reconsideration, the Eleventh Circuit pointed to several factors that might have indicated Stevens was entitled to a maritime lien: (1) that the government's representatives were aware of Steven's performance and the principal contract showed Stevens as a subcontractor having more than 15 percent of the contract's value; (2) that the government's representatives knew that Atlantic was not capable of full performance on its own; (3) that the contract covering the work was fully authorized by the government's representatives; (4) that the government's representatives worked directly with Stephens in discussing, testing, and inspecting Stephen's work; and (5) that all of the work was accepted and fully compensated to Atlantic. *Id.* at 1534–35.

Here, the majority opinion significantly understates Almi's involvement in the bunkering transaction when it describes it as a "one-off transaction in which the vessel owner was merely aware of the subcontractor's identity." To the contrary, the parallels to *Stevens,* in light of the standards adopted in *Lake Charles,* are clear: (1) during negotiations with O.W., Almi made a point to discover who would perform the bunkering; it did not object to Valero's selection and thus impliedly approved Valero prior to finalizing the bunkering **[—16—]** agreement; (2) Almi knew that O.W., as a "reputable bunker trader," could not bunker the vessel itself but would purchase bunkers from a physical supplier; (3) the contract with O.W., which designated Valero as the supplier, was fully authorized by a party with authority to bind the vessel; (4) the vessel's agents engaged directly with Valero and tested and approved of Valero's bunkers; and (5) the vessel's agents approved of the bunkers and signed a certificate confirming performance.

The majority opinion's reliance on *Barcliff, LLC v. M/V DEEP BLUE, IMO No. 9215359* is misplaced. *See* 876 F.3d 1063, 1071–73, 5 Adm. R. 518, 523–25 (11th Cir. 2017). As an initial matter, *Barcliff* determined that the central issue here was not properly before it, thus the commentary relied on by the majority opinion is mere dicta. *See id.* at 1073, 5 Adm. R. at 525. Even if it were not dicta, *Barcliff* does not mandate the result reached by the majority opinion. As already shown, similar to *Stevens,* Almi "was sufficiently aware of, and involved in, [Valero's services] that it might be said that [Valero] was working for [it]." *See id.* at 1071, 5 Adm. R. at 524 (quoting **{-300-}** *Galehead,* 183 F.3d at 1245). Moreover, *Barcliff* does not exclude one-off bunkering services that satisfy this rule. *Barcliff* indicated that the exception has not been applied where the owner's involvement was "minimal or non-existent," and then it observed that "[o]ne of those cases involved fuel provision." *Id.* at 1072, 5 Adm. R. at 524 (citing *Tramp Oil & Marine, Ltd. v. M/V Mermaid I,* 805 F.2d 42, 45 (1st Cir. 1986)). In *Tramp Oil,* however, no relationship existed between the vessel's owner and the fuel broker seeking the lien, and the vessel's owner did not know about the fuel broker (who was retained by an intermediary) until after its work was completed. *See Tramp Oil,* 805 F.2d at 45 ("In this case, however, no relationship existed between Tramp and the vessel, and neither the vessel owner nor the charterer even knew of Tramp until after Tramp had made the payment to Exxon."). **[—17—]**

Although a subcontractor, the interactions between the vessel and Valero are such that Valero is entitled to assert a maritime lien. That O.W. was expected to pay Valero is not the point; "[e]xpectations that payment for the services would be made by some party other than the vessel does not vitiate a lien by one who, as permitted under [the Act], is not required to prove reliance on the credit of the vessel."[2] *Stevens*, 913 F.2d at 1536.

For these reasons, I conclude Valero is entitled to relief. From the majority opinion's decision to the contrary, I therefore respectfully dissent.

[2] Verna argued in its brief and at oral argument that it has already paid OW Malta for the fuel in order to settle a contractual arbitration dispute in the United Kingdom; that this decision will result in Verna being forced to pay twice for the same fuel. That reality is one of Verna's own making—an attempt to extinguish O.W.'s claims while this action was pending. I note that Almi Tankers expressed concern to O.W. regarding the conglomerate's financial situation and reserved the right to pay Valero directly, ultimately deciding to pay O.W. Verna's unilateral decision does not control the outcome here.

United States Court of Appeals
for the Fifth Circuit

No. 16-30984

STEMCOR USA INC.
vs.
CIA SIDERURGICA DO PARA COSIPAR

Appeal from the United States District Court for the Eastern District of Louisiana

Decided: July 11, 2018

Citation: 895 F.3d 375, 6 Adm. R. 214 (5th Cir. 2018).

Before **HIGGINBOTHAM, GRAVES,** and **HIGGINSON,** Circuit Judges.

[—2—] {-377-} **HIGGINSON,** Circuit Judge:

We grant Intervenor Plaintiff–Appellees' Motion for Panel Rehearing and deny the Motion For Rehearing En Banc. We withdraw the prior opinion, 870 F.3d 370, 5 Adm. R. 306 (5th Cir. 2017), and substitute the following.

This case is a dispute between two creditors, each of which attached the same pig iron owned by America Metals Trading L.L.P. ("AMT"). Plaintiff- Appellant Daewoo International Corp. ("Daewoo") sued AMT in the Eastern District of Louisiana, seeking an order compelling AMT to arbitrate and an attachment of the pig iron. Daewoo invoked both maritime attachment and the Louisiana non-resident attachment statute, which allows attachments in aid of any "action for a money judgment." La. Code Civ. Proc. art. 3542. Citing both types of attachment, the district court granted Daewoo its attachment. Following Daewoo's attachment, Intervenor-Appellee Thyssenkrupp Mannex GMBH ("TKM") attached the same pig iron in Louisiana state court. TKM then intervened in the federal suit, arguing that Daewoo's attachment should be vacated because (1) maritime jurisdiction was improper and (2) Louisiana non-resident attachment was inapplicable.

The district court agreed with TKM and vacated Daewoo's attachment. Specifically, the district court found that because Daewoo's underlying suit sought to compel arbitration, it was not an "action for a money judgment" and therefore Daewoo could not receive a non-resident attachment writ. Daewoo appeals only the district court's conclusion that its Louisiana non-resident attachment writ was invalid. We affirm on slightly different grounds.

I

Daewoo is a South Korean trading company. In May 2012, Daewoo entered into a series of contracts with AMT for the purchase of pig iron, to be **[—3—]** delivered in New Orleans. The sale contracts contained arbitration clauses. Although Daewoo made payments under the contracts, AMT never shipped the pig iron. TKM is a German company. Between June 2010 and February 2011, TKM entered into six contracts to purchase pig iron from AMT. AMT never delivered. In response to the breach of contract, TKM and AMT negotiated a **{-378-}** settlement, which required AMT to make quarterly payments to TKM. AMT did not pay.

On December 14, 2012, Daewoo filed suit in the Eastern District of Louisiana, seeking attachment of AMT's pig iron on board the M/V Clipper Kasashio, and asserting maritime jurisdiction. The district court issued the attachment. On December 21, Daewoo amended its complaint to seek a writ of attachment under the Louisiana non-resident attachment statute. The writ was granted. On December 22, the U.S. Marshals Service served Daewoo's writ on the cargo, which was then anchored in Kenner Bend.

On December 28, 2012, TKM filed suit in Jefferson Parish state court seeking a writ of attachment over the same pig iron that Daewoo attached on December 22. TKM's state court writ of attachment was served on the cargo on December 29, 2012. TKM then moved to intervene in Daewoo's federal suit. TKM sought a federal writ of attachment over the pig iron, which was granted and served on the cargo on January 11.

That same day, all of the parties moved in federal court to sell the pig iron. The court approved the sale. The parties agreed that the proceeds of the sale would serve as substitute res, subject to TKM's jurisdictional attack on the federal attachments. **[—4—]**

On May 9, 2016, TKM moved to vacate Daewoo's attachment.[1] The district court agreed with TKM and vacated Daewoo's writ on August 4, 2016. With Daewoo's federal writ vacated, the first valid remaining writ was TKM's state court writ. Accordingly, the district court ordered that the proceeds from the pig-iron sale be transferred to the Jefferson Parish state court. On August 10, Daewoo moved to stay the district court's order, arguing that "[i]n the event that Daewoo's appeal is successful it would be difficult to retrieve the funds from the state court, assuming the state court has not already dispersed the funds, and would create serious issues of federal-state comity." The district court denied the stay request because it was filed after the district court had sent the money to the Jefferson Parish state court.

II

The district court found federal subject matter jurisdiction under the Convention on the Recognition and Enforcement of Foreign Arbitral Awards (the "Convention"). We agree.

For a federal court to have jurisdiction under the Convention two requirements must be met: (1) there must be an arbitration agreement or award that falls under the Convention, and (2) the dispute must relate to that arbitration agreement. These requirements flow from the text of two sections of the Convention. The explicit jurisdictional provision is Section 203, which gives federal courts jurisdiction over all "action[s] or proceeding[s] falling under the Convention." 9 U.S.C. § 203. "An arbitration agreement or arbitral award arising out of a legal relationship, whether contractual or not, which is considered as commercial, including a transaction, contract, or agreement described in section 2 of this title, falls under the Convention." 9 U.S.C. § 202. **[—5—]** Accordingly, the first step for determining jurisdiction is deciding whether the "arbitration agreement or award . . . falls under the Convention." *Id.* **{-379-}**

The next step, derived from Section 203, is to ask whether the "action or proceeding"—as opposed to the arbitration agreement or award—falls under the Convention. The Convention's removal statute offers guidance on what "falling under" means because "[g]enerally, the removal jurisdiction of the federal district courts extends to cases over which they have original jurisdiction." *Francisco v. Stolt Achievement MT*, 293 F.3d 270, 272 (5th Cir. 2002). Section 205 of the Convention allows for removal whenever "the subject matter of an action or proceeding pending in a State court relates to an arbitration agreement or award falling under the Convention." 9 U.S.C. § 205. We have read "relates to" to mean "has some connection, has some relation, [or] has some reference" to. *Acosta v. Master Maint. & Constr. Inc.*, 452 F.3d 373, 378–79 (5th Cir. 2006). And reading "falling under" to mean "relates to" makes sense grammatically. "Fall" means "to come within the limits, scope, or jurisdiction of something." Merriam-Webster's Collegiate Dictionary 418 (10th ed. 2002). Accordingly, the second step of the jurisdictional question is asking whether the "action or proceeding" "relates to" a covered arbitration agreement or award. *See Fred Parks, Inc. v. Total Compagnie*, 981 F.2d 1255, 1992 WL 386999, at *1–2 (5th Cir. 1992) (unpublished) (treating the question of original and removal jurisdiction under the Convention as identical).

This two-step jurisdictional inquiry is consistent with case law interpreting the Convention. *See, e.g., BP Expl. Libya Ltd. v. ExxonMobil Libya Ltd.*, 689 F.3d 481, 487 & n.4 (5th Cir. 2012) (finding jurisdiction where there was a covered arbitration agreement and the suit sought appointment of arbitrators); *Borden, Inc. v. Meiji Milk Prods. Co.*, 919 F.2d 822, 826 (2d Cir. 1990) (holding that jurisdiction over preliminary injunction in aid of covered arbitration was proper

[1] TKM successfully moved to vacate a number of parties' attachments. Only Daewoo appealed.

because the remedy sought did not try to "bypass **[—6—]** arbitration"); *Sunkyong Eng'g & Const. Co. v. Born, Inc.*, 149 F.3d 1174, 1998 WL 413537, at *5 (5th Cir. 1998) (unpublished) ("The FAA grants the United States district courts original federal question jurisdiction over arbitral awards and agreements to arbitrate that fall within the Convention."); *Venconsul N.V. v. Tim Int'l. N.V.*, 03Civ.5387(LTS)(MHD), 2003 WL 21804833, at *3 (S.D.N.Y. Aug. 6, 2003) ("*Borden* has been interpreted as recognizing a court's power to entertain requests for provisional remedies in aid of arbitration even where the request for remedies does not accompany a motion to compel arbitration or to confirm an award.").

Both jurisdictional requirements are met here. First, Daewoo's arbitration agreements with AMT are covered by the Convention. For an arbitration agreement to be covered by the Convention, four requirements must be met: (1) there must be an agreement in writing to arbitrate the dispute; (2) the agreement must provide for arbitration in the territory of a Convention signatory; (3) the agreement to arbitrate must arise out of a commercial legal relationship; and (4) at least one party to the agreement must not be an American citizen. *See Freudensprung v. Offshore Tech. Servs., Inc.*, 379 F.3d 327, 339 (5th Cir. 2004); *Sunkyong*, 149 F.3d 1174, 1998 WL 413537, at *5; *Sedco, Inc. v. Petroleos Mexicanos Mexican Nat'l Oil Co. (Pemex)*, 767 F.2d 1140, 1144–45 (5th Cir. 1985). All four requirements are met here:

- There is an agreement in writing to arbitrate Daewoo and AMT's dispute.
- That agreement provides for arbitration in New York, and the United States is a signatory to the Convention. **{-380-}**
- The agreement arises out of a commercial relationship between Daewoo and AMT.
- Both Daewoo and AMT are not American citizens.

Second, this suit is related to the AMT arbitration agreements because Daewoo seeks an attachment to facilitate the arbitration provided for in the AMT agreements. *See Borden*, 919 F.2d at 826 ("[T]he desire for speedy **[—7—]** decisions in arbitration is entirely consistent with a desire to make as effective as possible recovery upon awards, after they have been made, which is what provisional remedies do." (internal quotation marks and citation omitted)). Our decision in *E.A.S.T., Inc. of Stamford v. M/V Alaia*, 876 F.2d 1168 (5th Cir. 1989), strongly counsels towards recognizing subject matter jurisdiction based on the Convention to issue provisional remedies in aid of arbitration.[2]

[2] At one point at least, there was significant contrary authority on this issue. *See, e.g., Simula, Inc. v. Autoliv, Inc.*, 175 F.3d 716, 726 (9th Cir. 1999) ("Because the district court correctly concluded that all of Simula's claims were arbitrable and the ICC arbitral tribunal is authorized to grant the equivalent of an injunction *pendente lite*, it would have been inappropriate for the district court to grant preliminary injunctive relief."); *I.T.A.D. Assocs., Inc. v. Podar Bros.*, 636 F.2d 75, 77 (4th Cir. 1981) ("[T]he attachment obtained by I.T.A.D. and the superseding bond posted by Podar are contrary to the parties' agreement to arbitrate and the Convention[.]"); *McCreary Tire & Rubber Co. v. CEAT S.p.A.*, 501 F.2d 1032, 1038 (3d Cir. 1974) (finding that the Convention does not allow a court to issue provisional remedies). It appears, however, that the courts that read jurisdiction under the Convention restrictively have retreated from their views and now, at least in most circumstances, recognize subject matter jurisdiction to grant provisional remedies in aid of arbitration. *See Aggarao v. MOL Ship Mgmt. Co.*, 675 F.3d 355, 377 n.19 (4th Cir. 2012) ("Because the Supreme Court has rejected the *McCreary* premise, *Podar Bros.* has been effectively overruled by the Court on the jurisdictional point and is not controlling precedent with respect to [the] injunction request [in aid of arbitration]."); *Toyo Tire Holdings Of Americas Inc. v. Cont'l Tire N. Am., Inc.*, 609 F.3d 975, 980 (9th Cir. 2010) ("In contrast to *Simula*, [plaintiff] seeks an injunction to preserve the status quo until the arbitral panel can consider and rule upon Toyo's application for interim relief pending the arbitration panel's final decision. Allowing a district court to grant this type of relief is not contrary to the 'emphatic federal policy in favor of arbitral dispute resolution' of primary concern in *Simula*. To the contrary, in cases such as this,

The court in *E.A.S.T.*, albeit in the context of a maritime attachment, found that the "the arrest of a vessel prior to arbitration is not inconsistent with the Convention." *Id.* at 1173. And the court noted that the Convention "does not expressly forbid pre-arbitration attachment" and that pre-arbitration attachment "may 'serve[] . . . as a security device in aid of arbitration.'" *Id.* (alteration in original) (quoting *Atlas Chartering Servs., Inc. v. World Trade* **[—8—]** *Grp., Inc.*, 453 F. Supp. 861, 863 (S.D.N.Y. 1978)).

Indeed, *E.A.S.T.*'s reasoning mirrors the reasoning of courts that have found subject matter jurisdiction under the Convention to order state-law provisional remedies. Like the court in *E.A.S.T.*, those courts reason that "nothing in the Convention divests federal courts of jurisdiction to issue provisional remedies . . . such as an attachment, when appropriate in international arbitrations." *Bahrain Telecomms. Co. v. Discoverytel, Inc.*, 476 F. Supp. 2d 176, 181 (D. Conn. 2007); *see also China Nat'l Metal Prods. Imp./Exp. Co. v. Apex Dig., Inc.*, 155 F. Supp. 2d 1174, 1180 (C.D. Cal. 2001) ("Rather than conflicting with **{-381-}** the parties' agreement to arbitrate, provisional remedies such as attachment reinforce arbitration agreements by ensuring that assets from which an arbitration award would be satisfied are secured while arbitration is pending."). *E.A.S.T.* therefore strongly suggests that this court recognizes jurisdiction under the Convention to issue state-law preliminary remedies in aid of arbitration.[3] **[—9—]**

Applying *E.A.S.T.* and the cases that follow it, the Convention grants jurisdiction over Daewoo's request for an attachment. Like the plaintiff in *E.A.S.T.*, Daewoo sought to attach the pig iron in order to facilitate arbitration and increase its chance of recovering on any award. Because Daewoo sought attachment to bring about a covered arbitration—that is, because Daewoo's suit related to a covered arbitration agreement—this court has subject matter jurisdiction.[4]

III

The parties dispute whether Louisiana's non-resident attachment statute allows for attachment in aid of arbitration. The district court held that it does not. With great respect

---

judicial interim relief may be necessary to preserve the meaningfulness of the arbitral process." (internal citation omitted)); *Rhone Mediterranee Compagnia Francese Di Assicurazioni E Riassicurazoni v. Lauro*, 712 F.2d 50, 55 (3d Cir. 1983) (allowing district court to maintain jurisdiction pending arbitration).

[3] And there are compelling reasons against reading jurisdiction under Section 203 as narrowly limited to the three remedies expressly allowed by the Convention (compelling arbitration and appointing arbitrators in Section 206 and confirming awards in Section 207). Namely,

> [n]othing in § 206 or § 207 limits the subject matter jurisdiction of federal courts. These sections merely identify the remedies that federal courts may grant, and do not speak in jurisdictional terms or refer in any way to the jurisdiction of the district courts. . . . To grant the remedies provided in those sections, the Court must first determine that it has jurisdiction . . . .
>
> Treating §§ 206 and 207 as jurisdictional provisions confuses the subject matter jurisdiction of federal courts with their remedial authority. Although jurisdiction is a word of many . . . meanings, there is a difference between the two. The nature of the relief available after jurisdiction attaches is, of course, different from the question whether there is jurisdiction to adjudicate the controversy . . . . The breadth or narrowness of the relief which may be granted under federal law . . . is a distinct question from whether the court has jurisdiction over the parties and the **[—9—]** subject matter. Any error in granting or designing relief does not go to the jurisdiction of the court.

CRT Capital Grp. v. SLS Capital, S.A., 63 F. Supp. 3d 367, 374–75 (S.D.N.Y. 2014) (internal quotations marks, citations, and alterations omitted). Simply put, the question of what remedies are available in a Convention suit is distinct from the question of jurisdiction.

[4] We asked the parties to brief whether this court has personal jurisdiction under quasi in rem principles. We are satisfied that we have personal jurisdiction. *See Republic Nat'l Bank of Miami v. United States*, 506 U.S. 80, 88–89 (1992); *Nassau Realty Co., Inc. v. Brown*, 332 So. 2d 206, 210 (La. 1976).

for the district court, and cognizant of the lack of instructional case law and limited briefing on this issue below, we decline to adopt a categorical approach to this question. Louisiana's non-resident attachment statute allows for attachment in aid of suits to confirm monetary arbitration awards. Moreover, because Louisiana law allows for attachment in aid of yet-to-be-brought actions, non-resident attachment may be available in aid of arbitration when an eventual confirmation suit is contemplated. Nevertheless, we affirm the district court's vacatur because Daewoo did not strictly comply with the attachment statute's procedural requirements.

As always, statutory interpretation begins with "the plain language and **[—10—]** structure of the statute." *Coserv Ltd. Liab. Corp. v. Sw. Bell Tel. Co.*, 350 F.3d 482, 486 (5th Cir. 2003); *see also Arabie v. CITGO Petroleum Corp.*, 89 So. 3d 307, 312 (La. 2012) ("[A]ccording to the general **{-382-}** rules of statutory interpretation, our interpretation of any statutory provision begins with the language of the statute itself."). Louisiana's attachment statute provides that "[a] writ of attachment may be obtained in any action for a money judgment, whether against a resident or a nonresident, regardless of the nature, character, or origin of the claim, whether it is for a certain or uncertain amount, and whether it is liquidated or unliquidated." La. Code Civ. Proc. art. 3542. A "money judgment" is a "[a] judgment for damages subject to immediate execution, as distinguished from equitable or injunctive relief." Black's Law Dictionary 972 (10th ed. 2014). Accordingly, an "action for a money judgment" is a civil or criminal judicial proceeding seeking monetary damages.

Louisiana case law supports this interpretation. In *de Lavergne v. de Lavergne*, 244 So. 2d 698 (La. App. 4th Cir. 1971), a Louisiana court of appeals was asked to decide whether a suit for alimony was an "action for a money judgment" within the meaning of Article 3542. The court concluded that it was, reasoning:

> A proceeding for alimony is a suit for judgment ordering the payment of money just as any other suit which has for its object the recovery of money in damages or in enforcement of any obligation to pay a sum of money whether liquidated or not. The difference is that in a judgment ordering the payment of a sum of money as alimony or for child support in addition to the ordinary remedies available to the judgment creditor for execution, there is the additional remedy of a contempt proceeding and the imposition of a penalty for noncompliance with the court's order. We must reject the argument of appellants that the additional remedy makes the action something other than one for a money judgment. **[—11—]**

Id. at 704. The *de Lavergne* court's analysis aligns with the plain meaning of Article 3542. That is, the *de Lavergne* court first asked whether a suit for alimony sought an order compelling the payment of money. *Id.* Noting, however, that an alimony suit allowed for more than just a payment of money—because an alimony proceeding allowed "the additional remedy of a contempt proceeding and the imposition of a penalty for noncompliance with the court's order"—the court asked whether the additional remedy converted alimony into "something other" than an action "for a money judgment." *Id.* The court concluded that it did not because the additional contempt remedy was intended to make the money judgment more effective. *Id.*

And other sections of Louisiana law that refer to money judgments have similarly been interpreted to refer to judicial proceedings seeking judgments of money damages. *See Flowers v. S. Reg'l Physician Servs. Inc.*, 247 F.3d 229, 233 n.4 (5th Cir. 2001) ("[A]s a matter of statutory interpretation, in determining the meaning of a particular statutory provision, it is helpful to consider the interpretation of other statutory provisions that employ the same or similar language."). For example, Civil Code Article 3501 sets forth the prescriptive period for "money judgments": "A money judgment rendered by a trial court of this state is prescribed by the lapse of ten years . . . ." Courts interpreting Article 3501 have found that orders for "the payment of a sum of money" are money judgments, *see, e.g.*, *Eikert v. Beebe*, 188 So. 3d 1129, 1131 (La. App. 2d Cir. 2016), but that orders directing a party to take an action are not money judgments, *see, e.g.*, *Liquidator of Clinton & P.H.R. Co. v. Whitaker*, 22 La. Ann. 209, 209 (1870) ("The judgment directs the liquidator to discharge a duty attached to his office. It is not a money judgment."); **{-383-}** *Williams v. Perry*, 436 So. 2d 1268, 1269 (La. App. 1st Cir. 1983) (judgment of partition is not a money judgment). Courts interpreting Code of Civil Procedure Article 2291 **[—12—]** have similarly defined "money judgment." Article 2291 provides "[a] judgment for the payment of money may be executed by a writ of fieri facias directing the seizure and sale of property of the judgment debtor." The Article has been interpreted to distinguish between orders for the payment of money and orders directing a party to take an action. *See, e.g.*, *Madere v. Madere*, 660 So. 2d 1205, 1205 (La. 1995) (order of partition "did not create" a money judgment); *Lindy Invs., III, L.P. v. Shakertown Corp.*, 631 F. Supp. 2d 815, 821 & n.13 (E.D. La. 2008) (suit seeking declaration that condition precedent for payment was met was not a suit for money judgment).

Based on this definition of "action for a money judgment," we agree with the district court that a suit to compel arbitration (like this suit) is not directly an action for a money judgment. A motion to compel arbitration seeks an order requiring a party to take an action—namely, to arbitrate the dispute. Accordingly, a suit seeking to compel arbitration is not an "action for a money judgment," and Daewoo's suit seeking to compel arbitration cannot underlie a Louisiana non-resident attachment writ. On the arguments raised by Daewoo, its appeal ends here.

We further take the opportunity to note that Louisiana law provides, in limited circumstances, that an attachment may issue before the suit underlying the attachment is filed. Article 3502 of the Louisiana Code of Civil Procedure provides:

> A writ of attachment . . . may issue before the petition is filed, if the plaintiff obtains leave of court and furnishes the affidavit and security provided in Article 3501. In such a case the petition shall be filed on the first judicial day after the issuance of the writ of attachment . . . unless for good cause shown the court grants a longer delay.

Article 3502 allows for the possibility of attachments in suits like this one. In **[—13—]** Louisiana, arbitral awards are convertible into money judgments in confirmation proceedings. *See, e.g.*, *Matherne v. TWH Holdings, L.L.C.*, 136 So. 3d 854, 860 (La. App. 1st Cir. 2013) ("A confirmed arbitration award is considered to be a valid and final judgment for purposes of res judicata."); La. Stat. § 9:4212 ("Upon the granting of an order confirming, modifying, or correcting an award, judgment may be entered in conformity therewith in the court wherein the order was granted."); La. Stat. § 9:4214 (noting that when an award is converted to a judgment, "[t]he judgment so entered shall have the same force and effect, in all respects, as, and be subject to all the provisions of law relating to, a judgment in an action, and it may be enforced as if it had been rendered in an action in the court in which it is entered"). Thus, an action to confirm a money award is an action for a money judgment. And because a confirmation suit can be an action for a money judgment, Article 3502 allows for attachments to be issued before the contemplated underlying confirmation suit is brought.[5] **{-384-}**

---

[5] Reading Louisiana law to allow for pre-suit attachment in aid of arbitration makes sense of the statutory scheme as a whole because other provisions of Louisiana law assume that some state-law preliminary remedies are available to aid arbitration. Louisiana has adopted the UNCITRAL Model Law on interim measures in arbitration, which provides, "[i]t is not incompatible with an arbitration agreement for a party to request, before or during arbitral proceedings, from a court an interim measure of protection and for a court to grant the measure." La. Stat. § 9:4249. Moreover, the UNCITRAL Model Law indicates that

Put into context, Article 3502 allows for attachments to issue in aid of arbitration so long as the party seeking the attachment (1) complies with the **[—14—]** requirements of Article 3502 and (2) shows good cause for a pre-petition attachment, which will usually require showing that arbitration is likely to result in a confirmation suit and also showing a need for an immediate attachment (which may include an inquiry into the imminence of the arbitration or confirmation suit).

Although Daewoo's briefs did not rely on Article 3502 as a reason to reverse the district court, our independent review of the record confirms that Daewoo did not satisfy step one. Because attachment is a "harsh" remedy, the Louisiana statutes "providing for a Writ of Attachment . . . must be strictly and literally complied with." *Barnett Marine, Inc. v. Van Den Adel*, 694 So. 2d 453, 458 (La. App. 5th Cir. 1997); *accord Yorkwood Sav. & Loan Ass'n v. Thomas*, 379 So. 2d 798, 799 (La. App. 4th Cir. 1980). Failure to do so renders a granted writ a "nullity." *Lee v. Lee*, 38 So. 2d 66, 69 (La. 1948). The record does not disclose that Daewoo strictly and literally complied with Article 3502's requirements. We see no indication that Daewoo invoked Article 3502 when it sought a writ, that the district court granted Daewoo permission to file a petition on "the first judicial day after the issuance of the writ," or that the district court made the good-cause finding to permit a later filing. La. Code Civ. Proc. art. 3502.[6] **[—15—]**

Although Article 3502 allows parties to seek an Article 3542 attachment before commencing confirmation proceedings, **{-385-}** Daewoo neither invoked nor complied with Article 3502's requirements when it sought the attachment here.

We AFFIRM.

(Reporter's Note: Dissenting Opinion follows on p. 221).

---

attachment is one of the interim remedies that may aid an arbitration. It would be strange for Louisiana to have adopted the UNCITRAL Model Law without allowing for state law interim remedies in aid of arbitration. *See Food & Drug Admin. v. Brown & Williamson Tobacco Corp.*, 529 U.S. 120, 121 (2000) ("In determining whether Congress has specifically addressed the question at issue, the court should not confine itself to examining a particular statutory provision in isolation. Rather, it must place the provision in context, interpreting the statute to create a symmetrical and coherent regulatory scheme."); *Green v. La. Underwriters Ins. Co.*, 571 So. 2d 610, 616 (La. 1990) ("If two statutes can be reconciled by a fair and reasonable interpretation, we must read the statutes so as to give effect to each.").

[6] On this score, the dissent observes that Daewoo's compliance with Article 3502 "was not raised on appeal, [that] neither party presented any such argument, and [that] the district court made no such finding." Dissenting Opinion at 1. Indeed, but the forfeiture was Daewoo's, not TKM's. The court that issued the attachment did not address Article 3502 because Daewoo did not invoke that provision; nor did Daewoo rely on that law as ground to reverse the district court's judgment. As for the merits: true enough, "the statute *allows* the court to grant a longer delay" beyond Article 3502's default timeline, Dissenting Opinion at 2 (emphasis added), but the attachment order said nothing of deadline extensions or the required good-cause showing, *contra* La. Code Civ. Proc. art. 3502. Finally, forfeiture principles also work against the dissent's contention that "Louisiana law permits only the party whose assets were attached to raise procedural challenges to the attachment." Dissenting Opinion at 2. This argument implicates statutory, not constitutional, standing, *see Bd. of Miss. Levee Comm'rs v. EPA*, 674 F.3d 409, 417 (5th Cir. 2012) ("Unlike constitutional standing, prudential standing arguments may be waived."); *cf. Harold H.* **[—15—]** *Huggins Realty, Inc. v. FNC, Inc.*, 634 F.3d 787, 795 n.2 (5th Cir. 2011) (noting that constitutional standing, unlike statutory standing, is unwaivable), and Daewoo did not stake this position until its reply brief, *see, e.g., Flex Frac Logistics, L.L.C. v. N.L.R.B.*, 746 F.3d 205, 208 (5th Cir. 2014) ("Ordinarily, arguments raised for the first time in a reply brief are waived."); *United States v. Scroggins*, 599 F.3d 433, 446–47 (5th Cir. 2010) ("We look to an appellant's initial brief to determine the adequately asserted bases for relief." (quoting *Knatt v. Hosp. Serv. Dist. No. 1*, 327 F. App'x 472, 483 (5th Cir. 2009)).

[—16—] {-385-} **GRAVES,** Circuit Judge, dissenting:

I would conclude that the underlying action seeking to compel arbitration here is clearly an "action for a money judgment" under Louisiana's non-resident attachment statute. See La. Code Civ. P. art. 3542. Because I would vacate the judgment of the district court and remand, I respectfully dissent.

As the majority acknowledges, Daewoo has made it clear from the outset that it would be pursuing a money judgment. The "nature, character, or origin of the claim" just happens to be arbitration. La. Code Civ. P. art. 3542. The majority cites various cases for its conclusion that, under the definition of "action for a money judgment," a suit to compel arbitration is not directly an action for a money judgment. However, those cases are inapposite. The majority declares, incorrectly, that "[o]n the arguments raised by Daewoo, its appeal ends here." As the majority has previously conceded, the inquiry absolutely does not end there. The majority's declaration is wholly undermined by the analysis which immediately follows that declaration. Clearly that analysis continues to be the basis for the majority's decision on rehearing. Further, the majority correctly concedes that Article 3502 allows for attachments in suits like this. *See Matherne v. TWH Holdings, L.L.C.*, 136 So.3d 854, 860 (La. App. 1st Cir. 2013); *see also* La. Stat. § 9:4249.[1] This concession establishes that the district court erred in vacating the attachment on the basis that the underlying action was not an action for a money judgment.

Rather than properly concluding that the district court erred, the majority instead concludes that "[t]he record does not disclose that Daewoo [—17—] strictly and literally complied with Article 3502's requirements." Saying, "[w]e see no indication that Daewoo invoked Article 3502 when it sought a writ, that the district court granted Daewoo permission to file a petition 'on the first judicial day after the issuance of the writ,' or that the district court made the good-cause finding to permit a later filing. La. Code Civ. Proc. art. 3502." Yet that issue was not raised on appeal, neither party presented any such argument, and the district court made no such finding. Moreover, as TKM argues on rehearing, the majority fails to identify any exceptional circumstance to justify consideration of a new issue sua sponte. *See Martinez v. Tex. Dep't of Criminal Justice*, 300 F.3d 567, 574 (5th Cir. 2002).

Notwithstanding the lack of exceptional circumstances, I disagree with the majority's analysis of and conclusion that Daewoo failed to comply with the procedural requirements of Article 3502 of the Louisiana Code of Civil Procedure. As Daewoo asserts in its response to the petition for rehearing, the statute allows the court to grant a longer delay and Daewoo's application was based on an affidavit stating that it would be filing for arbitration within 30 days. Additionally, as Daewoo asserts, longstanding Louisiana law permits only the party whose assets were attached to raise procedural challenges to the attachment.

In {-386-} *Gilkerson-Sloss Commission Co. v. Bond*, 11 So. 220 (La. 1892)[2] the Supreme Court of Louisiana said:

> On the first point urged by the interveners it is elementary that in an attachment suit the intervener will not be permitted to urge defenses personal to the defendants. The formality and regularity of the proceedings, the rightful issuing of the attachment, in the absence of fraud and collusion between plaintiff and defendants, are matters pertaining exclusively to the [—18—] defendant. The intervener is limited to the assertion of his own rights, to show that the property attached is his; that he has a superior privilege on it, or, as alleged in this case,

[1] TKM's counsel has also conceded that an action to confirm an arbitration award would be an action for a money judgment.

[2] There appears to be a typographical error in the listing of this case which says "*Gilkeson.*" The caption and body of the opinion, as well as some other opinions involving the same company, indicate the spelling "*Gilkerson.*"

> the plaintiffs and defendants perpetrated a fraud in the issuing of the attachment in order to defeat his pursuit of the property. He has nothing to do with the irregularity of the affidavit, the insufficiency of the attachment bond, and other irregularities in the proceedings.

Id. at 221. *See also Gen'l Motors Acceptance Corp. v. Jordan*, 65 So.2d 627, (La. Ct. App. 1st Cir. 1953) ("All of o[u]r jurisprudence on this point shows a long standing and well-defined rule that an intervenor must take the case as he finds it, and he is not allowed to retard the progress of the main action."). *Id.* at 629; *Fleming v. Shields*, 21 La. Ann. 118, 119-20 (1869) ("In the absence of fraud and collusion, the intervenor will not be permitted to urge defenses which are personal to the defendant."); and *West v. His Creditors*, 8 Rob. 123, 128 (La. 1844) ("An intervenor who claims property in controversy between other parties, cannot interfere therein any further than to prove his right to the property. He cannot contest the plaintiff's claim against the defendant, nor urge any irregularities in the suit."). This court, in *Berger v. First Federal Savings and Loan Association of Warner Robbins, Ga.*, 824 F.2d 400, 402 (5th Cir. 1987), recognized the holding from *Gilkerson-Sloss*, cited above, that "wrongful attachment may not be raised by intervenor." Also, in *Fisher v. Jordan*, 116 F.2d 183, 185 (5th Cir. 1940), this court prohibited such a collateral attack on an attachment.

The majority does not conclude that there was fraud and collusion here, and the cases cited by the majority are easily distinguished. In *Barnett Marine, Inc. v. Van Den Ade*, 694 So.2d 453, 458 (La. App. 5th Cir. 1997), the matter involved the defendants whose assets were attached, not an intervenor. The majority also cites *Yorkwood Sav. & Loan Ass'n v. Thomas*, 379 So.2d 798, 799 (La. App. 4th Cir. 1980), and *Lee v. Lee*, 38 So.2d 66, 69 (La. 1948), but, **[—19—]** again, those cases did not involve an intervenor. The majority argues that Daewoo somehow forfeited the right to rebut any argument that it did not procedurally comply with Article 3502 even though TKM waived the very issue of Daewoo's procedural compliance by never raising it. That argument is illogical. The majority offers no authority for its statement that "forfeiture principles also work against the dissent's contention that 'Louisiana law permits only the party whose assets were attached to raise procedural challenges to the attachment.'" Instead, the majority concedes that "[t]his argument implicates statutory, not constitutional, standing" and then cites *Board of Mississippi Levee Commissioners v. Environmental Protection Agency*, 674 F.3d 409, 417 (5th Cir. 2012), for the proposition that, "[u]nlike constitutional standing, prudential standing arguments may be **{-387-}** waived."[3] In doing so, the majority acknowledges that any procedural compliance argument TKM may have against Daewoo's attachment is waived. It is wholly improper for the majority to raise, sua sponte, an issue that has been waived and then conclude that Daewoo forfeited the right to assert that the issue is waived.

Regardless, Daewoo did not fail to raise any constitutional or procedural argument in its initial brief. Daewoo also did not raise any new issue in its reply brief. Instead, Daewoo merely provided additional authority regarding the issues it raised in its initial brief. Moreover, Daewoo was not aware of its need to address TKM's lack of standing to raise a procedural challenge to the attachment as the dispositive issue until the majority decided the appeal on **[—20—]** this procedural issue rather than the issues actually raised or decided in the district court. This is particularly so when TKM still maintains that it is not challenging whether Daewoo complied with the procedural requirements.

---

[3] The majority also cites various other cases to support its propositions that "constitutional standing, unlike statutory standing, is unwaivable" and that this court should decline to address the merits of a constitutional argument not raised in the initial brief. *See Harold H. Huggins Realty, Inc. v. FNC, Inc.* 634 F.3d 787 (5th Cir. 2011*); see also Flex Frac Logistics, L.L.C. v. N.L.R.B.*, 746 F.3d 205, 208 (5th Cir. 2014); and *United States v. Scroggins*, 599 F.3d 433 (5th Cir. 2010). But none of these cases address the issue which is raised here.

TKM asserts on rehearing that the standing argument is "undiscerning" and argues that the language from *Gilkerson* "that he has a superior privilege," quoted above, gives it standing to raise a procedural challenge to the attachment. *Gilkerson-Sloss*, 11 So. At 221. Notwithstanding that the referenced language in no way confers standing to raise a procedural challenge to Daewoo's attachment, TKM then asserts that, under *Fleming*, it is not asserting a procedural irregularity. Instead, TKM argues that it is attacking the "very availability of an Article 3541 attachment" because the action "is not for a money judgment."[4] However, as the majority concedes, this is an action for which article 3541 attachment is proper, thus, TKM's argument is defeated. Further, like the majority, TKM fails to distinguish any of the cases on point and does not argue there was fraud and collusion.

For these reasons, I would vacate the judgment of the district court and remand. Accordingly, I respectfully dissent.

---

[4] Yet, the majority ignores TKM's concession on rehearing that it is not asserting a procedural irregularity.

United States Court of Appeals
for the Fifth Circuit

No. 16-31214

IN RE CRESCENT ENERGY SERVS., L.L.C.

Appeal from the United States District Court for the Eastern District of Louisiana

Decided: July 13, 2018

Citation: 896 F.3d 350, 6 Adm. R. 224 (5th Cir. 2018).

Before **HIGGINBOTHAM**, **SOUTHWICK**, and **COSTA**, Circuit Judges.

[—1—] **{-351-}** SOUTHWICK, Circuit Judge: **[—2—]** **{-352-}**

This appeal poses the question of whether a particular contract to plug and abandon three offshore oil wells is a maritime contract. The answer matters because it determines where to place financial liability for injuries to an employee of the contractor performing the work. Complicating the appeal is that after the district court ruled, this court altered the several decades-old test for determining whether such contracts were maritime or not. Applying the new test to the facts that are not in dispute in this record, we AFFIRM.

FACTUAL AND PROCEDURAL BACKGROUND

In 2015, Carrizo Oil & Gas, Incorporated, needed a contractor to plug and abandon three no longer producing wells located on small fixed platforms in coastal waters of Lafourche Parish, Louisiana. State law obligated Carrizo to decommission these wells. The parties, and so will we, refer to this activity as plugging and abandoning the wells, or "P&A work." We once described such work this way: "Cement plugs are inserted into the wells beneath the ocean floor and the casing pipe is removed." *St. Romain v. Indus. Fabrication & Repair Serv., Inc.*, 203 F.3d 376, 378 (5th Cir. 2000).[1]

Crescent Energy Services, LLC, an oil and gas industry contractor, submitted a bid for the work. In the bid letter, Crescent noted that the equipment it would use included the "5K P&A Equipment Package," "5K Sand Cutting Casing Cutter Package," a five-person crew to perform the P&A work, **[—3—]** and three vessels. The vessels included a quarters barge with a thirty-foot long crane, called the "OB 808"; a tug boat named the "SLYE JOSEPH"; and a cargo barge. The OB 808 was a barge that could operate in shallow water where its spuds or footings would be anchored in the mud to create a stable platform. The OB 808 provided living quarters **{-353-}** for the crew and operated as an additional platform for the P&A operations. The OB 808 spud barge required use of a tug boat because the barge was not motorized, and Crescent contracted with another entity for use of the SLYE JOSEPH.

Carrizo accepted Crescent's bid to plug and abandon the three wells, forming an agreement that we will refer to, because the parties do, as the Turnkey Bid. Those two companies already had an ongoing relationship under a Master Service Agreement, which provides general terms applicable to contracts between the parties "for the performance of work or the provision of services." Included were several paragraphs describing Crescent's obligation to indemnify Carrizo against any claims for bodily injury, death, or damage to property. The Turnkey Bid and the Master Service Agreement together formed Carrizo and Crescent's

[1] The parties' briefing has given little attention to whether Crescent was contractually tasked with removal of the fixed platforms themselves. Federal law requires removal to complete the decommissioning of a well on the Outer Continental Shelf. *See Cutting Underwater Techs. USA, Inc. v. Eni U.S. Operating Co.*, 671 F.3d 512, 519 (5th Cir. 2010). As to rules applicable to Louisiana's territorial waters, Carrizo refers us to state regulations which require operators to provide financial security for the eventual "site restoration" of plugged and abandoned wells. *See* LA. ADMIN. CODE tit. 43 XIX, § 104A (2017). Crescent's insurers cite Section 311 of Part IX of those regulations, which seem to require the removal of a production platform. Whether it was Crescent's chore would depend on the contract. Dismantling and salvaging the platform is not among the 13 tasks identified on a document entitled "P&A Procedure" discussed by both parties.

contract. A document detailing the P&A work breaks the tasks into thirteen steps.

On February 13, 2015, Crescent's employee Corday Shoulder was severely injured. Shoulder, a pump operator, was sitting on the fixed platform when he was injured. The district court described the event this way:

> Before the accident, Shoulder attached a piece of pipe to Carrizo's well and screwed the pipe into a flange. When Shoulder began releasing pressure from the well, the pipe separated from the flange, severely injuring Shoulder's leg.

In March 2015, Crescent filed a limitation of liability action in the United States District Court for the Eastern District of Louisiana. The suit was brought under Federal Rule of Civil Procedure 9(h) and Rule F of the Supplemental Rules for Admiralty and Maritime Claims, the latter rule **[—4—]** specifically governing maritime limitation of liability actions. Crescent asserted the seaworthiness of its vessel and its proper operation, disclaimed any negligence, identified the value of the vessel and offered security in that amount to the court, sought to require all who had claims arising out of the accident to file them in this suit, requested the enjoining of prosecution of claims elsewhere, and demanded exoneration from liability.

Carrizo in its answer rejected that Crescent had brought a valid limitation of liability action. It claimed the benefit of the insurance applicable to the incident, and also identified Crescent's agreement to indemnify it for claims such as these. Crescent and its insurers would deny that indemnity was owed despite the contractual language, arguing that Louisiana's Oilfield Anti-Indemnity Act applied. *See* LA. STAT. ANN. § 9:2780. As relevant here, that Act voids an agreement in a contract involving "a well for oil, gas, or water" which would require a contractor to indemnify its principal from the latter's own fault in causing death or bodily injury. *Id.*

Shoulder and Carrizo both filed claims along with their answers. Carrizo also filed claims against four companies that it alleged were Crescent's insurers. Of those, Liberty Mutual Insurance Company and Starr Indemnity & Liability Company are the only appellants here. Pursuant to an agreement with Carrizo, Crescent has been dismissed from the case. When referring collectively to the only appellants, we label them "Crescent's insurers."

The parties all filed for summary judgment. The district court granted Carrizo's motion and denied the others. The court relied on the provision in the Master Service Agreement in which Crescent agreed to indemnify Carrizo for injuries to Crescent employees. The court held that indemnification was enforceable against Crescent because the parties had entered a maritime contract. Such a contract made federal maritime law applicable and precluded **[—5—]** **{-354-}** application of the Louisiana Oilfield Anti-Indemnity Act. Crescent's insurers timely appealed.

DISCUSSION

We have either one or two issues to resolve. We know we must determine whether the relevant collection of agreements constitutes a maritime contract. If so, general maritime law applies, and the indemnity provision in the contract is enforceable.

We are also urged by Crescent's insurers to decide an issue that was not presented to the district court. That issue arises only if the contract in question is a maritime one. We start with that issue, then turn to whether this is a maritime contract.

A. Inherently local disputes

The Supreme Court, in a decision central to our resolution of whether the contract in question was a maritime one, observed preliminarily that even when maritime law would otherwise apply, some disputes could be inherently local and maritime law could be displaced:

> For not "every term in every maritime contract can only be controlled by some federally defined admiralty rule."

> *Wilburn Boat Co. v. Fireman's Fund Ins. Co.*, 348 U.S. 310, 313, 75 S.Ct. 368, 99 L.Ed. 337 (1955) (applying state law to maritime contract for marine insurance because of state regulatory power over insurance industry). A maritime contract's interpretation may so implicate local interests as to beckon interpretation by state law.

Norfolk S. Ry. Co. v. Kirby, 543 U.S. 14, 27 (2004). The Court stated that no specific local interest had been identified by the party seeking application of this rule. *Id.* Moreover, "when state interests cannot be accommodated without defeating a federal interest, *as is the case here*, then federal substantive law should govern." *Id.* (emphasis added). **[—6—]**

Thus, there are two requirements for what is being argued: (1) the contract in question is a maritime one, and (2) the dispute is so inherently local as to cause application of state law. That is the law Crescent's insurers want us to apply, despite their otherwise vigorous contention that the lawsuit does not concern a maritime contract. They acknowledge that the first time this issue was raised was in their opening brief on appeal. We generally consider waived any issue not first presented to the district court. *Tex. Commercial Energy v. TXU Energy, Inc.*, 413 F.3d 503, 510 (5th Cir. 2005). This inherently-local-dispute issue certainly is a candidate for waiver.

Crescent's insurers, though, point us to opinions where we have held that "when a question is one of pure law, and when refusal to consider it will lead to an incorrect result or a miscarriage of justice, appellate courts are inclined to consider questions first raised on appeal." *Murray v. Anthony Bertucci Constr.*, 958 F.2d 127, 128 (5th Cir. 1992) (quoting *Nilsen v. City of Moss Point*, 674 F.2d 379, 387 n.13 (5th Cir. 1982), *rev'd en banc on other grounds*, 701 F.2d 556 (5th Cir. 1983)). Further, our authority to consider late-breaking legal arguments has been recognized by the Supreme Court, which "characterized the matter of what issues a court of appeals may consider for the first time on appeal as 'one left primarily to the discretion of the courts of appeals, to be exercised on the facts of the individual cases.'" *Id.* (quoting *Singleton v. Wulff*, 428 U.S. 106, 121 (1976)).

The usual procedural rule that all issues must first be presented to the district **{–355–}** court, leaving us to review that court's determinations, is an efficient approach that allows a full consideration of all the parties' arguments in the district court. That is true even for purely legal arguments. A thorough ruling might avoid an appeal by making clearer the unlikelihood of appellate success based on the strengths of the district court decision. A clear reason to deviate **[—7—]** from the rule should be shown. We see no excuse for the late introduction of this issue. It is true that we altered some of the controlling law since the district court's ruling with our en banc decision in *In re Larry Doiron, Inc.*, 879 F.3d 568, 6 Adm. R. 160 (5th Cir. 2018). Nothing in that decision, though, affected the applicability of the issue tardily raised by Crescent's insurers.

Finally, it is doubtful this issue would alter the outcome of the case. In *Kirby* itself, the Court held both that no local interest had been identified but had a state interest been described, it "cannot be accommodated without defeating a federal interest," thus leaving maritime law in place. *Kirby*, 543 U.S. at 27. The federal interest is "for the uniform meaning of maritime contracts," which applies here as much as it did in *Kirby*. *Id.* at 28. If the contract here is maritime, the fact that it was to be performed in the territorial waters of Louisiana does not justify causing the outcome of this lawsuit to be different than if the contract was for work on the high seas. Consistency and predictability are hard enough to come by in maritime jurisprudence, but we at least should not intentionally create distortions. We do not exercise our discretion to consider this issue.

B. Maritime contracts

Thus, we do have only one issue to decide: did Crescent and Carrizo enter into a maritime contract? If the contract between Carrizo and Crescent is a maritime one, federal law applies and Louisiana's bar to indemnity provisions is inapplicable. The district court determined when granting summary judgment that the contract was maritime. Our review of the ruling is *de novo*. *James v. State Farm Mut. Auto. Ins. Co.*, 743 F.3d 65, 68 (5th Cir. 2014). Summary judgment is appropriate when "there is no genuine dispute as to any material fact and the movant is entitled to judgment as a matter of law." FED. **[—8—]** R. CIV. P. 56(a). The facts and evidence are viewed in the light most favorable to the nonmovant. *James*, 743 F.3d at 68.

This circuit has dealt particularly extensively with issues that arise in determining whether a contract applicable to offshore oil and gas exploration should be categorized as maritime. Recently, we concluded that a test we had created in 1990 for resolving those questions focused on incidentals that were not altogether relevant to the determination. Removing some clutter, our en banc opinion simplified the mission of identifying such contracts. We now only ask: (1) "is the contract one to provide services to facilitate the drilling or production of oil and gas on navigable waters?" and (2) "does the contract provide or do the parties expect that a vessel will play a substantial role in the completion of the contract?" *Doiron*, 879 F.3d at 576, 6 Adm. R. at 165 (revising the test announced in *Davis & Sons, Inc. v. Gulf Oil Corp.*, 919 F.2d 313 (5th Cir. 1990)). An affirmative answer to both questions is necessary before the label "maritime" may be applied to the contract. *Id.*, 6 Adm. R. at 165–66.

Significant parts of our prior law were explicitly unchanged. For example, "[o]il and gas drilling on navigable waters aboard a vessel is recognized to be maritime commerce." *Id.* at 575, 6 Adm. R. at 165 (quoting *Theriot v. Bay Drilling Corp.*, 783 F.2d 527, 538–39 (5th Cir. 1986)). Caselaw cited by **{-356-}** Crescent's insurers also remains in place, namely, that maritime law generally does not extend to events that are confined to fixed platforms, as those structures are not vessels. *See Rodrigue v. Aetna Cas. & Sur. Co.*, 395 U.S. 352, 360 (1969). From such caselaw, the insurers argue that the accident here, which occurred on the fixed platform that was being decommissioned and not on one of Crescent's vessels, is not covered by maritime law.

Using our *de novo* review standard, we now apply *Doiron* to these facts. **[—9—]**

1. *Was this a contract to provide services to facilitate the drilling or production of oil and gas on navigable waters?*

The *Doiron* test focuses the court on two separate questions: does the contract concern "the drilling and production of oil and gas on navigable waters," and if so, will the work be performed "from a vessel"? *Doiron*, 879 F.3d at 575, 6 Adm. R. at 165. We start with whether the activity concerns development of oil and gas offshore. In its post-*Doiron* supplemental brief, Crescent's insurers raise two arguments under this factor. First, the contract did not facilitate the drilling or production of oil and gas because decommissioning oil wells is more analogous to construction of offshore platforms, which they say is not maritime activity. Second, the services were not on "navigable waters" because the decommissioning work occurred from the fixed platform itself. In response, Carrizo argues its contract with Crescent does qualify because plugging and abandoning oil wells is "part of the total life cycle of oil and gas drilling."

The life-cycle characterization draws in part from the fact that Louisiana requires site restoration when an oil or gas well is to be abandoned. *See* LA. STAT. ANN. § 30:4, *et seq.* To obtain an initial permit to drill, an applicant must provide financial security. *Id.* § 30:4.3A. The financial security will only be released "after plugging and abandonment and associated site restoration is completed and inspection thereof indicates compliance with applicable regulations or upon transfer of such well to another operator." LA. ADMIN. CODE tit. 43 XIX, § 104F (2017). It is fair to say that state law regulates the exploration for and production of oil and gas starting from the initial exploratory drilling in a likely location, through production when the exploration is successful, until the process ends by plugging and abandoning the well and removing such structures as state law requires. We conclude this contract for P&A work involved the drilling and production of oil and gas. **[—10—]**

Crescent's insurers next argue that the plugging and abandoning work did not occur on "navigable waters." The focus is on caselaw concerning events that are confined to fixed offshore platforms and similar locations: "Admiralty jurisdiction has not been construed to extend to accidents on piers, jetties, bridges, or even ramps or railways running into the sea." *See Rodrigue*, 395 U.S. at 360. Liberty Mutual argues that similarly, the fixed platform on which Corday Shoulder was injured in this case was not on "navigable waters."

It is true that where Shoulder was located when injured would have been relevant under the *Davis* test, which inquired what the worker was doing when injured. *See Davis*, 919 F.2d at 316. *Doiron* rejected that concern: "The facts surrounding the accident are relevant to whether the worker was injured in a maritime tort, but they are immaterial in determining whether the worker's employer entered into a maritime contract." *Doiron*, 879 F.3d at 573–74, 6 Adm. R. at 163. We are no longer concerned about whether the **{-357-}** worker was on a platform or vessel. The question is whether this contract concerned the drilling and production of oil and gas on navigable waters from a vessel. All parties acknowledge that the wells were located within the territorial inland waters of Louisiana and that the vessels involved in this contract were able to navigate to them.

We conclude that the contract between Crescent and Carrizo was to facilitate the drilling or production of oil and gas on navigable waters.

Before turning to the second factor in the *Doiron* test, we examine Crescent's insurers' argument that *Doiron* must be read in conjunction with other law that was not even discussed in that decision. The insurers seek to place barriers to contain *Doiron*'s effluence by deploying precedents involving the construction or deconstruction of an offshore, fixed platform from which oil and gas wells are drilled, or of related devices attached to the sea floor. *See Petrobas Am., Inc. v. Vicinay Cadenas, S.A.*, 815 F.3d 211, 4 Adm. R. 199 (5th Cir.), *order* **[—11—]** *clarified on reh'g*, 829 F.3d 770, 4 Adm. R. 266 (5th Cir. 2016); *Texaco Exp. & Prod. v. Amclyde Engineered Prod.*, 448 F.3d 760 (5th Cir.), *amended on reh'g*, 453 F.3d 652 (5th Cir. 2006); *Union Texas Petroleum Corp. v. PLT Eng'g, Inc.*, 895 F.2d 1043 (5th Cir. 1990); *Laredo Offshore Constructors, Inc. v. Hunt Oil Co.*, 754 F.2d 1223 (5th Cir. 1985). Those cases support that torts occurring on and during the construction of fixed, offshore platforms for the drilling and production of oil and gas on the Outer Continental Shelf are generally not governed by maritime law. *See, e.g., Texaco,* 448 F.3d at 771.

The analysis comes at least in part from a Supreme Court decision involving a worker who fell from a derrick to the fixed, offshore platform's floor. *See Rodrigue*, 395 U.S. at 353. A second worker in a companion case decided in the same opinion died when the platform crane he was operating collapsed, causing him to fall onto the deck of an adjacent barge. *Id.*

A recent melding of both *Davis* and one of the cases from the Crescent insurers' preferred collection is *Tetra Tech., Inc. v. Continental Ins. Co.*, 814 F.3d 733, 4 Adm. R. 185 (5th Cir. 2016). The broader question was whether under the Outer Continental Shelf Lands Act's ("OCSLA") requirements, the court was to apply Louisiana law as surrogate federal law. *Id.* at 738, 4 Adm. R. at 186. A subordinate question was whether federal law, *i.e.,* maritime law, applied of its own force. *Id.*, 4 Adm. R. at 186–87 (citing *PLT*, 895 F.2d at 1047). The subject matter of the contract was the salvaging of a decommissioned well's platform on the Outer Continental Shelf. *Id.* at 740–42, 4 Adm. R. at 187–89. As the court explained, the contract in question, which unfortunately was not in the record, contained obligations both for work on the fixed platform and on vessels. *Id.* at 739–40, 4 Adm. R. at 187–88. Without knowing the details of the contract, we could not complete our analysis of the six factors of the then-relevant *Davis* test. *Id.* at 741, 4 Adm. R. at 188–89. **[—12—]**

Despite that the analysis was necessarily stunted, we find its progression to be helpful. It said there were two steps in deciding whether maritime law applied of its own accord: (1) identifying the historical treatment of contracts such as the one at issue, and (2) applying the six *Davis* factors. *Id.* at 740, 4 Adm. R. at 188 (citing *ACE Am. Ins. Co. v. M–I, LLC*, 699 F.3d 826, 832 (5th Cir. 2012)). Yes, the *Tetra* court said, as the insurers argue here, contracts for "decommissioning, deconstructing, or salvaging a fixed platform used for oil and gas exploration on the [Outer Continental Shelf] . . . are not 'historically treated' as maritime contracts, and maritime law thus generally would not apply of its own **{-358-}** force." *Id.* at 741, 4 Adm. R. at 188.[2] That general law was not conclusive on the overall issue, though, because also relevant was the parties' specific contract applicable to that specific dispute. A detailed understanding was needed of the relative scope of the work on the fixed platform and from vessels, which the evidence on appeal did not allow the court to discern; thus, summary judgment was improper. *Id.* at 741–42, 4 Adm. R. at 188–90.

We are not concerned here with those OCSLA issues of whether to borrow state law as surrogate federal law, which leads to analyzing whether maritime law applies of its own force, which requires determining the historical treatment of certain contracts. We do need to analyze, though, whether this is a maritime contract. *Doiron* now controls that endeavor.

We may not eliminate all doubt with a citation to learned commentary, but we conclude this issue by taking note of a comprehensive but unhappy article analyzing Fifth Circuit maritime law. Professor David Robertson **[—13—]** discussed three of the cases Crescent's insurers are arguing are the appropriate ones to apply here. David W. Robertson, *The Outer Continental Shelf Lands Act's Provisions on Jurisdiction, Remedies, and Choice of Law: Correcting the Fifth Circuit's Mistakes*, 38 J. MAR. L. & COM. 487, 541–42 (*PLT*), 562–64 (*Texaco*), 566 (*Laredo*) (2007). In *Doiron*, we cited the article as being helpful in our revisions to *Davis*. *Doiron*, 879 F.3d at 572 n.20, 6 Adm. R. at 162 n.20. The author also discussed the *Davis* opinion, expressed his disagreement with the need for most of the six elements of the *Davis* test, but never hinted there was an inconsistency between cases relying on *Rodrigue* and cases using *Davis* to classify contracts as maritime or not. Robertson, *supra*, at 542–49.

Professor Robertson described the purposes of *Davis* in a more limited way than would this court, but it is the purpose relevant to this case:

> The OCS [Outer Continental Shelf] oil patch is latticed with contracts and subcontracts. Litigation arising from injuries to OCS workers ordinarily entails claims for contractual indemnity among the putative tortfeasors. Whether a contract calling for indemnity is maritime or not is a recurrently dispositive question. "[I]f the contract is a maritime contract, federal maritime law applies of its own force, and state law does not apply." If the contract calling for indemnity is not a maritime contract, the governing law will be adjacent-state law made surrogate federal law by OCSLA § 1333(a)(2)(A). Very often the applicable adjacent-state law will be that of Texas or Louisiana.
>
> Both Texas and Louisiana have anti-indemnity statutes that will invalidate most indemnity contracts. Federal maritime law, on the other hand, shows no hostility to indemnity agreements[.]

[2] The historical treatment can be seen from the following. OCSLA gives jurisdiction to federal courts over claims arising from the development of minerals on the OCS. *Texaco*, 448 F.3d at 768. As to fixed platforms there, the Supreme Court held that "accidents on these structures, which under maritime principles would be no more under maritime jurisdiction than accidents on a wharf located above navigable waters, were not changed in character by the [OCSLA]." *Rodrigue*, 395 U.S. at 366. Thus, accidents on fixed platforms on the OCS are not generally matters for maritime law.

> . . .
>
> The Fifth Circuit regularly complains about how difficult it is to tell whether an OCS indemnity contract is maritime. In *Davis & Sons, Inc. v. Gulf Oil Corp.* Judge Rubin made a heroic effort to synthesize the circuit's jurisprudence into something that made sense . . . . **[—14—] {-359-}**

Id. at 542–43 (footnotes omitted). The good professor concluded that despite being heroic, the effort in *Davis* failed. The en banc court in *Doiron*, after 25-plus years of applying *Davis*, at least agreed that a change was due.

This reference to a scholarly effort to organize the caselaw is to show that *Davis* previously and *Doiron* now are performing the task of determining how to classify contracts. That classification has often been employed to determine whether indemnity provisions are enforceable but is not so limited. Our analysis in the past under *Davis* was consistent with the caselaw cited to us by Crescent's insurers. Consistent now is our application of *Doiron*.

Finally, regardless of what other Fifth Circuit caselaw there may be, nothing in such caselaw detracts from the clarity of our 2018 en banc decision in *Doiron*. We are here classifying a contract for a certain purpose, a judicial activity that has been done consistently with the 1969 *Rodrigue* decision at least since our 1990 *Davis* decision. We en banc eliminated most of the factors, narrowing our focus, but we did not fundamentally change the task. *Doiron* is the law we must apply.

2. *Does the contract provide or do the parties expect that a vessel will play a substantial role in the completion of the contract?*

We now examine whether the Crescent-Carrizo contract contemplated that a vessel would play a substantial role in the performance of the contract. Among the directions given by *Doiron* on what "substantial" means is that if "work is performed in part on a vessel and in part on a platform or on land, we should consider not only time spent on the vessel but also the relative importance and value of the vessel-based work to completing the contract." *Doiron*, 879 F.3d at 576 n.47, 6 Adm. R. at 165 n.47. We quoted part of the Supreme Court's *Kirby* discussion, from which the word "substantial" was taken: "Conceptually, so long as a bill of lading requires *substantial* carriage of goods by sea, its purpose **[—15—]** is to effectuate maritime commerce—and thus it is a maritime contract." *Id.* at 576, 6 Adm. R. at 166 (emphasis added) (quoting *Kirby*, 543 U.S. at 27). We also draw from our *Doiron* discussion a "rule of thumb" used in Jones Act cases:

> A worker who spends less than about 30 percent of his time in the service of a vessel in navigation should not qualify as a seaman under the Jones Act. This figure of course serves as no more than a guideline established by years of experience, and departure from it will certainly be justified in appropriate cases.

Id. at 576 n.47, 6 Adm. R. at 165 n.47 (quoting *Chandris, Inc. v. Latsis*, 515 U.S. 347, 371 (1995)). The court also declared that any determination of the significance of the vessel "would not include transportation to and from the job site." *Id.*, 6 Adm. R. at 165 n.47.

The Crescent insurers argue that measuring the anticipated use of the vessel should follow OCSLA caselaw where, for purposes of deciding the situs of the controversy, we are to consider where the majority of work was performed under "the focus-of-the-contract test." *Grand Isle Shipyard, Inc. v. Seacor Marine, LLC*, 589 F.3d 778, 781 (5th Cir. 2009) (en banc). We do not see the usefulness of that law to our task. *Doiron* did not hold that to be a maritime contract, the parties must have contemplated that a vessel will be used for a majority of the work. Such a rule would be inconsistent with the explicit suggestion in *Doiron* that "substantial" can mean 30 percent, considerably less than a majority.

We must remember that the contracting parties' expectations are central. It was not **{–360–}** enough in *Doiron* that a vessel ultimately had a key role in the completion of the needed work because that was unexpected and occurred only after initial efforts without a vessel failed. *Doiron,* 879 F.3d at 577, 6 Adm. R. at 167. In searching for expectations here, we start with examining the contractual obligations. The Turnkey Bid is the relevant document, as the Master Service Agreement's more general language does not address the details of the P&A work. The first page identifies the equipment being provided that would **[—16—]** perform the P&A work itself, the work crew details, and a description of three vessels. Thus, unlike in *Doiron*, a need for vessels was understood. The vessels were a tug, a cargo barge, and the OB 808 barge on which equipment and the quarters for the work crew were located. Our analysis of "substantial" ignores the need for vessels to transport equipment and crew to the platform and considers only the other roles the vessels played. *Id.* at 576 n.47, 6 Adm. R. at 165 n.47.

The Turnkey Bid included a daily charge for use of each of the three vessels. The daily charge for all three was $4,000. Crescent states that the vessels were used for 33 days, resulting in a total cost of $132,000. Liberty Mutual uses those numbers in its supplemental briefing to say the vessels' cost was 37 percent of the total contract bid of $360,735.20. Our precise fact issue, though, is what was anticipated when the contract was entered. The operations manager for Crescent testified that the time for completing the work "was way more than what we estimated." He was not asked what had been the estimated number of days.

We now examine the use of the key vessel, the OB 808. The only crane involved in the work was on the barge, moving equipment and materials back and forth from the cargo barge to the well platform. The injured worker, Corday Shoulder, testified that the three well platforms were small and there was not enough room for all the equipment. The wireline unit was among the equipment that remained on the barge. We mention the wireline unit in particular because its purpose is central to plugging and abandoning the well. We once described the work this way:

> A "wireline" is a continuous cable used to perform various subsurface functions in a well, including the lowering and raising of various tools, instruments, and other devices. One of the downhole tools used on a wireline is a "perforation gun," a device that originally used cartridges similar to rifle or pistol ammunition but evolved to use "shaped charges," cylinder-shaped ammunition **[—17—]** which is cone-shaped internally and fires directionally. It is formed in layers, one a brittle compound of explosive material and the other a metal alloy. When fired by any of several methods, this bazooka-like ammunition shoots a short, concentrated stream of molten alloy or "plasma" in the direction at which the open end of the charge's conically shaped interior is aimed. Generally, perforating guns are used either early in the life of a well to fractionate ("frac") a hydrocarbon-bearing formation or zone so as to commence or enhance production or, late in the life of a well or of a particular formation, to perforate casing or tubing in preparation for "squeezing" or sealing off the well or the zone to "plug and abandon" it.

Roberts v. Cardinal Servs., 266 F.3d 368, 371–72 (5th Cir. 2001). The district court's decision in *Roberts*, written by Judge Clement a year before she became a member of this court, called the wireline operation in P&A work an "essential component of the drilling process." *Roberts v. Cardinal Servs., Inc.*, 2000 WL 1300390, at *3 (E.D. La. 2000). **{–361–}**

The significance of the wireline operation is also highlighted in this record. Shoulder testified that about 50 percent of the P&A operation was wireline work. Further, in Crescent's statement of undisputed facts filed in the district court, it declared that the work on the well on which Shoulder was injured "involved primarily wireline services." Surely, wireline work was similarly dominant as to the other two wells.

Mentioning wireline operations requires us to acknowledge that for 30 years, Fifth Circuit law has been that such work from a vessel is not a maritime activity. *See Thurmond v. Delta Well Surveyors,* 836 F.2d 952, 955–56 (5th Cir. 1988). We recently criticized that opinion, criticism that matters because it was expressed en banc, because *Thurmond* and its descendants improperly focus on whether services were inherently maritime as opposed to whether a substantial amount of the work was to be performed from a vessel. *Doiron,* 879 F.3d at 573, 6 Adm. R. at 163. Indeed, almost "none of these services [for offshore oil and **[—18—]** gas operations] are inherently maritime." *Id.*, 6 Adm. R. at 163. What is important in the present case is that use of the wireline unit on the vessel was central to the entire P&A contract.

As to other uses of the OB 808, Shoulder drew a sketch of what was on the OB 808. He outlined crew quarters, a galley, some offices, the mud tank, the wireline unit, a crane, its generator, and a pump. There is no statement that leaving all this equipment on the barge had been originally planned, nor is it clear which features were structurally part of the OB 808. Still, surely the investigation Crescent performed in order to estimate its costs before bidding caused it to understand the space limitations and to plan in advance where equipment would need to be. Also relevant to the importance of this vessel, Carrizo adds that "Crescent designed and built the OB 808 for the specific purpose of decommissioning wells at the end of their productive cycle."

Certainly, then, the parties anticipated the OB 808 would be indispensably involved in performance of the contract. A vessel's being indispensable may not equate to its role being "substantial," though. In attempting to define "substantial role," Liberty Mutual and Starr argue that a vessel does not play a substantial role when it is being used as a "work platform" rather than as a navigable, self-propelled water vehicle. We do not see its role as being properly demeaned in this way, so long as the vessel is being used for more than transporting between land and the wellsite. Indeed, its necessity as a work platform is particularly relevant. To the extent there was not enough space on the fixed platform for the equipment, such as for the wireline unit, the role of the vessel becomes more significant. Its utility as a work platform comes from its being a vessel, as it could be positioned as needed at the well site, then proceed to the other wells to perform similar functions. According to Carrizo, the OB 808 was being used every day, certainly as crew **[—19—]** quarters but also for its crane, the wireline unit, and other equipment that could not be moved onto a platform.

In conclusion, this contract anticipated the constant and substantial use of multiple vessels. It was known that the OB 808 would be necessary as a work platform; that essential equipment would need to remain on that vessel, including a crane; that the most important component of the work, the wireline operation, would be substantially controlled from the barge; and that other incidental uses of the vessel would exist such as for crew quarters. This vessel and the other two vessels were expected to perform an important role, indeed, a substantial one, under the Crescent **{-362-}** and Carrizo contract. It was a maritime contract. The Louisiana Oilfield Anti-Indemnity Act does not apply.

AFFIRMED.

United States Court of Appeals
for the Fifth Circuit

No. 17-40584

UNITED STATES
vs.
ANCHUNDIA-ESPINOZA

Appeal from the United States District Court for the Eastern District of Texas

Decided: July 27, 2018

Citation: 897 F.3d 629, 6 Adm. R. 233 (5th Cir. 2018).

Before **CLEMENT**, **HIGGINSON**, and **HO**, Circuit Judges.

[—1—] {-630-} **CLEMENT**, Circuit Judge:

Roger Alfredo Anchundia-Espinoza pleaded guilty to conspiracy to possess, with the intent to distribute, cocaine while aboard a vessel subject to the jurisdiction of the United States, in violation of 46 U.S.C. §§ 70503(a)(1), 70506(a) & (b) and 21 U.S.C. § 960. The district court denied Anchundia-Espinoza's requests for safety-valve and minor participant reductions. Anchundia-Espinoza appeals those denials. For the reasons set forth below, we AFFIRM.

I.

Roger Alfredo Anchundia-Espinoza, a citizen of Ecuador, and three others were contracted by an unknown individual to transport cocaine. They **[—2—]** were each paid $1,000 up front for the service. They were also promised an additional $9,000 and a plane ticket once they reached their destination. On December 10, 2015, the group left the Esmeraldas area of Ecuador on a small boat. After traveling a number of miles in open waters and being provided additional fuel by two other boats, they met a larger boat, which contained the shipment of cocaine and two occupants. Anchundia-Espinoza and the three other men boarded the larger boat, and the two men on the larger boat took their smaller one (presumably back to Ecuador, although it is unclear). The four men traveled for five days, and each drove the boat at different times. **{-631-}**

On December 15, 2015, the group met up with a boat named *Imemsa* and transferred the shipment of cocaine and their equipment to it. They intentionally sank the boat they had been traveling on and drove the *Imemsa* toward Mexico at a high rate of speed. There was a total of seven occupants on the *Imemsa*. Within two hours, a U.S. Marine Patrol Aircraft detected the *Imemsa*, and the U.S. Coast Guard sought to intercept it. The boat failed to comply with numerous demands to stop; after two warning shots, however, it finally stopped approximately 95 nautical miles southwest of the Mexico/Guatemala boarder. The driver of the boat made no claim of nationality for the vessel, so it was treated as without nationality, and U.S. officials boarded the boat. They found 35 bales of cocaine on board and another bail floating in the water attached to a line over the side of the boat. A later laboratory report prepared by the DEA revealed that the cocaine weighed 681.6 kilograms.

In January 2016, Anchundia-Espinoza and the six other men were indicted for conspiring to possess, with intent to distribute, five or more kilograms of cocaine while aboard a vessel subject to the jurisdiction of the United States, in violation of 46 U.S.C. §§ 70503(a)(1), 70506(a) & (b), and 21 U.S.C. § 960. Anchundia-Espinoza pleaded guilty without a plea agreement. **[—3—]** The punishment guidelines for § 70503 are provided at 21 U.S.C. § 960(b)(1)(B)(ii); the offense carries a statutory minimum sentence of 10 years' imprisonment and a maximum of life.

Using the 2016 Sentencing Guidelines, the Pre-sentence Report ("PSR") determined that Anchundia-Espinoza had a base offense level of 38 because he was responsible for 681.6 kilograms of cocaine—well above the 450 kilogram minimum in U.S.S.G. § 2D1.1, the provision providing the base offense levels for conspiracies. The offense level was increased by two levels under U.S.S.G. § 2D1.1(b)(3), which provides for an adjustment when the defendant acted as a captain or navigator aboard a vessel carrying a controlled substance. The defendant was then lowered to an offense level of 37 for acceptance of responsibility, pursuant to U.S.S.G. § 3E1.1(a) and (b). Finally, he had a criminal history category of I, and faced an advisory sentencing range of 210 to 262 months of imprisonment. And relevant to this appeal, the PSR provided that, "[s]ince the defendant was convicted of a 46 U.S.C. § 70503(a)(1) offense, the safety valve does not apply."

Anchundia-Espinoza filed two objections to the PSR. First, he objected to the denial of the safety valve reduction. Second, he objected to the denial of the "minor participant" reduction under U.S.S.G. § 3B1.2. The probation office disagreed with both objections.

The district court denied Anchundia-Espinoza's first objection because the safety valve provision applies only to the five offenses specified in 18 U.S.C. § 3553(f), and 46 U.S.C. § 70503 is not one of those offenses. The district court similarly denied Anchundia-Espinoza's request for the "minor participant" adjustment. The district court concluded that the average participants in this offense were Anchundia-Espinoza and his co-defendants, rather than the unknown number of unidentified and uncharged participants in the **[—4—]** conspiracy. It found that he was not substantially less culpable than those co-defendants.

The district court ultimately varied downward from the 210-month advisory minimum and sentenced Anchundia-Espinoza to 175 months in prison.[1] **{-632-}**

II.

On appeal, Anchundia-Espinoza challenges the district court's denial of two sentencing reductions by erring in its application of two relevant statutes. The district court's legal interpretation of a statutory provision is reviewed de novo. *United States v. Flanagan*, 80 F.3d 143, 145 (5th Cir. 1996). Factual findings made during sentencing, however, are reviewed for clear error. *United States v. Kiekow*, 872 F.3d 236, 247 (5th Cir. 2017). "Whether a defendant 'was a minor or minimal participant is a factual determination that we review for clear error.'" *United States v. Torres-Hernandez*, 843 F.3d 203, 207 (5th Cir. 2016) (quoting *United States v. Gomez-Valle*, 828 F.3d 324, 327 (5th Cir. 2016)). "If the district court's account of the evidence is plausible in light of the record viewed in its entirety, this court may not reverse, even if, had we been sitting as trier of fact, we might have weighed the evidence differently." *Kiekow*, 872 F.3d at 247 (quoting *United States v. Harris*, 740 F.3d 956, 967 (5th Cir. 2014)).

III.

Anchundia-Espinoza first appeals the district court's denial of "safety valve" relief. The safety valve provision of U.S.S.G. § 5C1.2 allows a court to sentence a defendant below the statutory minimum sentence in certain instances. *United States v. Treft*, 447 F.3d 421, 426 (5th Cir. 2006). A defendant may qualify for a sentence below the statutory minimum if he meets the five **[—5—]** criteria set forth in 18 U.S.C. § 3553(f) (and also provided at § 5C1.2). *See United States v. Lopez*, 264 F.3d 527, 529–30 (5th Cir. 2001). In these circumstances, the defendant is also entitled to a two-level reduction in his offense level. *See id.* at 530; U.S.S.G. § 2D1.1(b)(17). The defendant bears the burden of establishing eligibility for the safety valve reduction. *Flanagan*, 80 F.3d at 146–47.

The safety valve provision set forth in 18 U.S.C. § 3553(f) provides:

> Notwithstanding any other provision of law, in the case of an offense under section 401, 404, or 406 of the Controlled Substances Act (21 U.S.C. 841, 844, 846) or section 1010 or 1013 of the Controlled Substances Import and Export Act (**21 U.S.C. 960**, 963), the court shall impose a sentence pursuant to guidelines promulgated by the United States Sentencing Commission under section 994 of title 28 without regard to any statutory minimum sentence, if the court finds at sentencing, after the Government has been afforded the

[1] The court expressed that it wanted to give him the same 168-month sentence that his co-defendants got, but it felt he should receive more time because he rejected the plea offer that his co-defendants accepted.

opportunity to make a recommendation, that —

(1) the defendant does not have more than 1 criminal history point, as determined under the sentencing guidelines;

(2) the defendant did not use violence or credible threats of violence or possess a firearm or other dangerous weapon (or induce another participant to do so) in connection with the offense;

(3) the offense did not result in death or serious bodily injury to any person;

(4) the defendant was not an organizer, leader, manager, or supervisor of others in the offense, as determined under the sentencing guidelines and was not engaged in a continuing criminal enterprise, as defined in section 408 of the Controlled Substances Act; and

(5) not later than the time of the sentencing hearing, the defendant has truthfully provided to the Government all information and evidence the defendant has concerning the offense or offenses that were part of the same course **{-633-}** of conduct or of a common scheme or plan, but the fact that the defendant has no relevant or useful other information to provide or that the Government is already aware of the information shall not **[—6—]** preclude a determination by the court that the defendant has complied with this requirement.

(Emphasis added). U.S.S.G. § 5C1.2(a) similarly explains that § 3553(f) applies to specific offenses, including 21 U.S.C. § 960. The crux of the issue here is whether § 70503 falls under the safety valve relief because 21 U.S.C. § 960—which provides the penalties for § 70503—is enumerated in § 3553(f). Importantly, § 70503 is not an "offense under" § 960; section 960 merely provides the penalties for § 70503.

This issue presents a case of first impression for this circuit. As a general matter, however, this court has strictly limited the safety valve's application to the statutes listed in § 3553(f). *See, e.g., United States v. Phillips*, 382 F.3d 489, 499–500 (5th Cir. 2004). Notably, the Eleventh and Ninth Circuits have addressed the issue presented here, and both courts held that the safety valve does not apply to violations of § 70503. *See United States v. Pertuz-Pertuz*, 679 F.3d 1327, 1328–29 (11th Cir. 2012); *United States v. Gamboa-Cardenas*, 508 F.3d 491, 496–97 (9th Cir. 2007). Anchundia-Espinoza argues that § 3553(f) is ambiguous, and he relies on the dissenting opinion in *Gamboa-Cardenas*, which reasoned that a plausible reading of § 3553(f) is that all of the crimes punishable under § 960 are subject to the safety valve. *See Gamboa-Cardenas*, 508 F.3d at 506–08 (Fisher, J., concurring in part and dissenting in part). The Eleventh Circuit rejected Anchundia-Espinoza's argument by explaining that the safety valve applies only to an "offense under" § 960 and not to a "sentence under" § 960. *Pertuz-Pertuz*, 679 F.3d at 1329.

The Supreme Court has instructed that "courts must presume that a legislature says in a statute what it means and means in a statute what it says there." *Conn. Nat'l Bank v. Germain*, 503 U.S. 249, 253–54 (1992). Our court, and other circuits, have confirmed "that there is no 'ambiguity concerning the **[—7—]** ambit of' § 3553(f)." *Phillips*, 382 F.3d at 500 (quoting *United States v. Kakatin*, 214 F.3d 1049, 1052 (9th Cir. 2000)). This court addressed a similar issue in *United States v. Phillips*. There, the defendant was convicted under 21 U.S.C. § 860. *Id.* at 492–93. Phillips urged that he was entitled to the safety valve reduction because his violation under § 860, although not enumerated in § 3553(f), was "merely a 'sentence enhancement,'" and § 21 U.S.C. § 841, which *is* specifically enumerated, is a lesser-included offense of § 860. *Id.* at 499. This court, similar to other circuits, rejected the argument. *Id.* at 499–500. It reasoned that it was "clear that § 841 and § 860 are separate substantive offenses, and that there is no ambiguity concerning the ambit of § 3553(f)." *Id.* at 500 (internal quotations omitted); *see also United States v. Anderson*, 200 F.3d 1344, 1348 (11th Cir. 2000) (reasoning that "[t]he selection of these five [enumerated] statutes reflects [a Congressional] intent to exclude others, including 21 U.S.C. § 860").

The Ninth Circuit, relying in part on this court's *Phillips* decision, addressed whether a conviction under § 70503[2] was entitled to the safety valve reduction. *Gamboa-Cardenas*, 508 F.3d at 496–99. It held that the statutes enumerated in **{-634-}** § 3553(f) presented an exhaustive list. *Id.* at 498. Moreover, it explained that § 3553(f) was codified *after* the statute in question, so "Congress could have included [§ 70503] as easily as it included the other statutes specifically listed in § 3553(f). The timing of Congress's actions indicates that it consciously chose *not* to include [§ 70503] offenses on the safety valve list." *Id.* at 497–98. Finally, § 3553(f) applies to offenses *under* the enumerated statutes. *See id.* at 497. Section 70503 is an offense *penalized* by an enumerated statute, and therefore it is not subject to the safety valve provision. *See id.* **[—8—]**

Likewise, the Eleventh Circuit held that, because the defendant was not convicted under a statute appearing in § 3553(f), the defendant was not entitled to its relief. *Pertuz-Pertuz*, 679 F.3d at 1328. It reiterated that the safety valve statute was to apply *only* to those statutes specifically provided in § 3553(f). *Id.* "The safety valve statute . . . refers to an 'offense under' section 960—not to an 'offense penalized under' section 960 and not to a 'sentence under' section 960." *Id.* at 1329. Accordingly, it concluded § 3553(f) was unambiguous and applied only to the statutes enumerated.

We decline to accept Anchundia-Espinoza's invitation to steer away from this court's strict interpretation of the statute—and the lead of circuits that have addressed this issue. Instead, we follow this court's precedent in strictly construing the safety valve provision. To hold otherwise would run afoul of this court's decision that § 3553(f) is unambiguous. Not only is § 70503 not specifically provided for under § 3553(f), but it is also not an "offense under" § 960, which does, in fact, list other statutes. *See* 21 U.S.C. § 960(a). As the Eleventh Circuit explained, § 3553(f) applies to "offenses under", *not* "offense[s] penalized under" and not "sentence[s] under." *See Pertuz-Pertuz*, 679 F.3d at 1329.

IV.

Anchundia-Espinoza also contends that he should have received a two-level reduction in his offense level for playing a minor role in the conspiracy. He argues, as he did in the district court, that the district court erred by comparing him only to the co-defendants who played the same role he did, rather than comparing him to all of the other participants in the conspiracy. He asserts that the district court committed, "at the very least, a legal error in the interpretation" of the Guidelines such that remand is required. Generally, the factual determination of whether a defendant played a minor role in the offense is reviewed for clear error. *See Torres-Hernandez*, 843 F.3d at 207. **[—9—]**

The defendant bears "the burden of proving by a preponderance of the evidence that the adjustment [was] warranted." *United States v. Castro*, 843 F.3d 608, 612 (5th Cir. 2016) (quoting *United States v. Miranda*, 248 F.3d 434, 446 (5th Cir. 2001)). "A minor participant adjustment is not appropriate simply because a defendant does less than other participants; in order to qualify as a minor participant, a defendant must have been peripheral to the advancement of the illicit activity." *Miranda*, 248 F.3d at 446–47.

Determining minor participation is a "sophisticated factual determination[]" to be made by the sentencing judge. *United States v. Gallegos*, 868 F.2d 711, 713 (5th Cir. 1989). Here, the district court meticulously compared Anchundia-Espinoza's participation to that of his co-defendants—the only members of the conspiracy about whom the district court had concrete knowledge. Indeed, the only reference to unindicted co-conspirators was defense counsel's statement and the government's **{-635-}** acknowledgement that there presumably were other participants in this conspiracy. The district court determined that Anchundia-Espinoza and his co-defendants all played similar roles by accepting money to complete a portion of this drug transaction and by captaining multiple boats to transport

[2] The court actually considered whether § 70503's predecessor, 46 U.S.C. § 1903, was applicable.

very substantial amounts of cocaine. None was the "mastermind" behind the operation, and all seemed to participate for the same amount of time and held the same type of responsibilities. Accordingly, there appears to be no clear error in the district court's fact-finding that Anchundia-Espinoza was not a minor participant. In fact, he appears to have been a part of the conspiracy for even longer than some of his co-defendants. As this court has explained, "[e]ven if [the defendant] played a relatively smaller role in the offense as compared to his other co-defendants, viewing the record[] as a whole[,] the district court did not commit clear error in finding that" Anchundia-Espinoza was "not deserving of a downward adjustment." *United States v. Angeles-Mendoza*, 407 F.3d 742, 754 **[—10—]** (5th Cir. 2005). Even if the district court misspoke that the minor-participant inquiry permits comparisons only among co-defendants, Anchundia-Espinoza did not meet his burden to prove his minor role because his participation was so substantial—captaining multiple boats to transport such substantial quantities of drugs—and because he failed to present any evidence challenging the government's denominator of co-conspirators. As such, Anchundia-Espinoza certainly has not met his burden to prove by a preponderance of the evidence that he should have received the minor participant reduction.

Accordingly, the judgment of the district court is AFFIRMED.

United States Court of Appeals
for the Fifth Circuit

No. 17-30543

ROYAL SMIT TRANSFORMERS
VS.
ONEGO SHIPPING & CHARTERING

Appeal from the United States District Court for the Eastern District of Louisiana

Decided: August 2, 2018

Citation: 898 F.3d 543, 6 Adm. R. 238 (5th Cir. 2018).

Before **HIGGINBOTHAM**, **SMITH**, and **CLEMENT**, Circuit Judges.

[—1—] **{–544–}** **CLEMENT**, Circuit Judge: **{–545–}**

Royal SMIT tried to ship a few of its transformers from the Netherlands to Louisiana. It contracted with an intermediary to arrange the transport. The transformers were damaged along the way, so Royal SMIT and its insurers tried to sue the carriers with whom the intermediary had contracted. But the district court concluded they were precluded from doing so because of a Himalaya Clause in the company's agreement with the intermediary. The court granted summary judgment in favor of the carriers. That decision was appealed, and we affirm. **[—2—]**

I.

Plaintiff Royal SMIT Transformers B.V. ("Royal") is a company based in the Netherlands that manufactures large power transformers. In November 2015, Royal sold three of its transformers to Entergy Louisiana, LLC, for use at one of its substations in St. Gabriel, Louisiana. The transformers were insured by the co-plaintiffs-appellants AXA Versicherung AG, HDI-Gerling Industrie-Versicherung AG, Basler Sachversicherung AG, and Ergo Versicherung AG.

One month later, Royal contracted with Central Oceans USA, LLC ("Central Oceans") to facilitate the delivery of the three transformers from the Port of Rotterdam to St. Gabriel. The arrangement was established by a multimodal through bill of lading[1] between the parties.

The delivery comprised three legs: ocean transportation from Rotterdam to New Orleans, rail transportation from New Orleans to St. Gabriel, and truck transportation to Entergy's substation. Central Oceans contracted with the defendants to carry out each part of the journey: Onego Shipping & Chartering, B.V. ("Onego") provided the ocean carriage to New Orleans; Illinois Central Railroad Company ("IC") provided rail carriage to St. Gabriel; and Berard Transportation, Inc. ("Berard") provided truck carriage to the final destination.

All of these arrangements were negotiated separately. The defendants were not involved in—nor aware of—the agreement between Central Oceans and Royal, and Royal was not a party to the contracts Central Oceans signed **[—3—]** with the defendants. Each defendant negotiated its agreement with Central Oceans independently and memorialized its terms in separate documents.

The terms of the agreement between Royal and Central Oceans were initially **{–546–}** set forth in a Request for Transport Quotation ("RFQ") issued by Royal, which incorporated terms from two other documents: a Shipment of Transformers Procedure and a General Terms and Conditions of Purchase. The Terms and Conditions stated that Central Oceans would be held liable "for all cases of loss or damage suffered by [Royal] . . . caused by [Central Oceans's] performance" of the contract. It also anticipated that Central

---

[1] "Multimodal" transport refers to a delivery that entails some combination of air, land, and sea travel. 1 T. Schoenbaum, *Admiralty and Maritime Law*, § 10-4 (5th ed. 2017). A "bill of lading" refers to a document that memorializes the terms of a shipping agreement. *Id.* § 10-11. And a "through bill of lading" refers to a bill of lading that allows cargo owners to contract with an intermediary for a multimodal transportation in a single transaction. *Norfolk S. Ry. Co. v. Kirby*, 543 U.S. 14, 25–26 (2004). The intermediary, in turn, arranges for the transportation with various carriers.

Oceans might subcontract with a third party to perform part of its duties. It warned that Central Oceans was "not release[d] . . . from any obligation or liability" as a result of subcontracting its duty, but was still required to "indemnify [Royal] in full against [resultant liability]." Further, Central Oceans was required to "bind [the] third party fully to the provisions of these terms and conditions." The Terms and Conditions did not, however, specify whether or to what extent the third parties were liable to Royal.

The Purchase Order between the parties noted that "[a]ll services provided" were pursuant to the RFQ, and "expressly den[ied] the applicability of any other terms and conditions." Notwithstanding this provision, the parties then executed the through bill of lading, which stated that its "provisions . . . apply to all claims against [Central Oceans] relating to the performance of the Multimodal Transport Contract."

Like the Terms and Conditions, the bill also anticipated that, as Royal's intermediary, Central Oceans would facilitate the transport by contracting with other entities. Those entities were designated as agents acting on behalf of Central Oceans. Central Oceans, in turn, was liable for their actions: **[—4—]**

> **10. Basis of Liability**
>
> . . . .
>
> (c) [Central Oceans] shall be responsible for the acts and omissions of his servants or agents when any such servant or agent is acting within the scope of his employment, or of any other person of whose services he makes use for the performance of the Contract, as if such acts and omissions were his own.

The bill of lading limited both the amount and source of Royal's recovery if something went wrong. Specifically, it set a per-package limitation on liability in accordance with requirements set by the Carriage of Goods by Sea Act ("COGSA"), 46 U.S.C. § 30701, note § 4(5). And, relevant to the present appeal, it also contained a Himalaya Clause, which prohibited Royal from suing Central Oceans's subcontractors:

> **15. Defenses and limits for [Central Oceans], Servants, etc.**
>
> . . . .
>
> (b) [Royal] undertakes that no claim shall be made against any servant, agent, or other persons whose services [Central Oceans] has used in order to perform the Multimodal Transport Contract and if any claim should nevertheless be made, to indemnify [Central Oceans] against all consequences thereof.
>
> (c) However, the provisions of this Contract apply whenever claims relating to the performance of the Multimodal Transport Contract are made against any servant, agent or other person whose services [Central Oceans] has used in order to perform the Multimodal Transport Contract, whether such claims are founded in contract or in tort. In entering into this Contract, [Central Oceans] . . . does so not only on his own behalf but also as agent or trustee for such persons. **{-547-}**

The transformers were delivered to the final destination in January 2016, where an inspection revealed that the transformers had been damaged **[—5—]** by "excessive vibration" somewhere along the journey.[2] Royal and its insurers[3] then sued Central Oceans and the defendants on September 12, 2016, for breach of contract, fault, and negligence, seeking over $1,600,000 in damages. Notably, the complaint alleged that "Royal . . . contracted with Central Oceans . . . pursuant to" the through bill of lading. It did not mention the RFQ or Purchase Order.

Central Oceans filed a motion to transfer venue three months later, relying on the mandatory forum selection clause in the

---

[2] The record does not establish where the damage occurred or which carrier caused it.

[3] For clarity, we will continue to use "Royal" to refer to these entities collectively.

multimodal through bill of lading. Royal's opposition again did not contest the applicability of the bill of lading; rather, it was based on convenience to the remaining defendants, who were "not privy to the contractual forum select clause" therein. Royal admitted, in fact, that its "claims against Central Oceans [were] under the" multimodal bill of lading, and it justified its opposition to transfer in part by relying on the bill.

The district court granted the motion in part, severing Royal's claims against Central Oceans and transferring them to the Western District of Virginia. The court noted that "[n]o one disputes the validity of the forum selection clause" in the bill of lading, and that Royal must abide by the terms it negotiated with Central Oceans. The court also concluded that the claims against the defendants could not be transferred because they were not bound by the clause.

The remaining defendants collectively filed a summary judgment motion on April 21, 2017, arguing that they were protected from suit by the Himalaya Clause. In response, Royal submitted an affidavit from Niek Vehreschild, its Strategic Procurement Manager, denying that Royal agreed to this clause. **[—6—]** Vehreschild asserted, "In engaging Central Oceans . . . for the transportation services at issue . . . [Royal] did not agree to be bound by any contractual terms barring [Royal] from filing any action and seeking recovery for damages sustained to its transformers from any . . . entities involved in their transport." Royal also submitted certain documents received from the defendants during discovery, which outlined the terms of their carrier agreements with Central Oceans.

The district court granted the defendants' motion. Relying on two Supreme Court opinions, *Norfolk Southern Railway Co. v. Kirby*, 543 U.S. 14 (2004) and *Kawasaki Kisen Kaisha, Ltd. v. Regal-Beloit Corp.*, 561 U.S. 89 (2010), the court concluded that "actual carriers who fall within the scope of Himalaya Clauses can rely on those clauses to limit their liability." The court also observed that enforcing Himalaya Clauses that shield downstream carriers from liability had become "common practice." Because the defendants fell within the scope of the Himalaya Clause's protection, they could not be sued. Royal timely appealed.

II.

This court reviews grants of summary judgment de novo, applying the same standard as the district court. *Star Fin. Servs., Inc. v. Cardtronics USA, Inc.*, 882 F.3d 176, 179 (5th Cir. 2018). Summary judgment is appropriate "if the movant shows that there is no genuine dispute **{–548–}** as to any material fact and the movant is entitled to judgment as a matter of law." Fed. R. Civ. P. 56(a). Once the movant carries its burden, the nonmovant must point to specific evidence that demonstrates a genuine dispute of material fact exists. *See Matsushita Elec. Indus. Co. v. Zenith Radio Corp.*, 475 U.S. 574, 587 (1986).

A.

We begin by addressing a preliminary legal question that is not contested by the parties, yet has never been addressed by our court: whether **[—7—]** the specific type of Himalaya Clause at issue here is enforceable. We hereby join our sister courts in the Second and Ninth Circuits in concluding that it is. *Cf. Sompo Japan Ins. Co. of Am. v. Norfolk S. Ry. Co.*, 762 F.3d 165, 2 Adm. R. 78 (2d Cir. 2014); *Fed. Ins. Co. v. Union Pac. R.R. Co.*, 651 F.3d 1175 (9th Cir. 2011).

As the Supreme Court has noted, through bills of lading are central to modern maritime commerce, which has embraced "door-to-door transport based on efficient use of all available modes of transportation by air, water, and land." *Kirby*, 543 U.S. at 25 (citation omitted); *see* William Coffey, *Multimodalism and the American Carrier*, 64 TUL. L. REV. 569, 593 (1989) (observing that the through bill of lading is the "dominant instrument of trade"). The through bill allows a cargo owner to arrange for a complex transportation of goods in a single transaction, "rather than [having] to negotiate a separate contract" for each leg. *Kirby*, 543 U.S. at 26;

see also Regal-Beloit, 561 U.S. at 109. Accordingly, through bills promote efficient contracting—a point of emphasis in this area of law. *See Regal-Beloit*, 561 U.S. at 109; *Kirby*, 543 U.S. at 29.

Himalaya Clauses "extend[] the bills' defenses and limitations on liability to parties that sign subcontracts to perform services contemplated by the bills." *Regal-Beloit*, 561 U.S. at 94. In other words, they operate much like the mountain range by the same name, creating a barrier between the cargo owner and downstream carriers that can be neither scaled nor circumvented.

The Supreme Court has twice enforced Himalaya Clauses in through bills. *See Kirby*, 543 U.S. at 31–32; *Regal-Beloit*, 561 U.S. at 109–10. *Kirby*, in particular, demonstrates the strong protection such Clauses afford. There, the Court held that two different Himalaya Clauses introduced by separate bills of lading within the same multimodal transportation were enforceable. 543 U.S. at 36. The two clauses limited the amount of damages the cargo owner could receive from the intermediary's subcontractors. *Id.* at 32. Despite the fact that **[—8—]** the Clauses did not specifically name to whom they applied (instead naming "any servant" of the intermediary), *id.* at 31, and the fact that the cargo owner was not even a party to one of bills, *id.* at 33–34, the Court held that both protected a downstream carrier from the cargo owner.

In *Regal-Beloit*, the Court enforced a Himalaya Clause that afforded a very different protection to downstream carriers: a forum selection clause negotiated between the cargo owner and intermediary. 561 U.S. at 109–10. Applying the terms of the through bill of lading, the Court held that "any suit relating to the cargo" filed by the cargo owner against downstream carriers had to be conducted in Japan, *id.* at 110–11, regardless of any practical difficulties this might cause. **{-549-}**

Here, the through bill of lading's Himalaya Clause protects downstream carriers from being sued by Royal. Although it offers a protection distinct from what was provided in *Kirby* and *Regal-Beloit*, we see no reason why the result should be different.

In reaching the same conclusion, both the Second and Ninth Circuits acknowledged a potential pitfall—namely, that such Himalaya Clauses implicate a longstanding policy in maritime law against agreements that improperly limit the recovery to which the cargo owner is entitled. *See Sompo Japan Ins. Co.*, 762 F.3d at 181, 2 Adm. R. at 89; *Fed Ins. Co.*, 651 F.3d at 1180. Indeed, COGSA itself states:

> Any clause, covenant, or agreement in a contract of carriage relieving the carrier or the ship from liability for loss or damage to or in connection with the goods, arising from negligence, fault, or failure in the duties and obligations provided in this section, or lessening such liability otherwise than as provided in this chapter [this note], shall be null and void and of no effect. **[—9—]**

46 U.S.C. § 30701, note § 3(8). As the Supreme Court has observed, this provision was enacted in response to abuses by common carriers that were able to leverage their bargaining advantage over the cargo owner by "insert[ing] clauses in bills of lading exempting themselves from liability for damage or loss . . . and capping any damages awards." *Vimar Seguros y Reaseguros, S.A. v. M/V Sky Reefer*, 515 U.S. 528, 534–35 (1995). Indeed the courts themselves had long before fashioned a similar rule to protect the cargo owner's "unquestioned right . . . to recover full damages from a noncarrying vessel." *United States v. Atl. Mut. Ins. Co.*, 343 U.S. 236, 239–42 (1952).

Both the Second and Ninth Circuits concluded that Himalaya Clauses shielding a common carrier's agents from suit did not run afoul of this general prohibition, though the justifications for this conclusion differed slightly. The Second Circuit observed that the Supreme Court had two major concerns about such clauses: (1) that the cargo owner might not receive full recovery, and (2) that actual carriers would not be properly incentivized to exercise due care. *Sompo Japan Ins. Co.*, 762 F.3d at 182–83, 2 Adm. R. at 90–91 (citing *Atl. Mut. Ins. Co.*, 343 U.S. at 241–42; *Hart v. Pa. R. Co.*, 112 U.S. 331, 340 (1884)). It noted that neither was violated because the Clause does not "exonerate[] a common carrier or its agent from liability for damages caused by their negligence." *Id.* at 182, 2 Adm. R. at 90. Instead, it is properly construed as "an ordering mechanism" that "regulate[s] who will be responsible to whom"—specifically, the common carrier to the cargo owner, and the actual carriers to the common carrier. *Id.* at 182–83, 2 Adm. R. at 90–91. Accordingly, the cargo owner would still receive the recovery to which it was entitled (albeit perhaps through more inconvenient means). And the actual carriers, which remain liable to the common carrier for mistakes, would still be incentivized to exercise due care. *Id.*, 2 Adm. R. at 90–91.

The Ninth Circuit relied on a single Supreme Court opinion, *Sky Reefer. Fed. Ins. Co.*, 651 F.3d at 1179–80. In *Sky Reefer*, the Supreme Court **[—10—]** established a distinction between limitations on liability, which are impermissible in certain cases, and "mechanisms for [the] enforcement" of that liability, which are permissible. *Sky Reefer*, 515 U.S. at 534–35. The Court then concluded the bill of lading's forum selection clause fell into the latter category, despite the fact that it would impose heightened transaction costs on the cargo owner's ability to vindicate its interests. *Id.* at 533–36. **{-550-}** The Ninth Circuit, relying on *Sky Reefer*, held that the Himalaya Clause was akin to a forum selection clause—that is, "an enforcement mechanism rather than a reduction of the carrier's obligations to the cargo owner below what COGSA guarantees." *Fed. Ins. Co.*, 651 F.3d at 1180 (quoting *Sky Reefer*, 515 U.S. at 539) (internal quotation marks omitted). Like the Second Circuit, the court acknowledged—and was unaffected by—the fact that the Himalaya Clause might "make it more difficult as a practical matter for [the cargo owner] to recover damages." *Id.*

As the reasoning of our sister courts highlights, the bottom line is this: a Himalaya Clause that protects downstream carriers from suit by a cargo owner does not, in and of itself, limit the cargo owner's ability to receive the recovery to which it is entitled. Here, for example, Royal agreed with Central Oceans to a COGSA-authorized damages limitation. The mere fact that Royal must recover its remedy only from Central Oceans does not prevent it from receiving the full measure of that bargain. Moreover, nothing in the Himalaya Clause precludes Central Oceans from suing the defendants to recoup its losses from Royal. Accordingly, the extension of *Kirby* and *Regal-Beloit* is appropriate. We hold that the downstream carriers are entitled to the protection of such Himalaya Clauses.

B.

As noted, Royal does not contest this legal conclusion. Instead, Royal contends that the Himalaya Clause was never meant to be enforced. Its **[—11—]** argument is notable for what it does not state. Royal does not contest that the Clause is part of a multimodal through bill of lading, which established other contractual obligations between itself and Central Oceans. It does not contest that the Himalaya Clause, by its clear terms, blocks Royal from suing the Clause's beneficiaries. Nor does Royal contest that the defendants qualify as those beneficiaries.

Instead, Royal argues that there is a material issue of fact as to whether the parties agreed to be bound by the Himalaya Clause within the bill of lading. It cites (1) evidence that allegedly shows Royal neither negotiated nor agreed to the Himalaya Clause and (2) evidence that allegedly suggests the defendants executed other agreements independent of the bill of lading.[4] The district

[4] Royal also notes in passing that there is a dispute as to whether Central Oceans should qualify as a freight forwarder or non-vessel operating common carrier ("NVOCC"), which are two types of intermediaries. The defendants assert that Central Oceans is an NVOCC, but Royal points out that Central Oceans referred to itself as a freight forwarder in a letter Royal received.

Both roles serve as middlemen between cargo owners and actual carriers in the negotiation of multimodal transports. Whereas the freight forwarder largely coordinates and organizes the various deals with the carriers, the NVOCC

court concluded that {-551-} neither strand of evidence should impact the enforcement of the Himalaya Clause. We agree. **[—12—]**

1.

As to the former, Royal highlights the Vehreschild affidavit, which asserted that Royal did not intend to be so bound; the provision in its purchase order that expressly denied terms or conditions not contained in the purchase order or RFQ; and specific provisions in the RFQ that, according to Royal, demonstrate that subcontractors were meant to be held liable to Royal. But, again, Royal does not dispute the validity of the through bill of lading itself as a binding maritime contract. Royal's complaint, in fact, asserted that it "contracted with Central Oceans . . . pursuant to" the multimodal through bill of lading.

Particularly in light of these concessions, we discern several problems with Royal's argument. First, this court has long held that, "by filing a lawsuit for damages under the bill of lading, [the party] has accepted the terms of the bill of lading, including . . . unnegotiated" clauses. *Mitsui & Co. (USA), Inc. v. Mira M/V*, 111 F.3d 33, 36 (5th Cir. 1997) (rejecting the party's claim that the bill in question was "a contract of adhesion which it did not negotiate and which therefore should not bind it"). As noted above, Royal's complaint plainly relied on the bill of lading as the basis for its suit, omitting all other documents that memorialized the agreement. And, as noted, Royal has not challenged the validity of the bill of lading itself as a binding agreement. Its attempt to disavow the application of the Himalaya Clause within this agreement because the clause was not part of its negotiations is foreclosed by *Mitsui*.

Furthermore, to the extent that Royal would have us look to extrinsic evidence to discern an intent contrary to the plain text of the bill of lading, basic principles of maritime law governing the interpretation of contracts foreclose such an argument. Specifically, much as for ordinary contract interpretation, we "may not look beyond the written language of the document to determine the intent of the parties unless the disputed contract provision **[—13—]** is ambiguous." *Corbitt v. Diamond M. Drilling Co.*, 654 F.2d 329, 332–33 (5th Cir. Unit A Aug. 1981); *cf. Kirby*, 543 U.S. at 31–32. Further, to the extent a bill of lading's terms differ from prior agreements, the bill of lading supersedes them. *See W. India Indus., Inc. v. Tradex*, 664 F.2d 946, 949–50 (5th Cir. 1981) (noting that parties may agree to terms in a bill of lading that are different from a prior agreement and "thereby make a new and different contract" (quoting *N. Pac. Ry. Co. v. Am. Trading Co.*, 195 U.S. 439, 463 (1904))); 1 T. Schoenbaum, *Admiralty and Maritime Law*, § 10-11 (5th ed. 2017) ("The terms of the bill of lading may supersede an earlier term or agreement negotiated between the parties unless it is specifically preserved in the bill of lading."). Accordingly, insofar as Royal would have us read out a clear provision in the bill of lading based on an affidavit concerning Royal's private intention or conflicting provisions in prior agreements, its argument must be rejected.[5] **{-552-}**

participates as a party to the transactions. *See* 1 Schoenbaum, § 10-7; *compare Constructores Tecnicos, S. de R.L. v. Sea-Land Serv., Inc.*, 945 F.2d 841, 846 (5th Cir. 1991) (defining the freight forwarder role), *with GIC Servs., L.L.C. v. Freightplus USA, Inc.*, 866 F.3d 649, 657, 5 Adm. R. 287, 290 (5th Cir. 2017) (defining the NVOCC role).

Admittedly, whether an intermediary participates as a freight forwarder or an NVOCC has some legal significance in other contexts. 1 Schoenbaum, § 10-7 (noting differences in their status as "carriers" under the law). But Royal fails to offer any explanation as to its impact on the interpretation of a through bill of lading, which can be issued by freight forwarders and NVOCCs alike. Michael Crowley, *The Limited Scope of the Cargo Liability Regime Covering Carriage of Goods by Sea: The Multimodal Problem*, 79 TUL. L. REV. 1461, 1462 (2005). Notably, *Kirby* concerned a bill of lading issued by a freight forwarder, 543 U.S. at 19, and *Sompo Japan Insurance Co.*, which relied on *Kirby*, concerned a bill of lading issued by an NVOCC, 762 F.3d at 168, 184, 2 Adm. R. at 78, 91. Accordingly, even if Royal's assertion that Central Oceans is a freight forwarder has merit, the dispute is immaterial.

[5] We add that, contrary to Royal's assertions, there does not appear to be any conflict between the bill of lading and the RFQ. In its sole references to the defendants, the RFQ only requires Central Oceans's agents to abide by its terms. These

Last, we agree with the district court that Royal's argument runs afoul of Supreme Court guidance. A point of emphasis in *Kirby* was the importance of protecting downstream carriers according to the text of through bills of lading. There, the Court applied the terms of a Himalaya Clause protecting a downstream carrier from the cargo owner despite the fact that the through bill of lading was negotiated between the common carrier and another actual carrier higher up in the chain—not the cargo owner. *Kirby*, 543 U.S. at 32–35. Rejecting the cargo owner's argument that it should not be bound by a Himalaya Clause to which it had not agreed, the Court highlighted the complexity of multimodal transactions and the extreme, "even impossible" **[—14—]** burden it would place on downstream carriers if they were required "to assure themselves that their contractual liability limitations provide true protection." *Id.* at 35.

The Supreme Court's reasoning looms large here. Royal seeks to override the plain text of *its own* through bill of lading based on private intentions and agreements between Royal and Central Oceans. The defendants were never made privy to either source. Yet, by Royal's logic, downstream carriers should not be able to rely on the plain text of a through bill of lading to which the cargo owner agreed; instead, they must conduct a thorough search for other agreements between the cargo owner and intermediary that might evince contradictory provisions or intent. As the district court noted, such a burden is, if anything, more extreme than what the Supreme Court concluded was untenable in *Kirby*. And it would certainly hinder the underlying policy goal of this area of the law generally and through bills specifically—namely, efficient contracting. *See id.* at 25–26, 29.

We therefore agree with the district court that Central Oceans's arguments seeking to undermine the plain terms of the through bill are irrelevant; the defendants are entitled to rely on that plain text.

provisions do not explicitly require that the defendants be liable to Royal. To the contrary, the RFQ merely states that Central Oceans remains liable for their actions. We discern no conflict between the Himalaya Clause and the RFQ's terms.

2.

Next we consider Royal's citation to documents that allegedly show the defendants did not understand the bill of lading as enforceable "to the exclusion" of their individual agreements. Royal cites documents that record these agreements for support, but have no binding legal authority.[6] Here again, we disagree. **[—15—]**

The key is Royal's concession that its bill of lading with Central Oceans is a through bill of lading. As noted, through bills have become the "dominant instrument of trade," Coffey, 64 TUL. L. REV. at 593, in international maritime commerce precisely because they allow cargo owners to avoid having to contract separately with actual carriers. *Kirby*, 543 U.S. at 25–26. Instead, that task is passed on to the intermediary, which must coordinate the network of shipping contracts required to complete the delivery. Accordingly, **{-553-}** the downstream carriers will come to specific agreements with the intermediary, but these agreements do not, in and of themselves, affect the terms of the Himalaya Clause in the through bill of lading. In other words, the contracts between downstream carriers and an intermediary do not impact the protections negotiated by that intermediary with the cargo owner. *Cf. id.* at 36 (defining—in a far more complex multimodal transport involving numerous, coordinated entities—the downstream carrier's protection from the cargo owner by sole reference to the through bills of lading).

[6] Royal also references in passing the defendants' arguments in response to Central Oceans's motion to transfer—i.e., that the bill of lading's forum selection clause did not apply to them because they were not parties to the contract. Royal does not explain what significance—legal or otherwise—this should have. We fail to see why the defendants **[—15—]** argument concerning a forum selection clause of the bill of lading should preclude or affect their argument that the Himalaya Clause expressly protects them from being sued.

In other words, it is not merely usual, but expected that the defendants would have come to separate arrangements regarding the transportation. And the existence of such agreements does not weaken the binding effect of a Himalaya Clause in applicable through bills of lading. Indeed, allowing such individual agreements to call into question the terms of the through bill of lading would seem to turn the industry practice on its head.

We add that all three of the documents highlighted by Royal are consistent with standard practice. The documents attributed to Berard and IC are copies of their bids to Central Oceans to serve as a carrier to the transport. Similarly, Onego's non-negotiable bill of lading is a common means by which **[—16—]** downstream carriers memorialize their contracts as part of a multimodal transport. *See* 1 Schoenbaum, § 10-11 (noting that such bills serve as mere receipts, not separate contracts).[7] We decline to deprive the defendants of the Himalaya Clause's protection on this basis.[8]

In short, Royal has again failed to articulate a basis for overriding the clear terms of the through bill of lading.

[7] Royal's argument that Onego's bill of lading is a separate contract with Royal itself is solely based on the fact that Royal is listed as a "shipper" on the document. To the extent this argument is relevant, its error is clear from the document itself. Central Oceans is listed as the Merchant on a signed page within the same document. That same page includes signatures only from representatives of the Carrier (Onego) and the Merchant (Central Oceans). This is immediately followed by the Conditions of Carriage between the Merchant and Carrier. Onego and Central Oceans are clearly the parties between which the bill of lading was formed. Moreover, Royal admitted in its response to the Defendants' Statement of Uncontested Material Facts that "the Defendants did not sign a contract with Royal."

[8] We also note that the presence of a through bill renders the sole case Royal cites for support—an unpublished district court opinion from another jurisdiction—inapplicable. *See LIG Ins. Co. v. ZP Transport, Inc.*, Civ. A. No. 14-4007, 2015 WL 4725004, at *4 (N.D. Ill. July 31, 2015) (noting that application of *Kirby* and *Regal-Beloit* was inappropriate because they involved through bills).

III.

The summary judgment is AFFIRMED.

United States Court of Appeals
for the Fifth Circuit

No. 17-30805

SCF WAXLER MARINE, L.L.C.
vs.
ARIS T M/V

Appeal from the United States District Court for the Eastern District of Louisiana

Decided: August 29, 2018
Revised: October 30, 2018

Citation: 902 F.3d 461, 6 Adm. R. 246 (5th Cir. 2018).

Before **STEWART,** Chief Judge, and **JONES** and **ENGELHARDT,** Circuit Judges.

[—2—] {-462-} STEWART, Chief Judge:

A stream of litigation followed a marine accident that resulted in damages estimated to exceed $60 million. The underlying fault or liability for that accident is not at issue on appeal. Rather, Valero, Shell, and Motiva ask this court to resolve whether the excess insurers of one of the involved vessels may limit their liability to that of the insured vessel. On a partial motion for summary judgment, the district court held that the Protection and Indemnity policy covering the vessel has a *Crown Zellerbach* clause thereby permitting the excess insurers to limit their liability to that of the insured vessel.

Valero, Shell, and Motiva timely appealed, asserting that this court has jurisdiction to hear an appeal of that interlocutory order under 28 U.S.C. §1292(a)(3). Because we lack appellate jurisdiction, we DISMISS. **[—3—]**

I. FACTUAL BACKGROUND AND PROCEDURAL HISTORY

On January 31, 2016, bulk carrier *Aris T* collided with a tank barge, a towing vessel, **{-463-}** and two facility structures along the Mississippi River upriver from New Orleans. Prior to the accident, the *Aris T* was proceeding upriver as two towing vessels, the *Elizabeth M. Robinson* and *Loretta G. Cenac*, were moving downriver toward their respective destinations. Both towing vessels were pushing ahead three loaded tank barges, each barge 300 feet long and 54 feet wide. Despite communications between the captains of each vessel about facilitating the *Loretta G. Cenac*'s attempted pass of the *Elizabeth M. Robinson*, an accident occurred after the *Aris T* struck the portside of an empty tank barge which in turn struck another tank barge. The barges were connected by the stern to the bow of towing vessel *SCF Vision* moored at a dock owned by Valero Refining – New Orleans ("Valero"). In the aftermath of this initial collision, the *Aris T*, still moving upriver, struck another towing vessel as well as multiple berths owned by Shell Chemical, L.P. ("Shell") and Motiva Enterprises ("Motiva"). Both tank barges, the facility dock, and the *SCF Vision* sustained damage.

On February 2, 2016, SCF Waxler Marine, LLC, owner and operator of damaged towing vessel *SCF Vision*, filed suit against the *Aris T* in the Eastern District of Louisiana. Soon thereafter, Valero, Shell, and Motiva also filed actions against the *Aris T*. Seeking to limit its liability for damages resulting from the accident, the *Aris T* filed a Verified Complaint in Limitation under the Limitation of Liability Act (46 U.S.C. §§ 30501–12), arguing that it was not at fault for the accident. The vessel most relevant to this appeal—the *Loretta G. Cenac* through its owner Cenac Marine Services, LLC ("Cenac")—similarly filed a Verified Complaint for Exoneration from or Limitation of Liability. The district court consolidated that action along with others related to the accident. The Exoneration Complaint sought declaratory relief from the district court **[—4—]** providing that Cenac was not liable or, if found liable, that its liability be limited to the value of Cenac's interest in the vessels involved—$14,602,365 (value of the vessels plus freight).

Louisiana's Direct Action Statute permits persons sustaining damages in accidents occurring in Louisiana to bring direct actions against insurers of the individual alleged to have caused the accident. LA. REV. STAT. ANN. 22:1269. Subject to a handful of exceptions not applicable here, a direct action may not be brought against the insurer alone. *See id.* at

B(1)(a)-(f). On January 24, 2017, Valero, Shell, and Motiva exercised this right, impleading Cenac's Primary[1] and Excess[2] Insurers pursuant to Federal Rule of Civil Procedure 14. They claimed that the Excess Insurers, by virtue of Louisiana's Direct Action Statute, were liable to Valero, Shell, and Motiva for all damages sustained in the accident that were the fault of Cenac.

Valero, Shell, Motiva, and the Excess **{-464-}** Insurers[3] then quarreled about whether the primary P&I policy, issued by the Primary Insurers and followed by all Excess Insurers, had language indicating that the insurers could limit their liability to that of the *Loretta G. Cenac*. That is, whether the P&I policy contains a "*Crown Zellerbach* clause." *See Crown Zellerbach Corp. v. Ingram Indus., Inc.* 783 F.2d 1296 (5th Cir. 1986) (en banc). **[—5—]**

Valero, Motiva, and Shell filed a motion for partial summary judgment to settle the *Crown Zellerbach* issue. On September 6, 2017, the district court sided with the Excess Insurers, denying the motion. More specifically, the district court concluded that the following provision satisfied *Crown Zellerbach's* requirements for an insurer to limit its liability:

> The Assurer hereby undertakes to make good to the Assured or the Assured's executors, administrators and/or successors, all such loss and/or expense ***as the Assured shall as owners of the vessel named herein have become liable to pay and shall pay*** on account of the liabilities, risks, events and/or happenings herein set forth . . . .

Valero, Motiva, and Shell timely appealed on October 5, 2017. They assert that this court has jurisdiction to hear the appeal pursuant to 28 U.S.C. § 1292(a)(3).

II. JURISDICTION

The Excess Insurers contend that this court lacks jurisdiction to hear this interlocutory appeal under § 1292(a)(3) because the district court's Order and Reasons fails to "determin[e] the rights and liabilities of the parties." We agree.

Although this court must satisfy itself of its own jurisdiction, Valero, Shell, and Motiva "'bear[] the burden of establishing this court's appellate jurisdiction over this appeal,' and there is no need to explore jurisdictional bases the appellant does not address." *Thibodeaux v. Vamos Oil & Gas Co.*, 487 F.3d 288, 293 (5th Cir. 2007). This court's appellate jurisdiction is ordinarily limited to "final decisions of the district courts of the United **[—6—]** States."[4] 28 U.S.C. § 1291. Where permitted by statute, however, this court may hear interlocutory appeals satisfying certain requirements.

Relevant here, § 1292(a)(3) provides that appellate courts may entertain appeals from a district court's "[i]nterlocutory decrees . . . determining the rights and liabilities of the parties to admiralty cases." This circuit has construed the grant narrowly, hewing closely to the statute's "original purpose of permitting appeals from orders finally determining one party's liability to another and referring the action for a computation of damages." *Hollywood Marine, Inc. v. M/V Artie James,*

---

1 Continental Insurance Company and AGCS Marine Insurance Company are Cenac's Primary insurers and provide a policy with $1 million in coverage. They will collectively be referred to as the Primary Insurers throughout this opinion.

2 New York Marine and General Insurance Company and Stonington Insurance Company National Specialty Insurance Company ("First Excess Insurers") are Cenac's First Excess Insurers and provide policies with $29 million in coverage. Certain Underwriters at Lloyd's of London ("Second Excess Insurers") are Cenac's Second Excess Insurers and provide policies with $70 million in coverage. The First and Second Excess Insurers will be collectively referred to as the Excess Insurers throughout this opinion.

3 The Primary Insurers did not oppose the partial motion for summary judgment. On appeal the Primary Insurers maintain a hands off approach. Their brief on appeal simply explains that they are unaffected by the outcome of this appeal because the limitation fund posted by Cenac exceeds the $1 million limit of their policy.

4 Notably, one of Appellants' counsel conceded during oral arguments that there was nothing precluding this court's review of the ruling at issue after a final judgment.

755 F.2d 414, 416 (5th Cir. 1985) (Rubin, J.). This court looks beyond the characterization of the ruling at issue and to the substance of what the lower court decided. *See Treasure Salvors, Inc. v. Unidentified Wrecked & Abandoned Sailing Vessel*, 640 F.2d 560, 564 (5th Cir. 1981).

We have clarified that appellate jurisdiction is generally appropriate "whenever an order in an admiralty case dismisses **{-465-}** a claim for relief on the merits." *Francis ex rel. Francis v. Forest Oil Corp.*, 798 F.2d 147, 149 (5th Cir. 1986) (per curiam). That is not to say that all claims (or rights and liabilities) of all parties must be determined before this court may invoke jurisdiction; rather, the heartland of this court's jurisdiction over an interlocutory appeal under § 1292(a)(3) is a conclusive determination of the rights and liabilities as to the claim on appeal. *See In re Complaint of Ingram Barge Co.*, 517 F.3d 246, 247 (5th Cir. 2008) ("Interpreting Section 1292(a)(3), we then held 'that in admiralty the liability of only one party need be determined for an interlocutory appeal to lie.'"). **[—7—]**

For example, in *In re Ingram Towing Co.*, this court concluded that jurisdiction was not proper under § 1292(a)(3) where the district court did not determine liability or determine that a party could never bring a claim against the opposing party. 59 F.3d 513, 516–17 (5th Cir. 1995). In other words, this court lacked jurisdiction to hear an appeal of a district court's determination of "how and where the rights and liabilities would be determined." *Id.* at 517. Similarly in *Hollywood Marine*, this court held that an order finding that an insurer could not deny coverage under its policy did not provide appellate jurisdiction under § 1292(a)(3). 755 F.2d at 415–16. The *Hollywood* panel explained that jurisdiction under the statute is not appropriate where "the party whose contention is rejected remains in the litigation and the issue of its liability on the claim asserted remains to be finally resolved." *Id.* at 416. The decision did not "completely cut off" a party's ability to pursue the claim. *See Crews v. Arundel Corp.*, 386 F.2d 528, 530 (5th Cir. 1967). As this court plainly stated in *Hollywood*, § 1292(a)(3) offers no appellate jurisdiction where the district court's order "does not conclusively determine [a party's] 'rights and liabilities' as to the claim asserted." *Hollywood Marine, Inc.*, 755 F.2d at 416.

The principle dispute on the jurisdictional question in this case revolves around the applicability of this court's per curiam decision in *Bucher-Guyer AG v. M/V Incontrans Spirit*, 868 F.2d 734 (5th Cir. 1989) (per curiam). The Excess Insurers argue that the decision governs this case. First, they note that *Bucher-Guyer* is particularly instructive because the court held that we lack jurisdiction over an appeal of a district court's order stating that a statutory limitation on damages was applicable to a case. The court would still have to remand the case to the district court for a decision on whether the party entitled to a cap on its liability was actually liable. The Excess Insurers press that the same logic applies here. Valero, Shell, and Motiva distinguish *Bucher-Guyer* by arguing that the court's decision there did not concern the grant of a **[—8—]** substantive right, as here, and concerned a statute—the U.S. Carriage of Goods by Sea Act—that has no bearing on this case. Lastly, Valero relies on *Wallis v. Princess Cruises, Inc.*, where the Ninth Circuit held that a district court's conclusion concerning an insurance contract provision was appealable because, among other things, a holding to the contrary "would make interlocutory appeals impossible in many admiralty cases, and would do so in precisely those cases where appeals are most needed." 306 F.3d 827, 834 (9th Cir. 2002). In the same vein as their approach to *Bucher-Guyer*, Valero, Shell, and Motiva argue that this court has appellate jurisdiction because the district court, in denying their motion for partial summary judgment, granted the Excess Insurers rights that did not exist before that decision. In other words, the district court determined that Cenac could actually limit that liability based on an insurance contract clause. This determination was the **{-466-}** final pronouncement on the extent of the Excess Insurers' liability in this case. That finality is not diminished, they urge, merely because the district court did not rule on the issue of liability. It is sufficient that the boundaries and limits of liability are now set in stone.

The Excess Insurers present a more persuasive view of this jurisdictional dispute. In *Bucher-Guyer*, this court held that the applicability of a $500 limitation on liability pursuant to the Carriage of Goods at Sea Act ("COGSA") was not a determination of a party's rights and liabilities for purposes of § 1292(a)(3). *Bucher-Guyer*, 868 F.2d at 735; *see also Hager v. Laurelton Welding Serv., Inc.*, 124 F. App'x 104, 106–07 (3d Cir. 2005) (unpublished) (Scirica, J.) (expressing agreement with Fifth Circuit approach to issue of "whether orders regarding limitations of damages are appealable under § 1292(a)(3)").

The fundamentals of *Bucher-Guyer* bear a striking resemblance to this case. There, the district court determined the boundaries of a party's liability—$500—based on the applicability of statutory language. Nevertheless, whether **[—9—]** the opposing party was entitled to anything and, if so, how much was still to be determined. In this case, the court decided the boundaries of a party's liability through determination of whether a contractual provision permitted them to do so. Whether Valero, Shell, and Motiva are legally permitted to recover anything from the Excess Insurers and, if so, how much remains to be determined. That question turns on the fault and or liability of the *Loretta G. Cenac*. Answering the important, but ancillary, question about the extent of the insurer's potential liability leaves the heart of the claim to be decided.

Valero, Shell, and Motiva attempt to dismiss the relevance of this decision because: (1) *Bucher-Guyer* does not address an insurance policy provision; (2) the statute at issue in that case—the U.S. Carriage of Goods Act—has no bearing on this case; and (3) here the district court did not find a statutory right to entitlement; rather, the focus was on a policy provision. Valero, Shell, and Motiva advance these arguments despite asking this court to instead rely on *Wallis*—a case that rejects the first two of their proffered distinguishing features.

In *Wallis*, the Ninth Circuit addressed whether that court had appellate jurisdiction over a district court's determination of the applicability of a contractual limitation of liability provision. In analyzing that issue, the Ninth Circuit explained that § 1292(a)(3) case law concerning the Carriage of Goods at Sea Act was instructive. 306 F.3d at 832–35.

Beyond not being helpful to Valero, Shell, and Motiva's attempt to distinguish *Bucher-Guyer*, *Wallis* expressly noted that the panel disagreed with and would not follow this court's interpretation of § 1292(a)(3). *Id.* at 833–34 (collecting cases from other circuits, including the Fifth Circuit, and stating "[w]e think that these other circuits have read § 1292(a)(3) too narrowly"). However, we stand by *Bucher-Guyer*. We also find persuasive the Eleventh **[—10—]** Circuit's reasoning in *Wajnstat v. Oceania Cruises, Inc.*, addressing a similar issue to the one we analyze here. 684 F.3d 1153 (11th Cir. 2012) (Carnes, J.).

In *Wajnstat*, the Eleventh Circuit analyzed whether § 1292(a)(3) permitted the appeal of a district court order determining whether a "limitation-of-liability provision in a cruise ticket contract was unenforceable and, as a result, inapplicable." *Id.* at 1155. Citing to this circuit's § 1292(a)(3) jurisprudence, the *Wajnstat* panel held that a district court's order denying a motion for partial summary judgment on a **{-467-}** limitation-of-liability affirmative defense failed to meet the requirements of § 1292(a)(3). *Id.* at 1155–56. Announcing a rule that is eminently reasonable, the Eleventh Circuit explained as follows:

> If, as [the Fifth Circuit in] *Ford Motor Co.* held, a district court does not determine the "rights and liabilities of the parties" when it decides the applicability of a statutory limitation of liability, it also does not determine the "rights and liabilities of the parties" when it determines the applicability of a contractual limitation of liability.

Id. at 1155.

We find no compelling reason to distinguish between a district court's determination of a contractual entitlement rather than statutory entitlement to limit liability.[5] Neither decision is reviewable on appeal under § 1292(a)(3). We join the Eleventh Circuit in so holding. **[—11—]**

If the district court had determined that the Excess Insurers via the shipowner's liability were not entitled to exoneration or limitation—requiring a determination of actual liability and having res judicata effect—jurisdiction would likely be appropriate. *See, e.g., Republic of France v. United States*, 290 F.2d 395, 397 (5th Cir. 1961) (exercising appellate jurisdiction over denial of exoneration or limitation of liability where the district court concluded that appealing party was negligent and thus not entitled to limitation). Similarly, the court has expressed willingness to hear appeals where indemnity or coverage by an insurer of an insured is altogether denied. *Thibodeaux*, 487 F.3d at 292–93 n.1 ("An order denying indemnity completely settles the third-party's liability as to both the plaintiff and the principal defendant, as it establishes that the third party has no liability whatsoever."). These scenarios are not present here.

Shell, Motiva, and Valero also rely on this court's decision in *Gabarick v. Laurin Maritime (America), Inc.*, when asserting that this court has exercised jurisdiction over interlocutory admiralty appeals under § 1292(a)(3) where, as here, the trial court interpreted part of a marine insurance policy before any liability determinations had been made. 649 F.3d 417, 420–21 (5th Cir. 2011). Notwithstanding that errant characterization, *Gabarick* does not govern the jurisdictional inquiry in this case. In *Gabarick*, excess underwriters filed an interpleader complaint in the district court seeking release from further liability under the excess policy upon deposit of their policy limit of $9 million into the court's registry. Upon deposit of this amount, all claims by and against the **{–468–}** excess underwriters would be dismissed. *Id.* at 420. The district court **[—12—]** concluded, contrary to the underwriters' contention, that they owed prejudgment interest on their policy limit. *Id.* The district court's decision conclusively determined what amount the excess insurers would be required to submit to be dismissed from the action. *Id.* Accordingly, the panel concluded that the district court's decision requiring the insurers to deposit more than they believed appropriate before they would be dismissed from the case "affected a 'liability.'" *Id.* at 421. Suffice it to say that whatever the import of *Gabarick* for its jurisdictional analysis, that case simply does not guide us where the underlying district court order determines a party's entitlement to a contractual limitation of liability.[6]

---

[5] It is true that *Crown Zellerbach* refers to the "*right* to assert [a] policy defense." 783 F.2d at 1300 (emphasis added). And thus, according to Valero, Shell, and Motiva, determination of the applicability of such a clause determines the Excess Insurers' rights. This argument is essentially what one of Appellants' counsel referred to as their "plain language" argument. This point is much too fine. Valero, Shell, and Motiva's argument that the district court determined the Excess Insurers' "right" to limit liability falls in the face of the simple fact that, distilled to its essence, the determination is about ascertaining whether a party is merely permitted to limit its liability should the insured be found able to do so. *Crown Zellerbach* acknowledged that even those insurers who can qualify for limitation of liability under the issued policy must demonstrate "a right to it by," among other things, **[—12—]** having the vessel owner "establish that the casualty occurred without the [vessel] owner's privity and fault." *Id.* at 1303. In other words, irrespective of the applicability of a limitation of liability insurance provision, under Louisiana's Direct Action Statute, "there must be a legal liability on part of the assured for the insurer to have a direct action liability." *Id.* at 1301. Section 1292(a)(3) does not confer jurisdiction under these circumstances.

[6] Our conclusion is not changed by the Federal Rule of Appellate Procedure 28(j) letter filed by Motiva and Shell after oral argument. The cases cited, similar to *Gabarick*, conclusively decided how much a party was required to deposit to satisfy their legal or policy obligations. It is fair for Motiva and Shell to make clear that this court has exercised jurisdiction prior to a final determination of liability in a case. But, again, the question preceding the determination of liability matters. Where the question, as here, is whether a potentially liable party may limit his liability, §1292(a)(3) does not afford this court jurisdiction

III. CONCLUSION

For the foregoing reasons, this appeal is DISMISSED for lack of jurisdiction.

where the underlying claim for liability has not been adjudicated. Moreover, as Motiva and Shell ostensibly concede, the cited decisions did not meaningfully analyze the jurisdictional question. Stated simply, where the district court answers the question of whether a party may, under a contractual provision, limit his liability should the liability question be determined in his or his insured's favor, we will not exercise jurisdiction.

United States Court of Appeals
for the Fifth Circuit

No. 16-60662

PARFAIT
VS.
DIRECTOR, OFFICE OF WORKERS' COMPENSATION PROGRAMS

Petition for Review of an Order of the Benefits Review Board

Decided: September 11, 2018

Citation: 903 F.3d 505, 6 Adm. R. 252 (5th Cir. 2018).

Before **DAVIS**, **OWEN**, and **ENGELHARDT**, Circuit Judges.

[—1—] {-506-} DAVIS, Circuit Judge:

McGill C. Parfait filed this Petition for Review to challenge a ruling by the Benefits Review Board ("BRB") in a proceeding in which Parfait sought benefits under the Longshore and Harbor Workers' Compensation Act ("LHWCA"). Parfait's employer, Performance Energy Services, L.L.C. ("Performance" or "Employer"), and its insurer, Signal Mutual Indemnity Association, Ltd. ("Signal" or "Insurer"), moved to dismiss the Petition for Review based on 33 U.S.C. § 933(f) and (g) of the LHWCA. The motion charged that Parfait had received funds in settlement of a tort action with a third party, **[—2—]** Apache Corporation ("Apache"), and a judgment against another third party, Wood Group PSN, Inc. ("Wood Group"), for the injuries for which he sought compensation benefits. The Employer and Insurer argued that Parfait failed to obtain approval or provide notice of the settlement and judgment as required by the above sections of the LHWCA. **{-507-}**

Based on written responses by Counsel for Parfait to questions posed by this Court, it is clear that Parfait received substantial sums from a settlement with and judgment against third parties and that the required notice was not given. Based on the plain language of the statute, we must dismiss this Petition for Review.

A. BACKGROUND

In December 2013, Petitioner filed a claim with the Office of Workers' Compensation Programs for total/permanent disability benefits under the LHWCA for back and chest injuries he sustained in an accident on June 30, 2013, while working for Performance. Following a formal hearing, the administrative law judge ("ALJ") awarded Petitioner $1,493.60 in temporary total and temporary partial disability benefits for his chest injury. The ALJ denied his claim for benefits for his back injury. The Petitioner then appealed the ALJ's award to the BRB, which affirmed. The Petitioner then lodged this Petition for Review challenging the BRB's ruling denying total/permanent disability benefits for his back injury.

Petitioner also filed a third-party tort action against Apache and Wood Group in the Southern District of Texas arising out of his June 30, 2013 accident. While Petitioner's appeal to the BRB was under submission, the Employer learned from counsel for Apache that Petitioner had settled a portion of the third-party tort action. The Employer also learned, after inquiring of Wood Group's counsel, that a judgment had been entered in favor of Petitioner **[—3—]** against Wood Group. After the appeal was lodged in this Court, the Employer and Insurer moved to dismiss the appeal alleging that Petitioner failed to obtain their approval of the third-party settlement, or to notify them of the third-party judgment, as required by § 33(g) of the LHWCA. In an effort to determine whether any factual issues were presented that required remand of this case to the BRB, we submitted questions to counsel for Petitioner and Respondents. On August 13, 2018, Counsel for Parfait, in response to questions from the Court, divulged that[1]:

---

[1] **Response of Petitioner to Question 1 (State the net amount the Claimant received in the two settlements that he made with third parties):**

On or about April 25, 2016, Claimant McGill Parfait entered into a release and indemnity agreement with Apache Corporation in order to settle the suit initiated by McGill Parfait

(1) On or about April 25, 2016, Petitioner compromised a suit he had pending against Apache in the Southern District of Texas, with Petitioner receiving $325,000. Petitioner reserved his right in his release with Apache to proceed against Wood Group. **[—4—] {–508–}**

(2) Following a jury trial in April 2017, Petitioner received a favorable verdict against Wood Group, and a judgment was entered on that verdict from which Petitioner enjoyed a net recovery of $41,542.17.

With respect to notice of this settlement and judgment to the Employer/Insurer, Petitioner's counsel responded to the Court's question as follows:

Question: Describe or furnish a copy of any notification Claimant or counsel gave to the employer or insurer of Claimant's intent to settle with either of the third parties with whom settlement was made.

Response:

> Counsel for Employer/Carrier were specifically invited to attend a mediation session that was held March 10, 2016, and was contacted during the mediation session by Claimant's counsel. This session was specifically called in order to resolve compensation issues and third-party claims. In addition, Parfait's claims against Wood Group were tried to a jury over five days in April of 2017, which resulted in a favorable verdict to Claimant, and which judgment was published by the District Court on June 2, 2017, and of which Respondents plainly were aware. Parfait's claims against Wood Group claims were not compromised by settlement.
>
> Claimant contends that counsel for Employer/Carrier received adequate notice of any settlement(s) for which any prior notice was legally required.

B. ANALYSIS

Section 33 of the LHWCA guarantees prompt payment of compensation to an employee injured through the negligence of a third party. Under this scheme,[2] **{–509–}** the

against Apache Corp., *et. al.* in the U.S. District Court for the Southern District of Texas – Galveston Division, C.A. No. 3:14-cv-00213. The net amount of this settlement was $325,000.00 (three-hundred twenty-five thousand dollars) to McGill Parfait. Expressly excepted from this settlement was Wood Group PSN, Inc., its parents, subsidiaries, affiliates and interrelated companies, against all of whom Claimant McGill Parfait expressly reserved his rights, actions and causes of action.

Following a jury trial in April 2017, on or about July 2017, McGill Parfait entered into a release and indemnity agreement with John Wood Group PLC ("Wood Group") in order to settle the suit initiated by McGill Parfait against Wood Group, et al., in the U.S. District Court for the Southern District of Texas–Galveston Division, C.A. No. 3:14-cv-00213. This 'settlement' did not represent a compromise of Parfait's claim, and followed a jury trial that was held in April 2017, which resulted in a favorable verdict for Parfait which was published as public record by the District Court on June 2, 2017, as Doc. No. 204 in that cause. The net amount of this post-verdict settlement was $41,542.17 (forty-one thousand, five-hundred forty-two dollars and 17 cents) to McGill Parfait.

[2] 33 U.S.C. § 933, Compensation for injuries where third persons are liable, provides:

(a) Election of remedies **[—5—]**

If on account of a disability or death for which compensation is payable under this chapter the person entitled to such compensation determines that some person other than the employer or a person or persons in his employ is liable in damages, he need not elect whether to receive such compensation or to recover damages against such third person.

. . . .

(f) Institution of proceedings by person entitled to compensation

employee may receive longshore benefits and still maintain a civil **[—5—]** action against a negligent third party. To ensure that the employee does not receive a double recovery, the employer is granted rights to full reimbursement of all benefits paid, including compensation and medical benefits, from net third-party recoveries. If such recoveries exceed benefits already paid, the employer is allowed to credit any remainder against its future liability under the LHWCA.

If the person entitled to compensation institutes proceedings within the period prescribed in subsection (b) the employer shall be required to pay as compensation under this chapter a sum equal to the excess of the amount which the Secretary determines is payable on account of such injury or death over the net amount recovered against such third person. Such net amount shall be equal to the actual amount recovered less the expenses reasonably incurred by such person in respect to such proceedings (including reasonable attorneys' fees).

(g) Compromise obtained by person entitled to compensation

(1) If the person entitled to compensation (or the person's representative) enters into a settlement with a third person referred to in subsection (a) for an amount less than the compensation to which the person (or the person's representative) would be entitled under this chapter, the employer shall be liable for compensation as determined under subsection (f) only if written approval of the settlement is obtained from the employer and the employer's carrier, before the settlement is executed, and by the person entitled to compensation (or the person's representative). The approval shall be made on a form provided by the Secretary and shall be filed in the office of the deputy commissioner within thirty days after the settlement is entered into.

(2) If no written approval of the settlement is obtained and filed as required by paragraph (1), or if the employee fails to notify the employer of any settlement obtained from or judgment rendered against a third person, all rights to compensation and medical benefits under this chapter shall be terminated, regardless of whether the employer or the employer's insurer has made payments or acknowledged entitlement to benefits under this chapter.

The Employer relies on § 33(g) of the LHWCA. Section 33(g)(1) provides: **[—6—]**

> If the person entitled to compensation (or the person's representative) enters into a settlement with a third person referred to in subsection (a) for an amount less than the compensation to which the person (or the person's representative) would be entitled under this chapter, the employer shall be liable for compensation as determined under subsection (f) only if written approval of the settlement is obtained from the employer and the employer's carrier, before the settlement is executed, and by the person entitled to compensation (or the person's representative). The approval shall be made on a form provided by the Secretary and shall be filed in the office of the deputy commissioner within thirty days after the settlement is entered into.

Subsection 33(g)(2) provides further:

> If no written approval of the settlement is obtained and filed as required by paragraph (1), or if the employee fails to notify the employer of any settlement obtained from or judgment rendered against a third person, all rights to compensation and medical benefits under this chapter shall be terminated, regardless of whether the employer or the employer's insurer has made payments or acknowledged entitlement to benefits under this chapter.

Section 33(g), quoted above, which requires the employee to obtain written approval of certain third-party settlements and to give notice of all third-party settlements and judgments, is designed to ensure that the employer's rights are protected in the settlement and to prevent the claimant from unilaterally bargaining away funds to which the employer or its carrier might be entitled under 33 U.S.C. § 933(b)-(f). In particular, the notice requirement enables an employer to protect its right to set off the settlement amount against its future obligations and its right to reimbursement of its previous payments from the settlement proceeds. Further, it ensures against fraudulent double recovery by the employee.

Parfait has conceded in the filings with the Court that he did not give notice to the Employer or Insurer of his settlement with Apache or the **[—7—]** judgment obtained from Wood Group. Specifically, with respect to the Apache settlement, Parfait argues that inviting counsel for the Employer/Insurer to a mediation session where settlement was being discussed with Apache put the Employer/Insurer on notice that a settlement might be made in the future. With respect to the judgment Petitioner obtained against Wood Group, Parfait contends that publication of the judgment on the verdict filed in the public records following the trial was sufficient to put the Employer/Insurer on notice of that judgment. We are unpersuaded that Parfait gave adequate notice as required under § 33(g)(2) with respect to either the settlement or judgment.

Estate of Cowart v. Nicklos Drilling Co. is the most relevant Supreme Court authority on the questions presented to us.[3] **{-510-}** In that case, Cowart hurt his hand while working for Nicklos Drilling Company ("Nicklos") on Transco Exploration Company's ("Transco") offshore drilling rig.[4] Although Cowart had received no formal award and was not receiving compensation, the Department of Labor notified Nicklos's carrier that it owed Cowart $35,592.77 for permanent partial disability.[5] Cowart made a third-party settlement with Transco in his tort action against the platform owner from which he received a net amount of $29,350.60.[6] The settlement was funded by Nicklos under an indemnity agreement with Transco.[7] Although Nicklos had notice of the settlement, Cowart did not obtain written approval from Nicklos to make this settlement.[8]

Because Subsection (g)(1) begins "[i]f the person entitled to compensation . . . enters into a settlement with a third person," the ALJ found that because **[—8—]** Cowart was not receiving compensation, the written approval requirement did not apply to him.[9] This Court reversed, holding that the approval requirement applied regardless of the fact that the employee was not receiving compensation and no award had been made in his favor.[10] The Supreme Court agreed and, in affirming this en banc Court's judgment, found that while § 33(g)(1) requires the employer's written approval of settlements for amounts less than the employee's compensation entitlement, only notice to the employer is required for other settlement amounts and for any judgment obtained against a third party. Specifically, the Court stated:

> An employee is required to provide notification to his employer, but is not required to obtain written approval, in two instances: (1) Where the employee obtains a judgment, rather than a settlement, against a third party; and (2) Where the employee settles for an amount greater than or equal to the employer's total liability. Under our construction the written-approval requirement of § 33(g)(1) is inapplicable in those instances, but the <u>notification requirement of § 33(g)(2) remains in force</u>. That is why subsection (g)(2) mandates that an employer be notified of 'any settlement.'[11]

The Court also explained the reasons that notice is sufficient in those instances:

> In cases where a judgment is entered . . . the employee does not determine the amount of his recovery, and employer approval, even if somehow feasible, would serve no purpose. And in cases where the employee settles for greater than the employer's liability, the employer is protected regardless of the

[3] 505 U.S. 469 (1992).

[4] *Id.* at 471.

[5] *Id.* at 471, 473-74.

[6] *Id.* at 471.

[7] *Id.* at 471-72.

[8] *Id.*

[9] *Id.* at 473-74.

[10] *See id.* at 471, 473-75. We affirmed this decision in an en banc opinion. *Id.* at 474.

[11] *Id.* at 475, 482 (emphasis added).

> precise amount of the settlement because his liability for compensation is wiped out. Notification provides full protection to the employer in these situations because it ensures against fraudulent double recovery by the employee.[12] **[—9—]**

Under the above language from the Supreme Court in *Cowart*, Parfait's rights to compensation and medical benefits under the LHWCA must be terminated. The Employee (Parfait) received $325,000 in **{-511-}** the settlement of his claim against Apache. He has appealed the ALJ's award of $1,493.60 and challenges the BRB's denial of benefits for his back injury. If the settlement amount is less than the compensation to which the Employee would ultimately be entitled, § 33(g)(1) required him to obtain his Employer's written approval (which he undisputedly did not obtain). And if the settlement amount is greater than the compensation to which he would ultimately be entitled, § 33(g)(2) required him to give his Employer notice of the settlement (which he did not give).

In addition, the Employee received sums in the amount of $41,542.17 by way of a judgment against another third party, Wood Group. Subsection 33(g)(2) required the Employee to give his Employer notice of this judgment (which he did not give).

Under the statutory scheme, if an employee makes a settlement with or obtains a judgment against a third party, at a bare minimum, the employee must give notice of the settlement or judgment to his employer. Here, the ultimate benefits to which the Employee is entitled have never been finally determined. That determination is not necessary here because whatever the outcome of this appeal, his failure to give notice of the settlement and judgment would terminate his right to compensation.

The Supreme Court's reasons outlining the consequences of Cowart's failure to obtain written approval from the employer of a settlement apply equally to the failure of Parfait to give notice of the sums he received in settlement and judgment from third parties. **[—10—]**

First, the Court stated that with respect to § 33(g)(1) (requiring the employee to obtain written approval for certain settlements), "Congress has spoken with great clarity to the precise question raised by this case. It is the duty of the courts to enforce the judgment by the Legislature."[13] The same can be said for the clarity of § 33(g)(2) to the question presented in this case relative to the requirement of the employee to give notice of judgment and settlement.

The Court also observed that accepting *Cowart's* interpretation would conflict with the goals of § 33(f). "It mandates that an employer's liability be reduced by the net amount a person entitled to compensation recovers from a third party."[14] The same difficulty would be presented by accepting Petitioner's argument in this case.

There is a dearth of federal circuit court opinions on the type of notice that must be given in order to satisfy § 33(g)(2). The BRB, however, has given a strict interpretation to that section. In *Fisher v. Todd Shipyards Corp.*, the employer challenged an ALJ's determination that compensation was not barred by § 33(g)(2) since the employer had denied liability for compensation and was not prejudiced by the settlement.[15] The BRB disagreed with the ALJ, stating:

> [T]he plain language of Section 33(g)(2) places on claimant an affirmative duty to notify employer, before the entry of an award of benefits, of any third-party settlement or judgment obtained by claimant. Employer's mere knowledge of settlements or the absence of prejudice to employer will not suffice to prevent the absolute bar to compensation from being invoked. To hold otherwise would

12 *Id.* at 482-83.

13 *Id.* at 483-84.

14 *Id.* at 479.

15 21 BRBS 323 (1988).

virtually read Section 33(g)(2) out of the statute.[16] **[—11—]**

Since *Cowart*, the BRB has consistently employed this strict interpretation, holding that if the employee settles for an amount **{-512-}** greater than the total liability of the employer and fails to give notice of that settlement, the employee suffers the termination of his benefits.[17] This is required to protect the employer's right to offset third-party recovery against its liability for compensation and also to prevent a fraudulent double recovery.

It is clear to us that Petitioner's counsel's telephonic notice on March 10, 2016 to Respondents' counsel that a mediation was being held to attempt to compromise the Petitioner's claim against Apache was just that -- notice that Parfait was trying to settle that case. That is clearly inadequate notice of the settlement that was ultimately made on April 25, 2016. Similarly, we reject the argument that the court's filing of the judgment obtained against Wood Group in the public record amounted to the required notice to the Employer. A finding that this constituted the requisite notice would, in the language of the Supreme Court in *Cowart*, be contrary to "the clear meaning"[18] of § 33(g)(2) as written,[19] and the "affirmative duty to notify." **[—12—]**

C. CONCLUSION

We find no reason to remand this case to the BRB for fact-finding. The Employee in this case did not comply with the approval and notice requirements of § 33(g) (1) and (2) with respect to his third-party settlement with Apache or his judgment against Wood Group. This failure requires termination of any right to compensation or medical benefits Petitioner might otherwise have under the LHWCA. We therefore grant Respondents' motion and dismiss this appeal.

---

[16] *Id.*

[17] *Edwards v. Marine Repair Servs., Inc.*, 49 BRBS 71 (2015) ("The Board has held that the plain language of subsection (g)(2) places on the claimant an affirmative duty to notify his employer of the third-party settlement, and the employer's mere knowledge of the settlement or the absence of prejudice to the employer will not suffice to prevent the bar to compensation from being invoked."); *Cooley v. Huntington Ingalls, Inc.*, 49 BRBS 45 (UBD) (2014) ("Although employer gained knowledge of agreements through the discovery process, the administrative law judge must address whether claimant satisfied his affirmative duty to notify employer . . . of any third-party judgment he obtained."); *H.S. v. Pacorini USA, Inc.*, No. 07-0991 (BRB June 30, 2008) (UBD) ("Pursuant to the Supreme Court's decision in *Cowart*, 505 U.S. 469, 26 BRBS 49 (CRT), if claimant *either* fails to comply with the written approval requirement of Section 33(g)(1) *or* fails to give notice to employer in the instances where written approval is not required, *i.e.*, a settlement exceeding compensation entitlement or a judgment, the forfeiture provision applies."); *Dilts v. Todd Shipyard Corp.*, No. 02-0434 (BRB Mar. 12, 2003) (UBD) ("There is no requirement under Section 33(g) that employer establish prejudice in order for Section 33(g) to bar a claim for compensation.").

[18] *Cowart*, 505 U.S. at 476.

[19] 33 U.S.C. § 933(g)(2) (requiring "*the employee* . . . to notify the employer of any settlement obtained from or judgment rendered against a third person").

United States Court of Appeals
for the Fifth Circuit

No. 17-60698

UNITED STATES
vs.
NATURE'S WAY MARINE, L.L.C.

Appeal from the United States District Court for the Southern District of Mississippi

Decided: September 21, 2018

Citation: 904 F.3d 416, 6 Adm. R. 258 (5th Cir. 2018).

Before **KING**, **ELROD**, and **HAYNES**, Circuit Judges.

[—1—] {-417-} ELROD, Circuit Judge:

This appeal presents us with a question of statutory interpretation. Specifically, we must determine whether the district court was correct in its summary judgment determination that Nature's Way, as the owner of a tugboat, was also "operating" an oil barge that the tugboat was moving at the time of a collision, as the term is **{-418-}** used in the Oil Pollution Act of 1990 (OPA).[1] **[—2—]** Because we agree that the ordinary and natural meaning of "operating" under the statute would apply to the exclusive navigational control that Nature's Way exercised over the barge at the time of the collision, we AFFIRM the judgment of the district court.[2]

I.

The relevant facts of this appeal are not in dispute. In January 2013, a tugboat owned by Nature's Way was moving two oil-carrying barges owned by Third Coast Towing down the Mississippi River. The barges were "dumb" barges lacking the ability for self-propulsion or navigation, and as such were reliant on the propulsion and navigation provided by the tugboat. The barges collided with a bridge, resulting in one of the barges discharging over 7,000 gallons of oil into the Mississippi River. Nature's Way and its insurer (collectively "Nature's Way"), as well as Third Coast Towing and its insurer (collectively "Third Coast") were all designated by the Coast Guard as "responsible parties" under the Oil Pollution Act. Nature's Way subsequently spent over $2.99 million on the clean-up, and various governmental entities spent over an additional $792,000.

Third Coast and Nature's Way settled a lawsuit between them in late 2014. In May 2015, Nature's Way submitted a claim to the National Pollution Funds Center (NPFC) seeking reimbursement of over $2.13 million on the grounds that its liability should be limited by the tonnage of the tugboat and not the tonnage of the barges.[3] Nature's Way also requested that it be relieved **[—3—]** of any obligation to reimburse the government for the additional $792,000-plus. Those claims were denied by the NPFC based upon its determination that Nature's Way was an "operator" of the oil-discharging barge at the time of the collision. In January 2016, the United States initiated this litigation, seeking recovery of the additional $792,000-plus from Nature's Way and Third Coast. Nature's Way answered that it was not liable for the additional $792,000-plus, and counterclaimed that the NPFC violated the Administrative Procedure Act (APA) by deeming it to be an "operator" of the barge and consequently ineligible for reimbursement of the $2.13 million-plus.

The government moved for partial summary judgment on the sole question of whether the NPFC violated the APA by declaring Nature's Way an "operator" of the

[1] Pub. L. No. 101-380, 104 Stat. 484 (codified as amended in 33 U.S.C. §§ 2701–2762).

[2] The parties also dispute on appeal whether Nature's Way waived any right to reimbursement from the oil spill trust fund by entering into a settlement deal with Third Coast Towing (the owner of the oil barge). However, because we affirm the judgment in the government's favor on the "operating" issue, we—like the district court—do not address that contention.

[3] The OPA limits the potential liability of a "responsible party" based on the tonnage of the vessels it was operating. *See* 33 U.S.C. § 2704(a). The NPFC manages a claims process **[—3—]** by which eligible responsible parties who are initially over-charged can subsequently request reimbursement from the federal government. *See id.* § 2708(a)(2); 26 U.S.C. § 9509.

barge and denying reimbursement of the $2.13 million-plus.[4] The district court granted the government's motion for partial summary judgment, concluding that a "common sense" understanding of the term "operator," as it is used in the statute, would include a tugboat that was moving **{-419-}** a barge through the water. Nature's Way timely appeals.[5] **[—4—]**

II.

A federal court will overturn an agency's ruling under the APA "only if it is arbitrary, capricious, an abuse of discretion, not in accordance with law, or unsupported by substantial evidence on the record[.]" *Buffalo Marine Servs. Inc. v. United States*, 663 F.3d 750, 753 (5th Cir. 2011) (citation omitted). Federal courts generally review an agency's legal conclusions *de novo*, unless precedent obligates that we follow one of several deference regimes. *Id.* at 753–54. Summary judgment is appropriate when "the movant shows that there is no genuine dispute as to any material fact and the movant is entitled to judgment as a matter of law." Fed. R. Civ. P. 56(a). Finally, this court reviews a district court's grant of summary judgment *de novo. Buffalo Marine*, 663 F.3d at 753.

Both parties dedicate considerable portions of their briefs disputing whether the NPFC's determination that Nature's Way was an "operator" should be entitled to *Chevron* deference.[6] Because we conclude that even under a *de novo* review Nature's Way was "operating" the barge in the ordinary and natural sense of the word as it is used in the statute, we do not make any determination as to whether *Chevron* deference would be proper in this case. However, in the appropriate case, a thorough examination of the procedural defects alleged against the NPFC in adjudicating claims such as the one here might be warranted.[7] **[—5—] {-420-}**

---

[4] In this appeal we do not address any other claims raised by any parties in the district court litigation.

[5] This court has interlocutory jurisdiction over the district court's grant of partial summary judgment pursuant to 28 U.S.C. § 1292(a)(3) because that order determined the rights and liabilities of the parties to an admiralty case. *See also MS Tabea Schiffahrtsgesellschaft MBH & Co. KG v. Board of Comm'rs of the Port of New Orleans*, 636 F.3d 161, 165 (5th Cir. 2011) ("[a]n order that dismisses on the merits only one of several separate claims for relief [in an admiralty case] is appealable under Section 1293(a)(3)") (citation omitted); *Foremost Ins. Co. v. Richardson*, 457 U.S. 668, 672 (1982) ("[i]f the wrong occurred on navigable waters, the action is within admiralty jurisdiction") (citation omitted).

[6] *See generally Chevron U.S.A., Inc. v. Nat. Res. Def. Council*, 467 U.S. 837 (1984); *United States v. Mead Corp.*, 533 U.S. 218 (2001) (holding that in certain cases an administrative agency's reasonable interpretation of an otherwise ambiguous statute should be given deference by the courts).

[7] "*Chevron* deference is not warranted where the regulation is 'procedurally defective'—that is, where the agency errs by failing to follow the correct procedures in issuing the regulation." *Encino Motorcars, LLC v. Navarro*, 136 S. Ct. 2117, 2125 (2016) (citing *Mead Corp.*, 533 U.S. at 227 (2001)). **[—5—]**

As alleged in this case, the NPFC considered the findings of a Marine Casualty Investigation Report in adjudicating the claim made by Nature's Way and determining Nature's Way to be an "operator" of the barges. However, 46 U.S.C. § 6308(a) clearly states that no part of a Marine Casualty Investigation Report, including its findings of facts, shall be admissible as evidence in "any civil or administrative proceedings."

The U.S. Coast Guard, which is both the parent agency of the NPFC and the entity that conducts Marine Casualty Investigations, has interpreted 46 U.S.C. § 6308(a) as inapplicable to the NPFC claims at issue here on the bases that such claims are an "internal, informal agency process" and that its prior interpretation of the statute—which it had read to exclude using Marine Casualty Investigation Reports as evidence in NPFC claims—was resulting in delays and duplicative efforts. *See* 71 Fed. Reg. 60,553 (Oct. 13, 2006); 72 Fed. Reg. 17,574-02 (Apr. 9, 2007).

The Coast Guard's interpretation of 46 U.S.C. § 6308(a) as inapplicable to the administrative proceeding of an NPFC claim is puzzling to say the least. The most natural reading of a statute that states no part of a Marine Casualty Investigation Report shall be admissible as evidence in "any civil or administrative proceedings" would be that such reports cannot be used as evidence in *any* civil or administrative proceedings—not that such reports cannot be used in any civil or administrative proceedings *except* for NPFC claims.

III.

Because this is a question of statutory interpretation, we begin with the text of the statute. *See Matter of Glenn*, 900 F.3d 187, 190 (5th Cir. 2018) ("We begin with the text of [the relevant statute]."). 33 U.S.C § 2702(a) establishes that each "responsible party" shall be liable for the removal costs and damages when oil is discharged into navigable waters or onto adjoining shorelines. Section 2701(32)(A) defines a "responsible party" as "[i]n the case of a vessel, any person owning, operating, or demise chartering the vessel." The statute does not define "operating," offering instead only the circular definition that an "owner or operator" is "in the case of a vessel, any person owning, operating, or chartering by demise, the vessel." *Id.* § 2701(26)(A)(i). It therefore falls to the **[—6—]** court to give the term its "ordinary or natural meaning." *United States v. Bestfoods*, 524 U.S. 51, 66 (1998) (citation omitted).

Defining the term "operating" in the context of an oil discharge is not *terra nova* for the courts. Indeed, the Supreme Court has already grappled with the term as it is used in the Comprehensive Environmental Response, Compensation, and Liability Act of 1980 (CERCLA),[8] which defines the term "operator" with the exact same language as is used in the OPA. *See* 42 U.S.C. § 9601(20)(A)(i). Given that the OPA and CERCLA have common purposes and a shared history, parallel language between the two statutes is significant. *See Buffalo Marine*, 663 F.3d at 756; *see also Gen. Elec. Co. v. United States Dep't of Commerce*, 128 F.3d 767, 769–70 (D.C. Cir. 1997) (noting that prior to passage of the OPA, damages resulting from oil spills were assessed pursuant to CERCLA). A unanimous Supreme Court has analyzed CERCLA's definition of "operator" as such:

> In a mechanical sense, to "operate" ordinarily means "[t]o control the functioning of; run: operate a sewing machine." American Heritage Dictionary 1268 (3d ed. 1992); *see also* Webster's New International Dictionary 1707 (2d ed. 1958) ("to work; as, to operate a machine"). And in the organizational sense more obviously intended by CERCLA, the word ordinarily means "[t]o conduct the affairs of; manage: operate a business." American Heritage Dictionary, *supra*, at 1268; *see also* Webster's New International Dictionary, *supra*, at 1707 ("to manage"). So, under CERCLA, an operator is simply someone who directs the workings of, manages, or conducts the affairs of a facility.[9]

Bestfoods, 524 U.S. at 66. **[—7—]**

It follows from that analysis that the ordinary and natural meaning of an "operator" of a vessel under the OPA would **{-421-}** include someone who directs, manages, or conducts the affairs of the vessel. Furthermore, it follows that the ordinary and natural meaning of "operating" a vessel under the OPA would thereby include the act of piloting or moving the vessel. It is undisputed that Nature's Way had exclusive navigational control over the barge at the time of the collision, and, as such, that it was a party whose direction (or lack thereof) caused the barge to collide with the bridge. Consequently, we—like the NPFC and district court—hold that Nature's Way was "operating" the barge at the time of the collision based on the ordinary and natural meaning of the term.

In an appropriate case, further examination is warranted on the question of whether the plain language of 46 U.S.C. § 6308(a) permits the Coast Guard's interpretation that the statute is inapplicable to NPFC claims, and, if that is not a permissible interpretation, whether the consideration of such reports in an NPFC claim would be a procedural defect precluding *Chevron* deference. However, this case is not the appropriate one to reach that issue because, without any deference whatsoever, we conclude that the NPFC's interpretation of the word "operating" is correct under the ordinary and natural meaning of the term.

[8] Pub. L. No. 96-510, 94 Stat. 2767 (codified as amended in 42 U.S.C. §§ 9601–9675).

[9] Technically, the Court in *Bestfoods* was referring specifically to the definition of an operator of a "facility" under 42 U.S.C. § 9601(20)(A)(ii), rather than an operator of a "vessel" under 42 U.S.C. § 9601(20)(A)(i); however, the analysis would apply with equal force were the word "vessel" to be substituted in for the word "facility."

Nonetheless, Nature's Way argues that the *Bestfoods* definition of "operator" should be understood differently. Nature's Way emphasizes language in another section of the *Bestfoods* opinion which states: "when [Congress] used the verb 'to operate,' we recognize that the statute obviously meant something more than mere mechanical activation of pumps and valves, and must be read to contemplate 'operation' as including the exercise of direction over the facility's activities." *Id.* at 71. According to Nature's Way, its conduct in moving the barge was more akin to the "mere mechanical activation of pumps," and it cannot be deemed to have been "operating" the barge because it was merely moving the barge as per Third Coast's directions, and it did not exercise control over its environmental affairs or inspections. In support of its argument, Nature's Way points to an order from the District of Kansas, where that court held that a vice-president with only general management responsibilities over a facility was not an "operator" of the facility under CERCLA because there was no showing that he actively managed or directed any of the facility's environmental operations. *See Harris v. Oil Reclaiming Co.*, 94 F. Supp. 2d 1210, 1213 (D. Kan. 2000). **[—8—]**

However, navigating a barge through a river entails a degree of discretion and judgment significantly different than that required for the "mere mechanical activation of pumps." Moreover, even if the District of Kansas case were applicable to the case at hand, it would appear to cut the other way. In that case, the vice-president was held not to be an "operator" of a facility because there was no showing that he personally engaged in the activities which caused the pollution; in this case, Nature's Way directed precisely the activity that caused the pollution—it literally was the party that crashed the barge into the bridge. To hold that Nature's Way was not "operating" the barge at the time of the collision would be to strain beyond the ordinary and natural meaning of the word.

* * * *

We therefore AFFIRM the district court's grant of partial summary judgment for the government.

United States Court of Appeals
for the Fifth Circuit

No. 16-30528

SHELL OFFSHORE, INC.
VS.
TESLA OFFSHORE, L.L.C.

Appeal from the United States District Court for the Eastern District of Louisiana

Decided: October 5, 2018

Citation: 905 F.3d 915, 6 Adm. R. 262 (5th Cir. 2018).

Before **CLEMENT**, **HIGGINSON**, and **HO**, Circuit Judges.

[—1—] {–918–} HIGGINSON, Circuit Judge:

On November 2, 2012, an underwater sonar device struck the mooring line of an offshore drilling rig in the Gulf of Mexico, causing substantial damage. Tesla Offshore, LLC was using the sonar device, known as a towfish, **[—2—]** to survey the ocean floor. Tesla had chartered a vessel from International Offshore Services, LLC to pull the towfish.

Shell Offshore, Inc., the owner of the drilling rig, sued Tesla and International for damages arising out of the accident.[1] After a trial on the merits, the jury returned a verdict in favor of Shell and apportioned 75% of the liability to Tesla and 25% to International. International and Tesla each appealed (No. 16-30528). While the appeal was pending, Tesla and Shell entered into a settlement agreement, and Shell executed a full satisfaction of judgment. After a limited remand from this court, the district court found that Tesla was entitled to contribution from **{–919–}** International toward the settlement amount. Another appeal followed (No. 17-30338).

Tesla and International are the sole remaining parties in this litigation, and we have consolidated their pending appeals. International disputes the district court's legal conclusion that its vessel was a towing vessel and subject to towing regulations. Tesla challenges the jury's allocation of fault and the district court's calculation of the contribution owed by International. We affirm on all issues.

I.

At the time of the accident, Tesla was undertaking a "high-resolution deeptow archaeological survey" of part of the Outer Continental Shelf in the Gulf of Mexico. Tesla hired two vessels to assist with the survey. International's vessel, the M/V INTERNATIONAL THUNDER, was the "mother ship" that pulled the sonar towfish. Another vessel served as the "chase vessel" and helped track the towfish. The captain of the THUNDER was **[—3—]** employed by International. The charter agreement between International and Tesla stated that Tesla would provide "towing and anchor handling gear," and would procure insurance for "each tow to be towed under" the agreement.

A team of five Tesla employees worked aboard the THUNDER. Tesla installed surveying equipment on the vessel, including a survey shack, electronics to monitor the towfish and receive data, a winch with 25,000 feet of cable, and the towfish itself. The towfish was about seven and a half feet long and resembled a torpedo. It is undisputed that Tesla personnel controlled the survey, including when to place the towfish in the water and how much cable to let out. Tesla also told the captain of the THUNDER what course to take within the survey grid.

On November 2, 2012, the THUNDER was pulling the towfish at the end of 14,000 feet of cable. The THUNDER approached the DEEPWATER NAUTILUS, a mobile offshore drilling rig owned by Shell. The rig was anchored by multiple submerged mooring lines. In February 2012, Shell had shared information about the NAUTILUS's position and mooring pattern with Tesla. Tesla did not

[1] Shell sued three International entities: International Offshore Services, LLC, International Boat Rentals, Inc., and International Marine, LLC. International Boat Rentals is no longer a party to this litigation. We refer to the other two International entities as "International."

provide this information to the captain of the THUNDER. According to Tesla, Shell informed it that the NAUTILUS would be operating in the area only until August 2012 and Tesla did not believe the information was relevant in October and November of 2012.

It is undisputed that, on the day of the allision, the crew of the THUNDER was unaware of the layout of the rig's mooring lines. Neither the THUNDER nor the NAUTILUS made radio contact with each other. But the captain of the chase vessel, the LADY JOANNA, testified that his vessel contacted the captain of the THUNDER to warn him that he was getting too close to the rig. Shortly afterward, the towfish hit one of the NAUTILUS's mooring lines. According to Shell, the allision caused the mooring line to lose **[—4—]** all tension and forced the NAUTILUS to temporarily suspend drilling operations.

The district court held a jury trial on Shell's claims against Tesla and International. The jury awarded Shell over $9 million in damages and determined that Tesla was 75% at fault and International was 25% at fault. The jury also found that the negligent acts or omissions of the THUNDER's crew were within the privity or knowledge of International. The district court entered final judgment holding Tesla and International jointly and severally liable for the full amount of judgment. Consistent with the jury verdict, the district court denied International's limitation of **{–920–}** liability defense. The district court also denied Tesla's post-trial motion for judgment as a matter of law, a new trial, and to alter or amend judgment.

II.

International challenges the district court's determination that the THUNDER was a "towing vessel" under 46 U.S.C. § 2101. The master of a towing vessel of 26 feet or more in length is required to hold a towing license. *See* 46 U.S.C. § 8904(a); 46 CFR §§ 15.805(a)(5), 15.910. It is undisputed that the captain of the THUNDER did not hold the relevant towing credential. International argued pre-trial that this credential was not required because the THUNDER was not a towing vessel as a matter of law. The district court denied International's motion for partial summary judgment on this issue. At trial, the court instructed the jury that the THUNDER was a towing vessel and that its captain did not have the requisite towing certification.

International maintains that this instruction was erroneous and argues that the instruction led the jury to reject its limitation of liability defense. Under the Limitation of Liability Act, a vessel owner is entitled to limit its liability only if the owner lacked "privity or knowledge" of the negligent acts or other fault that caused the damage. 46 U.S.C. § 30505; *see also In re Omega* **[—5—]** *Protein, Inc.*, 548 F.3d 361, 371 (5th Cir. 2008). International contends that the finding of privity or knowledge was likely based on the jury's belief that the captain of the THUNDER was improperly licensed. Jury "[i]nstructions that hinge on a question of statutory construction are reviewed de novo." *Janvey v. Dillon Gage, Inc. of Dall.*, 856 F.3d 377, 388 (5th Cir. 2017). We will reverse a jury verdict if "the charge as a whole leaves us with substantial and ineradicable doubt whether the jury has been properly guided in its deliberations and the challenged instruction affected the outcome of the case." *Jowers v. Lincoln Elec. Co.*, 617 F.3d 346, 352 (5th Cir. 2010) (internal citation omitted).

We invited the views of the U.S. Solicitor General on whether applicable laws and regulations at the time of the allision required the master of the THUNDER to have a towing license. The Government filed an amicus brief supporting the district court's legal conclusion that the THUNDER was a towing vessel whose captain was required to hold a towing license.

The U.S. Code defines a "towing vessel" as "a commercial vessel engaged in or intending to engage in the service of pulling, pushing, or hauling along side, or any combination of pulling, pushing, or hauling along side." 46 U.S.C. § 2101(50).[2] International does not

[2] This provision was recently renumbered. At the time of the relevant events, the same definition of towing vessel was at 46 U.S.C. § 2101(40).

seriously dispute that the THUNDER qualifies as a towing vessel under the plain language of the statute.[3] The **[—6—]** THUNDER is a commercial **{-921-}** vessel and it was hired by Tesla to pull the towfish. International contends, however, that the court must look beyond the statutory text to avoid absurd results. Specifically, International argues that a literal reading of the statute would transform any commercial vessel that pushes, pulls, or hauls anything into a towing vessel, including fishing boats as soon as someone hooks a fish.

But the statutory definition does not encompass *any* vessel that pushes, pulls, or hauls. Rather, it is limited to commercial vessels engaged "*in the service of* pulling, pushing, or hauling along side." 46 U.S.C. § 2101(50) (emphasis added). This provision defines a towing vessel in terms of the service it provides. We interpret this language to exclude vessels that engage in some incidental pulling, pushing, or hauling activities as part of a distinct commercial endeavor. A fishing vessel that pulls nets or cages in furtherance of its fishing activities would not qualify as a towing vessel because it is in the business of fishing, not "in the service of pulling." *See Mount v. Keahold Point Fish, LLC*, 147 F. Supp. 3d 1116, 1120-21 (D. Haw. 2015).

This is consistent with our familiar approach to determining what floating objects qualify as vessels. Like a towing vessel, a "vessel" is defined by its function. It must be "used, or capable of being used, as a means of transportation on water." 1 U.S.C. § 3. But a vessel's transportation function must be more than incidental to its primary purpose. *See Lozman v. City of Riviera Beach*, 568 U.S. 115, 121, 1 Adm. R. 2, 3 (2013) (distinguishing between a vessel "designed to a practical degree for carrying people or things over water" and a floating structure capable of "incidentally carrying" items while under tow); *Manuel v. P.A.W. Drilling & Well Service, Inc.*, 135 F.3d 344, 351 (5th Cir. 1998) (examining whether the transportation function of a craft was more than "merely incidental to its primary purpose of serving as a work platform"). By International's own account, the service provided by the THUNDER was to **[—7—]** pull the towfish as directed by Tesla. Tesla was responsible for all technical aspects of the survey itself. The THUNDER was therefore "in the service of pulling," and qualified as a towing vessel under the statute. 46 U.S.C. § 2101(50).

International argues that this result is illogical because sonar surveying is very different from traditional towing and, as the jury heard, existing towing regulations and licensing training programs do not address the towing of submerged objects like the towfish. We will avoid interpreting a statute to produce absurd results "if alternative interpretations consistent with legislative purpose are available." *Griffin v. Oceanic Contractors, Inc.*, 458 U.S. 564, 575 (1982). But our holding here produces no absurd results. As outlined above, the statutory definition of towing vessel is limited to vessels that engage in pulling, pushing, or hauling as a commercial service. Even if current towing industry practices are a poor fit for sonar surveying, applying towing regulations to the commercial towing of submerged objects is not "so bizarre that Congress 'could not have intended' it." *Demarest v. Manspeaker*, 498 U.S. 184, 191 (1991) (quoting *Griffin*, 458 U.S. at 575). Although International has described policy concerns, "it is not our task to assess the consequences of each approach and adopt the one that produces the least mischief." **{-922-}** *Lewis v. City of Chicago,* 560 U.S. 205, 217 (2010). We must "give effect to the law Congress enacted." *Id.*

[3] International briefly argues that the THUNDER is not a "commercial" vessel because it does not meet the statute's definition of "commercial service." "[C]ommercial service" is defined to include "any type of trade or business involving the transportation of goods or individuals, except service performed by a combatant vessel." 46 U.S.C. § 2101(4). International asserts that the THUNDER was not transporting personnel or cargo in commerce within the meaning of traditional maritime jurisprudence. But International failed to present this argument to the district court, and has therefore forfeited it on appeal. *See Celanese Corp. v. Martin K. Eby Constr. Co.*, 620 F.3d 529, 531 (5th Cir. 2010). Regardless, the term "commercial service" is broad enough to cover the THUNDER's commercial activity in transporting Tesla's equipment.

Moreover, we perceive no acceptable alternative offered by International's interpretation of the statute. International contends that the category of towing vessels should be limited to "traditional" towing activities, and specifically to one vessel helping another vessel make a voyage. This argument has no basis in the statutory text, and we find little support for such a restrictive definition of towing. Current Coast Guard regulations define a tow as "the barge(s), vessel(s), or object(s) being pulled, pushed, or hauled alongside **[—8—]** a towing vessel." 46 C.F.R. § 136.110. This definition expressly contemplates that a towing vessel may tow objects other than vessels.[4] The Supreme Court has similarly explained that a structure can "mov[e] under tow" without qualifying as a vessel. *Lozman*, 568 U.S. at 121-22, 1 Adm. R. at 3–4; *see also Evansville & Bowling Green Packet Co. v. Chero Cola Bottling Co.*, 271 U.S. 19, 20-22 (1926) (holding that a wharfboat towed each year to a winter location was not a vessel). As the Government notes in its brief, accepting the definition proposed by International would permit the transportation of large and potentially dangerous objects without a towing license.

International's reliance on *Sacramento Navigation Co. v. Salz*, 273 U.S. 326 (1927), is unavailing. In *Salz*, the Supreme Court considered whether a contract for the shipment of goods became a towage contract simply because the goods were placed on a barge towed by a steamer. *Id.* at 328. The shipping company owned both the barge and the steamer. *Id.* at 327. The Court reasoned that "the contract actually made with respondent was not to tow a vessel, but to transport goods, and plainly that contract was a contract of affreightment." *Id.* at 328. Although *Salz* refers to towage as "the employment of one vessel to expedite the voyage of another," the Court did not address whether pulling non-vessel objects through water would also constitute towing. *Id.* Our recent opinion in *Continental Insurance Co. v. L & L Transportation, Inc.*, 882 F.3d 566, 6 Adm. R. 187 (5th Cir. 2018), is similarly inapposite. On a question of contract interpretation, we held that one vessel was not the "tow" of another vessel because it did not receive any motive power and was not pushed or pulled in any way. *Id.* at 571-72, 6 Adm. R. at 190. The towing of non-vessels was not at issue in that case. **[—9—]** As noted above, the Supreme Court has recently made clear that non-vessels can be "towed." *Lozman*, 568 U.S. at 122, 1 Adm. R. at 4.

Nor do we accept International's alternative position that towing involves assisting the voyage of a vessel or object from one point to another rather than pulling equipment around a work area. The statute does not limit where or when the "pushing, pulling, or hauling along side" can occur. And whether the towfish was placed in the water at port or at sea has no apparent bearing on what regulations should apply. Finally, it is not determinative that the THUNDER was documented as an offshore supply vessel rather than a towing vessel. A vessel can fall into more than one statutory category. *See* 46 U.S.C. § 3302(a)(1). Accordingly, the district court did not err in instructing the jury that the THUNDER was a towing **{-923-}** vessel and that its captain lacked a towing credential.

III.

In its cross-appeal, Tesla challenges the jury's allocation of fault and the district court's calculation of International's contribution liability.

A.

Tesla filed a post-trial motion for judgment as a matter of law arguing that the jury erred in not finding International at least 50% at fault for Shell's damages. The district court denied this motion. We review de novo the denial of a motion for judgment as a matter of law. *E.E.O.C. v. Boh Bros. Constr. Co., LLC*, 731 F.3d 444, 451 (5th Cir. 2013) (en banc). We are "especially deferential" to jury verdicts. *Id.* Judgment as a matter of law is appropriate only if "the facts and inferences point 'so strongly and overwhelmingly in the

[4] Although this regulation was not in place at the time of the events in question, it supports the view that towing is not generally understood to be limited to towing other vessels.

movant's favor that reasonable jurors could not reach a contrary conclusion.'" *Id.* (quoting *Baisden v. I'm Ready Prods., Inc.*, 693 F.3d 491, 498 (5th Cir. 2012)). We will not disturb a jury verdict so long as there is "substantial evidence, in the light most favorable to the successful party, to support the **[—10—]** verdict." *Am. Home Assurance Co. v. United Space All., LLC*, 378 F.3d 482, 487 (5th Cir. 2004).

The jury's allocation of 75% fault to Tesla and 25% to International has ample support in the record. The jury heard testimony that Tesla had information from Shell regarding the location of the drilling rig and the layout of its submerged mooring lines but failed to share this information with the crew of the THUNDER. International also offered considerable evidence that its captain's lack of a towing license was unrelated to the cause of the accident. Tesla did not contest that it controlled the implementation of the survey. Further, a Shell employee testified at trial that Tesla failed to provide him with timely and accurate information about the accident, causing Shell to incur additional damages. Although Tesla maintains that it acted in good faith after the allision, the jury was free to weigh the evidence and reach its own conclusions regarding Tesla's actions.

Tesla argues that the jury should nevertheless have found International to be at least equally at fault for Shell's damages because the captain of the THUNDER lacked experience in sonar surveying, failed to pay attention to the location of the towfish and possible collision risks, and violated other legal duties. In support of this position, Tesla cites numerous cases in which vessels were found to be 50% or more at fault for accidents. The referenced cases are factually dissimilar from the circumstances here, and none involved the reversal of a jury verdict. It is for the jury, and not the court, "to weigh conflicting evidence and inferences, and determine the credibility of witnesses." *Boh Bros. Constr. Co.*, 731 F.3d at 452 (quoting *Roman v. W. Mfg., Inc.*, 691 F.3d 686, 692 (5th Cir. 2012)). Although there was some evidence of fault by International and its employees, a reasonable jury could nonetheless find Tesla more responsible for Shell's damages. **[—11—]**

B.

Tesla also appeals the district court's calculation of the contribution amount due by International. After trial, International paid Shell $244,918.99 in partial satisfaction of judgment. This payment was in lieu of posting a supersedeas bond, and without prejudice to International's right to challenge the judgment on appeal. Tesla and Shell later agreed to settle all of Shell's claims in exchange for **{-924-}** $8,771,918.99. The settlement agreement states that this sum resolves "any liability or damages owed by Tesla Offshore and International" and "is to be funded in two parts: (a) by $8,527,000 in new money from the Tesla Underwriters to be paid on or before December 19, 2016, and (b) by $244,918.99 in funds previously collected by Shell from International."

Following the settlement, Tesla argued that it was entitled to contribution from International. The district court entered summary judgment in favor of Tesla on its contribution claim and held that International owed Tesla $1,948.060.76. This represented 25% of the total settlement amount, minus the $244,918.99 previously paid by International. On appeal, Tesla argues that International is not entitled to credit for its earlier payment to Shell because this payment was conditional on the outcome of the appeal. As part of the settlement agreement, Tesla agreed to indemnify Shell if International prevails on appeal and becomes entitled to repayment of some of its money.

But Tesla does not dispute that International actually paid the amount in question, and that Shell kept the money. It is clear from the language of the settlement agreement that International's partial payment was credited toward the total amount due and therefore reduced the amount of new money owed by Tesla. There is no logical basis to require International to make the **[—12—]** same payment twice, especially when Tesla already received the benefit of the first payment.

In the alternative, Tesla argues that International's payment should be credited to both International and Tesla because the parties are jointly liable. Tesla offers no legal authority for this proposition. Notably, the district court gave Tesla sole credit for the $8,527,000 it contributed to the settlement. Tesla does not contest this decision, and does not explain why International's payment should be treated differently. We see no error in the district court's contribution calculations. AFFIRMED.

United States Court of Appeals
for the Fifth Circuit

No. 17-30792

STATE BANK & TRUST CO.
VS.
C&G LIFTBOATS, L.L.C.

Appeal from the United States District Court for the Eastern District of Louisiana

Decided: October 16, 2018

Citation: 906 F.3d 361, 6 Adm. R. 268 (5th Cir. 2018).

Before **KING, SOUTHWICK,** and **HO,** Circuit Judges.

[—1—] {-361-} SOUTHWICK, Circuit Judge:

The district court granted summary judgment to the plaintiff, holding that the plaintiff had a preferred ship mortgage under the Ship Mortgage Act. The defendants appealed. The district court's order, though, did not finally determine the rights or obligations of the parties in this dispute, which leaves us without jurisdiction.

The appeal is DISMISSED. **[—2—]**

FACTUAL AND PROCEDURAL BACKGROUND **{-362-}**

The plaintiff State Bank & Trust Company sought to foreclose on four ship mortgages and seize three vessels owned by defendants C&G Liftboats, LLC and AMC Liftboats, Inc. The defendants argued in the district court that there was no subject matter jurisdiction to hear the plaintiff's claim in admiralty because the underlying mortgages used to secure the vessels were invalid under Louisiana law, and therefore could not be valid preferred ship mortgages under the Ship Mortgage Act. The district court denied the defendants' motion to dismiss and granted in part the plaintiff's motion for summary judgment, holding that a collateral chattel mortgage, even if invalid under Louisiana law, meets the requirements of the Ship Mortgage Act. *See* 46 U.S.C. §§ 31321, 31322.

The limit of the district court's order was to recognize that the plaintiff had a preferred ship mortgage under the Ship Mortgage Act on the vessel "Lil Al," allowing the plaintiff to proceed in its foreclosure action in federal court. The district court did not grant judgment on the plaintiff's claim that the defendants defaulted nor hold that the relevant mortgage was enforceable. The defendants appealed the district court's order. Jurisdiction was claimed under 28 U.S.C. § 1292(a)(3). The district court stayed further proceedings pending our resolution of the appeal.

DISCUSSION

Under 28 U.S.C. § 1292(a)(3), "the courts of appeals . . . have jurisdiction of appeals from . . . interlocutory decrees of . . . district courts . . . determining the rights and liabilities of the parties to admiralty cases in which appeals from final decrees are allowed." Section 1292(a)(3) is construed narrowly; it does not "permit interlocutory appeals in admiralty except where the order . . . had the effect of ultimately determining the rights and obligations of the parties." **[—3—]** *Treasure Salvors, Inc. v. Unidentified Wrecked and Abandoned Sailing Vessel*, 640 F.2d 560, 564 (5th Cir. 1981). "Orders which do not determine parties' substantive rights or liabilities . . . are not appealable under section 1292(a)(3), even if those orders have important procedural consequences." *Celtic Marine Corp. v. James C. Justice Companies, Inc.*, 760 F.3d 477, 480, 2 Adm. R. 288, 290 (5th Cir. 2014) (quoting *Francis v. Forest Oil Corp.*, 798 F.2d 147, 150 (5th Cir. 1986)). An order which merely permits a party to proceed in an action is not sufficiently final to grant jurisdiction under Section 1292(a)(3). *Id.* at 480-81, 2 Adm. R. at 290.

In *Celtic Marine*, we held there to be no jurisdiction to hear an appeal of a district court order re-opening a case under Federal Rule of Civil Procedure 60(b). *Id.*, 2 Adm. R. at 290. The **{-363-}** motion sought to re-open the case in order to enforce a settlement agreement. *Id.* at 480, 2 Adm. R. at 289. The order granting the motion made a procedural ruling but was not a grant of final relief. *Id.* at 480-81, 2 Adm. R. at 290.

Here, the district court's order finally determined that the plaintiff has a preferred ship mortgage on "Lil Al," but deferred all other requests for relief. For example, the district court's order did not find that the defendants defaulted on the collateral mortgages. The defendants deny the allegation in the plaintiff's complaint that they were in default.

The district court's order holding that the plaintiff had a valid preferred ship mortgage on Lil Al merely allows the plaintiff to proceed on its foreclosure action in federal court. The district court did not finally determine the parties' rights as to Lil Al, and we therefore lack appellate jurisdiction under Section 1292(a)(3).

The defendants refer us to decisions in which we found jurisdiction under Section 1292(a)(3). In one case, we reviewed an order in which the district court held that one creditor's claim had priority over another against a vessel, the proceeds of which would satisfy only one of the debts. *Bank One, Louisiana N.A. v. Mr. Dean MV*, 293 F.3d 830, 831-32 (5th Cir. 2002). We had jurisdiction **[—4—]** because the summary judgment order disposed of the appealing party's rights in the vessel, as the question of priority was the final issue to be decided. *Id.* In the other case cited by the defendants, we held that interlocutory sale orders are appealable under Section 1292(a)(3). *Silver Star Enters., Inc. v. M/V Saramacca*, 19 F.3d 1008, 1012-13 (5th Cir. 1994). Jurisdiction exists in that circumstance because an interlocutory sale order extinguishes the owners' rights in a vessel, thus satisfying the finality requirement of Section 1292(a)(3). *Id.* at 1013.

In the present case, the district court's order permitted the plaintiff to continue in its foreclosure action and explicitly deferred all the plaintiff's other requests for relief. Therefore, the district court's order did not ultimately determine the "rights and liabilities of the parties." 28 U.S.C. § 1292(a)(3).

DISMISSED.

United States Court of Appeals
for the Fifth Circuit

No. 17-30122

IN RE DEEPWATER HORIZON

BARRERA
VS.
BP, P.L.C.

Appeals from the United States District Court for the Eastern District of Louisiana

Decided: October 18, 2018

Citation: 907 F.3d 232, 6 Adm. R. 270 (5th Cir. 2018).

Before **KING, ELROD,** and **HAYNES,** Circuit Judges.

[—2—] {-233-} PER CURIAM:

This case presents another in the line of cases related to the Deepwater Horizon oil spill. The 104 appellants here (collectively referred to as "Plaintiffs") appeal the district **{-234-}** court's order dismissing their claims with prejudice. We AFFIRM.

I. Background

Plaintiffs are individuals and associations located in Mexico that rely on the fishing industry as a primary source of income. They are a part of the remaining group of plaintiffs from multidistrict litigation ("MDL") 2179, which was created following the Deepwater Horizon accident in 2010 to ensure that the people and entities affected by the accident with legitimate claims could recover from appellees, various corporate entities of British Petroleum, collectively referred to as "BP."

Following settlements of certain claims in the MDL, the district court issued pretrial order 60 ("PTO 60"), which required that all remaining individuals or entities whose claims had not been settled file individual lawsuits with the district court. Plaintiffs, along with other foreign plaintiffs, **[—3—]** filed a complaint which was transferred to the MDL court in May 2013. Significantly, PTO 60 required individual lawsuits to have a wet-ink signature from each plaintiff, to be received by the court by May 2, 2016. PTO 60 warned that non-compliance would result in "dismissal of their claims with prejudice without further notice."

Plaintiffs' attorneys filed a motion for extension of time and requested an additional ninety days to comply with PTO 60. They stated that they needed the additional time because they represented 1510 plaintiffs and it would be logistically difficult to comply. The district court granted a fourteen-day extension, but emphasized that "[n]o further extensions of time will be granted."

Plaintiffs' attorneys then filed a second motion for extension of time and explained that they were having technical filing issues, and that they had "clients that [were] out of town, out of the country, or working offshore and unable to respond to counsel in the 48-day window and [could] not provide the sworn declaration." The district court did not rule on the motion, and Plaintiffs did not properly file their declarations by the deadline. The district court then issued a show cause order, mandating that plaintiffs that failed to comply with PTO 60 "show cause in writing on or before June 28, 2016, why this Court should not dismiss their B1 claim(s) with prejudice for failing to comply with the requirements of PTO 60."

Plaintiffs' attorneys argued that: (1) certain plaintiffs should be granted additional time to submit the signed declaration, (2) other plaintiffs had, since the deadline, filed an individual declaration and had an individual lawsuit filed, and (3) the plaintiffs in the mass joinder complaint needed additional time to comply because of a "lack of electronic means, working offshore, inaccessibility, and change of contact information." BP countered that any plaintiffs that had not complied with PTO 60 by that time should be dismissed. **[—4—]**

On December 16, 2016, the district court dismissed Plaintiffs' claims with prejudice. Plaintiffs filed a motion for reconsideration on January 13, 2017, and the district court denied that motion. Plaintiffs appeal the dismissal of their claims with prejudice and the denial of their Rule 59(e) and 60(b) motions.

II. Standard of Review

We review matters concerning docket management for an abuse of discretion. *See Garcia v. Woman's Hosp. of Tex.*, 143 F.3d 227, 229 (5th Cir. 1998) (per curiam). "A trial court abuses its discretion when its ruling is based on an erroneous view of the law or a clearly erroneous assessment of the evidence." **{-235-}** *Elementis Chromium v. Coastal States Petroleum*, 450 F.3d 607, 610 (5th Cir. 2006) (internal quotation marks omitted) (quoting *Bocanegra v. Vicmar Servs., Inc.*, 320 F.3d 581, 584 (5th Cir. 2003)).

III. Discussion

The parties agree that dismissal with prejudice is only permissible where there is "a clear record of delay or contumacious conduct by the plaintiff" and "where lesser sanctions would not serve the best interests of justice."[1] *Sealed Appellant v. Sealed Appellee*, 452 F.3d 415, 417 (5th Cir. 2006) (quoting *Rogers v. Kroger Co.*, 669 F.2d 317, 320 (5th Cir. 1982)). However, as two of our sister circuits have held, there is a special deference required in the context of an **[—5—]** MDL.[2] The ability for "judges to enforce orders pertaining to the progress of their cases" is most important in "[MDL] cases, where the very purpose of the centralization before the transferee judge is the efficient progress of the cases in preparation for trial." *In re Asbestos Prod. Liab. Litig. (No. VI)*, 718 F.3d 236, 248 (3d Cir. 2013).

A. *Clear Record of Delay or Contumacious Conduct*

Plaintiffs argue that the district court abused its discretion in making dismissal with prejudice the remedy for failing to comply with PTO 60. However, Plaintiffs repeatedly failed to provide the district court with any affidavits or other documentation to corroborate and explain their reasons for needing an extension of time. At first, Plaintiffs' attorneys stated that, "[l]ogistically, it is impossible to file each lawsuit individually after obtaining a signed declaration signed by each litigant by the deadline." But hundreds of other plaintiffs complied with PTO 60, demonstrating it was not logistically impossible. Despite receiving a fourteen-day extension with an explicit warning that no further extensions of time would be granted, Plaintiffs did not comply with PTO 60.

When Plaintiffs were ordered to show cause for why their claims should not be dismissed, they responded that "a number of the clients could not be reached within the time allotted by the Court," as they "were travelling, worked offshore for extended periods of time, do not have access to phones, computers, faxes, and/or are abroad." But Plaintiffs still did not submit any documentation or other evidence to the district court corroborating their **[—6—]** explanation for the delay, nor did they show that their attorneys had attempted to contact the non-compliant plaintiffs. Plaintiffs **{-236-}** were also given an opportunity to reply to BP's objections to their response to the show cause order, but provided the same explanation and once again, did not provide any corroborating

---

[1] Although our prior analysis surrounding whether a dismissal with prejudice is proper has predominantly been in the context of effectuating service and involuntary dismissal for failure to prosecute under Federal Rule of Civil Procedure 41(b), we have also indicated that the same standard applies in the case of dismissals with prejudice related to docket management. *See, e.g., Price v. McGathery*, 792 F.2d 472, 474–75 (5th Cir. 1986) (per curiam). There have been, however, variations in the standard's precise language. *Compare Sealed Appellant v. Sealed Appellee*, 452 F.3d 415, 417 (5th Cir. 2006) *with Tello v. C.I.R.*, 410 F.3d 743, 744 (5th Cir. 2005). We need not decide the exact parameters because, even assuming arguendo that we should apply the standard most favorable to the appellants here, they still do not prevail. Finally, aggravating factors are not required for a dismissal with prejudice. *Sealed Appellant*, 452 F.3d at 418.

[2] *See, e.g., In re Asbestos Prod. Liab. Litig. (No. VI)*, 718 F.3d 236, 243 (3d Cir. 2013) ("We review a district court's interpretation of its own orders with deference, particularly in the MDL context."); *In re Fannie Mae Sec. Litig.*, 552 F.3d 814, 822 (D.C. Cir. 2009) ("District judges must have authority to manage their dockets, especially during massive litigation such as this [MDL], and we owe deference to their decisions whether and how to enforce the deadlines they impose.").

documentation. In fact, aside from a few untimely individuals, Plaintiffs *never* filed sworn declarations that complied with PTO 60.[3] Nor have Plaintiffs provided records of calls or letters to show that their attorneys unsuccessfully attempted to contact them. Their attorneys have not procured affidavits from Plaintiffs, or representatives of Plaintiffs, indicating why a plaintiff could not be reached. Given the number of opportunities the district court gave Plaintiffs to either comply with PTO 60, explain why they could not do so, or show documentation of their attorneys' efforts, we hold Plaintiffs' failure to comply with PTO 60 constitutes a clear record of delay.[4]

B. *Lesser Sanctions and the Best Interests of Justice*

We next consider whether lesser sanctions would serve the best interests of justice. "Lesser sanctions include '[a]ssessments of fines, costs, or damages against the plaintiff . . . conditional dismissal, dismissal without prejudice, and explicit warnings.'" *Thrasher v. City of Amarillo*, 709 F.3d 509, 514 (5th Cir. 2013) (alterations in original) (quoting *Rogers*, 669 F.2d at 321–22). When it issued PTO 60, the district court expressly warned that non-compliance would lead to dismissal with prejudice. When the district court granted Plaintiffs' **[—7—]** extension request, it expressly stated no further extension would be granted. Even when Plaintiffs did not comply, the district court gave Plaintiffs multiple opportunities to explain why their claims should not be dismissed.

It is also unclear what lesser sanctions could have been appropriate following the district court's warnings and second chances. In issuing PTO 60, the district court sought to streamline proceedings by having all the remaining claims in the MDL filed in the same manner, each as an individual lawsuit. Any sanction other than dismissal would not achieve the desired effect of PTO 60, and would further delay the district court's efforts to adjudicate the MDL expeditiously. *See In re Asbestos*, 718 F.3d at 248.

In addition, unfortunately, there have been fraudulent claims filed on behalf of fictitious plaintiffs related to the Deepwater Horizon accident. *See, e.g., United States v. Warren*, 728 F. App'x 249, 251–52 (5th Cir. 2018) (per curiam), *cert. denied*, No. 17-9350, 2018 WL 3009122 (U.S. Oct. 1, 2018). Dismissal with prejudice is a proper remedy to prevent lawsuits from non-existent plaintiffs, which further hamper the resolution of meritorious claims by real plaintiffs. The district court's explicit warnings and second chances illustrate that lesser sanctions would not serve the best interests of justice.

For the reasons stated above, Plaintiffs' conduct satisfies both prongs of the standard for dismissing with prejudice. Thus, the district court did not abuse its discretion **{-237-}** in dismissing Plaintiffs' claims with prejudice.

AFFIRMED.

---

[3] The plaintiffs who filed untimely declarations still failed to provide any reasonable explanation for the delay, despite numerous opportunities to do so. Nor did they provide evidence showing their attorneys had attempted to contact them.

[4] We recently upheld the same district court's decision to dismiss other plaintiffs' claims with prejudice based on their failure to comply with PTO 60—even after being given numerous opportunities to do so. *In re Deepwater Horizon*, 713 F. App'x 360, 362 (5th Cir. 2018) (per curiam), *cert. denied, Perez v. B.P., P.L.C.*, No.18-59, 2018 WL 3377965 (U.S. Oct. 1, 2018).

United States Court of Appeals for the Fifth Circuit

No. 17-30949

BP EXPLORATION & PROD., INC.
vs.
CLAIMANT ID 100094497

Appeal from the United States District Court for the Eastern District of Louisiana

Decided: November 9, 2018

Citation: 910 F.3d 797, 6 Adm. R. 273 (5th Cir. 2018).

Before **JONES, BARKSDALE,** and **WILLETT,** Circuit Judges.

[—1—] {-798-} JONES, Circuit Judge:

Appellant BP unsuccessfully sought discretionary review of an Appeal Panel's calculation of lost profits owed to the Appellee under the Deepwater Horizon Economic and Property Damages Class Action Settlement Agreement ("E&P Settlement Agreement"). Because the Appeal Panels are split and this Appeal Panel misapplied the distinction between fixed and variable costs under the Business Economic Loss formula, the district court abused its discretion in failing to correct the significant legal error. We VACATE and REMAND for further proceedings consistent with this opinion. **[—2—]**

BACKGROUND

The E&P Settlement Agreement was negotiated between BP and various class action representatives in the aftermath of **{-799-}** the 2010 *Deepwater Horizon* oil spill and provides compensation for claimants harmed by the spill. The Court Supervised Settlement Program ("CSSP") is responsible for administering and processing claims made under the Settlement Agreement. Accounting firms including Price Waterhouse Cooper perform the initial analysis to verify and compute the claims. The Appellee, Texas Gulf Seafood, Inc. ("Texas Gulf Seafood"), is a Texas corporation that serves as an intermediary for Texas gulf shrimpers, freezing and packing shrimp and arranging for delivery to wholesalers. Texas Gulf Seafood filed a Business Economic Loss ("BEL") claim with the CSSP on August 2, 2012.

BEL claims are calculated using a two-step process prescribed by Exhibit 4C of the Settlement Agreement. We describe the pertinent provisions here without recapitulating the complete, more complex formula contained in the Settlement Agreement. Step 1 Compensation focuses on the claimant's "reduction in profit between the 2010 Compensation Period" and a "Benchmark Period" of comparable months before the spill. Step 2 Compensation provides for incremental profits a claimant might have generated in the period after the *Deepwater Horizon* spill if the incident had never occurred.

Variable Profit is central to calculating damages in a BEL Claim. Step 1 Compensation is determined by calculating "the difference in Variable Profit between the 2010 Compensation Period selected by the claimant and the Variable Profit over the comparable months of the Benchmark Period." Variable Profit, in turn, is defined as the sum of monthly revenue over the Benchmark Period minus variable costs identified in Exhibit 4D, among others. Thus, whether a cost is defined as "variable" (and factored into **[—3—]** Variable Profit calculations) or "fixed" (and excluded from such calculations) can significantly alter the size of an award.

Exhibit 4D of the Settlement Agreement contains a detailed list of costs stipulated by the parties to be "variable" or "fixed." Contract labor, consumable goods, freight, and fuel are among the items defined as "variable expenses," for example. *Id.* "Fixed" expenses include, inter alia, internet fees, postage, and uniforms. Notably, for purposes of this dispute supplies are deemed "fixed." *Id.*

The CSSP initially calculated a base compensation amount of $322,459.22 for Texas Gulf Seafood, resulting in a total award of $1.33 million.[1] Before generating this award, CSSP asked Texas Gulf Seafood to explain the large "supplies" category listed on the profits and loss statement the company submitted with its claim. Texas Gulf Seafood responded that the "supplies" in this case included "items which are used to unload, process, and package shrimp, such as packing bags and other materials." CSSP disagreed with Texas Gulf Seafood's classification of those materials as "fixed" and concluded that, because the expenses fluctuated based on the amount of shrimp the company shipped, the costs "appear[ed] to be more in line with consumable goods" than "supplies." The claims administrators therefore re-categorized Texas Gulf Seafood's expenses as "variable" rather than "fixed" and calculated Texas Gulf Seafood's award accordingly.

Texas Gulf Seafood sought reconsideration of the award, based on its assertion that the "supplies" line item referenced **{–800–}** more than just "packing bags and other materials." Upon review, CSSP found that Texas Gulf Seafood's "supplies" consisted primarily of "consumable goods" and recalculated the **[—4—]** award, increasing it slightly from $1.33 million to $1.34 million. Texas Gulf Seafood asked CSSP to visit the matter a third time, but CSSP declined.

Still dissatisfied, Texas Gulf Seafood appealed its CSSP award to an Appeal Panel, which, under the Settlement Agreement, reviews CSSP awards *de novo*. Texas Gulf Seafood argued that CSSP should have deferred to its business judgment when it categorized the costs as "supplies," or alternatively, that CSSP should have categorized some of the costs as fixed and some as variable. Texas Gulf Seafood proposed a base compensation award of $640,124.47. The Appeal Panel agreed with Texas Gulf Seafood, reversed the CSSP award, and granted Texas Gulf Seafood its requested base compensation of $640,124.47, nearly doubling the total award to $2.56 million. The Appeal Panel determined that only 31-45% of the "supplies" category related to the cost of goods sold cited by CSSP when it reclassified the materials. Therefore, Texas Gulf Seafood had a "rational basis" for classifying the costs the way it did and CSSP had "insufficient ground[s]" for reclassifying them.

BP sought discretionary review of the Appeal Panel's decision by the district court, but the district court denied the request. BP now appeals this denial.

STANDARD OF REVIEW

This court reviews a district court's denial of discretionary review for abuse of discretion. *See Claimant ID 100212278 v. BP Expl. & Prod. Inc.*, 848 F.3d 407, 410, 5 Adm. R. 202, 203 (5th Cir. 2017). A district court abuses its discretion if an Appeal Panel decision not reviewed by the district court contradicted or misapplied the Settlement Agreement, or had the clear potential to contradict or misapply the Settlement Agreement. *Holmes Motors v. BP Expl. & Prod., Inc.*, 829 F.3d 313, 315, 4 Adm. R. 263, 263 (5th Cir. 2016) (internal citation omitted). A district court also abuses its discretion if it denies a request for review that "raises a recurring issue on which the Appeal Panels are split if 'the resolution of the **[—5—]** question will substantially impact the administration of the Agreement.'" *Claimant ID 100212278*, 848 F.3d at 410, 5 Adm. R. at 203 (quoting *In re Deepwater Horizon*, 632 F. App'x 199, 203-04 (5th Cir. 2015)). Nevertheless, the district court need not grant review of all claims that raise questions about the proper interpretation of the Settlement Agreement and does not abuse its discretion if it denies a request for review that "involve[s] no pressing question of how the Settlement Agreement should be interpreted and implemented, but simply raise[s] the correctness of a discretionary administrative decision in the facts of a single claimant's case." *Id.*, 5 Adm. R. at 203 (quoting *In re Deepwater Horizon*, 641 F. App'x 405, 410 (5th Cir. 2016)); *Holmes*, 829 F.3d at 316, 4 Adm. R. at 264.

---

[1] The first award was remanded for reconsideration in light of an intervening Fifth Circuit decision, *In re Deepwater Horizon II*, 744 F.3d 370, 378, 2 Adm. R. 183, 187 (5th Cir. 2014), but it is unnecessary to repeat the entire procedural history here.

DISCUSSION

Texas Gulf Seafood characterizes this case as a garden-variety factual dispute among several hundred thousand claims processed under this Settlement Agreement. But the issue raised by BP implicates the core of the Settlement Agreement. This court must determine whether the Settlement Agreement allows Appeal Panels to classify expenses as "fixed" or "variable" based on the way claimants label the expenses in documents supporting their losses, or whether it requires Appeal Panels to use independent judgment to classify expenses according to their substantive nature. Texas Gulf Seafood argues for the former approach, while BP urges the latter. **{–801–}**

The Settlement Agreement must "be interpreted in accordance with General Maritime Law," rather than state law. *See In re Deepwater Horizon*, 785 F.3d 986, 994, 3 Adm. R. 341, 345 (5th Cir. 2015) (quoting Settlement Agreement 36.1); *Int'l Marine, L.L.C. v. Delta Towing, L.L.C.*, 704 F.3d 350, 354, 1 Adm. R. 188, 190 (5th Cir. 2013). A settlement agreement "is a contract." *E.E.O.C. v. Exxon Corp.*, 202 F.3d 755, 757 (5th Cir. 2000) (internal quotation marks omitted). Under admiralty law, contracts "should be read as a whole and [their] words given their plain meaning unless the provision is ambiguous." *Breaux v. Halliburton Energy* **[—6—]** *Servs.*, 562 F.3d 358, 364 (5th Cir. 2009) (quotation marks and citation omitted).

Here, the parties disagree about the correct process for classifying expenses as "fixed" or "variable" under the Settlement Agreement. BP asserts that "[t]he only reasonable interpretation of [Exhibit 4D's list of classifications] is that expenses must be classified as fixed or variable according to their nature." Under this interpretation, Texas Gulf Seafood's use of packing and shipping materials, labels, and carbon dioxide are properly categorized as variable expenses because they "all vary in proportion to the amount of shrimp processed by the company . . . ." Texas Gulf Seafood responds that the proper approach, followed by the Appeals Panel in this case, is to evaluate the claimants' own categorization of their expenses under a "rational basis" standard and then "appl[y] the Settlement Agreement as written."

When the expense category provided by a claimant contains a mix of variable costs and fixed costs, claims administrators have previously held that "[i]f an expense does not fit the description of the [v]ariable or [f]ixed expense categories in Exhibit 4D [], the [CSSP] will use discretion to apply the classification that best conforms to delineations made by the Parties . . . ." They have also recognized situations in which the CSSP "must make a determination whether an expense which Claimant labels as 'Supplies' is better classified as some other type of expense (such as variable cost of goods sold or consumable goods)." Further, when a party "uses a description that does not fit the actual expense, the description should be re-defined more accurately and a determination made based on what category most closely approximates that determination." *Id.* In other words, "[i]t is [the] duty [of] panelists to look beyond mere labelling of an item to discern in a *de novo* review whether it truly conforms to its label." 21 A.P.D 2015-1152. **[—7—]**

Both parties agree that the list of expenses in the "supplies" category of Texas Gulf Seafood's original profit and loss statements and tax returns was only partially accurate, because variable expenses, *i.e.*, costs that varied directly with the amount of shrimp handled by the company, comprised approximately 40% of the costs that Texas Gulf Seafood initially categorized as "fixed." Despite admitting that its initial classification was inaccurate, however, Texas Gulf Seafood argues for a claims regime that essentially takes claimants at their word and classifies items as they request. BP correctly notes that adopting such an approach would lead to "absurd results," in which the CSSP could find itself "classify[ing] identical costs enumerated in Exhibit 4D as fixed [in one claim and] variable" in another, depending on each claimant's choice.

In short, Texas Gulf Seafood wants the claims process to resemble a blank check that claimants fill out, panelists rubber stamp, and BP pays. That is not the arrangement prescribed in the Settlement Agreement. The Agreement provides for accountants from Price Waterhouse Cooper and other firms to review claims and **{-802-}** supporting documents and determine an appropriate level of compensation for the claimants. The parties would not have authorized accounting experts to review claims if they intended Appeal Panels simply to defer to claimants' descriptions. This structure is inconsistent with the permissive standard urged by Texas Gulf Seafood and applied by the Appeal Panel in this case.

As the Appellee acknowledges, "the Exhibit 4D expense classifications were the subject of intense and protracted negotiations by the parties, are tantamount to a stipulation and may not be lightly disregarded" because they are "binding upon the Settlement Program." Exhibit 4D characterizes forty-six separate types of expenses as "fixed" or "variable" (twenty-nine types of fixed expenses and seventeen types of variable expenses). It distinguishes, for **[—8—]** instance, between "maintenance" (a fixed cost) and "repairs (excluding maintenance)" (a variable cost), and between "supplies" (fixed cost) and "[cost of goods sold]" and "consumable goods" (both variable costs). These distinctions utilize the customary understanding of cost allocation in the accounting business.[2] The parties' attention to detail evinces a common understanding that the substantive nature of claimants' expenses is critical to determining a fair settlement. Exhibit 4D of the Settlement Agreement represents a categorical approach that is inconsistent with the approach advocated by Texas Gulf Seafood.

Texas Gulf Seafood asserts repeatedly that the Appeal Panels have used a rational basis test for evaluating claimants' classifications but cites no case using that language other than the case below. BP locates one other panel decision that takes the approach urged by Texas Gulf Seafood, *Claim Number 303174*. In that instance, an Appeal Panel ignored evidence that "Auto Expenses" listed as "fixed" by the claimant likely referenced mileage or fuel and should have been classified as "variable" instead. For that panel, the fact that the claimant described the expense as "fixed" was evidence enough that it was indeed fixed. The decision in *Claim Number 303174*, however, does not help Texas Gulf Seafood. That another Appeal Panel also deferred to the claimant's classification under the Settlement Agreement proves only that more than one panel has misapplied the Agreement and reinforces the need to clarify the proper standard for evaluating claimants' listed expenses. **[—9—]**

Thus, this court holds that the Settlement Agreement requires claims administrators to use their independent judgment and classify expenses as "fixed" or "variable" according to their substantive nature, rather than rational basis review of the claimants' own descriptions. Appeal Panels, too, are bound by the substantive nature of the expense claims under the Settlement Agreement rather than the claimants' inaccurate characterizations.

As applied here, Attachment A's categorical list of fixed and variable costs may require that some costs be allocated according to their substantive nature. For instance, the distinction accepted by the parties is that somewhere between 30-40% of Texas Gulf Seafood's claimed fixed cost "supplies" related to shrimp packaging and freezing costs that are actually variable **{-803-}** with its product output ("consumable supplies"). Whether the evaluative process is denominated allocation or reclassification, these costs should be placed in substantively correct categories.

CONCLUSION

Because the Appeal Panel here misapplied Exhibits 4C and 4D and Attachment A to 4D

---

[2] A "variable cost" is a business expense that "will vary in direct proportion to changes in the level of [a business] activity. For example, direct material, direct labor, sales commissions, fuel cost for a trucking company, and so on, may be expected to increase with each additional unit of output. . . . The opposite of variable costs are fixed costs. Fixed costs do not fluctuate with changes in the level of activity." LARRY WALTHER & CHRISTOPHER SKOUSEN, MANAGERIAL AND COST ACCOUNTING 37-38 (2009).

of the Settlement Agreement, and the district court erred in failing to review and correct this error of law, we **VACATE** the award and **REMAND** for further proceedings consistent with this opinion.

(Reporter's Note: Dissenting Opinion follows on p. 278).

[—10—] {-803-} BARKSDALE, Circuit Judge, dissenting in part:

I concur, *dubitante*, in holding the district court abused its discretion by not reviewing the appeal-panel's decision. But, in the many iterations of the Deepwater Horizon settlement-agreement litigation, our case law does not accord with the majority's decision to rule on the underlying legal issue, rather than reverse and remand, in the absence of *any* district-court decision on the merits of that issue. Nor is the issue a difference between questions of law and fact.

Here, our review is simply of the district court's decision not to review the appeal-panel's decision—a procedural issue involving abuse, *vel non*, of discretion. Moreover, it is well-settled "that [generally] a federal appellate court does not consider an issue not passed upon below". *Singleton v. Wulff*, 428 U.S. 106, 120 (1976); *see also Montano v. Texas*, 867 F.3d 540, 546 (5th Cir. 2017). Accordingly, I must respectfully dissent in part.

In the vast majority of these actions, our court has affirmed the denial of discretionary review; but, in a few instances, our court has remanded to the district court for both a more complete factual record and a decision on the contract-interpretation issue. "Contract interpretation, such as the meaning of the Settlement Agreement, is a question of law." *In re Deepwater Horizon*, 732 F.3d 326, 345, 1 Adm. R. 287, 301 (5th Cir. 2013) (citation omitted). If questions of law are at issue, the district court should first decide them, followed by our reviewing those decisions *de novo*. *BP Expl. & Prod., Inc. v. Claimant ID 100169608*, 682 F. App'x 256, 259 (5th Cir. 2017) (reviewing legal question of contract interpretation "effectively de novo", where district court granted discretionary review and decided issue); *Claimant ID 100197593 v. BP Expl. & Prod., Inc.*, 666 F. App'x 358, 360 (5th Cir. 2016) (same); *see also Claimant ID 100217021 v. BP Expl. & Prod., Inc.*, 693 F. App'x 272, 274 (5th Cir. 2017) (district court [—11—] reviews compliance with settlement agreement; our court reviews denial of discretionary review); *Claimant ID 100226366 v. BP Expl. & Prod., Inc.*, 671 F. App'x 940, 941 (5th Cir. 2016) ("It is only when the district court abuses its discretion that we will remand to require the court to review what the plan administrators have done." (citation omitted)).

Contrary to the majority's reviewing on the merits, our court has held a district court should have reviewed a decision by the appeal-panel, and remanded to the district court for review of a purely legal issue. *In re Deepwater Horizon*, 632 F. App'x 199, 204 (5th Cir. 2015). Our court held: appeal-panels were split over the interpretation of the settlement agreement; therefore, the district court abused its discretion in denying review; "the question of contract interpretation presented . . . would be best addressed first by the district court charged with administering the Agreement"; and, again, "the district court should have granted discretionary review to address this question". *Id.* On remand, the district court interpreted the settlement {-804-} agreement; and, in the second appeal, our court addressed that interpretation, because the district court had the opportunity to decide the legal issue in the first instance. *In re Deepwater Horizon*, 864 F.3d 360, 363, 5 Adm. R. 284, 285 (5th Cir. 2017) That should be the procedure for the appeal at hand.

The majority decides an underlying issue of law in the absence of a district-court decision on that issue; instead, it merely exercised its considerable discretion and decided *not* to review. In my view, in this instance, the extent of our prudential power is only to instruct the district court to undertake such review.

For these reasons, I respectfully dissent in part.

United States Court of Appeals
for the Fifth Circuit

No. 17-30963

RANDLE
vs.
CROSBY TUGS, L.L.C.

Appeal from the United States District Court for the Eastern District of Louisiana

Decided: December 19, 2018
Revised: January 7, 2019

Citation: 911 F.3d 280, 6 Adm. R. 279 (5th Cir. 2018).

Before **KING, ELROD,** and **HAYNES,** Circuit Judges.

[—1—] {–281–} PER CURIAM:

While working aboard the M/V DELTA FORCE, David J. Randle suffered a stroke. The nature of his injury was not immediately apparent, and the captain of the vessel called 911. The emergency responders took Randle to a nearby hospital, where physicians failed to diagnose his condition correctly. As a result, Randle did not receive medication that might have improved his post-stroke recovery. Randle sued the owner of the M/V DELTA FORCE, arguing that it breached its duty under the Jones Act to provide Randle with prompt and adequate medical care. The district court granted the vessel owner's motion for summary judgment. We AFFIRM. **[—2—]**

I.

Crosby Tugs, L.L.C. ("Crosby"), employed Randle as a seaman aboard the M/V DELTA FORCE. On the morning of Randle's stroke, the vessel was temporarily docked in Amelia, Louisiana. Randle had been unloading a grocery delivery onto the boat when he began to feel fatigued and lightheaded. He retreated to his cabin to rest. Shortly thereafter, a fellow crewmember heard a banging coming from Randle's cabin. The crewmember discovered Randle incapacitated on the **{–282–}** cabin floor and unable to communicate. The crewmember immediately notified the captain, who quickly called 911.

Acadian Ambulance Services ("Acadian") responded to the call. At the direction of the Louisiana Emergency Response Network ("LERN"), Acadian transported Randle to Teche Regional Medical Center ("TRMC"). Crosby did not instruct Acadian to take Randle to TRMC. Nor did Crosby hire, authorize, or otherwise contract with TRMC to administer medical care to its seamen.

Although the Acadian paramedics suspected that Randle was suffering from a stroke, the TRMC physicians failed to diagnose his condition as such. After performing a CT scan without contrast and consulting a telemedicine physician in New Orleans, the TRMC physicians diagnosed Randle with a brain mass and transferred him to another hospital for further treatment. Randle's medical expert testified that TRMC's physicians could have "easily" diagnosed the stroke if they had administered a CT scan with contrast.

Because the TRMC physicians failed to diagnose Randle's stroke correctly, they did not administer "tissue plasminogen activator," a medication that could have improved Randle's post-stroke recovery. To be effective, the medication must be administered within three hours of the stroke. By the time Randle's stroke was correctly diagnosed, it was too late for the medication to be effective. **[—3—]**

Randle is permanently disabled because of the stroke and needs constant custodial care. He brought suit against Crosby, arguing that Crosby negligently failed to provide prompt and adequate medical care; provided an unseaworthy vessel; and failed to provide maintenance-and-cure benefits.

The district court granted Crosby's motion for partial summary judgment on Randle's negligence and unseaworthiness claims. The parties settled Randle's maintenance-and-cure claim prior to this appeal. On Randle's motion, the district court certified the partial summary judgment as a partial final judgment pursuant to Federal Rule of Civil Procedure 54(b), from which Randle could appeal.

II.

"We review a district court's grant of summary judgment de novo, applying the same standard on appeal as that applied below." *Rogers v. Bromac Title Servs., L.L.C.*, 755 F.3d 347, 350 (5th Cir. 2014). Summary judgment is appropriate when "the movant shows that there is no genuine dispute as to any material fact and the movant is entitled to judgment as a matter of law." Fed. R. Civ. P. 56(a). A dispute about a material fact is genuine "if the evidence is such that a reasonable jury could return a verdict for the nonmoving party." *Anderson v. Liberty Lobby, Inc.*, 477 U.S. 242, 248 (1986).

III.

Randle appeals only the district court's entry of summary judgment on his negligence claims.[1] Under the Jones Act, "[a] seaman injured in the course of employment . . . may elect to bring a civil action at law . . . against [his] employer." 46 U.S.C. § 30104. A Jones Act seaman's **{-283-}** rights parallel those of a **[—4—]** railroad employee under the Federal Employers' Liability Act ("FELA"). *Id.* (making applicable all statutes "regulating recovery for personal injury to, or death of, a railway employee" to a seaman's Jones Act action); *Gautreaux v. Scurlock Marine, Inc.*, 107 F.3d 331, 335 (5th Cir. 1997) (en banc). "A seaman is entitled to recovery under the Jones Act, therefore, if his employer's negligence is the cause, in whole or in part, of his injury." *Gautreaux*, 107 F.3d at 335 (citing 45 U.S.C. § 51 (imposing liability on railroads for the negligence of their officers, agents, or employees)).

Randle argues that Crosby, through its employees, acted negligently by merely calling 911 in response to his stroke. Randle also argues that Crosby is vicariously liable for the TRMC physicians' alleged medical malpractice. We address each argument in turn.

A.

Randle contends that Crosby breached its duty to provide adequate medical care by merely calling 911 in response to his stroke. A shipowner has a nondelegable duty to provide prompt and adequate medical care to its seamen. *De Zon v. Am. President Lines*, 318 U.S. 660, 667 (1943); *De Centeno v. Gulf Fleet Crews, Inc.*, 798 F.2d 138, 140 (5th Cir. 1986). Thus, a shipowner is directly liable to its seaman under the Jones Act when it fails to provide proper medical care. *Cent. Gulf S.S. Corp. v. Sambula*, 405 F.2d 291, 298 (5th Cir. 1968).

The extent of the shipowner's duty to provide medical care depends on "the circumstances of each case" and "varies with the nature of the injury and the relative availability of medical facilities." *Id.* at 300. A shipowner breaches its duty to provide prompt and adequate medical care "when [it] fails to get a crewman to a doctor when it is reasonably necessary, and the ship is reasonably able to do so." *Olsen v. Am. S.S. Co.*, 176 F.3d 891, 896 (6th Cir. 1999); *see also De Centeno*, 798 F.2d at 140. A shipowner also violates this duty **[—5—]** when it takes its seaman to a doctor it knows is not qualified to care for its seaman's injury. *See Sambula*, 405 F.2d at 299-300.

Randle has not put forth evidence demonstrating a genuine issue of material fact as to whether Crosby fulfilled its duty to provide medical care under these circumstances. Randle was suffering an unknown but clearly urgent medical emergency in the service of a ship away from its home port. By calling 911, Crosby's employees selected the course of action reasonably calculated to get Randle to a medical facility that would be able to treat him. Randle acknowledges that TRMC could have properly diagnosed and treated his stroke by administering a CT scan with contrast. That the TRMC physicians may be faulted does not mean that Crosby is directly

[1] Randle only discusses unseaworthiness claims generally, using such claims as an analogy to his negligence claim. Because he does not challenge the district court's entry of summary judgment on his unseaworthiness claim, we consider this argument to be forfeited. *See United States v. Scroggins*, 599 F.3d 433, 447 (5th Cir. 2010) (finding argument not adequately presented where brief did not discuss the issue "in any depth").

liable for failing to procure adequate medical care. Under these circumstances, Crosby made reasonable efforts to secure appropriate medical treatment, and it was not negligent in its provision of medical care to Randle.[2] *Cf. id.* at 301 **{-284-}** (noting, in considering shipowner's treatment of seaman's severe eye injury, "[t]he law does not require prognostic omniscience of the master, but it does impose upon him a duty to make reasonable efforts to secure the treatment leading most naturally to sight rather than blindness"). **[—6—]**

Randle analogizes his case to *De Centeno* and *Sambula*, arguing that Crosby failed to take him to a capable medical provider. But neither case alters our conclusion that Crosby acted reasonably under the circumstances. Unlike *De Centeno*, this is not a case where the shipowner procured initial treatment and then did nothing as the seaman's condition continued to deteriorate. *See* 798 F.2d at 139-40. Nor is this case like *Sambula*, in which we concluded that the shipowner acted negligently by taking its seaman to a general practitioner, rather than an ophthalmologist. 405 F.2d at 300-01. In *Sambula*, the seaman's eye injury was "such that even a layman could have recognized the possibility of internal eye damage." *Id.* at 293. Here, Crosby's employees did not know what was wrong with Randle, nor was it obvious. Thus, unlike the shipowner in *Sambula* who provided its seaman with the incorrect type of care, Crosby properly sought out emergency medical services given the nature of Randle's illness.

Randle has not shown that there is a genuine issue of material fact as to whether Crosby acted negligently by calling 911. Therefore, we conclude that the district court properly granted summary judgment for Crosby on Randle's direct liability claim.

B.

Randle argues that Crosby should also be held vicariously liable for the TRMC physicians' alleged medical malpractice. A shipowner is liable "for the injuries negligently inflicted on its employees by its 'officers, agents, or employees.'" *Hopson v. Texaco, Inc.*, 383 U.S. 262, 263 (1966) (per curiam) (quoting 45 U.S.C. § 51). The word "agents" is given "an accommodating scope," requiring only that the "employee's injury [be] caused in whole or in part by the fault of others performing, under contract, operational activities of his employer." *Id.* at 264 (quoting *Sinkler v. Mo. Pac. R.R. Co.*, 356 U.S. 326, 329 (1958)). Thus, a shipowner is vicariously liable for the negligence of an on- **[—7—]** board physician in its employ. *De Zon*, 318 U.S. at 668. We have also held that a shipowner is vicariously liable for an on-shore physician "it chooses to treat its seaman." *De Centeno*, 798 F.2d at 140; *see also Sambula*, 405 F.2d at 299 (stating standard for vicarious liability for on-shore physician as "whether the ship was negligent in selecting and relying upon [the physician]").[3] **{-285-}**

---

[2] Randle also urges that he should have been taken to a stroke center, which would have been more likely to diagnose his stroke. But the test is not, with the benefit of hindsight, whether Randle received the *best* care, but instead, whether the care he received was reasonable under the circumstances. As discussed above, Randle's medical expert testified that TRMC was capable of properly treating his stroke. Moreover, Randle has not demonstrated that Crosby could have reasonably taken other action. Randle has not shown that there was a stroke center nearby, that Crosby was capable of extracting Randle from the vessel and taking him to a stroke center itself, or that Crosby could have instructed the ambulance to go to a specific hospital. In fact, Randle admitted that he did not believe there was anything else Crosby's employees could have done to help him, and that his own "instinct" would have been to call 911. Thus, there is no genuine issue of material fact that Crosby procured prompt and adequate care under the circumstances.

[3] Our sister circuits have similarly noted that shipowners may be held vicariously liable for physicians they affirmatively select, hire, or with whom they have a contract. *E.g., Dise v. Express Marine, Inc.*, 476 F. App'x 514, 521-22 (4th Cir. 2011) (unpublished) (holding tugboat owner not vicariously liable where it did not take an "affirmative act to select or otherwise engage the [physician]"); *Greenwell v. Aztar Ind. Gaming Corp.*, 268 F.3d 486, 492 (7th Cir. 2001), *abrogated on other grounds by McCarter v. Ret. Plan for Dist. Managers of Am. Family Ins. Grp.*, 540 F.3d 649, 653 (7th Cir. 2008) (finding casino boat owner not vicariously liable where doctors were neither employees of the boat nor acting on its behalf);

But this "accommodating scope" is not boundless—even in the context of FELA, the Supreme Court has defined an agent as one "performing, *under contract*, operational activities of [the] employer." *Hopson*, 383 U.S. at 264 (emphasis added) (quoting *Sinkler*, 356 U.S. at 329). We are not aware of any case holding that FELA overrides agency principles such that an employer will be liable for the acts of an unrelated third party. Accordingly, we have recognized that a shipowner will not be held vicariously liable for the negligence of a physician that the seaman chooses himself. *Joiner v. Diamond M. Drilling Co.*, 688 F.2d 256, 262 n.9 (5th Cir. 1982).

Therefore, although we must give the word "agent" an "accommodating scope," we cannot forget the basic principles of agency law. Randle argues that a shipowner's vicarious liability arises from its nondelegable duty to provide adequate medical care, regardless of whether the shipowner employs or affirmatively selects the medical provider. This reasoning misconstrues agency **[—8—]** principles: a nondelegable duty cannot create an agency relationship because such a duty presupposes an agency relationship. Put otherwise, an agency relationship is only formed when the principal takes an affirmative act to select the agent—regardless of the principal's duty to a third party. *See Crist v. Dickson Welding, Inc.*, 957 F.2d 1281, 1286 (5th Cir. 1992) ("For the doctrine of apparent authority to apply, the principal must first *act to manifest* to an innocent third party the alleged agent's authority." (emphasis added)); Restatement (Third) of Agency § 3.01 (Am. Law Inst. 2006) ("Actual authority . . . is created by a principal's *manifestation to an agent* that, as reasonably understood by the agent, expresses the principal's assent that the agent take action on the principal's behalf." (emphasis added)); *id.* at § 3.03 cmt. b (apparent authority "originates with expressive conduct by the principal toward a third party"). Thus, "[a] principal is subject to liability [for failure to perform a nondelegable duty] when the principal owes a duty to protect a third party and an agent *to whom the principal has delegated performance of the duty* fails to fulfill it." *Id.* at § 7.03 cmt. b (emphasis added).

As applied here, Crosby (the principal) had a nondelegable duty to provide adequate medical care to Randle; Crosby would be vicariously liable if it had "delegated performance of the duty" to an agent, and the agent acted negligently in carrying out the duty. But no such agency relationship was formed here because Crosby did not manifest authority to TRMC or its physicians, or otherwise express its assent that TRMC act on its behalf. Randle does not argue that Crosby directed the ambulance to go to TRMC, and it is not clear that Crosby had the power to do so. There is no evidence of a relationship between Crosby and TRMC. Thus, Randle has not demonstrated that Crosby, by calling 911, intended TRMC to act as its agent, and the district court properly granted summary judgment on this issue. **[—9—]**

Randle contends that the district court's holding is inconsistent with the Supreme Court's decision in *Hopson* and our decisions in *De Centeno* and *Sambula*. But these cases do not support Randle's position. **{-286-}** In *Hopson*, the Supreme Court held that a shipowner was liable for the negligence en route of a taxi it had hired to fulfill its statutory duty to take two ill seamen to the United States consulate. 383 U.S. at 264. Likewise, in *De Centeno*, we held a shipowner vicariously liable for its chosen physician's negligence in misdiagnosing its seaman's diabetes. 798 F.2d at 139-140. And in *Sambula*, we found a shipowner vicariously liable for the malpractice of a general practitioner it had negligently selected to treat its seaman's eye injury. 405 F.2d at 300-01.

Olsen v. Am. S.S. Co., 176 F.3d 891, 895-96 (6th Cir. 1999) (noting that "a shipowner is liable for the negligence of an on-shore physician that it hires to treat a crewman," and may be vicariously liable "when the shipowner selects a doctor who acts negligently" (citing *De Centeno*, 798 F.2d at 140)); *Fitzgerald v. A. L. Burbank & Co.*, 451 F.2d 670, 680 (2d Cir. 1971) (finding physician was shipowner's agent where services were provided under contract).

These cases support the proposition that medical providers that a shipowner *selects* "are deemed to be engaged in the ship's business as 'agents' despite the fact that the practitioner may be an independent contractor or completely unrelated to the ship." *Dise v. Express Marine, Inc.*, 476 F. App'x 514, 521 (4th Cir. 2011) (unpublished). But these cases do not override the basic principles of agency law requiring that an agency relationship arise from the principal's act in selecting the agent, rather than its nondelegable duty. And because Crosby did not select TRMC as its agent or otherwise express its assent that TRMC would act on its behalf, there was no agency relationship here. Crosby called 911. The 911 dispatcher sent Acadian to respond to the call. After responding to the call, Acadian called LERN, the state's emergency response network. LERN instructed Acadian to take Randle to TRMC. There is no evidence Crosby knew how this sequence of events would unfold, much less that it was aware that LERN would direct Acadian to take Randle to TRMC. Thus, TRMC was not Crosby's agent.

Therefore, we find that there is no genuine issue of material fact as to whether Crosby is vicariously liable for the TRMC physicians' alleged **[—10—]** malpractice, and we affirm the district court's grant of summary judgment on this issue.[4]

IV.

For the foregoing reasons, we AFFIRM the judgment of the district court.

---

[4] Randle also challenges the proper standard of care for his medical malpractice claims. Because we find that Crosby is not vicariously liable for TRMC's alleged medical malpractice, we do not reach this issue.

This page intentionally left blank

United States Court of Appeals for the Sixth Circuit

United States Court of Appeals
for the Sixth Circuit

No. 17-3679

BUCCINA
VS.
GRIMSBY

Appeal from the United States District Court for the Northern District of Ohio at Toledo

Decided: April 27, 2018

Citation: 889 F.3d 256, 6 Adm. R. 286 (6th Cir. 2018).

Before **BATCHELDER, SUTTON,** and **WHITE,** Circuit Judges.

[—1—] {-257-} SUTTON, Circuit Judge:

Linda Ann Grimsby invited her friend Nancy Buccina to take a boat trip on Lake Erie. Toward the end of the voyage, the boat hit a wave, jarring the passengers and injuring Nancy. Nancy and her husband Scot sued. A jury found that Grimsby was not negligent. But the district court granted Nancy and Scot's motion for a new trial on the ground that the evidence did not support the verdict. Grimsby filed an interlocutory appeal, and the Buccinas **{-258-}** cross-appealed. Both sides think we may entertain their appeals thanks to an **[—2—]** interlocutory exception to the final judgment rule that applies to admiralty cases. But the exception does not apply because the Buccinas chose to pursue their claims under ordinary civil procedures, as the relevant rule and case law permits. We dismiss the appeals for lack of jurisdiction.

I.

In June 2012, Linda Ann Grimsby invited Nancy Buccina and one other friend to join her on a 17-foot motor boat to waterski on Lake Erie. After skiing, the group decided to take a trip down the Maumee River, which runs into the lake at Toledo. Grimsby navigated the vessel while Nancy sat in the front. The vessel hit an unexpected wave, likely caused by the wake of other boats. Nancy bounced up from her seat and came down hard on it. Grimsby steered the boat to a local Coast Guard station where Nancy received medical attention.

Nancy and her husband Scot Buccina sued Grimsby in the United States District Court for the Northern District of Ohio for personal injury and loss of consortium, invoking the court's diversity and admiralty jurisdiction. At the same time, they pleaded that "this action is not to be deemed an 'admiralty and maritime claim' within the meaning of" Rule 9 of the Federal Rules of Civil Procedure, a choice that guaranteed them a jury trial as opposed to the bench trial that defendants may force plaintiffs to undergo in admiralty cases. R.1 at 1–2.

The trip through federal court has taken much longer than their voyage. It has prompted nearly a half-dozen district court opinions, a jury trial, and (to date) two opinions from our court. In 2015, the district court held that the incident fell within the court's admiralty jurisdiction, meaning that federal maritime law controlled the duty of care. In 2016, the court held that a boat hitting a wave did not count as a "collision" under the Coast Guard Navigation Rules. The district court certified the question for interlocutory appeal under 28 U.S.C. § 1292(b). But there was no "substantial ground for a difference of opinion" about the answer that would justify an interlocutory appeal, we determined, and thus we opted not to accept the appeal. *In re Buccina*, 657 F. App'x 350, 351 (6th Cir. 2016). **[—3—]**

On remand, a jury ruled for Grimsby, finding that she was not negligent. The Buccinas moved for a new trial under Civil Rule 59(a) or judgment notwithstanding the verdict under Civil Rule 50(b). The district court granted the motion for a new trial.

Grimsby appealed, and the Buccinas cross-appealed.

II.

Appellate jurisdiction typically extends only to final judgments. 28 U.S.C. § 1291. The district court's new-trial decision is the epitome of a non-final order. The case will not end until after the new trial. *See Allied Chem. Corp. v. Daiflon, Inc.*, 449 U.S. 33, 34 (1980) (per curiam).

That leaves the possibility that an exception to the final judgment rule applies. The parties might have asked the district court to certify the appeal for immediate review. 28 U.S.C. § 1292(b). But they did not, perhaps due to their last experience with that option.

The parties instead claim that we may review the appeal and cross appeal under an admiralty exception to the final judgment rule provided by statute. It permits litigants to appeal "[i]nterlocutory decrees . . . determining the rights and liabilities of **{-259-}** the parties to admiralty cases in which appeals from final decrees are allowed." *Id.* § 1292(a)(3).

But is this an "admiralty case" under this law? Yes and no.

Yes, the complaint permissibly invokes the court's diversity *and* admiralty jurisdiction. Diversity jurisdiction exists because the Buccinas live in Florida, Grimsby lives in Michigan, and the Buccinas have plausibly alleged that their damages exceed $75,000. *Id.* § 1332(a)–(b). Admiralty jurisdiction exists as well. Article III extends federal jurisdiction to admiralty and maritime cases, U.S. Const. art. III, § 2, cl. 1, and Congress granted federal courts jurisdiction over "[a]ny civil case of admiralty or maritime jurisdiction, saving to suitors in all cases all other remedies to which they are otherwise entitled." 28 U.S.C. § 1333(1).

An incident falls within our admiralty jurisdiction if it (1) occurs on a navigable waterway, (2) could potentially disrupt maritime commerce, and (3) bears a "substantial relationship to traditional maritime activity." *Jerome B. Grubart, Inc. v. Great Lakes Dredge & Dock Co.*, 513 U.S. 527, 533–34 (1995) (quotations omitted). This incident satisfies the test. **[—4—]** The Maumee River is a navigable waterway. The incident risked disrupting maritime commerce by clogging up a commercial waterway and diverting Coast Guard personnel from other duties. And a tort stemming from the negligent operation of a boat on navigable waters "has a sufficient nexus to traditional maritime activity to sustain admiralty jurisdiction." *Foremost Ins. Co. v. Richardson*, 457 U.S. 668, 674 (1982).

The "no" side of the answer is more complicated, as our diversity and admiralty jurisdiction over the case have substantive and procedural implications for the case. As a matter of substance, the Constitution "prescribe[s] uniformity" in admiralty and maritime law. *Am. Dredging Co. v. Miller*, 510 U.S. 443, 451 (1994). We treat admiralty and maritime law as "a uniform body of substantive *federal* law, applicable not only in federal admiralty courts but also binding upon the state courts" and federal courts exercising their civil law powers. Richard H. Fallon, Jr. et al., *Hart and Wechsler's the Federal Courts and the Federal System* 690 (7th ed. 2015). Once a claim comes within our admiralty jurisdiction, substantive federal maritime law thus applies. *See Kermarec v. Compagnie Generale Transatlantique*, 358 U.S. 625, 628 (1959); *Jerome B. Grubart, Inc.*, 513 U.S. at 545–46.

While uniformity of substance is required in an admiralty case, "[u]niformity of process . . . is assuredly not what the law of admiralty seeks to achieve." *Am. Dredging Co.*, 510 U.S. at 453. That leaves open two routes in a federal court case like this one.

Route A is to invoke federal admiralty procedures, which differ from ordinary civil procedures in several ways. The Supplemental Rules for Admiralty and Maritime Claims, for example, preserve the traditional maritime remedy of attachment and garnishment and create special procedures for actions brought against vessels or property. Fed. R. Civ. P. Supp. AMC Rules B, C.

(As a side note, the Admiralty Rules used to be separate from the Civil Rules. In 1966, the rules makers merged the Admiralty Rules with the Civil Rules, not unlike the earlier merger of law and equity. Comm. on the Rules of Practice & Procedure, Report to the Judicial Conference of the United States at 4–5 (Sept. **{-260-}** 1966); Fed. R. Civ. P. 9, 1966 cmt. Today, unless otherwise noted, the Civil Rules apply to admiralty actions, but there are several provisions in **[—5—]** the Civil Rules that spell out special admiralty procedures. *See, e.g.*, Fed. R. Civ. P. 14(c) (third-party impleader), 38(e) (no jury trial by right), 82 (venue); Fed. R. Civ. P. Supp. AMC Rules B (special attachment and garnishment rules), C (admiralty claims in rem), D (warrant of arrest of vessel, cargo, or other property in possessory, petitory, and partition actions), E (procedures for in rem and quasi in rem proceedings), F (liability limitation rules for owners of vessels and freight), G (forfeiture actions in rem).)

Route B is to invoke the traditional federal civil procedures for the case. Section 1333(1) "sav[es] to suitors in all cases all other remedies to which they are otherwise entitled." That gives plaintiffs the option of bringing an action sounding in admiralty under the general rules of civil procedure, including with the guarantee of a jury trial, as long as they can show that the matter arises under the court's diversity jurisdiction as well. *Atl. & Gulf Stevedores, Inc. v. Ellerman Lines, Ltd.*, 369 U.S. 355, 359–60 (1962); 14A Charles Alan Wright & Arthur R. Miller, Federal Practice and Procedure § 3672 (4th ed. 2018).

Plaintiffs like the Buccinas thus have two options. They may use admiralty procedures to govern a substantive admiralty claim. Or they may pursue a hybrid action in which customary civil procedures govern their substantive admiralty law action. *See Atl. & Gulf Stevedores, Inc.*, 369 U.S. at 359–64 (permitting a plaintiff to bring an unseaworthiness claim before a jury after asserting diversity jurisdiction); *Kermarec*, 358 U.S. at 628–29 (same); *Carey v. Bahama Cruise Lines*, 864 F.2d 201, 206–08 (1st Cir. 1988).

How do we know which route the plaintiffs have taken? Before the unification of admiralty and law in 1966, it was easy. The plaintiff would file one of two forms of action—a civil action or a suit in admiralty—that would trigger the attendant procedures. 5 Wright & Miller § 1211 (3d ed. 2018). Unification, however, created a single form of action for both types of lawsuits, Fed. R. Civ. P. 2 ("There is one form of action—the civil action"), meaning that the way that the plaintiff initiated the lawsuit no longer signaled which set of procedures to employ. *See* Fed. R. Civ. P. 9, 1966 cmt.; *see also* 5 Wright & Miller § 1211 (3d ed. 2018); Brainerd Currie, *Unification of the Civil and Admiralty Rules: Why and How*, 17 Me. L. Rev. 1, 9–10 (1965). The Advisory Committee for the Federal Rules of Civil Procedure provided an answer, blessed by the Standing Committee on Rules of Practice and Procedure, the Judicial **[—6—]** Conference of the United States, the United States Supreme Court, and Congress under the procedures created by the Rules Enabling Act, 28 U.S.C. § 2072. The Committee did not want to force plaintiffs to "forego mention of all available jurisdictional grounds" by having courts decide whether to apply admiralty or ordinary civil procedures based on the complaint's reference to one type of jurisdiction over the other. Fed. R. Civ. P. 9, 1966 cmt. It instead promulgated a rule under which plaintiffs could mention both types of jurisdiction but then decide which set of procedures would apply. Civil Rule 9(h) tells the plaintiff (the "suitor" in § 1333(1)) to designate how the case will proceed. *In re Lockheed Martin Corp.*, 503 F.3d 351, 355 (4th Cir. 2007); Fed. R. Civ. P. 9, 1966 cmt. The rule says:

> If a claim for relief is within the admiralty or maritime jurisdiction and also within the court's subject-matter jurisdiction on some other ground, the pleading **{-261-}** may designate the claim as an admiralty or maritime claim.

If a pleading designates a claim as an admiralty claim, the plaintiffs may use admiralty procedures (such as a guaranteed bench trial under Civil Rule 38(e)) but lose access to some procedures available in run-of-the-mine civil proceedings. And vice versa: If a pleading designates a claim as proceeding in diversity, the plaintiffs may use procedures available in ordinary civil cases (such as a guaranteed jury trial) but lose procedures unique to admiralty claims. *See Luera v. M/V Alberta*, 635 F.3d 181, 188–89 (5th Cir. 2011); *Cont'l Cas. Co. v. Anderson Excavating & Wrecking Co.*, 189 F.3d 512, 517 (7th Cir. 1999); *Bodden v. Osgood*, 879 F.2d 184, 186 (5th Cir. 1989); 5 Wright & Miller § 1211 (3d ed. 2018).

We are getting warmer. The Buccinas permissibly invoked both the admiralty and diversity jurisdiction of the federal courts. They then pleaded that "this action is not to be deemed an 'admiralty and maritime claim' within the meaning of" Civil Rule 9. R. 1 at 1–2. By opting not to proceed with the case as an admiralty claim, they told the defendant and the district court that ordinary civil procedures would apply. *See Cont'l Cas. Co.*, 189 F.3d at 517. The district court honored their wish and gave them the jury trial to which that choice entitled them.

The benefit of a guaranteed jury trial, however, comes with fewer rights to an immediate appeal. Civil Rule 9(h)(2) notes that a "case that includes an admiralty or maritime claim within **[—7—]** this subdivision (h) is an admiralty case within 28 U.S.C. § 1292(a)(3)." Had the Buccinas proceeded in admiralty, they could have invoked the statute in this interlocutory appeal. *See Williamson v. Recovery Ltd. P'ship*, 731 F.3d 608, 618–20, 1 Adm. R. 348, 354–56 (6th Cir. 2013). But they elected to pursue their action under the ordinary civil procedures, which left them with no "admiralty claim" as defined in Rule 9(h)(1). Lacking any admiralty claim, theirs is not a Rule 9(h)(2) "admiralty case." And having invoked the ordinary civil procedures available under diversity jurisdiction, "the parties are not entitled to invoke any of the special procedures or remedies of admiralty, including the right of interlocutory appeal under section 1292(a)(3)." *Cont'l Cas. Co.*, 189 F.3d at 517; *see Luera*, 635 F.3d at 188; *Alleman v. Bunge Corp.*, 756 F.2d 344, 346 (5th Cir. 1984); Currie, *supra*, at 12; 5A Wright & Miller § 1313 (3d ed. 2018).

All of this means that § 1292(a)(3)'s interlocutory-appeal opportunity does not apply. That leaves us with 28 U.S.C. § 1291. And in the absence of a final, appealable judgment or a cognizable exception to the final judgment rule, we lack jurisdiction over the appeals.

The cases mentioned by the parties do not lead to a contrary conclusion, as a sampling of them makes clear. Take *Foulk v. Donjon Marine Co.*, in which the Third Circuit dealt with a case that arose under admiralty and diversity jurisdiction. The problem with that case is that the plaintiff never specified which set of procedures he wanted to invoke. 144 F.3d 252, 255 n.2 (3d Cir. 1998). The Buccinas in marked contrast left no doubt about their preference.

Or consider *Southworth Machinery Co. v. F/V Corey Pride*. The First Circuit considered an interlocutory appeal from an in rem action against a vessel under § 1292(a)(3). 994 F.2d 37, 39–40 (1st Cir. 1993). But an in rem claim in this context, in contrast to a claim brought against an individual or entity, is always an admiralty proceeding. *See Am. Dredging Co.*, 510 U.S. at 446–47; *The Moses Taylor*, 71 U.S. 411 (1866); 14A Wright & Miller § 3672 (4th ed. 2018). Under that circumstance, **{-262-}** the court fairly inferred that the appeal arose from an admiralty case. *See also Martha's Vineyard Scuba Headquarters, Inc. v. Unidentified, Wrecked & Abandoned Steam Vessel*, 833 F.2d 1059, 1064 (1st Cir. 1987); *In re S.S. Tropic Breeze*, 456 F.2d 137 (1st Cir. 1972). **[—8—]**

Or consider *Bergeron v. Elliot*. The Fifth Circuit's per curiam opinion is brief but it does say that the case was "specified to be in admiralty" under Rule 9(h). 466 F.2d 514, 516 n.3 (5th Cir. 1972) (per curiam). So too of *O'Donnell v. Latham*, in which the complaint made clear that the principal claim arose under admiralty. 525 F.2d 650, 652 (5th Cir. 1976).

Grimsby claims that the Buccinas received a jury trial not because they pleaded their case in diversity, but because they brought the action in admiralty and both parties consented to a jury trial. She is correct that the parties *could* have taken that route. Although Civil Rule 38(e) says that litigants have no right to a jury trial for an admiralty claim, Civil Rule 39(c)(2) allows the district court to try an admiralty claim before a jury provided that both parties consent. But that is not what happened. The Buccinas pleaded that the entire action was "not to be deemed an 'admiralty and maritime claim'" within the meaning of Rule 9. R. 1 at 1–2. In their opposition to Grimsby's motion to dismiss, the Buccinas explained that they "opted not to invoke the provisions of Fed. R. Civ. P. Rule 9(h) in order to preserve a jury trial . . . under [the district court's] alternative diversity jurisdiction." R. 11 at 3. In his order denying the motion, Judge Carr explained that the Buccinas could have proceeded under admiralty procedures but "chose to proceed in diversity to procure a different procedural benefit: the right to a jury trial." *Buccina v. Grimsby*, 96 F. Supp. 3d 706, 710 (N.D. Ohio 2015). Nothing in the record shows that the jury trial arose by mutual consent under Civil Rule 39(c).

In a minor twist on this theme, the Buccinas say that the complaint's Civil Rule 9(h) statement was "withdrawn, abandoned and disregarded as the case proceeded." A.R. 57 at 6. A party, it is true, may revoke a Rule 9(h) designation. As the Advisory Committee commentary points out, plaintiffs may amend their complaint to excise or change their designation under Civil Rule 15. Fed. R. Civ. P. 9, 1966 cmt., 2007 cmt. But the Buccinas never amended their complaint or otherwise re-designated the case. It is too late now. *See Bhd. Shipping Co. v. St. Paul Fire & Marine Ins. Co.*, 985 F.2d 323, 326 (7th Cir. 1993) (expressing "profound[]" doubt that plaintiffs could change their Rule 9(h) designations after invoking the benefits of one set of procedures "so that the plaintiff can have the best of both procedural worlds").

For these reasons, we dismiss the appeal and cross-appeal for lack of jurisdiction and remand to the district court for further proceedings.

United States Court of Appeals for the Seventh Circuit

United States Court of Appeals
for the Seventh Circuit

No. 17-2324

ARMADA (SINGAPORE) PTE LTD.
vs.
AMCOL INT'L CORP.

Appeal from the United States District Court for the Northern District of Illinois, Eastern Division

Decided: March 26, 2018

Citation: 885 F.3d 1090, 6 Adm. R. 292 (7th Cir. 2018).

Before **BAUER, MANION,** and **ROVNER,** Circuit Judges.

[—1—] MANION, Circuit Judge: **{–1091–}**

The plaintiff in this case is a Singaporean shipping company. It entered into shipping contracts with an Indian mining company, but the Indian company breached those contracts. Now, the plaintiff believes that American businesses engaged in racketeering activity to divest the Indian company of assets so as to thwart the plaintiff's attempts to recover damages for the breached con- **[—2—]** tracts. Seeking redress for this alleged wrong, the plaintiff brought this lawsuit, claiming violations of the Racketeering Influenced and Corrupt Organizations Act ("RICO"). While the plaintiff's case was pending in the district court, the Supreme Court decided *RJR Nabisco, Inc. v. European Community*, 136 S. Ct. 2090 (2016). Addressing RICO's extraterritorial effect, the Supreme Court held that "[a] private RICO plaintiff ... must allege and prove a *domestic* injury to its business or property." *Id.* at 2106. After this decision came down, the American defendants moved for judgment on the pleadings, maintaining the plaintiff had not pleaded a domestic injury. The district court agreed and entered judgment on the RICO claims against the plaintiff, who now appeals. Because we also conclude the plaintiff has not pleaded a domestic injury, we affirm.

I.

As this case comes to us on appeal from judgment on the pleadings, we present the facts as stated in the plaintiff's amended complaint. *See Matrix IV, Inc. v. Am. Nat'l Bank and Trust Co. of Chicago*, 649 F.3d 539, 547 (7th Cir. 2011). Amcol International Corporation, an Illinois corporation with its principal place of business in Illinois, owns 100% of American Colloid Company and Volclay International Corporation (n/k/a Volclay International LLC). Both companies are also organized under the laws of Illinois with their principal places of business in Illinois. Given the extent of the three entities' affiliation, we will refer to them collectively as "Amcol." Amcol was the largest shareholder of Ashapura Minechem Limited ("Ashapura"), a foreign corporation with its principal place of business in Mumbai, India. **[—3—]**

Originally, Ashapura focused its business on the production and marketing of the mineral bentonite. But in 2007 and early 2008, Ashapura expected to sell large quantities of the mineral bauxite in China. Needing to get that bauxite to China, in April 2008 Ashapura entered into two long-term contracts of affreightment with Armada (Singapore) PTE Limited ("Armada"), a foreign corporation with its principal place of business in the Republic of Singapore. Unfortunately, Ashapura encountered problems with its bauxite suppliers, so it defaulted under the contracts with Armada at the end of September 2008. Ashapura failed to pay Armada for the shipment Armada had already carried and did not provide any further cargoes. **{–1092–}**

Armada subsequently initiated two arbitration actions in London against Ashapura, one for each contract. The arbitrator found for Armada and awarded more than $70,000,000 in two awards on February 16, 2010. About a year and a half later, Armada had the arbitration awards recognized by the United States District Court for the Southern District of New York, which entered a judgment for Armada. Armada had the judgment registered with the United States District Court for the Northern District of Illinois the next year. In addition to this activity, Armada sought to collect on its awards by filing maritime attachment proceedings in New York and Illinois, naming Amcol as garnishee. Through these actions, Armada was able to garnish and recover approximately $687,000 worth of debts that Amcol owed to Ashapura.

But Armada thinks Amcol obstructed its attempts to recover from Ashapura, and this brings us to the crux of the matter currently before the court. Armada alleges Amcol **[—4—]** used its influence as Ashapura's largest shareholder to engage in a number of schemes aimed at draining Ashapura of assets to thwart Armada's collection efforts. These plots ranged from routine collection avoidance—such as having Ashapura file for protection with the Board of Industrial and Financial Reconstruction in India and file a Chapter 15 bankruptcy petition in the United States—to more complicated methods—such as setting off debts owed by Ashapura affiliates against debts Amcol owed to Ashapura.

In 2013, Armada filed this lawsuit against Amcol, Ashapura, and five John Does. In July 2015, Armada filed an amended complaint setting out state-law claims for fraudulent transfer, wrongful dividend, and breach of fiduciary duties and a claim for maritime fraudulent transfer. Armada also made two claims pursuant to RICO's private right of action,[1] alleging Amcol engaged in racketeering activity and a racketeering conspiracy that harmed Armada's business or property.

While the case was pending, the Supreme Court decided *RJR Nabisco* and announced a domestic-injury requirement for civil RICO cases. Just over a month later, Amcol filed a motion for judgment on the pleadings. The district court entered judgment for Amcol on the state-law claims. The district court also entered judgment on the RICO claims, concluding that Armada's claimed injury—harm to its ability to collect on its judgment and other claims—was economic. Because economic injuries are felt at a corporation's principal place of business, and Armada's principal place of business is in Singapore, Armada had not pleaded a "domestic inju- **[—5—]** ry" as required by *RJR Nabisco*. However, the district court allowed the maritime fraudulent transfer claim to go forward, so it denied Amcol's motion to that extent. Armada now brings this interlocutory appeal, challenging only the district court's ruling concerning the RICO claims.

II.

Our review of the grant of a motion for judgment on the pleadings is *de novo*. *St. John v. Cach, LLC*, 822 F.3d 388, 389 (7th Cir. 2016). The standard for entering judgment on the pleadings is the same as that for dismissing a complaint for failure to state a claim: "the complaint must state a claim that is plausible on its face." *Id.* (quoting *Vinson v. Vermilion Cty., Ill.*, 776 F.3d 924, 928 (7th Cir. 2015)). In this appeal, the sole issue is whether Armada has pleaded a "domestic injury." **{-1093-}**

18 U.S.C. § 1964(c), colloquially referred to as "civil RICO," empowers private parties to bring lawsuits against those engaged in racketeering activity when that activity has caused them harm. *See generally Rotella v. Wood*, 528 U.S. 549, 557 (2000) ("The object of civil RICO is ... not merely to compensate victims but to turn them into prosecutors ... dedicated to eliminating racketeering activity."). By its terms, § 1964(c) requires that the plaintiff have suffered an injury to "his business or property by reason of" the racketeering activity. 18 U.S.C. § 1964(c). In this case, Armada claims that it suffered an injury to its property, namely its judgment and other claims against Ashapura. Armada claims that Amcol, by means of racketeering activity, injured that property by divesting Ashapura of assets, thereby making the judgment and other claims against Ashapura uncollectable. A cause of action is recognized as a property right **[—6—]** that can suffer injury. *See Pitts v. Unarco Indus., Inc.*, 712 F.2d 276, 279 (7th Cir. 1983); *cf. Malley-Duff & Assocs., Inc. v. Crown Life Ins. Co.*, 792 F.2d 341, 354 (3d Cir. 1986) (recognizing that an

[1] *See* 18 U.S.C. § 1964(c).

injury to a cause of action can be a "business injury" for RICO purposes). For Armada, so far so good.

But we do not ask only whether Armada has pleaded an injury. We also must determine, in light of *RJR Nabisco*, whether that injury is "domestic." Regrettably, the Supreme Court did not have occasion to elaborate on what it meant in *RJR Nabisco* by "domestic injury," as the plaintiffs in that case had specifically waived their claims for domestic injuries. *See* 136 S. Ct. at 2111. But the Court did provide some vague hints at what "domestic injury" might entail. For instance, it consistently referred to the location where an injury was *suffered*. *See, e.g., id.* at 2108 ("Nothing in § 1964(c) provides a clear indication that Congress intended to create a private right of action for injuries suffered outside of the United States."); *id.* at 2111 (directing the dismissal of the remaining claims because they "rest entirely on injury suffered abroad"). It also made a point of noting the domestic injury requirement does not categorically bar foreigners from recovering under the statute's provisions. *See id.* at 2110 n.12.

Having announced the domestic-injury requirement, but having declined to define the term, the Court cautioned that "application of this rule in any given case will not always be self-evident, as disputes may arise as to whether a particular injury is 'foreign' or 'domestic.'" *Id.* at 2111. Unsurprisingly, that statement has proved prescient. Since *RJR Nabisco* came down, many district courts have done their best to craft a rule for determining which injuries are domestic and which **[—7—]** are foreign. *See, e.g., Cevdet Aksüt Oğullari Koll. Sti v. Cavusoglu*, 245 F. Supp. 3d 650, 657 (D.N.J. 2017) ("These cases exhibit a wide array of factual scenarios and justifiable reasoning, with no clear victor in the 'domestic injury' debate."). These cases have only now begun percolating up to the courts of appeals.

In October of last year, the Second Circuit became the first court of appeals to address the "domestic injury" issue. In *Bascuñán v. Elsaca*, 874 F.3d 806 (2d Cir. 2017), the plaintiff, a resident of Chile, alleged that his cousin had stolen millions of dollars from him through various schemes. *Id.* at 809. The district court in that case, applying similar reasoning to the district court in this case, concluded that all of the plaintiff's injuries were economic, that economic injuries are suffered at a person's residence, and thus the injuries were Chilean, not domestic. *Id.*

On appeal, the Second Circuit rejected such a one-dimensional approach, noting that RICO's requirement that injury must be to business or property means *all* **{–1094–}** RICO claims are by nature based on "economic" injury. *See id.* at 817. In its place, the Second Circuit adopted an approach that addresses each individual injury alleged. *Id.* at 818. The court considered the four injuries pleaded by the plaintiff: the theft of dividends paid by a foreign corporation, the funneling of money into a private investment fund in Chile, the theft of money from a New York bank account, and the theft of physical bearer shares from a safe-deposit box in New York. *Id.* at 811–13. Concerning the theft of the dividends and the funneling of money into the investment fund, the only connection to the United States was that those funds either passed through or were placed in bank accounts in the **[—8—]** United States at some point in the scheme. *Id.* at 818. The court concluded that such minimal, defendant-initiated contacts with the United States were not sufficient to make the resulting injuries to the plaintiff "domestic." *Id.* On the other hand, the court held that the alleged theft of the bearer shares and the theft of the money in the New York bank account were "domestic injuries." *Id.* at 820. What set these injuries apart was the presence of harm to tangible property that was located in the United States. *Id.* at 820–24. The court held that "where the injury is to tangible property, we conclude that, absent some extraordinary circumstance, the injury is domestic if the plaintiff's property was located in the United States when it was stolen or harmed, even if the plaintiff himself resides abroad." *Id.* at 820–21. Because of the importance of the presence of *tangible* property to its conclusion, the court was quick to distinguish the situations in the case before it from those involving intangible harms. *See id.* at 823–24. For instance, concerning the theft of the bearer shares, the court pointed out the plaintiff was not alleging any harm to the *value* of those shares, but rather the harm caused by the defendant's theft of the physical shares themselves. *Id.* at 824.

Both Armada and Amcol tell us *Bascuñán* is a win for them. At oral argument, Armada maintained that its judgment and claims are tangible properties located in the United States. For its part, Amcol argued that there is no tangible property in this case, only "a bundle of litigation rights," and that the connections to the United States are too tenuous to make Armada's alleged injuries domestic. We agree with Amcol. **[—9—]**

To begin with, the property Armada claims Amcol has harmed is not tangible. A "tangible asset" is one "that has a physical existence and is capable of being assigned a value." *Tangible asset*, Black's Law Dictionary (9th ed. 2009). As much as a judgment or a cause of action is a piece of property, it does not have a "physical existence." The property at issue here, then, is an "intangible asset," which is one that "can be amortized or converted to cash, such as patents, ... or a right to something, such as services paid for in advance." *Intangible asset,* Black's Law Dictionary (9th ed. 2009); *see also Blodgett v. Silberman*, 277 U.S. 1, 12 (1928) (concluding that right to receive money was "a chose in action, and an intangible").

The Second Circuit's reasoning in *Bascuñán* focused on how to address situations involving tangible property. Here, we must determine where to locate an injury to intangible property. As we noted above, the Supreme Court directs us to focus on where the injury is *suffered.* To "suffer" is "[t]o experience or sustain ... [an] injury." *Suffer,* Black's Law Dictionary (9th ed. 2009). It is well understood that a party experiences or sustains injuries to its intangible property at its residence, which for a corporation like Armada is its principal place of business. *See, e.g.,* **{-1095-}** *Kamel v. Hill-Rom Co., Inc.*, 108 F.3d 799, 805 (7th Cir. 1997) ("The place of injury was clearly Saudi Arabia, where Kamel's business would suffer as a result of Hill-Rom's conduct."); *CMACO Auto. Sys., Inc. v. Wanxiang Am. Corp.*, 589 F.3d 235, 246 (6th Cir. 2009) (concluding "the economic injury suffered by [the plaintiff] ... was clearly felt at its corporate headquarters"); *Engine Specialties, Inc. v. Bombardier Ltd.*, 605 F.2d 1, 19 (1st Cir. 1979) ("The place of injury is where plaintiff suffered the harm ... at its place of business, Pennsylvania."). Here, Ar- **[—10—]** mada's principal place of business is in Singapore, so any harm to Armada's intangible bundle of litigation rights was suffered in Singapore. Thus, the injury is not domestic, and Armada has failed to plead a plausible claim under civil RICO.

III.

A plaintiff advancing a civil RICO claim must allege a domestic injury. Armada has not done so. Therefore, the district court's entry of judgment on the pleadings on the RICO counts of Armada's amended complaint is AFFIRMED.

United States Court of Appeals
for the Seventh Circuit

No. 18-1881

VESUVIUS USA CORP.
vs.
AMERICAN COMMERCIAL LINES LLC

Appeal from the United States District Court for the Southern District of Indiana, New Albany Division

Decided: December 6, 2018

Citation: 910 F.3d 331, 6 Adm. R. 296 (7th Cir. 2018).

Before **KANNE, HAMILTON,** and **ST. EVE,** Circuit Judges.

[—1—] {-332-} **KANNE,** Circuit Judge:

This breach of contract action comes to us in admiralty jurisdiction. Vesuvius USA Corporation contracted with American Commercial Lines LLC (now **[—2—]** known as American Commercial Barge Line LLC, or "ACBL") to transport olivine sand by river barge from Louisiana to Kentucky. But when one of those shipments arrived with apparent water damage, a dispute arose between the parties about who was to blame. After some back-and-forth, they seemed to drop the matter. Two years later, however, Vesuvius brought this suit. Because the contract contains a clear limitations provision requiring the parties to bring disputes within four months of an incident, we affirm the district court's dismissal of the case.

I. BACKGROUND

In 2014, Vesuvius and ACBL entered into a shipping contract to transport olivine sand from New Orleans, Louisiana to Vesuvius's facility in Wurtland, Kentucky by river barge. The January 2015 shipment arrived at the discharge port in Wurtland on February 20. Vesuvius's employees inspected the cargo upon arrival and found it damaged by excess moisture. They notified ACBL, and ACBL arranged for a surveyor to perform an inspection that same day. The surveyor found no structural defect in the barge. Instead, he concluded that the sand was wet when it was loaded. In transit, some of that water evaporated, condensed on the overhead portion of the cargo space, and dripped back onto the sand. (R. 14-2 at 2.) The surveyor filed his report with ACBL on February 23, and ACBL promptly contacted Vesuvius to disclaim any liability. **{-333-}**

There the matter sat for two years. But on February 1, 2017, Vesuvius filed suit to recover damages for its loss, alleging that ACBL had breached the contract by providing an unseaworthy vessel. ACBL moved to dismiss the complaint, pointing to the limitations provision in the contract: **[—3—]**

> 22. MISCELLANEOUS: ... This Contract will be interpreted and enforced under the general maritime laws of the United States and, to the extent applicable, the laws of the State of Indiana. The Parties agree that any action or proceeding arising out of or in connection with this Contract will be brought exclusively in a state or federal court in Clark or Floyd County, State of Indiana[,] and [Vesuvius] consents to personal jurisdiction in such court. ... Unless otherwise provided hereunder, *all disputes under this Contract ... must be brought within four (4) months of the act or occurrence giving rise to the claim.*

(R. 9-1 at 8) (emphasis added). Reading the plain language of this provision, the district court determined that the action was untimely and granted the motion to dismiss. This appeal followed.

II. ANALYSIS

Original jurisdiction to hear this case stemmed from 28 U.S.C. § 1333, which authorizes federal district courts to hear "[a]ny civil case of admiralty or maritime jurisdiction." Because the alleged breach occurred "on navigable waters," neither party disputes federal jurisdiction. *Weaver v. Hollywood Casino-Aurora, Inc.*, 255 F.3d 379, 382 (7th Cir. 2001). We review a motion to dismiss for failure to state a claim under Fed. R. Civ. P. 12(b)(6) *de novo*, drawing all reasonable inferences in favor of Vesuvius, the non-moving party. *Boucher v. Fin. Sys. of*

Green Bay, Inc., 880 F.3d 362, 365 (7th Cir. 2018).

This case turns on the interpretation of the limitations provision of the contract, and in particular on the meaning of the word "disputes." Vesuvius argues that the phrase is no more **[—4—]** than a notification requirement: Vesuvius was required to notify ACBL of the problem within four months of its occurrence, and it provided that notification immediately upon discovery of the issue. The provision requires no more, because a "dispute" is not necessarily a lawsuit, and a contractual requirement that the parties sue each other within four months of an incident would force unnecessary litigation of disputes that the parties might work out between themselves given sufficient time. In the alternative, Vesuvius contends that the language in the contract is at least ambiguous, and because its reading is just as plausible as any other reading, Vesuvius should get the benefit of the doubt at this stage in the litigation.

ACBL, on the other hand, believes that the provision requires the parties to bring lawsuits within four months. While it concedes that the provision might appear ambiguous on its own, it insists that other language in the contract provides context and demonstrates that the parties intended to contract for a short limitations period for any potential legal actions.

The parties selected Indiana law to govern their agreement. In Indiana, "[t]he general rules of contract interpretation are that, unless the terms of a contract are ambiguous, they will be given their plain and ordinary meaning." *Brockmann v. Brockmann*, 938 N.E.2d 831, 834 (Ind. Ct. App. 2010). "Clear and unambiguous terms in a contract are deemed conclusive, and we will not construe an unambiguous contract or look to extrinsic evidence, but will merely apply the contractual provisions." *Id.* The "ultimate goal" of our analysis is to determine the "parties' intent." **{-334-}** *BRC Rubber & Plastics, Inc. v. Cont'l Carbon Co.*, 804 F.3d 1229, 1231 (7th Cir. 2015) (citing *Brockmann*, 938 N.E.2d at 834–35). **[—5—]**

Both parties contend that the term "disputes" is unambiguous. ACBL points to legal dictionaries and various cases to demonstrate that the verb "to bring," when coupled with "claim" or "dispute," usually refers to filing suit in court. *See, e.g., Bring an Action, Black's Law Dictionary* (10th ed. 2014). In turn, Vesuvius cites other cases and statutes in which "dispute" had a broader meaning than simply a lawsuit, also encompassing a mere disagreement that may be resolved through negotiation or alternative dispute resolution. *See, e.g., City of New Albany v. Cotner*, 919 N.E.2d 125, 132 (Ind. Ct. App. 2009) (determining that the contractual phrase "sewer fee dispute" was ambiguous).

But "[t]erms are not ambiguous merely because the parties disagree as to the proper interpretation of those terms." *Brockmann*, 938 N.E.2d at 835. While we might get bogged down in an argument over dictionary definitions if we confine the scope of our analysis to the provision alone, under Indiana law, we must "construe the contract as a whole and consider all provisions of the contract, not just the individual words, phrases, or paragraphs." *Bhd. Mut. Ins. Co. v. Michiana Contracting, Inc.*, 971 N.E.2d 127, 131 (Ind. Ct. App. 2012). As the district court correctly noted, the other provisions contained in ¶ 22 relate to choice of law, choice of forum and venue, and consent to personal jurisdiction. Viewed in that context, an obligation to bring "disputes" seems more likely to refer to the lawsuits to be brought under the other rules established in the same paragraph.

Vesuvius, acknowledging this point, looks to linguistic inconsistencies within the paragraph. If "disputes" are lawsuits, it asks, then why does ¶ 22 also refer to a lawsuit as an "action or proceeding?" Fair enough, but when we expand our scope **[—6—]** once more, we see that the sentence at issue cannot be a mere notification requirement. Paragraph 9 of the contract includes just such a notification requirement: "[Vesuvius] will immediately notify [ACBL] in writing if a barge is reasonably determined to be unsuitable. Such notification will include the reason such barge is unsuitable." (R. 9-1 at 6.) If we were to read the limitations provision in ¶ 22 as a requirement for Vesuvius to notify ACBL of a problem with its barge within four months, then the notification provision in ¶ 9 would be superfluous. The more logical conclusion is that the parties knew how to write a notification requirement, and they inserted it in ¶ 9. Likewise, they knew how to write a limitations provision, and they inserted it in ¶ 22, right next to the other provisions spelling out how and where to bring suit in court. Vesuvius failed to comply with that unambiguous contractual obligation, and its suit is untimely.

On a final note, Vesuvius points to dicta in the district court's order dismissing its case in which it alleges that the district court improperly drew an inference against it:

> We might find Vesuvius's argument more persuasive if there had not been so long a time-lapse between ACBL's denial of responsibility for the cargo damage and its filing of this lawsuit. ... The reasonable inference from such silence is that Vesuvius had elected to acquiesce in, or at least chose not to contest, ACBL's rejection of their complaint about the condition of the cargo.

(R. 22 at 7.)

As we noted above, when considering a motion to dismiss under Rule 12(b)(6), a court must draw all reasonable inferences **{-335-}** in favor of the non-moving party. *Boucher*, 880 F.3d at **[—7—]** 365. In this case, it appears that the district court drew at least one inference *against* the non-moving party.

But any error was harmless. First, the district court had already stepped through the correct contractual analysis and made its conclusion before any discussion of inferences to draw from the parties' behavior after the incident had occurred. Second, and more importantly, even if we were to draw the opposite inference in Vesuvius's favor, it would make no difference. We might infer that Vesuvius genuinely believed that it had complied in full with its obligations under ¶ 22 by notifying ACBL of the problem on February 20, 2015. Vesuvius might then have genuinely believed that it had all the time in the world to bring suit, and it did so two years later. But because we find that the contract is not ambiguous, the parties' actions after they signed the contract are irrelevant to the meaning of the contract itself. Regardless of whether we were to infer from Vesuvius's actions that it genuinely believed its own position or whether it knew that its suit was untimely, the meaning of the contract is the same.

III. CONCLUSION

Standing on its own, perhaps the limitations provision of the contract might be ambiguous. But read in context with the rest of the contract, there is no question that Vesuvius was required to file suit no later than four months after it discovered the damage. Because Vesuvius waited two years to bring its claim, the district court properly dismissed it as untimely. Accordingly, we AFFIRM the judgment of the district court.

United States Court of Appeals for the Ninth Circuit

United States Court of Appeals
for the Ninth Circuit

No. 16-35474

GALILEA, LLC
vs.
AGCS MARINE INS. CO.

Appeal from the United States District Court for the District of Montana

Decided: January 16, 2018

Citation: 879 F.3d 1052, 6 Adm. R. 300 (9th Cir. 2018).

Before **BERZON**, **WATFORD**, and **OWENS**, Circuit Judges.

[—3—] **{-1053-}** **BERZON**, Circuit Judge: **{-1054-}**

"The sea, although an agreeable, is a dangerous companion," wrote Plato more than two millennia ago. Our case is about that danger; it concerns "a brave vessel . . . [d]ash'd all to pieces," like the ship Prospero hexed in *The Tempest*. William Shakespeare, *The Tempest* act 1, sc. 2.

Although the background has its drama, the primary legal issues are more mundane: Is an arbitration provision in a maritime insurance policy enforceable despite law in the forum state assertedly precluding its application? In addressing this question, we consider several questions concerning the intersection of the McCarran-Ferguson Act, 15 U.S.C. § 1012, which shields state insurance laws from federal preemption, and the Federal Arbitration Act ("FAA"), 9 U.S.C. § 1–16, which provides for enforcement of arbitration provisions in maritime contracts. After doing so, we conclude that the arbitration clause should be given effect. **[—4—]**

I. BACKGROUND

A. Contracting for Yacht Insurance

Montana residents Taunia and Chris Kittler are the sole members of Galilea, LLC ("Galilea"), a Nevada limited liability company. In 2014, Galilea purchased a sixty-foot yacht ("the Yacht"). This case concerns the scope of the insurance coverage Galilea bought for the Yacht.

About a year after purchasing the Yacht, the Kittlers submitted to Pantaenius America Ltd. ("Pantaenius") an online request for an insurance quote. Pantaenius specializes in obtaining and administering yacht insurance policies, acting as an agent for insurance underwriters. Following the quote request, the Kittlers electronically exchanged several documents with Pantaenius. According to Galilea, the Kittlers also spoke with a Pantaenius representative over the phone to discuss the materials needed to complete an insurance application. The Kittlers say they informed the Pantaenius representative on one call that it would be difficult to submit a hand-signed application because the Kittlers were, at the time, sailing the yacht in the Caribbean, en route from Florida to San Diego via the Panama Canal. Pantaenius nonetheless required a hand-signed application, so the Kittlers docked in Puerto Rico to locate the necessary equipment to print and scan a signed application.

The application for insurance listed three different underwriters: AGCS Marine Insurance Company, Liberty Mutual Insurance Company, and Torus National Insurance Company (collectively, "Underwriters"). The application **[—5—]** noted that one or more of these Underwriters would "be assigned at the time of binding [insurance] coverage."[1]

The application also included arbitration and choice-of-law terms. The arbitration term provided, in relevant part:

> Any dispute arising out of or relating to the relationship between Pantaenius America Ltd and/or our participating underwriters and the insured shall be settled by arbitration administered by the American Arbitration Association ["AAA"] in accordance with its Commercial Arbitration Rules. . . . The dispute shall be submitted to one

[1] All three companies are appellees and cross-appellants here.

> arbitrator. . . . The place of arbitration shall be New York, New York. **{–1055–}**

The application also provided that the "relationship" and the Agreement "shall be governed by the laws of New York."

A day after Galilea submitted the signed application, Pantaenius issued an insurance binder providing preliminary coverage for up to two weeks from the date of application.[2] The binder set a coverage limit of $1,566,500, based on the "total agreed fixed value" of the Yacht; established a covered "Cruising Area" that extended south to 30.5 degrees north latitude; named the three Underwriters as the issuing insurance companies; incorporated the forthcoming policy's **[—6—]** terms and conditions; and attached a document with those anticipated terms.

The formal insurance policy issued a day later. Pantaenius formally signed the insurance policy on behalf of the three Underwriters. The policy provided that it would be "effective only when the insured vessel(s) are within the 'cruising area' specified."

The choice-of-law and forum selection provisions in the policy's terms and conditions were different from those in the application. Both the policy and the application called for arbitration in New York pursuant to AAA rules. But the scope of the choice-of-law provision and arbitration clause differed. The policy provided:

> This insurance policy shall be governed by and construed in accordance with well established and entrenched principles and precedents of substantive United States Federal Maritime Law, but where no such established and entrenched principles and precedents exist, the policy shall be governed and construed in accordance with the substantive laws of the State of New York, without giving effect to its conflict of laws principles, and the parties hereto agree that any and all disputes arising under this policy shall be resolved exclusively by binding arbitration to take place within New York County, in the State of New York, and to be conducted pursuant to the Rules of the American Arbitration Association. **[—7—]**

The policy thus differed from the application by (i) identifying federal maritime law and, to fill its gaps, New York law, as the choice of law applicable to the policy, and (ii) including different language concerning the scope of arbitrable disputes—"any and all disputes arising under this policy," not "any dispute arising out of or relating to the relationship."

B. The Parties' Dispute and Procedural History

The Yacht ran ashore near Colón, Panama about a month after the insurance policy issued. Galilea submitted a claim for insurance coverage, but the Underwriters refused to pay it. Pantaenius explained that the Yacht had traveled south of the cruising area set forth in both the application and the policy. Galilea rejoined that the application and policy do not reflect the parties' actual agreement, and that Pantaenius and the Underwriters misrepresented the scope of the written policy.

After Galilea requested reconsideration of the coverage denial, the Underwriters initiated arbitration proceedings in New York. Galilea submitted objections and counterclaims in the arbitration proceedings, but also filed a separate action in federal court in the District of Montana, along with a motion to stay the arbitration proceedings. **{–1056–}**

In its Montana complaint, Galilea asserted twelve causes of action, all of which substantially overlapped with its arbitration counterclaims. The Underwriters responded with a motion to dismiss for failure to state a claim and a motion to compel arbitration. Separately, in federal court in the Southern

[2] An insurance binder provides preliminary, temporary coverage, often reflecting the terms of a forthcoming formal insurance policy should one be issued. *See* 16 Williston on Contracts § 49:53 (4th ed. 2017).

District of New York, the Underwriters filed a petition to compel arbitration. **[—8—]**

The Montana district court issued two orders from which the parties have lodged certified interlocutory cross-appeals. *See* 28 U.S.C. § 1292(b). In those orders, the court held: (1) the arbitration provision in Galilea's original insurance application was not relevant, because it was not included in the Underwriters' demand for arbitration; (2) claims arising under the insurance policy come within admiralty jurisdiction, and under relevant choice-of-law principles, federal maritime law governs the contract; (3) the FAA applies and requires enforcing the policy's arbitration provision; (4) questions relating to the enforceability and scope of the arbitration provision are properly determined by the court, not an arbitrator; and (5) the scope of the policy's arbitration clause did not extend to cover ten of Galilea's twelve claims. The district court thus granted the Underwriters' motion to compel arbitration as to two of Galilea's claims but denied it as to the others.

II. DISCUSSION

This case ultimately presents "gateway" arbitrability questions: whether a valid and enforceable agreement to arbitrate exists, and, if so, whether particular claims fall within the scope of the arbitration provision. *See Rent-A-Ctr., W., Inc. v. Jackson*, 561 U.S. 63, 70 (2010). But, before we reach those questions, we must decide whether there is an agreement to which the federal law of arbitrability could apply. *See Prima Paint Corp. v. Flood & Conklin Mfg. Co.*, 388 U.S. 395, 401 (1967). We conclude the parties' insurance policy is the governing contract and falls within the Federal Arbitration Act's scope. **[—9—]**

A. The FAA Applies to the Insurance Policy but Not the Insurance Application

The FAA cannot compel a party "to arbitrate the threshold issue of the existence of an agreement to arbitrate" unless there is an overarching agreement to do so within the FAA's scope. *Three Valleys Mun. Water Dist. v. E.F. Hutton & Co.*, 925 F.2d 1136, 1140–41 (9th Cir. 1991) (emphasis omitted); *see also Granite Rock Co. v. Int'l Bhd. of Teamsters*, 561 U.S. 287, 296–97 (2010). That is, "[a]lthough challenges to the validity of a contract with an arbitration clause are to be decided by the arbitrator, challenges to the very existence of the contract are, in general, properly directed to the court." *Kum Tat Ltd. v. Linden Ox Pasture, LLC*, 845 F.3d 979, 983 (9th Cir. 2017) (internal citations omitted). Accordingly, we "must first make a threshold finding that the document [evidencing an agreement] at least purports to be . . . a contract." *Republic of Nicaragua v. Standard Fruit Co.*, 937 F.2d 469, 476 (9th Cir. 1991).

1. The Insurance Application Is Not a Contract

As noted, Galilea submitted a signed application for insurance to the Underwriters. Among other terms, the application included choice-of-law and forum selection clauses. *See* p. 5, *supra*. The Underwriters suggest the application's arbitration provision should govern this dispute under the FAA; Galilea maintains, to the contrary, **{–1057–}** that the application does not evidence mutual assent to a contract or to arbitration.

We agree with Galilea on this point. Under the law made applicable by the policy and application, the application was not a contract. **[—10—]**

New York state law is made applicable under Galilea's insurance application, and also, if no established substantive principle or precedent of federal maritime law applies, under the insurance policy's choice-of-law provision. We have not uncovered any established federal maritime law rule on this issue, and so we proceed to the law of New York.

Under New York law, language from an application may be incorporated into an insurance policy only if the application was attached to the policy at the time of delivery. *See Smith v. Pruco Life Ins. Co. of N.J.*, 710 F.3d 476, 479–80 (2d Cir. 2013) (per curiam) (citing N.Y. Ins. Law § 3204(a)); *Cutler v. Hartford Life Ins. Co.*, 22 N.Y.2d 245, 250–52 (1968); *Berkshire Life Ins. Co. v. Weinig*, 290 N.Y. 6, 10 (1943); *see also* 16 Williston on Contracts at § 49:41 (4th ed. 2017); 2 Couch on Insurance § 18:6 (3d ed. 2017). The insurance policy "shall contain the entire contract between the parties," and no document may be incorporated by reference into the insurance contract unless a true copy is "endorsed upon or attached to the policy or contract when issued." *Smith*, 710 F.3d at 479–80 (quoting N.Y. Ins. Law § 3204(a)(1)).

Here, it does not appear that the application was attached to the policy when issued. Instead, some of the information provided in the application was reprinted in the policy, but the forum-selection and choice-of-law provisions were not incorporated. Even if attached to the policy, the application is not named in the policy as an incorporated document. Thus, because the application was not a contractual **[—11—]** agreement under New York law, the federal law of arbitrability cannot apply to its arbitration clause.[3]

2. The Insurance Policy Is a Contract Subject to the FAA

We now turn to whether the policy is subject to the FAA. Policies that insure maritime interests against maritime risks are contracts subject to admiralty jurisdiction and to federal maritime law. *La Reunion Francaise SA v. Barnes*, 247 F.3d 1022, 1025 (9th Cir. 2001). The insurance policy here is a maritime insurance contract and so would seem to be subject to federal maritime law.

Galilea asserts to the contrary—that under federal maritime law, the FAA does *not* apply to this contract, because Montana public policy overrides its arbitration provision and Montana law, preserved from federal preemption by the federal McCarran-Ferguson Act, precludes the FAA's application. We disagree, and hold that the FAA does apply.

[3] We do not consider the extent to which other representations made in the application are incorporated into the policy or may otherwise be considered when interpreting or enforcing the policy.

a. The Federal Arbitration Act Constitutes Established Federal Maritime Law for "Maritime Transactions"

The Supreme Court long ago established that where an "insurance policy . . . is a maritime contract the Admiralty Clause of the Constitution brings it within federal jurisdiction." *Wilburn Boat Co. v. Fireman's Fund Ins. Co.*, 348 U.S. 310, 313 (1955). At **{-1058-}** the same time, *Wilburn Boat* **[—12—]** instructed, "it does not follow . . . that every term in every maritime contract can only be controlled by some federally defined admiralty rule." *Id.* Rather, held *Wilburn Boat*, as insurance is traditionally an area of state regulation, federal maritime law leaves room for state insurance regulation if there is no established federal maritime law rule or need for federal uniformity. *Id.* at 316, 321; *see also id.* at 323–24 (Frankfurter, J., concurring in the judgment).

After *Wilburn Boat*, "the initial inquiry of the courts in interpreting a policy of marine insurance [is] to determine whether there is an established federal maritime law rule." *Certain Underwriters at Lloyds, London v. Inlet Fisheries Inc.*, 518 F.3d 645, 649–50 (9th Cir. 2008) (quoting Thomas J. Schoenbaum, Admiralty and Maritime Law § 17–6 (4th ed. 2004)) (internal quotation marks omitted). If so, "federal admiralty law [will] govern[]. . . ." *Suma Fruit Int'l v. Albany Ins. Co.*, 122 F.3d 34, 35 (9th Cir. 1997). "[S]tate law will control . . . only in the absence of a federal statute, a judicially fashioned admiralty rule, or a need for uniformity in admiralty practice." *Id.* (internal quotation marks omitted).

Here, there is an established federal maritime law rule concerning the enforcement of arbitration provisions in insurance policies, namely, the Federal Arbitration Act. The FAA specifically applies to "maritime transaction[s]." 9 U.S.C. § 2. "Maritime transactions" include, among other types of agreements, "agreements relating to . . . repairs to vessels, collisions, or any other matters in foreign commerce which, if the subject of controversy, would be embraced within admiralty jurisdiction." *Id.* § 1.[4] The parties' **[—13—]** insurance policy relates both to collisions and to repairs to the Yacht, and, as *Wilburn Boat* holds, 348 U.S. at 313, a dispute concerning a maritime insurance policy comes within federal admiralty jurisdiction. As the parties' dispute falls within the scope of the FAA and the FAA includes an applicable, specific federal maritime law rule, under *Wilburn Boat*, Montana state law does not govern the validity of the agreement's arbitration provision.

b. Federal Maritime Law Is Not Precluded by Montana Law under the McCarran-Ferguson Act

Galilea first attempts to navigate around *Wilburn Boat* with the McCarran-Ferguson Act, 15 U.S.C. § 1011 *et seq.*, which precludes the application of federal statutes if (1) a state law is "enacted . . . for the purpose of regulating the business of insurance;" (2) the federal law does not "specifically relat[e] to the business of insurance;" and (3) the federal statute's application would "invalidate, impair, or supersede" state insurance law. *Humana Inc. v. Forsyth*, 525 U.S. 299, 307 (1999) (internal quotation marks omitted). Galilea points to Montana's Uniform Arbitration Act, which renders unenforceable arbitration clauses in "insurance polices or annuity contracts except for those contracts between insurance companies," Mont. Code Ann. § 27-5-114(2)(c), and asserts that the McCarran-Ferguson Act requires that, notwithstanding *Wilburn Boat*, the Montana rule precluding arbitration of consumer insurance disputes applies here. Galilea also cites to non-maritime insurance cases holding arbitration agreements unenforceable under state anti-arbitration laws saved by the **{–1059–}** McCarran-Ferguson Act. *See Am. Bankers Ins. Co. of Fla. v. Inman*, 436 F.3d 490, 492 (5th Cir. 2006); *McKnight v. Chicago Title Ins. Co.*, 358 F.3d 854, 855 (11th Cir. 2004) (per curiam); *Standard* **[—14—]** *Sec. Life Ins. Co. of N.Y. v. West*, 267 F.3d 821, 823–24 (8th Cir. 2001); *Mut. Reinsurance Bureau v. Great Plains Mut. Ins. Co.*, 969 F.2d 931, 931–32 (10th Cir. 1992). This McCarran-Ferguson-based argument sails too far ahead too fast. Slowing down the analysis, it becomes apparent that there is no route for Montana law to apply as a competitor to the FAA here.

Under *Wilburn Boat*, Galilea's maritime insurance policy is within federal admiralty jurisdiction and governed by applicable maritime law if such law exists. Applying an established federal maritime law rule—such as the provision of the FAA directly mandating the enforcement of arbitration clauses in maritime transactions—thus does not "invalidate, impair, or supersede any law enacted by any State for the purpose of regulating the business of insurance." 15 U.S.C. § 1012(b). Rather, given *Wilburn Boat* and its progeny, any applicable maritime law rule is primary, and state law applies only if maritime law does not. Given the interstitial, contingent nature of state law in this setting, state insurance law is not "invalidate[d], impair[ed], or supersede[d]," *id.*, by applying a maritime law rule when, as here, there is one.

Alternatively, one reaches the same conclusion if one applies established maritime choice-of-law principles to the insurance policy's choice-of-law provisions. The parties here agreed to a choice-of-law term in the insurance policy—federal maritime law and, as needed, New York law. "[W]here the parties specify in their contractual agreement which law will apply, admiralty courts will generally give effect to that choice," *Chan v. Soc'y Expeditions, Inc.*, 123 F.3d 1287, 1296–97 (9th Cir. 1997), absent, as relevant here, "a state which has a materially greater interest than the **[—15—]** chosen state . . . and which . . . would be the state of the applicable law in the absence of an effective choice of law," *Flores v. Am. Seafoods Co.*, 335 F.3d 904, 917 (9th Cir. 2003) (quoting Restatement (Second) of Conflict of Laws § 187(2) (1991)).

Montana does not have a materially greater interest than federal maritime (or New York) law. There is no question that Montana law has relatively little to do with this dispute. Galilea is a Nevada limited

[4] "[C]ontracts of employment of seamen" are excepted from the FAA's coverage. 9 U.S.C. § 1.

liability corporation, and the Insurers have principal places of business or are incorporated under the laws of Delaware, New Jersey, Illinois, and Massachusetts. Although Galilea's members are Montana residents, they were in Florida, Puerto Rico, and the Caribbean Sea at the time of contracting, and the insured property appears never to have been in Montana. Moreover, landlocked Montana has relatively weak interests in maritime insurance law, particularly as compared to coastal states with more developed maritime law, including New York.

But, again—there *is* a federal maritime law rule here applicable, the FAA. Under the FAA, the arbitration provision is enforceable. The McCarran-Ferguson Act thus has no pertinence, as no state's law is applicable in the first instance.

c. *Federal Maritime Law Is Not Precluded by Montana Law under* The Bremen

Galilea also argues that the policy's choice-of-law provision is unenforceable under *M/S Bremen v. Zapata OffShore Co.* (*The Bremen*), 407 U.S. 1 (1972). We are not persuaded. **[—16—] {-1060-}**

The Bremen held that federal maritime law makes *forum* selection clauses presumptively enforceable. *Id.* at 13–14. At the same time, "[u]nder the directives of the Supreme Court in [*The*] *Bremen*, we will determine a forum selection clause is unenforceable 'if enforcement would contravene a strong public policy of the forum in which suit is brought, whether declared by statute or by judicial decision.'" *Doe 1 v. AOL LLC*, 552 F.3d 1077, 1083 (9th Cir. 2009) (per curiam) (quoting *The Bremen*, 407 U.S. at 15) (emphasis omitted). Galilea points to the strong public policy of Montana against enforcement of arbitration agreements in the context of this dispute, and argues that enforcement of the policy's arbitration agreement would contravene the policy of the state in which Galilea brought suit.

There are two critical problems with Galilea's reliance on *The Bremen*. First, that case did not discuss federal maritime law rules about *choice-of-law clauses*, but rather about forum selection clauses. *See The Bremen*, 407 U.S. at 2, 17–19. By contrast, Galilea and the Underwriters agreed to a kind of forum selection provision—arbitration[5]—and also to a separate choice-of-law provision—federal maritime law, and where that law has gaps, New York law. And as we have already established, here there is no gap in federal maritime law to fill with law from *any* state, Montana included, as the FAA supplies the governing arbitration law for maritime transactions. **[—17—]**

Second, and more foundationally, *The Bremen* considered whether the public policy of the forum where suit was brought—there, federal public policy as supplied by federal maritime law—outweighed the application of the law of other countries. *Id.* at 17–18. In other words, under the rule of *The Bremen* and its progeny, courts consider the application of the laws of otherwise equally situated fora in light of the "concerns of international comity, respect for the capacities of foreign and transnational tribunals, and sensitivity to the need of the international commercial system for predictability." *Mitsubishi Motors Corp. v. Soler Chrysler-Plymouth, Inc.*, 473 U.S. 614, 629 (1985). But here we encounter an unequal, hierarchical relationship between federal maritime law and state law; again, "[s]tate law governs disputes arising under marine insurance contracts only 'in the absence of a federal statute, a judicially fashioned admiralty rule, or a need for uniformity in admiralty practice.'" *Kiernan v. Zurich Cos.*, 150 F.3d 1120, 1121 (9th Cir. 1998) (citations omitted).

It does not make sense to apply the federal maritime choice-of-forum rule of *The Bremen* to invalidate *another* established federal maritime rule specifically addressing the appropriate forum—here, arbitration—because of a conflict with a forum *state's*

[5] In the context of international arbitration, the Supreme Court has noted, "An agreement to arbitrate before a specified tribunal is, in effect, a specialized kind of forum-selection clause." *Scherk v. Alberto-Culver Co.*, 417 U.S. 506, 519 (1974); *see also Polimaster Ltd. v. RAE Sys., Inc.*, 623 F.3d 832, 837 (9th Cir. 2010).

public policy. Within federal admiralty jurisdiction, conflicting state policy cannot override squarely applicable federal maritime law. Applying *The Bremen* in the way Galilea requests would distort the basic, gap-filling principles underlying federal maritime law's limited recognition of state insurance law. "[S]ince the effect of the application of [state] law here would be to invalidate the contract, this case can hardly be analogized to cases . . . where state law had the effect of supplementing **{-1061-}** the remedies available in admiralty for the vindication of maritime rights." **[—18—]** *Kossick v. United Fruit Co.*, 365 U.S. 731, 741–42 (1961) (citations omitted).[6] We thus conclude that Galilea's reliance on Montana law under *The Bremen* is misplaced.

For the foregoing reasons, Montana's law simply does not apply to the dispute here. So it cannot act, through *The Bremen* or any other avenue, to trump the FAA as an established federal maritime law rule.

B. The Parties Have Delegated Arbitrability Issues to an Arbitrator

We conclude by addressing whether arbitrability issues have been delegated to an arbitrator under the parties' agreement. Because the parties here are sophisticated, and because they incorporated AAA rules into their arbitration agreement, they have clearly and unmistakably indicated their intent to submit arbitrability questions to an arbitrator.

Under the FAA, "the usual presumption that exists in favor of the arbitrability of merits-based disputes is replaced by a presumption *against* the arbitrability of arbitrability." *Cape Flattery Ltd. v. Titan Maritime, LLC*, 647 F.3d 914, 920 (9th Cir. 2011) (citing *First Options of Chi., Inc. v. Kaplan*, 514 U.S. 938, 944 (1995)); *see also BG Group PLC v. Republic of Argentina*, 134 S. Ct. 1198, 1206–07 (2014) (summarizing the presumptions that guide "'threshold' **[—19—]** questions about arbitration"). Because the question of who should decide arbitrability issues "is rather arcane," ambiguity on this question cuts in favor of deciding the parties did *not* delegate these questions to an arbitrator. *First Options*, 514 U.S. at 945 (citation omitted). Presuming otherwise "might too often force unwilling parties to arbitrate a matter they reasonably would have thought a judge, not an arbitrator, would decide." *Id.* (citation omitted). Accordingly, the court maintains jurisdiction over these gateway arbitrability questions unless there is "'clear and unmistakable' evidence that the parties intended to delegate the arbitrability question to an arbitrator." *Brennan v. Opus Bank*, 796 F.3d 1125, 1130 (9th Cir. 2015).

In *Brennan*, we decided that, at least in a contract between sophisticated parties, the "incorporation of the AAA rules [into an arbitration agreement] constitutes clear and unmistakable evidence that contracting parties agreed to arbitrate arbitrability." *Id.* That is because the American Arbitration Association's rules provide that "[t]he arbitrator shall have the power to rule on his or her own jurisdiction, including any objections with respect to the existence, scope, or validity of the arbitration agreement or to the arbitrability of any claim or counterclaim." American Arbitration Association Commercial Arbitration Rule 7; *accord* American Arbitration Association Consumer Arbitration Rule 14.[7] **{-1062-}**

Here, the policy's arbitration provision states, in relevant part, that "the parties hereto agree that any and all disputes **[—20—]** arising under this policy shall be resolved exclusively by binding arbitration . . . conducted pursuant to the Rules of the American Arbitration Association." This policy

[6] More generally, applying *The Bremen* in the manner Galilea requests—which could invalidate FAA-covered arbitration clauses, insurance-related or not, inconsistent with a state's public policy against arbitration—would not be compatible with the contemporary law of domestic arbitration, which ordinarily disallows giving force to state law rules that "single[] out arbitration agreements for disfavored treatment." *Kindred Nursing Ctrs. Ltd. P'ship v. Clark*, 137 S. Ct. 1421, 1425 (2017).

[7] Galilea contends that it is unclear which set of American Arbitration Association rules apply here. But the same result obtains as to arbitrability under either potentially applicable set of rules.

language is comparable to that in the provision in *Brennan*. *See* 796 F.3d at 1128 (quoting agreement that relevant disputes "'be settled by binding arbitration in accordance with the Rules of the American Arbitration Association'").

As in *Brennan* itself, we need not decide whether the *Brennan* rule applies when one or more party is unsophisticated. Both parties here are sophisticated with respect to contracting for insurance policies. The Underwriters are, obviously, sophisticated parties; they underwrite maritime insurance policies. But so are Galilea and the Kittlers. Although they are Montana residents, Taunia and Chris Kittler formed a limited liability company under Nevada law to own and maintain a yacht worth more than a million dollars. In addition, Chris Kittler owns and operates a financial services company, also incorporated under Nevada law. In light of Galilea's and the Underwriters' sophistication, the agreement to arbitrate according to AAA rules is sufficient to show clear and unmistakable intent to resolve arbitrability questions in arbitration, rather than federal court. The district court therefore erred by declining to send those questions to arbitration and instead construing the scope of the parties' arbitration agreement itself.

III. CONCLUSION

The Underwriters' argument that the insurance application supplies an enforceable arbitration agreement fails. The parties' insurance *policy*'s arbitration clause concerns a maritime transaction falling under the FAA, and **[—21—]** Montana law is inapplicable under both federal maritime law choice-of-law principles and the policy itself, so it does not render the arbitration clause unenforceable. We further agree with the Underwriters that the arbitration agreement shows a clear and unmistakable intent to resolve arbitrability questions in arbitration. We thus affirm the district court's order finding the policy's arbitration clause enforceable, affirm the district court's order granting the Underwriters' motion to compel arbitration as to certain causes of action, reverse the district court's order denying the Underwriters' motion to compel arbitration as to Galilea's remaining causes of action, and remand to the district court with instructions to grant the Underwriters' motion to compel arbitration in its entirety.

AFFIRMED IN PART, REVERSED IN PART, and REMANDED.

United States Court of Appeals
for the Ninth Circuit

No. 15-56775

BATTERTON
vs.
DUTRA GROUP

Appeal from the United States District Court for the Central District of California

Decided: January 23, 2018

Citation: 880 F.3d 1089, 6 Adm. R. 308 (9th Cir. 2018).

Before **THOMAS**, Chief Judge, and **KLEINFELD** and **NGUYEN**, Circuit Judges.

[—3—] {-1090-} KLEINFELD, Senior Circuit Judge:

We address the availability of punitive damages for unseaworthiness.

This case comes to us on a 28 U.S.C. § 1292(b) certification for interlocutory appeal. The district court certified the appeal, and we granted permission for it. District courts within our circuit have divided on the **[—4—]** substantive issue,[1] as have the circuits,[2] and the issue is of considerable importance in maritime law.

Facts

The case comes to us on the pleadings and nothing else. The district court denied a motion to strike the portion of the prayer seeking punitive damages for unseaworthiness. We therefore take our facts from the complaint. They are not proved, and we intimate no view as to whether punitive damages may ultimately turn out to be appropriate.

The plaintiff, Christopher Batterton, was a deckhand on a vessel owned and operated by the defendant, Dutra Group. While Batterton was working on the vessel in navigable waters, a hatch cover blew open and crushed his left hand. Pressurized **{-1091-}** air was being pumped into a compartment below the hatch cover, and the vessel lacked an exhaust mechanism to relieve the pressure when it got too high. The lack of a mechanism for exhausting the pressurized air made the vessel unseaworthy and caused permanent disability and other damages to Batterton. **[—5—]**

Analysis

The only question before us is whether punitive damages are an available remedy for unseaworthiness claims. We answered it in *Evich v. Morris*.[3] That would be the end of the case, except that Dutra contends, and the Fifth Circuit agrees,[4] that the later Supreme Court decision in *Miles v. Apex Marine Corp.*[5] implicitly overrules *Evich*.

In *Evich* we squarely held that "[p]unitive damages are available under general maritime law for claims of unseaworthiness, and for failure to pay maintenance and cure."[6] We distinguished Jones Act claims, where punitive damages are unavailable.[7] The standard for punitive damages, we held, was "conduct which manifests 'reckless or callous disregard' for the rights of others . . . or 'gross negligence or actual malice [or] criminal indifference.'"[8]

[1] *Compare, e.g., Rowe v. Hornblower Fleet*, No. C-11-4979 JCS, 2012 WL 5833541, at *900 (N.D. Cal. Nov. 16, 2012) *and Wagner v. Kona Blue Water Farms, LLC*, 2010 A.M.C. 2469, 2483 (D. Haw. Sept. 13, 2010) *with Jackson v. Unisea, Inc.*, 824 F. Supp. 895, 897–98 (D. Alaska 1992) *and Complaint of Aleutian Enter., Ltd.*, 777 F. Supp. 793, 796 (W.D. Wash. 1991).

[2] *Compare Evich v. Morris*, 819 F.2d 256, 258 (9th Cir. 1987), *overruling on other grounds acknowledged by Saavedra v. Korean Air Lines Co.*, 93 F.3d 547, 553–54 (9th Cir. 1996) *and Self v. Great Lakes Dredge & Dock Co.*, 832 F.2d 1540, 1550 (11th Cir. 1987) *with McBride v. Estis Well Service*, 768 F.3d 382, 384, 2 Adm. R. 320, 320 (5th Cir. 2014) (en banc) *and Horsley v. Mobil Oil Corp.*, 15 F.3d 200, 203 (1st Cir. 1994).

[3] 819 F.2d at 258.

[4] *See McBride*, 768 F.3d at 384, 2 Adm. R. at 320.

[5] 498 U.S. 19 (1990).

[6] 819 F.2d at 258 (citations omitted).

[7] *Id.*

[8] *Id.* at 258–59 (quoting *Protectus Alpha Nav. Co. v. N. Pac. Grain Growers, Inc.*, 767 F.2d 1379, 1385 (9th Cir. 1985)).

Evich was a wrongful death case, not an injury case.[9] But we did not speak to whether there might be any distinction **[—6—]** regarding the availability of punitive damages according to whether the seaman had died. Generally, the availability of damages is more restricted in wrongful death cases than in injury cases. So without authority to the contrary, we have no reason to distinguish *Evich* and limit its holding to wrongful death cases. No party has suggested that we do so.

Under *Miller v. Gammie*,[10] we must follow *Evich* unless it is "clearly irreconcilable" with the Supreme Court's decision in *Miles*.[11] *Miles* holds that loss of society damages are unavailable in a general maritime action for the wrongful death of a seaman and that lost future earnings are unavailable in a general maritime survival action.[12] That is because wrongful death damages are limited to "pecuniary loss"[13] and because "[t]he Jones Act/[Federal Employers' Liability Act] survival provision limits recovery to losses suffered during the decedent's lifetime."[14]

The Supreme Court's more recent decision in *Atlantic Sounding Co. v. Townsend*[15] speaks broadly: "Historically, punitive damages have been available and awarded in general **[—7—]** maritime actions, including some in maintenance and cure."[16] Unseaworthiness is a general maritime cause of action.[17] *Townsend* reads *Miles* as **{–1092–}** limiting the availability of damages for loss of society and lost future earnings[18] and holds that *Miles* does not limit the availability of punitive damages in maintenance and cure cases.[19] By implication, *Townsend* holds that *Miles* does not limit the availability of remedies in other actions "under general maritime law,"[20] which includes unseaworthiness claims.

Arguably, *Townsend* leaves room for a distinction between maintenance and cure claims and unseaworthiness claims. The Court recognizes that "remedies for negligence, unseaworthiness, and maintenance and cure have different origins and may on occasion call for application of slightly different principles and procedures."[21] But nothing in *Townsend*'s reasoning suggests that such a distinction would mean that a limitation ought to be made on the availability of punitive damages as a remedy for general maritime unseaworthiness claims. **[—8—]**

So far our discussion suggests that *Miles* does not overturn *Evich*, that *Evich* remains in force as controlling circuit law, and that *Evich*'s holding that punitive damages are available as a remedy for unseaworthiness claims is undisturbed and binding. Appellant's arguments to the contrary, though, are given force by *McBride v. Estis Well Service*.[22]

McBride, a sharply divided Fifth Circuit en banc decision, holds that "punitive damages are non-pecuniary losses"[23] and therefore may not be recovered under the Jones Act or under the general maritime law.[24] We held in another context in *Kopczynski v. The Jacqueline* that "[p]unitive damages are non-pecuniary" and so are not allowable under the Jones Act.[25] *McBride* has five extensive and scholarly opinions addressing all sides of the question. Six dissenters note that *Miles* "addressed the availability of loss of society damages to non-seamen under general maritime law, not punitive damages,"[26] and that "*Townsend* announced the default rule that punitive damages are available for

---

9 *Id.* at 258.
10 335 F.3d 889 (9th Cir. 2003).
11 *Id.* at 893.
12 *Miles*, 498 U.S. at 37.
13 *Id.* at 32.
14 *Id.* at 36.
15 557 U.S. 404 (2009).
16 *Id.* at 407.
17 *See id.* at 419; *see also Miles*, 498 U.S. at 29.
18 *Townsend*, 557 U.S. at 419.
19 *Id.*
20 *Id.* at 421.
21 *Id.* at 423 (quoting *Fitzgerald v. U.S. Lines Co.*, 374 U.S. 16, 18 (1963)).
22 768 F.3d 382, 2 Adm. R. 320 (5th Cir. 2014) (en banc).
23 *Id.* at 384, 2 Adm. R. at 320.
24 *Id.*, 2 Adm. R. at 320.
25 742 F.2d 555, 561 (9th Cir. 1984).
26 768 F.3d at 408–09, 2 Adm. R. at 342 (Higginson, J., dissenting).

actions under the general maritime law (such as unseaworthiness)."[27] **[—9—]**

Well before our decision in *Evich*, the Supreme Court addressed in *Moragne v. States Marine Lines, Inc.*[28] whether the general maritime law affords a cause of action for wrongful death. The Court overruled its 1886 decision that it did not.[29] Though *Moragne* concerns the availability of a wrongful death action under the general maritime law, it matters in our case, where the seaman did not die, because it bears on how we should understand *Miles*.

Moragne holds that the denial of a wrongful death remedy "had little justification except in primitive English legal history."[30] Lord Ellenborough had held in *Baker v. Bolton* that in "a Civil court, the death of a human being could not be complained **{-1093-}** of as an injury."[31] The Court noted that there was no good reason to maintain this "barbarous" view,[32] let alone extend it to the maritime law, the principles of which "included a special solicitude for the welfare of those men who undertook to venture upon hazardous and unpredictable sea voyages."[33] In any event, the common law rule had been overturned in England by Lord Campbell's Act, in American states by wrongful death statutes, and in our federal law by the Federal Employers' Liability Act, the Death on the High **[—10—]** Seas Act, and the Jones Act.[34] The Court noted that its "transformation of the shipowner's duty to provide a seaworthy ship into an absolute duty not satisfied by due diligence" had made unseaworthiness doctrine "the principal vehicle for recovery by seamen for injury or death."[35] It concluded that the limitations of the Death on the High Seas Act did not preclude the availability of a wrongful death remedy under the general maritime law where the Act did not apply.[36]

Three years after our decision in *Evich*, the Supreme Court decided *Miles v. Apex Marine Corp.*[37] *Miles* was a wrongful death case.[38] The immediate issues before the Court were whether the parent of a deceased seaman could recover under the general maritime law for loss of society and whether a seaman's lost future earnings claim survived his death.[39] A fellow crew member had stabbed a seaman to death.[40] His mother brought a Jones Act negligence claim for failure to prevent the deadly assault and a general maritime unseaworthiness claim for hiring an unfit crew member.[41] **[—11—]** Among other things, she sought loss of society, lost future income, and punitive damages.[42] The jury, though it found negligence, rejected the unseaworthiness claim, returning a verdict that the ship was seaworthy.[43] The Fifth Circuit reversed, holding that because of the extraordinarily violent disposition of the fellow crewman, the ship was unseaworthy as a matter of law.[44]

Miles declined to limit *Moragne* to its facts.[45] The Court noted that the "Jones Act evinces no general hostility to recovery under maritime law."[46] It does not "disturb seamen's general maritime claims for injuries resulting from unseaworthiness."[47] Nor does it "preclude the recovery for wrongful death due to unseaworthiness."[48] The permissibility of a punitive damages award was not before the Court, just loss of society and of future earnings.[49] **{-1094-}**

---

27 *Id.* at 413 n.16, 2 Adm. R. at 347 n.16; *see id.* at 418, 2 Adm. R. at 350–51.

28 398 U.S. 375 (1970).

29 *Id.* at 409 (overruling *The Harrisburg*, 119 U.S. 199 (1886)).

30 *Id.* at 379.

31 *Id.* at 383 (quoting Baker v. Bolton, 1 Camp. 493, 170 Eng. Rep. 1033 (1808)).

32 *Id.* at 381.

33 *Id.* at 387.

34 *Id.* at 389–90, 394.

35 *Id.* at 399.

36 *Id.* at 402.

37 498 U.S. 19 (1990).

38 *Id.* at 21.

39 *Id.* at 23.

40 *Id.* at 21.

41 *Id.*

42 *Id.* at 21–22.

43 *Id.* at 22.

44 *Id.*

45 *Id.* at 27.

46 *Id.* at 29.

47 *Id.*

48 *Id.*

49 *See id.* at 23.

The basis for Dutra's argument that *Miles* implicitly overturns *Evich* is *Miles*'s discussion of damages. Noting that the Death on the High Seas Act limited the availability of **[—12—]** damages for wrongful death to "*pecuniary* loss sustained by the persons for whose benefit the suit is brought,"[50] the Court held that damages "for non-pecuniary loss, such as loss of society, in a general maritime action" are barred.[51] Likewise, Lord Campbell's Act, which is the basis for most state and federal statutes for wrongful death recovery, had long been interpreted to provide recovery only for pecuniary loss.[52] And so the Court concluded that the Jones Act, too, having inherited the Supreme Court's interpretation in *Vreeland* of Lord Campbell's Act and the Federal Employers' Liability Act, also limited recovery to "pecuniary loss."[53] The Court therefore held that "there is no recovery for loss of society in a general maritime action for the wrongful death of a Jones Act seaman."[54]

But it is not apparent why barring damages for loss of society should also bar punitive damages. *Miles* itself suggests no such broad interpretation of "pecuniary loss"—it expressly notes that the Jones Act "evinces no general hostility to recovery under maritime law" and "does not disturb seamen's general maritime claims for injuries **[—13—]** resulting from unseaworthiness."[55] Lord Campbell's Act and its progeny provide an opportunity for a sailor's widow and children to recover the money that they were deprived of by his death. That is what "pecuniary loss" means: loss of money.[56] Non-pecuniary damages have long been understood to mean claims for such injuries as physical pain, mental anguish, or humiliation,[57] as well as loss of consortium. Punitive damages, allowed by *Evich*, are not "pecuniary loss." Though they are pecuniary, that is, like all damages, for money, they are not for loss. They are punitive, not compensatory. Their relationship to loss is that they may not exceed some multiple of the compensatory damages.[58]

That a widow may not recover damages for loss of the companionship and society of her husband has nothing to do with whether a ship or its owners and operators deserve punishment for callously disregarding the safety of seamen. One might reasonably argue that loss of society is more important than such punishment, or that such punishment is more important than loss of society. However, it cannot reasonably be argued that they are both compensation for "loss." If they were, they would fall within the rubric of compensatory damages, not punitive damages. **[—14—]**

Following *Miles*, we held in *Smith v. Trinidad Corp.* that loss of consortium damages are unavailable to the wives of injured mariners in their own actions under the Jones Act or general admiralty law.[59] And we noted in *Chan v. Society Expeditions, Inc.* that neither the general **{-1095-}** maritime law nor the Jones Act permits recovery for loss of society for the wrongful death of a seaman, nor does the Jones Act permit it for injury.[60] Neither speaks to punitive damages.

Whatever room might be left to support broadening *Miles* to cover punitive damages was cut off by the Supreme Court's decision in *Atlantic Sounding Co. v. Townsend*.[61] The shipowner in *Townsend* argued that *Miles* barred punitive damages for willful failure to pay maintenance and cure.[62] The Court noted that "[h]istorically, punitive damages have been available and awarded in general maritime actions."[63] It found "that nothing in *Miles* or the Jones Act eliminates that

50 *Id.* at 31 (quoting then 46 U.S.C. App. § 762, now 46 U.S.C. App. § 30303).

51 *Id.*

52 *Id.* at 32.

53 *Id.* (citing *Michigan Cent. R. Co. v. Vreeland*, 227 U.S. 59, 69–71 (1913)).

54 *Id.* at 33.

55 *Id.* at 29.

56 *See Pecuniary* and *Pecuniary Damages*, BLACK'S LAW DICTIONARY (10th ed. 2014).

57 CHARLES T. MCCORMICK, HANDBOOK ON THE LAW OF DAMAGES 105 (West 1935).

58 *See, e.g., Exxon Shipping Co. v. Baker*, 554 U.S. 471, 513–15 (2008).

59 992 F.2d 996 (9th Cir. 1993).

60 39 F.3d 1398, 1407 (9th Cir. 1994).

61 557 U.S. 404 (2009).

62 *Id.* at 418–19.

63 *Id.* at 407.

availability."[64] Unseaworthiness is a general maritime action long predating the Jones Act.[65] **[—15—]**

It is true, as Dutra contends, that *Miles*, taken alone, might arguably be read to suggest that the available damages for a general maritime unseaworthiness claim by an injured seaman should be limited to those damages permissible under the Jones Act for wrongful death. But that is a stretch. The remark upon which Dutra relies is *Miles*'s justification for its narrower conclusion: "that there is no recovery for loss of society in a general maritime action for the wrongful death of a Jones Act seaman."[66] Dutra takes that narrow remark out of context and reads it expansively.[67] *Miles*'s juxtaposition of the terms "pecuniary" and "non-pecuniary loss" was with reference to loss of society, not punitive damages.[68] *Miles* did not address punitive damages. It expressly noted that the Jones Act "evinces no general hostility to recovery under **[—16—]** maritime law" and "does not disturb seamen's general maritime claims for injuries resulting from unseaworthiness."[69] *Miles* further holds that lost future earnings are unavailable in a general maritime survival action.[70] But that is because "[t]he Jones Act/[Federal Employers' Liability Act] survival provision limits recovery to losses suffered during the decedent's lifetime."[71]

It is also true, as Dutra argues, that if we were to interpret *Miles* broadly and *Townsend* narrowly, as the Fifth Circuit has in *McBride*, then we might infer that *Miles* implicitly overruled *Evich*. But we would then have to disregard *Miles*'s statement that the Jones Act "does not disturb **{-1096-}** seamen's general maritime claims for injuries resulting from unseaworthiness."[72] The Fifth Circuit's leading opinions in *McBride* are scholarly and carefully reasoned, but so are the dissenting opinions, which to us are more persuasive.

Starting with Lord Campbell's Act, and continuing through the Federal Employers' Liability Act, the Death on the High Seas Act, and the Jones Act, wrongful death is a statutory cause of action.[73] There is no way to compensate a dead seaman for the wrong done to him. Compensation for his survivors is generally limited by statute to their resulting **[—17—]** "pecuniary loss."[74] These limitations, based on the restrictive recoveries permitted for wrongful death, have no application to general maritime claims by living seamen for injuries to themselves. The *Townsend* Court made this distinction when addressing maintenance and cure actions,[75] and there is no persuasive reason to distinguish maintenance and cure actions from unseaworthiness actions with respect to the damages awardable. The purposes of punitive damages, punishment and deterrence,[76] apply equally to both of these general maritime causes of action. Nor are punitive damages compensation for a pecuniary or non-pecuniary "loss," as described in *Miles*.[77] They

---

64 *Id.*

65 *See id.* at 419; *see also Miles*, 498 U.S. at 29; *Tabingo v. Am. Triumph LLC*, 391 P.3d 434, 438–40 (Wash. 2017).

66 *Miles*, 498 U.S. at 33.

67 *Miles* states:

> The Jones Act also precludes recovery for loss of society in this case. The Jones Act applies when a seaman has been killed as a result of negligence, and it limits recovery to pecuniary loss. The general maritime claim here alleged that Torregano had been killed as a result of the unseaworthiness of the vessel. It would be inconsistent with our place in the constitutional scheme were we to sanction more expansive remedies in a judicially created cause of action in which liability is without fault than Congress has allowed in cases of death resulting from negligence. We must conclude that there is no recovery for loss of society in a general maritime action for the wrongful death of a Jones Act seaman.

Id. at 32–33.

68 *See id.* at 31–33.

69 *Id.* at 29.

70 *Id.* at 36.

71 *Id.*

72 *Id.* at 29.

73 *Id.* at 31–32.

74 *Id.* at 31, 32 (citing *Vreeland*, 227 U.S. at 69–71).

75 557 U.S. at 419–20.

76 *See Exxon Shipping Co.*, 554 U.S. at 492–93.

77 *See* 498 U.S. at 30–33.

are not compensation for loss at all. One might argue for or against the desirability of punitive damages, but unless Congress legislates on the matter, their availability is clearly established not only in *Townsend*[78] but also in *Baker*.[79] They have been recognized **[—18—]** as proper in appropriate circumstances since *The Amiable Nancy*.[80]

Conclusion

The district court correctly denied Dutra's motion to strike the prayer for punitive damages. They are indeed awardable to seamen for their own injuries in general maritime unseaworthiness actions. Under *Miller v. Gammie*,[81] we cannot treat *Evich* as overruled by *Miles* unless *Miles* is "fundamentally inconsistent with the reasoning"[82] of *Evich* and *Evich* is "clearly irreconcilable"[83] with *Miles*. It is not. Under the *Miller* standard, *Evich* remains good law. And under *Townsend*, we would reach the same conclusion *Evich* did, even if we were not bound by *Evich*.

AFFIRMED.

---

[78] 557 U.S. at 407 ("Historically, punitive damages have been available and awarded in general maritime actions . . . . We find that nothing in *Miles* or the Jones Act eliminates that availability.").

[79] 554 U.S. at 489–90, 515 (noting that the issue of punitive damages in maritime law "falls within a federal court's jurisdiction to decide in the manner of a common law court, subject to the authority of Congress to legislate otherwise if it disagrees with the judicial result," and allowing an award of punitive damages).

[80] 16 U.S. (3 Wheat.) 546 (1818).

[81] 335 F.3d 889 (9th Cir. 2003).

[82] *Id.* at 892.

[83] *Id.* at 893.

United States Court of Appeals
for the Ninth Circuit

No. 15-56352

NEWTON
VS.
PARKER DRILLING MANAGEMENT SERVS., LTD.

Appeal from the United States District Court for the Central District of California

Decided: February 5, 2018

Citation: 881 F.3d 1078, 6 Adm. R. 314 (9th Cir. 2018).

Before **PAEZ**, **BERZON**, and **CHRISTEN**, Circuit Judges.

[—3—] {-1081-} **CHRISTEN**, Circuit Judge:

This case presents the novel question whether claims under state wage and hour laws may be brought by workers employed on drilling platforms fixed on the outer Continental Shelf. Brian Newton worked on such a platform off the coast of Santa Barbara. His shifts lasted fourteen days and he regularly worked twelve hours per day. After Parker Drilling ("Parker") terminated him, Newton sued in state court for wage and hour violations under California law. Parker removed the case to federal district court and filed a motion for judgment on the pleadings. The district court granted the motion, concluding that the Fair Labor Standards Act is a comprehensive statutory scheme that is exclusive of California wage and hour laws. Newton appeals. We have jurisdiction pursuant to 28 U.S.C. § 1291. **[—4—]**

We hold that the absence of federal law is not, as the district court concluded, a prerequisite to adopting state law as surrogate federal law under the Outer Continental Shelf Lands Act, 43 U.S.C. § 1333(a)(2)(A). We thus reject the proposition that "necessity to fill a significant void or gap," *Cont'l Oil Co. v. London S.S. Owners' Mut. Ins. Ass'n*, 417 F. 2d 1030, 1036 (5th Cir. 1969), is required in order to assimilate "applicable and not inconsistent," **{-1082-}** 43 U.S.C. § 1333(a)(2)(A), state law into federal law governing drilling platforms affixed to the outer Continental Shelf. We therefore vacate the district court's dismissal of Newton's claims and remand for further proceedings consistent with this opinion.

I. FACTUAL & PROCEDURAL BACKGROUND

Newton worked as a roustabout and painter for Parker on drilling platforms in the Santa Barbara Channel from approximately January 2013 to January 2015. It is uncontested that the drilling platforms where he worked were located more than three miles offshore and fixed to the seabed of the outer Continental Shelf. His fourteen-day shifts, known in the industry as "hitches," comprised twelve hours on duty followed by twelve hours on "controlled standby." Newton was paid for twelve hours of work per day and he was not able to leave the platform during his shifts. Newton alleges that he usually took fifteen to thirty minutes during his shifts to eat without clocking out or ate while not working and remaining on call, and that Parker did not provide thirty-minute meal periods for each five hours worked, as required by California law. Parker paid Newton twice per month. In addition to compensation for twelve hours per day, his pay stubs showed pay for "two hours for the boat ride out, back and debriefing with the next crew." **[—5—]**

Newton filed a putative class action in California state court on February 17, 2015. Although Parker paid an hourly rate well above California and federal minimum wage, Newton maintained that California law required Parker to pay him for the twelve hours he was on controlled standby each day. The First Amended Complaint (FAC) alleged that Newton's final paycheck did not include all the wages owed to him, "including the overtime/doubletime and meal period wages." In all, Newton brought seven causes of action under California law for: (1) minimum wage violations; (2) failure to pay overtime and doubletime; (3) pay stub violations; (4) failure to pay timely final wages; (5) failure to provide lawful meal periods; (6) civil penalties under the Private Attorney General Act of 2004 (PAGA); and (7) unfair competition.

Parker removed the action to federal court and filed a motion for judgment on the pleadings. Parker argued that, under the Outer Continental Shelf Lands Act, 43 U.S.C. §§ 1331–1356b (OCSLA), the Fair Labor Standards Act (FLSA) is a comprehensive statutory scheme that leaves no room for state law to address wage and hour grievances arising on the OCS.[1] For his part, Newton contended that California's more protective wage and hour laws may be applied concurrently with the minimum guarantees of their federal counterpart. *See* 29 U.S.C. § 201, *et seq.* Newton's opposition did not explain the complaint's allegation that some of Parker's allegedly unlawful conduct occurred in California rather than on the OCS, but did request that if the **[—6—]** district court were to grant Parker's motion, it do so "without prejudice to allow Plaintiff to correct any deficiencies."[2] **{-1083-}**

The district court granted Parker's motion for judgment on the pleadings, reasoning that "under [the] OCSLA, federal law governs and state law only applies to the extent it is necessary 'to fill a significant void or gap' in federal law." Finding no significant voids or gaps in the FLSA, the district court held that Newton could not invoke California wage and hour laws as surrogate federal law. The district court reached this decision after considering the Department of Labor (DOL) regulations elaborating the FLSA. While recognizing that the FLSA has a savings clause that expressly allows for more protective state minimum wage and overtime laws, the district court nevertheless concluded that California wage and hour claims were unavailable to Newton. The district court did not address Newton's request for leave to amend. Newton timely appealed.

[1] We collectively refer to the outer Continental Shelf and the devices attached to it for the purposes enumerated in the statute as "the OCS."

[2] The FAC alleged, without elaboration, that "the unlawful employment practices complained of herein occurred in the City of Goleta, California, County of Santa Barbara." On appeal, Newton argues that "at least some of the alleged California wage-and-hour violations took place on vessels to and from California's coast and on the coast of California."

II. STANDARD OF REVIEW

A dismissal on the pleadings pursuant to Rule 12(c) is reviewed *de novo. Lyon v. Chase Bank USA, N.A.*, 656 F.3d 877, 883 (9th Cir. 2011). "Dismissal without leave to amend is improper unless it is clear, upon *de novo* review, that the complaint could not be saved by any amendment." *Thinket* **[—7—]** *Ink Info. Res., Inc. v. Sun Microsystems, Inc.*, 368 F.3d 1053, 1061 (9th Cir. 2004).

III. DISCUSSION

Except for any claims that may have arisen while Newton was transiting to and from the offshore drilling platforms where he worked, Newton's grievances relate to his employment on the OCS, and the parties agree that the fate of Newton's appeal rests on the OCSLA's choice of law provision. *See* 43 U.S.C. § 1333(a)(2)(A).

A. The Outer Continental Shelf Lands Act

1. OCSLA's Choice of Law Provision

The outer Continental Shelf generally refers to submerged lands lying more than three miles offshore, outside the territorial jurisdiction of the states. *See* 43 U.S.C. §§ 1331(a), 1301(a)(2); *Valladolid v. Pac. Operations Offshore, LLP*, 604 F.3d 1126, 1130 (9th Cir. 2010). Subject to certain exceptions and conditions, the OCSLA declares that the Constitution and laws of the United States extend to the outer Continental Shelf, as well as "*all artificial islands, and all installations and other devices permanently or temporarily attached to the seabed* . . . for the purpose of exploring for, developing, or producing resources therefrom . . . to the same extent as if the outer Continental Shelf were an area of exclusive Federal jurisdiction located within a State." 43 U.S.C. § 1333(a)(1) (emphasis added). OCSLA's assertion of jurisdiction is unique because it comprises the ocean floor but not the waters above it. "[T]he jurisdiction asserted is a 'horizontal jurisdiction' and does not affect the status of superjacent waters." Warren M. Christopher, *The* **[—8—]** *Outer Continental Shelf Lands Act: Key to a New Frontier*, 6 Stan. L. Rev. 23,

34 (1953) (citing S. Rep. No. 83-411, at 2 (1953)). The OCSLA's choice of law provision declares:

> To the extent that they are *applicable and not inconsistent* with this subchapter or with other Federal laws and regulations of the Secretary now in effect or hereafter adopted, *the civil and criminal laws of each adjacent State, now in effect or hereafter adopted, amended, or repealed are declared to be the law of the United States for that portion of the subsoil and seabed of the outer Continental Shelf, and artificial islands and fixed structures erected thereon, which would be within the area* **{-1084-}** *of the State if its boundaries were extended seaward to the outer margin of the outer Continental Shelf,* and the President shall determine and publish in the Federal Register such projected lines extending seaward and defining each such area.

43 U.S.C. § 1333(a)(2)(A) (emphasis added). Because the OCSLA makes plain that the laws of the adjacent state are to apply to drilling platforms fixed to the seabed of the outer Continental Shelf as long as state law is "applicable and not inconsistent with . . . Federal laws," the parties' dispute turns on the interpretation of the terms "applicable" and "not inconsistent." *Id.*

The Supreme Court has not been called upon to decide a case involving wage and hour laws on the OCS. Both Newton and Parker ask us to look to the Fifth Circuit's interpretation of the OCSLA for guidance. Though the **[—9—]** parties disagree as to the Fifth Circuit's prevailing test for choice of law on the OCS, they both argue that we ought to follow the Fifth Circuit's lead and adopt the approach it has taken in cases involving injury, wrongful death, and contract claims arising on the OCS. Newton urges that the Fifth Circuit's test is the one set out in *Union Texas Petroleum Corp. v. PLT Engineering, Inc.*, 895 F.2d 1043 (5th Cir. 1990) (*PLT*). According to Newton, platform workers may bring state wage and hour claims to the extent that state law is not inconsistent with existing federal law, *see Breton Energy, L.L.C. v. Mariner Energy Res., Inc.*, 764 F.3d 394, 398 (5th Cir. 2014), and California's wage and hour laws are not inconsistent with the FLSA insofar as they are preserved by the FLSA's savings clause. Relying on *Continental Oil*, 417 F.2d at 1036, Parker argues that the FLSA is a comprehensive statutory and regulatory scheme that leaves no voids or gaps for state law to fill, so state wage and hour laws do not apply on the OCS and Newton's grievances may be redressed only by the FLSA.

Having examined the text of the original OCSLA and its 1975 amendment, the legislative history, and the Supreme Court's case law addressing the Act, we hold that state wage and hour laws are adopted as surrogate federal law on the OCS as long as they are "applicable and not inconsistent" with existing federal law.

2. Origins of the OCSLA

"The OCSLA grew out of a dispute, which first developed in the 1930's, between the adjacent States and the Federal Government over territorial jurisdiction and ownership of the OCS and, particularly, the right to lease the submerged lands for oil and gas exploration." *Shell Oil Co. v. Iowa Dep't of* **[—10—]** *Revenue*, 488 U.S. 19, 26 (1988). Passed in 1953,"[t]he purpose of the [OCSLA] was to define a body of law applicable to the seabed, the subsoil, and the fixed structures such as [drilling platforms] on the outer Continental Shelf." *Rodrigue v. Aetna Cas. & Sur. Co.*, 395 U.S. 352, 355 (1969).

Congress initially considered extending maritime law to the OCS, but it envisioned that 10,000 or more people might eventually be employed on the OCS to develop mineral resources.[3] *See* 99 Cong. Rec. **{-1085-}** 6963–

[3] "[L]arge crews of men will work on the miraculous structures which will rise from the sea bed of the outer Continental Shelf. These men will die, leave wills, and pay taxes. They will fight, gamble, borrow money, and perhaps even kill. They will bargain over their working conditions and sometimes they will be injured on the job. . . . the whole circle of legal problems familiar to the

64 (1953); *Shell Oil*, 488 U.S. at 27 n.8. Anticipating a broad range of activity associated with this mineral resource development, Congress feared that federal law, standing alone, would be inadequate because it "was never designed to be a complete body of law in and of itself." 99 Cong. Rec. 6963 (1953). Congress also rejected the incorporation of the OCS into the boundaries of the several states, *see* S. Rep. No. 83-411, at 6 (1953), deciding instead that existing federal law and the law of the abutting state (except for state taxation laws)[4] were to comprise the body of law governing the OCS. Because the Department of Justice and several members of Congress voiced concerns that the prospective incorporation of state laws on the OCS might be an unconstitutional delegation of Congress's legislative authority, S. Rep. No. 83-411, at 33 **[—11—]** (1953); *see* 99 Cong. Rec. 6963–64 (1953), the OCSLA only borrowed state law then in existence.[5] Thus, as originally adopted in 1953, "applicable" state law for purposes of § 1333(a)(2)(A) referred to state non-tax law, in existence on the effective date of the Act, that bore on the relevant subject matter.

The "applicable" state law for purposes of § 1333(a)(2)(A) changed in 1975 when Congress enacted the Deepwater Port Act, 33 U.S.C. §§ 1501, *et seq*., and simultaneously amended the OCSLA, *see* Pub. L. No. 93-627, § 19(f), 88 Stat. 2176 (1975). By then, *United States v. Sharpnack*, 355 U.S. 286 (1958), had allayed the concern that the prospective adoption of state law might amount to an unconstitutional delegation of congressional legislative authority.[6] The 1975 amendment redefined state law in **[—12—]** § 1333(a)(2)(A) as "the civil and criminal laws of each adjacent State, now in effect *or hereafter adopted, amended, or repealed.*" § 1333(a)(2)(A) (emphasis added). This amendment ensured that the same law governed resource development structures on the OCS and deep water ports.[7] **{–1086–}** The OCSLA's choice of law provision has not undergone significant statutory amendments since 1975.

3. Judicial Interpretation of the OCSLA

The Supreme Court first applied the OCSLA's choice of law provision in *Rodrigue v. Aetna Casualty & Surety Co.*, 395 U.S. 352, 355 (1969). The families of two workers who perished on drilling rigs fixed to the outer Continental Shelf off the Louisiana coast brought claims pursuant to Louisiana state law and the Death on the High Seas Act (High Seas Act). 395 U.S. at 352–53 (1969); *see* 46 U.S.C. §§ 30301–08. The High Seas Act

upland could occur on these structures." Christopher, *supra*, at 37.

[4] 43 U.S.C. § 1333(a)(2)(A) provides: "State taxation laws shall not apply to the outer Continental Shelf."

[5] As explained by Senator Cordon while introducing the bill to the Senate: "The enactment as Federal law by reference of the laws of the several abutting States meets the major constitutional objection, in that the laws so adopted are the laws as they exist at the time of the enactment of S. 1901. Only already existing State laws will become the law of the United States, and the amendatory legislation by the States thereafter will not be applicable, unless made so by later Federal legislation." 99 Cong. Rec. 6963–64 (1953); *see also* Christopher, *supra*, at 42.

[6] In *Sharpnack*, the Supreme Court sustained the Assimilative Crimes Act of 1948 (Crimes Act) against the challenge that Congress, in enacting the Crimes Act, impermissibly delegated its legislative authority to the states. 18 U.S.C. § 13; 355 U.S. at 286. The Crimes Act makes the version of state law enforceable at the time of allegedly unlawful conduct applicable, in conjunction with federal criminal law, on federal enclaves. *Sharpnack* explained that Congress's "deliberate continuing adoption" of state criminal law for federal enclaves does not rise to an unconstitutional delegation of legislative authority to the states because Congress always has the power to exclude a state law from the scope of the Crimes Act. 355 U.S. at 294.

[7] As explained in the Joint Report of the Committees on Commerce, Interior and Insular Affairs, and Public Works to the Senate, the Department of Justice sought the 1975 amendment to the OCSLA because, "from an enforcement point of view," it wanted the same law applied to all deepwater ports and structures erected on the OCS, *see* S. Rep. No. 93-1217, at 76 (1974), and "no provision was made in the Outer Continental Shelf Lands Act to apply State laws as adopted, amended or repealed, *after* the date of enactment of that Act." *Id.* at 60.

provides an admiralty remedy for deaths resulting from traditional maritime activity on the high seas, i.e., in waters three or more nautical miles from shore. *See Rodrigue*, 395 U.S. at 359. The trial courts in the two cases that were consolidated in the *Rodrigue* appeal dismissed the state wrongful death claims, ruling that the federal statutory remedy was exclusive. *Id.* at 353–54. The Fifth Circuit affirmed that ruling, but the Supreme Court reversed. *Id.* at 355. The Supreme Court explained that the **[—13—]** OCSLA requires fixed drilling platforms to be treated as artificial islands or federal enclaves within a landlocked state, not as vessels. *Id.* As such, "the [federal] admiralty action under the [High] Seas Act no more applies to these accidents actually occurring on the islands than it would to accidents occurring in an upland federal enclave."[8] *Id.* at 366. Moreover, since the accidents befalling the workers "involved no collision with a vessel, and the structures were not navigational aids," their deaths were not attributable to traditional maritime activity. *Id.* at 360. Hence, the High Seas Act's maritime remedy was unavailable, and "any obstacle to the application of state law by incorporation as federal law through [§ 1333(a)(2)]" was "remove[d]." *Id.* at 366.

In reaching this result, *Rodrigue* first examined the language of § 1333(a)(2), which, as originally enacted, expressly incorporated then-existing state laws "[t]o the extent that they are applicable and not inconsistent" with federal law. *See id.* at 356 n.3 (quoting 43 U.S.C. § 1333(a)(2)(A)). The Supreme Court concluded from its analysis of the text that "federal law is 'exclusive' in its regulation of [the OCS], and that state law is adopted only as surrogate federal law." *Id.* at 357. From the Senate Committee Report, the Conference Report, and the debate on the floor of the Senate, the Court found support for "[t]he principles that federal law should prevail, and that state law **[—14—]** should be applied only as federal law and then only when no inconsistent federal law applie[s]". *Id.* at 357–59 (citing S. Rep. No. 83-411, at 11 (1953); H.R. Conf. Rep. No. 1031, 83d Cong., 1st Sess., 12 (1953); 99 Cong. Rec. 6962–63, 7164, 7232–36 (1953)). "This legislative history buttresse[d] the Court of Appeals'[s] finding that in view of the inconsistencies between the state law and the [High] Seas Act, the [High] Seas Act remedy would be exclusive if it applied." *Id.* at 359. **{-1087-}**

But the High Seas Act remedy did not apply. The Supreme Court recounted that while introducing the OCSLA bill to the Senate, Senator Cordon explained that the Committee on Interior and Insular Affairs initially attempted to "provide housekeeping law" for the OCS by treating drilling platforms as vessels subject to maritime law. *Rodrigue*, 395 U.S. at 361 (quoting 99 Cong. Rec. 6963 (1953)). The Committee, however, eschewed this approach because "[t]he so-called social laws necessary for protection of the workers and their families would not apply[, including] such things as unemployment laws, industrial-accident laws, fair-labor-standard laws, and so forth. Ultimately, instead, the whole body of Federal law was made applicable to the area as well as state law where necessary." *Id.* at 362 (original alterations and quotation marks omitted). The *Rodrigue* court concluded from its "[c]areful scrutiny of the hearings which were the basis for eliminating from the [OCSLA] the treatment of artificial islands as vessels . . . that the motivation for this change, together with the adoption of state law as surrogate federal law, was the view that maritime law was inapposite to these fixed structures." *Id.* at 363. In sum, *Rodrigue* dispelled the misconception that maritime law applied perforce to drilling platforms on the outer Continental Shelf. Since federal law made no provision for wrongful **[—15—]** death claims on the OCS,[9] the Supreme Court held

[8] "[A] state may not legislate with respect to a federal enclave unless it reserved the right to do so when the state gave its consent to the purchase by the United States[;] only state laws existing at the time of the acquisition remain enforceable. Subsequent state laws are only enforceable if Congress provides for assimilation of later-enacted state controls." 3 William J. Rich, *Modern Constitutional Law* § 34:49 (3d ed. 2016).

[9] The Longshore and Harbor Workers' Compensation Act (LHWCA), 33 U.S.C. § 901, *et seq.*, provides a federal remedy for a non-seaman maritime employee to recover against an employer

that the OCSLA adopted state law as the applicable surrogate federal law. *Id.* at 365–66.

Notably, *Rodrigue* did not require the court to address a situation where state law *and* existing federal law made provisions for the type of claim asserted; no relevant federal cause of action for wrongful death existed. *Rodrigue* is therefore of faint value for resolving a case like the instant one, where both state and federal law are potentially applicable to Newton's wage and hour grievances.

The Supreme Court revisited the OCSLA choice of law provision in *Chevron Oil Co. v. Huson*, 404 U.S. 97 (1971). Huson filed a personal injury suit against a non-employer defendant, Chevron, for damages arising from a back injury he suffered while working on Chevron's artificial island drilling rig on the outer Continental Shelf. *Id.* at 98. The parties' dispute centered on the timeliness of the plaintiff's claims. *Id.* The Fifth Circuit resorted to the federal admiralty doctrine of laches, but the Supreme Court reversed, holding that Louisiana's one-year statute of limitations should have controlled.[10] *Id.* at 105. The *Huson* court explained that in **[—16—]** enacting the OCSLA, Congress expressed an intent for courts to fill "gaps" in existing federal law by applying state law, not by creating federal common law. *Id.* at 104–05 (internal quotation marks omitted). Like *Rodrigue*, *Huson* did not resolve a claimed inconsistency between potentially applicable state and federal laws. Nor did *Offshore Logistics Inc. v. Tallentire*, 477 U.S. 207 (1986), which considered **{–1088–}** whether the High Seas Act or state law governed wrongful death actions brought after a helicopter transporting two OCS platform workers crashed into the sea. *Id.* at 209. Starting from the observation that the text of the OCSLA precludes its application to the high seas over the outer Continental Shelf, the Supreme Court rejected "the proposition that it is the decedent's status or his special relationship with the shore" that triggers OCSLA's choice of law provision in § 1333(a)(2)(A), "regardless of the location of the accident." *Id.* at 219. Locale is key, and because "the fatalities underlying [the] suit . . . occurred on the high seas" rather than on the OCS, the High Seas Act—not the OCSLA—controlled. *Id.* at 220.

Surveying the Supreme Court's OCSLA jurisprudence, we conclude that there are three questions that must be asked in any case involving choice of law under § 1333(a)(2)(A) of the OCSLA. First, the threshold question is whether the situs of the controversy is the OCS. *See Tallentire*, 477 U.S. at 218–19; *cf. Pac. Operators Offshore, LLP v. Valladolid*, 565 U.S. 207, 222 (2012) (holding that in contrast to § 1333(a)(2)(A), the OCSLA's provision for workers' compensation, § 1333(b), covers employees who can establish a "substantial-nexus" between their injury and extractive operations on the OCS). If the situs is not the OCS, the OCSLA's choice of law provision cannot apply. *See Tallentire*, 477 U.S. at 220. Second, if the situs is the **[—17—]** OCS, we then ask whether there is any federal law applicable to the dispute. *See Rodrigue*, 395 U.S. at 366. If there is not, then state law generally applies. *See id.*; *Huson*, 404 U.S. at 101. Third, if there is federal law applicable to the dispute, then we "must consider the content of both potentially applicable federal and state law" and ask whether any applicable state law is inconsistent with federal law. *Gulf Offshore Co. v. Mobil Oil Corp.*, 453 U.S. 473, 486 (1981). As a contemporary commentator on the OCSLA presciently warned, "[w]hich state laws 'are applicable and not inconsistent' with federal laws and regulations will be open to constant interpretation and controversy." Christopher, *supra*, at 42.

The "seemingly innocuous extension of state law raised to the status of surrogate federal law raises extremely complex questions of interpretation[,]" particularly in

for personal injuries. *See Figueroa v. Campbell Indus.*, 45 F.3d 311, 315 (9th Cir. 1995). The OCSLA extends the LHWCA to the OCS, 43 U.S.C. § 1333(b), but defendants in *Rodrigue* were not the workers' employers. *See Rodrigue*, 395 U.S. at 354.

10 Because Huson initiated his action before the Supreme Court announced its decision in *Rodrigue*, the Court declined to apply this holding to his claims. *Huson*, 404 U.S. at 99–100.

addressing choice of law. 1 Thomas J. Shoenbaum, *Admiralty & Maritime Law* § 3-9 (5th ed. 2016). The Fifth Circuit has elaborated two strands of jurisprudence stemming from *Rodrigue*. According to the Fifth Circuit's *Continental Oil* line of cases, "the recurring theme of *Rodrigue* 'requires that "applicable" [state law] be read in terms of necessity—necessity to fill a significant void or gap"' in existing federal law. *Nations v. Morris*, 483 F.2d 577, 585 (5th Cir. 1973) (quoting *Cont'l Oil*, 417 F.2d at 1036). The Fifth Circuit last applied the *Continental Oil* test in 1985 in *LeSassier v. Chevron USA, Inc.*, 776 F.2d 506, 509 (5th Cir. 1985) (per curiam),[11] where the court considered whether a **[—18—]** drilling platform worker could maintain a Louisiana retaliatory discharge action even though the Longshore and Harbor Workers' Compensation Act (LHWCA) provides a federal remedy for retaliatory discharge. LeSassier was a platform worker who had been injured on an outer Continental Shelf **{-1089-}** platform. *LeSassier*, 776 F.2d at 507. After filing a successful claim for benefits under the LHWCA, LeSassier was fired. *Id.* He brought a state law action against his former employer alleging retaliatory discharge, but the district court concluded LeSassier could not rely on state retaliatory discharge law. *Id.* The Fifth Circuit affirmed, holding that "no gap" in federal law existed because "Congress provided a specific statutory provision [in the LHWCA] (33 U.S.C. § 948a) to address retaliatory discharges." *Id.* at 509. The court of appeals declined to "selectively apply[] only those parts of the overall LHWCA statutory structure which [LeSassier] happen[ed] to favor and ignore less favorable provisions." *Id.* at 508. In Parker's view, *Continental Oil* and its progeny establishes that, at least in the Fifth Circuit, state law is only applicable on the OCS if it is necessary to resort to state law to fill a gap or void in federal law. Parker urges us to adopt such a rule.

Newton advocates for the adoption of the *PLT* test as applied in the Fifth Circuit's more recent lines of cases. The *PLT* test distills *Rodrigue* thus: "[F]or state law to apply as surrogate federal law, three conditions must be met: '(1) The controversy must arise on a situs covered by OCSLA (i.e. the subsoil seabed, or artificial structures permanently or temporarily attached thereto)[;] (2) Federal maritime law must not apply of its own force[;] (3) [t]he state law must not be inconsistent with Federal law.'" *Grand Isle Shipyard, Inc. v. Seacor Marine, LLC*, 589 F.3d 778, 783 (5th Cir. 2009) (en banc) (quoting *PLT*, 895 F.2d at 1047). The Fifth Circuit **[—19—]** applied the third prong of this test in *Hodgen v. Forest Oil Corp.*, 87 F.3d 1512 (5th Cir. 1996), *overruled on other grounds by Grand Isle Shipyard*, 589 F.3d at 788 n.8. *Hodgen* arose from an accident suffered by an operator while executing a swing rope transfer from a OCS platform to a vessel. 87 F.3d at 1516. The operator settled his personal injury claims against the defendants who then litigated questions of comparative fault and indemnity between themselves. *Id.* at 1517. An agreement between the operator's employer and the charterer contained a clause requiring the former to indemnify the latter for costs and damages, but the Louisiana Oilfield Indemnity Act (LOIA) forbade any such transfer of liability. *Id.* at 1522. The charterer argued that the LOIA should not be adopted as surrogate federal law because it was inconsistent with federal law. *Id.* at 1528. The Fifth Circuit, relying on its prior decision in *Knapp v. Chevron USA, Inc.*, 781 F.2d 1123 (5th Cir. 1986), summarily rebuffed this contention. *Hodgen*, 87 F.3d at 1528. *Knapp* concluded that because the 1984 amendments to the LHWCA were silent as to indemnity agreements addressing injuries caused by the negligence of non-vessels and nothing signaled Congress's intent that the amendments should "preempt the field," Louisiana's Oilfield Indemnity Act was not inconsistent with federal law and, therefore, the OCSLA "makes [the LOIA] the applicable surrogate law on fixed platforms offshore Louisiana." *Knapp*, 781 F.2d at 1131. *Hodgen* and *Knapp* suggest that the Fifth Circuit's *PLT* test looks to congressional intent regarding preemption

---

[11] The *Continental Oil* test was also briefly alluded to in the footnotes of two later cases: *Oceanic Butler, Inc. v. Nordahl*, 842 F.2d 773, 777 n.4 (5th Cir. 1988) and *Mesa Operating Ltd. v. U.S. Dep't of Interior*, 931 F.2d 318, 325 n.48 (5th Cir. 1991).

to determine whether state law is inconsistent with a federal statutory scheme.

It remains unclear whether the *PLT* test has superseded the *Continental Oil* test in the Fifth Circuit, or whether the Fifth Circuit views the *Continental Oil* test as a precursor to **[—20—]** the *PLT* test, such that the *PLT* conditions come into play only if there is a significant gap or void in federal law. *See Tetra Techs., Inc. v. Cont'l Ins. Co.*, 814 F.3d 733, 738, 4 Adm. R. 185, 186–87 (5th Cir. 2016). Despite questions about the *PLT* test, in **{-1090-}** respects not here pertinent,[12] Newton argues that the *PLT* test should be adopted as the law of the Ninth Circuit.

B. The Instant Case

1. Newton's Claims under California Minimum Wage and Overtime Law

Parker paid Newton an hourly rate well above the state and federal minimum wage, and also paid him premium rates for overtime hours. Newton's principal wage and hour objection is that he was not properly compensated for standby hours on the drilling platform. We know of no appellate case law examining whether, for the purposes of the OCSLA, state wage and hour laws are inconsistent with the federal Fair Labor Standards Act.[13] **[—21—]**

a. Text and Legislative History of the OCSLA

To resolve the issue of first impression presented by Newton's appeal, "[w]e start, as we must, with the language of the statute[,]" *Bailey v. United States*, 516 U.S. 137, 144 (1995). "[W]hen the statute's language is plain, the sole function of the courts—at least where the disposition required by the text is not absurd—is to enforce it according to its terms." *Lamie v. U.S. Tr.*, 540 U.S. 526, 534 (2004) (internal quotation marks omitted).

The OCSLA makes the laws of the adjacent state, "[t]o the extent that they are applicable and not inconsistent with this subchapter or with other Federal laws . . . the law of the United States." 43 U.S.C. § 1333(a)(2)(A). "[W]ords used in a statute are to be given their ordinary meaning in the absence of persuasive reasons to the contrary." *Burns v. Alcala*, 420 U.S. 575, 580 (1975). In its *ordinary* sense, "applicable" state law, as that term was employed in the 1953 version of the statute, meant the non-tax law of the abutting state—frozen in time—that pertained to the subject matter at hand. *See, e.g., Applicable*, Funk & Wagnalls Standard Dictionary of the English Language (1958) ("Capable of or suitable for application; relevant; fitting"). The 1975 amendment to the OCSLA did not change the significance of the word "applicable," except that the state laws to be **[—22—]** adopted became "the civil and criminal laws of each adjacent State, now in effect or hereafter adopted, amended, or repealed." 43 U.S.C. § 1333(a)(2)(A); *see,* **{-1091-}** *e.g., Applicable*, Webster's New World Dictionary of the American Language (1972) ("that can be applied; appropriate"). Thus, we first observe that the "ordinary,

---

[12] *See Barker v. Hercules Offshore, Inc.*, 713 F.3d 208, 214, 1 Adm. R. 206, 209 (5th Cir. 2013) (Clement, J., writing for herself) ("Although the application of maritime law under OCSLA may be contrary to the intention of Congress, we are bound by our precedent to apply maritime law as the substantive rule of decision where it otherwise applies 'of its own force.'"); *Demette v. Falcon Drilling Co.*, 280 F.3d 492, 505 n.2 (5th Cir. 2002) (DeMoss, J., dissenting) (noting that "there is no statutory basis" for examining whether maritime law applies of its own force under the second prong of the *PLT* test), *overruled on other grounds by Grand Isle Shipyard*, 589 F.3d at 788 n.8.

[13] District courts within the Ninth Circuit have considered whether California wage and hour laws apply as surrogate federal law on the OCS. *See, e.g., Williams v. Brinderson Constructors Inc.*, No. CV 15-2474-MWF(AGRx), 2015 WL 4747892 (C.D. Cal. Aug. 11, 2015); *Reyna v.* **[—21—]** *Venoco, Inc.*, No. CV 15-4525 PA (RAOx) (C.D. Cal. October 23, 2015); *Espinoza v. Beta Operating Co.*, No. CV 15-04659-RGK (ASx) (C.D. Cal. Oct. 29, 2015); *Jefferson v. Beta Operating Co.*, No. CV 15-04966 SJO (PLAx) (C.D. Cal. Nov. 3, 2015); *Garcia v. Freeport-McMoran Oil & Gas LLC*, No. CV 16-4320-R (C.D. Cal. Sept. 16, 2016). Except where parties contractually agreed for state law to control, these district courts concluded that California's wage and hour laws do not extend to OCS platform workers because the FLSA leaves no gap for state law to fill.

contemporary, common meaning," *Williams v. Taylor*, 529 U.S. 420, 431 (2000), of "applicable" does not lend itself to the notion that state laws have to fill a gap in federal law to qualify as surrogate federal law.

Moreover, we generally "presume [that] Congress says what it means and means what it says." *Simmons v. Himmelreich*, 136 S. Ct. 1843, 1848 (2016). Congress could have said "necessary," or employed words to that effect, in § 1333(a)(2)(A). In another statute, Congress authorized the courts to borrow state common law where "the laws of the United States . . . are not adapted to the object [of the applicable federal statutes], or are deficient in the provisions necessary to furnish suitable remedies and punish offenses against law[.]" 42 U.S.C. § 1988(a). Congress did not make any such qualification here.

Legislative history, however pellucid, cannot rewrite the language of a statute, *Am. Rivers v. FERC*, 201 F.3d 1186, 1204 (9th Cir. 1999), but "clear evidence of congressional intent may illuminate ambiguous text." *Milner v. Dep't of Navy*, 562 U.S. 562, 572 (2011).

The Fifth Circuit in *Continental Oil* navigated OCSLA's choppy waters by taking legislative history as its lodestar. 417 F.2d at 1034–36. *Continental Oil* noted the "deep political and emotional currents centered around the clash between national sovereignty and states' rights" during the passage of the OCSLA and Congress's "express reject[ion]" **[—23—]** of the "notion of supremacy of state law administered by state agencies." *Id.* at 1036. The Fifth Circuit concluded that "the deliberate choice of federal law, federally administered, requires that 'applicable' be read in terms of necessity—necessity to fill a significant void or gap." *Id.* (footnote omitted).

The legislative history indicates that Congress was solicitous to retain and indeed, assert, the federal government's civil and political jurisdiction over the OCS, but we are not persuaded that this consideration justifies judicial substitution of "necessary" for the actual statutory term, "applicable." These two terms are manifestly different, and the latter does not connote the former. The OCSLA commands us to give force to "applicable and not inconsistent" state laws as surrogate federal law. 43 U.S.C. § 1333(a)(2)(A). By following the course charted by the OCSLA, we do not accord state law supremacy over federal law, nor cede the United States' jurisdiction over the OCS to state agencies. We simply acknowledge, as the Supreme Court did in *Rodrigue*, 395 U.S. at 355–56, that Congress adopted state law as surrogate federal law for the OCS, so long as it is "applicable and not inconsistent with" existing federal law.

Nor do we find in the legislative history a clear intent on the part of Congress to require a "significant void or gap" in federal legislation or regulation, meaning the complete absence of any federal law, as a prerequisite to the application of state law. Indeed, Senator Cordon, the floor manager of the bill, noted that the contemplated extension of admiralty law to the OCS was unsatisfactory because: **[—24—]**

> The so-called social laws necessary for protection of the workers and their families would not apply. I refer to such things as unemployment laws, industrial-accident laws, fair-labor-standard laws, and so forth. It was necessary that the protection afforded by such laws be extended **{-1092-}** to the outer Shelf area because of the fact that ultimately some 10,000 or more men might be employed in mineral-resource development there.

99 Cong. Rec. 6963 (1953); *see Rodrigue*, 395 U.S. at 362. Read in context, Senator Cordon's statements emphasized the importance of having state law apply to the OCS, and do not indicate that state laws had to be necessary to fill gaps or voids in federal law *before* they would be adopted as surrogate federal law. *See Rodrigue*, 395 U.S. at 363. As Senator Cordon went on to explain:

> [T]he legal situation [of the OCS] is comparable to that in areas owned by the Federal Government under the exclusive jurisdiction of the Federal

Government and lying within the boundaries of a State in the uplands.

As a part of the same amendment, the [Senate Committee on Interior and Insular Affairs] provided, first, that the laws of abutting States should become a part of the Federal law within such areas opposite the States as would have been included in the States were their boundaries extended to the edge of the Continental Shelf. **[—25—]**

. . . .

The outer Continental Shelf will have the protection of the Constitution itself, *and will have the protection and provision for conduct of affairs as given by the laws of each of the abutting States* within the area immediately opposite that State.

99 Cong. Rec. 6963–64 (1953) (emphasis added); *see* S. Rep. No. 83-411, at 11 (1953).

Read in isolation, some remarks by Senators Anderson and Long seem to endorse the idea that state law was to speak as federal law only where existing federal law was "silent" or otherwise left a "void." 99 Cong. Rec. 7257, 7164 (1953). But "scattered floor statements by individual lawmakers . . . [are] 'among the least illuminating forms of legislative history.'" *Advocate Health Care Network v. Stapleton*, 137 S. Ct. 1652, 1661 (2017) (quoting *NLRB. v. SW General, Inc.*, 137 S. Ct. 929, 943 (2017)); *see Shell Oil*, 488 U.S. at 29 ("We . . . find that Shell's reliance on an isolated statement by Senator Long," who was a "vocal opponent of the OCSLA," "is misplaced."); *see also Hertzberg v. Dignity Partners, Inc.*, 191 F.3d 1076, 1082 (9th Cir. 1999) ("This circuit relies on official committee reports when considering legislative history, not stray comments by individuals . . . ."). Here, the legislative history is at best muddled, as illustrated by the following exchange between Senator Cordon, the floor manager of the bill, and Senator Daniel:

Mr. DANIEL: . . . *Since we have applied State laws in the fields which are not covered by Federal laws or by regulations* of the **[—26—]** Secretary of the Interior, I should like to ask the Senator from Oregon whether he understands that State laws relating to conservation will apply in this area until and unless the Secretary of the Interior writes some rule or regulation to the contrary.

Mr. CORDON: There can be no question about that; the Senator's statement is correct. *The language clearly adopts State law as Federal law where it is not inconsistent with existing Federal law or with the rules and regulations of the Secretary of the Interior*: and, of necessity, the inconsistency with respect to rules and regulations of the Secretary of the Interior must be in the case of those rules and regulations which it is within the power of the Secretary of the Interior to adopt. **{–1093–}**

When he has adopted them, those rules and regulations *must be inconsistent with or in conflict* with the conservation laws of the States, which are then the conservation laws of the United States with respect to that particular area, *or else the laws of the States, having been adopted by the United States, apply to that area.* There can be no question about it.

99 Cong. Rec. 7264 (1953) (emphasis added). We cannot allow "ambiguous legislative history . . . to control the ordinary meaning of [the] statutory language." *League to Save Lake Tahoe, Inc. v. Trounday*, 598 F.2d 1164, 1172 (9th **[—27—]** Cir. 1979) (citing *NLRB v. Plasterer's Local No. 79*, 404 U.S. 116, 129–30 (1971)); *see Milner*, 562 U.S. at 572. Reading the plain text of the OCSLA against the background of its inconclusive legislative history, we are not convinced that state law applies as surrogate federal law on the OCS only if "necess[ary]," *Cont'l Oil*, 417 F.2d at 1036, in the sense that there is no existing federal law on the subject.

We do not understand the Supreme Court to have instructed otherwise. Although the Fifth Circuit has sometimes described "necessity to fill a significant void or gap" as the "recurring theme of *Rodrigue*," *Nations*, 483 F.2d at 585 (internal quotation marks omitted); *Cont'l Oil*, 417 F.2d at 1036, the issue actually decided by *Rodrigue* was whether federal admiralty law applied on OCS platforms, 395 U.S. at 360, 366. *Rodrigue* established that, absent a maritime nexus, federal admiralty law does not extend to the OCS. *Id.* at 359–60. State law was deemed the law governing the two wrongful death actions in *Rodrigue*, but there was no competing applicable federal law, *id.* at 366, and the Supreme Court has not yet squarely confronted a situation where, as here, a state statutory scheme and an existing federal statutory scheme are both "potentially applicable" to a civil suit arising on the OCS. *Cf. Gulf Offshore*, 453 U.S. at 486–87.

b. The Meaning of "Not Inconsistent"

As we see it, because there are California and federal statutory schemes that are "applicable," in the ordinary sense of that term, to the parties' conflict, the determinative question in Newton's case is not which law is "applicable," but whether California wage and hour laws are "inconsistent with" existing federal law. 43 U.S.C. § 1333(a)(2)(A). If **[—28—]** they are not inconsistent, the OCSLA dictates that state wage and hour grievances should be redressable as federal claims on the OCS.

We recently examined the usual meaning of "inconsistent" in *Ecological Rights Foundation v. Pacific Gas & Electricity Co.*, 874 F.3d 1083 (9th Cir. 2017), where we concluded that laws are inconsistent if they are mutually "incompatible, incongruous, [or] inharmonious." *Id.* at 1095 (quoting Webster's Third New International Dictionary (1971)).[14]

To further articulate a framework for deciding whether a state law is inconsistent with federal law under the OCSLA, we draw on cases that have arisen in the context of two statutes involving the incorporation of state law into federal law: (1) the Assimilative Crimes Act ("Crimes Act"), 18 U.S.C. § 13, and (2) 42 U.S.C. § 1988. We look to the Crimes Act because it is an example of Congress applying state **{-1094-}** law in conjunction with federal law on enclaves. We also consider 42 U.S.C. § 1988, because at the time Congress enacted the civil rights statutes, it recognized that federal civil rights law was not sufficiently comprehensive and would have to rely, in part, on state law to effectuate its objectives. *See Burnett v. Grattan*, 468 U.S. 42, 47 (1984). Similar to § 1333(a)(2)(A) of the OCSLA, 42 U.S.C. § 1988 conditions the incorporation of state law on it being "not inconsistent with the Constitution and laws of the United States."

In *Rodrigue*, the Supreme Court emphasized that drilling platforms on the OCS are "to be treated as island[s] or as **[—29—]** federal enclaves within a landlocked State, not as vessels." 395 U.S. at 361. "The central principle of federal enclave doctrine is that Congress has exclusive legislative authority over . . . enclaves. But in the absence of applicable federal legislation displacing state law, those state laws that existed at the time that the enclave was ceded to the federal government remain in force." *Allison v. Boeing Laser Tech. Servs.*, 689 F.3d 1234, 1237 (10th Cir. 2012). State law postdating the creation of the enclave, however, is federal law on the enclave only if Congress so directs. *Id.*

The Assimilative Crimes Act is one such directive.[15] "The [Crimes Act] applies state criminal law to a defendant's acts or omissions [in federal enclaves] that are not made punishable by any enactment of Congress." *Lewis v. United States*, 523 U.S. 155, 159

---

[14] *Ecological Rights Foundation* involved inconsistency between federal statutes. 847 F.3d at 1095.

[15] 18 U.S.C. § 13(a), the Crimes Act, provides: "Whoever within or upon any [federal enclave] . . . is guilty of any act or omission which, although not made punishable by any enactment of Congress, would be punishable if committed or omitted within the jurisdiction of the State . . . in which such place is situated, . . . shall be guilty of a like offense and subject to a like punishment."

(1998) (emphasis and internal quotation marks omitted). Its "basic purpose is one of borrowing state law to fill gaps in the federal criminal law that applies on federal enclaves." *Id.* at 160. But as we have recognized, the Supreme Court has held that a void or gap—in the sense of a total absence of applicable federal law—is not a prerequisite to the application of state law under the Crimes Act. *See, e.g., United States v. Reed*, 734 F.3d 881, 888 (9th Cir. 2013) (citing *Lewis*, 523 U.S. at 166).

In *Lewis*, the Supreme Court formulated a two-step test for whether state law applies to a defendant accused of **[—30—]** committing an offense on an enclave. 523 U.S. at 164–65. The first question is the statutory one: whether the defendant's act or omission has been made punishable by any enactment of Congress. *Id.* at 164. If the act is not punishable by federal law, then the Crimes Act presumptively assimilates state law. *Id.* If Congress has legislated to make the defendant's conduct punishable, then "the court must ask the further question whether the federal statutes that apply to the 'act or omission' *preclude* application of the state law in question," that is, whether "applicable federal law indicate[s] an intent to punish conduct such as the defendant's to the exclusion of the particular state statute at issue?" *Id.* at 164, 166 (emphasis added). There is no "touchstone to provide an automatic general answer to this second question," and the "primary question . . . is one of legislative intent . . . ." *Id.* at 165–66.

Reed employed *Lewis*'s two-step test to hold that a federal DUI regulation did not bar assimilation of a Nevada drugged driving statute. 734 F.3d at 893. Reed was **{-1095-}** caught speeding in Lake Mead National Recreation Area. *Id.* at 884. He admitted to smoking marijuana and imbibing alcohol while driving, and failed three of the four field sobriety tests subsequently administered. *Id.* Reed was charged, *inter alia*, under a Nevada statute that penalized the operation of a vehicle while the concentration of marijuana in the operator's blood exceeded a statutorily established limit. Nev. Rev. Stat. § 484C.110(3)(g). Above that limit, a violation of the statute was established *per se*, i.e., without regard to actual impairment.

Reed moved to dismiss the state charge, arguing that Nevada's *per se* drugged driving law did not apply on the federal enclave where he was stopped because a federal **[—31—]** regulation, 36 C.F.R. § 4.23(a)(1), also "prohibit[ed] operating a vehicle while under the influence of alcohol *or* drugs to a degree that renders the operator incapable of safe operation." *Id.* at 886. In other words, Reed argued that because federal law made his conduct punishable, there was no gap in federal law for state law to fill. After a magistrate judge denied Reed's motion to dismiss, Reed pleaded guilty to the state law crime and appealed to our court. *Id.* at 884.

Applying the first step of the *Lewis* test, we agreed with the trial court that the federal enactment punished Reed's conduct. *Id.* at 887. But at step two, we concluded that federal law did not preclude application of the Nevada statute. *Id.* at 888. We noted that there is no "automatic general answer" to *Lewis*'s second question and that the primary inquiry is one of legislative intent. *Id.* Although "a state statute will not be assimilated if, for example, (1) its application would conflict with federal policy; (2) it would effectively rewrite an offense definition that Congress carefully considered; or (3) the federal statutes reveal an intent to occupy so much of a field as to exclude use of the particular state statute," we concluded that "the mere presence of the federal DUI regulation [did] not manifest a federal policy against assimilating Nevada's per se drugged driving law . . . ." *Id.* at 888, 892. *Reed* observed that federal law only included a *per se* provision for alcohol; it did not punish those who operated a vehicle under the influence of marijuana absent actual impairment. *Id.* at 886 (citing 36 C.F.R. § 4.23(a)(1)). Further, by providing elsewhere in the federal regulations that "State law that is now or may later be in effect is adopted and made a part of the regulations . . . [,]" 36 C.F.R. § 4.2, the National Park Service clearly expressed its intent for all nonconflicting state traffic laws to apply on federal enclaves. *Id.* at 889. Finding "no indication of an **[—32—]** overriding federal policy with which Nevada's per se drugged driving law interferes," we affirmed Reed's convictions. *Id.* at 893.

Although Congress has never provided for the wholesale assimilation of state civil law into federal law on all federal enclaves, it has the authority to do so, and it has done so for the OCS, "an area of exclusive Federal jurisdiction." 43 U.S.C. § 1333(a)(1). In legislating for the OCS, Congress used more precise language than in the Crimes Act, specifying that applicable state law is to apply unless "inconsistent" with federal law. *Reed*, however, remains instructive in two ways. First, it reinforces that where Congress has provided for the assimilation of state law into federal law governing a federal enclave, the "mere presence" of federal law is not enough to prevent application of state law. *Reed*, 734 F.3d at 892. Second, it illustrates the principle that determining whether the presence of federal law precludes the application of state law on an enclave is primarily a question of congressional intent. *Id.* at 888–89 (citing **{-1096-}** *Lewis*, 523 U.S. at 166); *see also United States v. Souza*, 392 F.3d 1050, 1054 (9th Cir. 2004). In *Reed*, there was not only considerable overlap between the federal and state DUI laws, but Reed's conduct was actually criminalized by existing federal law. Nevertheless, assimilating Nevada's drugged driving law was entirely consistent with federal law and policy, as the overlapping federal regulation expressly contemplated "assimilation of all nonconflicting state traffic laws." 734 F.3d at 888. **[—33—]**

We draw a similar lesson from the jurisprudence pertaining to 42 U.S.C. § 1988(a).[16] Notably, § 1988(a) does use the term "inconsistent." But unlike the OCSLA, it requires, before the assimilation of state law, not simply that the state law be "not inconsistent with the Constitution and laws of the United States," but that "the laws of the United States [be] . . . not adapted to the object, or . . . deficient in the provisions necessary to furnish suitable remedies and punish offenses against [the] law . . . ." 42 U.S.C. § 1988(a). In other words, unlike the OCSLA, § 1988 does require a gap in federal law as a prerequisite for assimilation of state law. Taking that substantial difference into account, judicial interpretation of the term "not inconsistent" in § 1988(a) remains instructive here. In enacting the federal civil rights acts, Congress recognized that federal law would not contain every rule that may be required to adjudicate suits brought under them. *Burnett*, 468 U.S. at 47. Accordingly, in § 1988(a), "Congress determined that gaps in [the] federal civil rights acts should be filled by state law, as long as that law is not inconsistent with federal law." *Hardin v. Straub*, 490 U.S. 536, 538 (1989) (footnote omitted). The Supreme Court has explained that "[i]n resolving questions of inconsistency between state and federal law raised under § 1988, courts must look not only at particular federal statutes and constitutional provisions, but also at the policies **[—34—]** expressed in them." *Robertson v. Wegmann*, 436 U.S. 584, 590 (1978) (alteration and internal quotation marks omitted).

An example of inconsistency between state and federal law is illustrated by *Burnett*. 468 U.S. at 55. Plaintiffs in *Burnett* were white employees of a predominantly black college who sued their employer for racial and gender discrimination after it refused to renew their contracts. *Id.* at 43–44. The district court borrowed the six-month statute of limitations for filing an employment discrimination complaint with the relevant Maryland administrative body, and dismissed the action. *Id.* at 45. The Fourth Circuit reversed, holding that Maryland's generic three-year statute of limitations applied, *id.* at 45–46, and the Supreme Court affirmed the Fourth Circuit's decision. *Id.* at 46. The Supreme Court observed that "[a] legislative definition of a statute of limitations also reflects a policy

[16] 42 U.S.C. § 1988(a) provides that in the event that the federal civil rights acts "are deficient in the provisions necessary to furnish suitable remedies and punish offenses against law, the common law, as modified and changed by the constitution and statutes of the State wherein the court having jurisdiction of such civil or criminal cause is held, *so far as the same is not inconsistent with the Constitution and laws of the United States*, shall be extended to and govern the said courts in the trial and disposition of the cause, and, if it is of a criminal nature, in the infliction of punishment on the party found guilty." (emphasis added.)

assessment of the state causes of action to which it applies." *Id.* at 52. Hence, insofar as state policies are "inconsistent with, or of marginal relevance to, **{–1097–}** the policies informing the Civil Rights Acts," their accompanying statutes of limitations may be unsuitable for use under § 1988(a). *Id.* at 53. Contrasting the broad remedial goals of the federal civil rights statutes—"compensation of persons whose civil rights have been violated, and prevention of the abuse of state power"—to the relatively modest ambitions of Maryland's administrative scheme for employment discrimination, the *Burnett* court found Maryland's policy to be "manifestly inconsistent with the central objective of the Reconstruction-Era civil rights statutes, which is to ensure that individuals whose federal constitutional or statutory rights are abridged may recover damages or secure injunctive relief." *Id.* at 53–55. **[—35—]**

While § 1988(a) is not textually parallel to § 1333(a)(2)(A) of the OCSLA, we glean from *Burnett* and similar cases, *see, e.g., Board of Regents v. Tomanio*, 446 U.S. 478 (1980), the principle that inconsistency between state and federal law is assessed by looking at Congress's objective in enacting the federal statutes at issue.

c. Whether California Minimum Wage and Overtime Laws are Inconsistent with Federal Law

We thus turn to the remaining question and the crux of Newton's appeal: whether California's minimum wage and overtime laws are inconsistent with the FLSA.

The FLSA was enacted to "protect all covered workers from substandard wages and oppressive working hours." *Encino Motorcars, LLC v. Navarro*, 136 S. Ct. 2117, 2121 (2016) (internal quotation marks omitted). It "seeks to prohibit 'labor conditions detrimental to the maintenance of the minimum standard of living necessary for health, efficiency, and general well-being of workers.'" *Kasten v. Saint-Gobain Performance Plastics Corp.*, 563 U.S. 1, 11 (2011) (quoting 29 U.S.C. § 202(a)). Critical to our analysis, the FLSA "establish[es] a national *floor* under which wage protections cannot drop." *Pac. Merch. Shipping Ass'n v. Aubry*, 918 F.2d 1409, 1425 (9th Cir. 1990); *see Wang v. Chinese Daily News, Inc.*, 623 F.3d 743, 759 (9th Cir. 2010) ("[T]he FLSA sets a floor rather than a ceiling on protective legislation."), *vacated on other grounds, Chinese Daily News, Inc. v. Wang*, 565 U.S. 801 (2011). The FLSA's savings clause expressly provides that states are free to adopt more protective standards for minimum wages or maximum hours in a work week: **[—36—]**

> No provision of this chapter or of any order thereunder shall excuse noncompliance with any Federal or State law or municipal ordinance establishing a minimum wage higher than the minimum wage established under this chapter or a maximum work week lower than the maximum workweek established under this chapter.

29 U.S.C. § 218(a). Since "the best evidence of Congress's intent is the statutory text," *Nat'l Fed'n of Indep. Bus. v. Sebelius*, 567 U.S. 519, 544 (2012), and the FLSA explicitly permits more protective state wage and hour laws, we reject Parker's suggestion that California's minimum wage and overtime laws are antagonistic to the remedial purposes of the FLSA simply because they establish different and more generous benchmarks than the floor set by the FLSA's statutory and regulatory scheme.[17] **{–1098–}**

[17] Newton asserts that "inconsistency with regulations promulgated by departments other than the Department of the Interior does not bar the application of the state law" on the OCS. As a general matter, "properly promulgated, substantive agency regulations have 'the force and effect of law'" such as "to pre-empt state law under the Supremacy Clause." *Chrysler Corp. v. Brown*, 441 U.S. 281, 295–96 (1979); *see Wyeth v. Levine*, 555 U.S. 555, 576 (2009). We have "turned to these longstanding DOL regulations in resolving FLSA . . . disputes." *Brigham v. Eugene Water & Elec. Bd.*, 357 F.3d 931, 940 (2004). The OCSLA does not preclude courts from looking beyond the bare text of the FLSA to DOL regulations for illumination as to the content of existing federal law.

Moreover, the application of California minimum wage and overtime laws as federal law on the OCS serves the purpose of the OCSLA. In *Huson*, the Supreme Court observed that "Congress . . . recognized that the special **[—37—]** relationship between the men working on these artificial islands and the adjacent shore to which they commute favored application of state law with which these men and their attorneys would be familiar." 404 U.S. at 103 (internal quotation marks omitted). Application of California's minimum wage and "hours worked" provisions does not vitiate the "special relationship between the men working on these [platforms] and the adjacent shore to which they commute to visit their families," *Rodrigue*, 395 U.S. at 365; if anything, this policy consideration indicates that the overlapping state and federal statutory schemes regulating employment on the California shore should also govern, as federal law, on the OCS.[18] Application of California's wage and hour laws also does not frustrate an interest in national uniformity, because in enacting OCSLA, Congress "specifically rejected national uniformity as a paramount goal." *Gulf Offshore*, 453 U.S. at 487 (quoting *Huson*, 404 U.S. at 104) (internal quotation marks omitted).

Parker cites numerous cases for its contention that the FLSA is inconsistent with California's minimum wage and overtime laws. In particular, Parker relies on *Mendiola v. CPS Security Solutions, Inc.*, 60 Cal. 4th 833 (2015). *Mendiola* involved California wage and hour claims brought by security guards who regularly patrolled construction sites for eight hours on weekdays and sixteen hours on weekends, and who were required to reside, uncompensated, in an employer-provided trailer for eight hours after each shift and **[—38—]** remain on-call. 60 Cal. 4th at 837. The *Mendiola* court held that these on-call hours were "hours worked" for the purposes of California's Wage Order 4, and that the employer "could not exclude 'sleep time'" from the compensable hours in the security guards' 24-hour shifts. *Id.* at 838. In reaching this result, the California Supreme Court rejected the employer's argument that federal DOL regulations furnished the appropriate definition for hours worked under California's wage order. *Id.* at 842–44. Emphasizing that it had previously "cautioned against confounding federal and state labor law," the California Supreme Court ruled that the language of Wage Order 4 did not evidence the state Industrial Welfare Commission's intent to incorporate, by reference, federal law and regulations. **{-1099-}** *Id.* at 843, 847 (internal quotation marks omitted). Parker argues that *Mendiola* illustrates that California law is inconsistent with the FLSA. *See Brigham*, 357 F.3d at 940–41. We disagree. *Mendiola* only establishes that California embraces a more protective standard for determining hours worked, not that California's standard is *inconsistent* with federal law. Indeed, the savings clause in the FLSA reflects Congress's express intent that states should be allowed to adopt more protective standards. *See* 29 U.S.C. § 218(a). Parker has failed to demonstrate that California's minimum wage and overtime laws are inconsistent with federal law, and we know of nothing else indicating that California's provisions for minimum wage and maximum hours worked are inconsistent with the FLSA.

We conclude the district court erred by dismissing the claims Newton brought pursuant to California's minimum wage and overtime laws, and that California's minimum wage and maximum hours worked provisions are "applicable and not inconsistent," 43 U.S.C. § 1333(a)(2)(A), with the **[—39—]** FLSA. We vacate the order dismissing these claims and remand to the district court.

2. Newton's Claims under California Meal Period, Final Pay, and Pay Stub Laws

The district court dismissed the claims Newton brought pursuant to California's meal period, final pay, and pay stub laws because it concluded that state law does not apply on the

---

[18] To be clear, this "special relationship with the shore community," alone, does not support claims brought pursuant to § 1333(a)(2)(A) of the OCSLA "regardless of the location of the accident." *See Tallentire*, 477 U.S. at 218–19. This policy consideration only applies for grievances that arise on the OCS. *Id.*

OCS unless there is a "significant void or gap" in federal law, and it found that there were no such voids or gaps. In reaching this ruling, the district court relied on its conclusion that the FLSA is a comprehensive scheme, rather than considering whether California's wage and hour laws are inconsistent with the FLSA. Because we hold that the absence of federal law is not a prerequisite for applicable and not inconsistent state law to become surrogate federal law on the OCS, we vacate the order dismissing these claims. The district court shall determine on remand whether California's meal period, final pay, and pay stub laws are "not inconsistent" with existing federal law. If they are, the OCSLA adopts them as federal law on the OCS.

3. Newton's Civil Penalties and Unfair Competition Claims

Newton's claims under California's Private Attorney General Act (PAGA) and Unfair Competition Law (UCL) were dismissed by the district court on the grounds that he had not demonstrated a violation of California's labor and employment laws. Because we vacate the dismissal of Newton's other claims under California law, we also vacate the dismissal of his PAGA and UCL claims. **[—40—]**

4. Leave to Amend

Newton's operative complaint suggests that some of Parker's allegedly unlawful conduct occurred in California. We cannot determine on the record before us whether Newton has any claim arising from the time he spent onshore or within California's territorial waters. This portion of the complaint is cryptic and it has not been addressed by the district court. Under our precedent, Newton is entitled to an opportunity to clarify these claims. *See Eminence Capital, LLC v. Aspeon, Inc.*, 316 F.3d 1048, 1051 (9th Cir. 2003) (observing that the rule that leave to amend shall be "freely given" is "to be applied with extreme liberality") (citing *Owens v. Kaiser Found. Health Plan, Inc.*, 244 F.3d 708, 712 (9th Cir. 2001)). **{–1100–}**

IV. CONCLUSION

We vacate the order dismissing Newton's claims and remand to the district court for further proceedings consistent with this opinion.[19]

VACATED and REMANDED.

(Reporter's Note: On April 27, 2018, the Ninth Circuit entered an Order denying rehearing en banc and amended this opinion by adding footnote 19. The denial of rehearing en banc is reported at 888 F.3d 1085).

[19] We reserve for the district court's consideration on remand the question whether our holding should be applied retrospectively. *See Huson*, 404 U.S. at 355.

United States Court of Appeals for the Ninth Circuit

No. 16-15023

BARNES
VS.
SEA HAWAII RAFTING, LLC

Appeal from the United States District Court for the District of Hawaii

Decided: March 28, 2018
Amended: April 19, 2018

Citation: 889 F.3d 517, 6 Adm. R. 330 (9th Cir. 2018).

Before **FISHER, PAEZ,** and **NGUYEN,** Circuit Judges.

[—5—] {–523–} **NGUYEN,** Circuit Judge:

Chad Barnes is a seaman who was injured when the boat on which he was working, the M/V Tehani, exploded. During his recovery, Barnes received some monetary assistance from either Sea Hawaii Rafting, LLC ("SHR"), which owned the Tehani, or Kris Henry, SHR's owner and manager, but those payments soon stopped. Seeking the **[—6—]** ancient maritime remedy of maintenance and cure,[1] among other relief, Barnes sued the Tehani in rem and SHR and Henry in personam to enforce his seaman's lien against the vessel. Although admiralty courts normally **{–524–}** handle such matters expeditiously, that did not happen here for two reasons.

First, the district court rejected Barnes's pretrial requests to enforce SHR's obligation to pay maintenance and cure. The court concluded that Barnes was entitled to maintenance and cure and had demonstrated his actual maintenance expenses. Nonetheless, despite undisputed evidence that Barnes was entitled to at least some of his actual expenses, the district court declined to award Barnes any maintenance until trial.

Second, when SHR declared bankruptcy after fifteen months of litigation and shortly before trial, the district court stayed Barnes's action. The district court concluded that the Tehani was an asset of the debtor's estate and that the automatic bankruptcy stay barred proceedings to enforce Barnes's maritime lien against the vessel. The bankruptcy court partially lifted the bankruptcy stay to allow the district court to evaluate Barnes's claims against SHR but expressly prohibited the district court from issuing any ruling that would affect the maritime lien's status.

Ultimately, the district court dismissed Barnes's claims against the Tehani. The court reasoned that it lacked in rem jurisdiction because, even though Barnes verified his **[—7—]** original complaint, he failed to verify the amended complaint. Then, while Barnes's appeal was pending, the bankruptcy trustee—with the bankruptcy court's approval—sold the Tehani purportedly free and clear of Barnes's maritime lien. The trustee subsequently moved to dismiss this appeal as moot.

We conclude that the district court erred by denying Barnes's maintenance requests in full, staying the action, and dismissing the Tehani. The district court obtained jurisdiction over the vessel Tehani when Barnes filed a verified complaint and the defendants appeared generally and litigated without contesting in rem jurisdiction. The district court did not lose in rem jurisdiction while the Tehani remained in its constructive custody. And the court's control over the vessel, once obtained, was exclusive. SHR's later-filed bankruptcy petition did not divest the district court of in rem jurisdiction. Moreover, the automatic bankruptcy stay did not affect Barnes's maritime lien against the Tehani, and the bankruptcy court had no authority to dispose of the lien through the application of bankruptcy law.

When, as here, a seaman establishes his entitlement to maintenance and provides some evidence of his actual living expenses, the burden shifts to the vessel's owner to produce evidence that the seaman's actual costs were unreasonable. Whether or not the

[1] "Maintenance" is a seaman's "right . . . to food and lodging if he falls ill or becomes injured while in the service of the ship. 'Cure' is the right to necessary medical services." 1 Thomas J. Schoenbaum, *Admiralty and Maritime Law* § 6-28 (5th ed. 2016) (footnote omitted).

vessel's owner provides such evidence, the seaman is entitled to a maintenance award in the amount of his actual costs up to the reasonable rate in his locality. Over three years after concluding that Barnes was entitled to maintenance and had sufficiently proven his actual costs, the district court has yet to award him any maintenance.

Accordingly, we deny the trustee's motion to dismiss, reverse the district court's dismissal of the Tehani, and issue a writ of mandamus to the district court to award Barnes **[—8—]** maintenance for his undisputed actual and reasonable expenses—$34 per day—subject to a potential increase after trial.

I.

A. Factual Background

Barnes worked for SHR for six years as a captain and crew member of the Tehani, a 25-foot rigid hull inflatable boat powered by twin outboard engines. Barnes took passengers from Honokohau Harbor on sightseeing and snorkeling trips along the **{–525–}** Kona coast. Henry paid Barnes under the table with personal checks made out to "cash."

On July 3, 2012, Henry and Barnes were launching the Tehani for a night snorkeling trip. Henry was in his truck, towing the Tehani on an attached trailer, and Barnes was onboard the boat. Henry backed the trailer down the launch ramp until the vessel was in the water. When Barnes started the starboard engine, the Tehani exploded. The hatch struck Barnes on his back and head, propelling him into the ocean.

A Coast Guard investigation found that the explosion was caused by a fuel tank with a missing screw in the fuel tank sender. Fuel leaked into the bilge, where vapors accumulated and ignited when Barnes started the engine. The investigator concluded that the incident might have been avoided if Henry had installed the required flammable vapor detector and mechanical exhaust system. *See* 46 C.F.R. §§ 182.460, 182.480. The boat, which was insured, was subsequently repaired and returned to service.

Barnes was less fortunate. SHR lacked insurance to cover his medical expenses for physical, psychological, and neurological treatment. Barnes required approximately **[—9—]** 12 staples to reattach parts of his scalp. Due to his head injuries, he can no longer drive a car or swim. He cannot afford rent and has been living on friends' couches. He receives approximately $300 per month in disability income from the State of Hawaii.[2]

B. Litigation in the District and Bankruptcy Courts

On January 1, 2013, Barnes filed a verified complaint in admiralty against Henry, SHR, and the Tehani, claiming unseaworthiness, various theories of negligence, and intentional infliction of emotional distress. Barnes sought maintenance and cure, damages, and attorney's fees. The three defendants answered the complaint. Despite denying Barnes's allegation that the Tehani was subject to the district court's in rem jurisdiction, they did not move to dismiss the Tehani on that basis but instead proceeded to litigate the dispute.

Barnes moved for "summary judgment for payment of maintenance and cure," requesting that the district court order defendants to pay his "reasonable, actual costs of food and lodging" and medical costs since the date of his injury until he reached "maximum medical cure." The district court granted Barnes's motion in part. Noting that defendants did not dispute that Barnes was injured in the service of the Tehani, the district court ruled that Barnes was entitled to maintenance and cure and had not yet reached maximum cure. Applying the standard for determining a **[—10—]** maintenance rate from *Hall v. Noble Drilling (U.S.) Inc.*, 242 F.3d 582 (5th Cir. 2001), the district court concluded that Barnes

[2] Barnes also received some assistance from Henry, but the parties dispute the exact amount. Barnes acknowledges that Henry paid him $500 to cover rent. It is unclear whether Henry made this payment in his personal capacity or on SHR's behalf.

had shown his actual food and lodging costs but not the reasonable amount for such costs in his locality or his actual medical expenses.[3] The court therefore declined to award either maintenance or cure.

About four months after the district court's order, Henry volunteered to pay **{-526-}** Barnes $962.83 per month towards maintenance but stopped after making two payments. Barnes moved two more times for summary judgment to determine a daily maintenance rate.[4] The district court denied both motions, concluding that there were triable issues of fact regarding reasonable food and lodging costs in Hawaii. The district court also denied Barnes's separate motion for summary judgment for payment of cure.

Meanwhile, Barnes filed an unverified amended complaint, adding a claim for negligence per se. In answering the amended complaint, defendants again stated a general denial of Barnes's allegation that the Tehani was subject to the district court's in rem jurisdiction but did not specifically challenge jurisdiction by filing a motion under Federal Rule of Civil Procedure 12(b) or otherwise bringing the issue to the district court's attention.

In yet another summary judgment motion, Barnes asked the district court to grant relief on his claims for **[—11—]** unseaworthiness, negligence per se, and Jones Act negligence. Two weeks before the hearing on this motion and just over a month before the scheduled trial, SHR and Henry filed for bankruptcy relief—Henry for reorganization under Chapter 13 and SHR for dissolution under Chapter 7. Pursuant to the automatic bankruptcy stay, 11 U.S.C. § 362(a), the district court stayed the proceedings against all three defendants.

The bankruptcy court, recognizing the district court's "experience and expertise . . . in matters in admiralty," partially lifted the stay as to Henry and SHR so that the district court could "adjudicate the validity, extent, amount, and date of perfection of any maritime lien claim by . . . Barnes against the [Tehani]."[5] However, the bankruptcy court expressly kept the stay in place "to bar the enforcement of any maritime lien." The bankruptcy court expressed concern that the "limited assets" of SHR's estate did not warrant the bankruptcy trustee's "participat[ion] in extended or unlimited litigation in the District Court."[6]

After the bankruptcy court partially lifted the stay, the district court reopened the case. In a subsequent minute **[—12—]** order addressing Barnes's outstanding summary judgment motions, the district court noted—sua sponte and parenthetically—that "it lack[ed] jurisdiction over the [Tehani], as [the vessel] was never arrested." Thereafter, Barnes attempted several times to verify the amended complaint—a verified complaint being a precondition of arrest, *see* Fed. R. Civ. P. Supp. Adm. & Mar. Cl. R. C(2)(a)—though Barnes made no attempt to arrest the Tehani. The trustee in SHR's bankruptcy case conceded to the district court that defendants' "pre-petition answer subjected [them] to the [district **{-527-}** court's] jurisdiction." The trustee acknowledged the district court's previous statement that it lacked in rem jurisdiction but did not seek dismissal on that ground. Rather, the trustee argued that

[3] Barnes originally presented the district court with evidence of reasonable costs in Honolulu but subsequently clarified that Kailua-Kona was the relevant locality.

[4] Barnes later moved a fourth time for summary judgment on the issue of a maintenance rate but withdrew the motion after the district court dismissed his claims against the Tehani.

[5] Initially, there was confusion as to which defendant—Henry or SHR—owned the Tehani. Defendants erroneously listed the Tehani as Henry's rather than SHR's asset in their bankruptcy cases. Under that misapprehension, the bankruptcy court first lifted only the stay in Henry's bankruptcy, though the order allowed the district court to "value to its conclusion the claim of [Barnes] arising from [the admiralty case]," which necessarily implicated Barnes's claim against SHR's property. When the Tehani's ownership was clarified, the district court refused to proceed further with SHR's bankruptcy stay still in place. The bankruptcy court then lifted that stay as well.

[6] The Tehani and its trailer, appraised to be worth $38,500 and $2,500, respectively, were the estate's only substantial assets.

Barnes had lost any maritime lien he had in the vessel through his failure to verify the amended complaint and invoke the district court's in rem jurisdiction. Henry also did not seek dismissal for lack of in rem jurisdiction.[7]

The district court nonetheless dismissed the Tehani for lack of in rem jurisdiction and, in the same order, granted Barnes partial summary judgment on his claim for negligence per se. In dismissing the Tehani, the district court reasoned that Barnes's unverified amended complaint—filed after more than 15 months of litigation—superseded the original verified complaint; Barnes's attempts to verify the amended complaint while the bankruptcy stay was in effect were invalid; verification of the amended complaint was **[—13—]** necessary for his maritime lien against the Tehani to attach; and Barnes's failure to verify the amended complaint deprived the district court of in rem jurisdiction.

Barnes appeals the district court's orders dismissing the Tehani and denying his request to set a maintenance amount. While his appeal was pending, the bankruptcy court approved, and SHR's bankruptcy trustee executed, the sale of the Tehani and its trailer to Henry's new company, Aloha Ocean Excursions, LLC, for $35,000.

II.

Jurisdiction

We begin by considering our own jurisdiction as to each issue raised on appeal. *See Ashcroft v. Iqbal*, 556 U.S. 662, 671 (2009) ("Subject-matter jurisdiction . . . should be considered when fairly in doubt." (citing *Arbaugh v. Y & H Corp.*, 546 U.S. 500, 514 (2006))); *Gupta v. Thai Airways Int'l, Ltd.*, 487 F.3d 759, 769–70 (9th Cir. 2007) ("[A]ppellate courts must examine each claim or issue presented separately to determine their jurisdiction on interlocutory appeal . . . ." (citing *Will v. Hallock*, 546 U.S. 345, 349 (2006))). The district court, sitting in admiralty, had jurisdiction under 28 U.S.C. § 1333(1). SHR's bankruptcy trustee asserts that if this appeal is not moot, we have appellate jurisdiction under 28 U.S.C. § 1291 to review the dismissal of the Tehani because "[a]n order of dismissal is a final order." But the district court dismissed only the Tehani. "'[A]ny order or other decision, however designated, that adjudicates fewer than all the claims or *the rights and liabilities of fewer than all the parties*' is not final" unless the district court determines there is no just reason for delay and enters judgment. *Hyan v. Hummer*, 825 F.3d 1043, 1046 (9th Cir. 2016) (per curiam) (quoting **[—14—]** Fed. R. Civ. P. 54(b)) (emphasis in *Hyan*). That did not happen here.[8] Thus, this appeal is interlocutory. **{-528-}**

Barnes and Henry suggest 28 U.S.C. § 1292(a)(3) as the source of our jurisdiction, which permits appeals from "[i]nterlocutory decrees of . . . district courts . . . determining the rights and liabilities of the parties to admiralty cases in which appeals from final decrees are allowed." This means orders that decide "the merits of the controversies between [the parties]," because "'rights and liabilities' . . . are substantive in nature—not adjective, tactical, or procedural." *Rogers v. Alaska S.S. Co.*, 249 F.2d 646, 649 (9th Cir. 1957) (quoting *In re Wills Lines*, 227 F.2d 509, 510 (2d Cir. 1955)). In determining whether a ruling decides the merits, we consider "financial realities," *All Alaskan Seafoods, Inc.*

[7] Less than a week before the hearing on Barnes's motion for summary judgment on his claims for unseaworthiness, negligence per se, and Jones Act negligence, Henry in a supplemental memorandum requested dismissal of the action for lack of *subject matter* jurisdiction based on Barnes's failure to verify the amended complaint. He cited no authority for this proposition, and we know of none.

[8] Barnes moved for leave to file an interlocutory appeal under 28 U.S.C. § 1292(a)(3) or (b). The district court, viewing its approval as unnecessary for an appeal pursuant to § 1292(a)(3), *see Seattle First Nat'l Bank v. Bluewater P'ship*, 772 F.2d 565, 569 (9th Cir. 1985), denied the motion as moot. Although we ultimately agree with the district court that we have appellate jurisdiction under § 1292(a)(3) to review the dismissal of the Tehani, the issue is close, and the better practice in that situation would be to make an alternative ruling under § 1292(b).

v. M/V Sea Producer, 882 F.2d 425, 428 (9th Cir. 1989), as well as other "practical matter[s]," *Kesselring v. F/T Arctic Hero*, 30 F.3d 1123, 1125 (9th Cir. 1994).

In *Melwire Trading Co. v. M/V Cape Antibes*, we concluded that 28 U.S.C. § 1292(a)(3) applied to an order dismissing a vessel for lack of in rem jurisdiction. 811 F.2d 1271, 1273 (9th Cir. 1987). In concluding that we had jurisdiction, however, we construed "the actual basis for the district court's dismissal" to be "its conclusion that none of [the plaintiff's] claims gave rise to a maritime lien **[—15—]** enforceable in an action in rem," a question that "involves the merits." *Id.* at 1273 n.1 (citing *The Resolute*, 168 U.S. 437, 440 (1897)). Here, there is no doubt that Barnes had a seaman's lien, and the Tehani's dismissal was due to Barnes's purported procedural shortcomings in invoking the district court's in rem jurisdiction. Because this type of dismissal is "not an adjudication upon the merits," *Neifeld v. Steinberg*, 438 F.2d 423, 432 (3d Cir. 1971); *cf. Kendall v. Overseas Dev. Corp.*, 700 F.2d 536, 539 (9th Cir. 1983) ("[A] dismissal for lack of *in personam* jurisdiction is not *res judicata* as to the merits of the claim."), it is not necessarily appealable.

The district court concluded that its dismissal order effectively "foreclose[d] the only forum in which Barnes may bring his admiralty claims against the Tehani." Thus, notwithstanding that the ruling was procedural, it affects Barnes's substantive rights and is the proper subject of an interlocutory appeal under 28 U.S.C. § 1292(a)(3). *See Royal Ins. Co. of Am. v. S.W. Marine*, 194 F.3d 1009, 1013 n.2 (9th Cir. 1999) (holding that an order denying leave to amend was appealable under § 1292(a)(3) because it "effectively dismissed" the plaintiff's claims); *see also MS Tabea Schiffahrtsgesellschaft MBH & Co. v. Bd. of Comm'rs*, 636 F.3d 161, 165 (5th Cir. 2011) (holding that "dismiss[al] . . . for lack of subject matter jurisdiction . . . conclusively determined the parties' rights and liabilities").

We lack jurisdiction, however, to consider whether the district court should have awarded maintenance. The court's partial summary judgment that defendants are liable to Barnes for maintenance payments is not at issue. Defendants did not appeal that ruling, and the time to do so on an interlocutory basis expired long before Barnes filed his notice of appeal. *See* 28 U.S.C. § 2107(a) (providing a 30- **[—16—]** day deadline to appeal "any judgment, order or decree"). Rather, Barnes is attempting to appeal the district court's denial of summary judgment as to a maintenance amount. Except in limited circumstances not applicable here, the denial of summary judgment is not appealable. *See, e.g., Thomas v. Dillard*, 818 F.3d 864, 874 (9th Cir. 2016) (citing **{-529-}** *Mueller v. Auker*, 576 F.3d 979, 987 (9th Cir. 2009)); *see also P.R. Ports Auth. v. Barge Katy-B*, 427 F.3d 93, 106–07 (1st Cir. 2005) (holding that § 1292(a)(3) permits interlocutory review of only the portion of an order determining the parties' rights and liabilities); *cf. EEOC v. Recruit U.S.A., Inc.*, 939 F.2d 746, 757 (9th Cir. 1991) (dismissing for lack of jurisdiction challenge to district court's failure to rule on sanctions request in otherwise appealable order granting preliminary injunction).

When appellate jurisdiction is lacking, "[w]e can . . . treat the notice of appeal as a petition for a writ of mandamus." *Miller v. Gammie*, 335 F.3d 889, 895 (9th Cir. 2003) (en banc). For reasons we will explain, we conclude that mandamus relief is warranted in these unique circumstances. First, however, we turn to the district court's dismissal of the Tehani for lack of in rem jurisdiction, which we review de novo. *See Ventura Packers, Inc. v. F/V Jeanine Kathleen*, 424 F.3d 852, 858 (9th Cir. 2005).

III.

A. The District Court's In Rem Jurisdiction over the Tehani

To commence an action in rem against a vessel, the plaintiff must file a verified complaint that describes the vessel "with reasonable particularity" and states that the vessel "is within the district" or will be so "while the action is pending." Fed. R. Civ. P. Supp. Adm. & Mar. Cl. R. C(2); **[—17—]** *see*

Madeja v. Olympic Packers, LLC, 310 F.3d 628, 637 (9th Cir. 2002). If the plaintiff meets these conditions, the district court must take the boat into custody—unless the plaintiff requests otherwise—by issuing an arrest warrant to be served by the marshal.[9] *See* Fed. R. Civ. P. Supp. Adm. & Mar. Cl. R. C(3)(a)–(b), E(3)(b).

"Once the district court issue[s] warrants for the arrest of the . . . vessels pursuant to Rule C, and the warrants [are] successfully served, 'jurisdiction [i]s complete.'" *F/V Jeanine Kathleen*, 424 F.3d at 858 (quoting *The Rio Grande*, 90 U.S. (23 Wall.) 458, 463 (1874)). However, "as with other forms of jurisdiction over the party, *see* Fed. R. Civ. P. 12(h)(1), a vessel may waive jurisdiction in rem by appearing in the action and failing to raise the defense of lack of jurisdiction over the party in a timely fashion." *United States v. Republic Marine, Inc.*, 829 F.2d 1399, 1402 (7th Cir. 1987); *see Cactus Pipe & Supply Co. v. M/V Montmartre*, 756 F.2d 1103, 1107–11 (5th Cir. 1985); *see also Hapag-Lloyd A.G. v. U.S. Oil Trading LLC*, 814 F.3d 146, 153–54, 4 Adm. R. 62, 67 (2d Cir. 2016) (noting "the many cases in which *in rem* jurisdiction has been held waived without seizure when the owner appears without contesting jurisdiction" (citing *Republic Marine* and *M/V Montmartre*)); *Porsche* **[—18—]** *Cars N.A., Inc. v. Porsche.net*, 302 F.3d 248, 256 (4th Cir. 2002) ("[I]n admiralty . . . cases, for years courts have held that objections to in rem jurisdiction may be waived."); *Farwest Steel Corp. v. Barge Sea Span 241*, 769 F.2d 620, 622 (9th Cir. 1985) ("[J]urisdiction to review an *in rem* decision **{–530–}** [can be derived] from the existence of either consent or *in personam* jurisdiction over a shipowner whose other contacts with the forum satisfied 'traditional notions of fair play and substantial justice.'" (quoting *Int'l Shoe Co. v. Washington*, 326 U.S. 310, 316 (1945)); *The Willamette*, 70 F. 874, 877–78 (9th Cir. 1895) (holding that challenge to in rem jurisdiction was waived where the shipowner appeared and answered the complaint).

Barnes's original complaint was verified and met the other prerequisites to invoke the district court's in rem jurisdiction. Barnes understandably found it advantageous not to seek the Tehani's arrest. He was unwilling to pay the associated costs,[10] which he estimated would be approximately $30,000; there was no risk that the vessel would leave the district; and, Barnes asserts, "allowing **[—19—]** Henry to continue to operate his ocean excursion business with the vessel was the only possible way that [Henry] could generate enough money to pay Barnes [m]aintenance." Barnes's failure to arrest the Tehani benefitted defendants as well. Had he arrested the Tehani, defendants not only would have had to put up security to obtain the vessel's release, *see* Fed. R. Civ. P. Supp. Adm. & Mar. Cl. R. E(5)(a)–(b), but would have endured the inconvenience of being unable to use the

---

[9] Supplemental Admiralty and Maritime Claims Rule C(3)(a)(i) provides that the district court "*must* review the complaint and any supporting papers" and, if satisfactory, "the court *must* issue an order directing the clerk to issue a warrant for the arrest of the vessel." (Emphasis added.) The District of Hawaii requires admiralty plaintiffs to *apply* for this review and places the burden on the applicant "to ensure that the application has been reviewed and, upon approval, presented to the clerk for issuance of the appropriate order." D. Haw. Adm. R. E.3(e). Barnes does not challenge the local rule as being inconsistent with the federal rule, and it is unnecessary for us to consider any tension between them.

[10] A party seeking to arrest a vessel must deposit sufficient funds to cover for at least 10 days the marshal's expenses, including dockage, keepers, maintenance, and insurance, and pay the marshal's ongoing expenses in advance until the vessel is released. *See* 28 U.S.C. § 1921; D. Haw. Adm. R. E.11. There is a split of authority over whether seamen are exempt from prepayment of these fees. *See* 28 U.S.C. § 1916 ("In all courts of the United States, seamen may institute and prosecute suits and appeals in their own names and for their own benefit for wages or salvage or the enforcement of laws enacted for their health or safety without prepaying fees or costs or furnishing security therefor."); *compare Thielebeule v. M/S Nordsee Pilot*, 452 F.2d 1230, 1232 (2d Cir. 1971) (holding seamen are exempt from prepayment), *with P.R. Drydock & Marine Terminals, Inc. v. Motor Vessel Luisa Del Caribe*, 746 F.2d 93, 94 (1st Cir. 1984) (holding seamen are not exempt), *and Araya v. McLelland*, 525 F.2d 1194, 1196 (5th Cir. 1976) (same).

vessel until its release was secured. *See* 4 Erastus Cornelius Benedict et al., *Benedict on Admiralty* § 2.15[C] (7th ed., rev. 2017).

When Barnes filed his verified complaint, the district court issued summonses for each of the defendants, including the Tehani. Four months after Henry and SHR were served, they and the Tehani answered the complaint without moving to dismiss for lack of in rem jurisdiction. The three defendants then actively participated in the litigation—providing discovery, opposing two summary judgment motions and two motions for reconsideration of orders denying summary judgment, and participating in two settlement conferences—without challenging the court's in rem jurisdiction. By the time Barnes filed his unverified amended complaint, defendants had clearly waived any objection to in rem jurisdiction by litigating the merits of Barnes's claims for more than 15 months. *See Peterson v. Highland Music, Inc.*, 140 F.3d 1313, 1318 (9th Cir. 1998) ("Most defenses, including the defense of lack of personal jurisdiction, may be waived as a result of the course of conduct pursued by a party during litigation."); *cf. Cont'l Bank, N.A. v. Meyer*, 10 F.3d 1293, 1297 (7th Cir. 1993) (holding that personal jurisdiction defense, even though raised in the answer sufficiently to avoid waiver under Rule 12(h), was waived where "the defendants fully participated **[—20—]** in litigation of the merits for over two-and-a-half years without actively contesting personal jurisdiction"). **{-531-}**

B. Barnes's Failure to Verify the Amended Complaint Did Not Divest the Court of In Rem Jurisdiction

The district court concluded that it lacked in rem jurisdiction because Barnes failed to verify the amended complaint. It reasoned that an "amended complaint supersedes the original, the latter being treated thereafter as non-existent," *Lacey v. Maricopa County*, 693 F.3d 896, 925 (9th Cir. 2012) (en banc) (quoting *Forsyth v. Humana, Inc.*, 114 F.3d 1467, 1474 (9th Cir. 1997)), and that Barnes's "failure to verify [his amended] complaint deprived the district court of *in rem* jurisdiction." *Madeja*, 310 F.3d at 637 (citing *United States v. $84,740.00 U.S. Currency*, 900 F.2d 1402, 1405 (9th Cir. 1990)). Neither *Lacey* nor *Madeja* support the district court's conclusion.

While an amended complaint supersedes the original, it normally does so only with regard to the pleading's substance, not its procedural effect. For example, *Lacey* involved "the [former] law of this circuit that a plaintiff waives all claims alleged in a dismissed complaint which are not realleged in an amended complaint." 693 F.3d at 925 (quoting *Forsyth*, 114 F.3d at 1474). *Lacey* overruled this "formalistic and harsh" rule, which was neither "prudent [n]or sufficiently justified." *Id.* at 927. Now, "claims dismissed with prejudice [or] without leave to amend [need not] be repled in a subsequent amended complaint to preserve them for appeal." *Id.* at 928. The procedural effect of the original complaint—preserving for appeal certain subsequently dismissed claims—survives its amendment. Relation back is another example. A timely-filed claim is not rendered untimely when included in an amended **[—21—]** complaint filed after the statute of limitations has passed. *See* Fed. R. Civ. P. 15(c).

In rem jurisdiction is no different. It is a "general principle" of admiralty law that in rem "jurisdiction, once vested, is not divested, although a state of things should arrive in which original jurisdiction could not be exercised." *Republic Nat'l Bank of Miami v. United States*, 506 U.S. 80, 85 (1992) (quoting *United States v. The Little Charles*, 26 F. Cas. 979, 982 (C.C.D. Va. 1818) (No. 15,612) (Marshall, C.J.)); *see Edlin v. M/V Truthseeker*, 69 F.3d 392, 393 (9th Cir. 1995) ("Although control of the res is required to *establish* jurisdiction, it is not required to *maintain* a court's jurisdiction."); *cf. J. Lauritzen A/S v. Dashwood Shipping, Ltd.*, 65 F.3d 139, 142 (9th Cir. 1995) (explaining that quasi in rem jurisdiction, "once obtained, will not be defeated by a change in circumstances"). Since Barnes's original, verified complaint established the court's in rem jurisdiction, his unverified amended complaint did not take it away.

"Unless a rule or statute *specifically states otherwise*, a pleading need not be verified or accompanied by an affidavit." Fed. R. Civ. P. 11(a) (emphasis added). Here, the relevant rule provides only that "the complaint" must be verified. *Id.*, Supp. Adm. & Mar. Cl. R. C(2). Supplemental Rule C says nothing about the necessity of verifying amended pleadings. Such a requirement would not serve its purpose, which is to provide procedural protections to the vessel's owner—whose property is arrested without prior notice or a hearing—in order "to eliminate any doubt as to the rule's constitutionality." *Id.*, Supp. Adm. & Mar. Cl. R. C, advisory committee's note to 1985 amendment; *see also Merchs. Nat'l Bank of Mobile v. Dredge Gen. G. L. Gillespie*, 663 F.2d 1338, 1349–50 (5th Cir. Unit A Dec. **[—22—]** 1981) ("[T]he verified complaint filed by a maritime lienor as well as the prayer for seizure constitute the 'process' that brings that entity into court. Together, the verified **{-532-}** complaint and the warrant constitute 'notice,' and the shipmaster (or person in charge) knows of the arrest and is in a position to notify the owner.").

After the vessel is arrested, the owner is entitled to "a prompt post-seizure hearing at which he can attack the verified complaint, the arrest, the security demanded, or any other alleged deficiency in the proceedings up to that point." *Gen. G. L. Gillespie*, 663 F.2d at 1351; *see* Fed. R. Civ. P. Supp. Adm. & Mar. Cl. R. E(4)(f). Once the owner has appeared, whether due to the vessel's arrest or because the owner learned of the proceeding through some other means, no further procedural purpose is served by requiring the verification of amended pleadings. To the extent the verification provides evidentiary value, the original complaint "does not lose its character as the equivalent of an affidavit just because a later, amended complaint, is filed." *Beal v. Beller*, 847 F.3d 897, 901 (7th Cir. 2017).

Madeja did not involve an amended complaint or a situation in which the defendants had waived objections to in rem jurisdiction. Rather, it involved an original complaint that was inadequately verified and defendants that successfully objected to in rem jurisdiction. *See Madeja*, 310 F.3d at 637; *see also Madeja v. Olympic Packer, LLC*, 155 F. Supp. 2d 1183, 1211 (D. Haw. 2001). It is inapplicable here. The district court erred in dismissing the Tehani for lack of in rem jurisdiction. **[—23—]**

C. The Bankruptcy Court Lacked Jurisdiction to Dispose of the Maritime Lien

SHR's bankruptcy trustee argues that even if the district court erred, Barnes's claims are now moot because the bankruptcy court authorized the Tehani's sale to be free and clear of any liens. This argument assumes that the bankruptcy court had jurisdiction to dispose of Barnes's maritime lien. It did not.

1.

The automatic bankruptcy stay applies to "any act to create, perfect, or enforce any lien against property of the estate." 11 U.S.C. § 362(a)(4). The district court concluded that Barnes's claims to enforce his maritime lien were subject to the bankruptcy stay. In *United States v. ZP Chandon*, we reversed a district court's similar ruling "that the automatic stay provisions of the Bankruptcy Act apply to [a maritime lien for] seamen's wages."[11] 889 F.2d 233, 238 (9th Cir. 1989).

Although *Chandon* involved a maritime lien for seaman's wages rather than for maintenance and cure, its reasoning applies equally to both. We "construe[d] Congress' omission of any reference to maritime law in [§] 362(a)(4) as evidence of its intention to limit the reach of that statute to land-based transactions where (1) a recording of a lien interest is required and (2) the creditor first in time is entitled to priority." *Id.* at 238. **[—24—]**

The trustee would distinguish *Chandon* as involving a post-petition claim in a Chapter 11

---

[11] A seaman's right to unearned wages while injured or ill on a voyage is "part of the doctrine of 'maintenance and cure.'" *Day v. Am. Seafoods Co.*, 557 F.3d 1056, 1058 (9th Cir. 2009) (citing *Lipscomb v. Foss Maritime Co.*, 83 F.3d 1106, 1109 (9th Cir. 1996)).

reorganization case rather than the pre-petition claim in a Chapter 7 dissolution case at issue here. Those are not material differences. *Chandon* decided, broadly, "whether the enactment of the Bankruptcy Act and the Congressional grant of jurisdiction to the bankruptcy courts restricts the district court's jurisdiction in admiralty or maritime cases." *Id.* at 236. In answering that question in the **{–533–}** negative, we reasoned that the automatic stay provision "does not expressly refer to *maritime* liens," which, when owed to seamen as a consequence of their service, "are 'sacred liens' entitled to protection 'as long as a plank of the ship remains.'" *Id.* at 238 (quoting *The John G. Stevens*, 170 U.S. 113, 119 (1898)).[12] We concluded that Congress would not have overruled this "sacred" principle of admiralty law in the Bankruptcy Act sub silentio.

Neither the timing of the bankruptcy petition relative to the maritime lien nor the nature of the bankruptcy proceeding—liquidation versus reorganization—factored into our decision. The trustee does not explain why they should. We therefore conclude that, under *Chandon*, the **[—25—]** bankruptcy stay did not apply to Barnes's efforts to enforce his maritime lien for maintenance and cure.

2.

The bankruptcy court lacked jurisdiction to adjudicate Barnes's maritime lien because the admiralty court had already obtained jurisdiction over the Tehani. "As between two courts of concurrent and co-ordinate jurisdiction, having like jurisdiction over the subject-matter in controversy, the court which first obtains jurisdiction is entitled to retain it without interference, and cannot be deprived of its right to do so because it may not have first obtained physical possession of the property in dispute." *Moran v. Sturges*, 154 U.S. 256, 283–84 (1894); *see also State Engr. v. S. Fork Band of Te-Moak Tribe of W. Shoshone Indians*, 339 F.3d 804, 809 (9th Cir. 2003) (discussing the "ancient and oft-repeated . . . doctrine of prior exclusive jurisdiction—that when a court of competent jurisdiction has obtained possession, custody, or control of particular property, that possession may not be disturbed by any other court" (quoting 14 Charles Alan Wright et al., *Federal Practice and Procedure* § 3631, at 8 (3d ed. 1998))).[13]

Here, the district court took constructive control of the Tehani in order to adjudicate Barnes's maritime lien at the time Barnes filed his verified complaint. SHR's bankruptcy **[—26—]** petition, filed nearly two years later, could not have vested the bankruptcy court with the same jurisdiction.

3.

Even if the bankruptcy court had in rem jurisdiction over the Tehani, it is an open question whether bankruptcy courts have "the effective ability to sell a vessel free and clear of maritime liens." 3B Benedict **{–534–}** et al., *supra*, § 43 (citing Jonathan M. Landers, *The Shipowner Becomes a Bankrupt*, 39 U. Chi. L. Rev. 490, 500 (1972)). Nonetheless, two principles are well-established.

First, a maritime lien "accompanies the property into the hands of a bona fide purchaser. It can be executed and divested

[12] *The John G. Stevens* involved a maritime lien for tort damages from a negligent collision. 170 U.S. at 119. Although the discussion of "sacred [maritime] liens" was in the context of liens for seaman's wages, *id.*, liens for maintenance and cure are given a similarly high priority. *See Fredelos v. Merritt-Chapman & Scott Corp.*, 447 F.2d 435, 440 (5th Cir. 1971) (per curiam on rehearing) ("[T]he shipowner's liability [for maintenance and cure] is among 'the most pervasive' of all." (quoting *Aguilar v. Standard Oil Co. of N.J.*, 318 U.S. 724, 730 (1943))). In both instances the reason for favoring a seaman's lien over all others "is that just as a seaman owes his first duty to his ship, so does she owe the same to him." *Id.* at 439.

[13] There is an exception to prior exclusive jurisdiction that is inapplicable here: "where the jurisdiction [of the two courts over the res] is not the same or concurrent, and the subject-matter in litigation in the one is not within the cognizance of the other, or there is no constructive possession of the property in dispute by the filing of a bill, it is the date of the actual possession of the receiver that determines the priority of jurisdiction." *Harkin v. Brundage*, 276 U.S. 36, 43 (1928).

only by a proceeding *in rem*." *Vandewater v. Mills*, 60 U.S. 82, 89 (1856); *see In re World Imports Ltd.*, 820 F.3d 576, 583, 4 Adm. R. 132, 136 (3d Cir.) ("[A maritime] lien attaches to the maritime property from the moment a debt arises, and adheres, even through changes in the property's ownership, until extinguished by operation of law."), *cert. denied sub nom. World Imports, Ltd. v. OEC Grp. N.Y.*, 137 S. Ct. 340 (2016); Grant Gilmore & Charles L. Black, Jr., *The Law of Admiralty* § 9-2, at 588 (2d ed. 1975) ("The maritime lien can be 'executed' (which is the admiralty terminology for 'foreclosed') only by an admiralty court acting *in rem*."). The bankruptcy proceeding that purportedly discharged Barnes's maritime lien was in rem. *See Tenn. Student Assistance Corp. v. Hood*, 541 U.S. 440, 447 (2004).

Second, a maritime lien cannot be extinguished except through the application of admiralty law. *See In re Millenium Seacarriers, Inc.*, 419 F.3d 83, 93 (2d Cir. 2005) (Sotomayor, J.) ("Traditional admiralty principles suggest that only a federal admiralty court acting in rem has the jurisdiction to quiet title to a vessel conclusively by **[—27—]** extinguishing its maritime liens."); Eric D. Grayson, *Maritime Arrest and Rule C: A Historical Perspective*, 6 Mar. Law. 265, 271 (1981) ("It is a basic tenet of American jurisprudence that a maritime lien is enforceable only by in rem process and by a federal court sitting in admiralty.").

There are good reasons why a bankruptcy court, if it can release a maritime lien at all, should be required to do so pursuant to admiralty law. "The central bankruptcy scheme of pro rata distribution among creditors deprives secured creditors of immediate enforcement" and "is obviously at odds with the complex maritime system providing for priorities between various creditors and distinguishing between maritime and nonmaritime creditors." 3B Benedict et al., *supra*, § 1[a][9]. *See generally* 2 Benedict et al., *supra*, § 51 (discussing priority of liens). Maritime creditors have "secret liens," enforceable "without . . . formal or substantial documentation," which are "antithetical" to bankruptcy practice. 3B Benedict et al., *supra*, § 1[a][9]. *See generally* Gilmore & Black, *supra*, § 9-1, at 586–89 (discussing differences between land-based liens and maritime liens).

Other "unique aspects" of maritime liens make them ill-suited for resolution under bankruptcy law; for example, "seamen have traditionally been recognized by maritime courts as 'the wards of admiralty,' placing them in a preferred position. A seaman, after settling a claim . . . under the general maritime law, even when represented by an attorney, may later contend either that he was under-represented or that his rights were not completely explained to him." 29 James Wm. Moore et al., *Moore's Federal Practice* § 707.01[12] (3d ed. 2017). A seaman without counsel can claim "that he failed to understand what he was **[—28—]** doing when he accepted money in exchange for a release." *Id.*

In *Millenium Seacarriers*, the Second Circuit held that a bankruptcy court could extinguish a maritime lien in an admiralty adversary proceeding to which the lienors voluntarily submitted. 419 F.3d at 95–96. Its decision turned on the lienors' consent to bankruptcy jurisdiction because "admiralty **{-535-}** law itself allows individual lien claims to be expunged when lienors have submitted their claims to the equitable jurisdiction of another court." *Id.* Here, in contrast, the bankruptcy court applied bankruptcy law rather than admiralty law and Barnes did not submit voluntarily to the court's jurisdiction. Its attempt to dispose of his maritime lien was ineffectual.

IV.

Barnes's Entitlement to Maintenance

Having determined that the dismissal of the Tehani was improper, we need not reach Barnes's constitutional arguments. As for the merits of the district court's decision not to award maintenance, we lack appellate jurisdiction to review the orders denying summary judgment on that issue. We therefore consider whether mandamus relief is warranted. *See Miller*, 335 F.3d at 895 ("We can . . . treat the notice of appeal as a petition for a writ of mandamus . . . ."). "Whether we construe the appeal as a writ of mandamus depends on whether mandamus is itself justified." *Hernandez v. Tanninen*, 604 F.3d 1095, 1099 (9th **[—29—]** Cir. 2010) (citing *Z-Seven Fund, Inc. v. Motorcar Parts & Accessories*, 231 F.3d 1215, 1219–20 (9th Cir. 2000)).[14]

We review a party's entitlement to mandamus relief by weighing five factors:

> (1) whether the petitioner has no other adequate means, such as direct appeal, to obtain the desired relief; (2) whether the petitioner will be damaged or prejudiced in a way not correctable on appeal; (3) whether the district court's order is clearly erroneous as a matter of law; (4) whether the district court's order is an oft-repeated error or manifests a persistent disregard of the federal rules; and (5) whether the district court's order raises new and important problems or issues of first impression.

United States v. U.S. Dist. Court, 694 F.3d 1051, 1057 (9th Cir. 2012) (citing *Bauman v. U.S. Dist. Court*, 557 F.2d 650, 654–55 (9th Cir. 1977)). "These factors are not exhaustive," *In re Bundy*, 840 F.3d 1034, 1041 (9th Cir. 2016) (citing *In* **[—30—]** *re Cement Antitrust Litig.*, 688 F.2d 1297, 1301 (9th Cir. 1982)), and need not all be met in order to grant mandamus relief, *In re Benvin*, 791 F.3d 1096, 1103 (9th Cir. 2015) (per curiam) (citing *Bauman*, 557 F.2d at 655). Where a district court has erroneously concluded that triable issues of fact exist, or "has misconceived the burden of proof at trial," the district court's denial of summary judgment "implicates *Bauman* factors." *Ho ex rel. Ho v. S.F. Unified Sch. Dist.*, 147 F.3d 854, 861 (9th Cir. 1998).

A. Other Adequate Means of Relief

Barnes could not have immediately appealed the district court's pretrial denials of summary judgment, which were not final orders.[15] *See* **{–536–}** *Thomas*, 818 F.3d at 874. Furthermore, although Barnes did not request certification of an interlocutory appeal under 28 U.S.C. § 1292(b), we seriously doubt that the district court would have granted such a request given the evidentiary nature of its rulings. In the district court's view, Barnes was not entitled to maintenance due to evidentiary insufficiency rather than a controlling question of law as required by § 1292(b). Nor can Barnes seek review of the district court's orders denying summary judgment after a trial on the merits and final judgment. *See Ortiz v. Jordan*, 562 U.S. 180, 183–84 (2011). Thus, the first *Bauman* factor favors relief. **[—31—]**

B. Damage or Prejudice Correctable on Appeal

The second *Bauman* factor, whether the petitioner will be damaged or prejudiced in a way not correctable on appeal, "is closely related to the first." *In re Henson*, 869 F.3d 1052, 1058 (9th Cir. 2017) (citing *Douglas v. U.S. Dist. Court*, 495 F.3d 1062, 1068 n.3 (9th Cir. 2007) (per curiam)). Without our intervention now, it is unclear whether there ever *will* be an appeal given Barnes's extremely limited resources—he is currently homeless. Moreover, even if there is an

[14] Although Barnes did not indicate in his notice of appeal that he intended to appeal the district court's failure to set a maintenance rate, he conspicuously raised the issue in his opening brief. Henry, in his answering brief, also addressed the issue. The trustee, although noting the issue, declined to address it, as it was not material to his arguments. We conclude that defendants therefore had notice of the appeal of the maintenance rate issue and are not prejudiced by our consideration of it. *See Levald, Inc. v. City of Palm Desert*, 998 F.2d 680, 691 (9th Cir. 1993) (concluding that the appellant's opening brief was "enough to demonstrate that the appellee had notice of the issue and did not suffer prejudice from the appellant's failure to specify the order in the notice of appeal" (citing *Meehan v. County of Los Angeles*, 856 F.2d 102, 105–06 (9th Cir. 1988))).

[15] Barnes sought permission to file an interlocutory appeal under § 1292(a)(3) from the district court's first order denying his motion for summary judgment to set a maintenance rate, but the district court denied this request after concluding that its ruling did not "finally determine . . . the parties' rights and liabilities."

appeal, relief will come long after Barnes was entitled to maintenance to cover his basic living expenses. Four years have passed since Barnes initiated this litigation, and over three years have passed since the district court concluded that he was entitled to maintenance and had sufficiently demonstrated his actual expenses. Relief in a few more years will not redress his current need for assistance.

Although the timeliness of relief on appeal is an ever-present concern when a case proceeds to trial, this concern is of special import in the context of maintenance and cure. The shipowner's duty to pay maintenance and cure is virtually automatic, regardless of negligence by the seaman or lack of negligence by the shipowner. *Bertram v. Freeport McMoran, Inc.*, 35 F.3d 1008, 1013 (5th Cir. 1994); *accord Sana v. Hawaiian Cruises, Ltd.*, 181 F.3d 1041, 1044 (9th Cir. 1999). It "extends during the period when [the seaman] is incapacitated to do a seaman's work and continues until he reaches maximum medical recovery." *Vaughan v. Atkinson*, 369 U.S. 527, 531 (1962). There are three main reasons why courts impose this duty: "[t]he protection of seamen, who, as a class, are poor, friendless and improvident, from the hazards of illness and abandonment while ill in foreign ports; the inducement to masters and **[—32—]** owners to protect the safety and health of seamen while in service; and maintenance of a merchant marine for the commercial service and maritime defense of the nation by inducing men to accept employment in an arduous and perilous service." *Id.* (quoting *Calmar S.S. Corp. v. Taylor*, 303 U.S. 525, 528 (1938)).

In line with these goals, admiralty procedure is designed to resolve a seaman's dispute quickly and flexibly. *See Cont'l Grain Co. v. The Barge FBL-585*, 364 U.S. 19, 25 (1960); *Farrell v. United States*, 336 U.S. 511, 516 (1949) ("[T]he seaman's right to maintenance and cure . . . is so inclusive as to be relatively simple, and can be understood and administered without technical considerations."); *Putnam v. Lower*, 236 F.2d 561, 568 (9th Cir. 1956) (observing that **{-537-}** "admiralty courts are flexible in operation"); *cf. Atl. Sounding Co. v. Townsend*, 557 U.S. 404, 423 (2009) ("[R]emedies for negligence, unseaworthiness, and maintenance and cure have different origins and may on occasion call for application of slightly different principles and procedures." (quoting *Fitzgerald v. U.S. Lines Co.*, 374 U.S. 16, 18 (1963))).

For example, a complaint in admiralty is required to "state the circumstances from which the claim arises with such particularity that the defendant or claimant will be able, without moving for a more definite statement, to commence an investigation of the facts and to frame a responsive pleading." Fed. R. Civ. P. Supp. Adm. & Mar. Cl. R. E(2)(a). In addition, "the special needs of expedition that often arise in admiralty justify . . . the practice" of allowing the plaintiff to serve interrogatories with the complaint and requiring the defendant to answer the interrogatories when answering the complaint. *Id.* R. C(6), advisory committee's note to 2000 amendment. These rules favoring expediency **[—33—]** supplant inconsistent provisions in the Federal Rules of Civil Procedure. *See id.* R. A(2).

In light of admiralty's singular concern for the expeditious resolution of a seaman's claims for maintenance and cure, and Barnes's current need for financial assistance to meet his daily living expenses, the second *Bauman* factor favors mandamus relief.

C. Clear Error

The third *Bauman* factor is whether the district court clearly erred as a matter of law. "Where a petition for mandamus raises an important issue of first impression, however, a petitioner need show only 'ordinary (as opposed to clear) error.'" *San Jose Mercury News, Inc. v. U.S. Dist. Court*, 187 F.3d 1096, 1100 (9th Cir. 1999) (quoting *Calderon v. U.S. Dist. Court*, 134 F.3d 981, 983 (9th Cir. 1998)). Even if we have never squarely addressed an issue, a district court's ruling still can be clearly erroneous if contrary to an "unbroken string of authorities" from other jurisdictions. *See id.* at 1102.

1.

A question that has divided district courts in this circuit is the appropriate legal standard to adopt in a pretrial motion for maintenance and cure. *See Best v. Pasha Haw. Transp. Lines, LLC,* No. 06-634, 2008 WL 1968334, at *1 (D. Haw. May 6, 2008) ("District Courts in the Ninth Circuit have not been consistent in their treatment of motions for maintenance and cure. Some courts apply the summary judgment standard, even when the seaman is the moving party, while other courts have found that the summary judgment standard is inappropriate in such circumstances because it does not account for the flexible approach courts **[—34—]** should take in admiralty law cases and the deference courts should provide to seamen."). There is inherent tension between the law of admiralty, with its solicitude for seamen, and the Federal Rules of Civil Procedure.[16]

Under the Federal Rules, a plaintiff seeking summary judgment on a claim "must offer evidence sufficient to support a finding upon every element of his [or her] claim" other than elements admitted by the defendants. *Watts v. United States*, 703 F.2d 346, 347 (9th Cir. 1983) **{-538-}** (quoting *United States v. Dibble*, 429 F.2d 598, 601 (9th Cir. 1970)). There cannot be a "genuine dispute as to any material fact." Fed. R. Civ. P. 56(a). Rule 56 "authorizes summary judgment only where . . . it is quite clear what the truth is." *Poller v. Columbia Broad. Sys., Inc.*, 368 U.S. 464, 467 (1962) (internal quotation marks omitted) (quoting *Sartor v. Ark. Natural Gas Corp.*, 321 U.S. 620, 627 (1944)). It is ordinarily a "heavy burden" for the plaintiff. *Ambat v. City & County of San Francisco*, 757 F.3d 1017, 1031 (9th Cir. 2014). "Reasonable doubts as to the existence of material factual issue are resolved against the moving part[y] and inferences are drawn in the light most favorable to the non-moving party." *Addisu v. Fred Meyer, Inc.*, 198 F.3d 1130, 1134 (9th Cir. 2000).

[16] The district court here, while commenting on this tension, found it unnecessary to resolve.

Admiralty's approach, on the other hand, is "to do justice with slight regard to formal matters." *Cont'l Grain*, 364 U.S. at 25 (quoting *Point Landing, Inc. v. Ala. Dry Dock & Shipbuilding Co.*, 261 F.2d 861, 866 (5th Cir. 1958)). The administration of maintenance should be "easy and ready," with "few exceptions or conditions to stir contentions, cause delays, and invite litigations." *Vella v. Ford Motor Co.*, **[—35—]** 421 U.S. 1, 4 (1975) (quoting *Farrell*, 336 U.S. at 516). Given these concerns, courts sometimes decline to resolve a pretrial motion for maintenance and cure under a summary judgment standard. *See, e.g., Connors v. Iqueque U.S.L.L.C.*, No. 05-334, 2005 WL 2206922, at *2 (W.D. Wash. Aug. 25, 2005) ("[T]he Supreme Court's instructions to construe claims for maintenance and cure liberally in favor of seamen counsel against applying the rigid standards of Rule 56 to a pretrial motion to compel maintenance and cure.").[17]

Despite the tension between Rule 56 and admiralty procedure, the two standards are not incompatible. Although it is ordinarily difficult for a plaintiff to prevail on a motion for summary judgment, the seaman seeking maintenance has an easier task as a result of the breadth of the shipowner's duty. To establish his entitlement to maintenance, the seaman need only prove that he "bec[ame] ill or . . . injured while in the service of the ship." *Vella*, 421 U.S. at 3. The shipowner's duty to

[17] In addition, several courts have deviated from the summary judgment standard where a shipowner unilaterally terminates maintenance payments upon the belief that the seaman has reached maximum cure, leading the seaman to move to reinstate such payments. *See Robb v. Jantran, Inc.*, No. 15-162, 2016 WL 2986233, at *2 (N.D. Miss. May 6, 2016) (collecting cases from the Ninth Circuit); *Dean v. Fishing Co. of Alaska, Inc.*, 300 P.3d 815, 824 (Wash. 2013) (adopting the approach of district courts in the Ninth Circuit). These courts take the approach that absent a trial, the shipowner must reinstate payments "unless the shipowner can provide unequivocal evidence that the seaman has reached maximum cure." *Dean*, 300 P.3d at 824. As we are not faced with a motion for reinstatement or a dispute over whether Barnes has reached maximum cure, we do not pass on the appropriateness of the standard adopted by these courts.

pay maintenance "arises irrespective of the absence of shipowner negligence and indeed irrespective of whether the illness or injury is suffered in the course of **[—36—]** the seaman's employment." *Id.* at 4. "[S]o broad is the shipowner's obligation" that even "negligence or acts short of culpable misconduct on the seaman's part will not relieve (the shipowner) of the responsibility." *Id.* (quoting *Aguilar*, 318 U.S. at 730–31).

In sum, the liberal admiralty policies and correspondingly rudimentary elements **{–539–}** of a maintenance claim mean that, in practice, a seaman will have little difficulty demonstrating his entitlement to maintenance under a summary judgment standard. Accordingly, "[a] seaman's initial entitlement to maintenance and cure . . . can properly be resolved on summary judgment," *Dean*, 300 P.3d at 822, as evidenced by the "numerous federal district courts" to have done so, *id.* at 821 (citing cases); *see also Glynn v. Roy Al Boat Mgmt. Corp.*, 57 F.3d 1495, 1505–06 (9th Cir. 1995) (upholding the denial of summary judgment where there was a factual dispute over whether the "alleged accident aboard the [vessel] even occurred"), *abrogated on other grounds by Atlantic Sounding*; *Robb*, 2016 WL 2986233, at *2 (collecting cases and adopting the approach of courts that construe pretrial requests for maintenance and cure under a summary judgment standard).[18] **[—37—]**

The summary judgment standard is also capable of governing disputes over the amount of maintenance. The burden-shifting framework we adopt is a familiar mode of analysis at the summary judgment stage in other contexts, *see, e.g., Hardie v. Nat'l Collegiate Athletic Ass'n*, 876 F.3d 312, 323–24 (9th Cir. 2017) (affirming grant of summary judgment where there was no genuine issue of material fact at each step of the disparate-impact analysis), and has been successfully employed by district courts in this circuit to determine a maintenance amount, *see, e.g., Sabow v. Am. Seafoods Co.*, 188 F. Supp. 3d 1036, 1044–45 (W.D. Wash. 2016).

We recognize that the denial of summary judgment as to a maintenance amount could delay the seaman's recovery of maintenance that is owed to him and thereby undermine the remedy's "easy and ready administration." *Vella*, 421 U.S. at 4. This problem, however, can be mitigated in two ways. First, as we explain, a seaman who demonstrates his entitlement to maintenance and actual expenses need not wait until trial to receive the portion of those expenses to which he is undisputedly entitled. *See* Fed. R. Civ. P. 56(g) ("If the court does not grant all the relief requested by the motion [for summary judgment], it may enter an order stating any material fact—*including an item of damages or other relief*—that is not genuinely in dispute and treating the fact as established in the case." (emphasis added)). Second, a district court may on its own or at the seaman's request sever the issue of maintenance and hold an expedited trial on that claim under Federal Rule of Civil Procedure 42(b). *See Tate v. Am. Tugs, Inc.*, 634 F.2d 869, 871 (5th Cir. Unit A **[—38—]** Jan. 1981) ("[The seaman] may . . . ask for severance of the maintenance claim and an expedited trial of it by the court." (citing *Caulfield v. AC&D Marine, Inc.*, 633 F.2d 1129, 1133 (5th Cir. Unit A Jan. 1981))).

In light of these safeguards, we conclude that the summary judgment standard **{–540–}** properly governs a pretrial request to set a maintenance amount. *See* 1B Benedict et al., *supra*, § 51 ("The amount to which an injured or ill seaman is entitled [for maintenance and

[18] The Supreme Court's statement that "ambiguities or doubts . . . are resolved in favor of the seaman," *Vaughan*, 369 U.S. at 532, concerned the seaman's entitlement to maintenance at trial, not at summary judgment. Because the summary judgment standard is compatible with a seaman's claim for maintenance, we see no reason to modify the summary judgment standard in this way. Any such modification would run contrary to the stated purpose of the 1966 integration of admiralty and civil rules. *See* 14A Wright et al., § 3671.4 ("[I]n view of the 1966 integration of admiralty and civil rules, procedure in admiralty . . . should be the same as in cases in law and equity unless **[—37—]** a strong policy or statute prevents this uniformity of treatment." (quoting *United States v. Article Consisting of 216 Cartoned Bottles, More or Less, Sudden Change*, 288 F. Supp. 29, 32 (E.D.N.Y. 1968))).

cure] . . . [may] be determined by the court on a motion for summary judgment where the 'extraneous materials' in support of the motion 'establish with certainty that there is no triable issue of fact.'"). We now turn to the application of that standard.

2.

In evaluating the amount of maintenance to award, the district court stated that it was applying the standard articulated by the Fifth Circuit in *Hall v. Noble Drilling (U.S.) Inc.*, 242 F.3d 582 (5th Cir. 2001). Under *Hall*, a seaman-plaintiff seeking maintenance "is entitled to the reasonable cost of food and lodging, provided he has incurred the expense." 242 F.3d at 587. The plaintiff's actual expenses are presumptively reasonable, subject to an adjustment upwards or downwards if the court determines that the actual costs were more or less than an objectively reasonable amount. *See id.* at 590.

The burden is on the plaintiff to "present evidence to the court that is sufficient to provide an evidentiary basis for the court to estimate his actual costs." *Id.* In light of admiralty's goal of an expedient remedy for the seaman, his evidentiary burden "is 'feather light,' and a court may award reasonable expenses, even if the precise amount of actual expenses is not conclusively proved." *Id.* at 588 (quoting *Yelverton v.* **[—39—]** *Mobile Labs., Inc.*, 782 F.2d 555, 558 (5th Cir. 1986)). "If the plaintiff presents no evidence of actual expenses," however, "the plaintiff may not recover maintenance." *Id.* at 590. But if the plaintiff *does* provide evidence of actual expenses, "the court must determine the maintenance award" by "compar[ing] the seaman's actual expenses to reasonable expenses," and awarding the lower amount unless "the plaintiff's actual expenses were inadequate to provide him with reasonable food and lodging." *Id.* Thus, a thrifty seaman will normally be entitled to his actual expenses.

Hall explained how the district court should calculate a reasonable maintenance rate:

> In determining the reasonable costs of food and lodging, the court may consider evidence in the form of the seaman's actual costs, evidence of reasonable costs in the locality or region, union contracts stipulating a rate of maintenance or per diem payments for shoreside food or lodging while in the service of a vessel, and maintenance rates awarded in other cases for seamen in the same region.

Id. Importantly, "[a] seaman *need not present evidence* of the reasonable rate; a court may take judicial notice of the prevailing rate in the district."[19] *Id.* **[—40—]**

Courts and commentators roundly cite the Fifth Circuit's approach. *E.g.*, *Block Island Fishing, Inc. v. Rogers*, 844 F.3d 358, 365, 4 Adm. R. 47, 53 (1st Cir. 2016) ("In this circuit, as in numerous sister circuits, the norm is to award an injured seaman maintenance and cure payments in the amount of his actual living expenses." (citing, inter alia, *Hall*)); 2 Robert Force & Martin J. Norris, *The Law of Seamen* § 26:27 (5th ed. 2016) (citing *Hall* with approval); 1B Benedict et **{-541-}** al., *supra*, § 51 (setting forth *Hall* standard). Some describe it as a burden-shifting test under which the plaintiff "must bring forth prima facie evidence of his expenses," and, if he does, "[t]he burden of rebuttal then shifts to the defendant." 1 Schoenbaum, *supra*, § 6-32; *accord Incandela v. Am. Dredging Co.*, 659 F.2d 11, 14 (2d Cir. 1981) (holding that "a seaman makes out a prima facie case on the maintenance rate question when he proves the actual living expenditures which he found it necessary to incur during his convalescence," at which point "the burden shift[s] to the defendant to demonstrate that plaintiff's actual expenditures were excessive, in light of any realistic alternatives for room and board available to him in [the locality]").

---

19 From the 1940s until the 1980s, the reasonable rate was generally held by courts to be eight dollars per day, despite the deteriorating value of that fixed amount over four decades. *See Gardiner v. Sea-Land Serv., Inc.*, 786 F.2d 943, 946 (9th Cir. 1986). More recently, "courts have allowed [a] seaman to prove that higher costs of living require a higher maintenance amount." 8 Benedict et al., *supra*, § 10.02[C][4].

We agree with *Hall* and expressly adopt *Incandela*'s burden-shifting framework for determining a maintenance amount.

3.

In ruling on Barnes's first motion for summary judgment, the district court found that he established both his entitlement to maintenance and his actual living expenses of $68 per day. Under *Hall*, a decision which has gained widespread acceptance outside this circuit and which the district court purported to apply, defendants had the burden of showing that $68 per day was *un*reasonable.

Defendants submitted no such evidence. Therefore, Barnes carried his summary judgment burden of establishing **[—41—]** that no genuine issue of material fact existed as to the reasonableness of his actual expenses. The district court should have awarded Barnes $68 per day unless it independently determined that that amount was unreasonable. *See Hall*, 242 F.3d at 590. Instead, the district court faulted Barnes for "fail[ing] . . . to provide . . . evidence regarding the current costs of food and lodging in [his locality] such that the Court can make a determination as to the reasonable costs in the area." This was clear error. *See Incandela*, 659 F.2d at 14 ("[T]o require every injured seaman seeking a court award for maintenance to go to the expense of putting on expert witnesses before he will be permitted to recover more than a fixed nominal maintenance rate would be to place an unfair burden on those whom the idea of maintenance was designed to assist.").

After the district court denied Barnes's motion for reconsideration, Barnes moved for summary judgment a second time. This time, defendants produced evidence that the reasonable cost of living in Barnes's locality was between $24 and $34 per day. Barnes, in contrast, produced evidence that the reasonable rate was between $43 and $61 per day. Citing *Glynn*, the district court concluded that the dispute over a reasonable daily maintenance rate precluded summary judgment. The court subsequently denied Barnes's motion for reconsideration, in which he requested maintenance at the rate of $24 per day—the lowest end of the range of reasonable rates offered by defendants—subject to modification after trial. Barnes repeated this request in his third motion for summary judgment, but the district court again denied it.

Like the denial of Barnes's first motion for summary judgment, these later denials of summary judgment constituted clear error. The district court reasoned that a **[—42—]** genuine issue of fact existed as to whether Barnes was entitled to maintenance at a rate of at least $24 per day because Barnes did not agree that $24 per day was reasonable. But *Hall*, which provided the applicable substantive standard at summary judgment, held that "seamen are entitled to maintenance in the amount of their actual expenses on food and lodging **{–542–}** *up to* the reasonable amount for their locality." 242 F.3d at 590 (emphasis added). Regardless of whether $24 per day is ultimately proven to be reasonable at trial, there is no dispute that the reasonable rate is at least $24 per day. Because Barnes is entitled to maintenance up to the reasonable rate, there is no dispute, let alone a genuine dispute, that he is entitled to maintenance at a rate of at least $24 per day.

In fact, Barnes is entitled to more than $24 per day. As we have explained, defendants had the burden of demonstrating that his actual expenses were unreasonable. Defendants produced evidence that the reasonable daily rate for living expenses in Barnes's locality ranges from $24 per day to $34 per day. Thus, defendants produced *no* evidence disputing the reasonableness of a maintenance award in the amount of $34 per day; to the contrary, the evidence produced by defendants supported the reasonableness of a $34 daily rate. Accordingly, there is no genuine issue of fact as to Barnes's entitlement to maintenance in the amount of at least $34 per day.[20] **[—43—]**

[20] To the extent that Barnes's specific requests for maintenance of $24 per day pending trial amounted to a form of concession, courts are "not bound by a party's concession as to the meaning of the law." *United States v. Calvillo-Palacios*, 860 F.3d 1285, 1289 n.4 (9th Cir. 2017) (quoting *United*

Glynn is not to the contrary. There, we recognized that summary judgment would have been premature because the district court concluded "there was a material issue of fact about whether Glynn was *entitled* to maintenance and cure." 57 F.3d at 1505 (emphasis added). In particular, we explained that "whether Glynn's alleged accident aboard the [vessel] even occurred was a disputed issue of fact that had to be determined before Glynn could prevail on his claim." *Id.* at 1505–06. *Glynn* is inapposite when, as here, it is undisputed that a seaman is entitled to maintenance and has sufficiently demonstrated his actual expenses.

Finally, we note that under the district court's view of *Hall*, an injured seaman would be faced with a Hobson's choice: He could either stipulate to the reasonableness of the rate supported by the shipowner's evidence and thereby give up the possibility of proving a higher rate at trial, or he could decline to do so, in which case he would not receive payments for basic living expenses until after trial. Such a predicament is antithetical to the admiralty policies underlying the seaman's right to maintenance and cure. We cannot countenance a rule under which "uncertainty would displace the essential certainty of protection against the ravages of illness and injury that encourages seamen to undertake their hazardous calling." *Vella*, 421 U.S. at 4.

Because the district court clearly erred in applying *Hall*, the third *Bauman* factor favors granting the writ.

D. Remaining Factors

The remaining factors also support mandamus relief. Barnes moved the district court to set a maintenance rate on four separate occasions. The district court denied the first three of these motions and deemed the fourth withdrawn in light of the bankruptcy stay. Thus, the district court's error **[—44—]** was "oft-repeated." And lastly, because we had not yet considered the application of *Hall* or expressly adopted the *Incandela* burden-shifting framework for determining a maintenance amount, the questions involved are ones of first impression. **{–543–}**

States v. Ogles, 440 F.3d 1095, 1099 (9th Cir. 2006) (en banc)).

V.

Conclusion

Barnes, having undertaken a dangerous profession at sea, was entitled to reimbursement from the Tehani for his living and medical expenses while recovering from his injuries in its service. More than that, he was entitled to be reimbursed quickly. "The adequate protection of an injured or ill seaman against suffering and want requires more than the assurance that he will receive payments at some time in the indefinite future. Payments must be promptly made, at a time contemporaneous to the illness or injury." *Crooks v. United States*, 459 F.2d 631, 634–35 (9th Cir. 1972) (quoting *Vaughan*, 369 U.S. at 537–38 (Stewart, J., dissenting on other grounds)). Yet after more than five years, Barnes is still waiting. We urge the district court to move quickly upon remand.

The trustee's motion to dismiss the appeal against the Tehani is denied. We reverse the district court's order dismissing the Tehani for lack of jurisdiction. We issue a writ of mandamus directing the district court to award **[—45—]** Barnes maintenance at the rate of $34 per day, subject to a potential upward modification after trial.[21]

REVERSED in part and REMANDED; MANDAMUS GRANTED.

[21] It appears that prior to this appeal, the district court was on track to sever the issue of maintenance and cure and set it for trial. We commend this approach and encourage the court and the parties to continue to pursue it expeditiously on remand.

United States Court of Appeals
for the Ninth Circuit

No. 14-71768

SANCHEZ
vs.
SESSIONS

On Petition for Review of an Order of the Board of Immigration Appeals

Decided: July 18, 2018

Citation: 895 F.3d 1101, 6 Adm. R. 347 (9th Cir. 2018).

ON PETITION FOR REHEARING AND REHEARING EN BANC

(Original Opinion: 870 F.3d 901, 5 Adm. R. 399 (9th Cir. 2017)

Before **WARDLAW**, **PAEZ**, and **CHRISTEN**, Circuit Judges.

[—1—] {-1101-}:

ORDER

The opinion and concurring opinions filed August 30, 2017, and appearing at 870 F.3d 901, 5 Adm. R. 399 (9th Cir. 2017), are withdrawn. They may not be cited by or to this court or any district court of the Ninth Circuit. A new disposition will be filed in due course. Accordingly, the government's petition for rehearing en banc is **DENIED** as moot. Subsequent **[—2—]** petitions for rehearing and petitions for rehearing en banc may be filed following the filing of a new disposition.

United States Court of Appeals
for the Ninth Circuit

No. 17-70853

CHRISTIE
VS.
GEORGIA-PACIFIC CO.

On Petition for Review of an Order of the Benefits Review Board

Decided: August 2, 2018

Citation: 898 F.3d 952, 6 Adm. R. 348 (9th Cir. 2018).

Before **SMITH, JR.** and **MURGUIA,** Circuit Judges, and **HELLERSTEIN,*** District Judge.

* The Honorable Alvin K. Hellerstein, United States District Judge for the Southern District of New York, sitting by designation.

[—3—] **{–954–}** MURGUIA, Circuit Judge:

Stanley Christie, a longtime employee of the Respondent Georgia-Pacific Company ("Georgia-Pacific") in Portland, Oregon, injured his back at work in 1999. He returned to work following his injury but he eventually required surgery, which he underwent in 2004. Christie now asks us to decide if he is entitled to permanent total disability benefits under the Longshore and Harbor Workers' Compensation Act, 33 U.S.C. §§ 901–50 (the "Act"), because of his work-related injury.

The parties do not contest that following his surgery, Christie faced physical limitations, and Georgia-Pacific reassigned Christie to less physically demanding safety inspection work sometime in 2006. In late 2010, Christie learned that the option to take early retirement would likely no longer exist beginning in January of 2011. Since Christie was still years away from reaching the retirement age of 62, in December of 2010 he decided to retire early and accepted an 18-percent reduction in monthly pension payments. **[—4—]**

Years after he retired, Christie sought permanent total disability benefits as permitted by the Act. The administrative law judge ("ALJ") who considered Christie's claim awarded Christie permanent total disability benefits. Georgia-Pacific appealed the ALJ's decision to the United States Department of Labor's Benefits Review Board ("Board"), which reversed the award of benefits. Christie subsequently appealed to our court. **{–955–}**

To determine Christie's eligibility for benefits, we interpret the language of 33 U.S.C. § 902(10), which defines "disability" under the Act. In particular, we consider whether Christie's decision to retire early prevents him from receiving permanent total disability benefits. After reviewing the plain language of § 902(10), we hold that Christie's decision to retire early does not make him ineligible for benefits. Our conclusion is in accord with a recent Fourth Circuit decision also interpreting § 902(10). Accordingly, we grant Christie's petition, and we reverse and remand.

I.

A.

In 1986, Christie began working for Georgia-Pacific in Portland, Oregon. Thirteen years later, Christie injured his back at work while moving bags of concrete. Although Christie returned to work following his injury, he eventually required surgery, which was performed in January of 2004. It is undisputed that Christie's back injury is a work-related injury.

In 2006, Georgia-Pacific assigned Christie to safety inspection duties in part to accommodate his physical limitations from his back injury. As safety inspector, Christie **[—5—]** was responsible for inspecting three Portland warehouses, which involved both active and sedentary tasks. Among other things, Christie created labels for materials in the warehouses detailing the contents and locations of items and who last inspected them. He also performed physical inspections, such as inspecting fire extinguishers, which sometimes involved lifting them. Due to his physical limitations, Christie had difficulty performing some of his job duties.

In late 2010, Christie learned from his labor union's director that Georgia-Pacific was likely eliminating early retirement in 2011. Under the early retirement option available to Christie in 2010, Christie could choose to retire after age 55 and accept a penalty reducing his monthly payments by 18 percent. Christie knew that without the early retirement option, he was ineligible for retirement income until age 62. Because Christie, then 56, believed he would be unable to continue working for another six years due to his physical limitations, he decided to retire early, effective December 1, 2010.

After Christie retired, several doctors evaluated him for multi-level back fusion surgery. Once the doctors determined that Christie should first pursue other treatment options before undergoing surgery, he began conservative pain treatment in May of 2012. By November of 2012, the doctor providing Christie with pain treatment believed Christie had reached his maximum medical improvement, meaning the injury had healed to the fullest extent possible. *See Stevens v. Dir., Office of Workers' Comp. Programs*, 909 F.2d 1256, 1257 (9th Cir. 1990). Christie's pain doctor also opined that Christie could not return to his regular job and was permanently restricted from several physical activities as of December 3, 2012. **[—6—]**

Eventually, because of his physical limitations and inability to work, Christie filed a claim seeking permanent total disability benefits under the Act.

B.

The ALJ held a hearing; heard testimony; reviewed the evidence presented, including Christie's medical records; and concluded that Christie was entitled to permanent total disability benefits. The ALJ ordered Georgia-Pacific to pay Christie these benefits from December 3, 2012 onward, because that was the date on which, according to the ALJ and based on the medical opinions in the record, Christie **{-956-}** became disabled. In so ordering, the ALJ found that Christie was not disabled at the time he retired in December of 2010. However, the ALJ also determined that Christie's decision to retire did not bar Christie from receiving permanent total disability benefits because Christie's retirement was involuntary. Distinguishing Christie's case from other Board case law, the ALJ found that Christie did not retire "solely" because the early retirement package that he would receive was financially beneficial or a "good deal." Instead, the ALJ determined that Christie "testified credibly that he retired, at least in part, because he believed his back problems would not allow him to work until the full retirement age of 62, and he feared losing the ability to retire early."

On administrative appeal, the Board disagreed with the ALJ's conclusion. Relying on the Board's 2016 decision in *Moody v. Huntington Ingalls, Inc.*, 50 Ben. Rev. Bd. Serv. (MB) 9 (2016) ("*Moody I*") the Board reversed the ALJ's decision. The Board issued *Moody I* on the same day as the ALJ issued his decision in Christie's case. In reversing the ALJ, the Board cited *Moody I* and two other Board decisions—*Burson v. T. Smith & Son, Inc.*, 22 Ben. Rev. Bd. Serv. (MB) 124 (1989), and *Hoffman v. Newport News* **[—7—]** *Shipbuilding & Dry Dock Co.*, 35 Ben. Rev. Bd. Serv. (MB) 148 (2001)—for the proposition that "an employee is not entitled to receive a total disability award after he retires for reasons unrelated to the work injury because there is no loss of wage-earning capacity due to the injury." In the Board's view "'[d]isability' [under the Act] means incapacity *because of injury* to earn the wages which the employee was receiving at the time of injury in the same or any other employment." In other words, an employee's injury must be the cause of the employee's inability to earn wages. And because the Board determined that Christie's loss of wages was due to his decision to retire early, and not because of his work-related injury, Christie was not entitled to benefits. This appeal followed.

II.

We have jurisdiction to review the Board's decisions pursuant to 33 U.S.C. § 921(c). "The Board is required to 'accept the ALJ's findings unless they are contrary to law, irrational, or unsupported by substantial evidence.'"

Stevedoring Servs. of Am. v. Dir., Office of Workers' Comp. Programs, 297 F.3d 797, 801 (9th Cir. 2002) (quoting *Todd Shipyards Corp. v. Black*, 717 F.2d 1280, 1284 (9th Cir. 1983)). We review the Board's decisions for "adherence to the [substantial evidence] standard." *Id.* (alteration in original) (quoting *Bumble Bee Seafoods v. Dir., Office of Workers' Comp. Programs*, 629 F.2d 1327, 1329 (9th Cir. 1980)). We also review the Board's interpretation of the Act de novo because such interpretations are questions of law. *Id.* Further, "[b]ecause the Board is not a policymaking agency, its interpretation of [the Act] is not entitled to any special deference." *Id.* (quoting *McDonald v. Dir., Office of Workers' Comp. Programs*, 897 F.2d 1510, 1512 (9th Cir. 1990)). **[—8—]**

III.

A.

Under the Act, employees are entitled to obtain compensation for a permanent disability arising out of a work-related injury. *See Gen. Constr. Co. v. Castro*, 401 F.3d 963, 968–69 (9th Cir. 2005) (citing 33 U.S.C. §§ 902(2), 902(10), 908). The Act defines disability as:

> *incapacity because of injury to earn the wages which the employee was receiving at the time of injury in the same or any* **{-957-}** *other employment;* but such term [disability] shall mean permanent impairment, determined (to the extent covered thereby) under the guides to the evaluation of permanent impairment promulgated and modified from time to time by the American Medical Association, in the case of an individual whose claim is described in section 910(d)(2) of this title.

33 U.S.C. § 902(10) (emphasis added).[1] A disability is permanent when a claimant has "attained 'maximum medical improvement.'" *Gen. Constr. Co.*, 401 F.3d at 968 **[—9—]** (quoting *Stevens*, 909 F.2d at 1258). "Maximum medical improvement is attained when the injury has healed to the full extent possible." *Stevens*, 909 F.2d at 1257. To obtain permanent total disability benefits under the Act, an employee must show: (1) he is disabled within the meaning of the Act, (2) the work-related injury he suffered that makes him disabled has healed to the fullest extent possible, and (3) he cannot return to prior employment. *See Gen. Constr.*, 401 F.3d at 968–69. In addition, for the employee to obtain benefits, the employer must fail to establish that alternative employment, which the employee can perform, is available to the employee. *Id.* at 969.

Whether the Board erred in reversing the ALJ's award of permanent total disability benefits to Christie turns on the proper interpretation of "disability" under § 902(10) of the Act. According to the Board, "[t]he only relevant inquiry [in determining disability under the Act] is whether claimant's work injury caused a loss of earning capacity." The Board answered this question by concluding that because Christie voluntarily retired, he was not disabled within the meaning of § 902(10).

In its decision reversing the ALJ's award of benefits, the Board relied heavily on its decision in *Moody I*, and stated that Christie's case was "not legally distinguishable from *Moody* [*I*]." In *Moody I*, claimant Russell Moody had sought temporary total disability benefits. *Moody I*, 50 Ben. Rev. Bd. Serv. (MB) at 9–10. There, the ALJ had awarded Moody temporary total disability benefits because the ALJ found that Moody's retirement prior to the time of his surgery was irrelevant. *Id.* at 10. In reversing the ALJ's benefit award, the

[1] The latter portion of § 902(10), beginning with "but such term," concerns "claim[s] based on a death or disability due to an occupational disease," *see* 33 U.S.C. § 910(d)(2), which are different from the disability claim at issue here. *See Gen. Constr. Co.*, 401 F.3d at 968 ("The [Act's] compensation scheme distinguishes between injury, which is a physical impairment, 'occupational disease[,] or infection,' and disability, which the [Act] defines as the 'incapacity because of injury to earn the wages which the employee was receiving at the time of injury in the same or other employment.'" (second alteration in original) (citations omitted) (quoting 33 U.S.C. § 902)). The latter portion of § 902(10) therefore does not apply to the present case.

Board concluded that the disability inquiry under § 902(10) of the Act, which defines disability for purposes of the Act, "encompasses both physical and economic **[—10—]** considerations." *Id.* The Board reasoned that Moody's decision to retire "had already resulted in his complete loss of earning capacity" and Moody was therefore not disabled within the meaning of the Act. *Id.* at 11. In short, the Board interpreted § 902(10) to mean that retirement necessarily *causes* a loss of wage-earning capacity.

However, because the proper interpretation of § 902(10) is a question of law, the Board's interpretation of § 902(10) in *Moody* is not binding and our review is de novo. *See Stevedoring Servs. of Am.*, 297 F.3d at 801. **{-958-}**

We begin our analysis with the relevant statutory language. *See United States ex rel. Hartpence v. Kinetic Concepts, Inc.*, 792 F.3d 1121, 1128 (9th Cir. 2015) (en banc) ("In construing the provisions of a statute, we begin by looking at the language of the statute to determine whether it has a plain meaning."). In a statute, a legislature says "what it means and means in a statute what it says there." *Id.* (quoting *BedRoc Ltd. v. United States*, 451 U.S. 176, 183 (2004)). If a statute's language is plain and unambiguous, our inquiry ends. *Id.* Where statutory language is ambiguous, however, we may consider legislative history and other extrinsic materials. *See Exxon Mobil Corp. v. Allapattah Servs., Inc.*, 545 U.S. 546, 568 (2005).

The Act specifically defines disability as "incapacity because of injury to earn the wages which the employee was receiving at the time of injury in the same or any other employment." 33 U.S.C. § 902(10). The "injury" must be an "accidental injury or death arising out of and in the course of employment." *Id.* § 902(2).

The plain language of § 902(10) makes no reference to retirement or its timing, nor to whether an employee decides **[—11—]** to retire voluntarily or involuntarily. Rather, § 902(10) states that disability under the Act means an inability, resulting from an injury suffered at work, to earn the wages an employee was earning from his employer at the time he was injured. Nowhere in § 902(10) is an employee's decision to retire mentioned.

Indeed, the Board's reading of § 902(10) assumes that retirement categorically results in a person's incapacity to work. Yet, the language of § 902(10) does not give any indication that retirement is to be treated in that manner. Neither is it the case that retirement, in all instances, means that a retiree is incapable of working. Retirement simply means that a person is no longer working a particular job. In short, although retirement and incapacity to work may be linked, they are not necessarily one and the same. We conclude that the Board's reading of § 902(10) is overly restrictive and unsupported by the plain language of the statute.

Georgia-Pacific urges that the Board is correct that § 902(10) precludes an employee from obtaining disability benefits after an employee voluntarily retires because the employee cannot establish a loss of wage-earning capacity resulting from a work-related injury. Georgia-Pacific cites to three Board decisions—*Burson*, *Hoffman*, and *Moody I*—to support its argument, asserting that the "Board's standard reasonably interprets § 902(10) of [the Act] and balances the interests of the injured worker and employer." Georgia-Pacific's arguments are unavailing. As discussed above, the plain language of § 902(10) belies the purported relevance of an employee's decision to retire.

Further, the Fourth Circuit's reasoning in *Moody v. Huntington Ingalls Inc.*, 879 F.3d 96, 6 Adm. R. 126 (4th Cir. 2018) ("*Moody II*")—which overruled the Board's decision in **[—12—]** *Moody I*—is persuasive. In *Moody II*, the Fourth Circuit interpreted the same statutory language at issue here, § 902(10) of the Act. *Id.* at 101, 6 Adm. R. at 129. The Fourth Circuit rejected the Board's interpretation of § 902(10). *Id.*, 6 Adm. R. at 129. In holding that voluntary retirement does not preclude the existence of a disability under the Act, the *Moody II* court looked to the text of § 902(10) and concluded that the Board and the employer in *Moody I* misconstrued the plain meaning of "incapacity" and "the real-world significance of retirement." *Id.* at 98, 6 Adm. R. at 127. Rejecting the Board's "interpretation that an employee's retirement necessarily makes him incapable of earning any wages," the *Moody II* court noted that **{-959-}** "incapacity" means "inability," "incompetence," and "incapability." *Id.* at 99, 6 Adm. R. at 127. The *Moody II* court further explained that retirement is not inherently debilitating and that the Board and the employer in *Moody I* "confuse being *unwilling* with being *unable* [to work]" by focusing on the voluntary nature of Moody's retirement. *Id.*, 6 Adm. R. at 127.

The *Moody II* court further held that the Board "erroneously equate[d] loss of earning capacity with loss of actual earnings," concluding that the "law compensates [an employee's inability to make the choice to work] when it is caused by workplace injury." *Id.* at 99–100, 6 Adm. R. at 127–28. The Fourth Circuit also held that "retirement status, standing alone, is *irrelevant* to earning capacity and the determination of 'disability' under 33 U.S.C. § 902(10)." *Id.* at 100, 6 Adm. R. at 128 (emphasis added).[2] Here, *Moody II* is particularly persuasive because **[—13—]** the Board relied on *Moody I* to overturn the ALJ's award of benefits to Christie.[3]

Accordingly, a plain reading of § 902(10) reveals that the Board committed legal error in reversing the ALJ's award of benefits to Christie. We therefore join the Fourth Circuit in rejecting the Board's interpretation of § 902(10).

B.

To obtain permanent total disability benefits, Christie must show that he is disabled within the meaning of the Act and that he has attained maximum medical improvement, meaning his injury has healed to the fullest extent possible. *See* 33 U.S.C. §§ 902(10), 908; *see also Gen. Constr. Co.*, 401 F.3d at 968; *Stevens*, 909 F.2d at 1257. Christie must also show that he cannot return to prior employment, and Georgia-Pacific must fail to establish that there is suitable alternative employment available to Christie. *Gen. Constr. Co.*, 401 F.3d at 968–69.

Here, the ALJ granted Christie permanent total disability benefits, payable from December 3, 2012, onward. The **[—14—]** Board was required to accept the ALJ's factual findings "unless they [were] contrary to law, irrational, or unsupported by substantial evidence." *Stevedoring Servs. of Am.*, 297 F.3d at 801 (quoting *Todd Shipyards Corp.*, 717 F.2d at 1284). We review the Board's decision for adherence to the substantial evidence standard. *See id.*

The ALJ's determination that Christie was disabled as of December 3, 2012, was based on numerous doctors' opinions. Most notably, Christie's back pain doctor concluded on December 3, 2012, that Christie could not return to work. The Board did not disagree with this factual finding. Nor did the Board disturb the ALJ's other **{-960-}** factual findings. Therefore, the ALJ's factual findings must be upheld since they are not "contrary to law, irrational, or unsupported by substantial evidence." *See id* (quoting *Todd Shipyards Corp.*, 717 F.2d at 1284).

---

[2] In addition, the *Moody II* court discussed the Act's purpose in reaching its decision. Acknowledging that the Supreme Court "has recognized that 'the [Act] represents a compromise between the competing interests of disabled laborers and their employers,'" the Fourth Circuit explained that it gave effect to that compromise by "applying the plain text" of the Act. *Moody II*, 879 F.3d at 100, 6 Adm. R. at 129 (quoting *Potomac Elec. Power Co. v. Dir., Office of Workers' Comp. Programs*, **[—13—]** 449 U.S. 268, 281–82 (1980)). We agree that the plain language of § 902(10) realizes the statute's purpose.

[3] The Board's reliance on *Burson* and *Hoffman* also does not change the outcome of this case. Both *Burson* and *Hoffman* erroneously relied on the voluntary retirement of the respective employees in those cases as the factual predicate for each employee's inability to establish their loss of wage-earning capacity. But, as discussed above, because the plain language of § 902(10) reflects that an employee's retirement is not dispositive to determining disability under the Act, *Burson* and *Hoffman* do not compel us to reach a different conclusion than the one we reach today. 33 U.S.C. § 902(10); *see Hoffman*, 35 Ben. Rev. Bd. Serv. (MB) at 150; *Burson*, 22 Ben. Rev. Bd. Serv. (MB) at 127.

Georgia-Pacific failed to establish that suitable alternative employment was available to Christie. Although the Board and Georgia-Pacific highlight that Christie was capable of working as a safety inspector at Georgia-Pacific with suitable accommodations at the time he retired, substantial evidence supports the ALJ's finding that Georgia-Pacific never actually offered these accommodations to Christie. Indeed, the ALJ concluded that no one at Georgia-Pacific told Christie that Christie could ask for help with conducting the physical inspections of the warehouses that were part of Christie's work tasks. In addition, the ALJ found that Georgia-Pacific had not documented any accommodations the company made for Christie. Georgia-Pacific therefore "fail[ed] to establish the availability of suitable alternative employment" because it failed to offer Christie a job that accounts for his physical limitations. *See Gen. Constr. Co.*, 401 F.3d at 968–69 **[—15—]** (explaining that an employer fails to establish the availability of suitable alternative employment by, among other things, failing to identify a job that an employee can perform considering his or her limitations).

Substantial evidence in the record therefore supports the ALJ's findings that Christie is disabled within the meaning of the Act: he attained maximum medical improvement, he can no longer return to his previous employment, and Georgia-Pacific has failed to establish that suitable alternative employment exists. Accordingly, the Board erred in reversing the ALJ's decision awarding benefits. *See Stevedoring Servs. of Am.*, 297 F.3d at 801.

IV.

In sum, we hold that retirement status alone, in and of itself, is not dispositive to determining disability under the Act. In reversing the ALJ's award of permanent total disability benefits to Christie, the Board erred in relying on *Moody I*, which misinterprets § 902(10). Further, the Board did not question the ALJ's factual findings and substantial evidence supports the ALJ's award of benefits. We therefore grant Christie's petition, reverse the Board's decision denying Christie benefits, and remand for a calculation of the permanent total disability benefits to be awarded to Christie.

PETITION GRANTED; REVERSED AND REMANDED.

United States Court of Appeals
for the Ninth Circuit

No. 16-15942

HOLZHAUER
vs.
GOLDEN GATE BRIDGE HIGHWAY & TRANSP. DIST.

Appeal from the United States District Court for the Northern District of California

Decided: August 10, 2018

Citation: 899 F.3d 844, 6 Adm. R. 354 (9th Cir. 2018).

Before **SCHROEDER** and **GOULD,** Circuit Judges, and **DU,*** District Judge.

* The Honorable Miranda M. Du, United States District Judge for the District of Nevada, sitting by designation.

[—4—] {-845-} **GOULD,** Circuit Judge: **{-846-}**

These two related appeals arise from a tragic and fatal boating accident when a recreational speedboat crashed into a passenger ferry. Harry Holzhauer (Mr. Holzhauer) was driving his life-long friend Defendant David Rhoades's speedboat. Mr. Holzhauer was looking in the opposite direction of where the speedboat was traveling when he crashed Rhoades's speedboat into the M/S San Francisco ferry. Mr. Houlzhauer died from his injuries and Rhoades was severely injured. Mary Holzhauer (Mrs. Holzhauer), as representative of her late husband's estate and in her individual capacity, sued Rhoades and the Golden Gate Bridge Highway and Transportation District (GGB), which owns the M/S San Francisco ferry. Rhoades filed a cross-claim against GGB and a counterclaim against the Holzhauer **[—5—]** estate. Likewise, GGB filed a cross-claim against Rhoades and a counterclaim against the Estate.

After trial Rhoades moved for judgment as a matter of law against Mrs. Holzhauer, and for judgment as a matter of law against GGB. The district court granted both motions, and Mrs. Holzhauer and GGB appeal. Because the accident occurred while the colliding boats were in San Francisco Bay on waters of the United States, we apply federal maritime law. We hold that a boat owner who is a passenger on his boat has no duty to keep a lookout unless the owner-passenger knows that the person operating his boat is likely to be inattentive or careless or the owner-passenger was jointly operating the boat at the time of the accident. We also hold that joint operation is not viewed over the course of the entire trip, but instead at the time immediately preceding and concurrent with the accident. We affirm the district court's grant of judgment as a matter of law in favor of Rhoades against Mrs. Holzhauer and against GGB.

I

On February 16, 2013, Mr. Holzhauer was driving Rhoades's speedboat in the bays in and around San Francisco, California. Rhoades was along for the ride and assisted Mr. Holzhauer in his operation of the boat at some times on the trip. While in Richardson Bay, where Sausalito and Belvedere meet San Francisco Bay, the speedboat collided with the M/V San Francisco, a ferry owned and operated by GGB. A witness testified that at the time of the collision, neither Rhoades nor Mr. Holzhauer was looking in the direction that the boat was headed. Mr. Holzhauer died because of his injuries, and Rhoades was seriously injured.

Mrs. Holzhauer, on behalf of herself and the Holzhauer estate, sued Rhoades and GGB for negligence in the death of **[—6—]** Mr. Holzhauer. Rhoades and GGB filed counter-claims against the estate for negligence and filed cross-claims against each other. The case went to trial.

After Mrs. Holzhauer's case in chief, Rhoades moved for judgment as a matter of law that Mrs. Holzhauer had not presented any evidence that Rhoades was "anything other than a cautious and reasonable recreational boat owner and occupant." The district court heard argument **{-847-}** on Rhoades's motion for judgment as a matter of law on Mrs. Holzhauer's negligence claim against him. Mrs. Holzhauer's attorney stated both in his opposition papers and at argument that "I'm going to argue tomorrow that Mr. Rhoades didn't do anything wrong" and that he "no longer intend[ed] to argue that Rhoades was negligent." This created an untenable position for the district court wherein a party did not want to pursue a claim but advocated that a jury nevertheless had sufficient facts to find liability.

Mrs. Holzhauer's attorney also stated that *Weissman v. Boating Magazine*, 946 F.2d 811, 814 (11th Cir. 1991) provided the correct standard for a passenger, but argued that a passenger was not defined to include the registered owner of a boat. Mrs. Holzhauer's attorney added that under either the standard applicable to passengers or the standard applicable to owners, there was sufficient evidence to create liability for Rhoades. Rhoades's attorney argued that even if there were a joint venture, that venture "could kind of come and go with the moment on the boat." The district court gave a tentative ruling granting the motion for judgment as a matter of law on Mrs. Holzhauer's claim against Rhoades for negligence. After the close of all evidence, the motion was renewed, and the district court granted the motion and entered a special instruction **[—7—]** notifying the jury that Rhoades was no longer a defendant and that his conduct should not be considered.

At the end of trial, Rhoades also moved for judgment as a matter of law on GGB's cross-claim for indemnity and contribution. No motion was made on GGB's third affirmative defense of comparative negligence. The district court granted Rhoades's motion on GGB's cross-claim for equitable indemnity and contribution and *sua sponte* granted judgment as a matter of law on GGB's affirmative defense of comparative negligence. Because of the judgments as a matter of law, the jury did not assess any shared responsibility of Rhoades in the boating accident.

The jury found Mr. Holzhauer 70% at fault for the accident and GGB 30% at fault. But because of the special instruction, the jury attributed no fault to Rhoades. The jury awarded Mrs. Holzhauer $546,747 in economic damages and $1,000,000 in non-economic damages. It also awarded Rhoades $2,229,559 in economic damages and $1,500,000 in non-economic damages. The estate and Mrs. Holzhauer appeal the district court's grant of Rhoades's motion. And GGB appeals the district court's ruling on its third affirmative defense and its cross-claim for equitable indemnity and contribution.

II

We have jurisdiction to review this case pursuant to 28 U.S.C. § 1292(a)(3). In reviewing the district court's grant of judgment as a matter of law under Rule 50, we review its findings of fact for clear error and its conclusions of law *de novo*. *Torres v. City of L.A.*, 548 F.3d 1197, 1205–06 (9th Cir. 2008). We view all evidence in the light most favorable to the nonmoving party without weighing evidence or making credibility determinations. *Id.* With **[—8—]** those legal standards in mind, we review the district court's grants of judgment as a matter of law in Rhoades's favor.

III

Both Mrs. Holzhauer and GGB argue that the district court erred by applying the incorrect legal standard when determining Rhoades's duty of care. The duty of care that applies to a boat owner riding as a passenger in his boat is a question of first impression. Relying on the principles **{–848–}** set forth in *Weissman v. Boating Magazine*, 946 F.2d 811, 814 (11th Cir. 1991), which we consider to be persuasive, we see no material difference between an ordinary boat passenger and a passenger who owns the boat being used, if the boat owner entrusts the boat to a competent operator. We consider each appeal in turn.

A

Mrs. Holzhauer contends that the district court erred by treating Rhoades as just a passenger and by resolving questions of fact in favor of the moving party. She argues that maritime law is clear that every vessel owner owes others a duty of reasonable care and that applying the *Weissman* passenger standard was a legal error. She argues that even if Rhoades were merely a passenger, the record shows that he was operating the speedboat jointly, so one of the *Weissman* exceptions would apply, permitting a finding of liability.

Rhoades responds that Mrs. Holzhauer made a choice to litigate her case against only GGB and now that Mr. Holzhauer was apportioned 70% liability, she attempts to call Rhoades's liability into question. Rhoades contends that the district court applied the correct legal standard: he urges that there is no distinction between a passenger and an owner-passenger for purposes of liability. Rhoades further argues that Mrs. Holzhauer had not provided any facts to **[—9—]** establish a duty on the part of Rhoades particularly because Mr. Holzhauer was an experienced boat operator and because Rhoades did not jointly operate the boat. We agree with Rhoades.

Every shipowner has a "duty of reasonable care under the circumstances." *Peters v. Titan Navigation Co.*, 857 F.2d 1342, 1344 (9th Cir. 1988); *see Kermarec v. Compagnie Generale Transatlantique*, 358 U.S. 625, 632 (1959) ("We hold that the owner of a ship in navigable waters owes to all who are on board for purposes not inimical to his legitimate interests the duty of exercising reasonable care under the circumstances of each case."). But as "a general rule, a passenger has no duty to keep a lookout on behalf of the operator of the vehicle." *Weissman*, 946 F.2d at 814. The passenger need only keep a lookout in two circumstances: when "he knows from past experience or from the manner in which the vessel is being operated on the particular trip, that the driver is likely to be inattentive or careless" and when the passenger "jointly operated" the vessel, meaning he "had active responsibility for and control over certain aspects of navigation of the boat." *Id.*

The novel question for us is what legal standard applies when an owner of a boat is also a passenger on his vessel. In tension are general duties of a ship owner to use reasonable care under the circumstances and a passenger's presumed lack of a duty to keep a lookout. Mrs. Holzhauer cites *Kermarec* for the general duty of a boat owner to act reasonably under the circumstances. 358 U.S. at 632. There the Supreme Court held "that the owner of a ship in navigable waters owes to all who are on board for purposes not inimical to his legitimate interests the duty of exercising reasonable care under the circumstances of each case." *Id.* **[—10—]**

Doubtless a boat owner owes a general duty of care, but that duty of care depends on the circumstances. Here, the circumstances involved a transfer in operation of the boat from Rhoades to Holzhauer. Rhoades, to be sure, had a duty to act reasonably in entrusting operation of the boat to Holzhauer. And yet there is no record evidence whatsoever that Rhoades was derelict in that duty. To the contrary, **{-849-}** the record suggests that Rhoades's decision to entrust operation of the boat to Holzhauer was reasonable because Holzhauer "was a safe, cautious, and experienced boat operator." No party disputes that fact. Further, the Eleventh Circuit is the only circuit to have considered when a passenger has a duty to keep a lookout, and we will not create a circuit split merely because Rhoades was also the boat owner. *See CTIA-The Wireless Ass'n v. City of Berkeley, Cal.*, 873 F.3d 774, 776 (9th Cir. 2017) ("[C]ircuit splits are generally to be avoided.").

Although a boat owner has a general duty of care, when that boat owner is functioning as a passenger it makes the most sense to define the scope of duty to align it, so far as boat operations are concerned, with that of a passenger. We conclude that the *Kermarec* and *Weissman* duties are not in conflict. The general reasonableness standard that applies to a boat owner is designed to accommodate the particular circumstances of the case. *Kermarec*, 358 U.S. at 632. When the circumstances are that the boat owner is a passenger on the boat, we hold that an owner-passenger has no duty to keep a lookout unless, as with an ordinary passenger, the person running the boat is known to the passenger to be inattentive or careless in their operation, or the passenger has been jointly operating the boat. *Weissman*, 946 F.2d at 814. We conclude that the district court did not err by applying this standard. **[—11—]**

While sitting as a passenger when the accident occurred, Rhoades does not fit within either of the two exceptions specified by the Eleventh Circuit as to when a passenger would have a duty to act as a lookout. *See Weissman*, 946 F.2d at 814. No party argues that Mr. Holzhauer was inattentive or careless on past boating excursions or while operating the speedboat before the accident, and so that exception to the general rule is not applicable here. We conclude that it would be artificial to suggest that there was joint operation of the boat because Rhoades had operated it earlier in the day. Although Rhoades was running the boat earlier that day, the joint operation inquiry properly asks if the boat was being jointly operated when the accident occurred. *See id.* at 814 (noting that both occupants were jointly operating the boat "at the time of the accident" because each "had active responsibility for and control over certain aspects of navigation"). The testimony at trial bore out that although Rhoades had helped Mr. Holzhauer earlier in their trip by explaining the rules-of-the-road for passing and had told Mr. Holzhauer to take another loop of the Bay, Rhoades was looking off into the distance at the San Francisco skyline when the accident occurred. Rhoades allowed Mr. Holzhauer to take a loop, but Rhoades did not direct the exact path that Mr. Holzhauer would take. We conclude that the district court did not err in concluding that Rhoades was not jointly operating the boat when the accident occurred.

While Rhoades did not give any negligent advice or negligently entrust Mr. Holzhauer with the speedboat, it could be argued that there was testimony that could support the idea that his omission to give advice at a critical time might have contributed to the accident. Rhoades testified that his general practices in boating were to be aware of boats around his vessel, to ensure that those who drove his boat **[—12—]** adhered to his safety standards, to watch over people who drove his boat, and to look out for traffic. But Rhoades failed here to look out for vessel traffic on the side of the speedboat, suggested that Mr. Holzhauer make a loop through the ferry lanes, did not warn Mr. Holzhauer about ferry traffic, did not take extra precautions **{-850-}** when entering ferry lanes, and did not supervise Mr. Holzhauer, who was found to be 70% at fault in killing himself and hurting Rhoades. But Mrs. Holzhauer's counsel was asked many times by the district court whether counsel thought Rhoades acted negligently. Counsel more than once told the district court that he did not think Rhoades was responsible. We are not persuaded, just as Mrs. Holzhauer's attorney and the district court were not persuaded, that the facts mentioned show negligence on Rhoades's part in the circumstances once one rejects the idea that he was jointly operating the boat and hence responsible as a lookout. Rhoades was reasonable in his decision to allow Mr. Holzhauer, an experienced boater, to operate the boat. Once Rhoades was not negligent in entrusting boat operation to Mr. Holzhauer, he stood in the position of a passenger on the speedboat. Although tragic, it is obvious that the key factor contributing to the accident was the inattention of the two drivers of the two boats that collided, not Rhoades.

B

GGB appeals the same issue with a slight twist. GGB argues that the lack of radar reflectors on Rhoades's speedboat limited the ferry's ability to detect it. The district court concluded that radar reflectors, while a good idea, were not required and did not constitute a basis for finding a breach of duty against Rhoades. GGB's expert at trial said that boat owners should equip their boats with reflectors, but did not state that the reflectors were required or even **[—13—]** common among small boat operators. Another expert had no opinion on whether a small boat should have radar equipment. Even if having radar reflectors is a good practice, good practice does not create liability absent facts to support that the practice is an operational standard in the relevant community of small boat owners.

GGB also argues that Rhoades was "complicit" in the collision because he had been directing Mr. Holzhauer's route throughout the day and chose the route of the loop where the accident occurred. Rhoades argues that the evidence supported the conclusion that he had acted reasonably on the day in question because Mr. Holzhauer was an experienced boater and had not done anything unsafe, and because Rhoades was not jointly operating the boat. As we held above, passengers generally have no duty to keep a lookout. *See Weissman*, 946 F.2d at 814. But, if the passenger has notice that the operator is inattentive or careless or the passenger has been operating the boat jointly, he may have a duty to keep a look out. *Id.*

The district court reasoned that Rhoades was not directing the travel of the vessel and that Mr. Holzhauer was an experienced boater. The district court concluded that even though Mr. Holzhauer did not have experience in the San Francisco Bay, there was no law giving rise to a special duty from that type of lack of experience. We reject the contention that Rhoades is a joint operator of the boat because he had assisted Mr. Holzhauer previously that day. There is no evidence in the record to support the conclusion that Rhoades was jointly operating the speedboat when the accident occurred. Therefore, none of the *Weissman* exceptions to the general rule for a passenger—that he has no duty to keep a lookout—apply. **[—14—]**

Golden Gate finally argues that comparative negligence is ordinarily a jury question, and that there were facts sufficient for a reasonable jury to conclude that Rhoades's conduct was not that of a reasonably prudent person. After hearing argument on Rhoades's motion, the district **{-851-}** court dismissed GGB's affirmative defense for comparative negligence against Rhoades and its cross-claim for equitable contribution and indemnity, although Rhoades had only moved for judgment as a matter of law on GGB's cross-claim for equitable contribution and indemnity. Rhoades's attorney had also said that "the comparative-negligence issue [was] not at issue in th[e] motion."

A claim for indemnity is not the same as an affirmative defense for comparative negligence. In this case, GGB sought indemnification from Rhoades for any liability GGB was ultimately apportioned for causing Mr. Holzhauer's death. Courts have recognized that under tort principles, "a passively negligent party in admiralty can recover indemnity damages from a primary negligent party." *SPM Corp. v. M/V MING MOON*, 22 F.3d 523, 526 (3d Cir. 1994). The affirmative defense of comparative negligence, however, would reduce any liability GGB may have had in the collision by the proportion of Rhoades's own negligence in the accident. *See United States v. Reliable Transfer Co., Inc.*, 421 U.S. 397, 411 (1975). The former causes Rhoades to share in the cost GGB pays for liability to Mr. Holzhauer, and the latter reduces any award GGB would pay in Mr. Rhoades's favor.

While these claims are separate and distinct, the distinction does not lead to different results here because comparative negligence requires some negligence on Rhoades's part. GGB points to the fact that "Rhoades admitted that his normal practice when someone else is **[—15—]** driving is that '[he] kind of check[s] to see how they're doing; how they're driving; if they seem to be capable of just looking out for other traffic. Are they exceeding any kind of speed that I wouldn't do.'" "He admitted that had he noticed that Mr. Holzhauer was not looking in the direction that he was steering, he would have corrected him." GGB points to the fact that there was evidence that Rhoades had a lot of experience operating his boat in San Francisco Bay, compared to Mr. Holzhauer who, while experienced at boating, had hardly any experience operating speedboats in the San Francisco Bay. This, GGB claims, supports the view that Rhoades breached a duty of care in the circumstances. GGB's argument is that even if Rhoades did not have a duty to operate as a lookout for other boats, he had some duty to watch Mr. Holzhauer to make sure he was driving safely. But there is no evidence that Rhoades behaved negligently at all in his duty under the circumstances. Rhoades's duty was to ensure that he entrusted the operation of his boat to a competent boater, and everyone agrees that Mr. Holzhauer met this criterion. Rhoades was available for Mr. Holzhauer when he needed assistance navigating, but Rhoades otherwise enjoyed the day of boating with his skilled friend at the helm. Rhoades watched for the aberrant behaviors noted above, but when Mr. Holzhauer did not exhibit them, Rhoades enjoyed the leisure cruise. It is not surprising that a small boat owner would do that after entrusting operations to an experienced boater. Rhoades did not act negligently in regards to himself or Mr. Holzhauer, so there is no basis to reduce Rhodes's recovery. We affirm the district court.

IV

We hold that a boat owner who is a passenger on his boat has no duty to keep a lookout unless the owner-passenger was jointly operating the boat or the owner-passenger knows **[—16—]** from past experience or from conduct that day that the person operating the boat is likely to be inattentive or careless. We hold that joint operation **{-852-}** is not viewed over the course of the entire trip, but that we instead look at the time immediately preceding the accident. The district court applied the correct legal standard by adopting the reasoning in *Weissman*, and we affirm.

AFFIRMED.

United States Court of Appeals
for the Ninth Circuit

No. 16-35314

ADAMSON
VS.
PORT OF BELLINGHAM

Appeal from the United States District Court for the Western District of Washington

Decided: August 14, 2018

Citation: 907 F.3d 1122, 6 Adm. R. 360 (9th Cir. 2018).

Before **GOULD** and **IKUTA,** Circuit Judges, and **TUNHEIM,*** Chief District Judge.

* The Honorable John R. Tunheim, Chief United States District Judge for the District of Minnesota, sitting by designation.

[—5—] {-1124-} **IKUTA,** Circuit Judge:

A crew member employed by the Alaska Marine Highway System (AMHS) was seriously injured while attempting to operate a permanent passenger ramp extending from the Port of Bellingham's terminal building to an AMHS ferry. Because the permanent passenger ramp in this case is an extension of the land, and the Admiralty Extension Act (AEA), 46 U.S.C. § 30101, does not apply to an injury caused by land-based equipment, we affirm the district court's ruling that maritime law does not apply.[1] **[—6—]**

I

AMHS, an entity of the State of Alaska, currently operates commercial ferries at 36 ports that it owns or leases. In 1988, the Port successfully submitted a proposal to AMHS to construct a marine terminal for AMHS's use in Bellingham, Washington. The Port designed the Bellingham Cruise Terminal (BCT) to meet AMHS's requirements. Per AMHS's specifications, the BCT included a passenger ramp and a vehicle ramp to load and unload ferries.

As part of the BCT's design, the passenger ramp is an integral part of the structure of the ferry berth facilities. *See* Appendix, p.2. The passenger ramp is built into the terminal building, with one end extending approximately 75 feet over the dock. *See* Appendix, p.2. A retractable "apron" connects the end of the ramp to a vessel. *See* Appendix, p.1. The ramp is controlled by 3/4-inch thick wire cables, which extend from a steel tower on the BCT dock to the far end of the ramp. The ramp is locked in place by pins that slot into two long bars. In order to change the ramp's position, an operator uses the ramp's control panel to unlock the pins and then raise and lower the cables. Attempting to lower the ramp when it is in the locked position creates slack in the cables. If the operator creates such slack and then unlocks the pins, the ramp will drop until the cables catch the slack.

The Port leased portions of the BCT facilities to AMHS under a 20-year lease agreement, beginning in 1989 when the BCT was completed. In 2009, the Port and AMHS renewed the lease for another 15 years. **{-1125-}**

On November 2, 2012, Shannon Adamson was working as a crew member on the AMHS ferry M/V Columbia, which **[—7—]** had docked at the BCT that morning. Adamson was asked to lower the passenger ramp to load passengers from the terminal to the ferry. While she was operating the ramp, it fell 15 feet, breaking the cables and collapsing all the way to the pier. Adamson suffered serious injuries from the incident.

Adamson filed this suit against the Port in federal district court under diversity jurisdiction, alleging that the Port negligently caused her injuries under maritime law.[2] In

[1] In a concurrently filed order, we certify to the Washington State Supreme Court a question related to the proper application of Washington law to Adamson's Washington law negligence claims. *See Adamson v. Port of Bellingham*, — F.3d —, 6 Adm. R. 370 (9th Cir. Aug. 13, 2018) (order).

[2] Adamson first sued the Port in Washington state court. The Port impleaded the State of Alaska, but the trial court dismissed those claims based on Alaska's sovereign immunity, and the Washington Court of Appeals affirmed. *See*

its answer, the Port asserted as an affirmative defense that negligent supervision and training by AMHS personnel, including the crew of the M/V Columbia, was partly responsible for Adamson's injuries. The Port then moved for partial summary judgment, arguing in part that maritime law did not apply to Adamson's claims. The district court agreed, and subsequently denied Adamson's motion for reconsideration. The case proceeded under Washington state law. After a ten-day trial in March and April 2016, a jury found the Port liable under various Washington law theories of negligence. The district court denied the Port's post-trial motions for judgment as a matter of law or a new trial.

The Port timely appealed the jury verdict and the district court's denial of its post-trial motions. Adamson timely cross **[—8—]** appealed, arguing that the district court's ruling that maritime law did not apply was erroneous.

II

Pursuant to Adamson's cross appeal, we consider here whether the district court correctly applied Washington law rather than maritime law.[3] We review de novo a district court's determination that maritime jurisdiction, and therefore substantive maritime law, does not extend to a tort claim. *H20 Houseboat Vacations Inc. v. Hernandez*, 103 F.3d 914, 916 (9th Cir. 1996). We have jurisdiction under 28 U.S.C. § 1291.

Adamson v. Port of Bellingham, 192 Wash. App. 921, 923–24 (2016). While the Port's appeal of its third-party claim against Alaska was pending, Adamson requested and received a dismissal of her state court claim without prejudice and refiled in federal court. Adamson also received workers' compensation from the State of Alaska. *See Adamson*, 192 Wash. App. at 924.

[3] Because Adamson seeks no additional relief beyond upholding the jury's verdict, she need not have presented this claim in a cross appeal. *See Jennings v. Stephens*, 135 S. Ct. 793, 798 (2015). Nonetheless, we consider her argument as an alternative ground on which to affirm the district court. *See Cassirer v. Thyssen-Bornemisza Collection Found.*, 862 F.3d 951, 974 (9th Cir. 2017).

A

We begin by reviewing the legal framework for determining whether maritime law applies to a tort claim.[4]

Plaintiffs may bring maritime law claims under either diversity jurisdiction, 28 U.S.C. § 1332, or admiralty **[—9—]** jurisdiction, 28 U.S.C. § 1333.[5] **{-1126-}** *Victory Carriers, Inc. v. Law*, 404 U.S. 202, 204 (1971). Under either jurisdictional statute, "federal maritime law govern[s]" if the claim comes "within the admiralty and maritime jurisdiction conferred on the district courts by the Constitution and the jurisdictional statutes." *Id.*; *see also Kermarec v. Compagnie Generale Transatlantique*, 358 U.S. 625, 628 (1959). In other words, if the district court could have maritime jurisdiction over a tort claim, "[s]ubstantive maritime law controls" the claim, "whatever the forum or asserted basis of jurisdiction." *Unigard Sec. Ins. Co. v. Lakewood Eng'g & Mfg. Corp.*, 982 F.2d 363, 366 n.1 (9th Cir. 1992).

Maritime law applies to a tort if two conditions are met. First, the "location" test requires us to determine "whether the tort occurred on navigable water or whether injury suffered on land was caused by a vessel on navigable water." *In re Mission Bay Jet Sports, LLC*, 570 F.3d 1124, 1126 (9th Cir. 2009) (quoting *Jerome B. Grubart, Inc. v. Great Lakes Dredge & Dock Co.*, 513 U.S. 527, 534 (1995)). While this test historically served "as the exclusive test of admiralty tort jurisdiction," the Supreme Court has recognized an additional requirement: a nexus to maritime activity. *Exec. Jet Aviation, Inc. v. City of Cleveland*, 409 U.S. 249, 261 (1972). The nexus requirement avoids sweeping into

[4] "We use the terms 'admiralty' and 'maritime' interchangeably, as the relevant caselaw often uses both words without apparent distinction." *Gruver v. Lesman Fisheries, Inc.*, 489 F.3d 978, 982 n.5 (9th Cir. 2007).

[5] 28 U.S.C. § 1333 provides, in relevant part, that "[t]he district courts shall have original jurisdiction, exclusive of the courts of the States, of: (1) [a]ny civil case of admiralty or maritime jurisdiction, saving to suitors in all cases all other remedies to which they are otherwise entitled."

admiralty jurisdiction wholly unrelated torts, such as airplane crashes over water. *Id.* at 268. Thus, maritime torts must also satisfy a "connection" test, which requires that the tort have a "significant relationship to traditional maritime activity." *In* **[—10—]** *re Mission Bay Jet Sports, LLC*, 570 F.3d at 1126 (quoting *Foremost Ins. Co. v. Richardson*, 457 U.S. 668, 674 (1982)). Here, the Port agrees that Adamson's tort claim bears the requisite connection to maritime activity, so we focus on the locality where the asserted tort occurred.

B

For purposes of maritime law, "[p]iers and docks [have been] consistently deemed extensions of land; injuries inflicted to or on them were held not compensable under the maritime law." *Victory Carriers*, 404 U.S. at 206–07 (footnote omitted). Structures such as "bridges, shore docks, protection piling, piers, etc., pertained to the land" because they were "connected with the shore and immediately concerned commerce upon land." *Cleveland Terminal & Valley R.R. Co. v. Cleveland S.S. Co.*, 208 U.S. 316, 321 (1908). "None of these structures were aids to navigation in the maritime sense, but extensions of the shore and aids to commerce on land as such." *Id.*; *see also Rodrigue v. Aetna Cas. & Sur. Co.*, 395 U.S. 352, 360 (1969) (concluding that admiralty jurisdiction did not extend to accidents on artificial islands because "the accidents had no more connection with the ordinary stuff of admiralty than do accidents on piers"); *Cope v. Vallette Dry-Dock Co.*, 119 U.S. 625, 627 (1887) (explaining that a fixed structure, such as a dry-dock, is not used for the purpose of navigation any more so than a wharf or warehouse that projects upon water).

While piers and docks are considered extensions of the land, a gangway or gangplank is part of a vessel; thus, injuries on gangplanks are deemed to have occurred on navigable waters. *The Admiral Peoples*, 295 U.S. 649, **[—11—]** 651–52 (1935).[6] In **{-1127-}** *The Admiral Peoples*, the steamship owner had placed a 2-foot by 18-foot plank from the vessel to the dock, and a passenger was injured in a fall from the plank. *Id.* at 650. *The Admiral Peoples* reasoned that the gangplank at issue "was a part of the vessel's equipment which was placed in position to enable its passengers to reach the shore," and that "[i]t was no less a part of the vessel because in its extension to the dock it projected over the land." *Id.* at 651–52. While the plaintiff "was on the gangplank, she had not yet left the vessel," *id.* at 652, and therefore, the plaintiff's injury was within maritime jurisdiction, *id.*; *see also Victory Carriers*, 404 U.S. at 207 (noting that while piers and docks are extensions of land, maritime law applied to gangplanks, which "served as a rough dividing line between the state and maritime regimes").

In light of *The Admiral Peoples*'s gangplank rule, we have deemed gangplank incidents to be subject to admiralty jurisdiction and maritime law. *See The Shangho*, 88 F.2d 42, 42 (9th Cir. 1937) (holding that maritime law applied to a longshoreman's claim that he was injured when he fell from a gangplank that had been unlashed from the ship because the "gangplank is part of the ship when it is being used for the purpose of furnishing ingress and egress to and from the ship"). We have applied this gangplank rule to such injuries even when the gangplank was not part of the ship's equipment. *See Solano v. Beilby*, 761 F.2d 1369, 1370–71 (9th Cir. 1985) (holding that maritime law applied to a **[—12—]** longshoreman's claim that he was injured on a ramp to a ship while attempting to load a vehicle from the dock, even though the ramp was provided by his employer, a stevedoring company).

We have not had much occasion, however, to consider when the gangplank rule applies to other sorts of connecting equipment used for access to vessels to and from the shore. Several courts have held that temporary connecting equipment used for such access is analogous to gangplanks and therefore subject

[6] At the time *The Admiral Peoples* was decided, a gangplank was defined as "a long narrow moveable platform or bridge, used in entering or leaving a ship, as from a wharf." Webster's Second New International Dictionary 1032 (1934). The same definition applies today. *See* Webster's Third New International Dictionary 934 (2002).

to admiralty jurisdiction. *See Tullis v. Fid. & Cas. Co. of N.Y.*, 397 F.2d 22, 24 (5th Cir. 1968) (reasoning that "a row of pilings connected to shore by a single plank over nine or ten feet of water" was not "in any way analogous to a fixed pier or wharf" and "could be considered a part of the vessel's equipment in lieu of the usual or customary gangplank"); *Mich. Mutual Liab. Co. v. Arrien*, 344 F.2d 640, 642, 644 (2d Cir. 1965) (determining that "a removable wooden, rectangular platform, approximately six feet by ten feet" was more analogous to a gangplank than a permanent pier or wharf).[7] **[—13—]**

By contrast, there is a circuit split on the question whether the gangplank rule applies to permanent, land-based equipment used for access to a vessel to and from the shore. In the leading circuit case **{–1128–}** on the issue, the Fifth Circuit held that the gangplank rule did not apply to a permanent land-based ramp. *See Parker v. S. La. Contractors, Inc.*, 537 F.2d 113, 115–16 (5th Cir. 1976). In *Parker*, a truck driver was injured on a ramp connecting a barge to a landing and sued the barge owner and lessee, as well as the owner of the landing and another third party. *Id.* at 115. The ramp "weighed several tons, rested on land and had an apron extending over the water's edge which could be raised and lowered by winches to permit ingress and egress from docking barges." *Id. Parker* contrasted this situation with those involving temporary gangplanks and analogous connecting structures, reasoning that the ramp "rested on land, and removing it would involve a major undertaking calling for heavy equipment." *Id.* at 116. Accordingly, the Fifth Circuit concluded that, "[u]nlike a gangplank, [the ramp] cannot reasonably be conceived as an appurtenance of the barges that use it for docking," and therefore the injury did not occur at a maritime locality. *Id.*

The Fourth Circuit reached the same conclusion regarding a moored fuel flat used to cross from the dock to vessels.[8] *Russell v. City Ice & Fuel Co. of Point Pleasant*, 539 F.2d 1318, 1319 (4th Cir. 1976). *Russell* reasoned that the flat "was floating, but more or less permanently moored to the shore, and it constituted the principal portion of the dock." *Id.* at 1320. While the flat was still capable of use as a vessel, the Fourth Circuit concluded that "[a]s long as such a **[—14—]** structure is securely affixed to the land and is in use as a component of the shore facilities, it is not a vessel in navigation, but a dock." *Id.* at 1321. Both the Fourth and Fifth Circuits thus rejected a per se rule that the gangplank rule applies to any equipment used to provide access to and from a vessel.

Contrary to these two circuits, the First Circuit held that the gangplank rule applies to any equipment providing the means of ingress to and egress from a vessel. *See Romero Reyes v. Marine Enters., Inc.*, 494 F.2d 866, 867 (1st Cir. 1974). In *Romero Reyes*, a longshoreman sued a barge owner for injuries suffered on a "gangway, which was permanently affixed to a pier-based tower and did not belong to the barge." *Id.* The gangway was "[s]uspended from a tower on pilings next to the dock" and "could be raised or lowered by cables attached to the tower." *Id.* at 869. *Romero Reyes* concluded that maritime law applied to this accident, reasoning that "[b]ecause the means of ingress or egress, by whomever furnished, are an 'appurtenance' of the vessel, the [vessel] owner has a duty of care regarding them." *Id.* at 870.[9]

---

[7] *Arrien* arose in the context of interpreting the scope of the Longshoremen's and Harbor Workers' Compensation Act (LHWCA), *see* 344 F.2d at 643–44, which at the time provided compensation for injuries "occurring upon the navigable waters of the United States (including any dry dock)" for which recovery could not be provided by state law, 33 U.S.C. § 903(a) (1964). This version of the LHWCA "specifically adopted the . . . line" traditionally drawn between maritime and state jurisdiction, *Nacirema Oper. Co. v. Johnson*, 396 U.S. 212, 220 (1969), making *Arrien* relevant to our inquiry. In 1972, Congress amended the LHWCA to extend beyond the reach of admiralty jurisdiction and cover additional employees involved in land-based operations related to marine activities. *Ne. Marine Terminal Co., Inc. v. Caputo*, 432 U.S. 249, 251–52 (1977).

[8] A "flat" is generally a "a flat-bottomed boat with a shallow draft and without keel." Webster's Third New International Dictionary 866 (2002).

[9] Other cases have employed broad language suggesting that the gangplank rule applies whenever a connecting structure is used for loading

Although we have not directly addressed this issue, we have indicated our disagreement with the First Circuit's per se rule. *See Scheuring v. Traylor Bros., Inc.*, 476 F.3d 781, 789–90 (9th Cir. 2007). In *Scheuring*, we considered a claim involving an injury suffered when the plaintiff was lifting a **[—15—]** "20-foot ramp leading from the water's edge to an offshore float," from which crew members would use a skiff to reach a barge. *Id.* at 784. The ramp, which weighed 180 pounds, "could not be affixed to the float, and, on average, a few times a **{-1129-}** week it would fall into the water." *Id.* We noted several cases enunciating a per se rule "that a gangway or ramp which is 'necessarily used for embarking or disembarking' becomes 'a basic appurtenance of the vessel.'" *Id.* at 790 (quoting *Sarauw v. Oceanic Navigation Corp.*, 655 F.2d 526, 528 (3d Cir. 1981) and citing *Romero Reyes*, 494 F.2d at 869). But rather than adopt this rule, we concluded that "[t]here is a genuine issue of material fact whether the ramp . . . is more like a gangway than a dock or pier." *Id.* at 789–90.

We now join the well-reasoned conclusion of the Fourth and Fifth Circuits, and reject the First Circuit's rule that any equipment used to access a vessel is a gangplank that is subject to admiralty jurisdiction. There are several reasons for doing so. First, our conclusion is consistent with Supreme Court precedent, which has not indicated that every case involving a structure or piece of equipment used for access to a vessel falls within admiralty jurisdiction. Specifically, in *T. Smith & Son v. Taylor*, the Supreme Court considered an accident that occurred when a longshoreman unloading a vessel was killed by a fall from "a stage that rested solely upon the wharf and projected a few feet over the water to or near the side of the vessel." 276 U.S. 179, 181 (1928). The plaintiff there conceded that both the stage and the wharf were extensions of land. *Id.* at 181–82. The Supreme Court agreed, concluding that maritime jurisdiction was lacking because the injured worker had been struck while on the stage, and therefore on land. *Id.* at 182. Further, admiralty jurisdiction does not necessarily apply to injuries caused by **[—16—]** equipment used to load or unload a ship. *See Nacirema Oper. Co. v. Johnson*, 396 U.S. 212, 213, 223 (1969) (admiralty jurisdiction does not apply to the injuries suffered by a longshoreman who was working on a pier permanently affixed to the shore and caused by pier-based crane being used to load a ship) (construing the pre-1972 LHWCA, *see* supra 12 n.7).

Moreover, the historical justification for the gangplank rule was that the gangplank was actually carried by the vessel as "a part of the vessel's equipment." *The Admiral Peoples*, 295 U.S. at 651–52; *see also Victory Carriers*, 404 U.S. at 213 (noting that a purported maritime claim was particularly attenuated where, in part, the plaintiff "was not injured by equipment that was part of the ship's usual gear or that was stored on board"); *O'Keefe v. Atl. Stevedoring Co.*, 354 F.2d 48, 50 (5th Cir. 1965) (explaining that a gangplank was "traditionally, if no[t] always so in fact, a part of the equipment of the ship"). Although courts, including ours, have extended this rationale to gangplanks and other analogous temporary equipment that is not carried by the vessel, *see, e.g., Solano*, 761 F.2d at 1371; *Tullis*, 397 F.2d at 24, we agree with the Fifth Circuit that when the ramp at issue is a permanent part of the shore facility, affixed to the shore, and bearing little resemblance to a "moveable platform or bridge" capable of being carried with a vessel, Webster's Second New International Dictionary 1032, it "cannot reasonably be conceived as an appurtenance of the [vessels]" that use it, *Parker*, 537 F.2d at 116.

Finally, the rationale for the per se rule in *Romero Reyes* derives in part from the vessel owner's duty to provide a safe means of access to and from the shore. *Romero Reyes* reasoned that the duty of seaworthiness "includes providing **[—17—]** [crew members] with a suitable means to board and disembark," and that this duty "extends to the gangway by

---

or unloading a vessel, but in those cases the ramps were not permanently affixed to land. *See White v. United States*, 53 F.3d 43, 47 (4th Cir. 1995) (wooden platform bridging gap between gangway and dock); *Sarauw v. Oceanic Navigation Corp.*, 655 F.2d 526, 527–28 (3d Cir. 1981) (gangway falling to dock).

whomever supplied, owned, or controlled." 494 F.2d at 869. *Romero Reyes* concluded that because **{-1130-}** this duty made the gangway at issue "an 'appurtenance' of the vessel," the vessel owner's duty of care required the owner to inspect the gangway and warn against apparent defects. *Id.* at 870. The duty of seaworthiness does not apply to the Port in this case. *See Fla. Fuels, Inc. v. Citgo Petroleum Corp.*, 6 F.3d 330, 332 (5th Cir. 1993) ("It is well-settled, however, that the doctrine of 'seaworthiness' is not applicable to a dock owner who does not occupy the position of owner or operator of the vessel.").

Having rejected the First Circuit's per se rule, we follow *Scheuring*'s guidance and hold that courts must consider, on a case-by-case basis, whether the equipment at issue is analogous to a gangplank and therefore subject to admiralty jurisdiction, or is a permanent land-based structure subject to state law.

C

While our analysis above can guide us in determining whether the asserted tort occurred over the water or on land, this is not the end of the voyage for admiralty jurisdiction. In 1948, Congress enacted the AEA, which provides that "[t]he admiralty and maritime jurisdiction of the United States extends to and includes cases of injury or damage, to person or property, caused by a vessel on navigable waters, even though the injury or damage is done or consummated on land." 46 U.S.C. § 30101(a). Congress passed this law "specifically to overrule or circumvent" a line of Supreme Court cases that had "refused to permit recovery in admiralty **[—18—]** even where a ship or its gear, through collision or otherwise, caused damage to persons ashore or to bridges, docks, or other shore-based property." *Victory Carriers*, 404 U.S. at 209.

Interpreting this Act, the Supreme Court has held that a tort may fall within the AEA regardless whether it is "committed by the ship itself" or "by the ship's personnel while operating it." *Gutierrez v. Waterman S.S. Corp.*, 373 U.S. 206, 210 (1963). In *Gutierrez*, a stevedore was injured on the dock while unloading defective cargo containers from a ship when he slipped on loose beans that had spilled from the containers. *Id.* at 207. *Gutierrez* held that the AEA applied to the stevedore's negligence claim, noting that the vessel owner "allowed the cargo to be discharged in dangerous and defective bagging," and reasoning that the impact of this action was "felt ashore at a time and place not remote from the wrongful act." *Id.* at 210–11.

Applying *Gutierrez*, we held in *Gebhard v. S.S. Hawaiian Legislator* that a longshoreman injured on a pier by pier-based equipment could bring a maritime negligence claim against the vessel owner under the AEA. 425 F.2d 1303, 1305–06 (9th Cir. 1970). In *Gebhard*, an employee of a stevedoring company was directing straddle carriers (large vehicles which moved container vans to the water's edge) into position beneath a crane used to hoist the vans aboard ship. *Id.* at 1305. The employee was injured when a straddle carrier ran into him and crushed his leg. *Id.* We reasoned that there was "no substantial difference for jurisdictional purposes between an allegation that the shipowner was negligent in allowing beans to be unloaded by means of dangerously defective bagging, [as in *Gutierrez*,] and one that **[—19—]** he was negligent in allowing vans to be loaded [on their way onto the vessel] by means of dangerously defective equipment." *Id.* at 1306. Therefore, we concluded that we had jurisdiction under the AEA. *Id.*

When we decided *Gebhard*, however, we did not have the benefit of *Victory Carriers*, which clarified and narrowed *Gutierrez*'s scope. **{-1131-}** 404 U.S. at 210–11. In *Victory Carriers*, a longshoreman was injured while driving a forklift loaded with cargo to a point on a pier where the cargo could be hoisted onto a vessel. *Id.* at 202–03. During this process, the overhead protection rack of the forklift (which was owned by his stevedore employer) came loose and struck him. *Id.* The Court held that because the longshoreman was injured by alleged defects in his employer's forklift while operating on a pier, federal maritime law did not apply even though the longshoreman was in the process of loading a vessel. *Id.* at 210–11. Distinguishing *Gutierrez*, the Court explained that the decision in that case "turned . . . upon the fact that [the stevedore's] injury was caused by an appurtenance of a ship, the defective cargo containers," which led to the on-shore injuries. *Id.* at 210–11. *Victory Carriers* emphasized that where an individual is "injured on a pier by pier-based equipment," the injury "remain[s] outside the" AEA. *Id.* at 211 (quoting *Nacirema*, 396 U.S. at 223). Noting that extending admiralty jurisdiction to the injury would "raise a host of new problems as to the standards for and limitations on the applicability of maritime law to accidents on land," *Victory Carriers* stressed that "[r]eliance upon the gangplank line as the presumptive boundary of admiralty jurisdiction, except for cases in which *a ship's appurtenance causes damage ashore*, recognizes the traditional limitations of admiralty jurisdiction, and decreases . . . arbitrariness and uncertainties . . . ." *Id.* at 214 & n.14 (emphasis added). **[—20—]**

After *Victory Carriers*, all circuits considering the issue have agreed that "to invoke maritime jurisdiction under the Admiralty Extension Act, a plaintiff injured on shore must allege that the injury was caused by a[n] . . . appurtenance of a ship on navigable waters." *Margin v. Sea-Land Servs., Inc.*, 812 F.2d 973, 975 (5th Cir. 1987); *see also Garret v. Gutzeit*, 491 F.2d 228, 232 (4th Cir. 1974) ("*Victory Carriers* and *Gutierrez*, read and considered together, combine to formulate the following rule: Admiralty jurisdiction extends to shorebased workers who are injured by an appurtenance of the ship at a time and place not remote from the wrongful act of the shipowner."). In other words, when read in light of *Victory Carriers*, *Gutierrez*'s statement that admiralty jurisdiction applies to torts committed "by the ship's personnel while operating it," 373 U.S. at 210, applies only where the injury is "caused by an appurtenance of [the] ship" or the ship itself, *Victory Carriers*, 404 U.S. at 211. As the First Circuit put it, "[t]he [Supreme] Court's later decision in *Victory Carriers* . . . headed off whatever inclination lower courts might have had to read *Gutierrez* in as unbounded a manner as the passage [regarding torts committed by the ship's personnel], taken literally, might have sanctioned." *Kinsella v. Zim Isr. Navigation Co., Ltd.*, 513 F.2d 701, 703–04 (1st Cir. 1975) (holding that the AEA did not apply where the object that caused the injury "was not an appurtenance in relation to plaintiff's injury"); *see also MLC Fishing, Inc. v. Velez*, 667 F.3d 140, 142 (2d Cir. 2011) (holding that the AEA did not apply when a vessel passenger slipped and fell on a ramp deemed to be an extension of land, and the accident was not "'caused by' the vessel or its appurtenances."); *Scott v. Trump Ind., Inc.*, 337 F.3d 939, 944–45 (7th Cir. 2003) (concluding that AEA jurisdiction depended on whether "an appurtenance of the" vessel "proximately caused" the injury); *Anderson v. United States*, **[—21—]** 317 F.3d 1235, 1237 (11th Cir. 2003) (reasoning that whether injuries caused by aircraft dropping bombs were "caused by a vessel" turned on "whether the aircraft is an appurtenance to the" aircraft carrier (first **{-1132-}** quoting *Grubart*, 513 U.S. at 534; and then citing *Victory Carriers*, 404 U.S. at 210–11)).

The Supreme Court's subsequent decision in *Grubart*, supports this reading of *Victory Carriers* and *Gutierrez*. *Grubart* involved allegations that a dredging company had negligently caused flooding in a tunnel and numerous buildings. 513 U.S. at 529. The dredging company had "used a crane, sitting on [its] barge in the river next to a bridge, to drive piles into the riverbed above the tunnel." *Id.* In examining whether the tort was committed "by a vessel," *Grubart* explained that "[t]he fact that the pile driving was done with a crane makes no difference under the location test, given the maritime law that ordinarily treats an 'appurtenance' attached to a vessel in navigable waters as part of the vessel itself." *Id.* at 535 (citing *Victory Carriers*, 404 U.S. at 210–11; *Gutierrez*, 373 U.S. at 209–10). The Court went on to hold that proximate causation was the appropriate standard by which to measure whether the damage was "caused" by the appurtenance of the barge. *Id.* at 537–38. Of course, had the AEA required only that the tort be "committed . . . by the ship's personnel while operating it,"

Gutierrez, 373 U.S. at 210, *Grubart's* discussion as to whether the crane was an appurtenance of the barge would have been unnecessary, as the AEA would have been satisfied by the allegations that the dredging company's employees were negligent in their pile driving, regardless whether the crane was an appurtenance.

In light of this intervening authority, we conclude that *Gebhard's* interpretation of "caused by a vessel" no longer **[—22—]** remains good law. *See Miller v. Gammie*, 335 F.3d 889, 893–94 (9th Cir. 2003) (en banc). We join our sister circuits in holding that, under the AEA, an injury must have been caused by a vessel or its appurtenance. *See, e.g., Scott*, 337 F.3d at 944–45. Therefore, the AEA does not extend to injuries "on a pier by pier-based equipment." *Victory Carriers*, 404 U.S. at 211 (quoting *Nacirema Oper.*, 396 U.S. at 211).[10]

III

We now apply these principles to Adamson's arguments.

Adamson first argues that her injury occurred on navigable waters because the BCT passenger ramp is analogous to a gangplank, and therefore subject to admiralty jurisdiction.

We disagree; there is no genuine issue of material fact as to whether the passenger ramp is a gangplank or analogous to one. Unlike a traditional gangplank, the passenger ramp at the BCT is not equipment carried with the ship. *See The Admiral Peoples*, 295 U.S. at 651; *O'Keefe*, 354 F.2d at 50. **[—23—]** Nor is it a temporary platform or piece of equipment that can be "placed in position to enable its passengers to reach the shore," *The Admiral Peoples*, 295 U.S. at 651; *see also Solano*, 761 F.2d at 1370–71. **{-1133-}** Rather, the BCT's passenger ramp is a permanent fixture of the onshore terminal facilities. The ramp itself is permanently extended partially over water and, though it is raised or lowered, remains roughly in the same place. Only the apron can be retracted to cover less of the water, and it still remains permanently affixed to land-and dock-based structures. Like the ramp in *Parker*, the passenger ramp here can only be moved mechanically, "and removing it would involve a major undertaking calling for heavy equipment." 537 F.2d at 116. Given these characteristics, the passenger ramp "cannot reasonably be conceived of as an appurtenance" of the M/V Columbia and other AMHS ferries. *Id.* Therefore, Adamson's injuries did not occur "on or over navigable waters." *Taghadomi v. United States*, 401 F.3d 1080, 1084 (9th Cir. 2005).

Alternatively, Adamson argues that even if the passenger ramp is part of the land, the AEA applies because the Port argued as an affirmative defense that AMHS personnel, including the crew of the M/V Columbia, were negligent in their training, supervision, and control of Adamson. Relying on *Gutierrez*, 373 U.S. at 210, and *Gebhard*, 425 F.2d at 1306–07, Adamson reasons that when the negligence of ship personnel causes injury on shore, the AEA extends admiralty jurisdiction to that injury. Again, we disagree.

Even assuming that the Port's allegations in an affirmative defense could form the basis for jurisdiction under the AEA, the substance of these allegations is **[—24—]** insufficient.[11]

---

[10] This conclusion is consistent with our holding in *Christensen v. Georgia-Pacific Corp.*, where we considered a claim that a dock owner's negligence in the construction and operation of its dock had allowed a ship to break free. 279 F.3d 807, 811 (9th Cir. 2002). A longshoreman injured his back while pulling on the ship's line to retie the ship. *Id.* We explained that this injury was covered by the AEA, reasoning that it "was caused by a vessel on navigable water breaking free from a dock and needing to be retied." *Id.* at 814–15 n.29. In *Christensen*, the vessel did not directly cause the injury by striking the longshoreman, but because he was injured while attempting to rein in the vessel, the vessel was clearly a proximate cause of the damage. *See Grubart*, 513 U.S. at 537–38.

[11] To the extent that Adamson contends that the Port is judicially estopped from asserting that maritime law does not apply, this argument is meritless because Adamson has not shown that "the court relied on, or accepted, [a] previous inconsistent position" of the Port, or that any of the other factors favoring judicial estoppel are present. *Hamilton v. State Farm Fire & Cas. Co.*, 270 F.3d

As explained above, Adamson's reliance on *Gutierrez* and *Gebhard* is unavailing because Adamson was injured by the collapse of the passenger ramp, which is an extension of land. Adamson's injuries were thus not proximately "caused by an appurtenance of a ship," *Victory Carriers*, 404 U.S. at 211; *see also MLC Fishing, Inc.*, 667 F.3d at 142; *Parker*, 537 F.2d at 116, making the officers' role in her injuries irrelevant to AEA jurisdiction. Therefore this case does not involve an injury "caused by a vessel on navigable waters." 46 U.S.C. § 30101.[12] **[—25—]**

Accordingly, we hold that maritime law does not apply to Adamson's claims, and we affirm the district court's grant of partial summary judgment on that issue.

AFFIRMED. [—1—]

778, 782–83 (9th Cir. 2001) (internal quotation marks and citation omitted). We **GRANT** the Port's contested motion for judicial notice of the briefing in a related state court case, *Adamson v. Port of Bellingham*, 192 Wash. App. 921 (2016). *See Burbank-Glendale-Pasadena Airport Auth. v. City of Burbank*, 136 F.3d 1360, 1364 (9th Cir. 1998).

[12] We reject Adamson's argument that maritime law applies because the passenger ramp's collapse also damaged the M/V Columbia. The locality of the tort depends on whether "the tort occurred on navigable water," *In re Mission Bay Jet Sports, LLC*, 570 F.3d at 1126 (citation omitted), and Adamson has provided no authority holding that damage to a ship which is on navigable water confers admiralty jurisdiction even when that damage is not part of the lawsuit. *Northern Insurance Co. of New York v. Chatham County*, on which Adamson relies, is inapposite because the plaintiff there sought to recover for damages to a vessel and the damage plainly occurred on navigable waters. 547 U.S. 189, 192 (2006).

APPENDIX

Bellingham Cruise Terminal and Passenger Ramp **{-1134-}**

[—2—] {-1135-}

C14
151

United States Court of Appeals
for the Ninth Circuit

No. 16-35314

ADAMSON
vs.
PORT OF BELLINGHAM

Order Certifying Question to Washington State Supreme Court

Decided: August 14, 2018

Citation: 899 F.3d 1047, 6 Adm. R. 370 (9th Cir. 2018).

Before **GOULD** and **IKUTA**, Circuit Judges, and **TUNHEIM,*** Chief District Judge.

* The Honorable John R. Tunheim, Chief United States District Judge for the District of Minnesota, sitting by designation.

[—3—] {-1048-}:

ORDER

We respectfully ask the Washington State Supreme Court to answer the certified question presented below, pursuant to Revised Code of Washington § 2.60.020, because we have concluded that maritime law does not apply to these claims, and therefore "it is necessary to ascertain the local law of [Washington] state in order to **{-1049-}** dispose of [this] proceeding and the local law has not been clearly determined."

This case involves a tort claim under Washington law for which a jury awarded approximately $16,000,000 in damages to Sharon Adamson, the plaintiff. Adamson's damages arose when a passenger ramp that she was operating at the Port of **[—4—]** Bellingham ("the Port") fell about 15 feet, snapping the cables that supported it, and causing her severe injuries. The Port claimed that it was not liable for the damages, because the ramp was under the exclusive control of its tenant, the Alaska Marine Highway System ("the Ferry"), at the time of the accident. On the Port's theory, it was liable only for notifying the Ferry of hidden defects, and had no duty as a possessor of land. *See* Restatement (Second) of Torts §§ 328E, 343, 343A, 356, 360. The plaintiffs claimed and the district court held, in contrast, that under the lease the Port was liable as a possessor of land for damages occurring on the ramp.

I

We summarize the material facts. At the time of the accident, Adamson, an employee of the Ferry, was operating a passenger ramp at the Port's Bellingham Cruise Terminal facility. The ramp was designed to be raised and lowered with three-quarter inch thick cables. But once the ramp was in the proper position for passengers to board or disembark from a ship, hydraulic pins would be inserted to hold the ramp in place, rather than requiring the cables to bear the weight of people crossing the ramp.

There was, however, a flaw in this system: Once the pins were in place, it was still possible to continue to unspool the cables. Although the pins would prevent the ramp from descending, slack would build up in the cables. And then if the pins were removed while there was slack in the cables, the ramp would drop precipitously until the cables caught the slack—assuming that the cables could withstand the force of the ramp's fall. **[—5—]**

While she was operating the ramp, Adamson attempted to lower the ramp while the pins were in place, putting slack in the cables. She then removed the pins and the ramp dropped about 15 feet, severing the cables, and causing Adamson's extensive injuries. Available evidence showed that the ramp could have been modified at little cost to prevent slack in the cables when the pins were in place, thus preventing the serious type of injury that occurred in this case. Evidence also showed that the Port was aware of the potential risk because a similar incident had occurred previously, but fortunately without any resulting injuries.

The district court held as a matter of law that based on the agreement between the Port and the Ferry, the Port had not conveyed exclusive possession to the Ferry and that the Port faced liability as a possessor of property. The district court instructed the jury in accordance with this holding, and the jury returned a verdict in favor of Adamson and against the Port.

The agreement between the Port and the Ferry contains the following provisions that are relevant to the issues on appeal:

(1) Section 1.2 describes the leased premises. It notes that the Ferry will have "exclusive use" of the "Reservation and Ticketing Office," the "Bellingham Cruise Terminal Manager's office," "the Warehouse space located in Warehouse No. 4," and "the Staging and pursuer booth." The Ferry will have "priority use" of "approximately 125 parking spaces" and "the Marine Facilities, including the vehicle ramp, passenger ramp, and Berth 1—Pier and Dolphins." The passenger ramp was the location of the injury. **[—6—] {-1050-}**

(2) Section 1.3 defines "exclusive use" to mean "the sole possession and control of Areas subject only to the terms and conditions of this Lease."

(3) Section 1.4 defines "priority use" to mean "the [Ferry] is entitled to superior but not exclusive right of use to the identified areas. The [Port] may allow other uses of the priority use areas so long as such use does not unreasonably interfere with [the Ferry's] use."

(4) Section 4.1 of the agreement states that "[t]he lessor will be solely responsible for keeping the leased premises in good repair and tenantable condition. The term 'repair' includes repairs of any type including but not limited to exterior and interior, structural and nonstructural, routine or periodic, except as in case of damage arising from the negligence of the [Ferry's] agents or employees."

(5) Section 5.1 of the lease allows the Ferry "to make alterations of additions in or to the premises only with written consent of the Lessor, which consent will not unreasonably be withheld."

II

On Appeal the Port contends vigorously that under Washington law, whenever the Ferry was in port, exclusive control of the ramp passed to the Ferry, and the Port was no longer liable to the Ferry's invitees. In support of this conclusion, the Port argues, first, that the priority use provision meant, as a practical matter, that the Ferry had exclusive control over the ramp whenever it was in port; only **[—7—]** one ship could be docked at the ramp at a time. And the Port argued second, that it never allowed a third party to use the ramp for docking purposes, so, in fact, only the Ferry ever used the ramp.[1]

As we understand Washington law, as a general rule property that is conveyed to a lessee becomes the responsibility of the lessee, and the landlord is no longer treated as a possessor of land. *See* Restatement (Second) of Torts § 328E (1965); *Regan v. City of Seattle*, 76 Wash. 2d 501, 504 (1969) ("the lessee takes the property subject to all apparent defects; and, with some exceptions, the lessor is not liable for injuries caused by apparent defects after exclusive control of the property has passed to the lessee . . . a lessor owes no greater duty to invitees, guests or sublessees of his tenant than he does to the tenant himself"); *Clemmons v. Fidler*, 58 Wash. App. 32, 38 (1990). But where property is given over to the use of a tenant, some parts of the property can be the responsibility of the tenant, while other parts of the property remain the responsibility of the landlord. *See Andrews v. McCutcheon*, 17 Wash. 2d 340 (1943) (upholding jury's conclusion that a landlord maintained control of a stairway that provided access to the leased premises and was liable for an injury occurring in the stairway, despite the fact that normally a stairway to the leased premises used exclusively by the tenant would be considered part of the leased premises and hence the responsibility of the tenant). As a general rule, the landlord has a responsibility "to exercise reasonable care to maintain common areas in

[1] Adamson cross-appealed, urging us to sustain the jury's verdict under a federal maritime negligence theory. We have rejected this argument in an opinion filed concurrently herewith.

a safe condition," *Mucsi v. Graoch Assocs. Ltd. P'ship No. 12,* **[—8—]** 144 Wash. 2d 847, 863 (2001), but not areas where "other tenants and the general public have no right of access." **{-1051-}** *Resident Action Council v. Seattle Hous. Auth.*, 162 Wash. 2d 773, 780–81 (2008).

Also, as we understand Washington law, property can become the responsibility of a lessee, even if rented only for a short period of time. *Hughes v. Chehalis Sch. Dist.*, 61 Wash. 2d 222, 224 (1963) (holding that a landlord tenant relationship had been created even where the property was only leased for an evening). And property can be the responsibility of the lessee even if the agreement between the parties includes some reservations regarding use. *See Regan,* 76 Wash. 2d at 504 ("If this control has passed, even though the use is restricted by limitations or reservations, then a landlord-tenant relationship is established").

But we find little guidance in the Washington precedents on how to assess which parts of the property given over to the use of a tenant count as parts of the property transferred into the tenant's control, rather than portions of the property "the tenant is entitled to use as appurtenant to the part leased to him." Restatement (Second) of Property: Landlord & Tenant, § 17.3 (1997). Here, for instance, the question of usage is mixed. As a practical matter, only the Ferry used the passenger ramp, and the priority use provision effectively gave the Ferry exclusive control of the ramp when it was in Port—no other ship could dock at that time. But the agreement also gave the Port control over the ramp when the Ferry was not in port. For example, the Port could allow third parties to use the ramp without material restriction when the Ferry was not there. The Port also had responsibilities for maintenance and repair of the ramp, and could have had access to the ramp to make such repairs at any time **[—9—]** throughout the lease term when the Ferry was not docked. And the Ferry could not unilaterally alter the ramp without the Port's consent.

Under these circumstances, this case offers the Washington State Supreme Court the opportunity to provide more clarity about the conditions under which a lessor is absolved of responsibility for injuries occurring on a part of the property subject to a mixed use by both lessor and lessee. Especially relevant here is the apportionment of responsibility where the lessee, as a practical matter, has exclusive use of a part of the property for intermittent periods of time, short of the entire term of the lease agreement.

Because we have concluded that this important question of Washington law is not entirely settled and involves matters of policy best left to resolution by the State of Washington's highest court, certification of a question to the Washington State Supreme Court is the most appropriate course of action. If the Washington State Supreme Court concludes that a lessee's right to priority usage of a part of a facility is sufficient to transfer responsibility for injuries entirely away from the lessor, we will reverse the district court with instructions to hold a new trial that appropriately instructs the jury on bases of liability not premised on the assumption that the Port is liable as a premises owner. If, however, the Washington State Supreme Court decides that a priority usage agreement does not absolve a landlord of liability as a possessor of property, we will affirm the district court.

III

In light of the foregoing discussion, and because the answer to this question is "necessary to ascertain the local law **[—10—]** of this state in order to dispose" of this appeal, RCW § 2.60.020, we respectfully certify to the Washington State Supreme Court the following question:

> Is party A (here, the Port) liable as a premises owner for an injury that occurs **{-1052-}** on part of a leased property used exclusively by party B (here, the Ferry) at the time of the injury, where the lease has transferred only priority usage, defined as a superior but not exclusive right to use that part of the

> property, to party B, but reserves the rights of party A to allow third-party use that does not interfere with party B's priority use of that part of the property, and where party A had responsibility for maintenance and repair of that part of the property?
>
> Perhaps stated more broadly, the question of Washington law presented is whether priority use can be considered to give exclusive control, and if so in what circumstances?

We do not intend our framing of this question to restrict the Washington State Supreme Court's consideration of any issues that it determines are relevant. If the Washington State Supreme Court decides to consider the certified question, it may in its discretion reformulate the question. *Broad v. Mannesmann Anlagenbau AG*, 196 F.3d 1075, 1076 (9th Cir. 1999).

If the Washington State Supreme Court accepts review of the certified question, we designate appellant Port of Bellingham as the party to file the first brief pursuant to **[—11—]** Washington Rule of Appellate Procedure ("WRAP") 16.16(e)(1).

The clerk of our court is hereby ordered to transmit forthwith to the Washington State Supreme Court, under official seal of the United States Court of Appeals for the Ninth Circuit, a copy of this order and all relevant briefs and excerpts of record pursuant to Revised Code of Washington §§ 2.60.010, 2.60.030 and WRAP 16.16.

Further proceedings in our court are stayed pending the Washington State Supreme Court's decision whether it will accept review, and if so, receipt of the answer to the certified question. This case is withdrawn from submission until further order from this court. The panel will resume control and jurisdiction on the certified question upon receiving an answer to the certified question or upon the Washington State Supreme Court's decision to decline to answer the certified question. When the Washington State Supreme Court decides whether or not to accept the certified question, the parties shall file a joint report informing this court of the decision. If the Washington State Supreme Court accepts the certified question, the parties shall file a joint status report every six months after the date of the acceptance, or more frequently if circumstances warrant.

It is so **ORDERED**.

United States Court of Appeals
for the Ninth Circuit

No. 14-71768

SANCHEZ
VS.
SESSIONS

On Petition for Review of an Order of the Board of Immigration Appeals

Decided: September 19, 2018

Citation: 904 F.3d 643, 6 Adm. R. 374 (9th Cir. 2018).

Before **WARDLAW, PAEZ,** and **CHRISTEN,** Circuit Judges.

[—6—] {-645-} PAEZ, Circuit Judge: **{-646-}**:

As Judge Pregerson poignantly described in our prior opinion: "This case is about Luis Sanchez, a small boat owner, who took some friends on a fishing trip within United States territorial waters, and ended up in removal proceedings before an immigration judge ("IJ") under section 240 of the Immigration and Nationality Act, 8 U.S.C. § 1229a." *Sanchez v. Sessions*, 870 F.3d 901, 904, 5 Adm. R. 399, 399 (9th Cir. 2017), *withdrawn*, 895 F.3d 1101, 6 Adm. R. 347 (9th Cir. 2018).[1]

Neither Sanchez nor his friends could have predicted the sequence of events that produced this outcome. Their plan had been to go fishing for a few hours, but after they had [—7—] been out for about thirty minutes, the boat unexpectedly lost power. Stranded and with an infant on board, Sanchez's friend called for emergency assistance. Some time later, United States Coast Guard ("Coast Guard") officers arrived and towed the boat safely into Channel Islands Harbor, a recreational harbor near Oxnard, California, where Sanchez and his friends were promptly detained, frisked, and asked for identification. Although Sanchez complied and produced his driver's license, the Coast Guard continued to hold him and his friends without explanation. The Coast Guard also contacted Customs and Border Protection ("CBP") because they suspected that Sanchez and his friends were "possib[ly]" "undocumented worker[] aliens."

Sanchez was eventually taken into custody by CBP and placed in removal proceedings, where he unsuccessfully sought to suppress the Government's evidence of both his alienage and his entry into the United States without inspection as the products of Fourth Amendment and regulatory violations. Sanchez petitions for review of the agency's decision to admit the Government's evidence. We grant the petition and conclude that Sanchez has made a prima facie showing that he was seized solely on the basis of his Latino appearance, which constitutes a particularly egregious regulatory violation. We remand for further proceedings before the IJ so that the Government may rebut Sanchez's prima facie showing. We hold that the agency may consider on remand after the Government's rebuttal whether the Coast Guard officers violated 8 C.F.R. § 287.8(b)(2) and if so, whether the violation was egregious and therefore warrants terminating Sanchez's removal proceedings without prejudice. [—8—]

I.

Sanchez is a forty-seven year old citizen of Mexico. He was seventeen years old when he entered the United States without inspection in 1988 and has lived in this country ever since. Until December 1, 1988, Sanchez's father was a legalized Special Agricultural Worker. This meant that Sanchez was eligible to apply for Family Unity Benefits, a program that grants unmarried children of such legalized workers authorization to reside and work in the United States. *See* 8 C.F.R. § 236.12(a)(1).

Sanchez submitted his Family Unity Benefits and Employment Authorization applications to the United States Citizenship and Immigration Service ("USCIS") on May 11, 2004. Both applications were granted, with his Family Unity Benefits set to expire on May 11, 2006. Sanchez applied for an extension in December 2008. This time,

[1] Following Judge Pregerson's death, Judge Wardlaw was drawn to replace him. The newly reconstituted panel withdrew the prior opinion. Portions of this opinion draw from Judge Pregerson's previous opinion in this case.

however, USCIS denied Sanchez's **{–647–}** applications. USCIS concluded that he was ineligible for Family Unity Benefits and that his prior application for benefits had been approved in error, because he had previously been convicted of several California Vehicle Code violations.[2] *See* 8 C.F.R. § 236.13(b).

As a result, Sanchez was without lawful status on February 25, 2010, the day he and his friends embarked on their ill-fated fishing trip from Channel Islands Harbor. The **[—9—]** weather was balmy and the group planned to go fishing for approximately two hours. The trip was not meant to be particularly arduous: one of Sanchez's friends brought his fourteen-month-old son and the small recreational boat they took out to sea never made it beyond two or three miles from the harbor—well within United States territorial waters. *See* Proclamation No. 5928, 54 Fed. Reg. 777 (Jan. 9, 1989) (extending U.S. territorial waters to twelve nautical miles from the baseline).

The friends had just settled into their trip when, approximately thirty minutes after leaving the harbor, the boat's engines lost power. Unable to make their way back to shore, one of Sanchez's friends called 911 to request assistance. The 911 operator, in turn, contacted the Coast Guard for assistance. The Coast Guard proceeded to tow the boat and its occupants back to Channel Islands Harbor. The Coast Guard officers, however, did not inform Sanchez and his friends that they would be detained once they reached the shore. When Sanchez disembarked from the boat around 5:00 p.m., he was confronted by approximately eight Coast Guard officers waiting to take him into custody. The officers frisked Sanchez and his friends and then ordered them to turn over their identification documents and belongings. Sanchez complied with the officers' orders and produced his driver's license, which the officers took. Sanchez later testified at his removal hearing that the Coast Guard officers only asked him two questions while he was detained: his name and address, both of which he provided.

Understandably alarmed by the turn of events, Sanchez tried to ask the Coast Guard officers why they were detaining him. Instead of answering, the officers ordered Sanchez to stop asking questions and to stay put until "some other people" came to speak with him. What Sanchez did not **[—10—]** know at the time was that the Coast Guard had already contacted CBP to report "the possibility of 4 undocumented worker[] aliens" and that the officers were simply waiting for CBP agents to arrive and take custody of Sanchez.[3] The CBP agents arrived approximately two hours later, at which point the Coast Guard officers allowed the group to release the infant to a relative. CBP then transported Sanchez and his two friends, also Latino, to a facility where they were strip searched and interrogated. The CBP officers also confiscated their identification documents. It was during this interrogation that Sanchez admitted he had entered the United States without inspection.

The CBP officers released Sanchez later that evening and advised him to try and retain an attorney. A CBP officer separately **{–648–}** prepared a Form I-213 (Record of Deportable/Inadmissible Alien), which noted that CBP had been contacted after the Coast Guard officers failed to "establish positive identity or nationality" for Sanchez and his companions. The form did not mention that Sanchez gave his driver's license to the Coast Guard, but it did note that subsequent Immigration and Naturalization Service ("INS") checks in four databases all returned "negative" results.[4]

---

[2] On September 16, 1993, Sanchez was convicted of violating California Vehicle Code § 23109(c) (speeding on a highway), § 12500(a) (driving without a license), and § 40508(b) (failing to pay a court fine arising from a Vehicle Code violation). On September 27, 1995, Sanchez was convicted of violating California Vehicle Code § 20002(a) (failing to stop a vehicle at the nearest location after an accident). On February 8, 2008, Sanchez was convicted again of violating California Vehicle Code § 12500(a).

[3] Sanchez's group consisted of his two friends, himself, and an infant. The infant was a United States citizen.

[4] The four databases were the Automated Fingerprint Identification System, the Consular Consolidated Database, the National Crime

Although Sanchez was released the same day he was detained, his reprieve was short lived. The United States **[—11—]** Department of Homeland Security ("DHS") ultimately served him with a Notice to Appear for removal proceedings.[5] At the hearing, the Government sought to establish Sanchez's nationality and entry without inspection by submitting CBP's Form I-213 into evidence. Sanchez responded by filing a motion to suppress and to terminate removal proceedings. He argued that the Coast Guard egregiously violated his Fourth Amendment rights because the detention was based solely on race.[6] He also argued that his detention violated 8 C.F.R. § 287.8(b), which requires that officers possess "reasonable suspicion" that a person is unlawfully present in the United States before detaining her or him. Sanchez contended that the Form I-213 was therefore inadmissible and requested that the IJ terminate removal proceedings.

The IJ denied Sanchez's motion because he had failed to attach an affidavit in support of his motion; nonetheless, the IJ scheduled a suppression hearing. At the suppression hearing, which was held before a different IJ after Sanchez submitted an affidavit, the Government introduced into evidence Sanchez's 2008 Family Unity Benefits and Employment Authorization applications. Although the IJ **[—12—]** found that Sanchez's testimony was consistent with his affidavit, she denied his motion and ordered Sanchez removed to Mexico. In her decision, the IJ found that Sanchez had failed to establish a prima facie case of either an egregious Fourth Amendment violation or a regulatory violation. The IJ also concluded that Sanchez's Family Unity Benefits and Employment Authorization applications were separately and independently admissible to prove Sanchez's identity.

Sanchez unsuccessfully appealed the IJ's decision to the Board of Immigration Appeals ("BIA"). In a brief, unpublished decision, the BIA concluded that even assuming the Coast Guard officers violated Sanchez's rights, the Government was entitled to rely on independent evidence—here, Sanchez's Family Unity Benefits and Employment Authorization applications—to establish his nationality and identity. The BIA therefore affirmed the IJ's decision denying Sanchez's motion to suppress **{-649-}** and terminate removal proceedings and the IJ's removal order.

Sanchez timely petitioned us for review.

II.

We have jurisdiction over final orders of removal pursuant to 8 U.S.C. § 1252. "Where, as here, the BIA adopts the IJ's decision while adding some of its own reasoning, we review both decisions." *Lopez-Cardona v. Holder*, 662 F.3d 1110, 1111 (9th Cir. 2011). "We review constitutional claims and questions of law *de novo*." *Id.*

III.

It is well-established that the exclusionary rule generally does not apply to removal proceedings. *See Chuyon Yon* **[—13—]** *Hong v. Mukasey*, 518 F.3d 1030, 1034 (9th Cir. 2008). There are, however, two critical exceptions to this rule: (1) when the agency violates a regulation promulgated for the benefit of petitioners and that violation prejudices the petitioner's protected interests, *see id.* at 1035; and (2) when the agency egregiously violates a petitioner's Fourth Amendment rights, *see Lopez-Rodriguez v. Mukasey*, 536 F.3d 1012, 1018 (9th Cir. 2008). Because Sanchez has made a prima facie showing that the Coast

Information Center, and the Treasury Enforcement Communications System.

[5] The Notice to Appear charged Sanchez as removable under 8 U.S.C. § 1182(a)(6)(A)(i) (entry without admission or parole), § 1182(a)(2)(A)(i)(II) (conviction of a controlled substance offense), and § 1182(a)(2)(A)(i)(I) (conviction of a crime involving moral turpitude).

[6] Sanchez argues that the Coast Guard officers engaged in ethnic profiling by detaining him based on his Hispanic or Latino appearance. Nonetheless, because courts have "also used the language of race when discussing the relevant constitutional principles in cases involving Hispanic persons," we "refer[] to the nature of the bias as racial in keeping with the primary terminology" used by the Supreme Court. *Pena-Rodriguez v. Colorado*, 137 S. Ct. 855, 863 (2017).

Guard officers violated 8 C.F.R. § 287.8(b)(2) when they detained him, we do not address Sanchez's constitutional argument.

A.

The subject regulation, 8 C.F.R. § 287.8(b)(2), states that "[i]f the immigration officer has a reasonable suspicion, based on specific articulable facts, that the person being questioned is, or is attempting to be, engaged in an offense against the United States or is an alien illegally in the United States, the immigration officer may briefly detain the person for questioning." As an initial matter, we reject the Government's argument that the Coast Guard officers who detained Sanchez were not acting as "immigration officers" within the meaning of the regulation.

The Coast Guard is required by law to "enforce or assist in the enforcement of all applicable Federal laws on, under, and over the high seas and waters subject to the jurisdiction of the United States." 14 U.S.C. § 2(1). This includes enforcing all applicable provisions of the Immigration and Nationality Act ("INA"). *See* Gary W. Palmer, *Guarding the Coast: Alien Migrant Interdiction Operations at Sea*, 29 Conn. L. Rev. 1565, 1567, 1570 (1997) (explaining that the Coast Guard "enforce[s] compliance with the [INA] on behalf of INS and the Attorney General" (footnote omitted)). The Coast Guard is thus empowered to search, seize, and **[—14—]** arrest anyone "for the prevention, detection, and suppression of violations of laws of the United States" as long as the individuals in question are located within the high seas and waters over which the United States has jurisdiction. 14 U.S.C. § 89(a).

The Coast Guard's broad law enforcement powers are not, however, without restriction. Because they are tasked with "enforcing any law of the United States," including all those for which they do not have primary enforcement authority, officers of the Coast Guard are considered "agents of the particular executive department or independent establishment charged with the administration of the particular law" subject to "all the rules and regulations promulgated by such department or independent establishment with respect to the enforcement of that law." *Id.* § 89(b). In practice, 14 U.S.C. § 89(b) ensures that when—as here—Coast Guard officers detain individuals in service of the INA, they act as immigration agents subject **{-650-}** to the same regulations as their counterparts in CBP and Immigration and Customs Enforcement ("ICE").[7] We therefore conclude that when the Coast Guard officers detained Sanchez, they were acting as "immigration officers" within the meaning of 8 C.F.R. § 287.8(b)(2).

B.

For nearly four decades, it has been the law in our circuit that evidence may be excluded for a regulatory violation as **[—15—]** long as three conditions are satisfied: (1) the agency violated one of its regulations; (2) the subject regulation serves a "purpose of benefit to the alien"; and (3) the violation "prejudiced interests of the alien which were protected by the regulation." *Matter of Garcia-Flores*, 17 I. & N. Dec. 325, 328 (BIA 1980) (quoting *United States v. Calderon-Medina*, 591 F.2d 529, 532 (9th Cir. 1979)); *see also Chuyon Yon Hong*, 518 F.3d at 1035. Sanchez has made a prima facie showing that all three of these conditions have been met here.

1.

Section 287.8(b)(2) requires that officers possess reasonable suspicion on the basis of "specific articulable facts" that a person is unlawfully present in the country before they detain the person. The record before us is devoid of any such specific articulable facts. CBP's Form I-213 is remarkably terse in its recitation of events surrounding Sanchez's detention. The form simply states, in relevant part, that "US Coast Guard was not able to

---

[7] Contrary to the Government's argument, it matters little that the DHS does not formally include Coast Guard officers in its non-exhaustive, regulatory definition of immigration officers. *See* 8 C.F.R. § 1.2. Lest there be any doubt, 14 U.S.C. § 89(b) declares that Coast Guard officers who act to enforce immigration laws "shall[] be deemed to be acting as agents" of the relevant immigration agency.

establish positive identity or nationality of the 3 adult males and 14 month infant on board the vessel" and that "US Customs and Border Protection was notified of the possibility of 4 undocumented worker[] aliens."

The narrative in the Form I-213 is troubling for two reasons. First, Sanchez consistently testified and maintained throughout his removal proceedings that he provided the Coast Guard with his driver's license when he was initially detained.[8] A valid driver's license would, of course, positively establish Sanchez's identity. Second, Sanchez **[—16—]** testified that he was *immediately* detained and met by a number of Coast Guard officers once they returned to the Channel Island Harbor. The Government has yet to dispute the veracity of Sanchez's testimony. Crediting both the information in the Form I-213 and Sanchez's testimony, the record indicates that the Coast Guard officers thought Sanchez was an "undocumented worker alien" before they returned to the harbor. In other words, as the record currently stands, the officers could not have reasonably suspected Sanchez was unlawfully present in this country for lack of identification because they detained him and called CBP *before* they asked for identification and obtained Sanchez's driver's license.

On these facts, we agree with Sanchez that it appears he was detained solely on the basis of his race. The Government has yet to offer specific and articulable facts that would support the Coast Guard officers' decision to detain Sanchez on the basis of reasonable suspicion that he was unlawfully present in this country or otherwise **{–651–}** engaged in illegal activity. There is no evidence, for instance, that Sanchez's boat contained contraband of any kind or that he informed the Coast Guard officers before his detention that he had entered the United States without inspection two decades ago. Because race and ethnicity are never grounds for reasonable suspicion, we conclude that Sanchez has made a prima facie showing that the Coast Guard officers who detained him violated 8 C.F.R. § 287.8(b)(2). *See United States v. Brignoni-Ponce*, 422 U.S. 873, 886 (1975) ("We cannot conclude that [the apparent Mexican ancestry of the occupants in a car] furnished reasonable grounds to believe that the three occupants were aliens."). **[—17—]**

2.

We also conclude that 8 C.F.R. § 287.8(b)(2) was promulgated to serve a "purpose of benefit" to petitioners like Sanchez. *Calderon-Medina*, 591 F.2d at 531.

The Department of Justice ("DOJ") proposed § 287.8(b)(2)—along with a number of other regulations—to "establish enforcement standards in the areas of force, interrogation and detention not amounting to arrest." 57 Fed. Reg. 47011, 47011 (Oct. 14, 1992). The goal was to "bring immigration officers in line with other Department of Justice law enforcement officers" and to "assure the continuance of disciplined and professional conduct by Service enforcement personnel." *Id.* During the notice and comment period, a number of commenters suggested amending the proposed regulation to "include current judicial precedent defining 'reasonable suspicion' and the general authority to interrogate and detain." 59 Fed. Reg. 441093, 42411 (Aug. 17, 1994).

DOJ ultimately declined to adopt the commenters' suggestions. *See id.* DOJ explained that it would not "be appropriate to codify" current judicial precedent defining reasonable suspicion because "*binding* judicial precedent . . . is subject to revision in the ongoing process of litigation." *Id.* (emphasis added) (citing *Brewer v. Williams*, 430 U.S. 387 (1977)). DOJ thus made clear that the regulation was intended to reflect constitutional restrictions on the ability of immigration officials to interrogate and detain persons in this country—a doctrine rooted in the Fourth Amendment. *See INS v. Lopez-Mendoza*, 468 U.S. 1032, 1044–45 (1984) (explaining that "the INS has its own comprehensive scheme for deterring Fourth Amendment violations by its officers," including "regulations requir[ing] that no one

---

[8] The IJ acknowledged that Sanchez's testimony at the suppression hearing was "consistent[] with his declaration."

be detained without reasonable suspicion of illegal alienage"). **[—18—]**

The Fourth Amendment guarantees that "[t]he right of the people to be secure in their persons . . . against unreasonable searches and seizures [] shall not be violated." U.S. Const. amend. IV. As the Supreme Court has long held, officers may not "stop and briefly detain a person for investigative purposes" under the Fourth Amendment unless they have "reasonable suspicion supported by articulable facts that criminal activity 'may be afoot.'" *United States v. Sokolow*, 490 U.S. 1, 7 (1989) (citing *Terry v. Ohio*, 392 U.S. 1, 30 (1968)). Section 287.8(b)(2) all but parrots this standard: it provides that immigration officers may not briefly detain a person for questioning unless the officer has a "reasonable suspicion, based on specific articulable facts, that the person being questioned is, or is attempting to be, engaged in an offense against the United States or is an alien illegally in the United States." **{-652-}**

The regulation and the Fourth Amendment standards it reflects are undoubtedly for the benefit of petitioners and not mere best-practices suggestions for immigration officers. We therefore conclude that § 287.8(b)(2) was promulgated for the benefit of petitioners like Sanchez.[9] **[—19—]**

3.

This brings us to the final condition that Sanchez must satisfy: prejudice. Ordinarily, it is the petitioner's responsibility to "'specifically' identify any prejudice from the violation" that potentially affected the outcome of the petitioner's removal proceeding. *Garcia-Flores*, 17 I. & N. Dec. at 328 (quoting *Calderon-Medina*, 591 F.2d at 532). But where, as here, "compliance with the regulation is mandated by the Constitution, prejudice may be presumed."[10] *Id.*; *see also Puc-Ruiz v. Holder*, 629 F.3d 771, 780 (8th Cir. 2010) ("'As a general rule, . . . prejudice will **[—20—]** have to be specifically demonstrated,' unless compliance with the regulation is mandated by the Constitution, in which case prejudice may be presumed." (alteration in original) (quoting *Garcia Flores*, 17 I. & N. Dec. at 328)); *Martinez Camargo v. INS*, 282 F.3d 487, 492 (7th Cir. 2002) (same). Because 8 C.F.R. § 287.8(b)(2) reflects the Fourth Amendment's requirement that brief detentions be supported by reasonable

---

[9] Our conclusion is not affected by 8 C.F.R. § 287.12, which states that all regulations within Part 287 of the Code of Federal Regulation "do not, are not intended to, shall not be construed to, and may not be relied upon to create any rights, substantive or procedural, enforceable at law by any party in any matter, civil or criminal."

Section 287.12's bark is worse than its bite. DOJ made clear when it first promulgated section 287.12—previously designated section 287.11—that the provision was "only intended to ensure that the regulations do not create rights not otherwise existing in law." 59 Fed. Reg. 42406, 42414 (Aug. 17, 1994). DOJ pushed back against concerns that the disclaimer would somehow "preclude victims of unlawful Service enforcement practices from pursuing remedies for regulatory **[—19—]** violations," adding that section 287.12 would not "prevent any party from pursuing relief for alleged violations of the Constitution or laws of the United States." *Id.* The agency also clarified that section 287.12 was wholly consistent with *United States v. Caceres*, 440 U.S. 741 (1979), *see* 59 Fed. Reg. 42406, 42414, which held that "[a] court's duty to enforce an agency regulation is most evident when compliance with the regulation is *mandated by the Constitution* or federal law." *Caceres*, 440 U.S. at 749 (emphasis added); *see also Bridges v. Wixon*, 326 U.S. 135, 152–53 (1945) (invalidating a deportation order because the INS violated a regulation designed to "afford [petitioners] due process of law").

Section 287.12 thus leaves in place all regulatory rights derived from the Constitution or federal law. This necessarily includes 8 C.F.R. § 287.8(b)(2), which was promulgated to effectuate the Fourth Amendment.

[10] The regulation need not explicitly invoke the Constitution for the Constitution to mandate compliance with the regulation. *See Bridges*, 326 U.S. at 153 (concluding that a number of regulations, including one requiring statements to be signed and delivered under oath, were "designed as safeguards against essentially unfair procedures" and that the agency's failure to abide by those regulations necessitated vacating the petitioner's order of deportation); *see also Garcia-Flores*, 17 I. & N. Dec. at 328 (citing *Bridges* approvingly).

suspicion, we presume that Sanchez was prejudiced by the Coast Guard officers' failure to abide by § 287.8(b)(2)'s requirements.

C.

The BIA erroneously concluded that there was "nothing unreasonable about the Coast Guard seeking assurances that the occupants of . . . a vessel are entitled to be present in the United States before allowing **{–653–}** them to enter the country."[11] That is not the test that applies here. The test for an alleged violation of § 287.8(b)(2) is whether the Coast Guard officers possessed reasonable suspicion that Sanchez was unlawfully present in the country when they detained him. Sanchez has made a prima facie showing that the Coast Guard officers did not.

IV.

We turn to the heart of this case. A successful prima facie showing of a regulatory violation for evidentiary suppression purposes would normally entitle the petitioner to a remand for the government to rebut the petitioner's showing. *See Matter of Barcenas*, 19 I. & N. Dec. 609, 611 **[—21—]** (BIA 1988) (explaining that a petitioner must establish a prima facie case for suppression "before the Service will be called on to assume the burden of justifying the manner in which it obtained the evidence"). This remedy, however, is beyond Sanchez's reach. The BIA correctly concluded in the alternative that Sanchez's unlawful status could be independently established through his Family Unity Benefits and Employment Authorization applications, both of which are admissible.[12] Put simply, the Government does not need Sanchez's Form I-213 to prove that he entered this country without inspection.

Were suppression of tainted evidence the only remedy available to Sanchez, our review—much like the BIA's—would end here. But that is not the case. In *Calderon-Medina*, we recognized that regulatory violations may invalidate deportation proceedings. *See* 591 F.2d at 531. At the time, we did not elaborate on what such an invalidation would entail. Today, we join the Second Circuit and hold **[—22—]** that petitioners may be entitled to termination of their removal proceedings without prejudice for egregious regulatory violations. *See Rajah v. Mukasey*, 544 F.3d 427, 446–47 (2d Cir. 2008) (holding that pre-hearing regulatory violations may be grounds for termination without prejudice if they resulted in "prejudice that may have affected the outcome of the proceeding, conscience-shocking conduct, or a deprivation of fundamental rights"). Because Sanchez has made a prima facie showing that he was detained solely on the basis of his race and that his detention was contrary to the requirements of § 287.8(b)(2), we grant his petition for review and remand for the agency to determine in the first instance **{–654–}** whether termination without prejudice is appropriate here.

A.

The roots of termination without prejudice may be traced back to *Calderon-Medina*, when

---

[11] Sanchez was seized at Channel Islands Harbor, which is not a United States port of entry. *See* 8 C.F.R. § 100.4; 19 C.F.R. §§ 101.1, 101.3. Nor is there any evidence in the record that Sanchez's boat entered United States territorial waters from international waters.

[12] It is well-established that "the simple fact of who a defendant is cannot be excluded, regardless of the nature of the violation leading to his identity." *United States v. Del Toro Gudino*, 376 F.3d 997, 1001 (9th Cir. 2004). Here, however, Sanchez seeks to suppress evidence that he entered the country without inspection. Accordingly, that aspect of Sanchez's Form I-213 is suppressible. Because his Family Unity Benefits and Employment Authorization applications predated the Coast Guard officers' actions, they are admissible. *See United States v. Crews*, 445 U.S. 463, 472 (1980) (concluding that evidence of the victim's identity was admissible because it "was known long before there was any official misconduct, and her presence in court [was] thus not traceable to any Fourth Amendment violation"). The fruit-of-the-poisonous-tree doctrine does not extend backwards to taint evidence that existed before any official misconduct took place. *See id.* at 475 ("The exclusionary rule enjoins the Government from benefiting from evidence it has unlawfully obtained; it does not reach backward to taint information that was in official hands prior to any illegality.").

we first held that regulatory violations could "invalidate a deportation proceeding." 591 F.2d at 531. *Calderon-Medina* concerned criminal indictments against two defendants for illegal re-entry following deportation. *See id.* at 530. The question was whether the defendants' original deportations had been the unlawful product of a regulatory violation, such that they could not serve as a basis for the defendants' criminal indictments. *See id.* We concluded that although the INS had violated its own regulation, remand was necessary to give the defendants an opportunity to show prejudice. *See id.* at 532. Because it was impossible to invalidate the defendants' original deportations, which were carried out long before the defendants were criminally indicted for subsequent re-entry, we instructed the district court to dismiss the criminal indictments if the defendants successfully demonstrated prejudice on remand. *See id.* Put **[—23—]** differently, invalidating the defendants' deportation proceedings in *Calderon-Medina* meant nullifying their deportations as a legal matter for purposes of their criminal proceedings. Our decision, however, did not limit invalidation of removal proceedings to criminal indictments.[13]

The BIA's decision in *Garcia-Flores* built upon *Calderon-Medina* and recognized that certain types of regulatory violations can "render *subsequent* agency actions invalid." 17 I. & N. Dec. at 328 (emphasis added). This suggests that the invalidation remedy turns on *when* in the process the regulatory violation occurred. Indeed, the Second Circuit has recognized as much. *See Rajah*, 544 F.3d at 446–47 (distinguishing between pre-hearing regulatory violations and regulatory violations that take place during a deportation hearing). In *Montilla v. INS*, 926 F.2d 162 (2d Cir. 1991), for example, the Second Circuit concluded that the IJ presiding over Montilla's hearing violated a regulation by failing to ask Montilla to state on the record whether he wished to procure representation. *See id.* at 169. The court then granted Montilla's petition and remanded for a new hearing. *See id.* at 170.

Montilla's remedy fits cleanly within *Garcia-Flores*'s framework for invalidating deportation proceedings: the regulatory violation took place *during* the hearing, thereby invalidating the agency's actions that took place from the hearing onwards—but, critically, not any action that took place before. Montilla was not entitled to termination with prejudice because his initial presence in removal **[—24—]** proceedings was not the product of a disqualifying regulatory violation. He was, however, entitled to a new hearing because the IJ's failure to properly inquire about representation at the start of his hearing rendered the hearing itself invalid. By remanding for a new hearing, the Second Circuit effectively afforded Montilla a new hearing devoid of any of the regulatory infirmities that had taken place at the first one.

Nor is the Second Circuit the only circuit to have recognized the importance of providing petitioners with a clean slate on remand. The Seventh Circuit emphasized in *Snajder v. INS*, 29 F.3d 1203 (7th Cir. 1994), that the agency's interference with the petitioner's regulatory right to counsel "call[s] for the prophylactic remedy of vacating the order of deportation and for **{-655-}** writing *thereafter on a clean slate*." *Id.* at 1207 (emphasis added) (quoting *Castaneda-Delgado v. INS*, 525 F.2d 1295, 1302 (7th Cir. 1975)). Because the agency's actions tainted Snajder's hearing, the Seventh Circuit concluded that Snajder's case "must be remanded for a new hearing." *Id.*

Applying our sister circuits' reasoning to this case, we agree with the Second Circuit that certain kinds of pre-hearing regulatory violations can be remedied only by termination without prejudice as opposed to a new hearing. *See Rajah*, 544 F.3d at 446–47. Accordingly, we conclude that a petitioner is entitled to termination of their proceedings without prejudice as long as the following requirements are satisfied: (1) the agency violated a regulation; (2) the regulation was promulgated for the benefit of petitioners; and (3) the violation was egregious, meaning that

---

[13] Since then, courts have invalidated removal proceedings by remanding for new hearings. *See, e.g.*, *Montilla v. INS*, 926 F.2d 162 (2d Cir. 1991).

it involved conscience-shocking conduct, deprived the petitioner of fundamental rights, or prejudiced the petitioner. *See Calderon-Medina*, 591 F.2d at 531; **[—25—]** *Rajah*, 544 F.3d at 447. For this rare subset of cases, simply remanding for a new hearing or for further proceedings will be insufficient because the agency's violations predate any hearing. Only full termination of the proceedings without prejudice can "effectively cure[] any procedural defect by putting the parties into the position they would have been had no procedural error taken place." *Batanic v. INS*, 12 F.3d 662, 667 (7th Cir. 1993).

We emphasize that this remedy is reserved for truly egregious cases. Termination without prejudice is undoubtedly burdensome; it effectively means that the agency must hit the reset button and begin deportation proceedings anew. We also acknowledge that the Supreme Court has expressed particular concern with the unique costs of "releas[ing] from custody persons who would then immediately resume their commission of a crime though their continuing, unlawful presence in this country." *Lopez-Mendoza*, 468 U.S. at 1050. Nonetheless, we conclude that the costs of termination without prejudice do not outweigh its considerable benefits when the Government crosses the line into conscience-shocking conduct.

"Careless observance by an agency of its own administrative processes weakens its effectiveness in the eyes of the public because it exposes the possibility of favoritism and of inconsistent application of the law." *Montilla*, 926 F.2d at 170. This is particularly true when the agency stands accused of singling out persons for detention and deportation based on race or ethnicity. In such circumstances, the Government cannot simply rely on the existence of untainted evidence to continue with removal proceedings that are "tainted from their roots." *Castaneda-Delgado v. INS*, 525 F.2d 1295, 1302 (7th Cir. 1975) (quoting *United States v. Robinson*, 502 F.2d 894, 896 (7th **[—26—]** Cir. 1974)). To permit the Government to pick up where it left off would not only do a great disserve to petitioners, who have been subjected to conscience-shocking racial and ethnic profiling, but also remove from the table an effective tool for deterrence, specifically, termination without prejudice. *See Lopez-Mendoza*, 468 U.S. at 1043 (acknowledging the reduced "deterrent value of the exclusionary rule in a civil deportation proceeding").

B.

Applying our test for termination without prejudice, we conclude that Sanchez has made a prima facie showing that the Coast Guard officers' violation of § 287.8(b)(2) was conscience-shocking and therefore egregious. *Cf. Omni Behavioral Health v. Miller*, 285 F.3d 646, 652 (8th Cir. 2002) ("If . . . Miller conducted his **{-656-}** investigation in order to harass Woodlawn employees because of their race, it is possible, if not likely, that such conduct would meet the 'shock the conscience' test."). As discussed earlier, *see supra* pp. 15–16, we agree with Sanchez that the record indicates that the Coast Guard detained him on the basis of his Latino appearance.[14] The Government, to date, has offered no explanation for why Coast Guard officers contacted CBP and detained Sanchez and his companions for two hours, even after Sanchez produced his driver's license. Nor does CBP's Form I-213 shed much light on the Coast Guard officers' motivations that afternoon beyond noting **[—27—]** that the officers suspected that Sanchez and his companions were "undocumented worker[] aliens."

It is beyond question that detentions and interrogations based on racial or ethnic profiling and stereotyping egregiously violate § 287.8(b)(2)'s requirement that all detentions be based on reasonable suspicion.[15] *See, e.g.*,

---

[14] Sanchez has also made a prima facie showing that the Coast Guard violated 8 C.F.R. § 287.8(b)(2) and that the regulation was promulgated for the benefit of petitioners. *See supra* pp. 13–20.

[15] The Government concedes in its brief that a "stop made solely on the basis of ethnicity constitutes an egregious Fourth Amendment violation." Because 8 C.F.R. § 287.8(b)(2) is premised on Fourth Amendment standards, it follows that such a stop would also egregiously violate the regulation.

Maldonado v. Holder, 763 F.3d 155, 159 (2d Cir. 2014) (explaining that a seizure "may nevertheless qualify as an egregious violation if the stop was based on race (or some other grossly improper consideration)" (quoting *Almeida-Amaral v. Gonzales*, 461 F.3d 231, 235 (2d Cir. 2006))). "[W]e have long regarded racial oppression as one of the most serious threats to our notion of fundamental fairness and consider reliance on the use of race or ethnicity as a shorthand for likely illegal conduct to be 'repugnant under any circumstances.'" *Gonzalez-Rivera v. INS*, 22 F.3d 1441, 1449 (9th Cir. 1994) (quoting *United States v. Martinez-Fuerte*, 428 U.S. 543, 571 n.1 (1976)). "[D]iscrimination on the basis of race is illegal, immoral, unconstitutional, inherently wrong, and destructive of democratic society." *City of Richmond v. J.A. Croson Co.*, 488 U.S. 469, 521 (1989) (Scalia, J., concurring). When the Government ignores this country's commitment to equality and fairness by engaging in racial and ethnic profiling, it betrays all of its people—citizens, lawful permanent residents, visitors, and migrants alike who live within its borders. **[—28—]**

We emphasize that race and ethnicity alone can never serve as the basis for reasonable suspicion. The violation alleged by Sanchez here is egregious both for its grotesque nature and its patent unlawfulness. We therefore conclude that Sanchez has made a prima facie showing of an egregious violation of 8 C.F.R. § 287.8(b)(2).[16]

V.

When Sanchez first decided to gather his friends for a fishing trip on his boat, he could never have imagined that the short excursion would ensnare him in removal proceedings. Sanchez has since introduced evidence suggesting that the Coast Guard's decision to detain him was based on his race alone in contravention of 8 C.F.R. § 287.8(b)(2)'s requirements. Nonetheless, because the Government has not yet had an opportunity to introduce evidence **{–657–}** rebutting Sanchez's prima facie showing that the Government egregiously violated the regulation, we grant Sanchez's petition and remand for further proceedings. On remand, the agency shall afford the Government an opportunity to rebut Sanchez's prima facie showing that there was both a regulatory violation and that the violation was egregious. If the Government fails to rebut Sanchez's showing that the violation was egregious, the agency shall consider whether Sanchez is entitled to termination without prejudice.

PETITION FOR REVIEW GRANTED AND REMANDED.

(Reporter's Note: Concurring Opinion follows on p. 384).

[16] Consequently, we need not consider whether the Coast Guard and CBP officers also violated other regulations.

[—29—] **{-657-}** PAEZ, Circuit Judge, concurring:

In our prior panel opinion, Judge Pregerson wrote a separate concurrence expressing his frustration with the Government practice of encouraging non-citizens to apply for immigration relief, and later using that information against noncitizens in removal proceedings. *See Sanchez v. Sessions*, 870 F.3d 901, 913–14, 5 Adm. R. 399, 407 (9th Cir. 2017) (Pregerson, concurring), *withdrawn*, 895 F.3d 1101, 6 Adm. R. 347 (9th Cir. 2018). I share these concerns about the dilemma created by the Government's contradictory positions.

On the one hand, when the Government enacts immigration relief programs—such as driver's licenses, deferred action, and work authorization—it encourages noncitizens to apply and thereby provide the Government with personal information. *See Plyler v. Doe*, 457 U.S. 202, 220 (1982) (noting there are "significant social costs borne by our Nation when select groups are denied the means to absorb the values and skills upon which our social order rests."). On the other hand, the Government could at a later date use that personal information against noncitizens—as was the case here with Sanchez. Maj. Op. at 21 fn.12. As a result, many noncitizens are reluctant to "com[e] out of the shadows" and "step[] into the potential net of immigration enforcement." *See* Angélica Cházaro, *Challenging the "Criminal Alien" Paradigm*, 63 UCLA L. Rev. 594, 642–43 (2016). I agree with Judge Pregerson that the Government's practice in this regard contradicts the nation's longstanding principle of welcoming immigrants into our communities.

Judge Pregerson's concurrence is quoted in full below:

> I write separately to explain why it is unfair for the Government to encourage noncitizens to apply for immigration relief, **[—30—]** and at a later date use statements in those relief applications against noncitizens in removal proceedings.
>
> The Government should not be permitted to use noncitizens' applications for immigration relief to remove noncitizens from their homes and their families in our country. When the Government enacts immigration relief programs, it encourages noncitizens to apply because there are "significant social costs borne by our Nation when select groups are denied the means to absorb the values and skills upon which our social order rests." *Plyler v. Doe*, 457 U.S. 202, 220 (1982).
>
> The Government asks noncitizens to provide personal information to receive benefits, such as driver's licenses, visas, deferred action, and work authorization. But because noncitizens are afraid that the Government could at a later date use that information against them, many are reluctant to apply. *See* Angélica Cházaro, *Challenging the "Criminal Alien" Paradigm*, 63 UCLA L. Rev. 594, 642–43 (2016) ("Coming out of the shadows to be counted and accounted for, however, while it may bring the benefits of work authorization and a social security number, involves stepping into the potential **{-658-}** net of immigration enforcement.").
>
> The Government's practice in this regard contradicts the principle of welcoming immigrants into our communities. This **[—31—]** practice also contradicts President Kennedy's view that our nation's "[i]mmigration policy should be generous; it should be fair; it should be flexible." John Fitzgerald Kennedy, *A Nation of Immigrants* (1964). We should encourage, not punish, noncitizens who come out of the shadows seeking avenues to lawful status.

I am also concerned about the Government's argument that the exclusionary rule does not apply to Sanchez's Family Unity Benefits and Employment Authorization applications because they predate the egregious constitutional violation. *See United*

States v. Del Toro Gudino, 376 F.3d 997 (9th Cir. 2004).

Categorically exempting applications that predate an egregious constitutional violation from the exclusionary rule allows immigration and other law enforcement agencies to prey on migrant and working-class communities. Law enforcement officers can unconstitutionally round up migrant-looking individuals, elicit their names, and then search through Government databases to discover incriminating information in pre-existing immigration records. *See* Eda Katharine Tinto, *Policing the Immigrant Identity*, 68 Fla. L. Rev. 819, 864 (2016).

Nothing prevents law enforcement from engaging in this unfair tactic if, as the Government contends, immigration records **[—32—]** that predate an egregious constitutional violation can never be the fruit of the poisonous tree. *See Elkins v. United States*, 364 U.S. 206, 217 (1960) ("[The] purpose [of the exclusionary rule] is . . . to compel respect for the constitutional guaranty in the only effectively available way—by removing the incentive to disregard it."); *United States v. Olivares-Rangel*, 458 F.3d 1104, 1120 (10th Cir. 2006) ("[T]he deterrence purpose of the exclusionary rule would effectively be served only by excluding the very evidence sought to be obtained by the primary illegal behavior, not just the means used to obtain that evidence.").

This troubling end-around the exclusionary rule corrupts our justice system. The Government should not be allowed to flout the protections of the Fourth Amendment and then use a noncitizen's application for immigration relief against her or him. We should foster communication, not distrust, between migrant communities and law enforcement.

See Sanchez, 870 F.3d at 913–14, 5 Adm. R. at 407 (Pregerson, concurring).

United States Court of Appeals
for the Ninth Circuit

No. 16-35539

BUNKER HOLDINGS LTD.
VS.
YANG MING LIBERIA CORP.

Appeal from the United States District Court for the Western District of Washington

Decided: October 11, 2018

Citation: 906 F.3d 843, 6 Adm. R. 386 (9th Cir. 2018).

Before **SMITH** and **WATFORD**, Circuit Judges, and **RAYES**,* District Judge.

* The Honorable Douglas L. Rayes, United States District Judge for the District of Arizona, sitting by designation.

[—4—] **{-844-}** **WATFORD**, Circuit Judge: **{-845-}**:

This is an *in rem* action for a maritime lien brought by Bunker Holdings Ltd. against the containership M/V YM Success. Bunker Holdings supplied bunkers (marine fuel) to the YM Success while the ship was docked in Nakhodka, Russia. Under United States law, which we will assume applies here, Bunker Holdings is entitled to a maritime lien if it "provid[ed] necessaries to a vessel on the order of the owner or a person authorized by the owner." 46 U.S.C. § 31342(a).

Bunker Holdings provided "necessaries" to a "vessel," as the statute requires, because bunkers are considered necessaries and the YM Success qualifies as a vessel. The only issue is whether Bunker Holdings provided the bunkers "on the order of the owner or a person authorized by the owner." On cross-motions for summary judgment, the district court held that Bunker Holdings could not satisfy this last requirement. We agree with that conclusion.

The relevant facts are not in dispute. The owner of the YM Success, Yang Ming Liberia Corp., ordered the bunkers from O.W. Bunker Far East (Singapore) Pte. Ltd., which we will refer to as OWB Far East for short. Under the terms of their contract (simplified somewhat), Yang Ming agreed to buy 3,500 metric tons of fuel oil from OWB Far East for delivery to the YM Success on specified dates at a price of $498.00 per metric ton. The contract designated OWB Far East as the "seller" and Yang Ming as the "buyer." Yang Ming knew that in all likelihood OWB Far East, a fuel broker, would not supply the bunkers itself, but it did not direct OWB Far East to select any particular supplier. OWB Far East decided to purchase the bunkers from Bunker **[—5—]** Holdings, and those two companies entered into their own separate contract. Under the terms of their contract, Bunker Holdings agreed to sell 3,500 metric tons of fuel oil to OWB Far East at a price of $480.33 per metric ton. Bunker Holdings then supplied the bunkers to the YM Success and billed OWB Far East for payment. Shortly thereafter, OWB Far East filed for bankruptcy, leading Bunker Holdings to pursue payment through this maritime lien action against the ship.

These facts make clear that Bunker Holdings did not provide bunkers to the YM Success "on the order of the owner" of the vessel. Yang Ming placed its order with OWB Far East, not Bunker Holdings.

Because it did not provide the bunkers on the order of the vessel's owner, Bunker Holdings is entitled to a maritime lien only if it can show that it provided the bunkers "on the order of . . . a person authorized by the owner." 46 U.S.C. § 31342(a). Bunker Holdings supplied the bunkers "on the order of" OWB Far East, so it must show that OWB Far East was "a person authorized by the owner" to bind the vessel. A separate statutory provision, § 31341(a), provides a list of persons who are "presumed to have authority to procure necessaries for a vessel" on the ship's credit. They include the owner, the master, and "a person entrusted with the management of the vessel at the port of supply." § 31341(a)(1)–(3). OWB Far East does not fall into any of those categories. The statute also includes, as relevant here, "an agent appointed by . . . the owner." § 31341(a)(4)(A). But Bunker Holdings submitted no evidence that OWB Far East was acting as Yang Ming's agent when OWB Far

East contracted with Bunker Holdings to purchase bunkers for the YM Success. **[—6—]**

Unable to rely on the statutory list of persons with presumed authority to bind **{-846-}** the vessel, Bunker Holdings grounds its claim on our decision in *Marine Fuel Supply & Towing, Inc. v. M/V Ken Lucky*, 869 F.2d 473 (9th Cir. 1988). There, we ruled that the plaintiff was entitled to a maritime lien in circumstances not unlike those present in this case. Bulkferts, the subcharterer of the Ken Lucky, placed an order for bunkers with Brook Oil, which in turn placed an order with the plaintiff, Marine Fuel. *Id.* at 475. Marine Fuel was the entity that actually supplied the bunkers to the vessel. *Id.* We held that Marine Fuel was entitled to a maritime lien, but we based our holding on a critical factual admission made by the defendant. The defendant admitted that Marine Fuel sold the bunkers *to Bulkferts*, pursuant to an order originating from Bulkferts. *Id.* at 476–77. Based on that admission, we treated the case as though Bulkferts had ordered the bunkers directly from Marine Fuel and hence assumed that Marine Fuel had supplied the bunkers "on the order of" Bulkferts. Since Bulkferts was one of the entities with presumed authority to bind the vessel, *see id.* at 476 & n.3, each of the statutory requirements for a maritime lien was satisfied. In ruling for Marine Fuel, we explicitly refused to consider whether Brook Oil was authorized to bind the ship as Bulkferts' agent. *Id.* at 477.

Bunker Holdings cannot rely on our decision in *Ken Lucky* because the critical factual admission present there is absent here. Yang Ming never admitted that it ordered the bunkers from Bunker Holdings; it has asserted throughout, and the undisputed facts confirm, that it ordered the bunkers from OWB Far East. In contrast to the single transaction we assumed was involved in *Ken Lucky*, two independent transactions are involved in this case: one between Yang Ming and OWB Far East, and a second transaction between **[—7—]** OWB Far East and Bunker Holdings. That key factual difference renders this case distinguishable from *Ken Lucky*.

In our view, this case is controlled not by *Ken Lucky*, but instead by our decisions in *Port of Portland v. M/V Paralla*, 892 F.2d 825 (9th Cir. 1989), and *Farwest Steel Corp. v. Barge Sea-Span 241*, 828 F.2d 522 (9th Cir. 1987). In both of those cases, ship owners entered into contracts with general contractors for repair of the vessels. The general contractors, in the course of performing their work, negotiated separate agreements with subcontractors for certain necessaries, which the subcontractors provided to the vessels. We held that the subcontractors were not entitled to a maritime lien because they had contractual relationships only with the general contractors, and in most cases "a general contractor does not have the authority to bind a vessel." *Port of Portland*, 892 F.2d at 828; *see Farwest Steel*, 828 F.2d at 526. There is one exception to that general rule, which applies when the vessel owner directs the general contractor to use a particular subcontractor. In that scenario, the general contractor essentially acts as the owner's agent and thus exercises authority to bind the vessel. *Farwest Steel*, 828 F.2d at 526.

The general rule stated in *Port of Portland* and *Farwest Steel* governs this case because OWB Far East occupied a position no different from that of a general contractor. Under its contract with Yang Ming, OWB Far East assumed the obligation to supply bunkers to the YM Success. OWB Far East entered into a separate contract with Bunker Holdings to assist OWB Far East in fulfilling its own contractual obligations to Yang Ming. OWB Far East was not acting as Yang Ming's agent and lacked authority to bind the vessel, so its contract with Bunker Holdings could not give rise to a maritime lien in Bunker Holdings' favor. The **[—8—]** exception **{-847-}** to the general rule does not apply because Yang Ming did not direct or require OWB Far East to purchase the bunkers from Bunker Holdings.

In sum, we agree with the district court's conclusion that Bunker Holdings is not entitled to a maritime lien against the YM Success. In so holding, we join three other circuits that have reached the same conclusion on nearly identical facts. *See Valero Marketing & Supply Co. v. M/V Almi Sun*, 893 F.3d 290, 294–95, 6 Adm. R. 205, 207–08 (5th Cir. 2018); *ING Bank N.V. v. M/V Temara*, 892 F.3d 511, 521–22, 6 Adm. R. 44, 49–50 (2d Cir. 2018); *Barcliff, LLC v. M/V Deep Blue*, 876 F.3d 1063, 1071, 5 Adm. R. 518, 523 (11th Cir. 2017).

The one remaining issue concerns the district court's award of costs. After Bunker Holdings arrested the YM Success at the outset of this action, the parties agreed that Yang Ming could secure the ship's release by posting substitute security in the form of a letter of undertaking for $2.4 million. *See* 28 U.S.C. § 2464(a); Supplemental Admiralty and Maritime Claims Rule E(5). Yang Ming paid approximately $54,000 to keep the letter of undertaking in place during the 17 months this action remained pending in the district court. The court awarded Yang Ming that amount as a taxable cost under Rule 54(d)(3)(B) of the Local Rules of Civil Procedure for the Western District of Washington, which provides that "[r]easonable premiums paid on undertakings or bonds or security stipulations shall be allowed where the same have been furnished by reason of express requirement of law, rule, or court order." The court viewed the cost of obtaining the letter of undertaking as "tantamount to a premium on an undertaking, bond, or security."

Bunker Holdings argues that the costs award is invalid because Local Rule 54(d)(3)(B) lacks statutory authorization, at least as applied in admiralty and maritime **[—9—]** cases. We agree with Bunker Holdings on this point. Federal courts may not award costs beyond those mentioned in 28 U.S.C. § 1920 unless another federal statute authorizes them to do so. *West Virginia University Hospitals, Inc. v. Casey*, 499 U.S. 83, 86 (1991); *see Taniguchi v. Kan Pacific Saipan, Ltd.*, 566 U.S. 560, 573 (2012). Premiums paid on undertakings or bonds are not included among the six categories of taxable costs mentioned in § 1920. A separate statute, 28 U.S.C. § 1925, does authorize the Supreme Court to promulgate rules specifying additional categories of costs that may be awarded in admiralty and maritime cases. But thus far the Supreme Court has not issued a rule allowing a party to recover as a taxable cost the expenses incurred in posting a bond or other security under 28 U.S.C. § 2464 and Supplemental Rule E(5). The district court therefore lacked authority to award Yang Ming the costs it incurred in posting the letter of undertaking in this case.

Although we are constrained by precedent to rule as we have, this strikes us as an undesirable result. When a ship is arrested and held in the marshal's custody, the marshal's expenses may be taxed as costs. 28 U.S.C. § 1921(a)(1)(E). Posting substitute security to allow for the vessel's release avoids those expenses, often at a lower cost. If the plaintiff can be forced to bear the marshal's expenses when the ship remains in custody, a district court should have the discretion to award a prevailing ship owner the expenses it incurs to post substitute security allowing for the ship's release. Courts sitting in admiralty have historically awarded such costs to prevailing ship owners, *see, e.g., The South Portland*, 95 F. 295, 296 (D. Wash. 1899), but that was before the Supreme Court held that each item of a costs award must be **{-848-}** grounded on an explicit grant of statutory authority. A return to that earlier tradition seems warranted, but it will require action either by Congress or by the **[—10—]** Supreme Court pursuant to its delegated rulemaking authority under 28 U.S.C. § 1925. Until then, we do not think district courts may allow prevailing ship owners to recover as a taxable cost the expenses incurred in posting substitute security, even if a local court rule purports to authorize such an award. Accordingly, we reverse the district court's award of costs to Yang Ming.

AFFIRMED in part; REVERSED in part.

The parties shall bear their own costs on appeal.

United States Court of Appeals
for the Ninth Circuit

No. 17-55441

CRUZ
VS.
NATIONAL STEEL & SHIPBUILDING CO.

Appeal from the United States District Court for the Southern District of California

Decided: December 19, 2018

Citation: 910 F.3d 1263, 6 Adm. R. 389 (9th Cir. 2018).

Before **WARDLAW, BYBEE,** and **IKUTA,** Circuit Judges.

[—3—] {-1265-} BYBEE, Circuit Judge:

In this case we are asked to determine whether a maritime worker who has collected statutory workers' compensation for her injuries may further recover against a so-called "borrowing employer." Sira Cruz suffered injuries to her ribs and lungs while working as a tank tester aboard a Navy ship that was docked for repairs. She collected workers' compensation from her primary employer, a staffing agency. Then, she brought a negligence action against general contractor National Steel and Shipbuilding Company ("Nassco") seeking recovery for the same injuries. Nassco, which had functioned as Cruz's borrowing employer for several years at the time of the accident, asserted that it was immune from suit pursuant to the "one recovery" policy at the heart of workers' compensation law. The district court granted Nassco's motion for summary judgment on these grounds. Cruz appeals from that judgment, and we affirm. In this, we join the Third, Fourth, Fifth, and Eleventh Circuits in holding that the borrowed employee doctrine applies to **[—4—]** "employees" under the Longshore and Harbor Workers' Compensation Act ("LHWCA"), 33 U.S.C. §§ 901–50.

I

Except where noted, Cruz and Nassco have stipulated to the following facts. **{-1266-}**

Nassco is a shipbuilding company that contracts with the U.S. government to build and repair Navy vessels. To carry out this work, Nassco also contracts with labor brokers, including Tradesmen International, Inc. ("Tradesmen"), for temporary personnel. The contract between Nassco and Tradesmen granted Nassco significant control over the temporary employees Tradesmen assigned to Nassco. Nassco could terminate the temporary employees at any time, Tradesmen was required to provide Nassco notice if a temporary employee resigned, and temporary employees needed to seek approval for vacation time from Nassco. Tradesmen employees assigned to Nassco received a badge bearing both companies' names enabling them to access Nassco job sites. These employees attended daily meetings led by Nassco employees who discussed task assignments. Tradesmen provided some general safety training to employees, but Nassco trained these employees on how to perform shipbuilding and ship repair roles, including "fire watch" and "tank tester." Tradesmen invoiced Nassco for its employees' services at a rate agreed upon between the companies, and Tradesmen then paid its employees a separately agreed-upon hourly rate. The contract also required Tradesmen to obtain workers' compensation coverage for each employee pursuant to the Longshore and Harbor Workers' Compensation Act ("LHWCA"). **[—5—]**

Sira Cruz, a Tradesmen employee assigned to Nassco, was injured while conducting repair work on the *USS Makin Island*—a Nassco work site—on February 20, 2013. Prior to working for Tradesmen, Cruz had worked at another temporary staffing agency and did some work at Nassco on behalf of that agency. Cruz began her work for Tradesmen in October 2010. In the two years immediately preceding her injury Tradesmen assigned Cruz to work exclusively for Nassco, with the exception of one week where it assigned her to work for another Tradesmen client. In support of its motion for summary judgment, Nassco submitted an August 16, 2016 screenshot of Cruz's Facebook profile, where she listed her employer as "Nasco" [sic] from March 2008 to the present.

Cruz started her work for Tradesmen at Nassco as a fire watch. She later asked a Nassco employee to move her to the position of tank tester. After many conversations with Nassco employees about this move, Nassco informed Cruz she would become a tank tester. Cruz learned how to test tanks on the job with instructions from another Nassco employee. She has stipulated that she would not have otherwise known how to do the work because Tradesmen did not provide her with tank-testing training. Cruz attended meetings led by Nassco employees each morning, and some of her work clothing had Nassco's name on it. However, Cruz alleges that even when Nassco gave her work assignments, she controlled the details of her work and Nassco employees did not supervise or direct her.

At the time of her injury on February 20, 2013, Cruz had worked as a tank tester for at least six months on approximately eight different ships that Nassco was repairing. On that day, Nassco employees instructed her to work in a **[—6—]** tank on the *USS Makin Island*. Cruz fell through an access hole in the tank while descending a ladder and suffered rib fractures and a collapsed lung.

Cruz collected LHWCA benefits from Tradesmen, which had obtained LHWCA insurance coverage for her in accordance with its contract with Nassco. She then filed a complaint in admiralty in the Central District of California alleging, among other charges, that Nassco's negligence **{-1267-}** caused her injuries. Nassco moved for summary judgment. It argued that it was immune from suit in tort under the LHWCA's single-recovery provisions. The district court granted summary judgment, holding that "as a matter of law[] . . . Cruz was Nassco's borrowed employee and is barred from suing her employer under [the LHWCA]." Cruz now appeals this judgment.

II

The district court had original jurisdiction over this suit in admiralty, 28 U.S.C. § 1333, and we have appellate jurisdiction to review the district court's final decision on the merits, 28 U.S.C. § 1291. We review the district court's grant of summary judgment de novo. *Bravo v. City of Santa Maria*, 665 F.3d 1076, 1083 (9th Cir. 2011). Viewing the evidence in the light most favorable to the nonmoving party, we consider whether there are any genuine issues of material fact and whether the district court correctly applied the relevant substantive law. *Frudden v. Pilling*, 877 F.3d 821, 828 (9th Cir. 2017). **[—7—]**

A

The district court correctly found no genuine issue of material fact and ruled as a matter of law that Nassco was immune from Cruz's tort claims under the LHWCA, 33 U.S.C. §§ 901–50. Enacted in 1927, the LHWCA establishes a mandatory framework for compensation of maritime employees injured on the navigable waters of the United States. A 1972 revision to the statute expanded its coverage to injuries suffered in "any . . . adjoining area customarily used by an employer in loading, unloading, [or] repairing . . . a vessel." LHWCA Amendments of 1972, Pub. L. No. 92-576, § 2(c), 86 Stat. 1251, 1251 (codified as amended at 33 U.S.C. § 903(a)). When a covered employee is injured, the employer is liable regardless of fault. 33 U.S.C. § 904(b). A general contractor is liable to the employee of a subcontractor only where the subcontractor fails to procure workers' compensation insurance or otherwise fails to pay compensation. *See id.* § 905(a).

An injured employee may file a claim for workers' compensation benefits with the Office of Workers' Compensation Programs, which has sole authority to investigate the claim and hold a hearing, and must either reject the claim or make an award. *Id.* § 919; 20 C.F.R. § 1.2(e). The LHWCA fixes the amount of compensation based on the nature and extent of the injury and the employee's weekly pay rate. *See* 33 U.S.C. §§ 906, 908–10.

When the LHWCA applies, its remedy is "exclusive and in place of all other liability of [the] employer to the employee." *Id.* § 905(a); *see Figueroa v. Campbell Indus.*, 45 F.3d 311, 314–15 (9th Cir. 1995) (applying the LHWCA's one-recovery rule). The Supreme Court described the **[—8—]** LHWCA's compensation scheme as a quid pro quo: "In return for the guarantee of compensation, the employees surrender common-law remedies against their employers for work-related injuries." *Wash. Metro. Area Transit Auth. v. Johnson*, 467 U.S. 925, 931 (1984) (*superseded on other grounds by statute*, LHWCA Amendments of 1984, Pub. L. No. 98-426, 98 Stat. 1639). An employer is thus immune from any suit seeking further recovery for the same injury. *See id.*

Tradesmen, which paid Cruz's LHWCA claim, was Cruz's contractual employer at the time of her injury. However, the district court held that Nassco was legally Cruz's employer at this time under the borrowed employee doctrine and thus was **{–1268–}** entitled to assert the defense of LHWCA immunity.

B

We have long recognized the borrowed employee—traditionally, "borrowed servant" or "loaned servant"—doctrine. *Parker v. Joe Lujan Enters., Inc.*, 848 F.2d 118, 120 (9th Cir. 1988); *United States v. Bissett-Berman Corp.*, 481 F.2d 764, 772 (9th Cir. 1973); *McCollum v. Smith*, 339 F.2d 348, 351–52 (9th Cir. 1964). "When one person puts his [employee] at the disposal and under the control of another for the performance of a particular service . . . [the employee] is to be dealt with as [that] of the latter and not of the former." *Denton v. Yazoo & Miss. Valley R.R. Co.*, 284 U.S. 305, 308 (1932). The relationship between a borrowing employer and borrowed employee carries "all the legal consequences" of a conventional employer-employee relationship. *See id.* (quoting *Standard Oil Co. v. Anderson*, 212 U.S. 215, 220 (1909)). "[A]uthoritative direction and **[—9—]** control" are the "critical factors" by which we resolve a borrowed employee inquiry. *Parker*, 848 F.2d at 120 (citing *McCollum*, 339 F.2d at 351); *see United States v. N.A. Degerstrom, Inc.*, 408 F.2d 1130, 1133 (9th Cir. 1969) ("The critical factual inquiry in determining whether the loaned-servant doctrine should be applied is the location of the power to control the servant. . . . [R]esponsibility is regarded as a correlative of power." (quoting *McCollum*, 339 F.2d at 351)); *see also Wolsiffer v. Atlantis Submarines, Inc.*, 848 F. Supp. 1489, 1495 (D. Haw. 1994) (applying *McCollum* and also considering "whether there was a written agreement by the employers regarding the loan of the employee, who paid the employee's wages and benefits, whether the employee assented to the transfer, and the length of time of the employment").

Here, the record establishes that Nassco was Cruz's borrowing employer because her work was subject to its direction and control at all relevant times. Cruz had been "loaned" from Tradesmen to Nassco for two nearly uninterrupted years prior to her injury, and she had worked for Nassco prior to that while she was affiliated with a different temporary staffing agency. Cruz attended daily morning meetings at which Nassco employees gave her tasks to perform. On site, she wore an ID badge identifying her as a Nassco employee. Cruz became a tank tester, the job she performed on the day of her injury and for the six months prior, only because she asked a Nassco employee to promote her to the position and because another Nassco employee trained her. Conversely, Tradesmen provided her with no training or direction on how to perform this job. Nassco had the authority to terminate Cruz's temporary employment at any time, and Cruz had to seek Nassco's approval for vacation time. On the day before her injury, Nassco **[—10—]** employees instructed Cruz to work in the tank where she was injured.

Cruz presents no compelling argument that she was not subject to Nassco's direction and control. Although she remained on the payroll of Tradesmen, payroll status is not dispositive in borrowed employee inquiries. *See N.A. Degerstrom*, 408 F.2d at 1132–33 (affirming a district court's holding that a loader operator was the borrowed employee of the government despite being on the payroll of the plaintiff company). Her signed declaration that she subjectively considered herself a Tradesmen employee is insufficient to put the matter in controversy: the borrowed employee inquiry is objective; and this declaration made for litigation purposes contradicts Cruz's personal Facebook profile, **{–1269–}** where she listed "Nasco" [sic] as her employer from March

2008 until at least August 2016. Finally, Cruz's assertion that she "sometimes worked in the Tradesmen office" is immaterial to our conclusion that Nassco functioned as her borrowing employer while she was performing repairs on the *USS Makin Island*.

C

We next review the district court's conclusion that Nassco, as a borrowing employer, was entitled to the same immunity as a conventional employer under the LHWCA. Until now, we have never directly addressed this question. *See Burnette v. Sierra Nev. Corp.*, No. 2:14-cv-2761, 2015 WL 5475262 at *6 (D. Ariz. Sept. 18, 2015) (commenting on the lack of Ninth Circuit precedent). We now expressly hold that a borrowed employee is an "employee" and a borrowing employer is an "employer" for purposes of the LHWCA, and accordingly, a borrowed employee who has been fully **[—11—]** compensated under the LHWCA by any party has no further remedy for the same injury against her borrowing employer.

Sound construction of the LHWCA compels this conclusion. Congress enacted the statute's current definition of the term "employee" in 1984. LHWCA Amendments of 1984, Pub. L. No. 98-426, § 2, 98 Stat. 1639, 1639 (codified as amended at 33 U.S.C. § 902(3)). An "employee," for purposes of the statute, is "any person engaged in maritime employment . . . including a ship repairman," but excluding eight enumerated categories of individuals. 33 U.S.C. § 902(3). Those Congress excluded from employee status include, among others, secretarial and marina personnel, certain types of laborers on small vessels, and "individuals who (i) are employed by suppliers, transporters, or vendors, (ii) are temporarily doing business on the premises of an employer . . . and (iii) are not engaged in work normally performed by employees of that employer . . . ." *Id.* § 902(3)(A)–(H).

Borrowed employees are not among the eight categories of laborers Congress chose to categorically exclude from coverage in § 902(3). Moreover, § 902(3)(D)'s exclusion of individuals (i) employed by suppliers, transporters, or vendors, (ii) temporarily doing business on the premises of an employer, and (iii) not engaged in work normally performed by employees of the employer further supports our conclusion. Section 902(3)(D) excludes only a narrow subset of borrowed employees: those who perform work for the borrowing employer distinct from the type of work that **[—12—]** employer's conventional employees perform.[1] This precise language reflects a policy decision by Congress to exclude some borrowed employees—but not all. *See also id.* § 905(a) (describing the conditions under which a subcontractor's employees will be deemed employees of the contractor).

We may assume that Congress understood in 1984 that the Supreme Court had long recognized the borrowed employee doctrine and that the statute's definitions thus reflect this understanding. *Denton*, 284 U.S. at 308; *see Merck & Co. v. Reynolds*, 559 U.S. 633, 648 (2010) ("We normally assume that, when Congress enacts statutes, it is aware of relevant judicial precedent."); *Miranda B. v. Kitzhaber*, 328 F.3d 1181, 1189 (9th Cir. 2003) ("Congress is presumed to know the law and to have incorporated judicial interpretations when adopting a preexisting remedial scheme . . . ."). Thus, applying the well-recognized canon of *expressio unius est* **{-1270-}** *exclusio alterius*, we conclude that the LHWCA reaches borrowed employees who otherwise fall within Congress's definition of "employee." *See Andrus v. Glover Constr. Co.*, 446 U.S. 608, 616–17 (1980) ("Where Congress explicitly enumerates certain exceptions to a general prohibition, additional exceptions are not to be implied, in the absence of evidence of a contrary legislative intent.").

Our conclusion places us in agreement with the other circuits to address this question. *See Langfitt v. Fed. Marine Terminals, Inc.*, 647 F.3d 1116, 1124 (11th Cir. 2011); *White v. Bethlehem Steel Corp.*, 222 F.3d 146, 149 (4th Cir. 2000); **[—13—]** *Peter v. Hess Oil Virgin Islands Corp.*, 903 F.2d 935, 940 (3d Cir. 1990); *Gaudet v. Exxon Corp.*, 562 F.2d 351, 355 (5th Cir. 1977). It is also consistent with

[1] Cruz, who performed the same type of work on the *USS Makin Island* as Nassco employees, does not argue that she qualifies for this exclusion.

the broader body of workers' compensation law. Borrowing employers are generally immune from borrowed employees' tort suits under various other workers' compensation schemes. *See* 1 Modern Workers Compensation § 103:30 (compiling state and federal statutes and cases to conclude that "[e]xcept when the loaned servant doctrine has been abrogated for this purpose, the loaned employee cannot maintain a tort action against the borrowing employer, even if the borrowing employer does not provide workers' compensation benefits to the loaned employee." (citations omitted)).

III

Cruz's remaining arguments are without merit. She alleges that Nassco waived its right to assert that she was its borrowed employee through its contract with Tradesmen, citing two vague provisions of the contract which do not address the borrowed employee doctrine. Under California law,[2] "waiver is the *intentional* relinquishment of a known right *after knowledge* of the facts." *Waller v. Truck Ins. Exch., Inc.*, 900 P.2d 619, 636 (Cal. 1995) (emphasis added) **[—14—]** (internal quotation marks and citation omitted). Cruz bears the burden to "prove [waiver] by clear and convincing evidence that does not leave the matter to speculation," and we resolve doubtful cases against the party asserting waiver. *Id.* She has not met this burden. Nothing in the contract suggests Nassco intentionally waived its right to assert the borrowed employee doctrine, and even so, a contract cannot alter the truth of an employment relationship by placing parties in different positions from those they actually held. *See Kowalski v. Shell Oil Co.*, 588 P.2d 811, 816 (Cal. 1979) (en banc) (citing *Martin v. Phillips Petroleum Co.*, 117 Cal. Rptr. 269, 271 (Ct. App. 1974)).

Cruz also argues that the district court improperly allowed Nassco to join another defendant's motion for summary judgment. This argument is irrelevant because Nassco filed its own motion for summary judgment—in which it asserted the defense of immunity under the LHWCA—and we may affirm the district court's grant of summary judgment on any ground supported by the record. **{–1271–}** *Campidoglio LLC v. Wells Fargo & Co.*, 870 F.3d 963, 973 (9th Cir. 2017).

IV

The LHWCA provides maritime employees one guaranteed recovery for covered injuries. Cruz received her recovery, and the district court was correct to preclude her from pursuing a second. For these reasons, the judgment of the district court is **AFFIRMED**.

---

[2] We interpret the agreement between Nassco and Tradesmen according to California contract law. As a general contract principle, the law of the situs state applies. *See Thompson v. Enomoto*, 915 F.2d 1383, 1388 (9th Cir. 1990). State law may apply in an admiralty case so long as it merely supplements federal maritime law and does not deprive a party of substantive admiralty rights. *Pope & Talbot v. Hawn*, 346 U.S. 406, 409–10 (1953). Waiver does not disrupt any admiralty right, and we have previously considered claims of contractual waiver while sitting in admiralty. *Dant & Russell, Inc. v. Dillingham Tug & Barge Corp.*, 895 F.2d 507, 511 (9th Cir. 1989).

This page intentionally left blank

United States Court of Appeals for the Tenth Circuit

United States Court of Appeals
for the Tenth Circuit

No. 17-1050

STRAUB
VS.
BNSF RY. CO.

Appeal from the United States District Court for the District of Colorado

Decided: December 3, 2018

Citation: 909 F.3d 1280, 6 Adm. R. 396 (10th Cir. 2018).

Before **BACHARACH, MURPHY,** and **MCHUGH,** Circuit Judges.

[—1—] {-1282-} MURPHY, Circuit Judge:

I. INTRODUCTION

George Straub, an employee of BNSF Railway Company ("BNSF"), injured his back and neck when, in the course and scope of his duties, he attempted to adjust the engineer's chair of Locomotive #6295. Straub brought suit, asserting **[—2—]** BNSF was, inter alia, strictly liable for his injuries under the provisions of the Federal Locomotive Inspection Act ("LIA"), 49 U.S.C. § 20701–20703, and its implementing regulations, 49 C.F.R. pt. 229. Upon BNSF's Fed. R. Civ. P. 12(b)(6) motion to dismiss, the district court concluded Straub's injuries did not implicate LIA. The district court ruled the adjustment mechanism of the engineer's seat was not an "integral or essential part of a completed locomotive." *Cf. S. Ry. Co. v. Lunsford*, 297 U.S. 398, 402 (1936) (describing the parts of a locomotive that are covered by LIA). Instead, according to the district court, the seat adjustment mechanism was a non-essential comfort device. In reaching this conclusion, the district court relied on this court's decision in *King v. Southern Pacific Transportation Co.*, 855 F.2d 1485, 1488–89 (10th Cir. 1988). Straub appeals, asserting the district court's reliance on *King* is misplaced. Exercising jurisdiction pursuant to 28 U.S.C. § 1291, this court **reverses** and **remands** the matter to the district court for further proceedings consistent with this opinion.

II. BACKGROUND

A. General Legal Background

Congress enacted the Federal Employers' Liability Act ("FELA"), 45 U.S.C. §§ 51–60, after it determined the railroad industry owed a duty to its employees who daily expose themselves to extreme hazards.[1] FELA provides that **[—3—]** "[e]very common carrier by railroad . . . shall be liable in damages to any person suffering injury while he is employed by such carrier . . . for such injury or death resulting in whole or in part from the negligence of any of the officers, agents, or employees of such carrier." *Id.* § 51. "[T]he general congressional intent was to provide liberal recovery for injured workers." **{-1283-}** *Kernan v. Am. Dredging Co.*, 355 U.S. 426, 432 (1958). Thus, FELA does "away with several common-law tort defenses that had effectively barred recovery by injured workers." *Consol. Rail Corp. v. Gottshall*, 512 U.S. 532, 542–43 (1994) (noting FELA rejects the doctrine of contributory negligence, prohibits employers from exempting themselves from coverage via contract, and abolishes the defense of assumption of risk). Given that Congress intended FELA to be a broad, remedial statute, the Supreme Court has adopted a standard of liberal construction to facilitate Congress's objective of compensating railroad workers who are injured on the job. *See, e.g., id.* at 543; *CSX Transp., Inc. v. McBride*, 564 U.S. 685, 691–92, 695 (2011). **[—4—]**

LIA is an amendment to FELA and the two statutes are to be construed together. *See Urie*

[1] *See Consol. Rail Corp. v. Gottshall*, 512 U.S. 532, 542–43 (1994)

(continued...) **[—3—]**

(...continued)

("[W]hen Congress enacted FELA in 1908, its attention was focused primarily upon injuries and death resulting from accidents on interstate railroads. Cognizant of the physical dangers of railroading that resulted in the death or maiming of thousands of workers every year, Congress crafted a federal remedy that shifted part of the human overhead of doing business from employees to their employers." (quotations and citations omitted)).

v. Thompson, 337 U.S. 163, 189 (1949).[2] LIA makes it unlawful for a carrier to use any locomotive on its railway lines unless the locomotive and its "parts and appurtenances are safe to operate." 49 U.S.C. § 20701(1).[3] As is true of FELA, LIA must be construed liberally to carry out its remedial and humanitarian purposes. *Urie*, 337 U.S. at 189, 191; *see also Garcia v. Burlington N. R.R. Co.*, 818 F.2d 713, 715 (10th Cir. 1987) (holding that because LIA is "a remedial statute, it should be construed liberally to protect railroad workers against harm caused by defective railroad equipment"). The remedial purposes of FELA and LIA are promoted through the imposition of different types of liability. Unlike FELA, where proof of negligence is required, **[—5—]** LIA imposes on railroad carriers an absolute duty to maintain the locomotive in proper condition and safe to operate. 49 U.S.C. § 20701; *Lilly v. Grand Trunk W. R.R.* Co., 317 U.S. 481, 485 (1943); *Matson v. Burlington N. Santa Fe R.R.*, 240 F.3d 1233, 1235 (10th Cir. 2001). Even if a railroad carrier complies with every regulation promulgated by the Federal Railroad Administration ("FRA"),[4] it will still violate LIA if a locomotive is not in proper condition and safe to operate without unnecessary danger of injury. *Lilly*, 317 U.S. at 485–86.

LIA does not create a private right of action. **{-1284-}** *Urie*, 337 U.S. at 188. A railroad employee injured due to a LIA violation brings an action through FELA; a LIA violation substitutes for "negligence" in 45 U.S.C. § 51 and creates strict liability. *Id.* at 188–89 (characterizing LIA as a supplement to FELA, which "dispense[s], for the purposes of employees' suits, with the necessity of proving that violations of the safety statutes constitute negligence; and mak[es] proof of such violations . . . effective to show negligence as a matter of law"). A railroad carrier can violate LIA either by (1) breaching the broad statutory duty to keep all parts and appurtenances of its locomotives in proper condition and safe to operate without unnecessary danger of personal injury (the general statutory duty) or (2) **[—6—]** failing to comply with regulations issued by the FRA (a specific regulatory duty). *Lilly*, 317 U.S. at 485–86; *King*, 855 F.2d at 1489 & n.2; *McGinn v. Burlington N. R.R. Co.*, 102 F.3d 295, 299 (7th Cir. 1996).

B. Factual Background

The relevant facts, as set out in Straub's First Amended Complaint, are as follows. *See Peterson v. Grisham*, 594 F.3d 723, 727 (10th Cir. 2010) (holding that in the context of reviewing the grant of a Fed. R. Civ. P. 12(b)(6) motion to dismiss, this court will "accept all well-pled factual allegations as true and view these allegations in the light most favorable to the nonmoving party"). Straub was injured on September 9, 2012, while working in the course and scope of his

[2] *Urie*, as well as many other cases cited in this opinion, were decided under the provisions of the predecessor to LIA, the Federal Boiler Inspection Act ("BIA"), 45 U.S.C. § 22–34. *Urie v. Thompson*, 337 U.S. 163, 188 (1949). The provisions of BIA have been carried forward in LIA without meaningful substantive change. *See Kurns v. R.R. Friction Prods. Corp.*, 565 U.S. 625, 629 (2012). That being the case, this court will cite cases interpreting BIA and LIA interchangeably. Furthermore, in resolving this appeal, we are bound by Supreme Court decisions and Tenth Circuit precedent interpreting BIA. *See United States v. Edward J.*, 224 F.3d 1216, 1220 (10th Cir. 2000) ("Under the doctrine of stare decisis, this panel cannot overturn the decision of another panel of this court barring en banc reconsideration, a superseding contrary Supreme Court decision, or authorization of all currently active judges on the court." (quotation omitted)).

[3] LIA provides as follows: "A railroad carrier may use or allow to be used a locomotive . . . on its railroad line only when the locomotive . . . and its parts and appurtenances . . . are in proper condition and safe to operate without unnecessary danger of personal injury . . . ." 49 U.S.C. § 20701(1).

[4] The FRA is an "Operating Administration" within the Department of Transportation. 49 C.F.R. § 1.2. It is responsible for promulgating regulations to enforce the provisions of LIA. *Id.* § 1.89(a) (delegating to the FRA authority to "[c]arry out the functions and exercise the authority vested in the Secretary [of Transportation] by 49 U.S.C. Subtitle V, Part A (Safety, chapter 201 et seq.)").

employment with BNSF. On that day, Straub was assigned to work as an engineer on Locomotive #6295, a coal train originating out of Gillette, Wyoming. Just prior to departure, Straub attempted to adjust the seat assembly. The seat moved initially, and then stopped abruptly and unexpectedly, causing injury to his back and neck. Straub reported the condition of the seat to BNSF. "A Mechanical Department employee responded to the locomotive, attempted to move the seat, experienced the same problem, inspected the adjustment mechanism, and then oiled the adjustment mechanism."

The adjustment mechanism on the engineer's seat is intended to allow the engineer to move the seat forward or backward, thereby providing a safe and a comfortable position for the engineer to operate the locomotive. The defective **[—7—]** condition of the adjustment mechanism made it unsafe to operate and created a risk of injury because, among other things, the seat moved some distance then stopped unexpectedly while pressure was being applied to move the heavy engineer's seat in a bent-over position. The seat and its adjustment mechanisms are one unit, and an essential and integral part of the locomotive. Attached to the operative complaint are pictures of the engineer's chair. *See Tellabs, Inc. v. Makor Issues & Rights, Ltd.*, 551 U.S. 308, 322 (2007) ("[C]ourts must consider the complaint in its entirety, as well as other sources courts ordinarily examine when ruling on Rule 12(b)(6) motions to dismiss, in particular, documents incorporated into the complaint by reference . . . ."). Those pictures include the operating instructions for the chair's various adjustment mechanisms, which instructions are attached to the back of the engineer's chair. The operating instructions include several diagrams that explain the various functions of the engineer's chair (e.g., "lumbar horizontal adjust handle," "seat back recline adjust handle," "track fore & aft adjust handle," and "footrest height adjust pedal"). A particularly relevant set of diagrams show that the "locomotive wall mounted channel," the mechanism that allows for the adjustment of the **{-1285-}** engineer's chair forward and backward in relation to the control panel, is also the mechanism **[—8—]** which attaches the engineer's chair to the locomotive. The relevant photographs are attached to this opinion as an appendix.[5] **[—9—]**

[5] Because of the way this case proceeded through litigation, the record contains significant additional information about the engineer's chair. *See infra* Section II.C. (describing the procedural history of this case). Notably, the district court considered this information in denying, on the basis of futility, Straub's motion to file a Second Amended Complaint. *Id.*

The engineer's chair is secured and mounted to the locomotive by a wall-mounted seat adjustment mechanism (i.e., a metal channel). That is, the chair is mounted to a channel on the wall of the locomotive and suspended in the air; it does not come into contact with the locomotive's floor. The chair consists of the seat, the base of which attaches to a tripod pedestal assembly, and the footrest. The seat-footrest-tripod pedestal mechanism slides forward and backward in the channel of the seat adjustment mechanism. The seat adjustment mechanism, thus, performs several integrated functions: (1) it permits the seat to be moved forward and backward, allowing proper entry and exit; (2) it allows safe and comfortable access to the engineer's control panel for tall and short engineers; and (3) it securely fixes the seat in place during operation. BNSF admitted: (1) the adjustment mechanism is a "component on a locomotive"; (2) the adjustment mechanism is the "component that securely mounts and braces [the seat]" to the locomotive; and (3) if the seat were in proper condition, it would not have stuck when Straub attempted to operate it to move the seat backward. The BNSF mechanic who responded to Straub's report that the seat did not function properly stated the condition of the seat was such that if the maintenance he performed had not corrected the problem, the locomotive would have been taken out of service so the seat would not be used.

BNSF asserts it is inappropriate to consider this evidence in the context of reviewing a motion to dismiss. *Cf. generally Gee v. Pacheco*, 627 F.3d 1178, 1186 (10th Cir. 2010) (limiting consideration to the contents of the complaint when ruling on a Rule 12(b)(6) motion to dismiss). As noted above, however, the district court specifically considered all of this evidence in concluding any attempt by Straub to file an amended complaint would be futile (i.e., even a complaint containing this information would fail to state a valid claim). The district court's futility ruling is subject to de novo

C. Procedural Background

Straub filed this action alleging five "claims" for relief. His first "claim" for relief alleged negligence under FELA. The second "claim" alleged a violation of LIA. The third, fourth, and fifth "claims" for relief alleged violations of regulations promulgated by the FRA, 49 C.F.R. §§ 229.7 (reiterating the duties LIA imposes on railroad operators), 229.21 (imposing a duty of daily inspections on railroad operators), and 229.45 (mandating that "[a]ll systems and components on a locomotive shall be free of conditions that endanger the safety of the crew, locomotive or train).[6] BNSF moved to dismiss all four of Straub's claims that **[—10—]** relied on LIA-based **{-1286-}** strict liability. In a footnote in its motion to dismiss, BNSF stated it was unnecessary to separately analyze Straub's strict liability claims based on LIA's regulations because those regulations did nothing more than restate the standard set out in LIA itself. *See* Appellant's App. at 18 ("The Third, Fourth, and Fifth Claims for Relief are not independent claims, but merely restatements of the same general LIA standard in his second claim. Accordingly, Plaintiff's Second, Third, Fourth, and Fifth Claims state one claim for relief, and will be referred to as such in this motion."). BNSF then argued "LIA applies only to those parts and appurtenances that are (1) prescribed by a specific FRA regulation, or (2) essential or integral parts of a completed locomotive." Focusing exclusively on the "seat adjustment mechanism," it argued the mechanism is not **[—11—]** integral or essential, nor required by regulation, and Straub could not, therefore, state a valid claim for strict liability.

The district court granted BNSF's motion to dismiss. Focusing exclusively on the seat adjustment mechanism, the district court concluded it was merely for comfort and not, therefore "an integral or essential part of a completed locomotive." In reaching that

---

review. *Miller ex rel. S.M. v. Bd. of Educ.*, 565 F.3d 1232, 1249 (10th Cir. 2009) ("We ordinarily review a denial of a motion to amend a pleading for abuse of discretion. However, when

(continued...) **[—9—]**

(continued...)

denial is based on a determination that amendment would be futile, our review for abuse of discretion includes de novo review of the legal basis for the finding of futility." (citations omitted)). Given all this, BNSF's argument is not particularly convincing. This court need not resolve this issue, however, because the result in this appeal would be the same even if this court limited its consideration strictly to the four corners of Straub's First Amended Complaint.

6 Straub's complaint sets out five discrete "claims," specifically including four LIA "claims." The parties litigated the validity of Straub's LIA "claims" in district court through the lens of BNSF's motion to dismiss. On appeal, the parties continue to refer to LIA "claims." As noted above, however, LIA does not create a private cause of action. *See supra* Section II.A. It is only FELA that provides such a cause of action. *Id.* That does not mean LIA and its regulations are irrelevant. Instead, a plaintiff bringing a FELA claim is excused from the ordinary obligation to show negligence (i.e., duty and breach) if he can establish a violation of LIA. *Id.* Thus, Straub's complaint, for all practical purposes, sets out a single FELA claim with five potential theories of recovery, one based on BNSF's alleged negligence in failing to properly maintain the engineer's chair and four alternate methods of obtaining strict liability based on BNSF's asserted violations of LIA and its implementing regulations. Straub appears to have recognized as much at one point in the district court proceedings. In initial

(continued...) **[—10—]**

(continued...)

consideration of BNSF's motion to dismiss, a magistrate judge noted as follows:

> The Court notes . . . [Straub's] Claims 2-5 appear to seek recovery of damages resulting from violations of the LIA and certain regulations governed by the LIA. But, the LIA does not provide a private right of action to employees injured by defective equipment; rather, an injured employee must bring an action against his employer under [FELA]. [Straub] concedes as much in his brief responding to the present motion. Thus, while [Straub] may not seek damages under the LIA, he may cite a violation of the LIA to establish negligence per se against railroad carriers. Accordingly, the Court will construe Claims 2-5 as negligence per se theories by which [Straub] seeks to recover under the FELA (*see* Claim 1).

Appellant's App. at 113–14 (citations and footnote omitted).

conclusion, the district court relied on this court's decision in *King*, 855 F.2d at 1488–89. The district court further concluded that because no regulation required that locomotives be fitted with seat adjustment mechanisms, Straub could not state a valid claim for relief under LIA. Notably, the district court did not address in any manner Straub's contention that 49 C.F.R. § 229.7 imposed upon BNSF a duty to maintain "the entire locomotive and its appurtenances," even assuming no regulation imposed upon BNSF a duty to install the seat adjustment device in the locomotive in the first instance. Thus, it appears the district court, sub silentio, agreed with BNSF's argument that the identified regulations did not impose upon BNSF any duty beyond the general duty set out in the language of LIA itself.[7]

Thereafter, the parties conducted discovery regarding Straub's negligence-based FELA claim. During that discovery, Straub developed significant evidence **[—12—]** supporting the assertion in his First Amended Complaint that the engineer's chair and the seat adjustment mechanism were part **{-1287-}** of one, single integrated unit. *See supra* n.5. Accordingly, Straub filed a motion to file an amended complaint to include additional allegations related to that evidence. The district court denied Straub's motion on the ground that proposed amendments were futile. This was so, according to the district court, because "the relevant seat adjustment mechanism is a legally inessential element of a completed locomotive."

III. ANALYSIS

A. Standard of Review

The legal sufficiency of a complaint is a question of law and a Rule 12(b)(6) dismissal is reviewed de novo. *Moore v. Guthrie*, 438 F.3d 1036, 1039 (10th Cir. 2006). As noted above, for purposes of resolving a Rule 12(b)(6) motion, this court accepts as true all well-pleaded factual allegations in a complaint and views those allegations in the light most favorable to the plaintiff. *Id.* To withstand a motion to dismiss, a complaint must contain enough allegations of fact "to state a claim to relief that is plausible on its face." *Bell Atl. Corp. v. Twombly*, 550 U.S. 544, 570 (2007). "[A] well-pleaded complaint may proceed even if it strikes a savvy judge that actual proof of those facts is improbable . . . ." *Id.* at 556. As noted above, in evaluating the propriety of a district court's grant of a Rule 12(b)(6) motion to dismiss, we may consider not **[—13—]** only the complaint itself, but also attached exhibits. *Indus. Constructors Corp. v. U.S. Bureau of Reclamation*, 15 F.3d 963, 964–65 (10th Cir. 1994).

B. Merits

Straub argues the district court made a series of interrelated errors in granting BNSF's motion to dismiss. First, according to Straub, the district court erred when it applied LIA's "parts and appurtenances" language to a part or function of the engineer's chair—the seat adjustment mechanism—rather than to the engineer's chair itself. Second, Straub argues, the district court erred in relying on case law analyzing "failure to install" claims, when the instant case alleges a "failure to maintain." Finally, Straub asserts the district court erred when if failed to separately consider whether, even assuming the defect set out in his complaint did not fall within the general duties set out in LIA, the complaint stated a claim under the duties set out in 49 C.F.R. §§ 229.7 and 229.45 of the regulations. For the reasons set out below, this court agrees with Straub's contentions under 49 U.S.C. § 20701 and 49 C.F.R. § 229.7 and concludes the district court erred when it granted BNSF's Rule 12(b)(6) motion to dismiss.[8] **[—14—]** **{-1288-}**

---

[7] In a later order directed to BNSF's motion for summary judgment on Straub's negligence-based FELA claim, the district court concluded 49 C.F.R. § 229.45 was inapplicable to Straub's claims because the regulation "specifically enumerate[s] the specific conditions that are covered, which does not include the seat adjustment mechanism."

[8] Because Mr. Straub is able to advance his FELA claim past the motion to dismiss stage by alleging that the seat adjustment mechanism was an improperly maintained part and appurtenance of the locomotive for purposes of 49 U.S.C. § 20701 and 49 C.F.R. § 229.7, we need not determine

In concluding the facts alleged in Straub's complaint failed to state a violation of the general statutory duty to maintain a safe locomotive, the district court focused exclusively on the question whether the seat adjustment mechanism, as either a feature or fixture of the engineer's chair, was an essential or integral **[—15—]** part of a complete locomotive.[9] *See, e.g.*, District Court Order at 4 (noting BNSF's argument was that "seat adjustment mechanisms are neither an integral nor essential part of a completed locomotive"); *id.* (agreeing with BNSF's arguments); *id.* at 5 ("Therefore, in order for seat fixtures to be covered by the LIA, the fixtures themselves must be an integral or essential part of a completed locomotive."). The district court answered that abstract question in the negative. As noted above, however, Straub's complaint asserts that it was the engineer's chair that was the part or appurtenance of Locomotive #6295 not "in proper condition and safe to operate without unnecessary danger of personal injury." *See* 49 U.S.C. § 20701(1). In particular, the complaint alleges "[t]he seat and its adjustment mechanisms are one unit." Pictures of the operating instructions for the engineer's chair's various adjustment mechanisms, which instructions are attached to the back of the engineer's chair, demonstrate the plausibility, if not veracity, of this allegation.[10] The pictures contain diagrams which show that the **[—16—]** "locomotive wall mounted channel," the mechanism that allows for the adjustment of the engineer's chair forward and backward in relation to the control panel,

---

whether the seat adjustment device is also a "component" of a locomotive for purposes of 49 C.F.R. § 229.45. But we are skeptical that the seat adjustment mechanism is a "component" of the locomotive. For sure, the list of items identified as (continued...) **[—14—]**

(continued...)
"components" that shall be kept free "of conditions that endanger the safety of the crew" is a non-exhaustive list. *See Diede v. Burlington N. R.R. Co.*, 772 F.2d 593, 594 (9th Cir. 1985) (concluding list of "components" in 49 C.F.R. § 229.45 is "merely illustrative" and "not exclusive"). However, applying the *noscitur a sociis* and *ejusdem generis* canons of statutory construction, we must consider the items actually identified as "components" by the regulation when determining if an unidentified item is also a component. *Cf. Yates v. United States*, 135 S. Ct. 1074, 1085–86, 3 Adm. R. 2, 8–9 (2015) (observing that (1) "we rely on the principles of *noscitur a sociis*–a word is known by the company it keeps–to 'avoid ascribing to one word a meaning so broad that it is inconsistent with its accompanying words'" (quoting *Gustafson v. Alloyd Co, Inc..* 513 U.S. 561, 576 (1995)) and (2) "[a] canon related to *noscitur a sociis, ejusdem generis*, counsels: 'Where general words follow specific words in a statutory enumeration, the general words are usually constructed to embrace only objects similar in nature to those objects enumerated by the preceding specific words'" (quoting *Wash. State Dept. of Soc. & Health Servs. v. Guardianship Estate of Keffeler*, 537 U.S. 371, 384 (2003))). All of the items identified in § 229.45 as "components" can be found in the engine compartment, electrical system, or gearing and wheel system of the locomotive rather than in the cabin of the locomotive such that the seat adjustment mechanism at issue in this matter does not resemble the items identified as "components" in the regulation. Furthermore, were we to construe "components" so broadly as to include the seat adjustment mechanism, it is difficult to imagine what item on a locomotive would qualify as an "appurtenance" but not a "component." Yet, we must strive to interpret the regulations as a whole in a manner so as to avoid a construction that renders a portion of the regulations superfluous. *See Marx v. Gen. Revenue Corp.*, 568 U.S. 371, 385 (2013) ("[T]he canon against surplusage is strongest when an interpretation would render superfluous another part of the same statutory scheme").

[9] To be clear, in analyzing LIA, the Supreme Court has explicitly held Congress did not intend "that every gadget placed upon a locomotive by a carrier, for experimental purposes, should become part thereof within the rule of absolute liability." *S. Ry. Co. v. Lunsford*, 297 U.S. 398, 402 (1936). Instead, "[w]hatever in fact is an integral or essential part of a completed locomotive, and all parts or attachments definitely prescribed by lawful order of the [FRA], are within the statute." *Id.* For that reason, a particular piece of equipment attached to a locomotive qualifies as a part or appurtenance under LIA only if it is "an integral or essential part of a completed locomotive." *Id.*

[10] The record evidence adduced in this case while Straub's negligence-based (continued...) **[—16—]**

(continued...)
FELA claim was litigated fully supports the contention that the seat adjustment mechanism is not an independent item of locomotive equipment but is, instead, an essential and integral part of the engineer's chair. *See supra* n.4.

is also the mechanism which attaches the engineer's chair to the locomotive. Thus, it is also the mechanism that allows the chair to comply with **{-1289-}** the regulatory requirement that the chair be "securely mounted and braced" to the locomotive. 49 C.F.R. § 229.119(a).

The district court did not cite in its order, and BNSF does not identify on appeal, any authority for the proposition that it is appropriate to disregard the integrated nature of the engineer's chair and, instead, focus on its component parts in analyzing whether a complaint states a viable violation of LIA. On the other hand, there exist numerous cases focusing their LIA statutory analysis on the engineer's chair, not on its component parts. *See, e.g., Oglesby v. S. Pac. Transp. Co.*, 6 F.3d 603, 604–05 (9th Cir. 1993) (focusing analysis on engineer's chair, rather than the aspects of the chair (bent arms, tilted nature, and improperly supported backrest) that allegedly violated the statute); *Heiselmoyer v. Penn. R.R. Co.*, 243 F.2d 773, 774–76 (3d Cir. 1957) (focusing analysis on engineer's chair, rather than the chair's "back-rest"); *Munns v. CSX Transp., Inc.*, 579 F. Supp. 2d 924, 934 (N.D. Ohio 2008) ("Though failure to maintain seat padding is not a **[—17—]** claim in and of itself under the LIA, an inquiry into whether a seat was kept in good order and repair may include consideration of the seat's general condition, including whether it was properly padded."). Furthermore, the approach adopted by the district court is at odds with the remedial purposes of LIA. *Urie*, 337 U.S. at 189, 191; *Garcia*, 818 F.2d at 715. Such a reductive mode of analysis would serve only to minimize the applicability of LIA by reducing every piece of equipment on a locomotive down to its most basic component parts and, thereby, making it less likely such components are essential or integral to a completed locomotive.

Nor is the district court's analytical approach supported by this court's decision in *King*. In *King*, a railroad brakeman was injured when a locomotive collided with a cattle truck. 855 F.2d at 1487. He asserted a LIA violation on the basis that the brakeman's seat lacked armrests and seatbelts. *Id.* In response to the brakeman's suit, the railroad argued that the only requirement concerning locomotive seats was that they "be securely mounted and braced." *Id.* at 1487. The district court agreed and dismissed the brakeman's strict liability claims on the basis that such safety devices were not required by regulation. *Id.*

On the brakeman's appeal, this court began by recognizing that "a carrier cannot be held liable under [LIA] for failure to install equipment on a locomotive unless the omitted equipment (1) is required by federal regulations . . ., or (2) constitutes an integral or essential part of a completed locomotive." *Id.* at **[—18—]** 1488–89 (footnote omitted). *King* further noted that the brakeman did not assert a violation of any of LIA's implementing regulations but, instead, argued "the chair was 'unsafe' because it lacked armrests." *Id.* at 1489. Thus, *King* held that the relevant question on appeal was "whether a locomotive chair can be 'unsafe' under [LIA] if it conforms to pertinent regulations, but lacks additional safety features." *Id.* In answering this question, *King* specifically emphasized "that a locomotive or its parts and appurtenances might satisfy federal regulations and still be 'unsafe' under [LIA]." *Id.* Then, in language particularly relevant to the resolution of this appeal, *King* noted that such a situation

> occurs when the railroad fails to maintain the locomotive or its parts and appurtenances so that the locomotive cannot be operated without unnecessary peril to life or limb.[11] Such "failure to **{-1290-}** maintain" claims have been widely recognized as meritorious. However, those claims are entirely different from claims that a railroad is liable for failing to install additional safety devices which the [FRA] has not seen fit to require. Such "failure to install" claims have been rejected.

[11] Although the BIA prohibited use of a locomotive unless all its parts and appurtenances were safe to operate "without unnecessary peril to life or limb," *see Lunsford*, 297 U.S. at 400, LIA utilizes the following language: "unnecessary danger of personal injury." 49 U.S.C. § 20701(1).

Id. (footnote and citations omitted). Finally, *King* again emphasized that its holding was limited to failure to install claims and did not excuse railroad carriers from maintaining items installed on a locomotive. *Id.* at 1490 (citing to the Eight Circuit's decision in *Herold* and noting that "cases that hold the railroad liable for **[—19—]** failing to maintain or keep in place a device already placed on the locomotive are distinguishable").

While it was perfectly natural in a failure to install case to focus narrowly on the safety item that it is alleged the railroad improperly omitted from a locomotive, nothing in *King* supports the notion that courts should break down an engineer's chair into its component parts or subsidiary functions when it is alleged an already-installed engineer's chair on a locomotive was not "safe to operate without unnecessary danger of personal injury." 49 U.S.C. § 20701(1). Several courts have ruled that a railroad carrier's failure to maintain its engineer's chair in a safe condition constitutes a violation of LIA's general duty to maintain a locomotive, as well as its parts and appurtenances, in safe condition. *See Oglesby*, 6 F.3d at 610; *Clemons v. Burlington N. Santa Fe Ry.*, No. cv–15–01788, 2016 WL 10586284, at *10 (C.D. Cal. April 8, 2016); *Stevenson v. Union Pac. R.R. Co.*, No. 4:07–cv–00522, 2009 WL 129916, at *2 (E.D. Ark. Jan. 20, 2009); *Terrell v. Soo Line R.R. Co.*, No. 2:04–cv–095, 2005 WL 4882750, at *5 (S.D. Ind. Sept. 1, 2005); *Spade v. CSX Transp., Inc.*, No. 5:02–cv–129, 2004 WL 2980740, at *4 (W.D. Mich. Jan. 30, 2004); *Kleeberg v. Norfolk S. Ry. Co.*, No. 00–C–963, 2001 WL 914460, at *2 (N.D. Ill. Aug. 13, 2001). We agree with these decisions in that narrow regard and hold that the allegations set out in Straub's complaint (i.e., that the engineer's chair failed when moved initially and stopped abruptly as Straub was attempting to adjust it) state a violation of LIA. **[—20—]**

Once BNSF installed an engineer's chair with a seat adjustment mechanism, 49 U.S.C. § 20701(1) mandated that BNSF maintain the chair so that the seat adjustment device be "in proper condition and safe to operate without unnecessary danger of personal injury" and 49 C.F.R. § 229.7 mandated that BNSF maintain the chair so that the seat adjustment mechanism was "in proper condition and safe to operate in service . . . without unnecessary peril to life or limb."[12]

IV. CONCLUSION

For those reasons set out above, the order of the United States District Court for the District of Colorado granting BNSF's motion to dismiss Straub's FELA claim to the extent it depends on LIA-based **{-1291-}** strict liability is, hereby, **REVERSED**. The matter is **REMANDED** to the district court for further proceedings consistent with this opinion. **[—21—]**

APPENDIX {-1292-}

[12] In noting § 229.7 supports the conclusion that an engineer's chair is a part or appurtenance of a complete locomotive for purposes of LIA, we express no opinion as to whether the regulations would independently support sending a LIA-based strict liability claim to the jury. *See supra* n.6 (discussing nature of the "claims" in Straub's complaint). That is, it is unnecessary to decide whether the regulation could reasonably be read as imposing strict liability for the unsafe condition of all parts and appurtenances of an operating locomotive.

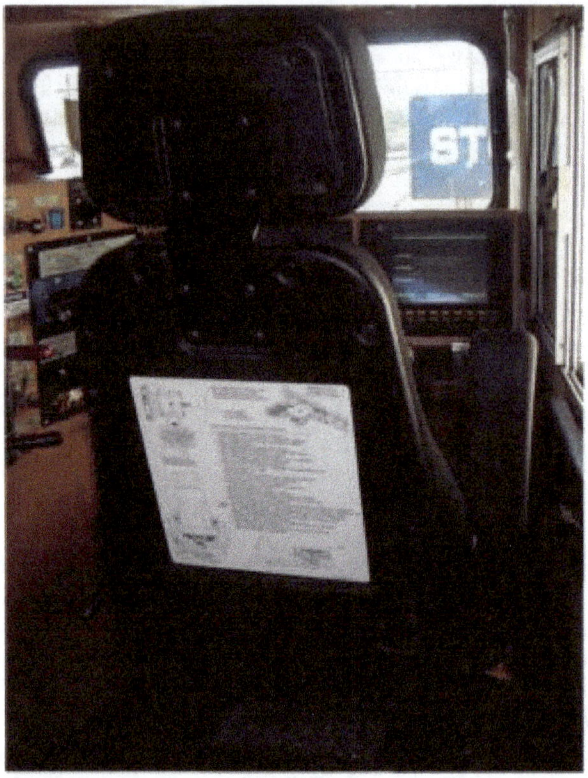

[—22—]

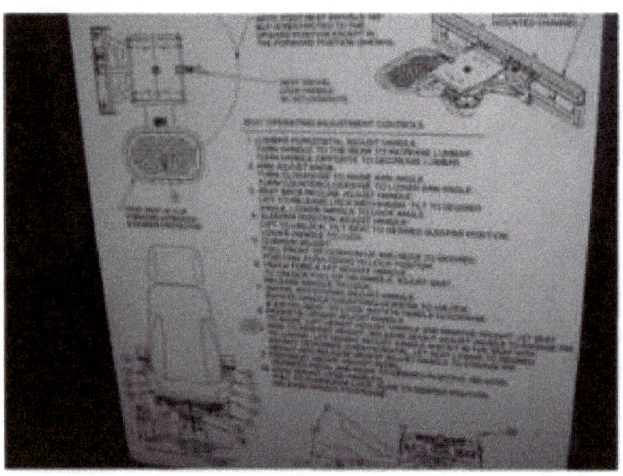

United States Court of Appeals
for the Tenth Circuit

No. 18-6003

SCHULENBERG
VS.
BNSF RY. CO.

Appeal from the United States District Court for the Western District of Oklahoma

Decided: December 27, 2018

Citation: 911 F.3d 1276, 6 Adm. R. 405 (10th Cir. 2018).

Before **MATHESON, PHILLIPS,** and **MCHUGH,** Circuit Judges.

[—1—] {-1279-} **MCHUGH,** Circuit Judge:

Terry Schulenberg, a train engineer for BNSF Railway Company, was injured when the train he was riding "bottomed out." Mr. Schulenberg filed suit against BNSF, alleging liability for negligence under the Federal Employers' Liability Act **[—2—]** (FELA), 45 U.S.C. §§ 51–60. BNSF filed motions to exclude Mr. Schulenberg's expert witness and for summary judgment, both of which the district court granted. **{-1280-}** Mr. Schulenberg appeals those decisions. We conclude the district court did not abuse its discretion in excluding the expert witness because there was no discernable methodology offered for his opinions. And we conclude the district court was correct in granting summary judgment to BNSF because Mr. Schulenberg failed to present a dispute of material fact on his sole theory of liability on appeal—negligence *per se*. Therefore, we affirm the district court.

I. BACKGROUND

On January 11, 2014, Mr. Schulenberg, along with Dewey Sutterfield, the conductor, was riding a train from Oklahoma City to Tulsa as part of his job as a locomotive engineer for BNSF. At a crossing between mileposts 485.8 and 485.5, the train hit rough track, causing the engine to "bounce[] and bottom[] out" and "hammer[]." Appellant's App. vol. I, at 172. The incident was so severe, Mr. Schulenberg testified it caused Mr. Sutterfield's water bottle to fly to the floor and almost caused Mr. Sutterfield to bounce out of his chair. Mr. Schulenberg grabbed onto the desk in front of him and braced himself with his legs and then felt a pain go down the back of his left leg and a cold sensation in his left thigh. Mr. Schulenberg continues to suffer from those feelings in his leg to this day.

At his deposition, Mr. Sutterfield testified that the incident was the worst bottoming out he had experienced in his forty-seven years riding trains for the **[—3—]** railroad. Mr. Sutterfield's statement after the incident reported the bouncing was so severe that he was bounced out of his seat.

At the time of the incident, the relevant track segment was classified as a Class 5 track under the Federal Railroad Administration (FRA) standards, permitting a maximum speed of eighty miles per hour. 49 C.F.R. § 213.9. However, BNSF had set a general internal timetable speed limit of fifty-five miles per hour for that segment. Additionally, on the day of the incident, there was a slow order in effect for that segment of track due to a report of "rough surface," lowering the speed limit to forty miles per hour. The train was traveling at thirty-eight miles per hour when the bottoming out occurred.

When the train arrived in Tulsa, Mr. Schulenberg completed a personal injury report for the incident. In response to the report, BNSF lowered the speed limit for that segment to twenty-five miles per hour and sent Lawrence Wallace to inspect the track. Mr. Wallace measured a deviation in the rail and found a deviation of 1 5/8 inches in a 62-foot chord.[1] After Mr. Wallace's inspection, BNSF raised the speed limit back to forty miles per hour.

[1] Mr. Schulenberg disputed this fact in the district court. However, on appeal, Mr. Schulenberg disputes only whether this measurement is accurate and takes the additional rail movement under load into consideration; he does not dispute that Mr. Wallace's actual static measurement was 1 5/8 inches.

Mr. Schulenberg filed three claims against BNSF: two claims alleging liability under FELA and a third claim alleging liability under the Locomotive Inspection Act. Mr. Schulenberg ultimately abandoned one of his FELA claims and his Locomotive **[—4—]** Inspection Act claim[2], leaving only his "single-event FELA negligence claim." Appellant's App. vol. III, at 168. **{-1281-}**

BNSF filed a motion to exclude the testimony of Mr. Schulenberg's expert witness, Alan Blackwell, and a motion for summary judgment on the remaining FELA claim. The district court granted the motion to exclude Mr. Blackwell's expert opinions, concluding the opinions lacked a reliable basis. Then, the district court granted summary judgment to BNSF, concluding that Mr. Schulenberg "ha[d] not submitted evidence sufficient to support an inference of negligence in the maintenance or inspection of the section of track at issue." *Id.* vol. III, at 168–72. Mr. Schulenberg appealed. Exercising jurisdiction pursuant to 28 U.S.C. § 1291, we conclude the district court did not abuse its discretion in excluding Mr. Blackwell's testimony or err in granting BNSF's motion for summary judgment. We therefore affirm.

II. DISCUSSION

On appeal, Mr. Schulenberg pursues only a theory of liability based on negligence *per se* for violation of FRA regulation 49 C.F.R. § 213.63. To put the exclusion of the expert witness and summary judgment issues in context, we begin with a brief discussion of liability under FELA and the relevant FRA regulations. **[—5—]** Next, we discuss whether the district court abused its discretion in excluding Mr. Blackwell's expert testimony. Finally, we review the district court's decision to grant summary judgment.

A. *Liability under FELA*

Mr. Schulenberg's FELA claim alleges that BNSF is liable for his injuries under 45 U.S.C. § 51. That section provides,

> Every common carrier by railroad . . . shall be liable in damages to any person suffering injury while he is employed by such carrier . . . for such injury or death resulting in whole or in part from the negligence of any of the officers, agents, or employees of such carrier, or by reason of any defect or insufficiency, due to its negligence, in its . . . track [or] roadbed . . . .

45 U.S.C. § 51. An employee can recover under FELA for the railroad's violation of a safety statute or regulation under the theory of negligence *per se*. *CSX Transp., Inc. v. McBride*, 564 U.S. 685, 703 n.12 (2011); *Straub v. BNSF Ry. Co.*, ___F.3d___, 2018 WL 6273359, at *4 n.6, 6 Adm. R. 396, 399 n.6 (10th Cir. 2018).

The FRA safety requirements are set out by "class" of track. The maximum allowable operating speed is eighty miles per hour for a Class 5 track, sixty miles per hour for a Class 4 track, and forty miles per hour for a Class 3 track. 49 C.F.R. § 213.9(a). If a segment of a track does not meet the necessary requirements for its intended class, it is reclassified as the class for which it does meet all the requirements. *Id.* § 213.9(b).

One of the safety requirements is the maximum deviation from uniform profile of the rail at the mid-ordinate of a 62-foot chord. *Id.* § 213.63. The maximum **[—6—]** allowable deviation is 1 1/4 inches for a Class 5 track, 2 inches for a Class 4 track, and 2 1/4 inches for a Class 3 track. *Id.* Importantly, when unloaded track is measured to determine compliance with these requirements, "the amount of rail movement, if any, that occurs while the track is loaded must be added to the measurements of the unloaded track." *Id.* § 213.13.

---

[2] Mr. Schulenberg labeled his cause of action as a Locomotive Inspection Act claim. However, as we have recently made clear, there is no independent private cause of action under the Locomotive Inspection Act. *Straub v. BNSF Ry. Co.*, ___F.3d ___, 2018 WL 6273359, at *4 n.6, 6 Adm. R. 396, 399 n.6 (10th Cir. Dec. 3, 2018). Instead, plaintiffs can bring FELA negligence per se claims based on violations of the Locomotive Inspection Act. *Id.*, 6 Adm. R. at 399 n.6.

Mr. Schulenberg alleges negligence *per se* based on a violation of § 213.63. Specifically, he argues Mr. Wallace's measurement of a 1 5/8 inch deviation in a 62-foot chord did not account for deflection under load, as required by § 213.13. And he contends the additional deflection under load, when added to the 1 5/8 inch static measurement, **{-1282-}** would exceed the 2 1/4 inch deviation permitted by § 213.63.

B. *Exclusion of Expert Witness*

Mr. Schulenberg submitted an expert report in support of his claim that BNSF violated § 213.63. The district court ultimately excluded the report and the expert's testimony. Mr. Schulenberg challenges that decision on appeal.

1. Standard of Review

Federal Rule of Evidence 702 "imposes on a district court a gatekeeper obligation to 'ensure that any and all scientific testimony or evidence admitted is not only relevant, but reliable.'" *Dodge v. Cotter Corp.*, 328 F.3d 1212, 1221 (10th Cir. 2003) (quoting *Daubert v. Merrell Dow Pharm., Inc.*, 509 U.S. 579, 589 (1993)). The district court has discretion in how it conducts its *Daubert* analysis, but enjoys no discretion in whether it performs such an analysis. "Accordingly, we review de novo the issue of whether the district court actually performed its gatekeeper role in the **[—7—]** first instance." *Adamscheck v. Am. Family Mut. Ins. Co.*, 818 F.3d 576, 586 (10th Cir. 2016) (internal quotation marks omitted)). But, where "the district court fulfilled its gatekeeping responsibility, [w]e then review the trial court's actual application of the standard in deciding whether to admit or exclude an expert's testimony for abuse of discretion." *Id.* (alteration in original) (internal quotation marks omitted); *see also Kumho Tire Co., Ltd. v. Carmichael*, 526 U.S. 137, 152 (1999).

Here, there is no dispute regarding the district court's performance of its gatekeeping function. Accordingly, "[t]he district court has 'wide latitude' in deciding whether to exclude expert testimony . . . ." *Hall v. Conoco Inc.*, 886 F.3d 1308, 1311 (10th Cir. 2018) (internal quotation marks omitted). In this regard, the district court abuses its discretion only if the decision "is arbitrary, capricious, whimsical or manifestly unreasonable, or when we are convinced that the district court made a clear error of judgment or exceeded the bounds of permissible choice in the circumstances." *United States v. Chapman*, 839 F.3d 1232, 1237 (10th Cir. 2016) (quotation marks omitted).

2. Rule 702 Standard

Federal Rule of Evidence 702 controls the admission of expert witness testimony. Rule 702 provides,

> A witness who is qualified as an expert by knowledge, skill, experience, training, or education may testify in the form of an opinion or otherwise if:
>
> (a) the expert's scientific, technical, or other specialized knowledge will help the trier of fact to understand the evidence or to determine a fact in issue;
> (b) the testimony is based on sufficient facts or data; **[—8—]**
> (c) the testimony is the product of reliable principles andmethods; and
> (d) the expert has reliably applied the principles and methods to the facts of the case.

Fed. R. Evid. 702.

In evaluating the admissibility of expert testimony, "the district court must satisfy itself that the proposed expert testimony is both reliable and relevant, in that it will assist the trier of fact, before permitting a jury to assess such testimony." *United States v. Nacchio*, 555 F.3d 1234, 1241 (10th Cir. 2009) (en banc) (quotation marks omitted). This requires a two-step process. First, the district court must "determine whether the expert is qualified 'by knowledge, skill, experience, training, or education' to render an opinion." *Id.* **{-1283-}** (quoting Fed. R. Evid. 702). Second, if the expert is sufficiently qualified, the district court "must determine whether the expert's opinion is reliable by assessing the underlying reasoning and methodology." *Id.* Importantly, the court is not required "to admit opinion evidence that is connected to existing data only by the *ipse dixit* of the expert. A court may conclude that there is simply too great an analytical gap between the data and the opinion proffered."[3] *Gen. Elec. Co. v. Joiner*, 522 U.S. 136, 146 (1997). **[—9—]**

3. Application to Mr. Blackwell's Testimony

BNSF "did not challenge Mr. Blackwell's qualifications in the areas of railroad track maintenance and inspections." BNSF's Br. at 17. Instead, the district court ultimately excluded Mr. Blackwell's testimony as not sufficiently reliable. Therefore, the only question on appeal is whether the district court abused its discretion in determining Mr. Blackwell's opinions were not based on reliable reasoning and methodology.

In answering that question, we begin by describing the district court's decision and rationale. Then, we explain why the district court did not abuse its discretion in excluding Mr. Blackwell's expert testimony.

a. *District court's opinion*

Mr. Blackwell filed a "lengthy" expert report "composed almost entirely of excerpts from federal railroad safety standards and various manuals." Appellant's App. vol. III, at 164. The district court found, "[t]he report made little or no effort to relate the various standards to Mr. Blackwell's conclusions." *Id.* Ultimately, the district court found Mr. Blackwell's report could be condensed to four specific opinions.

The district court concluded Mr. Blackwell should not be allowed to offer these four opinions because they "simply ignore[d] inconvenient facts," were based on evidence "so removed in time from the incident as to be essentially meaningless," and "lack[ed] the detail necessary to support [Mr. Blackwell's] conclusions." *Id.* vol. III, at 166. Additionally, the district court noted that "[Mr. Schulenberg's] response **[—10—]** to [BNSF's] motion makes virtually no effort to identify or defend Mr. Blackwell's methodology at all. Rather, [Mr. Schulenberg] relies only on Mr. Blackwell's experience in the area and his interpretation of deposition testimony from [Mr. Wallace that was] . . . taken after [Mr.] Blackwell's expert report was prepared." *Id.*

As part of Mr. Schulenberg's response to BNSF's motion to exclude Mr. Blackwell, Mr. Schulenberg attached an "addendum" to Mr. Blackwell's expert report based on the recent deposition of Mr. Wallace. Mr. Blackwell's addendum offered several additional opinions regarding BNSF's alleged failure to properly inspect and maintain the track. Most relevantly, Mr. Blackwell's addendum stated,

> Based on my specialized knowledge and experience that track deflection measurements under the running rails can substantially increase the collective deviation measurement under load, and based on BNSF Railway's knowledge that a locomotive bouncing up and down and bottoming out is an indication that there is a track surface crosslevel or profile dip defect, it is my opinion that the track surface was not in compliance with BNSF and **{-1284-}** Code of Federal Regulations Part 213.63 Track Safety Standard requirements at the time of the incident.

Id. vol. II, at 189.

The district court rejected the addendum because the opinions were "based on a forced and inaccurate characterization of what Mr. Wallace said" and the opinions were not "sufficiently reliable to be admissible when tested against" the evidentiary standards. *Id.* vol. III, at 166–67.

The district court ultimately summarized its reason for rejecting the totality of Mr. Blackwell's expert testimony: **[—11—]**

[3] "Ipse dixit" is roughly translated as "he himself said it" and refers to a dogmatic and unproven statement. *Ipse Dixit*, BLACK'S LAW DICTIONARY (10th ed. 2014).

> It is not enough to have a knowledgeable expert leap to the conclusions a party would like the jury to be exposed to. Rather, there must be a reliable and identifiable basis for the expert's opinions, grounded in the evidence and in the practices and standards of the particular discipline involved. That basis is lacking as to the proffered opinions of Mr. Blackwell.

Id. at 167.

b. *Abuse of discretion*

For purposes of appeal, Mr. Schulenberg abandons any argument that the district court improperly excluded Mr. Blackwell's specific opinions in all but one instance. But he argues the district court abused its discretion by excluding Mr. Blackwell's testimony in its entirety because Mr. Blackwell could have offered expert testimony about general safety standards. We therefore separately address whether the district court abused its discretion in excluding Mr. Blackwell's specific opinion and whether it abused its discretion in excluding his testimony in its entirety.

i. Mr. Blackwell's specific opinion

On appeal, the only specific opinion Mr. Schulenberg attempts to defend is Mr. Blackwell's conclusion that the deviation in the rail exceeded that which is permitted by 49 C.F.R. § 213.63. We conclude the trial court did not abuse its discretion in excluding this testimony. In his brief to this court, Mr. Schulenberg perpetuates the error he made in the district court: he "makes virtually no effort to identify or defend Mr. Blackwell's methodology at all." Appellant's App. vol. III, at 166. Instead, Mr. Schulenberg simply argues Mr. Blackwell should be able to "refer to FRSA regulations [in addition to] his industry experience, so long as his opinions **[—12—]** do not extend to whether [BNSF's] conduct actually violated the regulations," just as he was allowed to do in *Cowden v. BNSF Railway Co.* (*Cowden I*), No. 4:08-CV-01534-ERW, 2013 WL 5442926 (E.D. Mo. Sept. 30, 2013). Schulenberg's Br. at 43 (quoting *Cowden I*, 2013 WL 5442926, at *7). The problem with this argument is that before making this ruling, the district court in *Cowden I* had already determined Mr. Blackwell's opinions had a reliable factual foundation and used an acceptable methodology. *Cowden I*, 2013 WL 5442926, at *3–6. Here, Mr. Schulenberg has failed to identify any factual foundation or methodology behind Mr. Blackwell's opinions.

Mr. Schulenberg does not attempt to identify a methodology that supports any of Mr. Blackwell's opinions or to defend that methodology against an abuse of discretion standard. Accordingly, Mr. Schulenberg has offered nothing from which we could conclude the district court abused its discretion in excluding Mr. Blackwell's specific expert opinion.

ii. General safety and regulation testimony

The second issue is whether the district court abused its discretion in excluding Mr. Blackwell's testimony in its entirety because Mr. Blackwell could have provided **{–1285–}** general expert testimony that would "assist the jury in understanding track defects, the federal regulations[,] and BNSF standards with respect to defects and inspections, and the manner in which track is inspected." Schulenberg's Br. at 41. Specifically, Mr. Schulenberg argues that Mr. Blackwell should have been allowed to testify about **[—13—]** "the method of performing a proper inspection for deviations from uniform profile." *Id.* at 42.

As an initial matter, Mr. Schulenberg never argued to the district court that Mr. Blackwell should be permitted to provide general expert testimony on the applicable standards even if Mr. Blackwell's specific opinions were excluded. It is difficult to see how the district court's decision "is arbitrary, capricious, whimsical or manifestly unreasonable," or how we could be "convinced that the district court made a clear error of judgment or exceeded the bounds of permissible choice in the circumstances," *Chapman*, 839 F.3d at 1237 (quotation marks omitted), by failing to consider an argument with which the district court was never presented. Moreover, Mr. Schulenberg has not argued for plain error on appeal. Consequently, his claim fails for lack of preservation. *See United States v. Roach*, 896 F.3d 1185, 1192 (10th Cir. 2018) (noting that an appellant who fails to preserve an evidentiary objection must argue plain error on appeal or the argument is waived), *petition for cert. filed*, No. 18-6804 (Nov. 26, 2018).

And, even if the district court had abused its discretion in excluding Mr. Blackwell's general expert testimony, that error would be harmless. *Cf. Ho v. Michelin N. Am., Inc.*, 520 F. App'x 658, 666 (10th Cir. 2013) (applying a harmless error analysis to the exclusion of expert testimony). Mr. Schulenberg contends the proposed general expert testimony would "assist the jury in considering the adequacy of . . . the inspection performed by Mr. Wallace immediately after [Mr. Schulenberg's] injury." Schulenberg's Br. at 42. He further asserts this expert **[—14—]** testimony could help the jury conclude that Mr. Wallace failed to properly account for additional rail movement under load and that the 1 5/8 inch measurement therefore does not reflect the actual deviation of the rail in the 62-foot chord. For the reasons discussed in detail below, however, an inference that the 1 5/8 inch measurement does not account for additional deflection under load is not sufficient for Mr. Schulenberg's negligence *per se* claim to survive summary judgment. Therefore, any error in not admitting Mr. Blackwell's general standard testimony is harmless, even if Mr. Schulenberg had sought to admit it.

C. *Summary Judgment*

1. Standard of Review

We "review[] a district court's grant of summary judgment *de novo*, viewing the evidence in the light most favorable to the non-moving party." *Libertarian Party of N.M. v. Herrera*, 506 F.3d 1303, 1309 (10th Cir. 2007). Summary judgment is appropriate "if the movant shows that there is no genuine dispute as to any material fact and the movant is entitled to judgment as a matter of law." Fed. R. Civ. P. 56(a). "A party asserting that a fact cannot be or is genuinely disputed must support the assertion by: (A) citing to particular parts of materials in the record . . . ; or (B) showing that the materials cited do not establish the absence or presence of a genuine dispute, or that an adverse party cannot produce admissible evidence to support the fact." *Id.* 56(c)(1).

Where the nonmovant bears the burden of proof on an issue at trial, the movant has an "'initial responsibility of informing the district court of the basis for **[—15—] {-1286-}** its motion,' the absence of evidence establishing a fact on which the nonmovant had the burden of persuasion." *Felkins v. City of Lakewood*, 774 F.3d 647, 653 (10th Cir. 2014) (quoting *Celotex Corp. v. Catrett*, 477 U.S. 317, 323 (1986)). Importantly, "[a] movant that will not bear the burden of persuasion at trial need not negate the nonmovant's claim. Such a movant may make its prima facie demonstration simply by pointing out to the court a lack of evidence for the nonmovant on an essential element of the nonmovant's claim." *Id.* (quotation marks omitted). In response, the nonmovant bears the "burden to set forth specific facts that would be admissible in evidence in the event of trial from which a rational trier of fact could find for [him]." *Id.* (internal quotation marks omitted).

2. Standard of Proof for FELA Claims

"The standard applied by federal courts in determining whether there is sufficient evidence to send a FELA case to the jury is significantly broader than the standard applied in common law negligence actions." *Metcalfe v. Atchison, T. & S. F. Ry. Co.*, 491 F.2d 892, 895 (10th Cir. 1974). A FELA case can be taken from the jury "[o]nly when there is a complete absence of probative facts to support" the employee's claim. *Id.* (quoting *Lavender v. Kurn*, 327 U.S. 645, 653 (1946)). However, this standard must be considered against "[t]he essential requirement . . . that mere speculation be not allowed to do duty for probative facts after making due allowance for all reasonably possible inferences favoring the party whose case is attacked." *Id.* (quoting *Tennant v. Peoria & P.U. Ry. Co.*, 321 U.S. 29,

32–33 **[—16—]** (1944)).[4] Additionally, "in comparison to tort litigation at common law, 'a relaxed standard of causation applies under FELA.'" *CSX Transp.*, 564 U.S. at 692 (quoting *Consol. Rail Corp. v. Gottshall*, 512 U.S. 532, 542–43 (1994)). "Under [FELA] the test of a jury case is simply whether the proofs justify with reason the conclusion that employer negligence played any part, even the slightest, in producing the injury or death for which damages are sought." *Id.* (alteration in original) (quoting *Rogers v. Mo. Pac. R.R. Co.*, 352 U.S. 500, 506 (1957)).

3. Appropriateness of Summary Judgment

On appeal, Mr. Schulenberg's sole "theory of liability . . . is that BNSF's track violated the standards for maximum deviation from uniform profile provided for in 49 C.F.R. § 213.63." Schulenberg's Reply Br. at 1. It is undisputed that there was an internal slow order for the relevant segment of track at the time of Mr. Schulenberg's **{-1287-}** accident, reducing the speed limit to forty miles per hour. Based on the internal slow **[—17—]** order, BNSF would be required to comply with Class 3 track regulations. 49 C.F.R. § 213.9.

The district court granted summary judgment on Mr. Schulenberg's claim because BNSF's "inspection and industry maintenance records support [its] contention that the track in question complied with all necessary regulations." Appellant's App. vol. III, at 170. The district court rejected Mr. Schulenberg's argument that "the deposition testimony of the track inspector [Mr. Wallace] somehow shows that federal inspection standards were not followed." *Id.* And the district court found Mr. Schulenberg "offered no other evidence which would support an inference that the deflection/dip in the track was different from that reported by the inspector." *Id.* at 171. As a result, the district court concluded Mr. Schulenberg failed to "submit[] evidence sufficient to support an inference of negligence in the maintenance or inspections of the section of track at issue here." *Id.*at 172. Mr. Schulenberg challenges this conclusion on appeal.

We begin our analysis of whether the district court erred in granting summary judgment by reviewing the facts in the light most favorable to Mr. Schulenberg, including Mr. Schulenberg's challenges to the district court's statement of undisputed facts. Then we explain why those facts are insufficient to raise a dispute of material fact of negligence *per se*.

a. *Facts in the light most favorable to Mr. Schulenberg*

On January 9, 2014, BNSF lowered the speed limit for the relevant segment of track to forty miles per hour because of "rough surface." Appellant's App. vol. II, at **[—18—]** 180. This reduced speed limit was still in effect two days later when Mr. Schulenberg and Mr. Sutterfield rode over that segment of track on their way from Oklahoma City to Tulsa. Although they were traveling thirty-eight miles per hour—under the reduced speed limit—when the train hit rough track, the engine still "bounced and bottomed out" and "hammered."

Mr. Schulenberg testified that the bottoming out was so severe the engine bounced hard enough to knock Mr. Sutterfield's water bottle on the floor and almost caused Mr. Sutterfield to bounce out of

[4] Mr. Schulenberg cites *Metcalf v. Atchison, T. & S. F. Ry. Co.*, 491 F.2d 892 (10th Cir. 1974), and a series of cases from other circuits that establish the lower standard for FELA cases. BNSF argues Mr. Schulenberg waived these standards by failing to raise the specific language (and the cases) in the district court. But Mr. Schulenberg's brief to the district court stated that "a party moving for the equivalent of summary judgment in a FELA case should not prevail if there is even a minimum amount of evidence in the non-moving party's favor" and he cited cases in support of that standard. Appellant's App. vol. II, at 161. While we will not consider issues raised for the first time on appeal—whether "a bald-faced new issue or a new theory . . . that falls under the same general category as an argument presented at trial," *McDonald v. Kinder-Morgan, Inc.*, 287 F.3d 992, 999 (10th Cir. 2002) (internal quotation marks omitted)—Mr. Schulenberg is "simply offer[ing] new legal authority for the position that he . . . advanced before the district court," *United States v. Rapone*, 131 F.3d 188, 196 (D.C. Cir. 1997).

his chair.[5] Additionally, Mr. Sutterfield testified it was the worst bottoming out he has experienced in his forty-seven years working for the railroad.

After Mr. Schulenberg reported the incident, BNSF sent Mr. Wallace to inspect the track. Mr. Wallace measured a deflection and found a deviation in the rail of 1 5/8 inches in a 62-foot chord.

Mr. Schulenberg argues that he raised a dispute of material fact regarding whether Mr. Wallace's measurement took into account the additional deflection under load—a contention the district court rejected. In particular, Mr. Schulenberg relies on Mr. Wallace's deposition testimony as support for his position the load was not included in the measurement.

At Mr. Wallace's deposition, taken three years after the incident, he had no independent recollection of his inspection of the track after Mr. Schulenberg's **[—19—]** accident. Instead, Mr. Wallace testified as to his general practice for measuring a deviation of a rail in a 62-foot chord. Mr. Schulenberg argues that portions of Mr. Wallace's deposition testimony support an inference that Mr. Wallace failed to account for additional **{–1288–}** deflection under load when measuring the deviation in the rail. Ultimately, we need not decide whether the ambiguities in Mr. Wallace's deposition testimony create a dispute of fact regarding whether the 1 5/8 inch measurement included the deflection under load because, as we now explain, even granting Mr. Schulenberg that inference, he cannot survive summary judgment.[6] **[—20—]**

b. *Mr. Schulenberg's ability to show negligence* per se

Because Mr. Schulenberg bears the burden of proving BNSF was negligent *per se* based on a violation of the 2 1/4 inch deviation standard in 49 C.F.R. § 213.63, BNSF can prevail on summary judgment by establishing that Mr. Schulenberg "cannot produce admissible evidence to support the fact." Fed. R. Civ. P. 56(c)(1)(B). Mr. Schulenberg claims he has raised a dispute of material fact by pointing to Mr. Schulenberg's and Mr. Sutterfield's deposition testimony about the severity of the bottoming out incident and Mr. Wallace's failure to take proper measurements after the incident. Under the facts of this case, we disagree.

Based on Mr. Schulenberg's and Mr. Sutterfield's testimony, Mr. Schulenberg has raised at least a dispute of fact that the bottoming out incident was severe in comparison to other incidents those two men previously encountered. Additionally, as discussed above, we assume without deciding that Mr. Schulenberg has raised a dispute of

[5] Mr. Sutterfield's statement after the incident said he was bounced out of his seat.

[6] Mr. Schulenberg also argues that BNSF's reliance on the deposition of Roger Honeycutt is improper because Mr. Honeycutt lacked personal knowledge of the subject information. Similarly, Mr. Schulenberg contends the inspection report showing a deviation of 1 5/8 inches was not based on first-hand knowledge because it was completed by James Sadler with information supplied to him by Mr. Wallace. These arguments are unpreserved—while Mr. Schulenberg did assert the inspection report was based on hearsay, he did not make a personal knowledge challenge to the inspection report or Mr. Honeycutt's declaration. Therefore, in the absence of any claim of plain error, we will not consider these arguments on appeal. *See United States v. Roach*, 896 F.3d 1185, 1192 (10th Cir. 2018), *petition for cert. filed*, No. 18-6804 (Nov. 26, 2018).

Additionally, Mr. Schulenberg's challenge to this evidence does not create a dispute of material fact. "'[A] complete failure of proof concerning an essential element of the nonmoving party's case necessarily renders all other facts immaterial' and entitles the movant to judgment as a matter of law." *Digital Ally, Inc. v. Util. Assocs., Inc.*, 882 F.3d 974, 977 (10th Cir. 2018) (quoting *Celotex Corp. v. Catrett*, 477 U.S. 317, 322–23 (1986)). As discussed in the text, irrespective of Mr. Honeycutt's declaration and with the benefit of the deviation shown in the inspection report, Mr. Schulenberg has not put forth sufficient material facts to survive summary judgment. If we were to grant Mr. Schulenberg's challenge to the inspection report, Mr. Schulenberg would be in a worse position—asking the jury to infer a 2 1/4 inch deviation under load without the benefit of the measurement in the report, rather than asking the jury to infer there is an additional 5/8 inch deviation under load.

material fact that Mr. Wallace's 1 5/8 inch deviation measurement did not account for the track under load. Mr. Schulenberg argues that the combination of these facts is enough to survive summary judgment: "Taken with the description of the incident by [Mr. Schulenberg] and [Mr.] Sutterfield," Mr. Wallace's failure to properly measure the dip "leads to [the] inference that the dip was substantially greater [than] 1 5/8 inches and would permit a reasonable jury to conclude that the track at the time [Mr. Schulenberg] was injured was in violation of the maximum amount of deviation from 'uniform profile'" allowed by 49 C.F.R. § 263.13 (a). Schulenberg's Br. at 34–35. **[—21—]**

In support of this argument, Mr. Schulenberg cites to a district court case reaching a similar conclusion: **{-1289-}** *Cowden v. BNSF Ry. Co.* (*Cowden II*), 975 F. Supp. 2d 1005 (E.D. Mo. 2013). In *Cowden II*, the railroad inspector measured the rail deviation within the 62-foot chord at 2 1/4 inches—the exact deviation allowed by 49 C.F.R. § 213.63 for the Class 3 track at issue in that case. 975 F. Supp. 2d at 1016–17. The district court found the plaintiff had raised a genuine issue of material fact because "a reasonable jury could conclude that [the inspector's] measurements failed to account for potential deflection" and that based upon the expert's report, "a reasonable jury could conclude that the measurements would not have complied with § 213.63 if [the inspector] had taken deflection into account." *Id.* at 1018. In relevant part, the expert's opinion stated that if the inspector had measured the track under load, it would have certainly been greater than the 2 1/4 inch deviation measured not under load. *Id.* That is, deviation under load is greater than deviation when the track is not under load.

There are two significant differences between *Cowden II* and this case. First, the district court there held the expert's report satisfied Rule 702. *Id.* Second, and more importantly, the measurement taken when the track was not under load was the *exact* total deviation allowed for the track. *Id.* at 1016–17. Therefore, as long as the jury could reasonable infer that there is *any* additional deflection under load, the jury could also reasonably conclude the track did not meet the § 213.63 standards.

Such is not the case here. Mr. Wallace measured the deviation at 1 5/8 inches. Even assuming, as Mr. Schulenberg argues, this measurement did not include the **[—22—]** deflection under load, he must still come forward with evidence from which the jury could find the deviation under load was greater than 2 1/4 inches. The only evidence Mr. Schulenberg raises in support of that conclusion is the testimony about the relative severity of the bottoming out incident. Essentially, Mr. Schulenberg contends the jury could reasonably infer that the severity of the bottoming out shows the additional deviation under load exceeded 5/8 of an inch. We are not persuaded such an inference would be reasonable; to reach a conclusion as to the precise deflection under load, the jury would be forced to speculate.

"A long line of FELA cases reiterate the lesson that the statute vests the jury with broad discretion to engage in common sense inferences regarding issues of causation and fault." *Harbin v. Burlington N. R.R. Co.*, 921 F.2d 129, 132 (7th Cir. 1990). But "FELA claims, like common law negligence claims, must be supported by expert testimony where they involve issues . . . beyond the common experience and understanding of the average jury." *In re Amtrak "Sunset Ltd." Train Crash in Bayou Canot, Ala., on Sept. 22, 1993*, 188 F. Supp. 2d 1341, 1349 (S.D. Ala. 1999).

Mr. Schulenberg is not asking the jury to make "common sense inferences." From the anecdotal testimony about the severity of the bottoming out, Mr. Schulenberg expects the jury to infer (1) the severity of the bottoming out was caused by a deviation in the rail in a 62-foot chord measurement and (2) the severity of the bottoming out shows that the additional deviation under load exceeded 5/8 of an inch. But there is no evidence in the record establishing the relative severity of the bottoming out incident compared to the severity of other incidents where the **[—23—]** deflection under load was measured. Indeed, there is no evidence tying Mr. Sutterfield's past bottoming out experiences with a deviation in the rail in a 62-foot chord at all. Thus, there is no evidence from which the jury could infer that his prior bottoming out experiences were related to such a deviation, let alone that his past experiences had any **{–1290–}** bearing on whether this incident was caused by such a deviation. While a jury might make a common sense inference that there is *some* additional deviation in the rail in a 62-foot chord when the track is under load, there is no evidence from which a jury could reasonably infer that the additional deviation in this case exceeded 5/8 of an inch. Nor is the additional deviation under load within "the common experience and understanding of the average jury."

"[M]ere speculation [will] be not allowed to do duty for probative facts." *Metcalf*, 491 F.2d at 895 (quoting *Tennant*, 321 U.S. at 32–33). The anecdotal severity of the bottoming out incident does not supply the probative facts necessary to find that the additional deviation under load would have exceeded 5/8 of an inch without engaging in mere speculation. As a result, there is a "lack of evidence for [Mr. Schulenberg] on an essential element of [his] claim," *Felkins*, 774 F.3d at 653 (quotation marks omitted), and BNSF is entitled to judgment as a matter of law.

III. CONCLUSION

The district court did not abuse its discretion in excluding Mr. Blackwell as an expert witness. The district court also correctly granted summary judgment for BNSF because Mr. Schulenberg failed to present evidence from which the jury could find, **[—24—]** without speculation, that the track had a deviation of more than 2 1/4 inches in a 62-foot chord. Therefore, we AFFIRM the district court's rulings.

United States Court of Appeals for the Eleventh Circuit

United States Court of Appeals
for the Eleventh Circuit

No. 16-10261

UNITED STATES
vs.
MOSQUERA

Appeal from the United States District Court for the Middle District of Florida

Decided: March 30, 2018

Citation: 886 F.3d 1032, 6 Adm. R. 416 (11th Cir. 2018).

Before **MARCUS**, **MARTIN**, and **NEWSOM**, Circuit Judges.

[—3—] {–1037–} **MARCUS**, Circuit Judge:

In this large cocaine conspiracy, the appellants, Jesus Hernando Angulo-Mosquera ("Angulo"), Juan Rodriguez-Acosta ("Acosta"), Efrain Bilbao-Varela ("Varela"), and Arley Lopez-Enciso ("Lopez"), were charged, along with four other co-conspirators, with conspiring to possess and possessing cocaine with intent to distribute while aboard a vessel on the high seas and subject to United States jurisdiction. Before trial the four other co-conspirators pled guilty, and at trial they testified that all of the appellants knew there were drugs on the vessel they sailed and all were knowing participants in the conspiracy. Angulo, alone among the appellants, testified in his own defense. Each of the appellants was convicted by the jury and **{–1038–}** each was sentenced to a 235-month prison term.

The appellants argue that the district court's denial of their motions for a new trial amounted to an abuse of the district court's discretion because polygraph evidence offered by Angulo in support of his claimed lack of knowledge **[—4—]** prejudiced the remaining appellants in a joint trial and should have resulted in severance. They also claim that the prosecutor improperly cross-examined Angulo, that the district court erroneously allowed the introduction of hearsay evidence, and that the court erred in not including a particular jury instruction sought by Acosta, Varela, and Lopez. Finally, Varela and Acosta contest their sentences.

We can discern no error, and, accordingly, affirm the judgments of the district court.

I.

Angulo, Acosta, Varela, and Lopez were part of an eight-member crew on board the Hope II, a Panamanian-flagged cargo ship that departed from Cartagena, Colombia in August 2014 laden with nearly 1500 kilograms of cocaine secreted in a hidden compartment. The other four crewmembers were Simon Bolivar Ferreras-Trinidad, Euclides Tous-Calle, Manuel DeJesus Crespo-Marin, and Emerson Julio Carcedo.

Three of the appellants—Acosta, Varela, and Angulo—had been working on the Hope II for several months before the Coast Guard intercepted the vessel. Acosta was the ship's captain, Varela was its chief engineer, and Angulo claims to have been the cook. One of the co-conspirators, Crespo-Marin, testified that the August 2014 voyage was not the Hope II's first drug run. Rather, the Hope II had **[—5—]** sailed with cocaine at least one other time in February 2014, and according to Crespo-Marin, the entire crew for that voyage, including Acosta, Varela, and Angulo, had been involved in the drug conspiracy. Prior to that run, a secret compartment to house the drugs was built inside a fuel tank beneath the hallway outside the crew's cabins.

While the Hope II was undergoing repairs after the first run, the crew was told about an opportunity to participate in another drug run with about twice the cargo of cocaine; each crewmember would net between 50 and 120 million pesos for undertaking the task. Ferreras-Trinidad testified that everyone, including the four appellants, agreed to take part in the enterprise. Ferreras-Trinidad and Tous-Calle added that Angulo used the ship's crane to load some 61 boxes of cocaine onto the Hope II while Varela directed him from the deck, and Ferreras-Trinidad testified that Lopez detached the boxes from the crane when they got to the ship. The crew also stored some empty rice bags in the steering room—a type of bag often used to facilitate the delivery of drugs.

On August 28, 2014, a maritime patrol aircraft spotted the Hope II traveling in an area of "known drug-smuggling activity" some 47 nautical miles north of San Blas, Panama. The aircraft reported to a Coast Guard ship that it had encountered a vessel acting in a suspicious manner: the ship was seen changing course as soon as the aircraft approached, and its automated information system—which **[—6—]** broadcasts the ship's last port of call, next port of call, and purpose—was not active. A Coast Guard cutter hailed the Hope II and ultimately boarded it. Co-conspirator Tous-Calle testified that not long before the Hope II was boarded, Acosta tried to call someone on a satellite phone and ordered Tous-Calle to throw the phone overboard **{–1039–}** when the call did not go through "[s]o that it would not be seized."

Six Coast Guard personnel boarded the ship and began to conduct a safety sweep. They asked the captain, Acosta, to muster the crew on deck, and to produce documentation for the ship and its crew, along with the crew's passports. The Coast Guard then conducted an "at-sea space accountability" inspection—a visual inspection of "every single square inch of the vessel" to look for hidden compartments and drugs. They discovered the empty rice bags in the steering room, which added to their suspicions, because this kind of bag is often associated with contraband. Coast Guard personnel also discovered that the ship's automated information system worked but had been switched off. During the inspection, co-conspirator Carcedo overheard Varela warn Acosta that the Coast Guard was "right on top of the secret compartment."

The Coast Guard eventually found a hatch in the middle of the berthing area hallway that had been covered by two mats: a black rubber mat placed on top and a "welcome" mat found underneath. Coast Guard personnel assumed the hatch led **[—7—]** to a fuel hold, but one officer became suspicious because of its unusual location near the berthing area. Closer inspection revealed other oddities: the hatch was not airtight, which is highly unusual for a fuel hold; some of the bolts holding the hatch closed were shiny, indicating they had been manipulated recently; and there was caulking discerned around the access plate, which is not typically used for a fuel hold. The officer opened the hatch just a little bit to see if he could smell any fuel. Once he determined that he could not, he opened the hatch fully. Inside, the Coast Guard found 1483 kilograms of cocaine. Ion scans of the ship also revealed trace amounts of cocaine on the crane and in the galley area of the ship.

The crew was arrested, brought to Tampa, and each was indicted in the United States District Court for the Middle District of Florida for possessing cocaine with the intent to distribute while aboard a vessel subject to United States jurisdiction, under 46 U.S.C. §§ 70503(a) and 70506(a), and 21 U.S.C. § 960(b)(1)(B); and for conspiracy to possess cocaine with the intent to distribute, under 46 U.S.C. §§ 70503(a) and 70506(a)–(b), and 21 U.S.C. § 960(b)(1)(B)).

Four of the co-conspirators—Ferreras-Trinidad, Tous-Calle, Crespo-Marin, and Carcedo—pled guilty. One of them, Crespo-Marin, testified that after pleading guilty and returning to the holding area, Angulo came up to him and they had "a verbal fight." Angulo allegedly called Crespo-Marin a traitor, which Crespo-Marin took to be a reference to his decision to plead guilty. According to **[—8—]** Crespo-Marin, Angulo also said "that he [Angulo] was a man that demanded respect," and then Angulo threatened him by saying "[y]ou don't know who I am." Another co-conspirator, Ferreras-Trinidad, testified that Angulo and Varela "threatened to kill [him] 50 times over," observing "that [he] know[s] how [pleading guilty] is rewarded in Colombia," and that when Ferreras-Trinidad pled he "became a rat." A third co-conspirator, Carcedo, added that Angulo told him he had thrown away the gloves and clothing he had worn while loading the drugs on board the ship in order to dispose of any evidence against him. An unrelated prisoner, Jose Yamir Lopez-Marrero, testified that while the crew was incarcerated at Pinellas County Jail awaiting trial, Varela explained the Hope II operation to him, including that the vessel had been headed for San Andrés Island where the crew intended to drop off the dope and **{-1040-}** then sail on to Costa Rica in order to pick up a load of gravel.

For his part, Angulo swore before the jury that he never threatened anyone, and offered an entirely different version of the "verbal fight" with Crespo-Marin. According to Angulo, Crespo-Marin had been rude to him, and Angulo simply responded, "[b]e respectful to me because I've always been respectful to you." In fact, Angulo testified that it was Crespo-Marin who exclaimed that Angulo "didn't know who he [Crespo-Marin] was." As Angulo told it, this altercation had nothing to do with the criminal proceedings. **[—9—]**

Before trial, Lopez moved to sever his trial from Angulo's, based solely on the possible introduction by Angulo of rehabilitative polygraph evidence. Lopez claimed that the polygraph evidence would prejudice him because the jury might well assume that he either refused to take a lie detector test or, maybe, had failed a similar exam. The district court denied the motion to sever, explaining that severance in a conspiracy trial is particularly disfavored, that none of the exceptional reasons for severance applied in this case, and that a limiting instruction would cure any potential prejudice. During trial, Lopez renewed his motion to sever; Acosta and Varela joined in the application. Again, the trial court denied the motion.

Trial began on June 8, 2015. However, at the conclusion of the Government's case a mistrial was declared because one of the Government's witnesses commented on Acosta's decision not to testify, which, the trial court ruled, was a violation of Acosta's Fifth Amendment rights.

The re-trial began on October 13, 2015. Angulo testified. On direct examination, he swore that he did not know that there were any drugs on the vessel, had not been told anything about any drugs when he was hired or at any point thereafter, and had not been involved with the drug shipment in any way. Angulo also said that he had never before heard of the Hope II's prior drug run. He offered that he had only done maintenance work on the ship and later cooked **[—10—]** for the crew. He further observed that he had been in the process of obtaining a new mariner's license to replace his expired one. Finally, Angulo testified that he had never been convicted of a crime and that he had no criminal record involving narcotics, but acknowledged that he had been detained once before in the Bahamas in 1998.

On cross examination, the prosecutor elicited details surrounding Angulo's prior detention, which had involved a load of drugs found on another ship, and questioned him further about his role on the Hope II. Angulo then called as a rehabilitative witness a polygraph examiner he had hired to conduct a polygraph test in preparation for trial. The polygrapher did not testify about the substance of the examination, but did opine that Angulo had been "truthful when [he had] tested him on November 6th."

The jury deliberated for only two hours before finding all four defendants guilty on both counts. The district court denied the motion for a new trial, and sentenced each defendant who went to trial to a 235-month term of imprisonment on each of the counts, to be served concurrently, followed by a 5-year period of supervised release. As for the four co-conspirators who had pled guilty and testified on behalf of the Government, the court sentenced each of them to a 63-month term of imprisonment, followed by a 5-year period of supervised release. **[—11—]**

Angulo, Acosta, Varela, and Lopez now timely appeal from their convictions, and Acosta and Varela appeal from their sentences. **{-1041-}**

II.

The appellants argue that numerous prejudicial errors infected their trial, and, therefore, that the district court abused its discretion when it denied their motions for a new trial. We can discern no abuse of discretion in the trial court's determinations.

A.

Acosta, Varela, and Lopez[1] first claim that the district court abused its discretion by refusing to sever their trial from Angulo's on the ground that Angulo's intended introduction of polygraph testimony would prejudice them. But they have failed to show that there was any likelihood that impermissible prejudice would arise from the polygraph evidence, or that they were in fact prejudiced in any way.

The decision whether to grant a severance lies within the district court's sound and substantial discretion. *United States v. Lopez*, 649 F.3d 1222, 1235–36 (11th Cir. 2011). "We will not reverse the denial of a severance motion absent a clear abuse of discretion resulting in compelling prejudice against which the district court could offer no protection." *United States v. Ramirez*, 426 F.3d 1344, **[—12—]** 1352 (11th Cir. 2005) (quotation omitted). "Joint trials play a vital role in the criminal justice system and serve important interests: they reduce the risk of inconsistent verdicts and the unfairness inherent in serial trials, lighten the burden on victims and witnesses, increase efficiency, and conserve scarce judicial resources." *Lopez*, 649 F.3d at 1233. We have explained that "defendants who are indicted together are usually tried together." *Id.* at 1234 (quotation omitted). And "[t]hat rule is even more pronounced in conspiracy cases." *Id.* This rule is not ironclad. *Id.* Federal Rule of Criminal Procedure 14(a) explains that

> [i]f the joinder of offenses or defendants in an indictment, an information, or a consolidation for trial appears to prejudice a defendant or the government, the court may order separate trials of counts, sever the defendants' trials, or provide any other relief that justice requires.

The circumstances justifying severance are "few and far between"; a defendant seeking severance "must carry the heavy burden of demonstrating that compelling prejudice would result from a joint trial." *Lopez*, 649 F.3d at 1234 (quotation omitted and alteration adopted). To establish this level of prejudice, a defendant must show that "a joint trial would actually prejudice the defendant and that a severance is the only proper remedy for that prejudice—jury instructions or some other remedy short of severance will not work." *Id.*; *see also Zafiro v. United States*, 506 U.S. 534, 539 (1993) (noting that limiting instructions will often cure any potential prejudice resulting from a joint trial). It is not enough that a **[—13—]** defendant argues he may have a better result had the trials been severed. *Zafiro*, 506 U.S. at 540 ("[I]t is well settled that defendants are not entitled to severance merely because they may have a better chance of acquittal in separate trials.").

We have identified four discrete circumstances in which severance may be required: where defendants rely on mutually antagonistic defenses; where one defendant would exculpate another in a separate trial, but will not testify in a joint setting; **{–1042–}** where inculpatory evidence will be admitted against one defendant that is not admissible against another; and where a cumulative and prejudicial "spill over" may prevent the jury from sifting through the evidence to make an individualized determination of guilt as to each defendant. *United States v. Chavez*, 584 F.3d 1354, 1360–61 (11th Cir. 2009). The final category is limited in application, because "a court's cautionary instructions ordinarily will mitigate the potential 'spillover effect' of evidence of a co-defendant's guilt." *United States v. Kennard*, 472 F.3d 851, 859 (11th Cir. 2006).

The district court did not abuse its discretion when it declined to sever this trial. No antagonistic defenses, exculpatory testimony from co-defendants, or inculpatory evidence were at issue; the appellants can only argue that cumulative and prejudicial spillover warranted severance. But, for starters, our spillover precedent is generally concerned with circumstances in which "overwhelming evidence of [a co-defendant's] *guilt*" might bias another defendant—not **[—14—]** circumstances in which evidence of a

[1] Acosta, Varela, and Lopez have each adopted the others' arguments on appeal, and each has adopted Angulo's arguments as well.

co-defendant's innocence might spill over. *Lopez*, 649 F.3d at 1235 (emphasis added). In fact, as the Government points out, any spillover from the polygraph evidence suggesting Angulo's innocence might well have helped the other defendants in this case.

Moreover, the district court made it clear that Angulo's polygraph evidence would only be allowed under "very limited" circumstances: only if Angulo testified and his credibility was impeached could he then present evidence that he passed a polygraph test in an effort to rehabilitate his credibility. "[Testifying] [wa]s a prerequisite to the admission of [the polygraph] evidence"; a prerequisite none of the other defendants satisfied. The conditional and rehabilitative nature of the evidence in question made prejudicial spillover even less likely. We add that the trial court instructed the jury unambiguously to "consider the case of each Defendant separately and individually," and cautioned them that if they "find a Defendant guilty of one crime, that must not affect [the] verdict for any other crime or any other Defendant." And we have repeatedly said that "[a] jury is presumed to follow the instructions given to it by the district judge." *Ramirez*, 426 F.3d at 1352; *United States v. Mock*, 523 F.3d 1299, 1303 (11th Cir. 2008).

Finally, it is patently clear that Acosta, Varela, and Lopez cannot show the requisite prejudice to merit reversal. *See id.* ("We will not reverse the denial of a severance motion absent a clear abuse of discretion resulting in compelling **[—15—]** prejudice." (quotation omitted)). Their argument is built on the possibility that the introduction of the polygraph evidence drew a distinction between Angulo and the other defendants in the minds of the jury, to their demonstrable detriment. But Angulo ultimately was convicted on *both* charged counts, just as the others were. On this record the defendants cannot show that the polygraph evidence helped Angulo—much less that the jury's rejection of that evidence was likely considered in relation to, or had any deleterious effect on, their verdicts. The appellants have made no attempt to explain how Angulo's conviction (and the jury's concomitant rejection of his polygraph evidence) does not doom their allegation of prejudice, and so have failed to discharge their "heavy burden of demonstrating compelling prejudice." *United States v. Browne*, 505 F.3d 1229, 1268 (11th Cir. 2007). On this record, we can discern no abuse of discretion in rejecting the severance application. **{–1043–}**

B.

The same appellants, Acosta, Varela, and Lopez, also claim that the district court denied them their right to be present during trial when it failed to timely notify them of the pretrial evidentiary hearing to consider the admissibility of Angulo's polygraph evidence. The appellants did not make this argument before the district court, and so we can review it only for plain error. Under plain-error review, the defendant is required to show that there is "(1) error (2) that is plain **[—16—]** and (3) that affects substantial rights." *United States v. Monroe*, 353 F.3d 1346, 1349 (11th Cir. 2003) (quotation omitted). If all three conditions are met, we may exercise our discretion to notice a forfeited error, but only if "(4) the error seriously affects the fairness, integrity, or public reputation of judicial proceedings." *Id.* The district court committed no error, plain or otherwise.

The right of a criminal defendant to be present at his trial is axiomatic. "[It] has three bases: the Confrontation Clause of the Sixth Amendment, the Due Process Clause of the Fifth Amendment, and Federal Rule of Criminal Procedure 43." *United States v. Novaton*, 271 F.3d 968, 997 (11th Cir. 2001). Rule 43 itself explains that the defendant must be present at: "the initial appearance, the initial arraignment, and the plea"; "every trial stage, including jury impanelment and the return of the verdict"; and "sentencing." Considered in concert, the right to be present "extends to all hearings that are *an essential part of the trial*—i.e., to all proceedings at which the defendant's presence has a relation, reasonably substantial, to the fullness of his opportunity to defend against the charge." *Proffitt v. Wainwright*, 685 F.2d 1227, 1256 (11th Cir. 1982) (quotation omitted and emphasis added). However, it "does not confer upon the defendant the right to be present at *every* hearing or conference with the trial judge at which a matter relative to the case is discussed." *United States v. Pepe*, 747 F.2d 632, 654 (11th Cir. 1984) (quotation omitted, alterations adopted, and emphasis added). **[—17—]**

Our precedent suggests that there may be no general right to be present at all evidentiary hearings—let alone at an evidentiary hearing solely relating to the admissibility of exculpatory rehabilitative evidence proffered by another defendant in a joint trial. Thus, for example, in *United States v. Pepe* we held that a defendant had no right under the Sixth Amendment or Rule 43 to be present at a pretrial evidentiary hearing to consider whether certain evidence proffered by the Government was inadmissible hearsay. 747 F.2d 632, 652–54 (11th Cir. 1984). We observed that a hearing that does not "bind the court to make any particular evidentiary ruling at trial" is far from essential, and that Rule 43 "does not apply to hearings on motions made prior to or after trial." *Id.* at 653–54 (quoting Fed. R. Crim. P. 43, advisory committee n.1).

But we have no occasion to decide whether defendants have a right to be present at all evidentiary hearings concerning all of the defendants in a case; all we hold today is that the trial court did not commit plain error when it did not notify the other three appellants of Angulo's evidentiary hearing concerning the admissibility of exculpatory polygraph evidence offered by and relating to only one of the defendants. For starters, this hearing occurred well before trial began. And it did not concern the guilt or innocence of the other appellants. Indeed, Angulo's polygraph evidence was not directly relevant to them; the only possibility of prejudice was that the jury might draw adverse inferences from their failure to **[—18—]** produce similar **{-1044-}** evidence. Finally, the hearing did not result in a binding ruling—in fact, the court explicitly reserved ruling on the evidentiary question for trial. It is simply not plain that the appellants had a right to be present at that hearing.

But even if they did, there can be little question that they have failed to show that they were prejudiced by their absence, let alone that the fairness and integrity of the judicial process has been tainted. The appellants in no way suggest how their presence might have led the court to bar the limited admission of the polygraph evidence. Indeed, if they did have a colorable argument that they might have been able to exclude exculpatory evidence for another defendant, that would have been a ground for severance. But here the appellants do not point to any impact their presence may have had on the evidentiary hearing, and, as we've already said, the defendants cannot show that the admissibility of the polygraph evidence prejudiced them in any way.

Moreover, to the extent appellants suggest they suffered a Sixth Amendment violation because they were unable to cross-examine Angulo's polygraph expert at the pretrial hearing, we are unpersuaded. For one thing, no one introduced any testimony from the pretrial hearing at the trial itself, and, more importantly, the defendants had the opportunity to cross-examine the polygrapher and codefendant Angulo as well at trial. **[—19—]**

C.

Turning to the trial itself, the appellants claim reversible error in a discovery violation that occurred when the Government failed to turn over a report about Angulo's 1998 detention in connection with a different cocaine-smuggling ship, and then improperly asked Angulo questions based on the undisclosed report during cross-examination. But the district court properly limited the prosecution's questioning to asking only about information fully disgorged in a report that was available to the defense, and Angulo did not seek any further relief at trial. No prejudice can be shown from the discovery violation.

At the beginning of the Government's cross-examination of Angulo, this exchange occurred:

BY MR. RUDDY [prosecutor]:

Q: Mr. Angulo, let's talk about February 18th, 1998.

A (through interpreter): Yes, sir.

Q: You were on the Motor Vessel Sea Star II; is that right?

A (through interpreter): Yes, sir.

. . .

Q: And also on the vessel were 2236 kilograms of cocaine; right?

A (through interpreter): Correct.

Q: And there were also a lot of line throwing guns and polypropylene lines to be used for at-sea transfers of bales of cocaine; right? **[—20—]**

MR. KERR [defense counsel]: Your Honor, may we approach?

THE COURT: Yes.

At the bench conference conducted out of the presence of the jury, the court and the parties discussed whether the information underlying these questions had been properly disclosed to the defense. The court determined that the prosecutor was working from an undisclosed report of the 1998 incident, but that most of the information regarding the incident had previously been disclosed to the defense. The trial court thus agreed with defense counsel that the prosecutor could only ask questions based on information that had previously been disgorged, and defense counsel did not seek any further relief at that time. **{-1045-}**

After trial, Angulo moved for a new trial on various bases, including the discovery violation and attendant questioning regarding his prior apprehension. The district court denied that motion, finding as to the discovery violation that "there were no questions asked that . . . were unduly prejudicial."

In the context of Federal Rule of Evidence 404(b), the admission of extrinsic act evidence requires "the prosecution to provide notice of its intended use to the defense, regardless of how it intends to use the extrinsic act evidence at trial, i.e., during its case-in-chief, for impeachment, or for possible rebuttal." *United States v. Bradley*, 644 F.3d 1213, 1273 (11th Cir. 2011) (quoting the advisory committee's note to the 1991 amendments of Rule 404(b)) (alteration adopted). **[—21—]** The Government does not dispute that a discovery violation occurred here—rather, it argues that the court properly remedied the issue, and the appellants were in no way prejudiced by the error.

When a discovery violation occurs under Rule 404(b) or Federal Rule of Criminal Procedure 16, there is no automatic consequence—relief for the violation "lies within the discretion of the trial court." *United States v. Rodriguez*, 799 F.2d 649, 652 (11th Cir. 1986). "To support a claim for reversal . . . , the defendant must show prejudice to substantial rights." *See id.* (explaining the reversal standard for a Rule 16 violation); *Bradley*, 644 F.3d at 1273–74 (explaining the reversal standard for a Rule 404(b) violation). We have said that "[s]ubstantial prejudice exists when a defendant is unduly surprised and lacks an adequate opportunity to prepare a defense, or if the mistake substantially influences the jury." *United States v. Camargo-Vergara*, 57 F.3d 993, 998–99 (11th Cir. 1995).

The problem for the appellants is that they cannot show that the district court abused its discretion. The trial court was correct—and the defendants do not argue otherwise—that all of the information contained in the 1998 report, except for information concerning the line guns, had already been disclosed in the handwritten report about the incident that had been provided to Angulo. Thus any possible error or prejudice arising from the discovery violation could only be the result of the prosecutor's single question about the lines and line-throwing guns. **[—22—]**

No error or prejudice flowed from the singular question. In the first place, the question was never answered. The district court sustained the objection to the question before Angulo said anything, and prohibited the government from asking any questions drawn from a document that was not provided to the defense. Moreover, no follow up questions were asked about the line-throwing equipment. The jury never learned whether, according to Angulo, the information was correct or not. Instead, the bulk of the information the jury heard about the incident—including the size of the Sea Star II, the number of crew members on board, and most significantly, that 2200 kilograms of cocaine was found on the vessel—had been disclosed in the report that the Government had provided defense counsel earlier. Moreover, the district court properly instructed the jury that anything the attorneys said at trial—which included any questions they asked—was not evidence. *See United States v. Works*, 526 F.2d 940, 945 n.19 (5th Cir. 1976).

There is no showing that the single additional question drawn from the undisclosed report amounted to a surprise robbing defense counsel of the opportunity to prepare a defense. Angulo asserts that the decisions whether to testify and whether to raise the previous apprehension on direct **{–1046–}** examination were both difficult ones that would have been influenced by the additional information from the undisclosed report. While it may be the case that defense strategy decisions were close—as the decision whether to testify often is—there is **[—23—]** virtually no explanation how the singular piece of information used from the report to ask a question would have been significant in making those decisions, particularly in light of the inculpatory material that had been disclosed earlier about the prior voyage.

It's worth noting that on direct examination, defense counsel elicited from Angulo that he had no record of criminal history, and that in order to obtain his mariner's license, Angulo had to pass a test certifying that he had no problem in relation to narcotics. Indeed, defense counsel also elicited from Angulo that he was a crew member on the ship in 1998 and that he had been detained in the Bahamas. He was also asked by his lawyer whether he heard anything about whether drugs had been found on the ship and, indeed, whether he had ever seen any drugs onboard the vessel. On cross-examination, the prosecutor also asked, notably without any objection, about whether drugs were found on the vessel. Only when the prosecutor asked about the "line-throwing guns" did defense counsel object and only then did the court bar any inquiry about that singular piece of information.

Finally, it's worth observing that Angulo's counsel did not seek any further relief, such as an instruction to the jury to disregard the question itself, and so any claimed failure by the trial court is reviewable only for plain error. *See United States v. Marquardt*, 695 F.2d 1300, 1305 (11th Cir. 1983) (rejecting a challenge to **[—24—]** a question that was successfully objected to but still heard by the jury because "[the defendant] never moved to strike [the offending] statement and never moved for a mistrial. The trial court thus did all [the defendant] asked it to do by sustaining the objection."). It was not plain error—indeed, it was not error at all—for the court to not strike the question *sua sponte*.

Appellants also seem to suggest that the bench conference (conducted by the trial court out of the jury's presence) itself somehow was prejudicial because it may have made the jury think that counsel successfully convinced the trial court to bar incriminating evidence relating to Angulo's prior detention, but absent some extraordinary circumstance, a court's discussion of an evidentiary issue out of the presence of the jury (a very common trial procedure) cannot be deemed to be prejudicial.

D.

All of the defendants also assert error when the prosecutor asked Angulo whether he was the Hope II's "load guard"—the individual responsible for ensuring the drugs were safely delivered—without a good-faith basis. But the prosecutor had sufficient reason to ask the question, the district court did not abuse its broad discretion in allowing the inquiry, and regardless any claimed error would have been harmless. **[—25—]**

Toward the end of the cross-examination of Angulo, this exchange took place between the prosecutor and the defendant:

> Q: You know what a load guard is, Mr. Angulo?
>
> A (through interpreter): I don't know because I've never been into that.
>
> Q: You weren't on that vessel to ensure that all the drugs that were going—the 31 bales that were delivered the first time and the 31 bales that were going to be delivered on the August trip were delivered as planned at sea at night in **{-1047-}** the middle of the ocean? You were there to verify for the drug owners that those bales were delivered; correct?
>
> A (through interpreter): No, sir.
>
> Q: That's who you are; right?
>
> MR. KERR [defense counsel]: Objection, Your Honor. I assume counsel has a good-faith basis for asking the question.
>
> MR. RUDDY [prosecutor]: No further questions, Your Honor.
>
> THE COURT: The legal basis for the objection?
>
> MR. KERR: You can't ask questions on cross-examination for which you don't have a good-faith basis.
>
> THE COURT: All right, the objection is overruled.

In at least some circumstances, a prosecutor must have a good-faith basis for questions asked during trial. *See, e.g., United States v. Crutchfield*, 26 F.3d 1098, 1102 (11th Cir. 1994); *United States v. Glass*, 709 F.2d 669, 673 (11th Cir. 1983). Even if we assume a good-faith basis was required for the prosecutor's "load guard" question, the district court properly concluded that a sound basis existed, **[—26—]** and in any event, any claimed error would have been harmless. Where a good-faith basis is required, that basis "does not have to be definitive proof." *Coquina Investments v. TD Bank, N.A.*, 760 F.3d 1300, 1313 (11th Cir. 2014) (quotation omitted). Based on the testimony of the co-conspirators, there was powerful reason indeed to believe that Angulo had played a specific and substantial role in the drug scheme: among other things, he had been involved at least as a crew member on a different vessel that smuggled more than a ton of cocaine; he operated the crane to move a very large quantity of drugs onboard the vessel in this case; he knew enough to discard clothing and gloves that he had worn evidencing his participation in the drug conspiracy; he lacked a proper mariner's license and thus was less likely to be on the ship for a legitimate maritime reason; and, by one take, he appeared to threaten a co-conspirator with his status and power.

In order to show that the prosecutor could not have thought he was a load guard, Angulo submitted a sworn declaration from a former DEA special agent. The agent opined that "while the captain of this type of ship is almost always involved in the smuggling, crew members are often left in the dark." He further suggested that "it would be unheard of for the lowest-ranking crewmember, the cook, to assume any witting responsibility for the drugs and/or paid role in the overall transaction." He concluded that if there was a load guard, "this man, using drug trafficker logic, would have a considerable record of success in this area **[—27—]** before being hired, again, as security for such an immense undertaking"; "[h]is record and reputation would be visible, at minimum, in his life style"—a conclusion that ran contrary to reports of Angulo and his family living in a shack. But all of this at most only shows ultimately that the prosecutor may have been wrong; it does not establish that the prosecutor acted in bad faith when he asked the question of the defendant. Moreover, much of the evidence drawn from the co-conspirators' testimony flatly contradicts the picture the former DEA agent painted. Thus, for example, the co-conspirators testified that the entire crew was involved in the smuggling enterprise, and one testified that Angulo, the "lowest-ranking crewmember," insinuated by threat that he actually had significant status and power. There was no abuse of discretion in allowing the prosecutor to inquire of the defendant about his putative role as a load guard.

E.

The appellants also argue that the district court abused its discretion in allowing **{–1048–}** the prosecutor to introduce inadmissible hearsay evidence. The appellants say that the district judge erroneously allowed the prosecutor to ask one of its own witnesses leading questions based on an agent's summary of an earlier interview with the witness, and later improperly allowed the prosecutor to have sections of the report translated and read to the witness in order to refresh the witness's recollection. Because the appellants concede that these claimed errors do **[—28—]** not warrant reversal standing alone, we only review them to determine whether they might have contributed to a claim of cumulative prejudicial error. Here too the district court committed no error.

During the cross-examination of Crespo-Marin, one of the co-conspirators who pled guilty, defense counsel for Varela asked a number of questions regarding what he had told government agents during an interview conducted in January 2015. On re-direct examination, the prosecutor sought to read to Crespo-Marin four paragraphs from a summary of the interview. The defense objected; the prosecution then asserted that the rule of completeness allowed introduction of the remainder of the summary report, since "on cross-examination there were questions asked about details of the report that were published to the jury." The trial court limited the prosecutor to questioning Crespo-Marin only about the report. After asking a few more questions, the defense again objected, claiming that the prosecutor was improperly leading the witness. The court overruled the objection because the agent's report had "been called into question" during cross-examination. After a few more questions were asked, the defense again objected, claiming that the prosecutor was effectively trying to introduce the agent's summary as evidence. The court agreed that the prosecutor had improperly led the witness and sustained the objection. **[—29—]**

The prosecutor then asked Crespo-Marin whether he had told the agents how cocaine had been loaded onto the Hope II. When Crespo-Marin answered that he had not, the prosecutor asked that a sentence from the agent's report be translated into Spanish and read to Crespo-Marin, in order to refresh his recollection about that matter. The defense unsuccessfully objected. This happened once more, and again the defense unsuccessfully objected on the ground that the jury might overhear the read translation.

The exchange implicated two evidentiary rules on which the prosecution asserted it could, and to some extent was permitted to, use portions of the agent's report from Crespo-Marin's January 2015 interview, both of which the appellants cite as error. First, the appellants claim there was error in initially allowing questioning from the report under the rule of completeness. The appellants also claim error in allowing Crespo-Marin's recollection to be refreshed by having a portion of the report read to the witness in Spanish by the interpreter. Neither constituted an abuse of discretion.

i.

The evidentiary rulings made by a district court are made at the court's discretion. *See, e.g., Hessen ex rel. Allstate Ins. Co. v. Jaguar Cars, Inc.*, 915 F.2d 641, 645 (11th Cir. 1990). The "rule of completeness," as embodied in Federal Rule of Evidence 106, provides: "If a party introduces all or part of a writing or **[—30—]** recorded statement, an adverse party may require the introduction, at that time, of any other part . . . that in fairness ought to be considered at the same time." We have held that the policy behind Rule 106 applies "when a written document is admitted into **{–1049–}** evidence" or where "a document is used in such a way that it is 'tantamount' to introduction of the document itself." *United*

States v. Ramirez-Perez, 166 F.3d 1106, 1112–13 (11th Cir. 1999). Thus, for example, where a line of questioning led to publication of two paragraphs of a writing, those parts of the writing "effectively were introduced into evidence" and could be subject to the rule of completeness. *Id.* at 1113 (discussing *Rainey v. Beech Aircraft Corp.*, 784 F.2d 1523, 1529 n.11 (11th Cir. 1986), *reinstated on reh'g en banc*, 827 F.2d 1498 (11th Cir. 1987), *rev'd on other grounds*, 488 U.S. 153 (1988)).

Under Rule 106, additional admissions from a writing are allowable when "relevant and . . . necessary to qualify, explain, or place into context the portion already introduced." *United States v. Pendas-Martinez*, 845 F.2d 938, 944 (11th Cir. 1988). For example, where small portions of a writing are read out of context and give a misleading impression of the full contents of the writing, additional portions of the writing may be admitted to avoid misrepresentation. *See Rainey v. Beech Aircraft Corp.*, 784 F.2d 1523, 1529–30 (11th Cir. 1986). However, we have clarified that after introduction of part of a document, "Rule 106 does not automatically make the entire document admissible." *Pendas-Martinez*, 845 F.2d **[—31—]** at 944. We have previously overturned a district court's evidentiary decision to allow admission of an entire report into evidence when "the great majority of it was irrelevant to the issue [for which it was introduced]." *Id.* at 945.

The appellants say that Rule 106 does not apply here. That is, the rule of completeness did not allow introduction of the additional portions of the agent's report because the defense had not, in fact, read anything from the report during cross-examination. Thus, if we understand the argument, there was no "introduc[tion] . . . of a writing or recorded statement," as Rule 106 requires. Instead, appellants argue, the cross-examination used "information derived from" the report "without ever introducing any verbatim statements from" the report. The appellants also say that the portions of the report introduced by the prosecution were not relevant to any previous use of the report. Finally, they urge that the rule of completeness did not allow the prosecutor to ask leading questions based on additional contents found in the report.

The district court considered and limited the use of the report's contents on re-direct in response to the previous use of the report on cross-examination. It did not explicitly clarify whether it found both that the remainder of the report was subject to the rule of completeness and that the contents introduced by the prosecution were relevant to the explanation of the previously introduced portions. **[—32—]**

We need not determine whether the district court did, in fact, allow the limited use of the report because of the rule of completeness; whether the rule of completeness applied because the cross-examination use of the report was "tantamount" to the document's introduction; or whether the questioning by the prosecutor effectively introduced parts of the report that were properly relevant to the previously used portions. Instead, we conclude that even if there was any error in the evidentiary ruling, there was no prejudice nor any clear error to contribute to a showing of cumulative error. The first line of questioning from the report was otherwise admissible under Federal Rule of Evidence 801(d)(1)(B), which defines as nonhearsay Crespo-Marin's prior consistent statement "offered to rebut an express or implied charge that [he] recently fabricated [the **{-1050-}** testimony] . . . or to rehabilitate [his] credibility as a witness when attacked on another ground." *See also United States v. Ettinger*, 344 F.3d 1149, 1160–61 (11th Cir. 2003) (finding admissible under 801(d)(1)(B) a prior consistent statement of a witness contained in an FBI report offered to rebut an implied charge of recent fabrication during cross-examination). **[—33—]**

ii.

There was also no abuse of discretion in permitting the prosecutor to have a few sentences of the report read to Crespo-Marin in Spanish in order to refresh his memory. Under the Federal Rules of Evidence, any document may be used to refresh a witness's recollection. *See* Fed. R. Evid. 612. And "[w]hen there is careful supervision by the court, the testimony elicited through refreshing recollection may be proper, even though the document used to refresh the witness['s] memory is inadmissible." *United States v. Scott*, 701 F.2d 1340, 1346 (11th Cir. 1983). As the trial court explained, the difficulty here largely arose from examining a Spanish-speaking witness with a document that had been written in English; once the court was notified that the translation might be improperly overheard by the jury, it acted quickly to resolve the issue. The district court's supervision of the examination was careful and proper. The appellants also argue that the prosecution did not properly wait for a showing that the witness's memory of the interview had failed before attempting to refresh Crespo-Marin's recollection about the January 2015 interview. This is not supported by the record. Instead, the prosecution confirmed it was refreshing Crespo-Marin's recollection, and followed the appropriate procedure to do so, only after Crespo-Marin denied telling the agents a piece of information that was contained in the relevant report. Again, the record reveals no abuse of discretion. **[—34—]**

F.

Acosta, Varela, and Lopez further claim that the district court abused its discretion when it refused to give the following "blind mule" jury instruction:

> If you find from the evidence that a Defendant was unaware of the hidden packages of cocaine on the Hope II, then you must find him not guilty, because he could not have acted knowingly and willfully.
>
> An unknowing courier is not guilty of possessing cocaine nor is he guilty of a conspiracy to distribute cocaine.
>
> In order to find a Defendant guilty, you must be convinced that the government has proven beyond a reasonable doubt that the Defendant knew of the presence of the hidden packages of cocaine on the Hope II, and that he acted with the intent that the hidden cocaine be possessed and delivered.
>
> A Defendant's mere presence on the Hope II without actual knowledge of the hidden packages of cocaine does not constitute a conspiracy to distribute cocaine, nor does it constitute possession of cocaine with the intent to distribute it.
>
> Likewise, the requisite proof of knowledge on the part of the Defendant cannot be established by merely demonstrating that the Defendant was negligent, careless or foolish.

But this proposed instruction was repetitive of the instructions the trial court actually gave, and the court did not err in declining to include it.

"We review a district court's refusal to give a requested jury instruction for abuse of discretion." *United States v. Martinelli*, 454 F.3d 1300, 1309 (11th Cir. 2006) (quotation omitted). The refusal to **{-1051-}** give a requested instruction is reversible "if (1) the requested instruction was a correct statement of the law, (2) its subject **[—35—]** matter was not substantially covered by other instructions, and (3) its subject matter dealt with an issue in the trial court that was so important that failure to give it seriously impaired the defendant's ability to defend himself." *Id.* (quotation omitted).

The trial court unambiguously instructed the jury that the defendants were charged with "knowingly and willfully" conspiring to possess with intent to distribute and to distribute cocaine (Count 1), and with "knowingly and intentionally" possessing with intent to distribute cocaine (Count 2). The court properly defined "knowingly" and "willingly" using these words:

> The word "knowingly" means that an act was done voluntarily and intentionally and not because of a mistake or by accident.

> The word "willfully" means that the act was committed voluntarily and purposely, with the intent to do something the law forbids; that is, with the bad purpose to disobey or disregard the law. While a person must have acted with the intent to do something the law forbids before you can find that the person acted "willfully," the person need not be aware of the specific law or rule that his conduct may be violating.

As for the first count, the district court explained that in order to find a defendant guilty of conspiracy beyond a reasonable doubt, "the Defendant [must have known] the unlawful purpose of the plan and willfully joined in it," later reiterated that to find a defendant guilty that defendant must have "willfully joined in the plan on at least one occasion," and also clarified that "a person who doesn't know about a conspiracy but happens to act in a way that advances some purpose **[—36—]** of one doesn't automatically become a conspirator." And as for the second count, the district court explained that in order to find a defendant guilty of knowingly possessing cocaine with intent to distribute, the jury must find, beyond a reasonable doubt, that "the Defendant knowingly possessed cocaine" and "intended to distribute" it. The court emphasized that "[t]o 'possess with intent to distribute' means to knowingly have something while intending to deliver or transfer it to someone else." Finally, the court explained that while a defendant may be found guilty of a crime for aiding and abetting its commission, for this to be the case the jury "must find beyond a reasonable doubt that the Defendant was a willful participant and not merely a knowing spectator."

It is abundantly clear from the record of the court's instructions to the jury that the appellants' requested instruction was unnecessarily repetitive. The court explained in detail what "knowingly" and "willfully" mean, and expressly said that the defendants could not be convicted if these requirements were absent. All the proposed instruction would have done is connect the court's statements of the law about knowledge and specific intent to the facts at issue in this case. *Cf. United States v. Takhalov*, 827 F.3d 1307, 1318–19 (11th Cir. 2016) (explaining that when given instructions "substantially cover[ ]" more specific requested ones and the only difference is an easily bridged "logical gap," the requested instruction need not be given). The subject matter covered by the requested instruction was not a **[—37—]** technical point of law that might have been overlooked or misunderstood if not emphasized—rather, it was the entire defense of all of the defendants; was conceptually straightforward; and was discussed by the court at length. In a similar circumstance we have affirmed a district court's non-inclusion **{–1052–}** of "good faith" instructions explicating how the defendant's knowledge of the specific facts of the case could bear on his guilt, because "[those] concepts were substantially included in the instruction that the criminal act must be done 'knowingly' or 'willfully.'" *United States v. Jordan*, 582 F.3d 1239, 1248 (11th Cir. 2009). The appellants have offered no reason to think that the court's instructions were insufficient.

G.

The appellants also claim that even if all of the issues they have raised were harmless, their cumulative effect nevertheless deprived them of a fair trial. "The cumulative error doctrine provides that an aggregation of non-reversible errors (i.e., plain errors failing to necessitate reversal and harmless errors) can yield a denial of the constitutional right to a fair trial, which calls for reversal." *United States v. Baker*, 432 F.3d 1189, 1223 (11th Cir. 2005), *abrogated in part on other grounds by Davis v. Washington*, 547 U.S. 813 (2006) (internal quotation marks omitted). "We address claims of cumulative error by first considering the validity of each claim individually, and then examining any errors that we find in the **[—38—]** aggregate and in light of the trial as a whole to determine whether the appellant was afforded a fundamentally fair trial." *Morris v. Sec'y, Dep't of Corr.*, 677 F.3d 1117, 1132 (11th Cir. 2012). The appellants' cumulative error argument fails because they have been unable to identify any actual error. "This Court has made clear that where there is no error in any of the trial court's rulings, the argument that cumulative trial error requires that this Court reverse the defendant's convictions is without merit." *Id.* (quotation omitted and alterations adopted).

III.

Finally, Acosta and Varela urge us to vacate their sentences as being substantively unreasonable. The reasonableness of a sentence is reviewed for abuse of discretion. *Gall v. United States*, 552 U.S. 38, 51 (2007). On this record, there was no abuse of discretion in either case.

The district court imposed concurrent sentences of 235 months for both Acosta and Varela. As for Acosta, the court found that his total offense level was 40, his criminal history category was I, yielding an advisory guidelines range of 292–365 months' imprisonment along with five years' supervised release on each count. However, after considering the factors identified in 18 U.S.C. § 3553(a)—balancing Acosta's age (67), medical issues (including Type I diabetes, high blood pressure, and thyroid and kidney issues), light criminal history, and low likelihood of recidivism against the serious nature of the crime **[—39—]** (smuggling more than 1400 kilograms of cocaine)—the court varied the sentence downward two points, yielding a new advisory range of 235–293 months, and sentenced him at the low end to 235 months' imprisonment on each count, to run concurrently. The court explained that it was not imposing a life sentence, but acknowledged that, given Acosta's age and the length of sentence, the defendant may well be in custody for the rest of his life.

Acosta claims that his sentence is substantively unreasonable because he will be in excess of 86 years old when released, and that this effectively amounts to a life sentence. But a sentence which may result in a defendant passing away while in custody, however tragic, is neither automatically a life sentence nor presumptively unreasonable. *See, e.g., United States v. Joseph*, 709 F.3d 1082, 1105 (11th Cir. 2013) (affirming a 30-year sentence that **{-1053-}** the defendant argued "effectively amount[ed] to a life sentence"). On this record, we cannot say that the district court's sentence was substantively unreasonable. The court considered the § 3553(a) factors; it awarded Acosta a two-point downward variance; and then it sentenced him at the bottom of the new advisory range. Absent some other indication to the contrary, the sentence did not amount to an abuse of discretion.

As for Varela, the district court determined that his total offense level was 38 and his criminal history category was I, thus yielding an advisory range of 235–293 months' imprisonment, along with five years' supervised release. Again, the **[—40—]** court considered the § 3553(a) factors, and considered and declined Varela's request for a variance. The court sentenced him at the bottom of the guidelines range to 235 months on each count, also to be served concurrently.

Varela claims that his sentence was unreasonable, but he has abandoned this by failing to offer a single specific argument in support of this claim, as required by the Federal Rules of Appellate Procedure. *See* Fed. R. App. P. 28(a)(8) (explaining that an appellant's argument must contain the "contentions and the reasons for them, with citations to the authorities and parts of the record on which the appellant relies," along with "a concise statement of the applicable standard of review"). "We have long held that an appellant abandons a claim when he either makes only passing references to it or raises it in a perfunctory manner without supporting arguments and authority." *Sapuppo v. Allstate Floridian Ins. Co.*, 739 F.3d 678, 681 (11th Cir. 2014). But even if we were to address Varela's claim on the merits, we could discern no abuse of discretion. Again, the court considered the § 3553(a) factors and sentenced Varela at the very bottom of his recommended guideline range. The crime was a serious one, and the amount of cocaine was extraordinarily large. "Although we have not adopted a presumption that a sentence within the guideline range is reasonable, we have stated that ordinarily we would expect a sentence within the Guidelines range to be reasonable." *Joseph*, 709 F.3d at 1105 (quotation omitted). **[—41—]**

The long and short of it is that the district court managed this trial well. As we see it, the appellants can point to no instance where the trial court abused its discretion, and it's even more clear that they were not impermissibly prejudiced by any of the claimed errors. On this record, we find no ground to upset the jury's verdict or the court's sentences.

AFFIRMED.

(Reporter's Note: Concurring Opinion follows on p. 431).

[—42—] {-1053-} MARTIN, Circuit Judge, concurring:

I concur in large part with the majority opinion, but I have not arrived at my view with the ease the majority opinion displays. I find this to be a closer case. Also, in light of the seriousness of the crimes of which these men have been convicted, and the length of the sentences they will serve, I believe some of the problems with the prosecution and the trial merit further discussion.

The cargo ship known as the *Hope II* is a 165-foot freighter. About fifteen hundred kilograms of cocaine were found on the ship. The cocaine was hidden in a disguised fuel tank kept in a space accessible only by a single hatch. It took U.S. Coast Guard personnel 17 hours to find it. And these are people trained and experienced in conducting this type of drug search, and accustomed to using sophisticated drug-detection equipment capable of picking up any trace of cocaine. I emphasize these {-1054-} facts to explain (at least part of) the reason why I do not view the defendants' claim of lack of knowledge of the drugs to be so far-fetched as to be reflexively dismissed as untrue. I am also mindful that the defendants' claim of lack of knowledge of the presence of the drugs should be carefully evaluated against the only evidence the government presented as proof that they did know the drugs were there. That is, the testimony of the four cooperating witnesses who had been shipmates of the defendants whose case we consider here. [—43—]

I. MOTION TO SEVER & POLYGRAPH EVIDENCE

I ultimately agree with the majority that the convictions of Juan Rodriguez Acosta, Arley Lopez Enciso, and Efrain Bilbao Varela, are not due to be reversed on account of the fourth defendant's, Jesus Hernando Angulo Mosquera ("Mr. Angulo"),[1] presentation of evidence of his polygraph examination. But I read the majority to conclude that no possibility of prejudicial spillover existed from the introduction of Mr. Angulo's polygraph evidence. Maj. Op. at 14–16. My conclusion is different. I am well aware that conflicts routinely arise in multidefendant cases about evidence that might help one defendant, but hurt another. However, the speculation and inferences that necessarily arise from one of several defendants presenting polygraph evidence go beyond this type of run-of-the-mill conflict.

When one defendant presents evidence that he passed a polygraph test, surely a juror would be left to wonder: Why is only one defendant giving us evidence of his polygraph test? Did the other defendants refuse to submit to a polygraph test? Did they take one but fail it? A juror could logically infer from all this that the defendants not submitting polygraph evidence must be guilty. The only other court that I am aware of to have confronted this exact circumstance [—44—] noted that "[t]he admission of [polygraph] evidence as to one defendant does raise questions as to the inferences an unguided jury might draw about the other defendant regardless of whether or not that defendant testifies." *SEC v. Saul*, No. 90 C 2633, 1992 WL 3696, at *2 (N.D. Ill. Jan. 6, 1992).

Also in contrast to the majority's ruling, I believe the way the District Court conditionally admitted the polygraph evidence increased, rather than lessened, the possibility of prejudicial spillover to the no-lie-detector defendants. Maj. Op. at 14–15. The District Court admitted the polygraph evidence solely for rehabilitation purposes, and in doing so, tied the admission of the evidence to Mr. Angulo's decision to testify. This loaded more significance onto the decision the other defendants had to make about whether to testify. If they chose not to testify, Mr. Angulo would be not just the only defendant to testify, but his testimony could be backed up by polygraph evidence of his truthfulness. This starkly different presentation would certainly amplify any thoughts a juror might have about a defendant choosing not to testify because he is guilty. On the other hand, testifying would come with risks as well. Any codefendant who testified inevitably would draw more attention

[1] I refer to him as Mr. Angulo because that is the name he uses in his briefs.

to the fact that Mr. Angulo had polygraph evidence to rehabilitate his credibility while the testifying codefendant did not. Since this jury was presented with little more than a swearing match between the cooperating witnesses and the defendants (again, all shipmates), the credibility of **[—45—]** witnesses was mostly all the jury had to decide. Polygraph **{-1055-}** evidence takes on heightened importance in this circumstance.

For me, the government's argument that if the jury believed Mr. Angulo, there would have been an "innocence spillover," only underscores the relationship between Mr. Angulo's polygraph evidence and the jury's decision about the guilt or innocence of his codefendants. All four codefendants (including Mr. Angulo) offered the same "lack of knowledge" defense to the same charges. Thus, (1) Mr. Angulo's desire to put polygraph evidence before the jury; (2) the District Court's order allowing the polygraph evidence only if Mr. Angulo testified; (3) Mr. Angulo's decision to testify; and (4) the codefendants' resulting constrained decision not to testify, had the cumulative effect of making Mr. Angulo the de facto spokesperson for the group. That tied the codefendants' fates to Mr. Angulo's: If the jury believed him, his codefendants stood to benefit. If the jury rejected his testimony, his codefendants stood to suffer.

But as I've said, I ultimately agree with my colleagues that this issue does not require reversal of these convictions. Employing the standard that defendants must meet in this circuit, I cannot say they have shown that the dynamics surrounding the District Court's ruling on the polygraph issues rose to the level of "compelling prejudice," such that "severance [was] the only proper remedy." *See United States v. Lopez*, 649 F.3d 1222, 1234 (11th Cir. 2011). The defendants **[—46—]** point to this as a problem of an "unguided jury." *See Saul*, 1992 WL 3696, at *2. But we know that this jury was instructed to consider the evidence separately as to each defendant and not to use a defendant's exercise of his right to remain silent as a basis for deciding guilt or innocence. And we assume that juries follow the instructions they are given. *See Bruton v. United States*, 391 U.S. 123, 135, 88 S. Ct. 1620, 1627 (1968) (noting that in many cases "the jury can and will follow the trial judge's instructions"). Thus, while the introduction of polygraph evidence created a possibility of prejudicial spillover, I have concluded that the District Court did not abuse its discretion by denying the motion for severance.

II. ADMISSION OF INADMISSIBLE HEARSAY EVIDENCE

I next take up the government's argument that it was entitled to read from an agent's report to question a cooperating witness on re-direct examination under Federal Rule of Evidence 106, the "rule of completeness." I write only to address the propriety of the government's argument in this regard, which the majority does not decide. *See* Maj. Op. at 29–30, 32–33.

I do not read the government's argument to be consistent with the record. For example, the government's brief states that "[t]he prosecutor asked Marin about the portion of the report that defense counsel had not read." Gov't Br. at 44. Then, distinguishing this case from another, the government argued that in the other case counsel "had not read from the report to suggest that the witness's **[—47—]** testimony was inconsistent with the report or otherwise attacked the witness's credibility with the report" but "[t]hat is precisely [] what opposing counsel did here." *Id.* at 47 (alterations adopted). In making these statements, the government represents as a fact these defense lawyers took actions the record reveals they did not. Indeed, a review of the record makes it plain that no defense counsel read from the agent's report or even mentioned the *existence* of the report. Thus, this argument distorts the record, and the government should not have made it. See Fed. R. Evid. 106 ("If a party introduces all or part of a writing or **{-1056-}** recorded statement, an adverse party may require the introduction, at that time, of any other part—or any other writing or recorded statement—that in fairness ought to be considered at the same time."); *United States v. Ramirez-Perez*, 166 F.3d 1106, 1112–13 (11th Cir. 1999) (holding Rule 106 does not apply when counsel "questioned the agent only about what [a defendant] said rather than about what was written in the document" and "did not refer to th[e] writing").

III. GOVERNMENT CROSS-EXAMINATION OF MR. ANGULO

Finally, I address Mr. Angulo's argument that the government was improper in its cross-examination of him.[2] His first claim is based on the government's admitted discovery violation. At trial, the government used a report it had not disclosed to Mr. Angulo, when it questioned him about a 17-year-old incident **[—48—]** involving his presence on another ship. Maj. Op. at 19–21. The majority reduces that violation down to a single improper question about "the lines and line-throwing guns" and determines there was no prejudice. *Id.* at 22–24. Then the majority marshals evidentiary bits it says could qualify Mr. Angulo as a "load guard" and blesses that question entirely. *See id.* at 27. I disagree with both conclusions.

I believe Mr. Angulo was prejudiced by the question about the "line-throwing guns." This question was the last in a series designed to point out the similarities between the 1998 *Sea Star II* incident and the 2014 *Hope II* incident. The prosecutor's questions painted a picture for the jury, starting with the type of ship; the ship size; the crew size; Mr. Angulo's being there; the presence of over a ton of hidden cocaine; and, finally, the equipment referred to as "line throwing guns and polypropylene lines" necessary to make at-sea transfers of cocaine, which was apparently common to both ships. Two things become clear from this context. First, the jury could easily conclude that the last question about the line throwing equipment revealed more detail about Mr. Angulo's expertise and experience as a drug trafficker. Second, as a result of the government's admitted failure to turn over the report, Mr. Angulo was denied the opportunity to anticipate the question, **[—49—]** and be prepared to rebut it and all it implied.[3] Thus when Mr. Angulo stepped down from the witness stand, the jury was left to understand that Mr. Angulo had a long history of involvement with large cargo freighters equipped with specialized line throwing guns and polypropylene lines used to make at-sea transfers of thousands of kilograms of hidden cocaine. I don't believe the evidentiary record, as a whole, supports this. For this reason, I think Mr. Angulo was prejudiced by the government's failure to disclose the report which was the basis for its question about the specialized equipment on the *Sea Star II* in 1998.

I also believe the government's characterization of Mr. Angulo as a "load guard" during its cross-examination of him "waft[ed] an unwarranted innuendo into **{-1057-}** the jury box." *See United States v. Tucker*, 533 F.3d 711, 714 (8th Cir. 2008) (quotation omitted). In questioning Mr. Angulo before the jury, the prosecutor defined a "load guard" as one who is "there to verify for the drug owners that those [cocaine] bales were delivered." However, the evidence the government offers and which the majority accepts to justify the inquiry into this specialized role falls short in my opinion. Maj. Op. at 27. The government's basis for inquiring into Mr. **[—50—]** Angulo's role as a load guard could have qualified anyone on the ship as such.[4] The cooperating

[2] That is, I address only the two improper questions Mr. Angulo raises on appeal.

[3] Mr. Angulo's attorney argues that [h]aving never seen the report, the defense ha[d] no way to know how accurately the prosecutor recounted its contents for the jury. The defense had no opportunity to learn where the purported drug-smuggling equipment was stored on the large cargo ship, [or] whether Angulo would have had access to it or even reasonably *known* of its existence. There was no opportunity to investigate whether the equipment had legitimate uses that may have negated its sinister characterization by the prosecutor.

[4] Indeed, similar evidence would seem to apply to every member of the *Hope II* crew. For example, one of the cooperating witnesses, Simon Bolivar Ferreras-Trinidad, testified that he was supposed to be paid 10 million Columbian pesos more than the other crew members; that he served as "the deck supervisor" for one trip; and that he was involved in not only loading the crates containing the cocaine onto the ship, but also unpacking the crates and placing the individual bales in the hidden compartment. He also previously was imprisoned by Cuban authorities for trafficking in

witness's (disputed) statement about Mr. Angulo's threat of "status and power" never suggested he was a "load guard," or even used that term. *See id.* at 8–9, 27. And the government's agents' general knowledge about where load guards stand in the hierarchy of drug-trafficking organizations is not sufficient to turn Mr. Angulo's disputed taunt about his status, which the testimony characterized as general in nature, into a "well-reasoned suspicion." *See United States v. Beck*, 625 F.3d 410, 418 (7th Cir. 2010) (quotation omitted). A well-reasoned suspicion requires more than what the government had here. *Compare United States v. Crutchfield*, 26 F.3d 1098, 1101–02 (11th Cir. 1994) (faulting prosecutor for asking witness, who admitted only to personal marijuana use, about large-scale importation of drug when question was based only on prosecutor's "personal expertise in the prosecution of drug cases and . . . knowledge of many illegal activities in the area where the witness resided"), *with Tucker*, 533 F.3d at 714 (determining prosecutor had good-faith basis to ask about **[—51—]** defendant's knowledge of robberies based on FBI interview with other participant who said defendant knew of robberies and defendant's admission that she traveled with participant to places that were robbed). That the prosecutor abruptly ended his questioning after asking Mr. Angulo, twice, whether he was a "load guard," is consistent with a goal of leaving the jury with the impression that Mr. Angulo played a role on the ship, for which there was no real evidentiary support.

Within the confines of this record, I believe the government's discovery violation together with its unsupported characterization of Mr. Angulo as a "load guard" prejudiced him. *See United States v. Rodriguez*, 799 F.2d 649, 652 (11th Cir. 1986) (per curiam) ("The actual prejudice will often turn on the strength of the Government's case."). Aside from the cooperating witnesses' entirely self-serving testimony, the only evidence inculpating Mr. Angulo was his presence on the *Sea Star II* 17 years earlier when over a ton of cocaine was found there, and the fact of his expired mariner's license, which the majority treats as meaning he was less likely to have a "legitimate maritime reason" to be on the *Hope II*. *See* Maj. Op. at 5–11, 27. Mr. Angulo's guilt or innocence thus turned almost completely on his credibility compared to that of the cooperating **{–1058–}** witnesses. In cases that "turned entirely upon which biased witnesses the jury chose to believe," this Court has recognized that "[e]vidence that tended to erode [the defendant's] credibility and to prejudice the jury against him [] could have had a substantial—perhaps **[—52—]** overpowering—impact on the jury's deliberations." *United States v. Hands*, 184 F.3d 1322, 1332 (11th Cir. 1999).

Despite my view of the problems with the government's actions toward Mr. Angulo, I also think the District Court did the best it could to react to these actions. The court stopped more questions about the undisclosed report. And although the line-throwing question was left hanging, the District Court's failure to strike the question did not, in my view, amount to an abuse of discretion by the court. *See United States v. Kelly*, 888 F.2d 732, 745 (11th Cir. 1989) ("The abuse of discretion standard has been described as allowing a range of choice for the district court, so long as that choice does not constitute a clear error of judgment."). Finally, the court instructed the jury that what the lawyers say is not evidence. And we presume that juries follow their instructions. *See Bruton*, 391 U.S. at 135, 88 S. Ct. at 1627. While it's possible that the prosecutor's improper questioning of Mr. Angulo created a "risk that the jury will not, or cannot, follow instructions," *see id.*, Mr. Angulo has not shown that was in fact the case.

I therefore concur in the judgment affirming the convictions of Mr. Angulo, as well as his codefendants.

---

cocaine, and he had an expired license as well. Euclides Tous-Calle, another cooperating witness, testified that he saw the hidden compartment being built; that he helped load the cocaine into the compartment; and that he threw a satellite phone into the water to prevent its seizure (but allegedly on the captain's order).

United States Court of Appeals for the Eleventh Circuit

No. 16-16946

UNITED STATES vs. PLASENCIA

Appeal from the United States District Court for the Southern District of Florida

Decided: April 11, 2018

Citation: 886 F.3d 1336, 6 Adm. R. 435 (11th Cir. 2018).

Before **TJOFLAT**, **PRYOR**, and **ANDERSON**, Circuit Judges.

[—1—] {-1339-} PER CURIAM: **[—2—]**

Maikel Suarez Plasencia ("Suarez") appeals his convictions and fifty-one-month concurrent sentences for encouraging and inducing aliens to enter the United States, in violation of 8 U.S.C. § 1324(a)(1)(A)(iv), (v)(II). He contends that his convictions were based on evidence obtained from an unconstitutional search of his global positioning system ("GPS"), which linked him to the illegal entry of Cuban migrants, and that his sentence reflects an obstruction-of-justice enhancement applied contrary to his due process rights and against the merits. *See* U.S.S.G. § 3C1.1. After careful review, we affirm Suarez's convictions and sentence.

I.

On the morning of September 6, 2015, twenty-eight Cuban migrants were found on Loggerhead Key, Florida. Later that day, Suarez's boat broke down on Garden Key, an island three miles east of Loggerhead Key and seventy miles west of Key West. A park ranger, David Fuellner, responded to a report of Suarez's beached boat and located Suarez and the boat.[1] Fuellner asked Suarez for permission to search his boat, and Suarez consented orally and by signing a **[—3—]** consent form.[2] The signed form authorized Fuellner to perform a "complete" search of the vessel and to seize its contents for any "legitimate law enforcement purpose." Suarez then took a ferry to Key West to summon help with fixing his boat.

Fuellner conducted the search the next day and found a GPS which, once plugged into the boat's power source and turned on, showed a waypoint indicating that the boat had been just off of Cuba's shore on **{-1340-}** September 5, 2015.[3] Fuellner then powered off the GPS, seized it, and entered it into evidence. Later analysis of the GPS, performed by a Coast Guard analyst, revealed that Suarez left Key West around 1:30am on September 5, arrived off the coast of Cuba at about 4:30pm that day, and then reached the vicinity of Loggerhead and Garden Keys in the early morning of September 6. The trip from Cuba to the United States took about ten hours. No warrant was obtained for Fuellner's search or for this analysis.

Department of Homeland Security ("DHS") agents interviewed Suarez on September 8. Suarez claimed that he had taken his boat on a spear-fishing trip from Key West to the Dry Tortugas[4] and that he spent a night on the vessel. He denied knowledge of a migrant landing in the area. Months later, DHS agents **[—4—]** again interviewed Suarez. When they confronted Suarez with the GPS evidence linking him to the Cuban shore, he claimed that the agents had mixed up his GPS with someone else's. However, Suarez admitted that his wife and two of his children were among the migrants who landed on September 6, 2015.

---

[1] According to the Government, the report relayed that "a Spanish-speaking man had told a park supervisor that he had been camping and fishing for the previous two days, that he needed fuel for his boat, and that he needed to get . . . to Key West to get somebody to come back and bring him fuel."

[2] Fuellner spoke in Spanish, Suarez's native language. Also, the consent form provided to Suarez was written in Spanish.

[3] Fuellner's search yielded no camping equipment, operational fishing gear, extra clothing, or bait.

[4] Loggerhead Key and Garden Key are both within the Dry Tortugas.

On March 11, 2016, a federal grand jury sitting in the Southern District of Florida returned a twenty-eight-count indictment against Suarez, charging him with alien smuggling, in violation of 8 U.S.C. § 1324(a)(1)(A)(iv), (v)(II). Suarez filed a motion on June 8, 2016 to suppress the GPS evidence. The District Court denied the motion on two grounds. First, it held that by consenting to a search of his vessel without limitation, Suarez consented to a search of his GPS found onboard. Next, and in the alternative, the Court held that Suarez had abandoned the boat and its contents by leaving it on a public shore for "three to four days" before returning to fix it.

Suarez's case continued on to a jury trial, where Suarez presented as witnesses eight of the Cuban migrants found on September 6, 2015. The migrants testified generally that a "raft" with a single engine brought them from Cuba to the United States, that the trip took two nights and one day, that the raft was destroyed or lost, and that they waded to the United States shore from between fifteen and seventy-five feet out in the ocean. All of the migrant witnesses denied that Suarez assisted their journey in any way. The Government's witnesses testified that no **[—5—]** raft, or debris from a destroyed raft, was found and that the ocean's depth even fifteen feet from the shore at which the migrants claimed to have landed would have made wading impossible. The Government also presented testimony that the migrants did not appear hungry, dehydrated, disheveled, or wet—conditions typical of migrants who come from Cuba to the United States by raft. The jury found Suarez guilty of all twenty-eight counts of alien smuggling.

A presentence investigation report ("PSI") of Suarez was then issued. It set the Guidelines range of Suarez's sentence at thirty-three to forty-one months, which accounted for a two-point reckless-endangerment enhancement under U.S.S.G. § 2L1.1(b)(6). The PSI did not recommend a U.S.S.G. § 3C1.1 enhancement for obstruction of justice, stating, "The probation officer has no information indicating the defendant impeded or obstructed justice."

The Government did not object to the PSI for failing to recommend a sentencing **{-1341-}** enhancement for obstruction of justice, but it filed notice of its intent to seek an upward variance in Suarez's sentence due in part to the "full day's worth of conflicting, sworn testimony" Suarez presented at trial. Suarez did not respond to the Government's notice, citing a lack of time to do so as the reason.

At sentencing, the District Court applied U.S.S.G. § 2L1.1(b)(6)'s reckless-endangerment enhancement and then, *sua sponte*, added two more points to Suarez's total offense level under U.S.S.G. § 3C1.1 for knowingly suborning **[—6—]** perjury at trial. The Court noted that Suarez knew from his counsel's opening statement that numerous witnesses would lie on his behalf but Suarez nonetheless allowed them to testify.[5] This obstruction-of-justice enhancement increased the Guidelines range of Suarez's sentence to forty-one to fifty-one months. After relaying its decision to impose the enhancement, the Court stated that it "assume[s] that [defense counsel] makes an objection to the Court's analysis." Defense counsel confirmed that he objected, and the Court stated,

> So the record is clear. Defense counsel . . . has made a valid objection to all of this and objects to the Court's finding and he's fully protected to raise this on appeal. I think that protects the defendant. Do you have anything else? That's the finding.

The Court then heard arguments from the Government and defense counsel about whether the Court should vary from the

---

[5] Specifically, in his opening statement defense counsel announced to the jury,

> But what you're not going to hear from the government is the migrants. You're gonna hear that from the defense. You're gonna have the ability to look at the migrants, in that chair, and judge, hear what they say, hear them say that they didn't encounter [Suarez] out at sea; that he did not render aid, assist, or help them, in any way, get here to the United States.

applicable Guidelines range. The Government requested that Suarez receive sixty months' imprisonment, citing the seriousness of Suarez's offenses and the disrespect to the court that he promoted by presenting false testimony from numerous witnesses. Defense counsel then argued that Suarez deserved only fifteen months' imprisonment because, namely, the migrants Suarez smuggled into the United States were his friends and family and **[—7—]** he did not bring them over for profit. Defense counsel made no argument regarding Suarez's subornation of perjury. The Court then denied the Government's request for an upward variance and imposed a sentence of fifty-one months' imprisonment and three years' supervised release. Suarez appealed his convictions and sentence.

On appeal, Suarez first argues that the District Court erred in denying his motion to suppress evidence recovered from the search of his GPS. He contends that the consent he provided to Fuellner did not include consent to search his GPS and that he did not abandon his boat.[6] Next, Suarez makes two challenges to the District Court's decision to apply U.S.S.G. § 3C1.1's two-point obstruction-of-justice enhancement. First, he asserts that the Court violated his due process rights by applying the enhancement *sua sponte*, without offering him prior notice or an opportunity to argue against the enhancement. Second, he claims that the Court erred on the merits because he did not knowingly present perjured testimony. We start with the District Court's denial of Suarez's motion to suppress. **{-1342-}**

II.

When considering a district court's ruling on a motion to suppress, we review factual findings for clear error and application of law to the facts *de novo*. *United States v. Ramos*, 12 F.3d 1019, 1022 (11th Cir. 1994). Clear error lies only **[—8—]** where the record leaves us "with the definite and firm conviction that a mistake has been committed." *United States v. White*, 335 F.3d 1314, 1319 (11th Cir. 2003) (internal quotation marks omitted). Moreover, we construe all facts in the light most favorable to the party who prevailed below. *United States v. Bervaldi*, 226 F.3d 1256, 1262 (11th Cir. 2000).

"The Fourth Amendment protects the people against 'unreasonable' searches and seizures. A consensual search is manifestly reasonable so long as it remains within the scope of the consent." *United States v. Martinez*, 949 F.2d 1117, 1119 (11th Cir. 1992). Whether limitations were placed on the scope of consent, and whether the search conformed to those limitations, is a question of fact determined by the totality of the circumstances. *United States v. Blake*, 888 F.2d 795, 798 (11th Cir. 1989). The Government bears the burden of showing that its search was conducted within the scope of the consent received. *Id.* at 799–800. "When an individual gives a general statement of consent without express limitations," the scope "is constrained by the bounds of reasonableness: what a [law enforcement] officer could reasonably interpret the consent to encompass." *Martinez*, 949 F.2d at 1119.

Our decision in *United States v. Street*, a case analogous to Suarez's, is instructive. *See* 472 F.3d 1298 (11th Cir. 2006). There, the defendant consented to a "complete search" of his residence and to seizure of "any items" related to a **[—9—]** string of recent bank robberies. *Id.* at 1308. Law enforcement found a police radio on a bedroom floor, turned it on, and noticed that it was tuned to a radio zone covering where a robbery had occurred earlier. *Id.* at 1303. Because the radio was in plain view and the defendant did not limit the search, we concluded that law enforcement could reasonably believe that the radio was within the scope of the consent provided. *Id.* at 1308–09.

Here, via signed consent form, Suarez consented to a "complete" search of his boat and to seizure of its contents for any "legitimate law enforcement purpose." He did not limit the scope of his consent in any way. *Cf. United States v. Rich*, 992 F.2d 502, 507 (5th Cir. 1993) ("[The defendant], knowing the

[6] Because we conclude that the scope of Suarez's consent included the search and later analysis of his GPS, we do not review the Court's abandonment determination.

contents of [his] vehicle and its various containers at the time he gave his consent, had the responsibility to limit the scope of the consent if he deemed it necessary to do so."). Fuellner found the GPS in one of the boat's storage compartments, lying beneath some other items. Suarez's consent clearly covered the compartment where the GPS was found, despite Suarez's argument to the contrary. *See United States v. Strickland*, 902 F.2d 937, 942 (11th Cir. 1990) (holding that an officer's search of a spare-tire compartment was within the scope of the defendant's consent to a search of his "entire vehicle").

Suarez further argues that Fuellner exceeded the scope of Suarez's consent by powering up the GPS, which was off when Fuellner found it. *Street*, however, **[—10—]** guides the other way. *See* 472 F.3d at 1308–09. Moreover, in determining the scope of a search, we consider "what the parties knew at the time to be the object of the search." *Martinez*, 949 F.2d at 1119. Suarez's boat was beached seventy miles from Key West's shore. A reasonable person would understand that giving "complete" consent to a search of his boat, in **{-1343-}** this context, would include consenting to the search of a GPS on board that could indicate where the boat had been and shed light on why it is beached so far out in the ocean. This is especially so given that the consent form indicated that law enforcement was looking generally for items that could be used for any legitimate law enforcement purpose. Conversely, an officer receiving unbounded consent in this situation could reasonably believe that the consent covered a search of the GPS. Fuellner therefore did not violate Suarez's Fourth Amendment rights by searching the GPS. And, for the same reasons, nor did the Coast Guard analyst in performing a forensic analysis of the GPS. Accordingly, the District Court did not err in denying Suarez's motion to suppress.

III.

Suarez next argues that the District Court's application of U.S.S.G. § 3C1.1's two-point enhancement was both in violation of his due process rights and incorrect on the merits. When reviewing a district court's decision to apply an enhancement under § 3C1.1, we review factual findings for clear error and the **[—11—]** district court's application of the Guidelines to those facts *de novo*. *United States v. Bradberry*, 466 F.3d 1249, 1253 (11th Cir. 2006). In reviewing the district court's findings of fact, we provide "substantial deference" to the court's credibility determinations at sentencing. *United States v. Clay*, 483 F.3d 739, 744 (11th Cir. 2007).

A.

Suarez contends that the District Court violated his due process rights by imposing the § 3C1.1 enhancement *sua sponte*, without providing him adequate notice or an opportunity to be heard on the issue. We disagree.

Due process requires that a criminal defendant have adequate notice of, and an opportunity to contest, the facts used to support his criminal penalty. *United States v. Jules*, 595 F.3d 1239, 1243 (11th Cir. 2010). But "sentencing procedures are not required to be as exacting as those at trial." *Id.* The defendant's primary due process interest at sentencing is the "right not to be sentenced on the basis of invalid premises or inaccurate information." *See id.* Hence, the degree of due process protection required at sentencing is only that which is necessary "to ensure that the district court is sufficiently informed to enable it to exercise its sentencing discretion in an enlightened manner." *United States v. Stephens*, 699 F.2d 534, 537 (11th Cir. 1983). **[—12—]**

Federal Rule of Criminal Procedure 32 governs, *inter alia*, the issuance of PSIs. Rule 32(d) requires that a PSI "identify all applicable guidelines" and "any factor relevant to . . . the appropriate kind of sentence." But district courts are not bound by the facts and recommendations set forth in a PSI; they may choose not to adopt the facts as recited in the report or not to apply the Guidelines in the proposed manner. *United States v. Jones*, 899 F.2d 1097, 1102 (11th Cir. 1990), *overruled in part on other grounds*, *United States v. Morrill*, 984 F.2d 1136 (11th Cir. 1993) (en banc); *see United States v. Aguilar-Ibarra*, 740 F.3d 587, 591 (11th Cir. 2014) (noting that district courts have an obligation independent of the PSI to correctly calculate the defendant's Guidelines range). It follows that, with proper notice, a court may apply Guidelines enhancements not identified in the PSI.[7] **{-1344-}**

Here, defense counsel's opening statement indicated that the migrant witnesses would deny Suarez's involvement in their illegal entry into the United States. Then, Suarez sat idly as the witnesses told a similar story contradicting the record. This put Suarez on notice that the witnesses' apparently false testimony, and his own inaction, might later be cited by the Government or the Court as a reason for lengthening his sentence. Indeed, before Suarez's sentencing hearing, the Government provided notice that it intended to seek an upward variance in part **[—13—]** because of the witnesses' perjured testimony. Suarez thus cannot claim that he lacked adequate notice of the conduct underlying the Court's *sua sponte* decision to apply § 3C1.1's obstruction-of-justice enhancement.

The Guidelines, moreover, "define specific and finite factors warranting the application of an upward or downward adjustment to a defendant's otherwise applicable sentencing range." *United States v. Canada*, 960 F.2d 263, 266 (1st Cir. 1992). Therefore, when, as here, the circumstances afford a defendant notice that he engaged in conduct that may result in the application of a Guidelines enhancement, the court need not provide additional notice of its intention to apply the enhancement *sua sponte*—the Guidelines themselves provide adequate notice.[8]

Further supporting this conclusion are the Supreme Court's decisions in *Burns v. United States*, 501 U.S. 129, 111 S. Ct. 2182 (1991), and *Irizarry v. United States*, 553 U.S. 708, 128 S. Ct. 2198 (2008). In *Burns*, the Court held that **[—14—]** before a district court may issue an upward departure from the Guidelines, notice must be given in the PSI, in a prehearing submission by the Government, or by the district court itself. *Burns*, 501 U.S. at 138, 111 S. Ct. at 2187. Unlike with enhancements, "the Guidelines place essentially no limit on the number of potential factors that may warrant a departure." *Id.* at 136, 111 S. Ct. at 2186. Hence, notice is more important for defendants to prepare an argument against a departure than to prepare one against an enhancement.

In *Irizarry*, the Court then abrogated its holding in *Burns* by deciding that notice, although necessary for a court to issue an upward departure,[9] is not necessary **{-1345-}**

[7] It also follows that the Government's failure to object to the PSI for failing to recommend an applicable enhancement—here, § 3C1.1—does not preclude a district court from applying that enhancement.

[8] *See United States v. Sharp*, 436 F.3d 730, 738 (7th Cir. 2006) (stating that the defendant's awareness of his own false testimony put him "on notice that [his testimony] could result in a possible obstruction of justice enhancement"); *United States v. Knight*, 76 F.3d 86, 88 (5th Cir. 1996) ("[I]f the defendant has actual knowledge of the facts on which the district court bases an enhancement or a denial of a reduction, the Sentencing Guidelines themselves provide notice of the grounds relevant to the proceeding."); *United States v. Willis*, 997 F.2d 407, 416–17 (8th Cir. 1993) (affirming a district court's *sua sponte* imposition of an obstruction-of-justice enhancement, despite the PSI stating that the probation officer had "no information" regarding obstruction of justice, because the defendant was on notice that his perjured statements at trial might result in the enhancement); *Canada*, 960 F.2d at 266–67 (noting that even where a PSI states there is "no basis" for a particular sentencing enhancement, "the guidelines themselves provide notice to the defendant" that "he may be called upon to comment" on the enhancement); *United States v. Rucker*, 122 F.3d 1064 (4th Cir. 1997) (unpublished table decision) (holding that a defendant is not entitled to "advance notice of sua sponte adjustments to the guideline calculation, at least where the facts relevant to the adjustment are known to the defendant, because the bases for adjustments are limited and are set out in the guidelines").

[9] The *Irizarry* Court specified that "'[d]eparture' is a term of art under the Guidelines and refers only to non-Guidelines sentences imposed under the framework set out in the Guidelines." 553 U.S. at 714, 128 S. Ct. at 2202. The only departures relevant in *Burns* "were those authorized by 18 U.S.C. § 3553(b) (1988 ed.), which required 'an aggravating or mitigating circumstance of a kind, or to a degree, not adequately taken into

for a court to issue an upward *variance*. 553 U.S. at 716, 128 S. Ct. at 2203. It noted that because *United States v. Booker*, 543 U.S. 220, 125 S. Ct. 738 (2005), rendered the Guidelines advisory, there was no longer an "expectation subject to due process protection . . . that a criminal defendant would receive a sentence within the presumptively applicable Guidelines range." *Irizarry*, 553 U.S. at 713, 128 S. Ct. at 2202. Given that defendants are not entitled to notice of variances—and that Guidelines enhancements, unlike departures, are finite and **[—15—]** specific—Suarez, who had notice of § 3C1.1 and of his witnesses' conduct at trial, was not denied due process when the District Court applied § 3C1.1 *sua sponte*.

Suarez contends that a new sentencing hearing is nonetheless warranted because the District Court failed to allow his counsel to comment on the § 3C1.1 enhancement. *See United States v. Mylor*, 971 F.2d 706, 707 (11th Cir. 1992) (holding that the district court erred by refusing to hear argument by the defense concerning a Guidelines enhancement).[10] Although the District Court noticed a defense objection to the § 3C1.1 enhancement counsel without explicitly stating the basis of the objection, it did ask counsel whether there was "anything else" regarding the enhancements it applied. The Court then heard further argument from both parties regarding whether to deviate from the applicable Guidelines range in imposing Suarez's sentence. The Government argued for an upward variance in part because of the defense witnesses' false testimony—even stating that the District Court "succinctly summed up" the basis for its argument when imposing the § 3C1.1 enhancement. In his response, however, defense counsel did not attempt to counter the Government's argument or push back on the District Court's conclusion that Suarez suborned perjury. The Court did not refuse to hear **[—16—]** argument from counsel related to Suarez obstructing justice; rather, counsel failed to argue the point. A new sentencing hearing is therefore not warranted.[11]

B.

Suarez also contends that the District Court clearly erred in concluding that he suborned perjury and thus in applying § 3C1.1. We find no clear error.

Section 3C1.1 applies if "the defendant willfully obstructed or impeded, or attempted to obstruct or impede, the administration of justice with respect to the investigation, **{-1346-}** prosecution, or sentencing of the instant offense of conviction." Covered conduct includes "committing, suborning, or attempting to suborn perjury." U.S.S.G. § 3C1.1 cmt. n.4(B). Under § 3C1.1, "the defendant is accountable for the defendant's own conduct and for conduct that the defendant aided or abetted, counseled, commanded, induced, procured, or willfully caused." U.S.S.G. § 3C1.1 cmt. n.9; *Bradberry*, 466 F.3d at 1254.

Knowingly procuring another to commit perjury constitutes subornation of perjury. *Bradberry*, 466 F.3d at 1254. Perjury, for purposes of § 3C1.1, is defined as giving "false testimony concerning a material matter with the willful intent to provide false testimony, rather than as a result of confusion, mistake,

consideration by the Sentencing Commission in formulating the guidelines that should result in a sentence different from that described.'" *Irizarry*, 553 U.S. at 714, 128 S. Ct. at 2202 (quoting *Burns*, 501 U.S. at 141, 111 S. Ct. at 2189 (Souter, J., dissenting)).

[10] *See also* Fed. R. Crim. P. 32(i) (requiring courts to rule on any controverted matter at sentencing and give defense counsel an opportunity to speak on the defendant's behalf); U.S.S.G. § 6A1.3(a) ("When any factor important to the sentencing determination is reasonably in dispute, the parties shall be given an adequate opportunity to present information to the court regarding that factor.").

[11] Courts should still strive to provide notice of their intention to impose previously unnoticed enhancements and allow adequate opportunity for parties to debate relevant sentencing issues. As the *Irizarry* Court stated, "Sound practice dictates that judges in all cases should make sure that the [sentencing] information provided to the parties in advance of the hearing, and in the hearing itself, has given them an adequate opportunity to confront and debate the relevant issues." 553 U.S. at 715, 128 S. Ct. at 2203.

or faulty [—17—] memory." *Id.* (quoting *United States v. Singh*, 291 F.3d 756, 763 (11th Cir. 2002)). The Guidelines define material evidence as "evidence . . . that, if believed, would tend to influence or affect the issue under determination." U.S.S.G. § 3C1.1 cmt. n.6. Thus § 3C1.1's enhancement applies where a defendant knowingly calls a witness to testify on his behalf to produce false testimony tending to influence or affect the jury's verdict. *See Bradberry*, 466 F.3d at 1254.

Suarez became aware of the migrant witnesses' potential testimony no later than during his counsel's opening argument, when counsel stated that the witnesses would deny that Suarez aided their entry into the United States in any way. Then, spanning over more than a full day of trial, Suarez watched as each of the eight witnesses relayed a similar story denying his involvement and contradicting portions of the record. This testimony, moreover, served as Suarez's primary evidence of innocence. Under these circumstances, the District Court, which receives wide latitude in determining the credibility of evidence, *Clay*, 483 F.3d at 744, did not clearly err in concluding that Suarez knowingly suborned perjury, *cf. Bradberry*, 466 F.3d at 1254.

Finally, Suarez argues that because the Court applied § 3C1.1 *sua sponte* and without hearing from the Government, the Government could not have met its burden of proving the enhancement's applicability by a preponderance of the evidence. *See United States v. Ndiaye*, 434 F.3d 1270, 1300 (11th Cir. 2006) [—18—] ("The Government has the burden of proving the applicability of Guidelines that enhance a defendant's offense level.") But a "district court's factual findings for purposes of sentencing may be based on, among other things, evidence heard during trial." *Id.* (quoting *United States v. Polar*, 369 F.3d 1248, 1255 (11th Cir. 2004)). The Government presented testimony and other evidence at trial exposing the defense witnesses' perjury, and the District Court did not clearly err in crediting this evidence and determining that § 3C1.1 applied. *See Clay*, 483 F.3d at 744.

IV.

For the reasons discussed above, we affirm Suarez's convictions and sentence.

AFFIRMED.

United States Court of Appeals
for the Eleventh Circuit

No. 17-11202

UNITED STATES
vs.
OBANDO

Appeal from the United States District Court for the Southern District of Florida

Decided: June 1, 2018

Citation: 891 F.3d 929, 6 Adm. R. 442 (11th Cir. 2018).

Before **PRYOR**, **PRYOR**, and **BLACK**, Circuit Judges.

[—2—] {-930-} PRYOR, W., Circuit Judge:

This appeal requires us to decide whether a flag painted on the side of a vessel is "flying" for the purpose of making a "claim of nationality or registry" under the Maritime Drug Law Enforcement Act, 46 U.S.C. § 70502(e). When the United States Coast Guard stopped the vessel *Siempre Malgarita* in international waters on suspicion of drug trafficking, Alexander Obando, Laureano Roberto **[—3—]** Quiroz-Mendoza, and Alfonso Bitaliano Marcillo-Mera were aboard the vessel, but they failed to produce documents evidencing nationality or to make a verbal claim of nationality or registry. Coast guardsmen spotted a Colombian flag painted on the hull of the *Siempra Malgarita*, but the master of the vessel asserted that the flag was Ecuadorian. The guardsmen did not ask Colombian officials whether the vessel was registered in Colombia or whether Colombia consented **{-931-}** to the Coast Guard exercising jurisdiction. Guardsmen later boarded the vessel and arrested the crew members. In the district court, the crew members argued that the United States lacked jurisdiction because the painted Colombian flag constituted a claim of nationality under section 70502(e)(2) that obliged the Coast Guard to ask Colombian officials about the vessel. After the district court ruled that the vessel was stateless and subject to the jurisdiction of the United States, the crew members conditionally pleaded guilty. Because a painted flag does not fly, *id.* § 70502(e)(2), we affirm.

I. BACKGROUND

On November 17, 2016, the United States Coast Guard Cutter *Edmonton* spotted the *Siempre Malgarita*, a 32-foot "go-fast" vessel, in international waters approximately 208 nautical miles off the coast of Guatemala. A Marine Patrol Aircraft observed the crew of the *Siempre Malgarita* "jettison[ing] packages into **[—4—]** the water," and the *Edmonton* launched a small vessel to investigate these packages, which tested positive for cocaine. The *Edmonton* also launched a second small vessel that intercepted the *Siempre Malgarita*.

The parties stipulated to facts about the interception that we use to assess jurisdiction. *See United States v. Iguaran*, 821 F.3d 1335, 1337, 4 Adm. R. 457, 458 (11th Cir. 2016) ("Parties may . . . stipulate to facts that bear on our jurisdictional inquiry." (emphasis omitted) (citation and internal quotation marks omitted)). The guardsmen approached the *Siempre Malgarita* and identified her crew as Alexander Obando, Laureano Roberto Quiroz-Mendoza, and Alfonso Bitaliano Marcillo-Mera. The guardsmen also determined that Marcillo-Mera was the master of the vessel. All three crew members are citizens of Ecuador.

The guardsmen attempted to determine the nationality of the *Siempre Malgarita*, but none of the vessel's occupants made a verbal claim of nationality or registry for the vessel. Marcillo-Mera also failed to produce documents evidencing nationality or to identify the homeport of the vessel or its last port of call. Indeed, when asked, Marcillo-Mera told the guardsmen that "he did not know" the vessel's nationality. *See* 46 U.S.C. § 70502(d)(1)(B). **[—5—]**

The guardsmen noticed a flag painted on the hull of the vessel, and they "believed it was a Colombian flag." But when they asked Marcillo-Mera about the flag, he asserted that it was the flag of Ecuador.

The two national flags are similar in appearance. The flag of Ecuador consists of horizontal bands of yellow, blue, and red and has a coat of arms in its center.

The Flag of Ecuador **{-932-}**

The flag of Colombia does not have a coat of arms but is otherwise identical.

The Flag of Colombia

[—6—]

The Coast Guard sent a "Form 1: Action Request" to the government of Ecuador to determine whether the *Siempre Malgarita* was registered in Ecuador. On the form, the Coast Guard stated that the vessel lacked a "claimed nationality," but it acknowledged a "flag state claim via" "vessel markings." Ecuadorian officials could not confirm the nationality or registry of the vessel, and the Coast Guard never communicated with Colombian officials. The Coast Guard determined that the *Siempre Malgarita* was a vessel without nationality subject to the jurisdiction of the United States under the Maritime Drug Law Enforcement Act, *see* 46 U.S.C. § 70502(c)(1)(A), and the guardsmen arrested the crew members.

After the government charged the crew members with drug offenses, Marcillo-Mera moved to dismiss the charges on the basis that the United States lacked jurisdiction. He asserted that the Colombian flag painted on the *Siempre Malgarita* "was a claim of [Colombian] nationality in and of itself" and that "the Coast Guard contacted the incorrect flag state" when it instead communicated with Ecuadorian officials. A magistrate judge recommended that the district court deny the motion. The magistrate judge determined that the **{-933-}** vessel was stateless based on the parties' stipulation "that when the Coast Guard inquired as to the nationality of the vessel," Marcillo-Mera "either said nothing or said he did not know." And the **[—7—]** magistrate judge reasoned that the painted Colombian flag was not itself "a claim of nationality or registry" because a painted flag cannot fly.

The district court adopted the report and recommendation. All three crew members then conditionally pleaded guilty to conspiracy to possess with intent to distribute a controlled substance in violation of the Act, *see id.* §§ 70503(a), 70506(b), but reserved the right to challenge the jurisdiction of the United States on appeal.

II. STANDARD OF REVIEW

Whether the United States has extraterritorial jurisdiction under the Act is a question of law that we review *de novo*. *See Iguaran*, 821 F.3d at 1336, 4 Adm. R. at 457.

III. DISCUSSION

We divide our discussion in two parts. First, we explain that the United States has jurisdiction over the *Siempre Malgarita* and its crew because the painted Colombian flag on its hull was not "flying" for the purpose of making a "claim of nationality or registry." 46 U.S.C. § 70502(e). Second, we reject the crew members' alternative arguments about why the United States lacks jurisdiction.

A. A Flag Painted on a Vessel Does Not Fly.

The Maritime Drug Law Enforcement Act grants the United States extraterritorial jurisdiction over "vessel[s] without nationality." *Id.* **[—8—]** § 70502(c)(1)(A). The Act states that a vessel is without nationality if "the master or individual in charge fails, on request of an officer of the United States . . ., to make a claim of nationality or registry for that vessel." *Id.* § 70502(d)(1)(B). And the Act provides three exclusive methods for the master or individual in charge to make a "claim":

> (1) possession on board the vessel and production of documents evidencing the vessel's nationality as provided in article 5 of the 1958 Convention on the High Seas;
> (2) flying its nation's ensign or flag; or
> (3) a verbal claim of nationality or registry by the master or individual in charge of the vessel.

Id. § 70502(e). If the master of a vessel in international waters makes a claim of foreign nationality that is affirmed by the asserted nation, *see id.* § 70502(d)(1)(A) & (C), the United States ordinarily must obtain "consent[]" from that nation before exercising jurisdiction, *id.* § 70502(c)(1)(C).

Whether the United States has extraterritorial jurisdiction over a vessel is a "preliminary question[] of law" decided by the district court and "not an element of [the] offense." *Id.* § 70504(a); *see also United States v. Campbell*, 743 F.3d 802, 805, 2 Adm. R. 543, 543 (11th Cir. 2014). The answer to this question determines whether the district court may exercise subject matter jurisdiction, "for a district court . . . ha[s] adjudicatory authority over a charge that a defendant conspired to violate the substantive crime defined in the [Act]" only if "the conspira[tors'] vessel was, **[—9—]** when apprehended, subject to the jurisdiction of the United States." *Iguaran*, 821 F.3d at 1336, 4 Adm. R. at 457 (alteration adopted) (quoting *United States v. De La Garza*, 516 F.3d 1266, 1272 (11th Cir. 2008)). "[T]he government bears the burden of establishing . . . jurisdiction . . . ." *United States v. Tinoco*, 304 F.3d 1088, 1114 (11th Cir. 2002); *see also Iguaran*, 821 F.3d at 1338.

The crew members stipulated that the master of the *Siempre Malgarita* **{-934-}** failed to produce documents evidencing the vessel's nationality or to make a verbal "claim of nationality or registry," *see* 46 U.S.C. § 70502(e)(1) & (3), but they contend that the painted flag on the side of the vessel constituted a claim of Colombian nationality that obliged the Coast Guard to ask Colombian officials whether the vessel was registered there and whether Colombia consented to the exercise of jurisdiction by the United States. This argument fails if the Colombian flag painted on the hull was not "flying." *Id.* § 70502(e)(2). It was not.

The ordinary meaning of the word "flying" requires a flag to be capable of freely moving in the air. *See* Antonin Scalia & Bryan A. Garner, *Reading Law: The Interpretation of Legal Texts* 69 (2012) ("Words are to be understood in their ordinary, everyday meanings . . . ."). For example, Webster's New International Dictionary defines "fly" as "[t]o cause to fly or to float in the air as a . . . flag," and it offers the illustrative phrase of "the ship flew the flag of Spain." *Fly, Webster's* **[—10—]** *New International Dictionary* 976 (2d ed. 1961) (emphasis omitted). Webster's Third New International Dictionary gives a nearly identical definition. *Fly, Webster's Third New International Dictionary* 879 (3d ed. 1993) ("[T]o cause to fly or float in the air (as a bird, a flag) . . . ."). And the Oxford English Dictionary defines "fly" as, "[t]o set (a flag) flying; to *carry at the mast-head; to hoist*." *Fly, Oxford English Dictionary* (online ed.) (emphasis added). All of these definitions entail the movement of a physical object in the air. Indeed, the Oxford English Dictionary applies the same definition of "fly" to the act of "set[ting] (a sail) loosely." *Id.*

To be sure, the ordinary meaning of a term will yield when the term has "a technical meaning" or is a "term[] of art," *see* Scalia & Garner, *supra*, at 73 (emphasis omitted), but the meaning that the phrase "flying a flag" carries in the maritime context confirms that a vessel's flag must be able to move freely in the air. For example, the Oxford English Dictionary, in a section on "nautical phrases," defines "to keep the flag flying" as "to refuse to haul down one's flag and surrender." *Flag, Oxford English Dictionary, supra.* A painted flag cannot be "haul[ed] down." *Id.*

A maritime treatise confirms that a vessel's flag must be hoisted in the air. *See* H. Meyers, *The Nationality of Ships* (1967). It refers to the physical "hoisting **[—11—]** [of a] flag" to assert nationality, *id.* at 162, explains that "when [sea] traffic is heavy . . . [a] flag will have to be *flown from the stern*," *id.* at 163 (emphasis added), and cautions that a vessel's flag may not always be a reliable "indicator" of nationality because it can be "easily changed," *id.* at 140. It also explains that there may be times "when flying the flag cannot reasonably be required," such as in the presence of "heavy gales" or if a "flag[] [is] blown overboard." *Id.* at 164–65. Neither of these perils is relevant to painted flags. And the treatise presumes that vessels that are physically incapable of hoisting flags are similarly unable to "fly" flags when it discusses a hypothetical "deep sea research" submarine that, when "under water at all events . . ., will not fly a flag." *Id.* at 166.

Maritime etiquette supports the same definition. For example, a procedural guide published by the United States Navy offers extensive instructions for "hoisting and lowering" the flag. Department of the Navy, NTP 13(B), Flags, Pennants & Customs 3-1 (1986). It also explains that a vessel's crew must "haul[] [the ensign] down" after sunset, *id.* at 3-1, and that a vessel may "dip" its flag to salute another vessel, *id.* at 3-1 to 3-2. But the guide never suggests that a flag may be painted on a vessel. On the contrary, its discussion **{-935-}** of painted symbols is limited to non-flag "emblems," such as the medical cross. *Id.* at 17-11. It also specifically forbids service members from "paint[ing]" "[s]tars or *replicas* of personal flags . . . **[—12—]** on vehicles," *id.* at 14-1 (emphasis added), which suggests that *real* flags consist of more than paint. A Navy protocol handbook explains that "[t]he national ensign shall be displayed during daylight from the gaff (or from the triatic stay . . .)" and speaks in dynamic terms of "the hoisting, lowering[,] or flying of the ensign." Department of the Navy, 1710.7A, Social Usage and Protocol Handbook J-19 (2001); *see also id.* at J-20 (discussing "[d]ipping the national ensign" and "[h]alf-masting the national ensign"). The guide also fails to mention painted flags, and it distinguishes flags from the more general category of "distinctive mark[s]." *Id.* at J-19. And a flag guide published by a civilian group provides that even motorboats without a mast or rigging should still have a means of hoisting a flag. *See* United States Power Squadrons, *Flag Etiquette*, http://www.usps.org/f_stuff/etiquett.html (last visited May 31, 2018) (discussing the "United States Ensign").

Other federal statutes about the display of flags clearly imply that a flag flies only when hoisted in the air, and "laws dealing with the same subject . . . should if possible be interpreted harmoniously." Scalia & Garner, *supra*, at 252. For example, one statute provides that "[w]hen flags of two or more nations are displayed, they are to be *flown from separate staffs* of the same height," 4 U.S.C. § 7(g) (emphasis added), that when "flags are *flown from adjacent staffs*, the flag of the United States should be *hoisted first and lowered last*," *id.* § 7(f) (emphases **[—13—]** added), and that "[t]he flag, when *flown at half-staff*, should be first *hoisted to the peak*," *id.* § 7(m) (emphases added). And the statute does not use the term "flying" to refer to the display of flags that are not hoisted in the air. It instead uses different verbs like "drap[ing]," *id.* § 7(b), "display[ing]," *id.* § 7(i) & (k), and "cover[ing]," *id.* § 7(n), to describe that kind of use. And a related statute explains that the "flag patch" worn by military and emergency personnel should be "*affixed* to the[ir] uniform[s]." *Id.* § 8(j) (emphasis added). "Flying" refers to a particular method of displaying a flag, and the Maritime Drug Law Enforcement Act uses this specific word instead of the more general term "displaying."

The crew members contend that the phrase "flying a flag" refers to any kind of visual depiction of a flag that suggests the nationality of the vessel, and they highlight that the "Form 1" template used by the Coast Guard to communicate with foreign governments in this kind of maritime interception suggests the possibility of a "flag state claim via" a "flag *painted* on [the] stern" of the vessel. But whether the Coast Guard considers a painted flag to be an assertion of national affiliation is not the same question as whether that flag is "flying" under the Act.

That the Coast Guard may embrace a functionalist interpretation of how the master of a vessel may assert nationality in the interest of diplomatic caution cannot change the ordinary meaning of the statutory text. Indeed, the form permits **[—14—]** a "flag state claim" by means not included in the exclusive list provided in the Act, such as by a "homeport [marked] on [the] stern" or a "verbal" claim by a "*non*-master." *See* 46 U.S.C. § 70502(e) (explaining that "[a] claim of nationality or registry . . . includes *only* . . . (1) possession . . . and production of documents . . .; (2) flying [a] . . . flag; or (3) a verbal claim . . . by the master or individual in charge" (emphasis added)). The form also offers no suggestion that the Coast Guard has adopted a definitive or consistent interpretation of the phrase "flying a flag" worthy **{-936-}** of any kind of administrative deference. *Cf. Reno v. Koray*, 515 U.S. 50, 61 (1995) (explaining that an "internal agency guideline . . . is still entitled to some deference" when "it is a permissible construction of the statute" (citations and internal quotation marks omitted)). Indeed, the Coast Guard did not even check the "painted" flag box on the "Form 1" that it submitted to Ecuadorian officials after stopping the *Siempre Malgarita*, despite the stipulation that the guardsmen saw the painted flag. And the crew members offer no additional evidence that the Coast Guard credits painted flags as claims of nationality.

The crew members cite idioms that suggest that the phrase "[f]lying the flag" refers to a general invocation of a vessel's "association with a nation," but we are unpersuaded. They cite the Cambridge Idioms Dictionary, which defines "fly/show/wave the flag" as "to support or to represent [one's] country," *Flag*, **[—15—]** *Cambridge Idioms Dictionary* 145 (2006), and the Farlex Dictionary of Idioms, which defines the phrase "fly the flag" as to "represent or demonstrate support for [one's] country," *Fly the Flag, Farlex Dictionary of Idioms*, https://idioms.thefreedictionary.com/Flying+the+Flag (last visited May 31, 2018). And they cite the Oxford Living Dictionaries, which defines "fly the flag" "of a ship" as to "be registered in a particular country and sail under its flag." *Fly the Flag, Oxford Living Dictionaries*, https://en.oxforddictionaries.com/definition/fly_the_flag (last visited May 31, 2018). But were we to interpret the phrase "flying the flag" broadly to include a wide array of methods of signaling that a vessel is "registered in a particular country and sail[ing] under its flag," *id.*, we would render superfluous the other two specific methods of claiming nationality provided in the Act: the "possession . . . and production of documents evidencing the vessel's nationality," 46 U.S.C. § 70502(e)(1), and "a verbal claim of nationality . . . by the master," *id.* § 70502(e)(3). And the presumption against surplusage directs us to give effect to "every word and every provision" of a statute and not "giv[e] an interpretation [to one provision] that causes it to duplicate" other provisions. Scalia & Garner, *supra*, at 174. To be sure, the crew members modestly limit their definition of "flying a flag" to a visual "display [of] a flag" sufficient "to put [the] United States . . . on notice of another country's interests." But their **[—16—]** preferred idiomatic definitions encompass a wider range of expressive conduct that would swallow the three specific and exclusive methods outlined in the Act. *See* 46 U.S.C. § 70502(e)(1)–(3). In any event, extensive authorities on maritime practices trump the broader definitions cited by the crew members and confirm that "flying [a] . . . flag" is a distinct act that requires a flag to be hoisted in the air. *Id.* § 70502(e)(2).

The crew members also contend that statements in our precedents that addressed other questions about the Act suggest that the definition of "flag" includes any kind of visual symbol, but we disagree. For example, in

Campbell we mentioned that a "vessel lacked all indicia of nationality: it displayed no flag, port, or registration number." 743 F.3d at 804, 2 Adm. R. at 543. And in *United States v. de la Cruz* we explained that the stateless "vessel in question flew no flag, carried no registration paperwork, and bore no markings indicating its nationality." 443 F.3d 830, 832 (11th Cir. 2006). According to the crew members, this language suggests that any visual depiction of a flag is enough. But even if these statements addressed the question whether a painted flag can "fly," they would cut the other way. Our separate mentions of whether a vessel "flew [a] flag" or "bore . . . markings indicating its nationality," **{-937-}** *id.*, imply that a flying flag is *distinct* from other visual displays that also suggest nationality. **[—17—]**

To be sure, the only other decision to address this question assumed, for the sake of argument, the opposite conclusion. In *United States v. Prado*, 143 F. Supp. 3d 94 (S.D.N.Y. 2015), the Southern District of New York ruled that a "small emblem of what appear[ed] to be an Ecuadorian flag . . . affixed to [a] boat[]," *id.* at 97, was not "flying . . . within the meaning of the [Act]," *id.* at 101 (citation and internal quotation marks omitted). The district court declined to adopt the argument of the government "that a piece of fabric must wave in the air." *Id.* at 100. Instead, it explained that the phrase "'flying a nation's ensign or flag' . . . at a minimum refer[s] to a display sufficiently prominent as to put a United States official on notice of another country's interests" before it concluded that the particular emblem in question was "not remotely large or prominent enough." *Id.* (alteration adopted) (citation omitted).

Not only was this functionalist analysis unnecessary in the light of the ordinary meaning of the phrase "flying a flag," but the opinion in *Prado* also highlighted the inherent difficulty of dispensing with the requirement of a hoisted flag when it grappled with the question whether the "emblem" on the vessel in question was "enough to put a reasonable official on notice that [another country's] interests might be affected." *Id.* The district court began its analysis by "assuming" that the emblem was "an image of an Ecuadorian flag," *id.*, and it acknowledged **[—18—]** that the emblem, "[u]nlike a prominently displayed flag, . . . [is] easily confused with ornamentation . . . [and] difficult to see in any waters, not to mention . . . in the large waves of the high seas," *id.* at 100–01; *see also id.* at 97 ("[A] small emblem of *what appear[ed] to be* an Ecuadorian flag had been affixed to the boat's rear starboard side." (emphasis added)). It also underscored that "[t]he emblem [was] very much smaller than . . . nearby . . . images running the length of the boat's side," *id.* at 101, in concluding that this particular emblem was not "enough," *id.* at 100. In contrast, a flag hoisted in the air avoids these line-drawing problems and provides certainty to both American officials on the high seas and the courts that second-guess their decisions.

The ambiguities posed by painted flags also rebut the crew members' practical complaint that the requirement of a physical flag will "lead to absurd results" because "a postage-stamp size . . . flag hoisted on a ship's mast could constitute a claim of nationality but a flag several feet long by several feet wide painted on the . . . hull of a boat could not." Indeed, the Act has good reason to require an actual flag of any size instead of a painted representation. Consider a vessel painted with horizontal red, white, and blue stripes. Is this vessel flying the flag of the Netherlands? Or is it instead owned by a captain who only likes those colors? And as illustrated by *Prado*, static "emblems" require fact-intensive **[—19—]** inquiries into the size, location, and intended meaning of such markings. *See id.* at 100–01. A flag hoisted in the air avoids these questions and unambiguously asserts nationality.

The crew members also assert that our interpretation may create conflicts within international law because vessels registered in countries that permit painted flags will be "deemed stateless by American [vessels] and boarded," but this fear about micommunications on the high seas overlooks that the Act provides alternative methods of claiming nationality, including a simple "*verbal claim* of nationality or registry." 46 U.S.C. § 70502(e)(3) (emphasis **{-938-}**

added). Indeed, "the flying of the national flag [has] never [been] the cause of—or the condition for—allocation [of nationality]." Meyers, *supra*, at 162; *see also id.* at 140. The requirement that a vessel hoist a flag in the air will not render helpless foreign vessels that have only painted flags.

Finally, the crew members argue that we should invoke the rule of lenity because the statute is ambiguous, but the rule of lenity applies only when "traditional canons of statutory construction . . . [leave us] with an ambiguous statute." *Kasten v. Saint-Gobain Performance Plastics Corp.*, 563 U.S. 1, 16 (2011) (quoting *United States v. Shabani*, 513 U.S. 10, 17 (1994)). We have **[—20—]** already explained that the ordinary meaning of the term "flying" requires a flag to be hoisted in the air.

B. The Crew Members' Alternative Arguments Are Unpersuasive.

The crew members also assert several alternative and fact-bound reasons why we should hold that the United States lacks jurisdiction. None are persuasive. We reject each in turn.

The crew members contend that we should overlook the stipulation that no crew member made a claim of nationality and instead determine that Marcillo-Mera's "statement that the vessel's flag was 'Ecuadorian' . . . [was] tantamount to a claim of nationality" that obligated "the Coast Guard to contact the government of Colombia," but this reasoning is wholly unpersuasive. Parties may "stipulate to facts that bear on our jurisdictional inquiry." *Iguaran*, 821 F.3d at 1337, 4 Adm. R. at 458 (emphasis omitted) (citation and internal quotation marks omitted). And because the parties stipulated that no crewmember made a claim of nationality, we refuse to ignore this stipulation on appeal and act as a factfinder in the first instance.

The crew members also contend that the government is estopped from asserting "that there was never any claim of nationality" because the "Coast Guard's [decision to] contact[] . . . Ecuador" suggests that guardsmen thought that the defendants had asserted nationality, but this logic suffers from two flaws. First, **[—21—]** that the Coast Guard elected to communicate with Ecuadorian officials does not necessarily imply that the guardsmen thought that the defendants had satisfied their burden of asserting nationality under the Act. Indeed, the guardsmen may have acted out of an abundance of caution, and we see no reason to punish the government for doing more than the Act requires. Second, the crew members voluntarily stipulated to the fact that they made no verbal claim of nationality, and there is no suggestion that the government dishonestly induced this stipulation or changed its position mid-litigation.

Finally, the crew members contend that the guardsmen acted in bad faith because they "purposely chose not to contact the Colombian government" despite knowing that the flag painted on the vessel was Colombian. But this appeal to the subjective knowledge of the guardsmen again overlooks the stipulations that the crew members failed to make a verbal claim of nationality and that the only verbal suggestion of nationality was Marcillo-Mera's statement that the flag was Ecuadorian. As the master of the vessel, he owed the obligation to claim nationality. *See* 46 U.S.C. § 70502(d)(1)(A)–(C). And because the guardsmen knew that Marcillo-Mera was Ecuadorian, they had good reason to conclude that Ecuador was the correct target for their inquiry. **[—22—] {-939-}**

IV. CONCLUSION

We **AFFIRM** the judgments of conviction against Obando, Quiroz-Mendoza, and Marcillo-Mera.

(Reporter's Note: Concurring Opinion follows on p. 449).

[—23—] {-939-} BLACK, Circuit Judge, concurring:

I concur in the Court's opinion, but I write separately because there is an additional ground for affirmance. Section 70502(d) of the Act places the burden of claiming a vessel's nationality on "the master or individual in charge." *See* 46 U.S.C. § 70502(d)(1); *United States v. Rosero*, 42 F.3d 166, 171 (3d Cir. 1994). As the Court's opinion notes, the parties stipulated that the *Siempre Malgarita*'s master made no such claim. USDC Doc. 31 at ¶ 4 ("Neither the defendant Marcillo-Mera, as the master of the vessel, nor the co-defendants, Quiroz-Mendoza and Obando, as the crew members, made a claim of nationality or registry for the vessel."); *id.* at ¶ 5 ("When the boarding team asked about the vessel's nationality, the defendant Marcillo-Mera stated that he did not know . . . ."); *id.* at ¶ 6 ("The USCG Edmonton communicated the master's failure to make a claim of nationality or registry of vessel . . . ."). Thus, because "the master or individual in charge" did not make a claim of nationality or registry for the ship, the *Siempre Malgarita* was a "vessel without nationality" under the plain language of § 70502(d)(1). *See* 46 U.S.C. § 70502(d)(1).

The Act's focus on the words and actions of a vessel's master is consistent with longstanding principles of admiralty law. As Chief Justice John Marshall stated in 1818, "[t]he mere wood, iron, and sails of the ship, cannot, of themselves, **[—24—]** violate the law. But this body is animated and put in action by the crew who are guided by the master. *The vessel acts and speaks by the master. She reports herself by the master.*" *United States v. The Little Charles*, 26 F. Cas. 979, 982 (Marshall, Circuit Justice, D. Va. 1818) (No. 15,612) (emphasis added); *see also Dobbins's Distillery v. United States*, 96 U.S. 395, 402 (1877) (same); *United States v. Cargo of the Brig Malek Adhel*, 43 U.S. (2 How.) 210, 234 (1844) (same). Requiring the master to speak on behalf of the ship also makes sense for practical reasons. *See Rosero*, 42 F.3d at 171 (noting that by placing the burden of claiming nationality on the vessel's master, Congress alleviated the practical difficulties associated with requiring the Coast Guard to disprove all possible claims of nationality).

It was incumbent upon the *Siempre Malgarita*'s master to assert a claim of nationality on behalf of the ship. He did not, and Appellants' contention that the *Siempre Malgarita* spoke for itself[1] is contrary to both the statute's plain language **[—25—]** and established principles of admiralty law. Given the stipulated facts,[2] I would affirm the district court on the additional **{-940-}** basis that there was no claim of Colombian nationality or registry attributable to the vessel's master under § 70502(d)(1), regardless of whether the painted Colombian flag could otherwise support a claim of nationality or registry under § 70502(e).

---

[1] *See* Br. of Appellant Marcillo-Mera at 11 ("The Colombian flag painted on the side of the *Siempre Malgarita* put the Coast Guard on notice that *the vessel* claimed Colombian nationality . . . . *[T]he Siempre Malgarita* never claimed to be Ecuadorian . . . ." (second emphasis added)); USDC Doc. 20 at 7 ("[E]ffectively, the *Siempre Malgarita, speaking for herself,* told the boarding team she was Colombian." (emphasis added)).

[2] Appellants attempt to contradict the stipulated facts on appeal and argue that, to the extent an act attributable to the vessel's master is necessary, the master asserted a claim of Colombian nationality by setting out to sea in a vessel bearing the Colombian flag. The master, however, stated he believed the flag was Ecuadorian. Thus, even if we allowed Appellants to contradict the stipulated facts on appeal, the vessel's master could not have intentionally asserted a claim of Colombian nationality based on a flag he believed to be Ecuadorian, and it would be unreasonable to suggest he could have made such a claim accidentally.

United States Court of Appeals
for the Eleventh Circuit

No. 18-10374

MINOTT
vs.
M/Y BRUNELLO

Appeal from the United States District Court for the Southern District of Florida

Decided: June 6, 2018

Citation: 891 F.3d 1277, 6 Adm. R. 450 (11th Cir. 2018).

Before **MARCUS, PRYOR,** and **ROSENBAUM,** Circuit Judges.

[—2—] {-1279-} PRYOR, W., Circuit Judge:

This appeal from the denial of a warrant *in rem* for the arrest of a vessel requires us to decide whether we have interlocutory jurisdiction, and if so, whether John Minott established that the injury he allegedly suffered while boarding the *Brunello* entitles him to a warrant *in rem* for the arrest of the vessel. Minott filed a complaint against the *Brunello* and other parties alleging that he was entitled to enforce a maritime lien against the *Brunello* for damages arising from a maritime tort. He then moved the district court to direct the clerk to issue a warrant *in rem* for the arrest of the *Brunello*, but the district court denied the motion. In addition to expressing doubt about whether Minott's claim fell within its maritime jurisdiction, 28 U.S.C. § 1333, the district court ruled **{-1280-}** that Minott's claim did not "give[] rise to a 'maritime lien' supporting the *in rem* seizure of the [v]essel" based on the erroneous premise that maritime liens arise only by statute and not by operation of the general maritime law. It also denied Minott's motion for reconsideration. We have interlocutory jurisdiction, *id.* § 1292(a)(3), Minott's claim for a maritime tort against the *Brunello* falls within the admiralty jurisdiction of the district court, *id.* § 1333(1), and Minott is entitled to a warrant *in rem*, Fed. R. Civ. P. Supp. R. C(3)(a)(i). We reverse and remand with instructions to direct the clerk to issue a warrant *in rem* for the arrest of the *Brunello*. **[—3—]**

I. BACKGROUND

John Minott worked for Butch Kemp Designs, a marine engineering firm hired to perform maintenance and repairs aboard the *Brunello* while it was docked in navigable waters in Dania, Florida. Minott attempted to board the vessel, but when he was walking up the gangway "the [v]essel['s] captain or crew, suddenly and without warning, put the engines in gear, causing the gangway . . . to detach from the [v]essel and fall overboard, together with [Minott]." Minott suffered "severe injuries to his head, neck, and spine."

Minott filed a "verified complaint to enforce a maritime lien for damages arising from a maritime tort" in the district court. *See* Fed. R. Civ. P. 9(h); S.D. Fla. Adm. & Mar. R. B(2). The complaint asserted an *in rem* claim against the *Brunello* and *in personam* claims against other individual and corporate defendants. Minott then moved the district court to direct the clerk to issue a warrant *in rem* for the arrest of the vessel. *See* Fed. R. Civ. P. Supp. R. C(3)(a)(i); S.D. Fla. Adm. & Mar. R. B(3)(a). He explained that the tort was "cognizable under admiralty jurisdiction," that he was "entitled to a maritime lien," that he was "entitled to arrest the [v]essel and litigate directly against [it] *in rem*," and that the vessel was "transitory in nature and at risk of leaving the jurisdiction of [the district court] if not immediately arrested." **[—4—]**

The district court denied the motion without prejudice after finding that Minott failed to "establish good cause for the issuance of a warrant *in rem*." It concluded that a maritime tort cannot "form the basis for a maritime lien" and cited a federal statute, 46 U.S.C. § 31342, that grants a lien to "a person providing necessaries to a vessel." The district court also explained that its "uncertainty" whether Minott's "claim [fell] under maritime jurisdiction . . . weigh[ed] against issuing a warrant." Although it did not decide the question, the district court suggested that it lacked jurisdiction because Minott's "activity . . . [was] not significantly tied to maritime activity" and his accident had "minimal" potential to "disrupt[] . . . maritime commerce."

Minott moved for reconsideration and cited caselaw where plaintiffs filed *in rem* actions against vessels for maritime torts. The district court denied the motion. It explained that Minott's original motion sought a warrant only "based on 46 U.S.C. [section] 31301(5)(B)" and that he could not "raise [new] arguments" that he was "entitled to a warrant of arrest under [other] authorities." It also explained that these authorities "still . . . [failed to] convince [it] that alleged tort victims . . . are entitled to issuance of a warrant of arrest *in rem* upon filing a complaint."

Minott appealed and invoked our interlocutory jurisdiction, 28 U.S.C. § 1292(a)(3). **[—5—]**

II. STANDARD OF REVIEW

"Whether a party's claim[] give[s] rise to a maritime lien is a legal question that is reviewed *de novo*," **{-1281-}** *Salvors, Inc. v. Unidentified Wrecked & Abandoned Vessel*, 861 F.3d 1278, 1297, 5 Adm. R. 461, 474 (11th Cir. 2017), as is "[t]he [d]istrict [c]ourt's application of admiralty law and the local rules implementing that law," *Isbrandtsen Marine Servs. v. M/V Inagua Tania*, 93 F.3d 728, 733 (11th Cir. 1996). Under Federal Rule of Civil Procedure Supplemental Rule C, we review the facts alleged in the "complaint and . . . supporting papers" to determine "[i]f the conditions for an *in rem* action [and warrant] appear to exist." Fed. R. Civ. P. Supp. R. C(3)(a)(i) (italics added).

III. DISCUSSION

We divide our discussion in two parts. First, we explain that we have interlocutory jurisdiction over this appeal. Second, we explain that the district court erred when it refused to direct the clerk to issue a warrant *in rem* for the arrest of the *Brunello*.

A. We Have Interlocutory Jurisdiction.

We have interlocutory jurisdiction over appeals from "decrees of . . . district courts . . . [that] determin[e] the rights and liabilities of the parties to admiralty cases in which appeals from final decrees are allowed." 28 U.S.C. § 1292(a)(3). "As a general rule, a district court's order resolving one or more claims on the **[—6—]** merits is appealable under [section] 1292(a)(3), irrespective of any claims that remain pending." *Sea Lane Bahamas Ltd. v. Europa Cruises Corp.*, 188 F.3d 1317, 1321 (11th Cir. 1999). For example, we "ha[ve] jurisdiction over the appeal of an order dismissing on the merits one or more parties from an action." *Id.* (collecting cases); *see also Nichols v. Barwick*, 792 F.2d 1520, 1522 (11th Cir. 1986) ("Not all the rights and liabilities of the parties need be determined before such an order is appealable."); *Trinidad Foundry & Fabricating, Ltd. v. M/V K.A.S. Camilla*, 966 F.2d 613, 614 & n.1 (11th Cir. 1992). But we lack jurisdiction "when the order appealed from 'does not reach the merits of the claim and in no way determines, denies, or prejudices any substantive rights of the parties.'" *Sea Lane Bahamas*, 188 F.3d at 1321 (quoting *Jensenius v. Texaco, Inc.*, 639 F.2d 1342, 1343 (5th Cir. Unit A Mar. 1981)).

The refusal of the district court to issue a warrant *in rem* for the arrest of the *Brunello* falls within our interlocutory jurisdiction because it has the effect of a final order that "reach[es] the merits of the claim" and "prejudices [the] substantive rights of [Minott]." *Id.* (quoting *Jensenius*, 639 F.2d at 1343). To be sure, the decision refusing to arrest the *Brunello* did not resolve Minott's claims against the other defendants. But it resolved his claim against the vessel, and he is entitled to immediate review of that decision. **[—7—]**

The refusal to arrest the *Brunello* resolved the question of the vessel's liability because "[a]ttachment subjecting the *res* to the jurisdiction of the court is a prerequisite to a finding of *in rem* liability." *Dow Chem. Co. v. The Barge UM-23B*, 424 F.2d 307, 311 (5th Cir. 1970) (italics added). For example, in *The Pesaro* the Supreme Court exercised interlocutory jurisdiction over a "decree" that released a vessel from arrest but did not "formally" "dismiss the libel." 255 U.S. 216, 217 (1921). The Supreme Court explained that although the "decree . . . [did] not dismiss the libel," this detail was not "decisive" because "[t]he decree . . . declare[d] [that the vessel was] not subject to any such process[,] . . . direct[ed] her release . . ., [and] end[ed] the suit as effectually as if it formally dismissed the libel." *Id.* In short, although the question whether to arrest a vessel arises at the beginning of litigation, it also "reach[es] the merits of the claim," *Sea Lane Bahamas*, 188 F.3d at 1321 **{-1282-}** (quoting *Jensenius*, 639 F.2d at 1343), because it necessarily dictates jurisdiction and liability.

More importantly, a failure to arrest a vessel "prejudices [the] substantive rights of the parties" in the light of the mobile nature of vessels. *Id.* (quoting *Jensenius*, 639 F.2d at 1343). If a vessel leaves the jurisdiction while the district court is resolving claims against other defendants, the plaintiff risks forever losing his "substantive" right to "enforce a maritime lien," *Trinidad*, 966 F.2d at 615, because "where the *res* is no longer before the court, . . . *in rem* jurisdiction is **[—8—]** destroyed" and the district court "can[not] proceed to adjudication," *L.B. Harvey Marine, Inc. v. M/V River Arc*, 712 F.2d 458, 459 (11th Cir. 1983) (italics added). The Supreme Court highlighted this concern in *Swift & Co. Packers v. Compania Colombiana del Caribe, S.A.*, when it exercised interlocutory jurisdiction over "an order . . . vacating a foreign attachment of a vessel." 339 U.S. 684, 685 (1950); *see also id.* at 688–89. The Supreme Court explained that "[a]ppellate review of [an] order dissolving [an] attachment at a later date would be an empty rite after the vessel had been released and the restoration of the attachment only theoretically possible," *id.* at 689, and it underscored that the question of attachment "f[e]ll in that small class [of orders] which finally determine claims of right separable from . . . rights asserted in the action . . . [that are] too important to be denied review and too independent of the cause itself to require that appellate consideration be deferred," *id.* at 688–89 (quoting *Cohen v. Beneficial Indus. Loan Corp*, 337 U.S. 541, 546 (1949)); *see also Puerto Rico Ports Auth. v. Barge Katy-B*, 427 F.3d 93, 101 (1st Cir. 2005) (explaining that concerns of "effective finality" establish that "an order vacating an arrest finally determines the rights and liabilities of the parties within the meaning of section 1292(a)(3)"). Because Minott's present inability to proceed *in rem* against the *Brunello* may become permanent if the vessel departs the district, we have interlocutory jurisdiction. **[—9—]**

B. The District Court Erred when It Refused To Direct the Clerk To Issue a Warrant In Rem *for the Arrest of the* Brunello.

We divide this section in two parts. First, we explain that the tort alleged in the complaint falls within the admiralty jurisdiction of the district court. Second, we explain that this maritime tort entitles Minott to proceed *in rem* against the *Brunello* and obligates the district court to direct the clerk to issue a warrant *in rem* for the vessel's arrest.

1. The Alleged Incident Falls Within Admiralty Jurisdiction.

The Constitution grants federal courts power over "all Cases of admiralty and maritime Jurisdiction." U.S. Const. art. III, § 2; *cf.* 28 U.S.C. § 1333. Maritime jurisdiction over torts is based on the location of the incident and a nexus to maritime activity. *See* 1 Thomas J. Schoenbaum, Admiralty & Maritime Law § 3-5 (5th ed. 2017). A district court has jurisdiction if the tort "occurred on navigable water or . . . [occurred] on land [but] was caused by a vessel on navigable water," and if the tort "ha[d] sufficient connection with maritime activity." *Alderman v. Pac. N. Victor, Inc.*, 95 F.3d 1061, 1064 (11th Cir. 1996) (quoting *Jerome B. Grubart Inc. v. Great Lakes Dredge & Dock Co.*, 513 U.S. 527, 534 (1995)).

The "connection" element of this test for maritime-tort jurisdiction "raises two issues." *Id.* "First, we are required to assess the general features of **{-1283-}** the type of accident involved . . . to determine whether the incident has a potentially disruptive impact on maritime commerce." *Id.* (quoting *Grubart*, 513 U.S. at 534) (internal **[—10—]** quotation marks omitted). A plaintiff can satisfy this requirement by alleging "[u]nsafe working conditions aboard a vessel under repairs, maintenance, or conversion" because an accident caused by such conditions "could have the potential to disrupt further repairs of that vessel, vessels being worked on at the same dock, or vessels waiting to be worked upon." *Id.* "Second, we must determine whether the general character of the activity giving rise to the incident shows a substantial relationship to traditional maritime activity." *Id.* (quoting *Grubart*, 513 U.S at 534) (internal quotation marks omitted). This inquiry looks to "the activities of the tortfeasor" and encompasses a "broad" range of conduct, including "conversions, repairs, or maintenance aboard a vessel in navigable water." *Id.* at 1065.

The district court suggested, without deciding, that it lacked admiralty jurisdiction. It underscored that Minott's fall had "minimal" "potential[]" to "disrupt[] . . . maritime commerce . . . [because] any rescue effort would likely occur from land." And it explained that "[t]he general character of [Minott's] activity—walking to the boat—[was] not significantly tied to maritime activity." The district court concluded that its "uncertainty" about this question "weigh[ed] against issuing a warrant." We disagree.

Minott clearly alleged a maritime tort. The incident "occurred on navigable water," *id.* at 1064 (citation and internal quotation marks omitted), when the **[—11—]** *Brunello* was docked in Dania, Florida. Although Minott was not yet aboard the vessel when the gangway collapsed, "[i]t is well established that traditional maritime law encompasses the gangway." *White v. United States*, 53 F.3d 43, 46 (4th Cir. 1995). For example, in *The Admiral Peoples*, the Supreme Court explained that admiralty jurisdiction extended to an accident where a "disembarking . . . [passenger] was injured by falling from a gangplank leading from the vessel to the dock," 295 U.S. 649, 650 (1935), because the gangplank "was no less part of the vessel because in its extension to the dock it projected over the land," *id.* at 651–52. To be sure, the Supreme Court mentioned that "while [the passenger] was on the gangplank, she had not *yet left* the vessel." *Id.* at 652 (emphasis added). But this observation about the passenger's direction of travel does not affect the "basic fact . . . that the gangplank [is] a part of the vessel." *Id.* at 651. If anything, Minott's injury is a stronger candidate for admiralty jurisdiction because he fell into the water, unlike the passenger in *The Admiral Peoples* who "was violently thrown forward upon the dock." *Id.* at 652. Our predecessor circuit also explained in *O'Keeffe v. Atlantic Stevedoring Co.*, 354 F.2d 48 (5th Cir. 1965), that a plaintiff "sustained his injury over navigable water," *id.* at 50, when he was "lifted . . . from the dock" where he was working by a winch and struck either "the dock . . . [or] the side of the ship" before he fell into the water and drowned, *id.* at 49. And even if Minott's injury had occurred on land, it was **[—12—]** "caused by" the vessel, *Alderman*, 95 F.3d at 1064, when its "captain or crew . . . put the engines in gear." An injury caused by a vessel in navigable waters is a maritime tort.

The incident satisfied the first element of the "connection test" because the "general features of [this] type of accident . . . [had] a potentially disruptive impact on maritime commerce." *Id.* (citation and internal quotation marks omitted). Minott's employer had been hired to "perform maintenance and repairs aboard the **{-1284-}** . . . *Brunello*," and Minott's injury threatened "to disrupt further repairs of that vessel," not to mention the repairs of "vessels being worked on at the same dock . . . [and] vessels waiting to be worked upon." *Id.* The district court overlooked these consequences when it narrowly considered only the possibility of a "rescue effort [that] would likely occur from land" and failed to contemplate the *potential* impact of worker injuries on maritime commerce. To be sure, this particular accident may not have had widespread effects, but "[w]hether or not disruption resulted here is of no moment." *Id.*

On the second element, "the general character of the activity giving rise to [Minott's accident] shows a substantial relationship to traditional maritime activity." *Id.* (citation and internal quotation marks omitted). The district court focused on the activities of Minott when it explained that his "activity—walking to the boat—[was] not significantly tied to maritime activity." But this analysis **[—13—]** considered the actions of the incorrect party because we look instead to "the activities of the [alleged] *tortfeasor*"—in this case, the *Brunello*. *Id.* at 1065 (emphasis added). Minott alleged that the gangway fell when "the [v]essel captain or crew . . . put the engines in gear," and the operation and movement of a vessel in navigable waters are quintessential "maritime activit[ies]." *Id.* at 1064. That the incident occurred when the vessel was docked for "maintenance and repairs" also underscores its maritime quality, for "[w]ork upon ships . . . docked in navigable waterways is an indispensable maritime activity." *Id.* at 1065.

2. Minott is Entitled to a Warrant *In Rem* for the Arrest of the *Brunello*.

A vessel is "an entity apart from its owner" that "is liable . . . for torts," *Merchants Nat'l Bank of Mobile v. Dredge Gen. G. L. Gillespie*, 663 F.2d 1338, 1345 (5th Cir. Unit A Dec. 1981), and a maritime tort gives the victim a lien against the vessel "by operation of the general maritime law," Schoenbaum, *supra*, at § 9-1. This "lien is created as soon as the claim comes into being," and the "principle [of an automatic lien] . . . [is] equally applicable to all claims . . . which can be enforced in admiralty against the ship, whether arising out of tort or of contract." *The John G. Stevens*, 170 U.S. 113, 117 (1898); *see also The Bird of Paradise*, 72 U.S. 545, 554, 555 (1866) (explaining that "[s]hip-owners, unquestionably, as a general rule, have a lien upon the cargo for the freight" that "arises from the usages of commerce, independently of the agreement of the **[—14—]** parties, and not from any statutory regulations"); *Craddock v. M/Y The Golden Rule*, 110 F. Supp. 3d 1267, 1276 (S.D. Fla. 2015) ("A maritime lien attaches and is perfected by operation of law when the claim arises."); *Riverway Co. v. Spivey Marine & Harbor Serv.*, 598 F. Supp. 909, 912 (S.D. Ill. 1984) ("The creation of a maritime lien requires no judicial action; the lien is a right of the injured party which arises at the moment of the breach or tort and attaches to the *res*." (citing *The Bold Boccleaugh*, 13 Eng. Rep. 884 (1851))).

"Federal district courts obtain *in rem* jurisdiction over a vessel when a maritime lien attaches to it," *Crimson Yachts v. Betty Lyn II Motor Yacht*, 603 F.3d 864, 868 (11th Cir. 2010), and "[u]nder traditional admiralty law, maritime property is subject to arrest in order to enforce a maritime lien," *Merchants Nat'l Bank*, 663 F.2d at 1345. "Upon [the] filing [of] an *in rem* complaint, the clerk of court issues a warrant for the arrest of the *res*." *Crimson Yachts*, 603 F.3d at 868. This **{-1285-}** process is controlled by Supplemental Rule C, which provides that "[a]n action *in rem* may be brought . . . [t]o enforce any maritime lien," Fed. R. Civ. P. Supp. R. C(1) (italics added), and that, "[i]f the conditions for an *in rem* action appear to exist, the court *must issue* an order directing the clerk to issue a warrant for the arrest of the vessel," Fed. R. Civ. P. Supp. R. C(3)(a)(i) (emphasis and italics added); *see also* S.D. Fla. Adm. & Mar. R. B. **[—15—]**

The district court ruled that Minott "failed to establish that his negligence claim [gave] rise to a 'maritime lien' supporting the *in rem* seizure of the [v]essel." It ruled that maritime liens are exclusively "governed by 46 U.S.C. [section] 31342," which addresses materialmen's liens. It then underscored that this statute "provides that only a 'person providing necessaries to a vessel' has a maritime lien and corresponding right to bring a civil action *in rem*," and that "[t]he applicable statutes and rules do not expressly contemplate that a 'maritime tort' can form the basis for a 'maritime lien.'" The district court concluded that *in rem* proceedings for torts would be "untenable and contrary to the applicable law." And it chastised Minott for failing to cite more than one "authority that would allow for the arrest of a vessel [for a tort]."

The district court erred. The authority cited by Minott, *Craddock*, 110 F. Supp. 3d at 1276, correctly stated that a maritime tort gives the victim a lien against the vessel. *See id.* (explaining that the plaintiff "has alleged a maritime tort" and that "[i]t follows that [he] has a maritime lien" because "[a] maritime lien attaches and is perfected by operation of law when the claim arises"). Indeed, the "characteristic maritime liens recognized under United States law" include "[c]laims for maritime torts including personal injury." Schoenbaum, *supra*, at § 9-1. And contrary to the reasoning of the district court that section 31342 is the only font for maritime liens and *in rem* proceedings, "[m]ost maritime liens arise by **[—16—]** operation of the general maritime law." *Id.* To be sure, Congress can change maritime law, but nothing in section 31342, which addresses the completely different question of materialmen's liens, abrogates Minott's ability to assert a tort claim. *See* Antonin Scalia & Bryan A. Garner, *Reading Law: The Interpretation of Legal Texts* 318 (2012) ("A statute will be construed to alter the common law only when that disposition is clear."); *cf. Atl. Sounding Co. v. Townsend,* 557 U.S. 404, 416 (2009) (explaining that "Congress was envisioning the continued availability of . . . common-law causes of action" "for injured seamen" when it passed the Jones Act to confer additional statutory rights). Indeed, federal courts have long acknowledged a wide variety of maritime liens "arising out of services rendered to *or injuries caused by* [a vessel]." Schoenbaum, *supra*, at § 9-1 (emphasis added) (collecting cases). And Minott cited several authorities dating to the 1800s that establish that a vessel's tort grants the injured victim an automatic lien. *See, e.g., The Anaces*, 93 F. 240 (4th Cir. 1899). In short, his "prima facie showing that [he had] an action *in rem* against the [*Brunello*] . . . and that the [*Brunello*] [was] within the district," *Craddock,* 110 F. Supp. 3d at 1277, obligated the district court to "order . . . the clerk to issue a warrant for the arrest of the vessel," Fed. R. Civ. P. Supp. R. C(3)(a)(i). **[—17—]**

IV. CONCLUSION

We **REVERSE** and **REMAND** with instructions for the district court to enter an order directing the clerk to issue a warrant for the arrest of the *Brunello*.

United States Court of Appeals
for the Eleventh Circuit

No. 17-12164

INTERNAVES DE MEX. S.A. DE C.V.
vs.
ANDROMEDA S.S. CORP.

Appeal from the United States District Court for the Southern District of Florida

Decided: August 1, 2018

Citation: 898 F.3d 1087, 6 Adm. R. 456 (11th Cir. 2018).

Before **MARCUS, FAY,** and **HULL,** Circuit Judges.

[—1—] {-1089-} **MARCUS,** Circuit Judge: **[—2—] {-1090-}**

This case arises out of a battle over where the parties have agreed to arbitrate this admiralty and maritime dispute. Andromeda Steamship Corporation and Internaves de Mexico s.a. de C.V. entered into a shipping contract (the "Contract") whereby Andromeda agreed to furnish Internaves with a vessel to transport an electric transformer from Brazil to Mexico. Internaves claimed that Andromeda failed to tender the vessel on the agreed-upon date, while Andromeda countered that Internaves never delivered the transformer to the vessel. The Contract unambiguously required the parties to submit their dispute to arbitration. However, the Contract contained conflicting provisions regarding *where* the parties agreed to arbitrate. The district court could not ascertain the site of arbitration from the agreement itself and, therefore, resorted to the statutory default forum, compelling arbitration in its own district—the Southern District of Florida.

Andromeda appealed, arguing that the district court had erred in proclaiming the Contract hopelessly ambiguous as to the selection of a forum. Had the court waded through the Contract's interpretive tangles, Andromeda says, it would have discovered the parties' mutually agreed-upon intent to arbitrate in London, where it claims the arbitration must be held. Internaves suggests, however, that due to the Contract's murkiness, the district court properly ordered arbitration in Miami.

The Contract hardly represents a model of clarity. Nevertheless, we agree with Andromeda and discern from the document an agreement to arbitrate in **[—3—]** London. Accordingly, we reverse the judgment of the district court and remand with instructions to compel arbitration in London under English law.

I.

A.

Andromeda and Internaves entered into the Contract, a charter party agreement, in June 2016. A "charter party" is simply a contractual arrangement whereby a ship owner agrees to lend a ship to a charterer for the transportation of goods from one port to another. *See Hawkspere Shipping Co. v. Intamex, S.A.*, 330 F.3d 225, 228 (4th Cir. 2003); *see also* Soumyadipta Chanda, *A Comparison of Rights and Liabilities Under a Charter Party and a Bill of Lading*, 24 U.S.F. Mar. L.J. 65, 67–68 (2011).

The Contract is divided into two parts. Part I contains terms specific to the parties' particular transaction. Part II includes general boilerplate terms that are typically incorporated into shipping contracts of this kind. Part I includes Box 25, labeled "Law and Arbitration." Box 25 instructs, "[S]tate 19(a), 19(b) or 19(c) of Cl[ause] 19; if 19(c) agreed also state Place of Arbitration (if not filled in 19(a) shall apply)." Clause 19, in turn, also labeled "Law and Arbitration," appears in Part II of the agreement. Clause 19 is divided into sub-clauses 19(a) through 19(d). Affixed to each sub-clause is an asterisk, and the asterisk notation reads, "(a), (b) and (c) are alternatives; indicate alternative agreed in Box 25." Clause 19(a) **[—4—]** provides for arbitration in London under English law and imposes additional terms, including a scheme for appointing arbitrators. Clause **{-1091-}** 19(b) calls for arbitration in New York under U.S. law and prescribes similar supplemental conditions. Clause 19(c) reads this way: "Any dispute arising out of this Charter Party shall be referred to arbitration at the Place indicated in Box 25, subject to the procedures applicable there. The laws of the place indicated in Box 25 shall govern this Charter Party." Finally, 19(d) explains that if Box 25 is not filled in, then 19(a) governs. In sum, Clause 19 of the Contract, located in Part II, provides a list of forum alternatives and instructs the parties to indicate their selection among those alternatives in Box 25. Box 25, located in Part I, also directs the parties to write their selection among Clause 19's options within that space.

Inside Box 25, the parties clearly wrote these words: "London arbitration, English Law." However, in Clause 19, the parties crossed out 19(a), 19(c), and 19(d), leaving only 19(b)—New York arbitration under U.S. law—unstruck. Thus, while the parties wrote in the words "London arbitration, English Law" in Box 25 in Part I, they signaled some desire to arbitrate in New York under U.S. law in Part II. Finally, above the signature page, the Contract reads, "It is mutually agreed that this Contract shall be performed subject to the conditions contained in this Charter Party which shall include PART I as well as PART II. In the event of a **[—5—]** conflict of conditions, the provisions of Part I *shall* prevail over those of Part II to the extent of such conflict" (the "Conflict Clause") (emphasis added).

B.

In October 2016, Internaves sued Andromeda in the Southern District of Florida for breach of contract, conversion, and fraud. Internaves claimed that, although it prepaid Andromeda, Andromeda failed to tender the vessel on the agreed-upon date, in violation of the Contract. Andromeda moved to compel arbitration of the dispute in London under English law pursuant to the selection the parties made in Part I, Box 25. The district court granted Andromeda's motion in part, compelling arbitration, but concluded that it could not ascertain from the terms of the agreement where the parties had agreed to arbitrate the dispute. The court observed that, because Part I stipulated "London arbitration, English Law," while Part II indicated a contrary agreement to arbitrate any dispute arising from the Contract in New York under U.S. law, the Parts were hopelessly in conflict. The court continued this way: "This conflict is compounded by ambiguities in the very provisions ostensibly designed to resolve internal inconsistencies." Elaborating, the court recognized that, under the Conflict Clause, in the event of conflict, Part I superseded Part II. However, the court also observed that 19(c), "which also provide[d] for the supremacy of Part I," was crossed out. In light of that puzzle, the district court could not determine whether the Conflict Clause **[—6—]** remained applicable to the instant dispute. Accordingly, it held that the parties had failed to provide for a specific arbitral forum and, therefore, it could compel arbitration only within its own district pursuant to 9 U.S.C. § 4.

While Andromeda does not dispute its obligation to arbitrate, it contends that the district court should have compelled arbitration in London, as the parties had written into Box 25.

Andromeda timely appealed to this Court.

II.

Plainly, the site of arbitration turns on interpretation of the Contract's arbitration clauses, which we review *de novo*. **{-1092-}** *Inetianbor v. CashCall, Inc.*, 768 F.3d 1346, 1350 (11th Cir. 2014) ("This Court reviews *de novo* questions of law, such as a district court's interpretation of an agreement to arbitrate . . . ."). After thorough review, we hold that, despite the Contract's apparent conflict about choice of forum, under the Conflict Clause, the parties provided for arbitration in London, under English law, and the district court should have upheld the parties' forum selection under 9 U.S.C. § 206.

A.

Issues arising out of arbitration agreements are generally resolved by contract-law principles, pursuant to which we attempt to ascertain the parties' intent through the words they use. The Federal

Arbitration Act (FAA) provides that **[—7—]** written arbitration agreements in "any maritime transaction" "shall be valid, irrevocable, and enforceable, save upon such grounds as exist at law or in equity for the revocation of any contract." 9 U.S.C. § 2. "This provision reflects both a liberal federal policy favoring arbitration, and the fundamental principle that arbitration is a matter of contract." *Inetianbor*, 768 F.3d at 1349 (quotation omitted and alteration adopted). "In line with these principles, courts must place arbitration agreements on an equal footing with other contracts, and enforce them according to their terms." *Id.* (quotation omitted); *see also Am. Express Co. v. Italian Colors Rest.*, 570 U.S. 228, 233 (2013) ("[The FAA] reflects the overarching principle that arbitration is a matter of contract. And consistent with [its] text, courts must rigorously enforce arbitration agreements according to their terms . . . ." (quotations and citation omitted)).

International arbitration agreements are governed by the Convention on the Recognition and Enforcement of Foreign Arbitral Awards, commonly known as the "New York Convention," which the United Nations Economic and Social Council adopted in 1958. *Lindo v. NCL (Bahamas), Ltd.*, 652 F.3d 1257, 1262 (11th Cir. 2011). In 1970, the United States joined, by treaty, the New York Convention. 21 U.S.T. 2517; *see also Lindo*, 652 F.3d at 1262. Thereafter, Congress implemented the New York Convention into the United States Code as Chapter 2 of the Federal Arbitration Act, 9 U.S.C. § 201 *et seq.*, thereby **[—8—]** supplementing the original codification of the FAA contained in Chapter 1. The New York Convention requires that courts, *inter alia*, recognize written arbitration agreements and uphold freely negotiated forum-selection provisions. *Lindo*, 652 F.3d at 1262, 1266; *Mitsubishi Motors Corp. v. Soler Chrysler-Plymouth, Inc.*, 473 U.S. 614, 631 (1985). Specifically, under Chapter 2 of the FAA, courts "may direct that arbitration be held in accordance with the [arbitration] agreement at any place therein provided for, whether that place is within or without the United States." 9 U.S.C. § 206. By contrast, under Chapter 1, courts may compel arbitration only within their own districts. 9 U.S.C. § 4. Chapter 2 also applies Chapter 1 to all actions arising under Chapter 2 to the extent that the two Chapters do not conflict. 9 U.S.C. § 208. Therefore, if the parties to an international arbitration agreement "provided for" a forum, Chapter 2 establishes a "strong presumption" in favor of compelling arbitration in that forum. *Mitsubishi Motors Corp.*, 473 U.S. at 631. However, if the parties agreed to arbitrate, but failed to "provide[ ] for" a forum, then the court must compel arbitration, but only within its own district pursuant to the provisions found in Chapter 1. 9 U.S.C. § 4 ("The hearing and proceedings, under [an arbitration] agreement, shall be within the district in which the petition for **{-1093-}** an order directing such arbitration is filed."); *see also Jain v. de Mere*, 51 F.3d 686, 690 (7th Cir. 1995) ("[9 U.S.C.] § 4 not only permits but requires a court to compel arbitration in its own district when no other forum is specified."). **[—9—]**

Notably, "[w]hen a contract is a maritime one, and the dispute is not inherently local, federal law controls the contract interpretation." *Norfolk S. Ry. Co. v. Kirby*, 543 U.S. 14, 22–23 (2004). Specifically, our interpretation of maritime contracts sounds in federal common law, so we look to the general common law of contracts. *See AIG Centennial Ins. Co. v. O'Neill*, 782 F.3d 1296, 1302, 3 Adm. R. 643, 646 (11th Cir. 2015); *Interface Kanner, LLC v. JPMorgan Chase Bank, N.A.*, 704 F.3d 927, 932–33 (11th Cir. 2013); *Begner v. United States*, 428 F.3d 998, 1005 (11th Cir. 2005).

Five general principles of contract interpretation apply here. First, "[i]t is well settled that the actual language used in the contract is the best evidence of the intent of the parties and, thus, the plain meaning of that language controls." *Rose v. M/V "GULF STREAM FALCON"*, 186 F.3d 1345, 1350 (11th Cir. 1999). Additionally, "a [contract] should be read to give effect to all its provisions and to render them consistent with each other." *In re FFS Data, Inc.*, 776 F.3d 1299, 1305 (11th Cir. 2015) (quoting *Mastrobuono v. Shearson Lehman Hutton, Inc.*, 514 U.S. 52, 63 (1995)). Moreover, if contractual provisions conflict, but, significantly, the contract itself provides means for reconciling the conflict, we are obliged to apply the contract's internal conflict-resolution mechanism. *See Columbia Cas. Co. v. S. Flapjacks, Inc.*, 868 F.2d 1217, 1221 n.1 (11th Cir. 1989). Indeed, where a contract contains a conflict, but also includes a clause that expressly resolves the conflict, **[—10—]** "there is no ambiguity." *Lathem v. Sentry Ins.*, 845 F.2d 914, 916–17 (11th Cir. 1988). Further, "[w]hen general propositions in a contract are qualified by the specific provisions, the rule of construction is that the specific provisions in the agreement control." *Goldberg v. Bear, Stearns & Co.*, 912 F.2d 1418, 1421 (11th Cir. 1990). Finally, contracts must be interpreted with sensitivity to the reality that parties occasionally err or misprint in the course of contract drafting. *See Georgia R.R. Bank & Tr. Co. v. Fed. Deposit Ins. Corp.*, 758 F.2d 1548, 1551 (11th Cir. 1985) ("However unskillfully prepared a particular instrument or agreement may be, the courts are to discover and give effect to the intent of the parties if possible."); *see also Begner*, 428 F.3d at 1006 (noting that an apparent contractual error did not render the contract ambiguous).

Thus, when interpreting an international arbitration agreement, we ascertain the parties' intent through plain contractual language; we work to interpret the contract harmoniously to avoid conflict and give meaning to all of the provisions; we are obliged to apply any contractual clauses designed to resolve intra-contractual conflicts; we favor the specific terms over the more general language; and we strive to give the contract coherent meaning if we can, rather than capitulate in the face of apparent ambiguity. **[—11—]**

B.

As we see it, application of these principles yields the conclusion that the parties agreed to arbitrate their dispute in London. The Conflict Clause unambiguously establishes the superiority of Part I's enumeration of "London arbitration, English Law" over Part II's manifestation of the parties' preference for a New York forum. Moreover, Box 25's heading and instructions, coupled with Clause 19's **{-1094-}** asterisks, render Box 25 the Contract's authoritative forum-selection clause. Insertion of the written words "London arbitration, English Law" within that provision further evinces the parties' intent to arbitrate in London. The parties specifically wrote "London arbitration, English Law" into the Contract, whereas any indication of the parties' willingness to arbitrate in New York appears only among boilerplate script, and in that regard only by striking a provision with a line. The rule of construction subordinating general terms to specific ones also supports the selection of the London forum.

In Part I, the parties demonstrated their mutual desire to arbitrate in London by writing in their selection of "London arbitration, English Law" in Box 25, labeled "Law and Arbitration." In Part II, the parties indicated some inclination toward arbitrating in New York by crossing out all of Clause 19's sub-clauses except for 19(b), which, as we have already noted, provides for New York arbitration under U.S. law. Plainly, by choosing different arbitral forums in Parts I **[—12—]** and II—by writing in "London" in Part I and leaving 19(b) operative in Part II—the parties created an inter-Part conflict. Yet these parties anticipated and sought to resolve any such conflict by including a Conflict Clause, which, again, reads this way: "In the event of a conflict of conditions, the provisions of Part I shall prevail over those of Part II to the extent of such conflict." When parties author conflicting contractual provisions, but expressly provide for a contractual mechanism to resolve any conflict, we are bound by the mechanism they have chosen. *See Columbia Cas.*, 868 F.2d at 1221 n.1; *Lathem*, 845 F.3d at 916–17. Thus, under the Conflict Clause, Part I's designation "London arbitration, English Law" necessarily prevails over Part II.

Additionally, Box 25's heading and instructions, along with Clause 19's asterisks, militate in favor of London arbitration. Box 25, labeled "Law and Arbitration," instructs, "[S]tate 19(a), 19(b) or 19(c) of Cl. 19; if 19(c) agreed also state Place of Arbitration (if not filled in 19(a) shall apply)." Turning to Clause 19, also labeled "Law and Arbitration," an asterisk appears alongside sub-clauses 19(a) through 19(d), and the asterisk notation explains, "(a), (b), and (c) are alternatives; indicate alternative agreed in Box 25." The parties have designated in the Contract that Box 25 is the authoritative space within which to ascertain their forum selection. And inside that space, the parties wrote their preference. Box 25's "London arbitration, English Law" supersedes Clause 19's indication of their **[—13—]** preference of a forum. It is true that the parties neglected to stipulate one of "19(a)," "19(b)," or "19(c)" in Box 25, as the Contract had instructed. Nonetheless, the parties' omission essentially amounts to a small error that cannot undermine their manifest intent, as they wrote it, to arbitrate in London under English law. *See Georgia R.R. Bank & Tr. Co.*, 758 F.2d at 1551; *see also Begner*, 428 F.3d at 999–1000, 1006.

The canon of contract interpretation elevating specific terms over the more general ones also supports the selection of London. The parties' particular insertion of "London arbitration, English Law" prevails over the crossed-out boilerplate terms. *See United States v. Pielago*, 135 F.3d 703, 710 (11th Cir. 1998); *Faez v. Wells Fargo Bank, N.A.*, 745 F.3d 1098, 1106 n.4 (11th Cir. 2014); *McKinney Drilling Co. v. Collins Co.*, 701 F.2d 132, 135 (11th Cir. 1983). Internaves argues, nevertheless, that the specific-general canon is inapposite here because the parties also **{-1095-}** "specifically" crossed out 19(a), 19(c), and 19(d), thereby creating a conflict not between specific and general conditions, but rather between two specific terms. We are unpersuaded. As we see it, the specific written insertion of "London" entailed far greater specificity and particularity—and constitutes a far more powerful expression of intent—than striking 19(a), 19(c), and 19(d) from boilerplate script. **[—14—]**

Internaves advances several additional objections. First, it claims that, by crossing out 19(c), the parties rendered Box 25 ineffective, arguing that "[i]f the parties chose Paragraph 19(c), it would have provided for the selection in [B]ox 25 to prevail over the selection of London or New York. By striking out Paragraph 19(c) of Part II, [Andromeda] affirmatively rejected the effect of any designated forum within Part I and thereby exalted its choice in Part II over Part I and undermined the [Conflict Clause]." The district court agreed, similarly reasoning that, because 19(c) "provide[d] for the supremacy of Part I," having struck 19(c), the parties suggested that the Conflict Clause was inapplicable and Box 25 irrelevant.

Again, 19(c) reads, "Any dispute arising out of this Charter Party shall be referred to arbitration at the Place indicated in Box 25, subject to the procedures applicable there. The laws of the place indicated in Box 25 shall govern this Charter Party." Clause 19(c) does not "provide[ ] for the supremacy of Part I." Rather, what 19(c) does is offer a "write-in" forum option. Since parties to charter party agreements typically choose to arbitrate in London or New York, 19(a) and 19(b) provide shortcuts for selecting those forums. *See* Gu Weixia & Joshua A. Lindenbaum, *The NYPE 93 Arbitration Clause: Where Ends the Open-End?*, 37 J. Mar. L. & Com. 245, 259 (2006) ("The vast majority of charterparties contain arbitration clauses that call for arbitration in London or New York."). However, **[—15—]** since an alternative is occasionally preferred, 19(c) permitted the parties to insert a forum of their choosing. Clause 19(c)'s purpose, thus, was not to ensure Part I's primacy, but rather to afford a forum option other than London or New York. Meanwhile, none of the provisions that *do* establish Part I's supremacy are crossed out. The Conflict Clause expressly calls for Part I's terms to prevail over Part II's in the event of conflict. Likewise, Box 25's labeling and Clause 19's asterisk notation instructed the parties to insert their forum selection among Clause 19's alternatives—19(a), 19(b), or 19(c)—in Box 25. Each of those provisions was left intact, thereby rendering Box 25 the superseding and definitive forum-selection clause irrespective of the fact that the parties struck 19(c). Clause 19(c) does not implicate the Contract's inter-Part hierarchy, and striking 19(c) did not undermine either Part I's predominance over Part II or Box 25's status as the Contract's authoritative forum-selection clause.

Internaves also points to *Bauhinia Corp. v. China National Machinery & Equipment Import & Export Corp.*, 819 F.2d 247 (9th Cir. 1987). In *Bauhinia*, the parties entered into an arbitration agreement in which the only language pertaining to forum selection was the following:

> In case an arbitration is necessary and is to be held in Peking, the case in dispute shall then be submitted for arbitration to the Foreign Trade Arbitration Commission of the China Council for the Promotion of International Trade, Peking .... **[—16—]**
>
> In case the Arbitration is to take place at [BLANK] either party shall appoint one arbitrator, and the arbitrators thus appointed shall nominate a third person as umpire, to form an arbitration committee..... **{-1096-}**

Id. at 248. Because the agreement said nothing more about forum selection, the Ninth Circuit concluded that the agreement was ambiguous: "The clauses d[id] not expressly choose a forum" and "[t]he document lack[ed] any indication what forum the parties intended to select." *Id.* at 249. As a result, it determined, "The record permits only one conclusion, that the parties intended to leave the issue open." *Id.* at 249–50. Because the parties failed to provide for a forum in their agreement, the provisions of 9 U.S.C. § 206 were inapplicable and, pursuant to 9 U.S.C. § 4, the court could compel arbitration only within its own district. *Id.* at 250.

This case is different. Here, rather than providing *no* forum selection, the parties provided *conflicting* forum selections. But here, the parties created a contractual mechanism to resolve any ambiguity or conflict by declaring Part I superior to Part II in the event of conflict, and by designating Box 25 the conclusive forum selection provision. Thus, unlike in *Bauhinia*, in this case the parties provided for an arbitration forum by writing "London arbitration, English Law" in the Contract's superseding and authoritative forum-selection clause.

Finally, Internaves argues for the first time on appeal that the Contract retains some ambiguity because Part I includes an internal inconsistency. **[—17—]** Specifically, in Box 22, which is located in Part I and labeled "General Average to be adjusted at (Cl. 12)," the parties wrote "NEW YORK – USA." Clause 12, in turn, labeled "General Average and New Jason Clause," provides that "[g]eneral average shall be adjusted, stated and settled according [to] York-Antwerp rules 1994 or any subsequent modification thereof." Therefore, Internaves reasons, even if the Conflict Clause resolves conflicts between the Parts, the Contract still contains an intractable conflict within Part I itself, between Box 25 (which calls for London arbitration) and Box 22 (which provides for general-average adjustment in New York).

Again, we are unpersuaded. First, Internaves did not raise the argument in the district court, and we need not consider it on appeal. *Access Now, Inc. v. Sw. Airlines Co.*, 385 F.3d 1324, 1331 (11th Cir. 2004) ("This Court has repeatedly held that an issue not raised in the district court and raised for the first time in an appeal will not be considered by this court. . . . If we were to regularly address questions—particularly fact-bound issues—that district[ ] court[s] never had a chance to examine, we would not only waste our resources, but also deviate from the essential nature, purpose, and competence of an appellate court." (quotation and citations omitted)). To be sure, an appellate court may consider an issue not raised in the district court if it "involves a pure question of law, and if refusal to consider it would result in a miscarriage of justice." *Id.* at 1332 (quoting *Wright v.* **[—18—]** *Hanna Steel Corp.*, 270 F.3d 1336, 1342 (11th Cir. 2001). Although the argument raises a pure question of law, *see Inetianbor*, 768 F.3d at 1350, our failure to address it here would hardly create a miscarriage of justice. *See Blue Martini Kendall, LLC v. Miami Dade Cty.*, 816 F.3d 1343, 1349–50 (11th Cir. 2016).

But even if we were to consider the claim for the first time on appeal, it still would not help Internaves. The "ancient maritime doctrine" of general average holds that, if goods are thrown overboard in order to save a ship from impending catastrophe, the passenger who sacrificed his property for the common good is entitled to reimbursement by pro rata contributions from the other passengers onboard. *See* **{–1097–}** *Orient Mid-E. Lines, Inc. v. Shipment of Rice on Bd. S.S. Orient Transporter*, 496 F.2d 1032, 1034 (5th Cir. 1974).[1] General-average disputes are often resolved under the York-Antwerp Rules, which were designed to resolve issues stemming from general-average adjustment. *See Eagle Terminal Tankers, Inc. v. Ins. Co. of U.S.S.R.*, 637 F.2d 890, 894 (2d Cir. 1981).

The parties' insertion of "NEW YORK – USA" in Box 22 does not create an inconsistency within Part I. Mindful of our obligation to "give effect to all [the Contract's] provisions," and to discern incompatibility among them only if they cannot be construed harmoniously, we read Part I as requiring general-average **[—19—]** adjustment in New York under York-Antwerp Rules pursuant to Box 22, and arbitration of all other disputes in London under English law pursuant to Box 25. *See In re FFS Data, Inc.*, 776 F.3d at 1305; *Pielago*, 135 F.3d at 710; *Merrill Stevens Dry Dock Co. v. M/V YEOCOMICO II*, 329 F.3d 809, 814 (11th Cir. 2003). Indeed, the parties' use of separate Boxes—one labeled "Law and Arbitration" (Box 25) and the other labeled "General Average to be adjusted at (Cl. 12)" (Box 22)—strongly suggests that the parties sought to adjust general average in a location distinct from their arbitral forum. Those conditions are entirely compatible, and, as we see it, create no ambiguity. Moreover, this case does not in any way relate to general-average adjustment; the parties must arbitrate in London.

The only remaining question is which terms will govern the parties' arbitration. Recall that sub-clause 19(a) provides for arbitration in London under English law and prescribes supplemental conditions, including arbitration "in accordance with the arbitrations Acts 1950 and 1979 or any statutory modification or re-enactment thereof for the time being in force," and rules controlling the appointment of arbitrators. Yet the parties did not write "19(a)" in Box 25. Rather, they wrote only "London arbitration, English Law." "[C]ourts must take care not to alter or go beyond the express terms of the agreement, or to impose obligations on the parties that are not mandated by the unambiguous terms of the agreement itself." *Red Ball Interior Demolition Corp. v. Palmadessa*, 173 F.3d 481, 484 (2d **[—20—]** Cir. 1999). Thus, we bind the parties only to the terms on which they agreed—"London arbitration, English Law"—and do not impose 19(a)'s supplemental conditions. Rather, any terms governing the parties' arbitration that are not stipulated in the Contract must be supplied by English arbitration rules.

In short, because the parties' intention to arbitrate in London is discernible from the very terms they wrote into the Contract, the parties "provided for" a forum, which the district court was obliged to recognize and uphold. Accordingly, we reverse and remand with instructions to compel arbitration in London under English law.

REVERSED AND REMANDED

---

[1] "[T]he decisions of the United States Court of Appeals for the Fifth Circuit . . . as that court existed on September 30, 1981, handed down by that court prior to the close of business on that date, shall be binding as precedent in the Eleventh Circuit." *Bonner v. City of Prichard*, 661 F.2d 1206, 1207 (11th Cir. 1981).

United States Court of Appeals
for the Eleventh Circuit

No. 17-10830

UNITED STATES
vs.
CASTILLO

Appeal from the United States District Court for the Southern District of Florida

Decided: August 14, 2018

Citation: 899 F.3d 1208, 6 Adm. R. 463 (11th Cir. 2018).

Before **PRYOR** and **MARTIN,** Circuit Judges, and **WOOD,*** District Judge.

* The Honorable Lisa Wood, United States District Judge for the Southern District of Georgia, sitting by designation.

[—1—] {-1210-} **PRYOR,** Circuit Judge: **[—2—]**

This appeal requires us to decide three questions about Wuilson Estuardo Lemus **{-1211-}** Castillo's conviction and sentence for drug trafficking under the Maritime Drug Law Enforcement Act: whether the Fifth Amendment entitles Castillo to relief from his mandatory minimum sentence; whether the Act exceeds the powers of Congress; and whether the government violated Castillo's constitutional rights when it detained him for 19 days before presenting him to a magistrate judge. The Coast Guard stopped Castillo's vessel in international waters on suspicion of drug trafficking. The Coast Guard and the Department of Homeland Security then detained Castillo for over two weeks while they transported him to Florida, where he received a hearing before a magistrate judge. The government charged Castillo under the Act, and Castillo moved to dismiss the indictment on the grounds that the Act and his detention were unconstitutional. After the district court denied the motion, Castillo pleaded guilty without reserving the right to complain about his detention on appeal. The district court then sentenced him to 132 months of imprisonment after ruling that it could not give Castillo judicial relief from the statutory mandatory minimum sentence for his crimes. We affirm.

I. BACKGROUND

On August 20, 2016, the Coast Guard intercepted the *Cap Caleb* approximately 105 nautical miles from the western coast of Guatemala. When Coast guardsmen approached the *Cap Caleb,* its crew began to jettison neon green **[—3—]** bales that later tested positive for cocaine. Five people, including Wuilson Estuardo Lemus Castillo, were aboard the vessel, and all five asserted Guatemalan nationality. The Coast Guard informed Guatemala about the stop, and Guatemala confirmed the nationality of the vessel and gave the Coast Guard permission to board the *Cap Caleb.* Guardsmen then boarded the vessel and detained its crew members.

The government held Castillo between August 20 and September 9 while it transported him to the United States and coordinated prosecution with Guatemala. On September 8, the Coast Guard dropped Castillo at Guantanamo Bay, and the Department of Homeland Security airlifted Castillo to Florida on the same day. The next day, the government presented Castillo for an appearance before a magistrate judge.

After the government charged Castillo with drug-trafficking crimes under the Maritime Drug Law Enforcement Act, 46 U.S.C. §§ 70503(a)(1), 70506(b), Castillo moved to dismiss for lack of jurisdiction on three grounds. First, he contended that the Act "violates the Due Process Clause because it does not require proof of a nexus between the United States and a defendant." He underscored that the Coast Guard intercepted the *Cap Caleb* far from the United States and that he "is a Guatemalan national . . . [who] has no connection to the United States whatsoever." Second, he argued that the Act is "beyond the authority granted to **[—4—]** Congress under Article I." Third, he complained that his detention violated the Due Process Clause of the Fifth Amendment.

The district court denied Castillo's motion to dismiss, and Castillo pleaded guilty in a written agreement with the government. Castillo's plea agreement contained no reservation of a right to appeal any issue about his detention.

At the sentencing hearing, the district court explained that it could not give Castillo and his codefendants the benefit of a statutory safety valve, which permits relief from a mandatory minimum sentence for other kinds of drug offenses, *see* 18 U.S.C. § 3553(f), because this Court has held that the safety valve does not apply to the Act, *see United States v. Pertuz-Pertuz*, 679 F.3d 1327, 1329 (11th Cir. 2012). The district **{-1212-}** court stated that, had the safety valve applied, it "very well may have given" Castillo and his fellow crew members "less than [the] 120 month[] [mandatory minimum]." But it instead sentenced Castillo to 132 months of imprisonment. The district court explained that this sentence was necessary to punish Castillo more than other crew members who had received the minimum sentence after they "quickly" "accept[ed] responsibility" for their actions. **[—5—]**

II. STANDARD OF REVIEW

We review constitutional questions *de novo*. *See United States v. Osburn*, 955 F.2d 1500, 1503 (11th Cir. 1992).

III. DISCUSSION

We divide our discussion in three parts. First, we explain that Castillo is not entitled to judicial relief from the mandatory minimum sentence. Second, we explain that our precedents foreclose Castillo's arguments about the constitutionality of the Act and its application to him. Third, we explain that Castillo cannot object to his detention on appeal.

A. Castillo Is Not Entitled to the Safety Valve.

The Maritime Drug Law Enforcement Act grants the United States jurisdiction over "a vessel registered in a foreign nation if that nation has consented or waived objection to the enforcement of United States law by the United States," 46 U.S.C. § 70502(c)(1)(C), and it forbids individuals on such vessels from both "possess[ing] with intent to . . . distribute . . . a controlled substance," *id.* § 70503(a), and conspiring to do the same, *id.* § 70506(b). First-time offenders are subject to a mandatory minimum penalty of 10 years of imprisonment for a violation that "involv[es] . . . [five] kilograms or more of a mixture or substance containing a detectable amount of [cocaine]." 21 U.S.C. § 960(b)(1)(B); *see also* 46 U.S.C. § 70506(a). **[—6—]**

Other federal laws that concern domestic drug offenses provide similar mandatory minimums, *see, e.g.*, 21 U.S.C. §§ 841(a) & (b)(1)(A), 960(a) & (b), but a statutory safety valve grants courts the authority to impose sentences below the statutory minimum for certain less-culpable defendants, *see* 18 U.S.C. § 3553(f). This safety valve does not apply to offenses under the Act. *See id.* (specifying offenses eligible for the safety valve). As we explained in *Pertuz-Pertuz*, the "plain text" of the statute compels this disparate treatment, 679 F.3d at 1329, because "the safety valve provision applies only to convictions under five specified offenses," which do not include violations of the Act, *id.* at 1328 (citation and internal quotation marks omitted); *see also id.* ("No Title 46 offense appears in the safety-valve statute.").

Castillo contends that the equal protection guarantee of the Fifth Amendment entitles him to the kind of relief that the safety valve provides because "[t]here is no rational reason to subject defendants who commit drug trafficking offenses outside the United States to harsher penalties than those who traffic drugs within [its] borders." He underscores that "even defendants who import drugs into the country" or possess "illicit drug[s] while on board a vessel arriving in the United States" may benefit from the safety valve if they are convicted of a domestic trafficking offense, while "a defendant who commits a similar offense half a world away, without any direct effect on the United States, [is] denied the **[—7—]** same relief." Castillo concludes that the distinction between domestic and extraterritorial offenders is "at best . . . an oversight, and at worst an irrational and arbitrary distinction." We disagree. **{-1213-}**

The Due Process Clause of the Fifth Amendment, U.S. Const. amend. V, forbids the federal government from "denying to any person the equal protection of the laws," *United States v. Windsor*, 570 U.S. 744, 774 (2013), but not all allegations of discrimination are created equal. Instead, the rigor of judicial review depends on the kind of classification at issue. When "the classification infringes fundamental rights or concerns a suspect class," we apply heightened scrutiny. *Doe v. Moore*, 410 F.3d 1337, 1346 (11th Cir. 2005). But other kinds of classifications are subject to a weaker "rational basis test [that asks only] whether they are 'rationally related to a legitimate governmental purpose.'" *Id.* (quoting *City of Cleburne v. Cleburne Living Ctr.*, 473 U.S. 432, 446 (1985)).

Under rational basis review, we apply "a strong presumption of validity," *Heller v. Doe*, 509 U.S. 312, 319 (1993), and narrowly inquire if the "enacting government body *could* have been pursing" "a legitimate government purpose," *United States v. Ferreira*, 275 F.3d 1020, 1026 (11th Cir. 2001) (quoting *Joel v. City of Orlando*, 232 F.3d 1353, 1358 (11th Cir. 2000)). If we discern a legitimate goal, we then ask only "whether a rational basis exists for the enacting governmental body to believe that the legislation would further the hypothesized **[—8—]** purpose." *Id.* (quoting *Joel*, 232 F.3d at 1358). This inquiry occurs entirely in the abstract because "[t]he *actual* motivations of the enacting governmental body are entirely irrelevant," as is whether the legitimate "basis was actually considered by the legislative body." *Id.* (quoting *Joel*, 232 F.3d at 1358). Indeed, the government "has no obligation to produce evidence to sustain the rationality of a statutory classification," *Heller*, 509 U.S. at 320, and the complaining party has the burden to "negat[e] every conceivable basis which might support it," *id.* (quoting *Lehnhausen v. Lake Shore Auto Parts Co.*, 410 U.S. 356, 364 (1973)). Unsurprisingly, "[a]lmost every statute subject to the very deferential rational basis standard is found to be constitutional." *Moore*, 410 F.3d at 1346–47 (alteration adopted) (quoting *Williams v. Pryor*, 240 F.3d 944, 948 (11th Cir. 2001)).

Congress is entitled to deny the safety valve to offenders convicted under the Act. We apply rational basis review to the distinction between the Act and other statutes that punish domestic drug offenses because this distinction does not "infringe[] fundamental rights or concern[] a suspect class." *Id.* at 1346. And Congress has legitimate reasons to craft strict sentences for violations of the Act. In contrast with domestic drug offenses, international drug trafficking raises pressing concerns about foreign relations and global obligations. Indeed, the United States has signed a treaty that obliges it to "co-operate to the *fullest extent possible* to suppress illicit traffic by sea, in conformity with the international law of **[—9—]** the sea." United Nations Convention Against Illicit Traffic in Narcotic Drugs and Psychotropic Substances art. 17(1), Dec. 20, 1988, 1582 U.N.T.S. 95 (emphasis added). And the Act explains that "trafficking in controlled substances aboard vessels is a serious international problem" that is "universally condemned." 46 U.S.C. § 70501. In the light of these international concerns, Congress is entitled to mete out hefty sentences to maritime drug runners. Moreover, the inherent difficulties of policing drug trafficking on the vast expanses of international waters suggest that Congress could have rationally concluded that harsh penalties are needed to deter would-be offenders. **{-1214-}**

B. The Act and Its Application to Castillo Are Constitutional.

Castillo contends that the Act both "exceeds Congress'[s] enumerated powers" and "violates due process by subjecting foreign nationals to prosecution for offenses bearing no nexus to the United States," but our precedents foreclose his arguments. On the question of the constitutionality of the Act, "we have repeatedly held that Congress has the power, under the Felonies Clause, to proscribe drug trafficking on the high seas." *United States v. Campbell*, 743 F.3d 802, 812, 2 Adm. R. 543, 550 (11th Cir. 2014); *see also* U.S. Const. art. 1, § 8, cl. 10 (granting Congress the power "[t]o define and punish . . . Felonies committed on the high Seas"). And on the question of its application to Castillo despite his lack of connection to the United States, we have rejected the argument that the Due **[—10—]** Process Clause requires the government to prove a "nexus between the United States and a defendant" in a prosecution under the Act. *United States v. Wilchcombe*, 838 F.3d 1179, 1186 (11th Cir. 2016); *accord Campbell*, 743 F.3d at 812, 2 Adm. R. at 550. These precedents resolve Castillo's arguments because "only the court of appeals sitting en banc, an overriding United States Supreme Court decision, or a change in the statutory law can overrule a previous panel decision." *United States v. Hanna*, 153 F.3d 1286, 1288 (11th Cir. 1998) (italics omitted).

C. Castillo Cannot Challenge His Detention on Appeal.

Castillo invokes two constitutional amendments to challenge his detention. First, he contends that his detention violated the Due Process Clause of the Fifth Amendment. Second, he argues that his detention also violated his right under the Fourth Amendment to "a prompt judicial determination of probable cause." But we cannot consider either argument.

Castillo's guilty plea forecloses his argument "that the 19 day delay before [he] appeared before a magistrate [judge] . . . [was] unreasonable" and "violate[d] due process." As the Supreme Court recently explained in *Class v. United States*, "[a] valid guilty plea . . . renders irrelevant—and thereby prevents [a] defendant from appealing—the constitutionality of case-related government conduct that takes place before the plea is entered." 138 S. Ct. 798, 805 (2018). Castillo does **[—11—]** not dispute the validity of his plea, so he cannot complain about the specific facts of his detention.

Castillo nonetheless attempts to raise his detention on appeal by framing his complaint as a challenge to the constitutionality of the Act under the theory that "a guilty plea by itself [does not] bar[] a federal criminal defendant from challenging the constitutionality of the statute of conviction on direct appeal," *id.* at 803, but we reject his arguments. Castillo suggests that the Act facially "violates substantive due process because the pretrial detention it authorizes . . . constitutes impermissible punishment before trial." But this facial challenge fails because Castillo has not "establish[ed] that no set of circumstances exists under which the Act would be valid." *United States v. Salerno*, 481 U.S. 739, 745 (1987). Even assuming that the government occasionally enforces the Act in a manner that causes unconstitutional detentions, Castillo points to no evidence of detentions beyond the facts of this appeal. Castillo also suggests that the Act "as applied [to him] . . . violates substantive due process because it caused [him] to be detained a total of 19 days." But this challenge "focus[es] upon [a] case-related constitutional defect[] that occurred prior to the entry of the guilty plea." *Class*, 138 S. Ct. at 804–05 (citation **{-1215-}** and internal quotation marks omitted). His guilty plea bars this argument. **[—12—]**

Our colleague's concurring opinion would ignore the plea agreement and reach the merits of Castillo's detention, but "we can affirm the district court's judgment on any ground supported by the record." *United States v. Gill*, 864 F.3d 1279, 1280 (11th Cir. 2017). The effect of the plea agreement was raised at oral argument, where Castillo conceded that "if it's not jurisdictional . . . the guilty plea waives this issue." Oral Argument at 5:14–24. The government too agreed, *see id.* at 11:25–55, that Castillo's guilty plea waived non-jurisdictional issues about "case-related government conduct," *Class*, 138 S. Ct. at 805. And the detention of a particular defendant is case-related. Although the concurring opinion suggests that "unlawful detention" may not be "the kind of 'case-related government conduct' that cannot be challenged after a guilty plea," Concurring Op. at 3 (citation omitted), it nonetheless proceeds to explain why it would affirm the conviction *based on its analysis of the specific facts of Castillo's detention, see id.* at 4–6. For example, it considers the communications between the United States and Guatemala, *id.* at 5, the dates and length of the detention, *id.*, and the exact distance between where Castillo was apprehended and Key West, Florida, *id.* at 5–6. Castillo's guilty plea eliminates the need for this fact-specific inquiry.

Castillo also contends that his detention violated his right under the Fourth Amendment to "a prompt judicial determination of probable cause," but this argument fails for two reasons. First, Castillo failed to make this argument in his **[—13—]** opening brief, and "[a]n appellant in a criminal case may not raise an issue for the first time in a reply appellate brief." *United States v. Fiallo-Jacome*, 874 F.2d 1479, 1481 (11th Cir. 1989). Second, Castillo waived his right to complain about this "case-related government conduct" when he pleaded guilty. *Class*, 138 S. Ct. at 805. We need not address the merits of his argument.

IV. CONCLUSION

We **AFFIRM** Castillo's judgment of conviction and sentence.

(Reporter's Note: Concurring Opinion follows on p. 468).

[—14—] **{-1215-}** MARTIN, Circuit Judge, concurring:

I agree with the panel's treatment of Mr. Castillo's constitutional challenges to the Maritime Drug Law Enforcement Act. His challenges are foreclosed by Eleventh Circuit precedent. I also agree with the panel's ruling that there is a rational basis for the "safety valve" statute, which gives sentencing relief to certain defendants, to limit that relief to exclude those who commit drug trafficking offenses on the high seas. I am writing separately, however, because I do not join the majority's ruling that, by pleading guilty, Mr. Castillo waived his argument that his nineteen-day detention between his arrest and his first appearance violated the Due Process Clause of the Fifth Amendment. The government never made this argument and neither party briefed it. Because I believe the majority should have decided the issue of the pretrial detention on the merits, I do not join its opinion. Even so, I recognize my separate opinion has no real impact on Mr. Castillo. Despite my differences with one aspect of how the majority arrived at its result, I agree that Mr. Castillo's conviction and sentence should be affirmed.

I. The Panel Erred by Holding Mr. Castillo Waived Any Challenge to His Detention

Mr. Castillo entered into a plea agreement with the government, but it included **{-1216-}** no appeal waiver. Nothing in his plea agreement contemplated that Mr. Castillo would be barred from raising the issue of his pretrial detention on appeal. Perhaps because Mr. Castillo had no appeal waiver, the government never argued **[—15—]** in its brief that his plea agreement foreclosed his ability to bring his pretrial detention claim. To the contrary, the government argued that Mr. Castillo's 19-day detention was justified on the merits. But rather than reaching the merits of the government's argument regarding Mr. Castillo's nineteen-day detention, the panel concluded his claim was barred by his guilty plea.

In holding Mr. Castillo waived his right to challenge his pretrial detention, the panel opinion relies on and cites only to *Class v. United States*, 583 U.S. ___, 138 S. Ct. 798 (2018). But *Class* does not provide the basis for the majority's ruling. In fact, I read the central holding of *Class* to be that when a defendant pleads guilty, he *does not* waive his right to challenge the constitutionality of his statute of conviction. *Id.* at 803. In the *Class* opinion, the Supreme Court recounted the development of the idea that "a guilty plea bars appeal of many claims, including some antecedent constitutional violations related to events (say, grand jury proceedings) that had occurred prior to the entry of the guilty plea." *Id.* at 803 (quotations omitted). True, the *Class* opinion gave examples of rulings finding waivers in earlier cases, including objections to grand jury proceedings and "to challenge the admissibility of evidence obtained in violation of the Fourth Amendment." *Id.* at 803, 805 (quotation omitted) (citing *Haring v. Prosise*, 462 U.S. 306, 320, 103 S. Ct. 2368, 2377 (1983) and *Tollett v. Henderson*, 411 U.S. 258, 266–67, 93 S. Ct. 1602, 1607–08 (1973)). And the *Class* opinion generally **[—16—]** recognizes that certain constitutional claims may be raised after a guilty plea, although I acknowledge the opinion doesn't address claims regarding pretrial detention one way or the other. *Id.* at 806. I do not therefore read *Class* to opine on whether unlawful detention is the kind of "case-related government conduct" that cannot be challenged after a guilty plea. *See id.* Because the panel cites only to *Class* in making precisely that decision, I gather the panel does.

As for Eleventh Circuit precedent, we have said that "a guilty plea waives all non-jurisdictional defects occurring prior to the time of the plea." *Tiemens v. United States*, 724 F.2d 928, 929 (11th Cir. 1984) (per curiam). Yet I am not aware that this Court has ever ruled that a claim of unlawful detention for a defendant apprehended outside the United States is a non-jurisdictional defect that has occurred before the plea. Thus I do not read precedent from either our Circuit or the Supreme Court to require the ruling the majority opinion makes in this regard. I believe the better part of valor would have been to wait until one of the parties before us asked us to make this ruling, and to have the benefit of adversarial testing before taking this leap.

And in addition to valor, it seems worth mentioning that since the government never argued on appeal that Mr. Castillo had waived his right to raise his claims regarding pretrial detention, it is the government who faces a waiver. *See United States v. Jacobo Castillo*, 496 F.3d 947, 954–57 (9th Cir. 2007) (en **[—17—]** banc) (holding that the court could consider a claim that might otherwise be barred by entry of a guilty plea where the government failed to raise the issue on appeal and instead argued based on the underlying merits). While the majority seems to say the issue was raised because it came up at oral argument, this is not in keeping with our precedent. Arguments not raised in the initial briefs "are considered abandoned." *Allstate Ins. Co. v. Swann*, 27 F.3d 1539, 1542 (11th Cir. 1994). **{-1217-}**

II. Mr. Castillo's Pre-Trial Detention Does Not Warrant Reversal

Since I believe the panel should have addressed the merits of Mr. Castillo's argument about pretrial detention, I will do so here. Again, Mr. Castillo argues there was an unreasonable delay between when he was seized on board the *Cap Caleb* until his appearance before the Magistrate Judge in Miami. Mr. Castillo contends the delay violated substantive due process because it constituted punishment before trial.

While it is true that a person cannot be punished with imprisonment before an adjudication of guilt, it is also true that the government, "may detain [a defendant] to ensure his presence at trial . . . so long as th[e] conditions and restrictions [of detention] do not amount to punishment, or otherwise violate the Constitution." *Jacoby v. Baldwin Cty.*, 835 F.3d 1338, 1344–45 (11th Cir. 2016) (quoting *Bell v. Wolfish*, 411 U.S. 520, 536–37, 99 S. Ct. 1861, 1873 (1979)). "[W]hether a condition of pretrial detention amounts to punishment turns on **[—18—]** whether the condition is imposed for the purpose of punishment or whether it is incident to some legitimate government purpose." *Magluta v. Samples*, 375 F.3d 1269, 1273 (11th Cir. 2004).

Under Federal Rule of Criminal Procedure 5(a)(1)(B), a person arrested outside the United States must be brought before a Magistrate Judge "without unnecessary delay." In deciding whether there has been unnecessary delay, courts look to the distance from the place of arrest to the United States; the time between arrival in the United States and presentment to a magistrate; whether the defendant was improperly interrogated or otherwise mistreated; and whether exigent circumstances contributed to any delay. *See United States v. Purvis*, 768 F.2d 1237, 1239 (11th Cir. 1985) (per curiam).

The Coast Guard boarded the *Cap Caleb* and detained Mr. Castillo on August 20, 2016. On August 26, the United States asked Guatemala to waive its jurisdiction over the ship and its crew. On August 29, Guatemala agreed to waive jurisdiction. On September 8, the Coast Guard brought Mr. Castillo to Cuba, and he was flown to Miami that same day. On September 9, he appeared before a Magistrate Judge in Miami.

A 19-day total delay is reasonable in this case. This Court has previously affirmed a five-day delay for a defendant apprehended 350 miles from Key West, Florida, *Purvis*, 768 F.2d at 1239, and a five-day delay for a defendant arrested in **[—19—]** the Yucatan Straits, approximately 200 miles from the United States, *United States v. Odom*, 526 F.2d 339, 340, 343 (5th Cir. 1976).[1] The Pacific

[1] Other courts have allowed longer delays for defendants arrested further away from the United States. *See United States v. Zakhraov*, 468 F.3d 1174, 1180 (9th Cir. 2006) (allowing for 11-day delay for defendant apprehended "1620 nautical miles" from the United States); *United States v. Torres-Iturre*, No. 15CR2586-GPC, 2016 WL 2757283, at *3 (S.D. Cal. May 12, 2016) (finding 21-day delay was not unreasonable for defendant arrested "2439 nautical miles from San Diego"); *United States v. Savchenko*, 201 F.R.D. 503, 506 (S.D. Cal. 2001) ("[T]he [delay of] 16 days is more than reasonable for the transport of the fishing vessel from the high seas approximately 500 nautical miles from Mexico to this district."); *United States v. Greyshock*, 719 F. Supp. 927, 930–

coast of Guatemala is significantly further from the United States than the location discussed in these earlier cases. Indeed, even ignoring the need to go through the Panama Canal, Mr. Castillo was taken into custody approximately 1,000 miles from the port of Miami. And of course there was an added delay caused by **{–1218–}** the wait for the Guatemalan government to waive jurisdiction. Mr. Castillo does not allege he could have been taken to a closer port or that the journey could have been made more quickly. There is no allegation he was interrogated or mistreated during that time. And he was presented to a Magistrate Judge the day after his arrival in the United States. *See Purvis*, 768 F.2d at 1239 ("[T]he delay of less than one day after arriving at Key West was reasonable because of the magistrate's brief absence."). Therefore the pre-trial delay was reasonable, and Mr. Castillo's conviction should stand.

---

33 (D. Haw. 1989) (finding nine-day delay after arrest "600 miles northeast of Oahu" was reasonable because ship "proceeded directly to Honolulu").

United States Court of Appeals for the Eleventh Circuit

No. 17-15008

CARON
VS.
NCL (BAHAMAS), LTD.

Appeal from the United States District Court for the Southern District of Florida

Decided: December 13, 2018

Citation: 910 F.3d 1359, 6 Adm. R. 471 (11th Cir. 2018).

Before **TJOFLAT, MARTIN,** and **PRYOR,** Circuit Judges.

[—1—] {-1362-} TJOFLAT, Circuit Judge: **[—2—]**

This case arises from a drunken tumble down an escape hatch on a cruise ship. Olivier Caron, a Canadian citizen, was injured while a passenger on the *Star*, a vessel owned and operated by NCL. On the second day of his Baltic cruise, Caron bought an all-inclusive package, which allowed him unlimited beer and wine while on the cruise, and proceeded to drink beer late into the night. After leaving the bar, instead of returning to his room, Caron entered an area that was clearly marked with signs reading "CREW ONLY" and "RESTRICTED, CREW ACCESS ONLY." Pressing on, Caron entered another door labeled "CAUTION Only authorized crew beyond this sign," and fell several feet through an emergency-exit hatch, causing injuries for which he now seeks to recover. He filed suit in the District Court, claiming the cruise line was negligent in allowing him to fall down the hatch and in over-serving alcohol to him, which led to his fall. The District Court dismissed the over-service claim and granted summary judgment for NCL on the other negligence claim. Plaintiff appeals both rulings. After careful consideration, we affirm.

I.

This opinion is organized as follows. We discuss the facts and procedural history of the case in Part I, the subject-matter jurisdiction of the District Court in Part II, the dismissed over-service claim in Part III, and the other negligence claim in Part IV. Part V concludes. **[—3—] {-1363-}**

A.

Olivier Caron spent the evening of July 15, 2015, drinking with his fellow passengers aboard the *Star*. He became intoxicated to the point that he felt "completely disoriented." At about 3:37 a.m. on July 16, Caron descended a mid-ship flight of stairs into a passenger-elevator area. But instead of continuing on to his room on the ship, Caron opened a clearly marked crew-only door and proceeded into a restricted area of the ship. He walked down a hallway, where he was seen by two crewmembers who tried to talk to him; he did not respond. While the crewmembers called security, Caron moved away from them, such that they did not see where he went. He opened and walked through another door with obvious crew-only markings, where he fell into a hole, hitting the deck below and suffering an injury to his foot. The hole was an escape hatch from the bow-thruster room below, and the hole would have been clearly visible once the door was opened. Caron fell down the hole approximately four minutes after entering the crew-only area. About four and a half hours later, Caron climbed out of the hatch and, with assistance, went to the ship's medical center, where his injuries were treated.

B.

On July 14, 2016, Caron filed suit against NCL in the Southern District of Florida, asserting jurisdiction on the basis of diversity of citizenship and admiralty **[—4—]** jurisdiction. *See* 28 U.S.C. § 1332(a)(2), §1333(1).[1] His complaint made no mention of being served alcohol, but he did allege several other theories of negligence. He claimed, among other things, that NCL had failed to maintain its walkways and manholes in a safe condition, to remedy a known dangerous condition, and to warn Caron of a danger that was not open or obvious. Caron demanded a

[1] The District Court accepted jurisdiction but did not indicate expressly whether its jurisdiction lay under § 1332(a) or § 1333. In accepting Caron's demand for a jury trial, the Court purported to assume jurisdiction under § 1332(a) and not § 1333.

jury trial, and one was scheduled. Although Caron alleged that admiralty jurisdiction was proper, he did not make a Rule 9(h) election for his claim to proceed in admiralty. Fed. R. Civ. P. 9(h).

On September 30, 2016, Caron amended his complaint, adding an allegation that NCL was negligent in over-serving alcohol to him. NCL moved to dismiss this claim under Federal Rule of Civil Procedure 12(b)(6) and strike the allegation of over-service on the basis of a limitations provision in Caron's ticket contract, which required any personal-injury suits against NCL to be brought within one year of the incident giving rise to the injury. The District Court granted the motion, finding that the over-service claim was contractually barred and did not relate back to the initial complaint.

On November 3, 2017, the District Court granted NCL's Motion for Summary Judgment on the remaining negligence theories. It found that Caron had **[—5—]** not met his burden of production, as he had failed to produce evidence of the dangerousness of the escape hatch, of NCL's knowledge of such dangerousness, or of the unreasonableness of the crew's behavior in letting Caron escape further into the restricted area. This appeal followed.

II.

Whether subject matter jurisdiction exists is an issue of law that we review *de novo*. *Molinos Valle Del Cibao, C. por A. v. Lama*, 633 F.3d 1330, 1340 (11th Cir. 2011). The party seeking federal jurisdiction must prove, by a preponderance of the **{-1364-}** evidence, facts supporting the exercise of jurisdiction. *McCormick v. Aderholt*, 293 F.3d 1254, 1257 (11th Cir. 2002).

A.

The parties disagree as to whether the District Court had subject-matter jurisdiction. Caron contends that the alienage-diversity provision, which governs suits between aliens and citizens of a State, applies, and that the District Court thus entertained jurisdiction under this provision. *See* 28 U.S.C. § 1332(a)(2). Since Caron is a Canadian citizen and NCL is a Bermuda corporation with its principal place of business in Florida, Caron argues that NCL should be deemed a Florida citizen for diversity purposes. And even if alienage-diversity jurisdiction fails, Caron argues, as a fallback, that he sufficiently invoked the court's admiralty jurisdiction under 28 U.S.C. § 1333. **[—6—]**

NCL contends that Caron failed to adequately plead NCL's citizenship to invoke alienage-diversity jurisdiction, since he did not allege NCL's Bermuda citizenship or move to amend his complaint to do so. It also denies that admiralty jurisdiction is available, since Caron did not elect to proceed under admiralty per Federal Rule of Civil Procedure 9(h).

Alienage diversity, like general diversity under 28 U.S.C. § 1332(a)(1), must be complete; an alien on both sides of a dispute will defeat jurisdiction. *Lama*, 633 F.3d at 1340; *cf. Strawbridge v. Curtiss*, 3 Cranch 267 (1806) (requiring complete diversity under the predecessor statute to § 1332(a)(1)). This Court has never explicitly decided whether dual-citizen corporations, incorporated under the laws of a foreign state but with their principal place of business in a U.S. state, count as aliens in order to defeat complete diversity in suits against other aliens. Every other circuit court of appeals to consider the issue has concluded that alienage diversity is lacking in these cases, defeating subject-matter jurisdiction. *See, e.g.*, *Vantage Drilling Co. v. Hsin-Chi Su*, 741 F.3d 535, 537-38 (5th Cir. 2014); *Slavchev v. Royal Caribbean Cruises, Ltd.*, 559 F.3d 251, 254-55 (4th Cir. 2009); *Peninsula Asset Mgmt. (Cayman) Ltd. v. Hankook Tire Co.*, 509 F.3d 271, 272-73 (6th Cir. **[—7—]** 2007); *Creaciones Con Idea, S.A. de C. V. v. Mashreqbank PSC*, 232 F.3d 79, 82 (2d Cir. 2000).[2]

[2] A panel of this Court has suggested, in a footnote, that alienage-diversity jurisdiction was proper in a seemingly indistinguishable case. *Estate of Myhra v. Royal Caribbean Cruises, Ltd.*, 695 F.3d 1233, 1235 n.1 (11th Cir. 2012). We decline to follow *Myhra*, as it has been superseded by statute. The district court case reviewed in

The 2012 amendments to § 1332(c) bolster the rationale of these decisions. Section 1332(c) governs the citizenship of corporations for purposes of diversity jurisdiction. Previous versions of the statute referred only to corporations incorporated in, or with their principal place of business in, a "State." 28 U.S.C. § 1332(c) (2006); *see also Cabalceta v. Standard Fruit Co.*, 883 F.2d 1553, 1557 (11th Cir. 1989) (interpreting a prior version of § 1332). Before the recent amendments, the circuits were split on whether foreign states were "State[s]" within the meaning of the statute. *Compare Cabalceta,* 883 F.2d at 1557 *with Nike, Inc. v. Comercial Iberica de Exclusivas Deportivas, S.A.*, 20 F.3d 987, 990 (9th Cir. 1994). **{-1365-}**

In contrast, the 2012 amendments to § 1332(c) explicitly impute to corporations citizenship in every State or foreign state where the company is incorporated and in the State or foreign state where the company has its worldwide principal place of business. § 1332(c)(1) (2012). So a corporation incorporated in a **[—8—]** foreign state is specifically deemed a citizen of that foreign state when evaluating jurisdiction.

We therefore hold that § 1332(a)(2) does not grant jurisdiction over a suit between a corporation incorporated solely in a foreign state and another alien, regardless of the corporation's principal place of business.[3]

Myhra was originally filed before the 2012 amendments to § 1332, which clarified the citizenship of foreign corporations. *Myhra* gave no effect to the foreign incorporation of the defendant corporation, treating it as only a citizen of a state based on its principal place of business. This interpretation is clearly unavailable under the current text of the statute. *See* § 1332(c) (2012).

[3] We are not required to decide, and do not decide, whether a corporation incorporated in a State, but with its worldwide principal place of business abroad, can invoke alienage-diversity jurisdiction in a suit against an alien. This court held in *Cabalceta* that alienage-diversity jurisdiction was proper in that circumstance. 883 F.2d at 1557. Whether the 2012 amendments to § 1332 overruled *Cabalceta* is a question for another day.

Here, Caron is a Canadian citizen, and NCL is a Bermuda company with its principal place of business in Florida. Since both Caron and NCL are aliens, § 1332(a)(2) does not support the exercise of jurisdiction in this case.

B.

But all is not lost. Although alienage-diversity jurisdiction is lacking, the District Court validly exercised admiralty jurisdiction over the case pursuant to 28 U.S.C. § 1333(1).

Tort claims are within admiralty jurisdiction if 1) the incident occurred on navigable water, or the injury was caused by a vessel on navigable water, and 2) the incident is connected with maritime activity. *Broughton v. Fla. Int'l Underwriters, Inc.*, 139 F.3d 861, 865 (11th Cir. 1998). An incident is connected with maritime activity if, on an assessment of the general features of the type of **[—9—]** incident involved, it has "a potentially disruptive impact on maritime commerce," and "the general character of the activity giving rise to the incident shows a substantial relationship to traditional maritime activity." *Jerome B. Grubart, Inc. v. Great Lakes Dredge & Dock Co.*, 513 U.S. 527, 534, 115 S. Ct. 1043, 1048 (1995). Personal-injury claims by cruise ship passengers, complaining of injuries suffered at sea, are within the admiralty jurisdiction of the district courts. *See, e.g., Carnival Cruise Lines, Inc. v. Shute*, 499 U.S. 585, 587-88, 111 S. Ct. 1522, 1524 (1991) (exercising admiralty jurisdiction in a case alleging personal injury suffered aboard a cruise ship at sea).

In this tort case, Caron seeks to recover for a personal injury he suffered at sea. Furthermore, Caron alleged that admiralty jurisdiction was proper from the inception of the case and met his burden to prove facts showing a maritime nexus to his injury. The District Court therefore validly exercised jurisdiction over the case.[4]

[4] Since admiralty was the only proper source of jurisdiction, Caron was not required to elect it under Federal Rule of Civil Procedure 9(h). This election is not required for the exercise of admiralty jurisdiction unless " a claim for relief is within the

That the District Court mistakenly believed it had jurisdiction under § 1332 is troubling, but its lack of awareness does not invalidate the proceedings below. Before **{-1366-}** the union of law and admiralty under the 1966 revisions to the Federal **[—10—]** Rules of Civil Procedure, such a mistake would have required vacatur and remand with an instruction for the district court to decide whether transferring the case to its admiralty docket would be appropriate. *See Poole v. Lykes Bros. Steamship Co.*, 273 F.2d 423, 424 (5th Cir. 1960); 1 Thomas L. Schoenbaum & Jessica L. McClellan, *Admiralty & Maritime Law* § 3-2 (5th ed. 2011) (describing the 1966 union of law and admiralty). Nowadays, procedure in law and admiralty is much more similar, with only a few admiralty-specific rules remaining. *See* Fed. R. Civ. P. 9(h), 14(c), 38(e), 82 (special rules for admiralty claims); Supp. Adm. & Mar. Cl. R. (same). These rules do not generally require admiralty litigation to be conducted differently from other litigation in the district courts; rather, the admiralty rules mostly add strategy options for plaintiffs. Vacatur and remand are thus unnecessary.

The most salient difference that proceeding in admiralty creates is the absence of a right to a jury trial. Fed. R. Civ. P. 38(e); *St. Paul Fire & Marine Ins. Co. v. Lago Canyon, Inc.*, 561 F.3d 1181, 1187 (11th Cir. 2009) (setting out the "general rule that admiralty claims are to be tried without a jury"). Here, Caron made a jury demand, which would have been proper had the District Court had alienage-diversity jurisdiction, and the case had been scheduled for a jury trial. But even this does not cast doubt on the propriety of the proceedings below, since no **[—11—]** jury trial occurred; every claim in the case was finally adjudicated at either the pleading or summary judgment stage.

In his complaint, Caron alleged sufficient facts to support the District Court's exercise of admiralty jurisdiction, and all of the proceedings below were appropriate in light of this jurisdictional basis. We thus conclude that the District Court had jurisdiction to hear the case, and its mistake as to its basis was harmless. Having so concluded, we now address the District Court's rulings on each of Caron's negligence theories.

III.

Caron appeals the dismissal of his claim for negligent over-service of alcohol as contractually waived. We review the grant of a Federal Rule of Civil Procedure 12(b)(6) motion to dismiss *de novo*. *Mills v. Foremost Ins. Co.*, 511 F.3d 1300, 1303 (11th Cir. 2008).

A.

Caron's ticket contract contained a one-year limitations period on bringing personal-injury suits:

> The Guest agrees that no suit, whether brought in rem or in personam, shall be maintained against the Carrier for emotional or physical injury, illness or death of Guest unless written notice of the claim, including a complete factual account of the basis of such claim, is delivered to the Carrier within 185 calendar days from the date of the incident giving rise to such injury, illness or death; and no suit shall be maintainable unless commenced within one (1) year from the day of the incident giving rise to such injury, illness or **[—12—]** death, notwithstanding any provision of law of any state or country to the contrary.

Although Caron's original complaint was filed within this contractual limitations period, his over-service claim was not present in his original complaint; it was added in an amendment months later, after the one-year period had run. On NCL's Motion to Dismiss, the District Court held the waiver valid and enforceable, interpreting it to bar adding untimely claims to an already-filed suit, and held that Caron's **{-1367-}** allegations of over-

admiralty or maritime jurisdiction and also within the court's subject-matter jurisdiction on some other ground . . . . A claim cognizable only in the admiralty or maritime jurisdiction is an admiralty or maritime claim . . . whether or not so designated." Fed. R. Civ. P. 9(h)(1).

service did not relate back to his original filing date.

We address each of these holdings in turn.

B.

Under general maritime law, a valid waiver of a passenger's right to sue requires a waiver term that has been reasonably communicated to the passenger. *Nash v. Kloster Cruise A/S,* 901 F.2d 1565, 1567 (11th Cir. 1990). The two-factor test for reasonable communication evaluates the physical characteristics of the clause and the passenger's opportunity to become meaningfully informed of the contract terms. *Myhra*, 695 F.3d at 1244.

Caron does not object to the physical location or readability of the waiver language. Nor does he suggest that he lacked an opportunity to become informed of what the terms—the words constituting the contract—were. Rather, he suggests, the word "suit" is ambiguous and should be construed to permit claims first mentioned in an amended complaint more than one year after the incident, as long **[—13—]** as the initial complaint is filed within the year. Furthermore, according to Caron, if the waiver were interpreted to bar his claim, it would be invalid, since this meaning of "suit" was not reasonably communicated to him by the text of the contract.

We disagree because when read in context, the provision unambiguously bars a passenger from raising new claims in an amended complaint more than a year after an incident. *Cf. Kohlheim v. Glynn Cty.*, 915 F.2d 1473, 1479 (11th Cir. 1990) (finding that an initially ambiguous contract term was clarified by context). Under the subheading "Suits for Injury or Death," the contract features two clauses that bar personal-injury suits except as specified. The first clause provides in part "no *suit* . . . shall be maintained against the Carrier for emotional or physical injury . . . of Guest unless written notice of the *claim*, including a complete factual account of the basis of the claim, is delivered" within a specified time frame (emphasis added). The second clause imposes a limitations period requiring that a "suit" be "commenced within one (1) year from the day of the incident giving rise to such injury, illness or death."

The notice clause makes clear the relationship between a "claim" and a "suit." This clause requires a passenger to give written notice of each claim he alleges in the suit. It would make no sense to interpret this provision as allowing the passenger to give notice of one claim but then bring a lawsuit for different or additional claims. Our interpretation is bolstered by the notice clause's **[—14—]** specification that the passenger provide NCL with "a complete factual account of the basis of" his claim. It would likewise be nonsensical for this provision to permit the passenger to provide the factual basis of his claim to NCL before filing suit but then later change the factual basis to support a different claim.

The reference to "suit" in the second clause—the one that features the one year limitation at issue here—must be interpreted in light of and consistent with its earlier use. Thus, "suit" in this clause must refer to a lawsuit alleging a claim or claims for which notice was given.

Because of this language, the limitations provision is reasonably subject to only one interpretation: that it is to be read like a statute of limitations, barring not only untimely suits but also untimely claims added to already-filed suits. The word "suit," on its own and without considering the context, is susceptible of the meaning that Caron attaches to it. But our duty is to interpret the contract as a whole, not each term in a vacuum. *See* **{–1368–}** Restatement (Second) of Contracts § 202(b) (1981). Here, the context resolves any potential ambiguity about the meaning of "suit."

Since the limitations provision was unambiguous in context, and the presentation of its terms within the contract document was reasonable, its meaning was reasonably communicated to Caron. Caron objects to the specialized meaning of "suit" in its context in the contract. But Caron has not proposed a reasonable **[—15—]** alternative construction that would render the contract insufficiently communicative of NCL's proposed meaning. NCL's duty is *reasonable* communication; it has no responsibility to disabuse its customers of every imaginable-but-unreasonable interpretation of the contract terms.

So Caron's over-service claim is time-barred unless it relates back to his original filing date.

C.

Relation back is a legal fiction employed to salvage claims that would otherwise be unjustly barred by a limitations provision. *See McCurdy v. United States*, 264 U.S. 484, 487, 44 S. Ct. 345, 346 (1924); *Moore v. Baker*, 989 F.2d 1129, 1131 (11th Cir. 1993). Under Rule 15, a claim in an amended complaint relates back to the filing date of the original complaint if it "asserts a claim or defense that arose out of the conduct, transaction, or occurrence set out—or attempted to be set out—in the original pleading." Fed. R. Civ. P. 15(c)(1)(B). When the facts in the original complaint do not put the defendant "on notice that the new claims of negligence might be asserted," but the new claims instead "involve[] separate and distinct conduct," such that the plaintiff would have to prove "completely different facts" than required to recover on the claims in the original complaint, the new claims do not relate back. *Moore*, 989 F.2d at 1132. **[—16—]**

Here, the over-service claim does not relate back. The original complaint made no mention of alcohol and focused mostly on the physical condition of various areas of the ship, alleging various failures to maintain its "manholes, floors, walkways, or thresholds" in a safe condition. For example, Caron complained of inadequate lighting around hazards, unreasonably slippery floors, and failure to ensure proper drainage of liquids. Such allegations did nothing to put NCL on notice that Caron could complain of over-service of alcohol.

Nor are the complaint's generic allegations capacious enough to smuggle Caron's over-service claim into the case. The complaint alleges NCL's "failure to take proper precautions for the safety of passengers using its manholes, floors, walkways, or thresholds." This allegation, by its terms, could conceivably encompass serving more alcohol than passengers could safely consume before walking elsewhere on the ship. But the test for relation back is not whether the new facts alleged could substantiate an old, boilerplate claim but whether the old facts alleged could put the defendant on notice that the new claim might be part of the litigation. Here, Caron's original allegations did not put NCL on notice that over-service of alcohol (or anything involving alcohol, for that matter) could be relevant to the case.

Caron's over-service claim thus does not relate back and is barred by the limitations clause. **[—17—]**

IV.

The District Court granted summary judgment for NCL on Caron's other negligence theories. We review a district court's grant of summary judgment **{-1369-}** *de novo*. *Krutzig v. Pulte Home Corp.*, 602 F.3d 1231, 1234 (11th Cir. 2010). We will affirm "if we conclude that there is no genuine issue of material fact—that is, if no fair-minded jury could return a verdict for the plaintiff on the evidence presented." *Goodman v. Kimbrough*, 718 F.3d 1325, 1331 (11th Cir. 2013).

Federal maritime law provides the substantive law for this case. *Everett v. Carnival Cruise Lines*, 912 F.2d 1335, 1358 (11th Cir. 1990). Under the maritime law of negligence, Caron must prove that 1) NCL had a duty to protect him from a particular injury, 2) NCL breached that duty, 3) NCL's breach proximately caused his injury, and 4) he incurred damages. *Chaparro v. Carnival Corp.*, 693 F.3d 1333, 1336 (11th Cir. 2012). To survive summary judgment, Caron must produce evidence establishing the existence of a genuine issue of material fact as to each of the elements.

Caron included twenty-one separate allegations of negligence in his amended complaint, most of which asserted that the open escape hatch was dangerous. He also alleged that NCL was negligent in allowing him access to the area where he fell and failing to properly warn him of the area's hidden dangers. Still, the District Court concluded summary judgment was proper, since Caron did **[—18—]** not produce sufficient evidence that the hatch was dangerous, that NCL had notice of the danger, or that NCL's crewmembers acted unreasonably upon encountering him in the hallway.

A.

To survive summary judgment on his negligence claim based on a dangerous condition, Caron must produce evidence, sufficient for a jury to find for him, that the hatch was a dangerous condition of which NCL had notice. As the District Court correctly concluded, Caron did not do so.

Caron cannot show that the hatch he fell down was unreasonably dangerous. To get to the hatch, Caron had to pass through two clearly marked doors. The first indicated that the area was restricted and that only crewmembers were allowed in. The second indicated that persons passing through the door should use caution, and specified that only authorized crew were allowed in. Despite these measures that NCL took to keep passengers away from the hatch, Caron contends that they were insufficient to render the hatch reasonably non-dangerous. But the evidence Caron presents is insufficient to create a genuine issue of material fact on dangerousness.

Caron sought to prove dangerousness by expert and fact testimony about whether the doors to the crew-only areas and the hatch door itself should have been locked.[5] Caron's expert contended that the hatch door, as well as the marked crew- **[—19—]** only doors, should have had locking mechanisms installed, since those doors could have been locked without compromising their usability as emergency exits from the bow-thruster room, and since locking them would have been safer. Caron's fact witness, an assistant carpenter with NCL, stated his belief that emergency hatches on the ship are generally locked and cannot be accessed from the corridor.

We agree with the District Court that this testimony did not create a genuine issue of material fact on whether the absence of locks rendered the hatch dangerous. It may be safer to lock the doors than to leave them unlocked, but it does not follow that the absence of door locks rendered **{-1370-}** the hatch unreasonably unsafe. Additionally, one employee's perception that hatches are generally locked does not create a genuine issue of material fact on whether NCL had a policy of locking its hatch doors. Caron thus failed to meet his burden to produce sufficient evidence that the hatch was unreasonably dangerous, and summary judgment was proper on his dangerous-condition theory.

Even if Caron had produced evidence of dangerousness, summary judgment still would have been proper, as Caron failed to produce evidence that NCL was on notice of the dangerous condition. *See Keefe v. Bahama Cruise Line, Inc.*, 867 F.2d 1318, 1322 (11th Cir. 1989). NCL's uncontroverted records showed that no injuries similar to Caron's had been reported on any ship of NCL's in the last five years. None of Caron's proffered evidence on appeal, which mostly describes **[—20—]** NCL's efforts to keep passengers out of crew-only areas and remove them when they enter, suggests that NCL had actual or constructive notice that the hatch was dangerous. Summary judgment was thus proper on the notice issue as well.

B.

We similarly find no error in the District Court's treatment of the allegations of unreasonable behavior by NCL's crew.

Caron alleges that various crewmembers failed to follow NCL's policy on passengers in crew-only areas. Specifically, Caron alleges that crewmembers acted unreasonably after

[5] None of these doors had locking mechanisms installed at all.

encountering him in the crew-only area by failing to escort him back to his cabin, by losing track of him, and by calling off the search for him while he remained in the hatch.

None of these contentions can survive summary judgment. Caron presented testimony from crewmembers, suggesting that NCL's policy requires crew who find passengers in crew-only areas to escort the passengers back to the passenger area of the ship. Other crewmembers testified that NCL policy required crew to attempt to speak with the passenger and, if the passenger was unresponsive, to call security. It is undisputed that, when two crewmembers found Caron in the crew-only area and tried to talk with him, he did not respond. While the crew called security, Caron began to walk or run away. The crewmembers attempted to follow Caron, but he outpaced them and disappeared. Within two minutes of his initial **[—21—]** encounter with the crew, Caron had fallen down the hatch. Security arrived within a few minutes, after Caron had already fallen, and searched for Caron but did not find him.

We agree with the District Court that Caron has not presented sufficient evidence of negligence on the part of NCL's crew. Caron did not controvert the testimony that NCL crew were required to call security if a passenger was unresponsive when spoken to. While the crewmembers were calling security, Caron escaped down the hall and outpaced at least one crewmember who attempted to follow. Perhaps the crew could have physically blocked Caron from running down the hall or chased after him quickly enough not to lose sight, but Caron has presented no evidence that the standard of care is set that high. All available evidence suggests that the crewmembers tried to comply with NCL's policy and that they were not unreasonably lax in trying.

Caron contends as well that NCL's security personnel were negligent in calling off the search before finding him, leaving him to languish in the bow-thruster room for hours. We agree with the District Court that summary judgment is proper here as well, since Caron's injury had already occurred by the time NCL called off **{–1371–}** the search. Caron's eleventh-hour allegations, not fairly traceable to his complaint, of additional injury due to the time he spent in the bow-thruster room do not properly put the issue before the Court. *Miccosukee Tribe of Indians of Fla.* **[—22—]** *v. United States*, 716 F.3d 535, 559 (11th Cir. 2013) (refusing to consider allegations raised for the first time in a response to a motion for summary judgment).[6]

V.

NCL was entitled to dismissal of Caron's over-service claim and summary judgment on Caron's negligence claim. We thus AFFIRM the District Court's judgment and DENY AS MOOT Caron's Motion for Leave to File an Amended Complaint and his Motion to Supplement the Record.

SO ORDERED.

---

[6] Caron had additionally appealed several magistrate orders. As he did not address these orders in his opening brief, his contentions on the topic are waived. *Little v. T-Mobile USA, Inc.*, 691 F.3d 1302, 1306 (11th Cir. 2012).

United States Court of Appeals for the District of Columbia Circuit

United States Court of Appeals
for the District of Columbia Circuit

No. 17-1089

SANTA FE DISCOUNT CRUISE PARKING, INC.
vs.
FEDERAL MARITIME COMM'N

On Petition for Review of an Order of the Federal Maritime Commission

Decided: May 11, 2018

Citation: 889 F.3d 795, 6 Adm. R. 480 (D.C. Cir. 2018).

Before **KAVANAUGH** and **MILLETT**, Circuit Judges, and **SENTELLE**, Senior Circuit Judge.

[—2—] {-796-} **KAVANAUGH**, Circuit Judge:

This is not a complicated case. The Galveston Port charges commercial passenger vehicles such as taxis, limos, and shuttle buses for access to the Port's parking terminal. Petitioners operate shuttle buses. The Port charged Petitioners' shuttle buses more than the Port charged taxis and limos. Petitioners challenge that differential treatment.

Under the Shipping Act, a marine terminal operator such as the Galveston Port may not "give any undue or unreasonable preference or advantage or impose any undue or unreasonable prejudice or disadvantage with respect to any person." 46 U.S.C. § 41106(2). A disadvantaged party may bring a Section 41106(2) rate-discrimination complaint against the marine terminal operator before the Federal Maritime Commission. In adjudicating those complaints, the Commission applies a multi-part test that is not challenged by the parties here. To make out a Section 41106(2) claim, the complaining party must establish that the complainant and another party are similarly situated or in a competitive relationship; that the parties are accorded different treatment by the respondent marine terminal operator; and that the differential treatment injures the complaining party. If the **[—3—]** complaining party makes that showing, the respondent marine terminal operator has the burden of justifying the differential treatment based on legitimate transportation factors. *See Ceres Marine Terminal, Inc. v. Maryland Port Administration*, 27 S.R.R. 1251 (FMC 1997).

Here, Petitioners contend that they met their burden of showing that they were similarly situated to or in a competitive relationship with taxis and limos; that they were accorded different treatment; and that the differential treatment injured Petitioners. Petitioners argue that the burden **{-797-}** is therefore on the Galveston Port to justify the differential treatment based on legitimate transportation factors.

The Federal Maritime Commission accepted that Petitioners' shuttle buses were treated differently than taxis and limos. But the Commission then strangely concluded that Petitioners were not injured by being charged more. The Commission's conclusion is not sustainable. Petitioners were plainly injured when they were charged more than the other commercial passenger vehicles. To be sure, under the statute and the *Ceres* test, the Galveston Port may be able to show that the differential treatment of Petitioners' shuttle buses is justified by legitimate transportation factors. But the Commission never reached that step of the analysis. On remand, the Commission may consider the Port's argument to that effect.

We grant the petition, vacate the order of the Federal Maritime Commission, and remand for further proceedings consistent with this opinion.

So ordered.

United States Court of Appeals
for the District of Columbia Circuit

No. 15-1336

INTERNATIONAL LONGSHORE & WAREHOUSE UNION
VS.
NATIONAL LABOR RELATIONS BD.

On Petition for Review and Cross-Application for Enforcement of an Order of the National Labor Relations Board

Decided: May 29, 2018

Citation: 890 F.3d 1100, 6 Adm. R. 481 (D.C. Cir. 2018).

Before **HENDERSON**, **KAVANAUGH**, and **KATSAS**, Circuit Judges.

[—2—] {-1103-} HENDERSON, Circuit Judge:

The post-World War II growth in international maritime shipping has spawned a history of labor disputes along the West Coast of the United States between the Petitioner, the International Longshore and Warehouse Union (ILWU), and the Intervenor, the International Association of Machinists and Aerospace Workers, AFL-CIO (IAM). The battles between the two unions have played out in federal court, *see Int'l Ass'n of Machinists & Aerospace Workers v. NLRB*, 253 F. App'x 625 (9th Cir. 2007), and before the National Labor Relations Board (NLRB or Board), *see Pac. Mar. Ass'n*, 256 NLRB 769, 772 (1981). This case adds a chapter to the unions' protracted disputes. **[—3—]**

In 2002, the Pacific Crane Maintenance Company (PCMC) began using a subsidiary,[1] the Pacific Marine Maintenance Company (PMMC) (together, Employer or PCMC/PMMC), to provide loading and unloading services to Maersk, a large shipping company, at three West Coast ports: Oakland and Long Beach, California and Tacoma, Washington. PCMC created PMMC to perform the Maersk contract because Maersk had purchased the terminal operations from a company named Sealand, which, as a condition of sale, *required* Maersk to recognize IAM as the union representative for the employees performing maintenance and repair (M&R) work at the three ports. Because PCMC was already bound by a collective bargaining agreement (CBA) with ILWU, it could not recognize IAM itself. Thus, from 2002 to 2006, PCMC continued to recognize ILWU while its subsidiary, PMMC, recognized IAM as the representative of the M&R employees at the Oakland and Tacoma ports.[2]

In late 2004, in an effort to drive down costs, Maersk requested bids from both PCMC and PMMC for M&R work at the Oakland and Tacoma ports. PCMC responded with the lower bid and Maersk accepted it. As a result of losing the Oakland and Tacoma M&R work, on March 30, 2005, PMMC terminated its 100 M&R employees and shut down its operations completely. The next day, PCMC hired 76 of the former PMMC mechanics to do the **{-1104-}** same M&R work and hired **[—4—]** six additional former PMMC mechanics shortly thereafter. As a result of the change, however, PCMC ceased recognizing IAM and began recognizing ILWU as the former PMMC M&R employees' union. IAM responded with claims of unfair labor practices and the NLRB General Counsel brought charges against ILWU, PMMC and PCMC under the National Labor Relations Act, 29 U.S.C. §§ 151-169 (NLRA or Act). With a few exceptions no longer at issue, the administrative law judge (ALJ) recommended dismissing the charges. The Board disagreed, concluding that the Employer was obligated to bargain with IAM over the termination of PMMC's unit employees and that the Employer's recognition of ILWU was unlawful. Ultimately, PCMC and PMMC settled the claims, leaving ILWU as the sole Petitioner.

ILWU raises three challenges to the Board's Decision and Order. First, it contends that the Board erred in concluding that the

---

[1] PCMC joined with another company, Marine Terminals Corporation, to create PMMC. As discussed *infra*, the parties have stipulated that PCMC and PMMC are a "single employer" and, accordingly, Marine Terminals Corporation has no relevance to the case.

[2] For reasons discussed *infra*, the Long Beach terminal is no longer at issue.

Employer was obligated to bargain with IAM over its decision to shut down PMMC and terminate its workforce. Second, it argues that the Board improperly excluded evidence that the M&R employees merged by accretion into the ILWU West Coast-wide employee bargaining unit. Third, it disputes the propriety of the Board remedy. For the following reasons, we deny ILWU's petition and grant the Board's cross-application for enforcement.

I. BACKGROUND

Maersk, and companies like it, transport goods around the world in large container ships packed with 20-foot metal containers. At port terminals, the shipping containers are unloaded by cranes and transported to off-site locations where they are "stripped" and distributed to their final destinations. The inverse process includes "stuffing" containers off-site and eventually loading them onto the cargo ships for export at the **[—5—]** terminals. *See* Joint Appendix (JA) 693, 1218-19. The machinery and the containers used in this process periodically need maintenance and repair. Port-terminal contract repair companies, like the Employer, employ M&R mechanics to ensure the process runs smoothly.

The Board has previously chronicled the history of ILWU and IAM. *See, e.g., Shipowners' Ass'n of the Pac. Coast*, 7 NLRB 1002 (1938); *Pac. Mar. Ass'n*, 256 NLRB 769, 772 (1981). We note, however, that the two unions have different organizational models. In the port-terminal context, IAM represents only M&R mechanics and it usually does so on a local level, dividing its bargaining units either by terminal or by company. This was the case from the 1960s to the early 2000s, when IAM operated as the exclusive union representative for the single-employer, multi-terminal bargaining unit of M&R mechanics at Long Beach, Oakland and Tacoma.

ILWU is more inclusive. Its bargaining unit is composed of a West Coast-wide group of longshoremen, stevedores, marine clerks, planners and longshore mechanics. A single CBA, the Pacific Coast Longshore and Clerks Agreement (PCL&CA),[3] binds ILWU, on one side, and the Pacific Maritime Association (PMA), a collection of approximately 70 maritime employers along the Pacific Coast (including PCMC), on the other. Pursuant to the PCL&CA, ILWU and **[—6—]** PMA have established an employment **{-1105-}** dispatch system that is in effect along the Pacific Coast. The system operates through a series of "halls" that match employees to employers on a flexible basis so that labor can flow to the terminals that need it most. The Employer describes this system as its "lean staffing model." JA 412.

This chapter of the unions' story began in 1999, when Maersk purchased the Oakland, Tacoma and Long Beach port operations[4] from Sealand. As a condition of the sale, Sealand required Maersk to recognize IAM as the M&R mechanics' union in all three locations.

At that time, PCMC was performing M&R work for Maersk in Los Angeles and it was interested in expanding its work to the three newly acquired Maersk terminals.[5] Because PCMC was bound by the PCL&CA to recognize ILWU, however, Sealand's IAM-recognition requirement prevented PCMC from performing the work. In order to get

[3] The PCL&CA CBA comprises multiple documents, including (1) the Pacific Coast Clerks Contract Document (PCCCD), which governs marine clerks and planners; (2) the Pacific Coast Longshore Contract Document (PCLCD), which governs longshore workers, including stevedores and longshore mechanics; and (3) the Safety Code Contract. JA 479-82; 610-16. We refer to the documents together as the PCL&CA.

[4] Maersk leased terminals from the ports. For example, Maersk leased berths 20-24 at the Port of Oakland and contracted with PMMC to do its M&R work at those berths. *See Ports Am. Outer Harbor, LLC*, 366 NLRB No. 76, 2018 WL 2086090 (May 2, 2018) (deciding PCMC/PMMC successorship issues).

[5] PMMC's Oakland and Tacoma terminals served a second shipping company, Horizon Lines, which accounted for a small portion of PMMC's work. Horizon received the same services as Maersk through a contractual "me-too" relationship tied to Maersk's contract with PMMC. Maersk was the primary shipping company, however, and Horizon Lines had no role in the contract negotiations described herein.

around this obstacle, PCMC created PMMC. PMMC then bid on, and won, the Maersk contract. Thereafter, PMMC recognized IAM and **[—7—]** began performing the M&R work at the former Sealand terminals.

On March 31, 2002, the IAM-Sealand (now IAM-PMMC) CBA was set to expire. Around the same time, Maersk consolidated its Southern California operations by merging its M&R workforce into a single terminal (Pier 400) in the Port of Los Angeles. As a result of the consolidation, Maersk no longer needed PMMC's services at the Long Beach terminal and instead contracted with PCMC to do its M&R work at the new consolidated Los Angeles terminal. As for the Oakland and Tacoma terminals, PMMC and IAM agreed to a CBA extension from April 1, 2002 to March 31, 2005 but did so only after more than a dozen bargaining sessions and a strike vote of unit employees.

In late 2004, with the March 31, 2005 CBA expiration date looming, Maersk solicited bids from both PCMC and PMMC for work at the Oakland and Tacoma terminals. PCMC submitted a bid of $64.46 per hour and PMMC submitted a bid of $72.88 per hour. At the ALJ hearing, PCMC and PMMC representatives explained the difference in price. PCMC representative Joseph Gregorio testified that the discussion regarding the different bid prices "always was focused upon the concept that there was differences [sic] in labor costs," including "benefits and pensions." JA 92. Similarly, PMMC informed Maersk that its higher bid resulted from a "collection of [employee] benefits." JA 172.

Maersk selected PCMC to do the work. Accordingly, on January 25, 2005, Maersk terminated its maintenance contract with PMMC, effective March 31, 2005. On January 26, **[—8—]** PMMC notified IAM, informing it and its unit employees[6] that PMMC intended to terminate its operations on April 1. PMMC also explained how the unit employees could apply for employment with **{-1106-}** PCMC to continue working the same jobs. In early February, IAM requested that PMMC bargain over its decision to terminate work at the Oakland and Tacoma terminals. PMMC agreed to bargain over the effects of the terminations but asserted that it was Maersk's decision—not PMMC's—to use PCMC to perform the M&R work. Thus, PMMC refused to bargain about its decision to shut down operations.

Effective April 1, 2005, PMMC permanently "laid off" all of its M&R mechanics. JA 899-900 (Letter from Terry Murphy, PMMC Vice President, to IAM representatives). On March 31, PCMC hired 76 of the PMMC unit mechanics, requiring them to accept ILWU as their bargaining representative.[7] PCMC hired six more former PMMC mechanics shortly thereafter. For the most part, the mechanics continued to perform the same work at the same locations with the same tools and equipment. One difference was that PCMC began to transfer mechanics temporarily between the former- **[—9—]** PMMC terminals of Oakland and Tacoma and other nearby terminals in accordance with the PCL&CA hiring halls and its "lean staffing model."

In early 2005, IAM pressed unfair labor practice (ULP) charges against PMMC and PCMC as "a single employer" and alternatively as "alter egos" under sections 8(a)(1), (2), (3), and (5) of the NLRA[8]; it

---

[6] Although the January 26 letter was addressed to IAM representatives, it was also "[p]osted and distributed to employees covered by the 2002-2005 IAM/PMMC contract." JA 900.

[7] When PCMC extended employment offers to former PMMC mechanics, it made clear that "[a]ll of our operations are covered by our coast-wide contract with [ILWU]." JA 908. Specifically, the PCL&CA contained a "union security" clause providing that "[a]ny employee who becomes fully registered during the life of the Agreement shall . . . become and remain a member of the [ILWU] in good standing as a condition of employment." JA 665. Thus, ILWU membership was an explicit requirement of PCMC employment.

[8] Section 8(a) provides:

> It shall be an unfair labor practice for an employer . . . (1) to interfere with, restrain, or coerce employees in the exercise of the rights guaranteed in section 157 . . . (2) to dominate or interfere with the formation or administration of any labor organization or

subsequently filed ULP charges against ILWU under sections 8(b)(1)(A)[9] and (2).[10] In 2007, the **[—10—]** NLRB General Counsel filed a complaint alleging similar ULPs and moved to consolidate its charges with those filed by IAM. An ALJ granted the General Counsel's motion and heard the consolidated case in a 41-day hearing between September 13, 2007 and June 20, 2008. During the hearing, the parties narrowed the issues. First, PCMC and PMMC stipulated that they were a single employer. JA 608. The General Counsel disavowed any "successor" or "alter ego" theories of liability and agreed that the Employer had properly engaged in "effects bargaining." On February 12, 2009, the ALJ issued his opinion, recommending **{-1107-}** dismissal of all charges against ILWU and dismissal of all but one[11] charge against the Employer.

The Board rejected the ALJ's dismissal recommendations. It concluded that the Employer had violated sections 8(a)(5) and (2) of the NLRA, based largely on "the parties' stipulation that PMMC and PCMC were at all times material a single employer." *Pac. Crane Maint. Co., Inc. &/or Pac. Marine Maint. Co., LLC,* 359 NLRB 1206, 1207 (2013) (*PCMC/PMMC I*). The Board also held that ILWU violated sections 8(b)(1)(A) and (2) of the NLRA by accepting assistance and recognition from the Employer as the exclusive collective bargaining representative of the unit employees at a time when ILWU did not represent an uncoerced majority of unit employees. *Id.* at 1213. **[—11—]**

The Employer and ILWU originally sought review in the United States Court of Appeals for the Ninth Circuit. *Pac. Crane Maint. Co. v. NLRB,* No. 13-72463 (9th Cir. July 12, 2013). While that appeal was pending, the United States Supreme Court decided *NLRB v. Noel Canning,* 134 S. Ct. 2550 (2014), which led to the vacatur and remand of the original Board decision. On June 17, 2015, the Board reviewed the ALJ's opinion *de novo* and issued the Order *sub judice* in which it reached the same conclusions it had reached in its 2013 decision. *Pac. Crane Maint. Co., Inc. &/or Pac. Marine Maint. Co., LLC,* 362 NLRB No. 120, 2015 WL 3791632 (June 17, 2015) (*PCMC/PMMC II*). The Board Order requires ILWU, *inter alia*: (1) to cease and desist from the unfair labor practices found and from interfering with or coercing employees in the exercise of rights under section 7 of the Act; (2) to decline recognition as the exclusive bargaining representative unless and until it is certified by the Board; and (3) along with the Employer, to reimburse unit employees for all initiation fees, dues and other moneys paid to ILWU or withheld from their wages by the Employer. *Id.* at *8-9. PCMC/PMMC subsequently settled the claims against it for approximately $130,000 per employee. ILWU petitions this Court for review and the Board cross-applies for enforcement of its Order.

II. EMPLOYER'S DUTY TO BARGAIN

"We will uphold a decision of the Board unless it relied upon findings that are not supported by substantial evidence, failed to apply the proper legal standard, or departed from its precedent without providing a

> contribute financial or other support to it . . . (3) by discrimination in regard to hire or tenure of employment or any term or condition of employment to encourage or discourage membership in any labor organization . . . (5) to refuse to bargain collectively with the representatives of his employees . . . .

29 U.S.C. § 158(a).

[9] Section 8(b)(1)(A) provides, in relevant part, that it "shall be an unfair labor practice" for a union to "restrain or coerce . . . employees in the exercise of the rights guaranteed in section 157," 29 U.S.C. § 158(b)(1)(A), including, *inter alia,* the right to "self-organization" and the right to "bargain collectively through representatives of their own choosing," *id.* § 157.

[10] Section 8(b)(2) provides: "It shall be an unfair labor practice for a labor organization or its agents . . . to cause or attempt to cause an employer to discriminate against an employee in violation of subsection (a)(3) or to discriminate against an employee with respect **[—10—]** to whom membership in such organization has been denied or terminated . . . ." 29 U.S.C. § 158(b)(2).

[11] The ALJ found that the Employer violated sections 8(a)(1) and (5) of the NLRA by removing IAM material posted on a bulletin board at the Maersk terminal before March 31, 2005. That finding is not challenged here.

reasoned justification for doing so." *E.I. Du Pont De Nemours & Co. v. NLRB*, 682 F.3d 65, 67 (D.C. Cir. 2012). The Board's findings of fact are "conclusive" if supported by substantial evidence. 29 U.S.C. § 160(e). **[—12—]**

This case comes to us in an unusual posture. Because PCMC/PMMC settled its dispute with the Board and IAM, we are called upon to review only the Board's conclusion that ILWU violated sections 8(b)(1)(A) and (2) of the NLRA by accepting the Employer's recognition as the union representative of the M&R mechanics at the Oakland and Tacoma ports. To review that determination, however, we must first determine whether *the Employer* had an obligation to bargain with IAM under sections 8(a)(5) and (d) before it shut down PMMC's operations. As we discuss *infra*, we conclude that the Employer had such an obligation—and violated it. **{-1108-}**

A union violates section 8(b)(1)(A) by exercising exclusive bargaining authority when it does not, in fact, have the support of an uncoerced majority of the employees in the relevant bargaining unit. *Int'l Ladies' Garment Workers' Union v. NLRB*, 366 U.S. 731, 733 (1961) (applying 29 U.S.C. § 158(b)(1)(A)). Section 8(b)(2) prohibits a union from causing or attempting to cause "an employer to discriminate against an employee" by requiring the employee to adhere to a union-security clause imposed on behalf of a union that does not represent a majority of the employees in the appropriate bargaining unit. 29 U.S.C. § 158(b)(2); *Local Lodge No. 1424 v. NLRB*, 362 U.S. 411, 413-14 (1960). The purpose of both provisions is clear: neither an employer nor a union may unilaterally override the employees' organizational rights, including the right to select bargaining representatives of their choosing. *See* 29 U.S.C. § 157; *see also Radio Officers' Union of Commercial Telegraphers Union v. NLRB*, 347 U.S. 17, 40 (1954).

Key to our ultimate decision is whether IAM—rather than ILWU—continued as the appropriate representative of the M&R mechanics at the Oakland and Tacoma terminals once PMMC ceased operations. Put simply, if IAM remained the **[—13—]** appropriate union for the unit employees, ILWU was not permitted to accept the Employer's recognition. On this issue, ILWU has two arguments. First, it argues that the Employer properly terminated its relationship with IAM when it shut down PMMC's operations without bargaining and therefore PCMC—as a separate corporate entity—could hire employees without regard to their past IAM representation. Second, ILWU asserts that the employees formerly represented by IAM merged by accretion into the existing ILWU West Coast-wide bargaining unit. We address these arguments in turn.

A. Employer's Termination Decision

Under section 8(a)(5), an employer commits an unfair labor practice if it "refuse[s] to bargain collectively with the representatives of [its] employees." 29 U.S.C. § 158(a)(5). Under the NLRA, collective bargaining consists of a "mutual obligation of the employer and the representative of the employees to meet at reasonable times and confer in good faith with respect to wages, hours, and other terms and conditions of employment . . . ." *Id.* § 158(d). The subjects of mandatory bargaining are broad and the Supreme Court has explained that "Congress deliberately left the words 'wages, hours, and other terms and conditions of employment' without further definition, for it did not intend to deprive the Board of the power further to define those terms in light of specific industrial practices." *First Nat'l Maint. Corp. v. NLRB*, 452 U.S. 666, 675 (1981) (quoting 29 U.S.C. § 158(d)).

Under section 8(d), an employer's decision to replace employees in an "existing bargaining unit with those of an independent contractor to do the same work under similar conditions of employment" is a subject of mandatory bargaining. *Fibreboard Paper Prods. Corp. v. NLRB*, 379 U.S. 203, 215 (1964). Put differently, an employer may not **[—14—]** "unilaterally attempt to divert work away from a bargaining unit without fulfilling [its] statutory duty to bargain." *Rd. Sprinkler Fitters Local Union No. 669 v. NLRB*, 676

F.2d 826, 831 (D.C. Cir. 1982) ("double-breasted" employer has duty to bargain before diverting work from its union employees to its non-union employees). Accordingly, we have held that a movie theater employer had a **{-1109-}** duty to bargain with the union representing its movie-reel operators before transferring that work to its assistant managers. *Regal Cinemas, Inc. v. NLRB*, 317 F.3d 300, 307 (D.C. Cir. 2003). Our decision was based, in large part, on the fact that the employer "continued to operate the same business at the same locations and the only change [was] in the identity of the employees doing the work." *Id.* at 310 (quoting ALJ decision below). In other words, the nature of the theater's business itself was unchanged. *Id.* Thus, finding "no link" between a non-labor-cost reason for the change—*e.g.*, technological advances in the movie-projector business—and the theater's decision to reallocate work to assistant managers, we upheld the Board's conclusion that the reallocation of employee duties was based primarily on labor costs and therefore the subject of mandatory bargaining. *Id.* at 307.

At the same time, an employer's duty to bargain is not limitless and the NLRA does not prohibit a business from making independent economic decisions unrelated to labor relations. *First Nat'l Maint.*, 452 U.S. at 676-77. The duty to bargain "includes only issues that settle an aspect of the relationship between the employer and the employees." *Id.* at 676 (quoting *Chemical & Alkali Workers v. Pittsburgh Plate Glass Co.*, 404 U.S. 157, 178 (1971)). Bargaining is therefore mandatory "only if the benefit, for labor-management relations and the collective-bargaining process, outweighs the burden placed on the conduct of the business." *Id.* at 679. In *First National*, the Supreme Court held that the employer was not **[—15—]** required to bargain over its decision to shut down a portion of its maintenance business—and terminate many of its employees in the process—after the employer reduced its weekly rate from $500 to $250. 452 U.S. at 668. There, the employer made its strategic business decision "purely for economic reasons"—the reduced rate was not profitable and the client was not willing to pay the $500 rate—not in order to reduce labor costs or alter employee relations. *Id.* at 686.

When one company buys another, the transaction can qualify as a "core business decision" that falls outside the "terms and conditions" of employment contemplated by section 8(d). *See AG Comm'ns Sys. Corp.*, 350 NLRB 168 (2007), *pet. for review denied sub nom., Int'l Brotherhood of Elec. Workers, Local 21 v. NLRB*, 563 F.3d 418 (9th Cir. 2009) (*AG Communications*). *AG Communications* involved the merger of two telecommunication installation companies: AG and Lucent. *AG Comm'ns*, 563 F.3d at 421. Before the merger, the companies had CBAs with different unions: Lucent bargained with the Communications Workers of America (CWA) and AG bargained with the International Brotherhood of Electrical Workers, Local 21, AFL-CIO (Local 21). *Id.* After Lucent purchased AG, however, "Lucent began to merge AG into Lucent to streamline operations and to increase efficiency and profitability." *Id.* Following a period of integration, Lucent declared its intent to recognize only CWA. *Id.* Local 21 protested and demanded collective bargaining but the companies refused. *Id.* The Board sided with the merging companies, holding that the two companies became a single employer only *after* the merger took place and that the decision to merge was a "core business decision" motivated by operational efficiencies rather than labor costs. *Id.* at 422. The Ninth Circuit agreed with the Board. *Id.* at 421. **[—16—]**

We conclude that the Employer was required to bargain over its decision to shut down PMMC's operations and transfer them to PCMC. First, the record makes clear that the difference in bid **{-1110-}** prices was based almost exclusively on labor-related costs, which are "peculiarly suitable for resolution within the collective bargaining framework." *First Nat'l Maint.*, 452 U.S. at 680 (quoting *Fibreboard*, 379 U.S. at 214). During the ALJ hearing, the Employer's representative, Joseph Gregorio, testified that the difference between PCMC's and PMMC's respective bid prices was attributable to the wages and benefits the companies provided to their respective M&R employees. JA 92 (explaining that negotiations regarding the difference between bid prices "always was focused upon the concept that there was differences [sic] in labor costs"). Similarly, PMMC informed Maersk that its higher costs resulted from a "collection of [employee] benefits." JA 172. Driving this point home, Maersk representative Wayne Pighin testified that Maersk selected PCMC's bid principally on the basis of its lower bid price. JA 161, 172.

In arguing that the transition from PMMC to PCMC was a "core entrepreneurial decision" rather than a term or condition of employment, ILWU attempts to attribute PCMC's lower bid to its "lean staffing model." Pet'r's Br. 20-24. This argument ignores the fact that PCMC's "lean staffing model" is tied to its membership in the PMA and the PMA's CBA with ILWU's West Coast-wide bargaining unit. If PCMC had not recognized ILWU as the union representing the former PMMC employees, it would not have had access to the hiring hall or the flexible transfer policies of the PCL&CA. Accordingly, we do not view the "lean staffing model" as an independent business construct unique to PCMC but instead as a provision of the PCL&CA applicable to every PMA employer. *See Sw. Steel & Supply, Inc. v. NLRB*, 806 F.2d 1111, 1113 (D.C. Cir. 1986) (CBA's hiring hall provision is subject of mandatory bargaining). **[—17—]**

Our conclusion turns heavily on PMMC and PCMC's single-employer stipulation. *See Farmers Co-op. Elevator Ass'n Non-Stock of Big Springs, Neb. v. Strand*, 382 F.2d 224, 231 (8th Cir. 1967) ("The general rule is that parties are bound by stipulations voluntarily made . . . ."). By virtue of their stipulation, *both* PCMC and PMMC effectively conceded that they (together) were required to bargain with IAM about the "terms and conditions" of its members' employment at the Oakland and Tacoma terminals. *See RC Aluminum Indus., Inc. v. NLRB*, 326 F.3d 235, 239-40 (D.C. Cir. 2003) (explaining features of single-employer status in context of mandatory bargaining). The Employer's stipulation further distinguishes this case from *AG Communications*, where the merging companies became a single employer only *after* the two companies merged. 563 F.3d at 421. In light of the companies' single-employer status, ILWU's argument that PMMC simply made "a decision to close operations for economic reasons" on March 30, 2005 fails. Pet'r's Br. 20. As a single employer, PCMC/PMMC did not "close" its operations. Like the employer that reassigned duties in *Regal Cinemas*, 317 F.3d at 307, and the double-breasted employer that redistributed contract work from its union division to its non-union division in *Sprinkler Fitters*, 676 F.2d at 831, PCMC/PMMC unilaterally transferred work from one segment of its business to another, achieving its goal of lowered labor costs.

Nor did PMMC lose Maersk as a client, as was the case in *First National*. 452 U.S. at 669-70. Instead, the Employer's M&R work at the Maersk terminals continued uninterrupted the day after PMMC "closed." Except for a handful of employees, it was business as usual for the M&R mechanics at the Oakland and Tacoma terminals on March 31, 2005. The same M&R mechanics continued to work **{–1111–}** the same jobs in the same locations with the same equipment. *See Regal Cinemas*, 317 F.3d at 307. Indeed, the mechanics had the same customer **[—18—]** (Maersk). The only changes were their uniforms, JA 129-30, and the union representing them, JA 125-26. In every material sense, PCMC (as a single employer with PMMC) retained Maersk's business. Accordingly, we conclude that the Employer's decision to close PMMC was based primarily on labor costs and that it therefore had an obligation to bargain under sections 8(a)(5) and (d). When PCMC/PMMC refused IAM's bargaining request and unilaterally terminated its recognition of the Union, it breached that obligation.

B. Employees' Bargaining Unit

Having concluded that PCMC/PMMC had an obligation to bargain with IAM, we turn to ILWU's "accretion" argument and the Board's determination of the appropriate bargaining unit. *See S. Prairie Constr. Co. v. Local No. 627*, 425 U.S. 800, 805 (1976) (employee bargaining unit must be analyzed apart from single-employer determination).

Under section 9(b) of the NLRA, the Board has authority to delineate employee bargaining units. *Serramonte Oldsmobile, Inc. v. NLRB*, 86 F.3d 227, 236 (D.C. Cir. 1996). In doing so, it looks to the "community of interest" among employees, which includes factors such as "skills and duties; wages and benefits; interchange between sites; functional integration; geographic proximity; centralized control of management, supervision, and labor relations; and bargaining history." *RC Aluminum Indus., Inc.*, 326 F.3d at 239-40. Although no single factor is controlling, "a group of employees with a significant history of representation by a particular union presumptively constitute[s] an appropriate bargaining unit." *Cmty. Hosps. of Cent. Cal. v. NLRB*, 335 F.3d 1079, 1085 (D.C. Cir. 2003). The Board therefore demands that "a party challenging a historical unit show that 'compelling circumstances' warrant modification of the unit." *Dodge of* **[—19—]** *Naperville, Inc. v. NLRB*, 796 F.3d 31, 39 (D.C. Cir. 2015) (citations omitted). Moreover, "[b]ecause the assessment requires a fact-intensive inquiry and a balancing of various factors, the Board has broad discretion in making the determination." *United Food & Commercial Workers v. NLRB*, 519 F.3d 490, 494 (D.C. Cir. 2008).

In weighing the "community of interest" of a merged workforce, the Board sometimes applies the doctrine of "accretion." *Dean Transp., Inc. v. NLRB*, 551 F.3d 1055, 1067 (D.C. Cir. 2009). "Accretion is the addition of a group of employees to an existing union-represented bargaining unit without a Board election." *Id.* "[B]ecause accretion essentially deprives employees of their statutory right to choose their bargaining representative, the Board has historically followed a restrictive policy in applying the accretion doctrine." *Id.* The Board will not find accretion unless "the employees sought to be added to an existing bargaining unit have little or no separate identity and share an overwhelming community of interest with the preexisting unit to which they are accreted." *Id.* (internal quotation marks and citations omitted). Importantly, when evaluating "community of interest" factors—whether in the context of accretion or otherwise—we have held that the Board should ignore "any impermissible changes made unilaterally by the employer." *Dodge of Naperville*, 796 F.3d at 39. "To hold otherwise would allow [the employer] to benefit from its own unlawful conduct." *In re Comar, Inc.*, 339 NLRB 903, 911 (2003), *enfd.*, 111 F. App'x 1 (D.C. Cir. 2004). **{–1112–}**

The history of IAM's multi-terminal bargaining unit is plain. It covers a 40-year period with the M&R employees at the Oakland and Tacoma terminals. ILWU does not contest that IAM was the legitimate union representative of the M&R mechanics at those locations before March 31, 2005. Nor could it, as Sealand's insistence on the continuity of IAM as the **[—20—]** mechanics' union prompted PCMC to create PMMC to perform the Maersk contract in the first place. JA 23 (PCMC/PMMC co-owner Steve McLeod testifying that "purpose of creating [PMMC] was to have an entity to respond to a proposal to do maintenance work for [Maersk]"). Indeed, PCMC/PMMC was *required* to recognize the IAM bargaining unit as a condition of the Sealand contract.

Moreover, the Board found as a fact that, "[a]s of March 31 . . . the unit employees generally continued to perform the same work at the same location, with the same tools and equipment as they had before the merger, working under separate immediate supervision from the ILWU-represented employees." *PCMC/PMMC I*, 359 NLRB at 1211. In other words, PCMC did not hire new M&R employees to handle its new business; nor did PCMC use its "lean staffing model" to hire outside mechanics to staff the newly acquired terminals. Instead, on the date the change in ownership took place, the very same group of employees continued their daily work. *See* JA 73 (Joseph Gregorio testifying that PCMC "decided [to] hire only the former IAM mechanics"). In the face of the unchallenged bargaining history and the evident employee continuity, we uphold the Board's determination that the M&R mechanics at Tacoma and Oakland constituted a proper bargaining unit represented by IAM. *See Cmty. Hosps. of Cent. Cal.*, 335 F.3d at 1085.

We reject the argument that the PMMC M&R employees were merged by accretion into the West Coast-wide ILWU workforce. Moreover, we decline ILWU's invitation to look past March 31 at all for our "community of interest" assessment because any post-March 31 "accretion" necessarily occurred *after* the Employer violated section 8(a)(5) by failing to bargain over its decision to switch operations from PMMC to PCMC. In these circumstances, the Board correctly discounted any **[—21—]** evidence tied to "impermissible changes made unilaterally by the employer." *Dodge of Naperville*, 796 F.3d at 39.

In sum, we hold that substantial evidence supports the Board's conclusion that the M&R employees at the Oakland and Tacoma ports were not part of ILWU's West Coast-wide bargaining unit and the Employer's duty to bargain with the existing IAM bargaining unit was not extinguished by virtue of the accretion doctrine. Because IAM continued as the appropriate bargaining representative for the M&R mechanics at the Oakland and Tacoma terminals after March 31, 2005, ILWU violated sections 8(b)(1)(A) and (2) of the NLRA when it accepted recognition from the Employer.[12] **{-1113-}**

III. BOARD REMEDY

Finally, ILWU challenges the Board remedy. Specifically, ILWU points out that PCMC has ceased operations and paid roughly $130,000 to each of the approximately 100 unit employees formerly represented by IAM at the Oakland and Tacoma terminals as part of its settlement. Accordingly, it **[—22—]** argues that the Board remedy improperly provides a "windfall," or double recovery, to IAM. Pet'r's Br. 58.

Under section 10(e) of the NLRA, our review of Board decisions is limited to issues the parties in fact raised before the Board. 29 U.S.C. § 160(e) ("No objection that has not been urged before the Board . . . shall be considered by the court . . . [absent] extraordinary circumstances."). "Application of section 10(e) is mandatory, not discretionary." *Oldwick Materials, Inc. v. NLRB*, 732 F.2d 339, 341 (3d Cir. 1984). Accordingly, if a party wishes to challenge an issue first raised in a Board decision, it must move for reconsideration so that the Board—not this Court—can address the question in the first instance. *See Nova Se. Univ. v. NLRB*, 807 F.3d 308, 316 (D.C. Cir. 2015).

Before the Board, ILWU did not challenge the Board remedy in light of the Employer's settlement with IAM and its members. Nor did ILWU move for reconsideration once it learned of the Employer's settlement.[13] Therefore, under section 10(e), we cannot modify the relief granted absent "extraordinary circumstances." *See NLRB v. Ochoa Fertilizer Corp.*, 368 U.S. 318, 322 (1961) ("[I]n the absence of a showing within the statutory exception of 'extraordinary circumstances' the failure or neglect of the respondent to urge an objection in the Board's proceedings forecloses judicial consideration of the objection in enforcement proceedings."). Finding nothing "extraordinary" about ILWU's unexcused failure to raise its arguments before the Board, we conclude **[—23—]** that ILWU's remedial challenge is not properly before us and we decline to address it.

That said, ILWU has an opportunity to make its objection known at the compliance stage of the Board proceedings. *See Sure-Tan, Inc. v. NLRB*, 467 U.S. 883, 902 (1984). The

[12] It is undisputed that the PCMC-ILWU CBA contains a "union-security" clause that requires membership in ILWU as a condition of PCMC employment, JA 665, and that PCMC enforced the clause when it hired the former PMMC mechanics, *see PCMC/PMMC I*, 359 NLRB at 1207; *see also* JA 908 (PCMC employment offer letter). Because the Board correctly determined that IAM—not ILWU—was the proper union representative of the M&R employees at the Oakland and Tacoma terminals, it also correctly concluded that ILWU had violated section 8(b)(2) by applying its CBA—including the "union-security" clause—to those employees. *PCMC/PMMC I*, 359 NLRB at 1207; *see Local Lodge No. 1424 v. NLRB*, 362 U.S. 411, 413-14 (1960).

[13] The Employer moved for reconsideration regarding the merits of the Board Order. JA 1372. The Board denied the motion. *Id.* at 1376.

Board acknowledged as much in declaring that ILWU "may, in compliance proceedings, present evidence showing that particular remedial provisions are no longer appropriate . . . ." JA 1376 n.5 (March 1, 2016 Board Order Denying Reconsideration). This evidence will likely include, *inter alia*, the details of the Employer's settlement, which are not included in the record. *See* JA 1546-48 (letter explaining that ILWU does not have access to settlement documents). Thus, in any compliance proceeding, ILWU may make—and the Board may consider—the argument that the Employer's post-hearing settlement constitutes an offset of any amount the Board has determined ILWU owes.

For the foregoing reasons, we deny ILWU's petition for review and grant the Board's cross-application for enforcement against ILWU.

So ordered.

United States Court of Appeals for the District of Columbia Circuit

No. 17-1144

MATSON NAVIGATION CO.
VS.
UNITED STATES DEP'T OF TRANSP. & MARITIME ADMIN.

On Petition for Review of Decision and Order of the Maritime Administration

Decided: July 17, 2018

Citation: 895 F.3d 799, 6 Adm. R. 491 (D.C. Cir. 2018).

Before **ROGERS**, **GRIFFITH**, and **MILLETT**, Circuit Judges.

[—2—] {-800-} ROGERS, Circuit Judge: **{-801-}**

Matson Navigation Company, Inc., a competitor of APL Marine Services, Ltd., and APL Maritime, Ltd. (together, "APL"), petitions for review of three orders of the Maritime Administration approving APL's requested replacement vessels in the Maritime Security Fleet. For the following reasons, we dismiss the petition for review for lack of jurisdiction under 28 U.S.C. § 2342.

I.

The Maritime Security Fleet, established by the Secretary of Transportation, in consultation with the Secretary of Defense, is to consist of "active, commercially viable, militarily useful, privately owned vessels to meet national defense and other security requirements and maintain a United States presence in international commercial shipping." 46 U.S.C. § 53102(a). The Fleet is a part of the Merchant Marine "necessary for the national defense and the development of the domestic and foreign commerce." *Id.* § 50101(a). It is "owned and operated as vessels of the United States by citizens of the United States." *Id.* § 50101(a)(3). Fleet vessels must be covered by a Maritime Security Program Operating Agreement with the owner or operator. *Id.* § 53103(a). The owner or operator, known as a "contractor," must meet citizenship **[—3—]** requirements and, in turn, can receive operating subsidies for its vessels. *Id.* §§ 53101(2), 53102(b) & (c), 53105(b). As relevant here, "[a] contractor may replace a vessel under an operating agreement with another vessel that is eligible to be included in the Fleet under section 53102(b), if the Secretary, in conjunction with the Secretary of Defense, approves the replacement of the vessel." *Id.* § 53105(f).

The Maritime Security Program ("MSP") is administered by the Maritime Administration ("MARAD"). *See* 46 C.F.R. § 296.1. MARAD regulations provide that:

> A Contractor who disagrees with the findings, interpretations or decisions of the Maritime Administration or the Contracting Officer with respect to the administration of this part or any other dispute or complaint concerning MSP Operating Agreements may submit an appeal to the Administrator . . . within 60 days following the date of the document notifying the Contractor of the administrative determination . . . . Such an appeal is a prerequisite to exhausting administrative remedies.

Id. § 296.50(a). The regulations state a "contractor" refers to "the owner or operator of a vessel that enters into an MSP Operating Agreement for the vessel with the Secretary of Transportation (acting through MARAD)." *Id.* § 296.2.

APL, after reviewing its "total network of U.S. flag operations," requested MARAD on December 4, 2014, to approve, with regard to APL reinstating its U.S.-Guam shipping service, replacement of two "S-12" vessels, pursuant to **{-802-}** 46 U.S.C. § 53105(f). Letter from Eric L. Mensing, Chief Executive Officer of APL, to Paul N. Jaenichen, Sr., MARAD Administrator at 1, 3 (Dec. 4, 2014). The vessels were covered **[—4—]** under MSP Operating Agreements but no longer met the eligibility requirements in 46 U.S.C. § 53102(b) on "commercial viability" or requirements in the Operating Agreements on "militarily useful capability." *Id.* at 1. APL sought their replacement by two smaller "feeder" vessels that met those requirements, and sought MARAD's approval before proceeding with acquisition and U.S. flagging. After receiving approval in principle by MARAD and the U.S. Transportation Command, provided the replacement vessels met all MSP requirements, APL requested, on August 27, 2015, approval of the NEW DYNAMIC as a replacement vessel. On September 16, 2015, APL sought to rename that vessel as APL Guam, and to substitute its contractor under the Operating Agreement.

On October 22, 2015, MARAD approved APL Guam as a replacement, in light of the recommendation by the Commander of the U.S. Transportation Command that section 53102(b) requirements had been met and that those findings sufficed to fulfill the joint approval contemplated in 46 U.S.C. § 53105(f). MARAD's 2015 Approval Order stated that the replacement vessel's owner was "a citizen of the United States within the meaning of 46 U.S.C. § 50501"; that the "[r]eplacement vessel will provide transportation in foreign commerce pursuant to the requirements of 46 U.S.C. § 53102(b)(2)"; and that it is "commercially viable." 2015 Approval Order at 3.

Because APL Guam did not satisfy APL's shipping needs in the U.S.-Guam route, APL requested MARAD, on August 24, 2016, to approve replacement of another of its Fleet vessels with APL Saipan pursuant to 46 U.S.C. § 53105(f). On December 20, 2016, MARAD approved the replacement. The 2016 Approval Order stated that APL Saipan met statutory eligibility and citizenship requirements under 46 U.S.C. **[—5—]** § 53102(b)(1) & (c)(2); that it provided foreign commerce or mixed foreign commerce and domestic trade allowed under a registry endorsement, 46 U.S.C. § 12111, pursuant to the requirements of 46 U.S.C. §§ 53102(b)(2) and 53105(a)(1)(A); and that it met the commercial viability requirements, 46 U.S.C. § 53102(b)(4)(B). 2016 Approval Order at 1–2.

Matson also operates vessels in the U.S.-Guam route but does not have an MSP Operating Agreement with MARAD. Shortly before MARAD's approval of APL Saipan as a replacement vessel, Matson had urged MARAD not to allow APL to operate APL Guam and APL Saipan in the U.S.-Guam trade route because they did not meet the statutory requirements for "replacement vessels" and the operation of APL Guam was "distorting the market and creating an unlevel playing field" in service to Guam. Letter from Matthew J. Cox, President and Chief Executive Officer of Matson Navigation Co., Inc., to Paul N. Jaenichen, MARAD Administrator at 1–2 (Dec. 12, 2016); *see* Letter from Michael F. Scanlon, K&L Gates, to David J. Tubman, Jr., Chief Counsel of MARAD and Dep't of Transp. (Dec. 15, 2016). Matson also filed a protest, styled as "Amended Appeal of the Determinations under Maritime Security Program Operating Agreement Numbers MA/MSP-54 and MA/MSP-57," on February 17, 2017, as amended March 17. It raised the issue "whether assistance payments awarded to support U.S.-flag vessels operating in the international trades under the Maritime Security Program . . . can be used to subsidize vessels operating in regular service in Guam, a domestic trade." Am. Appeal at 1. Matson challenged **{-803-}** the 2015 and 2016 Approval Orders on the principal grounds that APL's replacement vessels did not operate in foreign commerce and were not commercially viable.

On April 7, 2017, the Acting Chief Counsel of MARAD rejected Matson's appeal on two grounds. First, because it was **[—6—]** not an MSP "contractor" under 46 C.F.R. § 296.2, Matson lacked standing to appeal the 2015 and 2016 Approval Orders pursuant to MARAD's regulation, 46 C.F.R. § 296.50(a). Second, on the merits, "the APL replacement vessels provide transportation in mixed foreign commerce and domestic trade, as authorized by 46 U.S.C. §§ 12111 and 53105(a)(1)(A)," and "APL's operation of the replacement vessels complies with the MSP statute, as did MARAD's approval of the vessel replacements." 2017 Appeal Decision at 3.

On June 2, 2017, Matson filed a petition for review in this court of MARAD's 2017 Appeal Decision, as well as its 2015 and 2016 Approval Orders.

II.

The Administrative Orders Review Act (known as the "Hobbs Act") provides that courts of appeals shall have

> exclusive jurisdiction to enjoin, set aside, suspend (in whole or in part), or to determine the validity of . . . all rules, regulations, or final orders of . . . the Secretary of Transportation *issued pursuant to* section 50501, 50502, 56101–56104, or 57109 of title 46 or pursuant to part B or C of subtitle IV, subchapter III of chapter 311, chapter 313, or chapter 315 of title 49.

28 U.S.C. § 2342(3)(A) (emphasis added). Petitions for review under the Hobbs Act must be filed "within 60 days" of the "entry" of the agency's final order. *Id.* § 2344; *see Energy Probe v. NRC*, 872 F.2d 436, 438 (D.C. Cir. 1989). The time limit "is jurisdictional in nature, and may not be enlarged or altered by the courts." *All. for Safe, Efficient & Competitive Truck Transp. v. Fed. Motor Carrier Safety Admin.*, 755 F.3d 946, 950 (D.C. Cir. 2014) (internal quotation marks and **[—7—]** citation omitted). This period can be tolled by "[t]he timely filing of a motion to reconsider," *Stone v. INS*, 514 U.S. 386, 392 (1995) (citing *ICC v. Bhd. of Locomotive Eng'rs*, 482 U.S. 270, 284 (1987)), but no "basis for tolling" exists where "there is no provision for rehearing or reconsideration" or administrative appeal available to the petitioner, *Laminators Safety Glass Ass'n v. Consumer Prod. Safety Comm'n*, 578 F.2d 406, 411 (D.C. Cir. 1978).

In the three challenged orders, MARAD made and upheld final determinations of APL's contractual obligations for the two approved replacement vessels. *See Citizens Ass'n of Georgetown v. Fed. Aviation Admin.*, 886 F.3d 130, 136 (D.C. Cir. 2018); *Adenariwo v. Fed. Mar. Comm'n*, 808 F.3d 74, 78, 3 Adm. R. 713, 714–15 (D.C. Cir. 2015); 46 U.S.C. § 53105. Unless the three orders were issued pursuant to a statute listed in the Hobbs Act vesting exclusive jurisdiction in the courts of appeals, 28 U.S.C. § 2342(3)(A), and the petition for their review is timely, *id.* § 2344, this court lacks jurisdiction to address Matson's petition for review. If the court lacks exclusive jurisdiction because an order was not issued pursuant to a statute listed in the Hobbs Act, then Matson is subject to the "'default rule'" and must "'go first to district court rather than to a court of appeals.'" *Watts v. SEC*, 482 F.3d 501, 505 (D.C. Cir. 2007) (quoting *Int'l Bhd. of Teamsters v. Peña*, 17 F.3d 1478, 1481 (D.C. Cir. 1994) ("*IBT*")). Here, Subtitle V (Merchant Marine) of Title 46 of the United States Code is silent on judicial review. **{-804-}**

In determining whether this court has exclusive jurisdiction over Matson's challenges to MARAD's three final orders, the Supreme Court's recent decision in *National Association of Manufacturers v. Department of Defense*, 138 S. Ct. 617 (2018) ("*NAM*"), is instructive. There, the Court considered a provision of the Clean Water Act, 33 U.S.C. **[—8—]** § 1369(b)(1), which enumerated seven categories of agency actions that must be challenged directly in the courts of appeals, including certain limitations issued under 33 U.S.C. § 1311. *NAM*, 138 S. Ct. at 626. The Court concluded that, viewed in context, the word "under" in "under section 1311" is "most naturally read to mean that the effluent limitation or other limitation must be approved or promulgated 'pursuant to' or 'by reason of the authority of' § 1311." *Id.* at 630 (citing *St. Louis Fuel & Supply Co. v. FERC*, 890 F.2d 446, 450 (D.C. Cir. 1989); BLACK'S LAW DICTIONARY 1368 (5th ed. 1979)). Further, the Court instructed, the provision pursuant to which an agency acts is the statute that "direct[s] or authorize[s]" the agency to take the relevant action. *Id.*

APL's requests that MARAD approve replacement vessels in the Fleet pursuant to 46 U.S.C. § 53105(f), MARAD's 2015 and 2016 Approval Orders, as well as the 2017 Appeal Decision suggest MARAD acted pursuant to its authority to "approve[] the replacement of the vessel[s]" under section 53105(f), which is not listed in the Hobbs Act. *Cf. Dist. No. 1, Pac. Coast Dist., Marine Eng'rs' Beneficial Ass'n v. Mar. Admin.*, 215 F.3d 37, 39, 42 (D.C. Cir. 2000). Matson contends, however, this court has jurisdiction because MARAD's "decisions involve regulations and programs that are 'interrelated' with citizenship determinations" in 46 U.S.C. § 50501. Appellant's Br. 26–27.

46 U.S.C. § 50501 identifies which organizations are "deemed citizens of the United States." It "groups corporations, partnerships, and associations into those deemed United States citizens and those deemed non-citizens." *Alaska Excursion Cruises, Inc. v. United States*, 595 F. Supp. 14, 16 (D.D.C. 1984) (describing then-section 802(a)). It does not "authorize" MARAD to act on a contractor's request for approval of a replacement vessel. *NAM*, 138 S. Ct. at 630. That **[—9—]** authority is provided in section 53105(f), which empowers MARAD, upon request of a contractor, to approve a vessel as a replacement if it meets the requirements of section 53102(b), which does not always require contractors to fit the definition of a U.S. citizen in section 50501. Insofar as section 53105(f) "direct[s] or authorize[s]" MARAD to approve replacement vessels, *NAM*, 138 S. Ct. at 630, the relevant consideration, assuming Matson acted timely, is whether MARAD's three orders were also issued pursuant to section 50501 or any other statute listed in the Hobbs Act vesting exclusive jurisdiction in the courts of appeals.

First, in its 2015 order approving APL Guam as a replacement, MARAD found the vessel was owned by a citizen of the United States "within the meaning of 46 U.S.C. § 50501," thus satisfying the owner's eligibility requirements in 46 U.S.C. § 53102(c)(2). 2015 Approval Order at 3. Then, in view of all of its findings, MARAD "determined" that APL Guam "meets the requirements of 46 U.S.C. § 53105(f) regarding replacement vessels." *Id.* at 4. MARAD's "explicit reliance" on section 50501 could provide this court with jurisdiction under the Hobbs Act over the 2015 approval. *See IBT*, 17 F.3d at 1482.

But the court has no occasion to decide this question because Matson failed to file a timely petition for review. Its **{-805-}** petition for review was not filed until June 2, 2017, long after the jurisdictional 60-day period in the Hobbs Act for seeking review of the 2015 Approval Order had run. 28 U.S.C. § 2344; *All. for Safe, Efficient & Competitive Truck Transp.*, 755 F.3d at 950. Matson maintains its administrative appeal tolled the 60-day clock. But even assuming Matson was eligible to file an administrative appeal under MARAD regulations, its appeal was untimely because it was filed more than a year after the approval order and MARAD's regulation sets a 60-day filing **[—10—]** period for seeking review, 46 C.F.R. § 296.50(a). Matson suggests that because the merits of its challenges were addressed in the 2017 Appeal Decision, MARAD eschewed reliance on any untimeliness principles. It relies on *Bowden v. United States*, 106 F.3d 433, 438–39 (D.C. Cir. 1997), where the court held on the particular facts that the agency had waived its timeliness defense by addressing the merits of a complaint and failing to mention timeliness on three occasions—during the administrative process and before two courts. Even if MARAD forfeited a timeliness defense, Matson has no vessels in the Fleet and is therefore not a "contractor," 46 C.F.R. § 296.2, for whom MARAD's regulations provide an administrative appeal, *see id.* § 296.50(a). "Because there is no provision for rehearing or reconsideration" applicable to Matson, there is no "basis for tolling the 60 day statutory period for judicial review in this case." *Laminators Safety Glass Ass'n*, 578 F.2d at 411.

Second, the 2016 Approval Order also does not trigger Hobbs Act jurisdiction. Matson's petition for review was not filed within sixty days of this Approval Order and it is likely untimely as well. Unlike the 2015 Approval Order, Matson timely filed an administrative appeal of the 2016 Approval Order. Matson therefore maintains that it would suffer "'unfair surprise'" if the Hobbs Act time limit were not thereby tolled. Pet'r's Reply Br. 23–24 (quoting *Christopher v. SmithKline Beecham Corp.*, 567 U.S. 142, 156 (2012)). In its view, MARAD's regulation on administrative appeals, 46 C.F.R. § 296.50, is ambiguous on whether non-contractors must file an administrative appeal in order to exhaust administrative remedies. The text of the regulation refers to contractors and

Matson has never claimed to be a contractor, for it has no MSP Operating Agreement covering its vessels in the U.S.-Guam trade. Matson suggests that even if its administrative appeal were defective, it was filed in good faith and merits tolling the [—11—] time limit. Pet'r's Reply Br. 24–25 (citing *Irwin v. Dep't of Veterans Affairs*, 498 U.S. 89, 90, 95–96 (1990)).

The court need not decide whether the Hobbs Act clock was tolled because even if Matson's petition for review were timely as to the 2016 Approval Order, this court lacks jurisdiction for another reason. *See Sinochem Int'l Co. v. Malaysia Int'l Shipping Corp.*, 549 U.S. 422, 431 (2007). In contrast to the 2015 Approval Order, MARAD never explicitly invoked section 50501 in reaching its eligibility determination in 2016. Nor is it apparent from its decision that it was addressing U.S. citizenship within the meaning of section 50501. The 2016 Approval Order stated that APL Saipan "will be owned by a U.S. Citizen Trust and demise chartered to a U.S. documentation citizen" and thereby "meets the citizenship requirements . . . established by 46 U.S.C. § 53102(c)." 2016 Approval Order at 1. That section references section 50501 and in some circumstances requires the entity chartering the vessel to be a section 50501 U.S. citizen. 46 U.S.C. § 53102(c)(2)(A)(ii)(II) & (B). In this order, **{-806-}** MARAD did not make an explicit finding that the entities involved were U.S. citizens within the meaning of section 50501.

Assuming that MARAD implicitly made a section 50501 finding in order to approve APL's second replacement request pursuant to section 53105(f), the 2016 Approval Order does not "interpret" section 50501 citizenship, unlike in *Conoco, Inc. v. Skinner*, 970 F.2d 1206, 1214–15 (3d Cir. 1992), and *Liberty Glob. Logistics LLC v. U.S. Mar. Admin.*, No. 13-cv-0399, 2014 WL 4388587, at *4 (E.D.N.Y. Sept. 5, 2014), on which Matson relies. Statutory grounds for jurisdiction are not to be given "a more expansive interpretation than their text warrants." *Exxon Mobil Corp. v. Allapattah Servs., Inc.*, 545 U.S. 546, 558 (2005). Absent explicit reference or its functional equivalent in the 2016 Approval Order to a statute **[—12—]** listed in the Hobbs Act, the court would expand its exclusive jurisdiction beyond that which Congress intended. *See Fla. Power & Light Co. v. Lorion*, 470 U.S. 729, 746 (1985); *cf. NAM*, 138 S. Ct. at 634; *Am. Portland Cement All. v. EPA*, 101 F.3d 772, 776 (D.C. Cir. 1996). Background principles relied on by the agency in making a final determination are insufficient to vest exclusive jurisdiction in the courts of appeals. *See NAM*, 138 S. Ct. at 631. Because there is no indication that the 2016 Approval Order was issued pursuant to section 50501 or other statute listed in the Hobbs Act, this court lacks exclusive jurisdiction to consider Matson's challenge, and it must initially pursue its challenge in the district court.

Finally, although Matson's petition for review of the 2017 Appeal Decision was timely, this court lacks jurisdiction to consider it. To the extent that decision rested on administrative standing, Matson has not challenged that aspect of the decision, so any challenge on that ground is forfeited. *U.S. Telecom Ass'n v. FCC*, 825 F.3d 674, 708 (D.C. Cir. 2016). The Decision also addressed the merits of Matson's challenges. Even if construed as a denial of a proper motion for reconsideration of the 2015 and 2016 Approval Orders, the Decision did not reopen or reference earlier determinations on citizenship or any portion of the Approval Orders issued pursuant to MARAD's authority under section 50501. *See Am. Ass'n of Paging Carriers v. FCC*, 442 F.3d 751, 756 (D.C. Cir. 2006). Nor does the Decision cite or rest its analysis on section 50501. *Cf. IBT*, 17 F.3d at 1482. To the extent the 2015 and 2016 Approval Orders are discussed, the Decision invokes only MARAD's authority to interpret and apply the meaning of "foreign commerce," as defined in 46 U.S.C. §§ 12111 and 53105(a)(1)(A), and to approve replacement vessels, as authorized by section 53105(f). Consequently, the Decision on the merits was not issued pursuant to section 50501 or other statute listed in the Hobbs Act, and this court lacks exclusive **[—13—]** jurisdiction to review it. Matson's challenge to the 2017 Appeal Decision must initially be pursued in the district court.

Accordingly, we dismiss the petition for review for lack of jurisdiction under the Hobbs Act.

United States Court of Appeals for the District of Columbia Circuit

No. 17-1160

GOOD FORTUNE SHIPPING SA
VS.
COMMISSIONER OF INTERNAL REVENUE SERV.

On Appeal from the Decision of the United States Tax Court

Decided: July 27, 2018

Citation: 897 F.3d 256, 6 Adm. R. 497 (D.C. Cir. 2018).

Before **GARLAND,** Chief Judge, and **GRIFFITH** and **SRINIVASAN,** Circuit Judges.

[—1—] {-258-} GRIFFITH, Circuit Judge:

In 2007, the foreign shipping corporation Good Fortune Shipping SA ("Good Fortune") **[—2—]** attempted to exempt some of its U.S.-based income from taxation. But in order to qualify for the exemption, a certain percentage of Good Fortune's stock needed to be owned by residents of a country that provided a reciprocal tax exemption. At that time, the Internal Revenue Service (IRS) categorically prohibited any consideration of bearer shares—securities owned by whoever holds physical certificates issued by the company—when assessing whether a sufficient amount of a foreign shipper's stock was owned by qualifying shareholders. The IRS refused to grant Good Fortune the exemption because all of the company's stock was made up of bearer shares. Good Fortune challenged the IRS's approach as inconsistent with the Internal Revenue Code, and the Tax Court ruled in favor of the IRS. Because the IRS's regulation prohibiting consideration of bearer shares unreasonably interpreted the Code, we reverse.

I

A

Under the Internal Revenue Code (the "Code"), foreign corporations generally must pay tax on any income derived from operating ships that transport goods to or from the United States (called "United States source gross transportation income"). I.R.C. § 887(a). However, the Code also historically exempted the income of certain foreign shippers from this tax. Prior to 1986, federal law exempted a foreign corporation's shipping income so long as the corporation registered its ships in a country that granted "equivalent tax exemptions to U.S. citizens and U.S. corporations." H.R. Rep. No. 99-841, at 597 (1986) (Conf. Rep.). This exemption applied "without regard to the residence of persons receiving the exemption or whether commerce is conducted in the country of registry." S. Rep. No. 99-313, at 340 (1986). **[—3—]**

This exemption did not work as effectively as Congress had anticipated. Members **{-259-}** of Congress had hoped that the registration-based exemption would encourage the "international adoption of uniform tax laws" that eliminated the prospect of double taxation from shippers' home countries and their countries of operation. S. Rep. No. 67-275, at 14 (1921). Although U.S. shippers were required to pay U.S. tax on their income, foreign shippers could avoid the U.S. tax by simply registering (or "flagging out") their ships in a country that provided a reciprocal exemption, regardless of whether the ships' owners had any connection to that country. *See* S. Rep. No. 99-313, at 340-41. Congress ultimately found that this registration-based exemption "place[d] U.S. persons with U.S.-based transportation . . . at a competitive disadvantage" compared to foreign shippers who claimed the U.S. exemption and were not taxed by either their countries of residence or registration. *Id.* at 340.

Congress therefore tightened the exemption in the Tax Reform Act of 1986, Pub. L. No. 99-514, § 1212, 100 Stat. 2085, 2536-37. After the 1986 Act, the Code places a four-percent tax on the U.S. source gross transportation income of nonresident alien individuals and foreign corporations. *See* I.R.C. § 887(a). Congress in 1986 replaced the registration-based exemption with a new residency-based exemption for foreign shippers. A foreign shipper can qualify for the new exemption only if it is "organized in a foreign country" that "grants an equivalent exemption to corporations organized in the

United States." *Id.* § 883(a)(1). However, even a foreign shipper organized in such a country is ineligible for the exemption "if 50 percent or more of the value" of its stock "is owned by individuals who are not residents" of a country providing a reciprocal exemption. *Id.* § 883(c)(1). **[—4—]**

In 2003, the IRS promulgated a regulation elaborating on the statutory requirement that residents of a country providing a reciprocal exemption own more than half of the foreign shipper's stock. *See* Exclusions from Gross Income of Foreign Corporations, 68 Fed. Reg. 51,394 (Aug. 26, 2003) (the "2003 Regulation"). To qualify as an exempted foreign corporation under the 2003 Regulation, a shipper must satisfy the "qualified shareholder test." Under that test, an exempted corporation must prove, among other things, that "more than 50 percent of the value of its outstanding shares is owned" by qualified shareholders, either directly or indirectly through application of attribution rules, "for at least half of the number of days in the foreign corporation's taxable year." 26 C.F.R. § 1.883-4(a) (2007). An individual is a "qualified shareholder" only if, among other things, he is a resident of a reciprocating country. *Id.* § 1.883-4(b)(1)(i)(A). And a foreign-corporation shareholder qualifies only if it is organized in a reciprocating country. *Id.* § 1.883-4(b)(1)(i)(C).

Generally, a foreign corporation claiming an exemption under the qualified shareholder test "must establish all the facts necessary to satisfy the [IRS] that more than 50 percent of the value of its shares is owned . . . by qualified shareholders." *Id.* § 1.883-4(d)(1). When it comes to establishing the facts necessary to demonstrate corporate ownership, the 2003 Regulation treats differently "bearer shares" and "registered shares" of corporate stock. Bearer shares are owned by the "physical bearer of the stock certificate" and traditionally have "no recorded ownership information." *Black's Law Dictionary* (10th ed. 2014). On the other hand, "registered shares" are securities "recorded in the issuer's books." *Id.* Under the 2003 Regulation, a corporation could prove it met § 883(c)(1)'s ownership requirement by submitting company records proving up registered shareholders' identities and countries of residence. *See* 26 C.F.R. § 1.883-4(d)(4). But a qualified **[—5—]** shareholder **{-260-}** may *not* "own its interest in the foreign corporation through bearer shares." *Id.* § 1.883-4(b)(1)(ii); *see also id.* § 1.883-4(c)(1) ("No attribution will apply to an interest held directly or indirectly through bearer shares."); *id.* § 1.883-4(d)(1) ("A foreign corporation cannot meet [the stock ownership] requirement with respect to any stock that is issued in bearer form. A shareholder that holds shares in the foreign corporation either directly or indirectly in bearer form cannot be a qualified shareholder."). The IRS drew this distinction and prohibited the use of bearer shares because of "the difficulty of reliably demonstrating the true ownership of bearer shares." 68 Fed. Reg. at 51,399. The 2003 Regulation provided no further explanation for the categorical exclusion of bearer shares.

B

Good Fortune is a corporation organized under the laws of the Republic of the Marshall Islands. The Marshall Islands offers a reciprocal exemption to U.S. shippers sufficient to satisfy § 883(a)(1). *See* Rev. Rul. 2001-48, tbl. I.A, 2001-2 C.B. 324; Rev. Rul. 2008-17, tbl. I.A, 2008-1 C.B. 626. During the 2007 tax year, all of Good Fortune's outstanding stock was composed of bearer shares, issued as physical certificates for which neither Good Fortune nor any financial institution maintained any formal records of ownership or transfer.

For the 2007 tax year, Good Fortune reported slightly less than $4.1 million in U.S. source gross transportation income. That income would have been taxable under I.R.C. § 887, unless it qualified for the exemption in § 883(a)(1). Good Fortune claimed that the income qualified for that exemption and provided documentation purporting to show that all of its bearer shares were indirectly owned by individuals residing in countries that provide a reciprocal exemption to U.S. corporations. Good Fortune also argued that the 2003 **[—6—]** Regulation prohibiting any consideration of bearer shares was unlawful.

The IRS sent Good Fortune a notice of deficiency for the 2007 tax year reflecting the IRS's determination that Good Fortune's U.S. source gross transportation income for that year was about $3.6 million, not $4.1 million. The IRS also determined that none of that income could be exempted presumably because all of Good Fortune's stock had been issued as bearer shares and the 2003 Regulation prohibited their consideration. The IRS accordingly determined that Good Fortune had an income tax deficiency of approximately $143,500 for the 2007 tax year.

Good Fortune then filed a petition in the Tax Court for a redetermination of its 2007 deficiency. The company conceded that it could not qualify for the § 883(a)(1) exemption under the 2003 Regulation but asserted that the regulation's categorical exclusion of bearer shares was an impermissible interpretation of § 883. The Commissioner filed a motion for summary judgment and Good Fortune filed a cross-motion for the same.

The Tax Court granted the Commissioner's motion and ordered Good Fortune liable on its 2007 tax deficiency. Applying the well-worn framework from *Chevron U.S.A. Inc. v. Natural Resources Defense Council, Inc.*, 467 U.S. 837 (1984), the Tax Court found that Congress had not "directly spoken to the precise question at issue," *id.* at 842, namely, "how to establish ownership by individuals for the purposes of section 883(c)(1)" or "how to establish ownership where the shares of the foreign corporation are owned in bearer form," *Good Fortune Shipping SA v. Comm'r*, 148 T.C. No. 10, slip op. at 32 (Mar. 28, 2017). **[—7—]**

Having found the statute silent or ambiguous on that question, the Tax Court **{-261-}** then considered whether the IRS's interpretation of § 883 was reasonable. *Id.* at 25. The Tax Court found the 2003 Regulation reasonable because it "provide[d] certainty and resolve[d] the difficult problems of proof associated with establishing ownership of bearer shares." *Id.* at 46. According to the Tax Court, the 2003 Regulation "set forth a sensible approach to effecting the intent of Congress in enacting section 883(c)(1) to ensure that abuse will not occur which will result in certain types of shipping transportation income described in section 883(a)(1) not being taxed." *Id.*

Good Fortune timely appealed the Tax Court's order.

II

The Tax Court had jurisdiction over Good Fortune's petition for a redetermination under I.R.C. §§ 6213(a), 6214(a), and 7442. We have appellate jurisdiction under I.R.C. § 7482(a)(1).

We review de novo the Tax Court's legal conclusions. *See, e.g.*, *Barnes v. Comm'r*, 712 F.3d 581, 582 (D.C. Cir. 2013).

III

A

The IRS does not argue that its interpretation of § 883 is compelled by the statute; rather the agency only maintains that "Congress has not directly spoken" to whether shippers may use bearer shares to satisfy § 883(c)(1)'s ownership requirement. IRS Br. 19. So for the IRS to prevail, it must demonstrate that § 883 is silent or ambiguous as to the treatment of bearer shares under § 883(c)(1) *and* that its **[—8—]** interpretation, as embodied in the 2003 Regulation, is reasonable. *See Chevron*, 467 U.S. at 842-43.

When we consider the lawfulness of an agency's statutory interpretation under *Chevron*, we usually ask first whether the statute at issue "unambiguously forecloses the agency's interpretation." *Nat'l Cable & Telecomms. Ass'n v. FCC*, 567 F.3d 659, 663 (D.C. Cir. 2009). However, we may also assume arguendo that the statute is ambiguous and proceed to *Chevron*'s second step. *See, e.g.*, *Lubow v. U.S. Dep't of State*, 783 F.3d 877, 884 (D.C. Cir. 2015); *U.S. Postal Serv. v. Postal Regulatory Comm'n*, 599 F.3d 705, 710 (D.C. Cir. 2010); *Aid Ass'n for Lutherans v. U.S. Postal Serv.*, 321 F.3d 1166, 1178 (D.C. Cir. 2003); *Hill v. Norton*, 275 F.3d

98, 99 (D.C. Cir. 2001); *Teicher v. SEC*, 177 F.3d 1016, 1021 (D.C. Cir. 1999).

We'll give the IRS the benefit of the doubt and assume that § 883 does not unambiguously foreclose its interpretation. We make this assumption because even proceeding to *Chevron* Step Two, we conclude that the IRS's interpretation of § 883 in the 2003 Regulation is unreasonable and cannot stand.

B

At *Chevron* Step Two, we ask whether the IRS's interpretation is "reasonable." *AT&T Corp. v. FCC*, 220 F.3d 607, 621 (D.C. Cir. 2000). That is, we consider whether the interpretation is "arbitrary or capricious in substance, or manifestly contrary to the statute." *Mayo Found. for Med. Educ. & Research v. United States*, 562 U.S. 44, 53 (2011) (quoting *Household Credit Servs., Inc. v. Pfennig*, 541 U.S. 232, 242 (2004)). Our focus is thus on "whether the [agency] has reasonably explained how the permissible interpretation it chose is 'rationally related to the goals of the statute." *Village of Barrington v. Surface Transp. Bd.*, 636 F.3d 650, 665 (D.C. **[—9—]** Cir. 2011) (quoting *AT&T Corp. v. Iowa Utils. Bd.*, 525 U.S. 366, 388 (1999)). **{-262-}**

Whether an agency's construction is reasonable depends, in part, "on the construction's 'fit' with the statutory language, as well as its conformity to statutory purposes." *Goldstein v. SEC*, 451 F.3d 873, 881 (D.C. Cir. 2006) (quoting *Abbott Labs. v. Young*, 920 F.2d 984, 988 (D.C. Cir. 1990)). Indeed, "[t]he starting place for any *Chevron* Step Two inquiry is the text of the statute." *Van Hollen v. FEC*, 811 F.3d 486, 492 (D.C. Cir. 2016).

Section 883(c)(1) states in relevant part that the exemption for foreign shippers introduced in § 883(a)(1) "shall not apply to any foreign corporation if 50 percent or more of the value of the stock of such corporation is owned by individuals who are not residents of" a country granting a reciprocal tax exemption. Congress has therefore determined that the tax exemption shall not be granted to foreign corporations if a certain percentage of their stock "is *owned* by individuals who are not residents of" a reciprocating country. I.R.C. § 883(c)(1) (emphasis added). The flipside of this prohibition is a mandate: If 50 percent or more of a shipper's stock "is owned by individuals" who *are* residents of reciprocating countries, then § 883(c)(1) poses no obstacle to an exemption. And if § 883(c)(1) poses no obstacle, then the relevant income "shall not be included in gross income of a foreign [shipping] corporation" and "shall be exempt from taxation." *Id.* § 883(a).

The IRS contends—and it is undisputed—that § 883(c)(1) is silent as to "what type of proof suffices to show any corporation's entitlement to the exemption." IRS Br. 19; *see also* Good Fortune Br. 31 (conceding that Good Fortune "does not contest" the IRS's "authority to issue regulations addressing attribution and proof of ownership"). That said, **[—10—]** § 883 implies that if a sufficient portion of a foreign corporation's stock is "owned" by qualified shareholders, the corporation will qualify for the exemption. Bearer shares are a valid form of ownership, and the 2003 Regulation acknowledged as much. *See* 26 C.F.R. § 1.883-4(b)(1)(ii) (2007) (requiring that a qualified shareholder "not *own* its interest in the foreign corporation through bearer shares" (emphasis added)). Nevertheless, the IRS claims that its refusal to consider bearer shares under the 2003 Regulation reasonably "treat[s] the ownership of bearer shares at a prior time as a fact not capable of sufficient proof." IRS Br. 28.

The IRS therefore attempts to characterize the 2003 Regulation as merely establishing modes of proving corporate ownership. But when the agency goes so far as to set an insurmountable burden of proof—in which no amount of relevant evidence could possibly suffice—the line between merely establishing a method of proving ownership and defining what counts as ownership begins to dissolve. As Good Fortune rightly notes, the IRS's abject refusal to attribute ownership for bearer shares risks "conflat[ing] proof of ownership with the meaning of ownership." Good Fortune Br. 28. Bearer shares are indisputably a legally valid form of corporate ownership, and yet the IRS's regulations categorically deny those shares any role in establishing ownership for the purposes of the § 883 exemption. This approach risks undercutting § 883(c)(1)'s use of the term "owned."

Even if § 883 grants the IRS significant discretion to establish how to prove ownership, it hardly authorizes the agency to categorically deny consideration of a recognized form of ownership based on only a single, undeveloped statement that it is "difficult[]" to reliably track the location of a given owner. 68 Fed. Reg. at 51,399. If the IRS found that the **[—11—]** transferable nature of bearer shares made substantiation impossible, we might conclude that the 2003 Regulation reasonably implemented that **{–263–}** finding. Indeed, a kind of stock that is entirely impossible to track might not constitute a form of ownership contemplated by § 883(c)(1). But the IRS has never made (much less adequately supported) such an absolute claim of impossibility with regard to bearer shares. The IRS's interpretation instead appears to rewrite § 883(c)(1) to require not only valid ownership, but ownership that is not "difficult" to track. Even if this regulatory amendment to § 883 is not unambiguously foreclosed by the statute's language, its unsubstantiated treatment of ownership "comes close to violating the plain language of the statute"—indicating that the 2003 Regulation is unreasonable at *Chevron* Step Two. *Goldstein*, 451 F.3d at 881.

Additionally, while the IRS's interpretation of § 883 is "entitled to no less deference . . . simply because it has changed over time," *Nat'l Home Equity Mortg. Ass'n v. Office of Thrift Supervision*, 373 F.3d 1355, 1360 (D.C. Cir. 2004), the agency must nevertheless engage in "'reasoned analysis' sufficient to command our deference under *Chevron*," *Ala. Educ. Ass'n v. Chao*, 455 F.3d 386, 396 (D.C. Cir. 2006). A sufficiently reasoned analysis requires the IRS to "display awareness that it *is* changing position" and "show that there are good reasons for the new policy." *FCC v. Fox Television Stations, Inc.*, 556 U.S. 502, 515 (2009); *see also Northpoint Tech., Ltd. v. FCC*, 412 F.3d 145, 156 (D.C. Cir. 2005) ("A statutory interpretation . . . that results from an unexplained departure from prior [agency] policy and practice is not a reasonable one."). Moreover, when assessing the reasonableness of the IRS's interpretation we look only to "what the agency said at the time of the rulemaking—not to its lawyers' post-hoc rationalizations." *Council for Urological Interests v. Burwell*, 790 F.3d 212, 222 (D.C. Cir. 2015). **[—12—]**

As early as 1991 the IRS presumed that bearer shares were "owned by individual residents of a foreign country which does not provide an equivalent exemption, for purposes of section 883(c)." Rev. Proc. 91-12, § 8.02(3), 1991-1 C.B. 473. But this presumption was only triggered "[i]n the absence of . . . documentation" demonstrating that more than 50 percent of the corporation's shares were owned by residents of a reciprocating country. *Id.* Therefore, between 1991 and 2003, the IRS apparently thought sufficient documentation regarding the ownership of bearer shares *could* secure a tax exemption under § 883. And yet in 2003 the agency concluded that the "difficulty of reliably demonstrating the true ownership of bearer shares" warranted the flat prohibition at issue here. 68 Fed. Reg. at 51,399. The IRS never explained how the pre-existing opportunity to provide substantiating documentation had somehow become unworkable since 1991. Nor did the agency explain if or how "reliably demonstrating the true ownership of bearer shares" was any more difficult in 2003 than in 1991.

Indeed, given the IRS's later recognition in 2010 that some forms of bearer shares were becoming *easier* to track over time, the agency's decision to treat bearer shares *less* favorably in 2003 than in 1991 is all the more inexplicable. In 2010, the IRS ultimately amended its treatment of bearer shares for purposes of the exemption in § 883(a)(1). Rather than categorically exclude bearer shares from consideration, the amended regulation allows bearer shares to count toward the § 883 exemption if they satisfy one of two conditions. First, they count toward the exemption if the shares are "dematerialized" or "represented only by book entries" with "no physical certificates . . . issued or transferred." 26 C.F.R. § 1.883-1(c)(3)(i)(G) (2010); *see also id.* § 1.883-4(b)(1)(ii). Second, the bearer shares **{-264-}** count toward the exemption if they are **[—13—]** "immobilized," in which "evidence of ownership is maintained on the books and records of the corporate issuer or by a broker or financial institution." *Id.* § 1.883-1(c)(3)(i)(G). While the IRS continued to maintain that it has "been difficult to reliably prove ownership of bearer shares," it nevertheless recognized in 2010 that dematerialized and immobilized bearer shares had "become increasingly common" and "provide the ability to reliably identify the beneficial owner of bearer shares." Exclusions from Gross Income of Foreign Corporations, 75 Fed. Reg. 56,858, 56,860 (Sept. 17, 2010).

The IRS abandoned the 2003 Regulation's categorical, exclusionary rule in 2010 in response to the "recent increase in the number of corporations switching to immobilized or dematerialized bearer shares." IRS Br. 34; *see also* 75 Fed. Reg. at 56,860. While the IRS maintained that dematerialized and immobilized bearer shares had become "increasingly common" by 2010, 75 Fed. Reg. at 56,860, at no time has the IRS ever argued that such bearer shares were nonexistent or obscure between 2003 and 2010, nor that they were less prevalent in 2003 than in 1991. Even if the IRS were correct that "there is no guarantee" that foreign shippers kept such records of bearer shares before 2010, IRS Br. 34, that skepticism alone does not justify the 2003 Regulation's categorical ban. If certain foreign shippers did not keep sufficient records, a substantiation requirement like those embraced by the IRS in 1991 or 2010 would have readily disposed of any such cases.

The 2003 Regulation also appears unreasonable because it treats bearer shares with disproportionate disfavor compared to other forms of corporate ownership sharing similar alleged problems. The IRS argues that § 883(c)(1) is an "anti-abuse provision" that would be undermined if the IRS accepted bearer shares as proof of ownership without any "reasonable **[—14—]** method of proving or disproving [a] statement of ownership." *Id.* at 21, 23. Even assuming that is true, there is a potential for abuse with other types of corporate shares, many of which the IRS accepts as proof of ownership under § 883(c)(1). For example, the IRS concedes that other financial arrangements—including the appointment of nominees and trustees—can "be used to obscure the identity of the beneficial owners." *Id.* at 37. Nevertheless, rather than promulgating broad, categorical prohibitions governing those financial instruments, the IRS instead established "safeguards against the use of trusts and nominees to obscure shareholders' identities in the regulations implementing § 883." *Id.* While the IRS has made it difficult to earn the exemption in § 883 with these financial instruments, the agency will find qualifying ownership if "the nominee or trustee submits to the IRS detailed statements substantiating the identity of the beneficial owners." *Id.* at 38 (citing 26 C.F.R. § 1.883-4(d)(4)(v)). Of course, the 2003 Regulation denies bearer shareholders this same opportunity to submit detailed, substantiating statements.

We've previously recognized that when an agency interprets a statute to afford disparate treatment between two different objects of concern, "we cannot defer to the [agency's] interpretation premised on such a difference unless the [agency] adequately supports it." *Northpoint Tech.*, 412 F.3d at 156. When the IRS promulgated the 2003 Regulation, it offered no justification for treating bearer shares differently than nominees and trustees under § 883. That's enough to render the distinction inadequate for purposes of *Chevron* Step Two. *See Envtl. Def. Fund, Inc. v. EPA*, 898 F.2d 183, 189 (D.C. Cir. 1990) ("We cannot sustain an action merely **{-265-}** on the basis of interpretive theories that the agency might have adopted and findings that (perhaps) it might have made."). **[—15—]**

In any event, the IRS's post-hoc attempt to distinguish nominees and trustees does not adequately support the agency's disparate treatment of bearer shares. The IRS argues that a "substantiation-based solution" is simply "inappropriate" for bearer shares because of their "transferable nature," a problem that is not as acute with nominees and trustees. IRS Br. 40-41. But while bearer shares' transferable nature might make it *more* difficult to substantiate the identity of their owners at any given time, the IRS has never explained why that difficulty alone makes a substantiation-based method of proving bearer-share ownership "inappropriate" relative to proving the ownership of nominees and trustees. Indeed, the agency even now concedes that "corporations might have formal records of the ownership of bearer shares even though there is no requirement that they keep such records." *Id.* at 34. Quite simply, the IRS's conclusory rejection in 2003 of any substantiation-based method for proving bearer-share ownership does not adequately reckon with analogous problems of proof facing other forms of ownership.

Finally, the categorical exclusion of bearer shares endorsed in the 2003 Regulation was even out of step with the IRS's treatment of bearer shares in similar contexts. For example, in another provision of the Code, some foreign corporations can receive comparably favorable tax treatment if their stock is regularly traded on an established securities market in their countries of residence. *See* I.R.C. § 884(e)(4)(B). However, stock that is otherwise regularly traded will not qualify for favorable treatment if the stock is "closely held." *See* Branch Profits Tax, 57 Fed. Reg. 41,644, 41,648 (Sept. 11, 1992). A foreign corporation is closely held if at least 50 percent of its stock is owned by a certain type of shareholder. *See* 26 C.F.R. § 1.884-5(d)(4)(iii) (2007). While the foreign corporation bore the burden of proving that it is not closely held, it can meet that burden "with either registered or **[—16—]** bearer shares . . . if it has no reason to know and no actual knowledge of facts that would cause the corporation's stock not to be treated as regularly traded . . . ." *Id.* § 1.884-5(d)(5); *see also* 57 Fed. Reg. at 41,648 ("[C]orporations with bearer shares can meet the burden of proof . . . as long as they have no knowledge and no reason to know their stock is closely held."). Therefore, the IRS recognizes that even if the owners of bearer shares are difficult to identify, a categorical prohibition on considering such shares is not necessary to cope with that challenge.

The IRS attempts to explain away these regulations implementing § 884 by focusing on the "impetus" for the restriction of bearer shares in § 883, explaining that "the abusive use of bearer shares to hide ownership constitutes a well-recognized problem in the shipping industry." IRS Br. 43. But that's entirely beside the point. What matters is that the IRS has recognized in the § 884 regulations that bearer shares are *capable* of proving ownership. The presence or absence of a risk of abuse has no effect on the ability of bearer shares to "reliably demonstrat[e]" who owns the share. 68 Fed. Reg. at 51,399. If bearer shares were reliable enough under § 884, we see no reason why they wouldn't have been reliable enough to justify their consideration under § 883. The IRS cannot reasonably rely on the risk of abuse to treat bearer shares as a form of second-class ownership in some contexts but not in others, especially without any contemporaneous explanation justifying the disparate treatment. The IRS's inconsistent approach to bearer shares is the last straw needed to break this camel's back. **{-266-}**

* * *

At the end of the day, the IRS here chose to "paint[] with such a broad brush" that it "failed adequately to justify" its **[—17—]** categorical rule excluding the use of bearer shares in qualifying for the tax exemption in § 883. *Goldstein*, 451 F.3d at 883. Even if the IRS reasonably concluded that sometimes—maybe oftentimes—bearer shares are incapable of proving the residence of their owners, the 2003 Regulation's categorical bar on considering bearer shares does not follow from that premise. The IRS has not justified treating *all* bearer shares as incapable of proving ownership. If *some* corporations' bearer shares are not kept in record form, and thus are not capable of proving the location of an owner, then the IRS "should have identified those [corporations' shares] and tailored its rule accordingly." *Id.* The 2003 Regulation is unreasonable and therefore invalid under *Chevron* Step Two.

IV

For the foregoing reasons, we reverse the Tax Court's order and direct the court to vacate the 2003 Regulation's provisions prohibiting the consideration of bearer shares.

So ordered.

United States Court of Appeals for the District of Columbia Circuit

No. 16-3096

UNITED STATES
vs.
MOSQUERA-MURILLO

Appeal from the United States District Court for the District of Columbia

Decided: August 24, 2018

Citation: 902 F.3d 285, 6 Adm. R. 505 (D.C. Cir. 2018).

Before **SRINIVASAN** and **MILLETT**, Circuit Judges, and **SENTELLE**, Senior Circuit Judge.

[—2—] **{-286-}** **SRINIVASAN**, Circuit Judge: **{-287-}**

In June 2012, the United States Coast Guard intercepted a Colombian vessel called the Mistby, which was transporting cocaine and marijuana to Panama. The three defendants in these consolidated cases pleaded guilty to conspiring to distribute, and possess with intent to distribute, the drugs on board the Mistby, in violation of the Maritime Drug Law Enforcement Act (MDLEA), 46 U.S.C. § 70501 et seq., and the Controlled Substances Import and Export Act, 21 U.S.C. § 951 et seq. Each defendant was sentenced to 10 years of imprisonment.

The defendants now appeal on two grounds. First, they argue that the district court lacked subject-matter jurisdiction over their prosecutions because they were not on board the Mistby when it was intercepted. In the defendants' view, Colombia's assent to U.S. jurisdiction over individuals associated with the Mistby was limited to persons found on board the vessel. Second, the defendants contend that their offense of conviction is covered by the so-called safety-valve provision, 18 U.S.C. § 3553(f). That provision, in certain circumstances, exempts covered offenses from mandatory-minimum sentences such as the 10-year sentences imposed against the defendants. **[—3—]**

We conclude that the district court had subject-matter jurisdiction over the defendants' prosecutions, but that the defendants' offense is covered by the safety-valve provision. We therefore vacate the defendants' sentences and remand for resentencing.

I.

The Coast Guard first spotted the Mistby on the high seas about 70 nautical miles off the coast of Panama. When the Coast Guard approached, the Mistby fled, and its crew began to dump cargo overboard. The cargo turned out to be 22 bales of drugs, containing more than 220 kilograms of cocaine and more than 120 kilograms of marijuana.

The Coast Guard eventually overtook the Mistby and boarded it to determine its nationality, at which point the Mistby's captain claimed the vessel was registered in Colombia. The United States and Colombia have agreed by treaty to "cooperate in combating illicit traffic by sea." Agreement to Suppress Illicit Traffic by Sea, Colom.-U.S., art. 2, Feb. 20, 1997, T.I.A.S. No. 12,835. Pursuant to that treaty, the Coast Guard asked the Colombian Navy (i) to verify that the Mistby was registered in Colombia, and (ii) to grant the Coast Guard permission to search the vessel. *See id.* art. 7. The Colombian Navy granted both requests. The Coast Guard then searched the Mistby and arrested the people on board, but the defendants were not among them.

The next day, the Coast Guard asked the Colombian Navy to confirm that, under Article 16 of the treaty, the United States had jurisdiction over the Mistby. The Colombian Navy did so on June 26, stating that, under the "agreement signed by the governments of the United States and Colombia, [the United States could] exercise their jurisdiction." Ardila M. Hector, **[—4—]** Colombian Naval Operations Ctr., Response to Request for Interpretation of Article 16(1) of the Maritime Agreement Col.-U.S. (June 26, 2012) (formatting modified). **{-288-}**

The Coast Guard memorialized the Colombian Navy's response in a certification, which reads, in relevant part:

> On June 26, 2012, Colombian authorities confirmed and concurred with the United States' interpretation of Article 16 of the Agreement, thereby waiving objection to the enforcement of United States law by the United States over the go-fast vessel MISTBY, all associated contraband, and persons on board.

Salvatore J. Fazio, U.S. Coast Guard, Certification for the Maritime Drug Law Enforcement Act Case Involving Go-Fast Vessel Mistby (Colombia) ¶ 4.e (Aug. 10, 2012) (hereinafter Coast Guard Certification). "Accordingly," the certification concludes, "the Government of the United States determined the go-fast vessel MISTBY was subject to the jurisdiction of the United States pursuant to 46 U.S.C. § 70502(c)(1)(C)." *Id.* ¶ 4.f.

Months later, the three defendants—Alfredo Mosquera-Murillo, Antonio Moreno-Membache, and Joaquin Chang-Rendon—were charged with conspiring to distribute, and possess with intent to distribute, the drugs transported on board the Mistby, in violation of 46 U.S.C. §§ 70503 and 70506(b), and 21 U.S.C. § 960(b)(1)(B) and (b)(2)(G). The government's theory as to each defendant's involvement was as follows: that Chang-Rendon (a civilian employee of the Colombian Navy) knew the patrol routes of Colombian and American law-enforcement vessels and passed that information along to Mosquera-Murillo; that Mosquera- **[—5—]** Murillo in turn conveyed the information to the people transporting the drugs; and that Moreno-Membache helped move the drugs to the Colombian coast and then load them onto the Mistby. At the time the defendants were charged, all three of them were still in Colombia. The United States thus requested extradition, which Colombia granted.

Chang-Rendon and Mosquera-Murillo moved to dismiss the indictment on the ground that the district court lacked subject-matter jurisdiction over their prosecutions. The government claimed that the district court had jurisdiction under 46 U.S.C. § 70502(c)(1)(C), which applies if the vessel on which an MDLEA offense was committed is "a vessel registered in a foreign nation [and] that nation has consented or waived objection to the enforcement of United States law by the United States." The defendants responded that, as shown by the Coast Guard's certification, Colombia waived objection to the United States exercising jurisdiction over the "MISTBY, all associated contraband, and persons on board"—but not persons like the defendants who never set foot on the vessel. Coast Guard Certification ¶ 4.e.

The district court rejected that argument. The court held that "a foreign government's waiver of jurisdiction over a particular vessel . . . establish[es a district] court's subject-matter jurisdiction over a subsequent prosecution of any land-based co-conspirators." *United States v. Mosquera-Murillo*, 153 F. Supp. 3d 130, 158 (D.D.C. 2015). And in any event, the court explained, the notion that Colombia had not consented to the defendants' prosecutions was difficult to square "with the Colombian government's subsequent extradition of the defendants to the United States." *Id.* at 159.

The defendants then pleaded guilty. In their plea agreements, they acknowledged that, given the quantity of **[—6—]** cocaine involved, the district court ordinarily would be required to impose a mandatory-minimum sentence of 10 years of imprisonment. *See* 21 U.S.C. § 960(b)(1)(B). But the defendants reserved their rights (i) to argue they were eligible for relief from that mandatory-minimum sentence under the safety-valve provision, **{-289-}** 18 U.S.C. § 3553(f), and (ii) to appeal any contrary determination by the district court.

The safety-valve provision states that sentencing relief is available only "in the case of an offense under" 21 U.S.C. §§ 841, 844, 846, 960 or 963. 18 U.S.C. § 3553(f). The government argued that, because that list does not include any provision of the MDLEA, the defendants' offense was not covered. The defendants responded that, because 21 U.S.C.

§ 960(b) supplied the penalties for their MDLEA violation, the violation qualified as "an offense under" § 960.

The district court agreed with the government, holding that the defendants were ineligible for safety-valve relief. *United States v. Mosquera-Murillo*, 172 F. Supp. 3d 24, 38 (D.D.C. 2016). The court thus sentenced each defendant to the mandatory-minimum sentence of 10 years. This appeal followed.

II.

In this appeal, the defendants renew two arguments they pressed unsuccessfully in the district court: that the district court lacked subject-matter jurisdiction over their prosecutions, and that they were eligible for safety-valve relief from the 10-year mandatory-minimum.

Despite the defendants' guilty pleas, they have not waived or forfeited either argument. Challenges to a district court's subject-matter jurisdiction can never be waived by plea. **[—7—]** *United States v. Miranda*, 780 F.3d 1185, 1188, 3 Adm. R. 676, 678 (D.C. Cir. 2015). Nor can such challenges be forfeited, so Moreno-Membache's failure to contest subject-matter jurisdiction in the district court does not preclude him from raising the challenge now. And although sentencing challenges can be waived, all three defendants entered conditional pleas reserving their right to appeal the district court's determination that they were ineligible for safety-valve relief. *See id.*, 3 Adm. R. at 677 (citing Fed. R. Crim. P. 11(a)(2)). We therefore consider both the district court's subject-matter jurisdiction and the defendants' safety-valve eligibility.

A.

The defendants initially argue that the district court lacked subject-matter jurisdiction over their prosecutions. The MDLEA criminalizes certain drug-related acts committed "on board a covered vessel," 46 U.S.C. § 70503(a), as well as conspiracies to commit those acts, *id.* § 70506(b). We have held that a defendant can violate the Act's conspiracy provision without personally setting foot "on board a covered vessel," *id.* § 70503(a), so long as a co-conspirator commits a prohibited act while "on board a covered vessel" and that act is attributable to the defendant under ordinary principles of conspiracy law. *United States v. Ballestas*, 795 F.3d 138, 145-46, 3 Adm. R. 698, 701–02 (D.C. Cir. 2015); *see Pinkerton v. United States*, 328 U.S. 640, 647 (1946).

The MDLEA defines "covered vessel" to include a vessel "subject to the jurisdiction of the United States." 46 U.S.C. § 70503(e)(1). Relatedly, the MDLEA provides that "[j]urisdiction of the United States with respect to a vessel . . . is not an element of an offense" but is instead a "preliminary question[] of law to be determined solely by the trial judge." *Id.* § 70504(a). Construing those provisions, we have held that, **[—8—]** "whether a vessel is 'subject to the jurisdiction of the United States' is a [question] of subject-matter jurisdiction." *Miranda*, 780 F.3d at 1192, 3 Adm. R. at 681.

In this case, the district court's subject-matter jurisdiction turns on the applicability of 46 U.S.C. § 70502(c)(1)(C), which provides that a vessel is "subject to **{-290-}** the jurisdiction of the United States"—and thus is a "covered vessel"—if it is "registered in a foreign nation [and] that nation has consented or waived objection to the enforcement of United States law by the United States." Under the MDLEA, "[c]onsent or waiver of objection by a foreign nation to the enforcement of United States law by the United States . . . is proved conclusively by certification of the [U.S.] Secretary of State or the Secretary's designee." *Id.* § 70502(c)(2)(B).

Here, the Secretary's designee—the Coast Guard's Liaison Officer to the State Department's Bureau of International Narcotics and Law Enforcement Affairs—certified that "Colombian authorities confirmed and concurred with the United States' interpretation of Article 16" of the treaty between the two countries, "thereby waiving objection to the enforcement of United States law by the United States over the go-fast vessel MISTBY, all associated contraband, and persons on board." Coast Guard

Certification ¶ 4.e. The certification concludes that, "[a]ccordingly, the Government of the United States determined the go-fast vessel MISTBY was subject to the jurisdiction of the United States pursuant to 46 U.S.C. § 70502(c)(1)(C)." *Id.* ¶ 4.f.

If, as the certification's conclusion seems to say, the Mistby is "subject to the jurisdiction of the United States pursuant to 46 U.S.C. § 70502(c)(1)(C)" for purposes of all MDLEA actions related to the vessel, *id.*, then the district court had subject-matter jurisdiction over the defendants' **[—9—]** prosecutions: in that event, the defendants' "charged conduct [would have] involved . . . one type of vessel 'subject to the jurisdiction of the United States,'" thus giving rise to subject-matter jurisdiction, *Miranda*, 780 F.3d at 1197, 3 Adm. R. at 685.

The defendants argue, however, that the language of the certification's conclusion sweeps more broadly than the scope of Colombia's consent to U.S. jurisdiction. The defendants submit that, if a foreign nation "consent[s] or waive[s] objection to the enforcement of United States law" over a vessel for purposes of proceedings against a specific person or item of property, 46 U.S.C. § 70502(c)(1)(C), then the vessel is "subject to the jurisdiction of the United States" for proceedings against that person or property—but is *not* "subject to the jurisdiction of the United States" for purposes of other MDLEA proceedings. And that, the defendants say, is exactly what occurred here.

The defendants emphasize that, according to the Coast Guard's certification, Colombia "waiv[ed] objection to the enforcement of United States law by the United States over the go-fast vessel MISTBY, all associated contraband, and *persons on board*." Coast Guard Certification ¶ 4.e (emphasis added). The reference to "persons on board," the defendants assert, means that Colombia denied consent to U.S. jurisdiction over the Mistby for purposes of proceedings against persons (like the defendants) who were *not* on board.

We think the defendants misunderstand the Coast Guard's certification. Assuming the defendants are correct that a foreign nation can grant consent to U.S. jurisdiction over a vessel for some purposes but deny it for others, and assuming also that a district court's subject-matter jurisdiction under the MDLEA would rise or fall correspondingly, we do not read the **[—10—]** Coast Guard's certification to indicate that is what happened here.

The certification's use of the term "persons on board," *id.* ¶ 4.e, tracks the language of the statute, which discusses its "prohibitions" in terms of individuals "on board a covered vessel." 46 U.S.C. § 70503(a). And the statute, as explained, nonetheless reaches land-based co-conspirators **{-291-}** because, pursuant to "well-established principle[s] of conspiracy law," the acts of a person who is on board the vessel can be attributed to a co-conspirator who remains on land. *Ballestas*, 795 F.3d at 145-46, 3 Adm. R. at 701–02. By the same token, the certification's reference to "persons on board" does not exclude persons who remain on land: the acts of persons on board the Mistby would be attributed to land-based co-conspirators like the defendants, such that they too would effectively be considered to have committed a prohibited act on board. The indictment correspondingly charges the defendants with "conspir[ing], and agree[ing] to . . . distribute, and possess with intent to distribute," cocaine and marijuana "*on board a vessel* subject to the jurisdiction of the United States." *United States v. Mosquera-Murillo*, No. 13-cr-00134-03, Indictment at 2 (D.D.C. May 9, 2013), ECF No. 1 (emphasis added).

That is not necessarily to say that a foreign nation is incapable of consenting to the enforcement of U.S. law against persons on board a vessel without also consenting to the enforcement of U.S. law against land-based co-conspirators. In theory, a foreign nation could say—and thus a certification from the Coast Guard could report—that the nation consented to U.S. jurisdiction over a vessel with respect to persons on board, but denied consent with respect to co-conspirators not on board. **[—11—]**

Here, though, the certification concludes by reporting, without qualification, that "the Government of the United States determined the go-fast vessel MISTBY was subject to the jurisdiction of the United States pursuant to 46 U.S.C. § 70502(c)(1)(C)." Coast Guard Certification ¶ 4.f. And the certification does not indicate that Colombia denied consent with respect to *any* particular class of MDLEA proceedings—including proceedings against co-conspirators not on board the Mistby. Rather, the certification confirms that Colombia's consent to U.S. jurisdiction encompasses persons on board the Mistby, whose conduct on board the vessel is attributable to co-conspirators like the defendants.

As a fallback argument, the defendants suggest that we should look behind the Coast Guard's certification and examine Colombian law for ourselves. If we do so, the defendants submit, we will find the following: (i) that the treaty contemplates the application of U.S. law only if Colombia's domestic law allows for it, T.I.A.S. No. 12,835 art. 16; and (ii) that Colombian law envisions the application of U.S. law only in the case of persons who are "on board" a Colombian vessel. Código Penal (Criminal Code) [C. Pen.] tit. II, § 217 (Colom.).

Even assuming, arguendo, that we should scrutinize Colombia's domestic law, we note that one provision of that law, introduced by the government in support of subject-matter jurisdiction, says that a "punishable act shall be deemed to have occurred" in "the place where the effect was produced or should have been produced." *Id.* § 201. That language mirrors the conspiracy-law principle under which a land-based conspirator in an enterprise that engages in prohibited conduct on board a vessel will be treated as having himself participated in the acts on board the vessel. **[—12—]**

Our understanding of the Coast Guard's certification (and of Colombian law) is reinforced by Colombia's decision to grant the United States' extradition request concerning the defendants. If Colombia had in fact intended to deny consent to U.S. jurisdiction over the Mistby with respect to proceedings against persons who never came on board the vessel, Colombia could have given effect to that intention by declining **{-292-}** to extradite the defendants. Colombia did not do so, however. That is not to say that the extradition itself gave rise to subject-matter jurisdiction. It is instead to say that the extradition fortifies our interpretation of the Coast Guard's earlier certification; and that certification substantiates the district court's subject-matter jurisdiction by demonstrating that the Mistby is a "vessel subject to the jurisdiction of the United States" for purposes of the defendants' prosecutions. 46 U.S.C. § 70502(c)(1).

In sum, we conclude that Colombia's waiver of objection to U.S. jurisdiction over the Mistby covers the defendants' MDLEA prosecutions. The district court therefore had subject-matter jurisdiction.

B.

The defendants next argue that the district court erred by holding that they were ineligible for safety-valve relief from the 10-year mandatory-minimum term to which they were sentenced. The safety-valve provision is entitled "Limitation on applicability of statutory minimums in certain cases." 18 U.S.C. § 3553(f). It provides that, "in the case of an offense under" one of five enumerated provisions—21 U.S.C. §§ 841, 844, 846, 960, or 963—"the court shall impose a sentence pursuant to [the sentencing] guidelines . . . without regard to any statutory minimum sentence, if the court finds at sentencing" that five specified requirements have been met. **[—13—]**

In these cases, the district court did not reach whether those five requirements had been satisfied. Rather, the court deemed the defendants ineligible for safety-valve relief at the threshold, ruling that they had not been convicted of "an offense under" any of the five enumerated provisions. The court rejected the defendants' argument that their cases involved "an offense under" one of those provisions, namely 21 U.S.C. § 960.

The sole question we face here is whether the defendants' crime is "an offense under" § 960 within the meaning of the safety-valve provision. 18 U.S.C. § 3553(f). Reviewing that question of statutory interpretation de novo, *see United States v. Cordova*, 806 F.3d 1085, 1098 (D.C. Cir. 2015) (per curiam), we agree with the defendants: they were convicted of "an offense under" § 960, and they therefore satisfy the threshold condition for safety-valve eligibility.

To see why, it is necessary to examine the relationship between § 960 and the MDLEA provisions the defendants pleaded guilty to violating. The MDLEA prohibits, as relevant here, distributing, and possessing with intent to distribute, drugs on board a covered vessel. 46 U.S.C. § 70503(a)(1). A separate MDLEA provision prohibits "conspiring to violate section 70503," and establishes that anyone who so conspires "is subject to the same penalties as provided for violating section 70503." *Id.* § 70506(b).

What are those penalties? That is where 21 U.S.C. § 960 comes into play. Under the MDLEA, the first time a person violates "paragraph (1) of section 70503(a)," she "shall be punished as provided in . . . 21 U.S.C. [section] 960." 46 U.S.C. § 70506(a). So the first time a person conspires to violate § 70503(a)(1), she likewise "shall be punished as provided in . . . 21 U.S.C. [section] 960." *Id.* § 70506(a)-(b). **[—14—]** Because this was the defendants' first conviction for conspiring to violate § 70503(a)(1), § 960 supplied the penalties applicable to their crime.

Does that mean that the defendants' crime is "an offense under" § 960 for purposes of safety-valve eligibility? 18 U.S.C. § 3553(f). We conclude it does.

As an initial matter, even if the precise meaning of the phrase, "an offense under **{–293–}** provision X" could be subject to some debate at the margins, there is no doubt about the following: a defendant's case involves "*an offense under*" provision X if the defendant has been convicted of *violating* provision X. So here, there is no dispute that the defendants' cases could be described as involving "an offense under" 46 U.S.C. §§ 70503(a)(1) and 70506(b). Indeed, the government, throughout its briefs, describes the defendants as having been "convicted of *violating* the MDLEA" or "*violating* a provision of the MDLEA," or, equivalently, as having been "convicted *under* the MDLEA" or of "an offense *under* the MDLEA." *E.g.*, Appellee's Br. 25, 27, 31-32, 34, 41, 43.

The defendants' crime of conviction, though, involved more than a violation of (or, equivalently, an offense under) the MDLEA. It also involved a violation of (or, equivalently, an offense under) 21 U.S.C. § 960. Offenses are defined by the provisions that supply their elements. *See Patterson v. New York*, 432 U.S. 197, 210 (1977). And here, the defendants' offense draws certain elements from the relevant MDLEA provisions, 46 U.S.C. §§ 70503(a)(1), 70506(b), and draws other elements from 21 U.S.C. § 960.

In particular, the MDLEA supplies the elements that make the defendants' conduct unlawful: (i) conspiring, (ii) to intentionally or knowingly, (iii) distribute or possess with **[—15—]** intent to distribute, (iv) a controlled substance, (v) while on board a vessel. 46 U.S.C. §§ 70503(a)(1), 70506(b). Meanwhile, § 960 supplies the offense elements of drug-type and drug-quantity—5 or more kilograms of cocaine, and 100 or more kilograms of marijuana—which bear on the degree of culpability and determine the statutory sentencing range. 21 U.S.C. § 960(b)(1)(B), (b)(2)(G). In that light, the defendants' crime is "an offense under" *both* the MDLEA *and* § 960, drawing offense elements from each.

The understanding that § 960 supplies offense elements coheres with the rule of *Apprendi v. New Jersey*, 530 U.S. 466 (2000). Under *Apprendi*, "any fact that increases the prescribed statutory maximum" penalty to which a defendant is exposed amounts to an offense element that "must be submitted to a jury, and proved beyond a reasonable doubt." *Id.* at 490; *see Alleyne v. United States*, 133 S. Ct. 2151, 2157 (2013) (plurality). The drug-type and drug-quantity elements set out in § 960(b) qualify as elements for purposes of *Apprendi* because they establish the maximum sentence. *See* 21 U.S.C. § 960(b)(1)(B)(ii) ("In the case of a violation . . . involving . . . 5 kilograms or more of . . . cocaine . . . the [defendant] shall be sentenced to a term of imprisonment of . . . not more than life."); *see also United States v. Fields*, 251 F.3d 1041, 1043 (D.C. Cir. 2001). And because the drug-type and drug-quantity criteria in § 960 constitute some of the elements of the defendants' offense (with the other elements supplied by the MDLEA), their cases involve "an offense under" § 960 for purposes of safety-valve eligibility. 18 U.S.C. § 3553(f).

As further confirmation that § 960 supplies elements of the defendants' offense, the government's indictment charged the defendants with violating both the MDLEA and § 960, not just the former. Specifically, the indictment charged the defendants with one count of conspiring to distribute, and possess with **[—16—]** intent to distribute, 5 or more kilograms of cocaine and 100 or more kilograms of marijuana on board a covered vessel, "all in violation of Title 46, United States Code, Sections 70503 and 70506(b)" *and "Title 21, United States Code, Sections 960(b)(1)(B) and* **{-294-}** *(b)(2)(G)." United States v. Mosquera-Murillo*, No. 13-cr-00134-03, Indictment at 2 (D.D.C. May 9, 2013), ECF No. 1 (emphasis added).

To the same effect, the government's plea agreement with each of the defendants stated that the defendant "agrees to plead guilty" to the charged conduct just described, once again "in violation of Title 46, United States Code, Sections 70503 and 70506(b)" *and "Title 21, United States Code, Sections 960(b)(1)(B) and (b)(2)(G)." E.g., United States v. Mosquera-Murrillo*, No. 13-cr-00134-03, Plea Agreement at ¶ 1 (D.D.C. Jan. 20, 2016), ECF No. 185. The judgments against the defendants therefore pronounce that they were "adjudicated guilty" of the charged offense in violation of both the relevant MDLEA provisions and § 960(b). *E.g., United States v. Mosquera-Murillo*, No. 13-cr-00134-03, Judgment at 1 (D.D.C. Aug. 1, 2016), ECF No. 250.

Despite the government's indictment and plea agreements describing the defendants as having violated § 960, the government now submits that the defendants were not convicted of "an offense under" § 960 for purposes of safety-valve eligibility. The government points out that § 960 consists of two subsections. The first, subsection (a), lists certain "unlawful acts" by reference to drug offenses set out elsewhere in the code—e.g., "bring[ing] or possess[ing] on board a vessel, aircraft, or vehicle a controlled substance" "contrary to section 955." 21 U.S.C. § 960(a)(2). The second subsection, subsection (b), sets out the penalties for the offenses listed in subsection (a) based on drug-type and drug-quantity—e.g., "[i]n the case of a violation of subsection **[—17—]** (a)" involving "1 kilogram or more of . . . heroin," the "person committing such violation shall be sentenced to a term of imprisonment of not less than 10 years and not more than life." 21 U.S.C. § 960(b)(1)(A).

According to the government, the safety-valve provision's reference to "an offense under" § 960 means only those specific offenses listed in § 960(a)—not other offenses defined in part by the drug-type and drug-quantity elements set out in § 960(b). And because no MDLEA offense is listed in § 960(a), the government argues, the defendants' cases do not involve "an offense under" § 960 within the meaning of the safety-valve provision.

The government's reading of the safety-valve provision is unpersuasive. The statute speaks in terms of an "offense under" § 960 without limitation—not an offense under only § 960(a). Plus, the structure of § 960 demonstrates that the defendants' crime qualifies as "an offense under" § 960 no less than the crimes listed in § 960(a).

Subsection (a) of § 960 does not lay out any element of—and thus does not define in whole or in part—any criminal offense. Instead, § 960(a) merely lists certain offenses established elsewhere in the code. It does so for one reason: to identify a set of offenses for which § 960(b) supplies the drug-type and drug-quantity elements, and, accordingly, the range of potential penalties.

The MDLEA offense of which the defendants were convicted interacts with § 960(b) in exactly the same way as the offenses listed in § 960(a). Just as those offenses are established outside of § 960 and "shall be punished as provided in subsection (b)" of § 960, *id.* § 960(a), the MDLEA also establishes offenses outside of § 960, which likewise are **[—18—]** punished under the penalty scheme set out in § 960(b). Indeed, the MDLEA uses precisely the same wording in linking certain of its offenses to § 960(b) as § 960(a) does in linking its listed offenses to § 960(b): the MDLEA states that, for first-time offenders **{-295-}** of 46 U.S.C. § 70503(a)(1), the defendant "shall be punished as provided in" § 960. 46 U.S.C. § 70506(a). *Compare id.*, *with* 21 U.S.C. § 960(a).

If both the offenses listed in § 960(a) and the relevant offenses under the MDLEA are (i) established outside of § 960, and (ii) make use of the drug-type and drug-quantity elements and associated penalties set forth in § 960(b), then there is no reason to conclude—as the government would—that the former qualify as "offenses under" § 960 for purpose of safety-valve eligibility whereas the latter do not. Nothing in the statutory text supports drawing such a distinction. Rather, just as a person who commits one of the offenses listed in § 960(a) violates both the provision establishing the offense (e.g., 21 U.S.C. § 955) and § 960(b), the defendants in these cases violated both the MDLEA and § 960(b). The government was right to describe the defendants' offenses in that manner in the indictment and plea agreements.

In addition, treating the defendants as having violated § 960, and thus as eligible for safety-valve relief, would align with Congress's nearly unbroken pattern of setting identical penalties for drug crimes committed in domestic waters and drug crimes committed on the high seas. When Congress criminalized opium possession on the high seas in 1914, it set the maximum penalty at two years, which at the time was the maximum penalty for importing opium into the United States. Act of Jan. 17, 1914, Pub. L. No. 63-46, §§ 2, 4, 38 Stat. 275, 276. In 1922, Congress simultaneously raised the maximum penalties for both offenses from two to ten years. Narcotic Drugs Import and Export Act, Pub. L. No. 67-227, § 2(c), 42 **[—19—]** Stat. 596, 596 (1922). Then, in 1951, Congress simultaneously decreased the maximum penalties for both offenses from ten to five years. Boggs Act, Pub. L. No. 82-255, § 2(c), 65 Stat. 767, 767 (1951).

In 1970, Congress overhauled the drug code, repealing the statutes that define the offenses discussed above, and establishing a new prohibition—codified at 21 U.S.C. § 955—against importing drugs via the customs waters of the United States. Comprehensive Drug Abuse Prevention and Control Act of 1970, Pub. L. No. 91-513, § 1007, 84 Stat. 1236, 1288. Congress provided that the penalties applicable to that offense were those set forth in 21 U.S.C. § 960. *Id.* § 1010, 84 Stat. at 1290. Shortly thereafter, Congress enacted what is now known as the MDLEA, including its prohibition against possession with intent to distribute on the high seas. Pub. L. No. 96-350, § 1, 94 Stat. 1159, 1159 (1980). And Congress provided that § 960 also supplied the penalties for that offense. *Id.* § 1(g)(1), 94 Stat. at 1159.

In light of the century-long pattern of identical penalties for drug offenses committed in domestic waters and on the high seas, it is notable that, as both parties agree, offenders who violate § 955 are eligible for safety-valve relief. 21 U.S.C. § 960(a) (listing violations of § 955 as offenses punishable under § 960(b)). So if offenders who violate the MDLEA were ineligible for safety-valve relief, then, by enacting the safety-valve provision, Congress would have broken its 100-year pattern of penalty parity. We do not understand Congress to have done so.

Two other circuits have considered whether MDLEA offenses penalized under § 960(b) qualify as "offenses under" § 960 for purposes of the safety-valve provision. Both courts have concluded that such offenses do not qualify. *See United* **[—20—]** *States v. Pertuz-Pertuz*, 679 F.3d 1327, 1329 (11th Cir. 2012) (per curiam); *United States v. Gamboa-Cardenas*, 508 F.3d 491, 496 (9th Cir. 2007). We respectfully reach the opposite **{-296-}**

conclusion. Neither of those decisions expressly assesses whether the drug-type and drug-quantity facts supplied by § 960(b) constitute offense elements, such that an MDLEA offender penalized under § 960(b) should be considered someone who has violated both the MDLEA and § 960. That consideration, as we have explained, is pivotal to our conclusion.

Our decision today, we note finally, does not necessarily resolve whether the safety valve covers a different provision to which both parties have directed our attention: 21 U.S.C. § 860. In defining the offense of "[d]istribution or manufacturing in or near schools and colleges," § 860 incorporates both the unlawful-act elements of 21 U.S.C. § 841(a) and the drug-type and drug-quantity elements of § 841(b). So one could argue that a violation of § 860 is an "offense under" § 841, in which case offenders who violate § 860 would be eligible for safety-valve relief, given that the safety valve lists § 841 as a covered provision. That said, § 860 restates in full the unlawful-act elements of § 841(a), and then modifies the penalties prescribed by § 841(b) by doubling or tripling them. That might mean that all the elements of an § 860 violation are supplied by § 860 itself, rather than by a combination of § 860 and § 841. If that is the case, then offenders who violate § 860 would be ineligible for safety-valve relief, given that the safety valve does not list § 860 as a covered provision. We need not decide the issue now; we simply note that today's decision does not necessarily answer the § 860 question either way. **[—21—]**

* * * * *

For the foregoing reasons, we vacate the defendants' sentences and remand for resentencing, at which the district court should consider whether the defendants meet the five remaining safety-valve requirements.

So ordered.

United States Court of Appeals
for the District of Columbia Circuit

No. 17-5269

ANGELEX, LTD.
VS.
UNITED STATES

Appeal from the United States District Court for the District of Columbia

Decided: November 2, 2018

Citation: 907 F.3d 612, 6 Adm. R. 514 (D.C. Cir. 2018).

Before **TATEL** and **MILLETT**, Circuit Judges, and **WILLIAMS**, Senior Circuit Judge.

[—1—] {-614-} **TATEL**, Circuit Judge:

Nearly forty years ago, Congress authorized the Coast Guard to detain ships suspected of **[—2—]** intentionally discharging oil and other contaminants into the sea. At the same time, Congress gave a ship "unreasonably detained or delayed" a cause of action to recover "any loss or damage suffered thereby." 33 U.S.C. § 1904(h). Until today, no circuit has considered the contours of this cause of action. Sailing into uncharted waters, we ask whether the Coast Guard acted reasonably in detaining a vessel for nearly six months pending a criminal trial after its owner and operator failed to meet the government's security bond demands. Measuring the reasonableness of the Coast Guard's actions by an objective standard, we find that the Coast **{-615-}** Guard set a reasonable monetary bond. We also conclude that the nonmonetary components of the bond demand contributed nothing to the owner's losses. We therefore affirm the district court's award of summary judgment to the government.

I.

The United States is a party to the 1973 International Convention for the Prevention of Pollution from Ships, as later supplemented by a protocol and several annexes (collectively, the "Convention"). *Watervale Marine Co. v. United States Department of Homeland Security*, 807 F.3d 325, 327, 3 Adm. R. 707, 707 (D.C. Cir. 2015). The Convention obliges member states to hold ships accountable for intentionally discharging oil and other contaminants into the ocean. *See id.*, 3 Adm. R. at 707.

Congress implemented the Convention through the Act to Prevent Pollution from Ships (the "Act"). *See* Pub. L. No. 96-478, 94 Stat. 2297 (1980) (codified as amended at 33 U.S.C. §§ 1901 et seq.). As amended, the Act authorizes the Department of Homeland Security to enforce the Convention and "prescribe any necessary or desired regulations to carry out" the Convention's obligations. 33 U.S.C. § 1903(c)(1). Pursuant to that authority, the Department requires ships to, **[—3—]** among other things, "maintain" an "Oil Record Book" that keeps track of the ship's oily discharges into the sea. 33 C.F.R. § 151.25(a), (d). "[K]nowingly violat[ing]" those regulations is a felony. 33 U.S.C. § 1908(a). It is undisputed in this case that a new violation occurs each time a ship enters a U.S. port with a non-compliant oil record book. "A ship operated in violation of" these rules is liable *in rem* for "any fine imposed under" the Act. *Id.* § 1908(d).

If the Coast Guard has "reasonable cause" to believe that a "ship, its owner, operator, or person in charge" may be liable under the Act, the Coast Guard may require Customs and Border Patrol ("Customs") to "refuse or revoke" the clearance required for a vessel to depart from American ports. *Id.* § 1908(e). While enforcement proceedings are pending, that clearance may nonetheless be granted "upon the filing of a bond or other surety satisfactory to the Secretary" of Homeland Security. *Id.* Consistent with the United States's obligations under the Convention—and central to this case—the Act, through section 1904(h), also creates a cause of action for a "ship unreasonably detained or delayed" to recover "compensation for any loss or damage suffered thereby." *Id.* § 1904(h); *see* International Convention for the Prevention of Pollution from Ships, art. 7(2), Nov. 2, 1973, 12 I.L.M. 1319, 1340 U.N.T.S. 184 (entered into force on Oct. 2, 1983).

Appellant, Angelex, Ltd., owns the Maltese-flagged *M/V Antonis G. Pappadakis*, a nearly 750-foot-long bulk carrier subject to the Convention. Kassian Maritime Navigation Agency, Ltd.—not a party to this lawsuit—chartered the vessel in 2013 to carry a load of coal. In the district court, Angelex conceded that Kassian was the ship's "operator," as the Act uses that term. *See* 33 U.S.C. § 1901(a)(9). Lambros Katsipis served as the ship's chief engineer during the 2013 voyage. **[—4—]**

In April 2013, the *Pappadakis* arrived at the port of Norfolk, and Coast Guard agents boarded for a routine inspection. A crewmember passed the inspectors a note confiding that the chief engineer was using a "magic pipe"—a device designed to covertly dump water containing oil residue—to avoid reporting discharges in the oil record book.

Investigating the allegation, the Coast Guard searched the ship and interviewed crew members. The on-board investigation **{-616-}** ended after one week, on April 19, and on the same day, the port captain sent Angelex and Kassian a letter saying that the investigation established "reasonable grounds" to believe that the *Pappadakis* had violated the oil record book requirements. The Coast Guard therefore directed Customs to withhold the ship's departure clearance.

Negotiations ensued to reach an agreement that would allow the *Pappadakis* to sail pending prosecution. Initially, the Coast Guard demanded "that Angelex and Kassian jointly and severally post a bond in the amount of $3 million." U.S. Statement of Material Facts ¶ 66, Joint Appendix (J.A.) 140. It also required Angelex and Kassian to agree to several nonmonetary bond conditions designed to facilitate further investigation and trial. These conditions included "expressly waiving all jurisdictional defenses, paying the salaries and expenses for several crewmembers to remain in the Eastern District of Virginia, stipulating to the authenticity of all documents and items seized from the *Pappadakis*, and assisting the United States in effecting service on foreign citizens not located in the United States." *Id.*

Angelex and Kassian both protested that, strapped for cash, they were unable to meet those demands. In particular, Angelex claimed in an email that it was "in a dire financial condition" and purported to attach its "most recent financial **[—5—]** statements" to prove that its free cash reserves topped out at $174,000, while its liabilities exceeded $10.5 million. Email from George M. Chalos, J.A. 93. Two days later, according to Angelex, it sent the Coast Guard updated financial documents, this time showing free cash reserves of nearly $800,000 and a ship mortgage of nearly $11 million. Both emails summarized the contents of the financial statements in no more than two sentences. The Coast Guard eventually reduced its demand to $2.5 million, but it would go no lower.

With negotiations at an impasse, and the *Pappadakis* stuck in Norfolk, Angelex took the Coast Guard to court. It filed an emergency petition for relief in the Eastern District of Virginia, and Senior District Judge Robert G. Doumar quickly convened a hearing. Halfway through, the court ordered a recess and urged the parties to settle. At first, that effort appeared to succeed: the parties agreed in principle for Angelex to comply with all of the Coast Guard's nonmonetary conditions and post a monetary bond of $1.5 million. But Coast Guard headquarters overruled its line negotiators, holding fast to the $2.5 million demand, and the deal fell through.

Two days later, Judge Doumar granted Angelex's petition. He did not mince words, saying of the Coast Guard's bond demands that he could "recall seeing no greater disregard for due process, nor any more egregious abdication of the reasonable exercise of discretion" in his over thirty-year judicial career. *Angelex Ltd. v. United States*, No. 2:13-cv-237, 2013 WL 1934490, at *9 (E.D. Va. May 8, 2013). He ordered the government to accept the terms negotiated during the recess: $1.5 million plus the Coast Guard's nonmonetary conditions. *Id.* at *10. The Fourth Circuit granted the government's motion for an emergency stay and eventually reversed on the ground that the district court lacked subject- **[—6—]** matter jurisdiction. *Angelex Ltd. v. United States*, 723 F.3d 500,

502, 505, 1 Adm. R. 169, 169, 172 (4th Cir. 2013).

Meanwhile, a grand jury returned an indictment charging Angelex, Kassian, and Katsipis with, among other things, three counts each of failing to maintain an accurate oil record book—one count each for three separate entries into U.S. ports. After a trial, the jury convicted Katsipis on the three oil record book counts, but acquitted **{–617–}** Angelex and Kassian of all charges.

The Coast Guard detained the *Pappadakis* in Norfolk until the trial ended, and the ship finally sailed just over three weeks after the jury's verdict. In total, the Coast Guard held the vessel for a little under six months.

In January 2015, Angelex filed this civil action alleging that the Coast Guard had unreasonably delayed the *Pappadakis* and seeking compensation for expenses and losses under section 1904(h). Following discovery, the parties cross-moved for summary judgment, and the district court granted the government's motion.

The court adopted a balancing approach to reasonableness under section 1904(h), "imposing an obligation on the Government to balance its own specific and legitimate enforcement interests with the interests of the vessel's other stakeholders." *Angelex Ltd. v. United States*, 272 F. Supp. 3d 64, 76 (D.D.C. 2017). The court then turned to Angelex's arguments that the Coast Guard acted unreasonably.

First, the district court rejected Angelex's contention that the Coast Guard should have given greater weight to the vessel's mortgage and the company's financial situation because Angelex failed to support those arguments with admissible evidence. Specifically, the court pointed out that Angelex had introduced into the record none of the financial **[—7—]** attachments that it supposedly sent the Coast Guard during the bond negotiations. That left the emails from Angelex's counsel to Coast Guard officials as the only evidence of the company's fiscal state. The district court also disregarded those emails because, in its view, they were "unqualified hearsay" and therefore inadmissible at trial. *Id.* at 78.

The court turned to the proposed $2.5 million monetary bond, holding that, as a matter of law, "any bond amount up to, and including, the maximum possible fines and penalties is necessarily within a range of reasonableness." *Id.* at 84. And, having found that the maximum fine in this case was $3 million, the court deemed the Coast Guard's $2.5 million demand *per se* reasonable.

Finally, as to the nonmonetary bond conditions, the district court read section 1904(h) to require the Coast Guard's conduct to have actually contributed to the length of time that the ship was detained or delayed, and it found that the nonmonetary conditions could not possibly have extended the *Pappadakis*'s delay, based in part on Angelex's admission "that, during the initial litigation before Judge Doumar," it was prepared to "accept *all* of the non-financial conditions if the Coast Guard would be willing to lower the bond amount to just $1.5 million." *Id.* at 87. Since Angelex had agreed to accept all of those conditions, the court reasoned, any additional delay could not be attributed to the nonmonetary conditions.

Having rejected all of Angelex's arguments that the Coast Guard harmed Angelex by behaving unreasonably, the district court entered judgment in favor of the government. Angelex timely appealed, and our review is de novo. *Jackson v. Finnegan, Henderson, Farabow, Garrett & Dunner*, 101 F.3d 145, 150 (D.C. Cir. 1996). **[—8—]**

II.

"[S]ummary judgment is proper if . . . there is no genuine issue as to any material fact . . . ." *Celotex Corp. v. Catrett*, 477 U.S. 317, 322 (1986) (internal quotation marks omitted). Once the moving party has met its "initial responsibility of informing **{–618–}** the . . . court of the basis for its motion," *id.* at 323, the party opposing summary judgment must point to "specific facts showing that there is a genuine issue for trial," *id.* at 324 (internal quotation marks omitted). To succeed, "the non-moving party must produce evidence capable of being converted into admissible evidence" that would allow a reasonable factfinder to return a verdict in its favor. *Greer v. Paulson*, 505 F.3d 1306, 1315 (D.C. Cir. 2007) (internal quotation marks and alterations omitted).

Section 1904(h) requires a party seeking damages to prove two elements. First, the Coast Guard must have "unreasonably detained or delayed" the ship. Whether the Coast Guard acted "unreasonably" is a question of law. *See Carter v. Bennett*, 840 F.2d 63, 64-65 (D.C. Cir. 1988) (whether facts satisfy a statutory standard of "reasonable" is a "conclusion of law"). Second, as a result of the detention or delay, the ship must have suffered "loss or damage." Therefore, summary judgment for the government is proper if the claimant fails to come forward with adequate evidence to support either of those elements as a matter of law.

With these principles in hand, we take up Angelex's several arguments that it is entitled to relief under section 1904(h). Broadly speaking, Angelex claims that it suffered losses because of the delay prompted by: (1) the Coast Guard's detention of the *Pappadakis* through trial despite the absence of an adequate evidentiary basis to do so; and (2) the government's unreasonable bond demands. We consider each contention in turn. **[—9—]**

A.

We begin with Angelex's argument that the protracted detention was unreasonable because it was unauthorized. Although Angelex does not challenge the Coast Guard's initial decision to detain the *Pappadakis*, it claims the Coast Guard had no basis for holding the ship all the way through the trial because, at some unspecified point in the investigation, it became clear "that there was no evidence which would support vicarious liability for Angelex (or Kassian)." Appellant's Br. 42. As Angelex sees it, the Coast Guard lost authority to continue holding the ship once the alleged absence of evidence became apparent. This argument misses the mark.

As this court recognized in *Watervale Marine Co. v. United States Department of Homeland Security*, when the Coast Guard has "reasonable cause" to believe a ship is being operated in violation of the Act, it may "hold the ship in port until legal proceedings are completed." 807 F.3d at 330, 3 Adm. R. at 709–10. And a validly obtained indictment generates in a subsequent civil proceeding a "rebuttable presumption" that the government had probable cause at the time of the indictment, which can be undermined only by "evidence that the indictment was produced by fraud, corruption, perjury, fabricated evidence, or other wrongful conduct undertaken in bad faith." *Moore v. Hartman*, 571 F.3d 62, 69 (D.C. Cir. 2009).

Here, a grand jury had sufficient basis to indict both Angelex and Kassian, and Angelex has given us no basis for distinguishing between the "reasonable cause" required to detain a ship and the "probable cause" necessary to indict. Thus, so long as the indictment was valid and there were no material post-indictment developments, the detention was authorized. **[—10—]**

The only evidence Angelex cites to question the extended detention's authorization is a single statement from the government's lead investigator, who testified that she did not "specifically" do anything "to investigate the basis to vicariously charge **{–619–}** Angelex." Appellant's Br. 44 (internal quotation marks omitted). At most, that statement implies that the government conducted no separate investigation focused on corporate liability; it does nothing to suggest "that the indictment was produced by . . . wrongful conduct undertaken in bad faith" or that the initial basis for detaining the ship had eroded. *Moore*, 571 F.3d at 69. We thus agree that the Coast Guard had section 1908(e) authority to detain the *Pappadakis* "until legal proceedings [were] completed." *Watervale*, 807 F.3d at 330, 3 Adm. R. at 710.

B.

Of course, a detention may be unreasonable even if authorized. Angelex's second, and more substantial, argument is that its case falls into that category because of the government's allegedly unreasonable bond demands.

Before considering the merits of that argument, we observe that the parties appear to agree on a threshold proposition, which we therefore assume is true for this case: that a detention or delay is unreasonable if the bond demand is excessive or otherwise inappropriate.

We start with the monetary demand. The district court thought that any bond amount below the statutory maximum fine for which the ship could be liable *in rem* is *per se* reasonable. We certainly agree that any bond amount below the maximum criminal fine will *often* be reasonable, but we are reluctant to adopt such a bright line rule. Calculation of the maximum fine is less straightforward than the district court assumed. *See* 18 U.S.C. § 3571(c), (d) (setting the maximum **[—11—]** fine at $500,000 per count, but authorizing an "[a]lternative fine based on" the defendant's "gain or loss"); 33 U.S.C. § 1908(b) (authorizing additional civil penalties per violation, per day). And a party may well be able to demonstrate, with appropriate evidence, that failure to deviate from the maximum—however calculated—was unreasonable. But this is not such a case: Angelex's arguments that a $2.5 million bond amount was unreasonable are meritless.

Angelex first argues that the Coast Guard should set bond based not on the maximum statutory fine, but rather on the fine the district court is likely to impose. As the district court rightly observed, that approach is often impractical: "there is . . . no reason to expect that anyone can accurately predict what fines or penalties a court might impose at some point in the future after trial." *Angelex*, 272 F. Supp. 3d at 84. It was thus perfectly reasonable for the Coast Guard to start by focusing instead on the maximum potential fine in formulating a bond demand.

Next, Angelex disputes that $3 million was the maximum fine that the *Pappadakis* could have been liable for *in rem*. Specifically, it claims that Kassian's potential liability cannot be included because Kassian had no "equitable interest" in the vessel. Appellant's Br. 28. That argument ignores how the statute's *in rem* liability scheme works. The Act makes "[a] ship operated in violation" of the oil record book regulations itself liable for "*any* fine imposed" as a result. 33 U.S.C. § 1908(d) (emphasis added). And it authorizes prosecution of any "person" who "knowingly violates" the regulations, a category of potential defendants that plainly includes a vessel's operator. *Id.* § 1908(a). The statute therefore puts the ship on the hook for Kassian's share. As for what that share comes to, the statute permits three alternatives: $500,000 per count, "twice the gross gain" derived by the defendant, or "twice the gross loss" to any third party. *See* 18 U.S.C. § 3571(c)(3), (d). **[—12—]** And that **{-620-}** leaves aside any civil penalties the government might seek, which the government can also pursue *in rem* against the ship. *See* 33 U.S.C. § 1908(b), (e). Given the six total counts against Angelex and Kassian, it was therefore no error for the district court to conclude that the maximum fine in this case was at least $3 million.

Angelex's next tack is to claim that the Coast Guard's demand was unreasonable given the company's financial state at the time. It argues that the Coast Guard had no hope of actually recovering *in rem* given the huge mortgage on the ship and that posting the bond would effectively have put Angelex out of business. For its part, the government argues that Angelex's ability to pay and the government's likelihood of actually recovering are entirely irrelevant to the reasonableness of the bond amount.

We can resolve this case without deciding whether those issues are relevant under section 1904(h). Assuming they are, to succeed on this argument Angelex would have to show that the information reasonably available to the Coast Guard reliably conveyed the relevant financial data. Any other approach would effectively require the Coast Guard to conduct its own independent investigation of a company's financial status—an unreasonable demand given the time and tools at the agency's disposal.

As the party opposing summary judgment, Angelex therefore had the burden of identifying the financial information that the Coast Guard could have relied on. It has failed to do so. As the district court accurately observed, Angelex entered into the record none of the financial documents that it supposedly sent the Coast Guard. *See Angelex*, 272 F. Supp. 3d at 78, 85 n.14. Although Angelex challenged that finding at oral argument, it never properly **[—13—]** anchored that claim in the record, *see* Fed. R. App. P. 28(a)(8)(A) (requiring "citations to the . . . parts of the record on which the appellant relies"); in any event, we have independently scoured the record and, like the district court, have come up empty.

Angelex's omission of those documents is fatal. Without them, the district court had no way of assessing whether the Coast Guard's $2.5 million demand reasonably took account of the information those documents contained. And regardless of whether the emails summarizing those documents would have been admissible at trial, the district court could not have relied solely on their bare-bones, self-serving statements to assess the information available to the Coast Guard. At oral argument, Angelex claimed that if the case went to trial, its own witnesses would corroborate those emails. Perhaps so, but counsel assertions at oral argument cannot create a genuine issue of material fact. *See* Fed. R. Civ. P. 56(c)(1)(A) (requiring a "party asserting that a fact . . . is genuinely disputed" to cite, among other things, "affidavits or declarations"). Anyway, that trial testimony would leave the core problem unaddressed: the district court would still be unable to review the documents available to the Coast Guard at the time of its decision.

Angelex repeatedly seeks to bolster its position by invoking Judge Doumar's observation that the Coast Guard's demands amounted to the most "egregious abdication of the reasonable exercise of discretion" he had ever seen. *Angelex*, 2013 WL 1934490, at *9. Although it is true, as the government argues, that the Fourth Circuit's reversal turns the order into a "*legal* nullity," *Khadr v. United States*, 529 F.3d 1112, 1116 (D.C. Cir. 2008) (emphasis added), the order remains part of the historical record, and a party might still be able to use it as evidence of what a reasonable contemporaneous observer might have concluded. **[—14—] {-621-}**

Nevertheless, under the circumstances of this case, the order affords Angelex no help. Judge Doumar's finding rested on two considerations that have not withstood the test of time. First, Judge Doumar believed that the only permissible reason to detain the ship was for eventual *in rem* recovery, and so he discounted the Coast Guard's interest in retaining custody of witnesses and evidence for trial. *Angelex*, 2013 WL 1934490, at *8. As we observed in *Watervale*, however, that is a false dichotomy: obviously the government cannot collect *in rem* without successfully prosecuting the case. 807 F.3d at 329–330, 3 Adm. R. at 709–10 ("[A] financial bond, given its limited use, is ordinarily not satisfactory" because "nothing prevents the ship, after posting the bond, from sailing away."). Moreover, the government's interest in enforcing environmental laws extends beyond merely collecting a fine. Second, Judge Doumar assumed that the maximum fine was only $1.5 million, apparently omitting Kassian's potential liability. *Angelex*, 2013 WL 1934490, at *8-9. As we have explained, however, the maximum fine in this case was at least $3 million. Finally, there is a crucial difference between this litigation and Angelex's emergency petition: Angelex presented Judge Doumar with the underlying financial documents that are missing here. *See Angelex*, No. 2:13-cv-237, ECF No. 4-8 (E.D. Va. Apr. 25, 2013). Given all these differences, Judge Doumar's finding has no appreciable probative value for the district court in this case.

Angelex also insists that the proposed bond amount was unreasonable when compared to other cases. It identifies only one: the *M/V Thetis*. Appellant's Br. 39. According to Angelex, the Coast Guard was willing to accept a lower bond in that case ($1 million) despite the "near-identical nature of the . . . charges." *Id.* at 39-40. But, as the government points out, that case differs from this one significantly: unlike the *Thetis*'s operators,

Kassian had a criminal history, having pled guilty to an oil record book violation in the past. *See United States v.* **[—15—]** *Kassian Maritime Navigation Agency, Ltd.*, No. 3:07-cr-48 (M.D. Fla. Aug. 17, 2007). Thus, the Coast Guard had a reasonable basis for suspecting that the *Pappadakis* was more likely to evade prosecution and potentially re-offend than the *Thetis*—possibilities that explain the higher bond demand in this case.

Lastly, Angelex objects to the process that the Coast Guard employed to formulate its bond demand. It alleges that the Coast Guard officers who handled the *Pappadakis* case failed to adequately consider or respond to various factors, such as the financial state of Angelex and Kassian and the detention's impact on crew members and the cargo owner. It also claims that confusion existed within the Coast Guard about who exactly held final decisionmaking authority to set bond. The government tersely responds that the test must be "objective," Appellee's Br. 35, which we take to mean that the test should give no consideration to these process-based concerns.

We agree with the government that the Act imposes an objective, outcome-oriented test, but we think some additional explanation is warranted. "Legal tests based on reasonableness are generally objective . . . ." *Kentucky v. King*, 563 U.S. 452, 464 (2011). In practice, this means that such tests usually disregard what government officers were thinking and instead focus on what they actually did in light of the information with which they can reasonably be charged. *See Whren v. United States*, 517 U.S. 806, 813 (1996) ("constitutional reasonableness" does not depend on a police **{–622–}** officer's "actual motivations"). And, as this court is acutely aware, Congress knows how to make an agency's decisionmaking processes subject to review when it wants to. *See, e.g.*, 5 U.S.C. § 706(2)(A) (review of "arbitrary" or "capricious" "findings" and "conclusions" in the Administrative Procedure Act); 42 U.S.C. § 4332(C) (requirement of a "detailed statement by the **[—16—]** responsible official" in the National Environmental Policy Act). Section 1904(h) contains no such language. Accordingly, we see no basis for believing that Congress intended to impose a reasoned decisionmaking requirement in that provision, meaning that Angelex cannot support its argument by pointing to the process the agency employed for setting bond.

Turning to the nonmonetary conditions, we agree with the district court that it is unnecessary to decide whether those conditions were reasonable because they caused Angelex no harm. But we arrive at that conclusion by a somewhat different route.

The district court held that section 1904(h) requires the "unreasonable terms and conditions" of the bond to have "resulted in a [detention or] delay." *Angelex*, 272 F. Supp. 3d at 87. But the statutory text sets up a slightly different causation question: whether the unreasonable detention or delay resulted in loss or damage. *See* 33 U.S.C. § 1904(h) (ships "unreasonably detained or delayed" are "entitled to compensation for any loss or damage suffered *thereby*" (emphasis added)).

In some cases, framing the question that way might yield different results, but this case is not one of them because Angelex's entire theory of loss stems from the *Pappadakis*'s delay. Thus, Angelex had to present evidence that the Coast Guard's nonmonetary conditions contributed to that delay to establish that they contributed to its claimed losses. At the hearing before Judge Doumar, however, Angelex agreed that it would have accepted all those nonmonetary conditions when combined with a $1.5 million bond. Oral Arg. Rec. 12:59-13:06 ("Angelex agreed" to all nonmonetary conditions). The record contains no evidence that Angelex ever retracted that agreement. Angelex now suggests that the total burden of **[—17—]** compliance with the nonmonetary conditions plus the cash bond led it to reject the settlement offer, but—as with the company's finances—we have no way to assess that claim because Angelex has made no specific argument regarding (much less produced any evidence of) the compliance cost. Thus, we are left with no basis for concluding that Angelex's losses resulted from the nonmonetary conditions.

In short, the record contains no evidence to support a finding that the Coast Guard acted unreasonably in demanding that Angelex and Kassian post a $2.5 million bond, or that the other nonmonetary assurances resulted in any additional loss or damage to Angelex.

C.

In a final bid to salvage its case, Angelex recites a list of supposedly "disputed" facts that it insists preclude summary judgment as a procedural matter. But Angelex's list primarily regurgitates all the facts we have just discussed: the nonmonetary bond conditions and the financial information Angelex supposedly provided to the Coast Guard. Those facts, however, are undisputed. What Angelex really disputes is whether those facts rendered the Coast Guard's actions unreasonable. But that determination—"whether the facts satisfy the statutory standard" of reasonableness—is a legal issue, not a factual one. *Carter*, 840 F.2d at 64-65 (internal quotation marks omitted). The only genuinely disputed factual issues relate to **{-623-}** who in the Coast Guard had decisionmaking authority and what those officers actually considered, and as explained above, those disputes are irrelevant because the legal test for reasonableness is objective. We therefore find meritless Angelex's contention that a trial is required to resolve any lingering factual disputes. **[—18—]**

III.

For the foregoing reasons, we affirm the district court's order awarding summary judgment to the government.

So ordered.

This page intentionally left blank

Tables of Authority

This page intentionally left blank

Table of Cases

This page intentionally left blank

TABLE OF CASES[1]

PAGE

A

[1] Cases named solely after ships, *see, e.g., The Pennsylvania,* 86 U.S. (19 Wall.) 125 (1873), are alphabetized under the letter "T." Cases where the United States is the plaintiff are alphabetized by defendant under the letter "U."

B

C

D

E

F

G

H

I

J

K

L

M

N

O

P

Q

R

S

T

U

V

W

Y

Z

Table of Statutes and Rules

This page intentionally left blank

TABLE OF STATUTES AND RULES[1]

PAGE

TREATIES/INTERNATIONAL

FEDERAL

CONSTITUTION

MISCELLANEOUS

[1] As cited in the opinions reported.

STATUTES

RULES

Regulations

State

This page intentionally left blank

Index

This page intentionally left blank

INDEX

PAGE

A

B

C

D

E

F

G

H

I

J

L

M

N

O

P

R

S

T

U

V

W

Z

This page intentionally left blank

www.ingramcontent.com/pod-product-compliance
Lightning Source LLC
LaVergne TN
LVHW060012210926
848481LV00013B/3693
* 9 7 8 1 7 3 3 7 7 9 0 0 5 *